# A SELECT LIBRARY

OF THE

# NICENE AND POST-NICENE FATHERS

OF

# THE CHRISTIAN CHURCH

*EDITED BY*

## PHILIP SCHAFF, D.D., LL.D.,

PROFESSOR OF CHURCH HISTORY IN THE UNION THEOLOGICAL SEMINARY, NEW YORK.

*IN CONNECTION WITH A NUMBER OF PATRISTIC SCHOLARS OF EUROPE AND AMERICA*

### VOLUME XIV

## SAINT CHRYSOSTOM:

### HOMILIES ON THE GOSPEL OF ST. JOHN

AND

### THE EPISTLE TO THE HEBREWS

---

T&T CLARK
EDINBURGH

WM. B. EERDMANS PUBLISHING COMPANY
GRAND RAPIDS, MICHIGAN

**British Library Cataloguing in Publication Data**

Nicene & Post-Nicene Fathers. — 1st series
1. Fathers of the church
I. Title   II. Schaff, Philip
230′.11     BR60.A62


T&T Clark ISBN 0 567 09403 0


Eerdmans ISBN 0-8028-8112-2

*Reprinted, May 1989*

PHOTOLITHOPRINTED BY EERDMANS PRINTING COMPANY
GRAND RAPIDS, MICHIGAN, UNITED STATES OF AMERICA

# CONTENTS OF VOL. XIV.

# PREFACE.

THIS volume closes the American edition of the Works of St. Chrysostom, and at the same time the First Series of the Nicene and Post-Nicene Library of the Christian Fathers.

The best works of St. Augustin and St. Chrysostom are thus brought within the reach of the English reader in a more complete form and at a lower price than ever before.

The Epistle to the Hebrews was the last volume of the Oxford "Library of the Fathers," published under the direction and with a Preface of the late Dr. Pusey, the chief originator of that valuable Library. His Preface is dated, Oxford, May, 1877. He died Sept. 16, 1882.

The American editor of the Homilies on the Hebrews has thoroughly revised the Oxford translation and enlarged it with a valuable introduction on the authorship of the Epistle (about which St. Chrysostom was mistaken), and a considerable number of explanatory footnotes. Unfortunately he died shortly before his MS. was sent to the printer, but his son read the proofs.

The Rev. Dr. Frederic Gardiner (born Sept. 11, 1822, died July 17, 1889) was for many years Professor in the Berkeley Episcopal Divinity School at Middletown, Conn., and President of the Society of Biblical Literature and Exegesis. He edited a Greek Harmony of the Four Gospels, and several exegetical works, and was a contributor to Lange's Commentary, Ellicott's Commentary for English Readers, and various periodicals. The revision of the Homilies on the Epistle to the Hebrews was his last work.

The Homilies on the Fourth Gospel appear as in the Oxford "Library of the Fathers," with a few additional notes. The Rev. Charles Marriott (1811–1858) edited them, and wrote the preface to the first volume. For fourteen years, from 1841 to 1855, he was associated with Dr. Pusey as working editor, and superintended the publication of at least twenty-four volumes (twelve of St. Chrysostom, eight of St. Augustin, four of St. Gregory I.), *i.e.* more than one-half of that Library. It was with both a labor of love and sacrifice, without fee or reward except the approval of their conscience and of good men. To their unselfish labors the American edition owes a great debt of gratitude. Mr. Marriott did most of the literary drudgery, as translator, corrector, and proof-reader, with untiring fidelity and painstaking zeal till he was struck down by paralysis in 1855, "to wait in stillness for his Lord's last call." Dean Burgon states these facts in an interesting account of his intimate friend (in *Lives of Twelve Good Men*, London and New York, 1888, vol. I. 296–376). He calls Marriott "a character unique, beautiful, and saint-like," and adds that he "lived quite above the world, and, like Enoch, walked habitually with God."

I feel very thankful that this Patristic Library has so far been finished, and I am happy to announce that the "Christian Literature Company" is sufficiently encouraged to publish the second series, which will contain the Greek Fathers from Eusebius to John of Damascus, and the Latin Fathers from Hilary to Gregory the Great. I secured the coöperation of eminent patristic scholars of England and America several years ago for the completion of this enterprise.

PHILIP SCHAFF

UNION THEOLOGICAL SEMINARY,
New York, Dec. 24, 1889.

# COMPARATIVE TABLE

OF THE

## WORKS OF ST. CHRYSOSTOM IN THE AMERICAN AND IN MIGNE'S EDITIONS.

# THE HOMILIES OF ST. JOHN CHRYSOSTOM,

## ARCHBISHOP OF CONSTANTINOPLE,

### ON THE

# GOSPEL OF ST. JOHN.

*The Oxford Translation Edited, with Additional Notes, by*

## REV. PHILIP SCHAFF, D.D., LL.D.

# PREFACE TO THE HOMILIES ON THE GOSPEL OF ST. JOHN.

THE Benedictine editor has already noticed the principal points in which these Homilies differ from others in which St. Chrysostom comments upon Holy Scripture. They are far more controversial than is usual with him, and the part devoted to moral exhortation is shorter. This may be partly owing to the number of passages in St. John which bear on the doctrine of our Lord's Person and His Divine and Human Natures. But it seems further that they were delivered to a select audience at an early hour of the day. For toward the latter part of Hom. XXXI. he contrasts the coolness of the morning, in which they were assembled, with the mid-day heat, in which the woman of Samaria listened to our Lord. And the character of the instruction given almost unquestionably marks the hearers as having been less miscellaneous, and less liable to be supposed wanting in points of common duty, than those whom he generally addressed.

They do not give their own date, but are referred to by the Author, while still at Antioch, as already published, in Hom. VII. on 1 Cor. ii. 8. "However, the manner of this way of knowledge and of that hath already been declared in the Gospel; and, not to be continually handling the same topic, thither do we refer our readers." The place is St. John viii. 19 treated in Hom. XLIX.

And since the three first years after St. Chrysostom was ordained Priest, A.D. 386–8, seem completely filled up, and the Homilies in St. Matthew were probably prior to these, it is most likely that they were not begun before A.D. 390, while those on some of the Epistles of St. Paul seem to have come after them, and still before the year 398, in which he was removed to Constantinople.

In either city there were numerous heretics of the sect against which he is most careful to supply arguments, the Anomœans, who held that the Son is not even of *like* [much less of the *same*] substance with the Father. And even in his less generally controversial works, we often meet with discussions of their tenets. But in these Homilies he is continually meeting with texts which they perverted to the maintenance of their heresy, and turning them into weapons for its confutation. And this he usually does with great success, since the Catholic doctrine of the true and perfect Godhead, united in One Person with true and perfect Manhood, affords a key that easily opens texts which most stubbornly resist any confused notion of an inferior Divinity, or an unreal Humanity. The texts urged by the heretic, put to this test, are found not really to belong to him. They are not even arguments *so far* for his view of the case, but perfectly consistent with the truth always held by the Church. There may remain a few cases, after attentive study, in which it is difficult to be sure what is the exact meaning, or even whether a given text speaks of the Godhead or of the Manhood, but as to the general doctrine of the whole Scripture, or the consistency of that doctrine with any and every text therein contained, there is no reasonable doubt. There are those whose faith seems to tremble on the balance when such a passage of Scripture is under discussion, but this must be either from an inveterate habit of doubting, or an imperfect apprehension of the real meaning of the Catholic doctrine. The most skillful commentator may occasionally fall into a critical error, but no one who has ever fairly entered into the sense of Holy Scripture will dream of the alternative being between such and such an exposition and the acceptance of heresy. Enough is clear to make us very sure what will be the doctrine of any difficult passage, though we may be in doubt of its interpretation. St. Chrysostom is usually right, and not only so, but most ingenious in detecting the rhetorical connection of sentiments and arguments.   If anywhere he fails, it is from some over-refinement in rhetorical analysis, and not from any want of apprehension of the main truths concerned.

In the first volume of the Benedictine edition there is a series of Homilies against the Ano-mœans, in the first of which he states that he had been unwilling for some time to enter on the controversy, for fear of driving away hearers who held those opinions, but that he had now taken it up at their earnest request.   These Homilies were delivered some time before those on St. John, beginning in the first year after his ordination with those " On the Incomprehensible Nature of God," in opposition to the pretensions of that sect to perfect knowledge of Divine things.   And the Benedictine Editor refers to them as containing a more complete array of the *positive* evidence of St. John to the Catholic doctrines than even this commentary affords.

The history of the woman taken in adultery is omitted in this commentary, and the Benedic-tine editor was not able to trace it in any of the works of St. Chrysostom.   It is suggested that his copies may have wanted the passage, or that he may have omitted it for fear it should be taken as an encouragement to vice.   But he was not the man to shrink from so slight a difficulty, nor would he have failed, in commenting on it, to leave an impression on the hearer by no means calculated to lessen his dread of sin.   Such a reason may have prevailed with some copy-ists to suppress the passage, and it is probable that it was not found in the copy which he used. It is omitted in like manner by St. Cyril of Alexandria.[1]

The text of Savile has been followed, except where the Benedictine edition has supplied improvements.   The Benedictine sections are numbered throughout : where the division seemed to be inconvenient, the number is given in the margin.   In the earlier Homilies a second series of numbers is employed to mark the sections in the translation ; this was discontinued as unnec-essary, and the Benedictine only retained.   In some of the references to the Psalms, where the Septuagint differs much from the Hebrew, the numbers given are those of the Greek.   Care will be taken in the Index of Texts to give always the reference to the Psalm and Verse according to the Hebrew reckoning followed in our own Version.

The editors are indebted for the present translation to the Rev. G. T. STUPART, M. A., late Fellow of Exeter College.   It has been kindly carried through the Press by the Rev. J. G. HICKLEY, B. D., Fellow of Trinity College, Oxford.   The translation of the remaining Homilies is completed, and will shortly be in the Press.[2]

C. M[ARRIOTT].

ORIEL COLLEGE,
*Feast of St. Andrew, 1848.*

---

[1] [The pericope John vii. 53–viii. 11 is considered by the best modern critics as an interpolation by a transcriber, but is probably based on a genuine apostolic tradition, perhaps taken from the lost work of Papias of Hierapolis, who collected from primitive disciples various discourses of our Lord, among others " a narrative concerning a woman maliciously accused before the Lord touching many sins." (Eusebius, *Hist. Eccl.* III. 39.)   The section is omitted in the oldest uncial and other Greek MSS. (א, B, etc.); it was unknown to Chrysostom and other Greek and early Latin fathers; it interrupts the context; it departs from the style of John, and presents an unusual number of various readings.   We find it first in Latin Gospel MSS. of the fourth century, but in different places, sometimes at the end of the Gospel of John as an appendix, sometimes at the end of Luke xxi.   It was also in the Gospel according to the Hebrews.   The R. V. properly retains it, but in brackets and with a marginal note.   The story, though no part of the Gospel of John, is eminently Christlike.   For details see Tischendorf (ed. viii.), Tregelles, Westcott and Hort, and the critical commentaries. — P. S.]

[2] [The second volume of the Oxford edition, containing Homilies 42–88 (John vi.–xxi.), was published in 1852 without a Preface. — P. S.]

# CONTENTS.

## HOMILIES ON JOHN.

these divine oracles. If a man cannot learn well a melody on pipe or harp, unless he in every way strain his attention; how shall one, who sits as a listener to sounds mystical, be able to hear with a careless soul?

[5.] Wherefore Christ Himself exhorted, saying, "Give not that which is holy unto the dogs, neither cast ye your pearls before swine." (Matt. vii. 6.) He called these words "pearls," though in truth they be much more precious than they, because we have no substance more precious than that. For this reason too He is wont often to compare their sweetness to honey, not that so much only is the measure of their sweetness, but because amongst us there is nothing sweeter. Now, to show that they very exceedingly surpass the nature of precious stones, and the sweetness of any honey, hear the prophet speaking concerning them, and declaring this superiority; "More to be desired are they," he saith, "than gold and much precious stone; sweeter are they also than honey and the honeycomb." (Ps. xix. 10.) But to those (only) who are in health; wherefore he has added, "For thy servant keepeth them." And again in another place calling them sweet he has added, "to my throat." For he saith, "How sweet are thy words unto my throat." (Ps. cxix. 103.) And again he insisteth on the superiority, saying, "Above honey and the honeycomb to my mouth." For he was in very sound health. And let not us either come nigh to these while we are sick, but when we have healed our soul, so receive the food that is offered us.

It is for this reason that, after so long a preface, I have not yet attempted to fathom[1] these expressions (of St. John), in order that every one having laid aside all manner of infirmity, as though he were entering into heaven itself, so may enter here pure, and freed from wrath and carefulness and anxiety of this life, of all other passions. For it is not otherwise possible for a man to gain from hence anything great, except he have first so cleansed anew his soul. And let no one say that the time to the coming communion[2] is short, for it is possible, not only in five days, but in one moment, to change the whole course of life. Tell me what is worse than a robber and a murderer, is not this the extremest kind of wickedness? Yet such an one arrived straight at the summit of excellence, and passed into Paradise itself, not needing days, nor half a day, but one little moment. So that a man may change suddenly, and become gold instead of clay. For since what belongs to virtue and to vice is not by nature, the change is easy, as being independent of any necessity. "If ye be willing and obedient," He saith, "ye

shall eat the good of the land." (Isa. i. 19.) Seest thou that there needs the will only? will — not the common wishing of the multitude — but earnest will. For I know that all are wishing to fly up to heaven even now; but it is necessary to show forth the wish by works. The merchant too wishes to get rich; but he doth not allow his wish to stop with the thought of it; no, he fits out a ship, and gets together sailors, and engages a pilot, and furnishes the vessel with all other stores, and borrows money, and crosses the sea, and goes away into a strange land, and endures many dangers, and all the rest which they know who sail the sea. So too must we show our will; for we also sail a voyage, not from land to land, but from earth to heaven. Let us then so order our reason, that it be serviceable to steer our upward course, and our sailors that they be obedient to it, and let our vessel be stout, that it be not swamped amidst the reverses and despondencies of this life, nor be lifted up by the blasts of vainglory, but be a fast and easy vessel. If so we order our ship, and so our pilot and our crew, we shall sail with a fair wind, and we shall draw down to ourselves the Son of God, the true Pilot, who will not leave our bark to be engulfed, but, though ten thousand winds may blow, will rebuke the winds and the sea, and instead of raging waves, make a great calm.

[6.] Having therefore ordered yourselves, so come to our next assembly, if at least it be at all an object of desire to you to hear somewhat to your advantage, and lay up what is said in your souls. But let not one of you be the "wayside," none the "stony ground," none the "full of thorns." (Matt. xiii. 4, 5, 7.) Let us make ourselves fallow lands. For so shall we (the preachers) put in the seed with gladness, when we see the land clean, but if stony or rough, pardon us if we like not to labor in vain. For if we shall leave off sowing and begin to cut up thorns, surely to cast seed into ground unwrought were extreme folly.

It is not meet that he who has the advantage of such hearing be partaker of the table of devils. "For what fellowship hath righteousness with unrighteousness?" (2 Cor. vi. 14.) Thou standest listening to John, and learning the things of the Spirit by him; and dost thou after this depart to listen to harlots speaking vile things, and acting viler, and to effeminates cuffing one another? How wilt thou be able to be fairly cleansed, if thou wallowest in such mire? Why need I reckon in detail all the indecency that is there? All there is laughter, all is shame, all disgrace, revilings and mockings, all abandonment, all destruction. See, I forewarn and charge you all. Let none of those who enjoy the blessings of this table destroy his own

---

[1] καθῆκα.      [2] συνάξεως.

soul by those pernicious spectacles. All that is said and done there is a pageant of Satan. But ye who have been initiated know what manner of covenants ye made with us, or rather ye made with Christ when He guided you into His mysteries, what ye spoke to Him, what speech ye had with Him concerning Satan's pageant ;[1] how with Satan and his angels ye renounced this also, and promised that you would not so much as cast a glance[2] that way. There is then no slight ground for fear, lest, by becoming careless of such promises, one should render himself unworthy of these mysteries.

[7.] Seest thou not how in king's palaces it is not those who have offended, but those who have been honorably distinguished,[3] that are called to share especial favor,[4] and are numbered among the king's friends. A messenger has come to us from heaven, sent by God Himself, to speak with us on certain necessary matters, and you leave hearing His will, and the message He sends to you, and sit listening to stage-players. What thunderings, what bolts from heaven, does not this conduct deserve ! For as it is not meet to partake of the table of devils, so neither is it of the listening to devils ; nor to be present with filthy raiment at that glorious Table, loaded with so many good things, which God Himself hath provided. Such is its power, that it can raise us at once to heaven, if only we approach it with a sober mind. For it is not possible that he who is continually under the influence of [7] the words of God, can remain in this present low condition, but he needs must presently take wing, and fly away to the land which is above, and light on the infinite treasures of good things ; which may it be that we all attain to, through the grace and lovingkindness of our Lord Jesus Christ, through whom and with whom be glory to the Father and the All-holy Spirit, now and ever, and world without end. Amen.

# HOMILY II.

JOHN i. 1.

"In the beginning was the Word."

WERE John about to converse with us, and to say to us words of his own, we needs must describe his family, his country, and his education. But since it is not he, but God by him, that speaks to mankind, it seems to me superfluous and distracting to enquire into these matters. And yet even thus it is not superfluous, but even very necessary. For when you have learned who he was, and from whence, who his parents, and what his character, and then hear his voice and all his heavenly wisdom,[5] then you shall know right well that these (doctrines) belong not to him, but to the Divine power stirring his soul.

From what country[6] then was he ? From no country ; but from a poor village, and from a land little esteemed, and producing no good thing. For the Scribes speak evil of Galilee, saying, "Search and look, for out of Galilee ariseth no prophet." (John vii. 52.) And "the Israelite indeed" speaks ill of it, saying, " Can any good thing come out of Nazareth ? " And being of this land, he was not even of any remarkable place in it, but of one not even distinguished by name. Of this he was,[8] and his father a poor fisherman, so poor that he took his sons to the same employment. Now you all know that no workman will choose to bring up his son to succeed him in his trade, unless poverty press him very hard, especially where the trade is a mean one. But nothing can be poorer, meaner, no, nor more ignorant, than fishermen. Yet even among them there are some greater, some less ; and even there our Apostle occupied the lower rank, for he did not take his prey from the sea, but passed his time on a certain little lake. And as he was engaged by it with his father and his brother James, and they mending their broken nets, a thing which of itself marked extreme poverty, so Christ called him.[9]

As for worldly instruction, we may learn from these facts that he had none at all of it. Besides, Luke testifies this when he writes not only that he was ignorant,[10] but that he was absolutely

[1] πομπῆς.
[2] παρακύψειν.
[3] τετιμημένοι.
[4] τῆς γνώμης ἐκείνης.
[5] φιλοσοφίας.
[6] πατρίδος.
[7] ἐπᾳδόμενον.
[8] One MS. " not even distinguished by name had he not been of it. His," &c.
[9] [On the other hand, the facts that John's father Zebedee had hired servants, that his mother Salome aided in the support of Jesus, that John was acquainted with the high-priest, and seems to have possessed a home in Jerusalem into which he took the mother of our Saviour after the crucifixion, prove that he was not the poorest among the fishermen, but in tolerably good circumstances. Comp. Mark ii. 20; Luke v. 10; viii. 3; Mark xvi. 1; John xviii. 15; xix. 27. — P. S.]
[10] ἰδιώτης.

unlettered.[1] (Acts iv. 13.) As was likely. For one who was so poor, never coming into the public assemblies, nor falling in with men of respectability, but as it were nailed to his fishing, or even if he ever did meet any one, conversing with fishmongers and cooks, how, I say, was he likely to be in a state better than that of the irrational animals? how could he help imitating the very dumbness of his fishes?

[2.] This fisherman then, whose business was about lakes, and nets, and fish; this native of Bethsaida of Galilee; this son of a poor fisherman, yes, and poor to the last degree; this man ignorant, and to the last degree of ignorance too, who never learned letters either before or after he accompanied Christ; let us see what he utters, and on what matters he converses with us. Is it of things in the field? Is it of things in rivers? On the trade in fish? For these things, perhaps, one expects to hear from a fisherman. But fear ye not; we shall hear nought of these; but we shall hear of things in heaven, and what no one ever learned before this man. For, as might be expected of one who speaks from the very treasures of the Spirit, he is come bringing to us sublime doctrines, and the best way of life and wisdom, [as though just arrived from the very heavens; yea, rather such as it was not likely that all even there should know, as I said before.[2]] Do these things belong to a fisherman? Tell me. Do they belong to a rhetorician at all? To a sophist or philosopher? To every one trained in the wisdom of the Gentiles? By no means. The human soul is simply unable thus to philosophize on that pure and blessed nature; on the powers that come next to it; on immortality and endless life; on the nature of mortal bodies which shall hereafter be immortal; on punishment and the judgment to come; on the enquiries that shall be as to deeds and words, as to thoughts and imaginations. It cannot tell what is man, what the world; what is man indeed, and what he who seems to be man, but is not; what is the nature of virtue, what of vice.

[3.] Some of these things indeed the disciples of Plato and Pythagoras enquired into. Of the other philosophers we need make no mention at all; they have all on this point been so excessively ridiculous; and those who have been among them in greater esteem than the rest, and who have been considered the leading men in this science, are so more than the others; and they have composed and written somewhat on the subject of polity and doctrines, and in all have been more shamefully ridiculous than children. For they have spent their whole life in making women common to all, in overthrowing the very order of life,[3] in doing away the honor of marriage, and in making other the like ridiculous laws. As for doctrines on the soul, there is nothing excessively shameful that they have left unsaid; asserting that the souls of men become flies, and gnats, and bushes,[4] and that God Himself is a soul; with some other the like indecencies.

And not this alone in them is worthy of blame, but so is also their ever-shifting current of words; for since they assert everything on uncertain and fallacious arguments, they are like men carried hither and thither in Euripus, and never remain in the same place.

Not so this fisherman; for all he saith is infallible; and standing as it were upon a rock, he never shifts his ground. For since he has been thought worthy to be in the most secret places, and has the Lord of all speaking within him, he is subject to nothing that is human. But they, like persons who are not held worthy even in a dream[5] to set foot in the king's palace, but who pass their time in the forum with other men, guessing from their own imagination at what they cannot see, have erred a great error, and, like blind or drunken men in their wandering, have dashed against each other; and not only against each other, but against themselves, by continually changing their opinion, and that ever on the same matters.

[4.] But this unlettered man, the ignorant, the native of Bethsaida, the son of Zebedee, (though the Greeks mock ten thousand times at the rusticity of the names, I shall not the less speak them with the greater boldness.) For the more barbarous his nation seems to them, and the more he seems removed from Grecian discipline, so much the brighter does what we have with us appear. For when a barbarian and an untaught person utters things which no man on earth ever knew, and does not only utter, (though if this were the only thing it were a great marvel,) but besides this, affords another and a stronger proof that what he says is divinely inspired, namely, the convincing all his hearers through all time; who will not wonder at the power that dwells in him? Since this is, as I said, the strongest proof that he lays down no laws of his own. This barbarian then, with his writing of the Gospel, has occupied all the habitable world. With his body he has taken possession of the center of Asia, where of old philosophized all of the Grecian party, shining forth in the midst of his foes, dispersing[6] their darkness, and breaking down the stronghold of

---

[1] ἀγράμματος.
[2] See above, p. 2 [4]. [From one MS. in the Bened. ed. — P.S.]
[3] βίον.
[4] Empedocles said this. Vid. Diog. Laert. viii. 2.
　'Ἤδη γάρ ποτ' ἐγὼ γενόμην κοῦρός τε κόρη τε
　Θάμνος τ' οἰωνός τε καὶ ἐξ ἁλὸς ἔμπυρος ἰχθύς.
[5] οὐδὲ ὄναρ.
[6] Lit. "quenching."

devils : but in soul he has retired to that place which is fit for one who has done such things.

[5.] And as for the writings of the Greeks, they are all put out and vanished, but this man's shine brighter day by day. For from the time that he (was) and the other fishermen, since then the (doctrines) of Pythagoras and of Plato, which seemed before to prevail, have ceased to be spoken of, and most men do not know them even by name. Yet Plato was, they say, the invited companion of kings, had many friends, and sailed to Sicily. And Pythagoras occupied Magna Græcia,[1] and practiced there ten thousand kinds of sorcery. For to converse with oxen, (which they say he did,) was nothing else but a piece of sorcery. As is most clear from this. He that so conversed with brutes did not in anything benefit the race of men, but even did them the greatest wrong. Yet surely, the nature of men was better adapted for the reasoning of philosophy ; still he did, as they say, converse with eagles and oxen, using sorceries. For he did not make their irrational nature rational, (this was impossible to man,) but by his magic tricks he deceived the foolish. And neglecting to teach men anything useful, he taught that they might as well eat the heads of those who begot them, as beans. And he persuaded those who associated with him, that the soul of their teacher had actually been at one time a bush, at another a girl, at another a fish.

Are not these things with good cause extinct, and vanished utterly? With good cause, and reasonably. But not so the words of him who was ignorant and unlettered ; for Syrians, and Egyptians, and Indians, and Persians, and Ethiopians, and ten thousand other nations, translating into their own tongues the doctrines introduced by him, barbarians though they be, have learned to philosophize. I did not therefore idly say that all the world has become his theater. For he did not leave those of his own kind, and waste his labor on the irrational creatures, (an act of excessive vainglory and extreme folly,) but being clear of this as well as of other passions, he was earnest on one point only, that all the world might learn somewhat of the things which might profit it, and be able to translate it from earth to heaven.

For this reason too, he did not hide his teaching in mist and darkness, as they did who threw obscurity of speech, like a kind of veil, around the mischiefs laid up within. But this man's doctrines are clearer than the sunbeams, wherefore they have been unfolded[2] to all men throughout the world. For he did not teach as Pythagoras did, commanding those who came to him to be silent for five years, or to sit like

senseless stones ; neither did he invent fables defining the universe to consist of numbers ; but casting away all this devilish trash and mischief, he diffused such simplicity through his words, that all he said was plain, not only to wise men, but also to women and youths. For he was persuaded that the words were true and profitable to all that should hearken to them. And all time after him is his witness ; since he has drawn to him all the world, and has freed our life when we have listened to these words from all monstrous display of wisdom ; wherefore we who hear them would prefer rather to give up our lives, than the doctrines by him delivered to us.

[6.] From this then, and from every other circumstance, it is plain, that nothing of this man's is human, but divine and heavenly are the lessons which come to us by this divine soul. For we shall observe not sounding sentences, nor magnificent diction, nor excessive and useless order and arrangement of words and sentences, (these things are far from all true wisdom,) but strength invincible and divine, and irresistible force of right doctrines, and a rich supply of unnumbered good things. For their over-care about expression was so excessive, so worthy of mere sophists, or rather not even of sophists, but of silly striplings, that even their own chief philosopher introduces his own master as greatly ashamed of this art, and as saying to the judges, that what they hear from him shall be spoken plainly and without premeditation, not tricked out rhetorically nor ornamented with (fine) sentences and words ; since, says he, it cannot surely be becoming, O men, that one at my age should come before you like a lad inventing speeches.[3] And observe the extreme absurdity of the thing ; what he has described his master avoiding as disgraceful, unworthy of philosophy and work for lads, this above all he himself has cultivated. So entirely were they given up to mere love of distinction.

And as, if you uncover those sepulchers which are whitened without you will find them full of corruption, and stench, and rotten bones ; so too the doctrines of the philosopher, if you strip them of their flowery diction, you will see to be full of much abomination, especially when he philosophizes on the soul, which he both honors and speaks ill of without measure. And this is the snare of the devil, never to keep due proportion, but by excess on either hand to lead aside those who are entangled by it into evil speaking. At one time he says, that the soul is of the substance of God ; at another, after having exalted it thus immoderately and impiously, he exceeds again in a different way, and treats it

---

[1] τὴν μεγίστην Ἑλλάδα.
[2] ἀνήπλωται.

[3] Plat. *Apol. Socr.* § 1, in init.

with insult, making it pass into swine and asses, and other animals of yet less esteem than these.

But enough of this; or rather even this is out of measure. For if it were possible to learn anything profitable from these things, we must have been longer occupied with them; but if it be only to observe their indecency and absurdity, more than requisite has been said by us already. We will therefore leave their fables, and attach ourselves to our own doctrines, which have been brought to us from above by the tongue of this fisherman, and which have nothing human in them.

[7.] Let us then bring forward the words, having reminded you now, as I exhorted you at the first, earnestly to attend to what is said. What then does this Evangelist say immediately on his outset?

"In the beginning was the Word, and the Word was with God." (Ver. 1.) Seest thou the great boldness and power of the words, how he speaks nothing doubting nor conjecturing, but declaring all things plainly? For this is the teacher's part, not to waver in anything he says, since if he who is to be a guide to the rest require another person who shall be able to establish him with certainty, he would be rightly ranked not among teachers, but among disciples.

But if any one say, "What can be the reason that he has neglected the first cause, and spoken to us at once concerning the second?" we shall decline to speak of "first" and "second," for the Divinity is above number, and the succession of times. Wherefore we decline these expressions; but we confess that the Father is from none, and that the Son is begotten of the Father. Yes, it may be said, but why then does he leave the Father, and speak concerning the Son? Why? because the former was manifest to all, if not as Father, at least as God; but the Only-Begotten was not known; and therefore with reason did he immediately from the very beginning hasten to implant the knowledge of Him in those who knew Him not.

Besides, he has not been silent as to the Father in his writings on these points. And observe, I beg of you, his spiritual wisdom. He knows that men most honor the eldest of beings which was before all, and account this to be God. Wherefore from this point first he makes his beginning, and as he advances, declares that God is, and does not like Plato assert, sometimes that He is intellect, sometimes that He is soul; for these things are far removed from that divine and unmixed Nature which has nothing common with us, but is separated from any fellowship with created things, I mean as to substance, though not as to relation.

And for this reason he calls Him "The Word." For since he is about to teach that this "Word"

is the only-begotten Son of God, in order that no one may imagine that His generation is passible, by giving Him the appellation of "The Word," he anticipates and removes beforehand the evil suspicion, showing that the Son is from the Father, and that without His suffering (change).

[8.] Seest thou then that as I said, he has not been silent as to the Father in his words concerning the Son? And if these instances are not sufficient fully to explain the whole matter, marvel not, for our argument is God, whom it is impossible to describe, or to imagine worthily; hence this man nowhere assigns the name of His essence, (for it is not possible to say what God is, as to essence,) but everywhere he declares Him to us by His workings. For this "Word" one may see shortly after called "Light," and the "Light" in turn named "Life."

Although not for this reason only did he so name Him; this was the first reason, and the second was because He was about to declare to us the things of the Father. For "all things," He saith, "that I have heard from my Father, I have made known unto you." (John xv. 15.) He calls Him both "Light" and "Life," for He hath freely given to us the light which proceeds from knowledge, and the life which follows it. In short, one name is not sufficient, nor two, nor three, nor more, to teach us what belongs to God. But we must be content to be able even by means of many to apprehend, though but obscurely, His attributes.

And he has not called Him simply "Word," but with the addition of the article, distinguishing Him from the rest in this way also. Seest thou then that I said not without cause that this Evangelist speaks to us from heaven? Only see from the very beginning whither he has drawn up the soul, having given it wings, and has carried up with him the mind of his hearers. For having set it higher than all the things of sense, than earth, than sea, than heaven, he leads it by the hand above the very angels, above cherubim and seraphim, above thrones and principalities and powers; in a word, persuades it to journey beyond all created things.

[9.] What then? when he has brought us to such a height as this, is he in sooth able to stop us there? By no means; but just as one by transporting into the midst of the sea a person who was standing on the beach, and looking on cities, and beaches, and havens, removes him indeed from the former objects, yet does not stay his sight anywhere, but brings him to a view without bound; so this Evangelist, having brought us above all creation, and escorted us towards the eternal periods which lie beyond it, leaves the sight suspended,[1] not allowing it to

---

[1] μετέωρον.

arrive at any limit upwards, as indeed there is none.

For the intellect, having ascended to "the beginning," enquires what "beginning"; and then finding the "was" always outstripping its imagination, has no point at which to stay its thought; but looking intently onwards, and being unable to cease at any point, it becomes wearied out, and turns back to things below. For this, "was in the beginning," is nothing else than expressive of ever being and being infinitely.

Seest thou true philosophy and divine doctrines? Not like those of the Greeks, who assign times, and say that some indeed of the gods are younger, some elder. There is nothing of this with us. For if God Is, as certainly He Is, then nothing was before Him. If He is Creator of all things, He must be first; if Master and Lord of all, then all, both creatures and ages, are after Him.

[10.] I had desired to enter the lists yet on other difficulties, but perhaps our minds are wearied out; when therefore I have advised you on those points which are useful [1] to us for the hearing, both of what has been said, and of what is yet to be said, I again will hold my peace. What then are these points? I know that many have become confused [2] by reason of the length of what has been spoken. Now this takes place when the soul is heavy laden with many burdens of this life. For as the eye when it is clear and transparent is keen-sighted also, and will not easily be tired in making out even the minutest bodies; but when from some bad humor from the head having poured into it, or some smoke-like fumes having ascended to it from beneath, a kind of thick cloud is formed before the ball, this does not allow it clearly to perceive even any larger object; so is naturally the case with the soul. For when it is purified, and has no passion to disturb it, it looks steadfastly to the fit objects of its regard; but when, darkened by many passions, it loses its proper excellence, then it is not easily able to be sufficient for any high thing, but soon is wearied, and falls back; and turning aside to sleep and sloth, lets pass things that concern it with a view to excellence and the life thence arising, instead of receiving them with much readiness.

And that you may not suffer this, (I shall not cease continually thus to warn you,) strengthen your minds, that ye may not hear what the faithful among the Hebrews heard from Paul. For to them he said that he had "many things to say, and hard to be uttered" (Heb. v. 11); not as though they were by nature such, but because, says he, "ye are dull of hear-

ing." For it is the nature of the weak and infirm man to be confused even by few words as by many, and what is clear and easy he thinks hard to be comprehended. Let not any here be such an one, but having chased from him all worldly care, so let him hear these doctrines.

For when the desire of money possesses the hearer, the desire of hearing cannot possess him as well; since the soul, being one, cannot suffice for many desires; but one of the two is injured by the other, and, from division, becomes weaker as its rival prevails, and expends all upon itself.

And this is wont to happen in the case of children. When a man has only one, he loves that one exceedingly. But when he has become father of many, then also his dispositions of affection being divided become weaker.

If this happens where there is the absolute rule and power of nature, and the objects beloved are akin one with another, what can we say as to that desire and disposition which is according to deliberate choice; especially where these desires lie directly opposed to each other; for the love of wealth is a thing opposed to the love of this kind of hearing. We enter heaven when we enter here; not in place, I mean, but in disposition; for it is possible for one who is on earth to stand in heaven, and to have vision of the things that are there, and to hear the words from thence.

[11.] Let none then introduce the things of earth into heaven; let no one standing here be careful about what is at his house. For he ought to bear with him, and to preserve both at home and in his business, what he gains from this place, not to allow it to be loaded with the burdens of house and market. Our reason for entering in to the chair of instruction is, that thence we may cleanse ourselves from [3] the filth of the outer world; but if we are likely even in this little space to be injured by things said or done without, it is better for us not to enter at all. Let no one then in the assembly be thinking about domestic matters, but let him at home be stirring with what he heard in the assembly. Let these things be more precious to us than any. These concern the soul, but those the body; or rather what is said here concerns both body and soul. Wherefore let these things be our leading business, and all others but occasional employments; for these belong both to the future and the present life, but the rest neither to the one nor the other, unless they be managed according to the law laid down for these. Since from these it is impossible to learn not only what we shall hereafter be, and how we

---

[1] al. "to you."          [2] ἰλιγγιάσαντας.          [3] al. "rub off."

shall then live, but how we shall rightly direct this present life also.

For this house is [1] a spiritual surgery, that whatever wounds we may have received without, here [2] we may heal, not that we may gather fresh ones to take with us hence. Yet if we do not give heed to the Spirit speaking to us, we shall not only fail to clear ourselves of our former hurts, but shall get others in addition.

Let us then with much earnestness attend to the book as it is being unfolded to us; since if we learn exactly its first principles and fundamental doctrines,[3] we shall not afterwards require much close study, but after laboring a little at the beginning, shall be able, as Paul says, to instruct others also. (Rom. xv. 14.) For this Apostle is very sublime, abounding in many doctrines, and on these he dwells more than on other matters.

Let us not then be careless hearers. And this is the reason why we set them forth to you by little and little, so that all may be easily intelligible to you, and may not escape your memory. Let us fear then lest we come under the condemnation of that word which says, " If I had not come and spoken unto them, they had not had sin." (John xv. 22.) For what shall we be profited more than those who have not heard, if even after hearing we go our way home bearing nothing with us, but only wondering at what has been said.

Allow us then to sow in good ground; allow us, that you may draw us the more to you. If any man hath thorns, let him cast the fire of the Spirit amongst them. If any hath a hard and stubborn heart, let him by employing the same fire make it soft and yielding. If any by the wayside is trodden down by all kind of thoughts, let him enter into more sheltered places, and not lie exposed for those that will to invade for plunder: that so we may see your cornfields waving with corn. Besides, if we exercise such care as this over ourselves, and apply ourselves industriously to this spiritual hearing, if not at once yet by degrees, we shall surely be freed from all the cares of life.

Let us therefore take heed that it be not said of us, that our [4] ears are those of a deaf adder. (Ps. lviii. 4.) For tell me, in what does a hearer of this kind differ from a beast? and how could he be otherwise than more irrational than any irrational animal, who does not attend when God is speaking? And if to be well-pleasing [5] to God is really to be a man, what else but a beast can he be who will not even hear how he may succeed in this? Consider then what a misfortune it would be for us to fall down [6] of our own accord from (the nature of) men to (that of) beasts, when Christ is willing of men to make us equal to angels. For to serve the belly, to be possessed by the desire of riches, to be given to anger, to bite, to kick, become not men, but beasts. Nay, even the beasts have each, as one may say, one single passion, and that by nature. But man, when he has cast away the dominion of reason, and torn himself from the commonwealth of God's devising, gives himself up to all the passions, is no longer merely a beast, but a kind of many-formed motley monster; nor has he even the excuse from nature, for all his wickedness proceeds from deliberate choice and determination.

May we never have cause to suspect this of the Church of Christ. Indeed, we are concerning you persuaded of better things, and such as belong to salvation; but the more we are so persuaded, the more careful we will be not to desist from words of caution. In order that having mounted to the summit of excellencies, we may obtain the promised goods. Which may it come to pass that we all attain to, through the grace and lovingkindness of our Lord Jesus Christ, by whom and with whom, to the Father and the Holy Ghost, be glory world without end. Amen.

---

[1] al. " is set."
[2] al. " hence."
[3] ὑποθέσεις.
[4] al. " their."
[5] al. " to be thankful."
[6] al. " to change."

# HOMILY III.

JOHN i. I.

"In the beginning was the Word."

[I.] ON the subject of attention in hearkening it is superfluous to exhort you any more, so quickly have you shown by your actions the effects of my advice. For your manner of running together, your attentive postures, the thrusting one another in your eagerness to get the inner places, where my voice may more clearly be heard by you, your unwillingness to retire from the press until this spiritual assembly be dissolved, the clapping of hands, the murmurs of applause; in a word, all things of this kind may be considered proofs of the fervor of your souls, and of your desire to hear. So that on this point it is superfluous to exhort you. One thing, however, it is necessary for us to bid and entreat, that you continue to have the same zeal, and manifest it not here only, but that also when you are at home, you converse man with wife, and father with son, concerning these matters. And say somewhat of yourselves, and require somewhat in return from them; and so all contribute to this excellent banquet.[1]

For let no one tell me that our children ought not to be occupied with these things; they ought not only to be occupied with them, but to be zealous about them only. And although on account of your infirmity I do not assert this, nor take them away from their worldly learning,[2] just as I do not draw you either from your civil business; yet of these seven days I claim that you dedicate one to the common Lord of us all. For is it not a strange thing that we should bid our domestics slave for us all their time, and ourselves apportion not even a little of our leisure to God; and this too when all our service adds nothing to Him, (for the Godhead is incapable of want,) but turns out to our own advantage? And yet when you take your children into the theaters, you allege neither their mathematical lessons, nor anything of the kind; but if it be required to gain or collect anything spiritual, you call the matter a waste of time. And how shall you not anger God, if you find leisure and assign a season for everything else, and yet think it a troublesome and unseasonable thing for your children to take in hand what relates to Him?

Do not so, brethren, do not so. It is this very age that most of all needs the hearing these things; for from its tenderness it readily stores up what is said; and what children hear is impressed as a seal on the wax of their minds. Besides, it is then that their life begins to incline to vice or virtue; and if from the very gates[3] and portals one lead them away from iniquity, and guide them by the hand to the best road, he will fix them for the time to come in a sort of habit and nature, and they will not, even if they be willing, easily change for the worse, since this force of custom draws them to the performance of good actions. So that we shall see them become more worthy of respect than those who have grown old, and they will be more useful in civil matters, displaying in youth the qualities of the aged.

For, as I before said, it cannot be that they who enjoy the hearing of such things as these, and who are in the company of such an Apostle, should depart without receiving some great and remarkable advantage, be it man, woman, or youth, that partakes of this table. If we train by words the animals which we have, and so tame them, how much more shall we effect this with men by this spiritual teaching, when there is a wide difference between the remedy in each case, and the subject healed as well. For neither is there so much fierceness in us as in the brutes, since theirs is from nature, ours from choice; nor is the power of the words the same; for the power of the first is that of the human intellect, the power of the second is that of the might and grace of the Spirit.[4] Let then the man who despairs of himself consider the tame animals, and he shall no longer be thus affected; let him come continually to this house of healing, let him hear at all times the laws of the Spirit, and on retiring home let him write down in his mind the things which he has heard; so shall his hopes be good and his confidence great, as he feels his progress by experience. For when the devil sees the law of God written in the soul, and the heart become tablets to write it on, he will not approach any more. Since wherever the king's writing is, not engraved on a pillar of brass, but stamped by the Holy Ghost on a mind loving God, and bright with abundant grace, that (evil one) will not be able even to look at it, but from afar will turn his back upon us. For nothing is so terrible to him and to the thoughts which are suggested by him as a mind careful

---

[1] ἔρανον, a feast to which all the guests contributed.
[2] al. "study."

[3] al. "beginning."
[4] i.e. Man is more tractable than brutes, the words of the Spirit more powerful than words of reason.

about Divine matters, and a soul which ever hangs over this fountain. Such an one can nothing present annoy, even though it be displeasing; nothing puff up or make proud, even though it be favorable; but amidst all this storm and surge it will even enjoy a great calm.

[2.] For confusion arises within us, not from the nature of circumstances, but from the infirmity of our minds; for if we were thus affected by reason of what befalls us, then, (as we all sail the same sea, and it is impossible to escape waves and spray,) all men must needs be troubled; but if there are some who stand beyond the influence of the storm and the raging sea, then it is clear that it is not circumstances which make the storm, but the condition of our own mind. If therefore we so order the mind that it may bear all things contentedly, we shall have no storm nor even a ripple, but always a clear calm.

After professing that I should say nothing on these points, I know not how I have been carried away into such a length of exhortation. Pardon my prolixity; for I fear, yes, I greatly fear lest this zeal of ours should ever become weaker. Did I feel confident respecting it, I would not now have said to you anything on these matters, since it is sufficient to make all things easy to you. But it is time in what follows to proceed to the matters proposed for consideration to-day; that you may not come weary to the contest. For we have contests against the enemies of the truth, against those who use every artifice to destroy the honor of the Son of God, or rather their own. This remains for ever as it now is, nothing lessened by the blaspheming tongue, but they, by seeking eagerly to pull down Him whom they say they worship, fill their faces with shame and their souls with punishment.

What then do they say when we assert what we have asserted? "That the words, 'in the beginning was the Word,' do not denote eternity absolutely, for that this same expression was used also concerning heaven and earth." What enormous shamelessness and irreverence! I speak to thee concerning God, and dost thou bring the earth into the argument, and men who are of the earth? At this rate, since Christ is called Son of God, and God, Man who is called Son of God must be God also. For, "I have said, Ye are Gods, and all of you are children of the Most High." (Ps. lxxxii. 6.) Wilt thou contend with the Only-Begotten concerning Sonship, and assert that in that respect He enjoys nothing more than thou? "By no means," is the reply. And yet thou doest this even though thou say not so in words. "How?" Because thou sayest that thou by grace art partaker of the adoption, and He in like manner. For

by saying that He is not Son by nature, thou only makest him to be so by grace.

However, let us see the proofs which they produce to us. "In the beginning," it is said, "God made the Heaven and the earth, and the earth was invisible and unformed." (Gen. i. 2.) And, "There 'was' a man of Ramathaim Zophim." (1 Sam. i. 1.) These are what they think strong arguments, and they are strong; but it is to prove the correctness of the doctrines asserted by us, while they are utterly powerless to establish their blasphemy. For tell me, what has the word "was" in common with the word "made"? What hath God in common with man? Why dost thou mix what may not be mixed? Why confound things which are distinct, why bring low what is above? In that place it is not the expression "was" only which denotes eternity, but that One "was in the beginning." And that other, "The Word was"; for as the word "being," when used concerning man, only distinguishes present time, but when concerning God, denotes eternity,[1] so "was," when used respecting our nature, signifies to us past time, and that too limited, but when respecting God it declares eternity. It would have been enough then when one had heard the words "earth" and "man," to imagine nothing more concerning them than what one may fitly think of a nature that came into being,[2] for that which came to be, be it what it may, hath come to be either in time, or the age before time was, but the Son of God is above not only times, but all ages which were before, for He is the Creator and Maker of them, as the Apostle says, "by whom also He made the ages." Now the Maker necessarily is, before the thing made. Yet since some are so senseless, as even after this to have higher notions concerning creatures than is their due, by the expression "He made," and by that other, "there was a man," he lays hold beforehand of the mind of his hearer, and cuts up all shamelessness by the roots. For all that has been made, both heaven and earth, has been made in time, and has its beginning in time, and none of them is without beginning, as having been made: so that when you hear that "he made the earth," and that "there was a man," you are trifling[3] to no purpose, and weaving a tissue of useless folly.

For I can mention even another thing by way of going further. What is it? It is, that if it had been said of the earth, "In the beginning was the earth," and of man, "In the beginning was the man," we must not even then have

---

[1] al. "one ever and through all time."
[2] τὰ ὄντα are opposed to τὰ γενόμενα in the Platonic philosophy. The reading here should be γενητῇ for γεννητῇ, as in the MS. Baroc. no. 210, in the Bodl. Library. Our Lord is γεννητὸς ἀγενήτως.
[3] al. "trifle not."

imagined any greater things concerning them than what we have now determined.[1] For the terms "earth" and "man" as they are presupposed, whatever may be said concerning them, do not allow the mind to imagine to itself anything greater concerning them than what we know at present. Just as "the Word," although but little be said of It, does not allow us to think (respecting It) anything low or poor. Since in proceeding he says of the earth, "The earth was invisible and unformed." For having said that "He made" it, and having settled its proper limit, he afterwards declares fearlessly what follows, as knowing that there is no one so silly as to suppose that it is without beginning and uncreated, since the word "earth," and that other "made," are enough to convince even a very simple person that it is not eternal nor increate, but one of those things created in time.

[3.] Besides, the expression "was," applied to the earth and to man, is not indicative of absolute existence. But in the case of a man (it denotes) his being of a certain place, in that of the earth its being in a certain way. For he has not said absolutely "the earth was," and then held his peace, but has taught how it was even after its creation, as that it was "invisible and unformed," as yet covered by the waters and in confusion. So in the case of Elkanah he does not merely say that "there was a man," but adds also whence he was, "of Armathaim Zophim." But in the case of "the Word," it is not so. I am ashamed to try these cases, one against the other, for if we find fault with those who do so in the case of men, when there is a great difference in the virtue of those who are so tried, though in truth their substance be one; where the difference both of nature and of everything else is so infinite, is it not the extremest madness to raise such questions? But may He who is blasphemed by them be merciful to us. For it was not we who invented the necessity of such discussions, but they who war against their own salvation laid it on us.

What then do I say? That this first "was," applied to "the Word," is only indicative of His eternal Being, (for "In the beginning," he saith, "was the Word,") and that the second "was," ("and the Word was with God,") denotes His relative Being. For since to be eternal and without beginning is most peculiar to God, this he puts first; and then, lest any one hearing that He was "in the beginning," should assert, that He was "unbegotten" also, he immediately remedies this by saying, before he declares what He was, that He was "with God." And he has prevented any one from supposing, that this

"Word" is simply such a one as is either uttered[2] or conceived,[3] by the addition, as I beforesaid, of the article, as well as by this second expression. For he does not say, was "in God," but was "with God": declaring to us His eternity as to person.[4] Then, as he advances, he has more clearly revealed it, by adding, that this "Word" also "was God."

"But yet created," it may be said. What then hindered him from saying, that "In the beginning God made the Word"? at least Moses speaking of the earth says, not that "in the beginning was the earth," but that "He made it," and then it was. What now hindered John from saying in like manner, that "In the beginning God made the Word"? For if Moses feared lest any one should assert that the earth was uncreated,[5] much more ought John to have feared this respecting the Son, if He was indeed created. The world being visible, by this very circumstance proclaims its Maker, (:"the heavens," says the Psalmist, "declare the glory of God" —Ps. xix. 1), but the Son is invisible, and is greatly, infinitely, higher than all creation. If now, in the one instance, where we needed neither argument nor teaching to know that the world is created,[6] yet the prophet sets down this fact clearly and before all others; much more should John have declared the same concerning the Son, if He had really been created.[7]

"Yes," it may be said, "but Peter has asserted this clearly and openly." Where and when? "When speaking to the Jews he said, that 'God hath made Him both Lord and Christ.'" (Acts ii. 36.) Why dost thou not add what follows, "That same Jesus whom ye have crucified"? or dost thou not know that of the words, part relate to His unmixed Nature, part to His Incarnation?[8] But if this be not the case, and thou wilt absolutely understand all as referring to the Godhead, then thou wilt make the Godhead capable of suffering; but if not capable of suffering, then not created. For if blood had flowed from that divine and ineffable Nature, and if that Nature, and not the flesh, had been torn and cut by the nails upon the cross, on this supposition your quibbling would have had reason; but if not even the devil himself could utter such a blasphemy, why dost thou feign to be ignorant with ignorance so unpardonable, and such as not the evil spirits themselves could pretend? Besides the expressions "Lord" and "Christ" belong not to His Essence, but to His dignity; for the one refers to His Power,[9] the other to his having been anointed. What then wouldest thou say con-

---

[1] al. "is now contained in them."

[2] προφορικὸν.
[3] ἐνδιάθετον.
[4] ὑπόστασιν.
[5] ἀγένητον.
[6] γενητός.
[7] κτισθείς.
[8] οἰκονομία signifies all that Christ did and suffered on earth for the salvation of mankind. Vide Euseb. *Hist. Ecc.* i. 1, Not. 11, ed. Heinichen.
[9] ἐξουσία.

cerning the Son of God? for if he were even, as you assert, created, this argument could not have place. For He was not first created and afterwards God chose Him, nor does He hold a kingdom which could be thrown aside, but one which belongs by nature to His Essence; since, when asked if He were a King, He answers, "To this end was I born." (c. xviii. 37.) But Peter speaks as concerning one chosen, because his argument wholly refers to the Dispensation.

[4.] And why dost thou wonder if Peter says this? for Paul, reasoning with the Athenians, calls Him "Man" only, saying, "By that Man whom He hath ordained, whereof He hath given assurance to all men, in that He hath raised Him from the dead." (Acts xvii. 31.) He speaks nothing concerning "the form of God" (Phil. ii. 6), nor that He was "equal to Him," nor that He was the "brightness of His glory." (Heb. i. 3.) And with reason. The time for words like these was not yet come; but it would have contented him that they should in the meanwhile admit that He was Man, and that He rose again from the dead. Christ Himself acted in the same manner, from whom Paul having learned, used this reserve.[1] For He did not at once reveal to us His Divinity, but was at first held to be a Prophet and a good man;[2] but afterwards His real nature was shown by His works and words. On this account Peter too at first used this method, (for this was the first sermon that he made to the Jews;) and because they were not yet able clearly to understand anything respecting His Godhead, he dwelt on the arguments relating to His Incarnation; that their ears being exercised in these, might open a way to the rest of his teaching. And if any one will go through all the sermon from the beginning, he will find what I say very observable, for he (Peter) calls Him "Man," and dwells on the accounts of His Passion, His Resurrection, and His generation according to the flesh. Paul too when he says, "Who was born of the seed of David according to the flesh" (Rom. i. 3), only teaches us that the word "made"[3] is taken with a view[4] to His Incarnation, as we allow. But the son of thunder is now speaking to us concerning His Ineffable and Eternal[5] Existence, and therefore he leaves the word "made" and puts "was"; yet if He were created, this point he needs must most especially have determined. For if Paul feared that some foolish persons might suppose that He shall be greater than the Father, and have Him who begat Him made subject to Him, (for this is the reason why the Apostle in send-

ing to the Corinthians writes, "But when He saith, All things are put under Him, it is manifest that He is excepted which did put all things under Him," yet who could possibly imagine that the Father, even in common with all things, will be subject to the Son?) if, I say, he nevertheless feared these foolish imaginations, and says, "He is excepted that did put all things under Him;" much more if the Son of God were indeed created, ought John to have feared lest any one should suppose Him uncreated, and to have taught on this point before any other.

But now, since He was Begotten, with good reason neither John nor any other, whether apostle or prophet, hath asserted that He was created. Neither had it been so would the Only-Begotten Himself have let it pass unmentioned. For He who spoke of Himself so humbly from condescension[6] would certainly not have been silent on this matter. And I think it not unreasonable to suppose, that He would be more likely to have the higher Nature, and say nothing of it, than not having it to pass by this omission, and fail to make known that He had it not. For in the first case there was a good excuse for silence, namely, His desire to teach mankind humility by being silent as to the greatness of His attributes; but in the second case you can find no just excuse for silence. For why should He who declined many of His real attributes have been, if He were created, silent as to His having been made? He who, in order to teach humility, often uttered expressions of lowliness, such as did not properly belong to Him, much more if He had been indeed created, would not have failed to speak of this. Do you not see Him, in order that none may imagine Him not to have been begotten,[7] doing and saying everything to show that He was so, uttering words unworthy both of His dignity and His essence, and descending to the humble character of a Prophet? For the expression, "As I hear, I judge" (v. 30); and that other, "He hath told Me what I should say, and what I should speak" (xii. 49), and the like, belong merely to a prophet. If now, from His desire to remove this suspicion, He did not disdain to utter words thus lowly, much more if He were created would He have said many like words, that none might suppose Him to be uncreated; as, "Think not that I am begotten of the Father; I am created, not begotten, nor do I share His essence." But as it is, He does the very contrary, and utters words which compel men, even against their will and desire, to admit the opposite opinion. As, "I am in the Father, and the Father in Me" (xiv. 11); and, "Have I been so long time with you, and yet hast thou

---

[1] οὕτω τὰ πράγματα ᾠκονόμει.
[2] al. "and Christ, simply a Man."
[3] "made," E. V.
[4] παρείληπται ἐπὶ τῆς οἰκονομίας, "adopted in reference to."
[5] προαιώνιος.

[6] συγκατάβασις.     [7] ἀγέννητον.

not known Me, Philip? he that hath seen Me, hath seen the Father." (xiv. 9.) And, "That all men should honor the Son, even as they honor the Father." (v. 23.) "As the Father raiseth up the dead and quickeneth them, even so the Son quickeneth whom He will." (v. 21.) "My Father worketh hitherto, and I work." (v. 17.) "As the Father knoweth Me, even so know I the Father." (x. 15.) "I and My Father are One." (x. 30.) And everywhere by putting the "as," and the "so," and the "being with the Father," He declares His undeviating likeness to Him.[1] His power in Himself He manifests by these, as well as by many other words; as when He says, "Peace, be still." (Mark iv. 39.) "I will, be thou clean." (Matt. viii. 3.) "Thou dumb and deaf spirit, I charge thee, come out of him." (Mark ix. 25.) And again, "Ye have heard that it was said by them of old time, Thou shalt not kill; but I say unto you, That whosoever is angry with his brother without a cause, shall be in danger." (Matt. v. 21, 22.) And all the other laws which He gave, and wonders which He worked, are sufficient to show His power, or rather, I should say, a very small part of them is enough to bring over and convince any, except the utterly insensate.

[5.] But vainglory[2] is a thing powerful to blind even to very evident truths the minds of those ensnared by it, and to persuade them to dispute against what is allowed by others; nay, it instigates[3] some who know and are persuaded of the truth to pretended ignorance and opposition. As took place in the case of the Jews, for they did not through ignorance deny the Son of God, but that they might obtain honor from the multitude; "they believed," says the Evangelist, but were afraid, "lest they should be put out of the synagogue." (xii. 40.) And so they gave up[4] their salvation to others.[5] For it cannot be that he who is so zealous a slave to the glory of this present world can obtain the glory which is from God. Wherefore He rebuked them, saying, "How can ye believe, which receive honor of men, and seek not the honor which cometh from God?" (v. 44.) This passion is a sort of deep intoxication, and makes him who is subdued by it hard to recover. And having detached the souls of its captives from heavenly things, it nails them to earth, and lets them not look up to the true light, but persuades them ever to wallow in the mire, giving them masters so powerful, that they have the rule over them without needing to use commands. For the man who is sick of this disease, does of his own accord, and without bidding, all that he

thinks will be agreeable to his masters. On their account he clothes himself in rich apparel, and beautifies his face, taking these pains not for himself but for others; and he leads about a train of followers through the market-place, that others may admire him, and all that he does he goes through, merely out of obsequiousness to the rest of the world. Can any state of mind be more wretched than this? That others may admire him, he is ever being precipitated[6] to ruin.

Would you learn what a tyrannous sway it exercises? Why surely, the words of Christ are sufficient to show it all. But yet listen to these further remarks.[7] If you will ask any of those men who mingle in state affairs and incur great expenses, why they lavish so much gold, and what their so vast expenditure means; you will hear from them, that it is for nothing else but to gratify the people. If again you ask what the people may be; they will say, that it is a thing full of confusion and turbulent, made up for the most part of folly, tossed blindly to and fro like the waves of the sea, and often composed of varying and adverse opinions. Must not the man who has such a master be more pitiable than any one? And yet strange though it be, it is not so strange that worldly men should be eager about these things; but that those who say that they have started away from the world should be sick of this same disease, or rather of one more grievous still, this is the strangest thing of all. For with the first the loss extends only to money, but in the last case the danger reaches to the soul. For when men alter a right faith for reputation's sake, and dishonor God that they may be in high repute themselves, tell me, what excess of stupidity and madness must there not be in what they do? Other passions, even if they are very hurtful, at least bring some pleasure with them, though it be but for a time and fleeting; those who love money, or wine, or women, have, with their hurt, a pleasure, though a brief one. But those who are taken captives by this passion, live a life continually embittered and stripped of enjoyment, for they do not obtain what they earnestly desire, glory, I mean, from the many. They think they enjoy it, but do not really, because the thing they aim at is not glory at all. And therefore their state of mind is not called glory,[8] but a something void of glory, vaingloriousness,[9] so have all the ancients named it, and with good reason; inasmuch as it is quite empty, and contains nothing bright or glorious within it, but as players' masks seem to be bright and lovely, but are hollow within, (for which cause, though they be more

---

[1] τὴν πρὸς αὐτὸν ἀπαραλλαξίαν.
[2] al. "love of rule."
[3] ἀλείφει.
[4] προέτειναν.
[5] i.e. gave up their salvation rather than offend others.

[6] κατακρημνίζεται.
[7] al. "but it may be seen from this."
[8] δόξα.
[9] κενοδοξία, lit. "empty glory."

# HOMILIES OF ST. JOHN CHRYSOSTOM,

## ARCHBISHOP OF CONSTANTINOPLE,

### ON THE

## GOSPEL ACCORDING TO

## ST. JOHN.

---

# HOMILY I

## PREFACE.

[1.] THEY that are spectators of the heathen games, when they have learned that a distinguished athlete and winner of crowns is come from any quarter, run all together to view his wrestling, and all his skill and strength; and you may see the whole theater of many ten thousands, all there straining their eyes both of body and mind, that nothing of what is done may escape them. So again these same persons, if any admirable musician come amongst them, leave all that they had in hand, which often is necessary and pressing business, and mount the steps, and sit listening very attentively to the words and the accompaniments, and criticising the agreement of the two. This is what the many do.

Again; those who are skilled in rhetoric do just the same with respect to the sophists, for they too have their theaters, and their audience, and clappings of hands, and noise, and closest criticism of what is said.

And if in the case of rhetoricians, musicians, and athletes, people sit in the one case to look on, in the other to see at once and to listen with such earnest attention; what zeal, what earnestness ought ye in reason to display, when it is no musician or debater who now comes forward to a trial of skill, but when a man is speaking from heaven, and utters a voice plainer than thunder? for he has pervaded the whole earth with the sound; and occupied and filled it, not by the loudness of the cry, but by moving his tongue with the grace of God.

And what is wonderful, this sound, great as it is, is neither a harsh nor an unpleasant one, but sweeter and more delightful than all harmony of music, and with more skill to soothe; and besides all this, most holy, and most awful, and full of mysteries so great, and bringing with it goods so great, that if men were exactly and with ready mind to receive and keep them, they could no longer be mere men nor remain upon the earth, but would take their stand above all the things of this life, and having adapted themselves to the condition of angels, would dwell on earth just as if it were heaven.

[2.] For the son of thunder, the beloved of Christ, the pillar of the Churches throughout the world, who holds the keys of heaven, who drank the cup of Christ, and was baptized with His baptism, who lay upon his Master's bosom with much confidence,[1] this man comes forward to us now; not as an actor of a play, not hiding his head with a mask, (for he hath another sort of words to speak,) nor mounting a platform,[2] nor striking the stage with his foot, nor dressed out with apparel of gold, but he enters wearing a robe of inconceivable beauty. For he will appear before us having "put on Christ" (Rom. xiii. 14; Gal. iii. 27), having his beautiful "feet shod with the preparation of the Gospel of peace" (Eph. vi. 15); wearing a girdle not about his waist, but about his loins, not made of scarlet leather nor daubed outside[3] with gold, but woven and composed of truth itself. Now will he appear before us, not acting a part, (for with him there is nothing counterfeit, nor fiction, nor fable,) but with unmasked head he

---

[1] παρρησίας πολλῆς.     [2] ὀκρίβαντος.     [3] ἄνωθεν ἠλειμμένην.

proclaims to us the truth unmasked; not making the audience believe him other than he is by carriage, by look, by voice, needing for the delivery of his message no instruments of music, as harp, lyre, or any other the like, for he effects all with his tongue, uttering a voice which is sweeter and more profitable than that of any harper or any music. All heaven is his stage; his theater, the habitable world; his audience, all angels; and of men as many as are angels already, or desire to become so, for none but these can hear that harmony aright, and show it forth by their works; all the rest, like little children who hear, but what they hear understand not, from their anxiety about sweetmeats and childish playthings; so they too, being in mirth and luxury, and living only for wealth and power and sensuality, hear sometimes what is said, it is true, but show forth nothing great or noble in their actions through fastening[1] themselves for good to the clay of the brickmaking. By this Apostle stand the powers from above, marveling at the beauty of his soul, and his understanding, and the bloom of that virtue by which he drew unto him Christ Himself, and obtained the grace of the Spirit. For he hath made ready his soul, as some well-fashioned and jeweled lyre with strings of gold, and yielded it for the utterance of something great and sublime to the Spirit.

[3.] Seeing then it is no longer the fisherman the son of Zebedee, but He who knoweth "the deep things of God" (1 Cor. ii. 10), the Holy Spirit I mean, that striketh this lyre, let us hearken accordingly. For he will say nothing to us as a man, but what he saith, he will say from the depths of the Spirit, from those secret things which before they came to pass the very Angels knew not; since they too have learned by the voice of John with us, and by us, the things which we know. And this hath another Apostle declared, saying, "To the intent that unto the principalities and powers might be known by the Church the manifold wisdom of God." (Eph. iii. 10.) If then principalities, and powers, and Cherubim, and Seraphim, learned these things by the Church, it is very clear that they were exceedingly earnest in listening to this teaching; and even in this we have been not a little honored, that the Angels learned things which before they knew not with us; I do not at present speak of their learning by us also. Let us then show much silence and orderly behavior; not to-day only, nor during the day on which we are hearers, but during all our life, since it is at all times good to hear Him. For if we long to know what is going on in the palace, what, for instance, the king has said, what he has done, what counsel he is taking

concerning his subjects, though in truth these things are for the most part nothing to us; much more is it desirable to hear what God hath said, especially when all concerns us. And all this will this man tell us exactly, as being a friend of the King Himself, or rather, as having Him speaking within himself, and from Him hearing all things which He heareth from the Father. "I have called you friends," He saith, "for all things that I have heard of My Father, I have made known unto you." (John xv. 15.)

[4.] As then we should all run together if we saw one from above bend down "on a sudden"[2] from the height of heaven, promising to describe exactly all things there, even so let us be disposed now. It is from thence that this Man speaketh to us; He is not of this world, as Christ Himself declareth, "Ye are not of the world" (John xv. 19), and He hath speaking within him the Comforter, the Omnipresent, who knoweth the things of God as exactly as the soul of man knoweth what belongs to herself, the Spirit of holiness, the righteous Spirit, the guiding Spirit, which leads men by the hand to heaven, which gives them other eyes, fitting them to see things to come as though present, and giving them even in the flesh to look into things heavenly. To Him then let us yield ourselves during all our life[3] in much tranquillity. Let none dull, none sleepy, none sordid, enter here and tarry; but let us remove ourselves to heaven, for there He speaketh these things to those who are citizens there. And if we tarry on earth, we shall gain nothing great from thence. For the words of John are nothing to those who do not desire to be freed from this swinish life, just as the things of this world to him are nothing. The thunder amazes our souls, having sound without significance;[4] but this man's voice troubles none of the faithful, yea, rather releases them from trouble and confusion; it amazes the devils only, and those who are their slaves. Therefore that we may know how it amazes them, let us preserve deep silence, both external and mental, but especially the latter; for what advantage is it that the mouth be hushed, if the soul is disturbed and full of tossing? I look for that calm which is of the mind, of the soul, since it is the hearing of the soul which I require. Let then no desire of riches trouble us, no lust of glory, no tyranny of anger, nor the crowd of other passions besides these; for it is not possible for the ear, except it be cleansed, to perceive as it ought the sublimity of the things spoken; nor rightly to understand the awful and unutterable nature of these mysteries, and all other virtue which is in

---

[1] προσηλοῦν.

[2] ἄθροον, comp. Eus. *Hist Eccl.* v. i. 29.
[3] πολλὴν παρέχωμεν τὴν ἡσυχίαν.
[4] ἄσημον.

beautiful than natural faces, yet they never draw any to love them,) even so, or rather yet more wretchedly, has the applause of the multitude tricked out for us this passion, dangerous as an antagonist, and cruel as a master. Its countenance alone is bright, but within it is no more like the mask's mere emptiness, but crammed with dishonor, and full of savage tyranny. Whence then, it may be asked, has this passion, so unreasonable, so devoid of pleasure, its birth? Whence else but from a low, mean soul? It cannot be that one who is captivated by love of applause should imagine readily anything great or noble; he needs must be base, mean, dishonorable, little. He who does nothing for virtue's sake, but to please men worthy of no consideration, and who ever makes account of their mistaken and erring opinions, how can he be worth anything? Consider; if any one should ask him, What do you think of the many? he clearly would say, "that they are thoughtless, and not to be regarded." Then if any one again should ask him, "Would you choose to be like them?" I do not suppose he could possibly desire to be like them. Must it not then be excessively ridiculous to seek the good opinion of those whom you never would choose to resemble?

[6.] Do you say that they are many and a sort of collective body? this is the very reason why you ought most to despise them. If when taken singly they are contemptible, still more will this be the case when they are many; for when they are assembled together, their individual folly is increased by numbers, and becomes greater. So that a man might possibly take a single one of them and set him right, but could not do so with them when together, because then their folly becomes intense, and they are led like sheep, and follow in every direction the opinions of one another. Tell me, will you seek to obtain this vulgar glory? Do not, I beg and entreat you. It turns everything upside down; it is the mother of avarice, of slander, of false witness, of treacheries; it arms and exasperates those who have received no injury against those who have inflicted none. He who has fallen into this disease neither knows friendship nor remembers old companionship, and knows not how to respect any one at all; he has cast away from his soul all goodness, and is at war with every one, unstable, without natural affection.

Again, the passion of anger, tyrannical though it be and hard to bear, still is not wont always to disturb, but only when it has persons that excite it; but that of vainglory is ever active, and there is no time, as one may say, when it can cease, since reason neither hinders nor restrains it, but it is always with us not only persuading us to sin, but snatching from our hands anything which we may chance to do aright, or sometimes not allowing us to do right at all. If Paul calls covetousness idolatry, what ought we to name that which is mother, and root, and source of it, I mean, vainglory? We cannot possibly find any term such as its wickedness deserves. Beloved, let us now return to our senses; let us put off this filthy garment, let us rend and cut it off from us, let us at some time or other become free with true freedom, and be sensible of the nobility[1] which has been given to us by God; let us despise vulgar applause. For nothing is so ridiculous and disgraceful as this passion, nothing so full of shame and dishonor. One may in many ways see, that to love honor, is dishonor; and that true honor consists in neglecting honor, in making no account of it, but in saying and doing everything according to what seems good to God. In this way we shall be able to receive a reward from Him who sees exactly all our doings, if we are content to have Him only for a spectator. What need we other eyes, when He who shall confer the prize is ever beholding our actions? Is it not a strange thing that, whatever a servant does, he should do to please his master, should seek nothing more than his master's observation, desire not to attract other eyes (though they be great men who are looking on) to his conduct, but aim at one thing only, that his master may observe him; while we who have a Lord so great, seek other spectators who can nothing profit, but rather hurt us by their observation, and make all our labor vain? Not so, I beseech you. Let us call Him to applaud and view our actions from whom we shall receive our rewards. Let us have nothing to do with human eyes. For if we should even desire to attain this honor, we shall then attain to it, when we seek that which cometh from God alone. For, He saith, "Them that honor Me, I will honor." (1 Sam. ii. 30.) And even as we are best supplied with riches when we despise them, and seek only the wealth which cometh from God ("Seek," he saith, "the kingdom of God, and all these things shall be added to you"—Matt. vi. 33); so it is in the case of honor. When the granting either of riches or honor is no longer attended with danger to us, then God gives them freely; and it is then unattended with danger, when they have not the rule or power over us, do not command us as slaves, but belong to us as masters and free men. For the reason that He wishes us not to love them, is that we may not be ruled by them; and if we succeed in this respect, He gives us them with great liberality. Tell me, what is brighter than Paul, when he says, "We seek not honor of men, neither of you, nor yet of others." (1 Thess. ii. 6.) What then is richer than him

---

[1] εὐγενεία, "high birth."

who hath nothing, and yet possesseth all things? for as I said, when we are not mastered by them, then we shall master them, then we shall receive them. If then we desire to obtain honor, let us shun honor, so shall we be enabled after accom-plishing the laws of God to obtain both the good things which are here, and those which are promised, by the grace of Christ, with whom, to the Father and the Holy Ghost, be glory for ever and ever. Amen.

# HOMILY IV.

## JOHN i. 1.

"In the beginning was the Word, and the Word was with God."

[1.] WHEN children are just brought to their learning, their teachers do not give them many tasks in succession, nor do they set them once for all, but they often repeat to them the same short ones, so that what is said may be easily implanted in their minds, and they may not be vexed at the first onset with the quantity, and with finding it hard to remember, and become less active in picking up what is given them, a kind of sluggish-ness arising from the difficulty. And I, who wish to effect the same with you, and to render your labor easy, take by little and little the food which lies on this Divine table, and instill it into your souls. On this account I shall handle again the same words, not so as to say again the same things, but to set before you only what yet remains. Come, then, let us again apply our discourse to the introduction.

"In the beginning was the Word, and the Word was with God." Why, when all the other Evangelists had begun with the Dispensation[1]; (for Matthew says, "The Book of the generation of Jesus Christ, the Son of David"; and Luke too relates to us in the beginning of his Gospel the events relating to Mary; and in like manner Mark dwells on the same narratives, from that point detailing to us the history of the Baptist;) why, when they began with these matters, did John briefly and in a later place hint at them, saying, "the Word was made flesh" (ver. 14.); and, passing by everything else, His conception, His birth, His bringing up, His growth, at once discourse to us concerning His Eternal Genera-tion?

I will now tell you what the reason of this is. Because the other Evangelists had dwelt most on the accounts of His coming in the flesh, there was fear lest some, being of grovelling minds, might for this reason rest in these doctrines alone, as indeed was the case with Paul of Samosata. In order, therefore, to lead away from this fondness for earth those who were like to fall into it, and to draw them up towards heaven, with good reason he commences his narrative from above, and from the eternal subsistence. For while Matthew enters upon his relation from Herod the king, Luke from Tiberius Cæsar, Mark from the Baptism of John, this Apostle, leaving alone all these things, ascends beyond all time or ·age.[2] Thither darting forward the imagination of his hearers to the "WAS IN THE BEGINNING," not allowing it to stay at any point, nor setting any limit, as they did in Herod, and Tiberius, and John.

And what we may mention besides as espe-cially deserving our admiration is, that John, though he gave himself up to the higher doc-trine,[3] yet did not neglect the Dispensation; nor were the others, though intent upon the relation of this, silent as to the subsistence before the ages. With good cause; for One Spirit It was that moved the souls of all; and therefore they have shown great unanimity in their narrative. But thou, beloved, when thou hast heard of "The Word," do not endure those who say, that He is a work; nor those even who think, that He is simply a word. For many are the words of God which angels execute, but of those words none is God; they all are prophe-cies or commands, (for in Scripture it is usual to call the laws of God His commands, and prophecies, words; wherefore in speaking of the angels, he says, "Mighty in strength, fulfilling His word") (Ps. ciii. 20), but this WORD is a Being with subsistence,[4] proceeding[5] without affection[6] from the Father Himself. For this, as I before said, he has shown by the term "Word." As therefore the expression, "In the beginning was the Word," shows His Eternity, so "was in the beginning with God," has declared to us His Co-eternity. For that you may not, when you hear "In the beginning was the Word," suppose Him to be Eternal, and yet imagine the life of

---

[1] οἰκονομίας.

[2] αἰῶνος.
[3] λόγον.
[4] οὐσία ἐνυπόστατος.

[5] προελθοῦσα.
[6] ἀπαθῶς.

the Father to differ from His by some interval and longer duration, and so assign a beginning to the Only-Begotten, he adds, " was in the beginning with God " ; so eternally even as the Father Himself, for the Father was never without the Word, but He was always God with God, yet Each in His proper Person.[1]

How then, one says, does John assert, that He was in the world, if He was with God? Because He was both[2] with God and in the world also. For neither Father nor Son are limited in any way. Since, if " there is no end of His greatness " (Ps. cxlv. 3), and if " of His wisdom there is no number " (Ps. cxlvii. 5), it is clear that there cannot be any beginning in time[3] to His Essence. Thou hast heard, that " In the beginning God made the heaven and the earth " (Gen. i. 1) ; what dost thou understand from this " beginning "? clearly, that they were created before all visible things. So, respecting the Only-Begotten, when you hear that He was " in the beginning," conceive of him as before all intelligible things,[4] and before the ages.

But if any one say, " How can it be that He is a Son, and yet not younger than the Father? since that which proceeds from something else needs must be later than that from which it proceeds " ; we will say that, properly speaking, these are human reasonings ; that he who questions on this matter will question on others yet more improper ;[5] and that to such we ought not even to give ear. For our speech is now concerning God, not concerning the nature of men, which is subject to the sequence and necessary conclusions of these reasonings. Still, for the assurance of the weaker sort, we will speak even to these points.

[2.] Tell me, then, does the radiance of the sun proceed from the substance[6] itself of the sun, or from some other source? Any one not deprived of his very senses needs must confess, that it proceeds from the substance itself. Yet, although the radiance proceeds from the sun itself, we cannot say that it is later in point of time than the substance of that body, since the sun has never appeared without its rays. Now if in the case of these visible and sensible bodies there has been shown to be something which proceeds from something else, and yet is not after that from whence it proceeds ; why are you incredulous in the case of the invisible and ineffable Nature? This same thing there takes place, but in a manner suitable to That Substance.[7] For it is for this reason that Paul too calls Him " Brightness " (Heb. i. 3) ; setting forth thereby His being from Him and His Co-eternity. Again, tell me, were not all the ages,

and every interval[8] created by Him? Any man not deprived of his senses must necessarily confess this. There is no interval[9] therefore between the Son and the Father ; and if there be none, then He is not after, but Co-eternal with Him. For " before " and " after " are notions implying time, since, without age or time, no man could possibly imagine these words ; but God is above times and ages.

But if in any case you say that you have found a beginning to the Son, see whether by the same reason and argument you are not compelled to reduce the Father also to a beginning, earlier indeed, but still a beginning. For when you have assigned to the Son a limit and beginning of existence, do you not proceed upwards from that point, and say, that the Father was before it? Clearly you do. Tell me then, what is the extent of the Father's prior subsistence? For whether you say that the interval is little, or whether you say it is great, you equally have brought the Father to a beginning. For it is clear, that it is by measuring the space that you say whether it is little or great ; yet it would not be possible to measure it, unless there were a beginning on either side ; so that as far as you are concerned you have given the Father a beginning, and henceforth, according to your argument, not even the Father will be without beginning. See you that the word spoken by the Saviour is true, and the saying everywhere discovers its force? And what is that word? It is, " He that honoreth not the Son, honoreth not the Father." (John v. 23.)

And I know indeed that what now has been said cannot by many be comprehended, and therefore it is that in many places we avoid[10] agitating questions of human reasonings, because the rest of the people cannot follow such arguments, and if they could, still they have nothing firm or sure in them. " For the thoughts of mortal men are miserable, and our devices are but uncertain." (Wisd. ix. 14.) Still I should like to ask our objectors, what means that which is said by the Prophet, " Before Me there was no God formed, nor is there any after Me "? (Isa. xliii. 10.) For if the Son is younger than the Father, how, says He, " Nor is there[11] any after me "? Will you take away the being of the Only-Begotten Himself? You either must dare this, or admit one Godhead with distinct Persons of the Father and Son.

Finally, how could the expression, " All things were made by Him," be true? For if there is an age older than He, how can that[12] which was before Him have been made by Him? See ye to what daring the argument has carried them,

---

1 ὑποστάσει.　　　4 νοητῶν.
2 al. " God with God."　　　5 ἀτοπώτερα.
3 χρονικῇ.　　　6 φύσεως.
7 Τὸ αὐτὸ δὴ τοῦτο ἐστιν οὕτως ὡς ἐκείνῃ τῇ οὐσίᾳ πρέπον ἦν.

8 διάστημα.　　　11 LXX. ἔστιν.
9 μέσον.　　　12 τὸ, al. ὁ.
10 ἀναβαλλόμεθα, " put off."

when once the truth has been unsettled? Why did not the Evangelist say, that He was made from things that were not, as Paul declares of all things, when he says, "Who calleth those things which be not as though they were"; but says, "Was in the beginning"? (Rom. iv. 17.) This is contrary to that; and with good reason. For God neither is made,[1] nor has anything older; these are words of the Greeks.[2] Tell me this too: Would you not say, that the Creator beyond all comparison excels His works? Yet since that which is from things that were not is similar to them, where is the superiority not admitting of comparison? And what mean the expressions, "I am the first and I am the last" (Isa. xliv. 6); and, "before Me was no other God formed"? (Isa. xliii. 10.) For if the Son be not of the same Essence, there is another God; and if He be not Co-eternal, He is after Him; and if He did not proceed from His Essence, clear it is that He was made. But if they assert, that these things were said to distinguish Him from idols, why do they not allow that it is to distinguish Him from idols that he says, "the Only True God"? (John xvii. 3.) Besides, if this was said to distinguish Him from idols, how would you interpret the whole sentence? "After Me," He says, "is no other God." In saying this, He does not exclude the Son, but that "After Me there is no idol God," not that "there is no Son." Allowed, says he; what then? and the expression, "Before Me was no other God formed," will you so understand, as that no idol God indeed was formed before Him, but yet a Son was formed before Him? What evil spirit would assert this? I do not suppose that even Satan himself would do so.

Moreover, if He be not Co-eternal with the Father, how can you say that His Life is infinite? For if it have a beginning from before,[3] although it be endless, yet it is not infinite; for the infinite must be infinite in both directions. As Paul also declared, when he said, "Having neither beginning of days, nor end of life" (Heb. vii. 3); by this expression showing that He is both without beginning and without end. For as the one has no limit, so neither has the other. In one direction there is no end, in the other no beginning.

[3.] And how again, since He is "Life," was there ever when He was not? For all must allow, that Life both is always, and is without beginning and without end, if It be indeed Life, as indeed It is. For if there be when It is not, how can It be the life of others, when It even Itself is not?

"How then," says one, "does John lay down a beginning by saying, 'In the beginning was'?" Tell me, have you attended to the "In the beginning," and to the "was," and do you not understand the expression, "the Word was"? What! when the Prophet says, "From everlasting[4] and to everlasting Thou art" (Ps. xc. 2), does he say this to assign Him limits? No, but to declare His Eternity. Consider now that the case is the same in this place. He did not use the expression as assigning limits, since he did not say, "had a beginning," but "was in the beginning"; by the word "was" carrying thee forward to the idea that the Son is without beginning. "Yet observe," says he, "the Father is named with the addition of the article, but the Son without it." What then, when the Apostle says, "The Great God, and our Saviour Jesus Christ" (Tit. ii. 13); and again, "Who is above all, God"? (Rom. ix. 5.) It is true that here he has mentioned the Son, without the article; but he does the same with the Father also, at least in his Epistle to the Philippians (c. ii. 6), he says, "Who being in the form of God, thought it not robbery to be equal with God"; and again to the Romans, "Grace to you, and peace, from God our Father, and the Lord Jesus Christ." (Rom. i. 7.) Besides, it was superfluous for it to be attached in that place, when close[5] above it was continually attached to "the Word." For as in speaking concerning the Father, he says, "God is a Spirit" (John iv. 24), and we do not, because the article is not joined to "Spirit," yet deny the Spiritual Nature of God; so here, although the article is not annexed to the Son, the Son is not on that account a less God. Why so? Because in saying "God," and again "God," he does not reveal to us any difference in this Godhead, but the contrary; for having before said, "and the Word was God"; that no one might suppose the Godhead of the Son to be inferior, he immediately adds the characteristics of genuine Godhead, including Eternity, (for "He was," says he, "in the beginning with God,") and attributing to Him the office of Creator. For "by Him were all things made, and without Him was not anything made that was made"; which His Father also everywhere by the Prophets declares to be especially characteristic of His own Essence. And the Prophets are continually busy on this kind of demonstration, not only of itself, but when they contend against the honor shown to idols; "Let the gods perish," says one "who have not made heaven and earth" (Jer. x. 11): and again, "I have stretched out the heaven with My hand" (Isa. xliv. 24); and it is as declaring it to be indicative of Divinity, that

---

1 γίνεται.
2 Heathens.
3 ἄνωθεν, "a parte ante."

4 ἀπὸ τοῦ αἰῶνος.          5 συνεχῶς.

He everywhere puts it.   And the Evangelist himself was not satisfied with these words, but calls Him " Life " too and " Light."   If now He was ever with the Father, if He Himself created all things, if He brought all things into existence, and keeps together[1] all things, (for, this he meant by " Life,") if He enlightens all things, who so senseless as to say, that the Evangelist desired to teach an inferiority of Divinity by those very expressions, by which, rather than by any others, it is possible to express its equality and not differing?   Let us not then confound the creation with the Creator, lest we too hear it said of us, that " they served the creature rather than the Creator" (Rom. i. 25) ; for although it be asserted that this is said of the heavens, still in speaking of the heavens he positively says, that we must not serve[2] the creature, for it is a heathenish[3] thing.

[4.] Let us therefore not lay ourselves under this curse.   For this the Son of God came, that He might rid us from this service ; for this He took the form of a slave, that He might free us from this slavery ; for this He was spit upon, for this He was buffeted, for this He endured the shameful death.   Let us not, I entreat you, make all these things of none effect, let us not go back to our former unrighteousness, or rather to unrighteousness much more grievous ; for to serve the creature is not the same thing as to bring down the Creator, as far at least as in us lies, to the meanness of the creature.   For He continues being such as He is ; as says the Psalmist, " Thou art the same, and Thy years shall not fail."   (Ps. cii. 27.)   Let us then glorify Him as we have received from our fathers, let us glorify Him both by our faith and by our works ; for sound doctrines avail us nothing to salvation, if our life is corrupt.   Let us then order it according to what is well-pleasing to God, setting ourselves far from all filthiness, unrighteousness, and covetousness, as strangers and foreigners and aliens to the things here on earth.   If any have much wealth and possessions, let him so use them as one who is a sojourner, and who, whether he will or not, shall shortly pass from them.   If one be injured by another, let him not be angry forever, nay rather not even for a time.   For the Apostle has not allowed us more than a single day for the venting of anger.

" Let not," says he, " the sun go down upon your wrath " (Eph. iv. 26) ; and with reason ; for it is matter for contentment that even in so short a time nothing unpleasant take place ; but if night also overtake us, what has happened becomes more grievous, because the fire of our wrath is increased ten thousand times by memory, and we at our leisure enquire into it more bitterly. Before therefore we obtain this pernicious leisure and kindle a hotter fire, he bids us arrest beforehand and quench the mischief.   For the passion of wrath is fierce, fiercer than any flame ; and so we need much haste to prevent the flame, and not allow it to blaze up high, for so this disease becomes a cause of many evils.   It has overturned whole houses, it has dissolved old companionships, and has worked tragedies not to be remedied in a short moment of time. " For," saith one, " the sway of his fury shall be his destruction."   (Ecclus. i. 22.)   Let us not then leave such a wild beast unbridled, but put upon him a muzzle in all ways strong, the fear of the judgment to come.   Whenever a friend grieves thee, or one of thine own family exasperates thee, think of the sins thou hast committed against God, and that by kindness towards him thou makest that judgment more lenient to thyself, (" Forgive," saith He, " and ye shall be forgiven") (Luke vi. 37), and thy passion shall quickly skulk away.[4]

And besides, consider this, whether there has been a time when thou wert being carried away into ferocity, and didst control thyself, and another time when thou hast been dragged along by the passion.   Compare the two seasons, and thou shalt gain thence great improvement.   For tell me, when didst thou praise thyself?   Was it when thou wast worsted, or when thou hadst the mastery?   Do we not in the first case vehemently blame ourselves, and feel ashamed even when none reproves us, and do not many feelings of repentance come over us, both for what we have said and done ; but when we gain the mastery, then are we not proud, and exult as conquerors?   For victory in the case of anger is not the requiting evil with the like, (that is utter defeat,) but the bearing meekly to be ill treated and ill spoken of.   To get the better is not to inflict but to suffer evil.   Therefore when angry do not say, " certainly I will retaliate," " certainly I will be revenged " ; do not persist in saying to those who exhort you to gain a victory, " I will not endure that the man mock me, and escape clear."   He will never mock thee, except when thou avengest thyself ; or if he even should mock thee he will do so as a fool.   Seek not when thou conquerest honor from fools, but consider that sufficient which comes from men of understanding.   Nay, why do I set before thee a small and mean body of spectators, when I make it up of men?   Look up straight to God : He will praise thee, and the man who is approved by Him must not seek honor from mortals.   Mortal honor often arises from flattery or hatred of others, and brings no profit ; but the

---

[1] συγκροτεῖ, al. συγκρατεῖ.
[2] λατρεύειν.
[3] Ἑλληνικὸν.

[4] δραπετεύσει.

decision of God is free from this inequality, and brings great advantage to the man whom He approves. This praise then let us follow after.

Will you learn what an evil is anger? Stand by while others are quarreling in the forum. In yourself you cannot easily see the disgrace of the thing, because your reason is darkened and drunken; but when you are clear from the passion, and while your judgment is sound, view your own case in others. Observe, I pray you, the crowds collecting round, and the angry men like maniacs acting shamefully in the midst. For when the passion boils up within the breast, and becomes excited and savage, the mouth breathes fire, the eyes emit fire, all the face becomes swollen, the hands are extended disorderly, the feet dance ridiculously, and they spring at those who restrain them, and differ nothing from madmen in their insensibility to all these things; nay, differ not from wild asses, kicking and biting. Truly a passionate man is not a graceful one.

And then, when after this exceedingly ridiculous conduct, they return home and come to themselves, they have the greater pain, and much fear, thinking who were present when they were angry. For like raving men, they did not then know the standers by, but when they have returned to their right mind, then they consider, were they friends? were they foes and enemies that looked on? And they fear alike about both; the first because they will condemn them and give them more shame; the others because they will rejoice at it. And if they have even exchanged blows, then their fear is the more pressing; for instance, lest anything very grievous happen to the sufferer; a fever follow and bring on death, or a troublesome swelling rise and place him in danger of the worst. And, "what need" (say they) "had I of fighting, and violence, and quarreling? Perish such things." And then they curse the ill-fated business which caused them to begin, and the more foolish lay on "wicked spirits," and "an evil hour," the blame of what has been done; but these things are not from an evil hour, (for there is no such thing as an evil hour,) nor from a wicked spirit, but from the wickedness of those captured by the passion; they draw the spirits to them, and bring upon themselves all things terrible. "But the heart swells," says one, "and is stung by insults." I know it; and that is the reason why I admire those who master this dreadful wild beast; yet it is possible if we will, to beat off the passion.

For why when our rulers insult us do we not feel it? It is because fear counterbalances the passion, and frightens us from it, and does not allow it to spring up at all. And why too do our servants, though insulted by us in ten thousand ways, bear all in silence? Because they too have the same restraint laid upon them. And think thou not merely of the fear of God, but that it is even God Himself who then insults thee, who bids thee be silent, and then thou wilt bear all things meekly, and say to the aggressor, How can I be angry with thee? there is another that restrains both my hand and my tongue; and the saying will be a suggestion of sound wisdom, both to thyself and to him. Even now we bear unbearable things on account of men, and often say to those who have insulted us, "Such an one insulted me, not you." Shall we not use the same caution in the case of God? How else can we hope for pardon? Let us say to our soul, "It is God who holds our hands, who now insults us; let us not be restive, let not God be less honored by us than men." Did ye shudder at the word? I wish you would shudder not at the word only, but at the deed. For God hath commanded us when buffeted not only to endure it, but even to offer ourselves to suffer something worse; and we withstand Him with such vehemence, that we not only refuse to offer ourselves to suffer evil, but even avenge ourselves, nay often are the first to act on the offensive,[1] and think we are disgraced if we do not the same in return. Yes, and the mischief is, that when utterly worsted we think ourselves conquerors, and when lying undermost and receiving ten thousand blows from the devil, then we imagine that we are mastering him. Let us then, I exhort you, understand what is the nature[2] of this victory, and this kind of nature[3] let us follow after. To suffer evil is to get the crown. If then we wish to be proclaimed victors by God, let us not in these contests observe the laws of heathen games, but those of God, and learn to bear all things with longsuffering; for so we may get the better of our antagonists, and obtain both present and promised goods, through the grace and lovingkindness of our Lord Jesus Christ, through whom and with whom to the Father and the Holy Spirit be glory, power, and honor, now and ever, and world without end. Amen.

---

1 ἄρχειν χειρῶν ἀδίκων.        3 τρόπου τὸ εἶδος.
2 τρόπος.

# HOMILY V.

## John i. 3.

"All things were made by Him; and without Him was not anything made that was made."

[1.] Moses in the beginning of the history and writings of the Old Testament speaks to us of the objects of sense, and enumerates them to us at length. For, "In the beginning," he says, "God made the heaven and the earth," and then he adds, that light was created, and a second heaven and the stars, the various kinds of living creatures, and, that we may not delay by going through particulars, everything else. But this Evangelist, cutting all short, includes both these things and the things which are above these in a single sentence; with reason, because they were known to his hearers, and because he is hastening to a greater subject, and has instituted all his treatise, that he might speak not of the works but of the Creator, and Him who produced them all. And therefore Moses, though he has selected the smaller portion of the creation, (for he has spoken nothing to us concerning the invisible powers,) dwells on these things;[1] while John, as hastening to ascend to the Creator Himself, runs by both these things, and those on which Moses was silent, having comprised them in one little saying, "All things were made by Him." And that you may not think that he merely speaks of all the things mentioned by Moses, he adds, that "without Him was not anything made that was made." That is to say, that of created things, not one, whether it be visible[2] or intelligible[3] was brought into being without the power of the Son.

For we will not put the full stop after "not anything," as the heretics do. They, because they wish to make the Spirit created, say, "What was made, in Him was Life"; yet so what is said becomes unintelligible. First, it was not the time here to make mention of the Spirit, and if he desired to do so, why did he state it so indistinctly? For how is it clear that this saying relates to the Spirit? Besides, we shall find by this argument, not that the Spirit, but that the Son Himself, is created by Himself. But rouse yourselves, that what is said may not escape you; and come, let us read for a while after their fashion, for so its absurdity will be clearer to us. "What was made, in Him was Life." They say that the Spirit is called "Life."

But this "Life" is found to be also "Light," for he adds, "And the Life was the Light of men." (Ver. 4.) Therefore, according to them the "Light of men" here means the Spirit. Well, but when he goes on to say, that "There was a man sent from God, to bear witness of that Light" (vers. 6, 7), they needs must assert, that this too is spoken of the Spirit; for whom he above called "Word," Him as he proceeds he calls "God," and "Life," and "Light." This "Word" he says was "Life," and this "Life" was "Light." If now this Word was Life, and if this Word and this Life became flesh, then the Life, that is to say, the Word, "was made flesh, and we beheld" Its "glory, the glory as of the Only-Begotten of the Father." If then they say that the Spirit is here called "Life," consider what strange consequences will follow. It will be the Spirit, not the Son, that was made flesh; the Spirit will be the Only-Begotten Son.

And those who read the passage so will fall, if not into this, yet in avoiding this into another most strange conclusion. If they allow that the words are spoken of the Son, and yet do not stop or read as we do, then they will assert that the Son is created by Himself. Since, if "the Word was Life," and "what was made in Him was Life"; according to this reading He is created in Himself and through Himself. Then after some words between, he has added, "And we beheld His glory, the glory as of the Only-Begotten of the Father." (Ver. 14.) See, the Holy Spirit is found, according to the reading of those who assert these things, to be also an only-begotten Son, for it is concerning Him that all this declaration is uttered by him. See when the word has swerved[4] from the truth, whither it is perverted, and what strange consequences it produces!

What then, says one, is not the Spirit "Light"? It is Light: but in this place there is no mention of the Spirit. Since even God (the Father) is called "Spirit," that is to say, incorporeal, yet God (the Father) is not absolutely meant wherever "Spirit" is mentioned. And why do you wonder if we say this of the Father? We could not even say of the Comforter, that wherever "Spirit" (is mentioned), the Comforter is absolutely meant, and yet this is His most distinctive name; still not always where Spirit (is mentioned is) the Comforter (meant). Thus Christ is called "the power of God" (1 Cor. i. 24),

---

[1] i.e. the visible creation.
[2] ὁρατὸν.
[3] νοητὸν.
[4] ἐκκυλίσθη, lit. "been rolled away."

and "the wisdom of God"; yet not always where "the power" and "the wisdom of God" are mentioned is Christ meant; so in this passage, although the Spirit does give "Light," yet the Evangelist is not now speaking of the Spirit.

When we have shut them out from these strange opinions, they who take all manner of pains to withstand the truth, say, (still clinging to the same reading,) "Whatever came into existence[1] by him was life, because," says one, "whatever came into existence was life." What then do you say of the punishment of the men of Sodom, and the flood, and hell fire, and ten thousand like things? "But," says one, "we are speaking of the material creation."[2] Well, these too belong entirely to the material creation. But that we may out of our abundance[3] refute their argument, we will ask them, "Is wood, life," tell me? "Is stone, life?" these things that are lifeless and motionless? Nay, is man absolutely life? Who would say so? he is not pure life,[4] but is capable of receiving life.

[2.] See here again, an absurdity; by the same succession of consequences we will bring the argument to such a point, that even hence you may learn their folly. In this way they assert things by no means befitting of the Spirit. Being driven from their other ground, they apply those things to men, which they before thought to be spoken worthily of the Spirit. However, let us examine the reading itself this way also. The creature is now called "life," therefore, the same is "light," and John came to witness concerning it. Why then is not he also "light"? He says that "he was not that light" (ver. 8), and yet he belonged to created things? How then is he not "light"? How was he "in the world, and the world was made by him"? (Ver. 10.) Was the creature in the creature, and was the creature made by the creature? But how did "the world know him not"? How did the creature not know the creature? "But as many as received him, to them gave he power to become the sons of God." (Ver. 12.) But enough of laughter. For the rest I leave it to you to attack these monstrous reasonings, that we may not seem to have chosen[5] to raise a laugh for its own sake, and waste the time without cause. For if these things are neither said of the Spirit, (and it has been shown that they are not,) nor of anything created, and yet they still hold to the same reading, that stranger conclusion than any which we before mentioned, will follow, that the Son was made by Himself. For if the Son is the true Light, and this Light was Life, and this Life was made in Him, this must needs be the result according to their own

reading. Let us then relinquish this reading, and come to the recognized reading and explanation.[6]

And what is that? It is to make the sentence end at "was made," and to begin the next sentence with, "In Him was Life." What (the Evangelist) says is this, "Without Him was not anything made that was made"; whatever created thing was made, says he, was not made without Him. See you how by this short addition he has rectified all the besetting[7] difficulties; for the saying, that "without Him was not anything made," and then the adding, "which was made," includes things cognizable by the intellect,[8] but excludes the Spirit. For after he had said that "all things were made by Him," and "without Him was not anything made," he needed this addition, lest some one should say, "If all things were made by Him, then the Spirit also was made." "I," he replies, "asserted that whatever was made was made by Him, even though it be invisible, or incorporeal, or in the heavens. For this reason, I did not say absolutely, 'all things,' but 'whatever was made,' that is, 'created things,' but the Spirit is uncreated."

Do you see the precision of his teaching? He has alluded to the creation of material things, (for concerning these Moses had taught before him,) and after bringing us to advance from thence to higher things, I mean the immaterial and the invisible, he excepts the Holy Spirit from all creation. And so Paul, inspired by the same grace, said, "For by Him were all things created." (Col. i. 16.) Observe too here again the same exactness. For the same Spirit moved this soul also. That no one should except any created things from the works of God because of their being invisible, nor yet should confound the Comforter with them, after running through the objects of sense which are known to all, he enumerates also things in the heavens, saying, "Whether they be thrones, or dominions, or principalities, or powers"; for the expression "whether" subjoined to each, shows to us nothing else but this, that "by Him all things were made, and without Him was not anything made that was made."

But if you think that the expression "by"[9] is a mark of inferiority, (as making Christ an instrument,) hear him say, "Thou, Lord, in the beginning, hast laid the foundation of the earth, and the heavens are the work of Thy hands." (Ps. cii. 25.) He says of the Son what is said of the Father in His character of Creator; which he would not have said, unless he had deemed of Him as of a Creator, and yet not subservient

---

[1] γέγονε.
[2] δημιουργίας.
[3] ἐκ περιουσίας.
[4] αὐτοζωή.
[5] Sav. and Ms. Bodl. προῃρῆσθαι.
[6] ἐξήγησιν.
[7] ὑφορμοῦντα, lit. "blockading."
[8] i.e. the things of the invisible world, opposed to ὁρατά.
[9] Or, through διά.

to any. And if the expression "by Him" is here used, it is put for no other reason but to prevent any one from supposing the Son to be Unbegotten. For that in respect of the title of Creator He is nothing inferior to the Father; hear from Himself, where He saith, "As the Father raiseth up the dead and quickeneth them, even so the Son quickeneth whom He will." (c. v. 21.) If now in the Old Testament it is said of the Son, "Thou, Lord, in the beginning hast laid the foundation of the earth," His title of Creator is plain. But if you say that the Prophet spoke this of the Father, and that Paul attributed to the Son what was said of the Father, even so the conclusion is the same. For Paul would not have decided that the same expression suited the Son, unless he had been very confident that between Father and Son there was an equality of honor; since it would have been an act of extremest rashness to refer what suited an incomparable Nature to a nature inferior to, and falling short of it. But the Son is not inferior to, nor falls short of, the Essence of the Father; and therefore Paul has not only dared to use these expressions concerning Him, but also others like them. For the expression "from Whom," which you decide to belong properly to the Father alone, he uses also concerning the Son, when he says, "from which all the body by joints and bands having nourishment ministered, and knit together, increaseth with the increase of God." (Col. ii. 19.)

[3.] And he is not content with this only, he stops your mouths in another way also, by applying to the Father the expression "by whom," which you say is a mark of inferiority. For he says, "God is faithful, by whom ye were called unto the fellowship of His Son" (1 Cor. i. 9): and again, "By His will" (1 Cor. i. 1, &c.); and in another place, "For of Him, and through Him, and to Him, are all things." (Rom. xi. 26.) Neither is the expression "from[1] whom," assigned to the Son only, but also to the Spirit; for the angel said to Joseph, "Fear not to take unto thee Mary thy wife, for that which is conceived in her is of the Holy Ghost." (Matt. i. 20.) As also the Prophet does not deem it improper to apply to the Father the expression "in whom,"[2] which belongs to the Spirit, when he says, "In[3] God we shall do valiantly." (Ps. lx. 12.) And Paul, "Making request, if by any means now at length I might have a prosperous journey, in the will of God, to come unto you." (Rom. i. 10.) And again he uses it of Christ, saying, "In Christ Jesus." (Rom. vi. 11, 23, &c.) In short, we may often and continually find these expressions interchanged;[4] now this would not have taken place, had not the same

Essence been in every instance their subject. And that you may not imagine that the words, "All things were made by Him," are in this case used concerning His miracles, (for the other Evangelists have discoursed concerning these;) he farther goes on to say, "He was in the world, and the world was made by Him"; (but not the Spirit, for This is not of the number of created things, but of those above all creation.)

Let us now attend to what follows. John having spoken of the work of creation, that "All things were made by Him, and without Him was not anything made that was made," goes on to speak concerning His Providence, where he saith, "In Him was Life." That no one may doubt how so many and so great things were "made by Him," he adds, that "In Him was Life." For as with the fountain which is the mother of the great deeps, however much you take away you nothing lessen the fountain; so with the energy of the Only-Begotten, however much you believe has been produced and made by it, it has become no whit the less. Or, to use a more familiar example, I will instance that of light, which the Apostle himself added immediately, saying, "And the Life was the Light." As then light, however many myriads it may enlighten, suffers no diminution of its own brightness; so also God, before commencing His work and after completing it, remains alike indefectible, nothing diminished, nor wearied by the greatness of the creation. Nay, if need were that ten thousand, or even an infinite number of such worlds be created, He remains the same, sufficient for them all not merely to produce, but also to control them after their creation. For the word "Life" here refers not merely to the act of creation, but also to the providence (engaged) about the permanence of the things created; it also lays down beforehand the doctrine of the resurrection, and is the beginning[5] of these marvelous good tidings.[6] Since when "life" has come to be with us, the power of death is dissolved; and when "light" has shone upon us, there is no longer darkness, but life ever abides within us, and death cannot overcome it. So that what is asserted of the Father might be asserted absolutely of Him (Christ) also, that "In Him we live and move and have our being." (Col. i. 16, 17.) As Paul has shown when he says, "By Him were all things created," and "by Him all things consist"; for which reason He has been called also "Root"[7] and "Foundation."[8]

But when you hear that "In Him was Life," do not imagine Him a compound Being, since

---

[1] ἐκ.　　[2] ἐν ᾧ.　　[3] ἐν.
[4] i.e. applied alike to the different Persons in the Holy Trinity.

[5] ἄρχεται.
[6] Or, "Gospels," Acts xvii. 28.
[7] Isa. xi. 10, as quoted Rom. xv. 12; Rev. xxii. 16.
[8] 1 Cor. iii. 11.

farther on he says of the Father also, "As the Father hath Life in Himself, so hath He given to the Son also to have Life" (John v. 26); now as you would not on account of this expression say that the Father is compounded, so neither can you say so of the Son. Thus in another place he says, that "God is Light" (1 John i. 5), and elsewhere (it is said), that He "dwelleth in light unapproachable" (1 Tim. vi. 16); yet these expressions are used not that we may suppose a compounded nature,[1] but that by little and little we may be led up to the highest doctrines. For since one of the multitude could not easily have understood how His life was Life Impersonate,[2] he first used that humbler expression, and afterwards leads them (thus) trained to the higher doctrine. For He who had said that "He hath given Him (the Son) to have life" (c. v. 26); the Same saith in another place, "I am the Life" (c. xiv. 6); and in another, "I am the Light." (c. viii. 12.) And what, tell me, is the nature of this "light"? This kind (of light) is the object not of the senses, but of the intellect, enlightening the soul herself. And since Christ should hereafter say, that "None can come unto Me except the Father draw him" (c. vi. 44); the Apostle has in this place anticipated an objection, and declared that it is He (the Son) who "giveth light" (ver. 9); that although you hear a saying like this concerning the Father, you may not say that it belongs to the Father only, but also to the Son. For, "All things," He saith, "which the Father hath are Mine." (c. xvi. 15.)

First then, the Evangelist hath instructed us respecting the creation, after that he tells us of the goods relating to the soul which He supplied to us by His coming; and these he has darkly described in one sentence, when he says, "And the Life was the Light of men." (Ver. 4.) He does not say, "was the light of the Jews," but universally "of men": nor did the Jews only, but the Greeks also, come to this knowledge, and this light was a common proffer made[3] to all. "Why did he not add 'Angels,' but said, 'of men'?" Because at present his discourse is of the nature of men, and to them he came bearing glad tidings of good things.

"And the light shineth in darkness." (Ver. 5.) He calls death and error, "darkness." For the light which is the object of our senses does not shine in darkness, but apart from it; but the preaching of Christ hath shone forth in the midst of prevailing error, and made it to disappear. And He by enduring death[4] hath so overcome death, that He hath recovered those already held by it. Since then neither death overcame it, nor

error, since it is bright everywhere, and shines by its proper strength, therefore he says,

"And the darkness comprehended it not." For it cannot be overcome, and will not dwell in souls which wish not to be enlightened.

[4.] But let it not trouble thee that It took not all, for not by necessity and force, but by will and consent[5] does God bring us to Himself. Therefore do not thou shut thy doors against this light, and thou shalt enjoy great happiness.[6] But this light cometh by faith, and when it is come, it lighteth abundantly him that hath received it; and if thou displayest a pure life (meet) for it, remains indwelling within continually. "For," He saith, "He that loveth Me, will keep My commandments; and I and My Father will come unto him, and make Our abode with him." (John xiv. 23; slightly varied.) As then one cannot rightly enjoy the sunlight, unless he opens his eyes; so neither can one largely share this splendor, unless he have expanded the eye of the soul, and rendered it in every way keen of sight.

But how is this effected? Then when we have cleansed the soul from all the passions. For sin is darkness, and a deep darkness; as is clear, because men do it unconsciously and secretly. For, "every one that doeth evil hateth the light, neither cometh to the light." (c. iii. 20.) And, "It is a shame even to speak of those things which are done of them in secret." (Eph. v. 12.) For, as in darkness a man knows neither friend nor foe, but cannot perceive any of the properties of objects; so too is it in sin. For he who desires to get more gain, makes no difference between friend and enemy; and the envious regards with hostile eyes the man with whom he is very intimate; and the plotter is at mortal quarrel with all alike. In short, as to distinguishing the nature of objects, he who commits sin is no better than men who are drunk or mad. And as in the night, wood, lead, iron, silver, gold, precious stones, seem to us all alike on account of the absence of the light which shows their distinctions; so he who leads an impure life knows neither the excellence of temperance nor the beauty of philosophy. For in darkness, as I said before, even precious stones if they be displayed do not show their luster, not by reason of their own nature, but because of the want of discernment in the beholders. Nor is this the only evil which happens to us who are in sin, but this also, that we live in constant fear: and as men walking in a moonless night tremble, though none be by to frighten them; so those who work iniquity cannot have confidence, though there be none to accuse them; but they are afraid of everything,

---

[1] σύνθεσιν.
[2] ἐνυπόστατος.
[3] κοινὸν προύκειτο.
[4] Lit. "having been in death."
[5] βουλήσει καὶ γνώμη.
[6] τρυφῆς, "spiritual enjoyment."

and are suspicious, being pricked by their conscience : all to them is full of fear and distress,[1] they look about them at everything, are terrified at everything. Let us then flee a life so painful, especially since after this painfulness shall follow death ; a deathless death, for of the punishment in that place there will be no end ; and in this life they (who sin) are no better than madmen, in that they are dreaming of things that have no existence. They think they are rich when they are not rich, that they enjoy when they are not enjoying, nor do they properly perceive the cheat until they are freed from the madness and have shaken off the sleep. Wherefore Paul exhorts all to be sober, and to watch ; and Christ also commands the same. For he who is sober and awake, although he be captured by sin, quickly beats it off; while he who sleeps and is beside himself, perceives not how he is held prisoner of it.

Let us then not sleep. This is not the season of night, but of day. Let us therefore "walk honestly[2] as in the day" (Rom. xiii. 13) ; and nothing is more indecent than sin. In point of indecency it is not so bad to go about naked as in sin and wrong doing. That is not so great matter of blame, since it might even be caused by poverty ; but nothing has more shame and less honor than the sinner. Let us think of those who come to the justice-hall on some account of extortion, or overreaching ;[3] how base and ridiculous they appear to all by their utter shamelessness, their lies, and audacity.[4] But we are such pitiable and wretched beings, that we cannot bear ourselves to put on a garment awkwardly or awry ; nay, if we see another person in this state, we set him right ; and yet though we and all our neighbors are walking on our heads, we do not even perceive it. For what, say, can be more shameful than a man who goes in to a harlot? what more contemptible than an insolent, a foul-tongued or an envious man? Whence then is it that these things do not seem so disgraceful as to walk naked? Merely from habit. To go naked no one has ever willingly endured ; but all men are continually venturing on the others without any fear. Yet if one came into an assembly of angels, among whom nothing of the sort has ever taken place, there he would clearly see the great ridicule (of such conduct). And why do I say an assembly of angels? Even in the very palaces among us, should one introduce a harlot and enjoy her, or be oppressed by excess of wine, or commit any other like indecency, he would suffer extreme punishment. But if it be intolerable that men should dare such things in palaces, much more when the King is everywhere present, and observes what is done, shall we if we dare them undergo severest chastisement. Wherefore let us, I exhort you, show forth in our life much gentleness, much purity, for we have a King who beholds all our actions continually. In order then that this light may ever richly enlighten us, let us gladly accept[6] these bright beams,[7] for so shall we enjoy both the good things present and those to come, through the grace and lovingkindness of our Lord Jesus Christ, by whom, and with whom, to the Father, and the Holy Spirit, be glory for ever and ever. Amen.

# HOMILY VI.

### JOHN i. 6.

"There was a man sent from God, whose name was John."

[1.] HAVING in the introduction spoken to us things of urgent importance[5] concerning God the Word, (the Evangelist) proceeding on his road, and in order, afterwards comes to the herald of the Word, his namesake John. And now that thou hearest that he was "sent from God," do not for the future imagine that any of the words spoken by him are mere man's words ; for all that he utters is not his own, but is of Him who sent him. Wherefore he is called[8] "messenger" (Mal. iii. 1), for the excellence of a messenger is, that he say nothing of his own. But the expression "was," in this place is not significative of his coming into existence, but refers to his office of messenger ; for "'there was' a man sent from God," is used instead of "a man 'was sent' from God."

How then do some say,[9] that the expression, "being in the form of God" (Phil. ii. 6) is not

---

[1] ἀγωνίας.
[2] εὐσχημόνως, "decently."
[3] πλεονεξίας.
[4] ἰταμευόμενοι.
[5] τὰ κατεπείγοντα.
[6] ἐπισπασώμεθα.
[7] ἀκτῖνα.
[8] al. προηγόρευται, "is foretold."
[9] Vid. supra, Hom. iv. 3.

used of His invariable likeness[1] to the Father, because no article is added?[2] For observe, that the article is nowhere added here. Are these words then not spoken of the Father? What then shall we say to the prophet who says, that, "Behold, I send My messenger before Thy face, who shall prepare Thy way" (Mal. iii. 1, as found in Mark i. 2)? for the expressions "My" and "Thy" declare two Persons.

Ver. 7. "The same came for a witness, to bear witness of that Light."

What is this, perhaps one may say, the servant bear witness to his Master? When then you see Him not only witnessed to by His servant, but even coming to him, and with Jews baptized by him, will you not be still more astonished and perplexed? Yet you ought not to be troubled nor confused, but amazed at such unspeakable goodness. Though if any still continue bewildered[3] and confused, He will say to such an one what He said to John, "Suffer it to be so now, for thus it becometh us to fulfill all righteousness" (Matt. iii. 15); and, if any be still further troubled, again He will say to him too[4] what he said to the Jews, "But I receive not testimony from man." (c. v. 34.) If now he needs not this witness, why was John sent from God? Not as though He required his testimony — this were extremest blasphemy. Why then? John himself informs us, when he says,

"That all men through him might believe."

And Christ also, after having said that "I receive not testimony from man" (c. v. 34), in order that He may not seem to the foolish to clash with[5] Himself, by declaring at one time, "There is another that beareth witness of Me, and I know that his[6] witness is true" (c. v. 32), (for He pointed to John;) and at another, "I receive not testimony from man" (c. v. 34); He immediately adds the solution of the doubt, "But these things I say" for your own sake,[7] "that ye might be saved." As though He had said, that "I am God, and the really-Begotten[8] Son of God, and am of that Simple and Blessed Essence, I need none to witness to Me; and even though none would do so, yet am not I by this anything diminished in My Essence; but because I care for the salvation of the many,[9] I have descended to such humility as to commit the witness of Me to a man." For by reason of the groveling nature and infirmity of the Jews, the faith in Him would in this way be more easily received, and more palatable.[10] As then

He clothed Himself with flesh, that he might not, by encountering men with the unveiled Godhead, destroy them all; so He sent forth a man for His herald, that those who heard might at the hearing of a kindred voice approach more readily. For (to prove) that He had no need of that (herald's) testimony, it would have sufficed that He should only have shown Himself who He was in His unveiled Essence, and have confounded them all. But this He did not for the reason I have before mentioned. He would have annihilated[11] all, since none could have endured the encounter of that unapproachable light.[12] Wherefore, as I said, He put on flesh, and entrusted the witness (of Himself) to one of our fellow-servants, since He arranged[13] all for the salvation of men, looking not only to His own honor, but also to what might be readily received by, and be profitable to, His hearers. Which He glanced at when He said, "These things I say" for your sake, "that ye might be saved." (c. v. 34.) And the Evangelist using the same language as his Master, after saying, "to bear witness of that Light," adds,

"That all men through Him might believe." All but saying, Think not that the reason why John the Baptist came to bear witness, was that he might add aught to the trustworthiness of his Master. No; (He came,) that by his means beings of his own class[14] might believe. For it is clear from what follows, that he used this expression in his anxiety to remove this suspicion beforehand, since he adds,

Ver. 8. "He was not that Light."

Now if he did not introduce this as setting himself against this suspicion, then the expression is absolutely superfluous, and tautology rather than elucidation of his teaching. For why, after having said that he "was sent to bear witness of that Light," does he again say, "He was not that Light"? (He says it,) not loosely or without reason; but, because, for the most part, among ourselves, the person witnessing is held to be greater, and generally more trustworthy than the person witnessed of; therefore, that none might suspect this in the case of John, at once from the very beginning he removes this evil suspicion, and having torn it up by the roots, shows who this is that bears witness, and who is He who is witnessed of, and what an interval there is between the witnessed of, and the bearer of witness. And after having done this, and shown His incomparable superiority, he afterwards proceeds fearlessly to the narrative which remains; and after carefully removing whatever strange (ideas) might secretly harbor[15] in the

---

[1] ἀπαραλλαξία, vid. supra, Hom. iii. 4 ad fin.
[2] i.e. to Θεοῦ.
[3] ἰλιγγιῶν, "dizzy."
[4] [καὶ πρὸς αὐτὸν], perhaps "and with reference to him (the Baptist), Sav. al. καὶ πρὸς σέ.
[5] περιπίπτειν.
[6] αὐτοῦ. ἣν μαρτυρεῖ περὶ ἐμοῦ. G. T.
[7] δι' ὑμᾶς (not in G. T.).
[8] γνήσιος, "genuine."
[9] τῶν πολλῶν.
[10] εὐκολωτέρα.
[11] ἠφάνισε.
[12] Lit. "unapproachable encounter of that light."
[13] ἐπραγματεύσατο.
[14] ὁμόφυλοι.
[15] ὑφορμοῦν.

minds of the simpler sort, so instills into all[1] easily and without impediment the word of doctrine in its proper order.

Let us pray then, that henceforth with the revelation of these thoughts and rightness of doctrine, we may have also a pure life and bright conversation,[2] since these things profit nothing unless good works be present with us. For though we have all faith and all knowledge of the Scriptures, yet if we be naked and destitute of the protection derived from (holy) living, there is nothing to hinder us from being hurried into the fire of hell, and burning for ever in the unquenchable flame. For as they who have done good shall rise to life everlasting, so they who have dared the contrary shall rise to everlasting punishment, which never has an end. Let us then manifest all eagerness not to mar the gain which accrues to us from a right faith by the vileness of our actions, but becoming well-pleasing to Him by these also, boldly to look on Christ. No happiness can be equal to this. And may it come to pass, that we all having obtained[7] what has been mentioned, may do all to the glory of God; to whom, with the Only-Begotten Son and the Holy Ghost, be glory for ever and ever. Amen.

# HOMILY VII.

## JOHN i. 9.

"That was the true Light, which lighteth every man that cometh into the world."

[1.] THE reason, O children greatly beloved, why we entertain you portion by portion with the thoughts taken from the Scriptures, and do not at once pour all forth to you, is, that the retaining what is successively set before you may be easy. For even in building, one who before the first stones are settled lays on others, constructs[3] a rotten wall altogether, and easily thrown down: while one who waits that the mortar may first get hard, and so adds what remains little by little, finishes the whole house firmly, and makes it strong, not one to last for a short time, or easily to fall to pieces. These builders we imitate,[4] and in like manner build up your souls. For we fear lest, while the first foundation is but newly laid, the addition of the succeeding speculations[5] may do harm to the former, through the insufficiency of the intellect to contain them all at once.

What now is it that has been read to us to-day?

"That was the true Light, which lighteth every man that cometh into the world." For since above in speaking of John he said, that he came "to bear witness of that Light"; and that he was sent in these our days;[6] lest any one at hearing this should, on account of the recent coming of the witness, conceive some like suspicion concerning Him, who is witnessed of, he has carried up the imagination, and transported it to that existence which is before all beginning, which has neither end nor commencement.

"And how is it possible," says one, "that being a Son, He should possess this (nature)?" We are speaking of God, and do you ask how? And do you not fear nor shudder? Yet should any one ask you, "How should our souls and bodies have endless life in the world to come?[8]" you will laugh at the question, on the ground that it does not belong to the intellect of man to search into such questions, but that he ought only to believe, and not to be over-curious on the subject mentioned, since he has a sufficient proof of the saying, in the power of Him who spake it. And if we say, that He, who created our souls and bodies, and who incomparably excels all created things, is without beginning, will, you require us to say "How?" Who could assert this to be the act of a well-ordered soul, or of sound reason? you have heard that "That was the true Light": why are you vainly and rashly striving to overshoot[9] by force of reasoning this Life which is unlimited? You cannot do it. Why seek what may not be sought? Why be curious about what is incomprehensible? Why search what is unsearchable? Gaze upon the very source of the sunbeams. You cannot; yet you are neither vexed nor impatient at your weakness; how then have you become so daring and headlong in greater matters? The son of thunder, John who sounds[10] the spiritual trumpet, when he had heard from the Spirit the WAS, enquired no farther. And are you, who share not in his grace, but speak from your own wretched

---

[1] al. "goes on and instills."
[2] πολιτεία.
[3] ὑφαίνει.
[4] al. "let us imitate."
[5] θεωρημάτων.
[6] νῦν.
[7] al. "living worthily of."
[8] μετὰ ταῦτα.
[9] ὑπερακοντίσαι.
[10] al. "holds."

reasonings, ambitious to exceed the measure of his knowledge? Then for this very reason you will never be able even to reach to the measure of his knowledge. For this is the craft of the devil: he leads away those who obey him from the limits assigned by God, as though to things much greater: but when, having enticed us by these hopes, he has cast us out of the grace of God, he not only gives nothing more, (how can he, devil as he is?) but does not even allow us to return again to our former situation, where we dwelt safely and surely, but leads us about in all directions wandering and not having any standing ground. So he caused the first created man to be banished from the abode of 'Paradise. Having puffed him up with the expectation of greater knowledge and honor, he expelled him from what he already possessed in security. For he not only did not become like a god as (the devil) promised him, but even fell beneath the dominion of death; having not only gained no further advantage by eating of the tree, but having lost no small portion of the knowledge which he possessed, through hope of greater knowledge. For the sense of shame, and the desire to hide himself because of his nakedness, then came upon him, who before the cheat was superior to all such shame; and this very seeing himself to be naked, and the need for the future of the covering of garments, and many other infirmities,[1] became thenceforth natural to him. That this be not our case, let us obey God, continue in His commandments, and not be busy about anything beyond them, that we may not be cast out from the good things already given us. Thus they have fared (of whom we speak). For seeking to find a beginning of the Life which has no beginning, they lost what they might have retained. They found not what they sought, (this is impossible,) and they fell away from the true faith concerning the Only-Begotten.

Let us not then remove the eternal bounds which our fathers set, but let us ever yield to the laws of the Spirit; and when we hear that "That was the true Light," let us seek to discover nothing more. For it is not possible to pass beyond this saying. Had His generation been like that of a man, needs must there have been an interval between the begetter and the begotten; but since it is in a manner ineffable and becoming God, give up the "before" and the "after," for these are the names of points in time, but the Son is the Creator even of all ages.[2]

[2.] "Then," says one, "He is not Father, but brother." What need, pray? If we had asserted that the Father and the Son were from a different root, you might have then spoken this well. But, if we flee this impiety, and say the Father, besides being without beginning, is Unbegotten also, while the Son, though without beginning, is Begotten of the Father, what kind of need that as a consequence of this idea, that unholy assertion should be introduced? None at all. For He is an Effulgence: but an effulgence is included in the idea of the nature whose effulgence it is. For this reason Paul has called Him so, that you may imagine no interval between the Father and the Son. (Heb. i. 3.) This expression[3] therefore is declaratory of the point; but the following part of the proof quoted, corrects an erroneous opinion which might beset simple men. For, says the Apostle, do not, because you have heard that he is an Effulgence, suppose that He is deprived of His proper person; this is impious, and belongs to the madness of the Sabellians, and of Marcellus' followers. We say not so, but that He is also in His proper Person. And for this reason, after having called Him "Effulgence," Paul has added that He is "the express image of His Person" (Heb. i. 3), in order to make evident His proper Personality, and that He belongs to the same Essence of which He is also the express image. For, as I before[4] said, it is not sufficient by a single expression to set before men the doctrines concerning God, but it is desirable that we bring many together, and choose from each what is suitable. So shall we be able to attain to a worthy telling of His glory, worthy, I mean, as regards our power; for if any should deem himself able to speak words suitable to His essential worthiness, and be ambitious to do so, saying, that he knows God as God knows Himself, he it is who is most ignorant of God.

Knowing therefore this, let us continue steadfastly to hold what "they have delivered unto us, which from the beginning were eye-witnesses, and ministers of the word." (Luke i. 2.) And let us not be curious beyond: for two evils will attend those who are sick of this disease, (curiosity,) the wearying themselves in vain by seeking what it is impossible to find, and the provoking God by their endeavors to overturn the bounds set by Him. Now what anger this excites, it needs not that you who know should learn from us. Abstaining therefore from their madness, let us tremble at His words, that He may continually build us up. For, "upon whom shall I look" (Isa. lxvi. 2, LXX.), saith He, "but upon the lowly, and quiet, and who feareth my words?" Let us then leave this pernicious curiosity, and bruise our hearts, let us mourn for our sins as Christ commanded, let us be pricked at heart[5] for our transgressions, let us reckon up exactly all the wicked deeds, which

---

[1] πάθη.   [2] αἰώνων.   [3] ἀπαύγασμα.   [4] Hom. ii. 4.   [5] κατανυγῶμεν.

in time past we have dared, and let us earnestly strive to wipe them off in all kinds of ways.

Now to this end God hath opened to us many ways. For, "Tell thou first," saith He, "thy sins, that thou mayest be justified" (Isa. xliii. 26[1]); and again, "I said, I have declared mine iniquity unto Thee, and Thou hast taken[2] away the unrighteousness of my heart" (Ps. xxxii. 5, LXX.); since a continual accusation and remembrance of sins contributes not a little to lessen their magnitude. But there is another more prevailing way than this; to bear malice against none of those who have offended against us, to forgive their trespasses to all those who have trespassed against us. Will you learn a third? Hear Daniel, saying, "Redeem thy sins by almsdeeds, and thine iniquities by showing mercy to the poor." (Dan. iv. 27, LXX.) And there is another besides this; constancy in prayer, and persevering attendance on the intercessions[3] made with God. In like manner fasting brings to us some, and that not small comfort and release from sins committed,[4] provided it be attended with kindness to others, and

quenches the vehemence of the wrath of God. (1 Tim. ii. 1.) For "water will quench a blazing fire, and by almsdeeds sins are purged away." (Ecclus. iii. 30, LXX.)

Let us then travel along all these ways; for if we give ourselves wholly to these employments, if on them we spend our time, not only shall we wash off our bygone transgressions, but shall gain very great profit for the future. For we shall not allow the devil to assault us with leisure either for slothful living, or for pernicious curiosity, since by these among other means, and in consequence of these, he leads us to foolish questions and hurtful disputations, from seeing us at leisure, and idle, and taking no forethought for excellency of living. But let us block up this approach against him, let us watch, let us be sober, that having in this short time toiled a little, we may obtain eternal goods in endless ages, by the grace and lovingkindness of our Lord Jesus Christ; by whom and with whom to the Father and the Holy Ghost, be glory for ever and ever. Amen.

# HOMILY VIII.

JOHN i. 9.

"That was the true Light, which lighteth every man that cometh into the world."

[1.] NOTHING hinders us from handling to-day also the same words, since before we were prevented by the setting forth of doctrines, from considering all that was read. Where now are those who deny that He is true God? for here He is called "the true Light" (c. xiv. 6), and elsewhere very "Truth" and very "Life." That saying we will discuss more clearly when we come to the place; but at present we must for a while be speaking to your Charity of that other matter.

If He "lighteth every man that cometh into the world," how is it that so many continue unenlightened? for not all have known the majesty of Christ. How then doth He "light every man"? He lighteth all as far as in Him lies. But if some, wilfully closing the eyes of their mind, would not receive the rays of that Light, their darkness arises not from the nature of the Light, but from their own wickedness, who wilfully deprive themselves of the gift. For the grace is shed forth upon all, turning itself back

neither from Jew, nor Greek, nor Barbarian, nor Scythian, nor free, nor bond, nor male, nor female, nor old, nor young, but admitting all alike, and inviting with an equal regard. And those who are not willing to enjoy this gift, ought in justice to impute their blindness to themselves; for if when the gate is opened to all, and there is none to hinder, any being wilfully evil[5] remain without, they perish through none other, but only through their own wickedness.

Ver. 10. "He was in the world."

But not as of equal duration with the world. Away with the thought. Wherefore he adds, "And the world was made by Him"; thus leading thee up again to the eternal[6] existence of the Only-Begotten. For he who has heard that this universe is His work, though he be very dull, though he be a hater, though he be an enemy of the glory of God, will certainly, willing or unwilling, be forced to confess that the maker is before his works. Whence wonder always comes over me at the madness of Paul of Samosata, who dared to look in the face so manifest a truth, and voluntarily threw himself down the preci-

---

[1] Slightly varied from LXX.
[2] al. "forgiven."
[3] ἐντεύξεσιν.
[4] λύσιν τῶν ἡμαρτημένων.
[5] ἐθελοκακοῦντες.
[6] προαιώνιον.

pice.[1] For he erred not ignorantly but with full knowledge, being in the same case as the Jews. For as they, looking to men, gave up sound faith, knowing that he was the only-begotten Son of God, but not confessing Him, because of their rulers, lest they should be cast out of the synagogue; so it is said that he, to gratify a certain woman,[2] sold his own salvation. A powerful thing, powerful indeed, is the tyranny of vainglory; it is able to make blind the eyes even of the wise, except they be sober; for if the taking of gifts can effect this, much more will the yet more violent feeling of this passion. Wherefore Jesus said to the Jews, "How can ye believe, which receive honor one of another, and seek not the honor that cometh from God only?" (c. v. 44.)

"And the world knew Him not." By "the world" he here means the multitude, which is corrupt, and closely attached[3] to earthly things, the common[4] turbulent, silly people. For the friends and favorites[5] of God all knew Him, even before His coming in the flesh. Concerning the Patriarch Christ Himself speaks by name, "that your father Abraham rejoiced to see My day, and he saw it, and was glad." (c. viii. 56.) And concerning David, confuting the Jews He said, "How then doth David in spirit call Him Lord, saying, the Lord said unto my Lord, Sit Thou on My right hand." (Matt. xxii. 43; Mark xii. 36; Luke xx. 42.) And in many places, disputing with them, He mentions Moses; and the Apostle (mentions) the rest of the prophets; for Peter declares, that all the prophets from Samuel knew Him, and proclaimed beforehand His coming afar off, when he says, "All the prophets from Samuel and those that follow after, as many as have spoken, have likewise foretold of these days." (Acts iii. 24.) But Jacob and his father, as well as his grandfather, He both appeared to and talked with, and promised that He would give them many and great blessings, which also He brought to pass.

"How then," says one, "did He say Himself, 'Many prophets have desired to see those things which ye see, and have not seen them; and to hear those things which ye hear, and have not heard them'? (Luke x. 24.) Did they then not share in the knowledge of Him?" Surely they did; and I will endeavor to make this plain from this very saying, by which some think that they are deprived of it. "For many," He saith, "have desired to see the things which ye see." So that they knew that He would come [to men]

from heaven, and would live and teach[6] as He lived and taught; for had they not known, they could have not desired, since no one can conceive desire for things of which he has no idea; therefore they knew the Son of Man, and that He would come among men. What then are the things which they did not hear? What those which they did not know? The things which ye now see and hear. For if they did hear His voice and did see Him, it was not in the Flesh, not among men; nor when He was living so familiarly, and conversing so frankly with them.[7] And indeed He to show this said not simply, "to see" "Me": but what? "the things which ye see"; nor "to hear" "Me": but what? "the things which ye hear."[8] So that if they did not behold His coming in the Flesh, still they knew that it would be, and they desired it, and believed on Him without having seen Him in the Flesh.

When therefore the Greeks bring charges such as these against us, and say; "What then did Christ in former time, that He did not look upon the race of men? And for what possible reason did He come at last to assist in our salvation, after neglecting us so long?" we will reply, that before this He was in the world, and took thought for His works, and was known to all who were worthy. But if ye should say, that, because all did not then know Him, because He was only known by those noble and excellent persons, therefore He was not acknowledged; at this rate you will not allow that He is worshiped even now, since even now all men do not know Him. But as at present no one, because of those who do not know Him, would refuse credit to those who do, so as regards former times, we must not doubt that He was known to many, or rather to all of those noble and admirable persons.

[2.] And if any one say, "Why did not all men give heed to Him? nor all worship Him, but the just only?" I also will ask, why even now do not all men know him? But why do I speak of Christ, when not all men knew His Father then, or know Him now? For some say, that all things are borne along by chance, while others commit the providence of the universe to devils. Others invent another God besides Him, and some blasphemously assert, that His is an opposing power,[9] and think that His laws are the laws of a wicked dæmon. What then? Shall we say that He is not God because their

---

[1] Paul of Samosata, Bishop of Antioch, denied the Personality of our Lord before His Birth of the Virgin Mary. His opinions were condemned, and himself deposed, at the second Council of Antioch, A.D. 270.
[2] Zenobia, Queen of Palmyra, who supported Paul against the Catholics after his deposition.
[3] προστετηκὸς, "melted to."    [4] χυδαῖον.    [5] θαυμαστοί.

[6] οἰκονομήσοντα, lit. "would dispense as He did dispense."
[7] μετ᾽ ἀδείας.
[8] al. "for they had both heard His voice, and seen Him, but not in the flesh."
[9] i.e. that the power which maintains the universe is a power opposed to the True God. The Gnostics accounted for the existence of evil, by supposing an evil Principle, to which they attributed the creation and support of the material world. The opinions here spoken of were maintained by Basilides, Valentinus, Marcion, Manes, and other supporters of that heresy.

are some who say so? And shall we confess Him to be evil? for there are some who even so blaspheme Him. Away with such mental wandering, such utter insanity. If we should delineate [1] doctrines according to the judgment of madmen, there is nothing to hinder us from being mad ourselves with most grievous madness. No one will assert, looking to those who have weak vision, that the sun is injurious to the eyes, but he will say that it is fitted to give light, drawing his judgments from persons in health. And no one will call honey bitter, because it seems so to the sense of the sick. And will any, from the imaginations of men diseased (in mind) decide that God either is not, or is evil; or that He sometimes indeed exerts His Providence, sometimes doth not so at all? Who can say that such men are of sound mind, or deny that they are beside themselves, delirious, utterly mad?

"The world," he says, "knew Him not"; but they of whom the world was not worthy knew Him. And having spoken of those who knew Him not, he in a short time puts the cause of their ignorance; for he does not absolutely say, that no one knew Him, but that "the world knew him not"; that is, those persons who are as it were nailed to the world alone, and who mind the things of the world. For so Christ was wont to call them; as when He says, "O Holy [2] Father, the world hath not known Thee." (c. xvii. 25.) The world then was ignorant, not only of Him, but also of His Father, as we have said; for nothing so darkens [3] the mind as to be closely attached [4] to present things.

Knowing therefore this, remove yourselves from the world, and tear yourselves as much as possible from carnal things, for the loss which comes to you from these lies not in common matters, but in what is the chief of goods. For it is not possible for the man who clings strongly to the things of the present life really [5] to lay hold on those in heaven, but he who is earnest about the one must needs lose the other. "Ye cannot," He says, "serve God and Mammon" (Matt. vi. 24), for you must hold to the one and hate the other. And this too the very experience of the things proclaims aloud. Those, for instance, who deride the lust of money, are especially the persons who love God as they ought, just as those who respect that sovereignty (of Mammon), are the men who above all others have the slackest [6] love for Him. For the soul when made captive once for all [7] by covetousness, will not easily or readily refuse doing or saying any of the things which anger God, as being the slave of another master, and one who gives all his commands in direct opposition to God. Return then at length to your sober senses, and rouse yourselves, and calling to mind whose servants we are, let us love His kingdom only; let us weep, let us wail for the times past in which we were servants of Mammon; let us cast off once for all his yoke so intolerable, so heavy, and continue to bear the light and easy yoke of Christ. For He lays no such commands upon us as Mammon does. Mammon bids us be enemies to all men, but Christ, on the contrary, to embrace and to love all. The one having nailed us [8] to the clay and the brickmaking, (for gold is this,) allows us not even at night to take breath a little; the other releases us from this excessive and insensate care, and bids us gather treasures in heaven, not by injustice towards others, but by our own righteousness. The one after our many toils and sufferings is not able to assist us when we are punished in that place, [9] and suffer because of his laws, nay, he increases the flame; the other, though He command us to give but a cup of cold water, never allows us to lose our reward and recompense even for this, but repays us with great abundance. How then is it not extremest folly to slight a rule so mild, so full of all good things, and to serve a thankless, ungrateful tyrant, and one who neither in this world nor in the world to come is able to help those who obey and give heed to him. Nor is this the only dreadful thing, nor is this only the penalty, that he does not defend them when they are being punished; but that besides this, he, as I before said, surrounds those who obey him with ten thousand evils. For of those who are punished in that place, one may see that the greater part are punished for this cause, that they were slaves to money, that they loved gold, and would not assist those who needed. That we be not in this case, let us scatter, let us give to the poor, let us deliver our souls from hurtful cares in this world, and from the vengeance, which because of these things is appointed for us in that place. Let us store up righteousness in the heavens. Instead of riches upon earth, let us collect treasures impregnable, treasures which can accompany us on our journey to heaven, which can assist us in our peril, and make the Judge propitious at that hour. Whom may we all have gracious unto us, both now and at that day, and enjoy with much confidence [10] the good things prepared in the heavens for those who love Him as they ought, through the grace and lovingkindness of our Lord Jesus Christ, with whom, to the Father and the Holy Ghost, be glory, now and ever, and world without end. Amen.

---

[1] χαρακτηρίζειν.          [2] Ἅγις (δίκαις G. T.).
[3] θολοῖ from θολὸς, " the ink of the cuttle fish." [4] προστετηκέναι.
[5] γνησίως ;, perhaps " as befits a rightful heir."
[6] al. ἀμβλυτέραν, " duller."          [7] καθάπαξ.

[8] προσηλώσας.          [9] ἐκεῖ.
[10] Or " with much openness," i.e. before angels and men.

# HOMILY IX.

John i. 11.

"He came unto His own, and His own received Him not."

[1.] If ye remember our former reflections, we shall the more zealously proceed with the building up [1] of what remains, as doing so for great gain. For so will our discourse be more intelligible to you who remember what has been already said, and we shall not need much labor, because you are able through your great love of learning to see more clearly into what remains. The man who is always losing what is given to him will always need a teacher, and will never know anything; but he who retains what he has received, and so receives in addition what remains, will quickly be a teacher instead of a learner, and useful not only to himself, but to all others also; as, conjecturing from their great readiness to hear, I anticipate that this assembly will specially be. Come then, let us lay up in your souls, as in a safe treasury, the Lord's money, and unfold, as far as the grace of the Spirit may afford us power, the words this day set before us.

He (St. John) had said, speaking of the old times, that "the world knew him not" (ver. 10); afterwards he comes down in his narrative to the times of the proclamation (of the Gospel), and says, "He came to His own, and His own received Him not," now calling the Jews "His own," as His peculiar people, or perhaps even all mankind, as created by Him. And as above, when perplexed at the folly of the many, and ashamed of our common nature, he said that "the world by Him was made," and having been made, did not recognize its Maker; so here again, being troubled beyond bearing [2] at the stupidity of the Jews and the many, he sets forth the charge in a yet more striking manner, saying, that "His own received Him not," and that too when "He came to them." And not only he, but the prophets also, wondering, said the very same, as did afterwards Paul, amazed at the very same things. Thus did the prophets cry aloud in the person of Christ, saying, "A people whom I have not known, have served Me; as soon as they heard Me, they obeyed Me; the strange children have dealt falsely with Me.[3] The strange children have waxed aged, and have halted from their paths." (Ps. xviii. 43-45, LXX.) And again, "They to whom it had not been told concerning Him, shall see, and they which had not heard, shall understand." And, "I was found of them that sought Me not" (Isa. lii. 15); "I was made manifest unto them that asked not after me." (Isa. xlv. 1, as quoted Rom. x. 20.) And Paul, in his Epistles to the Romans, has said, "What then? Israel hath not obtained that which he seeketh for: but the election hath obtained it." (Rom. xi. 7.) And again; "What shall we say then? That the Gentiles which followed not after righteousness, have attained unto righteousness: but Israel which followed after the law of righteousness, hath not attained to the law of righteousness." (Rom. ix. 30.)

For it is a thing indeed worthy of our amazement, how they who were nurtured in (knowledge of) the prophetical books, who heard Moses every day telling them ten thousand things concerning the coming of the Christ, and the other Prophets afterwards, who moreover themselves beheld Christ Himself daily working miracles among them, giving up His time [4] to them alone, neither as yet allowing His disciples to depart into the way of the Gentiles, or to enter into a city of Samaritans, nor doing so Himself, but everywhere [5] declaring that He was sent to the lost sheep of the house of Israel (Matt. x. 5): how, (I say), while they saw the signs, and heard the Prophets, and had Christ Himself continually putting them in remembrance, they yet made themselves once for all so blind and dull, as by none of these things to be brought to faith in Christ. (Matt. xv. 24.) While they of the Gentiles, who had enjoyed none of these things, who had never heard the oracles of God, not, as one may say, so much as in a dream, but ever ranging among the fables of madmen, (for heathen philosophy is this,) having ever in their hands [6] the sillinesses of their poets, nailed to stocks and stones, and neither in doctrines nor in conversation [7] possessing anything good or sound. (For their way of life was more impure and more accursed than their doctrine. As was likely; for when they saw their gods delighting in all wickedness, worshiped by shameful words, and more shameful deeds, reckoning this festivity and praise, and moreover honored by foul murders, and child-slaughters, how should not they emulate these things?) Still, fallen as they were as low as the very depth of wickedness, on a

---

[1] al. "the dispensing."
[2] δυσανασχετῶν.
[3] "lied unto me." LXX.
[4] al. "conversing with."
[5] ἄνω καὶ κάτω.
[6] ἀνελίττοντες, "unrolling."
[7] πολιτείας.

sudden, as by the agency of some machine, they have appeared to us shining from on high, and from the very summit of heaven.

How then and whence came it to pass? Hear Paul telling you. For that blessed person searching exactly into these things, ceased not until he had found the cause, and had declared it to all others. What then is it? and whence came such blindness upon the Jews? Hear him who was entrusted with this stewardship declare. What then does he say in resolving this doubt of the many? (1 Cor. ix. 17.) "For they," says he, "being ignorant of God's righteousness, and going about to establish their own righteousness, have not submitted themselves unto the righteousness of God." (Rom. x. 3.) Wherefore they have suffered this. And again, explaining the same matter in other terms, he says, "What shall we say then? That the Gentiles which followed not after righteousness, have attained unto righteousness, even the righteousness which is of faith; but Israel, which followed after the law of righteousness, hath not attained to the law of righteousness. Wherefore? Because they sought it not by faith. For they stumbled at that stumbling stone." (Rom. ix. 30, 32.) His meaning is this: "These men's unbelief has been the cause of their misfortunes, and their haughtiness was parent of their unbelief." For when having before enjoyed greater privileges than the heathen,[1] through having received the law, through knowing God, and the rest which Paul enumerates, they after the coming of Christ saw the heathen and themselves called on equal terms through faith, and after faith received one of the circumcision in nothing preferred to the Gentile, they came to envy and were stung by their haughtiness, and could not endure the unspeakable and exceeding lovingkindness of the Lord. So this has happened to them from nothing else but pride, and wickedness, and unkindness.

[2.] For in what, O most foolish of men, are ye injured by the care[2] bestowed on others? How are your blessings made less through having others to share the same? But of a truth wickedness is blind, and cannot readily perceive anything that it ought. Being therefore stung by the prospect of having others to share the same confidence,[3] they thrust a sword against themselves, and cast themselves out from the lovingkindness of God. And with good reason. For He saith, "Friend, I do thee no wrong, I will give to 'these also' even as unto thee." (Matt. xx. 14.) Or rather, these Jews are not deserving even of these words. For the man in the parable if he was discontented, could·yet speak of the labors and weariness, the heat and sweat, of a whole day. But what could these

men have to tell? nothing like this, but slothfulness and profligacy and ten thousand evil things of which all the prophets continued ever to accuse them, and by which they like the Gentiles had offended against God. And Paul declaring this says, "For there is no difference between the Jew and the Greek: For all have sinned, and come short of the glory of God: being justified freely by His grace." (Rom. x. 12; Rom. iii. 22–24.) And on this head he treats profitably and very wisely throughout that Epistle. But in a former part of it he proves that they are worthy of still greater punishment. "For as many as have sinned in the law shall be judged by the law" (Rom. ii. 12); that is to say, more severely, as having for their accuser the law as well as nature. And not for this only, but for that they have been the cause that God is blasphemed among the Gentiles: "My[4] Name," He saith, "is blasphemed among the Gentiles through you." (Rom. ii. 24; Isa. lii. 5.)

Since now this it was that stung them most, (for the thing appeared incredible even to those of the circumcision who believed, and therefore they brought it as a charge against Peter, when he was come up to them from Cesarea, that he "went in to men uncircumcised, and did eat with them" (Acts xi. 3); and after that they had learned the dispensation of God, even so still[5] they wondered how "on the Gentiles also was poured out the gift of the Holy Ghost" (Acts x. 45): showing by their astonishment that they could never have expected so incredible a thing,) since then he knew that this touched them nearest, see how he has emptied[6] their pride and relaxed[7] their highly swelling insolence. For after having discoursed on the case of the heathen,[8] and shown that they had not from any quarter any excuse, or hope of salvation, and after having definitely charged them both with the perversion[9] of their doctrines and the uncleanness of their lives, he shifts his argument to the Jews; and[10] after recounting all the expressions of the Prophet, in which he had said that they were polluted, treacherous, hypocritical persons, and had "altogether become unprofitable," that there was "none" among them "that seeketh after God," that they had "all gone out of the way" (Rom. iii. 12), and the like, he adds, "Now we know that what things soever the law saith, it saith to them who are under the law: that every mouth may be stopped, and all the world may become guilty before God." (Rom. iii. 19.) "For all have sinned, and come short of the glory of God." (Rom. iii. 23.)

---

1 Ἑλλήνων.　　2 κηδεμονίας.　　3 παρρησίας.

4 τοῦ Θεοῦ G. T.
5 al. " again."
6 al. " he does all things that he may empty."
7 al. " may relax."　　8 τῶν Ἑλληνίκων.
9 διαστροφή.　　10 al. " then."

Why then exaltest thou thyself, O Jew? why art thou high minded? for thy mouth also is stopped, thy boldness also is taken away, thou also with all the world art become guilty, and, like others, art placed in need of being justified freely. Thou oughtest surely even if thou hadst stood upright and hadst had great boldness with God, not even so to have envied those who should be pitied and saved through His loving-kindness. This is the extreme of wickedness, to pine at the blessings of others; especially when this was to be effected without any loss of thine. If indeed the salvation of others had been prejudicial to thy advantages, thy grieving might have been reasonable; though not even then would it have been so to one who had learned true wisdom.[1] But if thy reward is not increased by the punishment of another, nor diminished by his welfare, why dost thou bewail thyself because that other is freely saved? As I said, thou oughtest not, even wert thou (one) of the approved, to be pained at the salvation which cometh to the Gentiles through grace. But when thou, who art guilty before thy Lord of the same things as they, and hast thyself offended, art displeased at the good of others, and thinkest great things, as if thou alone oughtest to be partaker of the grace, thou art guilty not only of envy and insolence, but of extreme folly, and mayest be liable to all the severest torments; for thou hast planted within thyself the root of all evils, pride.

Wherefore a wise man has said, "Pride is the beginning of sin" (Ecclus. x. 13): that is, its root, its source, its mother. By this the first created was banished from that happy abode: by this the devil who deceived him had fallen from that height of dignity; from which that accursed one, knowing that the nature of the sin was sufficient to cast down even from heaven itself, came this way when he labored to bring down Adam from such high honor. For having puffed him up with the promise that he should be as a God, so he broke him down, and cast

him down into the very gulfs of hell.[2] Because nothing so alienates men from the lovingkindness of God, and gives them over to the fire of the pit,[3] as the tyranny of pride. For when this is present with us, our whole life becomes impure, even though we fulfill temperance, chastity, fasting, prayer, almsgiving, anything. For, "Every one," saith the wise man, "that is proud in heart is an abomination[4] to the Lord." (Prov. xvi. 5.) Let us then restrain this swelling of the soul, let us cut up by the roots this lump of pride, if at least we would wish to be clean, and to escape the punishment appointed for the devil. For that the proud must fall under the same punishment as that (wicked) one, hear Paul declare; "Not a novice, lest being lifted up with pride, he fall into the judgment, and the snare of the devil."[5] What is "the judgment"?[6] He means, into the same "condemnation," the same punishment. How then does he say, that a man may avoid this dreadful thing? By reflecting upon[7] his own nature, upon the number of his sins, upon the greatness of the torments in that place, upon the transitory nature of the things which seem bright in this world, differing in nothing from grass, and more fading than the flowers of spring. If we continually stir within ourselves these considerations, and keep in mind those who have walked most upright, the devil, though he strive ten thousand ways, will not be able to lift[8] us up, nor even to trip[9] us at all. May the God who is the God of the humble, the good and merciful God, grant both to you and me a broken and humbled heart, so shall we be enabled easily to order the rest aright, to the glory of our Lord Jesus Christ, by whom and with whom, to the Father and the Holy Ghost, be glory forever and ever. Amen.

---

[1] φιλοσοφεῖν.

[2] ᾅδου.

[3] γεέννης.

[4] "Unclean," LXX.

[5] 1 Tim. iii. 6, 7 (partially quoted).

[6] κρίμα, "condemnation," E. V.

[7] al. "calculating."

[8] ἐπᾶραι.

[9] ὑποσκελίσαι (a gymnastic term like the preceding).

# HOMILY X.

## John i. 11.

"He came unto His own, and His own received Him not."

[1.] BELOVED, God being loving towards man and beneficent, does and contrives all things in order that we may shine in virtue, and as desiring that we be well approved by Him. And to this end He draws no one by force or compulsion; but by persuasion and benefits He draws all that will, and wins them to Himself. Wherefore when He came, some received Him, and others received Him not. For He will have no unwilling, no forced domestic, but all of their own will and choice, and grateful to Him for their service. Men, as needing the ministry of servants, keep many in that state even against their will, by the law of ownership;[1] but God, being without wants, and not standing in need of anything of ours, but doing all only for our salvation, makes us absolute[2] in this matter, and therefore lays neither force nor compulsion on any of those who are unwilling. For He looks only to our advantage: and to be drawn unwilling to a service like this is the same as not serving at all.

"Why then," says one, "does He punish those who will not listen[3] to Him, and why hath He threatened hell to those who endure[4] not His commands?" Because, being Good exceedingly, He cares even for those who obey Him not, and withdraws not from them who start back and flee from Him. But when we[5] had rejected the first way of His beneficence, and had refused to come by the path of persuasion and kind treatment, then He brought in upon us the other way, that of correction and punishments; most bitter indeed, but still necessary, when the former is disregarded.[6] Now lawgivers also appoint many and grievous penalties against offenders, and yet we feel no aversion to them for this; we even honor them the more on account of the punishments they have enacted, and because though not needing a single thing that we have, and often not knowing who they should be that should enjoy the help afforded by their written laws,[7] they still took care for the good ordering of our lives, rewarding those who live virtuously, and checking by punishments the intemperate, and those[8] who would mar the

repose[9] of others. And if we admire and love these men, ought we not much more to marvel at and love God on account of His so great care? For the difference between their and His forethought regarding us is infinite. Unspeakable of a truth are the riches of the goodness of God, and passing all excess.[10] Consider; "He came to His own," not for His personal need, (for, as I said, the Divinity is without wants,) but to do good unto His own people. Yet not even so did His own receive Him, when He came to His own for their advantage, but repelled Him, and not this only, but they even cast Him out of the vineyard, and slew Him. Yet not for this even did He shut them out from repentance, but granted them, if they had been willing, after such wickedness as this, to wash off all their transgressions by faith in Him, and to be made equal to those who had done no such thing, but are His especial friends. And that I say not this at random, or for persuasion's sake, all the history of the blessed Paul loudly declares. For when he, who after the Cross persecuted Christ, and had stoned His martyr Stephen by those many hands, repented, and condemned his former sins, and ran to Him whom he had persecuted, He immediately enrolled him among His friends, and the chiefest of them, having appointed him a herald and teacher of all the world, who had been "a blasphemer, and persecutor, and injurious." (1 Tim. i. 13.) Even as he rejoicing at the lovingkindness of God, has proclaimed aloud, and has not been ashamed, but having recorded in his writings, as on a pillar, the deeds formerly dared by him, has exhibited them to all; thinking it better that his former life should be placarded[11] in sight of all, so that the greatness of the free gift of God might appear, than that he should obscure His ineffable and indescribable lovingkindness by hesitating to parade[12] before all men his own error. Wherefore continually[13] he treats of his persecution, his plottings, his wars against the Church, at one time saying, "I am not meet to be called an Apostle, because I persecuted the Church of God" (1 Cor. xv. 9); at another, "Jesus came into the world to save sinners, of whom I am chief." (1 Tim. i. 15.) And again, "Ye have heard of my conversation in time

---

1 δεσποτείας, i.e. "the law of master and slave."
2 κυρίους.        3 al. "submit."
4 al. "hear."        5 al. "they."
6 al. "For, when the former way is disregarded, the introduction of the second is necessary." Ben.
7 "Writings," al. "trouble."        8 al. "as those."

9 al. "settled state."        10 al. "beyond all thought."
11 στηλιτεύεσθαι. lit. "set on a pillar." al. στίζεσθαι, "be branded."
12 ἐκπομπεῦσαι.        13 ἄνω καὶ κάτω.

past in the Jews' religion, how that beyond measure I persecuted the church of God, and wasted it." (Gal. i. 13.)

[2.] For making as it were a kind of return to Christ for His longsuffering towards him, by showing who it was, what a hater and enemy that He saved, he declared with much openness the warfare which at the first with all zeal he warred against Christ; and with this he holds forth good hopes to those who despaired of their condition. For he says, that Christ accepted him, in order that in him first He " might show forth all longsuffering " (Tim. i. 16), and the abundant riches of His goodness, " for a pattern to them that should hereafter believe in Him to life everlasting." Because the things which they had dared were too great for any pardon; which the Evangelist declaring, said,

" He came to His own, and His own received Him not." Whence came He, who filleth all things, and who is everywhere present? What place did He empty of His presence, who holdeth and graspeth all things in His hand? He exchanged not one place for another; how should He? But by His coming down to us, He effected this. For since, though being in the world, He did not seem to be there, because He was not yet known, but afterwards manifested Himself by deigning to take upon Him our flesh, he (St. John) calls this manifestation and descent, " a coming." [1] One might wonder at [2] the disciple who is not ashamed of the dishonor of his Teacher, but even records the insolence which was used towards Him : yet this is no small proof of his truth-loving disposition. And besides, he who feels shame should feel it for those who have offered an insult, not for the person outraged. [3] Indeed He by this very thing shone the brighter, as taking, even after the insult, so much care for those who had offered it ; while they appeared ungrateful and accursed in the eyes of all men, for having rejected Him who came to bring them so great goods, as hateful to them, and an enemy. And not only in this were they hurt, but also in not obtaining what they obtained who received Him. What did these obtain?

Ver. 12. " As many as received Him, to them gave He power to become the sons of God," says the Evangelist. " Why then, O blessed one, dost thou not also tell us the punishment of them who received Him not? Thou hast said that they were ' His own,' and that when ' He came to His own, they received Him not ' ; but what they shall suffer for this, what punishment they shall undergo, thou hast not gone on to add. Yet so thou wouldest the more have terrified them, and have softened the hardness of their

insanity by threatening. Wherefore then hast thou been silent?" "And what other punishment," he would say, " can be greater than this, that when power is offered them to become sons of God, they do not become so, but willingly deprive themselves of such nobility and honor as this?" Although their punishment shall not even stop at this point, that they gain no good, but moreover the unquenchable fire shall receive them, as in going on he has more plainly revealed. But for the present he speaks of the unutterable goods of those who received Him, and sets these words in brief before us, [4] saying, " As many as received Him, to them gave He power to become sons of God." Whether bond or free, whether Greeks or barbarians or Scythians, unlearned or learned, female or male, children or old men, in honor or dishonor, rich or poor, rulers or private persons, all, He saith, are deemed worthy the same privilege ; for faith and the grace of the Spirit, removing the inequality caused by worldly things, hath moulded all to one fashion, and stamped them with one impress, the King's. What can equal this lovingkindness? A king, who is framed of the same clay with us, does not deign to enrol among the royal host his fellow-servants, who share the same nature with himself, and in character often are better than he, if they chance to be slaves ; but the Only-Begotten Son of God did not disdain to reckon among the company of His children both publicans, sorcerers, and slaves, nay, men of less repute and greater poverty than these, maimed in body, and suffering from ten thousand ills. Such is the power of faith in Him, such the excess of His grace. And as the element of fire, when it meets with ore from the mine, straightway of earth makes it gold, even so and much more Baptism makes those who are washed to be of gold instead of clay, the Spirit at that time falling like fire into our souls, burning up the " image of the earthy " (1 Cor. xv. 49), and producing " the image of the heavenly," fresh coined, bright and glittering, as from the furnace-mould.

Why then did he say not that " He made them sons of God," but that " He gave them power to become sons of God "? To show that we need much zeal to keep the image of sonship impressed on us at Baptism, all through without spot or soil [5] ; and at the same time to show that no one shall be able to take this power from us, unless we are the first to deprive ourselves of it. For if among men, those who have received the absolute control of any matters have well-nigh as much power as those who gave them the charge ; much more shall we, who have obtained such honor from God, be, if we do noth-

---

1 παρουσία, commonly so used in N. T.
2 al. " there is reason to wonder that."
3 παροινηθέντος, " insulted by men heated with wine."

4 al. " sets them in brief before us in these words."
5 ἀνέπαφον.

ing unworthy of this power, stronger than all; because He who put this honor in our hands is greater and better than all. At the same time too he wishes to show, that not even does grace come upon man irrespectively,[1] but upon those who desire and take pains for it. For it lies in the power of these to become (His) children; since if they do not themselves first make the choice, the gift does not come upon them, nor have any effect.

[3.] Having therefore everywhere excluded compulsion, and pointing to (man's) voluntary choice and free power, he has said the same now. For even in these mystical blessings,[2] it is, on the one hand, God's part, to give the grace, on the other, man's, to supply faith; and in after time there needs for what remains much earnestness. In order to preserve our purity, it is not sufficient for us merely to have been baptized and to have believed, but we must, if we will continually enjoy this brightness, display a life worthy of it. This then is God's work in us. To have been born the mystical Birth, and to have been cleansed from all our former sins, comes from Baptism; but to remain for the future pure, never again after this to admit any stain, belongs to our own power and diligence. And this is the reason why he reminds us of the manner of the birth, and by comparison with fleshly pangs shows its excellence, when he says,

Ver. 13. "Who were born, not of blood,[3] nor of the will of the flesh, but of God." This he has done, in order that, considering the vileness and lowness of the first birth, which is " of blood," and " the will of the flesh," and perceiving the highness and nobleness of the second, which is by grace, we may form from thence some great opinion of it, and one worthy of the gift of Him who hath begotten us, and for the future exhibit much earnestness.

For there is no small fear, lest, having sometime defiled that beautiful robe by our after sloth and transgressions, we be cast out from the inner room[4] and bridal chamber, like the five foolish virgins, or him who had not on a wedding garment. (Matt. xxv.; xxii.) He too was one of the guests, for he had been invited; but because, after the invitation and so great an honor, he behaved with insolence towards Him who had invited him, hear what punishment he suffers, how pitiable, fit subject for many tears. For when he comes to partake of that splendid table, not only is he forbidden the feast, but bound hand and foot alike, is carried into outer darkness, to undergo eternal and endless wailing and gnashing of teeth. Therefore, beloved, let not us either expect[5] that faith is sufficient to us for salvation; for if we do not show forth a pure life, but come clothed with garments unworthy of this blessed calling, nothing hinders us from suffering the same as that wretched one. It is strange that He, who is God and King, is not ashamed of men who are vile, beggars, and of no repute, but brings even them of the cross ways to that table; while we manifest so much insensibility, as not even to be made better by so great an honor, but even after the call remain in our old wickedness, insolently abusing[6] the unspeakable lovingkindness of Him who hath called us. For it was not for this that He called us to the spiritual and awful communion of His mysteries, that we should enter with our former wickedness; but that, putting off our filthiness, we should change our raiment to such as becomes those who are entertained in palaces. But if we will not act worthily of that calling, this no longer rests with Him who hath honored us, but with ourselves; it is not He that casts us out from that admirable company of guests, but we cast out ourselves.

He has done all His part. He has made the marriage, He has provided the table, He has sent men to call us, has received us when we came, and honored us with all other honor; but we, when we have offered insult to Him, to the company, and to the wedding, by our filthy garments, that is, our impure actions, are then with good cause cast out. It is to honor the marriage and the guests, that He drives off those bold[7] and shameless persons; for were He to suffer those clothed in such a garment, He would seem to be offering insult to the rest. But may it never be that one, either of us or of others, find this of Him who has called us! For to this end have all these things been written before they come to pass, that we, being sobered by the threats of the Scriptures, may not suffer this disgrace and punishment to go on to the deed, but stop it at the word only, and each with bright apparel come to that call; which may it come to pass that we all enjoy, through the grace and lovingkindness of our Lord Jesus Christ, by whom and with whom, to the Father and the Holy Ghost, be glory for ever and ever. Amen.

---

[1] ἁπλῶς.
[2] i.e. of Baptism.
[3] Lit. "bloods."
[4] παστάδος.
[5] al. "think."
[6] ἐμπαροινοῦντας.
[7] ἰταμούς.

# HOMILY XI.

John i. 14.

"And the Word was made Flesh, and dwelt among us."

[1.] I DESIRE to ask one favor of you all, before I touch on the words of the Gospel; do not you refuse my request, for I ask nothing heavy or burdensome, nor, if granted, will it be useful only to me who receive, but also to you who grant it, and perhaps far more so to you. What then is it that I require of you? That each of you take in hand that section of the Gospels which is to be read among you on the first day of the week, or even on the Sabbath, and before the day arrive, that he sit down at home and read it through, and often carefully consider its contents, and examine all its parts well, what[1] is clear, what obscure,[2] what seems to make for the adversaries,[3] but does not really so; and when you have tried,[4] in a word,[5] every point, so go to hear it read. For from zeal like this will be no small gain both to you and to us. We shall not need much labor to render clear the meaning of what is said, because your minds will be already made familiar with the sense of the words, and you will become keener and more clear-sighted not for hearing only, nor for learning, but also for the teaching of others. Since, in the way that now most of those who come hither hear, compelled to take in the meaning of all at once, both the words, and the remarks we make upon them, they will not, though we should go on doing this for a whole year, reap any great gain. How can they, when they have leisure for what is said as a bywork,[6] and only in this place, and for this short time? If any lay the fault on business, and cares, and constant occupation in public and private matters, in the first place, this is no slight charge in itself, that they are surrounded with such a multitude of business, are so continually nailed to the things of this life, that they cannot find even a little leisure for what is more needful than all. Besides, that this is a mere pretext and excuse, their meetings with friends would prove against them, their loitering in the theaters, and the parties[7] they make to see horse races, at which they often spend whole days, yet never in that case does one of them complain of the pressure of business. For trifles then you can without making any excuses, always find abundant leisure; but when you ought to attend to the things of God, do these seem to you so utterly superfluous and mean, that you think you need not assign even a little leisure to them? How do men of such disposition deserve to breathe or to look upon this sun?

There is another most foolish excuse of these sluggards; that they have not the books in their possession. Now as to the rich, it is ludicrous that we should take our aim at[8] this excuse; but because I imagine that many of the poorer sort continually use it, I would gladly ask, if every one of them does not have all the instruments of the trade which he works at, full and complete, though infinite[9] poverty stand in his way? Is it not then a strange thing, in that case to throw no blame on poverty, but to use every means that there be no obstacle from any quarter, but, when we might gain such great advantage, to lament our want of leisure and our poverty?

Besides, even if any should be so poor, it is in their power, by means of the continual reading of the holy Scriptures which takes place here, to be ignorant of nothing contained in them. Or if this seems to you impossible, it seems so with reason; for many do not come with fervent zeal to hearken to what is said, but having done this one thing[10] for form's sake[11] on our account,[12] immediately return home. Or if any should stay, they are no better disposed than those who have retired, since they are only present here with us in body. But that we may not overload you with accusations, and spend all the time in finding fault, let us proceed to the words of the Gospel, for it is time to direct the remainder of our discourse to what is set before us. Rouse yourselves therefore, that nothing of what is said escape you.

"And the Word was made Flesh," he saith, "and dwelt among us."

Having declared that they who received Him were "born of God," and had become "sons of God," he adds the cause and reason of this unspeakable honor. It is that "the Word became Flesh," that the Master took on Him the form of a servant. For He became Son of man, who was God's own[13] Son, in order that He might make the sons of men to be children of God. For the high when it associates with the low touches not at all its own honor, while it raises

---

[1] al. "let him mark what is clear, &c."
[2] al. "very plain."     [3] al. "to be contradictory."
[4] διακωδωνίσαντες, "having tried by ringing."
[5] ἁπλῶς.     [6] ἐκ παρέργου.     [7] συνέδρια.

[8] ἀποτείνεσθαι.     [11] ἀφοσιωσάμενοι.
[9] μυρία.     [12] al. "for the day."
[10] i.e. having come to the assembly.     [13] γνήσιος.

up the other from its excessive lowness; and even thus it was with the Lord. He in nothing diminished His own Nature by this condescension,[1] but raised us, who had always sat in disgrace and darkness, to glory unspeakable. Thus it may be, a king, conversing with interest and kindness with a poor mean man, does not at all shame himself, yet makes the other observed by all and illustrious. Now if in the case of the adventitious dignity of men, intercourse with the humbler person in nothing injures the more honorable, much less can it do so in the case of that simple and blessed Essence, which has nothing adventitious, or subject to growth or decay, but has[2] all good things immovable, and fixed for ever. So that when you hear that " the Word became Flesh," be not disturbed nor cast down. For that Essence did not change[3] to flesh, (it is impiety[4] to imagine this,) but continuing what it is, It so took upon It the form of a servant.

[2.] Wherefore then does he use the expression, " was made "? To stop the mouths of the heretics. For since there are some[5] who say that all the circumstances of the Dispensation were an appearance, a piece of acting, an allegory, at once to remove beforehand their blasphemy, he has put " was made "; desiring to show thereby not a change of substance, (away with the thought,) but the assumption of very flesh. For as when (Paul) says, " Christ hath redeemed us from the curse of the law, being made a curse for us," he does not mean that His essence removing from Its proper glory took upon It the being[6] of an accursed thing, (this not even devils could imagine, nor even the very foolish, nor those deprived of their natural understanding, such impiety as well as madness does it contain,) as (St. Paul) does not say this, but that He, taking upon Himself the curse pronounced against us, leaves us no more under the curse; so also here he (St. John) says that He " was made Flesh," not by changing His Essence to flesh, but by taking flesh to Himself, His Essence remained untouched.

If they say that being God, He is Omnipotent, so that He could lower Himself[7] to the substance of flesh, we will reply to them, that He is Omnipotent as long as He continues to be God. But if He admit of change, change for the worse, how could He be God? for change is far from that simple Nature. Wherefore the Prophet saith, "They all shall wax old as doth a garment, and as a vesture shalt Thou roll them

up, and they shall be changed; but Thou art the same, and Thy years shall not fail." (Ps. cii. 27, LXX.) For that Essence is superior to all change. There is nothing better than He, to which He might advance and reach. Better do I say? No, nor equal to, nor the least approaching Him. It remains, therefore, that if He change, He must admit a change for the worse; and this would not be God. But let the blasphemy return upon the heads of those who utter it. Nay, to show that he uses the expression, " was made," only that you should not suppose a mere appearance, hear from what follows how he clears the argument, and overthrows that wicked suggestion. For what does he add? "And dwelt among us." All but saying, " Imagine nothing improper from the word ' was made '; I spoke not of any change of that unchangeable Nature, but of Its dwelling[8] and inhabiting. But that which dwells[9] cannot be the same with that in which it dwells, but different; one thing dwells in a different thing, otherwise it would not be dwelling; for nothing can inhabit itself. I mean, different as to essence; for by an Union[10] and Conjoining[11] God the Word and the Flesh are One, not by any confusion or obliteration of substances, but by a certain union ineffable, and past[12] understanding. Ask not how[13]; for It was made, so as He knoweth."

What then was the tabernacle in which He dwelt? Hear the Prophet say; "I will raise up the tabernacle of David that is fallen." (Amos ix. 11.) It was fallen indeed, our nature had fallen an incurable fall, and needed only that mighty Hand. There was no possibility of raising it again, had not He who fashioned it at first stretched forth to it His Hand, and stamped it anew with His Image, by the regeneration of water and the Spirit. And observe, I pray you, the awful and ineffable nature[14] of the mystery. He inhabits this tabernacle for ever, for He clothed Himself with our flesh, not as again to leave it, but always to have it with Him. Had not this been the case, He would not have deemed it worthy of the royal throne, nor would He while wearing it have been worshiped by all the host of heaven, angels, archangels, thrones, principalities, dominions, powers. What word, what thought can represent such great honor done to our race, so truly marvelous and awful? What angel, what archangel? Not one in any place, whether in heaven, or upon earth. For such are the mighty works[15] of God, so great and marvelous are His benefits, that a right description of them exceeds not only the tongue of men, but even the power of angels.

---

[1] al. " descent."
[2] al. " possesses."
[3] μετέπεσεν, " fall from what It was into."
[4] al. " truly impious."
[5] The Docetæ, who maintained that our Lord *appeared* only to act and suffer in the Flesh, and that His Body was a phantom. Perhaps they are the heretics specially alluded to by St. John, 1 Ep. iv. 2, and 2 Ep. 7.
[6] οὐσιώθη.
[7] μεταπεσεῖν.

[8] Lit. " tabernacling."
[9] Lit. " which tabernacles."
[10] ἐνώσει.
[11] συναφείᾳ.
[12] ἀφράστου.
[13] al. " seek not accurately."
[14] al. " ineffable mystery."
[15] κατορθώματα.

Wherefore we will[1] for a while close our discourse, and be silent; only delivering to you this charge,[2] that you repay this our so great Benefactor by a return which again shall bring round to us all profit. The return is, that we look with all carefulness to the state of our souls. For this too is the work of His lovingkindness, that He who stands in no need of anything of ours, says that He is repaid when we take care of our own souls. It is therefore an act of extremest folly, and one deserving ten thousand chastisements, if we, when such honor has been lavished upon us, will not even contribute what we can, and that too when profit comes round to us again by these means, and ten thousand blessings are laid before us on these conditions. For all these things let us return[8] glory to our merciful God, not by words only, but much more by works, that we may obtain the good things hereafter, which may it be that we all attain to, through the grace and lovingkindness of our Lord Jesus Christ, by whom and with whom, to the Father and the Holy Ghost, be glory for ever and ever. Amen.

# HOMILY XII.

## JOHN i. 14.

"And we beheld His glory, the glory as of the Only-Begotten of the Father, full of grace and truth."

[1.] PERHAPS we seemed to you the other day[3] needlessly hard upon you and burdensome, using too sharp language, and extending too far our reproaches against the sluggishness of the many. Now if we had done this merely from a desire to vex you, each of you would with cause have been angry; but if, looking to your advantage, we neglected in our speech what might gratify you, if ye will not give us credit for our forethought, you should at least pardon us on account of such tender love.[4] For in truth we greatly fear, lest, if we are taking pains,[5] and you are not willing to manifest the same diligence in listening, your future reckoning may be the more severe. Wherefore we are compelled continually to arouse and waken you, that nothing of what is said may escape[6] you. For so you will be enabled to live for the present with much confidence, and to exhibit it at that Day before the judgment-seat of Christ. Since then we have lately sufficiently touched you, let us to-day at the outset enter on the expressions themselves.

"We beheld," he says, "His glory, the glory as of the Only-Begotten of the Father."

Having declared that we were made "sons of God," and having shown in what manner,[7] namely, by the "Word" having been "made Flesh," he again mentions another advantage which we gain from this same circumstance. What is it? "We beheld His glory, the glory as of the Only-Begotten of the Father"; which we could not have beheld, had it not been shown to us, by means of a body like to our own.[9] For if the men of old time could not even bear to look upon the glorified countenance of Moses, who partook of the same nature with us, if that just man needed a veil which might shade over the purity[10] of his glory, and show to them the face of their prophet mild and gentle;[11] how could we creatures of clay and earth have endured the unveiled Godhead, which is unapproachable even by the powers above? Wherefore He tabernacled[12] among us, that we might be able with much fearlessness to approach Him, speak to, and converse with Him.

But what means "the glory as of the Only-Begotten of the Father"? Since many of the Prophets too were glorified, as this Moses himself, Elijah, and Elisha, the one encircled by the fiery chariot (2 Kings vi. 17), the other taken up by it; and after them, Daniel and the Three Children, and the many others who showed forth wonders[13]; and angels who have appeared among men, and partly disclosed[14] to beholders the flashing light of their proper nature; and since not angels only, but even the Cherubim were seen by the Prophet in great glory, and the Seraphim also: the Evangelist leading us away from all these, and removing our thoughts from created things, and from the brightness of our fellow-servants, sets us at the very summit of good. For, "not of prophet," says[15] he, "nor angel, nor archangel, nor of the higher powers, nor of any other created nature," if other there

---

1 al. "let us."
2 παρεγγυάσαντες.
3 πρώην.
7 al. "that it was not otherwise than by."
4 φιλοστοργίας.
5 al. "speaking."
6 παραρρυῆναι.
8 ἀναπέμψωμεν.
9 συντρόφου.
11 Morel. "make the intolerable (brightness) of his countenance bearable to them."
12 ἐσκήνωσεν.
13 [were glorified.]
10 ἄκρατον
14 παρανοίξαντες.
15 al. "all but saying."

be, but of the Master Himself, the King Himself, the true Only-Begotten Son Himself, of the Very Lord[1] of all, did we "behold the glory."

For the expression "as," does not in this place belong to similarity or comparison, but to confirmation and unquestionable definition; as though he said, "We beheld glory, such as it was becoming, and likely that He should possess, who is the Only-Begotten and true Son of God, the King of all." The habit (of so speaking) is general, for I shall not refuse to strengthen my argument even from common custom, since it is not now my object to speak with any reference to beauty of words, or elegance of composition, but only for your advantage; and therefore there is nothing to prevent my establishing my argument by the instance of a common practice. What then is the habit of most persons? Often when any have seen a king richly decked, and glittering on all sides with precious stones, and are afterwards describing to others the beauty, the ornaments, the splendor, they enumerate as much as they can, the glowing tint of the purple robe, the size of the jewels, the whiteness of the mules, the gold about the yoke, the soft and shining couch. But when after enumerating these things, and other things besides these, they cannot, say what they will, give a full idea of[2] the splendor, they immediately bring in: "But why say much about it; once for all, he was like a king;" not desiring by the expression "like," to show that he, of whom they say this, resembles a king, but that he is a real king. Just so now the Evangelist has put the word AS, desiring to represent the transcendent nature and incomparable excellence of His glory.

For indeed all others, both angels and archangels and prophets, did everything as under command; but He with the authority which becomes a King and Master; at which even the multitudes wondered, that He taught as "one having authority." (Matt. vii. 29.) Even angels, as I said, have appeared with great glory upon the earth; as in the case of Daniel, of David, of Moses, but they did all as servants who have a Master. But He as Lord and Ruler of all, and this when He appeared in poor and humble form; but even so creation recognized her Lord. Now the star from heaven which called the wise men to worship Him, the vast throng pouring everywhere of angels attending the Lord,[3] and hymning His praise, and besides them, many other heralds sprang up on a sudden, and all, as they met,[4] declared to one another the glad tidings of this ineffable mystery; the angels to the shepherds; the shepherds to those of the city; Gabriel to Mary and Elisabeth; Anna and Simeon to those who came to the Temple. Nor were men and women only lifted up[5] with pleasure, but the very infant who had not yet come forth to light, I mean the citizen of the wilderness, the namesake of this Evangelist, leaped while yet in his mother's womb, and all were soaring[6] with hopes for the future. This too immediately after the Birth. But when He had manifested Himself still farther, other wonders, yet greater than the first, were seen. For it was no more star, or sky, or no more angels, or archangels, not Gabriel, or Michael, but the Father Himself from heaven above, who proclaimed Him, and with the Father the Comforter, flying down at the uttering of the Voice and resting on Him. Truly therefore did he say, "We beheld His glory, the glory as of the Only-Begotten of the Father."

[2.] Yet he says it not only on account of these things, but also on account of what followed them; for no longer do shepherds only, and widow women, and aged men, declare to us the good tidings, but the very voice[7] of the things themselves, sounding clearer than any trumpet, and so loudly, that the sound was straightway heard even in this land. "For," says one, "his fame went into[8] all Syria" (Matt. iv. 24); and He revealed Himself to all, and all things everywhere exclaimed, that the King of Heaven was come. Evil spirits everywhere fled and started away from Him, Satan covered his face[9] and retired, death[10] at that time retreated before Him, and afterwards disappeared altogether; every kind of infirmity was loosed, the graves let free the dead, the devils those whom they had maddened,[11] and diseases the sick. And one might see things strange and wonderful, such as with good cause the prophets desired to see, and saw not. One might see eyes fashioned (John ix. 6, 7), (might see) Him showing to all in short space and on the more noble portion of the body, that admirable thing which all would have desired to see, how God formed Adam from the earth; palsied and distorted limbs fastened and adapted to each other, dead hands moving, palsied feet leaping amain, ears that were stopped re-opened, and the tongue sounding aloud which before was tied by speechlessness. For having taken in hand the common nature of men, as some excellent workman might take a house decayed by time, He filled up what was broken off, banded together its crevices and shaken portions, and raised up again what was entirely fallen down.

And what should one say of the fashioning of

1 al. "and Master."
2 παράστησαι.
3 Morel. " and heavenly multitudes appearing on earth of Angels ministering."
4 al. "coming together."

5 ἐπτερώθησαν, "made winged."
6 μετέωροι.
7 al. "nature."
8 "Throughout," E. V.

9 ἐγκαλυψάμενος.
10 al "and death itself."
11 τοὺς μεμηνότας.

the soul, so much more admirable than that of the body? The health of our bodies is a great thing, but that of our souls is as much greater as the soul is better than the body. And not on this account only, but because our bodily nature follows whithersoever the Creator will lead it, and there is nothing to resist, but the soul being its own mistress, and possessing power over its acts, does not in all things obey God, unless it will to do so. For God will not make it beautiful and excellent, if it be reluctant and in a manner constrained by force, for this is not virtue at all; but He must persuade it to become so of its own will and choice. And so this cure is more difficult than the other; yet even this succeeded, and every kind of wickedness was banished. And as He re-ordered the bodies which He cured, not to health only, but to the highest vigor, so did He not merely deliver the souls from extremest wickedness, but brought them to the very summit of excellence. A publican became an Apostle, and a persecutor, blasphemer, and injurious, appeared as herald to the world, and the Magi became teachers of the Jews, and a thief was declared a citizen of Paradise, and a harlot shone forth by the greatness of her faith, and of the two women, of Canaan and Samaria, the latter who was another harlot, undertook to preach the Gospel to her countrymen, and having enclosed a whole city in her net,[1] so brought them[2] to Christ; while the former by faith and perseverance, procured the expulsion of an evil spirit from her daughter's soul; and many others much worse than these were straightway numbered in the rank of disciples, and at once all the infirmities[3] of their bodies and diseases of their souls were transformed, and they were fashioned anew to health and exactest virtue. And of these, not two or three men, not five, or ten, or twenty, or an hundred only, but entire cities and nations, were very easily remodeled. Why should one speak of the wisdom of the commands, the excellency of the heavenly laws, the good ordering of the angelic polity? For such a life hath He proposed to us, such laws appointed for us, such a polity established, that those who put these things into practice, immediately become angels and like to God, as far as is in our power, even though they[4] may have been worse than all men.

[3.] The Evangelist therefore having brought together all these things, the marvels in our bodies, in our souls, in the elements[5] (of our faith), the commandments, those gifts ineffable and higher than the heavens, the laws, the polity, the persuasion, the future promises, His sufferings, uttered that voice so wonderful and full of exalted docrine, saying, "We beheld His glory, the glory as of the Only-Begotten of the Father, full of grace and truth." For we admire Him not only on account of the miracles, but also by reason of the sufferings; as that He was nailed upon the Cross, that He was scourged, that He was buffeted, that He was spit upon, that He received blows on the cheek from those to whom He had done good. For even of those very things which seem to be shameful, it is proper to repeat the same expression, since He Himself called that action[6] "glory." For what then took place was (proof) not only of kindness and love, but also of unspeakable power. At that time death was abolished, the curse was loosed, devils were shamed and led in triumph and made a show of, and the handwriting of our sins was nailed to the Cross. And then, since these wonders were doing invisibly, others took place visibly, showing that He was of a truth the Only-Begotten Son of God, the Lord of all creation. For while yet that blessed Body hung upon the tree, the sun turned away his rays, the whole earth was troubled and became dark, the graves were opened, the ground quaked, and an innumerable multitude of dead leaped forth, and went into the city. And while the stones of His tomb were fastened upon the vault, and the seals yet upon them, the Dead arose, the Crucified, the nail-pierced One, and[7] having filled His eleven disciples with His mighty[8] power, He sent them to men throughout all the world, to be the common healers of all their kind,[9] to correct their way of living, to spread through every part of the earth the knowledge of their heavenly doctrines, to break down the tyranny of devils, to teach those great and ineffable blessings, to bring to us the glad tidings of the soul's immortality, and the eternal life of the body, and rewards which are beyond conception, and shall never have an end. These things then, and yet more than these, the blessed Evangelist having in mind, things which though he knew, he was not able to write, because the world could not have contained them (for if all things "should be written every one, I suppose that even the world itself could not contain the books that should be written"—c. xxi. 25), reflecting therefore on all these, he cries out, "We beheld His glory, the glory as of the Only-Begotten of the Father, full of grace and truth."

It behooves therefore those who have been deemed worthy to see and to hear such things, and who have enjoyed so great a gift, to display also a life worthy of the doctrines, that they may enjoy also the good things which are (laid up) there. For our Lord Jesus Christ came, not

---

[1] σαγηνεύσασα from σαγήνη, "a seine net."
[2] al. "brought them out."
[3] πάθη.   [4] al. "we."   [5] στοιχείοις.

[6] i.e. His Crucifixion.   [9] Or "of their whole nature."
[7] al. "then again."
[8] al. "a certain irresistible and divine."

only that we might behold His glory here, but also that which shall be. For therefore He saith, " I will that these [1] also be with Me where I am, that they may behold My glory." (c. xvii. 24.) Now if the glory here was so bright and splendid, what can one say of that (which shall be)? for it shall appear not on this corruptible earth, nor while we are in perishable bodies, but in a creation which is imperishable, and waxes not old, and with such brightness as it is not possible even to represent in words. O [2] blessed, thrice blessed, yea many times so, they who are deemed worthy to be beholders of that glory! It is concerning this that the prophet says, " Let the unrighteous be taken away, that he behold not the glory of the Lord." (Isa. xxvi. 10, LXX.) God grant that not one of us be taken away nor excluded ever from beholding it. For if we shall not hereafter enjoy it, then it is time to say of ourselves, " Good were it for " us, " if " we " had never been born." For why do we live and breathe? What are we, if we fail of that spectacle, if no one grant us then to behold our Lord? If those who see not the light of the sun endure a life more bitter than any death, what is it likely that they who are deprived of that light must suffer? For in the one case the loss is confined to this one privation; but in the other it does not rest here, (though if this were the only thing to be dreaded, even then the degrees of punishment would not be equal, but one would be as much severerer than the other, as that sun is incomparably superior to this,) but now

we must look also for other vengeance; for he who beholds not that light must not only be led into darkness, but must be burned continually, and waste away, and gnash his teeth, and suffer ten thousand other dreadful things. Let us then not permit ourselves by making this brief time a time of carelessness and remissness, to fall into everlasting punishment, but let us watch and be sober, let us do all things, and make it all our business to attain to that felicity, and to keep far from that river of fire, which rushes with a loud roaring before the terrible judgment seat. For he who has once been cast in there, must remain for ever; there is no one to deliver him from his punishment, not father, not mother, not brother. And this the prophets themselves declared aloud; one saying, " Brother delivers not brother. Shall man deliver?" ( Ps. xlix. 7, LXX.) And Ezekiel has declared somewhat more than this, saying, " Though Noah, Daniel, and Job were in it, they shall deliver neither sons nor daughters." (Ezek. xiv. 16.) For one defense [5] only, that through works,[6] is there, and he who is deprived of that cannot be saved by any other means. Revolving these things, then, and reflecting upon them continually, let us cleanse our life and make it lustrous, that we may see the Lord with boldness, and obtain the promised good things; through the grace and lovingkindness of our Lord Jesus Christ, by whom and with whom, to the Father and the Holy Spirit, be glory for ever and ever. Amen.

---

# HOMILY XIII.

## John i. 15.

" John beareth witness of Him, and crieth, saying, This is He of whom I spake, saying, He that cometh after me is preferred before me, for He was before me."

[1.] Do we then run and labor in vain? Are we sowing upon the rocks? Does the seed fall upon the rocks? Does the seed fall without our knowing it by the wayside, and among thorns? I am greatly troubled and fear, lest our husbandry be unprofitable; not [3] as though I shall be a loser as well as you, touching the reward of this labor. For it is not with those who teach as it is with husbandmen. Oftentimes the husbandman after his year's toil, his hard work and sweat, if the earth produce no suitable return for his pains, will be [4] able to find comfort for

his labors from none else, but returns ashamed and downcast from his barn to his dwelling, his wife and children, unable to require of any man a reward for his lengthened toil. But in our case there is [7] nothing like this. For even though the soil which we cultivate bring forth no fruit, if we have shown all industry, the Lord of it and of us will not suffer us to depart with disappointed hopes, but will give us a recompense; for, says St. Paul, " Every man shall receive his own reward according to his own labor " (1 Cor. iii. 8), not according to the event of things. And that it is so, hearken: " And Thou," he saith, " Son of man, testify unto this people, if

---

[1] οὗτοι κἀκεῖνοι (G. T.).
[2] al. " how."
[3] al. " nothing."
[4] al. " is."

[5] προστασία.
[6] There are places where he allows that the prayers of others may avail a man in the Judgment, when they are the consequence of his good deeds. See on Statues, Hom. ii. § 17.
[7] al. " shall be."

they will hear, and if they will understand."
(Ezek. ii. 5, not from LXX.) And Ezekiel says,[1]
" If the watchman give warning what it behooves
to flee from, and what to choose, he hath delivered his own soul, although there be none that
will take heed." (Ezek. iii. 18, and xxxiii. 9 ;
not quoted from LXX.) Yet although we have
this strong consolation, and are confident of the
recompense that shall be made us, still when we
see that the work in you does not go forward,
our state is not better than the state of those
husbandmen who lament and mourn, who hide
their faces and are ashamed. This is the sympathy of a teacher, this is the natural care of a
father. For Moses too, when it was in his
power to have been delivered from the ingratitude of the Jews, and to have laid the more
glorious foundation of another and far greater[2]
people, (" Let Me alone," said God, " that I
may consume them,[3] and make of thee a nation
mightier than this " — Ex. xxxii. 10,) because he
was a holy man, the servant of God, and a friend[4]
very true and generous, he did not endure even
to hearken to this word, but chose rather to
perish with those who had been once allotted to
him, than without them to be saved and be in
greater honor. Such ought he to be who has
the charge of souls. For it is a strange thing
that any one who has weak children, will not be
called the father of any others than those who
are sprung from him, but that he who has had
disciples placed in his hands should be continually changing one flock for another, that we
should be catching at the charge now of these,
then of those, then again of others,[5] having no
real affection for any one. May we never have
cause to suspect this of you. We trust that ye
abound more in faith in our Lord Jesus Christ,
and in love to one another and towards all men.
And this we say as desiring that your zeal may
be increased, and the excellence of your conversation[6] farther advanced. For it is thus that
you will be able to bring your understandings
down to the very depth of the words set before
us, if no film[7] of wickedness darken the eyes of
your intellect, and disturb its clearsightedness
and acuteness.

What then is it which is set before[8] us to-day?
" John bare witness of Him, and cried, saying,
This was He of whom I spake, He that cometh
after me is preferred before me, for He was before me." The Evangelist is very full in making
frequent mention of John, and often bearing
about his testimony. And this he does not without a reason, but very wisely ; for all the Jews

held the man in great admiration, (even Josephus
imputes the war to his death ;[9] and shows, that,
on his account, what once was the mother city,
is now no city at all,[10] and continues[11] the words
of his encomium to great length,) and therefore
desiring by his means to make the Jews ashamed,
he continually reminds them of the testimony
of the forerunner. The other Evangelists make
mention of the older prophets, and at each successive thing that took place respecting Him
refer the hearer to them. Thus when the Child
is born, they say, " Now all this was done, that
it might be fulfilled which was spoken by Esaias
the prophet, saying, Behold, a virgin shall be
with Child, and shall bring forth a Son " (Matt.
i. 22 ; Isa. vii. 14) ; and when He is plotted
against and sought for everywhere so diligently,
that even tender infancy is slaughtered by[12]
Herod, they bring in Jeremy, saying, " In Ramah
was there a voice heard, lamentation, and weeping, and great mourning, Rachel weeping for her
children " (Matt. ii. 18 ; Jer. xxxi. 15) ; and
again, when He comes up out of Egypt, they
mention[13] Hosea, saying, " Out of Egypt have I
called My Son " (Matt. ii. 15 ; Hosea xi. 1) ; and
this they do everywhere. But John providing
testimony more clear and fresh, and uttering a
voice more glorious than the others, brings continually forward not those only who had departed
and were dead, but one also who was alive and
present, who pointed Him out and baptized
Him, him he continually introduces, not desiring
to gain credit for the master[14] through the servant, but condescending to the infirmity of his
hearers.[15] For as unless He had taken the form
of a servant, He would not have been easily
received, so had He not by the voice of a
servant prepared the ears of his fellow-servants,
the many (at any rate) of the Jews would not[16]
have received the Word.

[2.] But besides this, there was another great
and wonderful provision. For because to speak
any great words concerning himself, makes a
man's witness to be suspected, and is often an
obstacle to many hearers, another comes to testify
of Him. And besides this, the many[17] are in a
manner wont to run more readily to a voice
which is more familiar and natural to them, as
recognizing it more than other voices ; and
therefore the Voice from heaven was uttered[18]
once or twice, but that of John oftentimes and

---

[9] No such passage is extant in Josephus. Probably the place
alluded to is *Antiq.* b. xviii. c. 5, § 2, where the destruction of the
troops of Herod the tetrarch by Aretas is attributed to the death of
John the Baptist.
[10] Ben. " the war through which the city of the Jews, which was
once the mother city, is no city." [11] al. " raises."
[12] Morel. καὶ πάντα τὰ αὐτοῦ ὄντως ἀνεζήτη, ὡς καὶ περὶ τῆς
ἀώρου ἡλικίας τῆς σφαττομένης. [13] al. " produce."
[14] Morel. inserts " hence, away with the thought."
[15] al. " of babes."
[16] al. " would not so."
[17] al. " because the many."
[18] γέγονεν.

---

[1] al. " this may be learnt from Ezekiel."
[2] al. " in a far greater way."
[3] Lit. " wipe out." [4] al. " very much a servant."
[5] al. " and others again with these."
[6] πολιτείας. [7] λήμη, al. λύμη, " defilement."
[8] al. " said to."

continually. For those[1] of the people who had surmounted the infirmity of their nature, and had been released from all the things of sense, could hear the Voice from heaven, and had no great need of that of man, but in all things obeyed[2] that other, and were led by it; but they who yet moved below, and were wrapt in many veils, needed that meaner (voice). In the same way John, because he had stripped himself in every way of the[3] things of sense, needed no other instructors,[4] but was taught from heaven. "He that sent me," saith he, "to baptize with water, the Same said unto me, Upon whom thou shalt see the Spirit" of God "descending, the same is He." (c. i. 33.) But the Jews who still were children, and could not as yet reach to that height, had a man for their teacher, a man who did not speak to them words of his own, but brought them a message from above.

What then saith he? He "beareth witness concerning Him, and crieth, saying." What means that word "crieth"? Boldly, he means, and freely, without any reserve,[5] he proclaims. What does he proclaim? to what does he "bear witness," and "cry"? "This is He of whom I said, He that cometh after me is preferred before me; for He was before me." The testimony is dark,[6] and contains besides much that is lowly. For he does not say, "This is the Son of God, the Only-begotten, the true Son"; but what? "He that cometh after me, is preferred before me; for He was before me." As the mother birds do not teach their young all at once how to fly, nor finish their teaching in a single day, but at first lead them forth so as to be just outside the nest, then after first allowing them to rest, set them again to flying,[7] and on the next day continue a flight much farther, and so gently, by little and little, bring them to the proper height; just so the blessed John did not immediately bring the Jews to high things, but taught them for a while to fly up a little above the earth, saying, that Christ was greater than he. And yet this, even this, was for the time no small thing, to have been able to persuade[8] the hearers that one who had not yet appeared nor worked any wonders was greater than a man, (John, I mean,) so marvelous, so famous, to whom all ran, and whom they thought to be an angel. For a while therefore he labored to establish this in the minds of his hearers, that He to whom testimony was borne was greater than he who bore it; He that came after, than he that

came before, He who had not yet appeared, than he that was manifest and famous. And observe how prudently he introduces his testimony; for he does not only point Him out when He has appeared, but even before He appears, proclaims Him. For the expression, "This is He of whom I spake," is the expression of one declaring this. As also Matthew says, that when all came to him, he said, "I indeed baptize you with water, but He that cometh after me is mightier than I, the latchet of whose shoes I am not worthy to unloose."[9] Wherefore then even before His appearance did he this? In order that when He appeared, the testimony might readily be received, the minds of the hearers being already prepossessed by what was said concerning Him, and the mean external appearance not vitiating it.[10] For if without having heard anything at all concerning Him they had seen the Lord,[11] and as they beheld Him had at the same time received the testimony of John's words, so wonderful and great, the meanness of His appearance[12] would have straightway been an objection to the grandeur of the expressions. For Christ took on Him an appearance so mean and ordinary, that even Samaritan women, and harlots, and publicans, had confidence boldly to approach and converse with Him. As therefore, I said, if they had at once heard these words and seen Himself, they might perhaps have mocked at the testimony of John; but now because even before Christ appeared, they had often heard and had been accustomed to[13] what was said concerning Him, they were affected in the opposite way, not rejecting the instruction of the words by reason of the appearance of Him who was witnessed of, but from their belief of what had been already told them, esteeming Him even more glorious.

The phrase, "that cometh after," means, "that" preacheth "after me," not "that" was born "after me." And this Matthew glances at when he says,[14] "after me cometh a man," not speaking of His birth from Mary, but of His coming to preach (the Gospel), for had he been speaking of the birth, he would not have said, "cometh," but "is come"; since He was born when John spake this. What then means "is before me"? Is more glorious, more honorable. "Do not," he saith, "because I came preaching first from this, suppose that I am greater than He; I am much inferior, so much inferior that I am not worthy to be counted in the rank of a servant." This is the sense of "is before me," which Matthew showing in a different manner, saith,[15] "The latchet of whose shoes I

[1] al. "those therefore."
[2] Morel. "as obeying it in all things: but they who yet moved below, needed also many other (things), because of their groveling on the ground, and being wrapt."
[3] al. "all the."                          [4] al. "men for inst."
[5] ὑποστολή.                          [6] Lit. "shaded over."
[7] Morel. and MS. Savile reads προστιθέασι τῇ πτήσει πάλιν καὶ . . . πλείονα συνάπτουσιν.
[8] al. "make believe."

[9] Matt. iii. 11, and Luke iii. 16.
[10] Some MSS. add, "but being able to possess the souls of the many with much fearlessness."
[11] al. "Christ Himself."
[12] σχῆμα.                    [13] Ben. "provoked (to curiosity) by."
[14] Matt. iii. 11 not verbally quoted.    [15] Not found in Matt.

am not worthy to unloose." (Luke iii. 16.) Again, that the phrase, "is before me," does not refer to His coming into Being, is plain from the sequel; for had he meant to say this, what follows, "for He was before me," would be superfluous. For who so dull and foolish as not to know that He who "was born before"[1] him "was before"[2] him? Or if the words refer to His subsistence[3] before the ages, what is said is nothing else than that "He who cometh after me came into being before me." Besides, such a thing as this is unintelligible, and the cause is thrown in needlessly; for he ought to have said the contrary, if he had wished to declare this, "that He who cometh after me was before me, since also He was born before me." For one might with reason assign this, (the "being born before") as the cause of "being before," but not the "being before," as the cause of "being born." While what we assert is very reasonable. Since you all at least know this, that they are always things uncertain, not things evident, that require their causes to be assigned. Now if the argument related to the production of substance,[4] it could not have been uncertain that he who "was born" first must needs "be" first; but because he is speaking concerning honor, he with reason explains what seems to be a difficulty. For many might well enquire, whence and on what pretext He who came after, became before, that is, appeared with great honor; in reply to this question therefore, he immediately assigns the reason; and the reason is, HIS BEING first. He does not say, that "by some kind of advancement he cast me who has been first behind him, and so became before me," but that "he was before me," even though he arrives after me.

But how, says one, if the Evangelist refers[5] to His manifestation to men, and to the glory which was to attend Him from them, does he speak of what was not yet accomplished, as having already taken place? for he does not say, "shall be," but "was." Because this is a custom among the prophets of old, to speak of the future as of the past. Thus Isaiah speaking of His slaughter, does not say, "He shall be led (which would have denoted futurity) as a sheep to the slaughter"; but "He was led as a sheep to the slaughter" (Isa. liii. 7); yet He was not yet Incarnate, but the Prophet speaks of what should be as if it had come to pass. So David, pointing to the Crucifixion, said not, "They shall pierce My hands and My feet," but "They pierced My hands and My feet, and parted My garments among them, and cast lots upon My vesture" (Ps. xxii. 16, 18); and discoursing

of the traitor as yet unborn, he says, "He which did eat of My bread, hath lifted up[6] his heel against Me" (Ps. xli. 9); and of the circumstances of the Crucifixion, "They gave Me gall for meat, and in My thirst they gave Me vinegar to drink." (Ps. lxix. 21.)

[4.] Do you desire that we adduce more examples, or do these suffice? For my part, I think they do; for if we have not dug over the ground in all its extent,[7] we have at least dug down to its bottom; and this last kind of work is not less laborious than the former; and we fear lest by straining your attention immoderately we cause you to fall back.

Let us then give to our discourse a becoming conclusion. And what conclusion is becoming? A suitable giving of glory to God; and that is suitable which is given, not by words only, but much more by actions. For He saith, "Let your light so shine before men, that they may see your good works, and glorify your Father which is in Heaven." (Matt. v. 16.) Now nothing is more full of light than a most excellent conversation. As one of the wise men has said, "The paths of the just shine like the light (Prov. iv. 18, LXX.); and they shine not for them alone who kindle the flame by their works, and are guides in the way of righteousness, but also for those who are their neighbors. Let us then pour oil into these lamps, that the flame become higher,[8] that rich light appear. For not only has this oil great strength now, but even when sacrifices were at their height,[9] it was far more acceptable than they could be. "I will have mercy,"[10] He saith, "and not sacrifice." (Matt. xii. 7; Hos. vi. 6.) And with good reason; for that is a lifeless altar, this a living; and all that is laid on that altar becomes the food of fire, and ends in dust, and it is poured forth as ashes, and the smoke of it is dissolved into the substance of the air; but here there is nothing like this, the fruits which it bears are different. As the words of Paul declare; for in describing the treasures of kindness to the poor laid up by the Corinthians, he writes, "For the administration of this service not only supplieth the want of the saints, but is abundant also by many thanksgivings unto God." (2 Cor. ix. 12.) And again; "Whiles they glorify God for your professed subjection unto the Gospel of Christ, and for your liberal distribution unto them, and unto all men; and by their prayer for you, which long after you. Dost thou behold it[11] resolving itself into thanksgiving and praise of God, and continual prayers of those

---

[1] γενόμενος ἔμπροσθεν.
[2] πρῶτος ἦν.
[3] ὑπάρξεως.
[4] οὐσιώσεως.
[5] al. "the reference is."

[6] al. "has magnified."    [7] al. "not much ground."
[8] al. "more soaring."
[9] lit. "flourished."
[10] ἔλεον. St. Chrysostom plays on the word, which was pronounced nearly as ἔλαιον, "oil." Thus on 2 Tim. ii. 25, Hom. vi.
[11] the "service," λειτουργία.

who have been benefited, and more fervent charity? Let us then sacrifice, beloved, let us sacrifice every day upon these altars. For this sacrifice is greater than prayer and fasting, and many things beside, if only it come from honest gain, and honest toils, and be pure from all covetousness, and rapine, and violence. For God accepts such [1] offerings as these, but the others He turns away from and hates; He will not be honored out of other men's calamities, such sacrifice is unclean and profane, and would rather anger God than appease Him. So that we must use all carefulness, that we do not, in the place of service, insult Him whom we would honor. For if Cain for making a second-rate offering,[2] having done no other wrong, suffered extreme punishment, how shall not we when we offer anything gained by rapine and covetousness, suffer yet more severely. It is for this that God has shown to us the pattern [3] of this commandment, that we might have mercy, not be severe to our fellow-servants; but he who takes what belongs to one and gives it to another, hath not shown mercy, but inflicted hurt, and done an extreme injustice. As then a stone cannot yield oil, so neither can cruelty produce humanity; for alms when it has such a root as this is alms [5] no longer. Therefore I exhort that we look not to this only, that we give to those that need, but also that we give not from other men's plunder. "When one prayeth, and another curseth, whose voice will the Lord hear?" (Ecclus. xxxiv. 24.) If we guide ourselves thus strictly, we shall be able by the grace of God to obtain much lovingkindness and mercy and pardon for what we have done amiss during all this long time, and to escape the river of fire; from which may it come to pass that we be all delivered, and [6] ascend to the Kingdom of Heaven, through the grace and lovingkindness of our Lord Jesus Christ, to whom, with the Father and the Holy Ghost, be glory for ever and ever. Amen.

# HOMILY XIV.

## John i. 16.

"And of His fullness have all we received, and grace for grace."

[1.] I SAID the other day, that John, to resolve the doubts of those who should question with themselves how the Lord, though He came after to the preaching, became before and more glorious than he, added, "for He was before me." And this is indeed one reason. But not content with this, he adds again a second, which now he declares. What is it? "And of his fullness," says he, "have all we received, and grace for grace." With these again he mentions another. What is this? That

Ver. 17. "The law was given by Moses, but grace and truth came by Jesus Christ."

And what means that, saith he, "Of His fullness have all we received"? for to this we must for a while direct our discourse. He possesseth not, says he, the gift by participation,[4] but is Himself the very Fountain and very Root of all good, very Life, and very Light, and very Truth, not retaining within Himself the riches of His good things, but overflowing with them unto all others, and after the overflowing remaining full, in nothing diminished by supplying others, but streaming ever forth, and imparting to others a share of these blessings, He remains in sameness of perfection. What I possess is by participation, (for I received it from another,) and is a small portion of the whole, as it were a poor [7] rain-drop compared with the untold abyss or the boundless sea; or rather not even can this instance fully express what we attempt to say, for if you take a drop from the sea, you have lessened the sea itself,[8] though the diminution be imperceptible. But of that Fountain we cannot say this; how much soever a man draw, It continues undiminished. We therefore must needs proceed to another instance, a weak one also, and not able to establish what we seek, but which guides us better than the former one to the thought now proposed to us.

Let us suppose that there is a fountain of fire; that from that fountain ten thousand lamps are kindled, twice as many, thrice as many, ofttimes as many; does not the fire remain at the same degree of fullness even after its imparting of its virtue to such members? It is plain to every man that it does. Now if in the case of bodies which are made up of parts, and are diminished by abstraction, one has been found of such a nature, that after supplying to others something from itself it sustains no loss, much more will

---

[1] al. "only such."
[2] τὰ δευτερεῖα προσενεγκών. St. Chrysostom implies, that the offering of Cain was not of his best.
[3] εἶδος.　　　　[4] μεθεκτὴν δωρεάν.

[5] ἐλεημοσύνη, (lit. "mercifulness,") whence our alms.
[6] Morel. "sit down in the heavenly bride-chamber."
[7] al. "little."　　　　[8] or, "just so much."

this take place with that incorporeal and un-compounded Power. If in the instance given, that which is communicated is substance and body, is divided yet does not suffer division, when our discourse is concerning an energy, and an energy too of an incorporeal substance, it is much more probable that this will undergo noth-ing of the sort. And therefore John said, "Of His fullness have all we received," and joins his own testimony to that of the Baptist; for the expression, "Of his fullness have we all received," belongs not to the forerunner but to the disciple; and its meaning is something like this: "Think not," he says, "that we, who long time com-panied with Him, and partook of His food[1] and table, bear witness through favor," since even John, who did not even know Him before, who had never even been with Him, but merely saw Him in company with others when he was bap-tizing, cried out, "He was before me," having from that source[2] received all; and all we the twelve, the three hundred, the three thousand, the five thousand, the many myriads of Jews, all the fullness of the faithful who then were, and now are, and hereafter shall be, have "received of His fullness." What have we received? "grace for grace," saith he. What grace, for what? For the old, the new. For there was a righteousness, and again a righteousness, ("Touching the right-eousness which is in the law," saith Paul, "blame-less.") (Phil. iii. 6.) There was a faith, there is a faith. ("From faith to faith.") (Rom. i. 17.) There was an adoption, there is an adop-tion. ("To whom pertaineth the adoption.") (Rom. ix. 4.) There was a glory, there is a glory. ("For. if that which was done away was glorious, much more that which remaineth is glorious.") (2 Cor. iii. 11.) There was a law, and there is a law. ("For the law of the Spirit of life hath made me free.") (Rom. viii. 2.) There was a service, and there is a service. ("To whom pertaineth the service" — Rom. ix. 4: and again: "Serving God in the Spirit.") (Phil. iii. 3.) There was a covenant, and there is a covenant. ("I will make with you[3] a new covenant, not according to the covenant which I made with your[4] fathers.") (Jer. xxxi. 31.) There was a sanctification, and there is a sancti-fication: there was a baptism, and there is a Baptism: there was a sacrifice, and there is a Sacrifice: there was a temple, and there is a tem-ple: there was a circumcision, and there is a cir-cumcision; and so too there was a "grace," and there is a "grace." But the words in the first case are used as types, in the second as realities, preserving a sameness of sound, though not of sense. So in patterns and figures, the shape of a man scratched with white lines[5] upon a black ground is called a man as well as that which has received the correct coloring; and in the case of statues, the figure whether formed of gold or of plaster, is alike called a statue, though in the one case as a model, in the other as a reality.

[2.] Do not then, because the same words are used, suppose that the things are identical, nor yet diverse either; for in that they were models they did not differ from the truth; but in that they merely preserved the outline, they were less than the truth. What is the difference in all these instances? Will you that we take in hand and proceed to examine one or two of the cases mentioned? thus the rest will be plain to you; and we shall see that the first were lessons for children, the last for high-minded full-grown men; that the first laws were made as for mor-tals, the latter as for angels.

Whence then shall we begin? From the son-ship itself? What then is the distinction between the first and second? The first is the honor of a name, in the second the thing goes with it. Of the first the Prophet says, "I have said, Ye are gods, and all of you are children of the Most High" (Ps. lxxxii. 6); but of the latter, that they "were born of God." How, and in what way? By the washing of regeneration, and renewing of the Holy Ghost. For they, even after they had received the title of sons, retained the spirit of slavery, (for while they remained slaves they were honored with this appellation,) but we being made free, received the honor, not in name, but in deed. And this Paul has de-clared and said, "For ye have not received the spirit of bondage again to fear, but ye have re-ceived the Spirit of adoption, whereby we cry, Abba, Father." (Rom. viii. 15.) For having been born again,[6] and, as one may say, thor-oughly remade,[7] we so are called "sons." And if one consider the character of the holiness, what the first was and what the second, he will find there also great[8] difference. They, when they did not worship idols, nor commit fornica-tion or adultery, were called by this name; but we become holy, not by refraining from these vices merely, but by acquiring things greater. And this gift we obtain first by means of the coming upon us of the Holy Ghost; and next, by a rule of life far more comprehensive[9] than that of the Jews. To prove that these words are not mere boasting, hear what He saith to them, "Ye shall not use divination,[10] nor make purification of your children, for ye are a holy people."[11] So that holiness with them consisted

---

[1] lit. " salt."     [2] or, " sight," ἐκεῖθεν.
[3] in Orig. " the house of Israel and Judah."
[4] in Orig. " their."

[5] al. " with black on white colors."
[6] or, " from above."
[7] ἀναστοιχειωθέντες, made up of fresh elements.
[8] So Morel. Ben. and MS. in Bodleian. Savile reads οὐ πολλὴν.
[9] μείζονος πολιτείας.
[10] or, " purify yourselves," φοιβάσεσθε.
[11] Perhaps from Deut. xviii. 10.

in being free from the customs of idolatry; but it is not so with us. "That she may be holy," saith Paul, "in body and spirit." (1 Cor. vii. 34.) "Follow peace, and holiness, without which no man shall see the Lord" (Heb. xii. 14) : and, "Perfecting holiness in the fear of God." (2 Cor. vii. 1.) For the word "holy" has not force to give the same meaning in every case to which it is applied; since God is called "Holy," though not as we are. What, for instance, does the Prophet say, when he heard that cry raised[1] by the flying Seraphim? "Woe is me ! because I am a man of unclean lips, and I dwell in the midst of a people of unclean lips" (Isa. vi. 5) ; though he was holy and clean; but if we be compared with the holiness which is above, we are unclean. Angels are holy, Archangels are holy, the Cherubim and Seraphim themselves are holy, but of this holiness again there is a double difference ; that is, in relation to us, and to the higher powers.[2] We might proceed to all the other points, but then the discussion would become too long, and its extent too great. We will therefore desist from proceeding farther, and leave it to you to take in hand the rest, for it is in your power at home to put these things together, and examine their difference, and in the same way to go over what remains. "Give," saith one, "a starting place to the wise, and he becometh wiser." (Prov. ix. 9, LXX.) The beginning is from us, but the end will be from you. We must now resume the connection.

After having said, "Of His fullness have all we received," he adds, "and grace for grace." For by grace the Jews were saved : "I chose you," saith God, "not because you were many in number, but because of your fathers." (Deut. vii. 7, LXX.) If now they were chosen by God not for their own good deeds,[3] it is manifest that by grace they obtained this honor. And we too all are saved by grace, but not in like manner ; not for the same objects, but for objects much greater and higher. The grace then that is with us is not like theirs. For not only was pardon of sins given to us, (since this we have in common with them, for all have sinned,) but righteousness also, and sanctification, and sonship, and the gift of the Spirit far more glorious[4] and more abundant. By this grace we have become the beloved of God, no longer as servants, but as sons and friends. Wherefore he saith, "grace for grace." Since even the things of the law were of grace, and the very fact of man[5] being created from nothing, (for we did not receive this as a recompense for past good deeds, how

could we, when we even were not? but from God who is ever the first to bestow His benefits,) and not only that we were created from nothing, but that when created, we straightway learned what we must and what we must not do, and that we received this law in our very nature, and that our Creator entrusted to us the impartial rule of conscience, these I say, are proofs of the greatest grace and unspeakable lovingkindness. And the recovery of this law after it had become corrupt, by means of the written (Law), this too was the work of grace. For what might have been expected to follow was, that they who falsified[6] the law once given should suffer correction and punishments ; but what actually took place was not this, but, on the contrary, an amending of our nature, and pardon, not of debt, but given through mercy and grace. For to show that it was of grace and mercy, hear what David saith ; "The Lord executeth righteousness and judgment for all that are oppressed ; He made known His ways unto Moses, His acts unto the children of Israel" (Ps. ciii. 6, 7) : and again ; "Good and upright is the Lord, therefore will He give laws to them that are in the way." (Ps. xxv. 8.)

[3.] Therefore that men received the law was of pity, mercies, and grace ; and for this reason he saith, "Grace for grace." But striving yet more fervently[7] to (express) the greatness of the gifts, he goes on to say,

Ver. 17. "The law was given by Moses, but grace and truth came by Jesus Christ."

See ye how gently, by a single word and by little and little, both John the Baptist and John the Disciple lead up their hearers to the highest knowledge, having first exercised them in humbler things? The former having compared to himself Him who is incomparably superior to all, thus afterwards shows His superiority, by saying, "is become before me," and then adding the words, "was before me" : while the latter has done much more than he, though too little for the worthiness of the Only-Begotten, for he makes the comparison, not with John, but with one reverenced by the Jews more than John, with Moses. "For the law," saith he, "was given by Moses, but grace and truth came by Jesus Christ."

Observe his wisdom. He makes enquiry not concerning the person, but the things ; for these being proved, it was probable that even the senseless would of necessity receive from them a much higher judgment and notion respecting Christ. For when facts bear witness, which cannot be suspected[8] of doing so either from favor to any, or from malice, they afford a means of judging which cannot be doubted even by the

---

[1] al. "sung."
[2] Morel. and MS. in Bodleian read the passage thus: "are holy, but the (Holiness) of God is greater than their holiness, and surpassing, as in comparison with us, so also with the powers which are above us."　　　[3] κατορθωμάτων.
[4] al. "stronger."　　　[5] al. "our."
[6] παραχαράττοντας.
[7] al. "clearly."
[8] al. "accused."

senseless; for they remain to open view just as their actors may have arranged them, and therefore their evidence is the least liable to suspicion of any. And see how he makes the comparison easy even to the weaker sort; for he does not prove the superiority by argument, but points out the difference by the bare words, opposing "grace and truth" to "law," and "came" to "was given." Between each of these there is a great difference; for one, "was given," belongs to something ministered, when one has received from another, and given to whom he was commanded to give; but the other, "grace and truth came," befits a king forgiving all offenses, with authority, and himself furnishing the gift. Wherefore He said, "Thy sins be forgiven thee" (Matt. ix. 2); and again, "But that ye may know that the Son of Man hath power on earth to forgive sins (He saith to the sick of the palsy), Arise, take up thy bed, and go unto thine house." (Ibid. v. 6.)

Seest[1] thou how "grace" cometh by Him? look also to "truth." His "grace" the instance just mentioned, and what happened in the case of the thief, and the gift of Baptism, and the grace of the Spirit given by Him[2] declare, and many other things. But His "truth" we shall more clearly know, if we understand the types. For the types like patterns anticipated and sketched beforehand the dispensations[3] which should be accomplished under the new covenant, and Christ came and fulfilled them. Let us now consider the types in few words, for we cannot at the present time go through all that relates to them; but when you have learned some points from those (instances) which I shall set before you,[4] you will know the others also.

Will you then that we begin with the Passion itself? What then saith the type? "Take ye a lamb for an house, and kill it, and do as he commanded and ordained." (Ex. xii. 3.) But it is not so with Christ. He doth not command this to be done, but Himself becomes It,[5] by offering Himself a Sacrifice and Oblation to His Father.

[4.] See how the type was "given by Moses," but the "Truth came by Jesus Christ." (Ex. xvii. 12.)

Again, when the Amalekites warred in Mount Sinai, the hands of Moses were supported, being stayed up by Aaron and Hur standing on either side of him (Ex. xvii. 12); but when Christ came, He of Himself stretched forth His Hands upon the Cross. Hast thou observed how the type "was given," but "the Truth came"?

Again, the Law said, "Cursed is every one that continueth not in all things that are written in this book." (Deut. xxvii. 26, LXX.) But what saith grace? "Come unto Me, all ye that labor and are heavy laden, and I will give you rest" (Matt. xi. 28); and Paul. "Christ hath redeemed us from the curse of the law, being made a curse for us." (Gal. iii. 13.)

Since then we have enjoyed such "grace" and "truth," I exhort you that we be not more slothful by reason of the greatness of the gift; for the greater the honor of which we have been deemed worthy, the greater our debt of excellence; for one who has received but small benefits, even though he makes but small returns, does not deserve the same condemnation; but he who has been raised to the highest summit of honor, and yet manifests groveling and mean dispositions, will be worthy of much greater punishment. May I never have to suspect this of you. For we trust in the Lord that you have winged your souls for heaven, that you have removed from earth, that being in the world ye handle not the things of the world; yet though so persuaded, we do not cease thus continually to exhort you. In the games of the heathen, they whom all the spectators encourage are not those who have fallen and lie supine, but those who are exerting themselves and running still; of the others, (since they would be doing what would be of no use,[7] and would not be able to raise up by their encouragements men once for all severed from victory,) they cease to take any notice. But in this case some good may be expected, not only of you who are sober, but even of those who have fallen, if they would but be converted. Wherefore we use every means, exhorting, reproving, encouraging, praising, in order that we may bring about your salvation. Be not then offended by our continual admonishing concerning the Christian conversation, for the words are not the words of one accusing you of sloth, but of one who has very excellent hopes respecting you. And not to you alone, but to ourselves who speak them, are these words said, yea, and shall be said, for we too need the same teaching; so though they be spoken by us, yet nothing hinders their being spoken to us, (for the Word, when it finds a man in fault, amends him, when clear and free, sets him as far off from it as possible,) and we ourselves are not pure from transgressions. The course of healing is the same for all, the medicines are set forth for all, only the application is not the same, but is made according to the choice of those who use the medicines; for one who will handle the remedy as he ought, gains some benefit from the application, while he who

---

[1] al. "see."
[2] Morel. and MS. in Bodleian, read, "and the adoption through the Spirit, given to us."
[3] οἰκονομίας.
[4] al. "having from a few learned the whole."
[5] αὐτὸς αὐτὸ γίγνεται.

[6] al. "so great."      [7] al. "senseless."

does not place it upon the wound, makes the evil greater, and brings it to the most painful end. Let us then not fret when we are being healed, but much rather rejoice, even though the system of discipline bring bitter pains, for hereafter it will show to us fruit sweeter than any. Let us then do all to this end, that we may depart to that world,[1] cleared of the wounds and strokes which the teeth of sin make in the soul, so that having become worthy to behold the countenance of Christ, we may be delivered in that day, not to the avenging and cruel powers, but to those who are able to bring us to that inheritance of the heavens which is prepared for them that love Him ; to which may it come to pass that we all attain, through the grace and lovingkindness of our Lord Jesus Christ, to whom be glory and dominion for ever and ever. Amen.

# HOMILY XV.

## JOHN i. 18.

"No man hath seen God at any time; the Only-begotten Son, which is in the bosom of the Father, He hath declared Him."

[1.] GOD will not have us listen to the words and sentences contained in the Scriptures carelessly, but with much attention. This is why the blessed David hath prefixed in many places to his Psalms the title "for understanding,"[2] and hath said, "Open Thou mine eyes, that I may behold wondrous things out of Thy Law." (Ps. xxxii. 42, &c. ; cxix. 18.) And after him his son again shows that we ought to "seek out wisdom as silver,[3] and to make merchandise of her rather than of gold." (Prov. ii. 4 and iii. 14 [partially quoted] ; John v. 39.) And the Lord when He exhorts the Jews to "search the Scriptures," the more urges us to the enquiry, for He would not thus have spoken if it were possible to comprehend them immediately at the first reading. No one would ever search for what is obvious and at hand, but for that which is wrapt in shadow, and which must be found after much enquiry ; and so to arouse us to the search He calls them "hidden treasure." (Prov. ii. 4 ; Matt. xiii. 44.) These words are said to us that we may not apply ourselves to the words of the Scriptures carelessly or in a chance way, but with great exactness. For if any one listen to what is said in them without enquiring into the meaning, and receive all so as it is spoken, according to the letter, he will suppose many unseemly things of God, will admit of Him that He is a man, that He is made of brass, is wrathful, is furious, and many opinions yet worse than these. But if he fully learn the sense that lies beneath, he will be freed from all this unseemli-

ness. (Rev. i. 15.) The very text which now lies before us says, that God has a bosom, a thing proper to bodily substances, yet no one is so insane as to imagine, that He who is without body is a body. In order then that we may properly interpret the entire passage according to its spiritual meaning, let us search it through from its beginning.

"No man hath seen God at any time." By what connection of thought does the Apostle come to say this? After showing the exceeding greatness of the gifts of Christ, and the infinite difference between them and those ministered by Moses, he would add the reasonable cause of the difference. Moses, as being a servant, was minister of lower things, but Christ being Lord and King, and the King's Son, brought to us things far greater, being ever with the Father, and beholding Him continually ; wherefore He saith, "No man hath seen God at any time." What then shall we answer to the most mighty of voice, Esaias, when he says, "I saw the Lord sitting upon a throne high and lifted up" (Isa. vi. 1) ; and to John himself testifying of Him, that "he said these things when he had seen His glory"? (c. xii. 41.) What also to Ezekiel? for he too beheld Him sitting above the Cherubim. (Ezek. i. and x.) What to Daniel? for he too saith, "The Ancient of days did sit" (Dan. vii. 9.) What to Moses himself, saying, "Show me Thy Glory, that I may see Thee so as to know Thee." (Ex. xxxiii. 13, partly from LXX.) And Jacob took his name from this very thing, being called[4] "Israel" ; for Israel is "one that sees God."[5] And others have seen him. How then saith John, "No man hath seen God at any time"? It is to declare, that all these were instances of (His) condescension, not the vision of the Essence itself unveiled. For had they

---

[1] αἰῶνα.
[2] εἰς σύνεσιν מַשְׂכִּיל Maschil, σύνεσις, intellectus, et ut Hieron. reddit, eruditio, aliqui, erudiens, vel intellectum præstans. Lorin. in tit. Ps. 31. (32).
[3] Some MSS. read "silver, and search for it as treasure; He would not have said Search, &c."

[4] γνωστῶς,
[5] Augus. De Civ. Dei, lib. 16, 39.

seen the very Nature, they would not have beheld It under different forms, since that is simple, without form, or parts, or bounding lines. It sits not, nor stands, nor walks : these things belong all to bodies. But how He Is, He only knoweth. And this He hath declared by a certain prophet, saying, " I have multiplied visions, and used similitudes[1] by the hands of the prophets " (Hos. xii. 10), that is, " I have condescended, I have not appeared as I really was." For since His Son was about to appear in very flesh, He prepared them from old time to behold the substance of God, as far as it was possible for them to see It ; but what God really is, not only have not the prophets seen, but not even angels nor archangels. If you ask them, you shall not hear them answering anything concerning His Essence, but sending up,[2] " Glory to God in the Highest, on earth peace, good will towards men." (Luke ii. 14.) If you desire to learn something from Cherubim or Seraphim, you shall hear the mystic song of His Holiness, and that " heaven and earth are full of His glory." (Isa. vi. 3.) If you enquire of the higher powers, you shall but find[3] that their one work is the praise of God. " Praise ye Him," saith David, " all His hosts." (Ps. cxlviii. 2.) But the Son only beholds Him, and the Holy Ghost. How can any created nature even see the Uncreated? If we are absolutely unable clearly to discern any incorporeal power whatsoever, even though created, as has been often proved in the case of angels, much less can we discern the Essence which is incorporeal and uncreated. Wherefore Paul saith, " Whom no man hath seen, nor can see." (1 Tim. vi. 16.) Does then this special attribute[4] belong to the Father only, not to the Son? Away with the thought. It belongs also to the Son ; and to show that it does so, hear Paul declaring this point, and saying, that He " is the Image of the invisible God." (Col. i. 15.) Now if He be the Image of the Invisible, He must be invisible Himself, for otherwise He would not be an " image." And wonder not that Paul saith in another place, " God was manifested in the Flesh " (1 Tim. iii. 16) ; because the manifestation[5] took place by means of the flesh, not according to (His) Essence. Besides, Paul shows that He is invisible, not only to men, but also to the powers above, for after saying, " was manifested in the Flesh," he adds, " was seen of angels."

[2.] So that even to angels He then became visible, when He put on the Flesh ; but before that time they did not so behold Him, because even to them His Essence was invisible.

" How then," asks some one, " did Christ say, ' Despise not one of these little ones, for I tell you, that their angels do always behold the face of My Father which is in heaven ' ? (Matt. xviii. 10.) Hath then God a face, and is He bounded by the heavens?" Who so mad as to assert this? What then is the meaning of the words? As when He saith, " Blessed are the pure in heart, for they shall see God" (Matt. v. 8), He means that intellectual vision which is possible to us, and the having God in the thoughts ; so in the case of angels, we must understand[6] that by reason of their pure and sleepless[7] nature they do nothing else, but always image to themselves God. And therefore Christ saith, that " No man knoweth the Father, save the Son." (Matt. x. 27.) What then, are we all in ignorance? God forbid ; but none knoweth Him as the Son knoweth Him. As then many[8] have seen Him in the mode of vision permitted to them, but no one has beheld His Essence, so many of us know God, but what His substance can be none knoweth, save only He that was begotten of Him. For by " knowledge " He here means an exact idea and comprehension, such as the Father hath of the Son. " As the Father knoweth Me, even so know I the Father." (c. x. 15.)

Observe, therefore, with what fullness[9] the Evangelist speaks ; for having said that " no man hath seen God at any time," he does not go on to say, " that the Son who hath seen, hath declared Him," but adds something beyond " seeing " by the words, " Who is in the bosom of the Father " ; because, " to dwell[10] in the bosom " is far more than " to see." For he that merely " seeth " hath not an in every way exact knowledge of the object, but he that " dwelleth in the bosom " can be ignorant of nothing. Now lest when thou hearest that " none knoweth the Father, save the Son," thou shouldest assert that although He knoweth the Father more than all, yet He knoweth not how great He is, the Evangelist says that He dwells in the bosom of the Father ; and Christ Himself declares, that He knoweth Him as much as the Father knoweth the Son. Ask therefore the gainsayer, " Tell me, doth the Father know the Son?" And if he be not mad, he will certainly answer "Yes." Then ask again ; " Doth He see and know Him with exact vision and knowledge? Doth He know clearly what He Is?" He will certainly confess this also. From this next collect the exact comprehension the Son has of the Father. For He saith, " As the Father knoweth me, even so know I the Father " (c. x. 15) ; and in another place, " Not that any man hath seen the

Father, save He which is of God." (c. vi. 46.) Wherefore, as I said, the Evangelist mentions " the bosom," to show all this to us by that one word ; that great is the affinity and nearness of the Essence, that the knowledge is nowise different, that the power is equal. For the Father would not have in His bosom one of another essence, nor would He have dared, had He been one amongst many servants, to live [1] in the bosom of his Lord, for this belongs only to a true Son, to one who has [2] much confidence towards His Father, and who is in nothing inferior to Him.

Wouldest thou learn also His eternity? Hear what Moses saith concerning the Father. When he asked what he was commanded to answer should the Jews enquire of him, " Who it was that had sent him," he heard these words : " Say, I AM hath sent me." (Ex. iii. 14.) Now the expression "I AM," [3] is significative of Being ever, and Being without beginning, of Being really and absolutely. And this also the expression, " Was in the beginning," declares, being indicative of Being ever ; so that John uses this word to show that the Son Is from everlasting to everlasting [4] in the bosom of the Father. For that you may not from the sameness of name, suppose that He is some one of those who are made sons by grace, first, the article is added, distinguishing Him from those by grace. But if this does not content you, if you still look earthwards, hear a name more absolute than this, " Only-Begotten." If even after this you still look below, " I will not refuse," says he, (St. John,) " to apply to God a term belonging to man, I mean the word ' bosom,' only suspect nothing degrading." Dost thou see the lovingkindness and carefulness of the Lord? God applies [5] to Himself unworthy expressions, that even so thou mayest see through them, and have some great and lofty thought of Him ; and dost thou tarry below? For tell me, wherefore is that gross and carnal word " bosom " employed in this place? Is it that we may suppose God to be a body? Away, he by no means saith so. Why then is it spoken? for if by it neither the genuineness of the Son is established, nor that God is not a body, the word, because it serves no purpose, is superfluously thrown in. Why then is it spoken? For I shall not desist from asking thee this question. Is it not very plain, that it is for no other reason but that by it we might understand the genuineness of the Only-Begotten, and His Co-eternity with the Father?

[3.] " He hath declared Him," saith John. What hath he declared? That " no man hath seen God at any time " ? That " God is one " ? But this all the other prophets testify, and Moses continually [6] exclaims, " The Lord thy God is one Lord " (Deut. vi. 4) ; and Esaias, " Before Me there was no God formed, neither shall there be after me." (Isa. xliii. 10.) What more then have we learned from " the Son which is in the bosom of the Father " ? What from " the Only-Begotten " ? In the first place, these very words were uttered by His working ; in the next place, we have received a teaching that is far clearer, and learned that " God is a spirit, and they that worship Him must worship Him in spirit and in truth " (c. iv. 24) ; and again, that it is impossible to see God ; " that no man knoweth " Him, " save the Son " (Matt. xi. 27) ; that He is the Father of the true and Only-Begotten ; and all other things that are told us of Him. But the word " hath declared " [7] shows the plainer and clearer teaching which He gave not to the Jews only but to all the world, and established. To the prophets not even all the Jews gave heed, but to the Only-Begotten Son of God all the world yielded and obeyed. So the " declaration " in this place shows the greater clearness of His teaching, and therefore also He is called " Word," and " Angel [8] of great counsel." [9]

Since then we have been vouchsafed a larger and more perfect teaching, God having no longer spoken by the prophets, but " having in these last days spoken to us by His Son " (Heb. i. 1), let us show forth a conversation far higher than theirs, and suitable to the honor bestowed on us. Strange would it be that He should have so far lowered Himself, as to choose to speak to us no longer by His servants, but by His own mouth, and yet we should show forth nothing more than those of old. They had Moses for their teacher, we, Moses' Lord. Let us then exhibit a heavenly wisdom [10] worthy of this honor, and let us have nothing to do with earth. It was for this that He brought His teaching from heaven above, that He might remove our thoughts thither, that we might be imitators of our Teacher according to our power. But how may we become imitators of Christ? By acting in everything for the common good, and not merely seeking our own. " For even Christ," saith Paul, " pleased not Himself, but as it is written, The reproaches of them that reproached Thee fell on Me." (Rom. xv. 3 ; Ps. lxix. 9.) Let no one therefore seek his own. In truth, a man (really) seeks his own good when he looks to that of his neighbor. What is their good is ours ; we are one body, and parts and limbs one of another. Let us not then be as though we were rent asunder. Let no one say, " such a person is no

---

[1] τρέφεσθαι, al. στρέφεσθαι, versari.
[2] lit. " uses."
[3] lit. " He Who Is." Another reading of the passage is, " if he were asked . . . and should answer, he is bidden to say that, &c."
[4] ἀνάρχως καὶ ἀϊδίως.          [5] al. " allows to be applied."
[6] ἄνω καὶ κάτω.          [7] ἐξηγήσατο.          [8] or, " Messenger."
[9] μεγάλης βουλῆς ἄγγελος. The LXX. version of the titles of Christ, Isa. ix. 6.
[10] φιλοσοφίαν.

friend of mine, nor relation, nor neighbor, I have nought to do with him, how shall I approach, how address him?" Though he be neither relation nor friend, yet he is a man, who shares the same nature with thee, owns the same Lord, is thy fellow-servant, and fellow-sojourner,[1] for he is born in the same world. And if besides he partakes of the same faith, behold he hath also become a member of thee : for what friendship could work such union, as the relationship of faith? And our intimacy one with another must not be such nearness only as friends ought to show to friends, but such as is between limb and limb, because no man can possibly discover any intimacy greater than this sort of friendship and fellowship.[2] As then you cannot say, "Whence arises my intimacy and connection with this limb?" (that would be ridiculous ;) so neither can you say so in the case of your brother. "We are all baptized into one body" (1 Cor. xii. 13), saith Paul. "Wherefore into one body?" That we be not rent asunder, but preserve the just proportions of that one body by our intercourse and friendship one with another.

Let us not then despise one another, lest we be neglectful of ourselves.[3] "For no man ever yet hated his own flesh, but nourisheth and cherisheth it." (Eph. v. 29.) And therefore God hath given to us but one habitation, this earth, hath distributed all things equally, hath lighted one sun for us all, hath spread above us one roof, the sky, made one table, the earth, bear[4] food for us. And another table hath He given far better than this, yet that too is one, (those who share our mysteries understand my words,) one manner of birth He hath bestowed on all, the spiritual, we all have one country, that in the heavens, of the same cup drink we all. He hath not bestowed on the rich man a gift more abundant and more honorable, and on the poor one more mean and small, but He hath called all alike. He hath given carnal things with equal regard to all,[5] and spiritual in like manner. Whence then proceeds the great inequality of conditions in life? From the avarice and pride of the wealthy. But let not, brethren, let not this any longer be ; and when matters of universal interest and more pressing necessity bring us together, let us not be divided by things earthly and insignificant : I mean, by wealth and poverty, by bodily relationship, by enmity and friendship ; for all these things are a shadow, nay less substantial than a shadow, to those who possess the bond of charity from above. Let us then preserve this unbroken, and none of those evil spirits[6] will be able to enter in, who cause division in so perfect union ;[7] to which may we all attain by the grace and lovingkindness of our Lord Jesus Christ, by whom and with whom, to the Father and the Holy Ghost, be glory, now and ever, and world without end. Amen.

---

# HOMILY XVI.

### JOHN i. 19.

"And this is the record of John, when the Jews sent priests and Levites from Jerusalem to ask him, Who art thou?"

[1.] A DREADFUL thing is envy, beloved, a dreadful thing and a pernicious, to the enviers, not to the envied. For it harms and wastes them first, like some mortal venom deeply seated in their souls ; and if by chance it injure its objects, the harm it does is small and trifling, and such as brings greater gain than loss. Indeed not in the case of envy only, but in every other, it is not he that has suffered, but he that has done the wrong, who receives injury. For had not this been so, Paul would not have enjoined the disciples rather to endure wrong than to inflict it, when he says, "Why do ye not rather take wrong? Why do ye not rather suffer yourselves to be defrauded?"

(1 Cor. vi. 7.) Well he knew, that destruction ever follows, not the injured party, but the injuring. All this I have said, by reason of the envy of the Jews. Because those who had flocked from the cities to John, and had condemned their own sins, and caused themselves to be baptized, repenting as it were after Baptism, send to ask him, "Who art thou?" Of a truth they were the offspring of vipers, serpents, and even worse if possible than this. O evil and adulterous and perverse generation, after having been baptized, do ye then become vainly curious, and question about the Baptist? What folly can be greater than this of yours? How was it that ye came forth? that ye confessed your sins, that ye ran to the Baptist? How was it that you asked him what you must do? when in all

---

[1] ὁμόσκηνος, " tent-fellow."  [2] al. " care."
[3] al. " let us then so care for our neighbors, as not neglecting each his own flesh."

[4] ἀνῆκεν.
[5] ὁμοτίμως.
[6] al. " passions."
[7] al. " union with Him."

this you were acting unreasonably, since you knew not the principle and purpose of his coming. Yet of this the blessed John said nothing, nor does he charge or reproach them with it, but answers them with all gentleness.

It is worth while to learn why he did thus. It was, that their wickedness might be manifest and plain to all men. Often did John testify of Christ to the Jews, and when he baptized them he continually made mention of Him to his company, and said, "I indeed baptize you with water, but there cometh One after me who is mightier than I; He shall baptize you with the Holy Ghost and with fire." (Matt. iii. 11.) With regard to him they were affected by a human feeling; for, tremblingly attentive[1] to the opinion of the world, and looking to "the outward appearance" (2 Cor. x. 7), they deemed it an unworthy thing that he should be subject to Christ. Since there were many things that pointed out John for an illustrious person. In the first place, his distinguished and noble descent; for he was the son of a chief priest. Then his conversation, his austere mode of life, his contempt of all human things; for despising dress and table, and house and food itself, he had passed his former time in the desert. In the case of Christ all was the contrary of this. His family was mean, (as they often objected to Him, saying, "Is not this the carpenter's son? Is not his mother called Mary? and his brethren James and Joses?") (Matt. xiii. 55); and that which was supposed to be His country was held in such evil repute, that even Nathanael said, "Can there any good thing come out of Nazareth?" (c. i. 46.) His mode of living was ordinary, and His garments not better than those of the many. For He was not girt with a leathern girdle, nor was His raiment of hair, nor did He eat honey and locusts. But He fared like all others, and was present at the feasts of wicked men and publicans, that He might draw them to Him. Which thing the Jews not understanding reproached Him with, as He also saith Himself, "The Son of Man came eating and drinking, and they say, Behold a gluttonous man and a winebibber, a friend of publicans and sinners." (Matt. xi. 19.) When then John continually sent them from himself to Jesus, who seemed to them a meaner person, being ashamed and vexed at this, and wishing rather to have him for their teacher, they did not dare to say so plainly, but send to him, thinking by their flattery to induce him to confess that he was the Christ. They do not therefore send to him mean men, as in the case of Christ, for when they wished to lay hold on Him, they sent servants, and then Herodians, and the like, but in this instance, "priests and Levites," and not merely "priests," but those "from Jerusalem," that is, the more honorable; for the Evangelist did not notice this without a cause. And they send to ask, "Who art thou?" Yet the manner of his birth was well known to all, so that all said, "What manner of child shall this be?" (Luke i. 66); and the report had gone forth into all the hill country. And afterwards when he came to Jordan, all the cities were set on the wing, and came to him from Jerusalem, and from all Judæa, to be baptized. Why then do they[2] now ask? Not because they did not know him, (how could that be, when he had been made manifest in so many ways?) but because they wished to bring him to do that which I have mentioned.

[2.] Hear then how this blessed person answered to the intention with which they asked the question, not to the question itself. When they said, "Who art thou?" he did not at once give them what would have been the direct answer, "I am the voice of one crying in the wilderness." But what did he? He removed the suspicion they had formed; for, saith the Evangelist, being asked, "Who art thou?"

Ver. 20. "He confessed, and denied not; but confessed, I am not the Christ."

Observe the wisdom of the Evangelist. He mentions this for the third time, to set forth the excellency of the Baptist, and their wickedness and folly. And Luke also says, that when the multitudes supposed him to be the Christ, he again removes their suspicion.[3] This is the part of an honest servant, not only not to take to himself his master's honor, but also to reject it[4] when given to him by the many. But the multitudes arrived at this supposition from simplicity and ignorance; these questioned him from an ill intention, which I have mentioned, expecting, as I said, to draw him over to their purpose by their flattery. Had they not expected this, they would not have proceeded immediately to another question, but would have been angry with him for having given them an answer foreign to their enquiry, and would have said, "Why, did we suppose that? did we come to ask thee that?" But now as taken and detected in the fact, they proceed to another question, and say,

Ver. 21. "What then? art thou Elias? And he saith, I am not."

For they expected that Elias also would come, as Christ declares; for when His disciples enquired, "How then do the scribes say that Elias must first come?" (Matt. xvii. 10) He replied, "Elias truly shall first come, and restore all

---

[2] al. "these therefore."
[3] Morel. "in like manner one may see in Luke, (iii. 16,) John saying to those who reasoned concerning him whether he was the Christ, that "One mightier than I cometh," and by his answer again removing such a suspicion."     [4] διακρούεσθαι.

things." Then they ask, "Art thou that prophet?
and he answered, No." (Matt. xvii. 10.) Yet
surely he was a prophet.  Wherefore then doth
he deny it? Because again he looks to the intention of his questioners.  For they expected
that some especial prophet should come, because Moses said, "The Lord thy God will
raise up unto thee a Prophet of thy brethren
like unto me, unto Him shall ye harken."
(Deut. xviii. 15.)  Now this was Christ. Wherefore they do not say, "Art thou a prophet?"
meaning thereby one of the ordinary prophets;
but the expression, "Art thou the prophet?"
with the addition of the article, means, "Art
thou that Prophet who was foretold by Moses?"
and therefore he denied not that he was a
prophet, but that he was "that Prophet."

Ver. 22. "Then said they unto him, Who art
thou? that we may give an answer to them that
sent us.  What sayest thou of thyself?"

Observe them pressing him more vehemently,
urging him, repeating their questions, and not
desisting; while he first kindly removes false
opinions concerning himself, and then sets before them one which is true.  For, saith he,

Ver. 23. "I am the voice of one crying in the
wilderness, Make straight the way of the Lord,
as said the prophet Esaias."

When he had spoken some high and lofty
words concerning Christ, as if (replying) to
their opinion, he immediately betook himself to
the Prophet to draw from thence confirmation
of his assertion.

Ver. 24, 25. "And [saith the Evangelist] they
who were sent were of the Pharisees.  And
they asked him, and said unto him, Why baptizest thou then, if thou be not that Christ,
neither Elias, neither that Prophet?"

Seest thou not without reason I said that they
wished to bring him to this? and the reason why
they did not at first say so was, lest they should
be detected by all men. And then when he said,
"I am not the Christ," they, being desirous to
conceal what they were plotting[1] within, go on to
"Elias," and "that Prophet." But when he said
that he was not one of these either, after that,
in their perplexity, they cast aside the mask, and
without any disguise show clearly their treacherous intention, saying, "Why baptizest thou
then, if thou be not that Christ?" And then
again, wishing to throw some obscurity over the
thing,[2] they add the others also, "Elias," and
"that Prophet." For when they were not able
to trip[3] him by their flattery, they thought that
by an accusation they could compel him[4] to
say the thing that was not.

What folly, what insolence, what ill-timed
officiousness! Ye were sent to learn who and
whence he might be, not to[5] lay down laws for
him also. This too was the conduct of men who
would compel him to confess himself to be the
Christ. Still not even now is he angry, nor
does he, as might have been expected, say to
them anything of this sort, "Do you give orders
and make laws for me?" but again shows great
gentleness towards them.

Ver. 26, 27. "I," saith he, "baptize with
water: but there standeth one among you, whom
ye know not; He it is, who coming after me is
preferred before me, whose shoe's latchet I am
not worthy to unloose."

[3.] What could the Jews have left to say to
this? for even from this the accusation against
them cannot be evaded, the decision against
them admits not of pardon, they have given sentence against themselves. How? In what way?
They deemed John worthy of credit, and so
truthful, that they might believe him not only
when he testified of others, but also when he spoke
concerning himself. For had they not been so
disposed, they would not have sent to learn from
him what related to himself. Because you know
that the only persons whom we believe, especially when speaking of themselves, are those
whom we suppose to be more veracious than any
others. And it is not this alone which closes
their mouths, but also the disposition with which
they had approached him; for they came forth
to, him at first with great eagerness, even though
afterwards they altered. Both which things
Christ declared, when He said, "He was a burning (and a shining) light, and ye were willing for
a season to rejoice in his light." Moreover, his
answer made him yet more worthy of credit.
For (Christ) saith, "He that seeketh not his
own glory,[6] the same is true, and no unrighteousness is in him." Now this man sought it not,
but refers the Jews to another. And those who
were sent were of the most trustworthy among
them, and of the highest rank, so that they could
have in no way any refuge or excuse, for the
unbelief which they exhibited towards Christ.
Wherefore did ye not receive the things spoken
concerning Him by John? you sent men who
held the first rank among you, you enquired by
them, you heard what the Baptist answered, they
manifested all possible officiousness, sought into
every point, named all the persons you suspected
him to be; and yet most publicly and plainly he
confessed that he was neither "Christ," nor
"Elias" nor "that Prophet." Nor did he stop
even there, but also informed them who he was,
and·spoke of the nature of his own baptism,
that it was but a slight and mean thing, nothing

[1] ἐτύρευον.
[2] Morel. and MS. in Bodl. "seest thou how, disguising what
they had, they add."   [3] ὑποσκελίσαι.
[4] Morel. and MS. in Bodl. "they attempt to involve him in an
accusation, compelling him."
[5] al. "will ye."
[6] τὴν δόξαν τοῦ πέμψαντος αὐτὸν, G. T.

more than some water, and told of the superiority of the Baptism given by Christ; he also cited Esaias the prophet, testifying of old very long ago, and calling Christ "Lord" (Isa. xl. 3), but giving him the names of "minister and servant." What after this ought they to have done? Ought they not to have believed on Him who was witnessed of, to have worshiped Him, to have confessed Him to be God? For the character and heavenly wisdom of the witness showed that his testimony proceeded, not from flattery, but from truth; which is plain also from this, that no man prefers his neighbor to himself, nor, when he may lawfully give honor to himself, will yield it up to another, especially when it is so great as that of which we speak. So that John would not have renounced[1] this testimony (as belonging) to Christ, had He not been God. For though he might have rejected it for himself as being too great for his own nature, yet he would not have assigned it to another nature that was beneath it.

"But there standeth One among you, whom ye know not." Reasonable it was that Christ should mingle among the people as one of the many, because everywhere He taught men not to be puffed up and boastful. And in this place by "knowledge" the Baptist means a perfect acquaintance with Him, who and whence He was. And immediately next to this he puts, "Who cometh after me"; all but saying, "Think not that all is contained in my baptism, for had that been perfect, Another would not have arisen after me to offer you a different One, but this of mine is a preparation and a clearing the way for that other. Mine is but a shadow and image, but One must come who shall add to this the reality. So that His very coming 'after me' especially declares His dignity: for had the first been perfect, no place would have been required for a second." "Is[2] before me," is more honorable, brighter. And then, lest they should imagine that His superiority was found by comparison, desiring to establish His incomparableness, he says, "Whose shoe's latchet I am not worthy to unloose"; that is, who is not simply "before me," but before me in such a way, that I am not worthy to be numbered among the meanest of His servants. For to loose the shoe is the office of humblest service.

Now if John was not worthy to "unloose the latchet" (Matt. xi. 11), John, than whom "among them that are born of women there hath not risen a greater," where shall we rank ourselves? If he who was equal to, or rather greater than, all the world,[3] (for saith Paul, " the world was not worthy" of them—Heb. xi. 38,) declares himself not worthy to be reckoned even among

the meanest of those who should minister unto Him, what shall we say, who are full of ten thousand sins, and are as far from the excellence of John, as earth from heaven.

[4.] He then saith that he himself is not "worthy so much as to unloose the latchet of His shoe"; while the enemies of the truth are mad with such a madness, as to assert[4] that they are worthy to know Him even as He knows Himself. What is worse than such insanity, what more frenized than such arrogance? Well hath a wise man said, "The beginning of pride is not to know the Lord."[5]

The devil would not have been brought down and become a devil, not being a devil before, had he not been sick of this disease. This it was that cast him out from that confidence,[6] this sent him to the pit of fire, this was the cause of all his woes. For it is enough of itself to destroy every excellence of the soul, whether it find almsgiving, or prayer, or fasting, or anything. For, saith the Evangelist, "That which is highly esteemed among men is impure before the Lord." (Luke xvi. 15—not quoted exactly.) Therefore it is not only fornication or adultery that are wont to defile those who practice them, but pride also, and that far more than those vices. Why? Because fornication though it is an unpardonable sin, yet a man may plead the desire; but pride cannot possibly find any cause or pretext of any sort whatever by which to obtain so much as a shadow of excuse; it is nothing but a distortion and most grievous disease of the soul, produced from no other source but folly. For there is nothing more foolish than a proud man, though he be surrounded with wealth, though he possess much of the wisdom of this world, though he be set in royal place, though he bear about with all things that among men appear desirable.

For if the man who is proud of things really good is wretched and miserable, and loses the reward of all those things, must not he who is exalted by things that are nought, and puffs himself up because of a shadow or the flower of the grass, (for such is this world's glory,) be more ridiculous than any, when he does just as some poor needy man might do, pining all his time with hunger, yet if ever he should chance one night to see a dream of good fortune, filled with conceit because of it?

O wretched and miserable! when thy soul is perishing by a most grievous disease, when thou art poor with utter poverty, art thou high-minded because thou hast such and such a number of talents of gold? because thou hast a multitude of slaves and cattle? Yet these are not thine;

---

[1] ἐξέστη.  [2] "is preferred," E. V.
[3] Morel. and MS. in Bodl. "for thus Paul speaks of the saints concerning whom he writes, 'of whom,' etc."

[4] Morel. and MS. in Bodl. "boldly speaking out, (ἀπαυθαδιαζομένους,) say that, &c."
[5] Ecclus. x. 12, LXX. ἀνθρώπου ἀφισταμένου ἀπὸ τοῦ K. Eng. ver. "when one departeth."  [6] παρρησίας.

and if thou dost not believe my words, learn from the experience of those who have gone before[1] thee. And if thou art so drunken, that thou canst not be instructed even from what has befallen others, wait a little, and thou shalt know by what befalls thyself that these things avail thee nothing, when gasping for life, and master not of a single hour, not even of a little moment, thou shalt unwillingly leave them[2] to those who are about thee, and these perhaps those whom thou wouldest not. For many have not been permitted even to give directions concerning them, but have departed suddenly,[3] desiring to enjoy them, but not permitted, dragged from them, and forced to yield them up to others, giving place by compulsion to those to whom they would not. That this be not our case, let us, while we are yet in strength and health, send forward our riches hence to our own city, for thus only and in no other way shall we be able to enjoy them; so shall we lay them up in a place inviolate and safe. For there is nothing, there is nothing there that can take them from us; no death, no attested wills,[4] no successors to inheritances,[5] no false informations, no plottings against us, but he who has departed hence bearing away great wealth with him may enjoy it there for ever. Who then is so wretched as not to desire to revel in riches which are his own throughout? Let us then transfer our wealth, and remove it thither. We shall not need for such a removal asses, or camels, or carriages, or ships, (God hath relieved even us from this difficulty,) but we only want the poor, the lame, the crippled, the infirm. These are entrusted with this transfer, these convey our riches to heaven, these introduce the masters of such wealth as this to the inheritance of goods everlasting. Which may it be that we all attain through the grace and lovingkindness of our Lord Jesus Christ, by whom and with whom, to the Father and the Holy Ghost, be glory, now and ever, and world without end. Amen.

# HOMILY XVII.

## JOHN i. 28, 29.

"These things were done in Bethany beyond Jordan, where John was baptizing. The next day he seeth Jesus coming unto him, and saith, Behold the Lamb of God, which taketh away the sin of the world."

[1.] A GREAT virtue is boldness and freedom of speech, and the making all things second in importance to the confessing of Christ; so great and admirable, that the Only-begotten Son of God proclaims such an one in the presence of the Father. (Luke xii. 8.) Yet the recompense is more than just, for thou confessest upon earth, He in heaven, thou in the presence of men, He before the Father and all the angels.

Such an one was John, who regarded not the multitude, nor opinion, nor anything else belonging to men, but trod all this beneath his feet, and proclaimed to all with becoming freedom the things respecting Christ. And therefore the Evangelist marks the very place, to show the boldness of the loud-voiced herald. For it was not in a house, not in a corner, not in the wilderness, but in the midst of the multitude, after that he had occupied Jordan, when all that were baptized by him were present, (for the Jews came upon him as he was baptizing,) there it was that he proclaimed aloud that wonderful confession concerning Christ, full of those sublime and great and mysterious doctrines, and that he was not worthy to unloose the latchet of His shoe. Wherefore he saith,[6] "These things were done in Bethany," or, as all the more correct copies have it, "in Bethabara." For Bethany was not "beyond Jordan," nor bordering on the wilderness, but somewhere nigh to Jerusalem.

He marks the places also for another reason. Since he was not about to relate matters of old date, but such as had come to pass but a little time before, he makes those who were present and had beheld, witnesses of his words, and supplies proof from the places themselves. For confident that nothing was added by himself to what was said, but that he simply and with truth described things as they were, he draws a testimony from the places, which, as I said, would be no common demonstration of his veracity.

"The next day he seeth Jesus coming to him, and saith, Behold the Lamb of God, which taketh away the sin of the world."

The Evangelists distributed the periods amongst them; and Matthew having cut short

---

[1] or, "received them before."
[2] al. "pass them on."
[3] ἄθροον.

[4] ἀληθεῖς διαθῆκαι.
[5] διάδοχοι κλήρων.
[6] al. "how then doth he this? adding and saying."

his notice of the time before John the Baptist was bound, hastens to that which follows, while the Evangelist John not only does not cut short this period, but dwells most on it. Matthew, after the return of Jesus from the wilderness, saying nothing of the intermediate circumstances, as what John spake, and what the Jews sent and said, and having cut short all the rest, passes immediately to the prison. "For," saith he, "Jesus having heard" that John was betrayed, "departed thence." (Matt. xiv. 13.) But John does not so. He is silent as to the journey into the wilderness, as having been described by Matthew; but he relates what followed the descent from the mountain, and after having gone through many circumstances, adds, "For John was not yet cast into prison." (c. iii. 24.)

And wherefore, says one, does Jesus now come to him? why does he come not merely once, but this second time also? For Matthew says that His coming was necessary on account of Baptism: since Jesus adds, that "thus it becometh us to fulfill all righteousness." (Matt. iii. 15.) But John says that He came again after Baptism, and declares it in this place, for, "I saw," saith he, "the Spirit descending from heaven like a dove, and It abode upon Him." Wherefore then did He come to John? for He came not casually, but went expressly to him. "John," saith the Evangelist, "seeth Jesus coming unto him." Then wherefore cometh He? In order that since John had baptized Him with many (others), no one might suppose that He had hastened to John for the same reason as the rest, to confess sins, and to wash in the river unto repentance. For this He comes, to give John an opportunity of setting this opinion right again, for by saying, "Behold the Lamb of God, that taketh away the sin of the world," he removes the whole suspicion. For very plain it is that One so pure as to be able to wash away[1] the sins of others, does not come to confess sins, but to give opportunity to that marvelous herald to impress what he had said more definitely on those who had heard his former words, and to add others besides. The word "Behold" is used, because many had been seeking Him by reason of what had been said, and for a long time. For this cause, pointing Him out when present, he said, "Behold," this is He so long sought, this is "the Lamb." He calls Him "Lamb," to remind the Jews of the prophecy of Isaiah, and of the shadow under the law of Moses, that he may the better lead them from the type to the reality. That Lamb of Moses took not at once away the sin of any one; but this took away the sin of all the world; for

when it was in danger of perishing, He quickly delivered it from the wrath of God.

Ver. 30. "This is He of whom I said, He that cometh after me is preferred before me."

[2.] Seest thou here also how he interprets the word "before"? for having called Him "Lamb," and that He "taketh away the sin of the world," then he saith that "He is preferred before me, for He was before me"; declaring that this is the "before," the taking upon Him the sins of the world, "and the baptizing with the Holy Ghost." "For my coming had no farther object than to proclaim the common Benefactor of the world, and to afford the baptism of water; but His was to cleanse all men, and to give them the power of the Comforter." "He is preferred before me," that is to say, has appeared brighter than I, because "He was before me." Let those who have admitted the madness of Paul of Samosata be ashamed when they withstand so manifest a truth.

Ver. 31. "And I knew Him not," he saith.

Here he renders his testimony free from suspicion, by showing that it was not from human friendship, but had been caused by divine revelation. "I knew Him not," he saith. How then couldest thou be a trustworthy witness? How shalt thou teach others, while thou thyself art ignorant? He did not say "I know Him not," but, "I knew Him not"; so that in this way he would be shown most trustworthy; for why should he have shown favor to one of whom he was ignorant?

"But that He should be made manifest unto Israel, therefore am I come baptizing with water."

He then did not need baptism, nor had that laver any other object than to prepare for all others a way to faith on Christ. For he did not say, "that I might cleanse those who are baptized," or, "that I might deliver them from their sins," but, "that He should be made manifest unto Israel." "And why, tell me, could he not without baptism have preached and brought the multitudes to Him?" But in this way it would not have been by any means easy. For they would not so all have run together, if the preaching had been without the baptism; they would not by the comparison have learned His superiority. For the multitude came together not to hear his words, but for what? To be "baptized, confessing their sins." But when they came, they were taught the matters concerning Christ, and the difference of His baptism. Yet even this of John was of greater dignity than the Jewish, and therefore all ran to it; yet even so it was imperfect.

"How then didst thou know Him?" "By the descent of the Spirit," he saith. But again, lest any one should suppose that he was in need

---

[1] al. "to redeem."

of the Spirit as we are, hear how he removes the suspicion, by showing that the descent of the Spirit was only to declare Christ. For having said, "And I knew Him not," he adds, "But He that sent me to baptize with water, the Same said unto me, Upon whom thou shalt see the Spirit descending and remaining on Him, the same is He which baptizeth with the Holy Ghost." (Ver. 33.)

Seest thou that this was the work of the Spirit, to point out Christ? The testimony of John was indeed not to be suspected, but wishing to make it yet more credible, he leads it up to God and the Holy Spirit. For when John had testified to a thing so great and wonderful, so fit to astonish all his hearers, that He alone took on Him the sins of all the world, and that the greatness of the gift sufficed for so great a ransom, afterwards he proves this assertion.[1] And the proof is that He is the Son of God, and that He needed not baptism, and that the object of the descent of the Spirit was only to make Him known. For it was not in the power of John to give the Spirit, as those who were baptized by him show when they say, "We have not so much as heard whether there be any Holy Ghost." (Acts xix. 2.) In truth, Christ needed not baptism, neither his nor any other;[2] but rather baptism needed the power of Christ. For that which was wanting was the crowning blessing of all, that he who was baptized should be deemed worthy of the Spirit; this free gift[3] then of the Spirit He added when He came.

Ver. 32–34. "And John bare record, saying, I saw the Spirit descending from the heaven like a dove, and It abode upon Him. And I knew Him not: but He that sent me to baptize with water, the Same said unto me, Upon whom thou shalt see the Spirit descending, and remaining on Him, the same is He which baptizeth with the Holy Ghost. And I saw, and bare record that this is the Son of God."

He puts the "I knew Him not" repeatedly.[4] On what account, and wherefore? He was His kinsman according to the flesh. "Behold," saith the angel, "thy cousin Elisabeth, she also hath received a son." (Luke i. 36.) That therefore he might not seem to favor Him because of the relationship, he repeats the "I knew Him not." And this happened with good reason; for he had passed all his time in the wilderness away from his father's house.

How then, if he knew Him not before the descent of the Spirit, and if he then for the first time recognized Him, did he forbid Him before baptism, saying, "I have need to be baptized of Thee, and comest Thou to me?" (Matt.

iii. 14), since this was a proof that he knew Him very well. Yet he knew Him not before or for a long time, and with good cause; for the marvels which took place when He was a child, as the circumstances of the Magi and others the like, had happened long before, while John himself was very young, and since much time had elapsed in the interval, He was naturally unknown to all. For had He been known, John would not have said, "That He should be made manifest to Israel, therefore am I come baptizing."

[3.] Hence it remains clear to us, that the miracles which they say belong to Christ's childhood, are false, and the inventions of certain who bring them into notice. For if He had begun from His early age to work wonders, neither could John have been ignorant of Him, nor would the multitude have needed a teacher to make Him known. But now he says, that for this he is come, "that He might be made manifest to Israel"; and for this reason he said again, "I have need to be baptized of Thee." Afterwards, as having gained more exact knowledge of Him, he proclaimed Him to the multitude, saying, "This is He of whom I said, After me cometh a Man which is preferred before me." For "He who sent me to baptize with water," and sent me for this end, "that He should be made manifest to Israel," Himself revealed Him even before the descent of the Spirit. Wherefore even before He came, John said, "One cometh after me who is preferred before me." He knew Him not before he came to Jordan and baptized all men, but when He was about to be baptized, then he knew Him; and this from the Father revealing Him to the Prophet, and the Spirit showing Him when He was being baptized to the Jews, for whose sake indeed the descent of the Spirit took place. For that the witness of John might not be despised who said, that "He was before me," and that "He baptizeth with the Spirit," and that "He judgeth the world," the Father utters a Voice proclaiming the Son, and the Spirit descends, directing[5] that Voice to the Head of Jesus. For since one was baptizing, the other receiving baptism, the Spirit comes to correct the idea which some of those present might form, that the words were spoken of John. So that when he says, "I knew Him not," he speaks of former time, not that near to His baptism. Otherwise how could he have forbidden Him, saying, "I have need to be baptized of Thee"? How could he have said such words concerning Him?

"But," says one, "how then did not the Jews believe? for it was not John only that saw the Spirit in the likeness of a dove." It was, because, even if they did see, such things require

---

[1] ἀπόφασιν.
[2] or, "of any other man."
[3] χορηγία.
[4] συνεχῶς.
[5] ἐπελκον.

not only the eyes of the body, but more than these, the vision of the understanding, to prevent men from supposing the whole to be a vain illusion. For if when they saw Him working wonders, touching with His own hands the sick and the dead, and so bringing them back to life and health, they were so drunk with malice as to declare the contrary of what they saw; how could they shake off their unbelief by the descent of the Spirit only? And some say, that they did not all see it, but only John and those of them who were better[1] disposed. Because, even though it were possible with fleshly eyes to see the Spirit descending as in the likeness of a dove, still not for this was it absolutely necessary that the circumstance should be visible to all. For Zacharias saw many things in a sensible form, as did Daniel and Ezekiel, and had none to share in what they saw; Moses also saw many things such as none other hath seen; nor did all the disciples enjoy[2] the view of the Transfiguration on the mount, nor did they all alike behold Him at the time of the Resurrection. And this Luke plainly shows, when he says, that He showed Himself "to witnesses chosen before of God." (Acts x. 41.)

"And I saw, and bare record that this is the Son of God."

Where did he "bear record that this is the Son of God?" he called Him indeed "Lamb," and said that He should "baptize with the Spirit," but nowhere did he say of Him, "Son of God." But the other Evangelists do not write that He said anything after the baptism, but having been silent as to the time intervening, they mention the miracles of Christ which were done after John's captivity,[3] whence we may reasonably conjecture that these and many others are omitted. And this our Evangelist himself has declared, at the end of his narrative. For they were so far from inventing anything great concerning Him, that the things which seem to bring reproach, these they have all with one voice[4] and with all exactness set down, and you will not find one of them omitting one of such circumstances; but of the miracles, part some have left for the others to relate,[5] part all have passed over in silence.

I say not this without cause, but to answer the shamelessness of the heathen.[6] For this is a sufficient proof of their truth-loving disposition, and that they say nothing for favor. And thus as well as in other ways you may arm yourselves for trial of argument[7] with them. But take heed. Strange were it that the physician, or the shoemaker, or the weaver, in short all artists, should be able each to contend correctly for his own art, but that one calling himself Christian should not be able to give a reason for his own faith; yet these things if overlooked bring only loss to men's property, these if neglected destroy our very souls. Yet such is our wretched disposition, that we give all our care to the former, and the things which are necessary, and which are the groundwork[8] of our salvation, as though of little worth, we despise.

[4.] That it is which prevents the heathen from quickly deriding his own error. For when they, though established in a lie, use every means to conceal the shamefulness of their opinions, while we, the servants of the truth, cannot even open our mouths, how can they help condemning the great weakness of our doctrine? how can they help suspecting our religion to be fraud and folly? how shall they not blaspheme Christ as a deceiver, and a cheat, who used the folly of the many to further his fraud? And we are to blame for this blasphemy, because we will not be wakeful in arguments for godliness, but deem these things superfluous, and care only for the things of earth. He who admires a dancer or a charioteer, or one who contends with beasts, uses every exertion and contrivance not to come off worst in any disputes concerning him, and they string together long panegyrics, as they compose their defense against those who find fault with them, and cast sneers without number at their opponents: but when arguments for Christianity are proposed, they all hang their heads, and scratch themselves, and gape, and retire at length the objects of contempt.

Must not this deserve excessive wrath, when Christ is shown to be less honorable in your estimation than a dancer? since you have contrived ten thousand defenses for the things they have done, though more disgraceful than any, but of the miracles of Christ, though they have drawn to Him the world, you cannot bear even to think or care at all. We believe in the Father, and the Son, and the Holy Ghost, in the Resurrection of bodies, and in Life everlasting. If now any heathen say, "What is this Father, what this Son, what this Holy Ghost? How do you who say that there are three Gods, charge us with having many Gods?" What will you say? What will you answer? How will you repel the attack of these arguments? But what if when you are silent, the unbeliever should again propose this other question, and ask, "What in a word is resurrection? Shall we rise again in this body? or in another, different from this? If in this, what need that it be dissolved?" What will you answer? And what, if he say, "Why did Christ come now and not in old time? Has it

---

seemed good to Him now to care for men, and did He despise us during all the years that are past?" Or if he ask other questions besides, more than these? for I must not propose many questions, and be silent as to the answers to them, lest, in so doing, I harm the simpler among you. What has been already said is sufficient to shake off your slumbers. Well then, if they ask these questions, and you absolutely cannot even listen to the words, shall we, tell me, suffer trifling punishment only, when we have been the cause of such error to those who sit in darkness? I wished, if you had sufficient leisure, to bring before you all the book of a certain impure heathen philosopher written against us, and that of another of earlier date, that so at least I might have roused you, and led you away from your exceeding slothfulness. For if they were wakeful that they might say these things against us, what pardon can we deserve, if we do not even know how to repel the attacks made upon us? For what purpose have we been brought forward?[1] Dost thou not hear the Apostle say, " Be ready to give an answer to every man that asketh you a reason of the hope that is in you"? (1 Pet. iii. 15.) And Paul exhorts in like manner, saying, " Let the word of Christ dwell in you richly." . (Col. iii. 16.) What do they who are more slothful[2] than drones reply to this? " Blessed is every simple soul," and, " he that walketh simply[3] walketh surely." (Prov. x. 8.) For this is the cause of all sorts of evil, that the many do not know how to apply rightly even the testimony of the Scriptures. Thus in this place, the writer does not mean (by "simple") the man who is foolish, or who knows nothing, but him who is free from wickedness, who is no evil-doer, who is wise. If it were not so, it would have been useless to say,[4] " Be ye wise as serpents, and harmless as doves." (Matt. x. 16.) But why should I name these things, when the discourse comes in quite out of place? For besides the things already mentioned, other matters are not right with us, those, I mean, which concern our life and conversation. We are in every way wretched and ridiculous, ever ready to find fault with each other, but slow to correct in ourselves things for which we blame and accuse our neighbor. Wherefore I exhort you, that now at least we attend to ourselves, and stop not at the finding fault, (this is not enough to appease God ;) but that we show forth a change in every way most excellent, in order that having lived here to the glory of God, we may enjoy the glory to come ; which may it come to pass that we will all attain, through the grace and lovingkindness of our Lord Jesus Christ, to whom be glory for ever and ever. Amen.

# HOMILY XVIII.

## JOHN i. 35–37.

" Again the next day after John stood, and two of his disciples; and looking upon Jesus as He walked, he saith, Behold the Lamb of God. And the two disciples heard him speak, and they followed Jesus."

[1.] THE nature of man is somehow a thing slothful, and easily declining to perdition, not by reason of the constitution of the nature itself, but by reason of that sloth which is of deliberate choice. Wherefore it needs much reminding. And for this cause Paul, writing to the Philippians, said, " To write the same things to you, to me indeed is not grievous, but for you it is safe." (Phil. iii. 1.)

The earth when it has once received the seed, straightway gives forth its fruits, and needs not a second sowing ; but with our souls it is not so, and one must be content, after having sown many times, and manifested much carefulness, to be able once to receive fruit. For in the first place, what is said settles in the mind with difficulty, because the ground is very hard, and entangled with thorns innumerable, and there are many which lay plots, and carry away the seed ; afterwards, when it has been fixed and has taken root, it still needs the same attention, that it may come to maturity, and having done so may remain uninjured, and take no harm from any. For in the case of seeds, when the ear is fully formed and has gained its proper strength, it easily despises rust, and drought, and every other thing ; but it is not so with doctrines ; in their case after all the work has been fully done, one storm and flood often comes on, and either by the attack of unpleasant circumstances, or by the plots of men skilled to deceive, or by various other temptations brought against them, brings them to ruin.

I have not said this without cause, but that when you hear John repeating the same words, you may not condemn him for vain talking,[5] nor

---

[1] παρήχθημεν. 　　[2] al. " irrational." 　　[3] " uprightly," E. V. 　　[4] al. " to hear." 　　[5] al. " want of taste."

deem him impertinent or wearisome. He desired to have been heard by once speaking, but because not many gave heed to what was spoken from the first, by reason of deep sleep, he again rouses them by this second call. Now observe; he had said, "He that cometh after me, is preferred before me": and that "I am not worthy to unloose the latchet of His shoe"; and that "He baptizeth with the Holy Ghost, and with fire"; and that he "saw the Spirit descending like a dove, and it abode upon Him," and he "bare record that this is the Son of God." No one gave heed, nor asked, nor said, "Why sayest thou these things? in whose behalf? for what reason?" Again he had said, "Behold the Lamb of God, which taketh away the sin of the world"; yet not even so did he touch their insensibility. Therefore, after this he is compelled to repeat the same words again, as if softening by tillage[1] some hard and stubborn soil, and by his word as by a[2] plow, disturbing the mind which had hardened into clods,[3] so as to put in the seed deep. For this reason he does not make his discourse a long one either; because he desired one thing only, to bring them over and join them to Christ. He knew that as soon as they had received this saying, and had been persuaded, they would not afterwards need one to bear witness unto Him. As also it came to pass. For, if the Samaritans could say to the woman after hearing Him, "Now we believe, not because of thy saying, for we know that this is indeed the Christ, the Saviour of the world," the disciples would be much more quickly subdued,[4] as was the case. For when they had come and heard Him but one evening, they returned no more to John, but were so nailed to Him, that they took upon them the ministry of John, and themselves proclaimed Him. For, saith the Evangelist, "He findeth his own brother Simon, and saith unto him, We have found the Messias, which is, being interpreted, the Christ." And observe, I pray you, this, how, when he said, "He that cometh after me is preferred before me"; and that, "I am not worthy to unloose the lachet of His shoe"; he caught no one, but when he spoke of the Dispensation, and lowered his discourse to a humbler tone, then the disciples followed Him.

And we may remark this, not only in the instance of the disciples, but that the many are not so much attracted when some great and sublime thing is said concerning God, as when some act of graciousness and lovingkindness, something pertaining to the salvation of the hearers, is spoken of. They heard that "He taketh away the sin of the world," and straightway they ran to Him. For, said they, "if it is possible to wash away[5] the charges that lie against us, why do we delay? here is One who will deliver us without labor of ours. Is it not extreme folly to put off accepting the Gift?" Let those hear who are Catechumens, and are putting off their salvation[6] to their latest breath.

"Again," saith the Evangelist, "John stood, and saith, Behold, the Lamb of God." Christ utters no word, His messenger saith all. So it is with a bridegroom. He saith not for a while anything to the bride, but is there in silence, while some show him to the bride, and others give her into his hands; she merely appears, and he departs not having taken her himself, but when he has received her from another who gives her to him. And when he has received her thus given, he so disposes her, that she no more remembers those who betrothed her. So it was with Christ. He came to join to Himself the Church; He said nothing, but merely came. It was His friend, John, who put into His the bride's right hand, when by his discourses he gave into His hand the souls of men. He having received them, afterwards so disposed them, that they departed no more to John who had committed them to Him.

[2.] And here we may remark, not this only, but something besides. As at a marriage the maiden goes not to the bridegroom, but he hastens to her, though he be a king's son, and though he be about to espouse some poor and abject person, or even a servant, so it was here. Man's nature did not go up,[7] but contemptible and poor as it was, He came to it, and when the marriage had taken place, He suffered it no longer to tarry here, but having taken it to Himself, transported it to the house of His Father.

"Why then doth not John take his disciples apart, and converse with them on these matters, and so deliver them over to Christ, instead of saying publicly to them in common with all the people, 'Behold the Lamb of God'?" That it may not seem to be a matter of arrangement; for had they gone away from him to Christ after having been privately admonished by him, and as though to do him a favor, they would perhaps soon have started away again; but now, having taken upon them the following Him, from teaching which had been general, they afterwards remained His firm disciples, as not having followed Him in order to gratify the teacher, but as looking purely to their own advantage.

The Prophets and Apostles then all preached Him absent; the Prophets before His coming according to the flesh, the Apostles after He was taken up; John alone proclaimed Him present.

---

[1] νεώσει.     [2] al. "a kind of."

[3] πεπιλημένην.

[4] Morel. and MS. in Bodleian, "much more would the disciples have been thus affected, and when they had come would have been subdued by His words."

[5] al. "to release ourselves from."

[6] i.e. their baptism.     [7] al. "depart."

Wherefore he calls himself the "friend of the Bridegroom" (c. iii. 29), since he alone was present at the marriage, he it was that did and accomplished all, he made a beginning of the work. And "looking upon Jesus walking, he saith, Behold the Lamb of God." Not by voice alone, but with his eyes·also he bore witness to, and expressed his admiration of, Christ, rejoicing and glorying. Nor does he for awhile address any[1] word of exhortation to his followers, but only shows wonder and astonishment at Him who was present, and declares to all the Gift which He came to give, and the manner of purification. For "the Lamb" declares both these things. And he said not, "Who shall take," or "Who hath taken"; but, "Who taketh away the sins of the world"; because this He ever doth. He took them not then only when He suffered, but from that time even to the present doth. He take them away, not being repeatedly[2] crucified, (for He offered One Sacrifice for sins,) but by that One continually purging them. As then THE WORD shows us His pre-eminence,[3] and THE SON His superiority in comparison with others, so "The Lamb, The Christ, that Prophet, the True Light, the Good Shepherd," and whatever other names are applied to Him with the addition of the article, mark a great difference. For there were many "Lambs," and "Prophets," and "Christs," and "sons," but from all these John separates Him by a wide interval. And this he secured not by the article only, but by the addition of "Only-Begotten"; for He had nothing in common with the creation.

If it seems to any unseasonable that these things should be spoken at "the tenth hour" (that was the time of day, for he says, "It was about the tenth hour" — (v. 39), such an one seems to me to be much mistaken. In the case indeed of the many, and those who serve the flesh, the season after feasting is not very suitable for any matters of pressing moment, because their hearts[4] are burdened with meats: but here was a man who did not even partake of common food, and who at evening was as sober as we are at morning, (or rather much more so; for often the remains of our evening food that are left within us, fill our souls with imaginations, but he loaded his vessel with none of these things;) he with good reason spake late in the evening of these matters. Besides, he was tarrying in the wilderness by Jordan, where all came to his baptism with great fear, and caring little at that time for the things of this life; as also they continued with Christ three days, and had nothing to eat. (Matt. xv. 32.) For this is the part of a zealous herald and a careful husbandman, not to desist before he see that the planted seed has got a firm hold.[5] "Why then did he not go about all the parts of Judæa preaching Christ, rather than stand by the river waiting for Him to come, that he might point Him out when He came?" Because he wished that this should be effected by His works; his own object being in the mean time only to make Him known, and to persuade some to hear of eternal life. But to Him he leaves the greater testimony, that of works, as also He saith, "I receive not testimony of men. The works which My Father hath given Me, the same bear witness of Me." (c. v. 34, 36.) Observe how much more effectual this was; for when he had thrown in a little spark, at once the blaze rose on high. For they who before had not even given heed to his words, afterwards say, "All things which John spake were true." (c. x. 41.)

[3.] Besides, if he had gone about saying these things, what was being done would have seemed to be done from some human motive, and the preaching to be full of suspicion.[6]

"And the two disciples heard him, and followed Jesus."

Yet John had other disciples, but they not only did not "follow Jesus," but were even jealously disposed towards him. "Rabbi," says one, "He that was with thee beyond Jordan, to whom thou barest witness, behold, the same baptizeth, and all men come unto him." (c. iii. 26.) And again[7] they appear bringing a charge against him; "Why do we fast, but thy disciples fast not?" (Matt. ix. 14.) But those who were better than the rest had no such feeling, but heard, and at once followed; followed, not as despising their teacher, but as being most fully persuaded by him, and producing the strongest proof that they acted thus from a right judgment of his reasonings. For they did not do so by his advice, that might have appeared suspicious; but when he merely foretold what was to come to pass, that "He should baptize with the Holy Ghost, [and with fire,]" they followed. They did not then desert their teacher, but rather desired to learn what Christ brought with Him more than John. And observe zeal combined with modesty. They did not at once approach and question Jesus on necessary and most important matters, nor were they desirous to converse with Him publicly, while all were present, at once and in an off-hand manner, but privately; for they knew that the words of their teacher proceeded not from humility, but from truth.

Ver. 40. "One of the two who heard, and followed Him, was Andrew, Simon Peter's brother."

---

[1] al. "even any."
[2] ἀεί.
[3] τὸ ἐξαίρετον.
[4] or, "stomachs."
[5] al. "is retained."
[6] Morel. reads: καὶ ὑποψίας ἦν μετὰ τὸ κήρυγμα λοιπόν.
[7] al. "these same."

Wherefore then has he not made known the name of the other also? Some say, because it was the writer himself that followed; others, not so, but that he was not one of the distinguished disciples; it behooved not therefore to say more than was necessary. For what would it have advantaged us to learn his name, when the writer does not mention the names even of the seventy-two? St. Paul also did the same.[1] "We have sent," says he, "with him the brother," (who has often in many things been forward,) "whose praise is in the Gospel." (2 Cor. viii. 18.) Moreover, he mentions Andrew for another reason. What is this? It is, that when you are informed that Simon having in company with him heard, "Follow Me, and I will make you fishers of men" (Matt. iv. 19), was not perplexed at so strange a promise, you may learn that his brother had already laid down within him the beginnings of the faith.

Ver. 38. "Then Jesus turned, and saw them following, and saith unto them, What seek ye?"

Hence we are taught, that God does not prevent our wills by His gifts, but that when we begin, when we provide the being willing, then He gives us many opportunities of salvation. "What seek ye?" How is this? He who knoweth the hearts of men, who dwelleth[2] in our thoughts, doth He ask? He doth; not that He may be informed; how could that be? but that by the question He may make them more familiar, and impart to them greater boldness, and show them that they are worthy to hear Him; for it was probable that they would blush and be afraid, as being unknown to him, and as having heard such accounts of Him from the testimony of their teacher. Therefore to remove all this, their shame and their fear, he questions them, and would not let them come all the way to the house in silence. Yet the event would have been the same had He not questioned them; they would have remained by following Him, and walking in His steps would have reached His dwelling. Why then did He ask? To effect that which I said, to calm their minds,[3] yet disturbed with shame and anxiety, and to give them confidence.

Nor was it by their following only that they showed their earnest desire, but by their question also: for when they had not as yet learned or even heard anything from Him, they call Him, "Master"; thrusting themselves as it were among His disciples, and declaring what was the cause of their following, that they might hear somewhat profitable. Observe their wisdom also. They did not say, "Teach us of Thy doctrines, or some other thing that we need to know"; but what? "Where dwellest Thou?"

Because, as I before said, they wished in quiet to say somewhat to Him, and to hear somewhat from Him, and to learn. Therefore they did not defer the matter, nor say, "We will come to-morrow by all means, and hear thee speak in public"; but showed the great eagerness they had to hear Him, by not being turned back even by the hour, for the sun was already near its setting, ("it was," saith John, "about the tenth hour.") And therefore Christ does not tell them the marks of His abode, nor its situation, but rather induces them to follow Him by showing them that He had accepted them. For this reason He did not say anything of this kind to them, "It is an unseasonable time now for you to enter into the house, to-morrow you shall hear if you have any wish, return home now";[4] but converses with them as with friends, and those who had long been with Him.

How then saith He in another place, "But the Son of Man hath not where to lay His head" (Luke ix. 58), while here He saith, "Come and see" (v. 39) where I abide? Because the expression "hath not where to lay His head," signifies that He had no dwelling place of His own, not that He did not abide in a house. And this too is the meaning of the comparison.[5] The Evangelist has mentioned that "they abode with Him that day," but has not added wherefore, because the reason was plain; for from no other motive did they follow Christ, and He draw them to Him, but only that they might have instruction; and this they enjoyed so abundantly and eagerly even in a single night, that they both proceeded straightway to the capture[6] of others.

[4.] Let us then also learn hence to consider all things secondary[7] to the hearing the word of God, and to deem no season unseasonable; and, though a man may even have to go into another person's house, and being a person unknown to make himself known to great men, though it be late in the day, or at any time whatever, never to neglect this traffic. Let food and baths and dinners and the other things of this life have their appointed time; but let the teaching of heavenly philosophy have no separate time, let every season belong to it. For Paul saith, "In season, out of season, reprove, rebuke, exhort" (2 Tim. iv. 2); and the Prophet too saith,[8] "In His law will he meditate day and night" (Ps. i. 3); and Moses commanded the Jews to do this always. For the things of this life, baths, I mean, and dinners, even if they are necessary, yet being continually repeated, render the body feeble;[9] but the teaching of the soul

1 Morel. and MS. in Bodl. " this also may be seen with Paul."
2 ἐμβατεύων.          3 λογισμὸν.

4 al. "for the present."          5 i.e. with the foxes and birds.
6 al. "the door."          7 πάρεργα.
8 Morel. and MS. in Bodl. "and David also glances at this, saying."          9 ἐξίτηλον.

the more it is prolonged, the stronger it renders the soul which receives it. But now we portion out all our time for trifles and unprofitable silly talking, and we sit together idly during the morning and afternoon,[1] midday and evening besides, and we have appointed places for this; but hearing the divine doctrines twice or thrice in the week we become sick,[2] and thoroughly sated. What is the reason? We are in a bad state of soul; its faculty of desiring and reaching after these things we have relaxed altogether. And therefore it is not strong enough to have an appetite for spiritual food. And this among others is a great proof of weakness, not to hunger nor thirst, but to be disinclined to both. Now if this, when it takes place in our bodies, is a sure sign of grievous disease, and productive of weakness, much more is it so in the soul.

" How then," says one, " shall we be able to renew it, thus fallen and relaxed, to strength? what doing, what saying?" By applying ourselves to the divine words of the prophets, of the Apostles, of the Gospels, and all the others; then we shall know that it is far better to feed on these than on impure food, for so we must term our unseasonable idle talking and assemblies. For which is best, tell me, to converse on things relating to the market, or things in the law courts, or in the camp, or on things in heaven, and on what shall be after our departure hence? Which is best, to talk about our neighbor and our neighbor's affairs, to busy ourselves in what belongs to other people, or to enquire into the things of angels, and into matters which concern ourselves? For a neighbor's affairs are not thine at all; but heavenly things are thine. " But," says some one, " a man may by once speaking finish these subjects altogether." Why do you not think this in matters on which you converse uselessly and idly, why though ye waste your lives on this have ye never exhausted the subject? And I have not yet named what is far more vile than this. These are the things about which the better sort converse one with the other; but the more indifferent and careless carry about in their talk players and dancers and charioteers, defiling men's ears, corrupting their souls, and driving

their nature into mad excesses by these narratives, and by means of this discourse introducing every kind of wickedness into their own imagination. For as soon as the tongue has uttered the name of the dancer, immediately the soul has figured to itself his looks, his hair, his delicate clothing, and himself more effeminate than all. Another again fans the flame in another way, by introducing some harlot into the conversation, with her words, and attitudes, and glances, her languishing looks and twisted locks, the smoothness of her cheeks, and her painted eyelids.[3] Were you not somewhat affected when I gave this description? Yet be not ashamed, nor blush, for the very necessity of nature requires this, and so disposes the soul according as the tendency of what is said may be. But if, when it is I that speak, you, standing in the church, and at a distance from these things, were somewhat affected at the hearing, consider how it is likely that they are disposed, who sit in the theater itself, who are totally free from dread, who are absent from this venerable and awful assembly, who both see and hear those things with much shamelessness. " And why then," perhaps one of those who heed not may say, " if the necessity of nature so disposes the soul, do you let go that, and blame us?" Because, to be softened[4] when one hears these things, is nature's work; but to hear them is not a fault of nature, but of deliberate choice. For so he who meddles with fire must needs be injured, so wills the weakness of our nature; yet nature does not therefore draw us to the fire and to the injury thence arising; this can be only from deliberate perversity. I beseech you, therefore, to remove and correct this fault, that you may not of your own accord cast yourself down the precipice, nor thrust yourselves into the pits of wickedness, nor run of yourselves to the blaze, lest we place ourselves in jeopardy of the fire prepared for the devil. May it come to pass, that we all being delivered both from this fire and from that, may go to the very bosom of Abraham, through the grace and lovingkindness of our Lord Jesus Christ, by whom and with whom, to the Father and Holy Ghost, be glory for ever and ever. Amen.

---

[1] δείλην.  [2] ναυτιῶμεν.

[3] ὑπογραφὰς.  [4] μαλάττεσθαι.

# HOMILY XIX.

John i. 41, 42.

"He first findeth his own brother Simon, and saith unto him, We have found the Messias, which is, being interpreted, the Christ. And he brought him to Jesus."

[1.] When God in the beginning made man, He did not suffer him to be alone, but gave him woman for a helpmate, and made them to dwell together, knowing that great advantage would result from this companionship. What though the woman did not rightly employ this benefit? still if any one make himself fully acquainted with the nature of the matter, he will see, that to the wise great advantage arises from this dwelling together; not in the cause of wife or husband only, but if brothers do this, they also shall enjoy the benefit. Wherefore the Prophet hath said, "What is good, what is pleasant, but that brethren should dwell together?" (Ps. cxxxiii. 1, LXX.) And Paul exhorted not to neglect the assembling of ourselves together. (Heb. x. 25.) In this it is that we differ from beasts, for this we have built cities, and markets, and houses, that we may be united one with another, not in the place of our dwelling only, but by the bond of love. For since our nature came imperfect[1] from Him who made it, and is not self-sufficient,[2] God, for our advantage, ordained that the want hence existing should be corrected by the assistance arising from mutual intercourse; so that what was lacking in one should be supplied by another,[3] and the defective nature thus be rendered self-sufficient; as, for instance, that though made mortal,[4] it should by succession for a long time maintain immortality. I might have gone into this argument at greater length, to show what advantages arise to those who come together from genuine and pure[5] intercourse with each other : but there is another thing which presses now, that on account of which we have made these remarks.

Andrew, after having tarried with Jesus and learned what He did, kept not the treasure to himself, but hastens and runs quickly to his brother, to impart to him of the good things which he had received.[6] But wherefore has not John said on what matters Christ conversed with them? Whence is it clear that it was for this that they "abode with Him"?[7]

It was proved by us the other day; but we may learn it from what has been read to-day as well. Observe what Andrew says to his brother; "We have found the Messias, which is, being interpreted, the Christ." You see how, as far as he had learned in a short time, he showed[8] the wisdom of the teacher who persuaded them, and their own zeal, who cared for these things long ago,[9] and from the beginning. For this word, "we have found," is the expression of a soul which travails[10] for His presence, and looks for His coming from above, and is made overjoyed when the looked-for thing has happened,[11] and hastens to impart to others the good tidings. This is the part of brotherly affection, of natural friendship, of a sincere disposition, to be eager to stretch out the hand to each other in spiritual things. Hear him besides speak with the addition of the article; for he does not say "Messias," but "the Messias"; thus they were expecting some one Christ,[12] having nothing in common with the others. And behold, I beg of you, the mind of Peter obedient and tractable from the very beginning; he ran to Him without any delay; "He brought him," saith St. John, "to Jesus." Yet let no one blame his easy temper if he received the word without much questioning, because it is probable that his brother had told him these things more exactly and at length; but the Evangelists from their care for conciseness constantly cut many things short. Besides, it is not said absolutely that "he believed," but that "he brought him to Jesus," to give him up for the future to Him, so that from Him he might learn all; for the other disciple also was with him, and contributed to this. And if John the Baptist, when he had said that He was "the Lamb," and that He "baptized with the Spirit," gave them over to learn the clearer doctrine concerning this thing from Him, much more would Andrew have done this, not deeming himself sufficient to declare the whole, but drawing him to the very fount of light with so much zeal and joy, that the other[13] neither deferred nor delayed at all.[14]

Ver. 42. "And when Jesus beheld him," saith

---

[1] ἐνδεής.　　　[2] αὐτάρκης.
[3] Ben. Morel. and MS. in Bodl. read the passage thus: "For this cause also marriage is arranged, in order that what is wanting," &c.
[4] καθάπερ οὖν καὶ θνητὴν γενομένην. Ben. and MS. in Bodl. read, ὡς αὑτὴν ἔχειν καὶ θ. γ.
[5] εἰλικρινοῦς.　　　[6] al. "shared."

[7] Morel. and MS. in Bodl. "conversed with them, when they straightway followed and abode with Him."
[8] Ben. Morel. and MS. in Bodl. "he showed hence, for he both establishes the wisdom," &c.
[9] ἄνωθεν.　　　　　　　[13] ἐκεῖνον.
[10] ὠδινούσης.
[11] al. "has appeared."　　[14] τὸ τυχόν.
[12] Anointed one.

the Evangelist, " He said, Thou art Simon, the son of Jonas ; thou shalt be called Cephas, which is, by interpretation, a stone."

[2.] He begins from this time forth to reveal the things belonging to His Divinity, and to open It out little by little by predictions. So He did in the case of Nathaniel and the Samaritan woman. For prophecies bring men over not less than miracles ; and are free from the appearance of boasting. Miracles may possibly be slandered among foolish men, (" He casteth out devils," said they, " by Beelzebub"—Matt. xii. 24), but nothing of the kind has ever been said of prophecy. Now in the case of Nathaniel and Simon He used this method of teaching, but with Andrew and Philip He did not so. Why was this? Because those [1] (two) had the testimony of John, no small preparation, and Philip received a credible evidence of faith, when he saw those who had been present.

" Thou art Simon, the son of Jonas." By the present, the future is guaranteed ; for it is clear that He who named Peter's father foreknew the future also. And the prediction is attended with praise ; but the object was not to flatter, but to foretell something future. Hear [2] at least in the case of the Samaritan woman, how He utters a prediction with severe reproofs ; [3] " Thou hast had," he saith, " five husbands, and he whom thou now hast is not thy husband." (c. iv. 18.) So also His Father makes great account of prophecy, when He sets Himself against the honor paid to idols : " Let them declare to you," saith He, " what shall come upon you " (Isa. xlvii. 13) ; and again, " I have declared, and have saved, and there was no foreign God amongst you " (Isa. xliii. 12, LXX.) ; and He brings this forward through all prophecy. Because prophecy is especially the work of God, which devils cannot even imitate, though they strive exceedingly. For in the case of miracles there may be delusion ; but exactly to foretell the future belongs to that pure Nature alone. Or if devils ever have done so, it was by deceiving the simpler sort ; whence their oracles are always easily detected.

But Peter makes no reply to these words ; as yet he knew nothing clearly, but still was learning. And observe, that not even the prediction is fully set forth ; for Jesus did not say, " I will change thy name to Peter, and upon this rock I will build My Church," but, " Thou shalt be called Cephas." The former speech would have expressed too great authority [4] and power ; for Christ does not immediately nor at first declare all His power, but speaks for a while in a hum-

bler tone ; and so, when He had given the proof of His Divinity, He puts it more authoritatively, saying,[5] " Blessed art thou, Simon, because My Father hath revealed it to thee " ; and again, " Thou art Peter, and upon this rock I will build My Church." (Matt. xvi. 17, 18.) Him therefore He so named, and James and his brother He called " sons of thunder." (Mark iii. 17.) Why then doth He this? To show that it was He who gave the old covenant, that it was He who altered names, who called Abram " Abraham," and Sarai " Sarah," and Jacob " Israel." To many he assigned names even from their birth, as to Isaac, and Samson, and to those in Isaiah and Hosea (Isa. viii. 3 ; Hos. i. 4, 6, 9) ; but to others He gave them after they had been named by their parents, as to those we have mentioned, and to Joshua the son of Nun. It was also a custom of the Ancients to give names from things, which in fact Leah also has done ; [6] and this takes place not without cause, but in order that men may have the appellation to remind them of the goodness of God, that a perpetual memory of the prophecy conveyed by the names may sound in the ears of those who receive it. Thus too He named John early,[7] because they whose virtue was to shine forth from their early youth, from that time received their names ; while to those who were to become great [8] at a later period, the title also was given later.

[3.] But then they received each a different name, we now have all one name, that which is greater than any, being called [9] " Christians," and " sons of God," and (His) " friends," and (His) " Body." For the very term itself is able more than all those others to rouse us, and make us more zealous [10] for the practice of virtue. Let us not then act unworthily of the honor belonging to the title, considering [11] the excess of our dignity, we who are called Christ's ; for so Paul hath named us. Let us bear in mind and respect the grandeur of the appellation. (1 Cor. iii. 23.) For if one who is said to be descended from some famous general, or one otherwise distinguished, is proud to be called this or that man's son, and deems the name a great honor, and strives in every way so as not to affix, by remissness of his own, reproach to him after whom he is called ; shall not we who are called after the name, not of a general, nor any of the princes upon earth, nor Angel, nor Archangel, nor Seraphim, but of the King of these Himself, shall

---

[1] i.e. those mentioned above, v. 40, who were present when St. John Baptist gave his testimony, one of whom was Andrew.
[2] al. " consider."
[3] al. " reproving with earnestness."
[4] αὐθεντίας.

[5] al. " And I say unto thee, ' Thou art Simon, thou shalt be called Cephas, which is by interpretation a stone.' "
[6] ὅπερ δήπου καὶ Ἡλίας πεποίηκε, and there are no various readings. Savile has in the margin ὅπερ οὖν καὶ Ἡλία. We may venture to read " ἡ Λεία," as he praises her for this, Hom. lvi. on Genesis. " Observe how she gave names to those she bore, not lightly nor at random."
[7] ἄνωθεν.
[8] ἐπιδίδοναι.
[9] al. " the being called."
[10] al. " more ready."
[11] al. " consider at least."

not we freely give even our very life, so as not to insult Him who has honored us? Know ye not what honor the royal bands of shield-bearers and spearmen that are about the king enjoy? So let us who have been deemed worthy to be near Him, and much closer, and as much nearer than those just named, as the body is closer to the head than they, let us, I say, use every means to be imitators of Christ.

What then saith Christ? "The foxes have holes, and birds of the air have nests; but the Son of man hath not where to lay His head." (Luke ix. 58.) Now if I demand this of you, it will seem perhaps to most of you grievous and burdensome; because therefore of your infirmity I speak not of[1] such perfection, but desire you not to be nailed to riches; and as I, because of the infirmity of the many, retire somewhat from (demanding) the excess of virtue, I desire that you do so and much more on the side of vice. I blame not those who have houses, and lands, and wealth, and servants, but wish them to possess[2] these things in a safe and becoming way. And what is "a becoming way"? As masters, not as slaves; so that they rule them, be not ruled by them; that they use, not abuse them. This is why they are called, "things to be used,"[3] that we may employ them on necessary services, not hoard them up; this is a domestic's office, that a master's; it is for the slave to keep them, but for the lord and one who has great authority to expend. Thou didst not receive thy wealth to bury, but to distribute. Had God desired riches to be hoarded, He would not have given them to men, but would have let them remain as they were in the earth; but because He wishes them to be spent, therefore He has permitted us to

have them, that we may impart them to each other. And if we keep them to ourselves, we are no longer masters of them. But if you wish to make them greater and therefore keep them shut up, even in this case the best plan of all is to scatter and distribute them in all directions; because there can be no revenue without an outlay, no wealth without expenditure. One may see that it is so even in worldly matters. So it is with the merchant, so with the husbandman, who put forth the one his wealth, the other his seed; the one sails the sea to disperse his wares, the other labors all the year putting in and tending his seed. But here there is no need of any one of these things, neither to equip a vessel, nor to yoke oxen, nor to plough land, nor to be anxious about uncertain weather, nor to dread a fall of hail; here are neither waves nor rocks; this voyage and this sowing needs one thing only, that we cast forth our possessions; all the rest will that Husbandman do, of whom Christ saith, "My Father is the Husbandman." (c. xv. 1.) Is it not then absurd to be sluggish and slothful where we may gain all without labor, and where there are many toils and many[5] troubles and cares, and after all, an uncertain hope, there to display all eagerness? Let us not, I beseech you, let us not be to such a degree senseless about our own salvation, but let us leave the more troublesome task, and run to that which is most easy and more profitable, that we may obtain also the good things that are to come; through the grace and lovingkindness of our Lord Jesus Christ, with whom to the Father and the Holy and quickening Spirit be glory, now and ever, and world without end. Amen.

---

# HOMILY XX.

## John i. 43, 44.

"The day following Jesus would go forth into Galilee, and findeth Philip, and saith unto him, Follow Me. Now Philip was of Bethsaida, the city of Andrew and Peter."

[1.] "To every careful thinker there is a gain"[4] (Prov. xiv. 23, LXX.), saith the proverb; and Christ implied more than this, when He said, "He that seeketh findeth." (Matt. vii. 8.) Wherefore it does not occur to me any more to wonder how Philip followed Christ. Andrew

was persuaded when he had heard from John, and Peter the same from Andrew, but Philip not having learned anything from any but Christ who said to him only this, "Follow Me," straightway obeyed, and went not back, but even became a preacher to others. For he ran to Nathanael and said to him, "We have found Him of whom Moses in the Law and the Prophets did write." Seest thou what a thoughtful[6] mind he had, how assiduously he meditated on the writings of Moses, and expected the Advent? for the expression, "we have found," belongs

---

[1] ἀφίημι.        [2] al. " to use."        [3] χρήματα.
[4] παντὶ τῷ μεριμνῶντι ἔνεστί τι περισσόν. In the next sentence Morel. Ben. and most MSS. read ὅθεν καὶ ἔπεισί μοι. Savile ὅθ. οὐδὲ ἐπ. μ. which seems the better reading.

[5] al. " more."        [6] μεμεριμνημένην.

always to those who are in some way seeking. "The day following Jesus went forth into Galilee." Before any had joined Him, He called no one; and He acted thus not without cause, but according to his own wisdom and intelligence. For if, when no one came to Him spontaneously, He had Himself drawn them, they might perhaps have started away; but now, having chosen this of themselves, they afterwards remained firm. He calls Philip, one who was better acquainted with Him; for he, as having been born and bred in Galilee, knew Him more than others. Having then taken the disciples, He next goes to the capture of the others, and draws to Him Philip and Nathanael. Now in the case of Nathanael this was not so wonderful, because the fame of Jesus had gone forth into all Syria. (Matt. iv. 24.) But the wonderful thing was respecting Peter and James and Philip, that they believed, not only before the miracles, but that they did so being of Galilee, out of which "ariseth no prophet," nor "can any good thing come"; for the Galilæans were somehow of a more boorish and dull disposition than others; but even in this Christ displayed forth His power, by selecting from a land which bore no fruit His choicest disciples. It is then probable that Philip having seen Peter and Andrew, and having heard what John had said, followed; and it is probable also that the voice of Christ wrought in him somewhat; for He knew those who would be serviceable. But all these points the Evangelist cuts short. That Christ should come, he knew; that this was Christ, he knew not, and this I say that he heard either from Peter or John. But John mentions his village also, that you may learn that "God hath chosen the weak things of the world." (1 Cor. i. 27.)

Ver. 45. "Philip findeth Nathanael, and saith unto him, We have found Him of whom Moses in the Law and the Prophets did write, Jesus of Nazareth, the son of Joseph."

He says this, to make his preaching credible, which it must be if it rests on Moses and the Prophets besides, and by this to abash his hearer. For since Nathanael was an exact[1] man, and one who viewed all things with truth, as Christ also testified and the event showed, Philip with reason refers him to Moses and the Prophets, that so he might receive Him who was preached. And be not troubled though he called Him "the son of Joseph"; for still he was supposed to be his son. "And whence, O Philip, is it plain that this is He? What proof dost thou mention to us? for it is not enough merely to assert this. What sign hast thou seen, what miracle? Not without danger is it to believe without cause in such matters. What proof then hast thou?"

"The same as Andrew," he replies; for he though unable to produce the wealth which he had found, or to describe his treasure in words, when he had discovered it, led his brother to it. So too did Philip. How this is the Christ, and how the prophets proclaimed Him beforehand, he said not; but he draws him to Jesus, as knowing that he would not afterwards fall off, if he should once taste His words and teaching.

Ver. 46, 47. "And Nathanael said unto him, Can there any good thing come out of Nazareth? Philip saith unto him, Come and see. Jesus saw Nathanael coming to Him, and saith of him, Behold an Israelite indeed, in whom is no guile."

He praises and approves the man, because he had said, "Can any good thing come out of Nazareth?" and yet he ought to have been blamed. Surely not; for the words are not those of an unbeliever, nor deserving blame, but praise. "How so, and in what way?" Because Nathanael had considered the writings of the Prophets more than Philip. For he had heard from the Scriptures, that Christ must come from Bethlehem, and from the village in which David was. This belief at least prevailed among the Jews, and the Prophet had proclaimed it of old, saying, "And thou, Bethlehem, art by no means the least among the princes of Judah, for out of thee shall come a Governor, that shall feed[2] My people Israel." (Matt. ii. 6; Mic. v. 2.) And so when he heard that He was "from Nazareth," he was confounded, and doubted, not finding the announcement of Philip to agree with the prediction of the Prophet.

But observe his wisdom and candor even in his doubting. He did not at once say, "Philip, thou deceivest me, and speakest falsely, I believe thee not, I will not come; I have learned from the prophets that Christ must come from Bethlehem, thou sayest 'from Nazareth'; therefore this is not that Christ." He said nothing like this; but what does he? He goes to Him himself; showing, by not admitting that Christ was "of Nazareth," his accuracy respecting the Scriptures, and a character not easily deceived; and by not rejecting him who brought the tidings, the great desire which he felt for the coming of Christ. For he thought within himself that Philip was probably mistaken about the place.

[2.] And observe, I pray you, his manner of declining, how gentle he has made it, and in the form of a question. For he said not, "Galilee produces no good"; but how said he? "Can any good thing come out of Nazareth?" Philip also was very prudent; for he is not as one perplexed, angry, and annoyed, but perseveres, wishing to bring over the[3] man, and manifesting

---

[1] ἀκριβής.

[2] or, "rule."

[3] al. "this."

to us from the first of his preaching[1] the firmness[2] which becomes an Apostle.　Wherefore also Christ saith, "Behold an Israelite indeed, in whom is no guile."　So that there is such a person as a false Israelite; but this is not such an one; for his judgment, Christ saith, is impartial, he speaks nothing from favor, or from ill-feeling.　Yet the Jews, when they were asked where Christ should be born, replied, "In Bethlehem" (Matt. ii. 5), and produced the evidence, saying, "And thou, Bethlehem, art by no means the least among the princes of Judah."　(Mic. v. 2.)　Before they had seen Him they bore this witness, but when they saw Him in their malice they concealed the testimony, saying, "But as for this fellow, we know not whence He is." (c. ix. 29.)　Nathanael did not so, but continued to retain the opinion which he had from the beginning, that He was not "of Nazareth."

How then do the prophets call Him a Nazarene?　From His being brought up and abiding there.　And He omits to say, "I am not 'of Nazareth,' as Philip hath told thee, but of Bethlehem," that He may not at once make the account seem questionable; and besides this, because, even if He had gained belief, He would not have given sufficient proof that He was the Christ.　For what hindered Him without being Christ, from being of Bethlehem, like the others who were born there?　This then He omits; but He does that which has most power to bring him over, for He shows that He was present when they were conversing.　For when Nathanael had said,

Ver. 48. "Whence knowest Thou me?"　He replies, "Before that Philip called thee, when thou wast under the fig-tree, I saw thee."

Observe a man firm and steady.[3]　When Christ had said, "Behold an Israelite indeed," he was not made vain by this approbation, he ran not after this open praise, but continues seeking and searching more exactly, and desires to learn something certain.　He still enquired as of a man,[4] but Jesus answered as God.　For He said, "I have known thee from the first,"[5] (him and the candor[6] of his character,[7] this He knew not as a man, from having closely followed him, but as God from the first,) "and but now I saw thee by the fig-tree"; when there was no one present there but only Philip and Nathanael who said all these things in private.　It is mentioned, that having seen him afar off, He said, "Behold an Israelite indeed"; to show,[8] that before Philip came near, Christ spoke these

words, that the testimony might not be suspected. For this reason also He named the time, the place, and the tree; because if He had only said, "Before Philip came to thee, I saw thee," He might have been suspected of having sent him, and of saying nothing wonderful; but now, by mentioning both the place where he was when addressed by Philip, and the name of the tree, and the time of the conversation, He showed that His foreknowledge[9] was unquestionable.

And He did not merely show to him His foreknowledge, but instructed him also in another way.　For He brought him to a recollection of what they then had said; as, "Can there any good thing come out of Nazareth?"　And it was most especially on this account that Nathanael received Him, because when he had uttered these words, He did not condemn, but praised and approved him.　Therefore he was assured that this was indeed the Christ, both from His foreknowledge, and from His having exactly searched out his sentiments, which was the act of One who would show that He knew what was in his mind; and besides, from His not having blamed, but rather praised him when he had seemed to speak against Himself.　He said then, that Philip had "called" him; but what Philip had said to him or he to Philip, He omitted, leaving it to his own conscience, and not desiring farther to rebuke him.

[3.] Was it then only "before Philip called him" that He "saw" him? did He not see him before this with His sleepless eye?　He saw him, and none could gainsay it; but this is what it was needful to say at the time.　And what did Nathanael?　When he had received an unquestionable proof of His foreknowledge, he hastened to confess Him, showing by his previous delay his caution,[10] and his fairness by his assent afterwards.　For, said the Evangelist,

Ver. 49. "He answered and saith unto Him, Rabbi, Thou art the Son of God, Thou art the King of Israel."

Seest thou how his soul is filled at once with exceeding joy, and embraces Jesus with words? "Thou art," saith he, "that expected, that sought-for One."　Seest thou how he is amazed, how he marvels? how he leaps and dances with delight?

So ought we also to rejoice, who have been thought worthy to know the Son of God; to rejoice, not in thought alone, but to show it also by our actions.　And what must they do who rejoice?　Obey Him who has been made known to them; and they who obey, must do whatever He willeth.　For if we are going to do what angers Him, how shall we show that we rejoice? See ye not in our houses when a man entertains

[1] προοιμίων.　　　[2] εὐτονίαν.　　　[3] βεβηκότα.
[4] ὡς ἄνθρωπον ἐξήταζεν.　So Morel. and MSS. in Bodleian.　Savile and the Bened. read ὡς ἄνθρωπος, "he enquired as a man."
[5] ἄνωθεν.
[6] ἐπιεικείαν.
[7] One MS. reads, οὐ γὰρ εἶπεν, ἄνωθέν σε οἶδα, καὶ τὸν τρόπον, καὶ τὴν ἐπ.
[8] ἵνα μάθῃ.　Savile conjectures ἵνα μάθῃς, but without authority.
[9] πρόρρησιν.　　　[10] ἀκρίβειαν.

one whom he loves, how gladly he exerts himself, running about in every direction, and though it be needful to spend all that he has, sparing nothing so that he please his visitor? But if one who invites should not attend to his guest,[1] and not do such things as would procure him ease, though he should say ten thousand times that he rejoices at his coming, he could never be believed by him. And justly; for this should be shown by actions. Let us then, since Christ hath come to us, show that we rejoice, and do nothing that may anger him; let us garnish the abode to which He has come, for this they do who rejoice; let us set before Him the meal[2] which He desires to eat, for this they do who hold festival. And what is this meal? He saith Himself; "My meat is, that I may do the will of Him that sent me." (c. iv. 34.) When He is hungry, let us feed Him; when He is thirsty, let us give Him drink: though thou give Him but a cup of cold water, He receives it; for He loves thee, and to one who loves, the offerings of the beloved, though they be small, appear great. Only be not thou slothful; though thou cast in but two farthings, He refuses them not, but receives them as great riches. For since He is without wants, and receives these offerings, not because He needs them, it is reasonable

that all distinction should be not in the quantity of the gifts, but the intention[3] of the giver. Only show that thou lovest Him who is come, that for His sake thou art giving all diligence, that thou rejoicest at His coming. See how He is disposed toward thee. He came for thee, He laid down His life for thee, and after all this He doth not refuse even to entreat thee. "We are ambassadors," saith Paul, "for Christ, as though God did beseech you by us." (2 Cor. v. 20.) "And who is so mad," saith some one, "as not to love his own Master?" I say so too, and I know that not one of us would deny this in words or intention; but one who is beloved desires love to be shown, not by words only, but by deeds also. For to say that we love, and not to act like lovers, is ridiculous, not only before God, but even in the sight of men. Since then to confess Him in word only, while in deeds we oppose Him, is not only unprofitable, but also hurtful to us; let us, I entreat you, also make confession by our works; that we also may obtain a confession from Him in that day, when before His Father He shall confess those who are worthy in Christ Jesus our Lord, by whom and with whom, to the Father and the Holy Ghost be glory, now and ever, and world without end. Amen.

---

# HOMILY XXI.

### JOHN i. 49, 50.

"Nathanael answered and saith unto Him, Rabbi, Thou art the Son of God, Thou art the King of Israel. Jesus answered, and said unto him, Because I said unto thee, I saw thee under the fig-tree, believest thou? Thou shalt see greater things than these."

[1.] BELOVED, we need much care, much watchfulness, to be able to look into the depth of the Divine Scriptures. For it is not possible to discover their meaning in a careless way, or while we are asleep, but there needs close search, and there needs earnest prayer, that we may be enabled to see some little way into the secrets of the divine oracles. To-day, for instance, here is no trifling question proposed to us, but one which requires much zeal and enquiry. For when Nathanael said, "Thou art the Son of God," Christ replies, "Because I said unto thee, I saw thee under the fig-tree, believest thou? Thou shalt see greater things than these."

Now what is the question arising from this passage? It is this.[4] Peter, when after so many miracles and such high doctrine he confessed that, "Thou art the Son of God" (Matt. xvi. 16), is called "blessed," as having received the revelation from the Father; while Nathanael, though he said the very same thing before seeing or hearing either miracles or doctrine, had no such word addressed to him, but as though he had not said so much as he ought to have said, is brought[5] to things greater still. What can be the reason of this? It is, that Peter and Nathanael both spoke the same words, but not both with the same intention. Peter confessed Him to be "The Son of God ' but as being Very God; Nathanael, as being mere man. And whence does this appear? Fron what he said after these words; for after, "Thou art the Son of God," he adds, "Thou art the King

---

[3] προαιρέσει.
[4] Morel. and MS. in Bodleian read the passage thus: πολλοὶ τῶν ἀναγινωσκόντων τὸ ῥητὸν τοῦτο διαποροῦντες φάσι· τί δήποτε Πέτρος κ.τ.λ. [5] al. " led forward."

of Israel." But the Son of God is not "King of Israel" only, but of all the world.

And what I say is clear, not from this only, but also from what follows. For Christ added nothing more to Peter, but as though his faith were perfect, said, that upon this confession of his He would build the Church; but in the other case He did nothing like this, but the contrary. For as though some large, and that the better, part were wanting to his confession, He added what follows. For what saith He?

Ver. 51. "Verily, verily I say unto you, Hereafter ye shall see heaven open, and the Angels of God ascending and descending upon the Son of Man."

Seest thou how He leads him up by little and little from the earth, and causes him no longer to imagine Him a man merely? for One to whom Angels minister, and on whom Angels ascend and descend, how could He be man? For this reason He said, "Thou shalt see greater things than these." And in proof of this, He introduces the ministry of Angels. And what He means is something of this kind: "Doth this, O Nathanael, seem to thee a great matter, and hast thou for this confessed me to be King of Israel? What then wilt thou say, when thou seest the Angels ascending and descending upon Me?" Persuading him by these words to own Him Lord also of the Angels. For on Him as on the King's own Son, the royal ministers ascended and descended, once at the season of the Crucifixion, again at the time of the Resurrection and the Ascension, and before this also, when they "came and ministered unto Him" (Matt. iv. 11), when they proclaimed the glad tidings of His birth, and cried, "Glory to God in the highest, and on earth peace" (Luke ii. 14), when they came to Mary, when they came to Joseph.

And He does now what He has done in many instances; He utters two predictions, gives present proof of the one, and confirms that which has to be accomplished by that which is so already. For of His sayings some had been proved, such as, "Before Philip called thee, under the fig-tree I saw thee"; others had yet to come to pass, and had partly done so, namely, the descending and ascending of the Angels, at the Crucifixion, the Resurrection, and the Ascension; and this He renders credible by His words even before the event. For one who had known His power by what had gone before, and heard from Him of things to come, would more readily receive this prediction too.

What then does Nathanael? To this he makes no reply. And therefore at this point Christ stopped His discourse with him, allowing him to consider in private what had been said; and not choosing to pour forth all at once, having cast seed into fertile ground, He then leaves it to shoot at leisure. And this He has shown in another place, where He saith, "The kingdom of heaven is like to a man that soweth good seed, but while he slept, his enemy cometh, and soweth tares among the wheat."[1]

Chap. ii. ver. 1, 2. "On the third day there was a marriage in Cana of Galilee. And Jesus was called to the marriage. And the mother of Jesus was there, and His brethren."[2]

I said before that He was best known in Galilee; therefore they invite Him to the marriage, and He comes; for He looked not to His own honor, but to our benefit. He who disdained not to "take upon Him the form of a servant" (Phil. ii. 7), would much less disdain to be present at the marriage of servants; He who sat down "with publicans and sinners" (Matt. ix. 13), would much less refuse to sit down with those present at the marriage. Assuredly they who invited Him had not formed a proper judgment of Him, nor did they invite Him as some great one, but merely as an ordinary acquaintance; and this the Evangelist has hinted at, when he says, "The mother of Jesus was there, and His brethren." Just as they invited her and His brethren, they invited Jesus.

Ver. 3. "And when they wanted wine, His mother saith unto Him, They have no wine."

Here it is worth while to enquire whence it came into His mother's mind to imagine anything great of her Son; for He had as yet done no miracle, since the Evangelist saith, "This beginning of miracles did Jesus in Cana of Galilee." (c. ii. 11.)

[2.] Now if any say that this is not a sufficient proof that it was the "beginning of His miracles," because there is added simply "in Cana of Galilee," as allowing it to have been the first done there, but not altogether and absolutely the first, for He probably might have done others elsewhere, we will make answer to him of that which we have said before. And of what kind? The words of John (the Baptist); "And I knew Him not; but that He should be made manifest to Israel, therefore am I come, baptizing with water." Now if He had wrought miracles in early age, the Israelites would not have needed another to declare Him. For He who came among men, and by His miracles was so made known, not to those only in Judæa, but also to those in Syria and beyond, and who did this in three years only, or rather who did not need even these three years to manifest Himself (Matt. iv. 24), for immediately and from the first His fame went abroad everywhere; He, I say, who in a short time so shone forth by the multitude of His miracles, that His name was

---

[1] Matt. xiii. 24, 25, slightly varying from G. T.
[2] The reading is different in G. T.

well known to all, was much less likely, if while a child He had from an early age wrought miracles, to escape notice so long. For what was done would have seemed stranger as done by a boy, and there would have been time for twice or thrice as many, and much more. But in fact He did nothing while He was a child, save only that one thing to which Luke has testified (Luke ii. 46), that at the age of twelve years He sat hearing the doctors, and was thought admirable for His questioning. Besides, it was in accordance with likelihood and reason that He did not begin His signs at once from an early age; for they would have deemed the thing a delusion. For if when He was of full age many suspected this, much more, if while quite young He had wrought miracles, would they have hurried Him sooner and before the proper time to the Cross, in the venom of their malice; and the very facts of the Dispensation would have been discredited.

"How then," asks some one, "came it into the mind of His mother to imagine anything great of Him?" He was now beginning to reveal ·Himself, and was plainly discovered by the witness of John, and by what He had said to His disciples. And before all this, the Conception itself and all its attending circumstances[1] had inspired her with a very great opinion of the Child; "for," said Luke, "she heard all the sayings concerning the Child, and kept them in her heart."[2] "Why then," says one, "did not she speak this before?"[3] Because, as I said, it was now at last that He was beginning to manifest Himself. Before this time He lived as one of the many, and therefore His mother had not confidence to say any such thing to Him; but when she heard that John had come on His account, and that he had borne such witness to Him as he did, and that He had disciples, after that she took confidence, and called Him, and said, when they wanted wine, "They have no wine." For she desired both to do them a favor, and through her Son to render herself more conspicuous; perhaps too she had some human feelings, like His brethren, when they said, "Show thyself to the world" (c. xvii. 4), desiring to gain credit from His miracles. Therefore He answered somewhat vehemently,[4] saying,

Ver. 4. "Woman, what have I to do with thee? Mine hour is not yet come."

To prove that He greatly respected His mother, hear Luke relate how He was "subject to" His parents (Luke ii. 51), and our own Evangelist declare how He had forethought for her at the very season of the Crucifixion. For where parents cause no impediment or hindrance in things belonging to God, it is our bounden duty to give way to them, and there is great danger in not doing so; but when they require anything unseasonably, and cause hindrance in any spiritual matter, it is unsafe to obey. And therefore He answered thus in this place, and again elsewhere, "Who is My mother, and who are My brethren?" (Matt. xii. 48), because they did not yet think rightly of Him; and she, because she had borne Him, claimed, according to the custom of other mothers, to direct Him in all things, when she ought to have reverenced and worshiped Him. This then was the reason why He answered as He did on that occasion. For consider what a thing it was, that when all the people high and low were standing round Him, when the multitude was intent on hearing[5] Him, and His doctrine had begun to be set forth, she should come into the midst and take Him away from the work of exhortation, and converse with Him apart, and not even endure to come within, but draw Him outside merely to herself. This is why He said, "Who is My mother and My brethren?" Not to insult her who had borne Him, (away with the thought!) but to procure her the greatest benefit, and not to let her think meanly of Him. For if He cared for others, and used every means to implant in them a becoming opinion of Himself, much more would He do so in the case of His mother. And since it was probable that if these words had been addressed to her by her Son, she would not readily have chosen even then to be convinced, but would in all cases have claimed the superiority as being His mother, therefore He replied as He did to them who spake to Him; otherwise He could not have led up her thoughts from His present lowliness to His future exaltation, had she expected that she should always be honored by Him as by a son, and not that He should come as her Master.

[3.] It was then from this motive that He said in this place, "Woman, what have I to do with thee?" and also for another reason not less pressing. What was that? It was, that His miracles might not be suspected. The request ought to have come from those who needed, not from His mother. And why so? Because what is done at the request of one's friends, great though it be, often causes offense to the spectators; but when they make the request who have the need, the miracle is free from suspicion, the praise unmixed, the benefit great. So if some excellent physician should enter a house where there were many sick, and be spoken to by none of the patients or their relations, but be

---

[1] al. "and all that took place after His birth."
[2] This is the common reading, but the passage (Luke ii. 51) is not so found in G. T.; Morel. and MS. in Bodleian read: τοῦτο καὶ ὁ Λουκᾶς ἡμῖν δείκνυσι λέγων· ἡ δὲ Μαριὰμ συνετήρει τὰ ῥήματα πάντα συμβάλλουσα ἐν τῇ κ.
[3] i.e. as she spoke at the marriage. [4] σφοδρότερον.
[5] lit. "hanging on the hearing."

directed only by his own mother, he would be suspected[1] and disliked by the sufferers, nor would any of the patients or their attendants deem him able to exhibit anything great or remarkable. And so this was a reason why He rebuked her on that occasion, saying, "Woman, what have I to do with thee?" instructing her for the future not to do the like; because, though He was careful to honor His mother, yet He cared much more for the salvation of her soul, and for the doing good to the many, for which He took upon Him the flesh.

These then were the words, not of one speaking rudely to his mother, but belonging to a wise dispensation, which brought her into a right frame of mind, and provided that the miracles should be attended with that honor which was meet. And setting other things aside, this very appearance which these words have of having been spoken chidingly, is amply enough to show that He held her in high honor, for by His displeasure He showed that He reverenced her greatly; in what manner, we will say in the next discourse. Think of this then, and when you hear a certain woman saying, "Blessed is the womb that bare Thee, and the paps which Thou hast sucked," and Him answering, "rather blessed are they that do the will of my Father"[2] (Luke xi. 27), suppose that those other words also were said with the same intention. For the answer was not that of one rejecting his mother, but of One who would show that her having borne Him would have nothing availed her, had she not been very good and faithful. Now if, setting aside the excellence of her soul, it profited Mary nothing that the Christ was born of her, much less will it be able to avail us to have a father or a brother, or a child of virtuous and noble disposition, if we ourselves be far removed from his virtue. "A brother," saith David, "doth not redeem, shall man redeem?" (Ps. xlix. 7, LXX.) We must place our hopes of salvation in nothing else, but only in our own righteous deeds (done) after[3] the grace of God. For if this by itself could have availed,[4] it would have availed the Jews, (for Christ was their kinsman according to the flesh,) it would have availed the town in which He was born, it would have availed His brethren. But as long as His brethren cared not for themselves, the honor of their kindred availed them nothing, but they were condemned with the rest of the world, and then only were approved, when they shone by their own virtue; and the city fell, and was burnt, having gained nothing from this; and His kinsmen according to the flesh were slaughtered and perished very miserably, having gained

nothing towards being saved from their relationship to Him, because they had not the defense of virtue. The Apostles, on the contrary, appeared greater than any, because they followed the true and excellent way of gaining relationship with Him, that by obedience. And from this we learn that we have always need of faith, and a life shining and bright, since this alone will have power to save us. For though His relations were for a long time everywhere held in honor, being called the Lord's kinsmen,[5] yet now we do not even know their names, while the lives and names of the Apostles are everywhere celebrated.

Let us then not be proud of nobleness of birth[6] according to the flesh, but though we have ten thousand famous ancestors, let us use diligence ourselves to go beyond their excellences, knowing that we shall gain nothing from the diligence of others to help us in the judgment that is to come; nay, this will be the more grievous condemnation, that though born of righteous parents and having an example at home, we do not, even thus, imitate our teachers. And this I say now, because I see many heathens,[7] when we lead them to the faith and exhort them to become Christians, flying to their kinsmen and ancestors and house, and saying, "All my relations and friends and companions are faithful Christians." What is that to thee, thou wretched and miserable? This very thing will be especially thy ruin, that thou didst not respect the number of those around thee, and run to the truth. Others again who are believers but live a careless life, when exhorted to virtue make the very same defense, and say, "my father and my grandfather and my great-grandfather were very pious and good men." But this will assuredly most condemn thee, that being descended from such men, thou hast acted unworthily of the root from whence thou art sprung. For hear what the Prophet says to the Jews, "Israel served for a wife, and for a wife he kept (sheep)" (Hos. xii. 12); and again Christ, "Your father Abraham rejoiced to see My day, and he saw it, and was glad." (c. viii. 56.) And everywhere they bring forward[8] to them the righteous acts of their fathers, not only to praise them, but also to make the charge against their descendants more heavy. Knowing then this, let us use every means that we may be saved by our own works, lest having deceived ourselves by vain trusting on others, we learn that we have been deceived when the knowledge of it will profit us nothing. "In the grave," saith David, "who shall give thee thanks?" (Ps. vi. 5.) Let us then repent here, that we may obtain the everlasting goods, which may God grant we all

---

1 [and tiresome] Morel.
2 ἀκούοντες τὸν λόγον τοῦ Θεοῦ, G. T.
3 or "next to," μετὰ with acc.
4 [the Virgin] Morel. and MS.

5 Δεσπόσυνοι, Eus. H. E. i. 7.
6 al. "relationship."
7 lit. "Greeks."
8 al. "apply."

do, through the grace and lovingkindness of our Lord Jesus Christ, with whom to the Father and the Holy Ghost be glory, for ever and ever. Amen.

---

# HOMILY XXII.

## JOHN ii. 4.

" Woman, what have I to do with thee? Mine hour is not yet come."

[1.] IN preaching the word there is some toil, and this Paul declares when he says, " Let the elders that rule well be counted worthy of double honor, especially they who labor in the word and doctrine." (1 Tim. v. 17.) Yet it is in your power to make this labor light or heavy ; for if you reject our words, or if without actually rejecting them you do not show them forth in your works, our toil will be heavy, because we labor uselessly and in vain : while if ye heed them and give proof of it by your works, we shall not even feel the toil, because the fruit produced by our labor will not suffer the greatness of that labor to appear. So that if you would rouse our zeal, and not quench or weaken it, show us, I beseech you, your fruit, that we may behold the fields waving[1] with corn, and being supported by hopes of an abundant crop, and reckoning up your[2] riches, may not be slothful[3] in carrying on this good traffic.

It is no slight question which is proposed to us also to-day. For first, when the mother of Jesus says, " They have no wine," Christ replies, " Woman, what have I to do with thee? Mine hour is not yet come." And then, having thus spoken, He did as His mother had said ; an action which needs enquiry no less than the words. Let us then, after calling upon Him who wrought the miracle, proceed to the explanation.

The words are not used in this place only, but in others also ; for the same Evangelist says, " They could not lay hands on Him,[4] because His hour was not yet come " (c. viii. 20) ; and again, " No man laid hands on Him, because His hour was not yet come " (c. vii. 30) ; and again, " The hour is come, glorify Thy Son." (c. xvii. 1.) What then do the words mean? I have brought together more instances, that I may give one explanation of all. And what is that explanation? Christ did not say, " Mine hour is not yet come," as being subject to the necessity of seasons, or the observance of an

" hour " ; how can He be so, who is Maker of seasons, and Creator of the times and the ages? To what else then did He allude? He desires to show[5] this ; that He works all things at their convenient season, not doing all at once ; because a kind of confusion and disorder would have ensued, if, instead of working all at their proper seasons, He had mixed all together, His Birth, His Resurrection, and His coming to Judgment. Observe this ; creation was to be, yet not all at once ; man and woman were to be created, yet not even these together ; mankind were to be condemned to death, and there was to be a resurrection, yet the interval between the two was to be great ; the law was to be given, but not grace with it, each was to be dispensed at its proper time. Now Christ was not subject to the necessity of seasons, but rather settled their order, since He is their Creator ; and therefore He saith in this place, " Mine hour is not yet come." And His meaning is, that as yet He was not manifest[6] to the many, nor had He even His whole company of disciples ; Andrew followed Him, and next to[7] him Philip, but no one else. And moreover, none of these, not even His mother nor His brethren, knew Him as they ought ; for after His many miracles, the Evangelist says of His brethren, " For neither did His brethren believe in Him." (c. vii. 5.) And those at the wedding did not know Him either, for in their need they would certainly have come to and entreated Him. Therefore He saith, " Mine hour is not yet come " ; that is, " I am not yet known to the company, nor are they even aware that the wine has failed ; let them first be sensible of this. I ought not to have been told it from thee ; thou art My mother, and renderest the miracle suspicious. They who wanted the wine should have come and besought Me, not that I need this, but that they might with an entire assent accept the miracle. For one who knows that he is in need, is very grateful when he obtains assistance ; but one who has not a sense

---

[1] κομῶντα.
[2] al. " our."
[3] lit. " numb," al. " be weary."
[4] οὐδεὶς ἐπίασεν αὐτόν, G. T.

[5] Ben. Morel. and MS. in Bodl. read: ἀλλὰ διὰ τῶν οὕτως εἰρημένων τοῦτο δηλῶσαι κ.τ.λ.
[6] Morel. and MS. in Bodl. read: ἀλλὰ Ἰωάννης ἐνταῦθα τὸ Οὔπω ἥκει ἡ ὥρα μου εἰσάγει τὸν Χριστὸν λέγοντα δεικνὺς ὅτι κ.τ.λ.
[7] al. " beside."

of his need, will never have a plain and clear sense of the benefit."

Why then after He had said, "Mine hour is not yet come," and given her a denial, did He what His mother desired? Chiefly it was, that they who opposed Him, and thought that He was subject to the "hour," might have sufficient proof that He was subject to no hour; for had He been so, how could He, before the proper "hour" was come, have done what He did? And in the next place, He did it to honor His mother, that He might not seem entirely to contradict and shame her that bare Him in the presence of so many; and also, that He might not be thought to want power,[1] for she brought the servants to Him.

Besides, even while saying to the Canaanitish woman, "It is not meet to take the children's bread, and to give[2] it unto dogs " (Matt. xv. 26), He still gave the bread, as considering her perseverance; and though after his 'first reply, He said, "I am not sent save unto the lost sheep of the house of Israel," yet even after saying this, He healed the woman's daughter. Hence we learn, that although we be unworthy, we often by perseverance make ourselves worthy to receive. And for this reason His mother remained by, and openly[3] brought to Him the servants, that the request might be made by a greater number; and therefore she added,

Ver. 5. "Whatsoever He saith unto you, do it."

For she knew that His refusal proceeded not from want of power, but from humility, and that He might not seem without cause[4] to hurry to[5] the miracle; and therefore she brought the servants.[6]

Ver. 6, 7. "And there were set there six waterpots of stone, after the manner of the purifying of the Jews, containing two or three firkins apiece. Jesus said unto them, Fill the waterpots with water; and they filled them up to the brim."

It is not without a reason that the Evangelist says, "After the manner of the purifying of the Jews," but in order that none of the unbelievers might suspect that lees having been left in the vessels, and water having been poured upon and mixed with them, a very weak wine had been made. Therefore he says, "after the manner of the purifying of the Jews," to show that those vessels were never receptacles for wine. For because Palestine is a country with but little water, and brooks and fountains were not everywhere to be found, they always used to fill waterpots with water, so that they might not have to hasten to the rivers if at any time they were defiled, but might have the means of purification at hand.

"And why was it, that He did not the miracle before they filled them, which would have been more marvelous by far? for it is one thing to change given matter to a different quality, and another to create matter out of nothing." The latter would indeed have been more wonderful, but would not have seemed so credible to the many. And therefore He often purposely lessens[7] the greatness of His miracles, that it may be the more readily received.

"But why," says one, "did not He Himself produce the water which He afterwards showed to be wine, instead of bidding the servants bring it?" For the very same reason; and also, that He might have those who drew it out to witness that what had been effected was no delusion; since if any had been inclined to be shameless, those who ministered might have said to them, "We drew the water, we filled the vessels." And besides what we have mentioned, He thus overthrows those doctrines which spring up against the Church. For since there are some who say that the Creator of the world is another, and that the things which are seen are not His works, but those of a certain other opposing god, to curb these men's madness He doth most of His miracles on matter found at hand.[8] Because, had the creator of these been opposed to Him, He would not have used what was another's to set forth His own power. But now to show that it is He who transmutes water in the vine plants, and who converts the rain by its passage through the root into wine, He effected that in a moment at the wedding which in the plant is long in doing. When they had filled the waterpots, He said,

Ver. 8–10. "Draw out now, and bear unto the governor of the feast; and they bare it. When the ruler of the feast had tasted the water that was made wine, and knew not whence it was, (but the servants which drew the water knew,) the governor of the feast called the bridegroom, and saith unto him, Every man at the beginning doth set forth good wine, and when men have well drunk, then that which is worst; but thou hast kept the good wine until now."

Here again some mock,[9] saying, "this was an assembly of drunken men, the sense of the judges was spoilt, and not able to taste[10] what was made, or to decide on what was done, so that they did not know whether what was made was water or wine: for that they were drunk," it is alleged, "the ruler himself has shown by what he said."

---

[1] This passage is wanting in the MS. in Bodleian.
[2] βαλεῖν, G. T.　　　　　[3] al. " wisely."
[4] ἁπλῶς.　　　　[5] ἐπιρρίπτειν.
[6] Morel. and MS. in Bodl. read: δι' ὁ καὶ τὴν ὑπακοὴν ἀναβάλλεται.

[7] lit. " clips round."
[8] ὑποκειμένων.
[9] al. " impeach."
[10] ἀντιλάβεσθαι.

Now this is most ridiculous, yet even this suspicion the Evangelist has removed. For he does not say that the guests gave their opinion on the matter, but "the ruler of the feast," who was sober, and had not as yet tasted anything. For of course you are aware, that those who are entrusted with the management[1] of such banquets are the most sober, as having this one business, to dispose all things in order and regularity; and therefore the Lord called such a man's sober senses to testify to what was done. For He did not say, "Pour forth to them that sit at meat," but, "Bear unto the governor of the feast."

"And when the ruler of the feast had tasted the water that was made wine, and knew not whence it was, (but the servants knew,) the governor of the feast called the bridegroom." "And why did he not call the servants? for so the miracle would have been revealed." Because Jesus had not Himself revealed what had been done, but desired that the power of His miracles should be known gently, little by little. And suppose that it had then been mentioned,[2] the servants who related it would never have been believed, but would have been thought mad to bear such testimony to one who at that time seemed to the many a mere man; and although they knew the certainty of the thing by experience, (for they were not likely to disbelieve their own hands,) yet they were not sufficient to convince others. And so He did not reveal it to all, but to him who was best able to understand what was done, reserving the clearer knowledge of it for a future time; since after the manifestation of other miracles this also would be credible. Thus when he was about to heal the nobleman's son, the Evangelist has shown that it had already become more clearly known; for it was chiefly because the nobleman had become acquainted with the miracle that he called upon Him, as John incidentally shows when he says, "Jesus came into Cana of Galilee, where He made the water wine." (c. iv. 46.) And not wine simply, but the best.

[3.] For such are the miraculous works of Christ, they are far more perfect and better than the operations of nature. This is seen also in other instances; when He restored any infirm member of the body, He made[3] it better than the sound.

That it was wine then, and the best of wine, that had been made, not the servants only, but the bridegroom and the ruler of the feast would testify; and that it was made by Christ, those who drew the water; so that although the miracle were not then revealed, yet it could not in the end be passed in silence, so many and constraining testimonies had He provided for the future. That He had made the water wine, He had the servants for witnesses; that the wine was good that had been made, the ruler of the feast and the bridegroom.

It might be expected that the bridegroom would reply to this, (the ruler's speech,) and say something, but the Evangelist, hastening to more pressing matters, has only touched upon this miracle, and passed on. For what we needed to learn was, that Christ made the water wine, and that good wine; but what the bridegroom said to the governor he did not think it necessary to add. And many miracles, at first somewhat obscure, have in process of time become more plain, when reported more exactly by those who knew them from the beginning.

At that time, then, Jesus made of water wine, and both then and now He ceases not to change our weak and unstable[4] wills. For there are, yes, there are men who in nothing differ from water, so cold, and weak, and unsettled. But let us bring those of such disposition to the Lord, that He may change their will to the quality of wine, so that they be no longer washy,[5] but have body,[6] and be the cause of gladness in themselves and others. But who can these cold ones be? They are those who give their minds to the fleeting things of this present life, who despise not this world's luxury, who are lovers of glory and dominion: for all these things are flowing waters, never stable, but ever rushing violently down the steep. The rich to-day is poor to-morrow, he who one day appears with herald, and girdle, and chariot, and numerous attendants, is often on the next the inhabitant of a dungeon, having unwillingly quitted all that show to make room for another. Again, the gluttonous and dissipated[7] man, when he has filled himself to bursting,[8] cannot retain even for a single day the supply[9] conveyed by his delicacies, but when that is dispersed, in order to renew it he is obliged to put in more, differing in nothing from a torrent. For as in the torrent when the first body of water is gone, others in turn succeed; so in gluttony, when one repast is removed, we again require another. And such is the nature and the lot of earthly things, never to be stable, but to be always pouring and hurrying by; but in the case of luxury, it is not merely the flowing and hastening by, but many other things that trouble us. By the violence of its course it wears away[10] the strength of the body, and strips the soul of its manliness, and the strongest currents of rivers do not so easily eat away their banks and make them sink down, as do luxury and wantonness sweep away

---

[1] διακονίαν.     [2] al. "examined."     [3] lit. "showed."

[4] lit. "flowing away."          [5] διαρρεῖν.
[6] τὸ ἐπεστυμμένον, "astringency."
[7] διασπώμενος.
[8] lit. "has burst his stomach."
[9] χορηγίαν.          [10] ἀποξύει, "abrades."

all the bulwarks of our health ; and if you enter a physician's house and ask him, you will find that almost all the causes of diseases arise from this. For frugality and a plain[1] table is the mother of health, and therefore physicians[2] have thus named it ; for they have called the not being satisfied " health," (because not to be satisfied with food is health,) and they have spoken of sparing diet as the " mother of health." Now if the condition of want[3] is the mother of health, it is clear that fullness is the mother of sickness and debility, and produces attacks which are beyond the skill even of physicians. For gout in the feet, apoplexy, dimness of sight, pains in the hands, tremors, paralytic attacks, jaundice, lingering and inflammatory fevers, and other diseases many more than these, (for we have not time to go over them all,) are the natural offspring, not of abstinence and moderate[4] diet, but of gluttony and repletion. And if you will look to the diseases of the soul that arise from them, you will see that feelings of coveting, sloth, melancholy, dullness, impurity, and folly of all kinds, have their origin here. For after such banquets the souls of the luxurious become no better than asses, being torn to pieces by such wild beasts as these (passions). Shall I say also how many pains and displeasures they have who wait upon luxury? I could not enumerate them all, but by a single principal point I will make the whole clear. At a table such as I speak of, that is, a sumptuous one, men never eat with pleasure ; for abstinence is the mother of pleasure as well as health, while repletion is the source and root not only of diseases, but of displeasure. For where there is satiety there desire cannot be, and where there is no desire, how can there be pleasure? And therefore we should find that the poor are not only of better understanding and healthier than the rich, but also that they enjoy a greater degree of pleasure. Let us, when we reflect on this, flee drunkenness and luxury, not that of the table alone, but all other which is found in the things of this life, and let us take in exchange for it the pleasure arising from spiritual things, and, as the Prophet says, delight ourselves in the Lord ; " Delight thyself in the Lord, and He shall give thee the desires of thine heart " (Ps. xxxvii. 4) ; that so that we may enjoy the good things both here and hereafter, through the grace and lovingkindness of our Lord Jesus Christ, by whom and with whom, to the Father and the Holy Ghost, be glory, world without end. Amen.

# HOMILY XXIII.

## John ii. 11.

" This beginning of miracles did Jesus in Cana of Galilee."

[1.] Frequent and fierce is the devil in his attacks, on all sides besieging our salvation ; we therefore must watch and be sober, and everywhere fortify ourselves against his assault, for if he but gain some slight vantage ground,[5] he goes on to make for himself a broad passage, and by degrees introduces all his forces. If then we have any care at all for our salvation, let us not allow him to make his approaches even in trifles, that thus we may check him beforehand in important matters ; for it would be the extreme of folly, if, while he displays such eagerness to destroy our souls, we should not bring even an equal amount in defense of our own salvation.

I say not this without a cause, but because I fear lest that wolf be even now standing unseen by us in the midst of the fold,[6] and some sheep become a prey to him, being led astray from the flock and from hearkening by its own carelessness and his craft. Were the wounds[7] sensible, or did the body receive the blows, there would be no difficulty in discerning his plots ; but since the soul is invisible, and since that it is which receives the wounds, we need great watchfulness that each may prove himself ; for none knoweth the things of a man as the spirit of a man that is in him. (1 Cor. ii. 11.) The word is spoken indeed to all, and is offered as a general remedy to those who need it, but it is the business of every individual hearer to take what is suited to his complaint. I know not who are sick, I know not who are well. And therefore I use every sort of argument, and introduce remedies suited to all maladies,[8] at one time condemning covetousness, after that touching on luxury, and again

---

[1] λιτὴ.
[2] lit. " children of phys."
[3] ἐνδεία.
[4] φιλοσόφου.
[5] ἀφορμῆς.
[6] or " sacred enclosure," σηκῶ.
[7] al. " words."
[8] Morel. and MS. in Bodl. read the passage thus: κινῶ, πᾶσιν ἀνθρώποις ὁμοίως ἁρμόζοντα, καὶ πᾶσιν ἐπιτήδειον πάθεσιν.

on impurity, then composing something in praise of and exhortation to charity, and each of the other virtues in their turn. For I fear lest when my arguments are employed on any one subject, I may without knowing it be treating you for one disease while you are ill of others. So that if this congregation were but one person, I should not have judged it so absolutely necessary to make my discourse varied; but since in such a multitude there are probably also many maladies, I not unreasonably diversify my teaching, since my discourse will be sure to attain its object when it is made to embrace you all. For this cause also Scripture is something multiform,[1] and speaks on ten thousand matters, because it addresses itself to the nature of mankind in common, and in such a multitude all the passions of the soul must needs be; though all be not in each. Let us then cleanse ourselves of these, and so listen to the divine oracles, and with contrite heart[2] hear what has been this day read to us.

And what is that? "This beginning of miracles did Jesus in Cana of Galilee." I told you the other day, that there are some who say that this is not the beginning. "For what," says one, "if 'Cana of Galilee' be added? This shows that this was 'the beginning' He made 'in Cana.'"[3] But on these points I would not venture to assert anything exactly. I before have shown that He began His miracles after His Baptism, and wrought no miracle before it; but whether of the miracles done after His Baptism, this or some other was the first, it seems to me unnecessary to assert positively.

"And manifested forth His glory."

"How?" asks one, "and in what way? For only the servants, the ruler of the feast, and the bridegroom, not the greater number of those present, gave heed to what was done." How then did he "manifest forth His glory"? He manifested it at least for His own part, and if all present hear not of the miracle at the time, they would hear of it afterwards, for unto the present time it is celebrated, and has not been unnoticed. That all did not know it on the same day is clear from what follows, for after having said that He "manifested forth His glory," the Evangelist adds,

"And His disciples believed on Him."

His disciples, who even before this regarded Him with wonder.[4] Seest thou that it was especially necessary to work the miracles at times when men were present of honest minds, and who would carefully give heed to what was

done? for these would more readily believe, and attend more exactly to the circumstances. "And how could He have become known without miracles?" Because His doctrine and prophetic powers were sufficient to cause wonder in the souls of His hearers, so that they took heed to what He did with a right disposition, their minds being already well affected towards Him. And therefore in many other places the Evangelists say, that He did no miracle on account of the perversity of the men who dwelt there. (Matt. xii. 38; ch. xiii. 58, &c.)

Ver. 12. "After this He went down to Capernaum, He, and His mother, and His brethren, and His disciples; and they continued there not many days."

Wherefore comes He with "His mother to Capernaum"? for He hath done no miracle there, and the inhabitants of that city were not of those who were rightminded towards Him, but of the utterly corrupt. And this Christ declared when He said, "And thou, Capernaum, which are exalted to heaven, shall be thrust down to hell." (Luke x. 15.) Wherefore then goes He? I think it was, because He intended a little after to go up to Jerusalem, that He then went to Capernaum, to avoid leading about[5] everywhere with Him, His mother and His brethren. And so, having departed and tarried a little while to honor His mother, He again commences His miracles after restoring to her home her who had borne Him. Therefore the Evangelist says, After "not many days,"

Ver. 13. "He went up to Jerusalem."

He received baptism then a few days before the passover. But on going up to Jerusalem, what did He, a deed full of high authority; for He cast out of the Temple those dealers and money changers, and those who sold doves, and oxen, and sheep, and who passed their time there for this purpose.

[2.] Another Evangelist writes, that as He cast them out, He said, Make not my Father's house[6] "a den of thieves," but this one,

Ver. 16. ("Make not My Father's house) an house of merchandise."

They do not in this contradict each other, but show that he did this a second time, and that both these expressions were not used on the same occasion, but that He acted thus once at the beginning of His ministry, and again when He had come to the very time of His Passion. Therefore, (on the latter occasion,) employing more strong expressions, He spoke of it as[7] (being made) "a den of thieves," but here at the commencement of His miracles He does not so, but uses a more gentle rebuke; from

---

[1] πολυειδής.
[2] Morel. and MS. in Bodleian read: οὕτω τοῖς θείοις λόγοις προσβάλλωμεν, καὶ οὕτω μετὰ συντετριμμένης σφόδρα τῆς διανοίας κ.τ.λ.
[3] Morel. and MS. in Bodleian read: τὶ γὰρ ἄτοπον προσκεῖσθαι ἐν Κανᾷ, καὶ μὴ ἀρχὴν εἶναι ταύτην τῶν τοῦ Ἰησοῦ σημείων.
[4] [admired and believed] Morel. and MS.

[5] ἐπισύρεσθαι.
[6] Luke xix. 46, ὑμεῖς ἐποιήσατε κ.τ.λ. G. T.
[7] lit. "called it."

which it is probable that this took place[1] a second time.

"And wherefore," says one, "did Christ do this same, and use such severity against these men, a thing which He is nowhere else seen to do, even when insulted and reviled, and called by them 'Samaritan' and 'demoniac'? for He was not even satisfied with words only, but took a scourge, and so cast them out." Yes, but it was when others were receiving benefit, that the Jews accused and raged against Him; when it was probable that they would have been made savage by His rebukes, they showed no such disposition towards Him, for they neither accused nor reviled Him. What say they?

Ver. 18. "What sign showest Thou unto us, seeing that Thou doest these things?"

Seest thou their excessive malice, and how the benefits done to others incensed them more (than reproofs)?

At one time then He said, that the Temple was made by them "a den of thieves," showing that what they sold was gotten by theft, and rapine, and covetousness, and that they were rich through other men's calamities; at another, "a house of merchandise," pointing to their shameless traffickings. "But wherefore did He this?" Since he was about to heal on the Sabbath day, and to do many such things which were thought by them transgressions of the Law, in order that He might not seem to do this as though He had come to be some rival God[2] and opponent of His Father, He takes occasion hence to correct any such suspicion of theirs. For One who had exhibited so much zeal for the House was not likely to oppose Him who was Lord of the House, and who was worshiped in it. No doubt even the former years during which He lived according to the Law, were sufficient to show His reverence for the Legislator, and that He came not to give contrary laws; yet since it was likely that those years were forgotten through lapse of time, as not having been known to all because He was brought up in a poor and mean dwelling, He afterwards does this in the presence of all, (for many were present because the feast was nigh at hand,) and at great risk. For he did not merely "cast them out," but also "overturned the tables," and "poured out the money," giving them by this to understand, that He who threw Himself into danger for the good order of the House could never despise his Master. Had He acted as He did from hypocrisy, He should only have advised them; but to place Himself in danger was very daring. For it was no light thing to offer Himself to the anger of so many market-folk,[3] to excite against Himself a most brutal mob of petty dealers by His reproaches and His blows, this was not the action of a pretender, but of one choosing to suffer everything for the order of the House.

And therefore not by His actions only, but by His words, He shows his agreement with the Father;[4] for He saith not "the Holy House," but "My Father's House." See, He even calls Him, "Father," and they are not wroth; they thought He spoke in a general way:[5] but when He went on and spoke more plainly, so as to set before them the idea of His Equality, then they become angry.

And what say they? "What sign showest Thou unto us, seeing that Thou doest these things?" Alas for their utter madness! Was there need of a sign before they could cease their evil doings, and free the house of God from such dishonor? and was it not the greatest sign of His Excellence that He had gotten such zeal for that House? In fact, the well-disposed[6] were distinguished by this very thing, for "They," His disciples, it says,

Ver. 17. "Remembered that it is written, The zeal of thine house hath eaten me up."

But the Jews did not remember the Prophecy, and said, "What sign showest Thou unto us?" (Ps. lxix. 9), both grieving that their shameful traffic was cut off, and expecting by these means to stop Him, and also desiring to challenge Him to a miracle, and to find fault with what He was doing. Wherefore He will not give them a sign; and before, when they came and asked Him, He made them the same answer, "A wicked and adulterous generation seeketh after a sign; and there shall no sign be given unto it, but the sign of the prophet Jonas." (Matt. xvi. 4.) Only then the answer was clear, now it is more ambiguous. This He doth on account of their extreme insensibility; for He who prevented[7] them without their asking, and gave them signs, would never when they asked have turned away from them, had He not seen that their minds were wicked and false, and their intention treacherous.[8] Think how full of wickedness the question itself was at the outset. When they ought to have applauded Him for His earnestness and zeal, when they ought to have been astonished that He cared so greatly for the House, they reproach Him, saying, that it was lawful to traffic, and unlawful for any to stop their traffic, except he should show them a sign. What saith Christ?

Ver. 19. "Destroy this Temple, and in three days I will raise it up."

Many such sayings He utters which were not intelligible to His immediate hearers, but which

---

[1] Or, "that He did this." ὅθεν εἰκὸς δεύτερον τοῦτο γεγενῆσθαι. al. πεποιηκέναι.
[2] or, "adversary of God."

[3] or, "base persons," ἀγοραίων.
[4] τὴν πρὸς αὐτὸν συμφωνίαν.
[5] ἁπλῶς.
[6] εὐγνώμονες.
[7] al. "took to Him."
[8] ὕπουλον.

were to be so to those that should come after. And wherefore doth He this? In order that when the accomplishment of His prediction should have come to pass, He might be seen to have foreknown from the beginning what was to follow; which indeed was the case with this prophecy. For, saith the Evangelist,

Ver. 22. "When He was risen from the dead, His disciples remembered that He had said this; and they believed the Scripture, and the word which Jesus had said."

But at the time when this was spoken, the Jews were perplexed as to what it might mean, and cast about to discover, saying,

Ver. 20. "Forty and six years was this Temple in building, and wilt thou rear it up in three days?"

"Forty and six years," they said, referring to the latter building, for the former was finished in twenty years' time. (Ezra vi. 15.)

[3.] Wherefore then did He not resolve the difficulty and say, "I speak not of that Temple, but of My flesh"? Why does the Evangelist, writing the Gospel at a later period, interpret the saying, and Jesus keep silence at the time? Why did He so keep silence? Because they would not have received His word; for if not even the disciples were able to understand the saying, much less were the multitudes. "When," saith the Evangelist, "He was risen from the dead, then they remembered, and believed the Scripture and His word." There were two things that hindered[1] them for the time, one the fact of the Resurrection, the other, the greater question whether He was God[2] that dwelt within; of both which things He spake darkly when He said, "Destroy this Temple, and I will rear it up in three days." And this St. Paul declares to be no small proof of His Godhead, when he writes, "Declared to be the Son of God with power, according to the Spirit of holiness, by the Resurrection from the dead." (Rom. i. 4.)

But why doth He both there, and here, and everywhere, give this for a sign, at one time saying,[3] "When ye have lifted up the Son of Man, then ye shall know that I Am" (c. viii. 28); at another, "There shall no sign be given you[4] but the sign of the prophet Jonas" (Matt. xii. 39); and again in this place, "In three days I will raise it up"? Because what especially showed that He was not a mere man, was His being able to set up a trophy of victory over death, and so quickly to abolish His long enduring tyranny, and conclude that difficult war. Wherefore He saith, "Then ye shall know." "Then." When? When after My Resurrection

I shall draw (all) the world to Me, then ye shall know that I did these things as God, and Very Son of God, avenging the insult offered to My Father.

"Why then, instead of saying, 'What need is there of "signs" to check evil deeds?' did He promise that He would give them a sign?" Because by so doing He would have the more exasperated them; but in this way He rather astonished them. Still they made no answer to this, for He seemed to them to say what was incredible, so that they did not stay even to question Him upon it, but passed it by as impossible. Yet had they been wise, though it seemed to them at the time incredible, still when He wrought His many miracles they would then have come and questioned Him, would then have intreated that the difficulty might be resolved to them; but because they were foolish, they gave no heed at all to part of what was said, and part they heard with evil frame of mind. And therefore Christ spoke to them in an enigmatical way.

The question still remains, "How was it that the disciples did not know that He must rise from the dead?" It was, because they had not been vouchsafed the gift of the Spirit; and therefore, though they constantly heard His discourses concerning the Resurrection, they understood them not, but reasoned with themselves what this might be. For very strange and paradoxical was the assertion that one could raise himself, and would raise himself in such wise. And so Peter was rebuked, when, knowing nothing about the Resurrection, he said, "Be it far from Thee." (Matt. xvi. 22.) And Christ did not reveal it clearly to them before the event, that they might not be offended at the very outset, being led to distrust His words on account of the great improbability of the thing, and because they did not yet clearly know Him, who He was. For no one could help believing what was proclaimed aloud by facts, while some would probably disbelieve what was told to them in words. Therefore He at first allowed the meaning of His words to be concealed; but when by their experience He had verified His sayings, He after that gave them understanding of His words, and such gifts of the Spirit that they received them all at once. "He," saith Jesus, "shall bring all things to your remembrance." (c. xiv. 26.) For they who in a single night cast off all respect for Him, and fled from and denied that they even knew Him, would scarcely have remembered what He had done and said during the whole time, unless they had enjoyed much grace of the Spirit.

"But," says one, "if they were to hear from the Spirit, why needed they to accompany Christ when they would not retain His words?" Be-

---

[1] al. "were proposed to."
[2] Savile, 'Ο Θεὸς, "whether He was the One God"; but the article is not found in Ben. Morel. or MSS.
[3] [ὅταν ὑψωθῶ] Ben.   [4] αὐτῇ [γενεᾷ] G. T.

cause the Spirit taught them not, but called to their mind what Christ had said before; and it contributes not a little to the glory of Christ, that they were referred to the remembrance of the words He had spoken to them. At the first then it was of the gift of God that the grace of the Spirit lighted upon them so largely and abundantly; but after that, it was of their own virtue that they retained the Gift. For they displayed a shining life, and much wisdom, and great labors, and despised this present life, and thought nothing of earthly things, but were above them all; and like a sort of light-winged eagle, soaring high by their works, reached [1] to heaven itself, and by these possessed the unspeakable grace of the Spirit.

Let us then imitate them, and not quench our lamps, but keep them bright by alms-doing, for so is the light of this fire preserved. Let us collect the oil into our vessels whilst we are here, for we cannot buy it when we have departed to that other place, nor can we procure it elsewhere, save only at the hands of the poor. Let us therefore collect it thence very abundantly, if, at least, we desire to enter in with the Bridegroom. But if we do not this, we must remain without the bridechamber, for it is impossible, it is impossible, though we perform ten thousand other good deeds, to enter the portals of the Kingdom without alms-doing. Let us then show forth this very abundantly, that we may enjoy those ineffable blessings; which may it come to pass that we all attain, by the grace and lovingkindness of our Lord Jesus Christ, with whom to the Father and the Holy Ghost be glory, for ever and ever. Amen.

# HOMILY XXIV.

### John ii. 23.

"Now when He was in Jerusalem at the Passover, in the feast, many believed on Him."

[1.] Of the men of that time some clung to their error, others laid hold on the truth, while of these last, some having retained it for a little while again fell off from it. Alluding to these, Christ compared them to seeds not deeply sown, but having their roots upon the surface of the earth; and He said that they should quickly perish. And these the Evangelist has here pointed out to us, saying,

"When He was in Jerusalem, at the Passover, in the feast, many believed on Him,[2] when they saw the miracles which He did."

Ver. 24. "But Jesus did not commit Himself unto them."

For they were the more perfect[3] among His disciples, who came to Him not only because of His miracles, but through His teaching also. The grosser sort the miracles attracted, but the better reasoners His prophecies and doctrines; and so they who were taken by His teaching were more steadfast than those attracted by His miracles. And Christ also called them "blessed," saying, "Blessed are they that have not seen, and yet have believed." (c. xx. 29.) But that these here mentioned were not real disciples, the following passage shows, for it saith, "Jesus did not commit Himself unto them." Wherefore?

"Because He knew all things," [4]

Ver. 25. "And needed not that any should testify of man, for He knew what was in man."

The meaning is of this kind. "He who dwells in men's hearts, and enters into their thoughts, took no heed of outward words; and knowing well that their warmth was but for a season, He placed not confidence in them as in perfect disciples, nor committed all His doctrines to them as though they had already become firm believers." Now, to know what is in the heart of men belongs to God alone, "who hath fashioned hearts one by one" (Ps. xxxiii. 15, LXX.), for, saith Solomon, "Thou, even Thou only, knowest the hearts" (1 Kings viii. 39); He therefore needed not witnesses to learn the thoughts of His own creatures, and so He felt no confidence in them because of their mere temporary belief. Men, who know neither the present nor the future, often tell and entrust all without any reserve to persons who approach them deceitfully and who shortly will fall off from them; but Christ did not so, for well He knew all their secret thoughts.

And many such now there are, who have indeed the name of faith, but are unstable,[5] and easily led away; wherefore neither now doth Christ commit Himself to them, but concealeth from them many things; and just as we do not place confidence in mere acquaintances but in real friends, so also doth Christ. Hear what He

---

[1] al. "were drawn away."
[2] εἰς τὸ ὄνομα αὐτοῦ, G. T.
[3] ἀκριβέστεροι, al. ἀσφαλέστεροι.

[4] πάντα [πάντας, G. T.].       [5] εὐρίπιστοι.

saith to His disciples, "Henceforth I call you not servants, ye are My friends." (c. xv. 14, 15.) Whence is this and why? "Because all things that I have heard of My Father I have made known unto you." And therefore He gave no signs to the Jews who asked for them, because they asked tempting Him. Indeed the asking for signs is a practice of tempters both then and now; for even now there are some that seek them and say, "Why do not miracles take place also at this present time?" If thou art faithful, as thou oughtest to be, and lovest Christ as thou oughtest to love Him, thou hast no need of signs, they are given to the unbelievers. "How then," asks one, "were they not given to the Jews?" Given they certainly were; and if there were times when though they asked they did not receive them, it was because they asked them not that they might be delivered from their unbelief, but in order the more to confirm their wickedness.

Chap. iii. 1, 2. "And there was a man of the Pharisees, named Nicodemus. The same came to Jesus by night."

This man appears also in the middle of the Gospel, making defense for Christ; for he saith, "Our law judgeth no man[1] before it hear him" (c. vii. 51); and the Jews in anger replied to him, "Search and look, for out of Galilee ariseth no prophet." Again after the crucifixion he bestowed great care upon the burial of the Lord's body: "There came also," saith the Evangelist, "Nicodemus, which came to the Lord[2] by night, and brought a mixture of myrrh and aloes, about an hundred pound weight." (c. xix. 39.) And even now he was disposed towards Christ,[3] but not as he ought, nor with proper sentiments respecting Him, for he was as yet entangled in Jewish infirmity. Wherefore he came by night, because he feared to do so by day. Yet not for this did the merciful God reject or rebuke him, or deprive him of His instruction, but even with much kindness conversed with him, and disclosed to him very exalted doctrines, enigmatically indeed, but nevertheless He disclosed them. For far more deserving of pardon was he than those who acted thus through wickedness. They are entirely without excuse; but he, though he was liable to condemnation, yet was not so to an equal degree. "How then does the Evangelist say nothing of the kind concerning him?" He has said in another place, that "of the rulers also many believed on Him, but because of the Jews[4] they did not confess (Him), lest they should be put out of the synagogue" (c. xii. 42); but here he has implied the whole by mentioning his coming "by night." What then saith Nicodemus?

"Rabbi, we know that Thou art a Teacher come from God: for no man can do the miracles that Thou doest, except God be with him."

[2.] Nicodemus yet lingers[5] below, has yet human thoughts concerning Him, and speaks of Him as of a Prophet, imagining nothing great from His miracles. "We know," he says, "that Thou art a Teacher come from God." "Why then comest thou by night and secretly, to Him that speaketh the things of God, to Him who cometh from God? Why conversest thou not with Him openly?" But Jesus said nothing like this to him, nor did He rebuke him; for, saith the Prophet, "A bruised reed shall He not break, and smoking flax shall he not quench; He shall not strive nor cry" (Isa. xlii. 2, 3; as quoted Matt. xii. 19, 20): and again He saith Himself, "I came not to condemn the world, but to save the world." (c. xii. 47.)

"No man can do these miracles, except God be with him."

Still here Nicodemus speaks like the heretics, in saying, that He hath a power working within Him,[6] and hath need of the aid of others to do as He did. What then saith Christ? Observe His exceeding condescension. He refrained for a while from saying, "I need not the help of others, but do all things with power, for I am the Very Son of God, and have the same power as My Father," because this would have been too hard for His hearer; for I say now what I am always saying, that what Christ desired was, not so much for a while to reveal His own Dignity, as to persuade men that He did nothing contrary to His Father. And therefore in many places he appears in words confined by limits,[7] but in His actions He doth not so. For when He worketh a miracle, He doth all with power, saying, "I will, be thou clean." (Matt. viii. 3.) "Talitha, arise." (Mark v. 41; not verbally quoted.) "Stretch forth thy hand." (Mark iii. 5.) "Thy sins be forgiven thee." (Matt. ix. 2.) "Peace, be still." (Mark iv. 39.) "Take up thy bed, and go unto thine house." (Matt. ix. 6.) "Thou foul spirit, I say unto thee, come out of him." (Mark ix. 25; not verbally quoted.) "Be it unto thee even as thou wilt." (Matt. xv. 28.) "If any one say (aught) unto you, ye shall say, The Lord hath need of him." (Mark xi. 3.) "This day shalt thou be with Me in Paradise." (Luke xxiii. 43.) "Ye have heard that it was said by them of old time, Thou shalt not kill; but I say unto you, that whosoever is angry with his brother without a cause, shall be in danger of the judgment." (Matt. v. 21, 22.) "Come ye after Me, and I will make you fishers of men." (Mark i. 17.) And everywhere we observe that His authority is great; for in His actions no one

---

[1] μὴ ὁ νόμος ἡμῶν κ.τ.λ. G. T.
[2] Ἰησοῦν, G. T.
[3] περὶ τὸν X.
[4] Φαρισαίους, G. T.
[5] στρέφεται.
[6] ἐνεργούμενον αὐτὸν.
[7] μετριάζων.

could find fault with what was done. How was it possible? Had His words not come to pass, nor been accomplished as He commanded, any one might have said that they were the commands of a madman; but since they did come to pass, the reality of their accomplishment stopped men's mouths even against their will. But with regard to His discourses, they might often in their insolence charge Him with madness. Wherefore now in the case of Nicodemus, He utters nothing openly, but by dark sayings leads him up from his low thoughts, teaching him, that He has sufficient power in Himself to show forth miracles; for that His Father begat Him Perfect and All-sufficient, and without any imperfection.

But let us see how He effects this. Nicodemus saith, "Rabbi, we know that Thou art a Teacher come from God, for no man can do the miracles that Thou doest, except God be with him." He thought he had said something great when he had spoken thus of Christ. What then saith Christ? To show that he had not yet set foot even on the threshold of right knowledge, nor stood in the porch, but was yet wandering somewhere without the palace, both he and whoever else should say the like, and that he had not so much as glanced towards true knowledge when he held such an opinion of the Only-Begotten, what saith He?

Ver. 3. "Verily, verily, I say unto thee, Except a man be born again, he cannot see the Kingdom of God."

That is, "Unless thou art born again and receivest the right doctrines, thou art wandering somewhere without, and art far from the Kingdom of heaven." But He does not speak so plainly as this. In order to make the saying less hard to bear, He does not plainly direct it at him, but speaks indefinitely, "Except a man be born again": all but saying, "both thou, and any other, who may have such opinions concerning Me, art somewhere without the Kingdom." Had He not spoken from a desire to establish this, His answer would have been suitable to what had been said. Now the Jews, if these words had been addressed to them, would have derided Him and departed; but Nicodemus shows here also his desire of instruction.[1] And this is why in many places Christ speaks obscurely, because He wishes to rouse His hearers to ask questions, and to render them more attentive. For that which is said plainly often escapes the hearer, but what is obscure renders him more active and zealous. Now what He saith, is something like this: "If thou art not born again, if thou partakest not of the Spirit which is by the washing[2] of Regeneration,

thou canst not have a right opinion of Me, for the opinion which thou hast is not spiritual, but carnal."[3] (Tit. iii. 5.) But He did not speak thus, as refusing to confound[4] one who had brought such as he had, and who had spoken to the best of his ability; and He leads him unsuspectedly up to greater knowledge, saying, "Except a man be born again." The word "again,"[5] in this place, some understand to mean "from heaven," others, "from the beginning." "It is impossible," saith Christ, "for one not so born to see the Kingdom of God"; in this pointing to Himself, and declaring that there is another beside the natural sight, and that we have need of other eyes to behold Christ. Having heard this,

Ver. 4. "Nicodemus saith, How can a man be born when he is old?"

Callest thou Him "Master," sayest thou that He is "come from God," and yet receivest thou not His words, but usest to thy Teacher a manner of speaking which expresses[6] much perplexity? For the "How," is the doubting question of those who have no strong belief, but who are yet of the earth. Therefore Sarah laughed when she had said, "How?" And many others having asked this question, have fallen from the faith.

[3.] And thus heretics continue in their heresy, because they frequently make this enquiry, saying, some of them, "How was He begotten?" others, "How was He made flesh?" and subjecting that Infinite Essence to the weakness of their own reasonings.[7] Knowing which, we ought to avoid this unseasonable curiosity, for they who search into these matters shall, without learning the "How," fall away from the right faith. On this account Nicodemus, being in doubt, enquires the manner in which this can be, (for he understood that the words spoken referred to himself,) is confused, and dizzy,[8] and in perplexity, having come as to a man, and hearing more than man's words, and such as no one ever yet had heard; and for a while he rouses himself at the sublimity of the sayings, but yet is in darkness, and unstable, borne about in every direction, and continually falling away from the faith. And therefore he perseveres in proving the impossibility, so as to provoke Him to clearer teaching.

"Can a man," he saith, "enter into his mother's womb, and be born?"

Seest thou how when one commits spiritual things to his own reasonings, he speaks ridiculously, seems to be trifling, or to be drunken, when he pries into what has been said beyond what seems good to God, and admits not the submission

---

[1] al. "of truth."　　　[2] or, "laver."

[3] ψυχική, "belonging to the natural life," opposed in N. T. to πνευματική.　　　[4] or, "strike."
[5] ἄνωθεν ("again," or "from above").
[6] lit. "introduces."
[7] Ben. transposes the clauses.　　　[8] ἰλιγγιᾷ.

of faith? Nicodemus heard of the spiritual Birth, yet perceived it not as spiritual, but dragged down the words to the lowness of the flesh, and made a doctrine so great and high depend upon physical consequence. And so he invents frivolities, and ridiculous difficulties. Wherefore Paul said, " The natural[1] man receiveth not the things of the Spirit." (1 Cor. ii. 14.) Yet even in this he preserved his reverence for Christ, for he did not mock at what had been said, but, deeming it impossible, held his peace. There were two difficulties; a Birth of this kind, and the Kingdom; for neither had the name of the Kingdom ever been heard among the Jews, nor of a Birth like this. But he stops for a while at the first, which most astonished[2] his mind.

Let us then, knowing this, not enquire into things relating to God by reasoning, nor bring heavenly matters under the rule of earthly consequences, nor subject them to the necessity of nature; but let us think of all reverently, believing as the Scriptures have said; for the busy and curious person gains nothing, and besides not finding what he seeks, shall suffer extreme punishment. Thou hast heard, that (the Father) begat (the Son) : believe what thou hast heard; but do ask not, " How," and so take away the Generation; to do so would be extreme folly. For if this man, because, on hearing of a Generation, not that ineffable GENERATION, but this which is by grace, he conceived nothing great concerning it, but human and earthly thoughts, was therefore darkened and in doubt, what punishment must they deserve, who are busy and curious about that most awful GENERATION, which transcends all reason and intellect? For nothing causes such dizziness[3] as human reasoning, all whose words are of earth, and which cannot endure to be enlightened from above. Earthly reasonings are full of mud, and therefore need we streams from heaven, that when the mud has settled, the clearer portion may rise and mingle with the heavenly lessons; and this comes to pass, when we present an honest soul and an upright life. For certainly it is possible for the intellect to be darkened, not only by unseasonable curiosity, but also by corrupt manners;

wherefore Paul hath said to the Corinthians, " I have fed you with milk, and not with meat; for hitherto ye were not able to bear it, neither yet now are ye able, for ye are yet carnal; for whereas there is among you envying, and strife, and divisions, are ye not carnal? " (1 Cor. iii. 2.) And also in the Epistle to the Hebrews, and in many places, one may see Paul asserting that this is the cause of evil doctrines; for that the soul possessed by passions[4] cannot behold anything great or noble, but as if darkened by a sort of film[5] suffers most grievous dimsightedness.

Let us then cleanse ourselves, let us kindle the light of knowledge, let us not sow among thorns. What the thorns are, ye know, though we tell you not; for often ye have heard Christ call the cares of this present life, and the deceitfulness of riches, by this name. (Matt. xiii. 22.) And with reason. For as thorns are unfruitful, so are these things; as thorns tear those that handle them, so do these passions; as thorns are readily caught by the fire, and hateful by the husbandman, so too are the things of the world; as in thorns, wild beasts, and snakes, and scorpions hide themselves, so do they in the deceitfulness of riches. But let us kindle the fire of the Spirit, that we may consume the thorns, and drive away the beasts, and make the field clear for the husbandman; and after cleansing it, let us water it with the streams of the Spirit, let us plant the fruitful olive, that most kindly of trees, the evergreen, the light-giving, the nutritious, the wholesome. All these qualities hath almsgiving, which is, as it were, a seal on[6] those that possess it. This plant not even death when it comes causes to wither, but ever it stands enlightening the mind, feeding the sinews[7] of the soul, and rendering its strength mightier. And if we constantly possess it, we shall be able with confidence to behold the Bridegroom, and to enter into the bridal chamber; to which may we all attain, through the grace and lovingkindness of our Lord Jesus Christ, with whom to the Father and the Holy Ghost be glory, for ever and ever. Amen.

---

[1] ψυχικὸς.　　[2] lit. "shook."　　[3] al. "dreadful darkness."

[4] ἐμπαθῆ.　　[5] λήμης.　　[6] lit. "with."　　[7] νεῦρα.

# HOMILY XXV.

John iii. 5.

"Verily I say unto thee, Except a man be born of water and of the Spirit, he cannot enter into the Kingdom of God."

[1.] Little children who go daily to their teachers receive their lessons, and repeat[1] them, and never cease from this kind of acquisition, but sometimes employ nights as well as days, and this they are compelled[2] to do for perishable and transient things. Now we do not ask of you who are come to age such toil as you require of your children; for not every day, but two days only in the week do we exhort you to hearken to our words, and only for a short portion of the day, that your task may be an easy one. For the same reason also we divide[3] to you in small portions what is written in Scripture, that you may be able easily to receive and lay them up in the storehouses of your minds, and take such pains to remember them all, as to be able exactly to repeat them to others yourselves, unless any one be sleepy, and dull, and more idle than a little child.

Let us now attend to the sequel of what has been before said. When Nicodemus fell into error and wrested the words of Christ to the earthly birth, and said that it was not possible for an old man to be born again, observe how Christ in answer more clearly reveals the manner of the Birth, which even thus had difficulty for the carnal enquirer, yet still was able to raise the hearer from his low opinion of it. What saith He? "Verily I say unto thee, Except a man be born of water and of the Spirit, he cannot enter into the Kingdom of God." What He declares is this: "Thou sayest that it is impossible, I say that it is so absolutely possible as to be necessary, and that it is not even possible otherwise to be saved." For necessary things God hath made exceedingly easy also. The earthly birth which is according to the flesh, is of the dust, and therefore heaven[4] is walled against it, for what hath earth in common with heaven? But that other, which is of the Spirit, easily unfolds to us the arches[5] above. Hear, ye as many as are unilluminated,[6] shudder, groan, fearful is the threat, fearful the sentence.[7] "It is not (possible)," He saith, "for one not born of water and the Spirit, to enter into the Kingdom of heaven"; because he wears the

raiment of death, of cursing, of perdition, he hath not yet received his Lord's token,[8] he is a stranger and an alien, he hath not the royal watchword. "Except," He saith, "a man be born of water and of the Spirit, he cannot enter into the Kingdom of heaven."

Yet even thus Nicodemus did not understand. Nothing is worse than to commit spiritual things to argument; it was this that would not suffer him to suppose anything sublime and great. This is why we are called faithful, that having left the weakness of human reasonings below,[9] we may ascend to the height of faith, and commit most of our blessings to her[10] teaching;[11] and if Nicodemus had done this, the thing would not have been thought by him impossible. What then doth Christ? To lead him away from his groveling imagination, and to show that He speaks not of the earthly birth, He saith, "Except a man be born of water and of the Spirit, he cannot enter into the Kingdom of heaven." This He spoke, willing to draw him to the faith by the terror of the threat, and to persuade him not to deem the thing impossible, and taking pains to move him from his imagination as to the carnal birth. "I mean," saith He, "another Birth, O Nicodemus. Why drawest thou down the saying to earth? Why subjectest thou the matter to the necessity of nature? This Birth is too high for such pangs as these; it hath nothing in common with you; it is indeed called 'birth,' but in name only has it aught in common, in reality it is different. Remove thyself from that which is common and familiar; a different kind of childbirth bring I into the world; in another manner will I have men to be generated: I have come to bring a new manner of Creation. I formed (man) of earth and water; but that which was formed was unprofitable, the vessel was wrenched awry;[12] I will no more form them of earth and water, but 'of water' and 'of the Spirit.'"

And if any one asks, "How *of water?*" I also will ask, How of earth? How was the clay separated into different parts? How was the material uniform, (it was earth only,) and the things made from it, various and of every kind? Whence are the bones, and sinews, and arteries, and veins? Whence the membranes, and vessels of the organs, the cartilages, the

---

[1] ἀποδίδωσι.
[2] al. [by you].
[3] διαξαίνομεν.
[4] lit. "things in heaven."
[5] ἀψῖδας.
[6] i.e. unbaptized.
[7] ἀπόφασις.
[8] σύμβολον.
[9] or, "which is below."
[10] al. "this."
[11] i.e. submit to the teaching of faith concerning them.
[12] διεστράφη.

tissues, the liver, spleen, and heart? whence the skin, and blood, and mucus, and bile? whence so great powers, whence such varied colors? These belong not to earth or clay. How does the earth, when it receives the seeds, cause them to shoot, while the flesh receiving them wastes them? How does the earth nourish what is put into it, while the flesh is nourished by these things, and does not nourish them? The earth, for instance, receives water, and makes it wine; the flesh often receives wine, and changes it into water. Whence then is it clear that these things are formed of earth, when the nature of the earth is, according to what has been said,[1] contrary to that of the body? I cannot discover by reasoning, I accept it by faith only. If then things which take place daily, and which we handle, require faith, much more do those which are more mysterious and more spiritual than these. For as the earth, which is soulless and motionless, was empowered by the will of God, and such wonders were worked in it; much more when the Spirit is present with the water, do all those things so strange and transcending reason, easily take place.

[2.] Do not then disbelieve these things, because thou seest them not; thou dost not see thy soul, and yet thou believest that thou hast a soul, and that it is a something different besides[2] the body.

But Christ led him not in by this example, but by another; the instance of the soul, though it is incorporeal, He did not adduce for that reason, because His hearer's disposition was as yet too dull. He sets before him another, which has no connection with the density of solid bodies, yet does not reach so high as to the incorporeal natures; that is, the movement of wind. He begins at first with water, which is lighter than earth, but denser than air. And as in the beginning earth was the subject material,[3] but the whole[4] was of Him who molded it; so also now water is the subject material, and the whole[5] is of the grace of the Spirit: then, "man became a living soul," (Gen. ii. 7); now he becomes "a quickening Spirit." But great is the difference between the two. Soul affords not life to any other than him in whom it is; Spirit not only lives, but affords life to others also. Thus, for instance, the Apostles even raised the dead. Then, man was formed last, when the creation had been accomplished; now, on the contrary, the new man is formed before the new creation; he is born first, and then the

world is fashioned anew. (1 Cor. xv. 45.) And as in the beginning He formed him entire, so He creates him entire now. Then He said, "Let us make for him a help" (Gen. ii. 18, LXX.), but here He said nothing of the kind. What other help shall he need, who has received the gift of the Spirit? What further need of assistance has he, who belongs to[6] the Body of Christ? Then He made man in the image of God, now He hath united[7] him with God Himself; then He bade him rule over the fishes and beasts, now He hath exalted our first-fruits above the heavens; then He gave him a garden for his abode,[8] now He hath opened heaven to us; then man was formed on the sixth day, when the world[9] was almost finished; but now on the first, at the very beginning, at the time when light was made before. From all which it is plain, that the things accomplished belonged to[10] another and a better life, and to a condition[11] having no end.

The first creation then, that of Adam, was from earth; the next, that of the woman, from his rib; the next, that of Abel, from seed; yet we cannot arrive at the comprehension of[12] any one of these, nor prove the circumstances by argument, though they are of a most earthly nature;[13] how then shall we be able to give account of the unseen[14] generation[15] by Baptism, which is far more exalted than these, or to require arguments[16] for that strange and marvelous Birth?[17] Since even Angels stand by while that Generation takes place, but they could not tell the manner of that marvelous working, they stand by only, not performing anything, but beholding what takes place. The Father, the Son, and the Holy Ghost, worketh all. Let us then believe the declaration of God; that is more trustworthy than actual seeing. The sight often is in error, it is impossible that God's Word should fail; let us then believe it; that which called the things that were not into existence may well be trusted when it speaks of their nature. What then says it? That what is effected is A GENERATION. If any ask, "How," stop his mouth with the declaration of God,[18] which is the strongest and a plain proof. If any enquire, "Why is water included?" let us also in return ask, "Wherefore was earth employed at the beginning in the creation of man?" for that it was possible for God to make man without earth, is quite plain to every one. Be not then over-curious.

---

1 κατὰ τὰ εἰρημένα. This seems to be the best reading, and is found in Morel. Ben. and MSS. Savile reads the passage thus: τὸ σῶμα; τὰ εἰρημένα λογισμῷ μὲν εὑρεῖν, κ.τ.λ.
2 παρά.          3 ὑπεκεῖτο στοιχεῖον.
4 τὸ πᾶν, i.e. the fabric of the human body.
5 i.e. the new man.

6 ὁ τελῶν εἰς τὸ σῶμα.          11 καταστάσεως.
7 ἥνωσε.          12 ἐφίκεσθαι.
8 δίαιταν.          13 παχύτατα.
9 αἰών.          14 νοητῆς.
10 al. "were the first-fruits of."          15 γεννήσεως.
16 Morel. and MS. in Bodl. "but if it is impossible to reply to these questions, how shall it not be more impossible to speak concerning the unseen and far higher Generation? or rather, how is it not superfluous to demand reasons," &c.
17 λοχείας.          18 al. "of Christ."

That the need of water is absolute and indispensable,[1] you may learn in this way. On one occasion, when the Spirit had flown down before the water was applied, the Apostle did not stay at this point, but, as though the water were necessary and not superfluous, observe what he says; "Can any man forbid water, that these should not be baptized, which have received the Holy Ghost as well as we?" (Acts x. 47.)

What then is the use of the water? This too I will tell you hereafter, when I reveal to you the hidden mystery.[2] There are also other points of mystical teaching connected with the matter, but for the present I will mention to you one out of many. What is this one? In Baptism are fulfilled the pledges of our covenant with God;[3] burial and death, resurrection and life; and these take place all at once. For when we immerse our heads in the water, the old man is buried as in a tomb below, and wholly sunk forever;[4] then as we raise them again, the new man rises in its stead.[5] As it is easy for us to dip and to lift our heads again, so it is easy for God to bury the old man, and to show forth the new. And this is done thrice, that you may learn that the power of the Father, the Son, and the Holy Ghost fulfilleth all this. To show that what we say is no conjecture, hear Paul saying, "We are buried with Him by Baptism into death": and again, "Our old man is crucified with Him": and again, "We have been planted together in the likeness of His death." (Rom. vi. 4, 5, 6.) And not only is Baptism called a "cross," but the "cross" is called "Baptism." "With the Baptism," saith Christ, "that I am baptized withal shall ye be baptized" (Mark x. 39): and, "I have a Baptism to be baptized with" (Luke xii. 50) (which ye know not); for as we easily dip and lift our heads again, so He also easily died and rose again when He willed, or rather much more easily, though He tarried the three days for the dispensation of a certain mystery.

[3.] Let us then who have been deemed worthy of such mysteries show forth a life worthy of the Gift, that is, a most excellent conversation;[6] and do ye who have not yet been deemed worthy, do all things that you may be so, that we may be one body, that we may be brethren. For as long as we are divided in this respect, though a man be father, or son, or brother, or aught else, he is no true kinsman, as being cut off from that relationship which is from above. What advantageth it to be bound by the ties of earthly family, if we are not joined by those of the spiritual? what profits nearness of kin on earth, if we are to be strangers in heaven? For the Catechumen is a stranger to the Faithful. He hath not the same Head, he hath not the same Father, he hath not the same City, nor Food, nor Raiment, nor Table, nor House, but all are different; all are on earth to the former, to the latter all are in heaven. One has Christ for his King; the other, sin and the devil; the food[7] of one is Christ, of the other, that meat which decays and perishes; one has worms' work for his raiment, the other the Lord of angels; heaven is the city of one, earth of the other. Since then we have nothing in common, in what, tell me, shall we hold communion? Did we remove the same pangs,[8] did we come forth from the same womb? This has nothing to do with that most perfect relationship. Let us then give diligence that we may become citizens of the city which is above. How long do we tarry over the border,[9] when we ought to reclaim our ancient country? We risk no common danger; for if it should come to pass, (which God forbid!) that through the sudden arrival of death we depart hence uninitiated,[10] though we have ten thousand virtues, our portion will be no other than hell, and the venomous worm, and fire unquenchable, and bonds indissoluble. But God grant that none of those who hear these words experience that punishment! And this will be, if having been deemed worthy of the sacred mysteries, we build upon that foundation gold, and silver, and precious stones; for so after our departure hence we shall be able to appear in that place rich, when we leave not our riches here, but transport them to inviolable treasuries by the hands of the poor, when we lend to Christ. Many are our debts there, not of money, but of sins; let us then lend Him our riches, that we may receive pardon for our sins; for He it is that judgeth. Let us not neglect Him here when He hungereth, that He may ever feed us there. Here let us clothe Him, that He leave us not bare of the safety which is from Him. If here we give Him drink, we shall not with the rich man say, "Send Lazarus, that with the tip of his finger he may drop water on my broiling[11] tongue." If here we receive Him into our house, there He will prepare many mansions for us; if we go to Him in prison, He too will free us from our bonds; if we take Him in when He is a stranger, He will not suffer us to be strangers to the Kingdom of heaven, but will give us a portion in the City which is above; if we visit Him when He is sick, He also will quickly deliver us from our infirmities.

Let us then, as receiving great things though

---

[1] ἀναγκαία καὶ ἀπαραίτητος.
[2] [as it is allowed me from above] Morel.
[3] θεῖα τελεῖται ἐν αὐτῷ σύμβολα. So in Euseb. *Hist. Ecc.* x. 3. Baptism is said to be σωτηρίον πάθους ἀπόρρητα σύμβολα. See also Rufinus. *de Constant.* 9. 9.
[4] Morel. "having been immersed below, is hidden wholly once for all." [The whole passage is important for the patristic view of the *mode* of baptism. — P. S.]    [5] πάλιν.    [6] πολιτείαν.

[7] al. "the delight."    [8] i.e. "were we twins."    [9] ὑπερορίας.
[10] i.e. unbaptized.    [11] ἀποτηγανιζομένη.

we give but little, still give the little that we may gain the great. While it is yet time, let us sow, that we may reap. When the winter overtakes us, when the sea is no longer navigable, we are no longer masters of this traffic. But when shall the winter be? When that great and manifest Day is at hand. Then we shall cease to sail this great and broad sea, for such the present life resembles. Now is the time of sowing, then of harvest and of gain. If a man puts not in his seed at seed time and sows in harvest, besides that he effects nothing, he will be ridiculous. But if the present is seed time, it follows that it is a time not for gathering together, but for scattering; let us then scatter, that we may gather in, and not seek to gather in now, lest we lose our harvest; for, as I said, this season summons us to sow, and spend, and lay out, not to collect and lay by. Let us not then give up the opportunity, but let us put in abundant seed, and spare none of our stores, that we may receive them again with abundant recompense, through the grace and lovingkindness of our Lord Jesus Christ, with whom to the Father and the Holy Ghost be glory, world without end. Amen.

# HOMILY XXVI.

### JOHN iii. 6.

"That which is born of the flesh is flesh: and that which is born of the Spirit is spirit."

[1.] GREAT mysteries are they, of which the Only-begotten Son of God has counted us worthy; great, and such as we were not worthy of, but such as it was meet for Him to give. For if one reckon our desert, we were not only unworthy of the gift, but also liable to punishment and vengeance; but He, because He looked not to this, not only delivered us from punishment, but freely gave us a life much more bright[1] than the first, introduced us into another world, made us another creature; "If any man be in Christ," saith Paul, "he is a new creature." (2 Cor. v. 17.) What kind of "new creature"? Hear Christ Himself declare; "Except a man be born of water and of the Spirit, he cannot enter into the Kingdom of God." Paradise was entrusted to us, and we were shown unworthy to dwell even there, yet He hath exalted us to heaven. In the first things we were found unfaithful, and He hath committed to us greater; we could not refrain from a single tree, and He hath provided for us the delights[2] above; we kept not our place in Paradise, and He hath opened to us the doors of heaven. Well said Paul, "O the depth of the riches, both of the wisdom and knowledge of God!" (Rom. xi. 33.) There is no longer a mother, or pangs, or sleep, or coming together, and embracings of bodies; henceforth all the fabric[3] of our nature is framed above, of the Holy Ghost and water, The water is employed, being made the Birth to him who is born; what the womb is to the embryo, the water is to the believer; for in the water he is fashioned and formed. At first it was said, "Let the waters bring forth the creeping things that have life" (Gen. i. 20, LXX.); but from the time that the Lord entered the streams of Jordan, the water no longer gives forth the "creeping thing that hath life," but reasonable and Spirit-bearing souls; and what has been said of the sun, that he is "as a bridegroom coming out of his chamber" (Ps. xviii. 6), we may now rather say of the faithful, for they send forth rays far brighter than he. That which is fashioned in the womb requires time, not so that in water, but all is done in a single moment. Here our life is perishable, and takes its origin from the decay of other bodies; that which is to be born comes slowly, (for such is the nature of bodies, they acquire perfection by time,) but it is not so with spiritual things. And why? Because the things made are formed perfect from the beginning.

When Nicodemus still hearing these things was troubled, see how Christ partly opens to him the secret of this mystery, and makes that clear which was for a while obscure to him. "That which is born," saith He, "of the flesh is flesh; and that which is born of the Spirit is spirit." He leads him away from all the things of sense, and suffers him not vainly to pry into the mysteries revealed with his fleshly eyes; "We speak not," saith He, "of flesh, but of Spirit, O Nicodemus," (by this word He directs him heavenward for a while,) "seek then nothing relating to things of sense; never can the Spirit appear to those eyes, think not that the Spirit bringeth forth the flesh." "How then," perhaps one may ask, "was the Flesh of the Lord brought forth?" Not of the Spirit only, but of flesh; as Paul de-

---

[1] al. "precious."
[2] τρυφὴν.
[3] κατασκευὴ.

clares, when he says, "Made of a woman, made under the Law" (Gal. iv. 4); for the Spirit fashioned Him not indeed out of nothing, (for what need was there then of a womb?) but from the flesh of a Virgin. How, I cannot explain unto you ; yet it was done, that no one might suppose that what was born is alien to our nature. For if even when this has taken place there are some who disbelieve in such a birth, into what impiety would they not have fallen had He not partaken of the Virgin's flesh.

"That which is born¹ of the Spirit is spirit." Seest thou the dignity of the Spirit? It appears performing the work of God ; for above he said of some, that, "they were begotten of God," (c. i. 13,) here He saith, that the Spirit begetteth them.

"That which is born of the Spirit is spirit." His meaning is of this kind ; "He that is born² of the Spirit is spiritual." For the Birth which He speaks of here is not that according to essence,³ but according to honor and grace. Now if the Son is so born also, in what shall He be superior to men so born? And how is He, Only-begotten? For I too am born of God, though not of His Essence, and if He also is not of His Essence, how in this respect does He differ from us? Nay, He will then be found to be inferior to the Spirit ; for birth of this kind is by the grace of the Spirit. Needs He then the help of the Spirit that He may continue a Son? And in what do these differ from Jewish doctrines?

Christ then having said, "He that is born of the Spirit is spirit," when He saw him again confused, leads His discourse to an example from sense, saying,

Ver. 7, 8. "Marvel not that I said unto thee, Ye must be born again.⁴ The wind bloweth where it listeth."

For by saying, "Marvel not," He indicates the confusion of his soul, and leads him to something lighter than body. He had already led him away from fleshly things, by saying, "That which is born of the Spirit is spirit" ; but when Nicodemus knew not what "that which is born of the Spirit is spirit" meant, He next carries him to another figure, not bringing him to the density of bodies, nor yet speaking of things purely incorporeal, (for had he heard he could not have received this,) but having found a something between what is and what is not body, namely, the motion of the wind, He brings him to that next. And He saith of it,

"Thou hearest the sound thereof, but canst not tell whence it cometh, and whither it goeth."

Though He saith, "it bloweth where it listeth," He saith it not as if the wind had any power of

choice, but declaring that its natural motion cannot be hindered, and is with power. For Scripture knoweth how to speak thus of things without life, as when it saith, "The creature was made subject to vanity, not willingly." (Rom. viii. 20.) The expression therefore, "bloweth where it listeth," is that of one who would show that it cannot be restrained, that it is spread abroad everywhere, and that none can hinder its passing hither and thither, but that it goes abroad with great might, and none is able to turn aside its violence.

[2.] "And thou hearest its voice,"⁵ (that is, its rustle, its noise,) "but canst not tell whence it cometh, and whither it goeth ; so is every one that is born of the Spirit."

Here is the conclusion of the whole matter. "If," saith He, "thou knowest not how to explain the motion nor the path of this wind⁶ which thou perceivest by hearing and touch, why art thou over-anxious about the working of the Divine Spirit, when thou understandest not that of the wind, though thou hearest its voice?" The expression, "bloweth where it listeth," is also used to establish the power of the Comforter ; for if none can hold the wind, but it moveth where it listeth, much less will the laws of nature, or limits of bodily generation, or anything of the like kind, be able to restrain the operations of the Spirit.

That the expression, "thou hearest its voice," is used respecting the wind, is clear from this circumstance ; He would not, when conversing with an unbeliever and one unacquainted with the operation of the Spirit, have said, "Thou hearest its voice." As then the wind is not visible, although it utters a sound, so neither is the birth of that which is spiritual visible to our bodily eyes ; yet the wind is a body, although a very subtle one ; for whatever is the object of sense is body. If then you do not complain because you cannot see this body, and do not on this account disbelieve, why do you, when you hear of "the Spirit," hesitate and demand such exact accounts, although you act not so in the case of a body? What then doth Nicodemus? still he continues in his low Jewish opinion, and that too when so clear an example has been mentioned to him. Wherefore when he again says doubtingly,

Ver. 9, 10. "How can these things be?" Christ now speaks to him more chidingly ; "Art thou a master in Israel, and knowest not these things?"

Observe how He nowhere accuses the man of wickedness, but only of weakness and simplicity. "And what," one may ask, "has this birth in common with Jewish matters?" Tell

---

¹ or, "begotten."      ³ οὐσίαν.
² or, "begotten."      ⁴ or, "from above."      ⁵ φωνήν.      ⁶ or, "spirit."

me rather what has it that is not in common with them? For the first-created man, and the woman formed from his side, and the barren women, and the things accomplished by water, I mean what relates to the fountain on which Elisha made the iron tool to swim, to the Red Sea which the Jews passed over, to the pool which the Angel troubled, to Naaman the Syrian who was cleansed in Jordan, all these proclaimed beforehand, as by a figure, the Birth and the purification which were to be. And the words of the Prophet allude to the manner of this Birth, as, " It shall be announced unto the Lord a generation which cometh, and they shall announce His righteousness unto a people that shall be born, whom the Lord hath made " (Ps. xxii. 30; xxx. 31, LXX.) ; and, "Thy youth shall be renewed as an eagle's " (Ps. ciii. 5, LXX.) ; and, "Shine, O Jerusalem ; behold, Thy King cometh ! " (Isa. lx. 1 ; Zech. ix. 9) ; and, " Blessed are they whose iniquities are forgiven." (Ps. xxxii. 1, LXX.) Isaac also was a type of this Birth. For tell me, Nicodemus, how was he born? was it according to the law of nature? By no means ; the mode of his generation was midway between this of which we speak and the natural ; the natural, because he was begotten by cohabitation ; the other, because he was begotten not of blood,[1] (but by the will of God.) I shall show that these figures[2] proclaimed beforehand not only this birth, but also that from the Virgin. For, because no one would easily have believed that a virgin could bear a child, barren women first did so, then such as were not only barren, but aged also. That a woman should be made from a rib was indeed far more wonderful than that the barren should conceive ; but because that was of early and old time, another figure, new and fresh, was given, that of the barren women; to prepare the way for belief in the Virgin's travail. To remind him then of these things, Jesus said, " Art thou a master in Israel, and knowest not these things?"

Ver. 11. "We speak that We do know, and testify that We have seen, and none receiveth[3] Our witness."

This He added, making His words credible by another argument, and condescending in His speech to the other's infirmity.

[3.] And what is this that He saith, " We speak that We do know, and testify that We have seen "? Because with us the sight is the most trustworthy of the senses, and if we desire to gain a person's belief, we speak thus, that we saw it with our eyes, not that we know it by hearsay ; Christ therefore speaks to him rather after the manner of men, gaining belief for His words by this means also. And that this is so,

and that He desires to establish nothing else, and refers not to sensual vision, is clear from this ; after saying, " That which is born of the flesh is flesh ; and that which is born of the Spirit is spirit," He adds, " We speak that we do know, and testify that we have seen." Now this (of the Spirit) was not yet born[4] ; how then saith He, " what we have seen "? Is it not plain that He speaks of a knowledge not otherwise than exact?

"And none receiveth our witness." The expression "we know," He uses then either concerning Himself and His Father, or concerning Himself alone ; and "no man receiveth," is the expression not of one displeased, but of one who declares a fact : for He said not, " What can be more senseless than you who receive not what is so exactly declared by us?" but displaying all gentleness, both by His works and His words, He uttered nothing like this ; mildly and kindly He foretold what should come to pass, so guiding us too to all gentleness, and teaching us when we converse with any and do not persuade them, not to be annoyed or made savage ; for it is impossible for one out of temper to accomplish his purpose, he must make him to whom he speaks still more incredulous. Wherefore we must abstain from anger, and make our words in every way credible by avoiding not only wrath, but also loud speaking[5] ; for loud speaking is the fuel of passion.

Let us then bind[6] the horse, that we may subdue the rider ; let us clip the wings of our wrath, so the evil shall no more rise to a height. A keen passion is anger, keen, and skillful to steal our souls ; therefore we must on all sides guard against its entrance. It were strange that we should be able to tame wild beasts, and yet should neglect our own savage minds. Wrath is a fierce fire, it devours all things ; it harms the body, it destroys the soul, it makes a man deformed[7] and ugly to look upon ; and if it were possible for an angry person to be visible to himself at the time of his anger, he would need no other admonition, for nothing is more displeasing than an angry countenance. Anger is a kind of drunkenness, or rather it is more grievous than drunkenness, and more pitiable than (possession of) a dæmon. But if we be careful not to be loud in speech,[8] we shall find this the best path to sobriety of conduct.[9] And therefore Paul would take away clamor as well as anger, when he says, " Let all anger and clamor be put away from you." (Eph. iv. 31.) Let us then obey this teacher of all wisdom, and when we are wroth with our servants, let us consider our own trespasses, and be ashamed at their

---

[1] lit. " of bloods," as in c. i. 13.　　[3] οὐ λαμβάνετε, G. T.
[2] τρόποι.

[4] or, " begotten."　　　　[7] or, " unpleasing."
[5] lit. " shouting."　　　　[8] κράζειν.
[6] lit. " tie the feet of."　　[9] φιλοσοφίαν.

forbearance.  For when thou art insolent, and thy servant bears thy insults in silence, when thou actest unseemly, he like a wise man, take this instead of any other warning.  Though he is thy servant, he is still a man, has an immortal soul, and has been honored with the same gifts as thee by your common Lord.  And if he who is our equal in more important and more spiritual things, on account of some poor and trifling human superiority so meekly bears our injuries, what pardon can we deserve, what excuse can we make, who cannot, or rather will not, be as wise through fear of God, as he is through fear of us?  Considering then all these things, and calling to mind our own transgressions, and the common nature of man, let us be careful at all times to speak gently, that being humble in heart we may find rest for our souls, both that which now is, and that which is to come ; which may we all attain, by the grace and lovingkindness of our Lord Jesus Christ, with whom to the Father and the Holy Ghost be glory, for ever and ever. Amen.

# HOMILY XXVII.

## John iii. 12, 13.

"If I have told you earthly things, and ye believe not, how shall ye believe, if I tell you of heavenly things? And no man hath ascended up to heaven, but He that came down from heaven, even the Son of Man which is in heaven."

[1.] WHAT I have often said I shall now repeat, and shall not cease to say.  What is that?  It is that Jesus, when about to touch on sublime doctrines, often contains Himself by reason of the infirmity of His hearers, and dwells not for a continuance on subjects worthy of His greatness, but rather on those which partake of condescension.  For the sublime and great, being but once uttered, is sufficient to establish that character, as far as we are able to hear it ; but unless more lowly sayings, and such as are nigh to[1] the comprehension of the hearers, were continually uttered, the more sublime would not readily take hold on a groveling listener.  And therefore of the sayings of Christ more are lowly than sublime.  But yet that this again may not work another mischief, by detaining the disciple here below, He does not merely set before men His inferior sayings without first telling them why He utters them ; as, in fact, He has done in this place.  For when He had said what He did concerning Baptism, and the Generation by grace which takes place on earth, being desirous to admit[2] them to that His own mysterious and incomprehensible Generation, He holds it in suspense for a while, and admits them not, and then tells them His reason for not admitting them.  What is that?  It is, the dullness and infirmity of His hearers.  And referring to this He added the words, "If I have told you earthly things, and ye believe not, how shall ye believe if I tell you of heavenly things?" so that wherever He saith anything ordinary and humble, we must attribute this to the infirmity of His audience.

The expression "earthly things," some say is here used of the wind ; that is, " If I have given you an example from earthly things, and ye did not even so believe, how shall ye be able to learn sublimer things?"  And wonder not if He here call Baptism an "earthly" thing, for He calls it so, either from its being performed on earth, or so naming it in comparison with that His own most awful Generation.  For though this Generation of ours is heavenly, yet compared with that true GENERATION which is from the Substance of the Father, it is earthly.

He does not say, "Ye have not understood," but, "Ye have not believed" ; for when a man is ill disposed towards those things which it is possible to apprehend by the intellect, and will not readily receive them, he may justly be charged with want of understanding ; but when he receives not things which cannot be apprehended by reasoning, but only by faith, the charge against him is no longer want of understanding, but unbelief.  Leading him therefore away from enquiring by reasonings into what had been said, He touches him more severely by charging him with want of faith.  If now we must receive our own Generation[3] by faith, what do they deserve who are busy with their reasonings about that of the Only-Begotten?

But perhaps some may ask, "And if the hearers were not to believe these sayings, wherefore were they uttered?"  Because though "they" believed not, those who came after would believe and profit by them.  Touching him therefore very severely, Christ goes on to show that He

---

[1] al. "touch."    [2] καθεῖναι.    [3] i.e. the new Birth.

knoweth not these things only, but others also, far more and greater than these. And this He declared by what follows, when He said, "And no man hath ascended up to heaven, but He that came down from heaven, even the Son of Man which is in heaven."

"And what manner of sequel is this?"[1] asks one. The very closest, and entirely in unison with what has gone before. For since Nicodemus had said, "We know that Thou art a teacher come from God," on this very point He sets him right, all but saying, "Think Me not a teacher in such manner as were the many of the prophets who were of earth, for I have come from heaven (but) now. None of the prophets hath ascended up thither, but I dwell there." Seest thou how even that which appears very exalted is utterly unworthy of his greatness? For not in heaven only is He, but everywhere, and He fills all things; but yet He speaks according to the infirmity of His hearer, desiring to lead him up little by little. And in this place He called not the flesh "Son of Man," but He now named, so to speak, His entire Self from the inferior substance; indeed this is His wont, to call His whole Person[2] often from His Divinity, and often from His humanity.

Ver. 14. "And as Moses lifted up the serpent in the wilderness, even so must the Son of Man be lifted up."

This again seems to depend upon what has gone before, and this too has a very close connection with it. For after having spoken of the very great benefaction that had come to man by Baptism, He proceeds to mention another benefaction, which was the cause of this, and not inferior to it; namely, that by the Cross. As also Paul arguing with the Corinthians sets down these benefits together, when he says, "Was Paul crucified for you? or were ye baptized into the name of Paul?" for these two things most of all declare His unspeakable love, that He both suffered for His enemies, and that having died for His enemies, He freely gave to them by Baptism entire remission of their sins.

[2.] But wherefore did He not say plainly, "I am about to be crucified," instead of referring His hearers to the ancient type? First, that you may learn that old things are akin to new, and that the one are not alien to the other; next, that you may know that He came not unwillingly to His Passion; and again, besides these reasons, that you may learn that no harm arises to Him from the Fact,[3] and that to many there springs from it salvation. For, that none may say, "And how is it possible that they who believe on one crucified should be saved, when he himself is holden of death?" He leads us to the ancient story. Now if the Jews, by looking to the brazen image of a serpent, escaped death, much rather will they who believe on the Crucified, with good reason enjoy a far greater benefit. For this[4] takes place, not through the weakness of the Crucified, or because the Jews are stronger than He, but because "God loved the world," therefore is His living Temple fastened to the Cross.

Ver. 15. "That whosoever believeth in Him should not perish, but have eternal life."

Seest thou the cause of the Crucifixion, and the salvation which is by it? Seest thou the relationship of the type to the reality? there the Jews escaped death, but the temporal, here believers the eternal; there the hanging serpent healed the bites of serpents, here the Crucified Jesus cured the wounds inflcted by the spiritual[5] dragon; there he who looked with his bodily eyes was healed, here he who beholds with the eyes of his understanding put off all his sins; there that which hung was brass fashioned into the likeness of a serpent, here it was the Lord's Body, builded by the Spirit; there a serpent bit and a serpent healed, here death destroyed and a Death saved. But the snake which destroyed had venom, that which saved was free from venom; and so again was it here, for the death which slew us had sin with it, as the serpent had venom; but the Lord's Death was free from all sin, as the brazen serpent from venom. For, saith Peter, "He did no sin, neither was guile found in His mouth." (1 Pet. ii. 22.) And this is what Paul also declares, "And having spoiled principalities and powers, He made a show of them openly, triumphing over them in it." (Col. ii. 16.) For as some noble champion by lifting on high and dashing down his antagonist, renders his victory more glorious, so Christ, in the sight of all the world, cast down the adverse powers, and having healed those who were smitten in the wilderness, delivered them from all venomous beasts[6] that vexed them, by being hung upon the Cross. Yet He did not say, "must hang," but, "must be lifted up" (Acts xxviii. 4); for He used this which seemed the milder term, on account of His hearer, and because it was proper to the type.[7]

Ver. 16. "God," He saith, "so loved the world that He gave His Only-begotten Son, that whosoever believeth in Him should not perish, but have everlasting life."

What He saith, is of this kind: Marvel not that I am to be lifted up that ye may be saved, for this seemeth good to the Father, and He hath so loved you as to give His Son for slaves, and ungrateful slaves. Yet a man would not do this even for a friend, nor readily even for a

---

[1] i.e. how is this connected with what has gone before?
[2] τὸ πᾶν.　　　　[3] i.e. of the Passion.
[4] i.e. the Crucifixion.　　　[6] θηρίων.
[5] νοητοῦ.　　　　[7] ἐγγὺς τοῦ τύπου.

righteous man; as Paul has declared when he said, "Scarcely for a righteous man will one die." (Rom. v. 7.) Now he spoke at greater length, as speaking to believers, but here Christ speaks concisely, because His discourse was directed to Nicodemus, but still in a more significant manner, for each word had much significance. For by the expression, "so loved," and that other, "God the world," He shows the great strength of His love. Large and infinite was the interval between the two. He, the immortal, who is without beginning, the Infinite Majesty, they but dust and ashes, full of ten thousand sins, who, ungrateful, have at all times offended Him; and these He "loved." Again, the words which He added after these are alike significant, when He saith, that "He gave His Only-begotten Son," not a servant, not an Angel, not an Archangel. And yet no one would show such anxiety for his own child, as God did for His ungrateful servants.

His Passion then He sets before him not very openly, but rather darkly; but the advantage of the Passion He adds in a clearer manner,[1] saying, "That every one that believeth in Him should not perish, but have everlasting life." For when He had said, "must be lifted up," and alluded to death, lest the hearer should be made downcast by these words, forming some mere human opinions concerning Him, and supposing that His death was a ceasing to be,[2] observe how He sets this right, by saying, that He that was given was "The Son of God," and the cause of life, of everlasting life. He who procured life for others by death, would not Himself be continually in death; for if they who believed on the Crucified perish not, much less doth He perish who is crucified. He who taketh away the destitution of others much more is He free from it; He who giveth life to others, much more to Himself doth He well forth life. Seest thou that everywhere there is need of faith? For He calls the Cross the fountain of life; which reason cannot easily allow, as the heathens now by their mocking testify. But faith which goes beyond the weakness of reasoning, may easily receive and retain it. And whence did God "so love the world"? From no other source but only from his goodness.

[3.] Let us now be abashed at His love, let us be ashamed at the excess of His lovingkindness, since He for our sakes spared not His Only-begotten Son, yet we spare our wealth to our own injury; He for us gave His Own Son, but we for Him do not so much as despise money, nor even for ourselves. And how can these things deserve pardon? If we see a man submitting to sufferings and death for us, we set him before all others, count him among our chief friends, place in his hands all that is ours, and deem it rather his than ours, and even so do not think that we give him the return that he deserves. But towards Christ we do not preserve even this degree of right feeling. He laid down His life for us, and poured forth His precious Blood for our sakes, who were neither well-disposed nor good, while we do not pour out even our money for our own sakes, and neglect Him who died for us, when He is naked and a stranger; and who shall deliver us from the punishment that is to come? For suppose that it were not God that punishes, but that we punished ourselves; should we not give our vote against ourselves? should we not sentence ourselves to the very fire of hell, for allowing Him who laid down His life for us, to pine with hunger? But why speak I of money? had we ten thousand lives, ought we not to lay them all down for Him? and yet not even so could we do what His benefits deserve. For he who confers a benefit in the first instance, gives evident proof of his kindness, but he who has received one, whatever return he makes, he repays as a debt, and does not bestow as a favor; especially when he who did the first good turn was benefiting his enemies. And he who repays both bestows his gifts on a benefactor, and himself reaps their fruit besides.[3] But not even this induces us; more foolish are we than any, putting golden necklaces about our servants and mules and horses, and neglecting our Lord who goes about naked, and passes from door to door, and ever stands at our outlets, and stretches forth His hands to us, but often regarding Him with unpitying eye; yet these very things He undergoeth for our sake. Gladly[4] doth He hunger that thou mayest be fed; naked doth He go that He may provide for thee the materials[5] for a garment of incorruption, yet not even so do ye give up any of your own. Some of your garments are moth-eaten, others a load to your coffers, and a needless trouble to their possessors, while He who gave you these and all else that you possess goeth naked.

But perhaps you do not lay them by in your coffers, but wear them and make yourself fine with them. And what gain you by this? Is it that the street people may see you? What then? They will not admire thee who wearest such apparel, but the man who supplies garments to the needy; so if you desire to be admired, by clothing others, you will the rather get infinite applause. Then too God as well as man shall praise thee; now none can praise, but all will grudge at thee, seeing thee with a body well arrayed, but having a neglected soul. So harlots

---

[1] al. "clearly and openly."   [2] ἀνυπαρξίαν.   [3] πάλιν.   [4] lit. "sweetly."   [5] ὑπόθεσιν.

have adornment, and their clothes are often more than usually expensive and splendid; but the adornment of the soul is with those only who live in virtue.

These things I say continually, and I will not cease to say them, not so much because I care for the poor, as because I care for your souls. For they will have some comfort, if not from you, yet from some other quarter; or even if they be not comforted, but perish by hunger, the harm to them will be no great matter. What did pov-erty and wasting by hunger injure Lazarus! But none can rescue you from hell, if you obtain not the help of the poor;[6] we shall say to you what was said to the rich man, who was continually broiling, yet gained no comfort. God grant that none ever hear those words, but that all may go into the bosom of Abraham; by the grace and lovingkindness of our Lord Jesus Christ, by whom and with whom, to the Father and the Holy Ghost, be glory for ever and ever. Amen.

# HOMILY XXVIII.

John iii. 17.

"For God sent not His Son[1] to condemn the world, but to save the world."[2]

[1.] Many of the more careless sort of persons, using the lovingkindness of God to increase the magnitude of their sins and the excess of their disregard, speak in this way, "There is no hell, there is no future punishment, God forgives us all sins." To stop whose mouths a wise man says, "Say not, His mercy is great, He will be pacified for the multitude of my sins; for mercy and wrath come from Him, and His indignation resteth upon sinners" (Ecclus. v. 6): and again, "As His mercy is great, so is His correction also." (Ecclus. xvi. 12.) "Where then," saith one, "is His lovingkindness, if we shall receive for our sins according to our deserts?" That we shall indeed receive "according to our deserts," hear both the Prophet and Paul declare; one says, "Thou shalt render to every man according to his work" (Ps. lxii. 12, LXX.); the other, "Who will render to every man according to his work." (Rom. ii. 6.) And yet we may see that even so the lovingkindness of God is great; in dividing our existence[3] into two periods,[4] the present life and that which is to come, and making the first to be an appointment of trial, the second a place of crowning, even in this He hath shown great lovingkindness.

"How and in what way?" Because when we had committed many and grievous sins, and had not ceased from youth to extreme old age to defile our souls with ten thousand evil deeds, for none of these sins did He demand from us a reckoning, but granted us remission of them by the washing[5] of Regeneration, and freely gave us Righteousness and Sanctification. "What then," says one, "if a man who from his earliest age has been deemed worthy of the mysteries, after this commits ten thousand sins?" Such an one deserves a severer punishment. For we do not pay the same penalties for the same sins, if we do wrong after Initiation.[7] And this Paul declares, saying, "He that despised Moses' law died without mercy under two or three witnesses; of how much sorer punishment, suppose ye, shall he be thought worthy, who hath trodden under foot the Son of God, and hath counted the blood of the Covenant an unholy thing, and hath done despite unto the Spirit of grace?" (Heb. x. 28, 29.) Such an one then is worthy of severer punishment.[8] Yet even for him God hath opened doors of repentance, and hath granted him many means for the washing away his transgressions, if he will. Think then what proofs of lovingkindness these are; by Grace to remit sins, and not to punish him who after grace has sinned and deserves punishment, but to give him a season and appointed space for his clearing.[9] For all these reasons Christ said to Nicodemus, "God sent not His Son to condemn the world, but to save the world."

For there are two Advents of Christ, that which has been, and that which is to be; and the two are not for the same purpose; the first came to pass not that He might search into our actions, but that He might remit; the object of the second will be not to remit, but to enquire. Therefore of the first He saith, "I came not to condemn the world, but to save the world" (c. iii. 17); but of the second, "When the

---

[1] [εἰς τὸν κόσμον, G. T.].
[2] ἵνα σωθῇ ὁ κόσμος δι' αὐτοῦ, G. T.
[3] τὰ ἡμέτερα.
[4] αἰῶνας.
[5] or, "laver."
[6] al. "the hungry."
[7] μυσταγωγίαν.
[8] Morel. "he then will be more severely punished who has sinned after grace."
[9] προθεσμίαν ἀπολογίας.

Son shall have come in the glory of His Father,[1] He shall set the sheep on His right hand, and the goats on His left." (Matt. xxv. 31 and 46.) And they shall go, these into life; and these into eternal punishment. Yet His former coming was for judgment, according to the rule of justice. Why? Because before His coming there was a law of nature, and the prophets, and moreover a written Law, and doctrine, and ten thousand promises, and manifestations of signs, and chastisements, and vengeances, and many other things which might have set men right, and it followed that for all these things He would demand account; but, because He is merciful, He for a while pardons instead of making enquiry. For had He done so, all would at once have been hurried to perdition. For "all," it saith, "have sinned, and come short of the glory of God." (Rom. iii. 23.) Seest thou the unspeakable excess of His loving-kindness?

Ver. 18. "He that believeth on the Son,[2] is not judged;[3] but he that believeth not, is judged already."

Yet if He "came not to judge the world," how is "he that believeth not judged already," if the time of "judgment" has not yet arrived? He either means this, that the very fact of disbelieving without repentance is a punishment, (for to be without the light, contains in itself a very severe punishment,) or he announces beforehand what shall be. For as the murderer, though he be not as yet condemned by the decision of the judge, is still condemned by the nature of the thing, so is it with the unbeliever. Since Adam also died on the day that he ate of the tree; for so ran the decree, "In the day that ye eat of the tree, ye shall die" (Gen. ii. 17, LXX.); yet he lived. How then "died" he? By the decree; by the very nature of the thing; for he who has rendered himself liable to punishment, is under its penalty, and if for a while not actually so, yet he is by the sentence.

Lest any one on hearing, "I came not to judge the world," should imagine that he might sin unpunished, and should so become more careless, Christ stops[4] such disregard by saying, "is judged already"; and because the "judgment" was future and not yet at hand, He brings near the dread of vengeance, and describes the punishment as already come. And this is itself a mark of great lovingkindness, that He not only gives His Son, but even delays the time of judgment, that they who have sinned, and they who believe not, may have power to wash away their transgressions.

"He that believeth on the Son, is not judged." He that "believeth," not he that is over-curious:

he that "believeth," not the busybody. But what if his life be unclean, and his deeds evil? It is of such as these especially that Paul declares, that they are not true believers at all: "They profess that they know God, but in works they deny Him." (Tit. i. 16.) But here Christ saith, that such an one is not "judged" in this one particular; for his works indeed he shall suffer a severer punishment, but having believed once, he is not chastised for unbelief.

[2.] Seest thou how having commenced His discourse with fearful things, He has concluded it again with the very same? for at first He saith, "Except a man be born of water and of the Spirit, he cannot enter into the Kingdom of God": and here again, "He that believeth not on the Son, is judged already." "Think not," He saith, "that the delay advantageth at all the guilty, except he repent, for he that hath not believed, shall be in no better state than those who are already condemned and under punishment."

Ver. 19. "And this is the condemnation, that light is come into the world, and men loved darkness rather than light."

What He saith, is of this kind: "they are punished, because they would not leave the darkness, and hasten to the light." And hence He goes on to deprive them of all excuse for the future: "Had I come," saith He, "to punish and to exact account of their deeds, they might have been able to say, 'this is why we started away from thee,' but now I am come to free them from darkness, and to bring them to the light; who then could pity one who will not come from darkness unto light? When they have no charge to bring against us, but have received ten thousand benefits, they start away from us." And this charge He hath brought in another place, where He saith, "They hated Me without a cause" (John xv. 25): and again, "If I had not come and spoken unto them, they had not had sin." (John xv. 22.) For he who in the absence of light sitteth in darkness, may perchance receive pardon; but one who after it is come abides by the darkness, produces against himself a certain proof of a perverse and contentious disposition. Next, because His assertion would seem incredible to most, (for none would prefer "darkness to light,") He adds the cause of such a feeling in them. What is that?

Ver. 19, 20. "Because," He saith, "their deeds were evil. For every one that doeth evil, hateth the light, neither cometh to the light, lest his deeds should be reproved."

Yet he came not to judge or to enquire, but to pardon and remit transgressions, and to grant salvation through faith. How then fled they?[5]

[1] τῇ δοξῇ αὐτοῦ, G. T.     [3] or, "condemned," E. V.
[2] εἰς αὐτὸν, G. T.     [4] lit. "walls off."
[5] Morel. "therefore they fled to their own hurt."

Had He come and sat in His Judgment seat, what He said might have seemed reasonable; for he that is conscious to himself of evil deeds, is wont to fly his judge. But, on the contrary, they who have transgressed even run to one who is pardoning. If therefore He came to pardon, those would naturally most hasten to Him who were conscious to themselves of many transgressions; and indeed this was the case with many, for even publicans and sinners sat at meat with Jesus. What then is this which He saith? He saith this of those who choose always to remain in wickedness. He indeed came, that He might forgive men's former sins, and secure them against those to come; but since there are some so relaxed,[1] so powerless for the toils of virtue, that they desire to abide by wickedness till their latest breath, and never cease from it, He speaks in this place reflecting[2] upon these. "For since," He saith, "the profession of Christianity requires besides right doctrine a sound conversation also, they fear to come over to us, because they like not to show forth a righteous life. Him that lives in heathenism none would blame, because with gods such as he has, and with rites as foul and ridiculous as his gods, he shows forth actions that suit his doctrines; but those who belong to the True God, if they live a careless life, have all men to call them to account, and to accuse them. So greatly do even its enemies admire the truth." Observe, then, how exactly He layeth down what He saith. His expression is, not "He that hath done evil cometh not to the light," but "he that doeth it always, he that desireth always to roll himself in the mire of sin, he will not subject himself to My laws, but chooses to stay without, and to commit fornication without fear, and to do all other forbidden things. For if he comes to Me, he becomes manifest as a thief in the light, and therefore he avoids My dominion." For instance, even now one may hear many heathen say, "that they cannot come to our faith, because they cannot leave off drunkenness and fornication, and the like disorders."

"Well," says some one, "but are there no Christians that do evil, and heathens that live discreetly?"[3] That there are Christians who do evil, I know; but whether there are heathens who live a righteous life, I do not yet know assuredly. For do not speak to me of those who by nature are good and orderly, (this is not virtue,) but tell me of the man who can endure the exceeding violence of his passions and (yet) be temperate.[4] You cannot. For if the promise of a Kingdom, and the threat of hell, and so much other provision,[5] can scarcely keep men in vir-

tue, they will hardly go after virtue who believe in none of these things. Or, if any pretend to do so, they do it for show; and he who doth so for show, will not, when he may escape observation, refrain from indulging his evil desires. However, that we may not seem to any to be contentious, let us grant that there are right livers among the heathen; for neither doth this go against my argument, since I spoke of that which occurs in general, not of what happens rarely.

And observe how in another way He deprives them of all excuse, when He saith that, "the light came into the world." "Did they seek it themselves," He saith, "did they toil, did they labor to find it? The light itself came to them, and not even so would they hasten to it." And if there be some Christians who live wickedly, I would argue that He doth not say this of those who have been Christians from the beginning, and who have inherited true religion from their forefathers, (although even these for the most part have been shaken from[6] right doctrine by their evil life,) yet still I think that He doth not now speak concerning these, but concerning the heathen and the Jews who ought to have come[7] to the right faith. For He showeth that no man living in error would choose to come to the truth unless he before had planned[8] for himself a righteous life, and that none would remain in unbelief unless he had previously chosen always to be wicked.

Do not tell me that a man is temperate, and does not rob; these things by themselves are not virtue. For what advantageth it, if a man has these things, and yet is the slave of vainglory, and remains in his error, from fear of the company of his friends? This is not right living. The slave of a reputation[9] is no less a sinner than the fornicator; nay, he worketh more and more grievous deeds than he. But tell me of any one that is free from all passions and from all iniquity, and who remains among the heathen. Thou canst not do so; for even those among them who have boasted great things, and who have, as they say,[10] mastered avarice or gluttony, have been, most of all men, the slaves of reputation,[11] and this is the cause of all evils. Thus it is that the Jews also have continued Jews; for which cause Christ rebuked them and said, "How can ye believe, which receive honor from men?" (c. v. 44.)

"And why, pray, did He not speak on these matters with Nathanael, to whom He testified of the truth, nor extend His discourse to any length?" Because even he came not with such zeal as did Nicodemus. For Nicodemus made

1 lit. "flaccid."   4 φιλοσοφοῦντα.   6 παρεσαλεύθησαν.   9 or, "glory."
2 ἐπισκώπτων.   5 al. "doctrine."   7 al. "shifted themselves."   10 or, "thou sayest."
3 ἐν φιλοσοφίᾳ.      8 ὑπογράψας. al. ἐπιγράψας.   11 or, "glory."

this his work,[1] and the season which others used for rest he made a season for hearing; but Nathanael came at the instance of another. Yet not even him did Jesus entirely pass by, for to him He saith, "Hereafter ye shall see heaven open, and the angels of God ascending and descending upon the Son of Man." (c. i. 51.) But to Nicodemus He spake not so, but conversed with him on the Dispensation and on eternal life, addressing each differently and suitably to the condition of his will. It was sufficient for Nathanael, because he knew the writings of the prophets, and was not so timid either, to hear only thus far; but because Nicodemus was as yet possessed by fear, Christ did not indeed clearly reveal to him the whole, but shook his mind so as to cast out fear by fear, declaring that he who did not believe was being judged,[2] and that unbelief proceeded from an evil conscience. For since he made great account of honor from men, more than he did of the punishment; ("Many," saith the Evangelist, " of the rulers believed on Him, but because of the Jews they did not confess " — c. xii. 42;) on this point Christ toucheth him, saying, "It cannot be that he who believeth not on Me disbelieveth for any other cause save that he liveth an unclean life." Farther on He saith, "I am the Light" (c. viii. 12), but here, "the Light came into the world"; for at the beginning He spoke somewhat darkly, but afterwards more clearly. Yet even so the man was kept back by regard for the opinion of the many, and therefore could not endure to speak boldly as he ought.

Fly we then vainglory, for this is a passion more tyrannical than any. Hence spring covet- ousness and love of wealth, hence hatred and wars and strifes; for he that desires more than he has, will never be able to stop, and he desires from no other cause, but only from his love of vainglory. For tell me, why do so many encircle themselves with multitudes of eunuchs, and herds of slaves, and much show? Not because they need it, but that they may make those who meet them witnesses of this unseasonable display. If then we cut this off, we shall slay together with the head the other members also of wickedness, and there will be nothing to hinder us from dwelling on earth as though it were heaven. Nor doth this vice merely thrust its captives into wickedness, but is even co-existent[3] with their virtues, and when it is unable entirely to cast us out of these, it still causeth us much damage in the very exercise of them, forcing us to undergo the toil, and depriving us of the fruit. For he that with an eye to this, fasts, and prays, and shows mercy, has his reward. What can be more pitiable than a loss like this, that it should befall man to bewail[4] himself uselessly and in vain, and to become an object of ridicule, and to lose the glory from above? Since he that aims at both cannot obtain both. It is indeed possible to obtain both, when we desire not both, but one only, that from heaven; but he cannot obtain both, who longs for both. Wherefore if we wish to attain to glory, let us flee from human glory, and desire that only which cometh from God; so shall we obtain both the one and the other; which may we all enjoy, through the grace and lovingkindness of our Lord Jesus Christ, by whom and with whom, to the Father and the Holy Ghost, be glory for ever and ever. Amen.

# HOMILY XXIX.

JOHN iii. 22.

"And He came and His disciples into the land of Judæa, and there He tarried with them (and baptized)."

[1.] NOTHING can be clearer or mightier than the truth, just as nothing is weaker than falsehood, though it be shaded by ten thousand veils. For even so it is easily detected, it easily melts away. But truth stands forth unveiled for all that will behold her beauty; she seeks no concealment, dreads no danger, trembles at no plots, desires not glory from the many, is accountable to no mortal thing, but stands above them all, is the object of ten thousand secret plots, yet remaineth unconquerable, and guards as in a sure fortress these who fly to her by her own exceeding might, who avoids secret lurking places, and setteth what is hers before all men. And this Christ conversing with Pilate declared, when He said, "I ever taught openly, and in secret have I said nothing." (c. xviii. 20.) As He spake then, so He acted now, for, "After this," saith the Evangelist, " He went forth and His disciples into the land of Judæa, and there He tarried with them and baptized." At the feasts He went up to the

---

[1] i.e. his one great object.    [2] κρίνεσθαι.    [3] παρυφέστηκε.    [4] κόπτεσθαι.

City to set forth in the midst of them His doctrines, and the help of His miracles; but after the feasts were over, He often went to Jordan, because many ran together there. For He ever chose the most crowded places, not from any love of show or vainglory, but because He desired to afford His help to the greatest number.

Yet the Evangelist farther on says, that "Jesus baptized not, but His disciples"; whence it is clear that this is his meaning here also. And why did Jesus not baptize? The Baptist had said before, "He shall baptize you with the Holy Spirit and with fire." Now he had not yet given the Spirit, and it was therefore with good cause that he did not baptize. But His disciples did so, because they desired to bring many to the saving doctrine.

"And why, when the disciples of Jesus were baptizing, did not John cease to do so? why did he continue to baptize, and that even until he was led to prison? for to say,

Ver. 23. 'John also was baptizing in Ænon'; and to add,

Ver. 24. 'John was not yet cast into prison,' was to declare that until that time he did not cease to baptize. But wherefore did he baptize until then? For he would have made the disciples of Jesus seem more reverend had he desisted when they began. Why then did he baptize?" It was that he might not excite his disciples to even stronger rivalry, and make them more contentious still. For if, although he ten thousand times proclaimed Christ, yielded to Him the chief place, and made himself so much inferior, he still could not persuade them to run to Him; he would, had he added this also, have made them yet more hostile. On this account it was that Christ began to preach more constantly when John was removed. And moreover, I think that the death of John was allowed, and that it happened very quickly, in order that the whole attention[1] of the multitude might be shifted to Christ, and that they might no longer be divided in their opinions concerning the two.

Besides, even while he was baptizing, he did not cease continually to exhort them, and to show them the high and awful nature of Jesus. For He baptized them, and told them no other thing than that they must believe on Him that came after him. Now how would a man who acted thus by desisting have made the disciples of Christ seem worthy of reverence? On the contrary, he would have been thought to do so through envy and passion. But to continue preaching gave a stronger proof; for he desired not glory for himself, but sent on his hearers to Christ, and wrought with Him not less, but

rather much more than Christ's own disciples, because his testimony was unsuspected and he was by all men far more highly esteemed than they. And this the Evangelist implies, when he says, "all Judæa and the country around about Jordan went out to him and were baptized." (Matt. iii. 5.) Even when the disciples were baptizing, yet many did not cease to run to him.

If any one should enquire, "And in what was the baptism of the disciples better than that of John?" we will reply, "in nothing"; both were alike without the gift of the Spirit, both parties alike had one reason for baptizing, and that was, to lead the baptized to Christ. For in order that they might not be always running about to bring together those that should believe, as in Simon's case his brother did, and Philip to Nathanael, they instituted baptism, in order by it to bring all men to them easily, and to prepare a way for the faith which was to be. But that the baptisms had no superiority one over the other, is shown by what follows. What is that?

Ver. 25. "There arose," saith the Evangelist, "a question (between some) of John's disciples and the Jews about purifying."

For the disciples of John being ever jealously disposed towards Christ's disciples and Christ Himself, when they saw them baptizing, began to reason with those who were baptized, as though their baptism was in a manner superior to that of Christ's disciples; and taking one of the baptized, they tried to persuade him of this; but persuaded him not. Hear how the Evangelist has given us to understand that it was they who attacked him, not he who set on foot the question. He doth not say, that "a certain Jew questioned with them," but that, "there arose a questioning from the disciples of John with a certain Jew,[2] concerning purification."

[2.] And observe, I pray you, the Evangelist's inoffensiveness. He does not speak in the way of invective, but as far as he is able softens the charge, merely saying, that "a question arose"; whereas the sequel (which he has also set down in an inoffensive manner) makes it plain that what was said was said from jealousy.

Ver. 26. "They came," saith he, "unto John, and said unto him, Rabbi, He that was with thee beyond Jordan, to whom thou barest witness, behold the same baptizeth, and all men come to Him."

That is, "He whom thou didst baptize"; for this they imply when they say, "to whom thou barest witness," as though they had said, "He whom thou didst point out as illustrious, and

---

[2] Ἰουδαίου τινός. This reading is found in the Complut. and in most of the Greek commentators: the plural in G. T., Vulgate, and Latin writers.

make remarkable, dares to do the same as thou." Yet they do not say, "He whom thou didst baptize" baptizeth; (for then they would have been obliged to make mention of the Voice that came down from heaven, and of the descent of the Spirit;) but what say they? "He that was with thee beyond Jordan, to whom thou barest witness"; that is, "He who held the rank of a disciple, who was nothing more than we, this man hath separated himself, and baptizeth." For they thought to make him jealous,[1] not only by this, but by asserting that their own reputation was now diminishing. "All," say they, "come to Him." Whence it is evident, that they did not get the better of the Jew with whom they disputed; but they spoke these words because they were imperfect in disposition, and were not yet clear from a feeling of rivalry. What then doth John? He did not rebuke them severely, fearing lest they should separate themselves again from him, and work some other mischief. What are his words?[2]

Ver. 27. "A man can receive nothing, except it be given him from above."

Marvel not, if he speak of Christ in a lowly strain; it was impossible to teach all at once, and from the very beginning, men so pre-occupied by passion. But he desires to strike them for a while with awe and terror, and to show them that they warred against none other than God Himself, when they warred against Christ. And here he secretly establishes that truth, which Gamaliel asserted, "Ye cannot overthrow it, lest haply ye be found even to fight against God." (Acts v. 39.) For to say, "None can receive anything, except it be given him from heaven," was nothing else than declaring that they were attempting impossibilities, and so would be found to fight against God. "Well, but did not Theudas and his followers 'receive' from themselves?" They did, but they straightway were scattered and destroyed, not so what belonged to Christ.

By this also he gently consoles them, showing them that it was not a man, but God, who surpassed them in honor; and that therefore they must not wonder if what belonged to Him was glorious, and if "all men came unto Him": for that this was the nature of divine things, and that it was God who brought them to pass, because no man ever yet had power to do such deeds. All human things are easily seen through, and rotten, and quickly melt away and perish; these were not such, therefore not human. Observe too how when they said, "to whom thou barest witness," he turned against themselves that which they thought they had put forward to lower Christ, and silences them after showing

that Jesus' glory came not from his testimony; "A man cannot," he saith, "receive anything of himself, except it be given him from heaven." "If ye hold at all to my testimony, and believe it to be true, know that by that testimony ye ought to prefer not me to Him, but Him to me. For what was it that I testified? I call you yourselves to witness."

Ver. 28. "Ye yourselves bear me witness that I said, I am not the Christ, but that I am sent before Him."

"If then ye hold to my testimony, (and ye even now produce it when ye say, 'to whom thou barest witness,') He is not only not diminished by receiving my witness, but rather is increased by it; besides, the testimony was not mine, but God's. So that if I seem to you to be trustworthy, I said this among other things, that 'I am sent before Him.'" Seest thou how he shows little by little that this Voice was divine? For what he saith is of this kind: "I am a servant, and say the words of Him that sent me, not flattering Christ through human favor, but serving His Father who sent me. I gave not the testimony as a gift,[3] but what I was sent to speak, I spake. Do not then because of this suppose that I am great, for it shows that He is great. He is Lord of all things." This he goes on to declare, and says,

Ver. 29. "He that hath the bride is the bridegroom; but the friend of the bridegroom which standeth and heareth him, rejoiceth greatly because of the bridegroom's voice."

"But how doth he who said, 'whose shoe's latchet I am not worthy to unloose,'[4] now call himself His 'friend'?" It is not to exalt himself, nor boastingly, that he saith this, but from desire to show that he too most forwards this, (i.e. the exaltation of Christ,) and that these things come to pass not against his will or to his grief, but that he desires and is eager for them, and that it was with a special view to them that all his actions had been performed; and this he has very wisely shown by the term "friend." For on occasions like marriages, the servants of the bridegroom are not so glad and joyful as his "friends." It was not from any desire to prove equality of honor, (away with the thought,) but only excess of pleasure, and moreover from condescension to their weakness that he calleth himself "friend." For his service he before declared[5] by saying, "I am sent before Him." On this account, and because they thought that he was vexed at what had taken place, he called himself the "friend of the Bridegroom," to show that he was not only not vexed, but that he even greatly rejoiced. "For," saith he, "I came to effect this, and am so far from grieving at what

---

[1] παρακνίζειν.
[2] Morel. "but he speaks in a manner reservedly."

[3] ἐχαρισάμην.     [4] c. i. 27.     [5] al. "implied."

has been done, that had it not come to pass, I should then have been greatly grieved. Had the bride not come to the Bridegroom, then I should have been grieved, but not now, since my task has been accomplished. When His servants[1] are advancing, we are they who gain the honor; for that which we desired hath come to pass, and the bride knoweth the Bridegroom, and ye are witnesses of it when ye say, 'All men come unto Him.' This I earnestly desired, I did all to this end; and now when I see that it has come to pass, I am glad, and rejoice, and leap for joy."

[3.] But what meaneth, "He which standeth and heareth Him rejoiceth greatly, because of the Bridegroom's voice"? He transfers the expression from the parable to the subject in hand; for after mentioning the bridegroom and the bride, he shows how the bride is brought home, that is, by a "Voice" and teaching. For thus the Church is wedded to God; and therefore Paul saith, "Faith cometh by hearing, and hearing by the word of God." (Rom. x. 17.) "At this 'Voice,'" saith he, "I rejoice." And not without a cause doth he put "who standeth," but to show that his office had ceased, that he had given over to Him "the Bride," and must for the future stand and hear Him; that he was a servant and minister; that his good hope and his joy was now accomplished. Therefore he saith,

"This my joy therefore is fulfilled."

That is to say, "The work is finished which was to be done by me, for the future I can do nothing more." Then, to prevent increase of jealous feeling, not then only, but for the future, he tells them also of what should come to pass, confirming this too by what he had already said and done.[2] Therefore he continues,

Ver. 30. "He must increase, but I must decrease."

That is to say, "What is mine has now come to a stand, and has henceforth ceased, but what is His increaseth; for that which ye fear shall not be now only, but much more as it advances. And it is this especially which shows what is mine the brighter; for this end I came, and I rejoice that what is His hath made so great progress, and that those things have come to pass on account of which all that I did was done." Seest thou how gently and very wisely he softened down their passion, quenched their envy, showed them that they were undertaking impossibilities, a method by which wickedness is best checked? For this purpose it was ordained, that these things should take place while John was yet alive and baptizing, in order that

his disciples might have him as a witness of the superiority of Christ, and that if they should not believe,[3] they might be without excuse. For John came not to say these words of his own accord, nor in answer to other enquirers, but they asked the question themselves, and heard the answer. For if he had spoken of himself, their belief would not have been equal to the self-condemning[4] judgment which they received when they heard him answer to their question; just as the Jews also, in that they sent to him from their homes, heard what they did, and yet would not believe, by this especially deprived themselves of excuse.

What then are we taught by this? That a mad desire of glory[5] is the cause of all evils; this led them to jealousy, and when they had ceased for a little, this roused them to it again. Wherefore they come to Jesus, and say, "Why do thy disciples fast not?" (Matt. ix. 14.) Let us then, beloved, avoid this passion; for if we avoid this we shall escape hell. For this vice specially kindles the fire of hell, and everywhere extends[6] its rule, and tyrannically occupies every age and every rank.[7] This hath turned churches upside down, this is mischievous in state matters, hath subverted houses, and cities, and peoples, and nations. Why marvelest thou? It hath even gone forth into the desert, and manifested even there its great power. For men who have bidden an entire farewell to riches and all the show of the world, who converse with no one, who have gained the mastery over the more imperious desires after the flesh, these very men, made captives by vainglory, have often lost all. By reason of this passion, one who had labored much went away worse off than one who had not labored at all, but on the contrary had committed ten thousand sins; the Pharisee than the Publican. However, to condemn the passion is easy enough, (all agree in doing that,) but the question is, how to get the better of it. How can we do this? By setting honor against honor. For as we despise the riches of earth when we look to the other riches, as we contemn this life when we think of that far better than this, so we shall be enabled to spit on this world's glory, when we know of another far more august than it, which is glory indeed. One is a thing vain and empty, has the name without the reality; but that other, which is from heaven, is true, and has to give its praise Angels, and Archangels, and the Lord of Archangels, or rather I should say that it has men as well. Now if thou lookest to that theater, learnest what crowns are there, transportest thyself into the applauses which come thence, never

---

¹ or, "affairs."
² So Savile and MSS. Morel.'s reading has the same sense, but is less clear and concise.

³ or, "obey."　　⁶ Ben. "so does it everywhere extend."
⁴ i.e. "if they believed not."　　⁷ ἀξίαν.
⁵ al. "vainglory."

will earthly things be able to hold thee, nor when they come wilt thou deem them great, nor when they are away seek after them. For even in earthly palaces none of the guards who stand around the king, neglecting to please him that wears the diadem and sits upon the throne, troubles himself about the voices of daws, or the noise of flies and gnats flying and buzzing about him; and good report from men is no better than these. Knowing then the worthlessness of human things,[4] let us collect our all into treasuries that cannot be spoiled, let us seek that glory which is abiding and immovable; which may we all attain, through the grace and loving-kindness of our Lord Jesus Christ, by whom, and with whom to the Father and the Holy Spirit be glory, now and ever, and world without end. Amen.

# HOMILY XXX.

## JOHN iii. 31.

"He that cometh from above is above all; he that is of the earth is earthly, and speaketh of the earth."

[I.] A DREADFUL thing is the love of glory, dreadful and full of many evils; it is a thorn hard to be extracted, a wild beast untamable and many headed, arming itself against those that feed it; for as the worm eats through the wood from which it is born, as rust wastes the iron whence it comes forth, and moths the fleeces, so vainglory destroys the soul which nourishes it; and therefore we need great diligence to remove the passion. Observe here how long a charm John uses over[1] the disciples affected by it, and can scarcely pacify them. For he softens[2] them with other words besides those already mentioned. And what are these others? "He that cometh from above," he saith, "is above all; he that is of the earth, is earthly, and speaketh of the earth." Since you make much ado with my testimony,[3] and in this way say that I am more worthy of credit than He, you needs must know this, that it is impossible for One who cometh from heaven to have His credit strengthened by one that inhabiteth earth.

And what means "above all," what is the expression intended to show to us? That Christ hath need of nothing, but is Himself sufficient for Himself, and incomparably greater than all; of himself John speaks as being "of the earth, and speaking of the earth." Not that he spake of his own mind, but as Christ said, "If I have told you of earthly things and ye believe not," so calling Baptism, not because it was an "earthly thing," but because He compared it when He spake with His own Ineffable Generation, so here John said that he spake "of earth," comparing his own with Christ's teaching. For the

"speaking of earth" means nothing else than this, "My things are little and low and poor compared with His, and such as it was probable that an earthly nature would receive. In Him 'are hid all the treasures of wisdom.'" (Col. ii. 5.) That he speaks not of human reasonings is plain from this. "He that is of the earth," saith he, "is earthly." Yet not all in him was earthly, but the higher parts were heavenly, for he had a soul, and was partaker of a Spirit which was not of earth. How then saith he that he is "earthly"? Seest thou not that he means only, "I am small and of no esteem, going on the ground and born in the earth; but Christ came to us from above." Having by all these means quenched their passion, he afterwards speaks more openly of Christ; for before this it was useless to utter words which could never have gained a place in the understanding of his hearers: but when he hath pulled up the thorns, he then boldly casts in the seed, saying,

Ver. 31, 32. "He that cometh from above is above all. And what He hath heard He speaketh, and what He hath seen He testifieth;[5] and no man receiveth His testimony."

Having uttered something great and sublime concerning Him, he again brings down his discourse to a humbler strain. For the expression, "what He hath heard and seen," is suited rather to a mere man. What He knew He knew not from having learned it by sight, or from having heard it, but He included the whole in His Nature, having come forth perfect from the Bosom of His Father, and needing none to teach Him. For, "As the Father," He saith, "knoweth Me, even so know I the Father." (c. x. 15.) What then means, "He speaketh that He hath heard, and testifieth that He hath seen"? Since

---

[1] ὅσα ἐπᾴδει.
[2] ἐπαντλεῖ, lit. "foments."
[3] ἄνω καὶ κάτω στρέφετε.
[4] al. "of men."
[5] ὃ ἑώρ. καὶ ἦκ. τοῦτο μ. G. T.

by these senses we gain correct knowledge of everything, and are deemed worthy of credit when we teach on matters which our eyes have embraced and our ears have taken in, as not in such cases inventing or speaking falsehoods, John desiring here to establish this point,[1] said, "What He hath heard and seen": that is, "nothing that cometh from Him is false, but all is true." Thus we when we are making curious enquiry into anything, often ask, "Didst thou hear it?" "Didst thou see it?" And if this be proved, the testimony is indubitable, and so when Christ Himself saith, "As I hear, I judge" (c. v. 30); and, "What I have heard from My Father, that I speak"[2] (c. xv. 15); and, "We speak[3] that We have seen" (c. iii. 11); and whatsoever other sayings He uttereth of the kind, are uttered not that we might imagine that He saith what He doth being taught of any, (it were extreme folly to think this,) but in order that nothing of what is said may be suspected by the shameless Jews. For because they had not yet a right opinion concerning Him, He continually betakes Himself to His Father, and hence makes His sayings credible.

[2.] And why wonderest thou if He betake Himself to the Father, when He often resorts to the Prophets and the Scriptures? as when He saith, "They are they that testify of Me." (c. v. 39.) Shall we then say that He is inferior to the Prophets, because He draws testimonies from them? Away with the thought. It is because of the infirmity of His hearers that He so orders His discourse, and saith that He spake what He spake having heard it from the Father, not because He needed a teacher, but that they might believe that nothing that He said was false. John's meaning is of this kind: "I desire to hear what He saith, for He cometh from above, bringing thence those tidings which none but He knoweth rightly; for 'what He hath seen and heard,' is the expression of one who declareth this."

"And no man receiveth His testimony." Yet He had disciples, and many besides gave heed to His words. How then saith John, "No man"? He saith "no man," instead of "few men," for had he meant "no man at all," how could he have added,

Ver. 33. "He that hath received His testimony, hath set to his seal that God is true."

Here he touches his own disciples, as not being likely for a time to be firm believers. And that they did not even after this believe in Him, is clear from what is said afterwards; for John even when dwelling in prison sent them thence to Christ, that he might the more bind them to Him. Yet even then they scarcely believed, to

which Christ alluded when He said, "And blessed is he whosoever shall not be offended in Me." (Matt. xi. 6.) And therefore now he said, "And no man receiveth His testimony," to make sure his own disciples; all but saying, "Do not, because for a time few shall believe on Him, therefore deem that His words are false; for, 'He speaketh that He hath seen.'" Moreover he saith this to touch also the insensibility of the Jews. A charge which the Evangelist at commencing[4] brought against them, saying, "He came unto His own, and His own received Him not." For this is no reproach against Him, but an accusation of those who received Him not. (c. i. 11.)

"He that hath received His testimony hath set to his seal that God is true." Here he terrifies them also by showing that he who believeth not on Him, disbelieveth not Him alone, but the Father also; wherefore he adds:

Ver. 34. "He whom God hath sent speaketh the words of God."

Since then He speaketh His words, he that believeth and he that believeth not, believeth or believeth not God. "Hath set to His seal," that is, "hath declared." Then, to increase their dread, he saith, "that God is true;" thus showing, that no man could disbelieve Christ without making God who sent Him guilty of a falsehood. Because, since He saith nothing save what is from the Father, but all that He saith is His, he that heareth not Him, heareth not Him that sent Him. See how by these words again he strikes them with fear. As yet they thought it no great thing not to hearken to Christ; and therefore he held so great a danger above the heads of the unbelievers, that they might learn that they hearken not to God Himself, who hearken not to Christ. Then he proceeds with the discourse, descending to the measure of their infirmity, and saying,

"For God giveth not the Spirit by measure."

Again, as I said, he brings down his discourse to lower ground, varying it and making it suitable to be received by those who heard it then; otherwise he could not have raised them and increased their fear. For had he spoken anything great and sublime concerning Jesus Himself, they would not have believed, but might even have despised Him. Therefore he leads up all to the Father, speaking for a while of Christ as of a man. But what is it that he saith, "God giveth not the Spirit by measure"? He would show that we all have received the operation of the Spirit, by measure, (for in this place he means by "Spirit" the operation of the Spirit, for this it is that is divided,) but that Christ hath all Its operation unmeasured and entire. Now if His operations be unmeasured,

[1] i.e. the credibility of Christ.　　[3] μαρτυροῦμεν, G. T.
[2] ἐγνώρισα ὑμῖν, G. T.

[4] or, "at the comm. of the Gospel."

much more His Essence. Seest thou too that the Spirit is Infinite? How then can He who hath received all the operation of the Spirit, who knoweth the things of God, who saith, "We speak that We have heard, and testify that We have seen" (c. iii. 11), be rightly suspected? He saith nothing which is not "of God," or which is not of "the Spirit." And for a while he uttereth nothing concerning God the Word,[1] but maketh all his doctrine credible by (reference to) the Father and the Spirit. For that there is a God they knew, and that there is a Spirit they knew, (even though they held not a right opinion concerning Him,) but that there is a Son, they knew not. It is for this reason that he ever has recourse to the Father and the Spirit, thence confirming his words. For if any one should take no account of this reason, and examine his language by itself, it[2] would fall very far short of the Dignity of Christ. Christ was not therefore worthy of their faith, because He had the operation of the Spirit, (for He needeth not aid from thence,) but is Himself Self-sufficient; only for a while the Baptist speaks to the understanding of the simpler[3] sort, desiring to raise them up by degrees from their low notions.

And this I say, that we may not carelessly pass by what is contained in the Scriptures, but may fully consider the object of the speaker, and the infirmity of the hearers, and many other points in them. For teachers do not say all as they themselves would wish, but generally as the state of their weak (hearers) requires. Wherefore Paul saith, "I could not speak unto you as unto spiritual, but as unto carnal; I have fed you with milk, and not with meat." (1 Cor. iii. 1, 2.) He means, "I desired indeed to speak unto you as unto spiritual, but could not"; not because he was unable, but because they were not able so to hear. So too John desired to teach some great things to the disciples, but they could not yet bear to receive them, and therefore he dwells for the most part on that which is lowlier.

It behooves us therefore to explore all carefully. For the words of the Scriptures are our spiritual weapons; but if we know not how to fit those weapons and to arm our scholars rightly, they keep indeed their proper power, but cannot help those who receive them. For let us suppose there to be a strong corselet, and helm, and shield, and spear; and let one take this armor and put the corselet upon his feet, the helmet over his eyes instead of on his head, let him not put the shield before his breast, but perversely tie it to his legs: will he be able to gain any advantage from the armor? will he not rather be harmed? It is plain to any one that he will. Yet not on account of the weakness of the weapons, but on account of the unskillfulness of the man who knows not how to use them well. So with the Scriptures, if we confound their order; they will even so retain their proper force, yet will do us no good. Although I am always telling you this both in private and in public, I effect nothing, but see you all your time nailed to the things of this life, and not so much as dreaming[4] of spiritual matters. Therefore our lives are careless, and we who strive for truth have but little power, and are become a laughing stock to Greeks and Jews and Heretics. Had ye been careless in other matters, and exhibited in this place the same indifference as elsewhere, not even so could your doings have been defended; but now in matters of this life, every one of you, artisan and politician alike, is keener than a sword, while in necessary and spiritual things we are duller than any; making by-work business, and not deeming that which we ought to have esteemed more pressing than any business, to be by-work even. Know ye not that the Scriptures were written not for the first of mankind alone, but for our sakes also? Hearest thou not Paul say, that "they are written for our admonition, upon whom the ends of the world are come; that we through patience and comfort of the Scriptures might have hope"? (1 Cor. x. 11; Rom. xv. 4.) I know that I speak in vain, yet will I not cease to speak, for thus I shall clear myself[5] before God, though there be none to hear me. He that speaketh to them that give heed hath this at least to cheer his speech, the persuasion of his hearers; but he that speaks continually and is not listened to, and yet ceaseth not to speak, may be worthy of greater honor than the other, because he fulfills the will of God, even though none give heed unto him, to the best of his power. Still, though our reward will be greater owing to your disobedience, we rather desire that it be diminished, and that your salvation be advanced, thinking that your being well approved of[6] is a great reward. And we now say this not to make our discourse painful and burdensome to you, but to show to you the grief which we feel by reason of your indifference. God grant that we may be all of us delivered from this, that we may cling to spiritual zeal and obtain the blessings of heaven, through the grace and lovingkindness of our Lord Jesus Christ, with whom to the Father and the Holy Ghost be glory, for ever and ever. Amen.

---

[1] τοῦ Θεοῦ λόγου.
[2] or, "he."
[3] ἀτελεστέρων.
[4] οὐδὲ ὄναρ μετέχοντας, al. οὐδένα λόγον ποιουμένους.
[5] ἀπολογήσομαι.
[6] εὐδοκίμησιν.

# HOMILY XXXI.

JOHN iii. 35, 36.

"The Father loveth the Son, and hath given all things into His hand. He that believeth on the Son hath everlasting life, and he that believeth not the Son shall not see life; but the wrath of God abideth on him."

[1] GREAT is shown to be in all things the gain of humility.[1] Thus it is that we have brought arts to perfection, not by learning them all at once from our teachers; it is thus that we have built cities, putting them together slowly, little by little; it is thus that we maintain[2] our life. And marvel not if the thing has so much power in matters pertaining to this life, when in spiritual things one may find that great is the power of this wisdom. For so the Jews were enabled to be delivered from their idolatry, being led on gently and little by little, and hearing from the first nothing sublime concerning either doctrine or life. So after the coming of Christ, when it was the time for higher doctrines, the Apostles brought over all men without at first uttering anything sublime. And so Christ appears to have spoken to most at the beginning, and so John did now, speaking of Him as of some wonderful man, and darkly introducing high matter.

For instance, when commencing he spake thus: "A man cannot receive anything of himself"[3] (c. iii. 27): then after adding a high expression, and saying, "He that cometh from heaven[4] is above all," he again brings down his discourse to what is lowly, and besides many other things saith this, that "God giveth not the Spirit by measure." Then he proceeds to say, "The Father loveth the Son, and hath given all things into His hand." And after that, knowing that great is the force of punishment,[5] and that the many are not so much led by the promise of good things as by the threat of the terrible, he concludes his discourse with these words; "He that believeth on the Son hath everlasting life; but he that believeth not the Son shall not see life; but the wrath of God abideth on him." Here again he refers the account of punishment to the Father, for he saith not "the wrath of the Son," (yet He is the Judge,) but sets over them the Father, desiring so the more to terrify them.

"Is it then enough," saith one, "to believe on the Son, that one may have eternal life?" By no means. And hear Christ Himself declaring this, and saying, "Not every one that saith unto Me, Lord, Lord, shall enter into the king-dom of heaven" (Matt. vii. 21); and the blasphemy against the Spirit is enough of itself to cast a man into hell. But why speak I of a portion of doctrine? Though a man believe rightly on the Father, the Son, and the Holy Ghost, yet if he lead not a right life, his faith will avail nothing towards his salvation. Therefore when He saith, "This is life eternal, that they may know Thee the only true God" (c. xvii. 3), let us not suppose that the (knowledge) spoken of is sufficient for our salvation; we need besides this a most exact life and conversation. Since though he has said here, "He that believeth on the Son hath eternal life," and in the same place something even stronger, (for he weaves his discourse not of blessings only, but of their contraries also, speaking thus: "He that believeth not the Son shall not see life, but the wrath of God abideth on him";) yet not even from this do we assert that faith alone is sufficient to salvation. And the directions for living given in many places of the Gospels show this. Therefore he did not say, "This by itself is eternal life," nor, "He that doth but believe on the Son hath eternal life," but by both expressions he declared this, that the thing[6] doth contain life, yet that if a right conversation follow not, there will follow a heavy punishment. And he did not say, "awaiteth him," but, "abideth on him," that is, "shall never remove from him." For that thou mayest not think that the "shall not see life," is a temporary death, but mayest believe that the punishment is continual, he hath put this expression to show that it rests[7] upon him continually. And this he has done, by these very words forcing them on[8] to Christ. Therefore he gave not the admonition to them in particular, but made it universal, the manner which best might bring them over. For he did not say, "if ye believe," and, "if ye believe not," but made his speech general, so that his words might be free from suspicion. And this he has done yet more strongly than Christ. For Christ saith, "He that believeth not is condemned already," but John saith, "shall not see life, but the wrath of God abideth on him." With good cause; for it was a different thing for a man to speak of himself and for another to speak of him. They would have thought that Christ spake often of these things from self-love, and that he was a boaster; but John was clear from all suspicion. And if at a later time, Christ also used stronger

---

[1] lit. "condescension."
[2] διακρατοῦμεν.
[3] [ἐὰν μὴ ᾖ δεδ. αὐτῷ.] G. T.
[4] ἄνωθεν, G. T.
[5] al. "of the mention of punishment."
[6] i.e. believing.
[7] lit. "sits upon."
[8] ὠθῶν.

expressions, it was when they had begun to conceive an exalted opinion of Him.

CHAP. IV. Ver. 1, 2, 3. "When therefore Jesus[1] knew how the Pharisees had heard that Jesus made and baptized more disciples than John, (though Jesus Himself baptized not but His disciples,) He left Judæa, and departed again into Galilee."

He indeed baptized not, but they who carried the news, desiring to excite their hearers to envy, so reported. "Wherefore then 'departed' He?" Not from fear, but to take away[2] their malice, and to soften their envy. He was indeed able to restrain them when they came against Him, but this He would not do continually, that the Dispensation of the Flesh might not be disbelieved. For had He often been seized and escaped, this would have been suspected by many; therefore for the most part, He rather orders matters after the manner of a man. And as He desired it to be believed that He was God, so also that, being God, He bore the flesh; therefore even after the Resurrection, He said to the disciple, "Handle Me and see, for a spirit hath not flesh and bones" (Luke xxiv. 39); therefore also He rebuked Peter when he said, "Be it far from Thee, this shall not be unto thee." (Matt. xvi. 22.) So much was this matter an object of care to Him.

[2.] For this is no small part of the doctrines of the Church; it is the chief point of the salvation wrought for us;[3] by which all has been brought to pass, and has had success, for it was thus that the bonds of death were loosed, sin taken away, and the curse abolished, and ten thousand blessings introduced into our life. And therefore He especially desired that the Dispensation should be believed, as having been the root and fountain of innumerable goods to us.

Yet while acting thus in regard of His Humanity,[4] He did not allow His Divinity to be overcast. And so, after His departure He again employed the same language as before. For He went not away into Galilee simply,[5] but in order to effect certain important matters, those among the Samaritans; nor did He dispense these matters simply, but with the wisdom that belonged to[6] Him, and so as not to leave to the Jews any pretense even of a shameless excuse for themselves. And to this the Evangelist points when he says,

Ver. 4. "And He must needs go through Samaria."

Showing that He made this the bye-work of the journey. Which also the Apostles did; for just as they, when persecuted by the Jews, came to the Gentiles; so also Christ, when the Jews drove Him out, then took the Samaritans in hand, as He did also in the case of the Syrophenician woman. And this was done that all defense might be cut away from the Jews, and that they might not be able to say, "He left us, and went to the uncircumcised." And therefore the disciples excusing themselves said, "It was necessary that the Word of God should first have been spoken unto you; but seeing ye judge yourselves unworthy of everlasting life, lo, we turn to the Gentiles." (Acts xiii. 46.) And He saith again Himself, "I am not come[7] but unto the lost sheep of the house of Israel" (Matt. xv. 24); and again, "It is not meet to take the children's bread, and to give[8] it to dogs." But when they drove Him away, they opened a door to the Gentiles. Yet not so did He come to the Gentiles expressly, but in passing.[9] In passing then,

Ver. 5, 6. "He cometh to a city of Samaria, which is called Sychar, near to the parcel of ground that Jacob gave to his son Joseph. Now Jacob's well was there."

Why is the Evangelist exact about the place? It is, that when thou hearest the woman say, "Jacob our father gave us this well," thou mayest not think it strange. For this was the place where Levi and Simeon, being angry because of Dinah, wrought that cruel slaughter. And it may be worth while to relate from what sources the Samaritans were made up; since all this country is called Samaria. Whence then did they receive their name? The mountain was called "Somor" from its owner (1 Kings xvi. 24): as also Esaias saith, "and the head of Ephraim is Somoron" (Isa. vii. 9, LXX.), but the inhabitants were termed not "Samaritans" but "Israelites." But as time went on, they offended God, and in the reign of Pekah, Tiglath-Pileser came up, and took many cities, and set upon Elah, and having slain him, gave the kingdom to Hoshea.[10] (2 Kings xv. 29.) Against him Shalmaneser came and took other cities, and made them subject and tributary. (2 Kings xvii. 3.) At first he yielded, but afterwards he revolted from the Assyrian rule, and betook himself to the alliance of the Ethiopians.[11] The Assyrian learnt this, and having made war upon them and destroyed their cities, he no longer allowed the nation to remain there, because he had such suspicions that they would revolt. (2 Kings xvii. 4.) But he carried them to Babylon and to the Medes, and having brought thence nations from divers places, planted them

---

1 ὁ Κύριος, G. T.
2 lit. "cut out,"
3 τῆς ὑπὲρ ἡμῶν σωτ.
4 οἰκονομῶν τὰ ἀνθρώπινα.
5 i.e. without an object, ἁπλῶς.
6 or, "became."
7 [οὐκ ἀπεστάλην] G. T.     8 [βάλλειν] G. T.
9 Morel. "having thus hinted that which he wished, he again begins, saying, Jesus therefore cometh," &c.
10 This account does not agree with the history, (2 Kings xv. 29, 30,) but there is no other reading.
11 i.e. the Egyptians.

in Samaria, that his dominion for the future might be sure, his own people occupying the place. After this, God, desiring to show that He had not given up the Jews through weakness, but because of the sins of those who were given up, sent lions against the foreigners,[1] who ravaged all their nation. These things were reported to the king, and he sent a priest to deliver to them the laws of God. Still not even so did they desist wholly from their impiety, but only by halves. But as time went on, they in turn abandoned[2] their idols, and worshiped God. And when things were in this state, the Jews having returned, ever after entertained a jealous feeling towards them as strangers and enemies, and called them from the name of the mountain, "Samaritans." From this cause also there was no little rivalry between them. The Samaritans did not use all the Scriptures, but received the writings of Moses only, and made but little account of those of the Prophets. Yet they were eager to thrust themselves into the noble Jewish stock, and prided themselves upon Abraham, and called[3] him their forefather, as being of Chaldæa; and Jacob also they called their father, as being his descendant. But the Jews abominated them as well as all (other nations). Wherefore they reproached Christ with this, saying, "Thou art a Samaritan, and hast a devil." (c. viii. 48.) And for this reason in the parable of the man that went down from Jerusalem to Jericho, Christ makes the man who showed pity upon him to have been "a Samaritan" (Luke x. 33), one who by them was deemed mean, contemptible, and abominable. And in the case of the ten lepers, He calls one a "stranger" on this account, (for "he was a Samaritan,") and He gave His charge to the disciples in these words, "Go not into the way of the Gentiles, and into any city of the Samaritans enter ye not." (Matt. x. 5.)

[3:] Nor was it merely to describe the place that the Evangelist has reminded us of Jacob, but to show that the rejection of the Jews had happened long ago. For during the time of their forefathers these Jews possessed the land, and not the Samaritans; and the very possessions which not being theirs, their forefathers had gotten, they being theirs, had lost by their sloth and transgressions. So little[4] is the advantage of excellent ancestors, if their descendants be not like them. Moreover, the foreigners when they had only made trial of the lions, straightway returned to the right worship[5] of the Jews, while they, after enduring such inflictions, were not even so brought to a sound mind.

To this place Christ now came, ever rejecting a sedentary and soft[6] life, and exhibiting[7] one laborious and active. He useth no beast to carry Him, but walketh so much on a stretch, as even to be wearied with His journeying. And this He ever teacheth, that a man should work for himself, go without superfluities, and not have many wants. Nay, so desirous is He that we should be alienated from superfluities, that He abridgeth many even of necessary things. Wherefore He said, "Foxes have holes, and birds of the air have nests, but the Son of Man hath not where to lay His head." (Matt. viii. 20.) Therefore He spent most of His time in the mountains, and in the deserts, not by day only, but also by night. And this David declared when he said, "He shall drink of the brook in the way" (Ps. cx. 7): by this showing His frugal[8] way of life. This too the Evangelist shows in this place.

Ver. 6, 7, 8. "Jesus therefore, being wearied with His journey, sat thus by the well; and it was about the sixth hour. There cometh a woman of Samaria to draw water. Jesus saith unto her, Give Me to drink. For His disciples were gone away into the city to buy meat."

Hence we learn His activity in journeying, His carelessness about food, and how He treated it as a matter of minor importance.[9] And so the disciples were taught to use the like disposition themselves; for they took with them no provisions for the road. And this another Evangelist declares, saying, that when He spake to them concerning "the leaven of the Pharisees" (Matt. xvi. 6), they thought that it was because they carried no bread; and when he introduces them plucking the ears of corn, and eating (Matt. xii. 1), and when he saith that Jesus came to the fig-tree by reason of hunger (Matt. xxi. 18), it is for nothing else but only to instruct us by all these to despise the belly, and not to deem that its service is anxiously to be attended to. Observe them, for instance, in this place neither bringing anything with them, nor because they brought not anything, caring for this at the very beginning and early part of the day, but buying food at the time when all other people were taking their meal.[10] Not like us, who the instant we rise from our beds attend to this before anything else, calling cooks and butlers, and giving our directions with all earnestness, applying ourselves afterwards to other matters, preferring temporal things to spiritual, valuing those things as necessary which we ought to have deemed of less importance.[11] Therefore all things are in confusion. We ought, on the

---

[1] βαρβάρους.
[2] lit. "started away from."
[3] lit. "registered."
[4] al. "truly little."
[5] εὐσεβείαν.

[6] βάναυσον καὶ ὑγρὸν.
[7] lit. "introducing."
[8] or "active."
[9] παρέργως.
[10] ἀριστοποιοῦνται. See on Stat. Hom. ix. 1, and note.
[11] πάρεργον.

contrary, making much account of all spiritual things, after having accomplished these, then to apply ourselves to the others.

And in this place it is not His laboriousness alone that is shown, but also His freedom from pride; not merely by His being tired, nor by His sitting by the way-side, but by His having been left alone, and His disciples having been separated[1] from Him. And yet it was in His power, if He had willed it, either not to have sent them all away, or when they departed to have had other ministers. But He would not; for so He accustomed His disciples to tread all pride beneath their feet.

"And what marvel," saith one, "if they were moderate in their wishes, since they were fishermen and tentmakers?" Yes! Fishermen and tentmakers they were; but they had in a moment[2] mounted even to the height of heaven, and had become more honorable than all earthly kings, being deemed worthy to become the companions of the Lord of the world, and to follow Him whom all beheld with awe. And ye know this too, that those men especially who are of humble origin, whenever they gain distinction, are the more easily lifted up to folly, because they are quite ignorant how to bear their sudden[3] honor. Restraining them therefore in their present humblemindedness, He taught them always to be moderate,[4] and never to require any to wait upon them.

"He therefore," saith the Evangelist, "being wearied with His journey, sat[5] thus at the well."[6]

Seest thou that His sitting was because of weariness? because of the heat? because of his waiting for His disciples? He knew, indeed, what should take place among the Samaritans, but it was not for this that He came principally; yet, though He came not for this, it behooved not to reject the woman who came to Him, when she manifested such a desire to learn. The Jews, when He was even coming to them, drove Him away; they of the Gentiles, when He was proceeding in another direction, drew Him to them. They envied, these believed on Him. They were angry with, these revered and worshiped Him. What then? Was He to overlook the salvation of so many, to send away such noble zeal? This would have been unworthy of His lovingkindness. Therefore He ordered all the matter in hand with the Wisdom which became Him. He sat resting His body and cooling It by the fountain; for it was the very middle of the day, as the Evangelist has declared, when he says,

"It was about the sixth hour."

He sat "thus." What meaneth "thus"?

Not upon a throne, not upon a cushion, but simply, and as He was,[7] upon the ground.

Ver. 7. "There cometh a woman of Samaria to draw water."

[4.] Observe how he declareth that the woman came forth for another purpose, in every way silencing the shameless gainsaying of the Jews, that none might say that He acted in opposition to His own command, bidding (His disciples) not to enter into any city of the Samaritans, yet conversing with Samaritans. (Matt. x. 5.) And therefore the Evangelist has put,

Ver. 8. "For His disciples were gone away into the city to buy meat."[8]

Bringing in many reasons for His conversation with her. What doth the woman? When she heard, "Give Me to drink,"[9] she very wisely makes the speech of Christ an occasion for a question, and saith,

Ver. 9. "How is it that thou, being a Jew, askest drink of me, which am a Samaritan? For the Jews have no dealings with the Samaritans."

And whence did she suppose Him to be a Jew? From His dress, perhaps, and from His dialect. Observe, I pray you, how considerate the woman was. If there was need of caution, Jesus needed it, not she. For she doth not say, "The Samaritans have no dealings with the Jews," but, "The Jews do not admit the Samaritans." Yet still, although free herself from blame,[10] when she supposed that another was falling into it she would not even so hold her peace, but corrected, as she thought, what was done unlawfully. Perhaps some one may ask how it was that Jesus asked drink of her, when the law[11] did not permit it. If it be answered that it was because He knew beforehand that she would not give it, then for this very reason He ought not to have asked. What then can we say? That the rejecting such observances as these was now a matter of indifference to Him; for He who induced others to do them away, would much more Himself pass them by. "Not that which goeth in," saith He, "defileth a man, but that which goeth out." (Matt. xv. 11.) And this conversation with the woman would be no slight charge against the Jews. For often did He draw them to Himself, both by words and deeds, but they would not attend; while observe how she is detained by a simple request.[12] For He did not as yet enter on the prosecution of this business,[13] nor the way,[14] yet if any came to Him He did not prevent them. And to the disciples also He said thus, "Into

---

[1] al. "having departed."
[2] ἄθροον.
[3] al. "so great."
[4] συνεστάλθαι.
[5] ἐκάθητο [ἐκαθέζετο] G. T.
[6] ἐπὶ τῇ πηγῇ.
[7] ὡς ἔτυχεν.
[8] al. "had not yet come."
[9] al. being asked for water by Christ; for, "Give Me to drink," the Evangelist tells us, was what Christ said to her. What then saith she? "How is it," &c.
[10] al. "sin."
[11] i.e. custom.
[12] al. "introduction."
[13] i.e. conversion.
[14] i.e. of salvation.

any city of the Samaritans enter ye not." He did not say, "And when they come to you, reject them"; that would have been very unworthy of His lovingkindness. And therefore He answered the woman, and said,

Ver. 10. "If thou knewest the gift of God, and who it is that saith to thee, Give Me to drink, thou wouldest have asked of Him, and He would have given thee living water."

First, He showeth that she is worthy to hear and not to be overlooked, and then He revealeth Himself. For she, as soon as she had learnt who He was, would straightway hearken and attend to Him; which none can say of the Jews, for they, when they had learned, asked nothing of Him, nor did they desire to be informed on any profitable matter, but insulted and drove Him away. But when the woman had heard these words, observe how gently she answers:

Ver. 11. "Sir, thou hast nothing to draw with, and the well is deep; from whence then hast thou that living water?"

Already He hath raised her from her low opinion of Him, and from deeming that He is a common man. For not without a reason doth she here call Him, "Lord";[1] but assigning to Him high honor. That she spake these words to honor Him, is plain from what is said afterwards, since she did not laugh nor mock, but doubted for a while. And wonder not if she did not at once perceive all, for neither did Nicodemus. What saith he? "How can these things be?" and again, "How can a man be born when he is old?" and again, "Can he enter the second time into his mother's womb, and be born?" But this woman more reverently: "Sir, thou hast nothing to draw with, and the well is deep; from whence then hast thou that living water?" Christ said one thing, and she imagined another, hearing nothing beyond the words, and as yet unable to form any lofty thought. Yet, had she spoken hastily, she might have said, "If thou hadst had that living water, thou wouldest not have asked of me, but wouldest rather have provided for thyself. Thou art but a boaster." But she said nothing like this; she answers with much gentleness, both at first and afterwards. For at first she saith, "How is it that thou, being a Jew, askest drink of me?" she saith not, as though speaking to an alien and an enemy, "Far be it from me to give to thee, who art a foe and a stranger to our nation." And afterwards again, when she heard Him utter great words, a thing at which enemies are most annoyed, she did not mock nor deride[2]; but what saith she?

Ver. 12. "Art thou greater than our father Jacob, which gave us the well, and drank thereof himself, and his children, and his cattle?"

Observe how she thrusts herself into the noble stock of the Jews. For what she saith is somewhat of this kind: "Jacob used this water, and had nothing better to give us." And this she said showing that from the first answer (of Christ) she had conceived a great and sublime thought; for by the words, "he drank thereof himself, and his children, and his cattle," she implies nothing else, than that she had a notion of a better Water, but that she[3] never found it, nor clearly knew it. More clearly to explain what she means to say, the sense of her words is this: "Thou canst not assert that Jacob gave us this well, and used another himself; for he and his children drank of this one, which they would not have done if they had had another and a better. Now of the water of this well it is not in thy power to give me, and thou canst not have another and a better, unless thou dost confess that thou art greater than Jacob. Whence then hast thou that water which thou promisest that thou wilt give us?" The Jews did not converse with Him thus mildly, and yet He spake to them on the same subject, making mention of the like water, but they profited nothing; and when He made mention of Abraham, they even attempted to stone Him. Not so does this woman approach Him; but with much gentleness, in the midst of the heat, at noon, she with much patience saith and hears all, and does not so much as think of what the Jews most probably would have asserted, that "This fellow is mad, and beside himself: he hath tied me to this fount and well, giving me nothing, but using big words"; no, she endures and perseveres until she has found what she seeks.

[5.] If now a woman of Samaria is so earnest to learn something profitable, if she abides by Christ though not as yet knowing Him, what pardon shall we obtain, who both knowing[4] Him, and being not by a well, nor in a desert place, nor at noon-day, nor beneath the scorching sunbeams, but at morning-tide, and beneath a roof like this, enjoying shade and comfort,[5] yet cannot endure to hear anything that is said, but are wearied[6] by it. Not such was that woman; so occupied was she by Jesus' words, that she even called others to hear them. The Jews, on the contrary, not only did not call, but even hindered and impeded those who desired to come to Him,[7] saying, "See, have any of the rulers believed on him? but this people, which knoweth not the Law, are cursed."[8] Let us then imitate this woman of Samaria; let us commune with Christ. For even now He standeth in the midst of us, speaking to us by the Prophets and Disciples; let us hear and obey. How long

---

[1] Κύριε, "Sir," E. V.　　　[2] διέσυρε.

[3] al. "not even he."
[4] al. "having seen."
[5] or, "coolness."
[6] ἀποκναίοντες, al. ἀποκνοῦντες.
[7] al. "to enter in."
[8] c. vii. 49. al. "is not this people," &c.

shall we live uselessly and in vain? Because, not to do what is well-pleasing to God is to live uselessly, or rather not merely uselessly, but to our own hurt; for when we have spent the time which has been given us on no good purpose, we shall depart this life to suffer severest punishment for our unseasonable extravagance. For it can never be that a man who has received money to trade with, and then has eaten it up, shall have it[1] required at his hands by the man who intrusted it to him; and that one who has spent such a life as ours to no purpose shall escape punishment. It was not for this that God brought us into this present life, and breathed into us a soul, that we should make use of the present time only,[2] but that we should do all our business with a regard to the life which is to come. Things irrational only are useful for the present life; but we have an immortal soul, that we may use every means to prepare ourselves for that other life. For if one enquire the use of horses and asses and oxen, and other such-like animals, we shall tell him that it is nothing else but only to minister to the present life; but this cannot be said of us; our best condition is that which follows on our departure hence; and we must do all that we may shine there, that we may join the choir of Angels, and stand before the King continually, through endless[4] ages. And therefore the soul is immortal, and the body shall be immortal too, that we may enjoy the never-ending blessings. But if, when heavenly things are proffered thee, thou remainest nailed to earth, consider what an insult is offered to thy Benefactor, when He holdeth forth to thee things above, and thou, making no great account of them choosest earth instead. And therefore, as despised by thee, He hath threatened thee with hell, that thou mayest learn hence of what great blessings thou deprivest thyself. God grant that none make trial of that punishment, but that having been well-pleasing to Christ, we may obtain everlasting blessings, through the grace and lovingkindness of our Lord Jesus Christ; to whom with the Father and the Holy Ghost be glory, now and ever, and world without end. Amen.

---

# HOMILY XXXII.

## John iv. 13, 14.

"Jesus answered and said unto her, Whosoever drinketh of this water shall thirst again: but whosoever drinketh of the water that I shall give him, shall never thirst; but the water that I shall give him, shall be in him a well of water springing up into everlasting Life."

[1.] SCRIPTURE calls the grace of the Spirit sometimes "Fire," sometimes "Water," showing that these names are not descriptive of its essence, but of its operation; for the Spirit, being Invisible and Simple, cannot be made up of different substances. Now the one John declares, speaking thus, "He shall baptize you with the Holy Ghost, and with Fire" (Matt. iii. 11): the other, Christ, "Out of his belly shall flow rivers of living water." (John vii. 38.) "But this," saith John, "spake He of the Spirit, which they should receive." So also conversing with the woman, He calleth the Spirit water;[3] for, "Whosoever shall drink of the water which I shall give him, shall never thirst." So also He calleth the Spirit by the name of "fire," alluding to the rousing and warming property of grace, and its power of destroying transgressions; but by that of "water," to declare the cleansing wrought by it, and the great refreshment which it affordeth to those minds which receive it. And with good reason; for it makes the willing soul like some[5] garden thick with all manner of trees fruitful and ever-flourishing, allowing it neither to feel despondency nor the plots of Satan, and quenches[6] all the fiery darts of the wicked one.

And observe, I pray you, the wisdom of Christ,[7] how gently He leads on[8] the woman; for He did not say at first, "If thou knewest who it is that saith to thee, Give Me to drink," but when He had given her an occasion of calling Him "a Jew," and brought her beneath the charge of having done so, repelling the accusation He saith, "If thou knewest who it is that saith to thee, Give Me to drink, thou wouldest have asked of Him"; and having compelled her by His great promises to make mention[9] of the Patriarch, He thus alloweth the woman to look through,[10] and then when she objects, "Art thou greater than our father Jacob?" He saith not,

---

[1] al. "an account."
[2] al. "live only for the present," κατὰ τὸ π.
[3] al. "saith the same now."

[4] al. "incorrupt."
[5] al. "some flourishing."
[6] al. "as quenching easily."
[7] al. "of God."

[8] al. "leads up."
[9] or, "to remember."
[10] or, "see clearly."

"Yea, I am greater," (for He would have seemed but to boast, since the proof did not as yet appear,) but by what He saith He effecteth this. For He said not simply, "I will give thee water," but having first set that given by Jacob aside, He exalteth that given by Himself, desiring to show from the nature of the things given, how great is the interval and difference between the persons of the givers,[1] and His own superiority to the Patriarch. "If," saith He, "thou admirest Jacob because he gave thee this water, what wilt thou say if I give thee Water far better than this? Thou hast thyself been first to confess that I am greater than Jacob, by arguing against Me, and asking, 'Art thou greater than Jacob, that thou promisest to give me better water?' If thou receivest that Water, certainly thou wilt confess that I am greater." Seest thou the upright judgment of the woman, giving her decision from facts, both as to the Patriarch, and as to Christ? The Jews acted not thus; when they even saw Him casting out devils, they not only did not call Him greater than the Patriarch, but even said that He had a devil. Not so the woman, she draws her opinion whence Christ would have her, from the demonstration afforded by His works. For by these He justifieth Himself, saying, "If I do not the works of My Father, believe Me not; but if I do, if ye believe not Me, believe the works." (c. x. 37, 38.) And thus the woman is brought over to the faith.

Wherefore also He, having heard, "Art thou greater than our father Jacob," leaveth Jacob, and speaketh concerning the water, saying, "Whosoever shall drink of this water, shall thirst again"; and He maketh His comparison, not by depreciating one, but by showing the excellence of the other; for He saith not, that "this water is naught," nor "that it is inferior and contemptible," but what even nature testifies that He saith: "Whosoever shall drink of this water shall thirst again; but whosoever shall drink of the Water which I shall give him, shall never thirst." The woman before this had heard of "living Water" (v. 10), but had not known its meaning. Since because that water is called "living" which is perennial and bubbles up unceasingly from uninterrupted springs, she thought that this was the water meant. Wherefore He points out this more clearly by speaking thus, and establishing by a comparison the superiority (of the water which He would give). What then saith He? "Whosoever shall drink of the Water that I shall give him, shall never thirst." This and what was said next especially showed the superiority, for material water possesses none of these qualities. And what is it that follows? "It shall be in him a well of water springing up into everlasting life." For

as one that hath a well within him could never be seized by thirst, so neither can he that hath this Water.

The woman straightway believed, showing herself much wiser than Nicodemus, and not only wiser, but more manly. For he when he heard ten thousand such things neither invited any others to this hearing, nor himself spake forth openly; but she exhibited the actions of an Apostle, preaching the Gospel to all, and calling them to Jesus, and drawing a whole city forth to Him. Nicodemus when he had heard said, "How can these things be?" And when Christ set before him a clear illustration, that of "the wind," he did not even so receive the Word. But the woman not so; at first she doubted, but afterwards receiving the Word not by any regular demonstration, but in the form of an assertion, she straightway hastened to embrace it. For when Christ said, "It shall be in him a well of water springing up into everlasting Life," immediately the woman saith,

Ver. 15. "Give me this water, that I thirst not, neither come hither to draw."

Seest thou how little by little she is led up to the highest doctrines? First she thought Him some Jew who was transgressing the Law; then when He had repelled that accusation, (for it was necessary that the person who was to teach[2] her such things should not be suspected,) having heard of "living water," she supposed that this was spoken of material water; afterwards, having learnt that the words were spiritual, she believed that the water could remove the necessity caused by thirst, but knew not yet what this could be; she still doubted, deeming it indeed to be above material things, but not being exactly informed. But here having gained a clearer insight, but not yet fully perceiving the whole, (for she saith, "Give me this water, that I thirst not, neither come hither to draw,") she for the time preferreth Him to Jacob. "For" (saith she) "I need not this well if I receive from thee that water." Seest thou how she setteth Him before the Patriarch? This is the act of a fairly-judging[3] soul. She had shown how great an opinion she had of Jacob, she saw One better than he, and was not held back by her prepossession. Thus this woman was neither of an easy temper, (she did not carelessly receive what was said, how can she have done so when she enquired with so great exactness?[4]) nor yet disobedient, nor disputatious, and this she showed by her petition. Yet to the Jews once He said, "Whosoever shall eat of My flesh[5] shall never hunger, and he that believeth on Me shall never thirst" (c. vi. 35); but they not only did not believe, but were offended at

[2] κατηχεῖν.
[3] εὐγνώμονος.
[4] al. "readiness."
[5] ὁ ἐρχόμενος πρός με, G. T.

Him. The woman had no such feeling, she remains and petitions. To the Jews He said, "He that believeth on Me shall never thirst"; not so to the woman, but more grossly, "He that drinketh of this Water shall never thirst." For the promise referred to spiritual and unseen[1] things. Wherefore having raised her mind by His promises, He still lingers among expressions relating to sense, because she could not as yet comprehend the exact expression of spiritual things. Since had He said, "If thou believest in Me thou shalt not thirst," she would not have understood His saying, not knowing who it could be that spake to her, nor concerning what kind of thirst He spake. Wherefore then did He not this in the case of the Jews? Because they had seen many signs, while she had seen no sign, but heard these words first. For which reason He afterwards reveals His power by prophecy, and does not directly introduce His reproof,[2] but what saith He?

Ver. 16–19. "Go, call thy husband, and come thither. The woman answered and said, I have no husband. Jesus saith unto her, Thou hast well said, I have no husband: for thou hast had five husbands, and he whom thou now hast is not thy husband: in that saidst thou truly. The woman saith unto Him, Sir, I perceive that Thou art a Prophet."

[2.] O how great the wisdom of the woman! how meekly doth she receive the reproof! "How should she not," saith some one? Tell me, why should she? Did He not often reprove the Jews also, and with greater reproofs than these? (for it is not the same to bring forward the hidden thoughts of the heart, as to make manifest a thing that was done in secret; the first are known to[3] God alone, and none other knoweth them but he who hath them in his heart; the second, all who were sharers in it know;) but still when reproved did not bear it patiently. When He said, "Why seek ye to kill me?" (c. vii. 19), they not only did not admire as the woman did but even mocked at and insulted Him; yet they had a demonstration from other miracles, she had only heard this speech. Still they not only did not admire, but even insulted Him, saying, "Thou hast a demon, who seeketh to kill thee?" While she not only doth not insult but admires, and is astonished at Him, and supposes Him to be a Prophet. Yet truly this rebuke touched the woman more than the other touched them; for her fault was hers alone, theirs was a general one; and we are not so much stung by what is general as by what is particular. Besides they thought they should be gaining a great object if they could slay Christ, but that which the woman had done was allowed

by all to be wicked; yet was she not indignant, but was astonished and wondered. And Christ did this very same thing in the case of Nathanael. He did not at first introduce the prophecy, nor say, "I saw thee under the fig-tree," but when Nathanael said, "Whence knowest thou me?" then He introduced this. For He desired to take the beginnings of His signs and prophecies from the very persons who came near to Him, so that they might be more attached[4] by what was done, and He might escape the suspicion of vainglory. Now this He doth here also; for to have charged her first of all that, "Thou hast no husband," would have seemed burdensome and superfluous, but to take the reason (for speaking) from herself, and then to set right all these points, was very consistent, and softened the disposition of the hearer.

"And what kind of connection," saith some one, "is there in the saying, 'Go, call thy husband'?" The discourse was concerning a gift and grace surpassing mortal nature: the woman was urgent in seeking to receive it. Christ saith, "Call thy husband," showing that he also must share in these things; but she, eager to receive[5] (the gift), and concealing the shamefulness of the circumstances, and supposing that she was conversing with a man, said, "I have no husband." Christ having heard this, now seasonably introduces His reproof, mentioning accurately both points; for He enumerated all her former husbands, and reproved her for him whom[6] she now would hide. What then did the woman? she was not annoyed, nor did she leave Him and fly, nor deem the thing an insult, but rather admired Him, and persevered the more. "I perceive," saith she, "that Thou art a Prophet." Observe her prudence; she did not straightway run to Him, but still considers Him, and marvels at Him. For, "I perceive," means, "Thou appearest to me to be a Prophet." Then when she suspected this, she asks Him nothing concerning this life, not concerning bodily health, or possessions, or wealth, but at once concerning doctrines. For what saith she?

Ver. 20. "Our fathers worshiped in this mountain," (meaning Abraham and his family, for thither they say that he led up his son,) "and how say ye[7] that in Jerusalem is the place where men ought to worship?"

[3.] Seest thou how much more elevated in mind she has become? She who was anxious that she might not be troubled for thirst, now questions concerning doctrines. What then doth Christ? He doth not resolve the question, (for to answer simply to men's words was not His care, for it was needless,[8]) but leads the woman on to the greater height, and doth not

---

[1] al. "not finite."
[2] ἔλεγχον.
[3] or, "is the work of."
[4] οἰκειοῦσθαι.
[5] al. "to be hidden."
[6] al. "the thing which."
[7] καὶ ὑμ. λέγετε, G. T.
[8] παρέλκον.

converse with her on these matters, until she has confessed that He was a Prophet, so that afterwards she might hear His Word with abundant belief; for having been persuaded of this, she could no longer doubt concerning what should be said to her.

Let us now after this be ashamed, and blush. A woman who had had five husbands, and who was of Samaria, was so eager concerning doctrines, that neither the time of day, nor her having come for another purpose, nor anything else, led her away from enquiring on such matters; but we not only do not enquire concerning doctrines, but towards them all our dispositions are careless and indifferent. Therefore everything is neglected. For which of you when in his house takes some Christian book[1] in hand, and goes over its contents, and searches the Scriptures? None can say that he does so, but with most we shall find draughts and dice, but books nowhere, except among a few. And even these few have the same dispositions as the many; for they tie up their books, and keep them always put away in cases, and all their care is for the fineness of the parchments, and the beauty of the letters, not for reading them. For they have not bought them to obtain advantage and benefit from them, but take pains about such matters to show their wealth and pride. Such is the excess of vainglory. I do not hear any one glory that he knows the contents, but that he hath a book written in letters of gold. And what gain, tell me, is this? The Scriptures were not given us for this only, that we might have them in books, but that we might engrave them on our hearts. For this kind of possession, the keeping the commandments merely in letter, belongs to Jewish ambition; but to us the Law was not so given[2] at all, but in the fleshy tables of our hearts.[3] And this I say, not to prevent you from procuring Bibles, on the contrary, I exhort and earnestly pray that you do this, but I desire that from those books you convey the letters and sense into your understanding, that so it may be purified when it receiveth the meaning of the writing.[4] For if the devil will not dare to approach a house where a Gospel is lying, much less will any evil spirit, or any sinful nature,[5] ever touch or enter a soul which bears about with it such sentiments as it contains. Sanctify then thy soul, sanctify thy body, by having these ever in thy heart, and on thy tongue. For if foul speech defiles and invites devils, it is clear that spiritual reading sanctifies and draws down the grace of the Spirit. The Scriptures[6] are divine charms, let us then apply to ourselves and[7] to the passions of our souls the remedies to be derived from them. For if we understand what it is that is read, we shall hear it with much readiness. I am always saying this, and will not cease to say it. Is it not strange that those who sit by the market can tell the names, and families, and cities of charioteers, and dancers, and the kinds of power possessed by each, and can give exact account of the good or bad qualities of the very horses, but that those who come hither should know nothing of what is done here, but should be ignorant of the number even of the sacred Books? If thou pursuest those worldly things for pleasure, I will show thee that here is greater pleasure. Which is sweeter, tell me, which more marvelous, to see a man wrestling with a man, or a man buffeting with a devil, a body closing with an incorporeal power, and him who is of thy race victorious? These wrestlings let us look on, these, which also it is seemly and profitable to imitate, and which imitating, we may be[8] crowned; but not those in which emulation brings shame to him who imitates them. If thou beholdest the one kind of contest, thou beholdest it with devils; the other, with Angels and Archangels, and the Lord of Archangels. Say now, if thou wert allowed to sit with governors and kings, and to see and enjoy the spectacle, wouldest thou not deem it to be a very great honor? And here when thou art a spectator in company with the King of Angels, when thou seest the devil grasped by the middle of the back,[9] striving much to have the better, but powerless, dost thou not run and pursue after such a sight as this? "And how can this be?" saith some one. If thou keep the Bible in thy hands; for in it thou shalt see the lists, and the long races, and his grasps,[10] and the skill of the righteous one. For by beholding these things thou shalt learn also how to wrestle so thyself, and shalt escape clear of devils; the performances of the heathen are assemblies of devils, not theaters of men. Wherefore I exhort you to abstain from these Satanic assemblies;[11] for if it is not lawful to enter into an idol's house, much less to Satan's festival. I shall not cease to say these things and weary you, until I see some change; for to say these things, as saith Paul, "to me indeed is not grievous, but for you it is safe." (Phil. iii. 1.) Be not then offended at my exhortation. If any one ought to be offended, it is I who often speak and am not heard, not you who are always

---

[1] πυκτίον.    [2] al. "this Law was not given."
[3] i.e. on the Day of Pentecost.
[4] al. "the reality of the matters."
[5] lit. "nature of sin."
[6] al. "the actions," i.e. of the Gospel.

[7] Morel. [let us prepare].
[8] al. "it were meet to be."
[9] Morel. "beholding the devil shamed by means of the Divine oracles, and greatly striving." Below Morel. reads, "run to such a sight."
[10] σκάμματα, διαύλους, λαβὰς, terms of the wrestling school. σκάμμα, the place dug out for the exercise, hence the exercise itself. δίαυλος, the double course. λαβὴ, the gripe of the wrestler. Thus of Job, on Stat. Hom. i. 16; of the Three Children, ib. Hom. iv. 8, &c.    [11] This clause is not found in Ben.

hearing and always disobeying. God grant that you be not always liable to this charge, but that freed from this shame you be deemed worthy to enjoy the spiritual spectacle,[1] and the glory which is to come, through the grace and loving-kindness of our Lord Jesus Christ, with whom to the Father and the Holy Ghost be glory for ever and ever. Amen.

# HOMILY XXXIII.

## John iv. 21, 22.

"Jesus saith unto her, Woman, believe Me, the hour cometh, when ye shall neither in this mountain, nor yet at Jerusalem, worship the Father. Ye worship ye know not what; we know what we worship, for salvation is of the Jews."

[1.] Everywhere, beloved, we have need of faith, faith the mother of blessings, the medicine of salvation; and without this it is impossible to possess any one of the great doctrines. Without this, men are like to those who attempt to cross[2] the open sea without a ship, who for a little way hold out by swimming, using both hands and feet, but when they have advanced farther, are quickly swamped by the waves: in like manner they who use their own reasonings, before they have learnt anything, suffer ship-wreck; as also Paul saith, "Who concerning faith have made shipwreck." (1 Tim. i. 19.) That this be not our case, let us hold fast the sacred anchor by which Christ bringeth over the Samaritan woman now. For when she had said, "How say ye[3] that Jerusalem is the place in which men ought to worship?" Christ replied, "Believe Me, woman, that the hour cometh, when ye shall neither in Jerusalem, nor yet in this mountain, worship the Father." An exceedingly great[4] doctrine He revealed to her, and one which He did not mention either to Nicodemus or Nathanael. She was eager to prove her own privileges more honorable than those of the Jews; and this she subtly argued from the Fathers, but Christ met not this question. For it was for the time distracting[5] to speak on the matter, and to show why the Fathers worshiped in the mountain, and why the Jews at Jerusalem. Wherefore on this point He was silent, and having taken away from both places priority in dignity, rouses her soul by showing that neither Jews nor Samaritans possessed anything great in comparison with that which was to be given; and then He introduceth the difference. Yet even thus He declared that the Jews were more honorable, not preferring place to place, but giving them the precedence because of their intention. As though He had said, "About the 'place' of worship ye have no need henceforth to dispute, but in the 'manner' the Jews have an advantage over you Samaritans, for 'ye,' He saith, 'worship ye know not what; we know what we worship.'"

How then did the Samaritans "know not" what they worshiped? Because they thought that God was local and partial; so at least they served Him, and so they sent to the Persians, and reported that "the God of this place is wroth with us" (2 Kings xxvi.), in this respect forming no higher opinion of Him than of their idols. Wherefore they continued to serve both Him and devils, joining things which ought not to be joined. The Jews, on the contrary, were free from this supposition, at least the greater part of them, and knew that He was God of the world. Therefore He saith, "Ye worship ye know not what; we know what we worship." Do not wonder that He numbereth Himself among Jews, for He speaketh to the woman's opinion of Him as though He were a Jewish Prophet, and therefore He putteth, "we worship." For that He is of the objects of worship is clear to every one, because to worship belongs to the creature, but to be worshiped to the Lord of the creature. But for a time He speaketh as a Jew; and the expression "we" in this place meaneth "we Jews." Having then exalted what was Jewish, He next maketh Himself credible, and persuadeth the woman to give the greater heed to His words, by rendering His discourse above suspicion, and showing that He doth not exalt what belongs to them by reason of relationship[6] to those of His own tribe. For it is clear, that one who had made these declarations concerning the place on which the Jews most prided themselves, and thought that they were superior to all, and who had taken away their high claims, would not after this[7] speak to get favor of any, but with truth and prophetic power. When therefore He had for a while removed her from such reasonings,[8] say-

---

[1] al. "of the Eternal Goods."
[2] διαβαλεῖν, al. διαλαβεῖν, al. διαπερᾶν.
[3] ὑμεῖς λέγετε, G. T.
[4] πολὺ μέγα.
[5] πάρελκον.
[6] al. "favor."
[7] al. "at this rate."
[8] al. "removed (her) reasoning from such things."

ing, "Woman, believe Me," and what follows, then He addeth, "for salvation is of the Jews." What He saith is of this kind: neither, that blessings to the world came from them, (for to know God and condemn idols had its beginning from them, and with you the very act of worship, although ye do it not rightly, yet received its origin from them,) or else, He speaketh of His own Coming. Or rather, one would not be wrong in calling both these things "salvation" which He said was "of the Jews"; which Paul implied when he said, "Of whom is Christ according to the flesh, who is God over all." (Rom. ix. 5.) Seest thou how He commendeth[1] the old Covenant, and showeth that it is the root of blessings, and that He is throughout not opposed to the Law, since He maketh the groundwork[2] of all good things to come from the Jews?

Ver. 23. "But the hour cometh, and now is, when the true worshipers shall worship the Father."

"We, O woman," He saith, "excel you in the manner of our worship, but even this shall henceforth have an end. Not the places only, but even the manner of serving God shall be changed. And this change is at your very doors. 'For the hour cometh, and now is.'"

[2.] For since what the Prophets said they said long before the event, to show that here it is not so,[3] He saith, "And now is." Think not, He saith, that this is a prophecy of such a kind as shall be accomplished after a long time, the fulfillment is already at hand and at your very doors, "when the true worshipers shall worship the Father in spirit and in truth." In saying "true,"[4] He excludeth Jews as well as Samaritans; for although the Jews be better than the Samaritans, yet are they far inferior to those that shall come, as inferior as is the type to the reality. But He speaketh of the Church, that she[5] is the "true" worship, and such as is meet for God.

"For the Father seeketh such to worship Him."

If then He in times past sought such as these, He allowed to those others their way of worship, not willingly,[6] but from condescension, and for this reason,[7] that He might bring them in also. Who then are "the true worshipers"? Those who confine not their service by place, and who serve God in spirit; as Paul saith, "Whom I serve in my spirit[8] in the Gospel of His Son": and again, "I beseech you that ye present your bodies a living sacrifice, acceptable unto God, your reasonable service." (Rom. i. 9 and xii. 1.) But when he saith,

Ver. 24. "God is a Spirit" [God is spirit].

He declareth nothing else than His incorporeal Nature. Now the service of that which is incorporeal must needs be of the same character, and must be offered by that in us which is incorporeal, to wit, the soul, and purity of mind. Wherefore He saith, "they that worship Him, must worship Him in spirit and in truth." For because both Samaritans and Jews were careless about the soul, but took great pains about the body, cleansing it in divers ways, it is not, He saith, by purity of body, but by that which is incorporeal in us, namely the mind, that the incorporeal One is served. Sacrifice then not sheep and calves, but dedicate thyself to the Lord; make thyself a holocaust, this is to offer a living sacrifice. Ye must worship "in truth"[9]; as former things were types, such as circumcision, and whole burnt offerings, and victims, and incense, they now no longer exist, but all is "truth." For a man must now circumcise not his flesh, but his evil thoughts, and crucify himself, and remove and slay his unreasonable desires." The woman was made dizzy by His discourse, and fainted[10] at the sublimity of what He said, and, in her trouble, hear what she saith:

Ver. 25, 26. "I know that Messias cometh, which is called Christ: when He is come, He will tell us all things. Jesus saith unto her, I am that speak unto thee."

And whence came the Samaritans to expect the coming of Christ, seeing that they received Moses only?[11] From the writings of Moses themselves. For even in the beginning He revealed the Son. "Let Us make man in Our Image, after Our Likeness" (Gen. i. 26), was said to the Son. It was He who talked with Abraham in the tent. (Gen. xviii.) And Jacob prophesying concerning Him said, "A ruler shall not fail from Judah, nor a leader from his thighs, until He come for whom it is reserved,[12] and He is the expectation of nations." (Gen. xviii.) And Moses himself saith, "The Lord thy God will raise up unto you a Prophet of your brethren like unto me, unto Him shall ye hearken." (Deut. xviii. 15.) And the circumstances attending the serpent, and the rod of Moses, and Isaac, and the sheep, and many other things they who chose might select as proclaiming His coming.

"And why, pray," saith one, "did not Christ lead on the woman by these means? why did He instance the serpent to Nicodemus, and

---

[1] συγκροτεῖ.
[2] ὑπόθεσιν.
[3] lit. "removing this."
[4] al. "truth."
[5] or, "this."
[6] The passage is read differently in the MS. in Bodl. "not willing them to continue in those ancient (practices)."
[7] al. "by these means."
[8] al. "in spirit. where? in," &c.
[9] MS. in Bodl. "this is to *worship in truth*."
[10] ἀπηγόρευσε.
[11] MS. in Bodl. "the law of Moses."          [12] ᾧ ἀπόκειται.

mention prophecy to Nathanael, but to her say nothing of the kind? For what reason, and why?" Because they were men, and were versed in these things, she a poor ignorant woman unpracticed in the Scriptures. Wherefore He doth not speak to her from them, but draweth her on by the "water" and by prophecy, and bringeth her to make mention of Christ, and then revealeth Himself; which had He at first told the woman when she had not questioned Him, He would have seemed to her to trifle and talk idly, while as it is by bringing her little by little to mention Him, at a fitting time He revealed Himself. To the Jews, who continually said, "How long dost Thou make us to doubt? tell us if Thou art the Christ" (c. x. 24), to them[1] He gave no clear answer, but to this woman He said plainly, that HE IS. For the woman was more fair-minded than the Jews; they did not enquire to learn, but always to mock at Him, for had they desired to learn, the teaching which was by His words, and by the Scriptures, and by His miracles would have been sufficient. The woman, on the contrary, said what she said from an impartial judgment and a simple mind, as is plain from what she did afterwards; for she both heard and believed, and netted[2] others also, and in every circumstance we may observe the carefulness and faith of the woman.

Ver. 27. "And upon this came His disciples," (very seasonably did they come when the teaching was finished,) "and marveled that He talked with the woman, yet no man said, What seekest Thou? or, Why talkest Thou with her?"

[3.] At what did they marvel? At His want of pride and exceeding humility, that looked upon as He was, He endured with such lowliness of heart to talk with a woman poor, and a Samaritan. Still in their amazement they did not ask Him the reason, so well were they taught to keep the station of disciples, so much did they fear and reverence Him. For although they did not as yet hold the right opinion concerning Him, still they gave heed unto Him as to some marvelous one, and paid Him much respect. Yet they frequently are seen to act confidently; as when John lay upon His bosom, when they came to Him and said, "Who is the greatest in the Kingdom of Heaven?" (Matt. xviii. 1), when the sons of Zebedee entreated Him to set one of them on His right hand, and the other on His left. Why then did they not here question Him? Because since all those instances related to themselves, they had need to enquire into them, while what here took place was of no such great importance to them. And indeed John did that a long time after towards

the very end, when He enjoyed greater confidence, and was bold in the love of Christ; for he it was,[3] he saith, "whom Jesus loved." What could equal such blessedness?

But, beloved, let us not stop at this, the calling the Apostle blessed, but let us do all things that we also may be of the blessed, let us imitate the Evangelist, and see what it was that caused such great love. What then was it? He left his father, his ship, and his net, and followed Jesus. Yet this he did in common with his brother, and Peter, and Andrew, and the rest of the Apostles. What then was the special[4] thing which caused this great love? Shall we discover it? He saith nothing of this kind about himself, but only that he was beloved; as to the righteous acts for which he was beloved he has modestly been silent. That Jesus loved him with an especial love was clear to every one; yet John doth not appear conversing with or questioning Jesus privately, as Peter often did, and Philip, and Judas, and Thomas, except only when he desired to show kindness and compliance to his fellow Apostle; for when the chief[5] of the Apostles by beckoning constrained him, then he asked. For these two had great love each for the other. Thus, for instance, they are seen going up together into the Temple and speaking in common to the people. Yet Peter in many places[6] is moved, and speaks more warmly than John. And at the end he hears Christ say, "Peter,[7] lovest thou Me more than these?" (c. xxi. 15.) Now it is clear that he who loved "more than these" was also beloved. But this in his case was shown by loving Jesus, in the case of the other by being beloved by Jesus.[8]

What then was it which caused this especial love? To my thinking, it was that the man displayed great gentleness and meekness, for which reason he doth not appear in many places speaking openly. And how great a thing this is, is plain also from the case of Moses. It was this which made him such and so great as he was. There is nothing equal to lowliness of mind. For which cause Jesus with this began the Beatitudes, and when about to lay as it were the foundation and base of a mighty building, He placed first lowliness of mind. Without this a man cannot possibly be saved; though he fast, though he pray, though he give alms, if it be with a proud spirit, these[9] things are abominable, if humility be not there; while if it be, all these things are amiable and lovely, and are

---

[1] al. "this."     [2] ἐσαγήνευσε.

[3] MS. in Bodleian, "for, saith the Evangelist, Peter looks on the disciple."
[4] ἐξαίρετον.     [5] κορυφαῖος.
[6] al. "all places."     [7] Σίμων Ἰωνᾶ, G. T.
[8] i.e. St. Peter loved his Lord, and therefore we *infer* that he was loved of Him; of St. John Scripture speaks expressly, as being "the Disciple whom Jesus loved."
[9] al. "all."

done with safety. Let us then be modest,[1] beloved, let us be modest; success is easy, if we be sober-minded. For after all what is it, O man, that exciteth thee to pride? Seest thou not the poverty of thy nature? the unsteadiness[2] of thy will? Consider thine end, consider the multitude of thy sins. But perhaps because thou doest many righteous deeds thou art proud. By that very pride thou shalt undo them all. Wherefore it behoveth not so much him that has sinned[3] as him that doeth righteousness to take pains to be humble. Why so? Because the sinner is constrained by conscience, while the other, except he be very sober, soon caught up as by a blast of wind is lifted on high, and made to vanish like the Pharisee. Dost thou give to the poor? What thou givest is not thine, but thy Master's, common to thee and thy fellow-servants. For which cause thou oughtest especially to be humbled, in the calamities of those who are thy kindred foreseeing thine own, and taking knowledge of thine own nature in their cases. We ourselves perhaps are sprung from such ancestors; and if wealth has shifted to you, it is probable that it will leave you again. And after all, what is wealth? A vain[5] shadow, dissolving smoke, a flower of the grass, or rather something meaner than a flower. Why then art thou high-minded over grass? Doth not wealth fall to thieves, and effeminates, and harlots, and tomb-breakers? Doth this puff thee up, that thou hast such as these to share in thy possesion? or dost thou desire honor? Towards gaining honor nothing is more serviceable than almsgiving. For the honors arising from wealth and power are compulsory, and attended with hatred, but these others are from the free will and real feeling of the honorers; and therefore those who pay them can never give them up. Now if men show such reverence for the merciful, and invoke all blessings upon them, consider what return, what recompense they shall receive from the merciful God. Let us then seek this wealth which endureth forever, and never deserts[6] us, that, becoming great here and glorious there, we may obtain everlasting blessings, through the grace and lovingkindness of our Lord Jesus Christ, with whom to the Father and the Holy Spirit be glory, now and ever, and world without end. Amen.

# HOMILY XXXIV.

### JOHN iv. 28, 29.

"The woman then left her water pot, and went her way into the city, and saith to the men, Come, see a Man which told me all things that ever I did; is not this the Christ?"

[1.] WE require much fervor and uproused zeal, for without these it is impossible to obtain the blessings promised to us. And to show this, Christ at one time saith, "Except a man take[4] up his cross and follow Me, he is not worthy of Me" (Matt. x. 38); at another, "I am come to send fire upon the earth, and what will I if it be already kindled?" (Luke xii. 49); by both these desiring to represent to us a disciple full of heat and fire, and prepared for every danger. Such an one was this woman. For so kindled was she by His words, that she left her water pot and the purpose for which she came, ran into the city, and drew all the people to Jesus. "Come," she saith, "see a Man which told me all things that ever I did."

Observe her zeal and wisdom. She came to draw water, and when she had lighted upon the true Well, she after that despised the material one; teaching us even by this trifling instance when we are listening to spiritual matters to overlook the things of this life, and make no account of them. For what the Apostles did, that, after her ability, did this woman also.[7] They when they were called, left their nets; she of her own accord, without the command of any, leaves her water pot, and winged by joy[8] performs the office of Evangelists. And she calls not one or two, as did Andrew and Philip, but having aroused a whole city and people, so brought them to Him.

Observe too how prudently she speaks; she said not, "Come and see the Christ," but with the same condescension[9] by which Christ had netted her she draws the men to Him; "Come," she saith, "see a Man who told me all that ever I did." She was not ashamed to say that He "told me all that ever I did." Yet she might have spoken otherwise, "Come, see one that prophesieth"; but when the soul is inflamed with holy fire, it looks then to nothing earthly, neither to glory nor to shame, but belongs to one thing alone, the flame which occupieth it.

---

[1] μετριάζωμεν.   [2] τὸ εὐόλισθον.   [3] al. "that sinneth."
[4] ὃς οὐ λαμβάνει κ.τ.λ. G. T.

[5] ἀδρανής.
[6] δραπετεύοντα.
[7] Ben. "in a higher degree."

[8] al. "by grace."
[9] i.e. to their infirmity.

"Is not this the Christ?" Observe again here the great wisdom of the woman; she neither declared the fact plainly, nor was she silent, for she desired not to bring them in by her own assertion, but to make them to share in this opinion by hearing Him; which rendered her words more readily acceptable to them. Yet He had not told all her life to her, only from what had been said she was persuaded (that He was informed) as to the rest. Nor did she say, "Come, believe," but, "Come, see"; a gentler[1] expression than the other, and one which more attracted them. Seest thou the wisdom of the woman? She knew, she knew certainly that having but tasted that Well, they would be affected in the same manner as herself. Yet any one of the grosser sort would have concealed the reproof which Jesus had given; but she parades her own life, and brings it forward before all men, so as to attract and capture all.

Ver. 31. "In the mean time His disciples asked[2] Him, saying, Master, eat." "Asked," here is "besought," in their native language; for seeing Him wearied with the journey, and the oppressive heat, they entreated Him; for their request concerning food proceeded not from hastiness, but from loving affection for their Teacher? What then saith Christ?

Ver. 32, 33. "I have meat to eat that ye know not of. Therefore" (saith the Evangelist) "said the disciples one to another, Hath any man brought Him aught to eat?"

Why now wonderest thou that the woman when she heard of "water," still imagined mere water to be meant, when even the disciples are in the same case, and as yet suppose nothing spiritual, but are perplexed? though they still show their accustomed modesty and reverence toward their Master, conversing one with the other, but not daring to put any question to Him. And this they do in other places, desiring to ask Him, but not asking. What then saith Christ?

Ver. 34. "My meat is to do the will of Him that sent Me, and to finish His work."

He here calleth the salvation of men "meat," showing what an earnest desire He hath of providing for us;[3] for as we long for food, so He that we may be saved. And hear how in all places He revealeth not all off-hand, but first throweth the hearer into perplexity, in order that having begun to seek the meaning of what has been said, and then being perplexed and in difficulty, he may when what he sought appears, receive it the more readily, and be made more attentive to listening. For wherefore said He not at once, "My meat is to do the will of My

Father?" (though not even this would have been clear, yet clearer than the other.) But what saith He? "I have meat to eat that ye know not of"; for He desireth, as I said, first to make them more attentive through their uncertainty, and by dark sayings like these to accustom them to listen to His words. But what is "the will of the Father"? He next speaketh of this, and explaineth.

Ver. 35. "Say ye not, that there are yet four months, and then cometh harvest? Behold, I say unto you, Lift up your eyes, and look upon the fields, for they are white already to harvest."

[2.] Behold, He again by familiar words leadeth them up to the consideration of greater matters; for when He spoke of "meat," He signified nothing else than the salvation of the men who should come to Him; and again, the "field" and the "harvest" signify the very same thing, the multitude of souls prepared for the reception of the preaching; and the "eyes" of which He speaketh are those both of the mind and of the body; (for they now beheld the crowd of Samaritans advancing;) and the readiness of their will He calleth, "fields already white." For as the ears of corn, when they have become white, and are ready for reaping, so these, He saith, are prepared and fitted for salvation.

And wherefore instead of calling them "fields" and "harvest," did He not plainly say, that "the men were coming to believe and were ready to receive the Word, having been instructed by the Prophets, and now bringing forth fruit"? What mean these figures used by Him? for this He doth not here only, but through all the Gospel; and the Prophets also employ the same method, saying many things in a metaphorical manner. What then may be the cause of this? for the grace of the Spirit did not ordain it to be so without a reason, but why and wherefore? On two accounts; one, that the discourse may be more vivid, and bring what is said more clearly before our eyes. For the mind when it has laid hold on a familiar image of the matters in hand, is more aroused, and beholding them as it were in a picture, is occupied by them to a greater degree. This is one reason; the other is, that the statement may be sweetened, and that the memory of what is said may be more lasting. For assertion does not subdue and bring in an ordinary hearer so much as narration by objects, and the representation of experience.[4] Which one may here see most wisely effected by the parable.

Ver. 36. "And he that reapeth receiveth wages, and gathereth fruit unto life eternal."

For the fruit of an earthly harvest profiteth

[1] al. "more fearful."
[2] ἠρώτων. E. V. prayed: Ben. and MS. in Bodl. ἠρώτων ἐνταῦθα παρεκαλοῦν ἐστι, τῇ ἐγχωρίῳ αὐτῶν φωνῇ.
[3] MS. in Bodl. "our salvation."
[4] i.e. given by means of things which are objects of experience. ὑπογραφὴ πείρας, al. πεῖρα.

not to life eternal, but to this which is for a time; but the spiritual fruit to that which hath neither age nor death. Seest thou that the expressions are of sense, but the thoughts spiritual, and that by the very words themselves He divideth things earthly from heavenly? For when in discoursing of water He made this the peculiar property of the heavenly Water, that " he who drinketh it shall never thirst," so He doth here also when He saith, " that this fruit is gathered unto eternal life."

" That both he that soweth and he that reapeth may rejoice together."

Who is " he that soweth"? Who " he that reapeth"? The Prophets are they that sowed, but they reaped not, but the Apostles. " Yet not on this account are they deprived of the pleasure and recompense of their labors, but they rejoice and are glad with us, although they reap not with us. For harvest is not such work as sowing. I therefore have kept you for that in which the toil is less and the pleasure greater, and not for sowing because in that there is much hardship and toil. In harvest the return is large, the labor not so great; nay there is much facility."[1] By these arguments He here desireth to prove, that " the wish of the Prophets is, that all men should come to Me." This also the Law was engaged in effecting; and for this they sowed, that they might produce this fruit.[2] He showeth moreover that He sent them also, and that there was a very intimate connection between the New Covenant and the Old, and all this He effecteth at once by this parable. He maketh mention also of a proverbial expression generally circulated.

Ver. 37. " Herein," He saith, " is that saying true, One soweth and another reapeth."

These words the many used whenever one party had supplied toil and another had reaped the fruits; and He saith, " that the proverb is in this instance especially true, for the Prophets labored, and ye reap the fruits of their labors." He said not " the rewards," (for neither did their great labor go unrewarded,) but " the fruits." This also Daniel did, for he too makes mention of a proverb, " Wickedness proceedeth from the wicked"; and David in his lamenting makes mention of a similar proverb.[3] Therefore He said beforehand, " that both he that soweth and he that reapeth may rejoice together." For since He was about to declare, that " one hath sowed and another reapeth," lest any one should deem that the Prophets were deprived of their reward, He asserteth something strange and

paradoxical, such as never chanceth in sensual things, but is peculiar to spiritual only. For in things of sense, if it chance that one sow and another reap, they do not " rejoice together," but those who sowed are sad, as having labored for others, and those who reap alone rejoice. But here it is not so, but those who reap not what they sowed rejoice alike with those who reap; whence it is clear that they too share the reward.

Ver. 38. " I sent you to reap that whereon ye bestowed no labor; other men labored, and ye are entered into their labors."

By this He the more encourageth them; for when it seemed a very hard matter to go through all the world and preach the Gospel, He showeth them that it is even most[4] easy. The very difficult work was that other, which required great labor, the putting in the seed, and introducing the uninitiated soul to the knowledge of God. But wherefore uttereth He these sayings? It is that when He sendeth them to preach they may not be confounded, as though sent on a difficult task. " For that of the Prophets," He saith, " was the more difficult, and the fact witnesseth to My word, that ye are come to what is easy; because as in harvest time the fruits are collected with ease, and in one moment the floor is filled with sheaves, which await[5] not the revolutions of the seasons, and winter, and spring, and rain, so it is now. The facts proclaim it aloud." While He was in the midst of saying these things, the Samaritans came forth, and the fruit was at once gathered together. On this account[6] He said, " Lift up your eyes, and look on the fields, that they are white." Thus He spake, and the fact was clear, and the words seen (true) by the event. For saith St. John,

Ver. 39. "Many of the Samaritans of that city believed on Him for the saying of the woman which testified, He told me all that ever I did."

They perceived[7] that the woman would not from favor have admired One who had rebuked her sins, nor to gratify another have paraded her own course of life.

[3.] Let us then also imitate this woman, and in the case of our own sins not be ashamed of men, but fear, as is meet, God who now beholdeth what is done, and who hereafter punisheth those who do not now repent. At present we do the opposite of this, for we fear not Him who shall judge us, but shudder at those who do not in anything hurt us, and tremble at the shame which comes from them. Therefore in the very thing which we fear, in this do we incur punishment. For he who now regards only the reproach of men, but when God seeth is not

---

[1] εὐκολία, al. ῥαστώνη.     [2] al. " by this."
[3] There is no authority for a different reading, but it seems to be rightly conjectured by Savile and Ben. that the names " Daniel" and " David" should be transposed. The proverb is that used by David, 1 Sam. xxiv. 13, and the other passage alluded to may be Dan. xii. 10, " the wicked shall do wickedly." MS. in Bodl. reads, ἀνομία ἐκ βαβυλῶνος for ἐξ ἀνόμων πλημμελεία.

[4] al. " more."     [5] al. " awaits."
[6] MS. in Bodl. " alluding to these."
[7] MS. in Bodl. " as soon as they heard the woman they believed, for they," &c.

ashamed to do anything unseemly, and who will not repent and be converted, in that day will be made an example, not only before one or two, but in the sight of the whole world. For that a vast assembly is seated there to behold righteous actions as well as those which are not such, let the parable of the sheep and the goats teach thee, as also the blessed Paul when He saith, "For we must all appear before the judgment-seat of Christ, that every one may receive the things done in his body, according to that he hath done, whether it be good or bad" (2 Cor. v. 10), and again, "Who will bring to light the hidden things of darkness." (1 Cor. iv. 5.) Hast thou done or imagined any evil thing, and dost thou hide it from man? yet from God thou hidest it not. But for this thou careth nothing; the eyes of men, these are thy fear. Think then that thou wilt not be able to escape the sight even of men in that day [1]; for all things as in a picture shall then be set before our very eyes, so that each shall be self-condemned. This is clear even from the instance of Dives, for the poor man whom he had neglected, Lazarus I mean, he saw standing before his eyes, and the finger which he had often loathed, he intreats may become a comfort to him then. I exhort you therefore, that although no one see what we do, yet that each of us enter into his own con-science, and set reason for his judge, and bring forward his transgressions, and if he desire them not to be exposed to public view then in that fearful day, let him now heal his wounds, let him apply to them the medicines of repentance. For it is in the power, yea, it is in the power of one full of ten thousand wounds to go hence whole. For "if ye forgive," He saith, "your sins are forgiven unto you." [2] (Matt. vi. 14, not verbally quoted.) For as sins buried [3] in Baptism appear no more, so these [4] also shall disappear, if we be willing to repent. And repentance is the not doing the same again; for he that again puts his hand to the same, is like the dog that returneth to his own vomit, and like him in the proverb who cards wool into the fire, [5] and draws water into a cask full of holes. It behoves therefore to de-part both in action and in thought from what we have dared to do, and having departed, to apply to the wounds the remedies which are the contra-ries of our sins. For instance: hast thou been grasping and covetous? Abstain from rapine, and apply almsgiving to the wound. Hast thou been a fornicator? Abstain from fornication, and apply chastity to the wound. Hast thou spoken

ill of thy brother, and injured him? Cease find-ing fault, [6] and apply kindness. Let us thus act with respect to each point in which we have offended, and let us not carelessly pass by our sins, for there awaiteth us hereafter, there awaiteth us a season of account. Wherefore also Paul said, "The Lord is at hand: be care-ful for nothing." (Phil. iv. 5, 6.) But we per-haps must add the contrary of this, "The Lord is at hand, be careful." For they might well hear, "Be careful for nothing," living as they did in affliction, and labors, and trials; but they who live by rapine, or in luxury, and who shall give a grievous reckoning, would in reason hear not this, but that other, "The Lord is at hand, be careful." Since no long time now remains until the consummation, but the world is hastening to its end; this the wars declare, this the afflictions, this the earthquakes, this the love which hath waxed cold. For as the body when in its last gasp and near to death, draws to itself ten thou-sand sufferings; and as when a house is about to fall, many portions are wont to fall beforehand from the roof and walls; so is the end of the world nigh and at the very doors, and therefore ten thousand woes are everywhere scattered abroad. If the Lord was then "at hand," much more is He now "at hand." If three hundred [7] years ago, when those words were used, Paul called that season "the fullness of time," much more would he have called the present so. But perhaps for this very reason some disbelieve, yet they ought on this account to believe the more. For whence knowest thou, O man, that the end is not "at hand," and the words shortly to be accomplished? For as we speak of the end of the year not as being the last day, but also the last month, though it has thirty days; so if of so many years I call even four hundred years "the end," I shall not be wrong; and so at that time Paul spoke of the end by anticipation. Let us then set ourselves in order, let us delight in the fear of God; for if we live here without fear of Him, His coming will surprise us suddenly, when we are neither careful, nor looking for Him. As Christ declared when He said, "For as in the days of Noah, and as in the days of Lot, so shall it be at the end of this world." (Matt. xxiv. 37, not verbally quoted.) This also Paul declared when he said, "For when they shall say, Peace and safety, then sudden destruction cometh upon them, as travail upon a woman with child." (1 Thess. v. 3.) What means, "as travail upon a woman with child"? Often have pregnant women when sporting, or at their meals, or in the bath or market-place, and foreseeing nothing of what was coming, been seized in a moment by their pains. Now since

---

[1] MS. in Bodleian reads here, "and be more careful than thy (present) self."
[2] MS. in Bodl. reads, "My Heavenly Father will also forgive you, but if ye forgive not, neither will He forgive you."
[3] καταχωννύμενα.
[4] i.e. sins done after Baptism.
[5] Εἰς πῦρ ξαίνοντι. Plat. *Legg.* vi. p. 750. "And like," &c. is not in the text of Savile.

[6] al. "speaking evil."
[7] al. "four hundred."

our case is like theirs, let us ever be prepared, for we shall not always hear these things, we shall not always have power to do them. "In the grave," saith David, "who shall give Thee thanks?"[1] (Ps. vi. 5.) Let us then repent here, that so we may find God merciful unto us in the day that is to come, and be enabled to enjoy abundant forgiveness; which may we all obtain, through the grace and lovingkindness of our Lord Jesus Christ, to whom be glory and dominion now and ever, and world without end. Amen.

# HOMILY XXXV.

## JOHN iv. 40–43.

"So when the Samaritans were come unto Him, they besought Him that He would tarry with them: and He abode there two days. And many more believed because of His own Word; and said unto the woman, Now we believe, not because of thy saying: for we have heard Him ourselves, and know that This is indeed the Christ, the Saviour of the world. Now after two days He departed thence, and went into Galilee."

NOTHING is worse than envy and malice, nothing more mischievous than vainglory; it is wont to mar ten thousand good things. So the Jews, who excelled the Samaritans in knowledge, and had been always familiar with[2] the Prophets, were shown from this cause inferior to them. For these believed even on the testimony of the woman, and without having seen any sign, came forth beseeching Christ to tarry[3] with them; but the Jews, when they had beheld His wonders, not only did not detain Him among them, but even drove Him away, and used every means to cast Him forth from their land, although His very Coming[4] had been for their sake. The Jews expelled Him, but these even entreated Him to tarry with them. Was it not then rather fitting, tell me, that He should receive those who asked and besought Him, than that He should wait upon those who plotted against and repulsed Him, while to those who loved and desired to retain Him He gave not Himself? Surely this would not have been worthy of His tender care;[5] He therefore both accepted[6] them, and tarried with them two days. They desired to keep Him among them continually, (for this the Evangelist has shown by saying, that "they besought Him that He would tarry with them,") but this He endured not, but stayed with them only two days; and in these many more believed on Him. Yet there was no likelihood that these would have believed, since they had seen no sign, and had hostile feelings towards the Jews; but still, inasmuch as they gave in sincerity their judgment on His words, this stood not in their way, but they received a notion which surmounted their hindrances, and vied with each other to reverence Him the more. For, saith the Evangelist, "they said to the woman, Now we believe, not because of thy saying: for we have heard Him ourselves, and know that this is indeed the Christ, the Saviour of the world." The scholars overshot their instructress. With good reason might they condemn the Jews, both by their believing on, and their receiving Him. The Jews, for whose sake He had contrived[7] the whole scheme,[8] continually were for stoning Him,[9] but these, when He was not even intending to come to them, drew Him to themselves. And they, even with signs, remain uncorrected; these, without signs, manifested great faith respecting Him, and glory in this very thing that they believe without them; while the others ceased not asking[10] for signs and tempting Him.

Such need is there everywhere of an honest soul; and if truth lay hold on such an one, she easily masters it; or if she masters it not, this is owing not to any weakness of truth, but to want of candor[11] in the soul itself. Since the sun too, when he encounters clear eyes, easily enlightens them; if he enlightens them not, it is the fault of their infirmity, not of his weakness.

Hear then what these say; "We know that this is of a truth the Christ, the Saviour of the world." Seest thou how they at once understood that He should draw the world to Him, that He came to order aright[12] our common salvation, that He intended not to confine His care to the Jews, but to sow His Word everywhere? The Jews did not so, but going about to establish their own righteousness, submitted not themselves to the righteousness of God; while these confess that all are deserving of punishment, declaring with the Apostle, that "all have sinned, and come short of the glory of God; being justified freely by His grace." (Rom. iii. 23, 24.)

---

1 or, "confess to Thee."
2 lit. "brought up with."
3 al. "to be."
4 Ben. "that coming."
5 κηδεμονίας.
6 al. "elected."
7 al. "instituted."
8 i.e. of Redemption. πᾶσαν τὴν πραγματείαν συνεστήσατο.
9 al. "them," i.e. the Prophets.
10 al. "seeking."
11 ἀγνωμοσύνην.
12 ἐπὶ διορθώσει.

For by saying that He was "the Saviour of the world," they showed that it was of a lost world,[1] and He not simply a Saviour, but one of the very mightiest. For many had come to "save," both Prophets and Angels[2]; but this, saith one, is the True Saviour, who affordeth the true salvation, not that which is but for a time. This proceeded from pure faith. And in both ways are they admirable; because they believed, and because they did so without signs, (whom Christ also calleth "blessed," saying, "Blessed are they that have not seen, and yet have believed,") (c. xx. 29,) and because they did so sincerely. Though they had heard the woman say doubtfully, "Is not this the Christ?" they did not also say, "we too suspect," or, "we think,"[3] but, "we know," and not merely, "we know," but, "we know that this is of a truth the Saviour of the world." They acknowledged Christ not as one of the many,[4] but as the "Saviour" indeed. Yet whom had they seen saved? They had but heard His words, and yet they spake as they would have spoken had they beheld many and great marvels. And why do not the Evangelists tell us these words, and that He discoursed admirably? That thou mayest learn that they pass by many important matters, and yet have declared the whole to us by the event. For He persuaded an entire people and a whole city by His words. When His hearers are not persuaded, then the writers are constrained to mention what was said, lest any one from the insensibility of the hearers should give a judgment against Him who addressed them.

"Now after two days He departed thence and went into Galilee."

Ver. 44. "For Jesus Himself testified that a Prophet hath no honor in his own country."

Wherefore is this added? Because He departed not unto Capernaum, but into Galilee, and thence to Cana. For that thou mayest not enquire why He tarried not with His own people, but tarried with the Samaritans, the Evangelist puts the cause,[5] saying that they gave no heed unto Him; on this account He went not thither, that their condemnation might not be the greater. For I suppose that in this place He speaketh of Capernaum as "His country." Now, to show that there He received no honor, hear Him say, "And thou, Capernaum, which art exalted unto heaven, shalt be brought down to hell." (Matt. xi. 23.) He calleth it "His own country," because there He set forth the Word of the Dispensation, and more especially dwelt upon it. "What then," saith some one,

"do we not see many admired among their kindred?" In the first place such judgments must not be formed from rare instances; and again, if some have been honored in their own, they would have been much more honored in a strange country, for familiarity is wont to make men easily despised.

Ver. 45. "Then when He was come into Galilee, the Galilæans received Him, having seen all the things that He did at Jerusalem at the feast, for they also came unto the feast."

Seest thou that these men so ill spoken of are found most to come to Him? For one said, "Can there any good thing come out of Nazareth?" (c. i. 46), and another, "Search and look, for out of Galilee ariseth no prophet." (c. vii. 52.) These things they said insulting Him, because He was supposed by the many to be of Nazareth, and they also reproached Him with being a Samaritan; "Thou art a Samaritan," said one, "and hast a devil." (c. viii. 48.) Yet behold, both Samaritans and Galilæans believe, to the shame of the Jews, and Samaritans are found better than Galilæans, for the first received Him through the words of the woman, the second when they had seen the miracles which He did.

Ver. 46. "So Jesus came again into Cana of Galilee, where He made the water wine."

The Evangelist reminds the hearer of the miracle to exalt the praise of the Samaritans. The men of Cana received Him by reason of the miracles which He had done in Jerusalem and in that place; but not so the Samaritans, they received Him through His teaching alone.

That He came then "to Cana," the Evangelist has said, but he has not added the cause why He came.[6] Into Galilee He had come because of the envy of the Jews; but wherefore to Cana? At first He came, being invited to a marriage; but wherefore now? Methinks to confirm by His presence the faith which had been implanted by His miracle, and to draw them to Him the more by coming to them self-invited, by leaving His own country, and by preferring them.

"And there was a certain nobleman whose son was sick at Capernaum."

Ver. 47. "When he heard that Jesus was come out of Judæa into Galilee, he went unto Him and besought Him that He would come down and heal his son."

This person certainly was of royal race, or possessed some dignity from his office, to which the title "noble" was attached. Some indeed think that this is the man mentioned by Matthew (Matt. viii. 5), but he is shown to be a different person, not only from his dignity, but also from his faith. That other, even when Christ was

---

[1] MS. in Bodl. reads, "and why say I of a lost world? of a world which was in evils great exceedingly."

[2] or, "messengers."

[3] al. "suppose."

[4] i.e. who had wrought deliverances.

[5] MS. in Bodl. "and this is, that 'a prophet hath no honor in his own country.'"

[6] MS. in Bodl. reads, "and why, saith some one, went He again to Cana?"

willing to go to him, entreats Him to tarry; this one, when He had made no such offer, draws Him to his house. The one saith, "I am not worthy that Thou shouldest come under my roof"; but this other even urges[1] Him, saying, "Come down ere my son die." In that instance He came down from the mountain, and entered into Capernaum; but here, as He came from Samaria, and went not into Capernaum but into Cana, this person met Him. The servant of the other was possessed by the palsy, this one's son by a fever.

"And he came and besought Him that He would heal his son: for he was at the point of death." What saith Christ?

Ver. 48. "Except ye see signs and wonders, ye will not believe."

Yet the very coming and beseeching Him was a mark of faith. And besides, after this the Evangelist witnesses to him,[2] declaring that when Jesus said, "Go, thy son liveth," he believed His word, and went. What then is that which He saith here? Either He useth the words as approving of[3] the Samaritans because they believed without signs; or, to touch Capernaum which was thought to be His own city, and of which this person was. Moreover, another man in Luke, who says, "Lord, I believe," said besides, "help Thou mine unbelief."[4] And so if this ruler also believed, yet he believed not entirely or soundly, as is clear from his enquiring "at what hour the fever left him," since he desired to know whether it did so of its own accord, or at the bidding of Christ. When therefore he knew that it was "yesterday at the seventh hour," then "himself believed and his whole house." Seest thou that he believed when his servants, not when Christ spake? Therefore He rebuketh the state of mind with which he had come to Him, and spoken as he did, (thus too He the more drew him on to belief,) because that before the miracle he had not believed strongly. That he came and entreated was nothing wonderful, for parents in their great affection are also wont to resort not only to physicians in whom they have confidence, but also to talk with those in whom they have no confidence, desiring to omit nothing whatever.[5] Indeed, that he came without any strong purpose[6] appears from this, that when Christ was come into Galilee, then he saw Him, whereas if he had firmly believed in Him, he would not, when his child was on the point of death, have hesitated to go into Judæa. Or if he was afraid, this is not to be endured either.[7]

Observe how the very words show the weakness of the man; when he ought, after Christ had rebuked his state of mind, to have imagined something great concerning Him, even if he did not so before, listen how he drags along the ground.

Ver. 49. "Sir," he saith, "come down ere my child die."

As though He could not raise him after death, as though He knew not what state the child was in. It is for this that Christ rebuketh him and toucheth his conscience, to show that His miracles were wrought principally for the sake of the soul. For here He healeth the father, sick in mind, no less than the son, in order to persuade us to give heed to Him, not by reason of His miracles, but of His teaching. For miracles are not for the faithful, but for the unbelieving and the grosser sort.

[3.] At that time then, owing to his emotion, the nobleman gave no great heed to the words, or to those only which related to his son,[8] yet he would afterwards recollect what had been said, and draw from thence the greatest advantage. As indeed was the case.

But what can be the reason why in the case of the centurion He by a free offer undertook to come, while here though invited, He goeth not? Because in the former case faith had been perfected, and therefore He undertook to go, that we might learn the rightmindedness of the man; but here the nobleman was imperfect. When therefore he continually[9] urged Him, saying, "Come down," and knew not yet clearly that even when absent He could heal, He showeth that even this was possible unto Him in order that this man might gain from Jesus not going, that knowledge which the centurion had of himself.[10] And so when He saith, "Except ye see signs and wonders, ye will not believe," His meaning is, "Ye have not yet the right faith, but still feel towards Me as towards a Prophet." Therefore to reveal Himself and to show that he ought to have believed even without miracles, He said what He said also to Philip, "Believest thou[11] that the Father is in Me and I in the Father?[12] Or if not, believe Me for the very works' sake." (c. xiv. 10, 11.)

Ver. 51-53. "And as he was now going down, his servants met him, and told him, saying, Thy son liveth. Then enquired he of them the hour when he began to amend. And they said unto him, Yesterday at the seventh hour the fever left him. So the father knew that it was at the same hour in the which Jesus said unto him, Thy son liveth; and himself believed, and his whole house."

---

[1] al. "brings on."
[2] al. "witnesses it."  [3] θαυμάζων.
[4] Mark ix. 24 [not found in St. Luke].
[5] MS. in Bodl. adds, "of things belonging to carefulness."
[6] ἐκ παρέργου.  [7] i.e. in a true believer.

[8] Morel. "and regarded only what was taking place concerning his son."
[9] ἄνω καὶ κάτω.
[10] οἴκοθεν.
[11] MS. in Bodl. reads, "He said this as (He said) to the disciples, 'Believe,'" &c.
[12] ἐγὼ ἐν τῷ Πατρὶ καὶ ὁ Πατὴρ ἐν ἐμοί. G. T. and Ben.

Seest thou how evident the miracle was? Not simply nor in a common way was the child freed from danger, but all at once, so that what took place was seen to be the consequence not of nature, but the working[1] of Christ. For when he had reached the very gates of death, as his father showed by saying, "Come down ere my child die"; he was all at once freed from the disease. A fact which roused the servants also, for they perhaps came to meet their master, not only to bring him the good news, but also deeming that the coming of Jesus was now superfluous, (for they knew that their master was gone there,) and so they met him even in the way. The man released from his fear, thenceforth escaped[2] into faith, being desirous to show that what had been done was the result of his journey, and thenceforth he is ambitious of appearing not to have exerted himself[3] to no purpose; so he ascertained all things exactly, and "himself believed and his whole house." For the evidence was after this unquestionable. For they who had not been present nor had heard Christ speak nor known the time, when they had heard from their master that such and such was the time, had incontrovertible demonstration of His power. Wherefore they also believed.

What now are we taught by these things? Not to wait for miracles, nor to seek pledges of the Power of God. I see many persons even now become more pious,[6] when during the sufferings of a child or the sickness of a wife they enjoy any comfort, yet they ought even if they obtain it not, to persist just the same in giving thanks, in glorifying God. Because it is the part of right-minded servants, and of those who feel such affection[7] and love as they ought for their Master, not only when pardoned, but also when scourged, to run to Him. For these also are effects of the tender care of God; "Whom the Lord loveth He chasteneth, and scourgeth," it says, "every son whom He receiveth." (Heb. xii. 6.) When therefore a man serves Him only in the season of ease, he gives proofs of no great love, and loves not Christ purely. And why speak I of health, or abundant riches, or poverty, or disease? Shouldest thou hear of the fiery pit or of any other dreadful thing, not even so must thou cease from speaking good of thy Master, but suffer and do all things because of thy love for Him. For this is the part of right-minded servants and of an unswerving soul; and he who is disposed after this sort will easily endure the present, and obtain good[8] things to come, and enjoy much confidence in the presence of[9] God; which may it be that we all obtain through the grace and lovingkindness of our Lord Jesus Christ, to whom with the Father and the Holy Ghost be glory, now and ever, and world without end. Amen.

# HOMILY XXXVI.

## John iv. 54; v. 1.

"This is again the second miracle that Jesus did, when He was come out of Judæa into Galilee. After this there was a feast of the Jews; and Jesus went up to Jerusalem."

[1.] As in gold mines one skilful in what relates to them would not endure to overlook even the smallest vein as producing much wealth, so in the holy Scriptures it is impossible without loss to pass by one jot or one tittle, we must search into all. For they all are uttered by the Holy Spirit, and nothing useless[4] is written in them.

Consider, for instance, what the Evangelist in this place saith, "This is again the second miracle that Jesus did, when He was come out of Judæa into Galilee." Even the word "second" he has added not without cause, but to exalt yet more the praise[5] of the Samaritans, by showing that even when a second miracle had been wrought, they who beheld it had not yet reached as high as those who had not seen one.

"After this there was a feast of the Jews." What "feast"? Methinks that of Pentecost. "And Jesus went up to Jerusalem." Continually at the feasts He frequenteth the City, partly that He might appear to feast with them, partly that He might attract the multitude that was free from guile; for during these days[10] especially, the more simply disposed ran together more than at other times.

Ver. 2, 3. "Now there is at Jerusalem a sheep pool,[11] called in the Hebrew tongue Bethesda, having five porches. In these lay a great multitude of impotent folk,[12] of halt, blind, withered, waiting for the moving of the water."

---

[1] ἐνεργείας.
[2] διέκυψε.
[3] lit. "been aroused."
[4] lit. "distracting."
[5] lit. "wonder."
[6] εὐλαβεστέρους.　　[7] al. "are stanch."　　[8] al. "all."
[9] al. "from."　　[10] al. "feasts."
[11] προβατικὴ κολυμβήθρα [ἐπὶ τῇ π. G. T.].
[12] [ἀσθενούντων] G. T. and Ben.

What manner of cure is this? What mystery doth it signify to us? For these things are not written carelessly, or without a purpose, but as by a figure and type they show in outline[1] things to come, in order that what was exceedingly strange might not by coming unexpectedly harm among the many the power of faith.[2] What then is it that they show in outline? A Baptism was about to be given, possessing much power, and the greatest of gifts, a Baptism purging all sins, and making men alive instead of dead. These things then are foreshown as in a picture by the pool, and by many other circumstances. And first is given a water which purges the stains of our bodies, and those defilements which are not, but seem to be, as those from touching the dead,[3] those from leprosy, and other similar causes; under the old covenant one may see many things done by water on this account. However, let us now proceed to the matter in hand.

First then, as I before said, He causeth defilements of our bodies, and afterwards infirmities of different kinds, to be done away by water. Because God, desiring to bring us nearer to faith in[4] baptism, no longer healeth defilements only, but diseases also. For those figures which came nearer [in time] to the reality, both as regarded Baptism, and the Passion, and the rest, were plainer than the more ancient;[5] and as the guards near the person of the prince are more splendid than those before,[6] so was it with the types. And "an Angel came down and troubled the water," and endued it with a healing power, that the Jews might learn that much more could the Lord of Angels heal the diseases[7] of the soul. Yet as here it was not simply the nature of the water that healed, (for then this would have always taken place,) but water joined to the operation[8] of the Angel; so in our case, it is not merely the water that worketh, but when it hath received the grace of the Spirit, then it putteth away[9] all our sins. Around this pool "lay a great multitude of impotent folk, of blind, halt, withered, waiting for the moving of the water"; but then infirmity was a hindrance to him who desired to be healed, now each hath power to approach, for now it is not an Angel that troubleth, it is the Lord of Angels who worketh all. The sick man cannot now say, "I have no man"; he cannot say, "While I am coming another steppeth down before me"; though the whole world should come, the grace is not spent, the power is not exhausted, but remaineth equally great as it was before. Just as the sun's beams

give light every day, yet are not exhausted, nor is their light made less by giving so abundant a supply; so, and much more, the power of the Spirit is in no way lessened by the numbers of those who enjoy it. And this miracle was done in order that men, learning that it is possible by water to heal the diseases of the body, and being exercised in this for a long time, might more easily believe that it can also heal the diseases of the soul.

But why did Jesus, leaving the rest, come to one who was of thirty-eight years standing? And why did He ask him, "Wilt thou be made whole?" Not that He might learn, that was needless; but that He might show[10] the man's perseverance, and that we might know that it was on this account that He left the others and came to him. What then saith he? "Yea Lord," he saith, but "I have no man when the water is troubled to put me into the pool, but while I am coming another steppeth down before me."

It was that we might learn these circumstances that Jesus asked, "Wilt thou be made whole?" and said not, "Wilt thou that I heal thee?" (for as yet the man had formed no exalted notions concerning Him,) but "Wilt thou be made whole?" Astonishing was the perseverance of the paralytic, he was of thirty and eight years standing, and each year hoping to be freed from his disease, he continued in attendance,[11] and withdrew not. Had he not been very persevering, would not the future,[12] if not the past, have been sufficient to lead him from the spot? Consider, I pray you, how watchful it was likely that the other sick men there would be since the time when the water was troubled was uncertain. The lame and halt indeed might observe it, but how did the blind see? Perhaps they learnt it from the clamor which arose.

[2.] Let us be ashamed then, beloved, let us be ashamed, and groan over our excessive sloth. "Thirty and eight years" had that man been waiting without obtaining what he desired, and withdrew not. And he had failed not through any carelessness of his own, but through being oppressed and suffering violence from others, and not even thus did he grow dull;[13] while we if we have persisted for ten days to pray for anything and have not obtained it, are too slothful afterwards to employ the same zeal. And on men we wait for so long a time, warring and enduring hardships and performing servile ministrations, and often at last failing in our expectation, but on our[14] Master, from whom we are sure to obtain a recompense greater than our labors, (for, saith the Apostle, "Hope maketh

---

[1] ὑπογράφει, al. προϋπ.
[2] al. "harm the faith of the hearers."
[3] ἀπὸ κηδείας, Num. v.    [4] lit. "faith of," al. "the gift of."
[5] Morel. and MS. in Bodl. "have more power to lead by the hand than the archetypes."
[6] al. "afar."    [7] al. "hindrances."
[8] ἐπὶ τῇ ἐνεργείᾳ, al. "at the coming down."
[9] λύει.

[10] al. "teach."
[11] al. "lay in wait."
[12] i.e. the manifest hopelessness of his being able to go down *first* into the pool.
[13] ἐνάρκα.    [14] al. "the kind."

not ashamed"—Rom. v. 5,) on Him we endure not to wait with becoming diligence. What chastisement doth this deserve! For even though we could receive nothing from Him, ought we not to deem the very conversing with Him continually the cause of[1] ten thousand blessings? "But continual prayer is a laborious thing." And what that belongs to virtue is not laborious? "In truth," says some one, "this very point is full of great difficulty, that pleasure is annexed to vice, and labor to virtue." And many, I think, make this a question. What then can be the reason?[2] God gave us at the beginning a life free from care and exempt from labor. We used not the gift aright, but were perverted by doing nothing,[3] and were banished from Paradise. On which account He made our life for the future one of toil, assigning as it were His reasons for this to mankind, and saying, "I allowed you at the beginning to lead a life of enjoyment,[4] but ye were rendered worse by liberty, wherefore I commanded that henceforth labor and sweat be laid upon you."[5] And when even this labor did not restrain us, He next gave us a law containing many commandments, imposing it on us like bits and curbs placed upon an unruly horse to restrain his prancings, just as horse breakers do. This is why life is laborious, because not to labor is wont to be our ruin. For our nature cannot bear to be doing nothing, but easily turns aside to wickedness. Let us suppose that the man who is temperate, and he who rightly performs the other virtues, has no need of labor, but that they do all things in their sleep, still how should we have employed our ease? Would it not have been for pride and boastfulness? "But wherefore," saith some one, "has great pleasure been attached to vice, great labor and toil to virtue?" Why, what thanks wouldest thou have had, and for what wouldest thou have received a reward, if the matter had not been one of difficulty? Even now I can show you many who naturally hate intercourse with women, and avoid conversation with them as impure; shall we then call these chaste, shall we crown these, tell me, and proclaim them victors? By no means. Chastity is self-restraint, and the mastering pleasures which fight, just as in war the trophies are most honorable when the contest is violent, not when no one raises a hand against us. Many are by their very nature passionless; shall we call these good tempered? Not at all. And so the Lord after naming three manners of the eunuch state, leaveth two of them uncrowned, and admitteth one into the kingdom

of heaven. (Matt. xix. 12.) "But what need," saith one, "was there of wickedness?" I say this too. "What is it then which made wickedness to be?" What but our willful negligence? "But," saith one, "there ought to be only good men." Well, what is proper to the good man? Is it to watch and be sober, or to sleep and snore? "And why," saith one, "seemed[6] it not good that a man should act rightly without laboring?" Thou speakest words which become the cattle or gluttons, or who make their belly their god. For to prove that these are the words of folly, answer me this. Suppose there were a king and a general, and while the king was asleep or drunk, the general should endure hardship and erect a trophy, whose would you count the victory to be? who would enjoy the pleasure of what was done? Seest thou that the soul is more especially disposed towards those things for which she hath labored? and therefore God hath joined labors to virtue, wishing to make us attached to her. For this cause we admire virtue, even although we act not rightly ourselves, while we condemn vice even though it be very pleasant. And if thou sayest, "Why do we not admire those who are good by nature more than those who are so by choice?" we reply, Because it is just to prefer him that laboreth to him that laboreth not. For why is it that we labor? It is because thou didst not bear with moderation the not laboring. Nay more, if one enquire exactly, in other ways also sloth is wont to undo us, and to cause us much trouble. Let us, if you will, shut a man up, only feeding and pampering him, not allowing him to walk nor conducting him forth to work, but let him enjoy table and bed, and be in luxury continually; what could be more wretched than such a life? "But," saith one, "to work is one thing, to labor is another."[7] Yea, but it was in man's power then[8] to work without labor. "And is this," saith he, "possible?" Yea, it is possible; God even desired it, but thou enduredst it not. Therefore He placed thee to work in the garden, marking out employment, but joining with it no labor. For had man labored at the beginning, God would not afterwards have put labor by way of punishment. For it is possible to work and not to be wearied, as do the angels. To prove that they work, hear what David saith; "Ye that excel in strength, ye that do His word." (Ps. ciii. 20, LXX.) Want of strength causeth much labor now, but then it was not so. For "he that hath entered into His rest, hath ceased," saith one, "from his works, as God from His" (Heb. iv. 10): not meaning here idleness, but the ceasing from labor. For God worketh even now,

---

[1] al. "worth."
[2] Morel. and MS. in Bodl. "but hear also the explanation, for this we will now say for love of you. What then," &c.
[3] ἀργίας.    [4] τρυφᾶν.
[5] Morel. and MS. in Bodl. "therefore I have done that which remained to do, I have encompassed (*or* clothed) you with labors and toils."

[6] al. "thoughtest thou."
[7] Some MSS. read, "was it then meet to work without toil? yea," &c.
[8] i.e. during the abode in Paradise.

as Christ saith, "My Father worketh hitherto, and I work." (c. v. 17.) Wherefore I exhort you that, laying aside all carelessness, you be zealous for virtue. For the pleasure of wickedness is short, but the pain lasting; of virtue, on the contrary, the joy grows not old, the labor is but for a season. Virtue even before the crowns are distributed animates[1] her workman, and feeds him with hopes; vice even before the time of vengeance punishes him who works for her, wringing and terrifying his conscience, and making it apt to imagine all (evils). Are not these things worse than any labors, than any toils? And if these things were not so, if there were pleasure, what could be more worthless than that pleasure? for as soon as it appears it flies away, withering and escaping before it has been grasped, whether you speak of the pleasure of beauty, or that of luxury, or that of wealth, for they cease not daily to decay. But when there is besides (for this pleasure) punishment and vengeance, what can be more miserable than those who go after it? Knowing then this, let us endure all for virtue, so shall we enjoy true pleasure, through the grace and lovingkindness of our Lord Jesus Christ, with whom to the Father and the Holy Ghost be glory, now and ever, and world without end. Amen.

# HOMILY XXXVII.

## JOHN v. 6, 7.

"Jesus saith unto him, Wilt thou be made whole? The impotent man answered Him, Yea, Sir, but I have no man, when the water is troubled, to put me into the pool."

[1.] GREAT is the profit of the divine Scriptures, and all-sufficient is the aid which comes from them. And Paul declared this when he said, "Whatsoever things were written aforetime, were written aforetime for our admonition upon whom the ends of the world are come, that we through patience and comfort of the Scriptures might have hope." (Rom. xv. 4, and 1 Cor. x. 11.) For the divine oracles are a treasury of all manner of medicines, so that whether it be needful to quench pride, to lull desire to sleep, to tread under foot the love of money, to despise pain, to inspire confidence, to gain patience, from them one may find abundant resource. For what man of those who struggle with long poverty or who are nailed to[2] a grievous disease, will not, when he reads the passage before us, receive much comfort? Since this man who had been paralytic for thirty and eight years, and who saw each year others delivered, and himself bound by his disease, not even so fell back and despaired, though in truth not merely despondency for the past, but also hopelessness for the future, was sufficient to overstrain[3] him. Hear now what he says, and learn the greatness of his sufferings.[4] For when Christ had said, "Wilt thou be made whole?" "Yea, Lord," he saith, "but I have no man, when the water is troubled, to put me into the pool." What can be more pitiable than these words? What more sad than these circumstances? Seest thou a heart[5] crushed through long sickness? Seest thou all violence subdued? He uttered no blasphemous word, nor such as we hear the many use in reverses, he cursed not his day, he was not angry at the question, nor did he say, "Art Thou come to make a mock and a jest of us, that Thou asketh whether I desire to be made whole?" but replied gently, and with great mildness, "Yea, Lord"; yet he knew not who it was that asked him, nor that He would heal him, but still he mildly relates all the circumstances and asks nothing further, as though he were speaking to a physician, and desired merely to tell the story of his sufferings. Perhaps he hoped that Christ might be so far useful to him as to put him into the water, and desired to attract Him by these words. What then saith Jesus?

Ver. 8. "Rise, take up thy bed, and walk."[6]

Now some suppose that this is the man in Matthew who was "lying on a bed" (Matt. ix. 2); but it is not so, as is clear in many ways. First, from his wanting persons to stand forward for him. That man had many to care for and to carry him, this man not a single one; wherefore he said, "I have no man." Secondly, from the manner of answering; the other uttered no word, but this man relates his whole case. Thirdly, from the season and the time; this man was healed at a feast, and on the Sabbath, that other on a different day. The places too were different; one was cured in a house, the other by the pool. The manner also of the cure was altered; there Christ said, "Thy sins be forgiven thee,"

---

[1] or, "releases."
[2] al. "held by."
[3] or, "throw him down."
[4] lit. "the tragedy."
[5] al. "endurance."
[6] al. "and go to thine house."

but here He braced[1] the body first, and then cared for the soul. In that case there was remission of sins, (for He saith, "Thy sins be forgiven thee,") but in this, warning and threats to strengthen the man for the future; "Sin no more, lest a worse thing come unto thee." (Ver. 14.) The charges also of the Jews are different; here they object to Jesus, His working on the Sabbath, there they charge Him with blasphemy.

Consider now, I pray you, the exceeding wisdom of God. He raised not up the man at once, but first maketh him familiar by questioning, making way for the coming faith; nor doth He only raise, but biddeth him "take up his bed," so as to confirm the miracle that had been wrought, and that none might suppose what was done to be illusion or a piece of acting. For he would not, unless his limbs had been firmly and thoroughly compacted, have been able to carry his bed. And this Christ often doth, effectually silencing those who would fain be insolent. So in the case of the loaves, that no one might assert that the men had been merely[2] satisfied, and that what was done was an illusion, He caused that there should be many relics of the loaves. So to the leper that was cleansed He said, "Go, show thyself to the priest" (Matt. viii. 4); at once providing most certain proof of the cleansing, and stopping the shameless mouths of those who asserted that He was legislating in opposition to God. This also He did in like manner in the case of the wine; for He did not merely show it to them, but also caused it to be borne to the governor of the feast, in order that one who knew nothing of what had been done, by his confession might bear to Him unsuspected testimony; wherefore the Evangelist saith, that the ruler of the feast "knew not whence it was," thus showing the impartiality of his testimony. And in another place, when He raised the dead, He said, "Give ye him to eat";[3] supplying this proof of a real resurrection, and by these means persuading even the foolish that He was no deceiver, no dealer in illusions,[4] but that He had come for the salvation of the common nature of mankind.

[2.] But why did not Jesus require faith of this man, as He did in the case of others, saying, "Believest thou that I am able to do this?"[5] It was because the man did not yet clearly know who He was; and it is not before, but after the working of miracles that He is seen so doing. For persons who had beheld His power exerted on others would reasonably have this said to them, while of those who had not yet learned who He was, but who were to know afterwards

by means of signs, it is after the miracles that faith is required. And therefore Matthew doth not introduce Christ as having said this at the beginning of His miracles, but when He had healed many, to the two blind men only.

Observe however in this way the faith of the paralytic. When he had heard,[6] "Take up thy bed and walk," he did not mock, nor say, "What can this mean? An Angel cometh down and troubleth the water, and healeth only one, and dost Thou, a man, by a bare command and word hope to be able to do greater things than Angels? This is mere vanity, boasting, mockery." But he neither said nor imagined anything like this, but at once he heard and arose, and becoming whole, was not disobedient to Him that gave the command;[7] for immediately he was made whole, and "took up his bed, and walked." What followed was even far more admirable. That he believed at first, when no one troubled him, was not so marvelous, but that afterwards, when the Jews were full of madness and pressed upon him on all sides, accusing[8] and besieging him and saying, "It is not lawful for thee to take up thy bed," that then he gave no heed to[9] their madness, but most boldly in the midst of the assembly[10] proclaimed his Benefactor and silenced their shameless tongues, this, I say, was an act of great courage. For when the Jews arose against him, and said in a reproachful and insolent manner to him,

Ver. 10. "It is the Sabbath day, it is not lawful for thee to carry thy bed"; hear what he saith:

Ver. 11. "He that made me whole, the Same said unto me, Take up thy bed, and walk."

All but saying, "Ye are silly and mad who bid me not to take Him for my Teacher who has delivered me from a long and grievous malady, and not to obey whatever He may command."[11] Had he chosen to act in an unfair manner, he might have spoke differently, as thus, "I do not this of my own will, but at the bidding of another; if this be a matter of blame, blame him who gave the order, and I will set down the bed." And he might have concealed the cure, for he well knew that they were vexed not so much at the breaking of the Sabbath, as at the curing of his infirmity. Yet he neither concealed this, nor said that, nor asked for pardon, but with loud voice confessed and proclaimed the benefit. Thus did the paralytic; but consider how unfairly they acted. For they said

---

1 ἔσφιγξε.　　2 i.e. not by real eating, ἁπλῶς.
3 The reference seems to be to Luke viii. 55.
4 φαντασιοκόπος.
5 Morel. and MSS. read, "as He did in the case of the blind men, (Matt. ix. 28,) saying, 'Believe ye,'" &c.

6 Morel. and MS. in Bodl. read, "for having heard that with authority, and as one commanding, He said to him, 'Arise,'" &c.
7 Morel. and MS. "who had commanded, 'Arise,'" &c.
8 Morel. and MS. "accusing, as the Evangelist shows by what follows, saying, 'And on the same day was the Sabbath. The Jews therefore said unto him that was cured, It is the Sabbath day, it is not lawful,'" &c.
9 al. "not only disregarded."
10 lit. "theater."　　11 see p. 132.

not, "Who is it that hath made thee whole?" on this point they were silent, but kept on bringing forward the seeming transgression.

Ver. 12, 13. "What man is that which said unto thee, Take up thy bed and walk? And he that was healed wist not who it was: for Jesus had conveyed Himself away,[1] a multitude being in that place."

And why did Jesus conceal Himself? First, that while He was absent, the testimony of the man might be unsuspected, for he who now felt himself whole was a credible witness of the benefit. And in the next place, that He might not cause the fury of the Jews to be yet more inflamed, for the very sight of one whom they envy is wont to kindle not a small spark in malicious persons. On this account He retired, and left the deed by itself to plead its cause among them, that He might not say anything in person respecting Himself, but that they might do so who had been healed, and with them also the accusers. Even these last for a while testify to the miracle, for they said not, "Wherefore hast thou commanded these things to be done on the Sabbath day?" but, "Wherefore doest thou these things on the Sabbath day?" not being displeased at the transgression, but envious at the restoration of the paralytic. Yet in respect of human labor, what the paralytic did was rather a work, for the other[2] was a saying and a word. Here then He commandeth another to break the Sabbath, but elsewhere He doth the same Himself, mixing clay and anointing a man's eyes (c. 9); yet He doth these things not transgressing, but going beyond the Law. And on this we shall hereafter speak. For He doth not, when accused by the Jews respecting the Sabbath, always defend Himself in the same terms, and this we must carefully observe.

[3.] But let us consider awhile how great an evil is envy, how it disables the eyes of the soul to the endangering his salvation who is possessed by it. For as madmen often thrust their swords against their own bodies, so also malicious persons looking only to one thing, the injury[3] of him they envy, care not for their own salvation. Men like these are worse than wild beasts; they when wanting food, or having first been provoked by us, arm themselves against us; but these men when they have received kindness, have often repaid their benefactors as though they had wronged them. Worse than wild beasts are they, like the devils, or perhaps worse than even those; for they against us indeed have unceasing hostility, but do not plot against those of their own nature, (and so by this Jesus silenced the Jews when they said that He cast out devils by Beelzebub,) but these men neither respect their common nature, nor spare their own selves. For before they vex those whom they envy they vex their own souls, filling them with all manner of trouble and despondency, fruitlessly and in vain. For wherefore grievest thou, O man, at the prosperity of thy neighbor? We ought to grieve at the ills we suffer, not because we see others in good repute. Wherefore this sin is stripped of all excuse. The fornicator may allege his lust, the thief his poverty, the man-slayer his passion, frigid excuses and unreasonable, still they have these to allege. But what reason, tell me, wilt thou name? None other at all, but that of intense wickedness. If we are commanded to love our enemies, what punishment shall we suffer if we hate our very friends? And if he who loveth those that love him will be in no better a state than the heathen, what excuse, what palliation shall he have who injures those that have done him no wrong? Hear Paul, what he saith, "Though I give my body to be burned, and have not charity, it profiteth me nothing" (1 Cor. xiii. 3); now it is clear to every one that where envy and malice are, there charity is not. This feeling is worse than fornication and adultery, for these go no farther than him who doeth them, but the tyranny of envy hath overturned entire Churches, and hath destroyed the whole world. Envy is the mother of murder. Through this Cain slew Abel his brother; through this Esau (would have slain) Jacob, and his brethren Joseph, through this the devil all mankind. Thou indeed now killest not, but thou dost many things worse than murder, desiring that thy brother may act unseemly, laying snares for him on all sides, paralyzing his labors on the side of virtue, grieving that he pleaseth the Master of the world. Yet thou warrest not with thy brother, but with Him whom he serves, Him thou insultest when thou preferest thy glory to His. And what is in truth worst of all, is that this sin seems to be an unimportant one, while in fact it is more grievous than any other; for though thou showest mercy and watchest and fastest, thou art more accursed than any if thou enviest thy brother. As is clear from this circumstance also. A man of the Corinthians was once guilty of adultery, yet he was charged with his sin and soon restored to righteousness; Cain envied Abel; but he was not healed, and although God Himself continually charmed[4] the wound, he became more pained and wave-tossed, and was hurried on to murder. Thus this passion is worse than that other, and doth not easily permit itself to be cured except we give heed. Let us then by all means tear it up by the roots, considering this, that as we offend God when we waste with envy at other men's blessings, so

---

[1] ἐξέκλινεν ἐξένευσεν, G. T. and Mor.
[2] i.e. that which Jesus did.
[3] al. "pain."
[4] ἐπ᾽ ᾄδοντος.

when we rejoice with them we are well pleasing to Him, and render ourselves partakers of the good things laid up for the righteous. Therefore Paul exhorteth us to "Rejoice with them that do rejoice, and weep with them that weep" (Rom. xii. 15), that on either hand we may reap great profit.

Considering then that even when we labor not, by rejoicing with him that laboreth, we become sharers of his crown, let us cast aside all envy, and implant charity in our souls, that by applauding those of our brethren who are well pleasing unto God, we may obtain both present and future good things, through the grace and lovingkindness of our Lord Jesus Christ, by whom and with whom, to the Father and the Holy Ghost, be glory, now and ever, world without end. Amen.

# HOMILY XXXVIII.

### John v. 14.

"Afterward Jesus findeth him in the Temple, and said unto him, Behold, thou art made whole; sin no more, lest a worse thing come unto thee."

[1.] A FEARFUL thing is sin, fearful, and the ruin of the soul, and the. mischief oftentimes through its excess has overflowed and attacked men's bodies also. For since for the most part when the soul is diseased we feel no pain, but if the body receive though but a little hurt, we use every exertion to free it from its infirmity, because we are sensible of the infirmity,[1] therefore God oftentimes punisheth the body for the transgressions of the soul, so that by means of the scourging of the inferior part, the better part also may receive some healing. Thus too among the Corinthians Paul restored the adulterer, checking the disease of the soul by the destruction of the flesh, and having applied the knife to the body, so repressed the evil (1 Cor. v. 5); like some excellent physician employing external cautery for dropsy or spleen, when they refuse to yield to internal remedies. This also Christ did in the case of the paralytic; as He showed when He said, "Behold, thou art made whole; sin no more, lest a worse thing come unto thee."

Now what do we learn from this? First, that his disease had been produced by his sins; secondly, that the accounts of hell fire are to be believed; thirdly, that the punishment is long, nay endless. Where now are those who say, "I murdered in an hour, I committed adultery in a little moment of time, and am I eternally punished?" For behold this man had not sinned for so many years as he suffered, for he had spent a whole lifetime in the length of his punishment; and sins are not judged by time, but by the nature of the transgressions. Besides this, we may see[2] another thing, that though we have suffered severely for former sins, if we afterwards fall into the same, we shall suffer much more severely. And with good reason; for he who is not made better even by punishment, is afterwards led as insensible and a despiser to still heavier chastisement. The fault should of itself be sufficient to check and to render more sober the man who once has slipped, but when not even the addition of punishment effects this, he naturally requires more bitter torments.[3] Now if even in this world when after punishment[4] we fall into the same sins, we are chastised yet more severely then before, ought we not when after sinning we have not been punished at all, to be then[5] very exceedingly afraid and to tremble, as being about to endure something irreparable? "And wherefore," saith some one, "are not all thus punished? for we see many bad men well in body, vigorous, and enjoying great prosperity." But let us not be confident, let us mourn for them in this case most of all, since their having suffered nothing here, helps them on[6] to a severer vengeance hereafter.[7] As Paul declares when he saith, "But now that we are judged, we are chastened of the Lord, that we should not be condemned with the world" (1 Cor. xi. 32); for the punishments here are for warning, there for vengeance.

"What then," saith one, "do all diseases proceed from sin?" Not all, but most of them; and some proceed from different kinds of loose living,[8] since gluttony, intemperance, and sloth,

---

[1] Sav. omits "because we are sensible of the infirmity."

[2] al. "learn."
[3] Ben. and MS. in Bodl. read the passage thus: "For the chastisement was of itself sufficient . . . but when not being sobered by the application of punishment, he again dares the same things, such an one will reasonably suffer some penalty, calling this as he does upon his own self."
[4] al. "have been punished here."      [5] al. "at this."
[6] ἐφόδιον γίγνεται. So Euseb. H. E. viii. 10, ἐφ. τῆς εἰς τὴν ζωὴν εἰσόδου.      [7] lit. "there."
[8] al. "from loose living," ῥαθυμίας.

produce such like sufferings. But the one rule we have to observe, is to bear every stroke thankfully; for they are sent because of our sins, as in the Kings we see one attacked by gout (1 Kings xv. 23); they are sent also to make us approved, as the Lord saith to Job, "Thinkest thou that I have spoken to thee, save that thou mightest appear righteous?" (Job xl. 8, LXX.)

But why is it that in the case of these paralytics Christ bringeth forward their sins? For He saith also to him in Matthew who lay on a bed, "Son, be of good cheer, thy sins are forgiven thee" (Matt. ix. 2): and to this man, "Behold, thou art made whole; sin no more."[1] I know that some slander this paralytic, asserting that he was an accuser of Christ, and that therefore this speech was addressed to him; what then shall we say of the other in Matthew, who heard nearly the same words? For Christ saith to him also, "Thy sins be forgiven thee." Whence it is clear, that neither was this man thus addressed on the account which they allege. And this we may see more clearly from what follows;[2] for, saith the Evangelist, "Afterward Jesus findeth him in the Temple," which is an indication of his great piety; for he departed not into the market places and walks, nor gave himself up to luxury and ease, but remained in the Temple, although about to sustain so violent an attack and to be harassed by all there.[3] Yet none of these things persuaded him to depart from the Temple. Moreover Christ having found him, even after he had conversed with the Jews, implied nothing of the kind. For had He desired to charge him with this, He would have said to him, "Art thou again attempting the same sins as before, art thou not made better by thy cure?" Yet He said nothing of the kind, but merely secureth him for the future.

[2.] Why then, when He had cured the halt and maimed, did He not in any instance make mention of the like? Methinks that the diseases of these (the paralytic) arose from acts of sin, those of the others from natural infirmity. Or if this be not so, then by means of these men, and by the words spoken to them, He hath spoken to the rest also. For since this disease is more grievous than any other, by the greater He correcteth also the less. And as when He had healed a certain other He charged him to give glory to God, addressing this exhortation not to him only but through him to all, so He addresseth to these, and by these to all the rest of mankind, that exhortation and advice which was given to them by word of mouth. Besides this we may also say, that Jesus perceived great endurance in his soul, and addressed the exhortation to him as to one who was able to receive His command, keeping him to health both by the benefit, and by the fear of future ills.

And observe the absence of boasting. He said not, "Behold, I have made thee whole," but, "Thou art made whole; sin no more." And again, not, "lest I punish thee," but, "lest a worse thing come unto thee"; putting both expressions not personally,[4] and showing that the cure was rather of grace than of merit. For He declared not to him that he was delivered after suffering the deserved amount of punishment, but that through lovingkindness he was made whole. Had this not been the case, He would have said, "Behold, thou hast suffered a sufficient punishment for thy sins, be thou steadfast for the future." But now He spake not so, but how? "Behold, thou art made whole; sin no more." Let us continually repeat these words to ourselves, and if after having been chastised we have been delivered, let each say to himself, "Behold, thou art made whole; sin no more." But if we suffer not punishment though continuing in the same courses, let us use for our charm that word of the Apostle, "The goodness of God leadeth [us] to repentance, but after [our] hardness and impenitent heart, [we] treasure up unto [ourselves] wrath." (Rom. ii. 4, 5.)

And not only by strengthening[5] the sick man's body, but also in another way, did He afford him a strong proof of His Divinity; for by saying, "Sin no more," He showed that He knew all the transgressions that had formerly been committed by him; and by this He would gain his belief as to the future.

Ver. 15. "The man departed, and told the Jews that it was Jesus that had made him whole."

Again observe him continuing in the same right feeling. He saith not, "This is he who said, Take up thy bed," but when they continually advanced this seeming charge, he continually puts forward the defense, again declaring his Healer, and seeking to attract and attach others to Him. For he was not so unfeeling as after such a benefit and charge to betray his Benefactor, and to speak as he did with an evil intention. Had he been a wild beast, had he been something unlike a man and of stone, the benefit and the fear would have been enough to restrain him, since, having the threat lodged within, he would have dreaded lest he should suffer "a worse thing," having already received the greatest pledges[6] of the power of his Physician. Besides, had he wished to slander Him, he would have said nothing about his own cure, but would have mentioned and urged against Him the breach of the Sabbath. But this is not the case, surely it is not; the words are words of great boldness and candor; he pro-

---

[1] See p. 129.
[2] al. "from another reason."
[3] al. "chased thence by all."
[4] ἀπροσώπως, i.e. not referring to Himself.
[5] σφίγξαι.
[6] al. "proofs."

caims his Benefactor no less than the blind man did. For what said he? "He made clay, and anointed mine eyes" (c. ix. 6) ; and so this man of whom we now speak, "It is Jesus who made me whole."

Ver. 16. "Therefore did the Jews persecute Jesus, and sought to slay Him, because He had done these things on the Sabbath day." What then saith Christ?

Ver. 17. "My Father worketh hitherto, and I work."

When there was need to make excuse for the Disciples, He brought forward David their fellow-servant, saying, "Have ye not read what David did when he was an hungered?" (Matt. xii. 2.) But when excuse was to be made for Himself, He betook Himself to the Father, showing in two ways His Equality, by calling God His Father peculiarly,[1] and by doing the same things which He did. "And wherefore did He not mention what took place at Jericho[2]?" Because He wished to raise them up from earth that they might no longer attend to Him as to a man, but as to God, and as to one who ought to legislate : since had He not been The Very Son and of the same Essence, the defense would have been worse than the charge. For if a viceroy who had altered a royal law should, when charged with so doing, excuse himself in this manner, and say, "Yea, for the king also has annulled laws," he would not be able to escape, but would thus increase the weight of the charge. But in this instance, since the dignity is equal, the defense is made perfect on most secure grounds. "From the charges," saith He, "from which ye absolve God, absolve Me also." And therefore He said first, "My Father," that He might per-suade them even against their will to allow to Him the same, through reverence of His clearly asserted Sonship.

If any one say, "And how doth the Father 'work,' who ceased on the seventh day from all His works?" let him learn the manner in which He "worketh." What then is the manner of His working? He careth for, He holdeth[3] to-gether all that hath been made. Therefore when thou beholdest the sun rising and the moon run-ning in her path, the lakes, and fountains, and rivers, and rains, the course of nature in the seeds and in our own bodies and those of irra-tional beings, and all the rest by means of which this universe is made up, then learn the cease-less working of the Father. "For He maketh His sun to rise upon the evil and the good, and sendeth rain on the just and on the unjust." (Matt. v. 45.) And again ; "If God so clothe

the grass of the field, which to-day is, and to-morrow is cast into the fire[4]" (Matt. vi. 30) ; and speaking of the birds He said, "Your Heav-enly Father feedeth them."

[3.] In that place[5] then He did all on the Sabbath day by words only, and added noth-ing more, but refuted their charges by what was done in the Temple and from their own prac-tice. But here where He commanded a work to be done, the taking up a bed, (a thing of no great importance as regarded the miracle,[6] though by it He showed one point, a manifest violation of the Sabbath,) He leads up His discourse to something greater, desiring the more to awe them by reference to the dignity of the Father, and to lead them up to higher thought. There-fore when His discourse is concerning the Sab-bath, He maketh not His defense as man only, or as God only, but sometimes in one way, some-times in the other ; because He desired to per-suade them both of the condescension of the Dispensation, and the Dignity of His Godhead. Therefore He now defendeth Himself as God, since had He always conversed with them merely as a man, they would have continued in the same low condition. Wherefore that this may not be, He bringeth forward the Father. Yet the creation itself "worketh" on the Sabbath, (for the sun runneth, rivers flow, fountains bubble, women bear,) but that thou mayest learn that He is not of creation, He said not, "Yea, I work, for creation worketh," but, "Yea, I work, for My Father worketh."

Ver. 18. "Therefore the Jews sought the more to kill Him, because He not only had broken the Sabbath, but said also that God was His Father, making Himself equal with God."

And this he asserted not by words merely, but by deeds, for not in speech alone, but also yet oftener by actions He declared it. Why so? Because they might object to His words and charge Him with arrogance, but when they saw the truth of His actions proved by results, and His power proclaimed by works, after that they could say nothing against Him.

But they who will not receive these words in a right mind assert, that "Christ made not Him-self equal to God, but that the Jews suspected this." Come then let us go over what has been said from the beginning. Tell me, did the Jews persecute Him, or did they not? It is clear to every one that they did. Did they persecute Him for this or for something else? It is again allowed that it was for this. Did He then break the Sabbath, or did He not? Against the fact that He did, no one can have anything to say. Did He call God His Father, or did He not call Him so? This too is true. Then the rest also

---

[1] ἰδιαζόντως.
[2] Jericho was taken on the seventh day by command of God. Josh. vi. 4, 15.
[3] lit. " weldeth." συγκροτεῖ. Sav. conjectures συγκρατεῖ, but the word is not uncommon for holding together a system.

[4] εἰς κλίβανον, G. T.
[5] Matt. xii.
[6] πρᾶγμα.

follows by the same consequence; for as to call God His Father, to break the Sabbath, and to be persecuted by the Jews for the former and more especially for the latter reason, belonged not to a false imagination, but to actual fact, so to make Himself equal to God was a declaration of the same meaning.[1]

And this one may see more clearly from what He had before said, for "My Father worketh, and I work," is the expression of One declaring Himself equal to God. For in these words He has marked[2] no difference. He said not, "He worketh, and I minister," but, "As He worketh, so work I"; and hath declared absolute Equality. But if He had not wished to establish this, and the Jews had supposed so without reason, He would not have allowed their minds to be deceived, but would have corrected this. Besides, the Evangelist would not have been silent on the subject, but would have plainly said that the Jews supposed so, but that Jesus did not make Himself equal to God. As in another place he doth this very thing, when he perceiveth that something was said in one way, and understood in another; as, "Destroy this Temple," said Christ, "and in three days I will raise It up" (c. ii. 19); speaking of His Flesh. But the Jews, not understanding this, and supposing that the words were spoken of the Jewish Temple, said, "Forty and six years was this temple in building, and wilt Thou rear it up in three days?" Since then He said one thing, and they imagined another, (for He spake of His Flesh, and they thought that the words were spoken of their Temple,) the Evangelist remarking on this, or rather correcting their imagination, goes on to say, "But He spake of the Temple of His Body." So that here also, if Christ had not made Himself equal with God, had not wished to establish this, and yet the Jews had imagined that He did, the writer would here also have corrected their supposition, and would have said, "The Jews thought that He made Himself equal to God, but indeed He spake not of equality." And this is done not in this place only, nor by this Evangelist only, but again elsewhere another Evangelist is seen to do the same. For when Christ warned His disciples, saying, "Beware of the leaven of the Pharisees and Sadducees" (Matt. xvi. 6), and they reasoned among themselves, saying, "It is because we have taken no bread," and He spake of one thing, calling their doctrine "leaven," but the disciples imagined another, supposing that the words were said of bread; it is not now the Evangelist who setteth them

right, but Christ Himself, speaking thus, "How is it that ye do not understand, that I spake not to you concerning bread?" But here there is nothing of the kind.

"But," saith some one, "to remove this very thought Christ has added,

Ver. 19. "'The Son can do nothing of Himself.'"

Man! He doth the contrary. He saith this not to take away, but to confirm,[3] His Equality. But attend carefully, for this is no common question. The expression "of Himself" is found in many places of Scripture, with reference both to Christ and to the Holy Ghost, and we must learn the force of the expression, that we may not fall into the greatest errors; for if one take it separately by itself in the way in which it is obvious to take it, consider how great an absurdity will follow. He said not that He could do some things of Himself and that others He could not, but universally,

[4.] "The Son can do nothing of Himself."

I ask then my opponent, "Can the Son do nothing of Himself, tell me?" If he reply, "that He can do nothing," we will say, that He hath done of Himself the very greatest of all goods. As Paul cries aloud, saying, "Who being in the form of God, thought it not robbery to be equal with God, but made Himself of no reputation, and took upon Him the form of a servant." (Phil. ii. 6, 7.) And again, Christ Himself in another place saith, "I have power to lay down My life, and I have power to take it again": and, "No man taketh it from Me, but I lay it down of Myself." (c. x. 18.) Seest thou that He hath power over life and death, and that He wrought of Himself so mighty a Dispensation? And why speak I concerning Christ, when even we, than whom nothing can be meaner, do many things of ourselves? Of ourselves we choose vice, of ourselves we go after virtue, and if we do it not of ourselves, and not having power, we shall neither suffer hell if we do wrong, nor enjoy the Kingdom if we do right.

What then meaneth, "Can do nothing of Himself"? That He can do nothing in opposition to the Father, nothing alien from, nothing strange to Him,[4] which is especially the assertion of One declaring an Equality and entire agreement. But wherefore said He not, that "He doeth nothing contrary," instead of, "He cannot do"? It was that from this again He might show the invariableness and exactness of the Equality, for the expression imputes not weakness to Him, but even shows[5] His great power; since in another place Paul saith of the Father, "That by two immutable things in which it was impos-

---

[1] τῆς αὐτῆς γνώμης ἀπόφασις, i.e. in saying that He was making Himself "equal to the Father," the Evangelist asserts a truth which had before been signified by His breaking the Sabbath, and saying that God was His Father.
[2] al. "given."

[3] lit. "to clench."　　　　　　　[5] al. "testifies."
[4] i.e. nothing *by* Himself.

sible for God to lie " (Heb. vi. 18) : and again, " If we deny Him — He abideth faithful," for " He cannot deny Himself." (2 Tim. ii. 12, 13.) And in truth this expression, " impossible," is not declaratory of weakness, but power, power unspeakable. For what He saith is of this kind, that " that Essence admitteth not such things as these." For just as when we also say, " it is impossible for God to do wrong," we do not impute to Him any weakness, but confess in Him an unutterable power ; so when He also saith, " I can of Mine own Self do nothing " (v. 30), His meaning is, that " it is impossible, nature admits not,[1] that I should do anything contrary to the Father." And that you may learn that this is really what is said, let us, going over what follows, see whether Christ agreeth with what is said by us, or among you. Thou sayest, that the expression does away with His Power and His proper Authority, and shows His might to be but weak ; but I say, that this proves His Equality, His unvarying Likeness,[2] (to the Father,) and the fact that all is done as it were by one Will[3] and Power and Might. Let us then enquire of Christ Himself, and see by what He next saith whether He interpreteth these words according to thy supposition or according to ours. What then saith He?

" For what things soever the Father[4] doeth, these also doeth the Son likewise."

Seest thou how He hath taken away your assertion by the root, and confirmed what is said by us? since, if Christ doeth nothing of Himself, neither will the Father do anything of Himself, if so be that Christ doeth all things in like manner to Him.[5] If this be not the case, another strange conclusion will follow. For He said not, that " whatsoever things He saw the Father do, He did," but, " except He see the Father doing anything, He doeth it not " ; extending His words to all time ; now He will, according to you, be continually learning the same things. Seest thou how exalted is the idea, and that the very humility of the expression compelleth even the most shameless and unwilling to avoid groveling thoughts, and such as are unsuited to His dignity? For who so wretched and miserable as to assert, that the Son learneth day by day what He must do? and how can that be true, " Thou art the same, and Thy years shall not fail "? (Ps. cii. 27), or that other, " All things were made by Him, and without Him was not anything made " (c. i. 3) ; if the Father doeth certain things, and the Son seeth and imitateth Him? Seest thou that from what was asserted above, and from what was said afterwards, proof is given of His inde-

pendent Power? and if He bringeth forward some expressions in lowly manner, marvel not, for since they persecuted Him when they had heard His exalted sayings, and deemed Him to be an enemy of God, sinking[6] a little in expression alone, He again leadeth His discourse up to the sublimer doctrines, then in turn to the lower, varying His teaching that it might be easy of acceptance even to the indisposed.[7] Observe, after saying, " My Father worketh, and I work " ; and after declaring Himself equal with God, He addeth, " The Son can do nothing of Himself, but what He seeth the Father do." Then again in a higher strain, " What things soever the Father doeth, these also doeth the Son likewise." Then in a lower,

Ver. 20. " The Father loveth the Son, and showeth Him all things that Himself doeth ; and He will show Him greater works than these."

Seest thou how great is the humility of this? And with reason ; for what I said before, what I shall not cease to say, I will now repeat, that when He uttereth anything low or humbly, He putteth it in excess, that the very poverty of the expression may persuade even the indisposed to receive the notions with pious understanding. Since, if it be not so, see how absurd a thing is asserted, making the trial from the words themselves. For when He saith, " And shall show Him greater works than these," He will be found not to have yet learned many things, which cannot be said even of the Apostles ; for they when they had once received the grace of the Spirit, in a moment both knew and were able to do all things which it was needful that they should know and have power to do, while Christ will be found to have not yet learned many things which He needed to know. And what can be more absurd than this?

What then is His meaning? It was because He had strengthened the paralytic, and was about to raise the dead, that He thus spake, all but saying, " Wonder ye that I have strengthened the paralyzed? Ye shall see greater things than these." But He spake not thus, but proceeded somehow in a humbler strain, in order that He might soothe[8] their madness. And that thou mayest learn that " shall show " is not used absolutely, listen again to what followeth.

Ver. 21. " For as the Father raiseth up the dead, and quickeneth them, even so the Son quickeneth whom He will."

Yet " can do nothing of Himself " is opposed to " whom He will " : since if He quickeneth " whom He will," He can do something " of Himself," (for to " will " implies power,) but if He " can do nothing of Himself," then He can-

---

[1] ἀνεγχώρητον.
[2] τὸ ἀπαράλλακτον.
[3] γνώμης.
[4] Ἐκεῖνος, G. T.
[5] Morel. and MS. in Bodl., " that the 'likewise' (τὸ ὁμοίως) may remain."
[6] καθυφεὶς.
[7] ἀγνώμοσι.
[8] al. " heal."

not " quicken whom He will." For the expression, " as the Father raiseth up," showeth unvarying resemblance in Power, and " whom He will," Equality of Authority. Seest thou therefore that " cannot do anything of Himself " is the expression of One not taking away His (own) authority, but declaring the unvarying resemblance of His Power and Will (to those of the Father) ? In this sense also understand the words, " shall show to Him "; for in another place He saith, " I will raise him up at the last Day." (c. vi. 40.) And again, to show that He doth it not by receiving an inward power[1] from above, He saith, " I am the Resurrection and the Life." (c. xi. 25.) Then that thou mayest not assert that He raiseth what dead He will and quickeneth them, but that He doth not other things in such manner, He anticipateth and preventeth every objection of the kind by saying, " What things soever He doeth, these also doeth the Son likewise," thus declaring that He doeth all things which the Father doeth, and as the Father doeth them ; whether thou speakest of the raising of the dead, or the fashioning[2] of bodies, or the remission of sins, or any other matter whatever, He worketh in like manner to Him who begat Him.

[5.] But men careless of their salvation give heed to none of these things ; so great an evil is it to be in love with precedence. This has been the mother of heresies, this has confirmed the impiety of the heathen.[3] For God desired that His invisible things should be understood by the creation of this world (Rom. i. 20), but they having left these and refused to come by this mode of teaching, cut out for themselves another way, and so were cast out from the true.[4] And the Jews believed not because they received honor from one another, and sought not the honor which is from God. But let us, beloved, avoid this disease exceedingly and with all earnestness ; for though we have ten thousand good qualities, this plague of vainglory is sufficient to bring them all to nought. (c. v. 44.) If therefore we desire praise, let us seek the praise which is from God, for the praise of men of what kind soever it·be, as soon as it has appeared has perished, or if it perish not, brings to us no profit, and often proceeds from a corrupt judgment. And what is there to be admired in the honor which is from men? which young dancers enjoy, and abandoned women, and covetous and rapacious men? But he who is approved of God, is approved not with these, but with those holy men the Prophets and Apos-

tles, who have shown forth an angelic life. If we feel any desire to lead multitudes about with us or be looked at by them, let us consider the matter apart by itself, and we shall find that it is utterly worthless. In fine, if thou art fond of crowds, draw to thyself the host of angels, and become terrible to the devils, then shalt thou care nothing for mortal things, but shalt tread all that is splendid underfoot as mire and clay ; and shalt clearly see that nothing so fits a soul for shame as the passion for glory ; for it cannot, it cannot be, that the man who desires this should live the crucified life, as on the other hand it is not possible that the man who hath trodden this underfoot should not tread down most other passions ; for he who masters this will get the better of envy and covetousness, and all the grievous maladies. " And how," saith some one, " shall we get the better of it ? " If we look to the other glory which is from heaven, and from which this kind strives to cast us out. For that heavenly glory both makes us honored here, and passes with us into the life which is to come, and delivers us from all fleshly slavery which we now most miserably serve, giving up ourselves entirely to earth and the things of earth. For if you go into the forum, if you enter into a house, into the streets, into the soldiers' quarters, into inns, taverns, ships, islands, palaces, courts of justice, council chambers, you shall everywhere find anxiety for things present and belonging to this life, and each man laboring for these things, whether gone or coming, traveling or staying at home, voyaging, tilling lands, in the fields, in the cities, in a word, all. What hope then of salvation have we, when inhabiting God's earth we care not for the things of God, when bidden to be aliens from earthly things we are aliens from heaven and citizens of earth? What can be worse than this insensibility, when hearing each day of the Judgment and of the Kingdom, we imitate the men in the days of Noah, and those of Sodom, waiting to learn all by actual experience? Yet for this purpose were all those things written, that if any one believe not that which is to come, he may, from what has already been, get certain proof of what shall be. Considering therefore these things, both the past and the future, let us at least take breath a little from this hard slavery, and make some account of our souls also,[5] that we may obtain both present and future blessings ; through the grace and lovingkindness of our Lord Jesus Christ, to whom, with the Father and the Holy Ghost, be glory, now and ever, and world without end. Amen.

---

[1] ἐνεργείαν.
[2] διάπλασιν.
[3] lit. " Greeks."
[4] τῆς οὔσης sub. ὁδοῦ.
[5] i.e. as well as of earthly things.

# HOMILY XXXIX.

## John v. 23, 24.

"For My Father judgeth no man, but hath committed all judgment to the Son; that all men should honor the Son, even as they honor the Father."

[1.] Beloved, we need great diligence in all things, for we shall render account of and undergo a strict enquiry both of words and works. Our interests stop not with what now is, but a certain other condition of life shall receive us after this, and we shall be brought before a fearful tribunal. "For we must appear before the Judgment-seat of Christ, that every one may receive the things done in his body, according to that he hath done, whether it be good or bad." (2 Cor. v. 10.) Let us ever bear in mind this tribunal, that we may thus be enabled at all times to continue in virtue; for as he who has cast out from his soul that day, rushes like a horse that has burst his bridle to precipices, (for "his ways are always defiled" [1] — Ps. x. 5,) and then assigning the reason the Psalmist hath added, "He putteth Thy judgments far away out of his sight";) so he that always retains this fear will walk soberly. "Remember," saith one, "thy last things, and thou shalt never do amiss." (Ecclus. vii. 40.) For He who now hath remitted our sins, will then sin in judgment; He who hath died for our sake will then appear again to judge all mankind. [2] "Unto them that look for Him," saith the Apostle, "shall He appear the second time without sin unto salvation." (Heb. ix. 28.) Wherefore in this place also He saith, "My Father judgeth no man, but hath committed all judgment unto the Son; that all men should honor the Son, even as they honor the Father."

"Shall we then," saith some one, "also call Him Father?" Away with the thought. He useth the word "Son" that we may honor Him still remaining a Son, as we honor the Father; but he who calleth Him "Father" doth not honor the Son as the Father, but has confounded the whole. Moreover as men are not so much brought to by being benefited as by being punished, on this account He hath spoken thus terribly, [3] that even fear may draw them to honor Him. And when He saith "all," His meaning is this, that He hath power to punish and to honor, and doeth either as He will. [4] The expression "hath given," is used that thou mayest

not suppose Him not to have been Begotten, and so think that there are two Fathers. For all that the Father is, this the Son is also, [5] Begotten, and remaining a Son. And that thou mayest learn that "hath given" is the same as "hath begotten," hear this very thing declared by another place. "As," saith Christ, "the Father hath life in Himself, so hath He given to the Son to have life in Himself." (Ver. 26.) "What then? Did he first beget and then give Him life? For he who giveth, giveth to something which is. Was He then begotten without life?" Not even the devils could imagine this, for it is very foolish as well as impious. As then "hath given life" is "hath begotten Him who is Life," so, "hath given judgment" is "hath begotten Him who shall be Judge."

That thou mayest not when thou hearest that He hath the Father for His cause imagine any difference [6] of essence or inferiority of honor, He cometh to judge thee, by this proving His Equality. [7] For He who hath authority to punish and to honor whom He will, hath the same Power with the Father. Since, if this be not the case, if having been begotten He afterwards received the honor, how came it that He was afterwards [thus] honored, by what mode of advancement reached He so far as to receive and be appointed to this dignity? Are ye not ashamed thus impudently to apply to that Pure [8] Nature which admitteth of no addition these carnal and mean imaginations?

"Why then," saith some one, "doth Christ so speak?" That His words may be readily received, and to clear the way for sublime sayings; therefore He mixeth these with those, and those with these. And observe how (He doth it); for it is good to see this from the beginning. He said, "My Father worketh, and I work" (c. v. 17, &c.) : declaring by this their Equality and Equal honor. But they "sought to kill Him." What doth He then? He lowereth His form of speech indeed, and putteth the same meaning when He saith, "The Son can do nothing of Himself." Then again He raiseth His discourse to high matters, saying, "What things soever the Father doeth, these also doeth the Son likewise." Then He returneth to what is lower, "For the Father loveth the Son, and showeth Him all things that Himself doeth;

---

[1] βεβηλοῦνται.　　[2] τὴν φύσιν ἅπασαν.
[3] al. "since men being benefited are not so sensible of it, He saith 'hath given all judgment to' Him, in order that," &c.
[4] al. "to punish and honor all whomsoever He will."

[5] al. "all things which belong to the Father, belong also to the Son."
[6] παραλλαγήν.　　[7] al. "high Birth."　　[8] ἀκηράτῳ.

and He will show Him greater things than these." Then He riseth higher, "For as the Father raiseth up the dead and quickeneth them, even so the Son quickeneth whom He will." After this again He joineth the high and the low together, "For neither doth the Father judge any one, but hath given all judgment to the Son"; then riseth again, "That all men should honor the Son, even as they honor the Father." Seest thou how He varieth the discourse, weaving it both of high and low words and expressions, in order that it might be acceptable to the men of that time, and that those who should come after might receive no injury, gaining from the higher part a right opinion of the rest? For if this be not the case, if these sayings were not uttered through condescension, wherefore were the high expressions added? Because one who is entitled to utter great words concerning himself, hath, when he saith anything mean and low, this reasonable excuse, that he doth it for some prudential purpose;[1] but if one who ought to speak meanly of himself saith anything great, on what account doth he utter words which surpass his nature? This is not for any purpose at all, but an act of extreme impiety.[2]

[2.] We are therefore able to assign a reason for the lowly expressions, a reason sufficient, and becoming to God, namely, His condescension, His teaching us to be moderate, and the salvation which is thus wrought for us. To declare which He said Himself in another place, "These things I say that ye might be saved." For when He left His own witness, and betook Himself to that of John, (a thing unworthy of His greatness,) He putteth the reason of such lowliness of language, and saith, "These things I say that ye might be saved." And ye who assert that He hath not the same authority and power with Him who begat Him, what can ye say when ye hear Him utter words by which He declareth His Authority and Power and Glory equal in respect of the Father? Wherefore, if He be as ye assert very inferior, doth He claim the same honor? Nor doth He stop even here, but goeth on to say,

"He that honoreth not the Son honoreth not the Father which hath sent Him." Seest thou how the honor of the Son is connected with that of the Father? "What of that?" saith one. "We see the same in the case of the Apostles; 'He,' saith Christ, 'who receiveth you receiveth Me.'" (Matt. x. 40.) But in that place He speaketh so, because He maketh the concerns of His servants His own; here, because the Essence and the Glory is One (with that of the Father). Therefore[3] it is not said of the

Apostles "that they may honor," but rightly He saith, "He that honoreth not the Son honoreth not the Father." For where there are two kings, if one is insulted the other is insulted also, and especially when he that is insulted is a son. He is insulted even when one of his soldiers is maltreated; not in the same way as in this case, but as it were in the person of another,[4] while here it is as it were in his own. Wherefore He beforehand said, "That they should honor the Son even as they honor the Father," in order that when He should say, "He that honoreth not the Son honoreth not the Father," thou mightest understand that the honor is the same. For He saith not merely, "he that honoreth not the Son," but "he that honoreth Him not so as I have said" "honoreth not the Father."

"And how," saith one, "can he that sendeth and he that is sent be of the same essence?" Again, thou bringest down the argument to carnal things, and perceivest not that all this has been said for no other purpose, but that we might know Him to be The Cause,[5] and not fall into the error[6] of Sabellius, and that in this manner the infirmity of the Jews might be healed, so that He might not be deemed an enemy of God;[7] for they said, "This man is not of God" (c. ix. 16), "This man hath not come from God." Now to remove this suspicion, high sayings did not contribute so much as the lowly, and therefore continually and everywhere He said that He had been "sent"; not that thou mightest suppose that expression to be[8] any lessening of His greatness, but in order to stop their mouths. And for this cause also He constantly betaketh Himself to the Father, interposing moreover mention of His own high Parentage.[9] For had He said all in proportion to His dignity, the Jews would not have received His words, since because of a few such expressions they persecuted and oftentimes stoned Him; and if looking wholly to them He had used none but low expressions, many in after times might have been harmed. Wherefore He mingleth and blendeth[10] His teaching, both by these lowly sayings stopping, as I said, the mouths of the Jews, and also by expressions suited to His dignity banishing[11] from men of sense any mean notion of what He had said, and proving that such a notion did not in any wise apply to Him at all.

The expression "having been sent" denoteth change of place — but God is everywhere present. Wherefore then saith He that He was

---

[1] οἰκονομίας τινὸς.
[2] al. "folly."
[3] al. "Besides."
[4] διὰ μεσίτου.    [5] τὸν αἴτιον.    [6] νόσον.
[7] For from their extreme senselessness He was counted among them an enemy of God. Morel.
[8] al. "not that He might by this show any lessening," &c.
[9] al. "absolute power."
[10] κιρνᾷ, generally of mixing wine with water.
[11] al. "correcting."

" sent "?   He speaketh in an earthly[1] way,[2] declaring His unanimity with the Father. At least He shapeth His succeeding words with a desire to effect this.

Ver. 24. " Verily, verily, I say unto you, He that heareth My word, and believeth on Him that sent Me, hath everlasting life."

Seest thou how continually He putteth the same thing to cure that feeling of suspicion, both in this place and in what follows by fear and by promises of blessings removing their jealousy of Him, and then again condescending greatly in words? For He said not, " he that heareth My words, and believeth on Me," since they would have certainly deemed that to be pride, and a superfluous pomp of words; because, if after a very long time, and ten thousand miracles, they suspected this when He spake after this manner, much more would they have done so then. It was on this account that at that later period[3] they said to Him, " Abraham is dead, and the prophets are dead, how sayest Thou,[4] If a man keep My saying, he shall never taste of death?" (c. viii. 52.)   In order therefore that they may not here also become furious, see what He saith, " He that heareth My word, and believeth on Him that sent Me, hath everlasting life."   This had no small effect in making His discourse acceptable, when they learned that those who hear Him believe in the Father also; for after having received this with readiness, they would more easily receive the rest. So that the very speaking in a humble manner contributed and led the way to higher things; for after saying, " hath everlasting life," He addeth,

" And cometh not into judgment, but is passed from death unto life."

By these two things He maketh His discourse acceptable; first, because it is the Father who is believed on, and then, because the believer enjoyeth many blessings. And the " cometh not into judgment " meaneth, " is not punished," for He speaketh not of death " here," but of death eternal, as also of the other " life " which is deathless.

Ver. 25. " Verily, verily, I say unto you, the hour cometh, and now is, when the dead shall hear the voice of the Son of God: and they that have heard shall live."

Having said the words, He speaketh also of the proof by deeds.[5] For when He had said, " As the Father raiseth up the dead and quick-eneth them, even so the Son quickeneth whom He will," that the thing may not seem to be mere boasting and pride, He affordeth proof[6]

by works, saying, " The hour cometh "; then, that thou mayest not deem that the time is long, He addeth, " and now is, when the dead shall hear the voice of the Son of God, and they that have heard shall live." Seest thou here His absolute and unutterable authority? For as it shall be in the Resurrection, even so, He saith, it shall be " now." Then too when we hear His voice commanding us we are raised; for, saith the Apostle, " at the command of God the dead shall arise."[7] " And whence," perhaps some one will ask, " is it clear that the words are *not* mere boast?" From what He hath added, " and now is "; because had His promises referred only to some future time, His discourse would have been suspected by them, but now He sup-plieth them with a proof: " While I," saith He, " am tarrying among you, this thing shall come to pass "; and He would not, had He not pos-sessed the power, have promised for that time, lest through the promise He should incur the greater ridicule. Then too He addeth an argu-ment demonstrative of His assertions, saying,

Ver. 26. " For as the Father hath life in Him-self, so hath He given to the Son to have life in Himself."

[3.] Seest thou that this declareth a perfect likeness save in one[8] point, which is the One being a Father, and the Other a Son? for the expression " hath given," merely introduceth this distinction, but declareth that all the rest is equal and exactly alike. Whence it is clear that the Son doeth all things with as much authority and power as the Father, and that He is not empowered from some other source, for He " hath life " so as the Father hath. And on this account, what comes after is straightway added, that from this we may understand the other also. What is this then?   It is,

Ver. 27. " Hath given Him authority to exe-cute judgment also."

And wherefore doth He continually[9] dwell upon " resurrection " and " judgment "? For He saith, " As the Father raiseth up the dead and quickeneth them, even so the Son quicken-eth whom He will ": and again, " the Father judgeth no man, but hath committed all judg-ment to the Son ": and again, " As the Father hath life in Himself so hath He given to the Son to have life in Himself "; and again, " They that have heard [the Voice of the Son of God] shall live "; and here again, " Hath given to Him authority to execute judgment." Wherefore doth He dwell on these things continually? I mean, on " judgment," and " life," and " resur-rection "?   It is because these subjects are able most of any to attract even the obstinate hearer.

---

[1] παχύτερα.
[2] Morel. reads: " for this reason He doth not decline to use a more earthly expression, declaring," &c.
[3] τότε.     [4] σὺ λέγεις, G. T.
[5] Morel. reads: " He spake those great things in words, after-wards He desireth to prove them by works also."
[6] al. " truth."

[7] 1 Thess. iv. 16 [not verbally quoted].
[8] τὸ ἀπαράλλακτον καὶ ἐνὶ μόνῳ τὴν διαφορὰν ἐμφαῖνον.
[9] ἄνω καὶ κάτω.

For the man who is persuaded that he shall both rise again and shall give account to Christ[1] of his transgressions, even though he have seen no other sign, yet having admitted this, will surely run to Him to propitiate his Judge.

"That He is the Son of Man (v. 28), marvel not at this."

Paul of Samosata rendereth it not so; but how? "Hath given Him authority to execute judgment, 'because' He is the Son of Man."[2] Now the passage thus read is inconsequent, for He did not receive judgment "because" He was man, (since then what hindered all men from being judges,) but because He is the Son of that Ineffable Essence, therefore is He Judge. So we must read, "That He is the Son of Man, marvel not at this." For when what He said seemed to the hearers inconsistent, and they deemed Him nothing more than mere man, while His words were greater than suited man, yea, or even angel, and were proper to God only, to solve this objection He addeth,

Ver. 28, 29. "Marvel not [that He is the Son of Man,[3]] for the hour is coming in the which they[4] that are in the tombs shall hear His voice and shall go forth, they that have done good to the resurrection of life, and they that have done evil to the resurrection of judgment."

And wherefore said He not, "Marvel not that He is the Son of Man, for He is also the Son of God," but rather mentioned the "resurrection"? He did indeed put this above, by saying, "shall hear the Voice of the Son of God." And if here He is silent on the matter, wonder not; for after mentioning a work which was proper to God, He then permitteth His hearers to collect from it that He was God, and the Son of God. For had this been continually asserted by Himself, it would at that time have offended them, but when proved by the argument of miracles, it rendered His doctrine less burdensome. So they who put together syllogisms, when having laid down their premises[5] they have fairly[6] proved the point in question, frequently do not draw the conclusion themselves, but to render their hearers more fairly disposed, and to make their victory more evident, cause the opponent himself to give the verdict, so that the by-standers may the rather agree with them when their opponents decide in their favor. When therefore He mentioned the resurrection of Lazarus, He spake not of the Judgment (for it was not for this that Lazarus arose) ; but when He spake generally He also added, that "they that have done good shall go forth unto the resurrection of life, and they that have done evil unto the resurrection of judgment." Thus also John led on

his hearers by speaking of the Judgment, and that "he that believeth not on the Son, shall not see life, but the wrath of God abideth on him" (c. iii. 36) : so too Himself led on Nicodemus : "He that believeth on the Son," He said to him, "is not judged, but he that believeth not is judged already" (c. iii. 18) ; and so here He mentioneth the Judgment-seat[7] and the punishment which shall follow upon evil deeds. For because He had said above, "He that heareth My words and believeth on Him that sent Me," "is not judged," lest any one should imagine that this alone is sufficient for salvation, He addeth also the result of man's life,[8] declaring that "they which have done good shall come forth unto the resurrection of life, and they that have done evil unto the resurrection of judgment." Since then He had said that all the world should render account to Him, and that all at His Voice should rise again, a thing new and strange and even now disbelieved by many who seem to have believed, not to say by the Jews at that time, hear how He goeth to prove it, again condescending to the infirmity of His hearers.

Ver. 30. "I can of Mine own self do nothing ; as I hear I judge, and My judgment is just, because I seek not Mine own will, but the will of Him[9] which sent Me."

Although He had but lately given no trifling proof of the Resurrection by bracing[10] the paralytic ; on which account also He had not spoken of the Resurrection before He had done what fell little short of resurrection. And the Judgment He hinted at after He had braced the body, by saying, "Behold, thou art made whole, sin no more, lest a worse thing come unto thee" ; yet still He proclaimed beforehand the resurrection of Lazarus and of the world. And when He had spoken of these two, that of Lazarus which should come to pass almost immediately, and that of the inhabited world which should be long after, He confirmeth the first by the paralytic and by the nearness of the time, saying, "The hour cometh and now is" ; the other by the raising of Lazarus, by what had already come to pass bringing before their sight what had not yet done so. And this we may observe Him do everywhere, putting (forth) two or three predictions, and always confirming the future by the past.

[4.] Yet after saying and doing so much, since they still were very weak[11] He is not content, but by other expressions calms their disputatious temper,[12] saying, "I can of Myself do nothing ; as I hear I judge, and My judgment is just, because I seek not Mine own will, but the will of Him which sent Me." For since He

---

[1] τούτῳ.
[2] As in our Auth. Version.
[3] τοῦτο, G. T.
[4] πάντες, G. T.
[5] τὰ μέρη.
[6] γενναίως.
[7] δικαστήριον.
[8] τὰ ἐκ τοῦ βίου.
[9] τοῦ Πατρὸς, G. T.
[10] σφίγξας.
[11] al. "even thus too gross."
[12] al. "shamelessness."

appeared to make some assertions strange and varying from those of the Prophets, (for they said that it is God who judgeth all the earth, that is, the human race; and this truth David everywhere loudly proclaimed, "He shall judge the people in righteousness," and, "God is a righteous Judge, strong and patient" (Ps. xcvi. 10, and vii. 11, LXX.); as did all the Prophets and Moses; but Christ said, "The Father judgeth no man, but hath committed all judgment to the Son":[1] an expression which was sufficient to perplex a Jew who heard it, and to make him in turn suspect Christ of being an enemy of God,) He here greatly condescendeth in His speech, and as far as their infirmity requireth, in order to pluck up by the roots this pernicious opinion, and saith, "I can of Myself do nothing"; that is, "nothing strange, or unlike,[2] or what the Father desireth not will ye see done or hear said by Me." And having before declared that He was "the Son of Man," and because they[3] supposed Him to be a man at that time, so also He putteth [His expressions] here. As then when He said above, "We speak that we have heard, and testify that we have seen"; and when John said, "What He hath seen He testifieth, and no man receiveth His testimony" (c. iii. 32); both expressions are used respecting exact knowledge, not concerning hearing and seeing merely; so in this place when He speaketh of "hearing," He declareth nothing else than that it is impossible for Him to desire anything, save what the Father desireth. Still He said not so plainly, (for they would not as yet have at once received it on hearing it thus asserted;) and how? in a manner very condescending and befitting a mere man, "As I hear I judge." Again He useth these words in this place, not with reference to "instruction," (for He said not, "as I am taught," but "as I hear";) nor as though He needed to listen, (for not only did He not require to be taught, but He needed not even to listen;) but it was to declare the Unanimity and Identity of [His and the Father's] decision, as though He had said, "So I judge, as if it were the Father Himself that judged." Then He addeth, "and I know that My judgment is just, because I seek not Mine own will, but the will of Him that sent Me." What sayest Thou? Hast Thou a will different from that of the Father? Yet in another place He saith, "As I and Thou are One," (speaking of will and unanimity,) "grant to these also that they may be one in Us" (c. xvii. 21; not verbally quoted); that is, "in faith concerning Us." Seest thou that the words which seem most humble are those which conceal a high meaning? For what He implieth

is of this kind: not that the will of the Father is one, and His own another; but that, "as one will in one mind, so is Mine own will and My Father's."

And marvel not that He hath asserted so close a conjunction; for with reference to the Spirit also Paul hath used this illustration: "What man knoweth the things of a man, save the spirit of man which is in him? even so the things of God knoweth no man, but the Spirit of God." Thus Christ's meaning is no other than this: "I have not a will different and apart from that of the Father,[4] but if He desireth anything, then I also; if I, then He also. As therefore none could object to the Father judging, so neither may any to Me, for the sentence of Each[5] is given from the same Mind." And if He uttereth these words rather as a man, marvel not, seeing that they still deemed Him to be mere man. Therefore in passages like these it is necessary not merely to enquire into the meaning of the words, but also to take into account the suspicion of the hearers, and listen to what is said as being addressed to that suspicion. Otherwise many difficulties will follow. Consider for instance, He saith, "I seek not Mine own will": according to this then His will is different (from that of the Father), is imperfect, nay, not merely imperfect, but even unprofitable. "For if it be saving, if it agree with that of the Father, wherefore dost Thou not seek it?" Mortals might with reason say so because they have many wills contrary to what seemeth good to the Father, but Thou, wherefore sayest Thou this, who art in all things like the Father? for this none would say is the language even of a "man" made perfect and crucified. For if Paul so blended himself[6] with the will of God as to say, "I live, yet no longer I, but Christ liveth in me" (Gal. ii. 20), how saith the Lord of all, "I seek not Mine own will, but the will of Him that sent Me," as though that will were different? What then is His meaning? He applieth[7] His discourse as if the case were that of a mere man, and suiteth His language to the suspicion of His hearers. For when He had, by what had gone before, given proof of His sayings, speaking partly as God, partly as a mere man, He again as a man endeavoreth to establish[8] the same, and saith, "My judgment is just." And whence is this seen? "Because I seek not Mine own will, but the will of Him that sent Me." "For as in the case of men, he that is free from selfishness cannot be justly charged with having given an unfair decision, so neither will ye now be able to accuse Me. He that desireth to establish his own, may perhaps by

---

[1] al. "I am [He] who judge."  [2] παρηλλαγμένον.
[3] So Morel. and MS. in Bodl. Savile reads, "having shown that they," &c.

[4] According to Savile's conjectural reading, παρὰ τὸ τοῦ Π. in place of παρὰ τοῦ Π. for which is also MS. authority.
[5] al. "each sentence."  [7] al. "brings forward."
[6] ἐκέρασε.  [8] κατασκευάζει.

many be suspected of corrupting justice with this intent; but he that looketh not to his own, what reason can he have for not deciding justly? Apply now this reasoning to My case. Had I said that I was not sent by the Father, had I not referred to Him the glory of what was done, some of you might perhaps have suspected that desiring to gain honor for Myself, I said the thing that is not; but if I impute and refer what is done to another, wherefore and whence can ye have cause to suspect My words?" Seest thou how He confirmed His discourse, and asserted that "His judgment was just" by an argument which any common man might have used in defending himself? Seest thou how what I have often said is clearly visible? What is that? It is that the exceeding humility of the expressions most persuadeth men of sense not to receive the words off hand[1] and then fall down [into low thoughts], but rather to take pains that they reach to the height of their meaning; this humility too with much ease then raiseth up those who were once groveling on the ground.

Now bearing all this in mind, let us not, I exhort you, carelessly pass by Christ's words, but enquire closely into them all, everywhere considering the reason of what has been said; and let us not deem that ignorance and simplicity will be sufficient to excuse us, for He hath bidden us not merely to be "harmless," but "wise." (Matt. x. 16.) Let us therefore practice wisdom with simplicity, both as to doctrines, and the right actions[2] of our lives; let us judge ourselves here, that we be not condemned with the world hereafter;[3] let us act towards our fellow-servants as we desire our Master to act towards us: for (we say), "Forgive us our debts, as we forgive our debtors." (Matt. vi. 12.) I know that the smitten soul endureth not meekly, but if we consider that by so doing we do a kindness not to him who hath grieved us but to ourselves, we shall soon let go the venom of our wrath; for he who forgave not the hundred pence to him who had transgressed against him, wronged not his fellow-servant but himself, by rendering himself liable for the ten thousand talents of which he had before received forgiveness. (Matt. xviii. 30–34.) When therefore we forgive not others, we forgive not ourselves. And so let us not merely say to God, "remember not our offenses"; but let each also say to himself, "let us not remember the offenses of our fellow-servants done against us." For thou first givest judgment on thine own sins, and God judgeth after;[4] thou proposest the law concerning remission and punishment, thou declarest thy decision on these matters, and therefore whether God shall or shall not remember, rests with thee. For which cause Paul biddeth us "forgive, if any one hath cause of complaint against any" (Col. iii. 13), and not simply forgive, but so that not even any remnants be left behind. Since Christ not only did not publish our transgressions, but did not put us the transgressors in mind of them, nor say, "in such and such things hast thou offended," but remitted and blotted out the handwriting, not reckoning our offenses, as Paul hath also declared. (Col. ii. 14.) Let us too do this; let us wipe away all [trespasses against us] from our minds; and if any good thing hath been done to us by him that hath grieved us, let us only reckon that; but if anything grievous and hard to bear, let us cast it forth and blot it out, so that not even a vestige of it remain. And if no good has been done us by him, so much the greater recompense and higher credit will be ours if we forgive. Others by watching, by making the earth their bed, by ten thousand hardships, wipe away their sins, but thou by an easier way, I mean by not remembering wrongs, mayest cause all thy trespasses to disappear. Why then thrustest thou the sword against thyself, as do mad and frantic men, and banishest thyself from the life which is to come, when thou oughtest to use every means to attain unto it? For if this present life be so desirable, what can one say of that other from which pain, and grief, and mourning, have fled away? There it needs not to fear death, nor imagine any end to those good things. Blessed, thrice blessed, yea, and this many times over, are they who enjoy that blessed rest, while they are miserable, thrice miserable, yea, ten thousand times miserable, who have cast themselves forth from that blessedness. "And what," saith some one, "is it that maketh us to enjoy that life?" Hear the Judge Himself conversing with a certain young man on this matter. When the young man said, "What shall I do to inherit eternal life?" (Matt. xix. 16) Christ, after repeating to him the other commandments, ended with the love of his neighbor. Perhaps, like that rich man, some of my hearers will say, "that we also have kept these, for we neither have robbed, nor killed, nor committed adultery"; yet assuredly thou wilt not be able to say this, that thou hast loved thy neighbor as thou oughtest to have loved him. For if a man hath envied or spoken evil of another, if he hath not helped him when injured, or not imparted to him of his substance, then neither hath he loved him. Now Christ hath commanded not only this, but something besides. What then is this? "Sell," he saith, "that thou hast, and give to the poor; and come, follow Me" (Matt. xix. 21): terming the imitating Him in our actions "following" Him. What learn we hence? First, that

---

[1] ἐκ προχείρου.
[2] κατορθωμάτων.
[3] τότε.
[4] ἕπεται.

he who hath not all these things cannot attain unto the chief places in " that " rest. For after the young man had said, "All these things have I done," Christ, as though some great thing were wanting to his being perfectly approved, replied, " If thou wilt be perfect, sell that thou hast, and give to the poor: and come, follow Me." First then we may learn this; secondly, that Christ rebuked the man for his vain boast; for one who lived in such superfluity, and regarded not others living in poverty, how could he love his neighbor? So that neither in this matter did he speak truly. But let us do both the one and the other of these things; let us be eager to empt out our substance, and to purchase heaven. Since if for worldly honor men have often expended their whole possessions, an honor which was to stay here below, and even here not to stay by us long, (for many even much before their deaths have been stripped of their supremacy, and others because of it have often lost their lives, and yet, although aware of this, they expend all for its sake;) if now they do so much for this kind of honor, what can be more wretched than we if for the sake of that honor which abideth and which cannot be taken from us we will not give up even a little, nor supply to others those things which in a short time while yet here we shall leave? What madness must it be, when it is in our power voluntarily to give to others, and so to take with us those things of which we shall even against our will be deprived, to refuse to do so? Yet if a man were being led to death, and it were proposed to him to give up all his goods and so go free, we should think a favor was conferred upon him; and shall we, who are being led on the way to the pit, shall we, when it is allowed us to give up half and be free, prefer to be punished, and uselessly to retain what is not ours even to the losing what is so? What excuse shall we have, what claim for pardon, who, when so easy a road has been cut for us unto life, rush down precipices, and travel along an unprofitable path, depriving ourselves of all things both here and hereafter, when we might enjoy both in security? If then we did not so before, let us at least stop now; and coming to ourselves, let us rightly dispose of things present, that we may easily receive those which are to come, through the grace and lovingkindness of our Lord Jesus Christ, with whom to the Father and the Holy Ghost be glory, for ever and ever. Amen.

# HOMILY XL.

## JOHN v. 31, 32.

" If I bear witness of Myself, My witness is not true; there is another that beareth witness of Me, and I know that the witness which he witnesseth of Me is true."

[1.] IF any one unpracticed in the art undertake to work a mine, he will get no gold, but confounding all aimlessly and together, will undergo a labor unprofitable and pernicious: so also they who understand not the method[1] of Holy Scripture, nor search out its peculiarities[2] and laws, but go over all its points carelessly and in one manner, will mix the gold with earth, and never discover the treasure which is laid up in it. I say this now because the passage before us containeth much gold, not indeed manifest to view, but covered over with much obscurity, and therefore by digging and purifying we must arrive at the legitimate sense. For who would not at once be troubled at hearing Christ say, " If I testify of Myself, My witness is not true"; inasmuch as He often appeareth to have testified of Himself? For instance, conversing with the Samaritan woman He said, " I Am that speak unto thee ": and in like manner to the blind man, "It is He that talketh with thee " (c. ix. 37); and rebuking the Jews, " Ye say,[3] thou blasphemest, because I said I am the Son of God." (c. x. 36.) And in many other places besides He doth this. If now all these assertions be false, what hope of salvation shall we have? And where shall we find truth when Truth Itself declareth, " My witness is not true " ? Nor doth this appear to be the only contradiction; there is another not less than this. He saith farther on, " Though I bear witness of Myself, yet My witness is true " (c. viii. 14); which then, tell me, am I to receive, and which deem a falsehood? If we take them out thus [from the context] simply as they are said, without carefully considering the person to whom nor the cause for which they are said, nor any other like circumstances, they will both be falsehoods. For if His witness be "not true," then this assertion is not true either, not merely the second, but the first also. What then is the meaning? We need great watchfulness, or rather the grace of God, that we rest not in the mere

---

[1] lit. " consequence."		[2] ἰδιώματα.		[3] Savile reads, " and to the Jews, How say ye," &c.

words; for thus the heretics err, because they enquire not into the object of the speaker nor the disposition of the hearers. If we add not these and other points besides, as times and places and the opinions of the listeners, many absurd consequences will follow.

What then is the meaning?[1] The Jews were about to object to Him, "If thou bearest witness[2] concerning thyself, thy witness is not true" (c. viii. 13): therefore He spake these words in anticipation; as though He had said, "Ye will surely say to Me, we believe thee not; for no one that witnesseth of himself is readily[3] held trustworthy among men." So that the "is not true" must not be read absolutely, but with reference to[4] their suspicions, as though He had said, "to you it is not true"; and so He uttered the words not looking to His own dignity, but to their secret thoughts. When He saith, "My witness is not true," He rebuketh their opinion of Him, and the objection about to be urged by them against Him; but when He saith, "Though I bear witness of Myself, My witness is true" (c. viii. 14), He declareth the very nature of the thing itself, namely, that as God they ought to deem Him trustworthy even when speaking of Himself. For since He had spoken of the resurrection of the dead, and of the judgment, and that he that believeth on Him is not judged, but cometh unto life, and that He shall sit to require account of all men, and that He hath the same Authority and Power with the Father; and since He was about again otherwise to prove these things, He necessarily put their objection first. "I told you," He saith, "that 'as the Father raiseth the dead and quickeneth them, so the Son quickeneth whom He will'; I told you that 'the Father judgeth no man, but hath committed all judgment unto the Son'; I told you that men must 'honor the Son as they honor the Father'; I told you that 'he that honoreth not the Son honoreth not the Father'; I told you that 'he that heareth My words and believeth them shall not see death, but hath passed from death unto life' (v. 24; not exactly quoted); that My voice shall raise the dead, some now, some hereafter; that I shall demand account from all men of their transgressions, that I shall judge righteously, and recompense those who have walked uprightly." Now since all these were assertions, since the things asserted were important, and since no clear proof of them had as yet been afforded to the Jews but one rather[5] indistinct, He putteth their objection first when He is about to proceed[6] to establish His assertions, speaking somewhat in this way if not in these very words:[7] "Perhaps

ye will say, thou assertest all this, but thou art not a credible witness, since thou testifiest of thyself." First then checking their disputatious spirit by setting forth what they would say, and showing that He knew the secrets of their hearts, and giving this first proof of His power, after stating the objection He supplieth other proofs clear and indisputable, producing three witnesses to what He said, namely, the works wrought by Him, the witness of the Father, and the preaching of John. And He putteth first the less important witness of John. For after saying, "There is another that beareth witness of Me, and I know that his witness is true," He addeth,

Ver. 33. "Ye sent unto John, and he bare witness unto the truth."

Yet if Thy witness be not true, how sayest Thou, "I know that the testimony of John is true, and that he hath borne witness to the truth"? and seest thou (O man) how clear it hence is, that the expression, "My witness is not true," was addressed to their secret thoughts?

[2.] "What then," saith some one, "if John bare witness partially."[8] That the Jews might not assert this, see how He removeth this suspicion. For He said not, "John testified of Me," but, "Ye first sent to John, and ye would not have sent had ye not deemed him trustworthy." Nay, what is more, they had sent not to ask him about Christ, but about himself, and the man whom they deemed trustworthy in what related to himself they would much more deem so in what related to another. For it is, so to speak, the nature of us all not to give so much credit to those who speak of themselves as to those who speak of others; yet him they deemed so trustworthy as not to require even concerning himself any other testimony. For they who were sent said not, "What sayest thou concerning Christ?" but, "Who art thou? What sayest thou of thyself?" So great admiration felt they for the man. Now to all this Christ made allusion by saying, "Ye sent unto John." And on this account the Evangelist hath not merely related that they sent, but is exact as to the persons sent that[9] they were Priests and of the Pharisees, not common or abject persons, nor such as might be corrupted or cheated, but men able to understand exactly what he said.

Ver. 34. "But I receive not testimony from man."

"Why then hast Thou brought forward that of John?" His testimony was not the "testimony of man," for, saith he, "He that sent me to baptize with water, He said unto me." (c. i. 33.) So that John's testimony was the testimony of God; for having learned from Him he said what he did. But that none should ask, "Whence is it

[1] al. "let us see then with what intent these words were said."
[2] σὺ μαρτυρεῖς, G. T.    [3] al. "ever."
[4] al. with the addition "to their," &c.
[5] al. "in every way."    [6] ὁρμᾶν, al. χωρεῖν. [saith."
[7] Morel. reads, "all but conclusively refuting them by what He

[8] χάριτι.    [9] al. "showing that."

clear that he learnt from God?" and stop at
this, He abundantly silences them by still addressing Himself to their thoughts. For neither
was it likely that many would know these things;
they had hitherto given heed unto John as to
one who spake of himself, and therefore Christ
saith, " I receive not testimony from man."
And that the Jews might not ask, "And if Thou
wert not about to receive the testimony of man,
and by it to strengthen Thyself, why hast Thou
brought forward this man's testimony ?" see
how He correcteth this contradiction by what
He addeth. For after saying, "I receive not
testimony from man," He hath added,

"But these things I say, that ye may be
saved."

What He saith is of this kind ; " I, being God,
needed not the witness of John which is man's
witness, yet because ye gave more heed to him,
believe him more trustworthy than any, ran to
him as to a prophet, (for all the city was poured
forth to Jordan,) and have not believed on Me,
even when working miracles, therefore I remind
you of that witness of his."

Ver. 35. "He was a burning and a shining
light, and ye were willing for a season to rejoice
in his light.'

That they may not reply, "What if he did
speak and we received him not," He showeth
that they did receive John's sayings : since they
sent not common men, but priests and Pharisees,
and were willing to rejoice ;[1] so much did they
admire the man, and at the same time had nothing to say against his words. But the "for a
season," is the expression of one noting their
levity,[2] and the fact that they soon started away
from him.

Ver. 36: "But I have greater witness than
that of John."

" For had ye been willing to admit faith according to the (natural) consequence of the
facts, I would have brought you over by My
works more than he by his words. But since ye
will not, I bring you to John, not as needing his
testimony, but because I do all 'that ye may be
saved.' For I have greater witness than that of
John, namely, that from My works; yet I do
not merely consider how I may be made acceptable to you by credible evidence, but how by
that (of persons) known[3] to and admired by
you." Then glancing at them and saying that
they rejoiced for a season in his (John's) light,
He declared that their zeal was but temporary
and uncertain.[4]

He called John a torch,[5] signifying that he
had not light of himself, but by the grace of the
Spirit ; but the circumstance which caused the

absolute distinction[6] between Himself and John,
namely, that He was the Sun of righteousness,
this He put not yet ; but merely hinting as yet
at this He touched[7] them sharply, by showing
that from the same disposition which led them
to despise John, neither could they believe in
Christ. Since it was but for a season that they
admired even the man whom they did admire,
and who, had they not acted thus, would soon
have led them by the hand to Jesus. Having
then proved them altogether unworthy of forgiveness, He went on to say, "I have greater
witness than that of John." "What is that?"
It is that from His works.

" For the works," He saith, "which the Father
hath given Me to finish, the same works that I
do bear witness of Me that the Father sent[8]
Me."

By this He reminded them of the paralytic
restored, and of many other things. The words
perhaps one of them might have asserted were
mere boast, and said by reason of John's friendship towards Him, (though indeed it was not in
their power to say even this of John, a man
equal to the exact practice of wisdom,[9] and on
this account admired by them,) but the works
could not even among the maddest of them
admit this suspicion ; therefore He added this
second testimony, saying, "The works which the
Father hath given Me to finish, the same works
that I do bear witness of Me that the Father sent
Me."

[3.] In this place He also meeteth the accusation respecting the violation of the Sabbath.
For since those persons argued, "How can he be
from God, seeing that he keepeth not the Sabbath?" (c. ix. 16), therefore He saith, "Which
My Father hath given unto Me." Yet in truth,
He acted with absolute power, but in order
most abundantly to show that He doth nothing
contrary to the Father, therefore He hath put the
expression of much inferiority. Since why did
He not say, "The works which the Father hath
given Me testify that I am equal to the Father"?
for both of these truths were to be learned from
the works, that He did nothing contrary, and
that He was equal to Him who begat Him ; a
point which He is establishing elsewhere, where
He saith, "If ye believe not Me, believe the
works : that ye may know and believe that I am
in the Father and the Father in Me."[10] (c. x. 38.)
In both respects, therefore, the works bare witness to Him, that He was equal to the Father,
and that He did nothing contrary to Him. Why
then said He not so, instead of leaving out the
greater and putting forward this? Because to
establish this was His first object. For although

---

[1] clause omitted in Ben.                    [3] al. "nearer."
[2] εὐκολίαν.
[4] This passage is read variously in Ben. and MS. but without
any variety of meaning.          [5] λύχνον.

[6] ἀντιδιαστολὴν.                          [7] al. "reaches."
[8] ἀπέστειλε [ἀπέσταλκε, G. T.].
[9] φιλοσοφεῖν.
[10] ἐν ἐμοὶ ὁ Πατὴρ, κἀγὼ ἐν αὐτῷ, G. T.

it was a far less thing to have it believed that He came from God, than to have it believed that God was equal with Him, (for that belonged to the Prophets also,[1] but this never,) still He taketh much pains as to the lesser point, as knowing that, this admitted,[2] the other would afterwards be easily received. So that making no mention of the more important portion of the testimony, He putteth[3] its lesser office, that by this they may receive the other also. Having effected this, He addeth,

Ver. 37. "And the Father Himself, which hath sent Me, hath borne witness of Me."

Where did He "bear witness of" Him? In Jordan: "This is My beloved Son, in whom I am well pleased" (Matt. iii. 16); hear Him.[4] Yet even this needed proof. The testimony of John then was clear, for they themselves had sent to him, and could not deny it. The testimony from miracles was in like manner clear, for they had seen them wrought, and had heard from him who was healed, and had believed; whence also they drew their accusation. It therefore remained to give proof to the testimony of the Father. Next in order to effect this, He added,

"Ye have neither heard His voice at any time":

How then saith Moses, "The Lord spake, and Moses answered"? (Ex. xix. 19); and David, "He had heard a tongue which he knew not" (Ps. lxxxi. 5); and Moses again, "Is there any such people which hath 'heard the voice of God'?" (Deut. iv. 33.)

"Nor seen His shape."

Yet Isaiah, Jeremiah, and Ezekiel, are said to have seen Him, and many others. What then is that which Christ saith now? He guideth them by degrees to a philosophical doctrine, showing that with God is neither voice nor shape, but that He is higher than such forms or sounds like these. For as when He saith, "Ye have not heard His voice," He doth not mean that God doth not indeed utter a voice, but one which cannot be heard; so when He saith, "Nor seen His shape," He doth not mean that God hath a shape though one invisible, but that neither of these things belongeth to God. And in order that they might not say, "Thou art a boaster, God spake to Moses only"; (this at least they did say, "We know that God spake with Moses: as for this fellow, we know not whence He is" — c. ix. 29;) on this account He spake as He did, to show that there is neither voice nor shape with God. "But why," He saith, "name I these things? Not only have ye 'neither heard His voice nor seen His shape,' but it is not even in your power to assert that of which you most boast and of which you are all most fully assured, namely, that ye have received and keep His commandments." Wherefore He addeth,

Ver. 38. "And ye have not His word abiding in you."

That is, the ordinances, the commandments, the Law, and the Prophets. For even if God ordained these, still they are not with you, since ye believe not on Me. Because, if the Scriptures everywhere say[5] that it is necessary to give heed to[6] Me, and yet ye believe not, it is quite clear that His word is removed from you. Wherefore again He addeth,

"For whom He hath sent, Him ye believe not."

Then that they may not argue, "How, if we have not heard His voice, hath He testified unto thee?" He saith,

Ver. 39. "Search the Scriptures, for they are they which testify of Me."

Since by these the Father gave His testimony. He gave it indeed by Jordan also and in the mount, but Christ bringeth not forward those voices; perhaps by doing so[7] He would have been disbelieved;[8] for one of them, that in the mount, they did not hear, and the other they heard indeed, but heeded not. For this reason He referreth them to the Scriptures, showing that from them cometh the Father's[9] testimony, having first removed the old grounds on which they used to boast, either as having seen God or as having heard His voice. For as it was likely that they would disbelieve His voice, and picture to themselves what took place on Sinai, after first correcting their suspicions on these points, and showing that what had been done was a condescension, He then referreth them to the testimony of the Scriptures.

[4.] And from these too let us also, when we war against heretics, arm and fortify ourselves. For "all Scripture is given by inspiration of God, and is profitable for doctrine, for reproof, for correction, for instruction in righteousness, that the man of God may be perfect, thoroughly furnished unto every good work" (2 Tim. iii. 16, 17); not that he may have some and not others, for such a man is not "perfect." For tell me what profit is it, if a man pray continually, but give not liberal alms? or if he give liberal alms, but be covetous or violent? or if he be not covetous nor violent, but (is liberal) to make a show before men, and to gain the praise of the beholders? or if he give alms with exactness and according to God's pleasure, yet be lifted up by this very thing, and be high-

---

[1] al. "the Prophets said."     [2] al. "said."
[3] al. "deems worthy of mention."
[4] The latter words heard at the Transfiguration.

[5] al. "teach."     [6] al. "believe."     [7] ἐντεῦθεν.
[8] al. "they would have disbelieved them."
[9] al. "of the Spirit."

minded? or if he be humble and constant in fasting, but covetous, greedy of gain,[1] and nailed to earth, and one who introduceth into his soul the mother of mischief? for the love of money is the root of all evils.[2] Let us then shudder at the action, let us flee the sin; this hath made the world a waste,[3] this hath brought all things into confusion, this seduceth us from the most blessed service of Christ. "It is not possible,"[4] He saith, "to serve God and mammon." For mammon giveth commands contradictory to those of Christ. The one saith, "Give to them that need"; the other, "Plunder the goods of the needy." Christ saith, "Forgive them that wrong thee"; the other, "Prepare snares against those who do thee no wrong." Christ saith, "Be merciful and kind"; mammon saith, "Be savage and cruel, and count the tears of the poor as nothing"; to the intent that he may render the Judge stern to us in that day. For then all our actions shall come[5] before our eyes, and those who have been injured and stripped by us, shutting us out from all excuse. Since if Lazarus, who received no wrong from Dives, but only did not enjoy any of his good things, stood forth at that time[6] as a bitter accuser and allowed him not to obtain any pardon, what excuse, tell me, shall they have, who, besides giving no alms of their own substance, seize that of others, and overthrow orphans' houses? If they who have not fed Christ when He hungered have drawn such fire upon their heads, what consolation shall they enjoy who plunder what belongs not to them at all, who weave ten thousand law-suits, who unjustly grasp the property of all men? Let us then cast out this desire; and we shall cast it out if we think of those before us who did wrongfully, who were covetous and are gone. Do[9] not others enjoy their wealth and labors while they lie in punishment, and vengeance, and intolerable woes? And how can this be anything but extreme folly, to weary and vex ourselves, that living we may strain ourselves with labor, and on our departure hence undergo intolerable punishments and vengeances, when we might have enjoyed ourselves here, (for nothing so much causeth pleasure as the consciousness of almsgiving,[10]) and departing to that place might have been delivered from all our woes, and obtained ten thousand blessings? For as wickedness is wont to punish those who go after it, even before (they arrive at) the pit, so also virtue, even before the (gift of) the Kingdom, provides delights for those who here practice it, making them to live in company with good hopes and continual pleasure. Therefore that we may obtain this, both here and in the life to come, let us hold fast to good works, so shall we gain the future crown; to which may we all reach through the grace and lovingkindness of our Lord Jesus Christ, by whom and with whom, to the Father and the Holy Ghost, be glory, now and ever, and world without end. Amen.

# HOMILY XLI.

JOHN v. 39, 40.

"Search the Scriptures; for in them ye think ye have eternal life; and they are they which testify of Me. And ye will not come to Me that ye might have [eternal[7]] life."

[I.] BELOVED, let us make great account of spiritual things, and not think that it is sufficient for us to salvation to pursue them anyhow. For if in things of this life a man can gain no great profit if he conduct them in an indifferent and chance way, much more will this be the case in spiritual things, since these require yet greater attention. Wherefore Christ when He referred the Jews to the Scriptures, sent them not to a mere reading, but a careful and considerate[8] search; for He said not, "Read the Scriptures," but, "Search the Scriptures." Since the sayings relating to Him required great attention, (for they had been concealed from the beginning for the advantage of the men of that time,) He biddeth them now dig down with care that they might be able to discover what lay in the depth below. These sayings were not on the surface, nor were they cast forth to open view, but lay like some treasure hidden very deep. Now he that searcheth for hidden things, except he seek them with care and toil, will never find the object of his search. For which cause He said, "Search the Scriptures, because in them ye think ye have eternal life." He said not, "Ye have," but "ye think," showing that they gained from them nothing great or high, expecting as they did to be saved by the mere reading, without the addi-

---

1 ἐμπορικὸς.
2 al. "for Paul has said," &c.
3 or, "revolted," ἀνάστατον.
4 οὐ δύνασθε, G. T.
5 al. "stand."
6 τότε.
7 not in G. T.
8 al. "inquisitive."
9 al. "shall."
10 al. "almsgiving and a clear conscience."

tion of[1] faith. What He saith therefore is of this kind: "Do ye not admire the Scriptures, do ye not think that they are the causes of all life? By these I confirm My claims now, for they are they which testify of Me, yet ye will not come to Me that ye may have eternal life." It was thus with good reason that He said, "ye think," because they would not obey, but merely prided themselves on the bare reading. Then lest owing to His very tender care He should incur among them the suspicion of vainglory, and because He desired to be believed by them, should be deemed to be seeking His own; (for He reminded them of the words of John, and of the witness of God, and of His own works, and said all He could to draw them to Him, and promised them "life";[2]) since, I say, it was likely that many would suspect that He spake these things from a desire of glory, hear what He saith:

Ver. 41. "I receive not honor from men."

That is, "I need it not": "My nature," He saith, "is not of such a kind as to need the honor which is from men, for if the sun can receive no addition from the light of a candle, much farther am I from needing the honor which is from men." "Why then," asks some one, "sayest thou these things, if thou needest it not?" "That ye may be saved." This He positively asserted above, and the same He implied here also, by saying, "that ye might have life." Moreover, He putteth another reason:

Ver. 42. "But I know you that ye have not the love of God in you."

For when under pretense of loving God they[3] persecuted Him because He made Himself equal with God, and He knew that they would not believe Him, lest any one should ask, "why speakest thou these words?" "I speak them," He saith, "to convict you of this, that it is not for the love of God that ye persecute Me, if it be so that He testifieth to Me both by works and by the Scriptures. For as before this when ye deemed Me an enemy of God ye drove Me away, so now, since I have declared these things, ye ought to have hastened to Me, if ye had really loved God. But ye love Him not. And therefore have I spoken these words, to show that you are possessed with excessive pride, that you are vainly boasting and shading over[4] your own enviousness." And the same He proveth not by these things only, but by those that should come to pass.

Ver. 43. "I am come in My Father's name, and ye receive Me not; if another shall come in his own name, him will ye receive."

[2.] Seest thou that He everywhere declareth that He hath been "sent," that judgment hath been committed to Him by the Father, that He can do nothing of Himself, in order that He may cut off all excuse for their unfairness? But who is it that He here saith shall come "in his own name"? He alludeth here to Antichrist, and putteth[5] an incontrovertible proof of their unfairness. "For if as loving God ye persecute Me, much more ought this to have taken place[6] in the case of Antichrist. For he will neither say that he is sent by the Father, nor that he cometh according to his will, but in everything contrariwise, seizing like a tyrant what belongeth not to him, and asserting that he is the very God over all, as Paul saith, 'Exalting himself above all that is called God, or that is worshiped, showing himself that he is God.' (2 Thess. ii. 4.) This is to 'come in his own name.' I do not so, but am come in the Name of My Father." That they received not One who said that He was sent of God, was a sufficient proof that they loved not God; but now from the contrary of this fact, from their being about to receive Antichrist, He showeth their shamelessness.[7] For when they received not One who asserteth that He was sent by God, and are about to worship one who knoweth Him not, and who saith that he is God over all, it is clear that their persecution proceeded from malice and from hating God. On this account He putteth two reasons for His words; and first the kinder one,[8] "That ye may be saved"; and, "That ye may have life": and when they would have mocked at Him, He putteth the other which was more striking, showing that even although His hearers should not believe, yet that God was wont always to do His own works. Now Paul speaking concerning Antichrist said prophetically, that "God shall send them strong delusion,— that they all might be judged who believed not the truth, but had pleasure in unrighteousness." (2 Thess. ii. 11, 12.) Christ said not, "He shall come"; but, "if He come," from tenderness for His hearers; and because all their obstinacy[9] was not yet complete. He was silent as to the reason of His coming; but Paul, for those who can understand, has particularly alluded to it. For it is he who taketh away all excuse from them.

Christ then putteth also the cause of their unbelief, saying,

Ver. 44. "How can ye believe, which receive honor one of another, and seek not the honor that cometh from God only?"

Hence again He showeth that they looked not to the things of God, but that under this pretense they desired to gratify private feeling, and were so far from doing this on account of

---

[1] al. "being destitute of."
[2] al. "and promised all those things so as to draw them to Himself."     [3] al. "they often."     [4] al. "veiling."

[5] al. "whom also He putteth."
[6] al. "ought ye to do this."
[7] al. "enviousness."

[8] al. "kindness, saying."
[9] al. "wickedness."

His glory, that they preferred honor from men to that which cometh from Him. How then were they likely to entertain[1] such hostility towards Him[2] for a kind of honor which they so despised, as to prefer to it the honor which cometh from men?

Having told them that they had not the love of God, and having proved it by what was doing in His case, and by what should be in the case of Antichrist, and having demonstrated that they were deprived of all excuse, He next bringeth Moses to be their accuser, going on to say,

Ver. 45–47. "Do not think that I will accuse you to the Father; there is one that accuseth you, even Moses, in whom ye trust. For had ye believed Moses, ye would have believed Me; for he wrote of Me. But if ye believe not his writings, how shall ye believe My words?"

What He saith is of this kind: "It is Moses[3] who has been insulted more than I[4] by your conduct towards Me, for ye have disbelieved him rather than Me." See how in every way He hath cast them out from all excuse. "Ye said that ye loved God when ye persecuted Me; I have shown that ye did so from hatred of Him: ye say[5] that I break the Sabbath and annul the Law; I have rid Me of this slander also: ye maintain[6] that ye believe in Moses by what ye dare to do against Me; I on the contrary show that this is most to disbelieve in Moses; for so far am I from opposing the Law, that he who shall accuse you is none other than the man who gave you the Law." As then He said of the Scriptures, in which "ye think ye have eternal life," so of Moses also He saith, "in whom ye trust"; everywhere conquering them by their own weapons.

"And whence," saith some one, "is it clear that Moses will accuse us, and that thou art not a boaster? What hast thou to do with Moses? Thou hast broken the Sabbath which he ordained that we should keep; how then should he accuse us? And how doth it appear that we shall believe on another who cometh in his own name? All these assertions thou makest without evidence." Now in truth all these points are proved above. "For" (Christ would reply) "since it is acknowledged that I came from God, both by the works, by the voice of John, and by the testimony of the Father, it is evident that Moses will accuse the Jews." For what saith he? "If a man come doing miracles and leading you to God, and truly foretelling things future, ye must hearken unto him with all readiness." Now Christ had done all this. He wrought miracles in very truth, He drew all

men to God, and (so that He[7]) caused accomplishment to follow His predictions.[8]

"But whence doth it appear that they will believe another?" From their hating Christ, since they who turn aside from Him who cometh according to the will of God will, it is quite plain, receive the enemy of God. And marvel not if He now putteth forward Moses, although He said, "I receive not witness from man," for He referreth them not to Moses, but to the Scriptures of God. However, since the Scriptures terrified them less, He bringeth round His discourse to the very person (of Moses), setting over against them their Lawgiver as their accuser, thus rendering the terror more impressive;[9] and each of their assertions He refuteth. Observe: they said that they persecuted Him through love for God, He showeth that they did so through hating God; they said that they held fast to Moses, He showeth that they acted thus because they believed not Moses. For had they been zealous for the law, they ought to have received Him who fulfilled it; if they loved God they ought to have believed One who drew them to Him, if they believed Moses they ought to have done homage to One of whom Moses prophesied. "But" (saith Christ) "if Moses is disbelieved before My coming, it is nothing unlikely that I, who am heralded by him, should be driven away by you." As then He had shown from their conduct towards Himself that they who admired John (really) despised him, so now He showeth that they who thought that they believed Moses, believed him not, and turneth back on their own head all that they thought to put forward in their own behalf. "So far," He saith, "am I from drawing you away from the Law, that I call your Lawgiver himself to be your accuser."

That the Scriptures testified of Him He declared, but where they testify He added not; desiring to inspire them with greater awe, and to prompt them to search, and to reduce them to the necessity of questioning. For had He told them readily and without their questioning, they would have rejected the testimony; but now, if they gave any heed to His words, they needed first of all to ask, and learn from Him what that testimony was.[10] On this account He dealeth the more largely in assertions and threats, not in proofs only, that even so He may bring them over by fear of what He saith; but they even so were silent. Such a thing is wickedness; whatsoever a man say or do it is not stirred to move, but remaineth keeping its peculiar venom.

---

[1] ἀναδέχεσθαι.
[2] or, "to take on them such hostility as they would have incurred by following Him."
[3] ἐκεῖνος.
[4] or, "before Me."
[5] al. "accuse."
[6] al. "profess."

[7] Not in all copies.
[8] Not found in so many words. The command is given with this test, Deut. xviii. 18–22; see also Deut. xiii. 1.
[9] al. "more horrible."
[10] al. "to enquire even if He held His peace."

Wherefore we must cast out all wickedness from our souls, and never more contrive any deceit; for, saith one, "To the perverse God sendeth crooked paths" (Prov. xxi. 8, LXX.); and, "The holy spirit of discipline[1] will flee deceit, and remove from thoughts that are without understanding." (Wisd. i. 5.) For nothing maketh men so foolish as wickedness; since when a man is treacherous, unfair,[2] ungrateful, (these are different forms of wickedness,) when without having been wronged he grieves another, when he weaves deceits, how shall he not exhibit an example of excessive folly? Again, nothing maketh men so wise as virtue; it rendereth them thankful and fair-minded, merciful, mild, gentle, and candid; it is wont to be the mother of all other blessings. And what is more understanding than one so disposed? for virtue is the very spring and root of prudence, just as all wickedness hath its beginning in folly. For the insolent man and the angry become the prey of their respective passions from lack of wisdom; on which account the prophet said, "There is no soundness in my flesh: my wounds stink and are corrupt because of my foolishness" (Ps. xxxviii. 3, 4): showing that all sin hath its beginning in folly: and so the virtuous man who hath the fear of God is more understanding than any; wherefore a wise man hath said, "The fear of the Lord is the beginning of wisdom." (Prov. i. 7.) If then to fear God is to have wisdom, and the wicked man hath not that fear, he is deprived of that which is wisdom indeed; —and deprived of that which is wisdom indeed, he is more foolish than any. And yet many admire the wicked as being able to do injustice and harm, not knowing that they ought to deem them wretched above all men, who thinking to injure others thrust the sword against themselves;—an act of extremest folly, that a man should strike himself and not even know that he doth so, but should think that he is injuring another while he is killing himself. Wherefore Paul, knowing that we slay ourselves when we smite others, saith, "Why do ye not rather take wrong? Why do ye not rather suffer yourselves to be defrauded?" (1 Cor. vi. 7.) For the not suffering wrong consists in doing none, as also the not being ill-used in not using others ill; though this assertion may seem a riddle to the many, and to those who will not learn true wisdom. Knowing this, let us not call wretched or lament for those who suffer injury or insult, but for such who inflict these things; these are they who have been most injured, who have made God to be at war with them, and have opened the mouths of ten thousand accusers, who are getting an evil reputation in the present life, and drawing down on themselves severe punishment in the life to come. While those who have been wronged by them, and have nobly borne it all, have God favorable to them, and all to condone with, and praise, and entertain them. Such as these in the present life, shall enjoy an exceeding good report, as affording the strongest example of true wisdom, and in the life to come shall share the good things everlasting; to which may we all attain through the grace and lovingkindness of our Lord Jesus Christ, with whom to the Father and the Holy Ghost be glory, now and ever, and world without end. Amen.

# HOMILY XLII.

### JOHN vi. 1, 4.

"After these things Jesus went over the sea of Galilee, into the parts of[3] Tiberias. And a great multitude followed Him, because they saw the[4] miracles which He did on them that were diseased. And Jesus departed[5] into a mountain, and there sat with His disciples. And the Passover of the Jews[6] was nigh."

[1.] BELOVED, let us not contend with violent men, but learn[7] when the doing so brings no hurt to our virtue to give place to their evil counsels; for so all their hardihood is checked. As darts when they fall upon a firm,[8] hard, and resisting substance, rebound with great violence on those who throw them, but when the violence of the cast hath nothing to oppose it, it soon becometh weaker and ceaseth, so is it with insolent men; when we contend with them they become the fiercer, but when we yield and give ground, we easily abate all their madness. Wherefore the Lord when He knew that the Pharisees had heard "that Jesus made and baptized more disciples than John," went into Galilee, to quench their envy, and to soften by His retirement the wrath which was likely to be engendered by these reports. And when He departed for the second time into Galilee, He cometh not to the same places as before; for He went not to Cana,

---

[1] σοφίας.
[2] ἀγνώμων.
[3] εἰς τὰ μέρη, not in G. T.
[4] αὐτοῦ, G. T.
[5] ἀπῆλθε [ἀνῆλ.] G. T.
[6] [ἡ ἑορτὴ τῶν 'I.] G. T.
[7] al. "be content."
[8] ἐντεταμένον, al. διατ.

but to "the other side of the sea," and [1] great multitudes followed Him, beholding "the miracles which He did." What miracles? Why doth he [2] not mention them specifically? Because this Evangelist most of all was desirous of employing the greater part of his book on the discourses and sermons [of Christ]. Observe, for instance, how for a whole year, or rather how even now at the feast of the Passover, he hath given us no more information on the head of miracles, than merely that He healed the paralytic and the nobleman's son. Because he was not anxious to enumerate them all, (that would have been impossible,) but of many and great to record a few.

Ver. 2. "A great multitude followed Him beholding the miracles that He did." What is here told marks not a very wise state of mind; [3] for when they had enjoyed such teaching, they still were more attracted by the miracles, which was a sign of the grosser state. For "miracles," It saith, "are not for believers, but for unbelievers." [4] The people described by Matthew acted not thus,[5] but how? They all, he saith, "were astonished at His doctrine, because He taught as one having authority." (Matt. vii. 28, 29.)

"And why doth He occupy the mountain now, and sit there with His disciples?" Because of the miracle which was about to take place. And that the disciples alone went up with Him, was a charge against the multitude which followed Him not. Yet not for this only did He go up into the mountain, but to teach us ever to rest at intervals from the tumults and confusion of common life.[6] For solitude is a thing meet for the study of wisdom. And often doth He go up alone into a mountain, and spend the night there, and pray, to teach us that the man who will come most near to God must be free from all disturbance, and must seek times and places clear of confusion.

Ver. 4. "And the Passover, a feast of the Jews, was nigh."

"How then," saith some one, "doth He not go up unto the feast, but, when all are pressing to Jerusalem, goeth Himself into Galilee, and not Himself alone, but taketh His disciples with Him, and proceedeth thence to Capernaum?" Because henceforth He was quietly annulling the Law, taking occasion from the wickedness of the Jews.

Ver. 5. "And as He lifted up His eyes, He beheld a great company." [7]

This showeth that He sat not at any time idly [8] with the disciples, but perhaps carefully conversing with them, and making them attend [9] and turn towards Him, a thing which peculiarly marks [10] His tender care, and the humility and condescension of His demeanor towards them. For they sat with Him, perhaps looking at one another; then having lifted up His eyes, He beheld the multitudes coming unto Him. Now the other Evangelists say, that the disciples came and asked and besought Him that He would not send them away fasting, while St. John saith, that the question was put to Philip by Christ. Both occurrences seem to me to be truly reported, but not to have taken place at the same time, the former account being prior to the other, so that the two are entirely different.

Wherefore then doth He ask "Philip"? He knew which of His disciples needed most instruction; for this is he who afterwards said, "Show us the Father, and it sufficeth us" (c. xiv. 8), and on this account Jesus was beforehand bringing him into a proper state.[11] For had the miracle simply been done, the marvel would not have seemed so great, but now He beforehand constraineth him to confess the existing want, that knowing the state of matters he might be the more exactly acquainted with the magnitude of the miracle about to take place. Wherefore He saith,[12]

"Whence shall we have so many loaves,[13] that these may eat?"

So in the Old [Testament] He spake to Moses, for He wrought not the sign until He had asked him, "What is that in thy hand?" Because things coming to pass unexpectedly and all at once,[14] are wont to throw us into forgetfulness of things previous, therefore He first involved him in a confession of present circumstances, that when the astonishment should have come upon him, he might be unable afterwards to drive away the remembrance of what he had confessed, and thus might learn by comparison the greatness of the miracle, which in fact takes place in this instance; for Philip being asked, replied,

Ver. 7, 6. "Two hundred pennyworth of bread is not sufficient for them, that every one of them may take a little. And this He said to prove him: for He Himself knew what He would do."

[2.] What meaneth, "to prove him"? Did not He know what would be said by him? We cannot assert that. What then is the meaning of the expression? We may discover it from the Old [Testament]. For there too it is said, "And it came to pass after these things that God did

---

[1] Ben. "wherefore also."  [2] al. "dost thou."
[3] al. "this kind of following belongs not to a settled mind."
[4] Not exactly quoted from 1 Cor. xiv. 22, where the words relate to the gift of tongues.
[5] al. "was not such."  [6] τῆς ἐν μέσω.
[7] ἀναβλέψας τοῖς ὀφθαλμοῖς ὁρᾷ ὄχλον πολύν. In G. T. the words are: ἐπάρας οὖν ὁ Ἰησοῦς τοὺς ὀφθαλμοὺς, καὶ θεασάμενος ὅτι πολὺς ὄχλος ἔρχεται πρὸς αὐτόν.

[8] ἁπλῶς.  [9] al. "teaching."
[10] Ben. Ed. reads: οὐ μάλιστα καὶ ἐντεῦθεν τὴν κηδεμονίαν ἐστι μαθεῖν.  [11] ἐρρύθμιζεν.  [12] Ben. "and see what he saith."
[13] In G. T. πόθεν ἀγοράσομεν ἄρτους ἵνα ἔρχεται, κ.τ.λ.
[14] ἀθρόον.

tempt Abraham, and said unto him, Take thy beloved son whom thou lovest " (Gen. xxii. 1, 2) ; yet it doth not appear in that place either, that when He saith this He waited to see the end of the trial, whether Abraham would obey or not, (how could He, who knoweth all things before they come into existence?[1]) but the words in both cases are spoken after the manner of men. For as when (the Psalmist[2]) saith that He "searcheth the hearts of men," he meaneth not a search of ignorance but of exact knowledge, just so when the Evangelist saith that He proved (Philip), he meaneth only that He knew exactly. And perhaps one might say another thing, that as He once made Abraham more approved, so also did He this man, bringing him by this question to an exact knowledge of the miracle. The Evangelist therefore, that thou mayest not stop at the feebleness of the expression, and so form an improper opinion of what was said, addeth, " He Himself knew what He would do."

Moreover we must observe this, that when there is any wrong suspicion, the writer straightway very carefully corrects[3] it. As then in this place that the hearers might not form any such suspicion, he adds the corrective, saying, " For He Himself knew what He would do" : so also in that other place, when He saith, that " the Jews persecuted Him, because He not only had broken the Sabbath, but said also that God was His Father, making Himself equal with God," had there not been the assertion of Christ Himself confirmed by His works, he would there also have subjoined this correction. For if even in words which Christ speaketh the Evangelist is careful that none should have suspicions, much more in cases where others were speaking of Him would he have looked closely, had he perceived that an improper opinion prevailed concerning Him. But he did not so, for he knew that this[4] was His meaning,[5] and immovable decree.[6] Therefore after saying, " making Himself equal with God," he used not any such correction ; for the matter spoken of was not an erroneous fancy of theirs, but His own assertion ratified by His works. Philip then having been questioned,

Ver. 8, 9. " Andrew, Simon's[7] brother, said, There is a lad here, which hath five barley loaves, and two small fishes : but what are they among so many?"

Andrew is higher minded than Philip, yet had not he attained to everything. Yet I do not think that he spake without an object, but as having heard[8] of the miracles of the Prophets, and how Elisha wrought a sign with the loaves (2 Kings iv. 43) ; on this account he mounted to a certain height,[9] but could not attain to the very top.

Let us learn then,[10] we who give ourselves to luxury, what was the fare of those great and admirable men ; and in quality and quantity[11] let us behold and imitate the thriftiness of their table.

What follows also expresses great weakness. For after saying, " hath five barley loaves," he addeth, " but what are they among so many?" He supposed that the Worker of the miracle would make less out of less, and more out of more. But this was not the case, for it was alike easy to Him to cause bread to spring forth[12] from more and from less, since He needed no subject-matter. But in order that the creation might not seem foreign to His Wisdom, as afterwards slanderers and those affected with the disease of Marcion[13] said, He used the creation itself as a groundwork for His marvels.

When both the disciples had owned themselves at a loss, then He wrought the miracle ; for thus they profited the more, having first confessed the difficulty of the matter, that when it should come to pass, they might understand the power of God. And because a miracle was about to be wrought, which had also been performed by the Prophets, although not in an equal degree, and because He would do it after first giving thanks, lest they should fall into any suspicion of weakness on His part, observe how by the very manner of His working He entirely raiseth their thoughts of it and showeth them the difference (between Himself and others). For when the loaves had not yet appeared,[14] that thou mayest learn, that things that are not are to Him as though they were, (as Paul saith, " who calleth the things that are not as though they were " — Rom. iv. 17,) He commanded them as though the table were prepared and ready, straightway to sit down, rousing by this the minds of His disciples. And because[15] they had profited by the questioning, they immediately obeyed, and were not confounded, nor said, " How is this, why dost Thou bid us sit down, when there is nothing before us?" The same men, who at first disbelieved so much as to say, "Whence shall we buy bread?" began so far to believe even before they saw the miracle,[16] that they readily made the multitudes to sit down.

---

[1] πρὶν γενέσεως, Hist. Susann. ver. 42.
[2] Ps. vii. 9, or St. Paul, Rom. viii. 27.
[3] al. " expels."
[4] i.e. the Equality of The Son with The Father.
[5] γνώμην.
[6] ψῆφον.
[7] Σίμωνος Πέτρου, G. T.

[8] al. " for I think that the miracles of the Prophets had entered his mind."    [9] al. " farther."
[10] al. " hence."    [11] [of that which is set on.] Morel. and Ben.
[12] πηγάσαι.    [13] See note, p. 30.
[14] In Ben. the reading is: " for when the loaves had not yet appeared, He doth the miracle." This looks like the gloss of a transcriber, surprised at the suspension of the sense.
[15] al. " when."    [16] al. " before the miracle."

[3.] But why when He was about to restore the paralytic did He not pray, nor when He was raising the dead, or bridling the sea, while He doth so here over the loaves? It was to show, that when we begin our meals, we ought to give thanks unto God. Moreover, He doth it especially in a lesser matter, that thou mayest learn that He doth it not as having any need; for were this the case, much more would He have done so in greater things; but when He did them by His own authority, it is clear that it was through condescension that He acted as He did in the case of the lesser. Besides, a great multitude was present, and it was necessary that they should be persuaded that He had come according to the will of God. Wherefore, when He doth miracles in the absence of witnesses, He exhibiteth nothing of the kind; but when He doth them in the presence of many, in order to persuade them that He is no enemy of God, no adversary of Him who hath begotten Him, He removeth the suspicion by thanksgiving.

"And He gave to them that were set down, and they were filled." [1]

Seest thou how great is the interval between the servants and the Master? They having grace by measure, wrought their miracles accordingly, but God, who acteth with free power, did all most abundantly.

Ver. 12. "And He said [2] unto His disciples, Gather up the fragments which remain; [3] — and they gathered them together, and filled twelve baskets."

This was not a superfluous show, but in order that the matter might not be deemed a mere illusion; and for this reason He createth [4] from matter already subsisting. "But why gave He not the bread to the multitudes to bear, but (only) to His disciples?" Because He was most desirous to instruct these who were to be the teachers of the world. The multitude would not as yet reap any great fruit from the miracles, (at least they straightway forgot this one and asked for another,) while these would gain no common profit. And what took place was moreover no ordinary condemnation of Judas, who bore a basket. And that these things were done for their instruction is plain from what is said afterwards, when He reminded them, saying, "Do ye not yet understand — how many baskets ye took up?" (Matt. xvi. 9.) And for

the same reason it was that the baskets of fragments were equal in number to the disciples; afterwards, when they were instructed, they took not up so many, but only "seven baskets." (Matt. xv. 37.) And I marvel not only at the quantity of loaves created, but besides the quantity, at the exactness of the surplus, that He caused the superabundance to be neither more nor less than just so much as He willed, foreseeing how much they would consume; a thing which marked unspeakable power. The fragments then confirmed the matter, showing both these points; that what had taken place [5] was no illusion, and that these were from the loaves by which the people had been fed. As to the fishes, they at this time were produced from those already subsisting, but at a later period, after the Resurrection, they were not made from subsisting matter. "Wherefore?" That thou mayest understand that even now He employed matter, not from necessity, nor as needing any base [6] (to work upon), but to stop the mouths of heretics. [7]

"And the multitudes said, that this is of a truth The Prophet." [8]

Oh, excess of gluttony! He had done ten thousand things more admirable than this, but nowhere did they make this confession, save when they had been filled. Yet hence it is evident that they expected some remarkable prophet; for those others had said (to John), "Art thou that Prophet?" [9] while these say, "This is that Prophet."

Ver. 15. "When Jesus therefore perceived that they would come and take Him by force to make Him a king, He departed again into a mountain." [10]

Wonderful! How great is the tyranny of gluttony, how great the fickleness of men's minds! No longer do they vindicate the Law, no longer do they care for the violation [11] of the Sabbath, no longer are they zealous for God; all such considerations are thrown aside, when their bellies have been filled; He was a prophet in their eyes, and they were about to choose Him for a king. But Christ fleeth. "Wherefore?" To teach us to despise worldly dignities, and to show us that He needed nothing on earth. For He who chose [12] all things mean, both mother and house and city and nurture and attire would not afterwards be made illustrious by things on earth. The things which (He had) from heaven were glorious and great, angels, a star, His Father loudly speaking, [13] the

---

[1] These words, which are not found in G. T., are quoted in place of v. 10. 11. "And Jesus said, Make the men sit down. Now there was much grass in the place. So the men sat down, in number about five thousand. And Jesus took the loaves; and when He had given thanks, He distributed to the disciples, and the disciples to them that were set down; and likewise of the fishes as much as they would."

[2] "When they were filled, He said." N. T.

[3] "That nothing be lost. Therefore they gathered them together, and filled twelve baskets with the fragments of the five barley loaves, which remained over and above unto them that had eaten." N. T.          [4] δημιουργεῖ.

[5] or, "had been made."          [6] ὑποβάθρας.

[7] i.e. the Gnostics, see note, p. 30.

[8] In place of ver. 14. "Then those men, when they had seen the miracle that Jesus did, said, This is of a truth that Prophet which should come into the world."

[9] al. "wherefore elsewhere they said, Is this," &c.

[10] [Himself alone] G. T.          [11] παραλύσεως, al. παραβάσεως.

[12] al. "showed."          [13] βοῶν.

Spirit testifying, and Prophets proclaiming Him from afar; those on earth were all mean, that thus His power might the more appear. He came also to teach us to despise the things of the world, and not be amazed or astonished by the splendors of this life, but to laugh them all to scorn, and to desire those which are to come. For he who admires things which are here, will not admire those in the heavens. Wherefore also He saith to Pilate, "My Kingdom is not of this world" (c. xviii. 36), that He may not afterwards appear to have employed mere human terror or dominion for the purpose of persuasion. Why then saith the Prophet, "Behold, thy King cometh unto thee, meek, and sitting upon an ass"? (Zech. ix. 9.) He spake of that Kingdom which is in the heavens, but not of this on earth; and on this account Christ saith, "I receive not honor from men." (c. v. 41.)

Learn we then, beloved, to despise and not to desire the honor which is from men; for we have been honored with the greatest of honors, compared with which that other is verily [1] insult, ridicule, and mockery. And as the riches of this world compared with the riches of that are poverty, as this life apart from that is deadness,[2] (for "let [3] the dead bury their dead"—Matt. viii. 28,) so this honor compared with that is shame and ridicule. Let us then not pursue it. If they who confer it are of less account than a shadow or a dream, the honor itself much more so. "The glory of man is as the flower of the grass" (1 Pet. i. 24); and what is meaner than the flower of the grass? Were this glory everlasting, in what could it profit the soul? In nothing. Nay, it very greatly injures us by making us slaves, slaves in worse condition than those bought with money, slaves who obey not one master only, but two, three, ten thousand, all giving different commands. How much better is it to be a free man than a slave, to be free from the slavery of men, and subject only to the dominion of God? In a word, if thou wilt desire glory, desire it, but let it be the glory immortal, for that is exhibited on a more glorious stage, and brings greater profit. For [4] the men here bid thee be at charges to please them, but Christ, on the contrary, giveth thee an hundredfold for what thou givest Him, and addeth moreover eternal life. Which of the two then is better, to be admired [5] on earth, or in heaven? by man, or by God? to your loss, or to your gain? to wear a crown for a single day, or for endless ages? Give to him that needeth, but give not to a dancer, lest thou lose thy money and destroy his soul. For thou art the cause of his (coming to) perdition through unseasonable

munificence.[6] Since did those on the stage know that their employment would be unprofitable, they would have long ago ceased to practice it; but when they behold thee applauding, crowding after them, spending and wasting thy substance upon them, even if they have no desire to follow (their profession), they are kept to it by the desire of gain. If they knew that no one would praise what they do, they would soon desist from their labors, by reason of their unprofitableness; but when they see that the action is admired by many, the praise of others becomes a bait to them. Let us then desist from this unprofitable expense, let us learn upon whom and when we ought to spend. Let us not, I implore you, provoke God in both ways, gathering whence we ought not, and scattering where we ought not; for what anger doth not thy conduct deserve, when thou passest by the poor and givest to a harlot? Would not the paying the hire of sin and the bestowing honor where it were meet to punish have been a charge against thee, even hadst thou paid out of thy just earnings? but when thou feedest thine uncleanness by stripping orphans and wronging widows, consider how great a fire is prepared for those who dare such things. Hear what Paul saith, "Who not only do these things, but also have pleasure in [7] them that do them." (Rom. i. 32.)

Perhaps we have touched you sharply, yet if we touch you not, there are actual [8] punishments awaiting those who sin without amendment. What then availeth it to gratify by words those who shall be punished by realities? Dost thou take pleasure [9] at a dancer, dost thou praise and admire him? Then art thou worse than he; his poverty affords him an excuse though not a reasonable one, but thou art stripped even of this defense. If I ask him, "Why hast thou left other arts and come to this accursed and impure one?" he will reply, "because I can with little labor gain great profits." But if I ask thee why thou admirest one who spends his time in impurity, and lives to the mischief of many, thou canst not run to the same excuse, but must bow down thy face and be ashamed and blush. Now if when called by us to give account, thou wouldest have nothing to reply,[10] when that terrible and inexorable Judgment cometh where we shall render account of thoughts and deeds and everything, how shall we stand? with what eyes shall we behold our Judge? what shall we say? what defense shall we make? what excuse reasonable or unreasonable shall we put forward? shall we allege the expense? the gratification? the perdition of others whom by means of his art we ruin? We can have nothing to say, but must be punished

---

1 al. "seems to be."
2 νέκρωσις.
3 al. "'let,' He saith."

4 al. "how? for."
5 Sav. reads "to be."

6 or, "love of praise."
7 or, "consent with."
8 διὰ τῶν πραγμάτων.

9 or, "consent with."
10 al. "couldest reply nothing."

with a punishment having no end, knowing no limit. That this come not to pass, let us henceforth guard all points, that having departed with a good hope, we may obtain the everlasting blessings ; to which may we all attain through the grace and lovingkindness of our Lord Jesus Christ, by whom and with whom to the Father and the Holy Ghost be glory, now and ever and world without end. Amen.

# HOMILY XLIII.

## John vi. 16–18.

"And when even was now come, His disciples went down unto[1] the sea and entered[2] into a ship, and went over[3] the sea toward Capernaum. And it was[4] now dark, and Jesus was not come unto them. And the sea arose by reason of a great wind that blew."

[1.] CHRIST provideth for the good of his disciples not only when He is present in the body, but also when far away; for having abundance of means and of skill, He effecteth one and the same end by contrary actions. Observe, for instance, what He hath done here. He leaveth His disciples, and goeth up into a mountain; and they,[5] when even was come, went down unto the sea. They waited for Him until evening, expecting that He would come unto them; but when even was come, they could no longer endure not to seek their Master;[6] so great a love possessed them. They said not, "It is now evening, and night hath overtaken us, whither shall we depart? the place is dangerous, the time unsafe"; but, goaded[7] by their longing, they entered into the ship. For it is not without a cause that the Evangelist hath declared[8] the time also, but by it to show the warmth of their love.

Wherefore then doth Christ let them go, and not show Himself?[9] And again,[10] wherefore doth He show Himself walking alone upon the sea? By the first He teacheth them how great (an evil) it is to be forsaken by Him, and maketh their longing greater; by the second, again, He showeth forth His power. For as in His teaching they heard not all in common with the multitude, so in the case of the miracles they saw them not all with the mass of people, since it was needful that they who were about to receive in charge the presidency[11] of the world, should have somewhat more than the rest. "And what sort of miracles," saith some one, "saw they by themselves?" The Transfiguration on the mount; this on the sea, and those after the Resurrection, which are many and important. And from these I conjecture that there were others also. They came to Capernaum without any certain information, but expecting to find Him there, or even in mid passage; this the Evangelist implies by saying that "it was now dark, and Jesus was not yet come to them."

"And the sea arose by reason of a great wind that blew." What did they? They were troubled, for there were many and various causes which forced them to be so. They were afraid by reason of the time for it was dark, of the storm for the sea had risen, of the place for they were not near land; but,

Ver. 19. "Had rowed about five and twenty[12] furlongs."

And, lastly, by reason of the strangeness of the thing, for,

"They see Him[13] walking upon the sea."

And when they were greatly troubled,

Ver. 20. "He saith unto them, It is I, be not afraid."

Wherefore then appeareth He? To show that it was He who would make the storm cease. For this the Evangelist hath shown, saying,[14]

Ver. 21. "They were willing to receive Him,[15] and immediately the ship was near the land."[16]

He not only gave them a safe passage, but also one with a fair wind.

To the multitude He showeth not Himself walking upon the sea, for the miracle was too great to suit their infirmity. Indeed, even by the disciples He was not seen long doing this, but He appeared, and at once retired.[17] Now this seems to me to be a different miracle from that found in Matthew xiv.; and that it is different is clear from many reasons. For He worketh often the same miracles, in order to cause the

---

[1] ἐπὶ [εἰς, G. T.].
[2] ἀναβάντες [ἐμβ. G. T.].
[3] πέραν [εἰς τὸ π. G. T.].
[4] ἐγένετο [ἐγεγόνει, G. T.].
[5] Ben. "they having been left behind by their Master, when," &c.
[6] Ben. "not to go to seek Him."
[7] al. "inflamed."
[8] al. "signifies."
[9] al. "and retire."
[10] al. "but rather."
[11] προστασίαν.
[12] "five and twenty or thirty," N. T.
[13] "they see Jesus," N. T.
[14] al. "is shown (or It shows by the Evangelist, saying," &c.).
[15] [into the ship,] N. T.
[16] "at the land whither they went," N. T.
[17] al. "withdrew from them."

beholders not merely to count them very strange,[1] but also to receive them with great faith.

"It is I, be not afraid." As He spake the word, He cast out fear from their souls. But at another time not so; wherefore Peter said, "Lord, if it be Thou, bid me to come unto Thee." (Matt. xiv. 28.) Whence then was it that at that time they did not straightway admit this,[2] but now were persuaded? It was because then the storm continued to toss the bark, but now at His voice the calm had come. Or if the reason be not this, it is that other which I have before mentioned, that oftentimes working the same miracles, He made the second to be readily received by means of the first. But wherefore went He not up into the ship? Because He would make the marvel greater, would more openly[3] reveal to them His Godhead, and would show them, that when He before gave thanks, He did not so as needing aid, but in condescension to them. He allowed the storm to arise, that they might ever seek Him; He stilled the storm, that He might make known to them His power; He went not up into the ship, that He might make the marvel greater.

Ver. 22. "And the people that were there saw that there was none other boat there save the one into which the disciples had entered, and that Jesus went not into the boat, but His disciples."[4]

And why is John so exact? Why said he not that the multitudes having passed over on the next day departed?[5] He desires to teach us something else, namely, that Jesus allowed the multitudes if not openly, at least in a secret manner, to suspect what had taken place. For, "They saw," saith he, "that there was none other boat there but one, and that Jesus went not into it with His disciples."

Ver. 24. And embarking in boats from Tiberias, they "came to Capernaum seeking Jesus."

What else then could they suspect, save that He had arrived there crossing the sea on foot? for it was not possible to say that He had passed over in another ship. For "there was one," saith the Evangelist, "into which His disciples entered." Still when they came to Him after so great a wonder, they asked Him not how He crossed over, how He arrived there, nor sought to understand so great a sign. But what say they?

Ver. 25. "Master, when camest Thou hither?"

[2.] Unless any one affirm that the "when" is here used by them in the sense of "how." But it is[6] worth while also to notice here the fickleness of their impulses.[7] For they who said, "This is that Prophet"; they who were anxious to "take Him and make Him a king," now when they have found Him take no such counsel, but having cast out their astonishment, they no longer admire Him for His former deeds. They sought Him, desiring again to enjoy a table like the first.

The Jews under the guidance of Moses passed over the Red Sea, but that case is widely different from this. He did all with prayer and as a servant, but Christ with absolute[8] power. There when the south wind[9] blew, the water yielded so as to make them pass over on dry land, but here the miracle was greater. (Ex. xiv. 21.) For the sea retaining its proper nature so bare its Lord upon its surface,[10] thus testifying to the Scripture which saith, "Who walketh upon the sea as upon a pavement." (Job ix. 8.)

And with reason, when He was about to enter into stubborn and disobedient Capernaum, did He work the miracle of the loaves, as desiring not only by what took place within, but also by the miracles which were wrought without the city, to soften its disobedience. For was it not enough to soften even any stone, that such multitudes should come with great eagerness to that city? Yet they had no such feeling, but again desired food for the body; for which also they are reproached by Jesus.

Let us then, beloved, knowing these things, give thanks to God for things of sense, but much more for things spiritual; for such is His will, and it is on account of the latter that He giveth the former, leading in, as it were, by these the more imperfect sort, and giving them previous teaching, because they are yet gaping upon the world. But when such persons having received these worldly things, rest in them, then are they upbraided and rebuked. For in the case of him that had the palsy, Christ wished first to give that which was spiritual, but they that were present endured it not; for when He said, "Thy sins be forgiven thee," they exclaimed, "This man blasphemeth." (Matt. ix. 2.) Let us not, I entreat you, be so affected, but let us make more[11] account of those (spiritual) things. Wherefore? Because when spiritual things are present with us, no harm ariseth from the absence[12] of fleshly things; but when they are not, what hope, what comfort, shall then remain to us? wherefore it is for these we ought always to call upon God, and entreat Him for them. And

---

[1] al. "so that the beholders might both marvel, and not count them very strange."
[2] i.e. that it was really Christ.
[3] lit. "more nakedly," al. "more clearly."
[4] N. T. ver. 22–24. "The day following, when the people which stood on the other side of the sea saw that there was none other boat there save that one whereinto His disciples were entered, and that Jesus went not with His disciples into the boat, but that His disciples were gone away alone; (howbeit there came other little boats from Tiberias nigh unto the place where they did eat bread, after that the Lord had given thanks;) when the people therefore saw that Jesus was not there, neither His disciples, they also took shipping, and came to Capernaum seeking for Jesus." The readings here vary, without variety of meaning.
[5] al. "came."

[6] al. "hence."
[7] εὐθραυστον ὁρμὴν, al. εὔκολον γνώμην.
[8] lit. "all."
[9] a strong east wind.
[10] lit. "back."
[11] al. "much."
[12] al. "lack."

for such hath Christ also taught us to pray; for if we unfold that Prayer, we shall find that there is nothing carnal in it, but all spiritual, and that even the small portion which seemeth to relate to sense, becometh by the manner spiritual. For to bid us ask no more than our "successive,"[1] that is, our "daily," bread, would mark a mind spiritual and truly wise. And consider what goeth before that, "Hallowed be Thy Name, Thy kingdom come, Thy will be done as in heaven so on earth"; then, after naming that temporal (need), He quickly leaveth it, and bringeth[2] us again to the spiritual doctrine, saying, "Forgive us our debts, as we forgive our debtors." Nowhere hath He put in the Prayer riches or glory or dominion, but all things contributing to the benefit of the soul; nothing earthly, but all things heavenly. If then we are bidden to refrain from the things of this present life, how could we help being wretched and miserable, asking from God those things which even having He biddeth us cast away, to free us from care about them, and for which He biddeth us take no pains.[4] This is the "using vain repetition"; and this is why we effect nothing by our prayers. "How then," saith some one, "do the wicked grow rich, how the unjust and impure, plunderers and covetous?" Not by God's giving; (away with the thought!) but by plundering, and taking more than their due.[5] "And how doth God allow them?" As He allowed that rich man, reserving him for greater punishment. (Luke xvi. 25.) Hear what (Abraham) saith to him; "Son, thou in thy lifetime receivedst thy good things, and likewise Lazarus evil things, but now he is comforted, and thou art tormented." Therefore that we also come not to hear that voice, by living softly and idly, and gathering together for ourselves many sins, let us choose the true riches and right wisdom, that we may obtain the promised good things; to which may we all arrive, through the grace and lovingkindness of our Lord Jesus Christ, by whom and with whom, to the Father and the Holy Ghost, be glory, now and ever and world without end. Amen.

# HOMILY XLIV.

### John vi. 26, 27.

"Jesus answered them, and said, Verily, verily, I say unto you, Ye seek Me, not because ye saw the miracles, but because ye did eat of the loaves and were filled. Labor not for the meat which perisheth, but for that meat which endureth unto everlasting life."

[1.] THE mild and gentle is not always useful, but there are times when the teacher needs sharper language. For if the disciple be dull and gross, then, in order to touch his dullness to the quick, we must rouse him with[3] a goad. And this the Son of God hath done in the present as well as in many other cases. For when the crowds had come and found Jesus, and were flattering Him, and saying, "Master, when camest Thou hither?" to show that He desireth not honor from men, but looketh to one thing only, their salvation, He answereth them sharply, wishing to correct them not in this way only, but also by revealing and exposing their thoughts. For what saith He? "Verily, verily, I say unto you," (speaking positively and with a confirmation,) "Ye seek Me, not because ye saw miracles, but because ye did eat of the loaves and were filled." He chideth and reproveth them by these words, yet doth not so abruptly or violently, but very sparingly. For He saith not, "O ye gluttons and belly-slaves, I have wrought so many wonders, and ye never have either followed Me, or marveled at My doings"; but mildly and gently somewhat in this manner; "Ye seek Me, not because ye saw miracles, but because ye did eat of the loaves and were filled"; speaking not only of the past, but also of the present miracle. "It was not," He saith, "the miracle of the loaves that astonished you, but the being filled."[6] And that He said not this of them by conjecture they straightway showed, for on this account they came the second time, as being about to enjoy the same (food) as before. Wherefore they said, "Our fathers did eat manna in the wilderness." Again they draw Him to (the subject of) carnal food, which was the chief accusation and charge against them. But He stoppeth not at rebukes, but addeth instruction also, saying, "Labor not for the meat which perisheth, but for that meat which endureth unto everlasting life."

"Which the Son of Man giveth[7] unto you; for Him hath God the Father sealed."

---

[4] al. "no pains, but rather neither to have nor to desire them."
[5] Ben. omits "but by plundering, and taking more than their due."
[6] al. For He all but saith this in what He directeth against them: "It was not," &c.
[7] "shall give," N. T.

---

[1] ἐπιούσιον, i.e. εἰς τὴν ἐπιοῦσαν ἡμ.
[2] al. "came."          [3] al. "use towards him."

What He saith, is of this kind: "Make ye no account of this earthly, but of that spiritual food." But since some of those who desire to live in doing nothing have abused this speech, as though Christ would entirely abolish working, it is seasonable to say somewhat to them. For they slander, so to speak, all Christianity, and cause it to be ridiculed on the score of idleness. First, however, we must mention that saying of Paul. What saith he? "Remember the Lord, how He said, It is more blessed to give than to receive." (Acts xx. 35.) Now how can it be possible for him to give who hath not? How then saith Jesus to Martha, "Thou art careful and troubled about many things, but one thing is needful, and Mary hath chosen that good part"? (Luke x. 41, 42); and again, "Take no thought for the morrow." (Matt. vi. 34.) For it is necessary now to resolve all these questions, not only that we may check men if they would be idle, but also that the oracles of God may not appear to bring in what is contradictory.

Now Paul in another place saith, "But we beseech you, brethren, that ye increase more and more, that ye study to be quiet, and to do your own business; that ye may walk honestly toward them that are without" (1 Thess. iv. 10, 11, 12); and again; "Let him that stole, steal no more; but rather let him labor, working with his own hands, that he may have to give to him that needeth." (Eph. iv. 28.) Here the Apostle bids not simply "work," but to work so vigorously and laboriously, as to have thereby somewhat to give to others. And in another place the same saith again; "These hands have ministered to my necessities, and to them that were with me." (Acts xx. 34.) And writing to the Corinthians he said, "What is my reward then? Verily, that when I preach the Gospel, I may make the Gospel of Christ without charge." (1 Cor. ix. 18.) And when he was in that city, he abode with Aquila and Priscilla, "and wrought, for by their occupation they were tentmakers." (Acts xviii. 3.)

These passages show a yet more decided opposition as to the letter;[1] we must therefore now bring forward the solution. What then must be our reply? That to "take no thought," doth not mean "not to work," but "not to be nailed to the things of this life"; that is, to take no care for to-morrow's ease, but to deem that superfluous. For a man may do no work, and (yet) lay up treasure for the morrow; and a man may work, yet be careful for nothing; for carefulness and work are not the same thing; it is not as trusting to his work that a man worketh, but, "that he may impart to him that needeth." And that too which was said to Martha refers

not to works and working, but to this, that it is our duty to know the right season, and not to spend on carnal things the time proper for listening. Thus Christ spake not the words as urging her to "idleness," but to rivet her to listening. "I came," saith He, "to teach you needful things, but thou art anxious about a meal. Dost thou desire to receive Me, and to provide for Me a costly table? Provide another sort of entertainment, by giving me a ready hearing, and by imitating thy sister's longing for instruction." He said not this to forbid her hospitality, (away with the thought! how could that be?) but to show that she ought not in the season for listening be busy about other matters. For to say, "Labor not for the meat that perisheth," is not the expression of one implying that we ought to be idle; (in fact, this most especially is "meat that perisheth," for idleness is wont to teach all wickedness;) but that we ought to work, and to impart. This is meat that never perisheth; but if any be idle and gluttonous, and careth for luxury, that man worketh for "the meat that perisheth." So too, if a man by his labor should feed Christ, and give Him drink, and clothe Him, who[2] so senseless and mad[3] as to say that such an one labors for the meat that perisheth, when there is for this the promise of the kingdom that is to come, and of those good things? This meat endureth forever. But at that time, since the multitudes made no account of faith, nor sought to learn who it was that did these things, and by what power, but desired one thing only, to fill their bellies without working; Christ with good reason called such food, "meat that perisheth." "I fed," He saith, "your bodies, that after this ye might seek that other food which endureth, which nourisheth the soul; but ye again run[4] after that which is earthy. Therefore ye do not understand that I lead you not to this imperfect food, but to that which giveth not temporal but eternal life, which nourisheth not the body but the soul." Then when He had uttered such great words concerning Himself, and had said that He would give this food, in order that what was spoken might not stand in their way, to make His saying credible He attributeth the supply to the Father. For after saying, "Which the Son of Man shall give you"; He addeth, "Him hath God the Father sealed," that is, "hath sent Him for this purpose, that He might bring the food to you." The saying also admits of another interpretation; for in another place Christ saith, "He that heareth My words, hath set to his seal that God is true" (c. iii. 33), that is, hath "showed forth undeniably." Which indeed the expression seems to me to hint at even in this place, for

---

[2] al. "none." 　　[3] al. "unschooled." 　　[4] al. "fall down."

" the Father hath sealed," is nothing else than " hath declared," " hath revealed by His testimony." He in fact declared Himself too, but since He was speaking to Jews, He brought forward the testimony of the Father.

[2.] Learn we then, beloved, to ask of God the things which it is meet for us to ask of Him. For those other things, those, I mean, which belong to this life, whichever way they may fall out, can do us no injury; for if we be rich, it is here only that we shall enjoy our luxury; and if we fall into poverty, we shall suffer nothing terrible. For neither the splendors nor the pains of the present life have much power in respect either of despondency or pleasure, they are contemptible, and slip away very swiftly. Wherefore they are called " a way," with reason, because they pass away, and by their very nature do not long endure,[1] but the things which are to come endure eternally, both those of punishment and those of the Kingdom. Let us then in regard of these things use much diligence to avoid the first and to choose the last. For what is the advantage of this world's luxury? To-day it is, and to-morrow it is not; to-day a bright flower, to-morrow scattered dust; to-day a burning fire, to-morrow smouldering ashes. But spiritual things are not so, they ever remain shining and blooming, and becoming brighter every day. That wealth never perishes,[2] never departs, never ceases, never brings with it care or envy or blame, destroys not the body, corrupts not the soul, is without ill will, heaps not up malice; all which things attend on the other kind of wealth. That honor lifts not men into folly, doth not make them puffed up, never ceases nor is dimmed. Again, the rest and delight of heaven endureth continually, ever being immovable and immortal, one cannot find its end or limit. This life then let us desire, for if we do so we shall make no account of present things, but shall despise and mock at them all, and though one should bid us enter into kingly halls, we shall not while we have this hope choose to do so; yet nothing (earthly) seems more near to happiness than such a permission; but to those who are possessed by love of heaven, even this seems little and mean, and worthy of no account. Nothing which comes to an end is to be much desired; whatever ceases, and to-day is and to-morrow is not, even though it be very great, yet seems to be very little and contemptible. Then let us not cling to fleeting things which slip away and depart, but to those which are enduring and immovable. To which may we all attain,[4] through the grace and lovingkindness of our Lord Jesus Christ, by whom and with whom, to the Father and the Holy Ghost, be glory, now and ever and world without end. Amen.

# HOMILY XLV.

## John vi. 28–30.

" Then said they unto Him, What shall we do,[3] that we might work the works of God? Jesus answered and said unto them, This is the work of God, that ye believe on Him whom He hath sent. They said therefore unto Him, What sign showest thou then, that we may see and believe thee? what dost thou work? "

[1.] There is nothing worse, nothing more shameful, than gluttony; it makes the mind gross, and the soul carnal; it blinds, and permits not to see clearly. Observe, for instance, how this is the case with the Jews; for because they were intent upon gluttony, entirely occupied with worldly things, and without any spiritual thoughts, though Christ leads them on by ten thousand sayings, sharp and at the same time forbearing, even thus they arise not, but continue groveling below. For consider; He said to them, " Ye seek Me, not because ye saw the miracles, but because ye did eat of the bread, and were filled "; He touched them by the reproof, He showed them what food they ought to seek, saying, " Labor not for the meat that perisheth "; He set before them the prize, saying, " but that which endureth unto everlasting life "; then provided a remedy for what might have been an objection, by declaring that He was sent from the Father.

What then did they? As though they had heard nothing, they said, " What shall we do, that we might work the works of God? " This they said, not that they might learn and do them, (as the sequel shows,) but to induce Him again to supply them with food, and desiring to persuade Him to satisfy them. What then saith Christ? " This is the work of God, that ye believe on Him whom He hath sent." On this they asked, " What sign showest thou, that we may see and believe? "

---

[1] al. " are called by God a way, for there is one broad, and one strait and narrow; but things to come," &c.

[2] al. " ceases."

[3] ποιῶμεν [ποιοῦμεν, G. T. ].

[4] al. " that we may also be able to attain them."

Ver. 31. "Our fathers did eat manna in the wilderness."

Nothing more senseless, nothing more unreasonable, than these men! While the miracle was yet in their hands,[1] as though none had been done, they spake after this manner, "What sign shewest thou?" and having thus spoken, they do not even allow Him the right of choosing the sign, but think to force Him to exhibit none other than such a one as was wrought in the days of their fathers; wherefore they say, "Our fathers did eat manna in the wilderness," thinking by this to provoke Him to work such a miracle as might supply them with carnal nourishment. Else why did they mention none other of the miracles of old, though many took place in those times, both in Egypt and at the sea and in the wilderness, but only that of the manna? Was it not because they greatly desired that one by reason of the tyranny of their bellies? Ye who when ye saw His miracle called him a Prophet, and attempted to make Him a king, how is that now, as though none had been wrought, ye have become thankless and ill-minded, and ask for a sign, uttering words fit for parasites, or hungry dogs? Does the manna now seem wonderful to you? Your soul is not now[2] parched up.

Mark too their hypocrisy. They said not, "Moses did this sign, what doest thou?" thinking it would annoy Him; but for a while they address Him with great reverence, through expectation of food. So they neither said, "God did this, what doest thou?" that they might not seem to make Him equal with God; nor did they bring forward Moses, that they might not seem to lower Him, but put the matter in an intermediate form, "Our fathers did eat manna in the wilderness." He indeed might have replied, "I, but now, have wrought greater wonders than did Moses, requiring no rod, having no need of prayer, but doing all of Myself; and, if ye call to remembrance the manna, see, I have given you bread." But this was not the season for such speeches; and the one thing He earnestly desired was, to bring them to spiritual food. And observe His infinite wisdom and His manner of answering.

Ver. 32. "Moses gave you not that bread from heaven; but My Father giveth you the true bread from heaven."

Why said He not, "It was not Moses that gave it to you, but I"; but putteth God in the place of Moses, and Himself instead of manna? Because the infirmity of His hearers was great. As is seen from what followeth. For not even when He had spoken thus did He secure their attention, although He said at first, "Ye seek Me, not because ye saw the miracle, but because ye did eat of the loaves, and were filled." (Ver. 26.) Now because they sought these (carnal) things, He would have corrected them by His succeeding words, yet not even so did they desist. When He promised the Samaritan woman that He would give her "the water," He made no mention of the Father. What saith He? "If thou knewest who it is that saith unto thee, Give Me to drink, thou wouldest have asked of Him, and He would have given unto thee living water" (c. iv. 10); and again, "The water which I shall give." He referreth her not to The Father. But here He maketh mention of The Father, that thou mayest understand how great was the faith of the Samaritan woman, and how great the infirmity of the Jews.

Was then the manna not from heaven? How then is it said to be from heaven? In the same manner as Scripture speaketh of "fowls of heaven" (Ps. viii. 8); and again, "The Lord thundered from heaven." (Ps. xviii. 13.) And He calleth that other the "true bread," not because the miracle of the manna was false, but because it was a type, and not the very truth. But in mentioning Moses, He doth not compare Himself to him, for the Jews did not as yet prefer Him to Moses, of whom they still had a higher opinion. So that after saying, "Moses gave not," He addeth not that "I give," but saith that The Father, and not Moses, giveth. They, when they heard this, replied, "Give us this bread to eat"; for they yet thought that it was something material, they yet expected to gratify their appetites, and so hastily ran to Him. What doth Christ? Leading them on[3] little by little, He saith,

Ver. 33. "The bread of God is He which cometh down from heaven, and giveth life unto the world."

Not, saith He, to Jews alone, but to all the "world," not mere food, but "life," another and an altered "life." He calleth it "life," because they all were dead in sins. Yet they still kept downward bent, saying,

Ver. 34. "Give us this bread."

Then He, to rebuke them, because while they supposed that the food was material they ran to Him, but not when they learned that it was a spiritual kind, said,

Ver. 35, 36. "I am the bread of life: he that cometh to Me shall never hunger, and he that believeth on Me shall never thirst. But I said unto you, that ye also have seen Me, and believe Me not."

[2.] Thus also John crieth, saying beforehand, "He speaketh that He knoweth, and testifieth that He hath seen, and no man receiveth

---

[1] al. "in their eyes."     [2] al. "when your soul is."     [3] al. "up."

His testimony" (c. iii. 32); and again Christ Himself, "We speak that We do know, and testify that We have seen" (c. iii. 11), "and ye believe not."[1] This He doth to prevent them, and to show them that the matter doth not trouble Him, that He desireth not honor, that He is not ignorant of the secrets of their minds, nor of things present, nor of things to come.

"I am the bread of life." Now He proceedeth to commit unto them mysteries. And first He discourseth of His Godhead, saying, "I am the bread of life." For this is not spoken of His Body, (concerning that He saith towards the end, "And the bread which I shall give is My flesh,") but at present it referreth to His Godhead. For That, through God the Word, is Bread, as this bread also, through the Spirit descending on it, is made Heavenly Bread. Here He useth not witnesses, as in His former address, for He had the miracle of the loaves to witness to Him, and the Jews themselves for a while pretending to believe Him; in the former case they opposed and accused Him. This is the reason why here He declareth Himself. But they, since they expected to enjoy a carnal feast, were not[2] disturbed until they gave up their hope. Yet not for that was Christ silent, but uttered many words of reproof. For they,[3] who while they were eating called Him a Prophet, were here offended, and called Him the carpenter's son; not so while they ate the loaves, then they said, "He is The Prophet," and desired to make Him a king. Now they seemed to be indignant at His asserting that He "came down from heaven," but in truth it was not this that caused their indignation, but the thought that they should not enjoy a material table. Had they been really indignant, they ought to have asked and enquired how He was the "bread of life," how He had "come down from heaven"; but now they do not this, but murmur. And that it was not this which offended them is plain from another circumstance. When He said, "My Father giveth you the bread," they exclaimed not, "Beseech Him that He give"; but what? "Give us that bread"; yet He said not, "I give," but, "My Father giveth"; nevertheless, they, from desire of the food, thought Him worthy to be trusted to for its supply. Now how should they, who deemed Him worthy of their trust for giving, be afterward offended when they also heard that "the Father giveth"? What is the reason? It is that when they heard that they were not to eat, they again disbelieved, and put forth by way of a cloak for their disbelief, that "it was a high saying." Wherefore He saith, "Ye have seen Me, and believe not" (c. v. 39); alluding partly to His miracles, partly

to the testimony from the Scriptures; "For they," He saith, "are they which testify of Me" (c. v. 43, 44); and, "I am come in My Father's Name, and ye receive Me not"; and, "How can ye believe which receive honor of men?"[4]

Ver. 37. "All that the Father giveth Me shall come to Me, and him that cometh to Me I will in nowise cast out."

Observe how He doeth all things for the sake of them that are saved; therefore He added this, that He might not seem to be trifling and speaking these things to no purpose. But what is it that He saith, "All that the Father giveth Me shall come unto Me" (ver. 37), and "I will raise it[5] up in the last day"? (Ver. 40.) Wherefore speaketh He of the common resurrection, in which even the ungodly have a part, as though it were the peculiar gift of those who believe on Him? Because He speaketh not simply of resurrection, but of a particular kind of resurrection. For having first said, "I will not cast him out, I shall lose nothing of it," He then speaketh of the resurrection. Since in the resurrection some are cast out,[6] ("Take him, and cast him into outer darkness," Matt. xxii. 13,) and some are destroyed. ("Rather fear Him who is able to destroy both soul and body in hell.") (Matt. x. 28.) And[7] the expression, "I give eternal life" (c. x. 28), declareth this; for they "that have done evil shall go forth to the resurrection of damnation, and they that have done good to the resurrection of life."[8] (c. v. 29.) This then, the resurrection to good things,[9] is that which He here designed. But what meaneth He by saying, "All that the Father giveth Me, shall come to Me"? He toucheth their unbelief, showing that whosoever believeth not on Him transgresseth the will of the Father. And thus He saith it not nakedly, but in a covert manner, and this He doth[10] everywhere, wishing to show that unbelievers are at variance with the Father, not with Him alone. For if this is His will, and if for this He came, that He might save man,[11] those who believe not transgress His will. "When therefore," He saith, "the Father guideth any man, there is nothing that hindereth him from coming unto Me"; and in another place, "No man can come unto Me, except the Father draw him." (Ver. 44.) And Paul saith, that He delivereth them up unto the Father; "When He shall have delivered up the kingdom to God, even the Father." (1 Cor. xv. 24.) Now as the Father when He giveth doth so without first depriving Himself, so the Son when He delivereth up doth so without excluding Himself. He

---

[1] al. "and ye receive not our witness," as in N. T.
[2] al. "remain and are not."    [3] Ben. "But they."

[4] al. "one of another?"
[5] Ben. "him."
[6] Ben. "as appears from," &c.
[7] al. "So that."
[8] clauses transposed.
[9] ἐπὶ τοῖς ἀγαθοῖς.
[10] al. "thou wilt see Him doing."
[11] al. "all the world."

is said to deliver us up, because through Him we have access (to the Father).

[3.] And the "by whom"[1] is also applied to the Father, as when the Apostle saith, "By whom ye were called unto the fellowship of His Son" (1 Cor. i. 9) : and,[2] "By the will of the Father." And again ; "Blessed art thou, Simon Barjona, for flesh and blood hath not revealed it unto thee." (Matt. xvi. 17.)   What He here intimateth is something of this kind,[3] that "faith in Me is no ordinary thing, but needeth an impulse[4] from above"; and this He establisheth throughout His discourse, showing that this faith requires a noble sort of soul, and one drawn on by God.

But perhaps some one will say, "If all that the Father giveth, and whomsoever He shall draw, cometh unto Thee; if none can come unto Thee except it be given him from above, then those to whom the Father giveth not are free from any blame or charges."   These are mere words and pretenses.   For we require our own deliberate choice also, because whether we will be taught is a matter of choice, and also whether we will believe.   And in this place, by the "which the Father giveth Me," He declareth nothing else than that "the believing on Me is no ordinary thing, nor one that cometh of human reasonings, but needeth a revelation from above, and a well-ordered soul to receive that revelation."   And the, "He that cometh to Me shall be saved," meaneth that he shall be greatly cared for. "For on account of these," He saith, "I came, and took upon Me the flesh, and entered into[5] the form of a servant."   Then He addeth ;

Ver. 38. "I came down from heaven not to do Mine own will, but the will of Him that sent Me."

What sayest Thou?   Why, is Thy will one, and His another?   That none may suspect this, He explaineth it by what follows, saying ;

Ver. 40. "And this is the will of Him that sent Me, that every one which seeth the Son, and believeth on Him, may have everlasting life."

Is not then this Thy will?   And how sayest Thou, "I am come to send fire upon the earth, and what have I desired to see,[6] if that be already kindled"?   (Luke xii. 49.)   For if Thou also desirest this, it is very clear that Thy will and the Father's is one.   In another place also He saith, "For as the Father raiseth up the dead and quickeneth them, even so the Son quickeneth whom He will."   (c. v. 21.)   But what is the will of the Father?   Is it not, that not so much as one of them should perish? This Thou willest also.   (Matt. xviii. 14.)   So

that the will of the One differeth not from the will of the Other.   So[7] in another place He is seen establishing yet more firmly His equality with the Father, saying, "I and My Father 'will come, and will make Our abode with him.'" (c. xiv. 23.)   What He saith then is this ; "I came not to do anything other than that which the Father willeth, I have no will of Mine own different from that of the Father, for all that is the Father's is Mine, and all that is Mine is the Father's."   If now the things of the Father and the Son are in common, He saith with reason, "Not that I might do Mine own will."   But here He speaketh not so, but reserveth this for the end.   For, as I have said, He concealeth and veileth for a while high matters, and desireth to prove that had He even said, "This is My will," they would have despised Him.   He therefore saith, that "I co-operate with that Will," desiring thus to startle them more ; as though He had said, "What think ye?   Do ye anger Me by your disbelief?   Nay, ye provoke My Father."   "For this is the will of Him that sent Me, that of all which He hath given Me I should lose nothing."   (Ver. 39.)   Here He showeth that He needeth not their service, that He came not for His own advantage,[8] but for their salvation ; and not to get honor from them. Which indeed He declared in a former address, saying, "I receive not honor from men" (c. v. 41) ; and again, "These things I say that ye may be saved."   (c. v. 34.)   Since He everywhere laboreth to persuade[9] them that He came for their salvation.   And He saith, that He obtaineth honor to the Father, in order that He may not be suspected by them.   And that it is for this reason He thus speaketh, He hath more clearly revealed by what follows.   For He saith, "He that seeketh his own will[10] seeketh his own glory ; but He that seeketh His glory that sent Him is true, and there is no unrighteousness in Him."   (c. vii. 18.)   "And this is the will of the Father, that every one which seeth the Son, and believeth on Him, may have everlasting life." (Ver. 40.)

"And I will raise him up at the last day." Why doth He continually dwell upon the Resurrection?   Is it that men may not judge of God's providence by present things alone ; that if they enjoy not results[11] here, they become not on that account desponding, but wait for the things that are to come, and that they may not, because their sins are not punished for the present, despise Him, but look for another life.

Now those men gained nothing, but let us

1 δι' οὗ.
2 al. "that is."
3 al. "all but this."
4 ῥοπῆς.                                          5 ὑπῆλθον.
6 S. C. here instead of τί θέλω ; reads τί ἤθελον ἰδεῖν.

7. In place of the passage which follows, Savile notices in the margin another reading: "Besides at a later time He said, (Luke xiii. 34,) 'How often would I have gathered thy children together, and ye would not!' what is it then that He saith?   Nothing else but," &c.
8 al. "ministering."            10 "that speaketh of himself," N. T.
9 al. "show."                      11 ἀπολαύωσι.

take pains to gain by having the Resurrection continually sounded in our ears ; and if we desire to be grasping, or to steal, or to do any wrong thing, let us straightway take into our thoughts that Day, let us picture to ourselves the Judgment-seat, for such reflections will check the evil impulse more strongly than any bit.  Let us continually say to others,[1] and to ourselves, "There is a resurrection, and a fearful tribunal awaiteth us."  If we see any man insolent and puffed up with the good things of this world, let us make the same remark to him, and show him that all those things abide here : and if we observe another grieving and impatient, let us say the same to him, and point out to him that his sorrows shall have an end ; if we see one careless and dissipated,[2] let us say the same charm over him, and show that for his carelessness he must render account.  This saying is able more than any other remedy to heal our souls.  For there is a Resurrection, and that Resurrection is at our doors, not afar off, nor at a distance.  "For yet a little while, and He that shall come will come, and will not tarry."  (Heb. x. 37.)  And again, "We must all appear before the judgment-seat of Christ" (2 Cor. v. 10) ; that is, both bad and good, the one to be shamed in sight of all, the other in sight of all to be made more glorious.  For as they who judge here punish the wicked and honor the good publicly, so too will it be there, that the one sort may have the greater shame, and the other more conspicuous glory.  Let us picture these things to ourselves every day.  If we are ever revolving them, no care for present things will be able to sting us.[3]  "For the things which are seen are temporal, but the things which are not seen are eternal."  (2 Cor. iv. 18.)  Continually let us say to ourselves and to others,[4] "There is a Resurrection, and a Judgment, and a scrutiny of our actions " ; and let as many as deem that there is such a thing as fate repeat this, and they shall straightway be delivered from the rottenness of their malady ; for if there is a Resurrection, and a Judgment, there is no fate, though they bring ten thousand arguments, and choke themselves to prove it.  But I am ashamed to be teaching Christians concerning the Resurrection : for he that needeth to learn that there is a Resurrection, and who hath not firmly persuaded himself that the affairs of this world go not on by fate, and without design, and as chance will have them, can be no Christian.  Wherefore, I exhort and beseech you, that we cleanse ourselves from all wickedness, and do all in our power to obtain pardon and excuse in that Day.

Perhaps some one will say, "When will be the consummation?  When will be the Resurrection?  See how long a time hath gone by, and nothing of the kind hath come to pass ?"  Yet it shall be, be sure.  For those before the flood spake after this manner, and mocked at Noah, but the flood came and swept away[5] all those unbelievers, but preserved him[6] who believed.  And the men of Lot's time expected not that stroke from God, until those lightnings and thunderbolts came down and destroyed them all utterly.  Neither in the case of these men, nor of those who lived in the time of Noah, was there any preamble[7] to what was about to happen, but when they were all living daintily, and drinking, and mad with wine, then came these intolerable calamities upon them.  So also shall the Resurrection be ; not with any preamble, but while we are in the midst of good times.[8]  Wherefore Paul saith, "For when they shall say, Peace and safety ; then sudden destruction cometh upon them, as travail upon a woman with child ; and they shall not escape."  (1 Thess. v. 3.)  God hath so ordered this, that we may be always struggling, and be not confident even in time of safety.  What sayest thou ?  Dost thou not expect that there will be a Resurrection and a Judgment?  The devils confess these, and art thou shameless ?[9]  "Art Thou come," they say, "to torment us before the time ?"  (Matt. viii. 29) ; now they who say that there will be " torment," are aware of the Judgment, and the reckoning, and the vengeance.  Let us not then besides daring evil deeds, anger God by disbelieving the word of the Resurrection.  For as in other things Christ hath been our beginning, so also hath He in this ; wherefore He is called "the first-born from the dead."  (Col. i. 18.)  Now if there were no Resurrection, how could He be "the first-born," when no one of "the dead " was to follow Him?  If there were no Resurrection, how would the justice of God be preserved, when so many evil men prosper, and so many good men are afflicted and die in their affliction?  Where shall each of these obtain his deserts, if so be that there is no Resurrection?  No one of those who have lived aright disbelieves the Resurrection, but every day they pray and repeat that holy sentence, "Thy Kingdom come."  Who then are they that disbelieve the Resurrection?  They who have unholy ways and an unclean life : as the Prophet saith, "His ways are always polluted.  Thy judgments are far above out of his sight."  (Ps. x. 5.)  For a man cannot possibly live a pure life without believing in the Resurrection ; since they who are conscious of no

---

[1] al. "one to another."  [2] διακεχυμένον.
[3] al. "none of the things present and perishable will be able to occupy us."  [4] al. "one to another."

[5] al. "seized."  [6] al. "him only."  [7] προοίμιον.

[8] lit. "fair weather."  [9] al. "dost thou not confess?"

iniquity both speak of, and wish for, and believe in it, that they may receive their recompense. Let us not then anger Him, but hear Him when He saith, "Fear Him which is able to destroy both body and soul in hell" (Matt. x. 28) ; that by that fear we may become better, and being delivered from that perdition, may be deemed worthy of the Kingdom of Heaven. Which may we all attain to, through the grace and loving-kindness of our Lord Jesus Christ, by whom and with whom to the Father and the Holy Ghost be glory, now and ever and to the endless ages of eternity. Amen.

---

# HOMILY XLVI.

### JOHN vi. 41, 42.

"The Jews then murmured at Him, because He said, I am the Bread which came down from heaven; and they said, Is not this Jesus, the son of Joseph, whose father and mother we know? How is it then that He saith, I came down from heaven?"

[1.] "WHOSE god is their belly, and whose glory is in their shame" (Phil. iii. 19), said Paul of certain persons, writing to the Philippians.[1] Now that the Jews were of this character is clear, both from what has gone before, and from what they came and said to Christ. For when He gave them bread, and filled their bellies, they said that He was a Prophet, and sought to make Him a King: but when He taught them concerning spiritual food, concerning eternal life, when He led them away from objects of sense, and spake to them of a resurrection, and raised their thoughts to higher matters, when most they ought to have admired, they murmur and start away. And yet, if He was that Prophet as they before asserted, declaring that he it was of whom Moses had said, "A Prophet shall the Lord your God raise up unto you of your brethren like unto me, unto Him shall ye hearken" (Deut. xviii. 15) ; they ought to have hearkened to Him when He said, "I came down from heaven"; yet they hearkened not, but murmured. They still reverenced Him, because the miracle of the loaves was recent, and therefore they did not openly gainsay Him, but by murmuring expressed their displeasure, that He did not give them the meal which they desired. And murmuring they said, "Is not this the son of Joseph?" Whence it is plain, that as yet they knew not of His strange and marvelous Generation. And so they still say that He is the son of Joseph, and are not rebuked ; and He saith not to them, "I am not the Son of Joseph" ; not because He was his son, but because they were not as yet able to hear of that marvelous Birth. And if they could not bear to hear in plain terms of His birth according to the flesh, much less could they hear of that ineffable Birth which is from above. If He revealed not that which was lower to them, much less would He commit to them the other. Although this greatly offended them, that He was born from a mean and common father, still He revealed not to them the truth, lest in removing one cause of offense He should create another. What then said He when they murmured?

Ver. 44. "No man can come unto Me, except the Father which hath sent Me draw Him."

The Manichæans spring upon these words, saying, "that nothing lies in our own power"; yet the expression showeth that we are masters of our will. "For if a man cometh to Him," saith some one, "what need is there of drawing?" But the words do not take away our free will, but show that we greatly need assistance. And He implieth not an unwilling[2] comer, but one enjoying much succor. Then He showeth also the manner in which He draweth ; for that men may not, again, form any material idea of God, He addeth,

Ver. 46. "Not that any man hath seen God,[3] save He which is of God, He hath seen the Father."

"How then," saith some one, "doth the Father draw?" This the Prophet explained of old, when he proclaimed beforehand, and said,

Ver. 45. "They shall all be taught of God." (Isa. liv. 13.)

Seest thou the dignity of faith, and that not of men nor by man, but by God Himself they shall[4] learn this? And to make this assertion credible, He referred them to their prophets. "If then 'all shall be taught of God,' how is it that some shall not believe?" Because the words are spoken of the greater number. Besides, the prophecy meaneth not absolutely all, but all that have the will. For the teacher sitteth ready to impart what he hath to all, and pouring forth his instruction unto all.

---

[1] al. "speaking concerning the Jews."

[2] Sav. ἄκοντα, Ben. τυχόντα.      [3] "The Father," N. T.
[4] Ben. "he foretold they shall."

Ver. 44. "And I will raise him up in the last day."

Not slight here is the authority of the Son, if so be that the Father leadeth, He raiseth up. He distinguisheth not His working from that of the Father, (how could that be?) but showeth equality[1] of power. As, therefore, after saying in that other place, "The Father which hath sent Me beareth witness of Me," He then, that they might not be over-curious about the utterance, referred them to the Scriptures; so here, that they may not entertain similar suspicions, He referreth them to the Prophets, whom He continually and everywhere quoteth, to show that He is not opposed to the Father.

"But what of those," saith some one, "who were before His time? Were not they taught of God? why then the special application of the words here?" Because of old they learned the things of God by the hands of men, but now by the Only-begotten Son of God, and by the Holy Ghost. Then He addeth, "Not that any man hath seen the Father, save He which is of God,"[2] using this expression here not with reference to the cause, but to the manner of being.[3] Since had He spoken in the former sense, we are all "of God." And where then would be the special and distinct nature of the Son? "But wherefore," saith some one, "did He not put this more clearly?" Because of their weakness. For if when He said, "I am come down from heaven," they were so offended, what would they have felt had He added this?

He calleth Himself, (ver. 48,) "the bread of life," because He maintaineth[4] our life both which is and which is to be, and saith, "Whosoever[5] shall eat of this bread shall live for ever." By "bread" He meaneth here either His saving doctrines and the faith which is in Him, or His own Body; for both nerve the soul. Yet in another place He said, "If a man hear[6] My saying, he shall never taste of death." (c. viii. 51.) And they were offended; here they had no such feeling perhaps, because they yet respected Him on account of the loaves which had been made.

[2.] And observe how He distinguisheth between His bread and the manna, by causing them to hear the result of each kind of food. For to show that the manna afforded them no unusual advantage, He added,

Ver. 49. "Your fathers did eat manna in the wilderness, and are dead."

He then establisheth a thing most likely to persuade them, that they were deemed worthy of greater things than their fathers, (meaning those marvelous men who lived in the time of Moses,) and so, after saying that they were dead who ate the manna, He addeth,

Ver. 51. "He that eateth[7] of this bread, shall live for ever."

Nor hath He put "in the wilderness" without a cause, but to point out that the supply of manna was not extended to a long time, nor entered with them into the land of promise. But this "bread" was not of the same kind.

"And the bread that I will give is My flesh, which I will give for the life of the world."

Here one might reasonably enquire, how this was a fit season for these words, which neither edified nor profited, but rather did mischief to those who had been edified; for "from that time," saith the Evangelist, "many of His disciples went back," saying, "This is a hard saying; who can hear it?" (ver. 60); since these things might have been entrusted to the disciples only, as Matthew hath told us that He discoursed with them apart. (Mark iv. 34: see Matt. xiii. 36.) What then shall we say? What is the profit of the words? Great is the profit and necessity of them. Because they pressed upon Him, asking for bodily food, reminding Him of the food provided in the days of their forefathers, and speaking of the manna as a great thing, to show them that all those things were but type and shadow, but that the very reality of the matter was now present with them, He mentioneth spiritual food. "But," saith some one, "he ought to have said, Your fathers did eat manna in the wilderness, but I have given you bread." But the interval between the two miracles was great, and the latter of them would have appeared inferior to the former, because the manna came down from heaven, but this, the miracle of the loaves, was wrought on earth. When therefore they sought food "coming down from heaven," He continually told them, "I came down from heaven." And if any one enquire why He introduced the discourse on the Mysteries, we will reply, that this was a very fitting time for such discourses; for indistinctness in what is said always rouses the hearer, and renders him more attentive. They ought not then to have been offended, but rather to have asked and enquired. But now they went back. If they believed Him to be a Prophet, they ought to have believed·His words, so that the offense was caused by their own folly, not by any difficulty in the words. And observe how by little and little He led them up to Himself. Here He saith that Himself giveth, not the Father;[8] "The

1 ἰσοστάσιον, al. ἰσότιμον.　　2 ἐκ Θεοῦ [παρὰ Θ. v. 46].
3 i.e. with reference, not to men who are "of God" as being their *Cause* by creation, but to Himself who is "of God" by His *Essence*.　　4 συγκρατεῖ, al. συγκροτεῖ.
5 Ver. 58, ὃς ἂν φάγῃ, [ὁ τρώγων, G. T.].
6 "keep," N. T.

7 "If any man eat," N. T.
8 al. "And observe how He bound the disciples to Himself; for these are they who say, 'Thou hast the words of life, whither shall we depart?' but here He bringeth in Himself giving, not the Father."

bread that I will give is My flesh, which I will give for the life of the world."

"But," saith some one, "this doctrine was strange to them and unusual."[1] And yet John at an earlier period alluded to it by calling Him "Lamb." (c. i. 29.) "But for all that, they knew it not." I know they did not; nay, neither did the disciples understand. For if as yet they had no clear knowledge of the Resurrection, and so knew not what, "Destroy this Temple, and in three days I will raise it up" (John ii. 19), might mean, much more would they be ignorant of what is said here. For these words were less clear than those. Since that prophets had raised men[2] from the dead, they knew, even if the Scriptures have not spoken so clearly on the subject, but not one of them ever asserted that any man had eaten flesh. Still they obeyed, and followed Him, and confessed that He had the words of eternal life. For this is a disciple's part, not to be over-curious about the assertions of his teacher, but to hear and obey him, and to wait the proper time for the solution of any difficulties. "How then," saith some one, "was it that the contrary came to pass, and that these men 'went back'?" It was by reason of their folly. For when questioning concerning the "how" comes in, there comes in with it unbelief. So Nicodemus was perplexed, saying, "How can a man enter into his mother's womb?" So also these are confounded, saying,

Ver. 52. "How can this man give us his flesh to eat?"

If thou seekest to know the "how," why askedst not thou this in the matter of the loaves, how He extended five to so great a number? Because they then only thought of being satisfied, not of seeing the miracle. "But," saith some one, "their experience then taught them." Then by reason of that experience these words ought to have been readily received. For to this end He wrought beforehand that strange miracle, that taught by it they might no longer disbelieve what should be said by Him afterwards.

[3.] Those men then at that time reaped no fruit from what was said, but we have enjoyed the benefit in the very realities. Wherefore it is necessary to understand the marvel of the Mysteries, what it is, why it was given, and what is the profit of the action. We become one Body, and "members of His flesh and of His bones." (Eph. v. 30.) Let the initiated[3] follow what I say. In order then that we may become this not by love only, but in very deed, let us be blended[4] into that flesh. This is effected by the food which He hath freely given us, desiring to show the love which He hath for us. On this account He hath mixed up Himself with us; He hath kneaded up[5] His body with ours, that we might be a certain One Thing,[6] like a body joined to a head. For this belongs to[7] them who love strongly; this, for instance, Job implied, speaking of his servants, by whom he was beloved so exceedingly, that they desired to cleave unto his flesh. For they said, to show the strong love which they felt, "Who would give us to be satisfied with his flesh?" (Job xxxi. 31.) Wherefore this also Christ hath done, to lead us to a closer friendship, and to show His love for us; He hath given to those who desire Him not only to see Him, but even to touch, and eat Him, and fix their teeth in His flesh, and to embrace Him, and satisfy all their love. Let us then return from that table like lions breathing fire, having become terrible to the devil; thinking on our Head, and on the love which He hath shown for us. Parents often entrust their offspring to others to feed; "but I," saith He, "do not so, I feed you with Mine own flesh, desiring that you all be nobly born,[8] and holding forth to you good hopes for the future. For He who giveth out Himself to you here, much more will do so hereafter. I have willed to become your Brother, for your sake I shared in flesh and blood, and in turn I give out to you the flesh and the blood by which I became your kinsman." This blood causeth the image of our King to be fresh[9] within us, produceth beauty unspeakable, permitteth not the nobleness of our souls to waste away, watering it continually, and nourishing it. The blood derived from our food becomes not at once blood, but something else; while this doth not so, but straightway watereth our souls, and worketh in them some mighty power. This[10] blood, if rightly taken, driveth away devils, and keepeth them afar off from us, while it calleth to us Angels and the Lord of Angels. For wherever they see the Lord's blood, devils flee, and Angels run together. This blood poured forth washed clean all the world; many wise sayings did the blessed Paul utter concerning it in the Epistle to the Hebrews. This blood cleansed the secret place, and the Holy of Holies. And if the type of it had such great power in the temple of the Hebrews, and in the midst of Egypt, when smeared on the door-posts, much more the reality. This blood sanctified the golden altar; without it the high priest dared not enter into the secret place. This blood consecrated[11] priests, this in types cleansed[12] sins. But if it had such power in the

---

[1] al. "'The bread which I will give.' But the multitudes not so, but contrariwise, 'This is a hard saying,' wherefore they go back. Yet it was no strange or unusual doctrine, for John," &c.
[2] or, "risen."     [3] i.e. communicants.     [4] ἀνακεραθῶμεν.

[5] ἀνέφυρε.
[6] ἕν π.
[7] al. "is proof of."
[8] i.e. by the New Birth.

[9] ἀνθηρὰν.
[10] al. "this mystical blood."
[11] ἐχειροτονεῖ.
[12] al. "washed away."

types, if death so shuddered at the shadow, tell me how would it not have dreaded the very reality? This blood is the salvation of our souls, by this the soul is washed,[1] by this is beautiful, by this is inflamed, this causeth our understanding to be more bright than fire, and our soul more beaming than gold; this blood was poured forth, and made heaven accessible.

[4.] Awful in truth are the Mysteries of the Church, awful in truth is the Altar. A fountain went up out of Paradise sending forth[2] material rivers, from this table springeth up a fountain which sendeth forth rivers spiritual. By the side of this fountain are planted not fruitless willows, but trees reaching even to heaven, bearing fruit ever timely and undecaying. If any be scorched with heat, let him come to the side of this fountain and cool his burning. For it quencheth drought, and comforteth[3] all things that are burnt up, not by the sun, but by the fiery darts. For it hath its beginning from above, and its source is there, whence also its water floweth. Many are the streams of that fountain which the Comforter sendeth forth, and the Son is the Mediator, not holding mattock to clear the way, but opening our minds. This fountain is a fountain of light, spouting forth rays of truth. By it stand the Powers on high looking upon the beauty of its streams, because they more clearly perceive the power of the Things set forth, and the flashings unapproachable. For as when gold is being molten if one should (were it possible) dip in it his hand or his tongue, he would immediately render them golden; thus, but in much greater degree, doth what here is set forth work upon the soul. Fiercer than fire the river boileth up, yet burneth not, but only baptizeth that on which it layeth hold. This blood was ever typified of old in the altars and sacrifices[4] of righteous men, This is the price of the world, by This Christ purchased to Himself the Church, by This He hath adorned Her all. For as a man buying servants giveth gold for them, and again when he desireth to deck them out doth this also with gold; so Christ hath pur-chased us with His blood, and adorned us with His blood. They who share this blood stand with Angels and Archangels and the Powers that are above, clothed in Christ's own kingly robe, and having the armor of the Spirit. Nay, I have not as yet said any great thing: they are clothed with the King Himself.

Now as this is a great and wonderful thing, so if thou approach it with pureness, thou approachest for salvation; but if with an evil conscience, for punishment and vengeance. "For," It saith, "he that eateth and drinketh unworthily" of the Lord, "eateth and drinketh judgment to himself" (1 Cor. xi. 29); since if they who defile the kingly purple are punished equally with those who rend it, it is not[5] unreasonable that they who receive the Body with unclean thoughts should suffer the same punishment as those who rent it with the nails. Observe at least how fearful a punishment Paul declareth, when he saith, "He that despised Moses' law dieth without mercy under two or three witnesses; of how much sorer punishment, suppose ye, shall he be thought worthy, who hath trodden under foot the Son of God, and hath counted the blood of the covenant, wherewith he was sanctified, an unholy thing?" (Heb. i. 28.) Take we then heed to ourselves, beloved, we who enjoy such blessings; and if we desire to utter any shameful word, or perceive ourselves hurried away by wrath or any like passion, let us consider of what things we have been deemed worthy, of how great a Spirit we have partaken, and this consideration shall be a sobering of our unreasonable passions. For how long shall we be nailed to present things? How long shall it be before we rouse ourselves? How long shall we neglect our own salvation? Let us bear in mind of what things Christ has deemed us worthy, let us give thanks, let us glorify Him, not by our faith alone, but also by our very works, that we may obtain the good things that are to come, through the grace and lovingkindness of our Lord Jesus Christ, by whom and with whom, to the Father and the Holy Ghost be glory, now and ever and world without end. Amen.

---

[1] al. "is delighted"
[2] al. "pouring forth."
[3] al. "cooleth."
[4] or, "slayings."

[5] al. "what is there."

# HOMILY XLVII.

### JOHN vi. 53, 54.

" Jesus therefore said unto them, Verily, verily, I say unto you, Except ye eat the flesh of the Son of Man, and drink His blood, ye have not eternal[1] life in yourselves. Whoso eateth My flesh, and drinketh My blood, hath life[2] in himself."

[1.] WHEN we converse of spiritual things, let there be nothing secular in our souls, nothing earthy, let all such thoughts retire, and be banished, and let us[3] be entirely given up to the hearing the divine oracles only. For if at the arrival of a king[4] all confusion is driven away, much more when the Spirit speaketh with us do we need[5] great stillness, great awe. And worthy of awe is that which is said to-day. How it is so, hear. " Verily I say unto you, Except a man eat My flesh, and drink My blood, he hath not eternal life in him." Since the Jews had before asserted that this was impossible, He showeth not only that it is not impossible, but that it is absolutely necessary. Wherefore He addeth, " He that eateth My flesh and drinketh My blood, hath eternal life."

" And I will raise him up at the last day." For since He had said, " He that eateth of this bread shall not die for ever " (ver. 50, not verbally quoted), and it was likely that this would stand in their way, (just as they before said, " Abraham is dead, and the prophets are dead ; and how sayest Thou, that he shall not taste of death ? " —c. viii. 52, not verbally quoted.) He bringeth forward the Resurrection to solve the question, and to show that (the man who eateth) shall not die at the last.[6] He continually handleth the subject of the Mysteries, showing the necessity of the action, and that it must by all means be done. Ver. 55. " For My flesh is true[7] meat, and My blood is true drink."

What is that He saith ?[8] He either desireth to declare that this is the true meat which saveth the soul, or to assure them concerning what had been said, that they might not suppose the words to be a mere enigma or parable, but might know that it is by all means needful to eat the Body. Then He saith,

Ver. 56. " He that eateth My flesh, dwelleth in Me."

This He said, showing that such an one is blended with[9] Him. Now what follows seems unconnected, unless we enquire into the sense ; for, saith some one, after saying, " He that eateth My flesh, dwelleth in Me," what kind of a consequence is it to add,

Ver. 57. " As the living Father hath sent Me, and I live by the Father " ?

Yet the words harmonize perfectly. For since He continually spake of " eternal life," to prove this point He introduceth the expression, " dwelleth in Me " ; for " if he dwelleth in Me, and I live, it is plain that he will live also." Then He saith, " As the living Father hath sent Me." This is an expression of comparison and resemblance, and its meaning is of this kind, " I live in like manner as the Father liveth." And that thou mayest not deem Him unbegotten, He immediately subjoineth, " by the Father," not by this to show that He needeth, in order to live, any power working in Him,[10] for He said before, to remove such a suspicion, " As the Father hath life in Himself, so hath He given to the Son also to have life in Himself " ; now if He needeth the working of another, it will be found that either the Father hath not given Him so to have it, and so the assertion is false, or if He hath so given it, then He will need no other one to support Him. What then means the, " By the Father " ? He here merely hinteth at the cause, and what He saith is of this kind : " As the Father liveth, so I live, and he that eateth Me shall live by Me." And the " life " of which He speaketh is not life merely, but the excellent[11] life ; for that He spake not simply of iife, but of that glorious and ineffable life, is clear from this. For all men " live," even unbelievers, and uninitiated, who eat not of that flesh. Seest thou that the words relate not to this life, but to that other? And what He saith is of this kind : " He that eateth My flesh, when he dieth shall not perish nor suffer punishment " ; He spake not of the general resurrection, (for all alike rise again,) but concerning the special, the glorious Resurrection, that which hath a reward.

Ver. 58. " This is that bread which came down from heaven ; not as your fathers did eat manna, and are dead ; he that eateth of this bread shall live for ever."

Continually doth He handle the same point, so as to imprint it on the understanding of the hearers, (for the teaching on these points was a

---

[1] " no life," N. T.       [2] " eternal life," N. T.
[3] al. " but having renounced all these things, and having banished all these things from our minds, let us," &c.
[4] Ben. adds, " in a city."
[5] al. " we must needs hear with."       [6] εἰς τέλος.
[7] " truly," N. T.
[8] al. " but what is the, ' is true meat '? " &c.

[9] ἀνακιρνᾶται.       [10] ἐνεργείας.       [11] εὐδόκιμον.

kind of final teaching,) and to confirm the doctrine of the Resurrection and of eternal life.
Wherefore He mentioneth the Resurrection
since He promiseth eternal life, showing that
that life is not now, but after the Resurrection.[1]
"And whence," saith some one, "are these
things clear?" From the Scriptures; to them
He everywhere referreth the Jews, bidding
them learn these things from them. And by
saying, "Which giveth life to the world," He
inciteth them to jealousy, that from very vexa-
tion that others should enjoy the gift, they may
not stay without. And continually He remindeth them of the manna, showing the difference,
(between it and His bread,) and guiding them
to the faith; for if He was able[2] to support
their life for forty years without harvest, or corn,
or other things in course;[3] much more now will
He be able to do so, as having come for greater
ends. Moreover, if those things were but types,
and yet men collected what came down without
sweat or labor; much more shall this be the
case, where the difference is great both in the
never dying, and in the enjoying the true life.
And rightly hath He spoken often of "life,"
since this is desired by men, and nothing is so
pleasing to them as not to die. Since even
under the old Covenant, this was the promise,
length of life and many days, but now it is not
length merely, but life having no end. He desireth at the same time to show, that He now
revoketh the punishment caused by sin, annulling that sentence which condemneth to death,
and bringing in not life merely, but life eternal,
contrariwise to the former things.[4]

Ver. 59. "These things said He in the synagogue, as He taught in Capernaum."

[2.] The place where most of His marvels
had been done, so that He ought there especially to have been listened to. But wherefore
taught He in the synagogue and in the Temple?
As well because He desired to catch the greatest
number of them, as because He desired to show
that He was not opposed to the Father.

Ver. 60. "But many of the disciples, when
they had heard this, said, This is a hard saying."

What means "hard"? Rough, laborious,
troublesome. Yet He said nothing of this kind,
for He spake not of a mode of life,[5] but of doctrines, continually handling the faith which is in
Him. What then means, "is a hard saying"?
Is it because it promiseth life and resurrection?
Is it because He said that He came down from
heaven? Or that it was impossible for one to
be saved who ate not His flesh? Tell me, are
these things "hard"? Who can assert that they

are? What then means "hard"? It means,
"difficult to be received," "transcending their
infirmity," "having much terror." For they
thought that He uttered words too high for His
real character, and such as were above Himself.
Therefore they said,

"Who can hear it?"

Perhaps making excuse for themselves, since
they were about to start away.

Ver. 61, 62. "When Jesus knew in Himself
that His disciples murmured at it," (for this is
an attribute of His Godhead to bring secret
things to light,) "He said unto them, Doth this
offend you? What and if ye shall see[6] the Son
of Man ascend up where He was before?"

This also He doth in the case of Nathanael,
saying, "Because I said unto thee, I saw thee
under the fig-tree, believest thou? Thou shalt
see greater things than these." (c. i. 50.) And
to Nicodemus, "No man hath ascended up to
heaven but the Son of man which is in heaven."
(c. iii. 13.) What then, doth He add difficulties
to difficulties? No, (that be far from Him,) but
by the greatness of the doctrines, and the number
of them, He desireth to bring them over. For
if one had said simply, "I have come down from
heaven," and added nothing more, he would
have been the more likely to offend them; but
He who said, "My body is the life of the
world"; He who said, "As the living Father
hath sent Me, so I live by the Father"; and
who said, "I have come down from heaven,"
solves the difficulty. For the man who utters
any one great thing concerning himself may
perhaps be suspected of feigning, but he who
connects together so many one after another
removes all suspicion. All that He doth and
saith is intended to lead them away from the
thought, that Joseph was His father. And it
was not with a wish to strengthen, but rather to
do away that stumbling-block, that He said this.
For whosoever deemed that He was Joseph's
son could not receive His sayings, while one
that was persuaded that He had come down
from heaven, and would ascend thither, might
more easily give heed to His words: at the
same time He bringeth forward also another
explanation, saying,

Ver. 63. "It is the Spirit that quickeneth,
the flesh profiteth nothing."

His meaning is, "Ye must hear spiritually
what relateth to Me, for he who heareth carnally
is not profited, nor gathereth any advantage."
It was carnal to question how He came down
from heaven, to deem that He was the son of
Joseph, to ask, "How can he give us His flesh
to eat?" All this was carnal, when they ought
to have understood the matter in a mystical and

---

[1] Ben. "both because He had said *eternal life*, and also showing."                                    [2] al. "it was possible."
[3] ἀκολουθίας.                         [4] or, "those before."
[5] πολιτείας.

[6] ἴδητε θεωρῆτε, G. T.

spiritual sense. "But," saith some one, "how could they understand what the ' eating flesh ' might mean?" Then it was their duty to wait for the proper time and enquire, and not to abandon Him.

"The words that I speak unto you, they are spirit and they are life."

That is, they are divine and spiritual, have nothing carnal about them, are not subject to the laws of physical consequence, but are free from any such necessity, are even set above the laws appointed for this world, and have also another and a different meaning. Now as in this passage He said "spirit," instead of " spiritual," so when He speaketh of "flesh," He meant not " carnal things," but " carnally hearing," and alluding at the same time to them, because they ever desired carnal things when they ought to have desired spiritual. For if a man receives them carnally, he profits nothing. "What then, is not His flesh, flesh?" Most certainly. "How then saith He, that the flesh profiteth nothing?" He speaketh not of His own flesh, (God forbid!) but of those who received His words in a carnal manner. But what is " understanding carnally "? It is looking merely to what is before our eyes, without imagining anything beyond. This is understanding carnally. But we must not judge thus by sight, but must look into all mysteries with the eyes within. This is seeing spiritually. He that eateth not His flesh, and drinketh not His blood, hath no life in him. How then doth " the flesh profit nothing," if without it we cannot live? Seest thou that the words, " the flesh profiteth nothing," are spoken not of His own flesh, but of carnal hearing?

Ver. 64. " But there are some of you that believe not."

Again, according to His custom, He addeth weight to His words, by foretelling what would come to pass, and by showing that He spake thus not from desire of honor from them, but because He cared for them. And when He said " some," He excepted the disciples. For at first He said, "Ye have both seen Me, and believe not " (ver. 36) ; but here, "There are some of you that believe not."

For He " knew from the beginning who they were that believed not, and who should betray Him."

Ver. 65. " And He said, Therefore said I unto you, that no man can come unto Me except it were given unto Him from above from My Father."

[3.] Here the Evangelist intimates to us the voluntary character of the Dispensation, and His endurance of evil. Nor is the, " from the beginning," put here without a cause, but that thou mayest be aware of His foreknowledge from the first, and that before the words were uttered, and not after the men had murmured nor after they had been offended, He knew the traitor, but before, which was an attribute of Godhead. Then He added, " Except it be given him from above from My Father"; thus persuading them to deem God His Father, not Joseph, and showing them that it is no common thing to believe in Him. As though He had said, " Unbelievers disturb Me not; trouble Me not, astonish Me not. I know of old before they were created, I know to whom the Father hath given to believe ; " and do thou, when thou hearest that " He hath given," imagine not merely an arbitrary distribution,[1] but that if any hath rendered himself worthy to receive the gift, he hath received it.

Ver. 66. " From that time many of His disciples went back, and walked no more with Him."

Rightly hath the Evangelist said, not that they " departed," but that they " went back "; showing that they cut themselves off from any increase in virtue, and that by separating themselves they lost the faith which they had of old. But this was not the case with the twelve; wherefore He saith to them,

Ver. 67. " Will ye also go away?"

Again showing that He needeth not their ministry and service, and proving to them that it was not for this that He led them about with Him. For how could He when He used such expressions even to them? But why did He not praise them? why did He not approve them? Both because He preserved the dignity befitting a teacher, and also to show them that they ought rather to be attracted by this mode of dealing. For had He praised them, they might, supposing that they were doing Him a favor, have had some human feeling ; but by showing them that He needed not their attendance, He kept them to Him the more. And observe with what prudence He spake. He said not, " Depart ye," (this would have been to thrust them from Him,) but asked them a question, " Will ye also go away?" the expression of one who would remove all force or compulsion, and who wished not that they should be attached to Him through any sense of shame, but with a sense of favor. By not openly accusing, but gently glancing at them, He showeth what is the truly wise course under such circumstances. But we feel differently ; with good reason, since we do everything holding fast our own honor, and therefore think that our estate is lowered by the departure of those who attend on us. But He neither flattered nor repulsed them, but asked them a question. Now this was

---

[1] ἀποκλήρωσιν.

not the act of one despising them, but of one wishing them not to be restrained by force and compulsion : for to remain on such terms is the same as to depart. What then saith Peter?

Ver. 68, 69. "To whom shall we go? Thou hast the words of eternal life. And we believe and are sure that Thou art the Christ, the Son of the living God."

Seest thou that it was not the words that caused offense, but the heedlessness, and sloth, and wrong-mindedness of the hearers? For even had He not spoken, they would have been offended, and would not have ceased to be ever anxious about bodily food, ever nailed to earth. Besides, the disciples heard at the same time with the others, yet they declared an opinion contrary to theirs, saying, "To whom shall we go?" An expression indicating much affection, for it shows that their Teacher[1] was more precious to them than anything, than father or mother, or any possessions,[2] and that if they withdrew from Him, they had not then whither to flee. Then lest it should seem that he had said, "to whom shall we go?" because there were none that would receive them, he straightway added, "Thou hast the words of eternal life." For the Jews listened carnally, and with human reasonings, but the disciples spiritually, and committing all to faith. Wherefore Christ said, "The words which I have spoken unto you are spirit"; that is, "do not suppose that the teaching of My words is subject to the rule of material consequences, or to the necessity of created things. Things spiritual are not of this nature, nor endure to submit to the laws of earth." This also Paul declareth, saying, "Say not in thine heart, Who shall ascend into heaven? (that is, to bring Christ down;) or, Who shall descend into the deep? (that is, to bring up Christ again from the dead.") (Rom. x. 6, 7.)

"Thou hast the words of eternal life." These men already admitted the Resurrection, and all the apportionment[3] which shall be there. And observe the brotherly and affectionate man, how he maketh answer for all the band. For he said not, "I know," but, "We know." Or rather, observe how he goes to the very words of his Teacher, not speaking as did the Jews. They said, "This is the son of Joseph"; but he said, "Thou art the Christ, the Son of the living God"; and, "Thou hast the words of eternal life"; having perhaps heard Him say,[4] "He that believeth on Me[5] hath eternal life, and I will raise him up at the last day." For he showed that he retained all that had been said, by recalling the very words. What then did Christ? He neither praised nor expressed admiration of

Peter, though He had elsewhere done so; but what saith He?

Ver. 70. "Have not I chosen you twelve, and one of you is a devil?"

For since Peter said, "We believe," Jesus excepteth Judas from the band. In the other place Peter made no mention of the disciples; but when Christ said, "Whom say ye that I am?" he replied, "Thou art the Christ, the Son of the living God" (Matt. xvi. 15); but here, since he said, "We believe," Christ with reason admitteth not Judas into that band. And this He did afar off, and long before the time, to check the wickedness of the traitor, knowing that He should avail nothing, yet doing His own part.

[4.] And remark His wisdom. He made not the traitor manifest, yet allowed him not to be hidden; that on the one hand he might not lose all shame, and become more contentious; and on the other, that he might not, thinking to be unperceived, work his wicked deed without fear. Therefore by degrees He bringeth plainer reproofs against him. First, He numbered him too among the others, when He said, "There are some of you that believe not," (for that He counted the traitor the Evangelist hath declared, saying, "For He knew from the beginning who they were that believed not, and who should betray Him;") but when he yet remained such, He brought against him a more severe rebuke, "One of you is a devil," yet made the fear common to them all, wishing to conceal him. And here it is worth while to enquire, why the disciples at this time said nothing, but afterwards were afraid and doubted, looking one upon another, and asking, "Lord, is it I?" (Matt. xxvi. 22), when Peter beckoned to John to find out the traitor, by enquiring of their Teacher which was he. What is[6] the reason? Peter had not yet heard, "Get thee behind me, Satan," wherefore he had no fear at all; but when he had been rebuked, and though he spoke through strong affection,[7] instead of being approved of, had even been called "Satan," he afterwards with reason feared when he heard, "One of you shall betray Me." Besides, He saith not even now, "One of you shall betray Me," but, "One of you is a devil"; wherefore they understood not what was spoken, but thought that He was only reflecting upon their wickedness.

But wherefore said He, "I have chosen you twelve, and one of you is a devil"? It was to show that His teaching was entirely free from flattery. For that they might not think that He would flatter them, because when all had left Him they alone remained, and confessed by Peter that He was the Christ, He leadeth them

---

1 al. "Christ."　　　　4 al. "often say."
2 or, "anything that is."　5 "Him (the Son)," N. T.
3 or, "rest," ληξιν.　　　6 al. "Is not this."　　7 διαθεσεως.

away from such a suspicion. And what He saith is of this kind. "Nothing abasheth Me from rebuking the bad; think not that because ye have remained I shall choose to flatter you, or that because ye have followed Me I shall not rebuke the wicked. For neither doth another circumstance abash Me, which is much more powerful than this to abash a teacher. For he that remaineth affordeth a proof of his affection, while one that hath been chosen by a teacher, being rejected, attacheth to him a character for folly among senseless persons. Still neither doth this cause Me to refrain from My reproofs." This at least even now the heathen frigidly and senselessly urge against Christ. For God is not wont to make men good by compulsion and force, neither is His election and choice compulsory on those who are called,[1] but persuasive.[2] And that thou mayest learn that the calling compelleth not, consider how many of these who have been called have come to perdition, so that it is clear that it lieth in our own will[3] also to be saved, or to perish.

[5.] Hearing therefore these things, learn we always to be sober and to watch. For if when he who was reckoned among that holy band, who had enjoyed so great a gift, who had wrought miracles, (for he too was with the others who were sent to raise the dead and to heal lepers,) if when he was seized by the dreadful disease of covetousness, and betrayed his Master, neither the favors, nor the gifts, nor the being with Christ, nor the attendance on Him, nor the washing the feet, nor the sharing His table, nor the bearing the bag, availed him, if these things rather served to help on[4] his punishment, let us also fear lest we ever through covetousness imitate Judas. Thou betrayest not Christ. But when thou neglectest the poor man wasting with hunger, or perishing with cold, that man draws upon thee the same condemnation.[5] When we partake of the Mysteries unworthily, we perish equally with the Christ-slayers. When we plunder, when we oppress[6] those weaker than ourselves, we shall draw down upon us severest punishment. And with reason; for how long shall the love of things present so occupy us, superfluous as they are and unprofitable? since wealth consists in superfluities, in which no advantage is. How long shall we be nailed to vanities? How long shall we not look through and away into heaven, not be sober, not be satiated with these fleeting things of earth, not learn by experience their worthlessness?

Let us think of those who before us have been wealthy; are not all those things a dream? are they not a shadow, a flower? are they not a stream which floweth by? a story and a tale? Such a man has been rich, and where now is his wealth? It has gone, has perished, but the sins done by reason of it stay by him, and the punishment which is because of the sins. Yea, surely if there were no punishment, if no kingdom were set before us, it were a duty to show regard for those of like descent and family, to respect those who have like feelings with ourselves. But now we feed dogs, and many of us wild asses, and bears, and different beasts, while we care not for a man perishing with hunger; and a thing alien to us is more valued than that which is of our kin, and our own family less honored than creatures which are not so, nor related to us.

Is it a fine thing to build one's self splendid houses, to have many servants, to lie and gaze at a gilded roof? Why then, assuredly, it is superfluous and unprofitable. For other buildings there are, far brighter and more majestic than these; on such we must gladden our eyes, for there is none to hinder us. Wilt thou see the fairest of roofs? At eventide look upon the starred heaven. "But," saith some one, "this roof is not mine." Yet in truth this is more thine than that other. For thee it was made, and is common to thee and to thy brethren; the other is not thine, but theirs who after thy death inherit it. The one may do thee the greatest service, guiding thee by its beauty to its Creator; the other the greatest harm, becoming thy greatest accuser at the Day of Judgment, inasmuch as it is covered with gold, while Christ hath not even needful raiment. Let us not, I entreat you, be subject to such folly, let us not pursue things which flee away, and flee those which endure; let us not betray our own salvation, but hold fast to our hope of what shall be hereafter; the aged, as certainly knowing that but a little space of life is left us; the young, as well persuaded that what is left is not much. For that day cometh so as a thief in the night. Knowing this, let wives exhort their husbands, and husbands admonish their wives; let us teach youths and maidens, and all instruct one another, to care not for present things, but to desire those which are to come, that we may be able also to obtain them; through the grace and lovingkindness of our Lord Jesus Christ, by whom and with whom, to the Father and the Holy Ghost be glory, now and ever and world without end. Amen.

---

[1] al. "for what is to come."
[2] προτρεπτική.
[3] γνώμῃ.
[4] ἐφόδια γέγονε.
[5] al. "vengeance."
[6] lit. "throttle."

# HOMILY XLVIII.

### John vii. 1, 2.

"After these things Jesus walked in Galilee; for He would not walk in Jewry, because the Jews sought to kill Him. Now the Jews' feast of tabernacles was at hand."

[1.] NOTHING is worse than envy and malice; through these death entered into the world. For when the devil saw man honored, he endured not his prosperity, but used every means to destroy him. (Wisd. ii. 24.) And from the same root one may everywhere see this same fruit produced. Thus Abel was slain; thus David, with many other just men, was like to have been so; from this also the Jews became Christ-slayers. And declaring this the Evangelist said, "After these things Jesus walked in Galilee; for He had not power[1] to walk in Jewry, because the Jews sought to kill Him." What sayest thou, O blessed John? Had not He "power," who was able to do all that He would? He that said, "Whom seek ye?" (c. xviii. 6) and cast them backward? He who was present, yet not seen (c. xxi. 4), had not He "power"? How then afterwards did He come among them in the midst of the temple, in the midst of the feast, when there was an assembly, when they that longed for murder were present, and utter those sayings which enraged them yet the more? Yea, this at least men marveled at, saying, "Is not this He, whom they seek to kill? And, lo, He speaketh boldly, and they say nothing unto Him." (Ver. 25, 26.) What mean these riddles? Away with the word![2] The Evangelist spake not so that he might be supposed to utter riddles, but to make it plain that He showeth proofs both of His Godhead and His Manhood. For when he saith, that "He had not power," he speaketh of Him as a man, doing many things after the manner of men; but when he saith, that He stood in the midst of them, and they seized Him not, he showeth to us the power of the Godhead, (as man He fled, as God He appeared,) and in both cases he speaks truly. To be in the midst of those who were plotting against Him, and yet not be seized by them, showed His unrivaled and irresistible nature; to yield strengthened and authenticated the Dispensation, that neither Paul of Samosata,[3] nor Marcion,[4] nor those affected with their maladies, might have anything to say. By this then he stoppeth all[5] their mouths.

"After these things was the Jews' feast of tabernacles." The words, "after these things," mean only, that the writer has here been concise, and has passed over a long interval of time, as is clear from this circumstance. When Christ sat[6] on the mountain, he saith, that it was the feast of the Passover;[7] while here the writer mentions the "feast of tabernacles," and during the five months hath neither related or taught us anything else, except the miracle of the loaves, and the sermon made to those who ate them. Yet He ceased not to work miracles, and to converse, both in the day, and in the evening, and oftentimes at night; at least, it was thus that He presided over His disciples, as all the Evangelists tell us. Why then have they omitted that interval? Because it was impossible to recount everything fully, and moreover, because they were anxious to mention those points which were followed[8] by any fault-finding or gainsaying of the Jews. There were many circumstances like those which here are omitted; for that He raised the dead, healed the sick, and was admired, they have frequently recorded;[9] but when they have anything uncommon to tell, when they have to describe any charge seemingly put forth against Him, these things they set down; such as this now, that "His brethren believed Him not." For a circumstance like this brings with it no slight suspicion, and it is worth our while to admire their truth-loving disposition, how they are not ashamed to relate things which seem to bring disgrace upon their Teacher, but have been even more anxious to report these than other matters. For instance, the writer having passed by many signs and wonders and sermons, has sprung at once to this.

Ver. 3–5. For, saith he, "His brethren said unto Him, Depart hence, and go into Judæa, that Thy disciples also may see the works that Thou doest; for there is no man that doeth anything in secret, and he himself seeketh to be known openly. Show thyself to the world. For neither did His brethren believe in Him."

[2.] What unbelief, saith some one, is here? They exhort[10] Him to work miracles. It is great deed; for of unbelief come their words, and their insolence, and their unseasonable freedom

---

[1] οὐ γὰρ εἶχεν ἐξουσίαν.
[2] al. "they are not riddles, God forbid! but this may be said, that," &c.
[3] p. 30.
[4] p. 30.
[5] al. "both."

[6] al. "when he showed Him sitting."
[7] "The Passover was nigh," c. vi. 4.
[8] al. "to be followed."
[9] al. "we have often heard."
[10] al. "what a word of unbelief, spake they, exhorting."

of speech. For they thought, that owing to their relationship, it was lawful[1] for them to address Him boldly. And their request seems forsooth to be that of friends, but the words were those of great maliciousness.[2] For in this place they reproach Him with cowardice and vainglory: since to say, "no man doeth anything in secret," is the expression of persons charging Him with cowardice, and suspecting the things done by Him as being not really done; and to add, that "he seeketh to be known," was to accuse Him of vainglory. But observe, I pray you, the power of Christ. Of those who said these things, one became first Bishop of Jerusalem, the blessed James, of whom Paul saith, "Other of the Apostles saw I none, save James, the Lord's brother" (Gal. i. 19); and Judas also is said to have been a marvelous man. And yet these persons had been present also at Cana, when the wine was made, but as yet they profited nothing. Whence then had they so great unbelief? From their evil mind,[3] and from envy; for superiority among kindred is wont somehow to be envied by such as are not alike exalted. But who are those that they call disciples here? The crowd that followed Him, not the twelve. What then saith Christ? Observe how mildly He answered; He said not, "Who are ye that counsel and instruct Me thus?" but,

Ver. 6. "My time is not yet come."

He here seemeth to me to hint at something other than He expresseth; perhaps in their envy they designed to deliver Him up to the Jews; and pointing out this to them, He saith, "My time is not yet come," that is, "the time of the Cross and the Death, why then hasten ye to slay Me before the time?"

"But your time is always ready."

As though He had said, "Though ye be ever with the Jews, they will not slay you who desire the same things with them; but Me they will straightway wish to kill. So that it is ever your time to be with them without danger, but My time is when the season of the Cross is at hand, when I must die." For that this was His meaning, He showed by what followed.

Ver. 7. "The world cannot hate you;" (how should it hate those who desire, and who run for the same objects as itself?) "but Me it hateth, because I testify of it, that the works thereof are evil."

"That is, because I upbraid and rebuke it, therefore I am hated." From this let us learn to master our anger, and not to give way to unworthy passion, though they be mean men who give us counsel. For if Christ meekly bore with unbelievers counseling Him, when their counsel was improper and not from any good intention,

what pardon shall we obtain, who being but dust and ashes, yet are annoyed with those who counsel us, and deem that we are unworthily treated, although the persons who do this may be but a little humbler than ourselves? Observe in this instance how He repelleth their accusation with all gentleness; for when they say, "Show Thyself to the world," He replieth, "The world cannot hate you, but Me the world hateth"; thus removing their accusation. "So far," He saith, "am I from seeking honor from men, that I cease not to reprove them, and this when I know that by this course hatred is produced against and death prepared for Me." "And where," asketh some one, "did He reprove men?" When did He ever cease to do so? Did He not say, "Think not that I will accuse you to the Father? There is one that accuseth you, even Moses." (c. v. 45.) And again; "I know you, that ye have not the love of God in you": and, "How can ye believe, who receive honor from men,[4] and seek not the honor that cometh from God only?" Seest thou how He hath everywhere shown, that it was the open rebuke, not the violation of the Sabbath, which caused the hatred against Him?

And wherefore doth He send them to the feast, saying,

Ver. 8. "Go ye up to the feast: I go not up yet"?

To show that He said these things not as needing them, or desiring to be flattered[5] by them, but permitting them to do what pertained to Jews. "How then," saith some one, "went He up after saying, 'I go not up'?" He said not, once for all,[6] "I go not up," but, "now," that is, "not with you."

"For My time is not yet fulfilled."

And yet He was about to be crucified at the coming Passover. "How then went He not up also? for if He went not up because the time was not yet come, He ought not to have gone up at all." But He went not up for this purpose, that He might suffer, but that He might instruct them. "But wherefore secretly? since He might by going openly both have been amidst them, and have restrained their unruly impulses as He often did." It was because He would not do this continually. Since had He gone up openly, and again blinded them,[7] He would have made His Godhead to shine through in a greater degree, which at present behooved not, but He rather concealed it.[8] And since they thought that His remaining was from cowardice, He showeth them the contrary, and that it was from

---

[1] al. "was fitting."
[2] al. "bitterness."
[3] al. "deliberate choice."
[4] "one of another," N. T.
[5] al. "desiring their company and honor."
[6] καθάπαξ.
[7] αὐτοὺς ἐπήρωσε.
[8] al. "He would have displayed greater signs of the Godhead, and revealed It in greater degree."

confidence, and a dispensation,[1] and that knowing beforehand the time when He should suffer, He would, when it should at length be at hand, be most desirous of going up to Jerusalem. And methinks by saying, "Go ye up," He meant, "Think not that I compel you to stay with Me against your will," and this addition of, "My time is not yet fully come," is the expression of one declaring that miracles must be wrought and sermons spoken, so that greater multitudes might believe, and the disciples be made more steadfast by seeing the boldness and the sufferings of their Master.

[3.] Learn we then, from what hath been said, His kindness and gentleness ; "Learn of Me, for I am meek and lowly of heart" (Matt. xi. 29) ; and let us cast away[2] all bitterness. If any exalt himself against us, let us be humble ; if any be bold, let us wait upon him ; if any bite and devour us with mocks and jests, let us not be overcome ; lest in defending ourselves we destroy ourselves. For wrath is a wild beast, a wild beast keen and angry. Let us then repeat to ourselves[3] soothing charms drawn from the holy Scripture, and say, "Thou art earth and ashes." "Why is earth and ashes proud?" (Ecclus. x. 9), and, "The sway of his fury shall be his destruction" (Ecclus. i. 22) : and, "The wrathful man is not comely" (Prov. xi. 25, LXX.) ; for there is nothing more shameful, nothing uglier than a visage inflamed with anger. As when you stir up mud there is an ill savor, so when a soul is disturbed by passion there is great indecency and unpleasantness. "But," saith some one, "I endure not insult from mine enemies." Wherefore? tell me. If the charge be true, then thou oughtest, even before the affront, to have been pricked at heart, and thank thine enemy for his rebukes ; if it be false, despise[4] it. He hath called thee poor, laugh at him ; he hath called thee base-born and foolish, then mourn for him ; for "He that saith to his brother, Thou fool, shall be in danger of hell fire." (Matt. v. 22.) Whenever therefore one insults thee, consider the punishment that he undergoeth ; then shalt thou not only not be angry, but shalt even shed tears for him. For no man is wroth with one in a fever or inflammation, but pities and weeps for all such ; and such a thing is a soul that is angry. Nay, if even thou desire to avenge thyself, hold thy peace, and thou hast dealt thine enemy a mortal blow ; while if thou addest reviling to reviling, thou hast kindled a fire. "But," saith some one, "the bystanders accuse us of weakness if we hold our peace." No, they will not condemn your weakness, but admire you for your wisdom. Moreover, if you are stung by insolence, you become insolent ; and being stung, compel men to think that what hath been said of you is true. Wherefore, tell me, doth a rich man laugh when he is called poor? Is it not because he is conscious that he is not poor? if therefore[5] we will laugh at insults, we shall afford the strongest proof that we are not conscious of the faults alleged. Besides, how long are we to dread the accounts we render to men? how long are we to despise our common Lord, and be nailed to the flesh? "For whereas there is among you strife, and envying, and divisions, are ye not carnal?" (1 Cor. iii. 3.) Let us then become spiritual, and bridle this dreadful wild beast. Anger differs nothing from madness, it is a temporary devil, or rather it is a thing worse than having a devil ; for one that hath a devil may be excused, but the angry man deserves ten thousand punishments, voluntarily casting himself into the pit of destruction, and before the hell which is to come suffering punishment from this already, by bringing a certain restless turmoil and never silent[6] storm of fury, through all the night and through all the day, upon the reasonings of his soul. Let us therefore, that we may deliver ourselves from the punishment here and the vengeance hereafter, cast out this passion, and show forth all meekness and gentleness, that we may find rest for our souls both here and in the Kingdom of Heaven. To which may we all attain, through the grace and lovingkindness of our Lord Jesus Christ, by whom and with whom, to the Father and the Holy Spirit be glory, now and ever and world without end. Amen.

---

[1] al. "at once a dispensation and a confidence."
[2] al. "cut up."     [3] al. "to it."     [4] al. "laugh at."
[5] al. "so also do ye ; if rather."     [6] al. "unbearable."

# HOMILY XLIX.

### JOHN vii. 9, 10.

"When He had said these words unto them, He abode still in Galilee. But when His brethren were gone up, then went He up also unto the feast, not openly, but as it were in secret."[1]

[1.] THE things done[2] by Christ after the manner of men, are not so done only to establish the Incarnation, but also to educate us for virtue. For had He done all as God, how could we have known, on falling in with such things as we wished not, what we must do? As, for instance, when He was in this very place, and the Jews would have killed Him, He came into the midst of them, and so appeased the tumult. Now had He done this continually, how should we, not being able to do so, and yet falling into the like case, have known in what way we ought to deal with the matter, whether to perish at once, or even to use some contrivance[3] in order that the word might go forward? Since, therefore, we who have no power could not have understood what to do on coming into the midst of our foes, on this account we are taught this very thing by Him. For, saith the Evangelist, Jesus, "when He had said these words, abode in Galilee; but when His brethren were gone up, then went He up also unto the feast, not openly, but as it were in secret." The expression, "when His brethren were gone up," is that of one showing that He chose not to go up with them. On which account He abode where He was, and manifested not Himself, although they in a manner urged[4] Him to do so. But why did He, who ever spake openly, do so now "as it were in secret"? The writer saith not "secretly," but, "as it were in secret." For thus, as I have said, He seemed[5] to be instructing us how to manage matters. And, apart from this,[6] it was not the same to come among them when heated and restive,[7] as to do so afterwards when the feast was ended.

Ver. 11. "Then the Jews sought Him,[8] and said, Where is He?"

Excellent truly the good deeds at their feasts! they are eager for murder, and wish to seize Him, even during the feast.[9] At least, in another place they speak thus, "Think ye that He will not come to the feast?" (John xi. 56); and here they said, "Where is He?" Through their ex-

cessive hatred and enmity they would not even call Him by name. Great was their reverence towards the feast, great their caution. By occasion of[10] the very feast they wished[11] to entrap Him!

Ver. 12. "And there was much murmuring among the people concerning Him."

I think they were exasperated by the place where the miracle had been wrought, and were[12] greatly infuriated and afraid, not so much from anger at what had gone before, as from fear lest He should again work something similar. But all fell out contrary to what they desired, and against their will they rendered Him conspicuous.

"And some said, He is a good man; others said, Nay, but He deceiveth the people."

Methinks the first of these opinions was that of the many, the other that of the rulers and priests. For to slander Him suited their malice and wickedness. "He deceiveth," say they, "the people." How, tell me? Was it by seeming to work, not really working miracles? But experience witnesses[13] the contrary.

Ver. 13. "Howbeit no man spake openly of Him for fear of the Jews."

Seest thou everywhere the ruling body corrupted, and the ruled sound indeed in judgment, but not having that proper courage[14] which a multitude especially lacketh?[15]

Ver. 14. "Now about the middle of the feast Jesus went up[16] and taught."

By the delay He made them more attentive; for they who had sought Him on the first days and said,[17] "Where is He?" when they saw Him suddenly present, observe how they drew near, and were like to press upon Him as He was speaking, both those who said that He was a good man, and those who said that He was not such;[18] the former so as to profit by and admire Him, the latter to lay hold on and detain Him. One party then said, "He deceiveth the people," by reason of the teaching and the doctrines, not understanding His meaning; the other on account of the miracles said, "He is a good man." He therefore thus came among them when He had slackened[19] their anger, so that they might

---

[1] al. "but secretly."
[2] lit. "dispensed."
[3] lit. "economize somewhat."
[4] al. "were eager."
[9] al. "they were always eager for murder, and by means of these (feasts) desired to catch Him."
[5] al. "it behooved."
[6] al. "besides, because."
[7] σφαδαζόντων, al. ἀκμαζόντων.
[8] "at the feast," N. T.
[10] or, "directly after."
[11] al. "were eager."
[14] al. "opinion."
[15] al. "which thing is especially characteristic of the multitude."
[16] "into the Temple," N. T.
[17] al. "they who seek Him and say."
[12] al. "and at the same time."
[13] al. "showed."
[18] al. "was wicked."
[19] χαλάσας, al. χαυνώσας.

hear His words at leisure, when passion no longer stopped their ears. What He taught, the Evangelist hath not told us; that He taught marvelously, this only he saith, and that He won[1] and brought them over. Such was the power of His speech. And they who had said, "He deceiveth the people," altered their opinion, "and marveled." Wherefore also they said,

Ver. 15. "How knoweth this man letters, having never learned?"

Observest thou how the Evangelist showeth here also their marveling to be full of wickedness? for he saith not, that they admired the teaching, or that they received the words, but simply that they "marveled." That is, were thrown into a state of astonishment, and doubted, saying, "Whence hath this man[2] these things"? when they ought from this very difficulty to have known that there was nothing merely human in Him. But because they would not confess[3] this, but stopped at wondering only, hear what He saith.

Ver. 16. "My doctrine is not Mine."

Again He answereth to their secret thoughts, referring them to the Father, and so desiring to stop their mouths.

Ver. 17. "If any man will do His will, he shall know of the doctrine, whether it be of God, or whether I speak of Myself."

What He saith is this, "Cast out from yourselves the malice and wrath and envy and hatred which has without cause been conceived against Me, then there is nothing to hinder you from knowing that My words are indeed the words of God. For at present these things cast a darkness over you, and destroy the light of right judgment, while if ye remove them this shall no longer be your case." Yet He spake not (plainly) thus, (for so He would have confounded them exceedingly,) but implied it all by saying, "He that doeth His will shall know of the doctrine, whether it is of God, or whether I speak of Myself"; that is, "whether I speak anything different and strange and contrary to God." For, "of Myself" is always put with this meaning, that "I say nothing except what seemeth good to Him, but all that the Father willeth, I will also."

"If any man do His will, he shall know of the doctrine."

"What meaneth," "If any man do His will?" "If any man be a lover of the life which is according to virtue, he shall know the power of the sayings." "If any man will give heed to the prophecies, to see whether I speak according to them or not."

[2.] But how is the doctrine His and not His? For He said not, "This doctrine is not Mine";

but having first said, "it is Mine," and having claimed it as His own, He then added, "it is not Mine." How then can the same thing be both "His" and not "His"? It is "His," because He spake it not as one who had been taught; and it is "not His," because it was the doctrine of the Father. How then saith He, "All that is the Father's is Mine, and Mine His"? (c. xvii. 10.[4]) "For if because the doctrine is the Father's, it is not thine, that other assertion is false, for according to that it ought to be thine." But the "is not Mine," affords a strong proof that His doctrine and the Father's are one; as if He had said, "It hath nothing different,[5] as though it were another's. For though My Person[6] be different, yet so do I speak and do as not to be supposed to speak or do anything contrary to the Father, but rather the very same things that the Father saith and doeth." Then He addeth another incontrovertible argument, bringing forward something merely human, and instructing them by things to which they were accustomed. And what is that?

Ver. 8. "He that speaketh of himself seeketh his own glory."

That is, "He that desireth to establish any doctrine of his own, desireth to do so only that he himself may enjoy the glory.[7] Now if I desire not to enjoy glory, wherefore should I desire to establish any doctrine of My own? He that speaketh of himself, that is, who speaketh anything peculiar or different from others, speaketh on this account, that he may establish his own glory; but if I seek the glory of Him that sent Me, wherefore should I choose to teach other[8] things?" Seest thou that there was a cause wherefore He said there too that He "did nothing of Himself"? (c. v. 19, and viii. 28.) What was it? It was that they might believe that He desired not the honor of the many. Therefore when His words are lowly, "I seek," He saith, "the glory of the Father," everywhere desiring to persuade them that He Himself loveth not glory. Now there are many reasons for His using lowly words, as that He might not be deemed unbegotten, or opposed to God, His being clothed with flesh, the infirmity of His hearers, that He might teach men to be modest, and to speak no great thing of themselves: while for speaking lofty words one could only find one reason, the greatness of His Nature. And if when He said, "Before Abraham was, I am" (c. viii. 58), they were offended, what would have been their case if they had continually heard high expressions?

---

[4] "all Mine are Thine," &c.　　[6] ὑποστάσις.
[5] i.e. from the Father's.
[7] al. "He that desires to speak of himself, desires it on no other account, but only to reap glory from this."
[8] i.e. other than He willeth.

---

[1] lit. "took."　　[2] al. "knoweth he."　　[3] al. "reveal."

Ver. 19. "Did not Moses give you the Law? and yet none of you keepeth the Law? Why go ye about to kill Me?"

"And what connection," saith some one, "has this, or what has this to do with what was said before?" The Jews brought against Him two accusations; one, that He broke the Sabbath; the other, that He called God His Father, making Himself equal with God. And that this was no imagination of theirs, but His own declared judgment,[1] and that He spake not as do the many, but in a special and peculiar sense, is clear from this circumstance. Many often called God their Father; as "Have we not all one Father, hath not one God created us?" (Mal. ii. 10), but not for that was the people equal to God, on which account the hearers were not offended. As then when the Jews said, "This man is not from God," He often healed them,[2] and made defense for the violation of the Sabbath; so now had the sense they assigned to His words been according to their imagination, not according to His intention, He would have corrected them, and said, "Why suppose ye Me equal to God? I am not equal"; yet He said nothing of the kind, but, on the contrary, declared by what followed, that He is equal. For, "As the Father raiseth up the dead, and quickeneth them, so also the Son" (c. v. 21); and "That all may honor the Son as they honor the Father"; and "The works which He doeth, the same doeth the Son likewise;" all these go to establish His equality. Again, concerning the Law He saith, "Think not that I am come to destroy the Law or the Prophets." (Matt. v. 17.) Thus He knoweth how to remove evil suspicions which are in their minds; but in this place He not only doth not remove, but even confirmeth their suspicion of His equality. On which account also, when they said in another place, "Thou makest thyself God," He did not remove their suspicion, but even confirmed it, saying, "That ye may know that the Son of Man hath power on earth to forgive sins, He saith to the sick of the palsy, Take up thy bed, and walk."[3] (Matt. ix. 6.) This then He first aimed at, to make Himself equal with God, showing that He was not God's adversary, but that He said the same and taught the same with Him, and afterwards He setteth Himself to[4] the breach of the Sabbath, saying, "Did not Moses give you the Law, and none of you keepeth the Law?" As though He had said, "The Law saith, Thou shalt not kill; but ye kill, and yet accuse Me as transgressing the Law." But wherefore saith He, "None of you"? Because they all sought to kill Him. "And if," He saith, "I even have broken the Law, it was in saving a man, but ye

transgress it for evil. And if My action was even a transgression, yet it was in order to save, and I ought not to be judged by you who transgress in the greatest matters. For your conduct is a subverting of the whole Law." Then also He presseth it farther, although He had said many things to them before, but at that former time He spake after a loftier manner, and more suitably to His own dignity, while now He speaketh more humbly. Wherefore? Because He would not continually irritate them. At present their anger had become intense, and they went on to murder. And therefore He continueth to check them in these two ways, by reproving their evil daring, and saying, "Why go ye about to kill Me?" and by modestly calling Himself, "A Man that hath told you the truth" (c. viii. 40), and by showing that murderers in heart are not worthy to judge others. And observe both the humility of Christ's question, and the insolence of their answer.

Ver. 20. "Thou hast a devil; who goeth about to kill thee?"

[3.] The expression is one of wrath and anger, and of a soul made shameless by an unexpected reproof, and put to confusion before their time, as they thought.[5] For just as a sort of robbers who sing over their plots, then when they desire to put him against whom they are plotting off his guard, effect their object by keeping silence, so also do these. But He, omitting to rebuke them for this, so as not to make them more shameless, again taketh in hand His defense with respect to the Sabbath, reasoning with them from the Law. And observe how prudently. "No wonder," He saith, "if ye disobey Me, when ye disobey the Law which ye think ye obey, and which ye hold to have been given you by Moses. It is therefore no new thing, if ye give not heed to My words." For because[6] they said, "God spake to Moses, but as for this fellow we know not whence he is" (c. ix. 29), He showeth that they were insulting Moses as well as Himself, for Moses gave them the Law, and they obeyed it not.

Ver. 21. "I have done one work, and ye all marvel."

Observe how He argueth, where it is necessary to defend Himself, and make His defense a charge against them.[7] For with respect to that which had been wrought, He introduceth not the Person of the Father, but His own: "I have done one work." He would show,[8] that not to have done it would have been to break the Law,

---

[1] γνώμης.
[2] i.e. of their error.
[3] "go to thine house," N. T.
[4] i.e. to meet the charge of.

[5] προκαταπληττομένης αὐτῶν ὡς ᾤοντο. This appears to be the meaning, if the text is correct. The passage is suspected, but there is no other reading.          [6] or, "when."
[7] al. "to admit what had taken place as a charge against Himself."
[8] i.e. by ver. 22. "Moses therefore gave you circumcision (not because it is of Moses, but the fathers) and ye on the Sabbath day circumcise a man."

and that there are many things more authoritative [1] than the Law, and that " Moses " endured to receive a command against [2] the Law, and more authoritative than the Law. For " circumcision " is more authoritative than the Sabbath, and yet circumcision is not of the Law, but of " the fathers." " But I," He saith, " have done that which is more authoritative and better than circumcision." Then He mentioneth not the command of the Law; for instance, that the Priests profane the Sabbath, as He had said already, but speaketh more largely. The meaning of, " Ye marvel " (Matt. xii. 5) is, " Ye are confused," " are troubled." For if the Law was to be lasting, circumcision would not have been more authoritative than it. And He said not, " I have done a thing greater than circumcision," but abundantly refuteth them by saying, [3]

Ver. 23. " If a man receive circumcision." [4]

" Seest thou that the Law is most established when a man breaketh it? Seest thou that the breaking of the Sabbath is the keeping of the Law? that if the Sabbath were not broken, the Law must needs have been broken? so that I also have established the Law." He said not, " Ye are wroth with Me because I have wrought a thing which is greater than circumcision," but having merely mentioned what had been done, He left it to them to judge, whether entire health was not a more necessary thing than circumcision. " The Law," He saith, " is broken, that a man may receive a sign which contributeth nothing to health; are ye vexed and indignant at its being broken, that one might be freed from so grievous a disease? "

Ver. 24. " Judge not according to appearance."

What is, " according to appearance "? " Do not, since Moses hath the greatest honor among you, give your decision according to your estimation of persons, but according to the nature of things; for this is to judge rightly. Wherefore hath no one of you reproved Moses? Wherefore hath no one disobeyed him when he ordereth that the Sabbath be broken by a commandment introduced from without into the Law? He alloweth a commandment to be of more authority than his own Law; a commandment not introduced by the Law, but from without, which is especially wonderful; while ye who are not lawgivers are beyond measure jealous for the Law, and defend it. Yet Moses, who ordereth that the Law be broken by a commandment which is not of the Law, is more worthy of confidence than you." By saying then, (I have made) " a whole man (healthy)," He showeth that circumcision also was " partial " health. And what was the health procured by circumcision? " Every soul," [5] It saith, " that is not circumcised, shall be utterly destroyed." (Gen. xvii. 14.) " But I have raised up a man not partially afflicted, but wholly undone." " Judge not," therefore, " according to appearance."

Be we persuaded that this is [6] said not merely to the men of that time, but to us also, that in nothing we pervert justice, but do all in its behalf; that whether a man be poor or rich, we give no heed to persons, but enquire into things. " Thou shalt not pity," [7] It saith, " the poor in judgment." (Ex. xxiii. 3.) What is meant? " Be not broken down, nor bent," It saith, " if he that doth the wrong be a poor man." Now if you may not favor a poor man, much less a rich. And this I say not only to you who are judges, but to all men, that they nowhere pervert justice, but preserve it everywhere pure. " The Lord," It saith, " loveth righteousness "; and, " he that loveth iniquity hateth his own soul." (Ps. xi. 7 and 5, LXX.) Let us not, I entreat, hate our own souls, nor love unrighteousness. For certainly its profit in the present world is little [8] or nothing, and for the world to come it brings great damage. [9] Or rather, I should say, that not even here can we enjoy it; for when we live softly, yet with an evil conscience, is not this vengeance and punishment? Let us then love righteousness, and never look aside [10] from that law. For what fruit shall we gain from the present life, if we depart without having attained unto excellence? What there will help us? Will friendship, or relations, or this or that man's favor? What am I saying? this or that man's favor? Though we have Noah, Job, or Daniel for a father, this will avail us nothing if we be betrayed by our own works. One thing alone we need, that is, excellency of soul. This will be able to carry you safe through, and to deliver you from everlasting fire, this will escort [11] you to the Kingdom of Heaven. To which may we all attain, through the grace and lovingkindness of our Lord Jesus Christ, by whom and with whom, to the Father and the Holy Ghost be glory, now and ever and world without end. Amen.

---

[1] κυριώτερα.
[2] κατὰ τοῦ ν.
[3] al. " but hinted by saying."
[4] ver. 23. " If a man on the Sabbath day receive circumcision, that the Law of Moses should not be broken; are ye angry at Me, because I have made a man every whit whole on the Sabbath day?"

[5] al. " soul of man."
[6] al. " but this is."
[7] ἐλεήσεις.
[8] al. " for how great is, &c. little."
[9] al. " and afterwards we perish miserably."
[10] al. " offend against."
[11] al. " escorts."

# HOMILY L.

John vii. 25–27.

"Then said some of them of Jerusalem, Is not this he, whom they seek to kill? But, lo, he speaketh boldly, and they say nothing unto him. Do the rulers know indeed that this is the very Christ? Howbeit we know this man whence he is."

[1.] Nothing is placed in the Holy Scriptures without a reason, for they were uttered by the Holy Ghost, therefore let us enquire exactly into every point. For it is possible from one expression to find out the entire meaning (of a passage), as in the case before us. "Many of them of Jerusalem said, Is not this he, whom they seek to kill? But, lo, he speaketh boldly, and they say nothing unto him." Now why is added, "them of Jerusalem"? The Evangelist by this shows, that they who had most enjoyed His mighty miracles were more pitiable than any; they who had beheld the greatest proof of His Godhead, and yet committed all to the judgment of their corrupt rulers. For was it not a great proof of it, that men furious and bent on murder, who went about and sought to kill Him, should be quiet of a sudden, when they had Him in their hands? Who could have effected this? who thus quenched their absolute fury? Still after such proofs, observe the folly and the madness of the men. "Is not this he, whom they seek to kill?" See how they accuse themselves; "whom," It saith, "they seek to kill, and yet they say nothing to him." And not only do they say nothing to Him, but nothing even when He "speaketh boldly." For one who spoke boldly and with all freedom would naturally have the more angered them; but they did nothing. "Do they know indeed that this is the very Christ?" "What think ye? What opinion give ye?" The contrary, It saith. On which account they said, "We know this man whence he is." What malice,[1] what contradiction! They do not even follow the opinion of their rulers, but bring forward another, perverse, and worthy of their own folly; "We know him whence he is."

"But when Christ cometh, no man knoweth whence He is." (Matt. ii. 4.)

"Yet your rulers when asked replied, that He should be born in Bethlehem." And others again said, "God spake unto Moses, but as for this fellow, we know not from whence he is." (c. ix. 29.) "We know whence he is," and "we know not whence He is"; observe the words of drunken men. And again, "Doth Christ come out of Galilee?" (Ver. 41.) Is He not of "the town of Bethlehem"? Seest thou that theirs is the decision of madmen? "We know," and, "we know not"; "Christ cometh from Bethlehem"; "When Christ cometh, no man knoweth whence He is." What can be plainer than this contradiction? For they only looked to one thing, which was, not to believe. What then is Christ's reply?

Ver. 28. "Ye both know Me, and ye know whence I am: and I am not come of Myself, but He that sent Me is true, whom ye know not."

[2.] And again, "If ye had known Me, ye should have known My Father also." (c. viii. 19.) How then saith He, that they both "know Him," and "whence He is," and then, "that they neither know Him, nor the Father"? He doth not contradict, (away with the thought,) but is very consistent with Himself. For He speaketh of a different kind of knowledge, when He saith, "ye know not"; as when He saith, "The sons of Eli were wicked sons, they knew not the Lord" (1 Sam. ii. 12); and again, "Israel doth not know Me." (Isa. i. 3.) So also Paul saith, "They profess that they know God, but in works they deny Him." (Tit. i. 16.) It is therefore possible, "knowing," "not to know." This then is what He saith: "If ye know Me, ye know that I am the Son of God." For the "whence I am" doth not here denote place. As is clear from what followeth, "I am not come of Myself, but He that sent Me is true, whom ye know not," referring here to the ignorance shown by their works. [As Paul saith, "They profess that they know God, but in works they deny Him."] For their fault came not merely of ignorance, but of wickedness, and an evil will; because even though they knew this, they chose to be ignorant. But what manner of connection is there here? How is it that He, reproving them, useth their own words? For when they say, "We know this man whence he is," He addeth, "ye both know Me." Was their expression, "We know him not"? Nay, they said, "We know him." But (observe), they by saying the, "We know whence he is," declared nothing else than that He was "of the earth," and that He was "the carpenter's son"; but He led them up to heaven, saying, "Ye know whence I am," that is, not thence whence ye suppose, but from that place whence He that

sent Me (hath sent Me). For to say, "I am
not come of Myself," intimateth to them, that
they knew that He was sent by the Father,
though they did not disclose it.[1] So that He
rebuketh them in a twofold manner; first, what
they said in secret He published aloud, so as to
put them to shame; after that He revealed also
what was in their hearts. As though He had
said, "I am not one of the abjects, nor of those
who come for nothing, but He 'that sent Me is
true, whom ye know not.'" What meaneth, "He
that sent Me is true"? "If He be true, He
hath sent Me for the truth; if He be true, it is
probable that He who is sent is true also." This
also He proveth in another way, vanquishing them
with their own words. For whereas they had
said, "When Christ cometh, no man knoweth
whence He is," He proveth from this that He
Himself is the Christ. They used the words,
"No man knoweth," with reference to distinction of some definite locality; but from the
same words He showeth Himself to be the
Christ, because He came from the Father; and
everywhere He witnesseth that He alone hath
the knowledge of the Father, saying, "Not that
any man hath seen the Father, save He which
is from the Father."[2] (c. vi. 46.) And His words
exasperated them; for to tell them, "Ye know
Him not," and to rebuke them because knowing
they pretended to be ignorant, was sufficient to
sting and annoy them.

Ver. 30. "Then they sought to take Him, and
no man laid his hand upon Him, because His
hour was not yet come."

Seest thou that they are invisibly restrained,
and their anger bridled? But wherefore saith
It not, that He had restrained them invisibly,
but, "Because His hour was not yet come"?
The Evangelist was minded to speak more
humanly and in a lowlier strain, so that Christ
might be deemed to be also Man. For because
Christ everywhere speaketh of sublime matters,
he therefore intersperseth expressions of this
kind. And when Christ saith, "I am from
Him," He speaketh not as a Prophet who
learneth, but as seeing Him, and being with
Him.

Ver. 29. "I know Him," He saith, "for I am
from Him, and He hath sent Me."

Seest thou how He continually seeketh to
prove the, "I am not come of Myself," and,
"He that sent Me is true," striving not to be
thought an enemy of God? And observe how
great is the profit of the humility of His words;
for, it saith, after this many said,

Ver. 31. "When Christ cometh, will He do
more miracles than these which this man hath
done?"

How many were the miracles? In truth,
there were three, that of the wine, that of the
paralytic, and that of the nobleman's son; and
the Evangelist hath related no more. From
which circumstance it is plain, as I have often
said, that the writers pass by most of them, and
discourse to us of those alone on account of
which the rulers ill-treated Him. "Then they
sought to take Him," and kill Him. Who
"sought"? Not the multitude, who had no
desire of rule, nor could be made captives by
malice; but the priests. For they of the multitude said, "When Christ cometh, will He do
more miracles?" Yet neither was this sound
faith, but, as it were, the idea of a promiscuous[3]
crowd; for to say, "When He cometh," was not
the expression of men firmly persuaded that He
was the Christ. We may either understand the
words thus, or that they were uttered by the
multitudes when they came together. "Since,"
they may have said, "our rulers are taking every
pains to prove that this man is not the Christ,
let us suppose that he is not the Christ; will the
Christ be better than he?" For, as I ever
repeat, men of the grosser sort are led in not
by doctrine, nor by preaching, but by miracles.

Ver. 32. "The Pharisees heard the people
murmuring,[4] and sent[5] servants to take Him."

Seest thou that the violation of the Sabbath
was a mere pretense? and that what most stung
them was this murmuring? For here, though
they had no fault to find with Him for anything
said or done, they desired to take Him because
of the multitude. They dared not do it themselves, suspecting danger, but sent their hired
servants.[6] Alas! for their tyranny and their
madness, or rather, I should say, for their folly.
After having often attempted themselves, and
not prevailed, they committed the matter to
servants, simply satisfying their anger. Yet He
had spoken much at the pool (c. v.), and they
had done nothing of the kind; they sought indeed occasion, but they attempted not, while
here they can endure it no longer, when the
multitude is about to run to Him. What then
saith Christ?

Ver. 33. "Yet a little while am I with you."

Having power to bow and terrify His hearers,
He uttereth words full of humility. As though
He had said, "Why are ye eager to persecute
and kill Me? Wait a little while, and even
though you should be eager to keep Me back,
I shall not endure it." That no one should (as
they did) suppose that the, "Yet a little while
am I with you," denoted a common death, that
no one might suppose this, or that He wrought[7]
nothing after death, He added,

---

[1] ἐξεκάλυπτον.     [2] " of God," N. T.

[3] χυδαίου.
[4] " murmuring such things concerning Him," N. T.
[5] " the Pharisees and Chief Priests sent," N. T.
[6] or, " sent their s. to be exposed " (ἐκδότους).     [7] ἐνήργει.

Ver. 34. "And where I am, thither ye cannot come."

Now had He been about to continue in death, they might have gone to Him, for to that place we all depart. His words therefore bent the simpler portion of the multitude, terrified the bolder, made the more intelligent anxious to hear Him, since but little time was now left, and since it was not in their power always to enjoy this teaching. Nor did He merely say, "I am here," but, "I am with you," that is, "Though ye persecute, though ye drive Me away, yet for a little while I shall not cease dispensing what is for your good, saying and recommending the things that relate to your salvation."

Ver. 33. "And I go unto Him that sent Me."

This was enough to terrify and throw them into an agony. For that they should stand in need of Him, He declareth also.

Ver. 34. "Ye shall seek Me," He saith, (not only "ye shall not forget Me," but ye shall even "seek Me,") "and shall not find Me."

[3.] And when did the Jews "seek Him"? Luke saith that the women mourned over Him, and it is probable that many others, both at the time and when the city was taken, remembered Christ and His miracles, and sought His presence. (Luke xxiii. 49.) Now all this He added, desiring to attract them. For the facts that the time left was short, that He should after His departure be regretfully desired by them, and that they should not then be able to find Him, were all together sufficient to persuade them to come to Him. For had it not been that His presence should with regret be desired by them, He would not have seemed to them to be saying any great thing; if, again, it was about to be desired, and they able to find Him, neither so would this have disturbed them. Again, had He been about to stay with them a long time, so also they would have been remiss. But now He in every way compelleth and terrifieth them. And the, "I go to Him that sent Me," is the expression of one declaring that no harm will happen to Him from their plotting, and that His Passion was voluntary. Wherefore now He uttered two predictions, that after a little while He should depart, and that they should not come to Him; a thing which belonged not to human intelligence, the foretelling His own death. Hear for instance, David saying, "Lord, make me to know mine end and the number of my days, what it is, that I may know what time I have."[1] (Ps. xxxix. 4.) There is no man at all that knoweth this; and by one[2] the other is confirmed. And I think that He speaketh this covertly to the servants, and direct-

eth His discourse to them, thus specially attracting them, by showing them that He knew the cause of their arrival. As though He had said, "Wait a little, and I shall depart."

Ver. 35. "Then said the Jews among themselves, Whither will he go?"

Yet they who wished to be rid of Him, who did all in their power not to see Him, ought not to have asked this question, but to have said, "we are glad of it, when will the departure take place?" but they were somewhat affected at His words, and with foolish suspicion question one another, "whither will he go?"

"Will he go unto the dispersion of the Gentiles?"[3]

What is, "the dispersion of the Gentiles"? The Jews gave this name to other nations, because they were everywhere scattered and mingled fearlessly with one another. And this reproach they themselves afterwards endured, for they too were a "dispersion." For of old all their nation was collected into one place, and you could not anywhere find a Jew, except in Palestine only; wherefore they called the Gentiles a "dispersion," reproaching them, and boasting concerning themselves. What then meaneth, "Whither I go ye cannot come"? For all nations at that time had intercourse with them, and there were Jews everywhere. He would not therefore, if He had meant the Gentiles, have said, "Where ye cannot come." After saying, "Will he go to the dispersion of the Gentiles?" they did not add, "and ruin," but, "and teach them." To such a degree had they abated their anger, and believed His words; for they would not, had they not believed, have enquired among themselves what the saying was.

These words were spoken indeed to the Jews, but fear there is lest they be suited to us also, that "where He is" we "cannot come" on account of our life being full of sins. For concerning the disciples He saith, "I will that they also be with Me where I am" (c. xvii. 24), but concerning ourselves, I dread lest the contrary be said, that, "Where I am, ye cannot come." For when we act contrary to the commandments, how can we go to that place? Even in the present life, if any soldier act unworthily towards his king, he will not be able to see the king, but being deprived of his authority will suffer the severest punishment; if therefore we steal, or covet, if we wrong or strike others, if we work not deeds of mercy, we shall not be able to go thither, but shall suffer what happened to the virgins. For where He was, they were not able to enter in, but retired, their lamps having gone out, that is, grace having left them. For we can, if we will, increase the brightness of that

---

[1] τὶ ὑστερῶ ἐγώ, LXX., thus rendered in margin of E. V.
[2] i.e. one prediction.

[3] lit. "Greeks."

flame which we received straightway[1] by the grace of the Spirit; but if we will not do this, we shall lose it, and when that is quenched, there will be nothing else than darkness in our souls; since, as while a lamp is burning the light is strong, so when it is extinguished there is nothing but gloom.   Wherefore the Apostle saith, "Quench not the Spirit."   (1 Thess. v. 19.) And It is quenched when It hath not oil, when there is any violent gust of wind, when It is cramped and confined, (for so fire is quenched,) and It is cramped by worldly cares, and quenched by evil desires.   In addition to the causes we have mentioned, nothing quencheth It so much as inhumanity, cruelty, and rapine.   For when, besides having no oil, we pour upon it cold water, (for covetousness is this, which chills with despondency the souls of those we wrong,) whence shall it be kindled again?   We shall depart, therefore, carrying dust and ashes with us, and having much smoke to convict us of having had lamps and of having extinguished them; for where there is smoke, there needs must have been fire which hath been quenched. May none of us ever hear that word, "I know you not."   (Matt. xxv. 12.)   And whence shall we hear that word, but from this, if ever we see a poor man, and are as though we saw him not? If we will not know Christ when He is an hungered, He too will not know us when we entreat His mercy.   And with justice; for how shall he who neglects the afflicted, and gives not of that which is his own, how shall he seek to receive of that which is not his own?   Wherefore, I entreat you, let us do and contrive everything, so that oil fail not us, but that we may trim our lamps, and enter with the Bridegroom into the bride-chamber.   To which may we all attain, through the grace and lovingkindness of our Lord Jesus Christ, by whom and with whom, to the Father and the Holy Ghost be glory, now and ever and world without end.   Amen.

# HOMILY LI.

## John vii. 37, 38.

" In the last day, the great day of the feast, Jesus stood and cried, saying, If any man thirst, let him come unto Me, and drink.   He that believeth on Me, as the Scripture hath said, out of his belly shall flow rivers of living water."

[1.]  THEY who come to the divine preaching and give heed to the faith, must manifest the desire of thirsty men for water, and kindle in themselves a similar longing; so will they be able also very carefully to retain what is said. For as thirsty men, when they have taken a bowl, eagerly drain it and then desist, so too they who hear the divine oracles if they receive them thirsting, will never be weary until they have drunk them up.   For to show that men ought ever to thirst and hunger, "Blessed," It saith, "are they which do hunger and thirst after right-eousness" (Matt. v. 6); and here Christ saith, "If any man thirst, let him come unto Me, and drink."   What He saith is of this kind, "I draw no man to Me by necessity and constraint; but if any hath great zeal, if any is inflamed with desire, him I call."

But why hath the Evangelist remarked that it was "on the last day, that great day"?   For both the first day and the last were "great," while the intermediate days they spent rather in enjoyment.   Wherefore then saith he, "in the last day"?   Because on that day they were all collected together.   For on the first day He came not, and told the reason to His brethren, nor yet on the second and third days saith He anything of this kind, lest His words should come to nought, the hearers being about to run into indulgence.   But on the last day when they were returning home He giveth them supplies[2] for their salvation, and crieth aloud, partly by this showing to us His boldness, and partly for the greatness of the multitude.   And to show that He spake not of material drink, He addeth, " He that believeth on Me, as the Scripture hath said, out of his belly shall flow rivers of living water."   By "belly" he here meaneth the heart, as also in another place It saith, "And Thy Law in the midst of my belly."   (Ps. xl. 10; Theodo-tion.)   But where hath the Scripture said, that " rivers of living water shall flow from his belly"? Nowhere.   What then meaneth, " He that believeth on Me, as the Scripture saith"?   Here we must place a stop, so that the, " rivers shall flow from his belly," may be an assertion of Christ.[3]   For because many said, "This is the Christ"; and, "When the Christ cometh will He do more miracles?"   He showeth that it be-hooveth to have a correct knowledge, and to be convinced not so much from the miracles as from

---

[1] i.e. in baptism.                [2] ἐφόδια.                [3] i.e. not of the Scripture.

the Scriptures. Many, in fact, who even saw Him working marvels received Him not as Christ, and were ready to say, "Do not the Scriptures say that Christ cometh of the seed of David?" and on this they[1] continually dwelt. He then, desiring to show that He did not shun the proof from the Scriptures, again referreth them to the Scriptures. He had said before, "Search the Scriptures" (c. v. 39); and again, "It is written in the Prophets, And they shall be taught of God" (c. vi. 45); and, "Moses accuseth you" (c. v. 45); and here, "As the Scripture hath said, rivers shall flow from his belly," alluding to the largeness and abundance of grace. As in another place He saith, "A well of water springing up unto eternal life" (c. iv. 14), that is to say, "he shall possess much grace"; and elsewhere He calleth it, "eternal life," but here, "living water." He calleth that "living" which ever worketh; for the grace of the Spirit, when it hath entered into the mind and hath been established, springeth up more than any fountain, faileth not, becometh not empty, stayeth not. To signify therefore at once its unfailing supply and unlimited[2] operation, He hath called it "a well" and "rivers," not one river but numberless; and in the former case He hath represented its abundance by the expression, "springing." And one may clearly perceive what is meant, if he will consider the wisdom of Stephen, the tongue of Peter, the vehemence of Paul, how nothing bare, nothing withstood them, not the anger of multitudes, not the risings up of tyrants, not the plots of devils, not daily deaths, but as rivers borne along with a great rushing sound, so they went on their way hurrying all things with them.

Ver. 39. "But this spake He of the Spirit, which they that believe on Him should receive; for the Holy Ghost was not yet given."

[2.] How then did the Prophets prophesy and work those ten thousand wonders? For the Apostles cast not out devils by the Spirit, but by power received from Him; as He saith Himself, "If I by Beelzebub cast out devils, by whom do your children cast them out?" (Matt. xii. 27.) And this He said, signifying that before the Crucifixion[3] not all cast out devils by the Spirit, but that some did so by the power received from Him. So when[4] He was about to send them, He said, "Receive ye the Holy Ghost" (c. xx. 22); and again, "The Holy Ghost came upon them" (Acts xix. 6), and then they wrought miracles. But when[5] He was sending them, the Scripture said not, that "He gave to them the Holy Ghost," but that He gave to them "power," saying, "Cleanse

the lepers, cast out devils, raise the dead, freely ye have received, freely give." (Matt. x. 1, 8.) But in the case of the Prophets, all allow that the Gift was that of the Holy Spirit. But this Grace was stinted and departed and failed from off the earth, from the day in which it was said, "Your house is left unto you desolate" (Matt. xxiii. 38); and even before that day its dearth had begun, for there was no longer any prophet among them, nor did Grace visit their holy[6] things. Since then the Holy Ghost had been withheld, but was for the future to be shed forth abundantly, and since the beginning of this imparting was after the Crucifixion, not only as to its abundance, but also as to the increased greatness of the gifts, (for the Gift was more marvelous, as when It saith, "Ye know not what Spirit ye are of" (Luke ix. 55); and again, "For ye have not received the Spirit of bondage, but the Spirit of adoption" (Rom. viii. 15); and the men of old possessed the Spirit themselves, but imparted It not to others, while the Apostles filled tens of thousands with It,) since then, I say, they were to receive this Gift, but It was not yet given, for this cause he addeth, "The Holy Ghost was not yet." Since then the Lord spoke of this grace,[7] the Evangelist hath said, "For the Holy Ghost was not yet," that is, "was not yet given,"

"Because Jesus was not yet glorified."

Calling the Cross, "glory." For since we were enemies, and had sinned, and fallen short of the gift of God, and were haters of God, and since grace was a proof of our reconciliation, and since a gift is not given to those who are hated, but to friends and those who have been well-pleasing; it was therefore necessary that the Sacrifice should first be offered for us, that the enmity (against God) which was in our flesh should be done away, that we should become friends of God, and so receive the Gift. For if this was done with respect to the promise made to Abraham, much more with respect to grace. And this Paul hath declared, saying, "If they which are of the Law be heirs, faith is made void—because the Law worketh wrath." (Rom. iv. 14, 15.) What he saith, is of this kind: God "promised that He would give the earth to Abraham and to his seed: but his descendants were unworthy of the promise, and of their own deeds could not be well-pleasing unto God. On this account came in faith, an easy action, that it might draw grace unto it, and that the promise might not fail. And It saith, "Therefore it is of faith, that it might be by grace, to the end the promise might be sure." (Rom. iv. 16.) Wherefore it is by grace, since by their own labors they prevailed not.

---

[1] al. "He dwelt desiring," &c.
[2] lit. "unspeakable."
[3] lit. "the Cross."
[4] i.e. after the Crucifixion.
[5] i.e. before the Crucifixion.
[6] al. "divine."
[7] In Ben. the reading is different, and the sense seems incomplete. "Since then speaking of this grace, the Ev."

But wherefore after saying, "according to the Scriptures,"[1] did He not add the testimony? Because their mind was corrupt; for,

Ver. 40–42.[2] "Some said, This is the Prophet. Others said, He deceiveth the people;[3] others said, Christ cometh not from Galilee, but from the village of Bethlehem."

Others said, "When Christ cometh, no man knoweth whence He is" (ver. 27); and there was a difference of opinion, as might be expected in a confused[4] multitude; for not attentively did they listen to His words, nor for the sake of learning. Wherefore He maketh them no answer; yet they said, "Doth Christ come out of Galilee?" And He had praised, as being "an Israelite indeed," Nathanael, who had said in a more forcible and striking manner, "Can there any good thing come out of Nazareth?" (c. i. 46.) But then these men, and they who said to Nicodemus, "Search and look, for out of Galilee ariseth no prophet" (ver. 52), said it not seeking to learn, but merely to overturn the opinion concerning Christ. Nathanael said this, being a lover of the truth, and knowing exactly all the ancient histories; but they looked only to one thing, and that was to remove the opinion that He was the Christ, on which account He revealed nothing to them. For they who even contradicted themselves, and said at one time, "No man knoweth whence He cometh," at another, "From Bethlehem," would manifestly even if they had been informed have opposed Him. For be it that they knew not the place of His birth, that He was from Bethlehem, because of His dwelling[5] in Nazareth, (yet this cannot be allowed, for He was not born there,) were they ignorant of His race also, that He was "of the house and lineage of David"? How then said they, "Doth not Christ come of the seed of David?" (Ver. 42.) Because they wished to conceal even this fact by that question, saying all that they said with malicious intent. Why did they not come to Him and say, "Since we admire thee in other respects, and thou biddest us believe thee according to the Scriptures, tell us how it is that the Scriptures say that Christ must come from Bethlehem, when thou art come from Galilee?" But they said nothing of the kind, but all in malice. And to show that they spoke not enquiringly, nor as desiring to learn, the Evangelist straightway hath added, that,

Ver. 44. "Some of them would have taken Him, but no man laid his hand upon Him."

This, if nothing else, might have been sufficient to cause compunction in them, but they felt it not, as the Prophet saith, "They were cleft asunder, and were not pricked in heart." (Ps. xxxv. 15, LXX.)

[3.] Such a thing is malice! it will give way to nothing, it looks to one thing only, and that is, to destroy the person against whom it plotteth. But what saith the Scripture? "Whoso diggeth a pit for his neighbor, shall fall into it himself." (Prov. xxvi. 27.) Which was the case then. For they desired to kill Him, to stop, as they thought, His preaching; the result was the opposite. For the preaching flourishes by the grace of Christ, while all that was theirs is quenched and perished; they have lost their country, their freedom, their security, their worship, they have been deprived of all their prosperity, and are become slaves and captives.

Knowing then this, let us never plot against others, aware that by so doing we whet the sword against ourselves, and inflict upon ourselves the deeper wound. Hath any one grieved thee, and desireth thou to avenge thyself on him? Avenge not thyself; so shalt thou be able to be avenged; but if thou avenge thyself, thou art not avenged. Think not that this is a riddle, but a true saying. "How, and in what way?" Because if thou avenge not thyself on him, thou makest God his enemy; but if thou avenge thyself, no longer so. "Vengeance is Mine, I will repay, saith the Lord." (Rom. xii. 19.) For if we have servants, and they having quarreled[6] with each other, do not give place to us for judgment and for punishment, but take it upon themselves; though they come to us ten thousand times, we not only shall not avenge them, but shall even be wroth with them, saying, "Thou runaway, thou flogging-post, thou oughtest to have submitted all to us, but since thou hast prevented us and avenged thyself, trouble us no farther"; much more shall God, who hath bidden us commit all unto Him, say this. For how can it be otherwise than absurd, when we demand from our servants so much minding of wisdom and obedience, but will not yield to our Master in those matters in which we desire our domestics to yield to us? This I say because of your readiness to inflict punishment one upon another. The truly wise man ought not to do this even, but to pardon and forgive offenses, though there were not that great reward proposed, the receiving in return forgiveness. For, tell me, if thou condemnest one who hath sinned, wherefore dost thou sin thyself, and fall into the same fault? Hath he insulted? Insult not thou again, or thou hast insulted thyself. Hath he struck? Strike not thou again, for then there is no difference between you. Hath he vexed thee? Vex him not again, for the profit is

---

[1] "as saith the Scripture," ver. 38.　[4] al. " not well ordered."
[2] not verbally quoted.　[5] al. " bringing up."
[3] ver. 12.

[6] al. " disputed."

nothing, and thou wilt in thy turn be placed on an equality with those who have wronged thee. Thus, if thou bear with meekness and gentleness, thou shalt be able to reprove thine enemy, to shame him, to weary[1] him of being wroth. No man cures evil with evil, but evil with good. These rules of wisdom give some of the heathen; now if there be such wisdom among the foolish heathen, let us be ashamed to show ourselves inferior to them. Many of them have been injured, and have borne it; many have been maliciously accused, and not defended themselves; have been plotted against, and have repaid by benefits. And there is no small fear lest some of them be found in their lives to be greater than we, and so render our punishment severer. For when we who have partaken of the Spirit, we who look for the Kingdom, who follow wisdom for the sake of heavenly things,[2] who fear (not) hell, and are bidden to become angels, who enjoy the Mysteries; when we reach not to the virtue unto which they have attained, what pardon[3] shall we have? If we must go beyond the Jews, (for, "Except your righteousness shall exceed the righteousness of the Scribes and Pharisees, ye shall in no case enter into the Kingdom of Heaven"—Matt. v. 20,) much more the heathen; if the Pharisees, much more the unbelievers. Since if when we go not beyond the righteousness of the Jews, the Kingdom is shut against us, how shall we be able to attain unto it when we prove ourselves worse than the heathen? Let us then cast out all bitterness, and wrath, and anger. To speak "the same things, to me indeed is not grievous, but for you it is safe." (Phil. iii. 1.) For physicians also often use the same remedy, and we will not cease from sounding the same things in your ears, reminding, teaching, exhorting, for great is the tumult of worldly things, and it causes in us forgetfulness, and we have need of continual teaching. Let us then, in order that we meet not together in this place uselessly and in vain, exhibit the proof[4] which is by works, that so we may obtain the good things to come, through the grace and lovingkindness of our Lord Jesus Christ, by whom and with whom, to the Father and the Holy Ghost be glory, now and ever and world without end. Amen.

# HOMILY LII.

### JOHN vii. 45, 46.

"Then came the officers to the Chief Priests and Pharisees; and they said unto them, Why have ye not brought him? The officers answered, Never man spake like this Man."

[1.] THERE is nothing clearer, nothing simpler than the truth, if we deal not perversely; just as (on the other hand) if we deal perversely, nothing is more difficult. For behold, the Scribes and Pharisees, who seemed forsooth to be wiser than other men, being ever with Christ for the sake of plotting against Him, and beholding His miracles, and reading the Scriptures, were nothing profited, but were even harmed; while the officers, who could not claim one of these privileges, were subdued by one single sermon, and they who had gone forth to bind Him, came back bound themselves by wonder. We must not only marvel at their understanding, that they needed not signs, but were taken by the teaching alone; (for they said not, "Never man wrought miracles thus," but, "Never man spake thus";) we must not, I say, merely marvel at their understanding, but also at their boldness, that they spake thus to those that had sent them, to the Pharisees, to His enemies, to men who were doing all with a view to gratify their enmity. "The officers," saith the Evangelist, "came, and the Pharisees said unto them, Why have ye not brought him?" To "come" was a far greater deed than to have remained, for in the latter case they would have been rid of the annoyance of these men, but now they become heralds of the wisdom of Christ, and manifested their boldness in greater degree. And they say not, "We could not become of the multitude, for they gave heed unto Him as unto a prophet"; but what? "Never man spake as this Man." Yet they might have alleged that, but they show their right feeling. For theirs was the saying not only of men admiring Him, but blaming their masters, because they had sent them to bind Him whom it behooved rather to hear. Yet they had not heard a sermon either, but a short one; for when the long mind is impartial, there is no need of long arguments. Such a thing is truth. What then say the Pharisees? When they ought to have been pricked at the heart, they, on the contrary, retort a charge on the officers, saying,

---

[1] or, "hinder."  [2] al. "the heavens."  [3] al. "hope of p."  [4] or, "display."

Ver. 47. "Are ye also deceived?"

They still speak them fair, and do not express themselves harshly, dreading lest the others should entirely separate themselves, yet nevertheless they give signs of anger, and speak sparingly. For when they ought to have asked what He spake, and to have marveled at the words, they do not so, (knowing that they might have been captivated,) but reason with them from a very foolish argument;

Ver. 48. "Wherefore," saith one, "hath none [1] of the rulers [2] believed on Him?"

Dost thou then make this a charge against Christ, tell me, and not against the unbelievers?

Ver. 49. "But the [3] people," saith one, "which knoweth not the Law, are accursed."

Then is the charge against you the heavier, because the people believed, and ye believed not. They acted like men that knew the Law; how then are they accursed? It is ye that are accursed, who keep not the Law, not they, who obey the Law. Neither was it right, on the evidence of unbelievers, to slander one in whom they believed not, for this is an unjust mode of acting. For ye also believed not God, as Paul saith; "What if some did not believe? shall their unbelief make the faith of God of none effect? God forbid." (Rom. iii. 3, 4.) For the Prophets ever rebuked them, saying, "Hear, ye rulers of Sodom"; and, "Thy rulers are disobedient" (Isa. i. 10, 23); and again, "Is it not for you to know judgment?" (Mic. iii. 1.) And everywhere they attack them vehemently. What then? Shall one blame God for this? Away with the thought. This blame is theirs. And what other proof can a man bring of your not knowing the Law than your not obeying it? For when they had said, "Hath any of the rulers believed on him?" and, "These who know not the Law," Nicodemus in fair consequence upbraids them, saying,

Ver. 51. "Doth our [4] law judge any man before it hear him?"

He showeth that they neither know the Law, nor do the Law; for if that Law commandeth to kill no man without first hearing him, and they before hearing were eager for this deed, they were transgressors of the Law. And because they said, "None of the rulers hath believed on him" (ver. 50), therefore the Evangelist informs us that Nicodemus was "one of them," to show that even rulers believed on Him; for although they showed not yet fitting boldness, still they were becoming attached [5] to Christ. Observe how cautiously he rebukes them; he said not, "Ye desire to kill him, and condemn the man for a deceiver without proof"; but spake in a milder

way, hindering their excessive violence, and their inconsiderate and murderous disposition. Wherefore he turns his discourse to the Law, saying, "Except it hear him carefully, and know what he doeth." So that not a bare "hearing," but "careful hearing" is required. For the meaning of, "know what he doeth," is, "what he intendeth," "on what account," "for what purpose," "whether for the subversion of the order of things and as an enemy." Being therefore perplexed, because they had said, "None of the rulers hath believed on him," they addressed him, neither vehemently, nor yet with forbearance. For tell me, after he had said, "The Law judgeth no man," how doth it follow that they should say,

Ver. 52. "Art thou also of Galilee?"

[2.] When they ought to have shown that they had not sent to summon Him without judgment, or that it was not fitting to allow Him speech, they take the reply rather in a rough and angry manner.

"Search, and look: for out of Galilee hath arisen no prophet."

Why, what had the man said? that Christ was a prophet? No; he said, that He ought not to be slain unjudged; but they replied insolently, and as to one who knew nothing of the Scriptures; as though one had said, "Go, learn," for this is the meaning of, "Search, and look." What then did Christ? Since they were continually dwelling upon Galilee and "The Prophet," to free all men from this erroneous suspicion, and to show that He was not one of the prophets, but the Master of the world, He said,

Chap. viii. ver. 12. [6] "I am the light of the world."

Not "of Galilee," not of Palestine, nor of Judæa. What then say the Jews?

Ver. 13. "Thou bearest record of thyself, thy record is not true."

Alas! for their folly, He continually referred them to the Scriptures, and now they say, "Thou bearest record of thyself." What was the record He bare? "I am the light of the world." A great thing to say, great of a truth, but it did not greatly amaze them, because He did not now make Himself equal to the Father, nor assert that He was His Son, nor that He was God, but for a while calleth Himself "a light." They indeed desired to disprove this also, and yet this was a much greater thing than to say,

"He that followeth Me, shall not walk in darkness."

Using the words "light" and "darkness" in a spiritual sense, and meaning thereby "abideth not in error." In this place He draweth on

---

[1] "Hath any," N. T.
[2] "or of the Pharisees," N. T.
[3] "this," N. T.
[4] al, "your."
[5] ῷκειοῦντο.

[6] The history of the woman taken in adultery is omitted by St. Chrysostom, and all the Greek commentators.

Nicodemus, and bringeth him in as having spoken very boldly, and praiseth the servants who had also done so. For to "cry aloud,"[1] is the act of one desirous to cause that they also should hear. At the same time He hinteth at these[2] who were secretly contriving treacheries, being both in darkness and error, but that they should not prevail over the light. And He remindeth Nicodemus of the words which He had uttered before, "Every one that doeth evil hateth the light, neither cometh to the light, lest his deeds should be reproved." (c. iii. 20.) For since they had asserted that none of the rulers had believed on Him, therefore He saith, that "he that doeth evil cometh not to the light," to show that their not having come proceedeth not from the weakness of the light, but from their own perverse will.

"They answered and said unto Him, Dost thou bear witness to thyself?"

What then saith He?

Ver. 14. "Though I bear record of Myself, My record is true; for I know whence I come, and whither I go; but ye cannot tell whence I come."

What He had before said,[3] these men bring forward as if it had been specially[4] asserted. What then doth Christ? To refute this, and to show that He used those expressions as suitable to them and to their suspicions, who supposed Him to be a mere man, He saith, "Though I bear record of Myself, My record is true, for I know whence I come." What is this? "I am of God, am God, the Son of God, and God Himself is a faithful witness unto Himself, but ye know Him not; ye willingly err,[5] knowing ye pretend not to know, but say all that ye say according to mere human imagination, choosing to understand nothing beyond what is seen."

Ver. 15. "Ye judge after the flesh."

As to live after the flesh is to live badly, so to judge after the flesh is to judge unjustly.

"But I judge no man."

Ver. 16. "And yet if I judge, My judgment is true."[6]

What He saith, is of this kind; "Ye judge unjustly." "And if," saith some one, "we judge unjustly, why dost Thou not rebuke us? why dost Thou not punish us? why dost Thou not condemn us?" "Because," He saith, "I came not for this." This is the meaning of, "I judge no man; yet if I judge, My judgment is true." "For had I been willing to judge, ye would have been among the condemned. And this I say, not judging you. Yet neither do I tell you that I say it, not judging you, as though I were not

confident that had I judged you, I should have convicted you; since if I had judged you, I must justly have condemned you. But now the time of judgment is not yet." He alluded also to the judgment to come, saying,

"I am not alone, but I and the Father that sent Me."

Here He hinted, that not He alone condemneth them, but the Father also. Then He concealed this, by leading them to His own testimony.

Ver. 17. "It is written in your Law, that the testimony of two men is true."

[3.] What would the heretics say here? (They would say,) "How is he better than man, if we take what he hath said simply? For this rule is laid down in the case of men, because no man by himself is trustworthy. But in the case of God, how can one endure such a mode of speaking? How then is the word 'two' used? Is it because they are two, or because being men they are therefore two? If it is because they are two, why did he not betake himself to John, and say, I bear witness of myself, and John beareth witness of me? Wherefore not to the angels? Wherefore not to the prophets? For he might have found ten thousand other testimonies." But he desireth to show not this only that there are Two, but also that they are of the same Substance.

Ver. 19. "Then said they unto Him, Who is thy father? Jesus answered, Ye neither know Me, nor My Father."

Because while they knew they spake as though they knew not, and as if trying Him, He doth not even deem them worthy of an answer. Wherefore henceforth He speaketh all more clearly and more boldly; drawing His testimony from signs, and from His teaching of them that followed Him, and[7] by the Cross being near. For, "I know," He saith, "whence I come." This would not greatly affect them, but the adding, "and whither I go," would rather terrify them, since He was not to remain in death. But why said He not, "I know that I am God," instead of, "I know whence I come"? He ever mingleth lowly words with sublime, and even these He veileth. For after saying, "I bear witness of Myself," and proving this, He descendeth to a humbler strain. As though He had said, "I know from whom I am sent, and to whom I depart." For so they could have had nothing to say against it, when they heard that He was sent from Him, and would depart to Him. "I could not have spoken," He saith, "any falsehood, I who am come from thence, and depart thither, to the true God. But ye know not God, and therefore judge according

---

[1] S. C. seems to refer to c. vii. 28. "Then cried Jesus in the Temple," &c.                    [2] i.e. the Pharisees.
[3] Ὅπερ φθάσας εἶπε, according to Savile's conjecture and a Vatican MS. The common reading is εἶπον.
[4] προηγουμένως.    [5] ἐθελοκακεῖτε.    [6] Ben. "just."

[7] Ben. omits "and."

to the flesh. For if having heard so many sure signs and proofs ye still say, 'thy witness is not true,' if ye deem Moses worthy of credit, both as to what he speaketh concerning others and what he speaketh concerning himself, but Christ not so, this is to judge according to the flesh." "But I judge no man." He saith indeed also that "the Father judgeth no man." (c. v. 22.) How then doth He here declare, that, "If I judge, My judgment is just, for I am not alone "? He again speaketh in reply to their thoughts. "The judgment which is Mine is the judgment of the Father. The Father, judging, would not judge otherwise than as I do, and I should not judge otherwise than as the Father." Wherefore did He mention the Father? Because they would not have thought that the Son was to be believed unless He received the witness of the Father. Besides, the saying doth not even hold good. For in the case of men when two bear witness in a matter pertaining to another, then their witness is true, (this is for two to witness,) but if one should witness for himself, then they are no longer two. Seest thou that He said this for nothing else but to show that He was of the same Substance, that He needed no other witness, and was in nothing inferior to the Father? Observe at least His independence[1];

Ver. 18. "I am One that bear witness of Myself; and the Father that sent Me beareth witness of Me."

Had He been of inferior substance, He would not have put this. But now that thou mayest not deem that the Father is included, to make up the number (of two), observe that His power hath nothing different (from the Father's). A man bears witness when he is trustworthy of himself, not when he himself needs testimony, and that too in a matter pertaining to another; but in a matter of his own, where he needs the witness of another, he is not trustworthy. But in this case it is all contrary. For He though bearing witness in a matter of His own, and saying that witness is borne to Him by another, asserteth that He is trustworthy, in every way manifesting His independence. For why, when He had said, "I am not alone, but I and the Father that sent Me," and, "The testimony of two men is true," did He not hold His peace, instead of adding, "I am One that bear witness of Myself"? It was evidently to show His independence. And He placeth Himself first; "I am One that bear witness of Myself." Here He showeth His equality of honor, and that they were profited nothing by saying that they knew God the Father, while they knew not Him. And He saith that the cause of this (ignorance) was that they were not willing to know Him. Therefore He telleth them that it was not possi-

ble to know the Father without knowing Him, that even so He might draw them to the knowledge of Him. For since leaving Him they even sought to get the knowledge of the Father, He saith, "Ye cannot know the Father without Me." (Ver. 19.) So that they who blaspheme the Son, blaspheme not the Son only, but Him that begat Him also.

[4.] This let us avoid, and glorify the Son. Had He not been of the same Nature, He would not have spoken thus. For had He merely taught, but been of different Substance, a man might not have known Him, and yet have known the Father; and again, it would not have been that one who knew Him, would have altogether known the Father; for neither doth one who knoweth a man know an Angel. "Yes," replieth some one, "he that knoweth the creation, knoweth God." By no means. Many, or rather I should say, all men know the creation, (for they see it,) but they know not God. Let us then glorify the Son of God, not with this glory (of words) only, but that also which is by works. For the first without the last is nothing. "Behold," saith St. Paul, "thou art called a Jew, and restest in the Law, and makest thy boast of God — thou therefore that teachest another, teachest[2] thou not thyself? Thou that makest thy boast of the Law, through breaking of the Law dishonorest thou God?" (Rom. ii. 17, 21, 23.) Beware lest we also who make boast of the rightness of our faith dishonor God by not manifesting a life agreeable to the faith, causing Him to be blasphemed. For He would have the Christian to be the teacher of the world, its leaven, its salt, its light. And what is that light? It is a life which shineth, and hath in it no dark thing. Light is not useful to itself, nor leaven, nor salt, but showeth its usefulness towards others, and so we are required to do good, not to ourselves only, but to others. For salt, if it salt not, is not salt. Moreover another thing is evident, that if we be righteous, others shall certainly be so also; but as long as we are not righteous, we shall not be able to assist others. Let there be nothing foolish or silly among us; such are worldly matters, such are the cares of this life. Wherefore the virgins were called foolish, because they were busy about foolish, worldly matters, gathering things together here, but laying not up treasure where they ought. Fear there is lest this be our case, fear lest we too depart clothed with filthy garments, to that place where all have them bright and shining. For nothing is more filthy, nothing more impure, than sin. Wherefore the Prophet declaring its nature cried out, "My wounds stink, and are corrupt." (Ps. xxxviii. 5.) And if thou wilt fully learn how ill-savored sin is, consider it after

---

[1] αὐθεντίαν.

[2] Sav. "judgest."

it hath been done ; when thou art delivered from the desire, when the fire no longer troubleth thee, then shalt thou see what sin is. Consider anger, when thou art calm ; consider avarice, when thou dost not feel it. There is nothing more shameful, nothing more accursed, than rapine and avarice. This we continually say, desiring not to vex you, but to gain some great and wonderful advantage. For he who hath not acted rightly after hearing once, may perhaps do so after hearing a second time ; and he who hath passed by the second time, may do right after the third. God grant that we, being delivered from all evil things, may have the sweet savor of Christ ; for to Him, with the Father and the Holy Ghost is glory, now and ever and world without end. Amen.

# HOMILY LIII.

### JOHN viii. 20.

" These words spake Jesus in the treasury, as He taught in the Temple; and no man laid hands on Him, for His hour was not yet come."

[1.] OH the folly of the Jews ! seeking Him as they did before the Passover, and then having found Him in the midst of them, and having often attempted to take Him by their own or by others' hands without being able ; they were not even so awed by His power, but set themselves to their wickedness, and desisted not. For it saith, that they continually made the attempt ; " These words spake He in the treasury, teaching in the Temple ; and no man laid hands on Him." He spake in the Temple, and in the character of teacher, which was more adapted to rouse them, and He spake those things because of which they were stung, and charged Him with making Himself equal to the Father. For " the witness of two men is true," proveth this. Yet still " He spake these words," It saith, " in the Temple," in the character of teacher, " and no man laid hands on Him, for His hour was not yet come " ; that is, it was not yet the fitting time at which He would be crucified. So that even then[1] the deed done was not of their power, but of His dispensation, for they had long desired, but had not been able, nor would they even then have been able, except He had consented.

Ver. 21. " Then said Jesus unto them, I go My way, and ye shall seek Me."

Why saith He this continually? To shame and terrify their souls ; for observe what fear this saying caused in them. Although they desired to kill Him that they might be rid of Him, they yet ask, " whither He goeth," such great things did they imagine from the matter. He desired also to show them another thing, that the deed would not be effected through their force ; but He showed it to them in a figure beforehand, and already foretold the Resurrection by these words.

Ver. 22. " Then said the Jews, Will he kill himself? "

What then doth Christ? To remove their suspicion, and to show that such an act is sin, He saith,

Ver. 23. " Ye are from beneath."

What He saith, is of this kind : " It is no wonder that ye imagine such things, ye who are carnal men, and have no spiritual thoughts, but I shall not do anything of the kind, for,

" I am from above ; ye are of the world."

Here again He speaketh of their worldly and carnal imaginations, whence it is clear that the, " I am not of this world," doth not mean that He had not taken upon Him flesh, but that He was far removed from their wickedness. For He even saith, that His disciples were " not of the world " (c. xv. 19), yet they had flesh. As then Paul, when he saith, " Ye are not in the flesh " (Rom. viii. 9), doth not mean that they are incorporeal, so Christ when He saith, that His disciples are " not of the world," doth nothing else than testify to their heavenly wisdom.

Ver. 24. " I said therefore unto you that . . . if ye believe not that I am He, ye shall die in your sins."

For if He came to take away the sin of the world, and if it is impossible for men to put that off in any other way except by the washing, it needs must be that he that believeth not must depart hence, having[2] the old man ; since he that will not by faith slay and bury that old man, shall die in him, and shall go away to that place to suffer the punishment of His former sins. Wherefore He said, " He that believeth not is judged already " (c. iii. 18) ; not merely through his not believing, but because he de-

---

[1] i.e. at the Crucifixion.					[2] al. " must have."

parteth hence having his former sins upon him.

Ver. 25. "Then said they unto Him, Who art thou?"

Oh folly! After so long a time, such signs and teaching, they ask, "Who art thou?" What then saith Christ?

"The same that I told you from the beginning."

What He saith, is of this kind; "Ye are not worthy to hear My words at all, much less to learn who I am, for ye say all that ye do, tempting Me, and giving heed to none of My sayings. And all this I could now prove against you." For this is the sense of,

Ver. 26. "I have many things to say and to judge of you."

"I could not only prove you guilty, but also punish you; but He that sent Me, that is, the Father, willeth not this. For I am come not to judge the world, but to save the world, since God sent not His Son to judge the world, He saith, but to save the world. (c. iii. 17.) If now He hath sent Me for this, and He is true, with good cause I judge no one now. But these things I speak that are for your salvation, not what are for your condemnation." He speaketh thus, lest they should deem that it was through weakness that on hearing so much from them He went not to extremities, or that He knew not their secret thoughts and scoffings.

Ver. 27. "They understood not that He spake to them of the Father."

Oh folly! He ceased not to speak concerning Him, and they knew Him not. Then when, after working many signs, and teaching them, He drew them not to Himself, He next speaketh to them of the Cross, saying,

Ver. 28, 29. "When ye have lifted up the Son of Man, then ye shall know that I Am, and that I speak not[1] of Myself, and that He that sent Me is with Me. And the Father hath not left Me alone."

[2.] He showeth that He rightly said, "the same that I said unto you from the beginning." So little heed they gave to His words. "When ye have lifted up the Son of Man." "Do ye not expect that ye then shall certainly rid yourselves of Me, and slay Me? But I tell you that then ye shall most know that I Am, by reason of the miracles, the resurrection, and the destruction (of Jerusalem)." For all these things were sufficient to manifest His power. He said not, "Then ye shall know who I am"; for, "when ye shall see," He saith, "that I suffer nothing from death, then ye shall know that I Am, that is, the Christ, the Son of God, who govern[2] all things, and am not opposed to

Him."[3] For which cause He addeth, "and of Myself I speak nothing." For ye shall know both My power and My unanimity with the Father. Because the, "of Myself I speak nothing," showeth that His Substance differeth not (from that of the Father), and that He uttereth nothing save that which is in the mind of the Father. "For when ye have been driven away from your place of worship, and it is not allowed you even to serve Him as hitherto, then ye shall know that He doth this to avenge Me, and because He is wroth with those who would not hear Me." As though He had said, "Had I been an enemy and a stranger to God, He would not have stirred up such wrath against you." This also Esaias declareth, "He shall give the wicked in return for His burial" (Isa. liii. 9, LXX.); and David, "Then shall He speak unto them in His wrath" (Ps. ii. 5); and Christ Himself, "Behold, your house is left unto you desolate." (Matt. xxiii. 38.) And His parables declare the same thing when He saith, "What shall the Lord of that vineyard do to those husbandmen? He shall miserably destroy those wicked men." (Matt. xxi. 40, 41.) Seest thou that everywhere He speaketh thus, because He is not yet believed? But if He will destroy them, as He will, (for, "Bring hither," It saith, "those which would not that I should reign over them, and slay them,") wherefore saith He that the deed is not His, but His Father's? He addresseth Himself to their weakness, and at the same time honoreth Him that begat Him. Wherefore He said not, "I leave your house desolate," but, it "is left"; He hath put it impersonally. But by saying, "How often would I have gathered your children together—and ye would not," and then adding, "is left," He showeth that He wrought the desolation. "For since," He telleth them, "when ye were benefited and healed of your infirmities, ye would not know Me, ye shall know by being punished who I am."

"And the Father is with Me." That they may not deem the "who sent Me" to be a mark of inferiority, He saith, "is with Me"; the first belongeth to the Dispensation, the second to the Godhead.

"And He hath not left Me alone," for I do always those things that please Him.

Again He hath brought down His discourse to a humbler strain, continually setting Himself against that which they asserted, that He was not of God, and that He kept not the Sabbath. To this He replieth, "I do always those things that are pleasing unto Him"; showing that it was pleasing unto Him even that the Sabbath should be broken. So, for instance, just before

---

[1] "do nothing," N. T.   [2] φέρων καὶ ἄγων.   [3] i.e. to The Father.

the Crucifixion He said, "Think ye that I cannot call upon My Father?" (Matt. xxvi. 53.) And yet by merely saying, "Whom seek ye?" (c. xviii. 4, 6) He cast them down backwards. Why then saith He not, "Think ye that I cannot destroy you," when He had proved this by deed? He condescendeth to their infirmity. For He took great pains to show that He did nothing contrary to the Father. Thus He speaketh rather after the manner of a man; and as "He hath not left Me alone," was spoken, so also was the, "I do always those things that are pleasing unto Him."

Ver. 30. "As He spake these words, many believed on Him."

When He brought down His speech to a lowly strain, many believed on Him. Dost thou still ask wherefore He speaketh humbly? Yet the Evangelist clearly alluded to this when he said, "As He spake these things, many believed on Him." By this all but proclaiming aloud to us, "Oh hearer, be not confounded if thou hear any lowly expression, for they who after such high teaching were not yet persuaded that He was of the Father, were with good reason made to hear humbler words, that they might believe." And this is an excuse for those things which shall be spoken in a humble way. They believed then, yet not as they ought, but carelessly and as it were by chance, being pleased and refreshed by the humility of the words. For that they had not perfect faith the Evangelist shows by their speeches after this, in which they insult Him again. And that these are the very same persons he has declared by saying,

Ver. 31. "Then said Jesus to those Jews which believed on Him, If ye continue in My word."

Showing that they had not yet received His doctrine, but only gave heed unto His words. Wherefore He speaketh more sharply. Before He merely said, "Ye shall seek Me" (c. vii. 34), but now He addeth what is more, "Ye shall die in your sins." (c. viii. 21.) And He showeth how; "because ye cannot when ye are come to that place afterwards entreat Me."

"These things which I speak unto the world."[1] By these words He showed that He was now going forth to the Gentiles. But because they still knew not that He spake to them of the Father, He again speaketh of Him, and the Evangelist hath put the reason of the humility of the expressions.

[3.] If now we will thus search the Scriptures, exactly and not carelessly, we shall be able to attain unto our salvation; if we continually dwell upon them, we shall learn right

doctrine and a perfect life. For although a man be very hard, and stubborn, and proud, and profit nothing at other times, yet at least he shall gain fruit from this time, and receive benefit, if not so great as to admit of his being sensible of it, still he shall receive it. For if a man who passes by an ointment-maker's shop, or sitteth in one, is impregnated with the perfume even against his will, much more is this the case with one who cometh to church. For as idleness is born of idleness, so too from working is generated a ready mind. Although thou art full of ten thousand sins, although thou art impure, shun not the tarrying here. "Wherefore," it may be said, "when hearing I do not?" It is no small profit to deem one's self wretched; this fear is not useless, this dread is not unseasonable. If only thou groanest that, "hearing I do not," thou wilt certainly come also to the doing at some time or other. For it cannot be that he who speaks with God, and hears God speak, should not profit. We compose ourselves at once and wash our hands when we desire to take the Bible into them. Seest thou even before the reading what reverence is here? And if we go on with exactness, we shall reap great advantage. For we should not, unless it served to place the soul in reverence, have washed our hands; and a woman if she be unveiled straightway puts on her veil, giving proof of internal reverence, and a man if he be covered bares his head. Seest thou how the outward behavior proclaims the inward reverence? Then moreover he that sits to hear groans often, and condemns his present life.

Let us then, beloved, give heed to the Scriptures, and if no other part be so, let the Gospels at least be the subjects of our earnest care, let us keep them in our hands. For straightway when thou hast opened the Book thou shalt see the name of Christ there, and shalt hear one say, "The birth of Jesus Christ was on this wise. When His mother Mary was espoused to Joseph, she was found with Child of the Holy Ghost." (Matt. i. 18.) He that heareth this will immediately desire virginity, will marvel at the Birth, will be freed from earthly things. It is not a little thing when thou seest the Virgin deemed worthy of the Spirit, and an Angel talking with her. And this upon the very surface; but if thou perseverest to go on unto the end, thou shalt loathe all that pertains to this life, shalt mock at all worldly things. If thou art rich, thou shalt think nothing of wealth, when thou hearest that she who was (the wife) of a carpenter, and of humble family, became the mother of thy Lord. If thou art poor thou shalt not be ashamed of thy poverty, when thou hearest that the Creator of the world was not ashamed of the meanest dwelling. Considering this, thou

---

[1] Savile connects these words with the clause preceding: with this reading it is difficult to see the sense of the clause which follows. The Bened. reading is as rendered above. The reference may be to c. vii. 33, 35.

wilt not rob, thou wilt not covet, thou wilt not take the goods of others, but wilt rather be a lover of poverty, and despise wealth. And if this be the case, thou shalt banish all evil. Again, when thou seest Him lying in a manger, thou wilt not be anxious to put golden garments about thy child, or to cause thy wife's couch to be inlaid with silver. And if thou carest not for these things, thou wilt not do either the deeds of covetousness and rapine, which are caused by them. Many other things you may gain which I cannot separately enumerate, but they will know who have made the trial. Wherefore I exhort you both to obtain Bibles, and to retain together with the Bibles the sentiments they set forth, and to write them in your minds. The Jews because they gave no heed were commanded to suspend their books from their hands;[1] but we place them not even in our hands but in our house, when we ought to stamp them on our heart. Thus cleansing our present life, we shall obtain the good things that are to come; to which may we all attain, through the grace and lovingkindness of our Lord Jesus Christ, by whom and with whom, to the Father and the Holy Ghost be glory, now and ever, and world without end. Amen.

# HOMILY LIV.

JOHN viii. 31, 32.

"Then said Jesus to those Jews which believed on Him, If ye continue in My word, then are ye My disciples indeed. And ye shall know the truth, and the truth shall make you free."

[1.] BELOVED, our condition needs much endurance; and endurance is produced when doctrines are deeply rooted. For as no wind is able by its assaults to tear up the oak, which sends down its root into the lower recesses of the earth, and is firmly clenched there; so too the soul which is nailed by the fear of God none will be able to overturn. Since to be nailed is more than to be rooted. Thus the Prophet prayeth, saying, "Nail my flesh by Thy fear" (Ps. cxix. 120, LXX.); "do Thou so fix and join me, as by a nail riveted into me." For as men of this kind are hard to be captured, so the opposite sort are a ready prey, and are easily thrown down. As was the case of the Jews at that time; for after having heard and believed, they again turned out of the way. Christ therefore desiring to deepen their faith that it might not be merely superficial, diggeth into their souls by more striking words. For it was the part of believers to endure even reproofs, but they immediately were wroth. But how doth He this? He first telleth them, "If ye continue in My word, ye are My disciples indeed: and the truth shall make you free." All but saying, "I am about to make a deep incision, but be not ye moved"; or rather by these expressions He allayed the pride of their imagination. "Shall make you free": from what, tell me? From your sins. What then say those boasters?

Ver. 33. "We be Abraham's seed, and were never in bondage to any man."

Immediately their imagination dropped, and this happened from their having been fluttered[2] about worldly things. "If ye continue in My word," was the expression of One declaring what was in their heart, and knowing that they had indeed believed, but had not continued. And He promiseth a great thing, that they should become His disciples. For since some had gone away from Him before this, alluding to them He saith, "If ye continue," because they also had heard and believed, and departed because they could not continue. "For many of His disciples went back, and walked no more openly with Him."[3] (c. vi. 66.)

"Ye shall know the truth," that is, "shall know Me, for I am the truth. All the Jewish matters were types, but ye shall know the truth from Me, and it shall free you from your sins." As to those others He said, "Ye shall die in your sins," so to these He saith, "shall make you free." He said not, "I will deliver you from bondage," this He allowed them to conjecture. What then said they?

"We be Abraham's seed, and were never in bondage to any man." And yet if they must needs have been vexed, it might have been expected that they would have been so at the former part of His speech, at His having said, "Ye shall know the truth"; and that they would have replied, "What! do we not now know the truth? Is then the Law and our knowledge a lie?" But they cared for none of these things, they are grieved at worldly things, and these were their notions of bondage. And certainly even now, there are many who feel shame at indifferent matters, and at this kind of bondage, but who feel none for the bondage of sin, and

---

[1] The Tephillim.　　[2] ἐπτοῆσθαι.　　[3] some omit "openly."

who would rather be called servants to this latter kind of bondage ten thousand times, than once to the former. Such were these men, and they did not even know of any other bondage, and they say, "Bondsmen callest thou those who are of the race of Abraham, the nobly born, who therefore ought not to be called bondsmen? For, saith one, we were never in bondage to any man." Such are the boastings of the Jews. "We are the seed of Abraham," "we are Israelites." They never mention their own righteous deeds. Wherefore John cried out to them, saying, "Think not to say that we have Abraham to our father." (Matt. iii. 9.) And why did not Christ confute them, for they had often been in bondage to the Egyptians, Babylonians, and many others? Because His words were not to gain honor for Himself, but for their salvation, for their benefit, and toward this object He was pressing. For He might have spoken of the four hundred years, He might have spoken of the seventy, He might have spoken of the years of bondage during the time of the Judges, at one time twenty, at another two, at another seven; He might have said that they had never ceased being in bondage. But He desired not to show that they were slaves of men, but that they were slaves of sin, which is the most grievous slavery, from which God alone can deliver; for to forgive sins belongeth to none other. And this too they allowed. Since then they confessed that this was the work of God, He bringeth them to this point, and saith,

Ver. 34. "Whosoever committeth sin is the servant of sin."

Showing that this is the freedom of which He speaketh, the freedom from this service.

Ver. 35. "The servant abideth not in the house, but the Son abideth forever."

Gently too from this He casts down the things of the Law,[1] alluding to former times. For that they may not run back to them and say, "We have the sacrifices which Moses commanded, they are able to deliver us," He addeth these words, since otherwise what connection would the saying have? For "all have sinned, and come short of the glory of God, being justified freely by His grace" (Rom. iii. 23, 24), even the priests themselves. Wherefore Paul also saith of the priest, that "he ought as for the people so also for himself to offer for sins, for that he also is compassed about with infirmity." (Heb. v. 3, 2.) And this is signified by His saying, "The servant abideth not in the house." Here also He showeth His equal honor with the Father, and the difference between slave and free. For the parable has this meaning, that is, "the servant hath no power," this is the meaning of "abideth not."

[2.] But why when speaking of sins doth He mention a "house"? It is to show that as a master hath power over his house, so He over all. And the, "abideth not," is this, "hath not power to grant favors, as not being master of the house"; but the Son is master of the house. For this is the, "abideth forever," by a metaphor drawn from human things. That they may not say, "who art thou?" "All is Mine, (He saith,) for I am the Son, and dwell in My Father's house," calling by the name of "house" His power. As in another place He calleth the Kingdom His Father's house, "In My Father's house are many mansions." (c. xiv. 2.) For since the discourse was of freedom and bondage, He with reason used this metaphor, telling them that they had no power to set free.[2]

Ver. 36. "If the Son therefore shall make you free."

Seest thou the consubstantiality of the Son with the Father, and how He declareth that He hath the same power as the Father? "If the Son make you free, no man afterwards gainsayeth, but ye have firm freedom." For "it is God that justifieth, who is He that condemneth?" (Rom. viii. 33, 34.) Here He showeth that He Himself is pure from sin, and alludeth to that freedom which reached only to a name; this even men give, but that God alone. And so he persuaded them not to be ashamed at this slavery, but at that of sin. And desiring to show that they were not slaves, except by repudiating that liberty, He the more showeth them to be slaves by saying,[3]

"Ye shall be free indeed."

This is the expression of one declaring that this freedom was not real. Then, that they might not say, "We have no sin," (for it was probable that they would say so,) observe how He bringeth them beneath this imputation. For omitting to convict all their life, He bringeth forward that which they had in hand, which they yet desired to do, and saith,

Ver. 37. "I know that ye are Abraham's seed but ye seek to kill Me."

Gently and by little doth He expel them from that relationship, teaching them not to be high-minded because of it. For as freedom and bondage depend on men's actions, so also doth relationship. He said not directly, "Ye are not the seed of Abraham, ye the murderers of the righteous"; but for a while He even goeth along with them, and saith, "I know that ye are Abraham's seed." Yet this is not the matter in question, and during the remainder of this speech He useth greater vehemence. For we

---

[1] Sav. "Gently and by help of the Law He casts them down."

[2] or, "forgive."

[3] This reading is from a Vatican MS. which has εἰ μὴ. Savile's is not grammatical. Ben. reads, "Then desiring to show that if they were not slaves, by repudiating that former slavery they were slaves the more, He straightway added."

may for the most part observe, that when He is about to work any great thing, after He hath wrought it, He useth greater boldness of speech, as though the testimony from His works shut men's mouths. "But ye seek to kill Me." "What of that," saith some one, "if they sought to do so justly." But this was not so either; wherefore also He puts the reason;

"Because My word hath no place in you."

"How then was it," saith some one, "that they believed on Him?" As I before said, they changed again. On which account He touched them sharply. "If ye boast the relationship of Abraham ye ought also to show forth his life." And He said not, "Ye do not contain[1] my words," but, "My word hath no place in you," thus declaring the sublimity of His doctrines. Yet not for this ought they to have slain, but rather to have honored and waited on Him so as to learn. "But what," saith some one, "if thou speakest these things of thyself?" On this account He added,

Ver. 38. "I speak that which I have seen with My Father, and ye do that which ye have heard from[2] your father."

"As," He saith, "I both by My words and by the truth declare the Father, so also do ye by your actions (declare yours). For I have not only the same Substance, but also the same Truth with the Father."

Ver. 39, 40. "They said unto Him, Abraham is our father. Jesus saith unto them, If ye had Abraham to your father, ye would do the works of Abraham. But now ye seek to kill Me."

He here repeatedly handleth their murderous intention, and maketh mention of Abraham. And this He doth desiring to draw off their attention from this relationship, and to take away their excessive boasting, and also to persuade them no longer to rest their hopes of salvation in Abraham, nor in the relationship which is according to nature, but in that which is according to the will.[3] For what hindered their coming to Christ was this, their deeming that relationship to be sufficient for them to salvation. But what is the "truth" of which He speaketh? That He is equal with the Father. For it was on this account that the Jews sought to slay Him; and He saith,

"Ye seek to kill Me because I have[4] told you the truth, which I have heard of My Father."[5]

To show that these things are not opposed to the Father, He again betaketh Himself to Him. They say unto Him,

Ver. 41. "We be not born of fornication, we have one Father, even God."

[3.] "What sayest thou? Ye have God for your Father, and do ye blame Christ for asserting this?" Seest thou that He said that God was His Father in a special manner? When therefore He had cast them out of their relationship to Abraham, having nothing to reply, they dare a greater thing, and betake themselves to God. But from this honor also He expelleth them, saying,

Ver. 42–44. "If God were your Father, ye would love Me; for I proceeded forth and came from God; neither came I of Myself, but He sent Me. Why do ye not understand My speech? Even because ye cannot hear My word. Ye are of your father the devil, and the lusts of your father ye will do: he was a murderer from the beginning, and abode not in the truth:[6] when he speaketh a lie, he speaketh of his own."

He had driven them out of their relationship to Abraham, and when they dared greater things, He then addeth a blow, telling them that they not only are not Abraham's children, but that they are even children of the devil, and inflicting a wound which might counterbalance their shamelessness; nor doth He leave it unsupported, but establisheth it by proofs. "For," He saith, "to murder[7] belongeth to the wickedness of the devil." And He said not merely, "ye do his works," but, "ye do his lusts," showing that both he and they hold to murder,[8] and that envy was the cause. For the devil destroyed Adam, not because he had any charge against him, but only from envy. To this also He alludeth here.

"And abode not in the truth." That is, in the right life. For since they continually accused Him of not being from God, He telleth them that this also is from thence.[9] For the devil first was the father of a lie, when he said, "In the day that ye eat thereof your eyes shall be opened" (Gen. iii. 5), and he first used it. For men use a lie not as a thing proper, but alien to their nature, but he as proper.

Ver. 45. "And because I tell you the truth, ye believe Me not."

What kind of consequence is this? "Having no charge against Me, ye desire to kill Me. For because ye are enemies of the truth, therefore ye persecute Me. Since had this not been the reason, ye would have named your charge." Wherefore He added,

Ver. 46. "Which of you convinceth Me of sin?"

Then they said, "We be not born of fornication." Yet in fact many of them were born of

---

1 χωρεῖτε.  
2 " seen with," N. T.  
3 κατὰ προαίρεσιν.  
4 "a man that hath," N. T.  
5 "of God," N. T.  
6 " because there is no truth in him," omitted.  
7 al. " be murderously minded."  
8 al. " are murderously minded."  
9 i.e. that this assertion of theirs being false is from the devil.

fornication, for they practiced unbefitting unions. Still He doth not convict them of this, but setteth Himself to the other point. For when He hath proved them to be, not of God, but of the devil, by all these signs, (for to do murder is of the devil, and to lie is of the devil, both which ye do,) then He showeth that to love is the sign of being of God. "Why do ye not understand My speech?" Since they were always doubting, saying, "What is it that he saith, 'Whither I go ye cannot come'?" therefore He telleth them, "Ye do not understand My speech," "because ye have not the word of God. And this cometh to you, because that your understanding is groveling, and because what is Mine is far too great for you." But what if they could not understand? Not to be able here means not to be willing; for " ye have trained yourselves to be mean, to imagine nothing great." Because they said that they persecuted Him as being themselves zealous for God, on this account He everywhere striveth to show, that to persecute Him is the act of those who hate God, but that, on the contrary, to love Him is the act of those who know God.

"We have one Father, even God." On this ground they pride themselves, on their honor, not their righteous deeds. "Therefore your not believing is no proof that I am an enemy to God, but your unbelief is a sign that you do not know God. And the reason is, from your being willing to lie and to do the works of the devil. But this is the effect of meanness of soul; (as the Apostle saith, ' For whereas there is among you envying and strife, are ye not carnal?') (1 Cor. iii. 3.) And why is it that ye cannot[1]? Because ye will to do the lusts of your father, ye are eager, ye are ambitious (to do them)." Seest thou that "ye cannot" express a want of will? For "this did not Abraham." "What are his works? Gentleness, meekness, obedience. But ye set yourselves on the contrary part, being hard and cruel."

But how came it into their thoughts to betake themselves to God? He had shown them unworthy of Abraham; desiring therefore to escape this charge, they mounted higher. For when He reproached them with murder, they said this,[2] making it, as it were, a kind of excuse for themselves that they were avenging God. Therefore He showeth that this very thing is the act of men opposing God. And the, " I came forth," showeth that He was from thence.[3] He saith, " I came forth," alluding to His arrival among us. But since they would probably say to Him, " Thou speaketh certain things strange and new,[4] " He telleth them that He was come from God. "And therefore with good reason ye hear them not, because ye are of the devil. For on what account would ye kill Me? What charge have ye to bring against Me? If there be none, why do ye not believe Me?" Thus then having proved them to be of the devil by their lying and their murder, He showeth them also to be alien from Abraham and from God, both because they hated One who had done no wrong, and because they would not hear His word; and in every way He proveth that He was not opposed to God, and that it was not on this account that they refused to believe, but because they were aliens from God. For when One who had done no sin, who said that He came from God and was sent of God, who spake the truth, and so spake it as to challenge all to the proof, after this was not believed, it is clear that He was not believed because of their being carnal. Since sins do use, yea they do use to debase a soul. Wherefore It saith, " Seeing ye are become dull of hearing." (Heb. v. 11.) For when a man cannot despise earthly things, how shall He ever be wise concerning heavenly things?

[4.] Wherefore, I exhort you, use we every means that our life may be righteous, that our minds may be cleansed, so that no filthiness be a hindrance to us; kindle for yourselves the light of knowledge, and sow not among thorns. For how shall one who knows not that covetousness is an evil, ever know the greater good? how shall one who refrains not from these earthly things ever hold fast to those heavenly? It is good to take by violence, not the things that perish, but the Kingdom of heaven. "The violent," it saith, "take it by force." (Matt. xi. 12.) It is then not possible to attain to it by sluggishness, but by zeal. But what meaneth " the violent"? There is need of much violence, (for strait is the way,) there is need of a youthful soul and a noble. Plunderers desire to outstrip all other, they look to nothing, neither to conviction, nor accusation, nor punishment, but are given up to one thing only, the getting hold of what they desire to seize, and they run past all that are before them in the way. Seize we then the Kingdom of heaven, for here to seize is no fault but rather praise, and the fault is the not seizing. Here our wealth comes not from another's loss. Haste we then to seize it. Should passion disquiet us, should lust disquiet us, let us do violence to our nature, let us become more gentle, let us labor a little, that we may rest forever. Seize not thou gold, but seize that wealth which showeth gold to be but mud. For tell me, if lead and gold were laid before thee, which wouldest thou take? Is it not clear that thou wouldest take the gold? Dost thou then, where one who seizes is punished, prefer that which is the more valuable, but where one who seizes is honored, give up what is the more

---

[1] i.e. cannot understand.
[2] i.e. that God was their Father.
[3] i.e. "from God."
[4] al. "empty."

valuable? If there were punishment in both cases, wouldest thou not rather aim at this latter [1]? But in this case there is nothing like punishment, but even blessedness. And, "How," saith some one, "may one seize it?" Cast away the things which thou hast already in thy hands; for so long as thou graspest them [2] thou wilt not be able to seize the other. For consider, I pray you, a man with his hands full of silver, will he be able, as long as he retains it, to seize on gold, unless he first cast away the silver, and be free? Because he that seizes a thing must be well-girt so as not to be detained. And even now there are adverse powers running down against us to rob us, but let us fly them, let us fly them, trail-ing after us nothing that may give a hold, let us cut asunder the cords, let us strip ourselves of the things of earth. What need of silken garments? How long shall we be unrolling this mockery? How long shall we be burying gold? I desired to cease from always saying these things, but ye will not suffer me, continually supplying me with occasions and arguments. But now at least let us desist, that having instructed others by our lives, we may obtain the promised good things, through the grace and lovingkindness of our Lord Jesus Christ, by whom and with whom to the Father and the Holy Ghost be glory, now and ever and world without end. Amen.

# HOMILY LV.

## JOHN viii. 48, 49.

"Then answered the Jews, and said unto Him, Say we not well that thou art a Samaritan, and hast a devil? Jesus answered, I have not a devil; but I honor My Father."

[1.] A SHAMELESS and a forward [3] thing is wickedness, and when it ought to hide itself, then is it the fiercer. As was the case with the Jews. For when they ought to have been pricked by what was said, admiring the boldness and conclusiveness [4] of the words, they even insult Him, calling Him a Samaritan, and saying that He had a devil, and they ask, "Said we not well that thou art a Samaritan, and hast a devil?" Because when He uttereth anything sublime, this is thought among the very senseless to be madness. Yet nowhere before did the Evangelist say that they called Him "a Samaritan"; but from this expression it is probable that this had been often asserted by them.

"Thou hast a devil," saith some one. Who is it that hath a devil? He that honoreth God, or he that insulteth Him that honoreth Him? What then saith Christ, who is very meekness and gentleness? "I have not a devil, but I honor Him [5] that sent me." Where there was need to instruct them, to pull down their excessive insolence, to teach them not to be proud because of Abraham, He was vehement; but when it was needful that He being insulted should bear it, He used much gentleness. When they said, "We have God and Abraham for our Father," He touched them sharply; but when they called Him a demoniac, He spake submis-sively, thus teaching us to avenge insults offered to God, but to overlook such as are offered to ourselves.

Ver. 50. "I seek not Mine own glory."

"These things," He saith, "I have spoken to show that it becometh not you, being murderers, to call God your Father; so that I have spoken them through honor for Him, and for His sake do I hear these reproaches, and for His sake do ye dishonor Me. Yet I care not for this insolence [6]; to Him, for whose sake I now hear these things, ye owe an account of your words. For 'I seek not Mine own glory.' Wherefore I omit to punish you, and betake Myself to exhortation, and counsel you so to act, that ye shall not only escape punishment, but also attain eternal life."

Ver. 51. "Verily, verily, I say unto you, If a man keep My saying, he shall never see death."

Here He speaketh not of faith only, but of a pure life. Above He said, "shall have everlasting life," but here, "shall not see death." (c. vi. 40.) At the same time He hinteth to them that they could do nothing against Him, for if the man that should keep His saying should not die, much less should He Himself. At least they understood it so, and said to Him,

Ver. 52. "Now we know that thou hast a devil; Abraham is dead, and the Prophets are dead."

That is, "they who heard the word of God are dead, and shall they who have heard thine not die?"

Ver. 53. "Art thou greater than our father Abraham?"

---

[1] i.e. at the Kingdom.
[2] al. "these present things."
[3] ἰταμὸν.
[4] ἀκολουθίαν.
[5] "My Father that," Ben.
[6] al. "insult."

Alas for their vainglory ! Again do they betake themselves to his relationship. Yet it would have been suitable to say, "Art thou greater than God? or they who have heard thee than Abraham?" But they say not this, because they thought that He was even less than Abraham. At first, therefore, He showed that they were murderers, and so led them away from the relationship ; but when they persevered, He contrived this in another way, showing that they labored uselessly. And concerning the "death," He said nothing to them, neither did He reveal or tell them what kind of death He meant, but in the meantime He would have them believe, that He is greater than Abraham, that even by this He may put them to shame. "Certainly," He saith, "were I a common man I ought not to die, having done no wrong ; but when I speak the truth, and have no sin, am sent from God, and am greater than Abraham, are ye not mad, do ye not labor in vain when ye attempt to kill Me?" What then is their reply? "Now we know that thou hast a devil." Not so spake the woman of Samaria. She said not to Him, "Thou hast a devil" ; but only, "Art thou greater than our father Jacob?" (c. iv. 12.) For these men were insolent and accursed, while she desired to learn ; wherefore she doubted and answered with proper moderation, and called Him, "Lord." For one who promised far greater things, and who was worthy of credit, ought not to have been insulted, but even admired ; yet these men said that He had a devil. Those expressions of the Samaritan woman were those of one in doubt ; these were the words of men unbelieving and perverse. "Art thou greater than our father Abraham?" so that this (which He had said) maketh Him to be greater than Abraham. "When therefore ye have seen Him lifted up,[1] ye shall confess that He is greater." On this account He said, "When ye have lifted Me[2] up, ye shall know that I Am." (Ver. 28.) And observe His wisdom. Having first rent them away from Abraham's kindred, He showeth that He is greater than Abraham, that so He may be seen to be very exceedingly greater than the Prophets also. Indeed it was because they continually called Him a prophet that He said, "My word hath no place in you." (Ver. 37.) In that other place[3] He declared that He raiseth the dead, but here He saith, "He that believeth shall never see death," which was a much greater thing than not to allow believers to be holden by death. Wherefore the Jews were the more enraged. What then say they?

"Whom makest thou thyself?"

And this too in an insulting manner. "Thou art taking somewhat upon thyself," saith one of them. To this then Christ replieth ;

Ver. 54. "If I honor Myself, My honor is nothing."

[2.] What say the heretics here? That He heard the question, "Art thou greater than our father Abraham?" and dared not to say to them, "Yea, I am greater," but did so in a covert manner. What then? Is His honor "nothing"? With respect to them[4] it is nothing. And as He said, "My witness is not true " (c. v. 31), with reference to the opinion they would form of it, so also doth He speak here.

"There is One[5] that honoreth Me."

And wherefore said He not, "The Father that sent Me," as He did before, but,

"Of whom ye say that He is your God."

Ver. 55. "Yet ye have not known Him."

Because He desired to show that they not only knew not His Father, but that they knew not God.

"But I know Him."

"So that to say, 'I know Him,' is not a boast, while to say, 'I know Him not,' would be a falsehood ; but ye when ye say that ye know Him, lie ; as then ye, when ye say that ye know Him, lie, so also should I, were I to say that I know Him not."

"If I honor Myself." Since they said, "Whom makest thou thyself?" He replieth, "If I make (Myself anything,) My honor is nothing. As then I know Him exactly, so ye know Him not." And as in the case of Abraham, He did not take away their whole assertion, but said, "I know that ye are Abraham's seed," so as to make the charge against them heavier ; thus here He doth not remove the whole, but what? "Whom ye say."[6] By granting to them their boast of words, He increaseth the force of the accusation against them. How then do ye "not know Him"? "Because ye insult One who saith and doeth everything that He[7] may be glorified, even when that One is sent from Him." This assertion is unsupported by testimony, but what follows serves to establish it.

"And I keep His saying."

Here they might, if at least they had anything to say, have refuted Him, for it was the strongest proof of His having been sent by God.

Ver. 56. "Your father Abraham rejoiced to see My day, and he saw it, and was glad."

Again, He showeth that they were aliens from the race of Abraham, if they grieved at what he rejoiced in. "My day," seems to me to mean the day of the Crucifixion, which Abraham foreshowed typically by the offering of the ram and of Isaac. What do they reply?

Ver. 57. "Thou art not yet forty[8] years old, and hast Thou seen Abraham?"

---

[1] al. " gone forth."   [2] " The Son of Man," N. T.   [3] c. vi. 39, 40.

[4] i.e. the Jews.                    [7] i.e. the Father.
[5] " It is My Father," N. T.        [8] " fifty," N. T.
[6] " that He is your God," N. T.

So that we conclude [1] that Christ was nearly forty.

Ver. 58, 59. "Jesus saith unto them, Before Abraham was, I Am. Then took they up stones to cast at Him."

Seest thou how He proved Himself to be greater than Abraham? For the man who rejoiced to see His day, and made this an object of earnest desire, plainly did so because it was a day that should be for a benefit, and belonging to one greater than himself. Because they had said, "The carpenter's son" (Matt. xiii. 55), and imagined nothing more concerning Him, He leadeth them by degrees to an exalted notion of Him. Therefore when they heard the words, "Ye know not God," they were not grieved; but when they heard, "before Abraham was, I Am," as though the nobility of their descent were debased, they became furious, and would have stoned Him.

"He saw My day, and was glad." He showeth, that not unwillingly He came to His Passion, since He praiseth him who was gladdened at the Cross. For this was the salvation of the world. But they cast stones at Him; so ready were they for murder, and they did this of their own accord, without enquiry.

But wherefore said He not, "Before Abraham was, I was," instead of "I Am"? As the Father useth this expression, "I Am," so also doth Christ; for it signifieth continuous Being, irrespective of all time. On which account the expression seemed to them to be blasphemous. Now if they could not bear the comparison with Abraham, although this was but a trifling one, had He continually made Himself equal to the Father, would they ever have ceased casting stones at Him?

After this, again He fleeth as a man, and concealeth Himself, having laid before them sufficient instruction: and having accomplished His work, He went forth from the Temple, and departed to heal the blind, proving by His actions that He is before Abraham. But perhaps some one will say, "Why did He not paralyze their strength? [2] So they would have believed." He healed the paralytic, yet they believed not; nay, He wrought ten thousand wonders; at the very Passion He cast them to the ground, and darkened their eyes, yet they believed not; and how would they have believed if He had paralyzed their strength? There is nothing worse than a soul hardened in desperation; though it see signs and wonders, it still perseveres in retaining the same shamelessness. Thus Pharaoh, who received ten thousand strokes, was sobered only while being punished, and continued of this character until the last day of his life, pursuing those whom

he had let go. Wherefore Paul continually saith, "Lest any of you be hardened by the deceitfulness of sin." (Heb. iii. 13.) For as the callosities [3] of the body, when formed, become dead, and possess no sensation; so the soul, when it is occupied by many passions, becomes dead to virtue; and apply what you will to it, it gets no perception of the matter, but whether you threaten punishment or anything else, continues insensible.

[3.] Wherefore I beseech you, while we have hopes of salvation, while we can turn, to use every means to do so. For men who have become past feeling, are after that in the blind state [4] of despairing pilots, who give up their vessel to the wind, and themselves contribute no assistance. Thus the envious man looks to one thing only, that is, to satisfy his lust, and though he be like to be punished or even slain, still he is possessed solely by that passion; and in like manner the intemperate and avaricious. But if the sovereignty of the passions be so great, much greater is that of virtue; if for them we despise death, much more for this; if they (sinners) regard not their own lives, much less ought we to do so in the cause of our salvation. For what shall we have to say, if when they who perish are so active about their own perdition, we for our own salvation manifest not even an equal activity, but ever continue wasting with envy? Nothing is worse than envy; to destroy another it destroys itself also. The eye of the envious wastes away in grief, he lives in a continual death, he deems all men, even those who have never wronged him, his enemies. He grieves that God is honored, he rejoices in what the devil rejoices in. Is any honored among men? This is not honor, envy him not. But is he honored by God? Strive and be thou like him. Thou wilt not? Why then dost thou destroy thyself too? Why castest thou away what thou hast? Canst thou not be like unto him, nor gain any good thing? Why then dost thou besides this take for thyself evil, when thou oughtest to rejoice with him, that so even if thou be not able to share his toils, thou mayest profit by rejoicing with Him? For often even the will is able to effect great good. At least Ezekiel saith, that the Moabites were punished because they rejoiced over the Israelites, and that certain others were saved because they mourned over the misfortunes of their neighbors. (Ezek. xxv. 8.) Now if there be any comfort for those who mourn over the woes of others, much more for those who rejoice at the honors of others. He charged the Moabites

---

[1] ὡς λοιπόν.        [2] i.e. so that they could not stone Him.

[3] οἱ τύλοι, a very happy emendation of Mr. Field's for στῦλοι, "pillars," of which former editors could make no sense. One MS. gives οἱ τυφλοὶ τοὺς ὀφθαλμοὺς, "those blind in their eyes," but the sense even so is not perfect.
[4] πηροῦνται, a conjecture of Dr. Heyse, for πειρῶνται.

with having exulted over the Israelites, yet it was God that punished them; but not even when He punisheth will He have us rejoice over those that are punished. For it is not His wish to punish them. Now if we must condole with those who are punished, much more must we avoid envying those who are honored. Thus, for example, Corah and Dathan perished with their company, making those whom they envied brighter, and giving themselves up to punishment. For a venomous beast is envy, an unclean beast, a deliberate vice which admits not of pardon, a wickedness stripped of excuse, the cause and mother of all evils. Wherefore let us pluck it up by the roots, that we may be freed from evil here, and may obtain blessings hereafter; through the grace and lovingkindness of our Lord Jesus Christ, by whom and with whom, to the Father and the Holy Ghost, be glory now and ever and world without end. Amen.

# HOMILY LVI.

### JOHN ix. 1, 2.

"And as Jesus passed by, He saw a man which was blind from his birth. And His disciples asked Him, saying, Master, who did sin, this man, or his parents, that he was born blind?"

[1.] "AND as Jesus passed by, He saw a man which was blind from his birth." Being full of love for man, and caring for our salvation, and desiring to stop the mouths of the foolish, He omitteth nothing of His own part, though there be none to give heed. And the Prophet knowing this saith, "That Thou mightest be justified when Thou speakest, and be clear when Thou art judged." (Ps. li. 4.) Wherefore here, when they would not receive His sublime sayings, but said that He had a devil, and attempted to kill Him, He went forth from the Temple, and healed the blind, mitigating their rage by His absence, and by working the miracle softening their hardness and cruelty, and establishing His assertions. And He worketh a miracle which was no common one, but one which took place then for the first time. "Since the world began," saith he who was healed, "was it not heard that any man opened the eyes of one that was born blind." (Ver. 32.) Some have, perhaps, opened the eyes of the blind, but of one born blind never. And that on going out of the Temple, He proceeded intentionally to the work, is clear from this; it was He who saw the blind man, not the blind man who came to Him; and so earnestly did He look upon him, that even His disciples perceived it. From this, at least, they came to question Him; for when they saw Him earnestly regarding the man, they asked Him, saying, "Who did sin, this man, or his parents?" A mistaken question, for how could he sin before he was born? and how, if his parents had sinned, would he have been punished? Whence then came they to put this question? Before, when

He healed the paralytic, He said, "Behold, thou art made whole, sin no more." (c. v. 14.) They therefore, having understood that he was palsied on account of sin, said, "Well, that other was palsied because of his sins; but concerning this man, what wouldest Thou say? hath he sinned? It is not possible to say so, for he is blind from his birth. Have his parents sinned? Neither can one say this, for the child suffers not punishment for the father." As therefore when we see a child evil entreated, we exclaim, "What can one say of this? what has the child done?" not as asking a question, but as being perplexed, so the disciples spake here, not so much asking for information, as being in perplexity. What then saith Christ?

Ver. 3. "Neither hath this man sinned, nor his parents."

This He saith not as acquitting them of sins, for He saith not simply, "Neither hath this man sinned, nor his parents," but addeth, "that he should have been born blind [1] — but that the Son of God should be glorified in him." "For both this man hath sinned and his parents, but his blindness proceedeth not from that." And this He said, not signifying that though this man indeed was not in such case, yet that others had been made blind from such a cause, the sins of their parents, since it cannot be that when one sinneth another should be punished. For if we allow this, we must also allow that he sinned before his birth. As therefore when He declared, "neither hath this man sinned," He said not that it is possible to sin from one's very birth, and be punished for it; so when He said, "nor his parents," He said not that one may be punished for his parents' sake. This supposition He re-

---

[1] not in N. T.

moveth by the mouth of Ezekiel; "As I live, saith the Lord, this proverb shall not be, that is used, The fathers have eaten sour grapes, and the children's teeth are set on edge." (Ezek. xviii. 3, 2.)    And Moses saith, "The father shall not die for the child, neither shall the child die for the father." (Deut. xxiv. 16.)    And of a certain king [1] Scripture saith, that for this very reason he did not this thing,[2] observing the law of Moses.    But if any one argue, "How then is it said, 'Who visiteth the sins of the parents upon the children unto the third and fourth generation'?" (Deut. v. 9); we should make this answer, that the assertion is not universal, but that it is spoken with reference to certain who came out of Egypt.    And its meaning is of this kind; " Since these who have come out of Egypt, after signs and wonders, have become worse than their forefathers who saw none of these things, they shall suffer," It saith, " the same that those others suffered, since they have dared the same crimes."    And that it was spoken of those men, any one who will give attention to the passage will more certainly know.    Wherefore then was he born blind?

"That the glory[3] of God should be made manifest,"[4] He saith.

Lo, here again is another difficulty, if without this man's punishment, it was not possible that the glory of God should be shown.    Certainly it is not said that it was impossible, for it was possible, but, " that it might be manifested even in this man."    "What," saith some one, "did he suffer wrong for the glory of God?"    What wrong, tell me?    For what if God had never willed to produce him at all?    But I assert that he even received benefit from his blindness : since he recovered the sight of the eyes within.    What were the Jews profited by their eyes?    They incurred the heavier punishment, being blinded even while they saw.    And what injury had this man by his blindness?    For by means of it he recovered sight.    As then the evils of the present life are not evils, so neither are the good things good; sin alone is an evil, but blindness is not an evil.    And He who had brought this man from not being into being, had also power to leave him as he was.

[2.] But some say, that this conjunction[5] is not at all expressive of cause, but relates to the consequence of the miracle; as when He saith, " For judgment I am come into this world, that they which see not might see, and that they which see might be made blind " (ver. 39); and yet it was not for this He came, that those who saw might be made blind.    And again Paul,

" Because that which may be known of God is manifested in them, that they may be without excuse" (Rom. i. 19, 20); yet He showed it not unto them for this, that they might be deprived of excuse, but that they might obtain excuse.    And again in another place, " The Law entered, that the offense might abound " (Rom. v. 20); yet it was not for this that it entered, but that sin might be checked.    Seest thou everywhere that the conjunction relates to the consequence?    For as some excellent architect may build part of a house, and leave the rest unfinished, so that to those who believe not he may prove, by means of that remnant, that he is author of the whole; so also God joineth together and completeth our body, as it were a house decayed, healing the withered hand, bracing the palsied limbs, straightening the lame, cleansing the lepers, raising up the sick, making sound the crippled, recalling the dead from death, opening the eyes that were closed, or adding them where before they were not; all which things, being blemishes [6] arising from the infirmity of our nature, He by correcting showed His power.

But when He said, "That the glory of God might be manifested," He spake of Himself, not of the Father; His[7] glory was already manifest.    For since they had heard that God made man, taking the dust of the earth, so also Christ made clay.    To have said, " I am He who took the dust of the earth, and made man," would have seemed a hard thing to His hearers; but this when shown by actual working, no longer stood in their way.    So that He by taking earth, and mixing it with spittle, showed forth His hidden glory; for no small glory was it that He should be deemed the Architect of the creation.

And after this the rest also followed; from the part, the whole was proved, since the belief of the greater also confirmed the less.    For man is more honorable than any created thing, and of our members the most honorable is the eye. This is the cause that He fashioned the eyes, not in a common manner, but in the way that He did.    For though that member be small in size, yet it is more necessary than any part of the body.    And this Paul showed when he said, " If the ear shall say, Because I am not the eye, I am not of the body; is it therefore not of the body?" (1 Cor. xii. 16.)    For all indeed that is in us is a manifestation of the wisdom of God, but much more the eye; this it is that guides the whole body, this gives beauty to it all, this adorns the countenance, this is the light of all the limbs.    What the sun is in the world, that the eye is in the body; quench the sun, and you destroy and confound all things; quench the

---

[1] Amaziah, 2 Kings xiv. 6.
[2] i.e. show not the children.
[3] " the works," N. T.
[4] " in Him," N. T.
[5] i.e. " that the glory," &c.
[6] πηρώματα.
[7] i.e. The Father's.

eyes, and the feet, the hands, the soul, are useless. When these are disabled, even knowledge is gone, since by means of these we know God. "For the invisible things of Him from the creation of the world are clearly seen, being understood by the things that are made." (Rom. i. 20.) Wherefore the eye is not only a light to the body, but beyond the body to the soul also. On which account it is established as in a royal fortress, obtaining the higher condition, and presiding over the other senses. This then Christ forms.

And that thou mayest not deem that He needeth matter when He worketh, and that thou mayest learn that He had not need at all of clay, (for He who brought into being the greater existences when as yet they were not, would much more have made this without matter,) that I say thou mayest learn that He did not this through necessity, but to show that He was the Creator at the beginning, when He had spread on the clay He saith, "Go, wash," "that thou mayest know that I need not clay to create eyes, but that My glory may be manifested hereby." For to show that He spake of Himself when He said, "That the glory of God may be manifested," He added,

Ver. 4. "I must work the works of Him that sent Me."

That is, "I must manifest Myself, and do the things which may show that I do the same things with the Father"; not things "similar," but "the same," an expression which marks greater unvaryingness, and which is used of those who do not differ ever so little. Who then after this will face Him, when he seeth that He hath the same power with the Father? For not only did He form or open eyes, but gave also the gift of sight, which is a proof that He also breathed in the soul. Since if that did not work, the eye, though perfected, could never see anything; so that He gave both the energy[1] which is from the soul, and gave the member also possessing all things, both arteries and nerves and veins, and all things of which our body is composed.

"I must work while it is day."

What mean these words? To what conclusion do they lead? To an important one. For what He saith is of this kind. "While it is day, while men may believe on Me, while this life lasteth, I must work."

"The night cometh," that is, futurity, "when no man can work."

He said not, "when I cannot work," but, "when no man can work": that is, when there is no longer faith, nor labors, nor repentance. For to show that He calleth faith, a "work," when they say unto Him, "What shall we do,

that we might work the works of God?" (c. vi. 28), He replieth, "This is the work of God, that ye believe on Him whom He hath sent." How then can no man work this work in the future world?[2] Because there faith is not, but all, willingly, or unwillingly, will submit. For lest any one should say that He acted as He did from desire of honor, He showeth that He did all to spare them who had power to believe "here" only, but who could no longer "there" gain any good thing. On this account, though the blind man came not to Him, He did what He did: for that the man was worthy to be healed, that had he seen he would have believed and come to Christ, that had he heard from any that He was present, he would not even so have been neglectful, is clear from what follows, from his courage, from his very faith. For it was likely that he would have considered with himself, and have said, "What is this? He made clay, and anointed my eyes, and said to me, 'Go, wash;' could he not have healed me, and then have sent me to Siloam? Often have I washed there with many others, and have gained no good; had he possessed any power, he would while present have healed me." Just as Naaman spake respecting Elisha; for he too being commanded to go wash in Jordan, believed not, and this too when there was such a fame abroad concerning Elisha. (2 Kings v. 11.) But the blind man neither disbelieved, nor contradicted, nor reasoned with himself, "What is this? Ought he to have put on clay? This is rather to blind one the more: who ever recovered sight so?" But he used no such reasonings. Seest thou his steadfast faith and zeal?

"The night cometh." Next He showeth, that even after the Crucifixion He would care for the ungodly, and bring many to Himself. For "it is yet day." But after that, He entirely cutteth them off, and declaring this, He saith,

Ver. 5. "As long as I am in the world, I am the Light of the world."

[3.] As also He said to others, "Believe while the light is with you."[3] (c. xii. 36.) Wherefore then did Paul call this life "night" and that other "day"? Not opposing Christ, but saying the same thing, if not in words yet in sense; for he also saith, "The night is far spent, the day is at hand." (Rom. xiii. 12.) The present time he calleth "night," because of those who sit in darkness, or because he compareth it with that day which is to come. Christ calleth the future "night," because there sin has no power to work;[4] but Paul calleth the present life night, because they are in darkness who continue in

---

[1] al. "noble birth."

[2] τότε.  [3] not verbally quoted.
[4] διὰ τὸ τῶν ἁμαρτημάτων ἀνενέργητον. Meaning, perhaps, "Because there is no place for the 'work' of repentance, faith, and obedience in the next world, when any through sin have neglected it in this."

wickedness and unbelief. Addressing himself then to the faithful he said, "The night is far spent, the day is at hand," since they should enjoy that light; and he calleth the old life, night. "Let us put away," he saith, "the works of darkness." Seest thou that he telleth them that it is "night"? wherefore he saith, "Let us walk honestly as in the day," that we may enjoy that light. For if this light be so good, consider what that will be; as much as the sunlight is brighter than the flame of a candle, so much and far more is that light better than this. And signifying this, Christ saith, that "the sun shall be darkened." Because of the excess of that brightness, not even the sun shall be seen.

If now in order to have here well-lighted and airy houses, we expend immense sums, building and toiling, consider how we ought to spend our very bodies themselves, that glorious houses may be built for us in the heavens where is that Light ineffable. Here there are strifes and contentions about boundaries and walls, but there will be nothing of the kind there, no envy, no malice, no one will dispute with us about settling boundaries. This dwelling too we assuredly needs must leave, but that abideth with us forever; this must decay by time, and be exposed to innumerable injuries, but that must remain without growing old perpetually; this a poor man cannot build, but that other one may build with two mites, as did the widow. Wherefore I choke with grief, that when so many blessings are laid before us, we are slothful, and despise them; we use every exertion to have splendid houses here, but how to gain in heaven so much as a little resting-place, we care not, we think not. For tell me, where wouldest thou have thy dwelling here? In the wilderness, or in one of the smaller cities? I think not; but in some of the most royal and grand cities, where the traffic is more, where the splendor is greater. But I will lead thee into such a City, whose Builder and Maker is God; there I exhort thee to found and build, at less cost [with less labor[1]]. That house the hands of the poor build, and it is most truly "building,"

just as the structures made here are the work of extreme folly. For if a man were to bring you into the land of Persia, to behold what is there and to return, and were then to bid you build houses there, would you not condemn him for excessive folly, as bidding you spend unseasonably? How then dost thou this very same thing upon the earth which thou shalt shortly leave? "But I shall leave it to my children," saith some one. Yet they too shall leave it soon after thee; nay, often even before thee; and their successors the same. And even here it is a subject of melancholy to thee that thou seest not thine heirs retain their possessions, but there thou needest apprehend nothing of the sort; the possession remaineth immovable, to thee, to thy children, and to their descendants, if they imitate the same goodness. That building Christ taketh in hand, he who buildeth that needs not to appoint care-takers, nor be thoughtful, nor anxious; for when God hath undertaken the work, what need of thought? He bringeth all things together, and raiseth the house. Nor is this the only thing wonderful, but also that He so buildeth it as is pleasing to thee, or rather even beyond what is pleasing, beyond what thou desirest; for He is the most excellent Artist, and careth greatly for thy advantage. If thou art poor, and desirest to build this house, it brings thee no envy, produces against thee no malice, for none of those who know how to envy behold it, but the Angels who know how to rejoice at thy blessings; none will be able to encroach upon it, for none dwell near it of those who are diseased with such passions. For neighbors thou hast there the saints, Peter and Paul with their company, all the Prophets, the Martyrs, the multitude[2] of Angels, of Archangels. For the sake then of all these things,[3] let us empty our substance upon the poor, that we may obtain those tabernacles;[4] which may we all obtain through the grace and lovingkindness of our Lord Jesus Christ, by whom and with whom to the Father and the Holy Ghost be glory, now and ever and world without end. Amen.

---

[1] om. in some MSS.

[2] δῆμον.   [3] or, "for all these reasons."   [4] al. "those [things]."

# HOMILY LVII.

John ix. 6, 7.

"When Jesus had thus spoken, He spat on the ground, and made clay of the spittle, and He anointed the eyes of the blind man with the clay, and said, Go, wash in the pool of Siloam."

[1.] Those who intend to gain any advantage from what they read, must not pass by even any small portion of the words ; and on this account we are bidden to "search" the Scriptures, because most of the words, although at first sight[1] easy, appear to have in their depth much hidden meaning. For observe of what sort is the present case. "Having said these words," It saith, "He spat on the ground." What words? "That the glory of God should be made manifest," and that, "I must work the works of Him that sent Me." For not without a cause hath the Evangelist mentioned to us His words, and added that, "He spat," but to show that He confirmed His words by deeds. And why used He not water instead of spittle for the clay? He was about to send the man to Siloam : in order therefore that nothing might be ascribed to the fountain, but that thou mightest learn that the power proceeding from His mouth, the same both formed and opened the man's eyes, He "spat on the ground"; this at least the Evangelist signified, when he said, "And made clay of the spittle." Then, that the successful issue might not seem to be of the earth, He bade him wash. But wherefore did He not this at once, instead of sending him to Siloam? That thou mayest learn the faith of the blind man, and that the obstinacy of the Jews might be silenced : for it was probable that they would all see him as he departed, having the clay spread upon his eyes, since by the strangeness of the thing he would attract to himself all, both those who did and those who did not know him, and they would observe him exactly. And because it is not easy to recognize a blind man who hath recovered sight, He first maketh by the length of way many to be witnesses, and by the strangeness of the spectacle exact observers, that being more attentive they may no longer be able to say, "It is he : it is not he." Moreover, by sending him to Siloam, He desireth to prove that He is not estranged from the Law and the Old (Covenant), nor could it afterwards be feared that Siloam would receive the glory, since many who had often washed their eyes there gained no such benefit ; for there also it was the power of Christ that wrought all. On which ac-count the Evangelist addeth for us the interpretation of the name ; for having said, "in Siloam," he addeth,

"Which is,[2] Sent."

That thou mayest learn that there also it was Christ who healed him. As Paul saith, "They drank of that spiritual Rock that followed them, and that Rock was Christ." (1 Cor. x. 4.) As then Christ was the spiritual Rock, so also was He the spiritual Siloam. To me also the sudden[3] coming in of the water seems to hint an ineffable mystery. What is that? The unlooked for (nature) of His appearance, beyond all expectation.

But observe the mind of the blind man, obedient in everything. He said not, "If it is really the clay or the spittle which gives me eyes, what need of Siloam? Or if there be need of Siloam, what need of the clay? Why did he anoint me? Why bid me wash?" But he entertained no such thoughts, he held himself prepared for one thing only, to obey in all things Him who gave the command, and nothing that was done offended him. If any one ask, "How then did he recover his sight, when he had removed the clay?" he will hear no other answer from us than that we know not the manner. And what wonder if we know it not, since not even the Evangelist knew, nor the very man that was healed? What had been done he knew, but the manner of doing it he could not comprehend. So when he was asked he said, that "He put clay upon mine eyes, and I washed, and do see" ; but how this took place he cannot tell them, though they ask ten thousand times.

Ver. 8, 9. "The neighbors therefore, and they which[4] had seen him, that he was a beggar,[5] Is not this he that sat and begged? Some said, This is he."

The strangeness of what had been brought to pass led them even to unbelief, though so much had been contrived[6] that they might not disbelieve. They said, "Is not this he that sat and begged?" O the lovingkindness of God ! Whither did He descend, when with great kindness He healed even beggars, and so silenced the Jews, because He deemed not the illustrious, nor the distinguished, nor the rulers, but men

---

[1] αὐτόθεν.

[2] "is being interpreted," N. T.    [4] "which before," N. T.
[3] τὸ ἀθρόον τῆς παρουσίας.
[5] "was blind," N. T. Vulgate, mendicus erat.
[6] lit. "dispensed."

of no mark to be fit objects of the same Providence. For He came for the salvation of all.

And what happened in the case of the paralytic, happened also with this man, for neither did the one or the other know who it was that healed him. And this was caused by the retirement of Christ, for Jesus when He healed always retired, that all suspicion might be removed from the miracles. Since how could they who knew not who He was flatter Him, or join in contriving what had been done? Neither was this man one of those who went about, but of those who sat at the doors of the Temple. Now when all were doubting concerning him, what saith he?

"I am he."

He was not ashamed of his former blindness, nor did he fear the wrath of the people, nor did he decline showing himself that he might proclaim his Benefactor.

Ver. 10, 11. "They said unto him, How were thine eyes opened? He answered and said, A man that is called Jesus."

What sayest thou? Doth "a man" work such deeds? As yet he knew nothing great concerning Him.

"A man that is called Jesus made clay, and anointed mine eyes."

[2.] Observe how truthful he is. He saith not whence He made it, for he speaks not of what he doth not know; he saw not that He spat on the ground, but that He spread it on he knew from sense and touch.

• "And said unto me, Go, wash in the pool of Siloam."

This too his hearing witnessed to him. But how did he recognize His voice? From His conversation with the disciples. And saying all this, and having received the witness by the works, the manner (of the cure) he cannot tell. Now if faith is needed in matters which are felt and handled, much more in the case of things invisible.

Ver. 12. "They said unto him, Where is he? He said, I know not."

They said, "Where is he?" having already murderous intentions against Him. But observe the modesty[1] of Christ, how He continued not with those who were healed; because He neither desired to reap glory, nor to draw a multitude, nor to make a show of Himself. Observe too how truthfully the blind man maketh all his answers. The Jews desired to find Christ to bring Him to the priests, but when they did not find Him, they brought the blind man to the Pharisees, as to those who would question him more severely. For which reason the Evangelist remarks, that it was "the Sabbath" (ver.

14), in order to point out their wicked thoughts, and the cause for which they sought Him, as though forsooth they had found a handle, and could disparage the miracle by means of what appeared to be a transgression of the Law. And this is clear from their saying immediately on seeing him nothing but, "How opened he thine eyes?"[2] Observe also the manner of their speech; they say not, "How didst thou receive thy sight?" but, "How opened he thine eyes?" thus affording him an excuse for slandering Jesus, because of His having worked. But he speaks to them shortly, as to men who had already heard; for without mentioning His name, or that "He said unto me, Go, wash," he at once saith,

Ver. 15. "He put clay upon my eyes, and I washed, and do see."

Because the slander was now become great, and the Jews had said, "Behold what work Jesus doth on the Sabbath day, he anointeth with clay!" But observe, I pray you, how the blind man is not disturbed. When being questioned he spake in the presence of those others without danger, it was no such great thing to tell the truth, but the wonder is, that now when he is placed in a situation of greater fear, he neither denies nor contradicts what he had said before. What then did the Pharisees, or rather what did the others also? They had brought him (to the Pharisees), as being about to deny; but, on the contrary, that befell them which they desired not, and they learned more exactly. And this they everywhere have to endure, in the case of miracles; but this point we will more clearly demonstrate in what follows. What said the Pharisees?

Ver. 16. "Some said," (not all, but the more forward,) "This man is not of God, because he keepeth not the Sabbath day; others said, How can a man that is a sinner do such miracles?"

Seest thou that they were led up[3] by the miracles? For hear what they say now, who before this had sent to bring Him. And if all did not so, (for being rulers through vainglory they fell into unbelief,) yet still the greater number even of the rulers believed on Him, but confessed Him not. Now the multitude was easily overlooked, as being of no great account in their synagogue, but the rulers being more conspicuous had the greater difficulty in speaking boldly, for some the love of rule restrained, others cowardice, and the fear of the many. Wherefore also He said, "How can ye believe who receive honor from men?"[4] (c. v. 44.) And these who were seeking to kill Him unjustly said that they

---

[1] τὸ ἀκόμπαστον.

[2] These words occur later, ver. 26. The account of the *first* examination of the blind man is different; ver. 15. "Then again the Pharisees asked him how he had received his sight."
[3] al. "taught."          [4] "one of another," N. T.

were of God, but that He who healed the blind could not be of God, because He kept not the Sabbath ; to which the others objected, that a sinner could not do such miracles. Those first, maliciously keeping silence about what had taken place, brought forward the seeming transgression ; for they said not, "He healeth on the Sabbath day," but, "He keepeth not the Sabbath." These, on the other hand, replied weakly, for when they ought to have shown that the Sabbath was not broken, they rely only upon the miracles ; and with reason, for they still thought that He was a man. If this had not been the case, they might besides have urged in His defense, that He was Lord of the Sabbath which Himself had made, but as yet they had not this opinion. Anyhow, none of them dared to say what he wished openly, or in the way of an assertion, but only in the way of doubt, some from not having boldness of speech, others through love of rule.

"There was therefore a division among them." This division first began among the people, then later among the rulers also, and some said, "He is a good man"; others, "Nay, but he deceiveth the people." (c. vii. 12.) Seest thou that the rulers were more void of understanding than the many, since they were divided later than they? and after they were divided, they did not exhibit any noble feeling, when they saw the Pharisees pressing upon them. Since had they been entirely separated from them, they would soon have known the truth. For it is possible to do well in separating. Wherefore also Himself hath said, "I am come not to bring peace upon the earth but a sword." (Matt. x. 34.) For there is an evil concord, and there is a good disagreement. Thus they who built the tower (Gen. xi. 4), agreed together to their own hurt ; and these same again were separated, though unwillingly, yet for their good. Thus also Corah and his company agreed together for evil, therefore they were separated for good ; and Judas agreed with the Jews for evil. So division may be good, and agreement may be evil. Wherefore It saith, "If thine eye offend thee, smite it out,[1] if thy foot, cut it off." (Matt. v. 29, and xviii. 8.) Now if we must separate ourselves from an ill-joined limb, must we not much more from friends united to us for evil[2]? So that agreement is not in all cases a good, just as division is not in all cases an evil.

[3.] These things I say, that we may shun wicked men, and follow the good ; for if in the case of our limbs we cut off that which is rotten and incurable, fearing lest the rest of the body should catch the same disease, and if we do this not as having no care for that part, but rather as desiring to preserve the remainder, how much more must we do this in the case of those who consent with us for evil? If we can set them right without receiving injury ourselves, we ought to use every means to do so ; but if they remain incorrigible and may injure us, it is necessary to cut them off and cast them away. For so they will often be[3] gainers rather (than losers). Wherefore also Paul exhorted, saying, "And ye shall put away from among yourselves that wicked person"; and, "that he that hath done this deed may be put away from among you." (1 Cor. v. 13, 2.) A dreadful thing, dreadful indeed, is the society of wicked men ; not so quickly doth the pestilence seize or the itch infect those that come in contact with such as are under the disease, as doth the wickedness of evil men. For "evil communications corrupt good manners." (1 Cor. xv. 33.) And again the Prophet saith, "Come out from among them, and be ye separate." (Isa. lii. 11.) Let no one then have a wicked man for his friend. For if when we have bad sons we publicly disclaim them, without regarding nature or its laws, or the constraint which it lays upon us, much more ought we to fly from our companions and acquaintances when they are wicked. Because even if we receive no injury from them, we shall anyhow not be able to escape ill report, for strangers search not into our lives, but judge us from our companions. This advice I address to young men and maidens. "Providing,"[4] It saith, "things honest," not only in the sight of the Lord, but also "in the sight of all men." (Rom. xii. 17.) Let us then use every means that our neighbor be not offended. For a life, though it be very upright, if it offend others hath lost all. But how is it possible for the life that is upright to offend? When the society of those that are not upright invests it with an evil reputation ; for when, trusting in ourselves, we consort with bad men, even though we be not harmed, we offend others. These things I say to men and women and maidens, leaving it to their conscience to see exactly how many evils are produced from this source. Neither I, perhaps, nor any of the more perfect, suspect any ill ; but the simpler brother is harmed by occasion of thy perfection ; and thou oughtest to be careful also for his infirmity. And even if he receive no injury, yet the Greek is harmed. Now Paul biddeth us be "without offense, both to Jews and Greeks, and to the Church of God." (1 Cor. x. 32.) (I think no evil of the virgin, for I love virginity, and "love thinketh no evil" (1 Cor. xiii. 5) ; I am a great admirer of that state of life,[5] and I cannot have so much as an unseemly thought about it.) How shall we per-

---

[1] "pluck it out," N. T.  [2] κακῶς ἡνωμένων.  [3] al. "often are."  [4] "provide," N. T.  [5] πολιτείας.

suade those that are without? For we must take forethought for them also. Let us then so order what relates to ourselves, that none of the unbelievers may be able even to find a just handle of accusation against us. For as they who show forth a right life glorify God, so they who do the contrary cause Him to be blasphemed. May no such persons be among [1] us;

but may our works so shine, that our Father which is in Heaven may be glorified, and that we may enjoy the honor which is from Him. To which may we all attain, through the grace and lovingkindness of our Lord Jesus Christ, by whom and with whom, to the Father and the Holy Ghost, be glory forever and ever. Amen.

# HOMILY LVIII.

### John ix. 17, 18.

"They say unto the blind man again, What sayest thou of him, that he hath opened thine eyes? He said, He is a Prophet. The Jews then did not believe."

[1.] WE must go over the Scriptures not in a chance way or carelessly, but with all exactness, that we be not entangled. Since even now in this place one might with show of reason question, how, when they had asserted, "This man is not of God, because he keepeth not the Sabbath," they now say to the man, "What sayest thou of him, that he hath opened thine eyes?" and not, "What sayest thou of him, that he hath broken the Sabbath?" but put now that which was the ground of the defense, not that of the accusation. What then have we to reply? That these (who speak) are not the men who said, "This man is not of God," but those who separated themselves from them, who also said, "A man that is a sinner cannot [2] do such miracles." For desiring to silence their opponents the more, in order that they may not seem to be partisans of Christ, they bring forward the man who had received proof of His power, and question him. Observe now the wisdom of the poor man, he speaketh more wisely than them all. First he saith, "He is a Prophet"; and shrank not from the judgment [3] of the perverse Jews who spake against Him and said, "How can this man be of God, not keeping the Sabbath?" but replied to them, "He is a Prophet."

"And they [4] did not believe that he had been blind, and received his sight, until they had called his parents." [5]

Observe in how many ways they attempt to obscure and take away the miracle. But this is the nature of truth, by the very means by which it seems to be assailed by men, by these it becomes stronger, it shines by means of that by which it is obscured. For if these things had

not taken place, the miracle might have been suspected by the many; but now, as if desiring to lay bare the truth, so do they use all means, and would not have acted otherwise, supposing they had done all in Christ's behalf. For they first attempted to cast Him down by occasion of this mode (of cure), saying, "How opened he thine eyes?" that is, "was it by some sorcery?" In another place also, when they had no charge to bring against Him, they endeavored to insult the mode of the cure, saying, "He doth not cast out devils save by Beelzebub." (Matt. xii. 24.) And here again, when they have nothing to say, they betake themselves to the time (of cure), saying, "He breaketh the Sabbath"; and again, "He is a sinner." Yet He asked you, who would slay [6] Him, and who were ready to lay hold of His actions, most plainly, saying, "Which of you convinceth Me of sin?" (c. viii. 46); and no man spake, nor said, "Thou blasphemest, because thou makest thyself without sin." But if they had had it in their power to say so, they would not have held their peace. For they who because they heard that He was before Abraham would have stoned Him, and said that He was not of God, who boasted that they, murderers as they were, were of God, but who said that One who did such wonders, after that He had wrought a cure, was not of God,[7] because He kept not the Sabbath, if they had had but a shadow of a charge against Him, would never have let it pass. And if they call Him a sinner because He seemed to break the Sabbath, this charge also is shown to be unsound, when those who are ranked with them condemn their great coldness and littleness of soul.[8] Being therefore entangled on every side, they afterwards betake themselves to something else more shameless and impudent. What is that? They "did not believe," It saith, "that

---

[1] Morel. "from among." [2] "How can a man," &c., N. T.
[3] al. "the judgment amazed him not." [4] "the Jews," N. T. [5] "the parents of him," &c., N. T.
[6] al. "who envied." [7] al. "was a sinner."
[8] μικροψυχίαν. The Bened. editor observes, that by the Fathers the word is used to signify "grudging"; "quarreling."

he had been blind, and received his sight." How then did they charge Christ with not keeping the Sabbath? Plainly, as having believed. But why gave ye not heed to the great number of people? to the neighbors who knew him? As I said, falsehood everywhere defeats itself by the very means by which it seems to annoy the truth, and makes the truth to appear more bright. Which was now the case. For that no one might say that his neighbors and those who had seen him did not speak with precision, but guessed from a likeness,[1] they bring forward his parents, by whom they succeeded against their will in proving that what had taken place was real,[2] since the parents best of all knew their own child. When they could not terrify the man himself, but beheld him with all boldness proclaim his Benefactor, they thought to wound the miracle by means of his parents. Observe the malice of their questioning. For what saith it? Having placed them in the midst so as to throw them into distress,[3] they apply the questioning with great severity and anger,

Ver. 19. "Is this your son?" (and they said not, "who once was blind," but) "of whom ye say that he was born blind?"

As if they were acting deceitfully, and plotting on behalf of[4] Christ. O ye accursed, utterly accursed! What father would choose to invent such falsehoods against his child? For they almost say, "Whom ye have made out blind, and not only so, but have spread abroad the report everywhere."

"How then doth he now see?"

[2.] O folly! "Yours," saith one, "is the trick[5] and the contrivance." For by these two things do they attempt to lead the parents to a denial; by using the words, "Whom ye say," and, "How then doth he now see?" Now when there were three questions asked, whether he was their son, whether he had been blind, and how he received his sight, the parents only acknowledged two of them, but do not add the third. And this came to pass for the sake of the truth, in order that none other save the man that was healed, who was also worthy[6] of credit, should acknowledge this matter. And how would the parents have favored (Christ), when even of what they knew some part they spake not through fear of the Jews? What say they?

Ver. 20, 21. "We know that this is our son, and that he was born blind; but by what means he now seeth we know not, or who hath opened his eyes we know not; he is of age, he shall speak for himself."

By making him to be worthy of credit, they begged off themselves; "He is not a child, say

they, nor incapable,[7] but able to testify for himself."

Ver. 22. "These words spake they,[8] because they feared the Jews."

Observe how the Evangelist again brings forward their opinion and thoughts. This I say, because of that speech which they before uttered, when they said, "He maketh Himself equal to God." (c. v. 18.) For had that also been the opinion of the Jews but not the judgment of Christ, he would have added and said, that "it was a Jewish opinion."[9] When therefore the parents referred them to him that had been healed, they called him again the second time, and did not say openly and shamelessly, "Deny that Christ healed thee," but would fain effect this under a pretense of piety.

Ver. 24. "Give,"[10] saith one, "the glory to God."

For to have said to the parents, "Deny that he is your son, and that he was born[11] blind," would have seemed very ridiculous. And again, to have said this to himself would have been manifest shamelessness. Wherefore they say not so, but manage the matter in another way, saying, "Give God the glory," that is, "confess that this man hath wrought nothing."

"We know that this man is a sinner."

"Why then did ye not convict Him when He said, 'Which of you convinceth Me of sin?' (c. viii. 46.) Whence know ye that He is a sinner?" After that they had said, "Give God the glory," and the man had made no reply, Christ meeting praised him, and did not rebuke him, nor say, "Wherefore hast thou not given glory to God?" But what said He? "Dost thou believe on the Son of God?"[12] (ver. 35), that thou mayest learn that this is "to give glory to God." Now had He not been equal in honor to the Father, this would not have been giving glory; but since he that honoreth the Son honoreth the Father also, the blind is with good reason not rebuked. Now while they expected that the parents would contradict and deny the miracle, the Pharisees said nothing to the man himself, but when they saw that they profited nothing by this, they again return to him, saying, "This man is a sinner."

Ver. 25. "He answered and said, Whether he be a sinner or no, I know not; one thing I know, that, whereas I was blind, now I see."

Surely the blind man was not terrified? That be far from him. How then doth he who said,

---

[1] ver. 9, "He is like him."
[2] al. "establishing what had been done."
[3] ἀγωνίαν.   [4] τὰ τοῦ Χριστοῦ συγκροτούντων, al. κατὰ τοῦ Χ.
[5] σκαιώρημα.   [6] al. "a witness worthy."

[7] ἀτελής.   [8] "his parents," N. T.
[9] Another reading has this sense: "For although that was the opinion of the Jews, yet he hath also added the judgment of Christ; and hath said that the sentence of the Jews was to put out of the synagogue those who confessed Him to be the Christ."
[10] N. T. ver. 22-24. "For the Jews had agreed already, that if any man did confess that He was Christ, he should be put out of the synagogue. Therefore said his parents, He is of age, ask him. Then again called they the man that was blind, and said unto him."
[11] lit. "that ye begot him."   [12] al. "Son of Man."

"He is a Prophet" (ver. 17), now say, "Whether he be a sinner, I know not"? He said so, not as being in such a state of mind, nor as having persuaded himself of this thing, but desiring to clear Him from their charges by the testimony of the fact, not by[1] his own declaration, and to make the defense credible, when the testimony of the good deed done should decide the matter against them. Since if after many words when the blind man said, "Except this were a righteous man he could not do such miracles" (ver. 33), they were so enraged as to reply, "Thou wast altogether born in sin, and dost thou teach us?" what would they not have said, if he had spoken so from the beginning; what would they not have done? "Whether he be a sinner or not, I know not"; as though he had said, "I say nothing in this man's favor, I make no declaration at present, yet this I certainly know and would affirm, that if he were a sinner he could not have done such things." Thus he kept himself free from suspicion, and his testimony uncorrupted, as not speaking from partiality, but as bearing witness according to the fact. When therefore they could neither upset nor remove what had been done, they again return to their former plan, making trifling enquiries about the manner of the cure, like men[2] who search on every side about a prey which is before them, and cannot be hurt,[3] hastening round now in one direction, now in another; and they recur to the man's former assertions, in order now to make them unsound by continual questions, and say,

Ver. 26. "What did he to thee? How opened he thine eyes?"

What was his reply? Having conquered and cast them down, he no longer speaks to them submissly. As long as the matter needed enquiry and arguments he spake guardedly, while he supplied the proof; but when he had conquered and gained a splendid victory, he then takes courage, and tramples upon them. What saith he?

Ver. 27. "I have told you once,[4] and ye did not hear; wherefore would ye hear it again?"

Seest thou the bold-speaking of a beggar towards Scribes and Pharisees? So strong is truth, so weak is falsehood. Truth, though she take hold but of ordinary men, maketh them to appear glorious; the other, even though it be with the strong, shows them weak.[5] What he saith is of this kind: "Ye give no heed to my words, therefore I will no longer speak or answer you continually, who question[6] me to no purpose, and who do not desire to hear in order to learn, but that you may insult over my words."

"Will ye also be His disciples?"

[3.] Now he hath ranked[7] himself among the band of disciples, for the "will ye also?" is the expression of one who is declaring himself to be a disciple. Then he mocked and annoyed them abundantly. For since he knew that this struck them hard, he said it, wishing to upbraid them with exceeding severity; the act of a soul courageous, soaring on high and despising their madness, pointing out the greatness of this dignity, in which he was very confident, and showing that they insulted him who was a man worthy to be admired, but that he took not the insult to himself, but grasped as an honor what they offered as a reproach.

Ver. 28. "Thou art his disciple, but we are Moses' disciples."

"But this cannot be. Ye are neither Moses' nor this Man's; for were ye Moses', ye would become this Man's also." Wherefore Christ before said unto them, because they were continually betaking themselves to these speeches, "Had ye believed Moses, ye would have believed Me, for he wrote of Me." (c. v. 46.)

Ver. 29. "We know that God spake unto Moses."[8]

By whose word, whose report? "That of our forefathers," saith one. Is not He then more to be believed than your forefathers, who confirmeth by miracles that He came from God, and that He speaketh things from above? They said not, "We have heard that God spake to Moses," but, "We know." Do ye affirm, O Jews, what ye have by hearing, as knowing it, but deem what ye have by sight as less certain than what ye have by hearing? Yet the one ye saw not, but heard, the other ye did not hear, but saw. What then saith the blind man?

Ver. 30. "Why herein is a marvelous thing, that ye know not whence He is, and He doeth such miracles."[9]

"That a Man, who is not one of the distinguished or noble or illustrious among you, can do such things; so that it is in every way clear that He is God, needing no human aid."

Ver. 31. "We know that God heareth not sinners."

Since they had been the first to say, "How can a man that is a sinner do such miracles?" (ver. 16), he now brings forward even their judgment, reminding them of their own words. "This opinion," saith he, "is common to me and you. Stand fast now to it." And observe, I pray you, his wisdom. He turns about the miracle in every way, because they could not

---

[1] Mor. "and by."
[2] al. "dogs."
[3] al. "surely enclosed."
[4] "already," N. T.
[5] al. "weaker."
[6] al. "trouble."
[7] al. "reckoned."
[8] "as for this fellow, we know not whence He is," N. T.
[9] "and yet He hath opened mine eyes," N. T.

do away with it, and from it he draws his inferences. Seest thou that at first he said, "Whether he be a sinner or not, I know not"? not doubting (God forbid!) but knowing that He was not a sinner. At least now, when he had an opportunity, see how he defended Him. "We know that God heareth not sinners":

"But if any man be a worshiper of God, and doeth His will."[1]

Here he not only hath cleared Him from sin, but declareth that He is very pleasing to God, and doeth all His will. For since they called themselves[2] worshipers of God, he added, "and doeth His will"; "since," saith he, "it is not sufficient to know God: men must also do His will." Then he magnifies what had been done, saying,

Ver. 32. "Since the world began was it not heard that any man opened the eyes of one that was born blind."[3]

"If now ye acknowledge[4] that God heareth not sinners, and this Person hath wrought a miracle, and such a miracle as no man ever wrought, it is clear that He hath surpassed all things in[5] virtue, and that His power is greater than belongeth to man." What then say they?

Ver. 34. "Thou wast altogether born in sins, and dost thou teach us?"

As long as they expected that he would deny Christ, they deemed him trustworthy, calling upon him once and a second time. If ye[6] deemed him not trustworthy, why did ye call and question him a second time? But when he spake the truth, unabashed, then, when they ought most to have admired, they condemned him. But what is the, "Thou wast altogether born in sins"? They here unsparingly reproach him with his very blindness, as though they had said, "Thou art in sins from thy earliest age"; insinuating that on this account he was born blind; which was contrary to reason. On this point at least Christ comforting him said, "For judgment I am come into the world, that they which see not might see, and that they which see might be made blind." (c. ix. 39.)

"Thou wast altogether born in sins, and dost thou teach us?" Why, what had the man said? Did he set forth his private opinion? Did he not set forth a common judgment, saying, "We know that God heareth not sinners"? Did he not produce your own words?

"And they cast him out."

Hast thou beheld the herald of the truth, how poverty was no hindrance to his true wisdom? Seest thou what reproaches, what sufferings he

bare from the beginning, and how by word and by deed he testified?

[4.] Now these things are recorded, that we too may imitate them. For if the blind man, the beggar, who had not even seen Him, straightway showed such boldness even before he was encouraged by Christ, standing opposed to a whole people, murderous, possessed, and raving, who desired by means of his voice to condemn Christ, if he neither yielded nor gave back, but most boldly stopped their mouths, and chose rather to be cast out than to betray the truth; how much more ought we, who have lived so long in the faith, who have seen ten thousand marvels wrought by faith, who have received greater benefits than he, have recovered the sight of the eyes within, have beheld the ineffable Mysteries, and have been called to such honor, how ought we, I say, to exhibit all boldness of speech towards those who attempt to accuse, and who say anything against the Christians, and to stop their mouths, and not to acquiesce without an effort. And we shall be able to do this, if we are bold,[7] and give heed to the Scriptures, and hear them not carelessly. For if one should come in here regularly, even though he read not at home, if he attends to what is said here, one year even is sufficient to make him well versed in them; because we do not to-day read one kind of Scriptures, and to-morrow another, but always and continually the same. Still such is the wretched disposition of the many, that after so much reading, they do not even know the names of the Books, and are not ashamed nor tremble at entering so carelessly into a place where they may hear God's word. Yet if a harper, or dancer, or stage-player call the city, they all run eagerly, and feel obliged to him for the call, and spend the half of an entire day in attending to him alone; but when God speaketh to us by Prophets and Apostles, we yawn, we scratch ourselves, we are drowsy. And in summer, the heat seems too great, and we betake ourselves to the market place; and again, in winter, the rain and mire are a hindrance, and we sit at home; yet at horse races, though there is no roof over them to keep off the wet, the greater number, while heavy[8] rains are falling, and the wind is dashing the water into their faces, stand like madmen, caring not for cold, and wet, and mud, and length of way, and nothing either keeps them at home, or prevents their going thither. But here, where there are roofs over head, and where the warmth is admirable, they hold back instead of running together; and this too, when the gain is that of their own souls. How is this tolerable, tell me? Thus it happens, that while we are

---

1 "him He heareth," N. T.
2 al. "he (al. they) said that Christ was a worshiper of God."
3 ver. 33. "If this Man were not of God, He could do nothing."
4 al. "Then he draws an inference also. 'If this Man were not of God, He could do nothing.' If therefore it is acknowledged," &c.
5 or, "prevailed in all by."    6 al. "if they," &c.

7 i.e. through a good conscience.    8 al. "heavy and violent."

more skilled than any in those matters, in things necessary we are more ignorant than children. If a man call you a charioteer, or a dancer, you say that you have been insulted, and use every means to wipe off the affront; but if he draw you to be a spectator of the action, you do not start away, and the art whose name you shun, you almost in every case pursue. But where you ought[1] to have both the action and the name, both to be and to be called a Christian, you do not even know what kind of thing the action is. What can be worse than this folly?[2] These things I have desired continually to say to you, but I fear lest I gain hatred in vain and unprofitably. For I perceive that not only the young are mad, but the old also; about whom I am especially ashamed, when I see a man venerable from his white hairs, disgracing those white hairs, and drawing a child after him. What is worse than this mockery? What more shameful than this conduct? The child is taught by the father to act unseemly.

[5.] Do the words sting? This is what I desire, that you should suffer the pain caused by the words, in order to be delivered from the disgrace caused by the actions. For there are some too far colder than these, who are not even ashamed at the things spoken of, nay, who even put together[3] a long argument in defense of the action. If you ask them who was Amos or Obadiah, or what is the number of the Prophets or Apostles, they cannot even open their mouth; but for horses and charioteers, they compose excuses more cleverly than sophists or rhetoricians, and after all this, they say, "What is the harm? what is the loss?" This is what I groan for, that ye do not so much as know that the action is a loss, nor have a sense of its evils. God hath given to thee an appointed space of life for serving Him, and dost thou while thou spendest it vainly, and at random, and on nothing useful, still ask, "What loss is there?" If thou hast spent a little money to no purpose, thou callest it a loss: when thou spendest whole days of thine upon the devil's pageants, thinkest thou that thou art doing nothing wrong? Thou oughtest to spend all thy life in supplications[4] and prayers, whereas thou wastest thy life and substance[5] heedlessly, and to thine own hurt, on shouts, and uproar, and shameful words, and fighting, and unseasonable pleasure, and actions performed by trickery, and after all this thou askest, "What is the loss?" not knowing thou shouldest be lavish of anything rather than time.[6] Gold, if thou shalt have spent, thou

mayest get again; but if thou lose time, thou shalt hardly recover that. Little is dealt out to us in this present life; if therefore we employ it not as we ought, what shall we say when we depart "there"? For tell me, if thou hadst commanded one of thy sons to learn some art, and then he had continually stayed at home, or even passed his time somewhere else, would not the teacher reject him? Would he not say to thee, "Thou hast made an agreement with me, and appointed a time; if now thy son will not spend this time with me but in other places, how shall I produce him to thee as a scholar?"[7] Thus also we must speak. For God will say also to us, "I gave you time to learn this art of piety, wherefore have ye foolishly and uselessly wasted that time? Why did ye neither go constantly to the teacher, nor give heed to his words?" For to show that piety is an art, hear what the Prophet saith, "Come, ye children, hearken unto me; I will teach you the fear of the Lord." (Ps. xxxiv. 11.) And again, "Blessed is the man whom Thou instructest, Lord, and teachest him out of Thy Law." (Ps. xciv. 12.) When therefore thou hast spent this time in vain, what excuse wilt thou have? "And why," saith some one, "did He deal out to us but little time?" O senselessness and ingratitude! That for which thou wert most bounden to give thanks to Him, for that He hath cut short thy labors and abridged thy toils, and made the rest long and everlasting, for this dost thou find fault, and art discontented?

But I know not how we have brought our discourse to this point, and have made it so long; we must therefore shorten it now. For this too is a part of our wretchedness, that here if the discourse be long, we all become careless, while there[8] they begin at noon, and retire by torch and lamp light. However, that we be not always chiding, we now entreat and beseech you, grant this favor to us and[9] to yourselves; and getting free from all other matters, to these let us rivet ourselves. So shall we gain from you joy and gladness, and honor on your account, and a recompense for these labors; while ye will reap all the reward, because having been aforetime so madly riveted to the stage, ye tore yourselves away, through fear of God, and by our exhortations, from that malady, and brake your bonds, and hastened unto God. Nor is it "there" alone that ye shall receive your reward, but "here" also ye shall enjoy pure pleasure. Such a thing is virtue; besides giving us crowns in heaven, even here it maketh life pleasant to us. Let us then be persuaded by what has been

---

[1] al. "desire."　　　　　　　　[2] al. "lawlessness."
[3] al. "are not even ashamed at what takes place at the theaters, but raise."
[4] al. "alms-deeds."　　　[5] βίον.
[6] al. "that thou wilt rather have required of thee the husbandry of time than any other thing."

[7] al. "an artist."
[8] i.e. in the theater.
[9] al. "or rather, both to us and."

said, that we may obtain the blessings both here and hereafter, through the grace and lovingkindness of our Lord Jesus Christ, by whom and with whom, to the Father and the Holy Ghost be glory, now and ever and world without end. Amen.

# HOMILY LIX.

### John ix. 34–36.

" And they cast him out. And Jesus heard that they had cast him out; and when He had found him, He said unto him, Dost thou believe on the Son of God? He answered and said, Who is He, Lord, that I might believe on Him?" And the rest.

[1.] They who for the sake of the truth and the confession of [1] Christ suffer anything terrible and are insulted, these are especially honored. For as he who loseth his possessions for His sake, the same it is who most findeth them; as he who hateth his own life, the same it is who most loveth it; so too he who is insulted, is the same who is most honored. As fell out in the case of the blind man. The Jews cast him out from the Temple, and the Lord of the Temple found him; he was separated from that pestilent company, and met with the Fountain of salvation; he was dishonored by those who dishonored Christ, and was honored by the Lord of Angels. Such are the prizes of truth. And so we, if we leave our possessions in this world, find confidence in the next; if here we give to the afflicted, we shall have rest in heaven; if we be insulted for the sake of God, we are honored both here and there.

When they had cast him out from the Temple, Jesus found him. The Evangelist shows, that He came for the purpose of meeting him. And observe how He recompenseth him, by that which is the chiefest of blessings. For He made Himself known to him who before knew Him not, and enrolled him into the company of His own disciples. Observe also how the Evangelist describes the exact circumstances; for when Christ had said, "Dost thou believe on the Son of God?" the man replied, "Lord, who is He?" For as yet he knew Him not, although he had been healed; because he was blind before he came to his Benefactor, and after the cure, he was being worried by those dogs. Therefore, like some judge at the games, He receiveth the champion who had toiled much and gained the crown. And what saith He? "Dost thou believe on the Son of God?" What is this, after so much arguing against the Jews, after so many words, He asketh him, "Dost thou believe?"

He spake it not from ignorance, but desiring to make Himself known, and showing that He greatly valued the man's faith. "This great multitude," He saith, "hath insulted Me, but of them I make no account; for one thing I care, that thou shouldest believe. For better is one who doeth the will of God, than ten thousand transgressors." "Dost thou believe on the Son of God?" As having both been present, and as approving what had been said by him, He asketh this question; and first,[2] He brought him to a state of longing for Himself. For He said not directly, "Believe," but in the way of an enquiry. What then said the man? "Lord, who is He, that I might believe on Him?" The expression is that of a longing and enquiring soul. He knoweth not Him in whose defense he had spoken so much, that thou mayest learn his love of truth. For he had not yet seen Him.

Ver. 37. "Jesus saith unto him, Thou hast both seen Him, and it is He that talketh with thee."

He said not, "I am He," but as yet in an intermediate [3] and reserved manner, "Thou hast both seen Him." This was still uncertain; therefore He addeth more clearly, "It is He that talketh with thee."

Ver. 38. "He saith, Lord, I believe; and he worshiped Him" (straightway [4]).

He said not, "I am He that healed thee, that bade thee, Go, wash in Siloam"; but keeping silence on all these points, He saith, "Dost thou believe on the Son of God?" and then the man, showing his great earnestness, straightway worshiped; which few of those who were healed had done; as, for instance, the lepers, and some others; by this act declaring His divine power. For that no one might think that what had been said by him was a mere expression, he added also the deed. When he had worshiped, Christ said,

Ver. 39. "For judgment I am come into the world, that they which see not might see, and that they which see might be made blind."

So also saith Paul; "What shall we say then?

---

[1] lit. "to."

[2] i.e. before revealing Himself.
[3] μέσως, al. μέσος.
[4] not in G. T.

That the Gentiles which followed not after righteousness have attained to righteousness, even
the righteousness which is of the faith of Jesus;
but Israel, which followed after the law of righteousness, hath not attained to the law of righteousness." (Rom. ix. 30, 31.) By saying, "For
judgment I am come into this world," He both
made the man stronger respecting the faith, and
aroused those who followed Him; for the Pharisees were following Him. And the, "For judgment," He spake with reference to a greater
punishment; showing that they who had given
sentence against Him, had received sentence
against themselves; that they who had condemned Him as a sinner, were themselves the
persons condemned. In this passage He speaketh of two recoveries of sight, and two blind-
nesses; one sensible, the other spiritual.

Ver. 40. "Some of them that followed Him,
say unto Him,[1] Are we also blind?"

As in another place they said, "We were never
servants to any man"; and, "We be not born
of fornication" (c. viii. 33, 41); so now they
gape on material things alone, and are ashamed
of this kind of blindness. Then to show that it
was better for them to be blind than seeing, He
saith,

Ver. 41. "If ye were blind, ye should have
no sin."

Since they deemed the calamity a matter to
be ashamed of, He turneth this back upon their
own head, telling them, that "this very thing
would have rendered your punishment more
tolerable"; cutting away on every side their
human thoughts, and leading them to a notion
high and marvelous.

"But now ye say, We see."

As He saith in that other place, "Of whom ye
said that He was your God" (c. viii. 54); so too
here, "Now ye say that ye see,[2] but ye see not."
He showeth that what they deemed a great
matter for praise, brought punishment upon
them. He also comforted him who was blind
from his birth, concerning his former maimed
state, and then speaketh concerning their blindness. For He directeth His whole speech to
this end, that they may not say, "We did not
refuse to come to thee owing to our blindness,
but we turn away and avoid thee as a deceiver."

[2.] And not without a cause hath the Evangelist mentioned, that they of the Pharisees who
were with Him heard these things, and said,
"Are we blind also?" but to remind thee that
these were the men who first withdrew from and
then stoned Him, for they were persons who
followed Him superficially, and who easily
changed to the contrary opinion. How then

doth He prove that He is not a deceiver, but a
Shepherd? By laying down the distinguishing
marks both of the shepherd, and of him who is
a deceiver and a spoiler, and from these affording them opportunity of searching into the truth
of the matter. And first He showeth who is a
deceiver and a spoiler, calling him so from the
Scriptures, and saying,

Chap. x. ver. 1. "Verily, verily, I say unto
you, he that entereth not by the door into the
sheepfold, but climbeth up some other way, the
same is a thief and a robber."

Observe the marks of a robber; first, that he
doth not enter openly; secondly, not according
to the Scriptures, for this is the, "not by the
door." Here also He referreth to those who
had been before, and to those who should be
after Him, Antichrist and the false Christs, Judas
and Theudas, and whatever others there have
been of the same kind. And with good cause
He calleth the Scriptures "a door," for they
bring us to God, and open to us the knowledge
of God, they make the sheep, they guard them,
and suffer not the wolves to come in after them.
For Scripture, like some sure door, barreth the
passage against the heretics, placing us in a state
of safety as to all that we desire, and not allowing us to wander; and if we undo it not, we
shall not easily be conquered by our foes. By
it we can know all, both those who are, and those
who are not, shepherds. But what is "into the
fold"? It refers to the sheep, and the care of
them. For he that useth not the Scriptures,
but "climbeth up some other way," that is, who
cutteth out for himself another and an unusual[3]
way, "the same is a thief." Seest thou from
this too that Christ agreeth with the Father, in
that He bringeth forward the Scriptures? On
which account also He said to the Jews, "Search
the Scriptures" (c. v. 39); and brought forward
Moses, and called him and all the Prophets witnesses, for "all," saith He,[4] "who hear the
Prophets shall come to Me"; and, "Had ye believed Moses, ye would have believed Me." But
here He hath put the same thing metaphorically.
And by saying, "climbeth up some other way,"
He alluded to the Scribes, because they taught
for commandments the doctrines of men, and
transgressed the Law (Matt. xv. 9); with which
He reproached them, and said, "None of you
doeth the Law." (c. vii. 19.) Well did He say,
"climbeth up," not "entereth in," since to climb
is the act of a thief intending to overleap a wall,
and who doeth all with danger. Hast thou seen
how He hath sketched the robber? now observe
the character of the shepherd. What then is it?

Ver. 2–4. "He that entereth in by the door,
the same is the shepherd of the sheep; to him

---

[1] "And some of the Pharisees which were with Him heard these
words, and said unto Him," N. T.
[2] "ye say, We see, therefore your sin remaineth," N. T.

[3] or, "unlawful."                          [4] or, "It saith."

the doorkeeper openeth, and the sheep hear his voice, and he calleth his own by name.[1] And when he hath brought them out, he goeth before them."

[3.] He hath set down the marks of the shepherd, and of the evil doer; let us now see how He hath fitted to them what followeth. "To him," He saith, "the doorkeeper openeth"; He continueth in the metaphor to make the discourse more emphatic. But if thou shouldest be minded to examine the parable word by word, there is nothing to hinder thee from supposing Moses to be the doorkeeper, for to him were entrusted the oracles of God. "Whose voice the sheep hear, and he calleth his own by name." Because they everywhere said that He was a deceiver, and confirmed this by their own unbelief, saying, "Which[2] of the rulers hath believed on him?" (c. vii. 48.) He showeth that they ought not on account of the unbelief of those persons to call Him a spoiler and deceiver, but that they, because they gave no heed to Him, were consequently even excluded from the rank of sheep. For if a shepherd's part is to enter through the usual door, and if He entered through this, all they who followed Him might be sheep, but they who rent themselves away, hurt not the reputation of the Shepherd, but cast themselves out from the kindred of the sheep. And if farther on He saith that He is "the door," we must not again be disturbed, for He also calleth Himself "Shepherd," and "Sheep," and in different ways proclaimeth His dispensations. Thus, when He bringeth us to the Father, He calleth Himself "a Door," when He taketh care of us, "a Shepherd"; and it is that thou mayest not suppose, that to bring us to the Father is His only office, that He calleth Himself a Shepherd. "And the sheep hear his voice, and he calleth his own sheep, and leadeth them out, and goeth before them." Shepherds indeed do the contrary, for they follow after them; but He to show that He will lead all men to the truth, doeth differently; as also when He sent the sheep, He sent them, not out of the way of wolves, but "in the midst of wolves." (Matt. x. 16.) For far more wonderful is this manner of keeping sheep than ours. He seemeth to me also to allude to the blind man, for him too, having "called," He "led out" from the midst of the Jews, and the man heard "His voice," and "knew" it.

Ver. 5. "And[3] a stranger will they not follow, for they know not the voice of strangers."

Certainly here He speaketh of Theudas and Judas, (for "all, as many as believed on them, were scattered" [Acts v. 36], It saith,) or of the false Christs who after that time should deceive.

For lest any should say that He was one of these, He in many ways separateth Himself from them. And the first difference He setteth down is His teaching from the Scriptures; for He by means of these led men to Him, but the others did not from these draw men after them. The second is, the obedience of the sheep; for on Him they all believed, not only while He lived, but when He had died; the others they straightway left. With these we may mention a third difference, no trifling one. They did all as rebels,[4] and to cause revolts, but He placed Himself so far from such suspicion, that when they would have made Him a king, He fled; and when they asked, "Is it lawful to give tribute unto Cæsar?" He bade them pay it, and Himself gave the two drachm piece. (Matt. xvii. 27.) Besides this, He indeed came for the saving of the sheep, "That they might have life, and that they might have more abundantly" (ver. 10), but the others deprived them even of this present life. They betrayed those who were entrusted to them and fled, but He withstood so nobly as even to give up His life. They unwillingly, and by compulsion, and desiring to escape, suffered what they suffered, but He willingly and by choice endured all.

Ver. 6. "This parable spake Jesus unto them, but they understood not what things they were which He spake unto them."

And wherefore spake He obscurely? Because He would make them more attentive; when He had effected this, He removes the obscurity, saying,

Ver. 9. "I am[5] the door, by Me if any man enter in, he[6] shall go in and out, and find pasture."

As though He had said, "shall be in safety and security," (but by "pasture," He here meaneth His nurturing and feeding the sheep, and His power[7] and Lordship,) that is, "shall remain within, and none shall thrust him out." Which took place in the case of the Apostles, who came in and went out securely, as having become lords of all the world, and none was able to cast them out.

Ver. 8. "All that ever came before Me are thieves and robbers, but the sheep did not hear them."

He doth not here speak of the Prophets, (as the heretics assert,) for as many as believed on Christ did hear them also, and were persuaded by them; but of Theudas and Judas, and the other exciters of sedition. Besides, He saith, "the sheep did not hear them," as praising them; now nowhere is He seen to praise those who refused to hearken to the Prophets, but, on the contrary, to reproach and accuse them vehe-

---

1 " and leadeth them out," N. T.     2 " Hath any," N. T.
3 ver. 4. " for they know his voice, and," N. T.

4 τύραννοι, assuming royalty.
5 " Verily, verily, I say unto you, I am," &c., N. T.
6 " he shall be saved, and," &c., N. T.
7 or, " power over them."

mently; whence it is evident that the, "did not hear," refers to those leaders of sedition.

Ver. 10. "The thief cometh not but for to steal, and to kill, and to destroy."

Which then took place when all (their followers) were slain and perished.

"But I am come that they might have life, and that they might have more."[1]

And what is "more" than life, tell me? The kingdom of heaven. But He doth not as yet say this, but dwelleth on the name of "life," which was known to them.

Ver. 11. "I am the good Shepherd."

Here He next speaketh concerning the Passion, showing that this should be for the salvation of the world, and that He came to it not unwillingly. Then again He mentioneth the character of the shepherd and the hireling.

"For the shepherd[2] layeth down his life."[3]

Ver. 12. "But he that is an hireling and not a shepherd, whose own the sheep are not, seeth the wolf coming, and leaveth the sheep and fleeth, and the wolf cometh and catcheth them."[4]

Here He declareth Himself to be Master even as the Father, if so be that He is the Shepherd, and the sheep are His. Seest thou how He speaketh in a more lofty tone in His parables, where the sense is concealed; and giveth no open handle to the listeners? What then doth this hireling? He "seeth the wolf coming, and leaveth the sheep, and the wolf cometh, and scattereth them." This those false teachers did, but He the contrary. For when He was taken, He said, "Let these go their way, that the saying might be fulfilled" (c. xviii. 8, 9), that not one of them was lost. Here also we may suspect a spiritual[5] wolf to be intended; for neither did Christ allow him to go and seize the sheep. But he is not a wolf only, but a lion also. "Because our[6] adversary the devil," It saith, "walketh about as a roaring lion." (1 Pet. v. 8.) He is also a serpent, and a dragon; for, "Tread ye[7] on serpents and scorpions." (Luke x. 19.)

[4.] Wherefore, I beseech you, let us remain pasturing beneath this Shepherd; and we shall remain, if we obey Him, if we hear His voice, if we follow not a stranger. And what is His voice? "Blessed are the poor in spirit, blessed are the pure in heart, blessed are the merciful." (Matt. v. 3, 8, 7.) If thus we do, we shall remain beneath the Shepherd, and the wolf will not be able to come in; or if he come against us, he will do so to his own hurt. For we have a Shepherd who so loveth us, that He gave even His life for us. When therefore He is both powerful and loveth us, what is there to hinder us from being saved? Nothing, unless we ourselves revolt from Him. And how can we revolt? Hear Him saying, "Ye cannot serve two masters, God and mammon." (Matt. vi. 24.) If then we serve God, we shall not submit to the tyranny of mammon. And truly a bitterer thing than any tyranny is the desire of riches; for it brings no pleasure, but cares, and envyings, and plottings, and hatred, and false accusations, and ten thousand impediments to virtue, indolence, wantonness, greediness, drunkenness, which make even freemen slaves, nay, worse than slaves bought with money, slaves not to men, but even to the most grievous of the passions, and maladies of the soul. Such a one dares many things displeasing to God and men, dreading lest any should remove from him this dominion. O bitter slavery, and devlish tyranny! For this is the most grievous thing of all, that when entangled in such evils we are pleased and hug our chain, and dwelling in a prison house full of darkness, refuse to come forth to the light, but rivet evil upon ourselves, and rejoice in our malady. So that we cannot be freed, but are in a worse state than those that work the mines, enduring labors and affliction, but not enjoying the fruit. And what is in truth worse than all, if any one desire to free us from this bitter captivity, we do not suffer it, but are even vexed and displeased, being in this respect in no better case than madmen, or rather in a much more miserable state than any such, inasmuch as we are not even willing to be delivered from our madness. What? was it for this, O man, that thou wast brought into the world? Was it for this that thou wast made a man, that thou mightest work in these mines, and gather gold? Not for this did God create thee in His Image, but that thou mightest please Him, that thou mightest obtain the things to come, that thou mightest join the choir of Angels. Why now dost thou banish thyself from such a relationship, and thrust thyself into the extreme of dishonor and meanness?[8] He who came by the same birth pangs with thee, (the spiritual birth pangs I mean,) is perishing with hunger, and thou art bursting with fullness: thy brother goeth about with naked body, but thou providest garments even for thy garments, heaping up all this clothing for the worms. How much better would it have been to put them on the bodies of the poor; so would they have remained undestroyed, would have freed thee from all care, and have won for thee the life to come. If thou wilt not have them to be moth-eaten, give them to the poor, these are they who know how to shake these garments well. The Body of Christ is more precious and more secure than the coffer, for not only doth It keep the garments safe, not

---

[1] περισσὸν ἔχωσι. E. V. "have (it) more abundantly."
[2] "good shepherd."     [3] "life for the sheep."
[4] "them, and scattereth the sheep," N. T.
[5] νοητὸν.        [6] "your," N. T.
[7] "I give you power to tread," N. T.
[8] lit. "low birth."

only doth It preserve them unconsumed, but even rendereth them brighter. Oftentimes the coffer taken with the garments causeth thee the utmost loss, but this place of safety not even death can harm. With It we need neither doors nor bolts, nor wakeful servants, nor any other such security, for our possessions are free from all treacherous attacks, and are laid up under guard, as we may suppose things laid up in heaven would be; for to all wickedness that place is inaccessible. These thing we cease not continually to say to you, and you hearing are not persuaded. The reason is, that we are of a soul which is mean, gaping upon the earth, groveling on the ground. Or rather, God forbid that I should condemn you all of wickedness, as though all were incurably diseased. For even if those who are drunk with riches stop their ears against my words, yet they who live in poverty will be able to look clearly to what I say. "But what," saith some one, "hath this to do with the poor? for they have no gold, or any such garments." No, but they have bread and cold water, but they have two obols, and feet to visit the sick, but they have a tongue and speech to comfort the bedridden, but they have house and shelter to make the stranger their inmate. We demand not from the poor such and such a number of talents of gold, these we ask from the rich. But if a man be poor, and come to the doors of others, our Lord is not ashamed to receive even an obol, but will say that He hath received more from the giver, than from those who cast in much. How many of those who now stand here would desire to have been born at that time, when Christ went about the earth in the flesh, to have conversed and sat at meat with Him? Lo, this may be done now, we may invite Him more than then to a meal, and feast with Him, and that to greater profit. For of those who then feasted with Him many even perished, as Judas and others like him; but every one of those who invite Him to their houses now, and share with Him table and roof, shall enjoy a great blessing. "Come," it saith, "ye blessed of My Father, inherit the Kingdom prepared for you from the foundation of the world. For I was an hungered, and ye gave Me meat: I was thirsty, and ye gave Me drink: I was a stranger, and ye took Me in; sick, and ye visited Me; I was in prison, and and ye came unto Me." (Matt. xxv. 34–36.) That then we may hear these words, let us clothe the naked, let us bring in the stranger, feed the hungry, give the thirsty drink, let us visit the sick, and look upon him that is in prison, that we may have boldness and obtain remission of our sins, and share those good things which transcend both speech and thought. Which may we all obtain, through the grace and lovingkindness of our Lord Jesus Christ, to whom be the glory and the might[1] forever. Amen.

# HOMILY LX.

### John x. 14, 15.

"I am the Good Shepherd, and know My sheep, and am known of Mine. As the Father knoweth Me, even so know I the Father; and I lay down My life for the sheep."

[1.] A GREAT matter, beloved, a great matter it is to preside over a Church: a matter needing wisdom and courage as great as that of which Christ speaketh, that a man should lay down his life for the sheep, and never leave them deserted or naked; that he should stand against the wolf nobly. For in this the shepherd differs from the hireling; the one always looks to his own safety, caring not for the sheep; the other always seeks that of the sheep, neglecting his own. Having therefore mentioned the marks of a shepherd, Christ hath put two kinds of spoilers; one, the thief who kills and steals; the other, one who doth not these things, but who when they are done doth not give heed nor hinder them. By the first, pointing to Theudas and those like him; by the second, exposing the teachers of the Jews, who neither cared for nor thought about the sheep entrusted to them. On which account Ezekiel of old rebuked them, and said, "Woe,[2] ye shepherds of Israel! Do the shepherds feed themselves? Do not the shepherds feed the sheep?" (Ezek. xxxiv. 2, LXX.) But they did the contrary, which is the worst kind of wickedness, and the cause of all the rest. Wherefore It saith, "They have not turned back the strayed, nor sought the lost, nor bound up the broken, nor healed the sick, because they fed themselves and not the sheep." (Ezek. xxxiv. 4.) As Paul also hath declared in another passage, saying, "For all seek their own, not the things which are Jesus Christ's" (Phil. ii. 21); and again, "Let no man seek his own, but every man his neighbor's." (1 Cor. x. 24.)

---

[1] al. "with whom to the Father and the Holy Ghost be glory."
[2] al. "O."

From both Christ distinguisheth Himself; from those who came to spoil, by saying, "I am come that they might have life, and that they might have more abundantly" (ver. 10); and from those who cared not for the sheep being carried away by wolves, by never deserting them, but even laying down His life for them, that the sheep might not perish.  For when they desired to kill Him, He neither altered His teaching, nor betrayed those who believed on Him, but stood firm, and chose to die.  Wherefore He continually said, "I am the good Shepherd." Then because His words appeared to be unsupported by testimony, (for though the, "I lay down My life," was not long after proved, yet the, "that they might have life, and that they might have more abundantly," was to come to pass after their departure hence in the life to come,) what doth He?  He proveth one from the other; by giving His mortal life[1] (He proveth) that He giveth life immortal.[2]  As Paul also saith, "If when we were enemies we were reconciled to God by the death of His Son, much more being reconciled we shall be saved." (Rom. v. 10.)  And again in another place, "He that spared not His own Son, but delivered Him up for us all, how shall He not with Him also freely give us all things?" (Rom. viii. 32.)

But wherefore do they not now bring against Him the charge which they did before, when they said, "Thou bearest witness of thyself, thy witness is not true?" (c. viii. 13.)  Because He had often stopped their mouths, and because His boldness towards them had been increased by His miracles.  Then because He said above, "And the sheep hear his voice, and follow him," lest any should say, "What then is this to those who believe not?" hear what He addeth, "And I know My sheep, and am known of Mine."  As Paul declared when he said, "God hath not rejected His people whom He foreknew" (Rom. xi. 2); and Moses, "The Lord knew those that were His" (2 Tim. ii. 19; comp. Num. xvi. 5); "those," He saith, "I mean, whom He[3] foreknew."  Then that thou mayest not deem the measure of knowledge to be equal, hear how He setteth the matter right by adding, "I know My sheep, and am known of Mine."  But the knowledge is not equal. "Where is it equal?"  In the case of the Father and Me, for there, "As the Father knoweth Me, even so know I the Father."  Had He not wished to prove this, why should He have added that expression?  Because He often ranked Himself among the many, therefore, lest any one should deem that He knew as a man knoweth, He added, "As the Father knoweth Me, even so know I the Father."  "I know Him as

exactly as He knoweth Me."  Wherefore He said, "No man knoweth the Son[4] save the Father, nor the Father save the Son" (Luke x. 22), speaking of a distinct kind of knowledge, and such as no other can possess.

[2.] "I lay down My life."  This He saith continually, to show that He is no deceiver. So also the Apostle, when he desired to show that he was a genuine teacher, and was arguing against the false apostles, established his authority by his dangers and deaths, saying, "In stripes above measure, in deaths oft." (2 Cor. xi. 23.) For to say, "I am light," and "I am life," seemed to the foolish to be a matter of pride; but to say, "I am willing to die," admitted not any malice or envy.  Wherefore they do not say to Him, "Thou bearest witness of thyself, thy witness is not true," for the speech manifested very tender care for them, if indeed He was willing to give Himself for those who would have stoned Him. On this account also He seasonably introduceth mention of the Gentiles;

Ver. 16.  "For other sheep also I have," He saith, "which are not of this fold, them also must I bring."

Observe again, the word "must," here used, doth not express necessity, but is declaratory of something which will certainly come to pass. As though He had said, "Why marvel ye if these shall follow Me, and if My sheep shall hear My voice?  When ye shall see others also following Me and hearing My voice, then shall ye be astonished more."  And be not confounded when you hear Him say, "which are not of this fold" (Gal. v. 6), for the difference relateth to the Law only, as also Paul saith, "Neither circumcision availeth anything, nor uncircumcision."

"Them also must I bring."  He showeth that both these and those were scattered and mixed, and without shepherds, because the good Shepherd had not yet come.  Then He proclaimeth beforehand their future union, that,

"They shall be one fold."[5]

Which same thing also Paul[6] declared, saying, "For to make in Himself of twain one new man." (Eph. ii. 15.)

Ver. 17.  "Therefore doth My Father love Me, because I lay down My life, that I might take it again."

What could be more full of humanity than this saying, if so be that on our account our Lord shall be beloved, because He dieth for us? What then? tell me, was He not beloved during the time before this; did the Father now begin to love Him, and were we the causes of His love? Seest thou how He used condescension?  But what doth He here desire to prove?  Because

---

[1] ψυχήν.          [2] ζωήν.          [3] Ben "I."

[4] "who the Son is," &c., N. T.
[5] "and there shall be one fold, one shepherd," N. T.
[6] al. "Which Paul also himself."

they said that He was alien from the Father, and a deceiver, and had come to ruin and destroy, He telleth them, "This if nothing else would persuade Me to love you, namely, your being so beloved by the Father, that I also am beloved by Him, because I die for you." Besides this, He desireth also to prove that other point, that He came not to the action unwillingly, (for if unwillingly, how could what was done cause love?) and that this was especially known to the Father. And if He speaketh as a man, marvel not, for we have often mentioned the cause of this, and to say again the same things is superfluous and unpleasant.

"I lay down My life, that I might take it again."

Ver. 18. "No man taketh it from Me, but I lay it down of Myself. I have power to lay it down, and I have power to take it again."

Because they often took counsel to kill Him, He telleth them, "Except I will, your labor is unavailing." And by the first He proveth the second, by the Death, the Resurrection. For this is the strange and wonderful thing. Since both took place in a new way, and beyond ordinary custom. But let us give heed exactly to what He saith, "I have power to lay down My life." And who hath not "power to lay down his life"? Since it is in the power of any that will, to kill himself. But He saith it not so, but how? "I have in such a way the power to lay it down, that no one can effect this against My will." And this is a power not belonging to men; for we have no power to lay it down in any other way than by killing ourselves. And if we fall into the hands of men who plot against us, and have the power to kill us, we no longer are free to lay it down or not, but even against our will they take it from us. Now this was not the case with Christ, but even when others plotted against Him, He had power not to lay it down. Having therefore said that, "No man taketh it from Me," He addeth, "I have power to lay down My life," that is, "I alone can decide as to laying it down," a thing which doth not rest with us,[1] for many others also are able to take it from us. Now this He said not at first, (since the assertion would not have seemed credible,) but when He had received the testimony of facts, and when, having often plotted against Him, they had been unable to lay hold on Him, (for He escaped from their hands ten thousand times,) He then saith, "No man taketh it from me." But if this be true, that other point follows, that He came to death voluntarily. And if this be true, the next point is also certain, that He can "take it again" when He will. For if the dying[2] was a greater thing than man could do, doubt no more about the other. Since the

fact that He alone was able to let go His life, showeth that He was able by the same power to take it again. Seest thou how from the first He proved the second, and from His death showed that His Resurrection was indisputable?

"This commandment have I received of My Father."

What commandment was this? To die for the world. Did He then wait first to hear, and then choose, and had He need of learning it? Who that had sense would assert this? But as before when He said, "Therefore doth My Father love Me," He showed that the first motion was voluntary, and removed all suspicion of opposition to the Father; so here when He saith that He received a commandment from the Father, He declared nothing save that, "this which I do seemeth good to Him," in order that when they should slay Him, they might not think that they had slain Him as one deserted and given up by the Father, nor reproach Him with such reproaches as they did, "He saved others, himself he cannot save"; and, "If thou be the Son of God, come down from the cross" (Matt. xxvii. 42, 40); yet the very reason of His not coming down was, that He was the Son of God.

[3.] Then lest on hearing that, "I have received a command from the Father," thou shouldest deem that the achievement[3] doth not belong to Him, He hath said preventing the, "The good Shepherd layeth down His life for the sheep"; showing by this that the sheep were His, and that all which took place was His achievement, and that He needed no command. For had He needed a commandment, how could He have said, "I lay it down of Myself"? for He that layeth it down of Himself needeth no commandment. He also assigneth the cause for which He doeth this. And what is that? That He is the Shepherd, and the good Shepherd. Now the good Shepherd needeth no one to arouse him to his duty; and if this be the case with man, much more is it so with God. Wherefore Paul said, that "He emptied Himself." (Phil. ii. 7.) So the "commandment" put here means nothing else, but to show His unanimity with the Father; and if He speaketh in so humble and human a way, the cause is the infirmity of His hearers.

Ver. 19. "There was a division therefore[4] among the Jews.[5] And some[6] said, He hath a devil (and is mad[7]). Others said, These are not the words of him that hath a devil: can a devil open the eyes of the blind?"

For because His words were greater than belonged to man, and not of common use, they

---

[1] Ben. "you."  [2] i.e. as He died.

[3] τὸ κατόρθωμα.  [4] "therefore again," N. T.
[5] "the Jews for these sayings," N. T.
[6] "many of them," N. T.
[7] "is mad, why hear ye him?" N. T.

said that He had a devil, calling Him so now for the fourth time. For they before had said, "Thou hast a devil, who seeketh to kill thee?" (c. vii. 20) ; and again, "Said we not well that thou art a Samaritan, and hast a devil?" (c. viii. 48) ; and here, "He hath a devil and is mad, why hear ye him?" Or rather we should say, that He heard this not for the fourth time, but frequently. For to ask, "Said we not well that thou hast a devil?" is a sign that they had said so not twice or thrice, but many times. "Others said, These are not the words of him that hath a devil: can a devil open the eyes of the blind?" For since they could not silence their opponents by words, they now brought proof from His works. "Certainly neither are the words those of one that hath a devil, yet if ye are not persuaded by the words, be ye shamed by the works. For if they are not the acts of one that hath a devil, and are greater than belong to man, it is quite clear that they proceed from some divine power." Seest thou the argument? That they were greater than belonged to man is plain, from the Jews saying, "He hath a devil"; that He had not a devil, He showed by what He did.

What then did Christ? He answered nothing to these things. Before this He had replied, "I have not a devil"; but not so now; for since He had afforded proof by His actions, He afterwards held His peace. For neither were they worthy of an answer, who said that He was possessed of a devil, on account of those actions for which they ought to have admired and deemed Him to be God. And how were any farther refutations from Him needed, when they opposed and refuted each other? Wherefore He was silent, and bore all mildly. And not for this reason alone, but also to teach us all meekness and long-suffering.

[4.] Let us now imitate Him. For not only did He now hold His peace, but even came among them again,[1] and being questioned answered and showed the things relating to His foreknowledge ; and though called "demoniac" and "madman," by men who had received from Him ten thousand benefits, and that not once or twice but many times, not only did He refrain from avenging Himself, but even ceased not to benefit them. To benefit, do I say? He laid down His life for them, and while being crucified spake in their behalf to His Father. This then let us also imitate, for to be a disciple of Christ, is the being gentle and kind. But whence can this gentleness come to us? If we continually reckon up our sins, if we mourn, if we weep ; for neither doth a soul that dwelleth in the company of so much grief endure to be provoked

or angered. Since wherever there is mourning, it is impossible that there should be anger ; where grief is, all anger is out of the way ; where there is brokenness of spirit, there is no provocation. For the mind, when scourged by sorrow, hath not leisure to be roused, but will groan[2] bitterly, and weep yet more bitterly. I know that many laugh on hearing these things, but I will not cease to lament for the laughers. For the present is a time for mourning, and wailings, and lamentations, since we do many sins both in word and deed, and hell awaiteth those who commit such transgressions, and the river boiling with a roaring stream of fire, and banishment from the Kingdom, which is the most grievous thing of all. When these things then are threatened, tell me, dost thou laugh and bear thee proudly? And when thy Lord is angered and threatening, dost thou stand careless,[3] and fearest thou not lest by this thou light for thyself the furnace to a blaze? Hearest thou not what He crieth out every day? "Ye saw Me[4] an hungered, and gave Me no meat ; thirsty, and ye gave Me no drink ; depart ye into the fire prepared for the devil and his angels." (Matt. xxv.) And these things He threatened every day. "But," saith some one, "I did give Him meat." When, and for how many days? Ten or twenty? But He willeth it not merely for so much time as this, but as much as thou spendest upon earth. For the virgins also had oil, yet not sufficient for their salvation ; they too lighted their lamps, yet they were shut out from the bridechamber. And with reason, since the lamps had gone out before the coming of the Bridegroom. On this account we need much oil, and abundant lovingkindness. Hear at least what the Prophet saith, "Have mercy upon me, O God, according to Thy great mercy." (Ps. li. 1.) We therefore must so take pity upon our neighbor, according to His great mercy towards us. For such as we are towards our fellow-servants, such shall we find our Lord towards ourselves. And what kind of "mercy" is "great"? When we give not of our abundance, but of our deficiency. But if we give not even of our abundance, what hope shall there be for us? Whence shall we have deliverance from those woes? Where shall we be enabled to flee and to find salvation? For if the virgins after so many and so great toils found no comfort anywhere, who shall stand forth for us when we hear those fearful words of the Judge Himself, addressing and reproaching us, because "I was an hungered, and ye gave Me no meat ; for inasmuch," It saith, "as ye did it not unto one of the least of these, ye did it not unto Me" ; saying this not

---

[1] πάλιν ἐπέστη.

[2] al. "groans."
[3] ἀναπεπτωκώς, lit. "reclined," or "despondent."
[4] "I was," &c., N. T.

merely of His disciples, nor of those who have taken upon themselves the ascetic life, but of every faithful man. For such an one though he be a slave, or one of those that beg in the market-place, yet if he believeth in God, ought by right to enjoy all our good will. And if we neglect such an one when naked or hungry, we shall hear those words. With reason. For what difficult or grievous thing hath He demanded of us? What that is not of the very lightest and easiest? He saith not, "I was sick, and ye restored Me not," but, "and ye visited Me not." He saith not, "I was in prison, and ye delivered Me not," but, "and ye came not unto Me." In proportion therefore as the commands are easy, so is the punishment greater to them that disobey. For what is easier, tell me, than to walk forth and enter into a prison? And what more pleasant? For when thou seest some bound, others covered with filth, others with uncut hair and clothed in rags, others perishing with hunger, and running like dogs to your feet, others with deep ploughed sides,[1] others now returning in chains from the market-place, who beg all day and do not collect even necessary sustenance, and yet at evening are required by those set over them to furnish that wicked and savage service;[2] though thou be like any stone, thou wilt certainly be rendered kinder; though thou livest a soft and dissipated life, thou wilt certainly become wiser, when thou observest the nature of human affairs in other men's misfortunes; for thou wilt surely gain an idea of that fearful day, and of its varied punishments. Revolving and considering these things, thou wilt certainly cast out both wrath and pleasure, and the love of worldly things, and wilt make thy soul more calm than the calmest harbor; and thou wilt reason concerning that Judgment seat, reflecting that if among men there is so much forethought, and order, and terror, and threatenings, much more will there be with God. "For there is no power but from God." (Rom. xiii. 1.) He therefore who permitteth rulers to order these things thus, will much more do the same Himself.

[5.] And certainly were there not this fear, all would be lost, when though such punishments hang over them, there are many who go over to the side of wickedness. These things if thou wisely observe, thou wilt be more ready-minded towards alms-doing, and wilt reap much pleasure, far greater than those who come down from the theater. For they when they remove from thence are inflamed and burn with desire. Having seen those women hovering[3] on the stage,

and received from them ten thousand wounds, they will be in no better condition than a tossing sea, when the image of the faces, the gestures, the speeches, the walk, and all the rest, stand before their eyes and besiege their soul. But they who come forth from a prison will suffer nothing of this kind, but will enjoy great calm and tranquillity. For the compunction arising from the sight of the prisoners, quenches all that fire. And if a woman that is an harlot and a wanton meet a man coming forth from among the prisoners, she will work him no mischief. For becoming for the time to come, as it were, incapable of molding,[4] he will thus not be taken by the nets of her countenance, because instead of that wanton countenance there will then be placed before his eyes the fear of the Judgment. On this account, he who had gone over every kind of luxury said, "It is better to go into the house of mourning than into the house of mirth." (Eccl. vii. 2.) And so "here" thou wilt show forth great wisdom, and "there" wilt hear those words which are worth ten thousand blessings. Let us then not neglect such a practice and occupation. For although we be not able to bring them food, nor to help them by giving money, yet shall we be able to comfort them by our words, and to raise up the drooping spirit, and to help them in many other ways by conversing with those who cast them into prison, and by making their keepers kinder, and we certainly shall effect either small or great good. But if thou sayest that the men there are neither men of condition,[5] nor good, nor gentle, but man-slayers, tomb-breakers, cut-purses, adulterers, intemperate, and full of many wickednesses, by this again thou showest to me a pressing reason for spending time there. For we are not commanded to take pity on the good and to punish the evil, but to manifest this lovingkindness to all men. "Be ye," It saith, "like to My Father[6] which is in heaven, for He maketh His sun to rise on the evil and on the good, and sendeth rain on the just and on the unjust." (Matt. v. 45.) Do not then accuse other men's faults bitterly, nor be a severe judge, but mild and merciful. For we also, if we have not been adulterers, or tomb-breakers, or cutpurses, yet have we other transgressions which deserve infinite punishment. Perchance we have called our brother "fool," which prepares[7] for us the pit; we have looked on women with unchastened eyes, which constitutes absolute adultery; and what is more[8] grievous than all, we partake not worthily of the Mysteries, which maketh us guilty of the Body and Blood of

---

[1] πλευρὰς διωρυγμένους.
[2] λειτουργίαν seems to mean a daily contribution demanded by the keepers out of the sum which prisoners gained by begging.
[3] lit. "winged."

[4] ἄπλαστος, possibly a corrupt form for ἀπέλαστος. Dr. Heyse conjectures ἄπλατος, "unapproachable."
[5] εὐδαίμονες.
[6] "That ye may be the children of," &c., N. T.
[7] προξενεῖ.                [8] al. "most."

Christ. Let us then not be bitter enquirers into the conduct of others, but consider our own state, so shall we desist from this inhumanity and cruelty. Besides this, it may be said that we shall there find many good men, and often men worth as much as all the city. Since even that prison-house in which Joseph was had in it many evil men, yet that just man had the care of them all, and was, with the rest, concealed as to his real character; for he was worth as much as all the land of Egypt, yet still he dwelt in the prison-house, and no one knew him of those that were within it. Thus also even now it is likely that there are[1] many good and virtuous men, though they be not visible to all men, and the care thou takest of such as these gives thee a return for thy exertions in favor of the whole. Or if there be none such, still even in this case great is thy recompense; for thy Lord conversed not with the just only, while He avoided the unclean, but received with kindness both the Canaanitish woman, and her of Samaria, the abominable and impure; another also who was a harlot, on whose account the Jews reproached Him, He both received and healed, and allowed His feet to be washed by the tears of the polluted one, teaching us to condescend to those that are in sin, for this most of all is kindness. What sayest thou? Do robbers and tomb-breakers dwell in the prison? And, tell me, are all they just men that dwell in the city? Nay, are there not many worse even than these, robbing with greater shamelessness? For the one sort, if there be no other excuse for them, at least put before themselves the veil of solitude and darkness, and the doing these things clandestinely; but the others throw away the mask, and go after their wickedness with uncovered head, being violent, grasping, and covetous. Hard it is to find a man pure from injustice.

[6.] If we do not take by violence gold, or such and such a number of acres of land, yet we bring about the same end by deceit and robbery in lesser matters, and where we are able to do so. For when in making contracts, or when we must buy or sell anything, we dispute and strive to pay less than the value, and use our utmost endeavors to have it so, is not the action robbery? Is it not theft and covetousness? Tell not me that thou hast not wrested away houses or slaves, for injustice is judged not by the measure of the things taken, but by the intention of those who commit the robbery. Since "just" and "unjust" have the same force in great and in little things; and I call cut-purses alike the man who cuts through a purse and takes the gold, and him who buying from any of the market people deducts something from the proper price; nor

is he the only house-breaker who breaks through a wall and steals anything within, but that man also who corrupts justice, and takes anything from his neighbor.

Let us not then pass by our own faults, and become judges of other men's; nor let us, when it is time for lovingkindness, be searching out their wickedness; but considering what our own state was once, let us now be gentle and kind. What then was our state? Hear Paul say; "For we ourselves also were sometime foolish, disobedient, deceived, serving divers lusts and pleasures, hateful, and hating one another" (Tit. iii. 3); and again, "We were by nature children of wrath." (Eph. ii. 3.) But God seeing us as it were confined in a prison-house, and bound with grievous chains, far more grievous than those of iron, was not ashamed of us, but came and entered the prison, and, though we deserved ten thousand punishments, both brought us out from hence, and brought us to a kingdom, and made us more glorious than the heaven, that we also might do the same according to our power. For when He saith to His disciples, "If I, your Lord and Master, have washed your feet, ye also ought to wash one another's feet; for I have given you an example, that ye should do as I have done to you" (c. xiii. 14), He writeth this law not merely for the washing the feet, but also in all the other acts which He manifested towards us. Is it a manslayer who inhabits the prison? Yet let not us be weary in doing Him good. Is it a tomb-breaker, or an adulterer? Let us pity not his wickedness, but his calamity. But often, as I before said, one will be found there worth ten thousand; and if thou goest continually to the prisoners, thou shalt not miss so great a prize. For as Abraham, by entertaining even common guests, once met with Angels, so shall we meet with great men too, if we make the action a business. And if I may make a strange assertion, he who entertains a great man is not so worthy of praise as he who receives the wretched and miserable. For the former hath, in his own life, no slight occasion of being well treated, but the other, rejected and given up by all, hath one only harbor, the pity of his benefactor; so that this most of all is pure kindness. He, moreover, who shows attention to an admired and illustrious man, doth it often for ostentation among men, but he who tends the abject and despairing, doth it only because of the command of God. Wherefore, if we make a feast, we are bidden to entertain the lame and halt, and if we do works of mercy, we are bidden to do them to the least and meanest. "For," It saith, "inasmuch as ye have done it unto one of the least of these, ye have done it unto Me." (Matt. xxv. 45.) Knowing, therefore, the treasure which

---

[1] i.e. "in prison."

is laid up in that place,[1] let us enter continually, and make it our business, and turn[2] there our eager feelings about theaters. If thou hast nothing to contribute, contribute the comfort of thy words. For God recompenseth not only him that feedeth, but him also who goeth in. When thou enterest and arouseth the trembling and fearful soul, exhorting, succoring, promising assistance, teaching it true wisdom, thou shalt thence reap no small reward. For if thou shouldest speak in such manner outside the prison, many will even laugh, being dissipated[3] by their excessive luxury: but those who are in adversity, having their minds humbled, shall meekly attend to thy words, and praise them, and become better men. Since even when Paul preached, the Jews often derided him, but the prisoners listened with much stillness. For nothing renders the soul so fit for heavenly wisdom as calamity and temptation, and the pressure of affliction. Considering all these things, and how much good we shall work both to those within the prison, and to ourselves, by being continually mixed[4] up with them, let us there spend the time we used to spend in the market-place, and in unseasonable occupations, that we may both win them and gladden ourselves, and by causing God to be glorified, may obtain the everlasting blessings, through the grace and lovingkindness of our Lord Jesus Christ, by whom and with whom, to the Father and the Holy Ghost, be glory for ever and ever. Amen.

# HOMILY LXI.

### JOHN x. 22–24.

"And it was at Jerusalem, the Feast of the dedication, and it was winter. And Jesus walked in the temple in Solomon's porch. Then came the Jews round about Him, and said unto Him, How long dost thou make us to doubt?"

[1.] EVERY virtue is a good thing, but most of all gentleness and meekness. This showeth us men; this maketh us to differ from wild beasts; this fitteth us to vie with Angels. Wherefore Christ continually expendeth many words about this virtue, bidding us be meek and gentle. Nor doth He merely expend words about it, but also teacheth it by His actions; at one time buffeted and bearing it, at another reproached and plotted against; yet again coming to those who plotted against Him. For those men who had called Him a demoniac, and a Samaritan, and who had often desired to kill Him, and had cast stones at Him, the same surrounded and asked Him, "Art thou the Christ?" Yet not even in this case did He reject them after so many and so great plots against Him, but answered them with great gentleness.

But it is necessary rather to enquire into the whole passage from the beginning.

"It was," It saith, "at Jerusalem, the Feast of the dedication, and it was winter." This feast was a great and national one. For they celebrated with zeal the day on which the Temple was rebuilt, on their return from their long captivity in Persia. At this feast Christ also was present, for henceforth He continually abode in Judæa, because the Passion was nigh.[5] "Then came the Jews round about Him, and said, How long dost thou make us to doubt?"

"If thou be the Christ, tell us plainly."

He did not reply, "What enquire ye[6] of Me? Often have ye called Me demoniac, madman, and Samaritan, and have deemed me an enemy of God, and a deceiver, and ye said but now, Thou bearest witness of thyself, thy witness is not true; how is it then that ye seek and desire to learn from Me, whose witness ye reject?" But He said nothing of the kind, although He knew that the intention with which they made the enquiry was evil. For their surrounding Him and saying, "How long dost thou make us to doubt?" seemed to proceed from a certain longing and desire of learning, but the intention with which they asked the question was corrupt and deceitful. For since His works admitted not of their slander and insolence, while they might attack His sayings by finding out in them a sense other than that in which they were spoken, they continually proposed questions, desiring to silence Him by means of His sayings; and when they could find no fault with His works, they wished to find a handle in His words. Therefore they said, "Tell us"; yet He had often told them. For He said to the woman of Samaria, "I Am that speak unto thee" (c. iv. 26); and to the blind man, "Thou hast both seen Him, and it is He that

---

[1] i.e. the prison.　[2] al. "feed," al. "bury."　[3] διακεχυμένοι.　[4] al. "we mix."　[5] lit. "at the doors."　[6] or, "What seek ye."

talketh with thee." (c. ix. 37.) And He had told them also, if not in the same, at least in other words. And indeed, had they been wise, and had they desired to enquire aright, it remained for them to confess Him by words, since by works He had often proved the point in question. But now observe their perverse and disputatious temper. When He addresseth them, and instructeth them by His words, they say, "What sign showest thou us?" (c. vi. 30.) But when He giveth them proofs by His works, they say to Him, "Art thou the Christ? Tell us plainly"; when the works cry aloud, they seek words, and when the words teach, then they betake themselves to works, ever setting themselves to the contrary. But that they enquired not for the sake of learning, the end showed. For Him whom they deemed to be so worthy of credit, as to receive His witness of Himself, when He had spoken a few words they straightway stoned; so that their very surrounding and pressing upon Him was done with ill intent.

And the mode of questioning was full of much hatred. "Tell us plainly, Art thou the Christ?" Yet He spake all things openly, being ever present at their feasts, and in secret He said nothing; but they brought forward words of deceit, "How long dost thou make us to doubt?" in order that having drawn Him out, they might again find some handle against Him. For that in every case they questioned Him not in order to learn, but to find fault with His words, is clear, not from this passage only, but from many others also. Since when they came to Him and asked, "Is it lawful to give tribute unto Cæsar or not?" (Matt. xxii. 17), when they spake about putting away a wife (Matt. xix. 3), when they enquired about her who, they said, had had seven husbands (Matt. xxii. 23), they were convicted of bringing their questions to Him, not from desire of learning, but from an evil intention. But there He rebuked them, saying, "Why tempt ye Me, ye hypocrites?" showing that He knew their secret thoughts, while here He said nothing of the kind; teaching us not always to rebuke those who plot against us, but to bear many things with meekness and gentleness.

Since then it was a sign of folly, when the works proclaimed Him aloud, to seek the witness of words, hear how He answereth them, at once hinting to them that they made these enquiries superfluously, and not for the sake of learning, and at the same time showing that He uttered a voice plainer than that by words, namely, that by works.

Ver. 25. "I told you often," [1] He saith, "and ye believe not: the works that I do in My Father's Name, they are they that bear witness of Me."

[2.] A remark which the more tolerable among them continually made to one another; "A man that is a sinner cannot [2] do such miracles." And again, "A devil cannot open the eyes of the blind": and, "No man can do such miracles except God be with him." (c. iii. 2.) And beholding the miracles that He did, they said, "Is not this the Christ?" Others said, "When Christ cometh, will He do greater miracles than those which this Man hath done?" (c. vii. 31.) And these very persons as many as then desired to believe on Him, saying, "What sign showest thou us, that we may see, and believe thee?" (c. vi. 30.) When then they who had not been persuaded by such great works, pretended that they should be persuaded by a bare word, He rebuketh their wickedness, saying, "If ye believe not My works, how will ye believe My words? so that your questioning is superfluous."

Ver. 26. "But," He saith, "I told you, and ye [3] believe not, because ye are not of My sheep." [4]

"For I on My part have fulfilled all that it behooved a Shepherd to do, and if ye follow Me not, it is not because I am not a Shepherd, but because ye are not My sheep."

Ver. 27–30. "For My sheep hear My voice, [5] and follow Me; and I give unto them eternal life [6]; neither can [7] any man pluck them out of My hand. The Father, [8] which gave them Me, is greater than all, and no man is able to pluck them out of My Father's hand. I and the Father are One."

Observe how in renouncing He exciteth them to follow Him. "Ye hear Me not," He saith, "for neither are ye sheep, but they who follow, these are of the flock." This He said, that they might strive to become sheep. Then by mentioning what they should obtain, He maketh these men jealous, so as to rouse them, and cause them to desire such things.

"What then? Is it through the power of the Father that no man plucketh them away, and hast thou no strength, but art too weak to guard them?" By no means. And in order that thou mayest learn that the expression, "The Father which gave them to Me," is used on their account, that they might not again call Him an enemy of God, therefore, after asserting that, "No man plucketh them out of My hand," He proceedeth to show, that His hand and the Father's is One. Since had not this been so, it would have been natural for Him to say, "The Father which gave them to Me is greater than all, and no man can

---

2 "How can," &c., N. T.  
3 " But ye," &c.  
4 " as I said unto you."  
5 "and I know them."  
6 " and they shall never perish."  
7 " shall."  
8 " My Father," N. T.

pluck them out of My hand." But He said not so, but, "out of My Father's hand." Then that thou mayest not suppose that He indeed is weak, but that the sheep are in safety through the power of the Father, He addeth, "I and the Father are One." As though He had said, "I did not assert that on account of the Father no man plucketh them away, as though I were too weak to keep the sheep. For I and the Father are One." Speaking here with reference to Power, for concerning this was all His discourse; and if the power[1] be the same, it is clear that the Essence is also. And when the Jews used ten thousand means, plotting and casting men out of their synagogues, He telleth them that all their contrivances are useless and vain; "For the sheep are in My Father's hand"; as the Prophet saith, "Upon My hand I have pictured thy walls." (Isa. xlix. 16.) Then to show that the hand is One, He sometimes saith that it is His own, sometimes the Father's. But when thou hearest the word "hand," do not understand anything material, but the power, the authority. Again, if it was on this account that no one could pluck away the sheep, because the Father gave Him power, it would have been superfluous to say what follows, "I and the Father are One." Since were He inferior to Him, this would have been a very daring saying, for it declares nothing else than an equality of power; of which the Jews were conscious, and took up stones to cast at Him. (Ver. 31.) Yet not even so did He remove this opinion and suspicion; though if their suspicion were erroneous, He ought to have set them right, and to have said, "Wherefore do ye these things? I spake not thus to testify that my power and the Father's are equal"; but now He doth quite the contrary, and confirmeth their suspicion, and clencheth it, and that too when they were exasperated. For He maketh no excuse for what had been said, as though it had been said ill, but rebuketh them for not entertaining a right opinion concerning Him. For when they said,

Ver. 33–36.[2] "For a good work we stone thee not, but for blasphemy; and because that thou being a man makest thyself God"; hear His answer;[3] "If the Scripture called[4] them gods unto whom the word of God came,[5] how say ye that I blaspheme, because I said, I am the Son of God?"

What He saith is of this kind: "If those who

have received this honor by grace, are not found fault with for calling themselves gods, how can He who hath this by nature deserve to be rebuked?" Yet He spake not so, but proved it at a later time, having first relaxed and yielded somewhat in His discourse, and said, "Whom the Father hath sanctified and sent." And when He had softened their anger, He bringeth forward the plain assertion. For a while, that His speech might be received, He spoke in a humbler strain, but afterwards He raised it higher, saying,

Ver. 37, 38. "If I do not the works of My Father, believe Me not; but if I do, though ye believe not Me, believe the works."

Seest thou how He proveth what I said, that He is in nothing inferior to the Father, but in every way equal to Him? For since it was impossible to see His Essence, from the equality and sameness of the works He affordeth a proof of unvaryingness as to Power. And what, tell me, shall we believe?

[3.] "That I am in the Father, and the Father in Me."[6]

"For I am nothing other than what the Father is, yet still Son; He nothing other than what I am, yet still Father. And if any man know Me, he knoweth the Father, and if he knoweth the Father,[7] he hath learnt also the Son." Now were the power inferior, then also what relateth to the knowledge would be false, for it is not possible to become acquainted with one substance or power by means of another.

Ver. 39–41. "Therefore they sought again to take Him, but He escaped out of their hands, and went away again beyond Jordan, into the place where John at first baptized.[8] And many resorted unto Him, and said, John did no miracle, but all things that John spake of this man were true."

When He hath uttered anything great and sublime, He quickly retireth, giving way to their anger, so that the passion may abate and cease through His absence. And thus He acted at that time. But wherefore doth the Evangelist mention the place? That thou mayest learn that He went there to remind them of the things there done and said by John, and of his testimony; at least when they came there, they straightway remembered John. Wherefore also they said, "John indeed did no miracle," since how did it follow that they should add this, unless the place had brought the Baptist to their memory, and they had come to remember his testimony. And observe how they form incontrovertible syllogisms. "John indeed did no

---

[1] i.e. of the Father and the Son.
[2] Ver. 31, 32, omitted. "Then the Jews took up stones again to stone Him. Jesus answered them, Many good works have I showed you from My Father; for which of those works do ye stone Me?"
[3] Ver. 34, omitted. "Jesus answered them, Is it not written in your Law, I said, Ye are gods?"
[4] "It called."
[5] "And the Scripture cannot be broken: say ye of Him whom the Father hath sanctified and sent into the world, Thou blasphemest," &c., N. T. The comment looks as if this had been read.

[6] "that ye may know and believe that the Father is in Me, and I in Him," N. T.
[7] Ben. omits, "if He knoweth the Father."
[8] "and there He abode," N. T.

miracle," " but this man doth," saith some one ; " hence therefore his superiority is shown. If therefore men[1] believed him who did no miracles, much more must they believe this man." Then, since it was John who bore the witness, lest his having done no miracle might seem to prove him unworthy of being a witness,[2] they added, " Yet if he did no miracle, still he spake all things truly concerning this man " ; no longer proving Christ to be trustworthy by means of John, but John to be so by what Christ had done.

Ver. 42. " Many therefore believed on Him."[3]

There were many things that attracted them. They remembered the words which John had spoken, calling Christ " mightier than himself," and " light," and " life," and " truth," and all the rest. They remembered the Voice which came down from heaven, and the Spirit which appeared in the shape of a dove, and pointed Him out to all ; and with this they recollected the demonstration afforded by the miracles, looking to which they were for the future established. " For," saith some one, " if it was right that we should believe John, much more ought we to believe this man ; if him without miracles, much more this man, who besides the testimony of John, hath also the proof[4] from miracles." Seest thou how much the abiding in this place, and the being freed from the presence of evil men, profited them ? wherefore Jesus continually leadeth and draweth them away from the company of those persons ; as also He seemeth to have done under the old Covenant, forming and ordering the Jews in all points, in the desert, at a distance from the Egyptians.

And this He now adviseth us also to do, bidding us avoid public places, and tumults, and disturbances, and pray peacefully in the chamber. For the vessel which is free from confusion, sails with a fair wind, and the soul which is separated from worldly matters rests in harbor. Wherefore women ought to have more true wisdom than men, because they are for the most part riveted to keeping at home. So, for instance, Jacob was a plain[5] man, because he dwelt at home, and was free from the bustle of public life ; for not without a cause hath Scripture put this, when It saith, " dwelling in a house." (Gen. xxv. 27.) " But," saith some woman, " even in a house there is great confusion." Yes, when thou wilt have it so, and bringest about thyself a crowd of cares. For the man who spends his time in the midst of the market-places and courts of justice is overwhelmed, as if by waves, by external troubles ; but the women who sits in her house as in some school of true wisdom, and collects her thoughts within herself, will be enabled to apply herself to prayers, and readings, and other heavenly wisdom. And as they who dwell in deserts have none to disturb them, so she being continually within can enjoy a perpetual calm. Nor even if at any time she need to go forth, is there then any cause for confusion. For the necessary occasions for a women to leave her house are, either for the purpose of coming hither, or when the body need to be cleansed in the bath ; but for the most part she sits at home, and it is possible for her both to be herself truly wise, and receiving her husband when agitated to calm and compose him, to abate the excess and fierceness of his thoughts, and so to send him forth again, having put off all the mischiefs which he collected from the market-place, and carrying with him whatever good he learnt at home. For nothing, nothing is more powerful than a pious and sensible women to bring a man into proper order, and to mould his soul as she will. For he will not endure friends, or teachers, or rulers, as he will his partner advising and counseling him, since the advice carries even some pleasure with it, because she who gives the counsel is greatly loved. I could tell of many hard and disobedient men who have been softened in this way. For she who shares his table, his bed, and his embraces, his words and secrets, his comings in and goings out, and many other things, who is entirely given up[6] and joined to him, as it is likely that a body would be joined to a head, if she happen to be discreet and well attuned, will go beyond and excel all others in the management of her husband.

[4.] Wherefore I exhort women to make this their employment, and to give fitting counsel. For as they have great power for good, so have they also for evil. A women destroyed Absalom, a woman destroyed Amnon, a woman was like to have destroyed Job, a woman rescued Nabal from the slaughter. Women have preserved whole nations ; for Deborah and Judith exhibited successes worthy of men ; so also do ten thousand other women. Wherefore Paul saith, " For what knowest thou, O wife, whether thou shalt save thy husband?" (1 Cor. vii. 16.) And in those times we see Persis and Mary and Priscilla taking part in the labors[7] of the Apostles (Rom. 16) ; whom we[8] also needs must imitate, and not by words only, but also by actions, bring into order him that dwelleth with us. But how shall we instruct him by our actions? When he sees that thou art not evilly disposed, not fond of expense or ornament, not demanding extravagant supplies of money, but content with what

---

1 al. " we."          2 al. " the testimony unworthy."
3 " on Him there," N. T.
4 al. " after the proof of his testimony and," &c.
5 ἄπλαστος.

6 al. " bound."
7 σκαμμάτων, " the arena," hence any severe labor.
8 Ben. " you."

thou hast, then will he endure thee counseling him. But if thou art wise in word, and in actions doest the contrary, he will condemn thee for very foolish talking. But when together with words thou affordest him also instruction by thy works, then will he admit thee and obey thee the more readily; as when thou desirest not gold, nor pearls, nor costly clothing, but instead of these, modesty, sobriety, kindness; when thou exhibitest these virtues on thy part and requirest them on his. For if thou must needs do somewhat to please thy husband, thou shouldest adorn thy soul, not adorn and so spoil thy person. The gold which thou puttest about thee will not make thee so lovely and desirable to him, as modesty and kindness towards himself, and a readiness to die for thy partner; these things most subdue men. Indeed, that splendor of apparel even displeases him, as straitening his means, and causing him much expense and care; but those things which I have named will rivet a husband to a wife; for kindness and friendship and love cause no cares, give rise to no expense, but quite the contrary. That outward adornment becomes palling by use, but that of the soul blooms day by day, and kindles a stronger flame. So that if thou wouldest please thy husband, adorn thy soul with modesty, piety, and management of the house. These things both subdue him more, and never cease. Age destroys not this adornment, sickness wastes it not. The adornment of the body length of time is wont to undo, sickness and many other things to waste, but what relates to the soul is above all this. That adornment causes envy, and kindles jealousy, but this is pure from disease, and free from all vainglory. Thus will matters at home be easier, and your income without trouble, when the gold is not laid on about your body or encircling your arms, but passes on [1] to necessary uses, such as the feeding of servants, the necessary care of children, and other useful purposes. But if this be not the case, if the (wife's) face be covered with ornaments, while the (husband's) heart is pressed by anxiety, what profit, what

kind of advantage is there? The one being grieved allows not the marvelous beauty of the other to be seen. For ye know, ye know that though a man see the most beautiful of all women, he cannot feel pleasure at the sight while his soul is sorrowful, because in order to feel pleasure a man must first rejoice and be glad. And when all his gold is heaped together to adorn a woman's body, while there is distress in his dwelling, her partner can have no pleasure. So that if we desire to be agreeable to our husbands, let us give them pleasure; and we shall give them pleasure, if we remove our ornaments and fineries. For all these things at the actual time of marriage appear to afford some delight, but this afterwards fades by time. Since if when the heaven is so beautiful, and the sun, to which thou canst not name any body that is equal, so bright, we admire them less from habitually seeing them, how shall we admire a body tricked out with gewgaws? These things I say, desiring that you should be adorned with that wholesome adornment which Paul enjoined; "Not with gold, or pearls, or costly array; but (which becometh women professing godliness) with good works." (1 Tim. ii. 9, 10.) But dost thou wish to please strangers, and to be praised by them? Then assuredly this is not the desire of a modest woman. However, if thou wishest it, by doing as I have said, thou wilt have strangers also to love thee much, and to praise thy modesty. For the woman who adorns her person no virtuous and sober person will praise, but the intemperate and lascivious; nay, rather neither will these praise her, but will even speak vilely of her, having their eyes inflamed by the wantonness displayed about her; but the other all will approve, both the one sort and the other, because they receive no harm from her, but even instruction in heavenly wisdom. And great shall be her praise from men, and great her reward with God. After such adornment then let us strive, that we may live here without fear, and may obtain the blessings which are to come; which may we all obtain through the grace and lovingkindness of our Lord Jesus Christ, to whom be glory for ever and ever. Amen.

---

[1] al. "goes forward."

# HOMILY LXII.

John xi. 1, 2.

"Now a certain man was sick, named Lazarus, of Bethany, of the town of Mary and her sister Martha. It was that Mary which anointed the Lord with ointment."[1]

[1.] MANY men, when they see any of those who are pleasing to God suffering anything terrible, as, for instance, having fallen into sickness, or poverty, and any other the like, are offended, not knowing that to those especially dear to God it belongeth to endure these things; since Lazarus also was one of the friends of Christ, and was sick. This at least they who sent said, "Behold, he whom Thou lovest is sick." But let us consider the passage from the beginning. "A certain man," It saith, "was sick, Lazarus of Bethany." Not without a cause nor by chance hath the writer mentioned whence Lazarus was, but for a reason which he will afterwards tell us. At present let us keep to the passage before us. He also for our advantage informeth us who were Lazarus' sisters; and, moreover, what Mary had more (than the other), going on to say, "It was that Mary which anointed the Lord with ointment." Here some doubting[2] say, "How did the Lord endure that a woman should do this?" In the first place then it is necessary to understand, that this is not the harlot mentioned in Matthew (Matt. xxvi. 7), or the one in Luke (Luke vii. 37), but a different person; they were harlots full of many vices, but she was both grave and earnest; for she showed her earnestness about the entertainment of Christ. The Evangelist also means to show, that the sisters too loved Him, yet He allowed Lazarus to die. But why did they not, like the centurion and the nobleman, leave their sick brother, and come to Christ, instead of sending? They were very confident in Christ, and had towards Him a strong familiar feeling. Besides, they were weak women, and oppressed with grief; for that they acted not in this way as thinking slightly of Him, they afterwards showed. It is then clear, that this Mary was not the harlot. "But wherefore," saith some one, "did Christ admit that harlot?" That He might put away her iniquity; that He might show His lovingkindness; that thou mightest learn that there is no malady which prevaileth over His goodness. Look not therefore at this only, that He received her, but consider the other point also, how He changed her. But, (to return,) why doth the Evangelist

relate this history to us? Or rather, what doth he desire to show us by saying,

Ver. 5.[3] "Jesus loved Martha, and her sister, and Lazarus."

That we should never be discontented or vexed if any sickness happen to good men, and such as are dear to God.

Ver. 3.[4] "Behold, he whom thou lovest is sick."

They desired to draw on Christ to pity, for they still gave heed to Him as to a man. This is plain from what they say, "If thou hadst been here, he[5] had not died," and from their saying, not, "Behold, Lazarus is sick," but "Behold, he whom thou lovest is sick." What then said Christ?

Ver. 4. "This sickness is not unto death, but for the glory of God, that the Son of God might be glorified thereby."

Observe how He again asserteth that His glory and the Father's is One; for after saying "of God," He hath added, "that the Son of God might be glorified."

"This sickness is not unto death." Since He intended to tarry two days where He was, He for the present sendeth away the messengers with this answer. Wherefore we must admire Lazarus' sisters, that after hearing that the sickness was "not unto death," and yet seeing him dead, they were not offended, although the event had been directly contrary. But even so they came to Him,[6] and did not think that He had spoken falsely.

The expression "that" in this passage denotes not cause, but consequence; the sickness happened from other causes, but He used it for the glory of God.

Ver. 6. "And having said this, He tarried two days."[7]

Wherefore tarried He? That Lazarus might breathe his last, and be buried; that none might be able to assert that He restored him when not yet dead, saying that it was a lethargy, a fainting, a fit,[8] but not death. On this account He tarried so long, that corruption began, and they said, "He now stinketh."

Ver. 7. "Then saith He to his disciples, Let us go into Judea."[9]

---

[1] ["and wiped His feet with her hair, whose brother Lazarus was sick."] N. T.          [2] al. "make a question."

[3] Transposed.
[4] "Therefore his sisters sent unto Him, saying," &c., N. T.
[5] "our brother," N. T.          [6] al. "to the Lord."
[7] v. 6. "When He had heard therefore that he was sick, He abode two days still in the same place where He was." N. T.
[8] καταγωγή.          [9] ["again"] N. T.

Why, when He never in other places told them beforehand where He was going, doth He tell them here? They had been greatly terrified, and since they were is this way disposed, He forewarneth them, that the suddenness might not trouble them. What then say the disciples?

Ver. 8. "The Jews of late sought to stone Thee, and goest Thou thither again?"

They therefore had feared for Him also, but for the more part rather for themselves; for they were not yet perfect. So Thomas, shaking with fear, said, "Let us go, that we also may die with Him" (ver. 16), because Thomas was weaker and more unbelieving[1] than the rest. But see how Jesus encourageth them by what He saith.

Ver. 9. "Are there not twelve hours of the day?"[2]

He either saith this,[3] that "he who is conscious to himself of no evil, shall suffer nothing dreadful; only he that doeth evil shall suffer, so that we need not fear, because we have done nothing worthy of death"; or else that, "he who 'seeth the light of this world' is[4] in safety; and if he that seeth the light of this world is in safety, much more he that is with Me, if he separate not himself from Me." Having encouraged them by these words, He addeth, that the cause of their going thither was pressing, and showeth them that they were about to go not unto Jerusalem, but unto Bethany.

Ver. 11, 12. "Our friend Lazarus," He saith, "sleepeth, but I go that I may awake him out of sleep."

That is, "I go not for the same purpose as before, again to reason and contend with the Jews, but to awaken our friend."

Ver. 12. "Then said His disciples, Lord, if he sleep he shall do well."

This they said not without a cause, but desiring to hinder the going thither. "Sayest Thou," asks one of them, "that he sleepeth? Then there is no urgent reason for going." Yet on this account He had said, "Our friend," to show that the going there was necessary. When therefore their disposition was somewhat reluctant, He said,

[2.] Ver. 14.[5] "He is dead."

The former word He spake, desiring to prove that He loved not boasting; but since they understood not, He added, "He is dead."

Ver. 15. "And I am glad for your sakes."

Why "for your sakes"? "Because I have forewarned you of his death, not being there, and because when I shall raise him again, there will be no suspicion of deceit." Seest thou how the disciples were yet imperfect in their disposition, and knew not His power as they ought? and this was caused by interposing terrors, which troubled and disturbed their souls. When He said, "He sleepeth," He added, "I go to awake him"; but when He said, "He is dead," He added not, "I go to raise him"; for He would not foretell in words what He was about to establish certainly by works, everywhere teaching us not to be vainglorious, and that we must not make promises without a cause. And if He did thus in the case of the centurion when summoned, (for He said, "I will come and heal him — Matt. viii. 7,) it was to show the faith of the centurion that He said this. If any one ask, "How did the disciples imagine sleep? How did they not understand that death was meant from His saying, 'I go to awake him?' for it was folly if they expected that He would go fifteen stadia to awake him"; we would reply, that they deemed it to be a dark saying, such as He often spake to them.

Now they all feared the attacks of the Jews, but Thomas above the rest; wherefore also he said,

Ver. 16. "Let us go, that we also may die with Him."

Some say that he desired himself to die; but it is not so; the expression is rather one of cowardice. Yet he was not rebuked, for Christ as yet supported his weakness, but afterwards he became stronger than all, and invincible.[6] For the wonderful thing is this; that we see one who was so weak before the Crucifixion, become after the Crucifixion, and after having believed in the Resurrection, more zealous than any. So great was the power of Christ. The very man who dared not go in company with Christ to Bethany, the same while not seeing Christ ran[7] well nigh through the inhabited world, and dwelt in the midst of nations that were full of murder, and desirous to kill him.

But if Bethany was "fifteen furlongs off," which is two miles, how was Lazarus "dead four days"?[8] Jesus tarried two days, on the day before those two one had come with the message,[9] (on which same day Lazarus died,) then in the course of the fourth day He arrived. He waited to be summoned, and came not uninvited on this account, that no one might suspect what took place; nor did those women who were beloved by Him come themselves, but others were sent.

---

[1] al. "more cowardly."
[2] ver. 9, 10. "If any man walk in the day, he stumbleth not, because he seeth the light of this world. But if a man walk in the night, he stumbleth, because there is no light in him." N. T.
[3] al. "and this He said desiring to show."
[4] al. "shall be."
[5] ver. 13-15. "Howbeit, Jesus spake of his death, but they thought that He had spoken of taking of rest in sleep. Then said Jesus unto them plainly, Lazarus is dead. And I am glad for your sakes that I was not there, to the intent ye may believe; nevertheless, let us go to him." N. T.

[6] ἄληπτος.
[7] al. "alone ran."
[8] ver. 17. "Then when Jesus came, He found that he had lain in the grave four days already." [9] i.e. that Lazarus was sick.

Ver. 18. "Now Bethany was[1] about fifteen furlongs off."

Not without cause doth he mention this, but desires to inform us that it was near, and that it was probable on this account that many would be there. He therefore declaring this adds,

Ver. 19. "Many of the Jews came[2] to comfort them."[3]

But how should they comfort women beloved of Christ, when[4] they had agreed, that if any should confess Christ, he should be put out of the synagogue? It was either because of the grievous nature of the calamity, or that they respected them as of superior birth, or else these who came were not the wicked sort, many at least even of them believed. The Evangelist mentions these circumstances, to prove that Lazarus was really dead.

[3.] But why did not [Martha,] when she went to meet Christ,[5] take her sister with her? She desired to meet with Him apart, and to tell Him what had taken place. But when He had brought her to good hopes, she went and called Mary, who met Him while her grief was yet at its height. Seest thou how fervent her love was? This is the Mary of whom He said, "Mary hath chosen that good part." (Luke x. 42.) "How then," saith one, "doth Martha appear more zealous?" She was not more zealous, but it was because the other had not yet been informed,[6] since Martha was the weaker. For even when she had heard such things from Christ, she yet speaks in a groveling manner, "By this time he stinketh, for he hath been dead four days." (Ver. 39.) But Mary, though she had heard nothing, uttered nothing of the kind, but at once believing,[7] saith,[8]

Ver. 21. "Lord, if Thou hadst been here, my brother had not died."

See how great is the heavenly wisdom of the women, although their understanding be weak. For when they saw Christ, they did not break out into mourning and wailing and loud crying, as we do when we see any of those we know coming in upon our grief; but straightway they reverence their Teacher. So then both these sisters believed in Christ, but not in a right way; for they did not yet certainly know[9] either that He was God, or that He did these things by His own power and authority; on both which points He taught them. For they showed their ignorance of the former, by saying, "If thou hadst

been here, our brother had not died"; and of the latter, by saying,[10]

Ver. 22. "Whatsoever[11] thou wilt ask of God, He will give it thee."

As though they spoke of some virtuous and approved mortal. But see what Christ saith;

Ver. 23. "Thy brother shall rise again."

He thus far refuteth the former saying, "Whatsoever thou wilt ask"; for He said not, "I ask," but what? "Thy brother shall rise again." To have said, "Woman, thou still lookest below, I need not the help of another, but do all of Myself," would have been grievous, and a stumblingblock in her way, but to say, "He shall rise again," was the act of one who chose a middle mode of speech.[12] And by means of that which follows, He alluded to the points I have mentioned; for when Martha saith,

Ver. 24. "I know that he shall rise again[13] in the last day," to prove more clearly His authority, He replieth,

Ver. 25. "I am the Resurrection and the Life."

Showing that He needed no other to help Him, if so be that He Himself is the Life; since if He needed another,[14] how could He be "the Resurrection and the Life"? Yet He did not plainly state this, but merely hinted it. But when she saith again, "Whatsoever thou wilt ask," He replieth,

"He that believeth in Me, though he were dead, yet shall he live."

Showing that He is the Giver of good things, and that we must ask of Him.

Ver. 26. "And whosoever liveth and believeth in Me, shall never die."

Observe how He leadeth her mind upward; for to raise Lazarus was not the only thing sought; it was necessary that both she and they who were with her should learn the Resurrection. Wherefore before the raising of the dead He teacheth heavenly wisdom by words. But if He is "the Resurrection," and "the Life," He is not confined by place, but, present everywhere, knoweth how to heal. If therefore they had said, as did the centurion, "Speak the word, and my servant shall be healed" (Matt. viii. 8), He would have done so; but since they summoned Him to them, and begged Him to come, He condescendeth in order to raise them from the humble opinion they had formed of Him, and cometh to the place. Still while condescending, He showed that even when absent He had power to heal. On this account also He delayed, for the mercy would not have been appar-

---

[1] "nigh unto Jerusalem," N. T.
[2] ["To Martha and Mary"] N. T.
[3] ["concerning their brother"] N. T.
[4] Ben. has a different reading, with no variety of sense.
[5] Ver. 20. "Then Martha, when she heard that Jesus was coming, went and met Him, but Mary sat in the house."
[6] al. "had not yet heard."
[7] al. "but believed, saying."
[8] The words are used by Martha also; but she afterwards implies want of faith.
[9] al. "they know not yet."

[10] al. and that they knew not, is manifest from their saying, "If Thou," &c., and from their adding, "Whatsoever," &c.
[11] "But I know that even now, whatsoever," &c., N. T.
[12] Ben. "fitly made the saying of a middle character."
[13] ["in the Resurrection"] N. T.
[14] al. "other help," al. "helper."

ent as soon as it was given, had there not been first an ill savor (from the corpse). But how did the woman know that there was to be a Resurrection? They[1] had heard Christ say many things about the Resurrection, yet still she now desired to see Him. And observe how she still lingers below; for after hearing, "I am the Resurrection and the Life," not even so did she say, "Raise him," but,

Ver. 27. "I believe that Thou art the Christ, the Son of God."

What is Christ's reply? "He that believeth on Me, though he were dead, yet shall he live,"[2] (here speaking of this death which is common to all.[3]) "And whosoever liveth and believeth on Me, shall never die" (ver. 26), signifying that other death. "Since then I am the Resurrection and the Life, be not thou troubled, though thy brother be already dead, but believe, for this is not death." For a while He comforted her on what had happened, and gave her glimpses of hope, by saying, "He shall rise again," and, "I am the Resurrection"; and that having risen[4] again, though he should again die, he shall suffer no harm, so that it needs not to fear this death. What He saith is of this kind: "Neither is this man dead, nor shall ye die." "Believest thou this?" She saith, "I believe that Thou art the Christ, the Son of God."

"Which should come into the world."

The woman seems to me not to understand the saying; she was conscious that it was some great thing, but did not perceive the whole meaning, so that when asked one thing, she answered another. Yet for a while at least she had this gain, that she moderated her grief; such was the power of the words of Christ. On this account Martha went forth first, and Mary followed. For their affection to their Teacher did not allow them strongly to feel their present sorrow; so that the minds of these women were truly wise as well as loving.

[4.] But in our days, among our other evils there is one malady very prevalent among our women; they make a great show in their dirges and wailings, baring[5] their arms, tearing their hair, making furrows down their cheeks. And this they do, some from grief, others from ostentation and rivalry, others from wantonness; and they bare their arms, and this too in the sight of men. Why doest thou, woman? Dost thou strip thyself in unseemly sort, tell me, thou who art a member of Christ, in the midst of the market-place, when men are present there? Dost thou pluck thy hair, and rend thy garments, and wail loudly,[6] and join the dance, and keep throughout a resemblance to Bacchanalian

women, and dost thou not think that thou art offending God? What madness is this? Will not the heathen[7] laugh? Will they not deem our doctrines fables? They will say, "There is no resurrection — the doctrines of the Christians are mockeries, trickery, and contrivance. For their women lament as though there were nothing after this world; they give no heed to the words engraven in their books; all those words are fictions, and these women show that they are so. Since had they believed that he who hath died is not dead, but hath removed to a better life, they would not have mourned him as no longer being, they would not have thus beaten themselves,[8] they would not have uttered such words as these, full of unbelief, 'I shall never see thee more, I shall never more regain thee,' all their religion is a fable, and if the very chief of good things is thus wholly disbelieved by them, much more the other things which are reverenced among them." The heathen[9] are not so womanish, among them many have practiced heavenly wisdom; and a woman hearing that her child had fallen in battle, straightway asked, "And in what state are the affairs of the city?" Another truly wise, when being garlanded[10] he heard that his son had fallen for his country, took off the garland, and asked which of the two; then when he had learnt which it was, immediately put the garland on again. Many also gave their sons and their daughters for slaughter in honor of their evil deities; and Lacedæmonian women exhort their sons either to bring back their shield safe from war, or to be brought back dead upon it. Wherefore I am ashamed that the heathen show true wisdom in these matters, and we act unseemly. Those who know nothing about the Resurrection act the part of those who know; and those who know, the part of those who know not. And ofttimes many do through shame of men what they do not for the sake of God. For women of the higher class neither tear[11] their hair nor bare their arms; which very thing is a most heavy charge against them, not because they do not strip themselves, but because they act as they do not through piety, but that they may not be thought to disgrace themselves. Is their shame stronger than grief, and the fear of God not stronger? And must not this deserve severest censure? What the rich women do because of their riches, the poor ought to do through fear of God; but at present it is quite the contrary; the rich act wisely through vainglory, the poor through littleness of soul act unseemly. What is worse than this anomaly? We do all for men, all for the

---

[1] al. "she."
[2] from ver. 25.
[3] or, "of this death."
[6] al. "and raise loud wailings, and leap."
[4] or, "one who has risen."
[5] al. "making bloody."

[7] lit. "Greeks."
[8] al. "have been thus inflamed."
[9] lit. "Greeks."
[10] i.e. about to sacrifice.
[11] al. "loose n."

things of earth. And these people utter words full of madness and much ridicule. The Lord saith indeed, "Blessed are they that mourn" (Matt. v. 4), speaking of those who mourn[1] for their sins; and no one mourneth that kind of mourning, nor careth for a lost soul; but this other we were not bidden to practice, and we practice it.[2] "What then?" saith some one, "Is it possible being man not to weep?" No, neither do I[3] forbid weeping, but I forbid the beating yourselves, the weeping immoderately.[4] I am neither brutal nor cruel. I know that our nature asks[5] and seeks for its friends and daily companions; it cannot but be grieved. As also Christ showed, for He wept over Lazarus. So do thou; weep, but gently, but with decency, but with the fear of God. If so thou weepest, thou dost so not as disbelieving the Resurrection, but as not enduring the separation. Since even over those who are leaving us, and departing to foreign lands, we weep, yet we do this not as despairing.

[5.] And so do thou weep, as if thou wert sending one on his way to another land. These things I say, not as giving a rule of action, but as condescending (to human infirmity). For if the dead man have been a sinner, and one who hath in many things offended God, it behooveth to weep; (or rather not to weep only, since that is of no avail to him, but to do what one can to procure[6] some comfort for him by almsgivings and offerings;[7]) but it behooveth also to rejoice at this, that his wickedness hath been cut short. If he have been righteous, it again[8] behooveth to be glad, that what is his is now placed in security, free from the uncertainty of the future; if young, that he hath been quickly delivered from the common evils of life; if old, that he hath departed after taking to satiety that which is held desirable. But thou, neglecting to consider these things, incitest thy handmaidens to act as mourners, as if forsooth thou wert honoring the dead, when it is an act of extreme dishonor.[9] For honor to the dead is, not wailings and lamentings, but hymns and psalmodies and an excellent life. The good man when he departeth, shall depart with angels, though no man be near his remains; but the corrupt, though he have a city to attend his funeral, shall be nothing profited. Wilt thou honor him who is gone? Honor him in another way, by alms-deeds, by acts of beneficence and public service.[10] What avail the many lamentations? And I have heard also another grievous thing, that many women attract lovers by their sad cries, acquiring by the fervor of their wailings a reputation for affection to their husbands. O devilish purpose! O Satanic invention![11] How long are we but dust and ashes, how long but blood and flesh? Look we up to heaven, take we thought of spiritual things.[12] How shall we be able to rebuke the heathen,[13] how to exhort them, when we do such things? How shall we dispute with them concerning the Resurrection? How about the rest of heavenly wisdom? How shall we ourselves live without fear? Knowest not thou that of grief[14] cometh death? for grief darkening[15] the seeing part of the soul not only hindereth it from perceiving anything that it ought, but also worketh it great mischief. In one way then we offend God, and advantage neither ourselves nor him who is gone; in the other we please God, and gain honor among men. If we sink not down ourselves, He will soon remove the remains of our despondency; if we are discontented, He permitteth us to be given up to grief. If we are thankful, we shall not despond. "But, how," saith some one, "is it possible not to be grieved, when one has lost a son or daughter or wife?" I say not, "not to grieve," but "not to do so immoderately." For if we consider that God hath taken away, and that the husband or son which we had was mortal, we shall soon receive comfort. To be discontented is the act of those who seek for something higher than their nature. Thou wast born man, and mortal; why then grievest thou that what is natural hath come to pass? Grievest thou that thou art nourished by eating? Seekest thou to live without this?[16] Act thus also in the case of death, and being mortal seek not as yet for immortality. Once for all this thing hath been appointed. Grieve not therefore, nor play the mourner, but submit to laws laid on all alike. Grieve for thy sins; this is good mourning, this is highest wisdom. Let us then mourn for this cause continually, that we may obtain the joy which is there, through the grace and lovingkindness of our Lord Jesus Christ, to whom be glory for ever and ever. Amen.

---

[1] al. "bewail."
[2] al. "to mourn, and we mourn it."
[3] al. "why, do I."
[4] al. "I forbid not to grieve, but I forbid to act unseemly."
[5] or, "is overcome."      [6] al. "give."
[7] see Hom. XII. p. 43, and note.
[8] al. "more."          [9] al. "folly," al. "madness."
[10] λειτουργίας.          [14] al. "for of grief."
[11] al. "thought."        [15] al. "it darkens."
[12] al. "consider the spiritual."   [16] al. "without meat."
[13] lit. "Greeks."

# HOMILY LXIII.

John xi. 30, 31.

"Now Jesus was not yet come into the town, but was in that place where Martha met Him. The Jews then which were with her," and what follows.[1]

[1.] A great good is philosophy; the philosophy, I mean, which is with us. For what the heathen have is words and fables only; nor have these fables anything truly wise[2] in them; since everything among those men is done for the sake of reputation. A great good then is true wisdom, and even here[3] returns to us a recompense. For he that despises wealth, from this at once reaps advantage,[4] being delivered from cares which are superfluous and unprofitable;[5] and he that tramples upon glory from this at once receives his reward, being the slave of none, but free with the real freedom; and he that desires heavenly things hence receives his recompense, regarding present things as nothing, and being easily superior to every grief. Behold, for example, how this woman by practicing true wisdom even here received her reward. For when all were sitting by her as she mourned and lamented, she did not wait that the Master should come to her, nor did she maintain what might have seemed her due, nor was she restrained by her sorrow, (for, in addition to the other wretchedness, mourning women have this malady, that they wish to be made much of on account of their case,) but she was not at all so affected; as soon as she heard, she quickly came to Him.[6] "Jesus was not yet come into the town."[7] He proceeded somewhat slowly, that He might not seem to fling Himself upon the miracle, but rather to be[8] entreated by them. At least, it is either with an intention of implying this that the Evangelist has said the, "riseth up quickly," or else he showeth that she ran so as to anticipate Christ's arrival. She came not alone, but drawing after her the Jews that were in the house. Very wisely did her sister call[9] her secretly, so as not to disturb those who had come together, and not mention the cause either; for assuredly many would have gone back, but now as though she were going to weep, all followed her. By these means again it is proved[10] that Lazarus was dead.

Ver. 32. "And she fell at His feet."[11]

She is more ardent than her sister. She regarded not the multitude, nor the suspicion which they had concerning Him, for there were many of His enemies, who said, "Could not this man, which opened the eyes of the blind, have caused that even this man should not have died?" (ver. 37); but cast out all mortal things in the presence of her Master, and was given up to one thing only, the honor of that Master. And what saith she?

"Lord, if Thou hadst been here, my brother had not died."

What doth Christ? He converseth not at all with her for the present, nor saith to her what He said to her sister, (for a great multitude was by, and this was no fit time for such words,) He only acteth measurably and condescendeth; and to prove His human nature, weepeth in silence, and deferreth the miracle for the present. For since that miracle was a great one, and such as He seldom wrought, and since many were to believe[12] by means of it, lest to work it without their presence should prove a stumbling-block to the multitude, and so they should gain nothing by its greatness, in order that He might not lose the quarry,[13] He draweth to Him many witnesses by His condescension, and showeth proof of[14] His human nature. He weepeth, and is troubled; for grief is wont to stir up the feelings. Then rebuking those feelings, (for He "groaned[15] in spirit" meaneth, "restrained His trouble,") He asked,

Ver. 34. "Where have ye laid him?"

So that the question might not be attended with lamentation. But why doth He ask? Because He desired not to cast Himself on (the miracle), but to learn all from them, to do all at their invitation, so as to free the miracle from any suspicion.

"They say unto Him, Come and see."

Ver. 35. "Jesus wept."

Seest thou that He had not as yet shown any sign of the raising, and goeth not as if to raise Lazarus, but as if to weep? For the Jews show that He seemed to them to be going to bewail, not to raise him; at least they said,

---

[1] ver. 31. "The Jews then which were with her, when they saw Mary that she rose up hastily and went out, followed her, saying, She goeth unto the grave to weep there."
[2] al. "any real wisdom."      [4] al. "good."
[3] ἐντεῦθεν.      [5] al. "senseless."
[6] al. "but rising straightway went to meet Him."
[7] al. "the place."      [9] al. "speak to."
[8] al. "being."      [10] al. "perhaps it is proved."

[11] Ver. 32, 33. "Then when Mary was come where Jesus was, and saw Him, she fell down at His feet, saying unto Him, Lord, if Thou hadst been here, my brother had not died. When Jesus therefore saw her weeping, and the Jews also weeping which came with her, He groaned in the spirit, and troubled Himself."
[12] al. "they were about to gain much."      [13] τὴν θήραν.
[14] al. "showeth for a time."      [15] Ἐνεβριμήσατο.

Ver. 36, 37. "Behold how he loved him ! And some of them said, Could not this man, which opened the eyes of the blind, have caused that even this man should not have died ? "

Not even amid calamities did they relax their wickedness. Yet what He was about to do was a thing far more wonderful ; for to drive away death when it hath come and conquered, is far more than to stay it when coming on. They therefore slander Him by those very points through which they ought to have marveled at His power. They allow for the time that He opened the eyes of the blind, and when they ought to have admired Him on account of that miracle, they, by means of this latter case, cast a slur upon it, as though it had not even taken place. And not from this only are they shown to be all corrupt, but because when He had not yet come, nor exhibited any action, they prevent Him with their accusations without waiting the end of the matter. Seest thou how corrupt was their judgment?

[2.] He cometh then to the tomb ; and again[1] rebuketh His feelings. Why doth the Evangelist carefully in several places mention that " He wept," and that, " He groaned "?[2] That thou mayest learn that He had of a truth put on our nature. For when this Evangelist is remarkable for uttering great things concerning Christ more than the others, in matters relating to the body, here he also speaketh much more humbly than they.[3] For instance, concerning His death he hath said nothing of the kind ; the other Evangelists declare that He was exceedingly sorrowful, that He was in an agony ; but John, on the contrary, saith, that He even cast the officers backwards. So that he hath made up here what is omitted there, by mentioning His grief. When speaking of His death, Christ saith, " I have power to lay down My life " (c. x. 18), and then He uttereth no lowly word ; therefore at the Passion they[4] attribute to Him much that is human, to show the reality of the Dispensation. And Matthew proves this by the Agony, the trouble, the trembling,[5] and the sweat ; but John by His sorrow. For had He not been of our nature, He would not once and again have been mastered by grief. What did Jesus? He made no defense with regard to their charges ; for why should He silence by words those who were soon to be silenced by deeds? a means less annoying, and more adapted to shame them.

Ver. 39. " He saith, Take ye away the stone."

Why did not He when at a distance summon Lazarus, and place him before their eyes? Or rather, why did He not cause him to arise while the stone yet lay on the grave? For He who was able by His voice to move a corpse, and to show it again endowed with life, would much more by that same voice have been able to move a stone ; He who empowered by His voice one bound and entangled in the grave-clothes to walk, would much more have been able to move a stone ; why then did He not so? In order to make them witnesses of the miracle ; that they might not say as they did in the case of the blind man, " It is he," " It is not he." For their hands[6] and their coming to the tomb testified that it was indeed he. If they had not come, they might have deemed that they saw a vision, or one man in place of another. But now the coming to the place, the raising the stone, the charge given them to loose the dead man bound in grave-clothes from his bands ; the fact that the friends who bore him from the tomb, knew from the grave-clothes[7] that it was he ; that his sisters were not left behind ; that one of them said, " He now stinketh, for he hath been dead four days " ; all these things, I say, were sufficient to silence the ill-disposed, as they were made witnesses of the miracle. On this account He biddeth them take away the stone from the tomb, to show that He raiseth the man. On this account also He asketh, " Where have ye laid him? " that they who said, " Come and see," and who conducted Him, might not be able to say that He had raised another person ; that their voice and their hands might bear witness, (their voice by saying, " Come and see," their hands by lifting the stone, and loosing the grave-clothes,) as well as their eyes and ears, (the one by hearing His voice, the other by seeing Lazarus come forth,) and their smell also by perceiving the ill-odor, for Martha said, " He now stinketh, for he hath been dead four days."

Therefore I said with good reason, that the woman did not at all understand Christ's words, " Though he were dead, yet shall he live." At least observe, that she speaketh as though the thing were impossible on account of the time which had intervened. For indeed it was a strange thing to raise a corpse which had been dead four days, and was corrupt. To the disciples Jesus said, " That the Son of Man may be glorified," referring to Himself ; but to the woman, " Thou shalt see the glory of God," speaking of the Father. Seest thou that the weakness of the hearers is the cause of the difference of the words? He therefore remindeth her of what He had spoken unto her, well nigh rebuking her, as being forgetful. Yet He did not wish at present to confound the spectators, wherefore He saith,[8]

---

[1] Ver. 38. " Jesus therefore, again groaning in Himself, cometh to the grave. It was a cave, and a stone lay upon it."
[2] al. " rebuked."　　　[4] i.e. the other Evangelists.
[3] al. " all things more humble."　　　[5] Ben. omits " the trembling."
[6] i.e. which raised the stone.　　　[8] al. " saith gently."
[7] al. " garments."

Ver. 40. "Said I not unto thee, that if thou wouldest believe, thou shouldest see the glory of God?"

[3.] A great blessing truly is faith, great, and one which makes great those who hold it rightly with (good) living.[1] By this men (are enabled) to do the things of God in His[2] name. And well did Christ say,[3] "If ye have faith ye shall say unto this mountain, Remove, and it shall remove" (Matt. xvii. 20); and again, "He that believeth on Me, the works that I do shall he do also, and greater works than these shall he do." (c. xiv. 12.) What meaneth He by "greater"? Those which the disciples are seen after this to work. For even the shadow of Peter raised a dead man; and so the power of Christ was the more proclaimed. Since it was not so wonderful that He while alive should work miracles, as that when He was dead others should be enabled to work in His name greater than He wrought. This was an indisputable proof of the Resurrection; nor if (that Resurrection) had been seen by all, would it have been equally believed. For men might have said that it was an appearance, but one who saw that by His name alone greater miracles were wrought than when He conversed with men, could not disbelieve unless he were very senseless. A great blessing then is faith when it arises from glowing feelings, great love,[4] and a fervent soul; it makes us truly wise, it hides our human meanness, and leaving reasonings beneath, it philosophizes about things in heaven; or rather what the wisdom of men cannot discover,[5] it abundantly comprehends and succeeds in. Let us then cling to this, and not commit to reasonings[6] what concerns ourselves. For tell me, why have not the Greeks been able to find out anything? Did they not know all the wisdom of the heathen?[7] Why then could they not prevail against fishermen and tentmakers, and unlearned persons? Was it not because the one committed all to argument, the others to faith? and so these last were victorious over Plato and Pythagoras, in short, over all that had gone astray; and they surpass those whose lives had been worn out in[8] astrology and geometry, mathematics and arithmetic, and who had been thoroughly instructed in[9] every sort of learning, and[10] were as much superior to them as true and real philosophers are superior to those who are by nature foolish and out of their senses.[11] For observe, these men asserted that the soul was immortal, or rather, they did not merely assert this, but persuaded others of it.

The Greeks, on the contrary, did not at first know what manner of thing the soul was, and when they had found out, and had distinguished it from the body, they were again in the same case, the one asserting that it was incorporeal, the other that it was corporeal and was dissolved with the body. Concerning heaven again, the one said that it had life and was a god, but the fishermen both taught and persuaded that it was the work and device[12] of God. Now that the Greeks should use reasonings is nothing wonderful, but that those who seem to be believers, that "they" should be found carnal,[13] this is what may justly be lamented.[14] And on this account they have gone astray, some saying that they know God as He knoweth Himself, a thing which not even any of those Greeks have dared to assert: others that God cannot beget without passion, not even allowing Him any superiority over men;[15] others again, that a righteous life and exact[16] conversation avail nothing. But it is not the time to refute these things now. [4.] Yet that a right faith availeth nothing if the life be corrupt, both Christ and Paul declare, having taken the more care for this latter part; Christ when He teacheth,[17] "Not every one that saith unto Me, Lord, Lord, shall enter into the kingdom of heaven" (Matt. vii. 21); and again, "Many will say unto Me in that day, Lord, have we not prophesied in Thy Name? And I will profess unto them, I never knew you; depart from Me, ye that work iniquity"[18] (Matt. xxii. 23); (for they who take not heed to themselves, easily slip away[19] into wickedness, even though they have a right faith;) and Paul, when in his letter to the Hebrews he thus speaks and exhorts them; "Follow peace with all men, and holiness, without which no man shall see the Lord." (Heb. xii. 14.) By "holiness," meaning chastity, so that it behooved each to be content with his own wife, and not have to do with[20] any other woman; for it is impossible that one not so contented should be saved; he must assuredly perish though he have ten thousand right actions, since with fornication it is impossible to enter into the kingdom of heaven. Or rather, this is henceforth[21] not fornication but adultery; for as a woman who is bound to a man, if she come together with[22] another man, then hath committed adultery, so he that is bound to a woman, if he have another, hath committed adultery. Such an one shall not inherit the kingdom of heaven, but shall fall into the pit. Hear what Christ

---

[1] Ben. " great and causing many blessings."
[2] " Jesus."
[3] " If ye believe," It saith, &c.
[4] φίλτρου.
[5] al. " discover, but slips off."
[6] al. " strip off by."
[7] τὴν ἔξωθεν.
[8] al. " who were familiar with."
[9] al. " had got together."
[10] al. " these they cast as dust, and."
[11] al. " so that these appeared henceforward to be truly philosophers, but those fools by nature and out of their senses."

[12] al. " devices."
[13] lit. " having only the natural life," ψυχικὸς, opposed in G. T. to πνευματικὸς.
[14] al. " is the ridiculous thing."
[15] al. " the many."
[16] al. " right."
[17] al. " Christ discourseth the more about this, and saith."
[18] al. " I never knew you": and again, " Rejoice not that the devils are subject to you": for, &c.
[19] al. " often turn aside."
[20] al. " attend to."
[21] i.e. after marriage.
[22] al. " lie with."

saith concerning these,[1] "Their worm shall not die,[2] and the fire shall not be quenched." (Mark ix. 44.) For he can have no pardon, who after (possessing) a wife, and the comfort of a wife, then acts shamelessly towards another woman; since this is henceforth wantonness.[3] And if the many abstain even from their wives when it be a season of fast or prayer, how great a fire doth he heap up for himself who is not even content with his wife, but mingleth with another; and if it is not permitted one who has put away and cast out his own wife to mingle with another, (for this is adultery,) how great evil doth he commit who, while his wife is in his house, brings in another. Let no one then allow this malady to dwell in his soul; let him tear it up by the root. He doth not so much wrong his wife as himself. For so grievous and unpardonable is this offense, that if a woman separate herself from a husband which is an idolater without his consent, God punisheth her; but if she separate herself from a fornicator, not so. Seest thou how great an evil this is? "If," It saith, "any faithful woman have[4] a husband that believeth not, and if he be pleased to dwell with her, let her not leave him." (1 Cor. vii. 13.) Not so concerning a harlot; but what? "If any man[5] put away his wife, saving for the cause of fornication, he causeth her to commit adultery." (Matt. v. 32.) For if the coming together maketh one body, he who cometh together with a harlot must needs become one body with her. How then shall the modest woman, being a member of Christ, receive such an one, or how shall she join to herself the member of an harlot. And observe the excess of the one (fornication) over the other (idolatry). The woman who dwelleth with an unbeliever is not impure; ("for," It saith, "the unbelieving husband is sanctified by the wife" — 1 Cor. vi. 15 ;) not so with the harlot; but what? "Shall I then make the members of Christ the members of an harlot?" In the one case sanctification remains, and is not removed though the unbeliever dwell-

eth with his wife; but in the other case it departeth. A dreadful, a dreadful thing is fornication, and an agent for[6] everlasting punishment; and even in this world it brings with it ten thousand woes. The man so guilty is forced to lead a life of anxiety and toil; he is nothing better off than those who are under punishment, creeping[7] into another man's house with fear and much trembling, suspecting all alike[8] both slave and free. Wherefore I exhort you to be[9] freed from this malady, and if you obey[10] not, step not on the sacred threshold.[11] Sheep that are covered with the scab, and full of disease, may not herd with those that are in health; we must drive them from the fold until they get rid of the malady. We have been made members of Christ; let us not, I entreat, become members of an harlot. This place is not a brothel but a church; if then thou hast the members of an harlot, stand not in the church, lest thou insult the place. If there were no hell, if there were no punishment, yet, after those contracts, those marriage torches, the lawful bed, the procreation of children, the intercourse, how couldest thou bear to join[12] thyself to another? How is it that thou art not ashamed nor blushest? Knowest thou not that they who after the death of their own wife, introduce another into their own house, are blamed by many? yet this action hath no penalty attached to it : but thou bringest in another while thy wife is yet alive. What lustfulness is this! Learn what hath been spoken concerning such men, "Their worm," It saith, "shall not die, and the fire shall not be quenched." (Mark ix. 44.) Shudder at the threat, dread the vengeance. The pleasure here is not so great as the punishment there, but may it not came to pass that any one (here) become liable to that punishment, but that exercising holiness they may see Christ, and obtain the promised good things, which may we all enjoy, through the grace and lovingkindness of our Lord Jesus Christ, to whom with the Father and the Holy Ghost be glory, for ever and ever. Amen.

---

[1] al. " for of such saith God."
[2] "dieth not," &c.
[3] al. " stupidity."
[4] " the woman which hath."
[5] " whosoever shall."
[6] προξενοῦσα, al. ἐπάγουσα.
[7] al. " introducing himself."
[8] al. " everywhere."
[9] al. " give diligence to be."
[10] al. " will."
[11] al. " sanctuary."
[12] al. " place."

# HOMILY LXIV.

John xi. 41, 42.

" Jesus lifted up His eyes, and said, Father, I thank Thee that Thou hast heard Me; and I knew that Thou hearest Me always, but because of the people which stand by, I said it." And what follows.

[1.] What I have often said, I will now say, that Christ looketh not so much to His own honor as to our salvation; not how He may utter some sublime saying, but how something able to draw us to Him. On which account His sublime and mighty sayings are few, and those also hidden, but the humble and lowly are many, and abound[1] through His discourses. For since by these men were the rather brought over, in these He continueth; and He doth not on the one hand utter these[2] universally, lest the men that should come after should receive damage, nor, on the other hand, doth He entirely withhold those,[3] lest the men of that time should be offended. Since they who have passed from lowmindedness unto perfection,[4] will be able from even a single sublime doctrine to discern the whole, but those who were ever lowminded, unless they had often heard these lowly sayings,[5] would not have come to Him[6] at all. In fact, even after so many such sayings they do not remain firm, but even stone and persecute Him, and try to kill Him, and call Him blasphemer. And when He maketh Himself equal with God, they say, " This man blasphemeth " (Matt. ix. 3); and when He saith, " Thy sins be forgiven thee " (c. x. 20), they moreover call Him a demoniac. So when He saith that the man who heareth His words is stronger than death, or, " I am in the Father and the Father in Me " (c. viii. 51), they leave Him; and again, they are offended when He saith that He came down from heaven. (c. vi. 33, 60.) If now they could not bear these sayings, though seldom uttered, scarcely, had His discourse been always sublime, had it been of this texture, would they have given heed to Him? When therefore He saith, " As the Father commanded Me, so I speak "[7] (c. xiv. 31); and, " I am not come[8] of Myself " (c. vii. 28), then they believe. That they did believe then is clear, from the Evangelist signifying this besides, and saying, " As He spake these words, many believed on Him." (c. v. 30.) If then lowly speaking drew men to[9] faith, and high speaking scared

them away,[10] must it not be a mark of extreme folly not to see at a glance how to reckon[11] the sole reason of those lowly sayings, namely, that they were uttered because of the hearers. Since in another place when He had desired to say some high thing, He withheld it, adding this reason, and saying, " Lest we should offend them, cast a hook into the sea." (Matt. xvii. 27.) Which also He doth here; for after saying, " I know that Thou hearest Me always," He addeth, " but because of the multitude which standeth around I said it, that they might believe." Are these words ours? Is this a human conjecture? When then a man will not endure to be persuaded by what is written, that[12] they were offended at sublime things, how, when he heareth Christ saying that He spake in a lowly manner that they might not be offended, how, after that, shall he suspect that the mean sayings belonged to His nature, not to His condescension?[13] So in another place, when a voice came down from heaven, He said, " This voice came not because of Me, but for your sakes." (c. xii. 30.) He who is exalted may be allowed to speak lowly things of himself, but it is not lawful for the humble to utter concerning himself anything grand or sublime. For the former ariseth from condescension, and has for its cause the weakness of the hearers; or rather (it has for its cause) the leading them to[14] humblemindedness, and His being clothed in flesh, and the teaching the hearers to say nothing great concerning themselves, and His being deemed an enemy of God, and not being believed to have come from God, His being suspected of breaking the Law, and the fact that the hearers looked on Him with an evil eye, and were ill disposed towards Him, because He said that He was equal to God.[15] But that a lowly man should say any great thing of Himself, hath no cause either reasonable or unreasonable;[16] it can only be folly, impudence, and unpardonable boldness. Wherefore then doth Christ speak humbly, being of that ineffable and great Substance? For the reasons mentioned, and that He might not be deemed unbegotten; for Paul seems to have

---

[1] lit. " overflow."　　[2] αὐτά.　　[3] αὐτὰ, i.e. higher sayings.
[4] al. " have passed to perfection,"[4] al. " have passed from low-mindedness."　　[5] ταῦτα.　　[6] al. " have been held."
[7] " so I do," N. T.　　[8] al. " I speak nothing."
[9] al. " caused."

[10] ἀπεσοβεῖ.　　[11] al. " not to reckon."　　[12] or, " because."
[13] al. for when we are persuaded from the actions that the men are offended at high sayings, and when He saith Himself, that " on this account I speak in a lowly way, lest they should be offended," who will yet suspect, &ç.
[14] al. " to look to."
[15] al. and the maliciousness of the hearers, and its being continually said in the Old (Covenant), " The Lord thy God is One Lord."
[16] al. " hath no cause at all that is specious."

feared some such thing as this; wherefore he saith, "Except Him who did put all things under Him." (1 Cor. xv. 27.) This it is impious even to think of. Since if being less than Him who begat Him, and of a different Substance, He had been deemed equal, would He not have used every means that this might not be thought? But now He doth the contrary, saying, "If I do not the works of Him that sent Me,[1] believe Me not." (c. x. 37.) Indeed His saying, that "I am in the Father and the Father in Me" (c. xiv. 10), intimateth to us the equality. It would have behooved, if He had been inferior, to refute this opinion with much vehemence, and not at all to have said, "I am in the Father and the Father in me" (c. x. 30), or that, "We are One," or that, "He that hath seen Me, hath seen the Father." (c. xiv. 9.) Thus also, when His discourse was concerning power, He said, "I and the Father are One"; and when His discourse was concerning authority, He said again, "For as the Father raiseth up the dead and quickeneth them, even so the Son quickeneth whom He wilt" (c. v. 21); which it would be impossible that He should do were He of a different substance; or even allowing that it were possible, yet it would not have behooved to say this, lest they should suspect that the substance was one and the same. Since if in order that they may not suppose Him to be an enemy of God, He often even uttereth words unsuited to Him, much more should He then have done so; but now, His saying, "That they should honor the Son even as they honor the Father" (c. v. 23); His saying, "The works which He doeth, I do also" (c. v. 19); His saying that He is "the Resurrection, and the Life, and the Light of the world" (c. xi. 25; c. viii. 12), are the expressions of One making Himself equal to Him who begat Him, and confirming the suspicion which they entertained. Seest thou[2] how He maketh this speech and defense, to show that He broke not the Law, and that He not only doth not remove, but even confirmeth the opinion of His equality with the Father? So also when they said, "Thou blasphemest, because thou makest thyself God" (c. x. 33), from equality of works He established this thing.

[2.] And why say I that[3] the Son did this, when the Father also who took not[4] the flesh doeth the same thing? For He also endured that many lowly things should be said concerning Him for the salvation of the hearers. For the, "Adam, where art thou?" (Gen. iii. 9), and, "That I may know whether they have done altogether according to the cry of it" (Gen. xviii. 21); and, "Now I know that thou fearest God" (Gen. xxii. 12); and, "If they will hear" (Ezek. iii. 11); and, "If they will understand" (Deut. v. 29); and, "Who shall give the heart of this people to be so?" and the expression, "There is none like unto Thee among the gods, O Lord" (Ps. lxxx. 29); these and many other like sentences in the Old Testament, if a man should pick them out, he will find to be unworthy of the dignity of God. In the case of Ahab it is said, "Who shall entice Ahab for Me?" (2 Chron. xviii. 19.) And the continually preferring Himself to the gods of the heathen in the way of comparison, all these things are unworthy of God. Yet in another way they are made worthy of Him, for He is so kind, that for our salvation He careth not for expressions which become His dignity. Indeed, the becoming man is unworthy of Him, and the taking the form of a servant, and the speaking humble words, and the being clothed in[5] humble (garments), unworthy if one looks to His dignity, but worthy if one consider the unspeakable riches[6] of His lovingkindness. And there is another cause of the humility of His words. What is that? It is that they knew and confessed[7] the Father, but Him they knew not. Wherefore He continually betaketh Himself to the Father as being confessed by them, because He Himself was not as yet deemed worthy of credit; not on account of any inferiority of His own, but because of the folly and infirmity of the hearers. On this account He prayeth, and saith, "Father, I thank Thee that Thou hast heard Me." For if He quickeneth whom He will, and quickeneth in like manner as doth the Father, wherefore doth He call upon Him?

But it is time now to go through the passage from the beginning.[8] "Then they took up the stone where the dead man lay. And Jesus lifted up His eyes, and said, Father, I thank Thee that Thou hast heard Me. And I knew that Thou hearest Me always, but because of the people that stand by I said it, that they might believe that Thou hast sent Me." Let us then ask the heretic, Did He receive an impulse[9] from the prayer, and so raise the dead man? How then did He work other miracles without prayer? saying, "Thou evil spirit, I charge thee, come out of him" (Mark ix. 25); and, "I will, be thou clean" (Mark i. 41); and, "Arise, take up thy bed" (c. v. 8); and, "Thy sins be forgiven thee" (Matt. ix. 2); and to the sea, "Peace, be still." (Mark iv. 39.) In short, what hath He more than the Apostles, if so be that He also worketh by[10] prayer? Or rather I should say, that neither did they work all with prayer, but often they wrought without prayer,

---

[1] "My Father," N. T.
[2] al. "now to show that," &c.
[3] al. "if."
[4] al. "put not on."

[5] al. "enduring mean things."
[6] al. "greatness."
[7] al. "admired."
[8] al. "to enter on the passage itself."
[9] ρομὴν.
[10] al. "upon."

calling upon the Name of Jesus. Now, if His Name had such great power, how could He have needed prayer? Had He needed prayer, His Name would not have availed. When He wholly made man, what manner of prayer did He need? was there not then great equality of honor? "Let Us make," It saith, "man." (Gen. i. 26.) What could be greater sign of weakness, if He needed prayer? But let us see what the prayer was; " I thank Thee that Thou hast heard Me." Who now ever prayed in this manner? Before uttering any prayer, He saith, " I thank Thee," showing that He needed not prayer.[1] "And I knew that Thou hearest Me always." This He said not as though He Himself were powerless, but to show that His will and the Father's is one. But why did He assume the form of prayer? Hear, not me, but Himself, saying, " For the sake of the people which stand by, that they may believe that Thou hast sent Me." He said not, " That they may believe that I am inferior, that I have need of an impulse from above, that without prayer I cannot do anything; but, " That Thou hast sent Me." For all these things the prayer declareth, if we take it simply. He said not, " Thou hast sent me weak, acknowledging servitude, and doing nothing of Myself"; but dismissing all these things, that thou mayest have no such suspicions, He putteth the real cause of the prayer, " That they may not deem Me an enemy of God; that they may not say, He is not of God, that I may show them that the work hath been done according to Thy will." All but saying, " Had I been an enemy of God, what is done would not have succeeded," but the, " Thou heardest Me," is said in the case of friends and equals. " And I knew that Thou hearest Me always," that is, " in order that My will be done I need no prayer, except to persuade men that to Thee and Me belongeth one will." " Why then prayest Thou?" For the sake of the weak and grosser[2] sort.

Ver. 43. " And when He had thus spoken, He cried with a loud voice."

Why said He not, " In the name of My Father come forth"? Or why said He not, " Father, raise him up "? Why did he omit all these expressions, and after assuming the attitude of one praying, show by His actions His independent authority? Because this also was a part of His wisdom, to show condescension by words, but by His deeds, power. For since they had nothing else to charge Him with except that He was not of God, and since in this way they deceived many, He on this account most abundantly proveth this very point by what He saith, and in the way that their infirmity required. For it was in His power by other

means to show at once His agreement with the Father and His own dignity, but the multitude could not ascend so far. And He saith, " Lazarus, come forth."

[3.] This is that of which He spake, " The hour is coming, when the dead shall hear the voice of the Son of God, and they that hear shall live." (c. v. 28.) For, that thou mightest not think that He received the power of working from another, He taught thee this before, and gave proof by deeds, and said not, Arise, but, " Come forth," conversing with the dead man as though living. What can be equal to this authority? And if He doth it not by His own strength, what shall He have more than the Apostles, who say, " Why look ye so earnestly on us as though by our own power or holiness we had made this man to walk?" (Acts iii. 12.) For if, not working by His own power, He did not add what the Apostles said concerning themselves, they will in a manner be more truly wise than He, because they refused the glory. And[3] in another place, " Why do ye these things? We also are men of like passions as you." (Acts xiv. 15.) The Apostles since they did nothing of themselves, spoke in this way to persuade men of this; but He when the like opinion was formed concerning Him, would He not have removed the suspicion, if at least He did not act by His own authority? Who would assert this? But in truth Christ doeth the contrary, when He saith,[4] " Because of the people which stand by I said it, that they might believe"; so that had they believed, there would have been no need of prayer. Now if prayer were not beneath His dignity, why should He account them the cause of His praying? Why said He not, " I do it in order that they may believe that I am not equal to Thee"; for He ought on account of the suspicion to have come to this point. When He was suspected of breaking the Law, He used the very expression, even when they had not said anything, " Think not that I am come to destroy the Law " (Matt. v. 17); but in this place He establisheth their suspicion. In fact, what need was there at all of going such a round, and of using such dark sayings? It had been enough to say, " I am not equal," and to be rid of the matter. " But what," saith some one, " did He not say that, I do not My own will?" Even this He did in a covert way, and one suited to their infirmity, and from the same cause through which the prayer was made. But what meaneth " That Thou hast heard Me"? It meaneth,[5] " That there is nothing on My part opposed to Thee." As then the, " That Thou hast heard Me," is not

---

[1] al. some MSS. add, "for Thou doest all things, whatsoever I will, He saith."          [2] al. "meaner."

[3] al. again, "why look ye," &c., "we also," &c.
[4] al. but He even saith the contrary "because," &c.
[5] al. so then the "hearing Me always" meaneth, &c.

the saying of one declaring, that of Himself He had not the power, (for were this the case, it would be not only impotence but ignorance, if before praying He did not know that God would grant the prayer ; and if He knew not, how was it that He said, " I go that I may awake him," instead of, " I go to pray My Father to awake him ? ") As then this expression is a sign, not of weakness, but of identity of will, so also is the, " Thou hearest Me always." We must then either say this, or else that it was addressed to their suspicions. If now He was neither ignorant nor weak, it is clear that He uttereth these lowly words, that thou mayest be persuaded by their very excess, and mayest be compelled to confess, that they suit not His dignity, but are from condescension. What then say the enemies of truth ? " He spake not those words, Thou hast heard me," saith some one, " to the infirmity of the hearers, but in order to show a superiority." Yet this was not to show a superiority,[1] but to humble Himself greatly, and to show Himself as having nothing more than man. For to pray is not proper to God, nor to the sharer of the Throne. Seest thou then that He came to this[2] from no other cause than their unbelief ? Observe at least that the action beareth witness to His authority.

" He called, and the dead man came forth wrapped."[3] Then that the matter might not seem to be an appearance, (for his coming forth bound did not seem to be less marvelous than his resurrection,) Jesus commanded to loose him, in order that having touched and having been near him, they might see that it was really he. And He saith,

" Let him go."

Seest thou His freedom from boastfulness ? He doth not lead him on, nor bid him go about[4] with Him, lest He should seem to any to be showing him ; so well knew He how to observe moderation.

When the sign had been wrought, some wondered, others went and told it to the Pharisees.[5] What then did they ? When they ought to have been astonished and to have admired Him, they took counsel to kill Him who had raised the dead. What folly ! They thought to give up to death Him who had overcome death in the bodies of others.

Ver. 47. " And they said, What do we ? for this man doeth many miracles."

They still call Him " man," these who had received such proof of His divinity. " What do we ? " They ought to have believed, and served, and bowed down to Him, and no longer to have deemed Him a man.

Ver. 58. " If we let him thus alone, the Romans will come,[6] and will take away both our nation and city."[7]

What is it which they counsel to do ?[8] They wish to stir up the people, as though they themselves would be in danger on suspicion of establishing a kingdom. " For if," saith one of them, " the Romans learn[9] that this Man is leading the multitudes, they will suspect us,[10] and will come and destroy our city." Wherefore, tell me ? Did He teach revolt ? Did He not permit you to give tribute to Cæsar ? Did not ye wish to make Him a king, and He fly from you ? Did He not follow[11] a mean and unpretending[12] life, having neither house nor anything else of the kind ? They therefore said this, not from any such expectation, but from malice. Yet it so fell out contrary to their expectation, and the Romans took their nation and city when they had slain Christ. For the things done by Him were beyond all suspicion. For He who healed the sick, and taught the most excellent way of life, and commanded men to obey their rulers, was not establishing but undoing a tyranny. " But," saith some one, " we conjecture from former (impostors)." But they taught revolt, He the contrary. Seest thou that the words were but a pretense ? For what action of the kind did He exhibit ? Did He lead about with Him[13] pompous[14] guards ? had He a train of chariots ? Did He not seek the deserts ? But they, that they may not seem to be speaking from their own ill feeling,[15] say that all the city is in danger, that the common weal is being plotted against, and that they have to fear the worst. These were not the causes of your captivity, but things contrary to them ; both of this last, and of the Babylonish, and of that under Antiochus which followed : it was not that there were worshipers among you, but that there were among you those who did unjustly, and excited God to wrath, this caused you to be given up into bondage. But such a thing is envy, allowing men to see nothing which they ought to see, when it has once for all blinded the soul. Did He not teach men to be meek ? Did He not bid them when smitten on the right cheek to turn the other also ? Did He not bid them when injured to bear it ? to show greater readi-

---

[1] i.e. a mere superiority of the Father.    [2] i.e. to use prayer.
[3] Ver. 44. " And he that was dead came forth, bound hand and foot with grave clothes: and his face was bound about with a napkin." N. T. " Jesus saith unto them, Loose him." N. T.
[4] al. " walk."
[5] Ver. 45-47. " Then many of the Jews which came to Mary, and had seen the things which Jesus did, believed on Him. But some of them went their ways to the Pharisees, and told them what things Jesus had done. Then gathered the Chief Priests and Pharisees a council." N. T.

[6] al. " are coming."
[7] N. T. " All men will believe on Him, and the Romans shall come and take away both our place and nation."
[8] al. " which they mean to say ? "    [9] al. " see."
[10] al. " us about a kingdom."    [11] al. " exhibit."
[12] al. " plain."
[13] al. " did He surround Himself with."  [14] σοβοῦντας.
[15] ἀπὸ παθοῦς τοῦ ἑαυτῶν. Sav. reads τὸ π. τοῦ ἑ.

ness to endure evil, than others have to inflict it? Are these, tell me, the signs of one establishing a tyranny, and not rather of one pulling a tyranny down?

[4.] But, as I said, a dreadful thing is malice, and full of hypocrisy; this hath filled the world with ten thousand evils; through this malady the law courts are filled, from this comes the desire of fame and wealth, from this the love of rule, and insolence,[1] through this the roads have wicked robbers and the sea pirates,[2] from this proceed the murders through the world, through this our race is rent asunder, and whatever evil thou mayest see, thou wilt perceive to arise from this. This hath even burst into[3] the churches, this hath caused ten thousand dreadful things from the beginning, this is the mother of avarice, this malady hath turned all things upside down, and corrupted justice. For "gifts," It saith, "blind the eyes of the wise, and as a muzzle on the mouth turn away reproofs." (Ecclus. xx. 29, LXX. and marg. of E. V.) This makes slaves of freemen, concerning this we talk every day, and no good comes of it, we become worse than wild beasts; we plunder orphans, strip widows, do wrong to the poor, join woe to woe. "Alas! that the righteous hath perished from the earth!" (Mic. vii. 1, 2.) It is our part too henceforth to mourn, or rather we have need to say this every day. We profit nothing by our prayers, nothing by our advice and exhortation, it remaineth therefore that we weep. Thus did Christ; after having many times exhorted those in Jerusalem, when they profited nothing, He wept at their hardness.[4] This also do the Prophets, and this let us do now. Henceforth is the season for mourning and tears and wailing; it is seasonable for us also to say now, "Call for the mourning women, and send for the cunning women, that they may cry aloud" (Jer. ix. 17); perhaps thus we shall be able to cast out the malady of those who build splendid houses, of those who surround themselves with lands gotten by rapine. It is seasonable to mourn; but do ye take part with me in the mourning, ye who have been stripped and injured, by your mournings bring down my tears. But while mourning we will mourn, not for ourselves but for them; they have not injured you, but they have destroyed themselves; for you have

the Kingdom of heaven in return for the injustice done you, they hell in return for their gain. On this account it is better to be injured than to injure. Let us bewail them with a lamentation not of man's making,[5] but that from the Holy Scriptures with which the Prophets also wailed. With Isaiah let us wail bitterly, and say, "Woe, they that add house to house, that lay field to field, that they may take somewhat from their neighbor; will ye dwell alone upon the earth? Great houses and fair, and there shall be no inhabitants in them." (Isa. v. 8, 9.)

Let us mourn with Nahum, and say with him, "Woe to him that buildeth his house on high." (Perhaps Jer. xxii. 13.) Or rather let us mourn for them as Christ mourned for those of old. "Woe to you that are rich, for ye have received your consolation." (Luke vi. 24.) Let us, I beseech you, not cease thus lamenting, and if it be not unseemly, let us even beat our breasts for the carelessness of our brethren. Let us not weep for him who is already dead, but let us weep for the rapacious man, the grasping, the covetous, the insatiable. Why should we mourn for the dead, in whose case it is impossible henceforth to effect anything? Let us mourn for these who are capable even of change. But while we are lamenting, perhaps they will laugh. Even this is a worthy cause for lamentation, that they laugh when they ought to mourn. For had they been at all affected by our sorrows, it would have behooved us to cease from sorrowing on account of their promise of amendment; but since they are of an insensible disposition, let us continue to weep, not merely for the rich, but for the lovers of money, the greedy, the rapacious. Wealth is not an evil thing, (for we may use it rightly when we spend it upon those who have need,) but greediness is an evil, and it prepares[6] deathless punishments. Let us then bewail them; perhaps there will be some amendment; or even if they who have fallen in do not escape, others at least will not fall into the danger, but will guard against it. May it come to pass that both they may be freed from their malady, and that none of us may ever fall into it, that we all may in common obtain the promised goods, through the grace and lovingkindness of our Lord Jesus Christ, to whom be glory for ever and ever. Amen.

---

[1] al. "vainglory."
[2] al. "the roads and the sea are beset."
[3] εἰσεκώμασε.
[4] al. "misfortune."
[5] al. "not the common."
[6] προξενοῦσα.

# HOMILY LXV.

John xi. 49, 50.

"And one of them, Caiaphas, being the High Priest that same year, said unto them, Ye know nothing at all, nor consider that it is expedient that one man should die for the people, and that the whole nation perish not," &c.

[1.] "The heathen are stuck fast in the destruction which they made; in the trap which they hid is their foot taken." (Ps. ix. 15, LXX.) This hath been the case with the Jews. They said that they would kill Jesus, lest the Romans should come and take away their place and nation; and when they had killed Him, these things happened unto them, and when they had done that by doing which they thought to escape, they yet did not escape. He who was slain is in Heaven, and they who slew have for their portion hell. Yet they did not consider these things; but what? "They desired," It saith, "from that day forth to kill Him" (ver. 53), for they said, "The Romans will come, and will take away our nation; and a certain one of them, Caiaphas, being High Priest that year, said," (being more shameless than the rest,) "Ye know nothing." What the others made matter of doubt, and put forth in the way of deliberation, this man cried aloud, shamelessly, openly, audaciously. For what saith he? "Ye know nothing, nor consider that it is expedient that one man should die, and that the whole nation perish not."

Ver. 51. "And this spake he not of himself, but being High Priest he prophesied."[1]

Seest thou how great is the force of the High Priest's authority? for, since he had in any wise been deemed worthy of the High Priesthood, although unworthy thereof, he prophesied, not knowing what he said; and the grace merely made use of his mouth, but touched not his accursed heart. Indeed many others have foretold things to come, although unworthy to do so, as Nebuchadnezzar, Pharaoh, Balaam; and the reason of all is evident. But what he saith is of this kind. "Ye still sit quiet, ye give heed but carelessly to this matter, and know not how to despise one man's safety for the sake of the community." See how great is the power of the Spirit; from an evil imagination It was able to bring forth words full of marvelous prophecy. The Evangelist calleth the Gentiles "children

of God," from what was about to be: as also Christ Himself saith, "Other sheep I have" (c. x. 16), so calling them from what should afterwards come to pass.

But what is, "being High Priest that year"? This matter as well as the rest had become corrupt; for from the time that offices became matters of purchase, they were no longer priests for the whole period of their lives, but for a year. Notwithstanding, even in this state of things the Spirit was still present. But when they lifted up their hands against Christ, then It left them, and removed to the Apostles. This the rending of the veil declared, and the voice of Christ which said, "Behold, your house is left unto you desolate." (Matt. xxiii. 38.) And Josephus, who lived a short time after, saith, that certain Angels who yet remained with them, (to see) if they would alter their ways, left them.[2] While the vineyard stood, all things[3] went on; but when they had slain the Heir, no longer so, but they perished. And God having taken it from the Jews, as a glorious garment from an unprofitable son, gave it to right-minded servants of the Gentiles, leaving the others desolate and naked. It was, moreover, no small thing that even an enemy should prophesy this. This might draw over others also. For in respect of his[4] will, matters fell out contrariwise, since,[5] when He died, the faithful were on this account delivered from the punishment to come. What meaneth, "That He might gather together those near and those afar off" (ver. 52)? He made them one Body. The dweller in Rome deemeth the Indians a member of himself. What is equal to this "gathering together"? And the Head of all is Christ.

Ver. 53. "From that day forth the Jews[6] took counsel to put Him to death."

And, in truth, had sought to do so before; for the Evangelist saith, "Therefore the Jews sought to kill Him" (c. v. 18); and, "Why seek ye to kill Me?" (c. vii. 19.) But then they only sought, now they ratified their determination, and treated the action as their business.

Ver. 54. "But Jesus walked no more openly in Jewry."[7]

---

[1] "Being High Priest that year, he prophesied that Jesus should die for that nation," ver. 52, "and not for that nation only, but that also He should gather together in one the children of God that were scattered abroad." G. T.

[2] De Bell. Jud. l. 6, 31. "During the Festival called Pentecost, the Priests having come by night into the Inner Temple to perform their services, as was their custom, reported that they perceived a motion and noise, and after that a voice as of a multitude, Let us depart hence."　　[3] πάντα ἐγίνετο.
[4] "Caiaphas."　　[5] al. "and."　　[6] "they," N. T.
[7] Ver. 54. "Jesus therefore walked no more openly among the Jews; but went thence unto a country near to the wilderness, into

[2.] Again He saveth Himself in a human manner, and this He doth continually. But I have mentioned the reason for which He often departed and withdrew. And at this time He dwelt in Ephratah, near the wilderness, and there He tarried with His disciples. How thinkest thou that those disciples were confounded when they beheld Him saving Himself after the manner of a man? After this no man followed Him. For since the Feast was nigh, all were running to Jerusalem; but they,[1] at a time when all others were rejoicing and holding solemn assembly, hide themselves, and are in danger. Yet still they tarried with Him. For they hid themselves in Galilee, at the time of the Passover and the Feast of Tabernacles; and after this again during the Feast, they only of all were with their Master in flight and concealment, manifesting their good will to Him. Hence Luke recordeth that He said, "I abode with you in temptations";[2] and this He said, showing that they were strengthened by His influence.[3]

Ver. 55.[4] "And many went up from the country to purify themselves."

Ver. 57. "And the High Priests and Pharisees had commanded that they should lay hands on Him."

A marvelous purification, with a murderous will, with homicidal intentions, and blood-stained hands!

Ver. 56. "And they said, Think ye that he will not come to the feast?"

By means of the Passover they plotted against Him, and made the time of feasting a time of murder, that is, He there would fall into their hands, because the season summoned Him. What impiety! When they needed greater carefulness, and to forgive those who had been taken for the worst offenses, then they attempted to ensnare One who had done no wrong. Yet by acting thus they had already not only profited nothing, but become ridiculous. For this end coming among them continually He escapeth, and restraineth them when they take counsel[5] to kill Him, and maketh them to be in perplexity, desiring to prick them by the display of His power; that when they took Him, they might know that what had been done was done, not by their power, but by His permission. For not even at that time could they take Him, and this though Bethany was near; and when they did take Him, He cast them backwards.

Ch. xii. ver. 1, 2. "Then six days before the Passover He came to Bethany, where Lazarus was, and feasted with them; and Martha served, but Lazarus sat at meat."[6]

This was a proof of the genuineness of his resurrection, that after many days he both lived and ate. "And Martha ministered"; whence it is clear that the meal was in her house, for they received Jesus as loving and beloved. Some, however, say, that it took place in the house of another. Mary did not minister, for she was a disciple. Here again she acted in the more spiritual manner. For she did not minister as being invited, nor did she afford her services to all alike. But she directeth[7] the honor to Him alone, and approacheth Him not as a man, but as a God. On this account she poured out the ointment,[8] and wiped (His feet) with the hairs of her head, which was the action of one who did not entertain the same opinion concerning Him as did others; yet Judas rebuked her, under the pretense forsooth of carefulness. What then saith Christ? "She hath done a good work for My burying."[9] But why did He not expose the disciple in the case of the woman, nor say to him what the Evangelist hath declared, that on account of his own thieving he rebuked her? In His abundant longsuffering He wished to bring him to a better mind.[10] For because He knew that he was a traitor, He from the beginning often rebuked him, saying, "Not all believe," and, "One of you is a devil." (c. vi. 64.) He showed them that He knew him to be a traitor, yet He did not openly rebuke him, but bare with him, desiring to recall him. How then saith another Evangelist, that all the disciples used these words? (Matt. xxvi. 70.) All used them, and so did he, but the others not with like purpose. And if any one ask why He put the bag of the poor in the hands of a thief, and made him steward who was a lover of money, we would reply, that God knoweth the secret reason; but that, if we may say something by conjecture, it was that He might cut off from him all excuse. For he could not say that he did this thing[11] from love of money, (for he had in the bag sufficient to allay his desire,) but from excessive wickedness which Christ wished to restrain, using

a city called Ephraim, and there continued with his disciples." 55. "And the Jews' Passover was nigh at hand." N. T.
[1] i.e. the disciples.
[2] Luke xxii. 28. "Ye are they which have continued with Me in My temptations." [3] ῥοπῆς.
[4] Ver. 55-57. "And many went out of the country up to Jerusalem before the Passover to purify themselves. Then sought they for Jesus, and spake among themselves as they stood in the Temple, What think ye, that He will not come to the feast? Now both the Chief Priests and Pharisees had given a commandment, that if any man knew where He were, he should show it, that they might take Him." N. T. [5] al. "wish."

[6] Ch. xii. ver. 1, 2. "Then Jesus, six days before the Passover, came to Bethany, where Lazarus was which had been dead, whom He raised from the dead. There they made Him a supper, and Martha served, but Lazarus was one of them that sat at the table with Him." N. T. [7] περίστησι.
[8] Ver. 3-6. "Then took Mary a pound of ointment of spikenard, very precious, and anointed the feet of Jesus, and wiped His feet with her hair: and the whole house was filled with the odor of the ointment. Then saith one of His disciples, Judas Iscariot, Simon's son, which should betray Him, Why was not this ointment sold for three hundred pence, and given to the poor? This he said, not that he cared for the poor, but because he was a thief, and had the bag, and bare what was put therein."
[9] These words are from St. Matthew or St. Mark. In St. John we read, ver. 7, "Then said Jesus, Let her alone, against the day of My burying hath she kept this."
[10] ἐντρέπειν. [11] i.e. the betrayal.

much condescension towards him. Wherefore He did not even rebuke him as stealing, although aware of it, stopping the way to his wicked desire, and taking from him all excuse. " Let her alone," He saith, " for against the day of My burying hath she done¹ this." Again, He maketh mention of the traitor in speaking of His burial. But him the reproof reacheth not, nor doth the expression soften² him, though sufficient to inspire him with pity : as if He had said, " I am burdensome and troublesome, but wait a little while, and I shall depart." This too he intended in saying,

Ver. 8. " But Me ye have not always."³

But none of these things turned back⁴ that savage madman ; yet in truth Jesus said and did far more than this, He washed his feet that night, made him a sharer in the table and the salt, a thing which is wont to restrain even the souls of robbers, and spake other words, enough to melt a stone, and this, not long before, but on the very day, in order that not even time might cause it to be forgotten. But he stood out against all.

[3.] For a dreadful, a dreadful thing is the love of money, it disables both eyes and ears, and makes men worse to deal with than a wild beast, allowing a man to consider neither conscience, nor friendship, nor fellowship, nor the salvation of his own soul, but having withdrawn them at once from all these things, like some harsh mistress,⁵ it makes those captured by it its slaves. And the dreadful part of so bitter a slavery is, that it persuades them even to be grateful for it ; and the more they become enslaved, the more doth their pleasure increase ; and in this way especially the malady becomes incurable, in this way the monster becomes hard to conquer. This made Gehazi a leper instead of a disciple and a prophet ; this destroyed Ananias and her with him ;⁶ this made Judas a traitor ; this corrupted the rulers of the Jews, who received gifts, and became the partners of thieves. This hath brought in ten thousand wars, filling the ways with blood, the cities with wailings and lamentations. This hath made meals to become impure, and tables accursed, and hath filled food with transgression ; therefore hath Paul called it " idolatry " (Col. iii. 5), and not even so hath he deterred men from it. And why calleth he it " idolatry " ? Many possess wealth, and dare not use it, but consecrate it, handing it down untouched, not daring to touch it, as though it were some dedicated thing. And if at any time they are forced to do so, they feel as though they had done something unlawful. Besides, as the Greek carefully tends

his graven image,⁷ so thou entrusteth thy gold to doors and bars ; providing a chest instead of a shrine, and laying it up in silver vessels. But thou dost not bow down to it as he to the image? Yet thou showest all kind of attention to it.

Again, he would rather give up his eyes or his life than his graven image. So also would those who love gold. " But," saith one, " I worship not the gold." Neither doth he, he saith, worship the image, but the devil that dwelleth in it ; and in like manner thou, though thou worship not the gold, yet thou worshipest that devil who springeth on thy soul, from the sight of the gold and thy lust for it. For more grievous than an evil spirit is the lust of money-loving, and many obey it more than others do idols. For these last in many things disobey, but in this case they yield everything, and whatever it telleth them to do, they obey. What saith it ? " Be at war with all," it saith, " at enmity with all, know not nature, despise God, sacrifice to me thyself," and in all they obey. To the graven images they sacrifice oxen and sheep, but avarice saith, Sacrifice to me thine own soul, and the man obeyeth. Seest thou what kind of altars it hath, what kind of sacrifices it receiveth ? The covetous shall not inherit the Kingdom of God, but not even so do they fear. (1 Cor. vi. 10.) Yet this desire is⁸ weaker than all the others, it is not inborn, nor natural, (for then it would have been placed in us at the beginning ;) but there was no gold at the beginning, and no man desired gold. But if you will, I will tell you whence the mischief entered. By each man's envying the one before him, men have increased the disease, and he who has gotten in advance provokes him who had no desire. For when men see splendid houses, and extensive lands, and troops of slaves, and silver vessels, and great heaps of apparel, they use every means to outdo them ; so that the first set of men are causes of the second, and these of those who come after. Now if they would be sober-minded, they would not be teachers (of evil) to others ; yet neither have these any excuse. For others there are also who despise riches. " And who," saith one, " despises them ? " For the terrible thing is, that, because wickedness is so general, this seems to have become impossible, and it is not even believed that one can act aright. Shall I then mention many both in cities and in the mountains ? And what would it avail ? Ye will not from their example become better. Besides, our discourse hath not now this purpose, that you should empty yourselves of your substance ; I would that ye could do so ; however, since the burden is too

---

¹ " kept," N. T.
² al. " nor will the expression check."
³ " For the poor always ye have with you, but Me," &c., N. T.
⁴ or, " bent."　　⁵ τυραννίς.　　⁶ τοὺς περί.
⁷ al. " as one the graven image of stone, so thou," &c.
⁸ i.e. in itself.

heavy for you, I constrain you not ; only I advise you that you desire not what belongs to others, that you impart somewhat of your own. Many such we shall find, contented with what belongs to them, taking care of their own, and living on honest labor. Why do we not rival and imitate these? Let us think of those who have gone before us. Do not their possessions stand, preserving nothing but their name ; such an one's bath, such an one's suburban seat and lodging? Do we not, when we behold them, straightway groan, when we consider what toil he endured, what rapine committed? and now he is nowhere seen, but others luxuriate in his possessions, men whom he never expected would do so, perhaps even his enemies, while he is suffering extremest punishment. These things await us also ; for we shall certainly die, and shall certainly have to submit to the same end. How much wrath, tell me, how much expense, how many enmities these men incurred ; and what the gain? Deathless punishment, and the having no consolation ; and the being not only while alive, but when gone, accused by all? What? when we see the images of the many laid up in their houses, shall we not weep the more? Of a truth well said the Prophet, "Verily, every man living disquieteth himself in vain" (Ps. xxxix. 11, LXX.) ; for anxiety about such things is indeed disquiet, disquiet and superfluous trouble. But it is not so in the everlasting mansions, not so in those tabernacles. Here one hath labored, and another enjoys ; but there each shall possess his own labors, and shall receive a manifold reward. Let us press forward to get that possession, there let us prepare for ourselves houses, that we may rest in Christ Jesus our Lord, with whom to the Father and the Holy Ghost be glory, for ever and ever. Amen.

# HOMILY LXVI.

JOHN xii. 8.

"Much people of the Jews therefore knew that He was there, and they came, not for Jesus' sake only, but that they might see Lazarus also, whom He had raised from the dead."

[1.] As wealth is wont to hurl into destruction [1] those who are not heedful, so also is power ; the first leads into covetousness, the second into pride. See, for instance, how the subject multitude of the Jews is sound, and their rulers corrupt ; for that the first of these believed Christ, the Evangelists continually assert, saying, that "many of the multitude believed on Him" (c. vii. 31, 48) ; but they who were of the rulers, believed not. And they themselves say, not the multitude,[2] "Hath any of the rulers believed on Him?" But what saith one? "The multitude who know not God [3] are accursed" (c. vii. 49) ; the believers they call accursed, and themselves the slayers, wise. In this place also, having beheld the miracle, the many believed ; but the rulers were not contented with their own evil deeds,[4] they also attempted to kill Lazarus.[5] Suppose they did attempt to slay Christ because He broke the Sabbath, because He made Himself equal to the Father, and because of the Romans whom ye allege, yet what charge had they against Lazarus, that they sought to kill him? Is the having received a benefit a crime? Seest thou how murderous is their will? Yet He had worked many miracles ; but none exasperated them so much as this one, not the paralytic, not the blind. For this was more wonderful in its nature, and was wrought after many others, and it was a strange thing to see one, who had been dead four days, walking and speaking. An honorable action, in truth, for the feast, to mix up the solemn assembly with murders. Besides, in the one case [6] they thought to charge Him concerning the Sabbath, and so to draw away the multitudes ; but here, since they had no fault to find with Him, they make the attempt on the man who had been healed. For here they could not even say that He was opposed to the Father, since the prayer stopped their mouths. Since then the charge which they continually brought against Him was removed, and the miracle was evident, they hasten to murder. So that they would have done the same in the case of the blind man, had it not been in their power to find fault respecting the Sabbath. Besides, that man was of no note, and they cast him out of the temple ; but Lazarus was a person of distinction, as is clear, since many came to comfort his sisters ; and the miracle was done in the sight of all, and most marvelously. On

---

[1] ἐκτραχηλίζειν.
[2] or, "is it not the multitude."　　　[3] "the Law," N. T.
[4] οἰκείοις ἀκοῖς, i.e. in matters affecting themselves.
[5] Ver. 10, 11. "But the Chief Priests consulted that they might put Lazarus also to death, because that by reason of him many of the Jews went away, and believed on Jesus."

[6] i.e. that of the blind man.

which account all ran to see. This then stung them, that while the feast was going on, all should leave it and go to Bethany. They set their hand therefore to kill him, and thought they were not[1] daring anything, so murderous were they. On this account the[2] Law at its commencement opens with this, "Thou shalt not kill" (Ex. xx. 13) ; and the Prophet brings this charge against them, "Their hands are full of blood." (Isa. i. 15.)

But how, after not walking openly in Jewry, and retiring into the wilderness, doth He again enter openly?[3] Having quenched their anger by retiring, He cometh to them when they were stilled. Moreover, the multitude which went before and which followed after was sufficient to cast them into an agony ; for no sign so much attracted the people as that of Lazarus. And another Evangelist saith, that they strewed their garments under His feet[4] (Matt. xxi. 8), and that "the whole city was moved" (Matt. xxi. 10) ; with so great honor did He enter. And this He did, figuring one prophecy and fulfilling another ; and the same act was the beginning of the one and the end of the other. For the, "Rejoice, for thy King cometh unto thee meek" (Zech. ix. 9), belonged to Him as fulfilling a prophecy, but the sitting upon an ass was the act of one prefiguring a future event, that He was about to have the impure race of the Gentiles subject to Him.

But how say the others, that He sent disciples, and said, "Loose the ass and the colt" (Matt. xxi. 2), while John saith nothing of the kind, but that "having found a young ass, He sat upon it"? Because it is likely that both circumstances took place, and that He after the ass was loosed, while the disciples were bringing it, found (the colt), and sat upon it. And they took the small branches of palm trees and olives, and strewed their garments in the way, showing that they now had a higher opinion concerning Him than of a Prophet, and said,

Ver. 13. "Hosannah, blessed is He that cometh in the name of the Lord."

Seest thou that this most choked them, the persuasion which all men had that He was not an enemy of God? And this most divided the people, His saying that He came from the Father. But what meaneth,

Ver. 15. "Rejoice greatly,[5] daughter of Zion"?

Because all their kings had for the most part been an unjust and covetous kind of men, and

had given them over to their enemies, and had perverted the people, and made them subject to their foes ; "Be of good courage," It saith, "this is not such an one, but meek and gentle " ; as is shown by the ass, for He entered not with an army in His train, but having an ass alone.

Ver. 16. "But this," saith the Evangelist, "the disciples knew not, that it was written of Him."[6]

[2.] Seest thou that they were ignorant on most points, because He did not reveal to them? For when He said, "Destroy this Temple, and in three days I will raise it up" (c. ii. 19), neither then did the disciples understand.[7] And another Evangelist saith, that "the saying was hid from them" (Luke xviii. 34), and they knew not that He should rise from the dead. Now this was with reason concealed from them, (wherefore another Evangelist saith, that as they heard it from time to time, they grieved and were dejected,[8] and this because they understood not the saying concerning the Resurrection,) it was with reason concealed, as being too high for them : but why was not the matter of the ass revealed to them? Because this was a great thing also. But observe the wisdom of the Evangelist, how he is not ashamed to parade their former ignorance. That it was written they knew, that it was written of Him they knew not. For it would have offended them if He being a King were about to suffer such things, and be so betrayed. Besides, they could not at once have taken in the knowledge of the Kingdom of which He spake ; for another Evangelist saith, that they thought the words were spoken of a kingdom of this world. (Matt. xx. 21.)

Ver. 17. "But the multitude bare witness that He had raised Lazarus."[9]

For so many would not have been suddenly changed, unless they had believed in the miracle.

Ver. 19. "The Pharisees therefore said among themselves, Perceive ye how ye prevail nothing? behold, the world is gone after Him."

Now this seems to me to be said by those who felt rightly, but had not courage to speak boldly, and who then would restrain the others by pointing to the result, as though they were attempting impossibilities. Here again they call the multitude "the world." For Scripture is wont to call by the name "world" both the creation, and those who live in wickedness ; the one, when It saith, "Who bringeth out His world[10] by number" (Isa. xl. 26) ; the other when It saith, "The

---

[1] Ben. "did not so much as think they were."
[2] i.e. the second Table.
[3] Ver. 12-15. "On the next day, much people that had come to the feast, when they heard that Jesus was coming to Jerusalem, took branches of palm trees, and went forth to meet Him, and cried, Hosanna, Blessed is the King of Israel that cometh in the name of the Lord. And Jesus, when He had found a young ass, sat thereon, as it is written, Fear not, daughter of Sion ; behold, thy King cometh, sitting on an ass's colt."
[4] "in the way," N. T.       [5] "Fear not," N. T.

[6] Ver. 16. "These things understood not the disciples at the first: but when Jesus was glorified, then remembered they that these things were written of Him, and that they had done these things unto Him." N. T.
[7] al. "neither did they know this."       [8] ἐν κατηφείᾳ.
[9] Ver. 17, 18. "The people therefore that was with Him when He called Lazarus out of his grave, and raised him from the dead, bare record. For this cause the people also met Him, for that they heard that He had done this miracle." N. T.
[10] E. V. "host."

world hateth not[1] you, but Me it hateth." (c. vii. 7.) And these things it is necessary to know exactly, that we may not through the signification of words afford a handle to the heretics.

Ver. 20. "And there were certain of the Greeks that came up to worship at the Feast."

Being now near to become proselytes, they were at[2] the Feast. When therefore the report concerning Him was imparted to them, they say,

Ver. 21. "We would see Jesus."[3]

Philip gives place to Andrew as being before him, and communicates the matter to him. But neither doth he at once act with authority; for he had heard that saying, "Go not into the way of the Gentiles" (Matt. x. 5): therefore having communicated with the disciple, he refers the matter to his Master. For they both spoke to Him. But what saith He?

Ver. 23, 24. "The hour is come, that the Son of Man should be glorified. Verily, verily, I say unto you, Except a corn of wheat fall into the ground and die, it abideth alone."

What is, "The hour is come"? He had said, "Go not into the way of the Gentiles," (thus cutting away all excuse of ignorance from the Jews,) and had restrained the disciples. When therefore the Jews continued disobedient, and the others desired to come to Him, "Now," saith He, "it is time to proceed to My Passion, since all things are fulfilled. For if we were to continue to wait for those who are disobedient and not admit these who even desire to come, this would be unbefitting our tender care." Since then He was about to allow the disciples to go to the Gentiles after the Crucifixion, and beheld them springing on before, He said, "It is time to proceed to the Cross." For He would not allow them to go sooner, that it might be for a testimony unto them.[4] Until that by their deeds the Jews rejected Him, until they crucified Him, He said not, "Go and make disciples of all nations" (Matt. xxviii. 19), but, "Go not into the way of the Gentiles" (Matt. x. 5), and, "I am not sent but unto the lost sheep of the house of Israel" (Matt xv. 24), and, "It is not meet to take the children's bread and give it unto dogs." (Matt. xv. 26.) But when they hated Him, and so hated as to kill Him, it was superfluous to persevere while they repulsed Him. For they refused Him, saying, "We have no king but Cæsar." (c. xix. 15.) So that at length He left them, when they had left Him. Therefore He saith, "How often would I have gathered your children together, and ye would not?" (Matt. xxiii. 37.)

What is, "Except a grain of corn fall into the ground and die"? He speaketh of the Cross, for that they might not be confounded at seeing, that just when Greeks also came to Him, then He was slain, He saith to them, "This very thing specially causeth them to come, and shall increase the preaching of Me." Then since He could not so well persuade them by words, He goeth about to prove this from actual experience, telling them that this is the case with corn; it beareth the more fruit when it hath died. "Now," saith He, "if this be the case with seeds, much more with Me." But the disciples understood not what was spoken. Wherefore the Evangelist continually putteth this,[5] as making excuse for their flight afterwards. This same argument Paul also hath raised when speaking of the Resurrection.

[3.] What sort of excuse then will they have who disbelieve the Resurrection, when the action is practiced each day, in seeds, in plants, and in the case of our own generation? for first it is necessary that the seed die, and that then the generation take place. But, in short, when God doeth anything, reasonings are of no use; for how did He make us out of those things that were not? This I say to Christians, who assert that they believe the Scriptures; but I shall also say something else drawn from human reasonings. Of men some live in vice, others in virtue; and of those who live in vice, many have attained to extreme old age in prosperity, many of the virtuous after enduring the contrary. When then shall each receive his deserts? At what season? "Yea," saith some one, "but there is no resurrection of the body." They hear not Paul, saying, "This corruptible must put on incorruption." (1 Cor. xv. 53.) He speaks not of the soul, for the soul is not corrupted; moreover, "resurrection" is said of that which fell, and that which fell was the body. But why wilt thou have it that there is no resurrection of the body? Is it not possible with God? But this it were utter folly to say. Is it unseemly? Why is it unseemly, that the corruptible which shared the toil and death, should share also the crowns? For were it unseemly,[6] it would not have been created at the beginning, Christ would not have taken the flesh again. But to show that He took it again and raised it up, hear what He saith: "Reach[7] hither thy fingers" (c. xx. 27); and, "Behold, a spirit hath not bones and sinews."[8] (Luke xxiv. 39.) But why did He raise Lazarus again, if it would have been better to rise without a body? Why doth He this, classing it as a miracle and a benefit? Why did He give nourishment at all? Be not therefore deceived

---

1 "cannot hate," N. T.
2 perhaps, "went to," ἤεσαν, conj. for ἦσαν.
3 Ver. 21, 22. "The same came therefore to Philip, which was of Bethsaida in Galilee, and desired him, saying, Sir, we would see Jesus. Philip cometh and telleth Andrew, and again Andrew and Philip tell Jesus." N. T.　　　4 i.e. to the Jews.

5 i.e. that they did not understand.　7 βάλε [φέρε, G. T.].
6 i.e. the body.　8 "flesh and bones," N. T.

by the heretics, beloved : for there is a Resurrection and there is a Judgment, but they deny these things, who desire not to give account of their actions.   For this Resurrection must be such as was that of Christ, for He was the first fruits, the first born of the dead.   But if the Resurrection is this,[1] a purifying of the soul, a deliverance from sin, and if Christ sinned not, how did He rise again?   And how have we been delivered from the curse, if so be that He also sinned?   And now saith He, " The prince of this world cometh, and had nothing in Me "? (c. xiv. 30.)   They are the words of One declaring His sinlessness.   According to them therefore He either did not rise again ; or that He might rise,[2] He sinned before His Resurrection.   But He both rose again, and did no sin.   Therefore He rose in the Body, and these wicked doctrines are nothing else than the offspring of vainglory.   Let us then fly this malady.   For, It is saith, " evil communications corrupt good manners."   (1 Cor. xv. 33.) These are not the doctrines of the Apostles ; Marcion and Valentius have newly invented them.   Let us then flee them, beloved, for a pure life profits nothing when doctrines are corrupt ; as on the other hand neither do sound doctrines, if the life be corrupt.   The heathen were the parents of these notions, and those heretics reared them, having received them from Gentile philosophers, asserting that matter is uncreated, and many such like things.   As then they asserted that there could be no Artificer[3] unless there were some uncreated subject matter, so also they disallowed the Resurrection.   But let us not heed them, as knowing that the power of God is all sufficient.[4]   Let us not heed them. To you I say this ; for *we* will not decline the battle with them.   But the man who is unarmed and naked, though he fall among the weak, though he be the stronger, will easily be vanquished.   Had you given heed to the Scriptures, had you sharpened yourselves each day, I would not have advised you to flee the combat with them, but would have counseled you to grapple with them ; for strong is truth.   But since you know not how to use the Scriptures, I fear the struggle, lest they take you unarmed and cast you down.   For there is nothing, there is nothing weaker than those who are bereft of the aid of

the Spirit.   If these heretics employ the wisdom of the Gentiles, we must not admire, but laugh at them, because they employ foolish teachers. For those men were not able to find out anything sound, either concerning God or the creation, and things which the widow among us is acquainted with, Pythagoras did not yet know, but said that the soul becomes a bush, or a fish, or a dog.   To these, tell me, ought you to give heed?   And how could it be reasonable to do so?   They are great men in their district,[5] grow beautiful curls, and are enfolded in cloaks ; thus far goes their philosophy ; but if you look within there is dust and ashes and nothing sound, but " their throat is an open sepulcher " (Ps. v. 9), having all things full of impurity and corruption,[6] and all their doctrines (full) of worms.   For instance, the first of them said that water was God, his successor fire, another one air, and[7] they descended to things corporeal ; ought we then, tell me, to admire these, who never even had the thought of the incorporeal God?  and if they did ever gain it afterwards, it was after conversing in Egypt with our people.   But, that we bring not upon you much confusion, let us here close our discourse.   For should we begin to set before you their doctrine, and what they have said about God, what about matter, what about the soul, what about the body, much ridicule will follow.   And they will not even require to be accused by us, for they have attacked each other ; and he who wrote against us the book concerning matter, made away with himself.   Therefore that we may not vainly delay you, nor wind together[8] a labyrinth of words, leaving these things we will bid you keep fast hold of the listening to the Holy Scriptures, and not fight with[9] words to no purpose ; as also Paul exhorteth Timothy (2 Tim. 2, 14), filled though he was with much wisdom, and possessing the power of miracles.   Let us now obey him, and leaving trifling let us hold fast to real works, I mean to brotherly-kindness and hospitality ; and let us make much account of almsgiving, that we may obtain the promised good things, through the grace and lovingkindness of our Lord Jesus Christ, to whom be glory for endless ages.[10]   Amen.

---

[1] i.e. which heretics say it is.
[2] al. " if He rose."
[3] δημιουργὸς.
[4] al. " almighty."

[5] κώμη.
[6] ἰχώρος.
[7] al. " and all."
[8] or, " unwind."
[9] or, " about."
[10] al. " To whom with the Father and the Holy Ghost be glory now and for the endless ages of eternity."

# HOMILY LXVII.

JOHN xii. 25, 26.

" He that loveth his life shall lose it, and he that hateth
his life in this world shall keep it unto life eternal.
If any man serve Me, let him follow Me."

[1.] SWEET is the present life, and full of much
pleasure, yet not to all, but to those who are
riveted to it. Since, if any one look to heaven
and see the beauteous things there, he will soon
despise this life, and make no account of it.
Just as the beauty of an object is admired while
none more beautiful is seen, but when a better
appears, the former is despised. If then we
would choose to look to that beauty, and observe
the splendor of the kingdom there, we should
soon free ourselves from our present chains; for
a kind of chain it is, this sympathy with present
things. And hear what Christ saith to bring us
in to this, " He that loveth his life shall lose it,
and he that hateth his life in this world shall
keep it unto life eternal; if any man serve Me,
let him follow Me "; and, " Where I am, there
is[1] My servant also." The words seem like a
riddle, yet they are not so, but are full of much
wisdom. But how shall " he that loveth his life,
lose it "? When he doeth its unseemly desires,
when he gratifies it where he ought not. Wherefore one exhorteth us, saying, " Walk not in the
desires of thy soul " (Ecclus. xviii. 30); for so
wilt thou destroy it since it leadeth away from
the path leading to virtue; just as, on the contrary, " he that hateth it in this world, shall save
it." But what meaneth, " He that hateth it "?
He who yields not to it when it commands what
is pernicious. And He said not, " he that yieldeth not to it," but, " He that hateth it "; for as
we cannot endure even to hear the voice of
those we hate, nor to look upon them with pleasure, so from the soul also we must turn away
with vehemence, when it commands things contrary to what is pleasing to God. For since He
was now about to say much to them concerning death, His own death, and saw that they
were dejected[2] and desponding, He spake very
strongly, saying, " What say I? If ye bear not
valiantly My death? Nay, if ye die not yourselves, ye will gain nothing." Observe also how
He softens the discourse. It was a very grievous
and sad thing to be told, that the man who loves
life should die. And why speak I of old times,
when even now we shall find many gladly enduring to suffer anything, in order to enjoy the

present life, and this too when they are persuaded
concerning things to come; who when they behold buildings, and works of art, and contrivances, weep, uttering the reflection, " How many
things man inventeth, and yet becometh dust!
So great is the longing after this present life."
To undo these bonds then, Christ saith, " He
that hateth his soul in this world, shall keep it
unto life eternal." For that thou mayest know
that He spake as exhorting them, and dissipat-
ing their fear, hear what comes next.
" If any man serve Me, let him follow Me."
Speaking of death, and requiring the following
which is by works. For certainly he that serveth
must follow him who is served. And observe at
what time He said these things to them; not
when they were persecuted, but when they were
confident; when they thought they were in
safety on account of the honor and attention of
the many, when they might rouse themselves and
hear, " Let him take up his cross, and follow
Me " (Matt. xvi. 24); that is, " Be ever,"[3] He
saith, " prepared against dangers, against death,
against your departure hence." Then after He
had spoken what was hard to bear, He putteth
also the prize. And of what kind was this? The
following Him, and being where He is; showing
that Resurrection shall succeed death. For,
saith He,
" Where I am, there is[4] My servant also."
But where is Christ? In heaven. Let us
therefore even before the Resurrection remove
thither in soul and mind.
" If any man serve Me, the Father shall love[5]
him."
Why said He not, " I "? Because they did
not as yet hold a right opinion concerning Him,
but held a higher opinion of the Father. For
how could they imagine anything great concerning Him, who did not even know that He was
to rise again? Wherefore He said to the sons of
Zebedee, " It is not mine to give, but it shall be
given to them for whom it is prepared by my
Father " (Mark x. 40), yet He it is that judgeth. But in this passage He also establisheth
His genuine sonship.[6] For as the servants of
His own Son, so will the Father receive them.
Ver. 27. " Now is My soul troubled; and
what shall I say? Father, save me from this
hour."

---

[1] " shall be," N. T.
[2] al. " looking down," or, " disdainful."
[3] lit. " in battle array."
[4] " shall be," N. T.
[5] " honor," N. T.
[6] τὸ γνήσιον.

"But surely this is not[1] the expression of one urging them to go even to death." Nay, it is that of one greatly so urging them. For lest they should say, that "He being exempt from mortal pains easily philosophizes on death, and exhorts us being himself in no danger," He showeth, that although feeling its agony,[2] on account of its profitableness He declineth it not. But these things belong to the Dispensation, not the Godhead. Wherefore He saith, "Now is My soul troubled"; since if this be not the case, what connection hath that which was spoken, and His saying, "Father, save Me from this hour"? And so troubled, that He even sought deliverance from death, if at least it were possible to escape. These were the infirmities of His human nature.

[2.] "But," He saith, "I have not what to say, when asking for deliverance."

"For for this cause came I unto this hour."

As though He had said, "Though we be confounded, though we be troubled, let us not fly from death, since even now I though troubled do not speak of flying; for it behooveth to bear what is coming on. I say not, Deliver Me from this hour," but what?

Ver. 28. "Father, glorify Thy Name."

"Although My trouble urges Me to say this,[3] yet I say the opposite, 'Glorify Thy Name,' that is, Lead Me henceforth to the Cross"; which greatly shows His humanity, and a nature unwilling to die, but clinging to the present life, proving that He was not exempt from human feelings. For as it is no blame to be hungry, or to sleep, so neither is it to desire the present life; and Christ indeed had a body pure from sin, yet not free from natural wants, for then it would not have been a body. By these words also He taught something else. Of what kind is that? That if ever we be in agony and dread, we·even then start not back from that which is set before us; and by saying,[4] "Glorify Thy Name," He showeth that He dieth for the truth, calling the action, "glory to God." And this fell out after the Crucifixion. The world was about to be converted, to acknowledge the Name of God, and to serve Him, not the Name of the Father only, but also that of the Son; yet still as to this He is silent.

"There came therefore a Voice from Heaven, I have both glorified it, and will glorify it again."

When had He "glorified it"? By what had been done before; and "I will glorify it again" after the Cross. What then said Christ?

Ver. 30.[5] "This Voice came not because of Me, but for your sakes."

They thought that it thundered, or that an Angel spake to Him. And how did they think this? Was not the voice clear and distinct? It was, but it quickly flew away from them as being of the grosser sort, carnal and slothful. And some of them caught the sound only,[6] others knew that the voice was articulate, but what it meant, knew not. What saith Christ? "This Voice came not because of Me, but for your sakes." Why said He this? He said it, setting Himself against what they continually asserted, that He was not of God. For He who was glorified by God, how was He not from that God whose name by Him was glorified? indeed for this purpose the Voice came. Wherefore He saith Himself, "This Voice came not because of Me, but for your sakes," "not that I may learn by it anything of which I am ignorant, (for I know all that belongeth to the Father,) but for your sakes." For when they said, "An Angel hath spoken unto Him," or "It hath thundered," and gave not heed to Him, He saith, "it was for your sakes," that even so ye might be led to enquire what the words meant. But they, being excited, did not even so enquire, though they heard that the matter related to them. For to one who knew not wherefore it was uttered, the Voice naturally appeared indistinct. "The Voice came for your sakes." Seest thou that these lowly circumstances take place on their account, not as though the Son needeth help?

Ver. 31. "Now is the judgment of this world, now shall the prince of this world be cast down."[7]

What connection hath this with, "I have glorified, and will glorify"? Much, and closely harmonizing. For when God saith, "I will glorify," He showeth the manner of the glorifying. What is it? That one[8] should be cast down. But what is, "the judgment of this world"? It is as though He said, "there shall be a tribunal and a retribution." How and in what way? "He[9] slew the first man, having found him guilty of sin, (for 'by sin death entered'—Rom. v. 12;) but in Me this he found not. Why then did he spring upon Me and give Me over to death? Why did he put into the mind of Judas to destroy Me?" (Tell me not that it was God's dispensation, for this belongeth not to the devil, but His wisdom; for the present let the disposition of that evil one be enquired into.) "How then is the world judged in Me?" It shall be said, as if a court of justice were sitting, to Satan, "Well, thou hast slain all men, because thou didst find them guilty of sin. But why didst thou slay Christ? Is it not clear that thou didst it wrongfully?" Therefore in Him the whole world shall be avenged. But, that this may be still more clear, I will make it plain by an exam-

---

[1] al. "is no longer."  
[2] ἀγωνιῶν αὐτόν.  
[3] i.e. "Save Me," &c.  
[4] Ben. omits "and by saying."  
[5] Ver. 29 omitted. "The people therefore that stood by, and heard it, said that it thundered; others said, An Angel spake to Him."  
[6] Ben. omits "only."  
[7] "cast out," N. T.  
[8] i.e. the prince of this world.  
[9] i.e. Satan.

ple. Suppose there is some cruel tyrant, bringing ten thousand evils on all those who fall into
his hands. If such a one engaging with a king,
or a king's son, slay him unjustly, his death will
have power to get revenge for the others also.
Suppose there is one who demands payment of
his debtors, that he beats them and casts them
into prison; then from the same recklessness
that he leads to the same dungeon one who
owes him nothing: such a man shall suffer punishment for what he hath done to the others.
For that one shall destroy him.

[3.] So also it is in the case of the Son; for
of those things which the devil hath done against
us, of these shall the penalty be required by
means of what he hath dared against Christ.
And to show that He implieth this, hear what
He saith; "Now shall the prince of this world
be cast down," "by My Death."

Ver. 32. "And I, if I be lifted up, will draw
all men unto Me."

That is, "even those of the Gentiles." And
that no one may ask, "How shall he be cast
down, if he is stronger even than Thou art?"
He saith, "He is not stronger; how can he be
stronger than One who draweth others to Him?"
And He speaketh not of the Resurrection, but
of what is more than the Resurrection, "I will
draw all men to Myself." For had He said, "I
shall rise again," it was not yet clear that they
would believe; but by His saying, "they shall
believe," both are proved at once, both this, and
also that He must rise again. For had He continued dead, and been a mere man, no one would
have believed. "I will draw all men to Myself." (c. vi. 44.) How then said He that the
Father draweth? Because when the Son draweth, the Father draweth also. He saith, "I will
draw them," as though they were detained by a
tyrant, and unable of themselves alone to approach Him, and to escape the hands of him
who keepeth hold of them. In another place
He calleth this "spoiling; no man can[1] spoil a

strong man's goods, except he first bind the
strong man, and then spoil his goods." (Matt.
xii. 29.) This He said to prove His strength,
and what there He calleth "spoiling," He hath
here called "drawing."

Knowing then these things, let us rouse ourselves, let us glorify God, not by our faith alone,
but also by our life, since otherwise it would not
be glory, but blasphemy. For God is not so
much blasphemed by an impure heathen, as by a
corrupt Christian. Wherefore I entreat you to
do all that God may be glorified; for, "Woe," it
saith, "to that servant by whom the Name of
God is blasphemed," (and wherever there is a
"woe," every punishment and vengeance straightway follows,) "but blessed is he by whom that
Name is glorified." Let us then not be as in
darkness, but avoid all sins, and especially those
which tend to the hurt of others, since by these
God is most blasphemed. What pardon shall
we have, when, being commanded to give to
others, we plunder the property of others?
What shall be our hope of salvation? Thou art
punished if thou hast not fed the hungry; but if
thou hast even stripped one who was clothed,
what sort of pardon shalt thou obtain? These
things I will never desist from saying, for they
who have not heard to-day perhaps will hear to-
morrow, and they who take no heed to-morrow
perhaps will be persuaded the next day; and
even if any be so disposed as not to be persuaded, yet for us there will be no account to give
of them at the Judgment. Our part we have fulfilled; may we never have cause to be ashamed
of our words, nor you to hide your faces, but
may all be able to stand with boldness before
the judgment-seat of Christ, that we also may
be able to rejoice over you, and to have some
compensation of our own faults, in your being
approved in Christ Jesus our Lord, with whom
to the Father and the Holy Ghost be glory for
ever. Amen.

---

[1] "how can," &c., N. T.

# HOMILY LXVIII.

## JOHN xii. 34.

"The people answered Him, We have heard out of the Law that Christ abideth for ever; and how sayest thou, The Son of Man must be lifted up? Who is this Son of Man?"

[1.] DECEIT is a thing easily detected, and weak, though it be daubed outside with ten thousand colors. For as those who whitewash decayed walls, cannot by the plastering make them sound, so too those who lie are easily found out, as in fact was the case here with the Jews. For when Christ said to them, "If I be lifted up I will draw all men unto Me; We have heard," saith one of them, "out of the Law, that Christ remaineth forever; and how sayest thou, that the Son of Man must be lifted up? Who is this Son of Man?" Even they then knew that Christ was some Immortal One, and had life without end. And therefore they also knew what He meant; for often in Scripture the Passion and the Resurrection are mentioned in the same place. Thus Isaiah puts them together, saying, "He was led as a sheep to the slaughter" (Isa. liii. 7), and all that follows. David also in the second Psalm, and in many other places, connects these two things. The Patriarch too after saying, "He lay down, He couched as a lion," addeth, "And as a lion's whelp, who shall raise Him up?" (Gen. xlix. 9.) He showeth at once the Passion and the Resurrection. But these men when they thought to silence Him, and to show that He was not the Christ, confessed by this very circumstance that the Christ remaineth forever. And observe their evil dealing; they said not, "We have heard that Christ neither suffereth nor is crucified," but that "He remaineth forever." Yet even this which has been mentioned, would have been no real objection, for the Passion was no hindrance to His Immortality. Hence we may see that they understood many of the doubtful points, and deliberately went wrong. For since He had before spoken about death, when they now heard in this place the, "be lifted up," they guessed that death was referred to. Then they said, "Who is this Son of Man?" This too they did deceitfully. "Think not, I pray," saith one, "that we say this concerning thee, assert not that we oppose thee through enmity, for, lo, we know not concerning whom thou speakest, and still we declare our opinion." What then doth Christ? To silence them, and to show that the Passion is no impediment to His enduring forever, He saith,

Ver. 35. "Yet a little while," He saith, "is the light with you."

Signifying that His death was a removal;[1] for the light of the sun is not destroyed, but having retired for a while appears again.

"Walk while ye have the light."[2]

Of what season doth He here speak? Of the whole present life, or of the time before the Crucifixion? I for my part think of both, for on account of His unspeakable lovingkindness, many even after the Crucifixion believed. And He speaketh these things to urge them on to the faith, as He also did before, saying, "Yet a little while I am with you." (c. vii. 33.)

"He that walketh in darkness knoweth not whither he goeth."

How many things, for instance, even now do the Jews, without knowing what they do, but walking as though they were in darkness? They think that they are going the right way, when they are taking the contrary; keeping[3] the Sabbath, respecting the Law and the observances about meats, yet knowing not whither they walk. Wherefore He said,

Ver. 36. "Walk in the light,[4] that ye may become children of the light."

That is, "My children." Yet in the beginning the Evangelist saith, "Were born, not of bloods, nor of the will of the flesh, but of God" (c. i. 13); that is, of the Father; while here Himself[5] is said to beget them; that thou mayest understand that the operation of the Father and the Son is One. "Jesus having spoken these things," departed from them, and did hide Himself.[6]

Why doth He now "hide Himself"? They took not up stones against Him, nor did they blaspheme Him in any such manner as before; why then did He hide Himself? Walking in men's hearts, He knew that their wrath was fierce, though they said nothing; He knew it boiling and murderous, and waited not till it issued into action, but hid Himself, to allay their ill-will. Observe how the Evangelist has alluded to this feeling; he has immediately added,

Ver. 37. "Though He had done so many miracles,[7] they believed not on Him."

---

[1] i.e. temporary.
[2] "Lest darkness come upon you," N. T.
[3] Savile reads κατηγορούντες, conject. τηρούντες, which is the Ben. reading.
[4] "While ye have light, believe in the light," N. T.
[5] i.e. Christ.
[6] "departed and did hide Himself from them," N. T.
[7] "before them," N. T.

[2.] What "so many"? So many as the Evangelist hath omitted. And this[1] is clear also from what follows. For when He had retired, and given in, and had come to them again, He speaketh with them in a lowly manner, saying, "He that believeth on Me, believeth not on Me, but on Him that sent Me." (Ver. 44.) Observe what He doeth. He beginneth with humble and modest expressions, and betaketh Himself to the Father; then again He raiseth His language, and when He seeth that they are exasperated, He retireth; then He cometh to them again, and again beginneth with words of humility. And where hath He done this? Nay, where hath He not done it? See, for instance, what He saith at the beginning, "As I hear, I judge." (c. v. 30.) Then in a loftier tone, "As the Father raiseth up the dead, and quickeneth them, so also the Son quickeneth whom He will" (c. v. 21); again, "I judge you not, there is another that judgeth." Then again He retireth. Then coming to Galilee, "Labor not," He saith, "for the meat that perisheth" (c. vi. 27); and after having said great things of Himself, that He came down from Heaven, that He giveth eternal life, He again withdraweth Himself. And He cometh in the Feast of Tabernacles also, and doth the same. And one may see Him continually thus varying His teaching, by His presence, by His absence, by lowly, by high discourses. Which He also did here. "Though He had done so many miracles," it saith, "they believed not on Him."

Ver. 38. "That the saying of Esaias[2] might be fulfilled which he spake, Lord, who hath believed our report, and to whom hath the arm of the Lord been revealed?" And again,

Ver. 39–41. "They[3] could not believe," it saith, "because that Esaias said,[4] Ye shall hear with your ears, and not understand.[5] These things he said,[6] when he saw His glory, and spake of Him."

Here again observe, that the "because," and "spake," refer not to the cause of their unbelief, but to the event. For it was not "because" Isaiah spake, that they believed not; but because they were not about to believe, that he spake. Why then doth not the Evangelist express it so, instead of making the unbelief proceed from the prophecy, not the prophecy from the unbelief? And farther on he putteth this very thing more positively, saying, "Therefore they could not believe, because that Esaias said." He desires hence to establish by many proofs the unerring truth of Scripture, and that

what Isaiah foretold fell not out otherwise, but as he said. For lest any one should say, "Wherefore did Christ come? Knew he not that they would give no heed to him?" he introduces the Prophets, who knew this also. But He came that they might have no excuse for their sin; for what things the Prophet foretold, he foretold as certainly to be; since if they were not certainly to be, he could not have foretold them; and they were certainly to be, because these men were incurable.

And if, "they could not," is put, instead of, "they would not," do not marvel,[7] for He saith also in another place, "He that is able to receive it, let him receive it." (Matt. xix. 12.) So in many places He is wont to term choice, power. Again, "The world cannot hate you, but Me it hateth." (c. vii. 7.) This one may even see observed in common conversation; as when a man saith, "I cannot love this or that person," calling the force of his will, power. And again, "this or that person cannot be a good man." And what saith the Prophet? "If the Ethiopian shall change his skin, or the leopard his spots, this people also shall be able to do good, having learned evil." (Jer. xiii. 23, LXX.) He saith not that the doing of virtue is impossible to them, but that because they will not, therefore they cannot. And by what he saith the Evangelist means, that it was impossible for the Prophet to lie; yet it was not on that account impossible that they should believe. For it was possible, even had they believed, that he should remain true; since he would not have prophesied these things if they had been about to believe. "Why then," saith some one, "did he not say so?" Because Scripture hath certain idiomatic phrases of this kind, and it is needful to make allowance for its laws.

"The seethings he spake when he saw His glory." Whose? The Father's. How then doth John speak of the Son? and Paul of the Spirit? Not as confounding the Persons, but as showing that the Dignity is one, they say it.[8] For that which is the Father's is the Son's also, and that which is the Son's is the Spirit's.[9] Yet many things God spake by Angels, and no one saith, "as the Angel spake," but how? "as God spake." Since what hath been said by God through the ministry of Angels would be of God; yet not therefore is what is of God, of the Angels also. But in this place John saith that the words are the Spirit's.

"And spake of Him." What spake he? "I saw the Lord sitting upon a high throne" (Isa. vi. 1), and what follows. Therefore he there

---

[1] i.e. that Christ withdrew from the malice of the Jews.
[2] "Esaias the prophet," N. T.
[3] "therefore they," N. T.     [4] "said again," N. T.
[5] Ver. 40. "He hath blinded their eyes, and hardened their heart: that they should not see with their eyes, nor understand with their heart, and be converted, and I should heal them." N. T.
[6] "said Esaias," N. T.

[7] Ben. "and if 'they could not' is put, it is put instead of 'they would not.' And do not marvel."
[8] al. "saith one."     [9] al. "the Father's."

calleth "glory," that vision, the smoke, the hearing unutterable Mysteries, the beholding the Seraphim, the lightning which leaped from the throne, against which those powers could not look. "And spake of Him." What said he? That he heard a voice, saying, "Whom shall I send? who shall go? And I said, Here am I, send me. And He said, Ye shall hear with your ears, and shall not understand, and seeing ye shall see, and not perceive." (Isa. vi. 8, 10.) For,

Ver. 40. "He hath blinded their eyes, and hardened their heart, lest they at any time should see with their eyes, and understand with their heart."

Here again is another question, but it is not so if we rightly consider it. For as the sun dazzles the eyes of the weak, not by reason of[1] its proper nature, so it is with those who give not heed to the words of God. Thus, in the case of Pharaoh, He is said to have hardened his heart, and so it is with those who are at all contentious against the words of God. This is a peculiar mode of speech in Scripture, as also the, "He gave them over unto a reprobate mind" (Rom. i. 28), and the, "He divided them to the nations,"[2] that is, allowed, permitted them to go. For the writer doth not here introduce God as Himself working these things, but showeth that they took place through the wickedness of others. For, when we are abandoned by God, we are given up to the devil, and when so given up, we suffer ten thousand dreadful things. To terrify the hearer, therefore, the writer saith, "He hardened," and "gave over." For to show that He doth not only not give us over, but doth not even leave us, except we will it, hear what He saith, "Do not your iniquities separate between Me and you?" (Isa. lix. 2, LXX.). And again, "They that go far away from Thee shall perish." (Ps.

lxxiii. 27, LXX.) And Hosea saith, "Thou hast forgotten the law of thy God, and I will also forget thee" (Hos. iv. 6, LXX.) ; and He saith Himself also in the Gospels, "How often would I have gathered your children — and ye would not." (Luke xiii. 34.) Esaias also again, "I came, and there was no man ; I called, and there was none to hearken." (Isa. l. 2, LXX.) These things He saith, showing that we begin the desertion, and become the causes of our perdition ; for God not only desireth not to leave or to punish us, but even when He punisheth, doth it unwillingly ; "I will not," He saith, "the death of a sinner, so much as that he should turn and live." (Ezek. xviii. 32, LXX.) Christ also mourneth over the destruction of Jerusalem,[3] as we also do over our friends.

[3.] Knowing this, let us do all so as not to remove from God, but let us hold fast to the care of our souls, and to the love towards each other ; let us not tear our own members, (for this[4] is the act of men insane and beside themselves,) but the more we see any ill disposed, the more let us be kind to them. Since we often see many persons suffering[5] in their bodies from difficult or incurable maladies, and cease not to apply remedies. What is worse than gout in foot or hand? Are we therefore to cut off the limbs? Not at all, but we use every means that the sufferer may enjoy some comfort, since we cannot get rid of the disease. This also let us do in the case of our brethren, and, even though they be diseased incurably, let us continue to tend them, and let us bear one another's burdens. So shall we fulfill the law of Christ, and obtain the promised good things, through the grace and lovingkindness of our Lord Jesus Christ, with whom to the Father and the Holy Ghost be glory for ever and ever. Amen.

---

[1] παρά.

[2] ἀπένειμε τοῖς ἔθνεσι. The words are found in Deut. iv. 19, LXX., but are there spoken concerning the heavenly bodies.

[3] al. "being about to destroy Jerusalem even weepeth."

[4] al. "which."        [5] al. "persons suffering many."

# HOMILY LXIX.

### JOHN xii. 42, 43.

"Nevertheless among the chief rulers also many believed on Him; but because of the Pharisees they did not confess Him, lest they should be put out of the synagogue: for they loved the praise of men more than the praise of God."

[1.] IT is necessary for us to avoid alike all the passions which corrupt the soul, but most especially those, which from themselves generate numerous sins. I mean such as the love· of money. It is in truth of itself a dreadful malady, but it becomes much more grievous, because it is the root and mother of all mischiefs. Such also is vainglory. See, for instance, how these men were broken off from the faith through their love of honor. "Many," it saith, "of the chief rulers also believed on Him, but because of the Jews[1] they did not confess Him, lest they should be put out of the synagogue." As He said also to them before, "How can ye believe which receive honor one of another, and seek not the honor that cometh from God only?" (c. v. 44.) So then they were not rulers, but slaves in the utmost slavery. However, this fear was afterwards done away, for nowhere during the time of the Apostles do we find them possessed by this feeling, since in their time both rulers and priests believed. The grace of the Spirit having come, made them all firmer than adamant. Since therefore this was what hindered them from believing at this time, hear what He saith.

Ver. 44. "He that believeth on Me, believeth not on Me, but on Him that sent Me."

As though He had said, "Why fear ye to believe on Me? Faith passeth to the Father through Me, as doth also unbelief." See how in every way He showeth the unvaryingness of His Essence.[2] He said not, He that believeth "Me," lest any should assert that He spake concerning His words; this might have been said in the case of mere men, for he that believeth the Apostles, believeth not them, but God. But that thou mightest learn that He speaketh here of the belief on His Essence, He said not, "He that believeth My words," but, "He that believeth on Me." "And wherefore," saith some one, "hath He nowhere said conversely, He that believeth on the Father, believeth not on the Father but on Me?" Because they would have replied, "Lo, we believe on the Father, but we believe not on thee." Their disposition was as yet too infirm. Anyhow, conversing with the

disciples, He did speak thus: "Ye believe on the Father,[3] believe also on Me" (c. xiv. 1); but seeing that these men were too weak to hear such words, He leadeth them in another way, showing[4] that it is not possible to believe on the Father, without believing on Him. And that thou mayest not deem that the words are spoken as of man, He addeth,

Ver. 45. "He that seeth Me, seeth Him that sent Me."

What then! Is God a body? By no means. The "seeing" of which He here speaketh is that of the mind, thence showing the Consubstantiality. And what is, "He that believeth on Me"? It is as though one should say, "He that taketh water from the river, taketh it not from the river but from the fountain"; or rather this image is too weak, when compared with the matter before us.

Ver. 46. "I am come a light into the world."[5]

For since the Father is called by this name everywhere both in the Old (Testament) and in the New, Christ useth the same name also; therefore Paul also calleth Him, "Brightness" (Heb i. 3), having learnt to do so from this source. And He showeth here His close relationship with the Father, and that there is no separation[6] between them, if so be that He saith that faith on Him is not on Him, but passeth on to the Father. And He called Himself "light," because He delivereth from error, and dissolveth mental darkness.

Ver. 47. "If any man hear not Me, and believe not, I judge him not, for I came not to judge the world, but to save the world."

[2.] For lest they should think, that for want of power He passed by the despisers, therefore spake He the, "I came not to judge the world." Then, in order that they might not in this way be made more negligent, when they had learned that "he that believeth is saved, and he that disbelieveth is punished,"[7] see how He hath also set before them a fearful court of judgment, by going on to say,

Ver. 48. "He that rejecteth Me, and receiveth not My words, hath One to judge him."

"If the Father judgeth no man, and thou art not come to judge the world, who judgeth him?" "The word that I have spoken, the

---

[1] "Pharisees," N. T.
[2] i.e. in respect of that of the Father.

[3] "on God," N. T.                    [4] al. "He showeth."
[5] "that whosoever believeth on Me should not abide in darkness," N. T.                    [6] οὐδὲν τὸ μέσον.
[7] The sense seems to require, "is not punished," and so Sav. and Ben. conjecture.

same shall judge him." [1]  For since they said, "He is not from God," He saith this,[2] that, "they shall not then be able to say these things, but the words which I have spoken now, shall be in place of an accuser, convicting them, and cutting off all excuse."  "And the word which I have spoken."  What manner of word?

Ver. 49. "For I have not spoken of Myself, but the Father which sent Me, He gave Me a commandment what I should say, and what I should speak."  And other such like.[3]

Surely these things were said for their sakes, that they might have no pretense of excuse. Since if this were not the case, what shall He have more than Isaiah? for he too saith the very same thing, "The Lord God giveth me the tongue of the learned, that I should know when I ought to speak a word." (Isa. l. 4, LXX.) What more than Jeremiah? for he too when he was sent was inspired. (Jer. i. 9.) What then Ezekiel? for he too, after eating the roll, so spake. (Ezek. iii. 1.) Otherwise also, they who were about to hear what He said shall be found to be causes of His knowledge. For if when He was sent, He then received commandment what He should say, thou wilt then argue that before He was sent He knew not. And what more impious than these assertions? if (that is) one take the words of Christ in this sense, and understand not the cause[4] of their lowliness? Yet Paul saith, that both he and those who were made disciples knew "what was that good and acceptable and perfect will of God" (Rom. xii. 2), and did the Son not know until He had received commandment? How can this be reasonable? Seest thou not that He bringeth His expressions to an excess of humility, that He may both draw those men over, and silence those who should come after. This is why He uttereth words befitting a mere man, that even so He may force us to fly the meanness of the sayings, as being conscious that the words belong not to His Nature, but are suited to the infirmity of the hearers.

Ver. 50. "And I know that His commandment is life everlasting; whatsoever I speak therefore, even as the Father said unto Me, so I speak."

Seest thou the humility of the words? For he that hath received a commandment is not his own master. Yet He saith, "As the Father raiseth up the dead and quickeneth them, even so the Son quickeneth whom He will." (c. v. 21.) Hath He then power to quicken whom He will, and to say what He will hath He not power? What He intendeth then by the words is this;[5] "The action hath not natural possi-

bility,[6] that He should speak one set of words, and I should utter another." "And I know that His commandment is life everlasting." He said this to those that called Him a deceiver, and asserted that He had come to do hurt. But when He saith, "I judge not," He showeth that He is not the cause of the perdition of these men.[7] By this He all but plainly testifies, when about to remove from, and to be no more with, them, that "I converse with you, speaking nothing as of Myself, but all as from the Father." And for this cause He confined His discourse to them to humble expressions, that He might say, "Even until the end did I utter this, My last word, to them." What word was that? "As the Father said unto Me, so I speak." "Had I been opposed to God I should have said the contrary, that I speak nothing of what is pleasing to God, so as to attract the honor to Myself, but now I have so referred all things to Him, as to call nothing My own.[8] Why then do ye not believe Me when I say that 'I have received a commandment,' and when I so vehemently remove your evil suspicion respecting rivalry? For as it is impossible for those who have received a commandment to do or say anything but what their senders wish, as long as they fulfill the commandment, and do not forge[9] anything; so neither is it possible for Me to say or do anything except as My Father willeth. For what I do He doeth, because He is with Me, and 'the Father hath not left Me alone.'" (c. viii. 29.) Seest thou how everywhere He showeth Himself connected with Him who begat Him, and that there is no separation?[10] For when He saith, "I am not come of Myself," He saith it not, as depriving Himself of power, but as taking away all alienation or opposition.[11] For if men are masters of themselves, much more the Onlybegotten Son. And to show that this is true, hear what Paul saith,[12] "He emptied Himself, and gave Himself for us." (Phil. ii. 7.) But, as I said, a terrible thing is vainglory, very terrible (Eph. v. 2); for this made these men not to believe, and others to believe ill, so that the things which were said for the sake of those men, through lovingkindness, they turned to[13] impiety.

[3.] Let us then ever flee this monster : various and manifold it is, and everywhere sheds its peculiar venom, in wealth, in luxury, in beauty of person. Through this we everywhere go beyond needful use;[14] through this arises extravagance in garments, and a great swarm of domestics; through this the needful use is every-

---

[1] al. "in the last day," N. T.　　　[3] Morel. "such like works."
[2] al. "thus showing."　　　[4] al. "pretext."
[5] al. "what then, saith one, meaneth this saying, that he hath not?"
[6] οὐκ ἔχει φύσιν τὸ πρᾶγμα.
[7] "I am not, &c.　He saith, but themselves."
[8] al. "a thing peculiar (to Myself)."
[9] παραχαράττωσι.　　　[10] οὐδὲν τὸ μέσον.
[11] i.e. between Himself and the Father.
[12] al. "yet this is true, for Paul showeth by what he saith."
[13] al. "drew to."　　　[14] χρείαν.

where despised, in our houses, our garments, our table; and extravagance prevails. Wilt thou enjoy glory? Do alms-deeds, then shall Angels praise thee, then shall God receive thee. Now the admiration goes no farther than the gold-smiths and weavers, and thou[1] departest without a crown, often seeing that thou receivest curses. But if thou put not these things about thy body, but expend them in feeding the poor, great will be the applause from all sides, great the praise. Then shalt thou have them, when thou givest them to others; when thou keepest them to thyself, then thou hast them not. For a house is a faithless treasury, but a sure treasury are the hands of the poor. Why adornest thou thy body, while thy soul is neglected, possessed by unclean-ness? Why bestowest thou not so much thought on thy soul, as thy body? Thou oughtest to bestow greater; but anyhow, beloved,[2] we ought to bestow equal care upon it. For tell me, if any one asked thee which thou wouldest choose, that thy body should be fresh and of good habit and surpassing in beauty, and wear mean raiment, or having the body deformed and full of diseases, to wear gold and finery; wouldest thou not much prefer to have beauty depending on the nature of thy person, than on the raiment with which thou art clothed? And wilt thou choose this in the case of thy body, but the contrary in the case of thy soul; and, when thou hast that ugly and unsightly and black, dost thou think to gain anything from golden ornaments? What mad-ness is this! Shift this adorning within, put these necklaces about thy soul. The things that are put about thy body help neither to its health nor to its beauty, for it will not make black white, nor what is ugly either beautiful or good looking. But if thou put them about thy soul,

thou shalt soon make it white instead of black, instead of ugly and unsightly, thou shalt make it beautiful and well-favored. The words are not mine, but those of the Lord Himself, who saith, "Though thy sins be as scarlet, I will make them white as snow" (Isa. i. 18, LXX.); and, "Give alms — and all things shall be clean unto you" (Luke xi. 41); and by such a disposition thou shalt beautify not thyself only, but thy husband. For they if they see you putting off these outward ornaments, will have no great need of expense, and not having it, they will abstain from all covetousness, and will be more inclined to give alms, and ye too will be able boldly to give them fitting counsel. At present ye are deprived of all such authority. For with what mouth will ye speak of these things? with what eyes will ye look your husbands in the face, asking money for alms, when ye spend most upon the covering of your bodies? Then wilt thou be able boldly to speak with thy husband concerning alms-giving, when thou layest aside thine ornaments of gold. Even if thou accomplish nothing, thou hast fulfilled all thy part; but I should rather say, that it is impossible that the wife should not gain the husband, when she speaks by the very actions.[4] "For what knowest thou, O woman, whether thou shalt save thy husband?" (1 Cor. vii. 16.) As then now thou shalt give account both for thyself and for him, so if thou put off all this vanity thou shalt have a double crown, wearing thy crown and triumphing[5] with thy husband through those unalloyed[6] ages, and enjoying the everlasting good things, which may we all obtain, through the grace and loving-kindness of our Lord Jesus Christ, to whom be glory for ever and ever. Amen.

---

# HOMILY LXX.

## JOHN xiii. 1.

"Now before the feast of the Passover, when Jesus knew that His hour was come that He should depart out of this world unto the Father, having loved His own which were in the world, He loved them unto the end."

[1.] "BE ye imitators of me," said Paul, "as I also am of Christ." (1 Cor. xi. 1.) For on this account He took also flesh of our substance,[3] that by means of it He might teach us virtue. For ("God sending His own Son) in the like-

ness of sinful flesh," it saith, "and for sin con-demned sin in the flesh." (Rom. viii. 3.) And Christ Himself[7] saith, "Learn of Me, for I am meek and lowly in heart." (Matt. xi. 29.) And this He taught, not by words alone, but by actions also. For they called Him a Samaritan, and one that had a devil, and a deceiver, and cast stones at Him; and at one time the Phari-sees sent servants to take[8] Him, at another they sent plotters against Him; and they continued

---

[1] addressed to women.
[2] al. "we might be content if ye did but."
[3] lit. "our lump."

[4] al. "with him by actions."
[5] πομπεύουσα.
[6] ἀκηράτους.
[7] al. "and Himself."
[8] al. "in order to kill."

also insulting Him themselves, and that when they had no fault to find, but were even being continually benefited. Still after such conduct He ceaseth not to do well to them both by words and deeds. And, when a certain domestic smote Him on the face, He said, "If I have spoken evil, bear witness of the evil, but if well, why smitest thou Me?" (c. xviii. 23.) But this was to those who hated and plotted against Him. Let us see also what He doeth now towards the disciples, or rather what actions He now exhibiteth[1] towards the traitor. The man whom most of all there was reason[2] to hate, because being a disciple, having shared the table and the salt, having seen the miracles and been deemed worthy of such great things, he acted more grievously than any, not stoning indeed, nor insulting Him, but betraying and giving Him up, observe in how friendly sort He receiveth this man, washing his feet; for even in this way He desired to restrain him from that wickedness. Yet it was in His power, had He willed it, to have withered him like the fig-tree, to have cut him in two as He rent the rocks, to have cleft him asunder like the veil; but He would not lead him away from his design by compulsion, but by choice. Wherefore He washed his feet; and not even by this was that wretched and miserable man shamed.

"Before the feast of the Passover," it saith, "Jesus knowing that His hour was come." Not then "knowing," but (it means) that He did what He did having "known" long ago. "That He should depart." Magnificently[3] the Evangelist calleth His death, "departure." "Having loved His own, He loved them unto the end." Seest thou how when about to leave them He showeth greater love? For the, "having loved, He loved them unto the end," showeth that he omitted nothing of the things which it was likely that one who earnestly loved would do. Why then did He not this from the beginning? He worketh[4] the greatest things last, so as to render more intense their attachment, and to lay up for them beforehand much comfort, against the terrible things that were about to fall on them. St. John calls them "His own," in respect of personal attachment, since he calls others also "His own," in respect of the work of creation; as when he saith, "His own received Him not." (c. i. 11.) But what meaneth, "which were in the world"? Because the dead also were "His own," Abraham, Isaac, Jacob, and the men of that sort,[5] but they were not in the world. Seest thou that He is the God both of the Old and New (Testament)? But what meaneth, "He loved them unto the end"? It stands for,

"He continued loving them unceasingly," and this the Evangelist mentions as a sure proof of great affection. Elsewhere indeed He spake of another (proof), the laying down life for His friends; but that had not yet come to pass. And wherefore did He this thing "now"? Because it was far more wonderful at a time when He appeared more glorious in the sight of all men. Besides, He left them no small consolation now that He was about to depart, for since they were going to be greatly grieved, He by these means introduceth also comfort to the grief.

Ver. 2. "And supper being ended, the devil having now put it into the heart of Judas[6] to betray Him."

This the Evangelist hath said[7] amazed, showing that Jesus washed the man who had already chosen to betray Him. This also proves his great wickedness, that not even the having shared the salt restrained him, (a thing which is most able to restrain wickedness;) not the fact that even up to the last day, his Master continued to bear with him.[8]

Ver. 3. "Jesus knowing that the Father had given[9] all things into His hands, and that He was come from God, and went to God."

Here the Evangelist saith, even[10] wondering, that one so great, so very great, who came from God and went to Him, who ruleth over all, did this thing, and disdained not even so to undertake such an action. And by the "giving over," methinks St. John means the salvation of the faithful. For when He saith, "All things are given over[11] to Me of My Father" (Matt. xi. 27), He speaketh of this kind of giving over; as also in another place He saith, "Thine they were, and Thou gavest them Me" (c. xvii. 6); and again, "No man can come unto Me except the Father draw him" (c. vi. 44); and, "Except it be given him from heaven." (c. iii. 27.) The Evangelist then either means this, or that Christ would be nothing lessened by this action, since He came from God, and went to God, and possessed all things. But when thou hearest of "giving over," understand it in no human sense, for it showeth how He honoreth the Father, and His unanimity with Him. For as the Father giveth over to Him, so He to the Father. And this Paul declares, saying, "When He shall have given over[12] the kingdom to God, even the Father." (1 Cor. xv. 24.) But St. John hath said it here in a more human sense, showing His great care for them, and declaring His unutterable love, that He now cared for them as for His own; teaching them the mother of all good, even

[1] al. "doeth."
[2] ἐχρῆν.
[3] al. "magniloquently."
[4] al. "added."
[5] οἱ κατ' ἐκείνους.
[6] "Judas Iscariot, Simon's son," N. T.
[7] al. "hath put in by the way."
[8] διαβαστάζοντα.
[9] al. "given over."
[10] al. "either he saith this."
[11] E. V. "delivered."
[12] "delivered up," E. V.

humblemindedness, which He said was both the beginning and the end of virtue. And not without a reason is added the,[1] "He came from God and went to God": but that we may learn that He did what was worthy[2] of One who came thence and went thither, trampling down all pride.

Ver. 4. "And having risen[3] from supper, and laid aside His garments."[4]

[2.] Observe how not by the washing only, but in another way also He exhibiteth humility. For it was not before reclining, but after they had all sat down, then He arose. In the next place, He doth not merely wash them, but doth so, putting off His garments. And He did not even stop here, but girded Himself with a towel. Nor was He satisfied with this, but Himself filled (the basin), and did not bid another fill it; He did all these things Himself, showing by all that we must do such things, when we are engaged in well doing, not merely for form's sake,[5] but with all zeal. Now He seemeth to me to have washed the feet of the traitor first, from its saying,

Ver. 5. "He began to wash the disciples' feet,"[6] and adding,

Ver. 6. "Then cometh He to Simon Peter, and Peter saith unto Him, Lord, dost Thou wash my feet?"

"With those hands," he saith, "with which Thou hast opened eyes, and cleansed lepers, and raised the dead?" For this (question) is very emphatic; wherefore He needed not to have said any more than the, "Thou"; for even of itself this would have sufficed to convey the whole. Some one might reasonably enquire, how none of the others forbade Him, but Peter only, which was a mark of no slight love and reverence. What then is the cause? He seemeth to me to have washed the traitor first, then to have come to Peter, and that the others were afterwards instructed from his case.[7] That He washed some one other before him is clear from its saying, "But when He came[8] to Peter." Yet the Evangelist is not a vehement accuser,[9] for the "began," is the expression of one imply- ing this. And even if Peter were the first,[10] yet it is probable that the traitor, being a forward person, had reclined even before the chief.[11] For by another circumstance also his forward- ness is shown, when He dippeth with his Master in the dish, and being convicted, feels no com-

punction; while Peter being rebuked but once on a former occasion, and for words which he spake from loving affection, was so abashed, that being even distressed and trembling, he begged another to ask a question. But Judas, though continually convicted, felt not. (Ver. 24.) When therefore He came to Peter, he saith unto Him, "Lord, dost Thou wash my feet?"

Ver. 7. "He saith unto him, What I do thou knowest not now, but thou shalt know here- after."

That is, "thou shalt know how great is the gain from this, the profit of the lesson, and how it is able to guide us into all humbleminded- ness." What then doth Peter? He still hinders Him, and saith,

Ver. 8. "Thou shalt never wash my feet."

"What doest thou, Peter? Rememberest thou not those former words? Saidst thou not, 'Be merciful to Thyself,'[12] and heardest thou not in return, 'Get thee behind Me, Satan'? (Matt. xvi. 22.) Art thou not even so sobered, but art thou yet vehement?" "Yea," he saith, "for what is being done is a great matter, and full of amazement." Since then he did this from exceeding love, Christ in turn subdueth him by the same; and as there He effected this by sharply rebuking him, and saying, "Thou art an offense unto Me," so here also by saying,

"If I wash thee not, thou hast no part with Me." What then saith that hot and burning one?

Ver. 9. "Lord, not my feet only, but also my hands and my head."

Vehement in deprecation, he becometh yet more vehement in acquiescence; but both from love. For why said He not wherefore He did this, instead of adding a threat? Because Peter would not have been persuaded. For had He said, "Suffer it, for by this I persuade you to be humbleminded," Peter would have promised it ten thousand times, in order that his Master might not do this thing. But now what saith He? He speaketh of that which Peter most feared and dreaded, the being separated from Him; for it is he who continually asks, "Whither goest Thou?" (Ver. 36.) Wherefore also he said, "I will give[13] even my life for Thee." (Ver. 37.) And if, after hearing, "What I do thou knowest not now, but thou shalt know hereafter," he still persisted, much more would he have done so had he learnt (the meaning of the action). Therefore said He, "but thou shalt know here- after," as being aware, that should he learn it immediately he would still resist. And Peter said not, "Tell me, that I may suffer Thee," but (which was much more vehement) he did not even endure to learn, but withstands Him,[14]

---

[1] al. "what then is added?"
[2] al. "went to God," that is, did what was worthy.
[3] ἀναστὰς (ἐγείρεται, G. T.).
[4] "He riseth," &c., "and took a towel, and girded Himself."
[5] "After that He poureth water into a basin." N. T.
[5] ἀφοσιουμένους.
[6] "and to wipe them with the towel wherewith He was girded," N. T.
[7] ἀπ' ἐκείνου, al. ὑπ' ἐκ. "by him."
[8] "He cometh therefore," οὖν, N. T.
[9] i.e. of Judas.
[10] i.e. in dignity.
[11] κορυφαίου.

[12] "that be far from Thee," E. V.
[13] "lay down," N. T.
[14] al. "Him again."

saying, "Thou shalt never wash my feet." But as soon as He threatened, he straightway relaxed his tone. But what meaneth, "Thou shalt know after this"? "After this?" When? "When in My Name thou shalt have cast out devils; when thou shalt have seen Me taken up into Heaven, when thou shalt have learnt from the Spirit[1] that I sit[2] on His right hand, then shalt thou understand what is being done now." What then saith Christ? When Peter said, "not my feet only, but also my hands and my head," He replieth,

Ver. 10, 11. "He that is washed, needeth not save to wash his feet, but is clean every whit; and ye are clean,[3] but not all. For He knew who should betray Him."[4]

"And if they are clean, why washeth He[5] their feet?" That we may learn to be modest.[6] On which account He came not to any other part of the body, but to that which is considered more dishonorable than the rest. But what is, "He that is washed"? It is instead of, "he that is clean." Were they then clean, who had not[7] yet been delivered from their sins, nor deemed worthy of the Spirit, since sin still had the mastery, the handwriting of the curse still remaining, the victim not having yet been offered? How then calleth He them "clean"? That thou mayest not deem them clean, as delivered from their sins, He addeth,[8] Behold, "ye are clean through the word that I have spoken unto you." That is, "In this way ye are so far[9] clean; ye have received the light, ye have been freed from Jewish error. For the Prophet also saith, 'Wash you, make you clean, put away the wickedness from your souls' (Isa. i. 16, LXX.); so that such a one is washed and is clean." Since

then these men had cast away all wickedness from their souls, and had companied with Him with a pure mind, therefore He saith according to the word of the Prophet, "he that is washed is clean already." For in that place also It meaneth not the "washing" of water, practiced by the Jews; but the cleansing of the conscience.[10]

[3.] Be we then also clean; learn we to do well. But what is "well"? "Judge for the fatherless, plead for the widow; and come, let us reason together, saith the Lord." (Isa. i. 7.) There is frequent mention in the Scriptures of widows and orphans, but we make no account of this. Yet consider how great is the reward. "Though," it saith, "your sins be as scarlet, I will whiten them as snow; though they be red like crimson, I will whiten them as wool." For a widow is an unprotected being, therefore He[11] taketh much care for her. For they, when it is even in their power to contract a second marriage, endure the hardships of widowhood through fear of God. Let us then all, both men and women, stretch forth our hands to them, that we may never undergo the sorrows of widowhood; or if we should have to undergo them, let us lay up[12] a great store of kindness for ourselves. Not small is the power of the widow's tears, it is able to open heaven itself. Let us not then trample on them, nor make their calamity worse, but assist them by every means. If so we do, we shall put around[13] ourselves much safety, both in the present life, and in that which is to come. For not here alone, but there also will they be our defenders, cutting away most of our sins by reason of our beneficence towards them, and causing us to stand boldly before the judgment-seat of Christ. Which[14] may it come to pass that we all obtain, through the grace and lovingkindness of our Lord Jesus Christ, to whom be glory for ever and ever. Amen.

---

[1] Ben. and MSS. Sav. "the Father."
[2] Sav. "He sitteth."
[3] al. "clean through the word which I have spoken unto you" (from c. xv. 3).
[4] "Him, therefore said He, Ye are not all clean," N. T.
[5] al. "washest thou."
[6] μετριάζειν.
[7] al. "yet they had not."
[8] from c. xv. 3.
[9] τέως.
[10] al. "of the creation."
[11] or, "It."
[12] al. "but we shall not undergo them, if we lay up."
[13] al. "putting around."
[14] οὖ, al. ἧς, "which boldness."

# HOMILY LXXI.

## John xiii.

"And He took[1] His garments, and having sat down again, said unto them, Know ye what I have done to you?" And what follows.

[1.] A grievous thing, beloved, a grievous thing it is to come to the depths of wickedness; for then the soul becomes hard to be restored. Wherefore we should use every exertion not to be taken at all;[2] since it is easier not to fall in,[3] than having fallen to recover one's self. Observe, for instance, when Judas had thrown himself into sin, how great assistance he enjoyed, yet not even so was he raised. Christ said to him, "One of you is a devil" (c. vi. 71); He said, "Not all believe" (c. vi. 65); He said, "I speak not of all," and, "I know whom I have chosen" (c. xiii. 18); and not one of these sayings doth he feel. Now when He had washed their feet, and taken His garments, and sat down, He said, "Know ye what I have done unto you?" He no longer addresseth Himself to Peter only, but to them all.

Ver. 13. "Ye call Me Lord[4] and Master,[5] and ye say well, for so I am."

"Ye call Me." He taketh to Him their judgment, and then that the words may not be thought to be words of their kindness, He addeth, "for so I am." By introducing a saying of theirs,[6] He maketh it not offensive, and by confirming it Himself when introduced from them, unsuspected. "For so I am," He saith. Seest thou how when He converseth with the disciples, He speaketh revealing more what belongeth unto Himself? As He saith, "Call no man master on earth,[7] for One is your guide"[8] (Matt. xxiii. 8, 9), so also, "And call no man father upon earth." But the "one" and "one"[9] is spoken not of the Father only, but of Himself also. For had He spoken excluding Himself, how saith He, "That ye may become the children of the light"? And again, if He called the Father only, "Master," how saith He, "For so I am"; and again, "For one is your Guide, even Christ"? (c. xii. 26.)

Ver. 14, 15. "If I then," He saith, "your Lord[10] and Master have washed your feet, ye ought also to wash one another's feet. For I have given you an example, that ye should do as I have done to you."

And yet it is not the same thing, for He is Lord and Master, but ye are fellow-servants one of another. What meaneth then the "as"? "With the same zeal." For on this account He taketh instances from greater actions that we may, if so be, perform the less. Thus schoolmasters write the letters for children very beautifully, that they may come to imitate them though but in an inferior manner. Where now are they who spit on their fellow-servants? where now they who demand honors? Christ washed the feet of the traitor, the sacrilegious, the thief, and that close to the time of the betrayal, and incurable as he was, made him a partaker of His table; and art thou highminded, and dost thou draw up thine eyebrows? "Let us then wash one another's feet," saith some one, "then we must wash those of our domestics." And what great thing if we do wash even those of our domestics? In our case[11] "slave" and "free" is a difference of words; but there an actual reality. For by nature He was Lord and we servants, yet even this[12] He refused not at this time to do. But now it is matter for contentment if we do not treat free men as bondmen, as slaves bought with money. And what shall we say in that day,[13] if after receiving proofs of such forbearance, we ourselves do not imitate them at all, but take the contrary part, being in diametrical opposition, lifted up, and not discharging the debt? For God hath made us debtors one to another, having first so done Himself, and hath made us debtors of a less amount. For He was our Lord, but we do it, if we do it at all, to our fellow-servants, a thing which He Himself implied by saying, "If I then your Lord and Master — so also do ye." It would indeed naturally have followed to say, "How much more should ye servants," but He left this to the conscience of the hearers.

[2.] But why hath He done this "now"? They were for the future to enjoy, some greater, some less honor. In order then that they may not exalt themselves one above the other, and say as they did before, "Who is the greatest" (Matt. xviii. 1), nor be angry one against the other, He taketh down[14] the high thoughts of them all, by saying, that "although thou mayest

---

[1] "So when He had washed their feet, and had taken," &c., N. T.
[2] τὴν ἀρχήν.
[3] al. "fall away."
[4] al. "the Christ."
[5] "Master and Lord," N.T.
[6] al. "among them."
[7] "be not ye called Rabbi," N. T.
[8] καθηγητῆς.
[9] i.e. one Master, one Father.
[10] al. "the Christ."
[11] ἐνταῦθα.
[12] i.e. this humble office.
[13] τότε.
[14] al. "purgeth."

be very great, thou oughtest to have no high thoughts towards thy brother." And He ·mentioned not the greater action, that "if I have washed the feet of the traitor, what great matter if ye one another's?" but having exemplified this by deeds, He then left it to the judgment of the spectators. Therefore He said, "Whosoever shall do and teach, the same shall be called great" (Matt. v. 19); for this is "to teach" a thing, actually to do it. What pride should not this remove? what kind of folly and insolence should it not annihilate!¹ He who sitteth upon the Cherubim washed the feet of the traitor, and dost thou, O man, thou that art earth and ashes and cinders and dust, dost thou exalt thyself, and art thou highminded? And how great a hell wouldest thou not deserve? If then thou desirest a high state of mind, come, I will show thee the way to it; for thou dost not even know what it is. The man then who gives heed to the present things as being great, is of a mean soul, so that there can neither be humility without greatness of soul, nor conceit except from littleness of soul. For as little children are eager for trifles, gaping upon balls and hoops and dice,² but cannot even form an idea of important matters; so in this case, one who is truly wise, will deem present things as nothing, (so that he will neither choose to acquire them himself, nor to receive them from others;) but he who is not of such a character will be affected in a contrary way, intent upon cobwebs and shadows and dreams of things less substantial than these.

Ver. 16-18. "Verily I say unto you, the servant is not greater than his lord, neither he that is sent greater than he that sent him. If ye know these things, happy are ye if ye do them. I speak not of you all³—but that the Scripture may be fulfilled, He that eateth bread with Me hath lifted up his heel against Me."

What He said before, this He saith here also, to shame them; "For if the servant is not greater than his master, nor he that is sent greater than him that sent him, and these things have been done by Me, much more ought they to be done by you." Then, lest any one should say, "Why now sayest Thou these things? Do we not already know them?" He addeth this very thing, "I speak not to you as not knowing, but that by your actions ye may show forth the things spoken of." For "to know," belongeth to all; but "to do," not to all. On this account He said, "Blessed are ye if ye do them"; and on this account I continually and ever say the same to you, although ye know it, that I may set you on the work. Since even Jews "know," but yet

they are not "blessed"; for they do not what they know.⁴

"I speak not," He saith, "of you all." O what forbearance! Not yet doth He convict the traitor, but veileth the matter, hence giving him room for repentance. He convicteth and yet doth not convict him when He saith thus, "He that eateth bread with Me hath lifted up his heel against Me." It seems to me that the, "The servant is not greater than his lord," was uttered for this purpose also, that if any persons should at any time suffer harm either from domestics or from any of the meaner sort, they should not be offended; looking to the instance of Judas, who having enjoyed ten thousand good things, repaid his Benefactor with the contrary. On this account He added, "He that eateth bread with Me," and letting pass all the rest, He hath put that which was most fitted to restrain and shame him; "he who was fed by Me," He saith, "and who shared My table." And He spake the words, to instruct them to benefit those who did evil to them, even though such persons should continue incurable.

But having said, "I speak not of you all," in order not to attach fear to more than one,⁵ He at last separateth the traitor, speaking thus; "He that eateth bread with Me." For the, "not of you all," doth not direct the words to any single one, therefore He added, "He that eateth bread with Me"; showing to that wretched one that He was not seized in ignorance, but even with full knowledge; a thing which of itself was most of all fitted to restrain him. And He said not, "betrayeth Me," but, "hath lifted up his heel against Me," desiring to represent the deceit, the treachery, the secrecy of the plot.

[3.] These things are written that we bear not malice towards those who injure us; but rebuke them and weep for them; for the fit subjects of weeping are not they who suffer, but they who do the wrong. The grasping man, the false accuser, and whoso worketh any other evil thing, do themselves the greatest injury, and us the greatest good, if we do not avenge ourselves. Such a case as this: some one has robbed thee; hast thou given thanks for the injury, and glorified God? by that thanksgiving thou hast gained ten thousand rewards, just as he hath gathered for himself fire unspeakable. But if any one say, "How then, if I 'could' not defend myself against him who wronged me, being weaker?" I would say this, that thou couldest have put into action the being discontented, the being impatient, (for these things are in our power,) the praying against him, who grieved you, the uttering ten thousand curses against him, the speaking ill

---

¹ κενώσειε.
² ἀστραγάλους, square bones used as dice.
³ " I speak not of you all, I know whom I have chosen," N.T.

⁴ αὐτά.        ⁵ lit. "to many."

of him to every one. He therefore who hath not done these things shall even be rewarded for not defending himself, since it is clear that even if he had had the power, he would not have done it. The injured man uses any weapon that comes to hand, when, being little of soul, he defends himself against one who has injured him, by curses, by abuse, by plotting. Do thou then not only not do these things, but even pray for him; for if thou do them not, but wilt even pray for him, thou art become like unto God. For, "pray," it saith, "for them, that despitefully use you — that ye may be like unto[1] your Father which is in Heaven." (Matt. v. 44, 45.) Seest thou how we are the greatest gainers from the insolence of others? Nothing so delighteth God, as the not returning evil for evil? But what say I? Not returning evil for evil? Surely we are enjoined to return the opposite, benefits, prayers. Wherefore Christ also repaid him who was about to betray Him with everything opposite. He washed his feet, convicted him secretly, rebuked him sparingly, tended[2] him, allowed him to share His table and His kiss, and not even by these[3] was he made better; nevertheless (Christ) continued doing His own part.

But come, let us teach thee even from the example of servants, and (to make the lesson stronger) those in the Old (Testament), that thou mayest know that we have no ground of defense when we remember a wrong. Will you then that I tell you of Moses, or shall we go yet farther back? For the more ancient the instances that can be pointed out, the more are we surpassed. "Why so?" Because virtue was then more difficult. Those men had no written precepts, no patterns of living, but their nature fought, unarmed, by itself,[4] and was forced to float in all directions unballasted.[5] Wherefore also when praising Noah, God called him not simply perfect, but added, "in his generation" (Gen. vii. 1); signifying, "at that time," when there were many hindrances, since many others shone after him, yet will he have nothing less than they; for in his own time he was perfect. Who then before Moses was patient? The blessed and noble Joseph, who having shone by his chastity, shone no less by his long suffering. He was sold when he had done no wrong, but was waiting on others, and serving, and performing all the duties of domestics. They brought against him an evil accusation, and he did not defend himself, though he had his father on his side. Nay, he even went to carry food to them in the desert, and when he found them not, he did not despair or turn back, (yet he had an excuse for doing so had he chosen,) but remained near the wild beasts and those savage men, preserving the feeling of a true brother. Again, when he dwelt in the prison house, and was asked the cause, he spake no evil of them, but only, "I have done nothing," and, "I was stolen out of the land of the Hebrews"; and after this again, when he was made lord, he nourished them, and delivered them from ten thousand dangers. If we be sober, the wickedness of our neighbor is not strong enough to cast us out of our own virtue. But those others were not like him; they both stripped him, and endeavored to kill him, and reproach him with his dream, though they had even received their meat from him, and planned to deprive him of life and of liberty. And they ate, and cared not for their brother lying naked in the pit. What could be worse than such brutality? Were they not worse than any number of murderers? And after this, having drawn him up, they gave him over to ten thousand deaths, selling him to barbarian and savage men, who were on their journey to barbarians. Yet he, when he became ruler, not only remitted them their punishment, but even acquitted them, as far at least as relating to himself, of their sin, calling what had been done a dispensation of God, not any wickedness of theirs; and the things which he did against them he did not as remembering evil, but in all these he dissembled, for his brother's[6] sake. After this, when he saw them clinging to him, he straightway threw away the mask, and wept aloud, and embraced them, as though he had received the greatest benefits, he, who formerly was made away with by them, and he brought them all down into Egypt, and repaid them with ten thousand benefits. What excuse then shall we have, if after the Law, and after grace, and after the addition of so much heavenly wisdom, we do not even strive to rival him who lived before grace and before the Law? Who shall deliver us from punishment? For there is nothing, there is nothing more grievous than the remembrance of injuries. And this the man hath showed that owed ten thousand talents; from whom payment was at one time not demanded, at another time again demanded; not demanded, because of the lovingkindness of God; but demanded, because of his own wickedness, and because of his malice toward his fellow-servant. Knowing all which things, let us forgive our neighbors their trespasses, and repay them by deeds of an opposite kind, that we too may obtain mercy from God, through the grace and lovingkindness of our Lord Jesus Christ, to whom be glory and dominion for ever and ever. Amen.

---

[1] "the children of," N. T.
[2] ἐθεράπευσε.
[3] al. "by this."

[4] or, in its own way, καθ' ἑαυτὴν
[5] ἀνερμάτιστος.

[6] i.e. Benjamin's.

# HOMILY LXXII.

## JOHN xiii. 20.[1]

" Verily, verily, I say unto you, He that receiveth whomsoever I send, receiveth Me: and He that receiveth Me, receiveth Him that sent Me."

[1.] GREAT is the recompense[2] of care bestowed upon the servants of God, and of itself[3] it yieldeth to us its fruits. For, "he that receiveth you," it saith, "receiveth Me, and he that receiveth Me, receiveth Him that sent Me." (Matt. x. 40.) Now what can be equal to the receiving Christ and His Father? But what kind of connection hath this with what was said before? What hath it in common with that which He had said, "If ye do these things happy are ye," to add, "He that receiveth you"? A close connection, and very harmonious.[4] Observe how. When they were about to go forth and to suffer many dreadful things, He comforteth them in two ways; one derived from Himself, the other derived from others. "For if," He saith, "ye are truly wise, ever keeping Me in mind, and bearing about all both what I said, and what I did, ye will easily endure terrible things. And not in this way only, but also from your enjoying great attention from all men." The first point He declared when He said, "If ye do these things happy are ye"; the second when He said, "He that receiveth you receiveth Me." For He opened the houses of all men to them, so that both from the sound wisdom of their manners, and the zeal of those who would tend them, they might have twofold comfort. Then when He had given these directions to them as to men about to run through all the world, reflecting that the traitor was deprived of both of these things, and would enjoy neither of them, neither patience in toils, nor the service of kind entertainers, He again was troubled. And the Evangelist to signify this besides, and to show that it was on his[5] account that He was troubled, adds,

Ver. 21. "When Jesus had thus said, He was troubled in spirit, and testified, and said, Verily, verily, I say unto you, that one of you shall betray Me."

Again He bringeth fear on all by not mentioning (the traitor) by name.

Ver. 22. "But they are in doubt";[6] although

conscious to themselves of nothing evil; but they deemed the declaration of Christ more to be believed than their own thoughts. Wherefore they "looked one on another." By laying the whole upon one, Jesus would[7] have cut short their fear, but by adding, "one of you," He troubled all. What then? The rest looked upon one another; but the ever fervent Peter "beckoneth"[8] to John. Since he had been before rebuked, and when Christ desired to wash him would have hindered Him, and since he is everywhere found moved indeed by love, yet blamed; being on this account afraid, he neither kept quiet, nor did he speak, but wished to gain information by means of John. But it is a question worth asking, why when all were distressed, and trembling, when their leader was afraid, John like one at ease[9] leans on Jesus' bosom, and not only leans, but even (lies) on His breast? Nor is this the only thing worthy of enquiry, but that also which follows. What is that? What he saith of himself, "Whom Jesus loved." Why did no one else say this of himself? yet the others were loved too. But he more than any. And if no other hath said this about him, but he about himself, it is nothing wonderful. Paul too does the same,[10] when occasion calls, saying thus, "I knew a man fourteen years ago"; yet in fact he[11] has gone through other no trifling praises of himself. Seems it to thee a small thing that, when he had heard, "Follow Me,"[12] he straightway left his nets, and his father, and followed; and that Christ took him alone with Peter into the mountain, (Matt. xvii. 1,) and another time again when He went into a house?[13] (Luke viii. 51.) What high praise also has he himself passed on Peter without concealment, telling us that Christ said, "Peter,[14] lovest thou Me more than these?" (c. xxi. 15), and everywhere he showeth him warm, and nobly disposed towards himself;[15] for instance, when he said, "Lord, and what shall this man do?" he spake from great love. But why did[16] no other say (this[17]) concerning him? Because he would not himself have said it, unless

---

[1] Ver. 19 omitted. "Now I tell you before it come, that when it is come to pass ye may believe that I am."
[2] al. "return." 　　　[3] ἐντεῦθεν.
[4] al. "one may see even a close connection, since," &c.
[5] i.e. the traitor's.
[6] "Then the disciples looked one on another, doubting of whom He spake." N. T.

[7] al. "The laying, &c., would."
[8] Ver. 23-25. "Now there was leaning on Jesus' bosom one of His disciples, whom Jesus loved. Simon Peter therefore beckoned to him, that he should ask who it should be of whom He spake. He then, lying on Jesus' breast, saith unto Him, Lord, who is it?"
[9] ἐντρυφῶν. 　　　[10] i.e. speaks of himself.
[11] St. John.
[12] not in St. John, but see Matt. iv. 21.
[13] of Jairus. 　　　[15] or, "Christ," αὐτόν.
[14] "Simon, son of Jonas." 　　[16] al. "on this account then."
[17] i.e. that Jesus loved him.

he had come to this passage.[1] For if after telling us that Peter beckoned to John to ask, he had added nothing more, he would have caused considerable doubt, and have compelled us to enquire into the reason. In order therefore himself to solve this difficulty, he saith, " He lay on the bosom of Jesus." Thinkest thou that thou hast learnt a little thing when thou hast heard that " he lay," and that their Master allowed such boldness to them?[2] If thou desirest to know the cause of this, the action was of love ;[3] wherefore he saith, " Whom Jesus loved."[4] I suppose also that John doth this for another reason, as wishing to show that he was exempt from the charge ; and so he speaks openly and is confident. Again, why did he use these words, not at any other point of time,[5] but only when the chief of the Apostles beckoned? That thou mightest not deem that Peter beckoned to him as being greater, he saith that the thing took place because of the great love (which Jesus bare him). But why doth he even lie on His bosom? They had not as yet formed any high surmises concerning Him ; besides, in this way He[6] calmed their despondency ; for it is probable that at this time their faces were overclouded. If they were troubled in their souls, much more would they be so in their countenances. Soothing them therefore by word and by the question, He makes a way beforehand, and allows him to lean on His breast. Observe too his modesty; he mentions not his own name, but, " whom He loved." As also Paul, when he said, " I knew a man about fourteen years ago." Now for the first time Jesus convicted the traitor, but not even now by name ; but how?

Ver. 26. " He it is, to whom I shall give a sop when I have dipped it."[7]

Even the manner (of the rebuke) was calculated to put him to shame. He respected not the table, though he shared the bread ; be it so ; but the receiving the sop from His own hand, whom would not that have won over? yet him it won not.

Ver. 27. " Then[8] Satan entered into him."

Laughing at him for his shamelessness. As long as he belonged to the band of disciples he dared not spring upon him, but attacked[9] him from without ; but when Christ made him manifest and separated him, then he sprang upon him without fear. It was not fitting to keep within one of such a character, and who so long had remained incorrigible. Wherefore He henceforth cast him out, and then that other

seized him when cut off, and he leaving them went forth by night.[10]

" Jesus saith unto him, Friend,[11] that thou doest, do quickly."

Ver. 28. " Now no man at the table knew with what intent He spake this unto him."[12]

[3.] Wonderful insensibility ! How could it be that he was neither softened nor shamed ; but rendered yet more shameless, " went out." The " do quickly," is not the expression of one commanding, nor advising, but of one reproaching, and showing him that He desired to correct him, but that since he was incorrigible, He let him go. And this, the Evangelist saith, " no man of those that sat at the table knew." Some one may perhaps find here a considerable difficulty, if, when the disciples had asked, " Who is it ? " and He had answered, " He to whom I shall give a sop when I have dipped it," they did not even so understand ; unless indeed He spake it secretly, so that no man should hear. For John on this very account, leaning by His breast, asked Him almost close to His ear, so that the traitor might not be made manifest ; and Christ answered in like manner, so that not even then did He discover him. And though He spake emphatically,[13] " Friend, that thou doest, do quickly," even so they understood not. But he spake thus to show that the things were true which had been said by Him to the Jews concerning His death. For He had said to them, " I have power to lay down My life, and I have power to take it again " : and, " No man taketh it from Me." (c. x. 18.) As long then as He would retain it, no man was able (to take it) ; but when He resigned it, then the action became easy. All this He implied when He said, " That thou doest, do quickly." Yet not even then did He expose him,[14] for perhaps the others might have torn him in pieces, or Peter might have killed him. On this account " no man at the table knew." Not even John? Not even he : for he could not have expected that a disciple would arrive[15] at such a pitch of wickedness. For since they were far from such iniquity themselves, they could not suspect such things concerning others. As before He had told them, " I speak not of you all " (ver. 18), yet did not reveal the person ; so here, they thought that it was said concerning some other matter.

" It was night," saith the Evangelist, when he went out. " Why tellest thou me the time ? " That thou mayest learn his forwardness, that not even the time restrained him from his purpose. Yet not even did this make him quite manifest,

---

[1] i.e. in his Gospel history.    [4] ἐφίλε.
[2] Sav. conject. " him."    [5] χωρίῳ.
[3] ἀγάπης.    [6] or, " Christ."
[7] " And when He had dipped the sop, He gave it to Judas Iscariot, the son of Simon." N. T.
[8] " after the sop," N. T.
[9] al. " put forward."

[10] al. " went forth out."    [11] " unto him, That," &c., N. T.
[12] Ver. 29, 30. " For some of them thought, because Judas had the bag, that Jesus had said unto him, Buy those things that we have need of against the feast, or that he should give something to the poor. He then having received the sop, went immediately out."
[13] al. " more plainly."    [14] Judas
[15] al. " have gone out."

for the others were at this time in confusion, occupied by fear and great distress, and they knew not the true reason of what had been said, but supposed[1] that He spake thus, in order that Judas might give somewhat to the poor. For He cared greatly for the poor, teaching us also to bestow much diligence on this thing. But they thought this, not without a cause, but "because he had the bag." Yet no one appears to have brought money to Him; that the female disciples nourished Him of their substance, it has said, but this[2] it hath nowhere intimated. (Luke viii. 3.) But how did He who bade His disciples bear neither scrip, nor money, nor staff, Himself bear a bag to minister to the poor? That thou mayest learn, that it behooveth even him who is exceedingly needy and crucified, to be very careful on this point. For many things He did in the way of dispensation[3] for our instruction. The disciples then thought that He said this, that Judas should give something to the poor; and not even this shamed him, His not being willing even to the last day to make him a public example. We too ought to do the like, and not parade the sins of our companions, though they be incurable. For even after this He gave a kiss to the man who came to betray Him, and endured,[4] such an action as that was, and then proceeded to a thing of far greater daring,[5] the Cross itself,[6] to the death of shame, and there again He manifested His lovingkindness. And here He calleth it "glory," showing us that there is nothing so shameful and reproachful which makes not brighter him who goeth to it, if it be done according to the will of God. At least after the going forth of Judas to the betraying, He saith,

Ver. 31. "Now is the Son of Man glorified."[7]

In this way rousing the dejected thoughts of the disciples, and persuading them not only not to despond, but even to rejoice. On this account He rebuked Peter at the first, because for one who has been in death to overcome death, is great glory. And this is what He said of Himself, "When I am lifted up,[8] then ye shall know that I Am" (c. viii. 28); and again, "Destroy this Temple" (c. ii. 19); and again, "No sign shall be given unto you[9] but the sign of Jonas." (Matt. xii. 39.) For how can it be otherwise than great glory, the being able even after death to do greater things than before death? for in order that the Resurrection might be believed, the disciples did work greater things. But unless He had lived, and had been God, how could these men have wrought such things in His Name?

Ver. 32. "And God shall glorify Him."[10]

What is, "And God shall glorify Him in Himself"? It is "by means of[11] Himself, not by means of another."

"And shall straightway glorify Him."

[4.] That is, "simultaneously with the Cross." "For it will not be after much time," He saith, "nor will He wait for the distant season of the Resurrection, nor will He then show Him glorious, but straightway on the Cross itself His glories shall appear." And so the sun was darkened,[12] the rocks rent, the veil of the temple was parted asunder, many bodies of saints that slept arose, the tomb had its seals, the guards sat by, and while a stone lay over the Body, the Body rose; forty days passed by, and the Gift of the Spirit came, and they all straightway preached Him. This is, "shall glorify Him in Himself, and shall straightway glorify Him"; not by Angels or Archangels, not by any other power, but by Himself. But how did He also glorify Him by Himself? By doing all for the glory of the Son. Yet the Son did all. Seest thou that He referreth to the Father the things done by Himself?

Ver. 33. "Little children, yet a little while I am with you — and[13] as I said unto the Jews, Whither I go ye cannot come, so now I say to you."

He now begins words of sorrow after the supper. For when Judas went forth it was no longer evening, but night. But since they[14] were about to come shortly, it was necessary to set all things before the disciples, that they might have them in remembrance; or rather, the Spirit recalled all to their minds. For it is likely that they would forget many things, as hearing for the first time, and being about to undergo such temptations. Men who were weighed down to sleep, (as another Evangelist saith, — Luke xxii. 45,) who were possessed by despondency, as Christ saith Himself, "Because I have said these things unto you, sorrow hath filled your hearts" (c. xvi. 6), how could they retain all these things exactly? Why then were they spoken? It became no little gain to them with respect to their opinion of[15] Christ, that in after times when reminded,[16] they certainly knew that they had long ago heard these things from Christ. But wherefore doth He first cast down their souls, saying, "Yet a little while I am with you"? "To the Jews indeed it was said with reason, but wherefore dost Thou place us in just the same class with those obstinate ones?" He by no means did so. "Why then said He, 'As I said to the Jews'?" He reminded them that

---

[1] al. "thought it saith."
[2] the carrying of money.
[3] οἰκονομῶν.
[4] κατεδέξετο.
[5] al. "far more grievous."
[6] al. "His Cross."
[7] "And God is glorified in Him." N. T.
[8] "When ye have lifted up the Son of Man." N. T.
[9] "this generation," N. T.
[10] "If God be glorified in Him, God shall also glorify," &c., N. T.
[11] διὰ.
[12] al. "turned away."
[13] "Ye shall seek Me, and," &c., N. T. and Ben.
[14] i.e. they who were to take Him.
[15] or, "the glory of."
[16] i.e. by the Spirit.

He did not now, because troubles were upon them, warn them of these things, but that He had foreknown them from the first, and that they were witnesses who had heard that He had said these things to the Jews. Wherefore He added also the word, "little children," that when they heard, "As I said to the Jews," they might not deem that the expression was used in like sense towards themselves. It was not then to depress but to comfort them that He thus spake, that their dangers might not, by coming upon them suddenly, trouble them to excess.

"Whither I go, ye cannot come." He showeth that His death is a removal, and a change for the better[1] to a place which admits not corruptible bodies. This He saith, both to excite their love towards Him, and to make it more fervent. Ye know that when we see any of our dearest friends departing from us, our affection is warmest, and the more so, when we see them going to a place to which it is not even possible for us to go. These things then He said, terrifying the Jews, but kindling longing in the disciples. "Such is the place, that not only not they, but not even you, My best beloved, can come there." Here He showeth also His Own dignity.

"So now I say to you." Why "now"? "In one way to them, to you in another way"; that is, "not with them." But when did the Jews seek Him, when the disciples? The disciples, when they fled; the Jews, when they suffered miseries unendurable and surpassing all description at the capture of their city, when the wrath of God was borne down upon them from every side. To the Jews therefore He[2] spake then, because of their unbelief, "but to you now, that troubles might not come upon you unexpected."

Ver. 34. "A new commandment I give unto you."[3]

For since it was likely that they would be troubled when they heard these things, as though they were about to be deserted, He comforteth them, investing them with that which was the root of all blessings and a safeguard, love. As though He had said, "Grieve ye at My departure? Nay, if ye love one another, ye shall be the stronger." Why then said He not this? Because He said what profited them more than this.

Ver. 35. "By this shall all men know that ye are My disciples."[4]

[5.] By this He at the same time showed that the company[5] should never be extinguished, when He gave them a distinguishing token. This He said when the traitor was cut off from them. But how calleth He that a new com-

mandment which is contained also in the Old (covenant)? He made it new Himself by the manner; therefore He added, "As I have loved you." "I have not paid back to you a debt of good deeds first done by you, but Myself have begun," He saith. "And so ought you to benefit your dearest ones, though you owe them nothing"; and omitting to speak of the miracles which they should do, He maketh their characteristic, love. And why? Because it is this which chiefly shows men holy; it is the foundation of all virtue; by this mostly we are all even saved. For "this," He saith, "is to be a disciple; so shall all men praise you, when they see you imitating My Love." What then? Do not miracles much more show this? By no means. For "many will say, Lord, have we not in Thy Name cast out devils?" (Matt. vii. 22.) And again, when they rejoice that the devils obey them, He saith, "Rejoice not that the devils obey[6] you, but that your names are written in heaven." (Luke x. 20.) And[7] this indeed brought over the world, because that[8] was before it; had not that been, neither would this have endured. This then straightway made them perfect,[9] the having[10] all one heart and one soul. But had they separated one from the other, all things would have been lost.

Now He spake this not to them only, but to all who should believe on Him; since even now, there is nothing else that causes the heathen[11] to stumble, except that there is no love. "But," saith some one, "they also urge against us the absence of miracles." But not in the same way. "But where did the Apostles manifest their love?" Seest thou Peter and John inseparable from one another, and going up to the Temple? (Acts iii. 1.) Seest thou Paul disposed in a like way towards them, and dost thou doubt? If they had gained the other blessings, much more had they the mother of them all. For this is a thing that springs from a virtuous soul; but where wickedness is, there the plant withers away. For "when," it saith, "iniquity shall abound, the love of many shall wax cold." (Matt. xxiv. 12.) And miracles do not so much attract the heathen as the mode of life; and nothing so much causes a right life as love. For those who wrought miracles they often even called deceivers; but they could have no hold upon a pure life. While then the message of the Gospel was not yet spread abroad, miracles were with good reason marveled at, but now men must get to be admired by their lives. For nothing so raises respect in the heathen as virtue, nothing so offends them as vice.

---

[1] μετάθεσις ἀμείνων.　　　[2] al. "I."
[3] "That ye love one another; as I have loved you, that ye also love one another." N. T.
[4] "if ye have love one to another," N. T.
[5] i.e. of Christian people, χορὸς.

[6] "are subject to," N. T.
[7] the working of miracles.
[8] love.
[9] καλοὶς κἀγαθοὺς, beautiful and good.
[10] al. "and to have."
[11] lit. "Greeks."
[12] "because," N. T.

And with good reason. When one of them sees the greedy man, the plunderer, exhorting others to do the contrary, when he sees the man who was commanded to love even his enemies, treating his very kindred like brutes, he will say that the words are folly. When he sees one trembling at death, how will he receive the accounts of immortality? When he sees us fond of rule, and slaves to the other passions, he will more firmly remain in his own doctrines, forming no high opinion of us. We, we are the cause of their remaining in their error. Their own doctrines they have long condemned, and in like manner they admire ours, but they are hindered by our mode of life. To follow wisdom in talk is easy, many among themselves have done this ; but they require the proof by works. "Then let them look to the ancients of our profession." But about them they by no means believe ; they enquire concerning those now living. For, " show me," it saith, " thy faith by thy works "[1] (Jas. ii. 18) ; but this is not the case ; on the contrary, seeing us tear our neighbors worse than any wild beast, they call us the curse of the world. These things restrain the heathen, and suffer them not to come over to our side. So that we shall be punished for these also ; not only for what we do amiss ourselves, but because the name of God is blasphemed. How long shall we be given up to wealth, and luxury, and the other passions? For the future let us leave them. Hear what the Prophet saith of certain foolish ones, " Let us eat and drink, for to-morrow we die." (Isa. xxii. 31.) But in the present case we cannot even say this,[5] so " many " gather round themselves what belongs to all. So chiding them also, the Prophet said, " Will ye dwell alone upon the earth? " (Isa. v. 8.) Wherefore I fear lest some grievous thing come to pass, and we draw down upon us heavy vengeance from God. And that this may not come to pass, let us be careful of[6] all virtue, that we may obtain the future blessings, through the grace and lovingkindness of our Lord Jesus Christ, by whom and with whom, to the Father and the Holy Ghost, be glory now and forever, and world without end. Amen.

# HOMILY LXXIII.

## JOHN xiii. 36.

" Simon Peter said unto Him, Lord, whither goest thou? Jesus answered him, Whither I go thou canst not follow Me now, but thou shalt follow Me afterwards."

[1.] A GREAT thing[2] is love, and stronger than fire itself, and it goeth up to the very heaven ; there is[3] no hindrance which can restrain its tearing[4] force. And so the most fervent Peter, when he hears, " Whither I go ye cannot come," what saith he? " Lord, whither goest thou? " and this he said, not so much from wish to learn, as from desire to follow. To say openly, " I go," he dared not yet, but, " Whither goest thou? " Christ answered, not to his words, but to his thoughts. For that this was his wish, is clear from what Christ said, " Whither I go thou canst not follow Me now." Seest thou that he longed for the following Him, and therefore asked the question? And when he heard, " thou shalt follow Me afterwards," not even so did he restrain his longing, and, though he had gained good hopes, he is so eager as to say,

Ver. 37. " Why cannot I follow Thee now? I will lay down my life for Thee."

When he had shaken off the dread of being the traitor, and was shown to be one of His own,[7] he afterwards asked boldly himself, while the others held their peace. " What sayest thou, Peter? He said, ' thou canst not,' and thou sayest, ' I can '? Therefore thou shalt know from this temptation that thy love is nothing without the presence of the impulse[8] from above." Whence it is clear that in care for him He allowed even that fall. He desired indeed to teach him even by the first words, when he continued in his vehemence, He did not indeed throw or force him into the denial, but left him alone, that he might learn his own weakness. Christ had said that He must be betrayed ; Peter replied, " Be it far from Thee, Lord ; this shall not happen unto Thee." (Matt. xvi. 22.) He was rebuked, but not instructed. On the contrary, when Christ desired to wash his feet, he said, " Thou shalt never wash my feet."[9] (Ver. 8.) Again, when he hears, " Thou canst not follow Me now," he saith, " Though all deny Thee, I will not deny Thee." Since then it was likely that he would be lifted up to folly by his

---

1 so read in some copies.　3 al. " whence neither shall there be."
2 al. " a great good."　4 ῥᾳγδαῖον.

5 i.e. " certain " foolish ones.　7 τῶν γνησίων.
6 al. " lay hold on."　8 ῥοπῆς.
9 al. " Thou shalt never do this thing."

practice of contradiction, Jesus next teacheth him not to oppose Him. This too Luke implies, when he telleth us that Christ said, "And I have prayed for thee, that thy faith fail not" (Luke xxii. 32); that is, "that thou be not finally lost." In every way teaching him humility, and proving that human nature by itself is nothing. But, since great love made him apt for contradiction, He now sobereth him, that he might not in after times be subject to this, when he should have received the stewardship of the world, but remembering what he had suffered, might know himself. And look at the violence of his fall; it did not happen to him once or twice, but he was so beside himself, that in a short time thrice did he utter the words of denial, that he might learn that he did not so love as he was loved. And yet, to one who had so fallen He saith again, "Lovest thou Me more than these?" So that the denial was caused not by the cooling of his love, but from his having been stripped of aid from above. He accepteth then Peter's love, but cutteth off the spirit of contradiction engendered by it. "For if thou lovest, thou oughtest to obey Him who is beloved. I said[1] to thee and to those with thee, 'Thou canst not'; why art thou contentious? Knowest thou what a thing it is to contradict God? But since thou wilt not learn in this way that it is impossible that what I say should not come to pass, thou shalt learn[2] it in the denial." And yet this appeared to thee to be much more incredible. For this thou didst not even understand, but of that thou hadst the knowledge[3] in thy heart. Yet still that came to pass which was not even[4] expected.

"I will lay down my life for Thee." For since he had heard, "Greater love than this hath no man,"[5] he straightway sprang forward, insatiably eager and desirous to reach even to the highest pitch of virtue. But Christ, to show that it belonged to Himself alone to promise these things with authority, saith,

Ver. 39. "Before the cock crow."[6]

That is, "now"; there was but a little interval. He spake when it was late at night, and the first and second watch was past.

Chap. xiv. ver. 1. "Let not your heart be troubled."

This He saith, because it was probable that when they heard they would be troubled. For if the leader of their band, one so entirely fervent, was told that before the cock crew he should thrice deny his Master, it was likely that they would expect to have to undergo some

great reverse, sufficient to bend even souls of adamant. Since then it was probable that they considering these things would be astounded, see how He comforteth them, saying, "Let not your heart be troubled." By this first word showing the power of His Godhead, because, what they had in their hearts He knew and brought to light.

"Ye believe in God, believe also in Me."

That is, "All dangers shall pass you by, for faith in Me and in My Father is more powerful than the things which come upon you, and will permit no evil thing to prevail against you." Then He addeth,

Ver. 2. "In My Father's house are many mansions."

As He comforteth Peter when bewildered[7] by saying, "but thou shalt follow afterwards," so also He gives this glimpse of hope to the others. For lest they should think that the promise was given to him alone, He saith, "In My Father's house are many mansions."

"If it were not so I would have said to you, I go[8] to prepare a place for you."

That is, "The same place which receiveth Peter shall receive you." For a great abundance of dwellings is there, and it may not be said that they need preparation. When He said, "Ye cannot follow Me now," that they might not deem that they were finally cut off, He added,

Ver. 3.[9] "That where I am, there ye may be also." "So earnest have I been concerning this matter,[10] that I should already have been given up to it,[11] had not preparation been made long ago for you." Showing them that they ought to be very bold and confident. Then that He may not seem to speak as though enticing them, but that they may believe the thing to be so, He addeth,

[2.] Ver. 4. "And whither I go ye know, and the way ye know."

Seest thou that He giveth them proof that these things were not said without a meaning? And He used these words, because He knew in Himself that their souls now desired to learn this. For Peter said what he said, not in order to learn, but that he might follow. But when Peter had been rebuked, and Christ had declared[12] that to be possible which for the time seemed impossible,[13] and when the apparent impossibility led him to desire to know the matter exactly, therefore He saith to the others, "And the way ye know." For as when He hath said, "Thou shalt deny Me," before any one spake a word, searching into their hearts, He said, "Be

1 in the Greek, "He said."    3 al. "the consciousness."
2 al. "shalt know."    4 al. "was not."
5 the words occur later, c. xv. 13.
6 "Jesus answered him, Wilt thou lay down thy life for Me? Verily, verily, I say unto thee, the cock shall not crow till thou hast denied Me thrice." N. T.

7 ἀλύοντα.    8 al. "shall go."
9 Ver. 3. "And if I go and prepare a place for you, I will come again, and receive you unto Myself, that where," &c. N. T.
10 i.e. the preparing a place for disciples.
11 ἤδη ἂν τούτου ἐγενόμην.    12 al. "had showed."
13 i.e. that the disciples should follow.

not troubled," so here also by saying, "Ye know," He disclosed the desire which was in their heart, and Himself giveth them an excuse for questioning. Now the, "Whither goest Thou?" Peter used from a very loving affection, Thomas from cowardice.

Ver. 5. "Lord,[1] we know not whither Thou goest." [2]

"The place," he saith, "we know not, and how shall we know the way leading thither?" And observe with what submissiveness he speaks; he saith not, "tell us the place," but, "we know not whither Thou goest"; for all had long yearned to hear this. If the Jews questioned among themselves when they heard (of His departure), although desirous to be rid of Him, much more would those desire to learn, who wished never to be separated from Him. They feared therefore to ask Him, but yet they asked Him, from their great love and anxiety. What then saith Christ?

Ver. 6. "I am the Way, and the Truth, and the Life; no man cometh unto the Father, but by Me."

"Why then, when He was asked by Peter, 'Whither goest Thou,' did He not say directly, 'I go to the Father, but ye cannot come now'? Why did He put in a circuit of so many words, placing together questions and answers? With good reason He told not this to the Jews; but why not to these?" He had indeed said both to these and to the Jews, that He came forth from God, and was going to God, now He saith the same thing more clearly than before. Besides, to the Jews He spake not so clearly; for had He said, "Ye cannot come to the Father but by Me," they would straightway have deemed the matter mere boasting; but now by concealing this, He threw them[3] into perplexity. "But why," saith some one, "did He speak thus both to the disciples and to Peter?" He knew his great forwardness, and that he would by reason of this[4] the more press on and trouble Him; in order therefore to lead him away, He hideth the matter. Having then succeeded in what He wished by the obscurity and by veiling His speech, He again discloseth the matter. After saying, "Where I am, no man can come," He addeth, "In My Father's house are many mansions"; and again, "No man cometh to the Father but by Me." This He would not tell them at first, in order not to throw them into greater despondency, but, now that He hath soothed them, He telleth them. For by Peter's rebuke He cast out[5] much of their despondency; and dreading lest they should be addressed in the same way, they were the more restrained. "I am the Way." This is the proof of the, "No man cometh to the Father but by Me"; [6] and, "the Truth, and the Life," of this, "that these things shall surely be." "There is then no falsehood with Me, if I am 'the Truth'; if I am 'Life' also, not even death shall be able to hinder you from coming to Me. Besides; if I am 'the Way,' ye will need none to lead you by the hand; if I am also 'the Truth,' My words are no falsehoods; if I am also 'Life,' though ye die ye shall obtain what I have told you." Now His being "the Way," they both understood and allowed, but the rest they knew not. They did not indeed venture to say what they knew not. Still they gained great consolation from His being "the Way." "If," saith He, "I have sole authority to bring[7] to the Father, ye shall surely come thither; for neither is it possible to come by any other way." But by saying before, "No man can come to Me except the Father draw him"; and again, "If I be lifted up from the earth, I shall draw all men unto Me" (c. xii. 32); and again, "No man cometh to the Father but by Me" (c. xiv. 6); He showeth Himself equal to Him who begat Him. But how after saying, "Whither I go ye know, and the way ye know," hath He added,

Ver. 7. "If ye had known Me, ye should have known My Father also; and from henceforth ye know Him, and have seen Him"?

He doth not contradict Himself; they knew Him indeed, but not so as they ought. God they knew, but the Father not yet. For afterwards, the Spirit having come upon them wrought[8] in them all knowledge. What He saith is of this kind. "Had ye known My Essence and My Dignity, ye would have known that of the Father also; and henceforth ye shall know Him, and have seen Him," (the one belonging to the future, the other to the present,) that is, "by Me." By "sight," He meaneth knowledge by intellectual perception. For those who are seen we may see and not know; but those who are known we cannot know and not know. Wherefore He saith, "and ye have seen Him"; just as it saith, "was seen also of Angels." (1 Tim. iii. 16.) Yet the very Essence was not seen; yet it saith that He "was seen," that is, as far as it was possible for them to see. These words are used, that thou mayest learn that[9] the man who hath seen Him[10] knoweth Him who begat Him. But they beheld Him not in His unveiled Essence, but clothed with flesh. He is wont elsewhere to put "sight" for "knowledge"; as when He saith, "Blessed are the pure in heart, for they shall see God." (Matt. v. 8.) By "pure," He meaneth not those who are free

---

[1] "Thomas saith unto Him, Lord," &c.
[2] "and how shall we know the way?" N. T.
[3] or, "these" (the disciples).
[4] i.e. if He had so spoken.　　　[5] al. "cast off."

[6] al. "that is, that ye come by Me."　　　[9] al. "showing that."
[7] Κύριος εἰμὶ τοῦ ἄγειν.　　　[10] the Son.
[8] κατεσκεύασεν.

from fornication only, but from all sins. For every sin brings filth upon the soul.

[3.] Let us then use every means to wipe off the filthiness. But first the font cleanseth, afterwards other ways also, many and of all kinds. For God, being merciful, hath even after this[1] given to us various ways of[2] reconciliation, of all which the first is that by alms-doing. "By alms-deeds," it saith, "and deeds of faith sins are cleansed away." (Ecclus. iii. 30.) By alms-doing I do not mean that which is maintained by injustice, for this is not alms-doing, but savageness and inhumanity. What profits it to strip one man and clothe another? For we ought to begin the action with mercy, but this is inhumanity. If we give away everything that we have got from other people, it is no gain to us. And this Zacchæus shows, who on that occasion said, that he propitiated God by giving four times as much as he had taken. (Luke xix. 8.) But we, when we plunder unboundedly, and give but little, think that we make God propitious, whereas we do rather[3] exasperate Him. For tell me, if thou shouldest drag a dead and rotten ass from the waysides and lanes, and bring it to the altar, would not all stone thee as accursed and polluted?[4] Well then, if I prove that a sacrifice procured by plunder is more polluted than this, what defense shall we obtain? Let us suppose that some article has been obtained by plunder, is it not of fouler scent than a dead ass? Wouldest thou learn how great is the rottenness of sin? Hear the Prophet saying, "My wounds stank, and were corrupt." (Ps. xxxviii. 5, LXX.) And dost thou in words entreat God to forget thy misdeeds, and dost thou by what thou thyself doest, robbing and grasping, and placing thy sin upon the altar, cause Him to remember them continually? But now, this is not the only sin, but there is one more grievous than this, that thou defilest the souls of the saints.[5] For the altar is but a stone, and is consecrated, but they ever bear with them Christ Himself; and darest thou to send thither any of such impurity? "No," saith one, "not the same money, but other." Mockery this, and trifling. Knowest thou not, that if one drop of injustice fall on a great quantity of wealth, the whole is defiled? And just as a man by casting dung into a pure fountain makes it all unclean, so also in the case of riches, anything ill-gotten entering in makes

them to be tainted with the ill savor from itself. Then we wash our hands when we enter into church, but our hearts not so. Why, do our hands send forth a voice? It is the soul that utters[6] the words: to that God looketh; cleanness of the body is of no use, while that is defiled. What profits it, if thou wipe clean thine outward hands, while thou hast those within impure? For the terrible thing and that which subverts all good is this, that while we are fearful about trifles, we care not for important matters. To pray with unwashed hands is a matter indifferent; but to do it with an unwashed mind, this is the extreme of all evils. Hear what was said to the Jews who busied themselves about such outward impurities. "Wash thine heart from wickedness, how long shall there be in thee thoughts of thy labors?"[7] (Jer. iv. 14.) Let us also wash ourselves, not with mire, but with fair water, with alms-doing, not with covetousness. First get free from rapine, and then show forth alms-deeds. Let us "decline from evil, and do good." (Ps. xxxvii. 27.) Stay thy hands from covetousness, and so bring them to alms-giving. But if with the same hands we strip one set of persons,[8] though we may not clothe the others with what has been taken[9] from them, yet we shall not thus escape punishment. For that which is the groundwork[10] of the propitiation is made the groundwork of all wickedness. Better not show mercy, than show it thus; since for Cain also it had been better not to have[11] brought his offering at all. Now if he who brought too little angered God, when one gives what is another's, how shall not he anger Him? "I commanded thee," He will say, "not to steal, and honorest thou Me from that thou hast stolen? What thinkest thou? That I am pleased with these things?" Then shall He say to thee, "Thou thoughtest wickedly that I am even such an one as thyself; I will rebuke thee, and set before thy face thy sins." (Ps. l. 21, LXX.) But may it not come to pass that any one of us hear this voice, but having wrought pure alms-deeds, and having our lamps burning, so may we enter into the bride-chamber by the grace and lovingkindness of our Lord Jesus Christ, to whom with the Father and the Holy Ghost[12] be glory for ever and ever. Amen.

---

1 after baptism.
2 Ben. "ways of various."
3 al. "not knowing that we."
4 al. "abominable."
5 i.e. of communicants.
6 al. "offers."
7 E. V. "How long shall thy vain thoughts lodge within thee?"
8 al. "the poor."     9 al. "given."     10 ὑπόθεσις.
11 al. "Cain would have been better if he had not."
12 Ben. omits, "with the Father and the Holy Ghost."

# HOMILY LXXIV.

## JOHN xiv. 8, 9.

"Philip saith unto Him, Lord, show us the Father, and it sufficeth us. Jesus saith unto him, Have I been so long time with you, and yet hast thou not known Me, Philip? He who hath seen Me, hath seen the Father."[1]

[1.] THE Prophet said to the Jews, "Thou hadst the countenance of a harlot, thou wert shameless towards all men." (Jer. iii. 3, LXX.) Now it seems fitting to use this expression not only against that city,[2] but against all who shamelessly set their faces against the truth. For when Philip said to Christ, "Show us the Father," He replied, "Have I been so long time with you, and hast thou not known Me, Philip?" And yet there are some who even after these words separate the Father from the Son. What proximity dost thou require closer than this? Indeed, from this very saying some have fallen into the malady of Sabellius. But let us, leaving both these and those as involved in directly opposite error, consider the exact meaning of the words. "Have I been so long time with you, and hast thou not known Me, Philip?" He saith. What then? replieth Philip, "Art thou the Father after whom I enquire?" "No," He saith. On this account He said not, "hast thou not known Him," but, "hast thou not known Me," declaring nothing else but this, that the Son is no other than what the Father is, yet continuing to be a Son. But how came Philip to ask this question? Christ had said, "If ye had known Me, ye should have known My Father also" (c. xiv. 7), and He had often said the same to the Jews. Since then Peter and the Jews had often asked Him, "Who is the Father?" since Thomas had asked Him, and no one had learnt anything clear, but His words were still not understood; Philip, in order that He might not seem to be importunate, and to trouble Him by asking in his turn after the Jews, "Show us the Father," added, "and it sufficeth us," "we seek no more." Yet Christ had said, "If ye had known Me, ye should have known My Father also," and by Himself He declared the Father. But Philip reversed the order, and said, "Show us the Father," as though knowing Christ exactly. But Christ endureth him not, but putteth him in the right way, persuading him to gain the knowledge of the Father through Himself, while Philip desired to see Him with these bodily eyes, having perhaps heard concerning the Prophets, that they "saw God."

But those cases, Philip, were acts of condescension. Wherefore Christ said, "No man hath seen God at any time" (c. i. 18); and again, "Every man that hath heard and hath learned from God cometh unto Me." (c. vi. 45.) "Ye have neither heard His voice at any time, nor seen His shape." (c. v. 37.) And in the Old Testament, "No man shall see My face, and live." (Ex. xxxiii. 20.) What saith Christ? Very reprovingly He saith, "Have I been so long time with you, and hast thou not known Me, Philip?" He said not, "hast thou not seen," but, "hast thou not known Me." "Why," Philip might say, "do I wish to learn concerning Thee? At present I seek to see Thy Father, and Thou sayest unto me, hast thou not known Me?" What connection then hath this with the question? Surely a very close one; for if He is that which the Father is, yet continuing a Son, with reason He showeth in Himself Him who begat Him. Then to distinguish the Persons He saith, "He that hath seen Me hath seen the Father," lest any one should assert that the same is Father, the same Son. For had He been the Father, He would not have said, "He that hath seen Me hath seen Him." Why then did He not reply, "thou askest things impossible, and not allowed to man; to Me alone is this possible"? Because Philip had said, "it sufficeth us," as though knowing Christ, He showeth that he had not even seen Him. For assuredly he would have known the Father, had he been able to know the Son.[3] Wherefore He saith, "He that hath seen Me, hath seen the Father." "If any one hath seen Me, he shall also behold Him." What He saith is of this kind: "It is not possible to see either Me or Him." For Philip sought the knowledge which is by sight, and since he thought that he had so seen Christ, he desired in like manner to see the Father; but Jesus showeth him that he had not even seen Himself. And if any one here call knowledge, sight, I do not contradict him, for, "he that hath known Me," saith Christ, "hath known the Father." Yet He did not say this, but desiring to establish the Consubstantiality, declared, "he that knoweth My Essence, knoweth that of the Father also." "And what is this?" saith some one; "for he who is acquainted with creation knoweth also God." Yet all are acquainted with creation, and have seen it, but all do not know God. Besides, let us consider what Philip

[1] "And how sayest thou then, Show us the Father?" N. T.
[2] i.e. Jerusalem.
[3] al. "to do this."

seeks to see. Is it the wisdom of the Father? Is it His goodness? Not so, but the very whatever God is, the very Essence. To this therefore Christ answereth, "He that hath seen Me." Now he that hath seen the creation, hath not also seen the Essence of God. "If any one hath seen Me, he hath seen the Father," He saith. Now had He been of a different Essence, He would not have spoken thus. But to make use of a grosser argument, no man that knows not what gold is, can discern the substance of gold in silver. For one nature is not shown by another. Wherefore He rightly rebuked him, saying, "Am I so long with you?" Hast thou enjoyed such teaching, hast thou seen miracles wrought with authority, and all belonging to the Godhead, which the Father alone worketh, sins forgiven, secrets published, death retreating, a creation wrought from earth,[1] and hast thou not known Me? Because He was clothed with flesh, therefore He said, "Hast thou not known Me?"

[2.] Thou hast seen the Father; seek not to see more; for in Him thou hast seen Me. If thou hast seen Me, be not over-curious; for thou hast also in Me known Him.

Ver. 10. "Believest thou not that I am in the Father?"[2]

That is, "I am seen in that Essence."

"The words that I speak, I speak not of Myself."

Seest thou the exceeding nearness, and the proof of the one Essence?

"The Father that dwelleth in Me, He doeth the works."

How, beginning with words, doth He come to works? for that which naturally followed was, that He should say, "the Father speaketh the words." But He putteth two things here, both concerning doctrine and miracles. Or it may have been because the words also were works. How then doeth He[3] them? In another place He saith, "If I do not the works of My Father, believe Me not." (c. x. 37.) How then saith He here that the Father doeth them? To show this same thing, that there is no interval between the Father and the Son. What He saith is this: "The Father would not act in one way, and I in another." Indeed in another place both He and the Father work; "My Father worketh hitherto, and I work" (c. v. 17); showing in the first passage the unvaryingness of the works,[4] in the second the identity. And if the obvious meaning of the words denotes humility, marvel not; for after having first said, "Believest thou not?" He then spake thus, showing that He so modeled His words to bring him to the faith; for He walked in their hearts.

Ver. 11. "Believe[5] that I am in the Father and the Father in Me."

"Ye ought not, when ye hear of 'Father' and 'Son,' to seek anything else to the establishing of the relationship[6] as to Essence, but if this is not sufficient to prove to you the Condignity and Consubstantiality, ye may learn it even from the works." Had the, "he that hath seen Me, hath seen My Father," been used with respect to works, He would not afterwards have said, "Or else believe Me for the very works' sake."

And then to show that He is not only able to do these things, but also other much greater than these, He putteth them with excess. For He saith not, "I can do greater things than these," but, what was much more wonderful, "I can give to others also to do greater things than these."

Ver. 12. "Verily, verily, I say unto you, He that believeth on Me, the works that I do shall he do also; and greater works than these shall he do, because I go to the Father."

That is, "it now remaineth for you to work miracles, for I go away." Then when He had accomplished what His argument intended, He saith,

Ver. 13. "Whatsoever ye shall ask in My Name, that will I do, that the Father may be glorified in Me."

Seest thou again that it is He who doeth it? "I," saith He, "will do it"; not, "I will ask of the Father," but, "that the Father may be glorified in Me." In another place He said, "God shall glorify Him in Himself" (c. xiii. 32), but here, "He shall glorify the Father"; for when the Son shall appear with great power, He who begat shall be glorified. But what is, "in My Name"? That which the Apostles said, "In the Name of Jesus Christ, arise and walk." (Acts iii. 6.) For all the miracles which they did He wrought in them, and "the hand of the Lord was with them." (Acts xi. 21.)

Ver. 14. "I will do[7] it," He saith.

Seest thou His authority? The things done by means of others Himself doeth; hath He no power for the things done by Himself, except as being wrought in by the Father? And who could say this? But why doth He put it second? To confirm His own words, and to show that the former sayings were of condescension. But the, "I go to the Father," is this: "I shall not perish, but remain in My own proper Dignity, and Am in Heaven." All this He said, comforting them. For since it was likely that they, not yet understanding His discourses concerning the Resurrection, would imagine something dismal, He in other discourses promiseth that He will give them such things, soothing them in

---

[1] i.e. eyes given by means of the clay.
[2] "and the Father in Me?" N. T.
[3] the Father.   [4] i.e. those of the Father and the Son.
[5] "Believe Me," N. T.
[6] τῆς κατὰ τὴν οὐσίαν συγγενείας.
[7] "If ye shall ask anything in My Name, I," &c., N. T.

every way, and showing that He abideth continually; and not only abideth, but that He will even show forth greater power.

[3.] Let us then follow Him, and take up the Cross. For though persecution be not present, yet the season for another kind of death is with us. "Mortify," it saith, "your members which are upon earth." (Col. iii. 5.) Let us then quench concupiscence, slay anger, abolish envy. This is a "living sacrifice." (Rom. xii. 1.) This sacrifice ends not in ashes, is not dispersed in smoke, wants neither wood, nor fire, nor knife. For it hath both fire and a knife, even the Holy Spirit. Using this knife, circumcise the superfluous and alien portion of thy heart; open the closedness of thine ears, for vices[1] and evil desires are wont to stop the way against the entrance of the word. The desire of money, when it is set before one, permits not to hear the word concerning almsgiving; and malice when it is present raises a wall against the teaching concerning love; and some other malady falling on in its turn, makes the soul yet more dull to all things. Let us then do away these wicked desires; it is enough to have willed, and all are quenched. For let us not, I entreat, look to this, that the love of wealth is a tyrannical thing, but that the tyranny is that of our own slackmindedness. Many indeed say that they do not even know what money is. For this desire is not a natural one; such as are natural were implanted in us from the first, from the beginning, but as for gold and silver, for a long time not even what it is was known. Whence then grew this desire? From vainglory and extreme slackmindedness. For of desires some are necessary, some natural, some neither the one nor the other. For example, those which if not gratified destroy the creature are both natural and necessary, as the desire of meat and drink and sleep; carnal desire is natural indeed but not necessary, for many have got the better of it, and have not died. But the desire of wealth is neither natural nor necessary, but superfluous; and if we choose we need not admit its beginning. At any rate, Christ speaking of virginity saith, "He that is able to receive it, let him receive it." (Matt. xix. 12.) But concerning riches not so, but how? "Except a man forsake all that he hath, he is not worthy of Me." (Luke xiv. 33.) What was easy He recommended, but what goes beyond the many He leaveth to choice. Why then do we deprive ourselves of all excuse? The man who is made captive by some more tyrannical passion shall not suffer a heavy punishment, but he who is subdued by a weak one is deprived of all defense. For what shall we reply when He saith, "Ye saw Me hungry and fed Me not"? (Matt. xxv. 42); what excuse shall we have? We shall certainly plead poverty; yet we are not poorer than that widow, who by throwing in two mites overshot all the rest. For God requireth not the quantity of the offering, but the measure of the mind; and that He doth so, comes from His tender care. Let us then, admiring His lovingkindness, contribute what is in our power, that having both in this life and in that which is to come obtained in abundance the lovingkindness of God, we may be able to enjoy the good things promised to us, through the grace and lovingkindness of our Lord Jesus Christ, to whom be glory for ever and ever. Amen.

# HOMILY LXXV.

## John xiv. 15–17.

"If ye love Me, keep My commandments. And I will pray the Father, and He shall give you another Comforter, that He may abide with you forever; even the Spirit of truth, whom the world cannot receive, because it seeth Him not, neither knoweth Him."[2]

[1.] WE need everywhere works and actions, not a mere show of words. For to say and to promise is easy for any one, but to act is not equally easy. Why have I made these remarks? Because there are many at this time who say that they fear and love God, but in their works show the contrary; but God requireth that love which is shown by works. Wherefore He said to the disciples, "If ye love Me, keep My commandments." For after He had told them, "Whatsoever ye shall ask,[3] I will do it," that they might not deem the mere "asking" to be availing, He added, "If ye love Me," "then," He saith, "I will do it." And since it was likely that they would be troubled when they heard that, "I go[4] to the Father," He telleth them "to be troubled now is not to love, to love is to

---

[1] lit. "maladies."
[2] "But ye know Him, for He dwelleth with you, and shall be with you." N. T.
[3] "in My Name," N. T.    [4] al. "depart."

obey My words. I have given you a commandment that ye love one another, that ye do so to
each other as I have done to you; this is love,
to obey these My words, and to yield to Him
who is the object of your love."

"And I will ask the Father, and He shall give
you another Comforter." Again His speech is
one of condescension. For since it was probable,
that they not yet knowing Him would eagerly
seek His society, His discourse, His presence
in the flesh, and would admit of no consolation
when He was absent, what saith He? "I will
ask the Father, and He shall give you another
Comforter," that is, "Another like unto Me."
Let those be ashamed who have the disease of
Sabellius,[1] who hold not the fitting opinion
concerning the Spirit. For the marvel of this
discourse is this, that it hath stricken down
contradictory heresies with the same blow. For
by saying "another," He showeth the difference
of Person, and by "Paraclete," the connection
of Substance. But why said He, "I will ask the
Father"? Because had He said, "I will send
Him," they would not have so much believed,
and now the object is that He should be believed.
For afterwards He declares that He Himself sendeth Him, saying, "Receive ye the Holy Ghost"
(c. xx. 22); but in this place He telleth them
that He asketh the Father, so as to render His
discourse credible to them. Since John saith
of Him, "Of His fullness have all we received"
(c. i. 16); but what He had, how receiveth He
from another? And again, "He shall baptize
you with the Holy Ghost and with fire." (Luke
iii. 16.) "But what had He more than the
Apostles, if He was about to ask It of His Father
in order to give It to others, when they often
even without prayer appear to have done thus?"
And how,[2] if It is sent according to request
from the Father, doth It descend of Itself? And
how is that which is everywhere present sent
by Another, that which "divideth to every man
severally as He will" (1 Cor. xii. 11), and which
saith with authority, "Separate Me Paul and
Barnabas"? (Acts xiii. 2.) Those ministers
were ministering unto God, yet still It called
them authoritatively to Its own work; not that It
called them to any different work, but in order
to show Its power. "What then," saith some
one, "is, 'I will ask the Father'?" (He saith
it) to show the time of Its coming. For when
He had cleansed them by the sacrifice,[3] then
the Holy Ghost lighted upon them. "And why,
while He was with them, came it not?" Because the sacrifice was not yet offered. But
when afterwards sin had been loosed, and they

were being sent forth to dangers, and were
stripping themselves for the contest, then need
was that the Anointer[4] should come. "But
why did not the Spirit come immediately after
the Resurrection?" In order that being greatly
desirous of It, they might receive It with great
joy. For as long as Christ was with them, they
were not in tribulation; but when He departed,
being made defenseless and thrown into much
fear, they would receive It with much readiness.
"He remaineth with you." This showeth
that even after death It departeth not. But lest
when they heard of the "Paraclete," they should
imagine a second Incarnation, and expect to see
It with their eyes, He setteth them right by saying, "Whom the world cannot receive, because
it seeth Him not." "He will not be with you
as I have been, but will dwell in your very
souls"; for this is the, "shall be in you."[5] He
calleth it the "Spirit of truth"; thus explaining the types in the Old Testament. "That He
may be[6] with you." What is, "may be with
you"? That which He saith Himself, that "I
am with you." (Matt. xxviii. 20.) Besides, He
also implieth something else, that "the case of
the Spirit shall not be the same as Mine, He
shall never leave you." "Whom the world cannot receive, because it seeth Him not." "Why,
what is there belonging to the other Persons that
is visible?" Nothing; but He speaketh here
of knowledge; at least He addeth, "neither
knoweth Him." For He is wont, in the case
of exact knowledge, to call it "sight"; because
sight is clearer than the other senses, by this
He always representeth exact knowledge. By
"world," He here speaketh of "the wicked,"
thus too comforting the disciples by giving to
them a special gift. See in how many particulars He raised His discourse concerning It. He
said, "He is Another like unto Me"; He said,
"He will not leave you"; He said, "Unto you
alone He cometh, as also did I"; He said,
that "He remaineth in you"; but not even so
did He drive out their despondency. For they
still sought Him and His society. To cure then
this feeling, He saith,

Ver. 18. "I will not leave you orphans, I will
come unto you."

[2.] "Fear not," He saith, "I said not that
I would send you another Comforter, as though
I were Myself withdrawing from you for ever; I
said not that He remaineth with you, as though
I should see you no more. For I also Myself
will come to you, I will not leave you orphans."
Because when commencing He said, "Little
children," therefore He saith also here, "I will
not leave you orphans." At first then He told
them, "Ye shall come whither I go"; and, "In

---

[1] Sabellius was a bishop in Upper Egypt in the third century.
The heresy which bears his name denies the Personality of the Son
and the Holy Spirit, and holds that they are manifestations or characters of the Godhead.
[2] The objection is met by other questions.     [3] i.e. of Himself.

[4] ἀλείφοντα.                    [6] "may abide," N. T.
[5] al. "remaineth in you."

My Father's house there are many mansions"; but here, since that time was long, He giveth them the Spirit; and when, not knowing what it could be of which He spake, they were not sufficiently comforted, "I will not leave you orphans," He saith; for this they chiefly required. But since the, "I will come to you," was the saying of one declaring a "presence," observe how in order that they might not again seek for the same kind of presence as before, He did not clearly tell them this thing, but hinted at it; for having said,

Ver. 19. "Yet a little while, and the world seeth Me not"; He added, "but ye see Me."

As though He had said, "I come indeed to you, but not in the same way as before, ever being with you day by day." And lest they should say, "How then saidst Thou to the Jews, Henceforth ye shall not see Me?" He solveth the contradiction by saying, "to you alone"; for such also is the nature of the Spirit.

"Because I live, ye shall live also."

For the Cross doth not finally separate us, but only hideth for a little moment; and by "life" He seemeth to me to mean not the present only, but the future also.

Ver. 20. "At that day ye shall know that I am in the[1] Father, and you in Me, and I in you."

With regard to the Father, these words refer to Essence; with regard to the disciples, to agreement of mind and help from God. "And how, tell me, is this reasonable?" saith some one. And how, pray, is the contrary reasonable? For great and altogether boundless is the interval between Christ and the disciples. And if the same words are employed, marvel not; for the Scripture is often wont to use in different senses the same words, when applied to God and to men. Thus we are called "gods," and "sons of God," yet the word hath not the same force when applied to us and to God. And the Son is called "Image," and "Glory"; so are we, but great is the interval between us. Again, "Ye are Christ's, and Christ is God's" (1 Cor. iii. 23), but not in like manner as Christ is God's are we Christ's. But what is it that He saith? "When I am arisen," He saith, "ye shall know that I am not separated from the Father, but have the same power with Him, and that I am with you continually, when facts proclaim the aid which cometh to you from Me, when your enemies are kept down, and you speak boldly, when dangers are removed from your path, when the preaching of the Gospel flourisheth day by day, when all yield and give ground to the word of true religion. "As the Father hath sent Me, so send I you." (c. xx. 21.) Seest thou that here also the word hath not the same force? for if we

take it as though it had, the Apostles will differ in nothing from Christ. But why saith He, "Then ye shall know"? Because then they saw Him risen and conversing with them, then they learnt the exact faith; for great was the power of the Spirit, which taught them all things.

[3.] Ver. 21. "He that hath My commandments and keepeth them, he it is that loveth Me."

It is not enough merely to have them, we need also an exact keeping of them. But why doth He frequently say the same thing to them? as, "If ye love Me, ye will keep[2] My commandments" (ver. 15); and, "He that hath My commandments and keepeth them"; and, "If any one heareth My word and keepeth it, he it is that loveth Me — he that heareth not My words, loveth Me not." (Ver. 24.) I think that He alluded to their despondency; for since He had uttered many wise sayings to them concerning death, saying, "He that hateth his life in this world shall save it unto life eternal" (c. xii. 25); and, "Unless a man take[3] his cross andf ollow Me, he is not worthy of Me" (Matt. x. 38); and is about to say other things besides, rebuking them, He saith, "Think ye that ye suffer sorrow from love? The not sorrowing would be a sign of love." And because He wished all along to establish this, as He went on He summed up His discourse in this same point; "If ye loved Me," He saith, "ye would have rejoiced, because — I go to My Father" (ver. 28), but now ye are in this state through cowardice. To be thus disposed towards death is not for those who remember My commandments; for you ought to be crucified, if you truly loved Me, for My word exhorteth you not to be afraid of those that kill the body. Those that are such both the Father loveth and I. "And I will manifest Myself unto him.[4] Then saith Judas,[5]

Ver. 22. "How is it that Thou wilt manifest Thyself unto us?"[6]

Seest thou that their soul was close pressed[7] with fear? For he was confounded and troubled, and thought that as we see dead men in a dream, so He also would be seen. In order therefore that they might not imagine this, hear what He saith.

Ver. 23. "I and the Father will come unto him, and make Our abode with him."[8]

All but saying, "As the Father revealeth Himself, so also do I." And not in this way only He removed the suspicion, but also by saying, "We will make Our abode with him," a thing

2 "If ye love Me, keep," &c.
3 "He that taketh not," &c.
4 "And he that loveth Me shall be loved of My Father, and I will love him, and will manifest," &c.  N. T.
5 "not Iscariot," N. T.
6 "and not unto the world," N. T.
7 πεπληγμένην, "crushed like felt."
8 Ver. 23. "Jesus answered and said unto him, If a man love Me, he will keep My words; and My Father will love him, and We will come," &c.

which doth not belong to dreams. But observe, I pray you, the disciple confounded, and not daring to say plainly what he desired to say. For he said not, "Woe to us, that Thou diest, and will come to us as the dead come"; he spake not thus; but, "How is it that Thou wilt show Thyself to us, and not unto the world?" Jesus then saith, that "I accept you, because ye keep My commandments." In order that they might not, when they should see Him afterwards,[1] deem Him to be an apparition, therefore He saith these things beforehand. And that they might not deem that He would appear to them so as I have said, He telleth them also the reason, "Because ye keep My commandments"; He saith that the Spirit also will appear in like manner. Now if after having companied with Him so long time, they cannot yet endure that Essence, or rather cannot even imagine It, what would have been their case had He appeared thus to them at the first? on this account also He ate with them, that the action might not seem to be an illusion. For if they thought this when they saw Him walking on the waters, although His wonted form was seen by them, and He was not far distant, what would they have imagined had they suddenly seen Him arisen whom they had seen taken[2] and swathed? Wherefore He continually telleth them that He will appear, and why He will appear, and how, that they may not suppose Him to be an apparition.

Ver. 24. "He that loveth Me not keepeth not My sayings; and the word which ye hear is not Mine, but the Father's which sent Me."

"So that he that heareth not these sayings not only doth not love Me, but neither doth he love the Father." For if this is the sure proof of love, the hearing the commandments, and these are of the Father, he that heareth them loveth not the Son only, but the Father also. "And how is the word 'thine' and 'not thine'?" This means, "I speak not without the Father, nor say anything of Myself contrary to what seemeth good to Him."

Ver. 25. "These things have I spoken unto you, being yet present with you."

Since these sayings were not clear, and since some they did not understand, and doubted about the greater number, in order that they might not be again confused, and say, "What commands?" He released them from all their perplexity, saying,

Ver. 26. "The Comforter, whom the Father shall send in My Name, He shall teach you."[3]

"Perhaps these things are not clear to you now, but 'He'[4] is a clear teacher of them." And the, "remaineth with you" (ver. 17), is the expression of One implying that Himself will depart. Then that they may not be grieved, He saith, that as long as He should remain with them and the Spirit should not come, they would be unable to comprehend anything great or sublime. And this He said to prepare them to bear nobly His departure, as that which was to be the cause of great blessings to them. He continually calleth Him "Comforter," because of the afflictions which then possessed them. And since even after hearing these things they were troubled, when they thought of the sorrows, the wars, His departure, see how He calmeth them again by saying,

Ver. 27. "Peace I leave to you."[5]

All but saying, "What are ye harmed by the trouble of the world, provided ye be at peace with[6] Me? For this peace is not of the same kind as that. The one is external, is often mischievous and unprofitable, and is no advantage to those who possess it; but I give you peace of such a kind that ye be at peace with one another, which thing rendereth you stronger." And because He said again, "I leave," which was the expression of One departing, and enough to confound them, therefore He again saith,

"Let not your heart be troubled, neither let it be afraid."

Seest thou that they were affected partly by loving affection, partly by fear?

Ver. 28. "Ye have heard how I said unto you, I go away, and come again unto you. If ye loved Me, ye would rejoice because I said, I go unto the Father; for My Father is greater than I."

[4.] And what joy would this bring to them? What consolation? What then mean the words? They did not yet know concerning the Resurrection, nor had they right opinion concerning Him; (for how could they, who did not even know that He would rise again?) but they thought that the Father was mighty. He saith then, that "If ye are fearful for Me, as not able to defend Myself, and if ye are not confident that I shall see you again after the Crucifixion, yet when ye heard that I go to the Father, ye ought then to have rejoiced because I go away to One that is greater, and able to undo all dangers." "Ye have heard how I said unto you." Why hath He put this? Because, He saith, "I am so firmly confident about the things which come to pass, that I even foretell them, so far am I from fearing." This also is the meaning of what follows.

Ver. 29. "And now I have told you before

---

[1] i.e. after the Resurrection.　　[2] κατεχόμενον.
[3] Ver. 26. "But the Comforter, the Holy Ghost, whom the Father will send in My Name, He shall teach you all things, and bring all things to your remembrance whatsoever I have said unto you."

[4] ἐκεῖνος.
[5] Ver. 27. "Peace I leave with you. My peace I give unto you; not as the world giveth give I unto you," N. T.　　[6] πρὸς.

it come to pass, that when it is come to pass, ye might believe that I Am." [1]  As though He had said, "Ye would not have known, had I not told you. And I should not have told you, had I not been confident."  Seest thou that the speech is one of condescension? for when He saith, "Think ye that I cannot pray to the Father, and He shall presently give Me more than twelve legions of Angels" (Matt. xxvi. 53), He speaketh to the secret thoughts of the hearers; since no one, even in the height of madness, would say that He was not able to help Himself, but needed Angels; but because they thought of Him as a man, therefore He spoke of "twelve legions of Angels." Yet in truth He did but ask those who came to take Him a question, and cast them backwards. (c. xviii. 6.) (If any one say that the Father is greater, inasmuch as [2] He is the cause of the Son, we will not contradict this. But this doth not by any means make the Son to be of a different Essence.)  But what He saith, is of this kind: "As long as I am here, it is natural that you should deem that I am [3] in danger; but when I am gone 'there,' [4] be confident that I am in safety; for Him none will be able to overcome." All these words were addressed to the weakness of the disciples, for, " I Myself am confident, and care not for death." On this account, He said, "I have told you these things before they come to pass"; "but since," He saith, "ye are not yet able to receive the saying concerning them, I bring you comfort even from the Father, whom ye entitle great." Having thus consoled them, He again telleth them sorrowful things.

Ver. 30. "Hereafter I will not talk [5] with you." Wherefore? "For the ruler of this world cometh, and hath nothing in Me."

By "ruler of this world," He meaneth the devil, calling wicked men also by the same name. For he ruleth not heaven and earth, since he would have been subverted, and cast down all things, but he ruleth over those who give themselves up to him. Wherefore He calleth him, "the ruler of the darkness of this world," in this place again calling evil deeds, "darkness." "What then, doth the devil slay Thee?" By no means; "he hath nothing in Me." "How then do they kill Thee?" "Because I will it, and,

Ver. 31. "'That the world may know that I love the Father.'" [6]

"For being not subject," He saith, "to death, nor a debtor to it, I endure it through My love to the Father." This He saith, that He may again rouse their souls, and that they may learn

that not unwillingly but willingly He goeth to this thing, and that He doth it despising the devil. It was not enough for Him to have said, "Yet a little while I am with you" (c. vii. 33), but He continually handleth this painful subject, (with good reason,) until He should make it acceptable to them, by weaving along with it pleasant things. Wherefore at one time He saith, "I go, and I come again"; and, "That where I am, there ye may be also"; and, "Ye cannot follow Me now, but afterwards ye shall follow Me"; and, "I go to the Father"; and, "The Father is greater than I"; and, "Before it come to pass, I have told you"; and, "I do not suffer these things from constraint, but from love for the Father." So that they might consider, that the action could not be destructive nor hurtful, if at least He who greatly loved Him, and was greatly loved by Him, so willed. On this account, while intermingling these pleasant words, He continually uttered the painful ones also, practicing their minds. For both the, "remaineth with you" (c. xvi. 7), and, "My departure is expedient for you," were expressions of One giving comfort. For this reason He spake by anticipation ten thousand sayings concerning the Spirit, [7] the, "Is in you," and, "The world cannot receive," and, "He shall bring all things to your remembrance," and, "Spirit of truth," and, "Holy Spirit," and, "Comforter," and that "It is expedient for you," in order that they might not despond, as though there would be none to stand before and help them. "It is expedient," He saith, showing that It [8] would make them spiritual.

[5.] This at least, we see, was what took place. For they who now trembled and feared, after they had received the Spirit sprang into the midst of dangers, and stripped themselves for the contest against steel, and fire, and wild beasts, and seas, and every kind of punishment; and they, the unlettered and ignorant, discoursed so boldly as to astonish their hearers. For the Spirit made them men of iron instead of men of clay, gave them wings, and allowed them to be cast down by nothing human. For such is that grace; if it find despondency, it disperses it; if evil desires, it consumes them; if cowardice, it casts it out, and doth not allow one who has partaken of it to be afterwards mere man, but as it were removing him to heaven itself, causes him to image to himself all that is there. (Acts iv. 32, and ii. 46.) On this account no one said that any of the things that he possessed was his own, but they continued in prayer, in praise, and in singleness of heart. For this the Holy Spirit most requireth, for "the fruit of the Spirit is joy, peace — faith, meek-

---

[1] The words " that I Am " are not read here, but in c. xiii. 19.
[2] καθ' ὅ.          [4] i.e. to the Father.
[3] Gr. "we are."          [5] "talk much," N. T.
[6] " And as the Father gave Me commandment, even so I do."
N. T.

[7] al. "concerning It."          [8] i.e. the Holy Spirit.

ness." (Gal. v. 22, 23.) "And yet spiritual persons often grieve," saith some one. But that sorrow is sweeter than joy. Cain was sorrowful, but with the sorrow of the world; Paul was sorrowful, but with godly sorrow. Everything that is spiritual brings the greatest gain, just as everything that is worldly the utmost loss. Let us then draw to us the invincible aid of the Spirit, by keeping the commandments, and then we shall be nothing inferior to the Angels. For neither are they therefore of this character,[1] because they are incorporeal, for were this the case, no incorporeal being would have become wicked, but the will is in every case the cause of all. Wherefore among incorporeal beings some have been found worse than men or things irrational, and among those having bodies some better than the incorporeal. All just men, for instance, whatever were their righteous deeds, did them while dwelling on earth, and having bodies. For they dwelt on earth as those who were pilgrims and strangers; but in heaven, as citizens. Then say not thou either, "I am clothed with flesh, I cannot get the mastery, nor undertake the toils[2] which are for the sake of virtue." Do not accuse the Creator. For if the wearing the flesh make virtue impossible, then the fault is not ours. But that it does not make it impossible, the band of saints has shown. A nature of flesh did not prevent Paul from becoming what he was, nor Peter from receiving the keys of heaven; and Enoch also, having worn flesh, was translated, and not found. So also Elias was caught up with the flesh. Abraham also with Isaac and his grandson shone brightly, having the flesh; and Joseph in the flesh struggled against that abandoned woman. But why speak I of the flesh? For though thou place a chain upon the flesh, no harm is done. "Though I am bound," saith Paul, yet "the word of God is not bound." (2 Tim. ii. 9.) And why speak I of bonds and chains? Add to these the prison,[6] and bars, yet neither are these any hindrance to virtue; at least so Paul hath instructed us. For the bond of the soul is not iron but cowardice, and the desire of wealth, and the ten thousand passions. These bind us, though our body be free. "But," saith some one, "these have their origin from the body." An excuse this, and a false pretense. For had they been produced from the body, all would have undergone them. For as we cannot escape weariness, and sleep, and hunger, and thirst, since they belong to our nature; so too these, if they were of the same kind, would not allow any one to be exempt from their tyranny; but since many escape them, it is clear that such things are the faults of a careless soul. Let us then put a stop to this, and not accuse the body, but subdue it to the soul, that having it under command, we may enjoy the everlasting good things, through the grace and lovingkindness of our Lord Jesus Christ, to whom be glory for ever and ever. Amen.

---

# HOMILY LXXVI.

### JOHN xiv. 31; xv. 1.

"Arise, let us go hence. I am the true Vine, (ye are the branches,[3]) and My Father is the Husbandman."

[1.] IGNORANCE makes the soul timid and unmanly, just as instruction in heavenly doctrines makes it great and sublime. For when it has enjoyed no care, it is in a manner timid, not by nature but by will.[4] For when I see the man who once was brave,[5] now become a coward, I say that this latter feeling no longer belongs to nature, for what is natural is immutable. Again, when I see those who but now were cowards all at once become daring, I pass the same judgment, and refer all to will. Since even the disciples were very fearful, before they had learned what they ought, and had been deemed worthy of the gift of the Spirit; yet afterwards they became bolder than lions. So Peter, who could not bear the threat of a damsel, was hung with his head downwards, and was scourged, and though he endured ten thousand dangers, would not be silent, but enduring what he endured as though it were a dream, in such a situation spake boldly; but not so before the Crucifixion. Wherefore Christ said, "Arise, let us go hence." "But why, tell me? Did he not know the hour at which Judas would come upon Him? Or perhaps He feared lest he should come and seize them, and lest the plotters should be upon him before he had furnished his most excellent teaching." Away with the thought! these things are far from His dignity. "If then He did not fear, why did He remove them, and then after finish-

---

[1] i.e. keeping God's commands.
[2] al. "I cannot master the toils."
[3] from ver. 5.
[4] προαίρεσιν.
[5] al. "a brave darer."
[6] al. "prisons."

ing His discourse lead them into a garden known to Judas? And even had Judas come, could He not have blinded their eyes, as He also did when the traitor was not present?[1] Why did He remove them?" He alloweth the disciples a little breathing time. For it was likely that they, as being in a conspicuous place, would tremble and fear, both on the account of the time and the place, (for it was the depth of night,) and would not give[2] heed to His words, but would be continually turning about, and imagining that they heard those who were to set upon them; and that more especially when their Master's speech made them expect evil. For, "yet a little while," He saith, "and I am not with you," and, "the ruler of this world cometh." Since now when they heard these and the like words they were troubled, as though they should certainly be taken immediately, He leadeth them to another place, in order that thinking themselves in safety, they might listen to Him without fear. For they were about to hear lofty doctrines. Therefore He saith, "Arise, let us go hence." Then He addeth, and saith,[3] "I am the Vine, ye are the branches." What willeth He to imply by the comparison? That the man who gives no heed to His words can have no life, and that the miracles about to take place, would be wrought by the power of Christ. "My Father is the Husbandman." "How then? Doth the Son need a power[4] working within?" Away with the thought! this example does not signify this. Observe with what exactness He goeth through the comparison. He saith not that the "root" enjoys the care of the Husbandman, but, "the branches." And the root is brought in in this place for no other purpose, but that they may learn that they can work nothing without His power, and that they ought to be united with Him by faith as the branch with the vine.

Ver. 2. "Every branch in Me that beareth not fruit the Father[5] taketh away."

Here He alludeth to the manner of life, showing that without works it is not possible to be in Him.

"And every branch that beareth fruit, He purgeth it."[6]

That is, "causeth it to enjoy great care." Yet the root requires care rather than the branches, in being dug about, and cleared, yet about this He saith nothing here, but all about the branches. Showing that He is sufficient to Himself, and that the disciples need much help from the Husbandman, although they be very excellent. Wherefore He saith, "that which beareth fruit,

He purgeth it." The one branch, because it is fruitless, cannot even remain in the Vine, but for the other, because it beareth fruit, He rendereth it more fruitful. This, some one might assert, was said with relation also to the persecutions then coming upon them. For the "purgeth it," is "pruneth," which makes the branch bear better. Whence it is shown, that persecutions rather make men stronger. Then, lest they should ask concerning whom He said these things, and lest He should throw them back into anxiety, He saith,

Ver. 3. "Now ye are clean through the word which I have spoken unto you."

Seest thou how He introduceth Himself as tending the branches? "I have cleansed you," He saith; yet above He declareth that the Father doth this. But there is no separation[7] between the Father and the Son. "And now your part also must be performed." Then to show that He did not this as needing their ministry,[8] but for their advancement, He addeth,

Ver. 4.[9] "As the branch cannot bear fruit of itself except it abide in the vine, so neither can he who abideth not in Me."[10]

For that they might not be separated from Him by timidity, He fasteneth and glueth to Himself their souls slackened through fear, and holdeth out to them good hopes for the future. For the root remains, but to be taken away, or to be left, belongs to the branches. Then having urged them on in both ways, by things pleasant and things painful, He requireth first what is to be done on our side.

Ver. 5. "He that abideth in Me, and I in him."[11]

Seest thou that the Son contributeth not less than the Father towards the care of the disciples? The Father purgeth, but He keepeth them in Himself. The abiding in the root is that which maketh the branches to be fruit-bearing. For that which is not purged, if it remain on the root, bears fruit, though perhaps not so much as it ought; but that which remains not, bears none at all. But still the "purging" also hath been shown to belong to the Son, and the "abiding in the root," to the Father, who also begat the Root. Seest thou how all is common,[12] both the "purging," and the enjoying the virtue which is from the root?

[2.] Now it were a great penalty, the being able to do nothing, but He stayeth not the punishment at this point, but carrieth on His discourse farther.

---

[1] al. "to persons present."
[2] al. "and it was not even possible to give."
[3] al. "having led them away, He saith."
[4] ἐνεργείας.   [5] "He," N. T.
[6] "that it may bring forth more fruit," N. T.

[7] μέσον.   [8] al. "teaching."
[9] Ver. 4. "Abide in Me, and I in you. As," &c. N. T.
[10] "so neither can ye, except ye abide in Me." N. T.
[11] Ver. 5. "I am the Vine, ye are the branches. He that abideth in Me, and I in him, the same bringeth forth much fruit; for without Me ye can do nothing." N. T.
[12] i.e. to the Father and the Son.

Ver. 6. "He is cast forth,"[1] He saith.

No longer enjoying the benefit of the husbandman's hand. "And is withered." That is, if he had aught of the root, he loses it; if any grace, he is stripped of this, and is bereft of the help and life which proceed from it. And what the end? "He is cast into the fire." Not such he who abideth with Him. Then He showeth what it is to "abide," and saith,

Ver. 7. "If My words abide in you."[2]

Seest thou that with reason I said above, that He seeketh the proof by works? For when He had said, "Whatsoever ye shall ask I will do it" (c. xiv. 14, 15), He added, "If ye love Me, ye will keep[3] My commandments." And here, "If ye abide in Me, and My words abide in you."

"Ye shall ask what ye will, and it shall be done unto you."

This He said to show that they who plotted against Him should be burnt up, but that "they" should bear fruit. Then transferring the fear from them to the others, and showing that they should be invincible, He saith,

Ver. 8. "Herein is My Father glorified, that ye be My disciples, and bear much fruit."

Hence He maketh His discourse credible, for if the bearing fruit pertains to the glory of the Father, He will not neglect His own glory. "And ye shall be My disciples." Seest thou how he that beareth fruit, he is the disciple? But what is, "In this is the Father glorified"? "He rejoiceth when ye abide in Me, when ye bear fruit."

Ver. 9. "As the Father hath loved Me, so have I loved you."

Here at length He speaketh in a more human manner, for this, as spoken to men,[4] has its peculiar force. Since what a measure of love did He manifest, who chose to die, who counted worthy of such honor those who were His slaves, His haters, His open enemies, and led them up to the heavens! "If then I love you, be bold; if it be the glory of My Father that ye bear fruit, imagine nothing ill." Then that He may not make them supine, observe how He braceth them again,

"Continue ye in My love."

"For this ye have the power to do." And how shall this be?

Ver. 10. "If ye keep My commandments, even as I have kept my Father's commandments."[5]

Again, His discourse proceedeth in a human way; for certainly the Lawgiver would not be subject to commandments. Seest thou that here also, as I am always saying, this is declared because of the infirmity of the hearers? For He chiefly speaketh to their suspicions, and by every means showeth them that they are in safety, and that their enemies are being lost, and that all, whatever they have, they have from the Son, and that, if they show forth a pure life, none shall ever have the mastery over them. And observe that He discourseth with them in a very authoritative manner, for He said not, "abide in the love of My Father," but, "in Mine"; then, lest they should say, "when Thou hast set us at war with all men, Thou leavest us, and departest," He showeth that He doth not leave them, but is so joined to them if they will, as the branch in the vine. Then, lest from confidence they should become supine, He saith not that the blessing cannot be removed if they are slackminded. And in order not to refer the action to Himself, and so make them more apt to fall, He saith, "Herein is My Father glorified." For everywhere He manifesteth His own and His Father's love towards them. Not the things of the Jews, then, were "glory," but those which they[6] were about to receive. And that they might not say, "we have been driven from the possessions of our fathers, we have been deserted, we have become naked, and destitute of all things," "Look," He saith, "on Me. I am loved by the Father, yet still I suffer these things appointed. And so I am not now leaving you because I love you not. For if I am slain, and take not this for a proof of not being loved by the Father, neither ought ye to be troubled. For, if ye continue in My love, these dangers shall not be able to do you any mischief on the score of love."

[3.] Since then love is a thing mighty and irresistible, not a bare word, let us manifest it by our actions. He reconciled us when we were His enemies, let us, now that we have become His friends, remain so. He led the way, let us at least follow; He loveth us not for His own advantage, (for He needeth nothing,) let us at least love Him for our profit; He loved us being His enemies, let us at least love Him being our friend. At present we do the contrary; for every day God is blasphemed through us, through our plunderings, through our covetousness. And perhaps one of you will say, "Every day thy discourse is about covetousness." Would that I could speak about it every night too; would that I could do so, following you about in the market-place, and at your table; would that both wives, and friends, and children, and domestics, and tillers of the soil, and neighbors, and the very pavement and walls, could ever

---

[1] Ver. 6. "If a man abide not in Me, he is cast forth as a branch, and is withered; and men gather them, and cast them into the fire, and they are burned." N. T.

[2] "If ye abide in Me, and My words," &c. N. T.

[3] "If ye love me, keep," &c. N. T.

[4] al. "suitably to a man."

[5] Ver. 10. "If ye keep," &c., "ye shall abide in My love; even as," &c., "and abide in His love." N. T.

[6] i.e. the disciples.

shout forth this word, that so we might perchance have relaxed a little. For this malady hath seized upon all the world, and occupies the souls of all, and great is the tyranny of Mammon. We have been ransomed by Christ, and are the slaves of gold. We proclaim the sovereignty of the one, and obey the other. Whatever "he" commands we readily obey, and we have refused to know family, or friendship, or nature, or laws, or anything, for him. No one looks up to Heaven, no one thinks about things to come. But there will be a time, when there will be no profit even in[1] these words. "In the grave," it saith, "who shall confess to Thee?" Gold is a desirable thing, and procures us much luxury, and makes us to be honored, but not in like manner as doth Heaven. For from the wealthy man many even turn aside, and hate him, but him who lives virtuously they respect and honor. "But," saith some one, "the poor man is derided, even though he be virtuous." Not among men, but brutes.[2] Wherefore he ought not so much as to notice them. For if asses were to bray and daws chatter at us, while all wise men commended us, we should not, losing sight of this latter audience, have regard to clamors of the brutes; for like to daws, and worse than asses, are they who admire present things. Moreover, if an earthly king approve thee, thou makest no account of the many, though they all deride thee; but if the Lord of the universe praise thee, seekest thou the good words of beetles and gnats? For this is what these men are, compared with God, or rather not even this, but something viler, if there be aught such. How long do we wallow in the mire? How long do we set sluggards and belly-gods for our judges? They can prove dicers well, drunkards, those who live for the belly, but as for virtue and vice,

they cannot imagine so much as a dream. If any one taunt thee because thou hast not skill to draw the channels of the watercourses,[3] thou wilt not think it any terrible thing, but wilt even laugh at him who objects to thee ignorance of this kind; and dost thou, when thou desirest to practice virtue, appoint as judges those who know nothing of it? On this account we never reach that art. We commit our case not to the practiced, but to the unlearned, and they judge not according to the rules of art, but according to their own ignorance. Wherefore, I exhort you, let us despise the many; or rather let us desire neither praises, nor possessions, nor wealth, nor deem poverty any evil. For poverty is to us a teacher of prudence, and endurance, and all true wisdom. Thus Lazarus lived in poverty, and received a crown; Jacob desired to get bread only; and Joseph was in the extreme of poverty, being not merely a slave, but also a prisoner; and on this account we admire him the more, and we do not so much praise him when he distributed the corn, as when he dwelt in the dungeon; not when he wore the diadem, but when the chain; not when he sat upon the throne, but when he was plotted against and sold.[4] Considering then all these things, and the crowns twined for us after the conflicts, let us admire not wealth, and honor, and luxury, and power, but poverty, and the chain, and bonds, and endurance in the cause of virtue. For the end of those things is full of troubles and confusion, and their lot is bound up with this present life; but the fruit of these, heaven, and the good things in the heavens, which neither eye hath seen, nor ear heard; which may we all obtain, through the grace and lovingkindness of our Lord Jesus Christ, to whom be glory for ever. Amen.

# HOMILY LXXVII.

### John xv. 11, 12.

"These things have I spoken unto you, that My joy might remain in you, and that your joy might be full. This is My commandment, that ye love one another, as I have loved you."

[1.] ALL things good then have their reward, when they arrive at their proper end, but if they be cut off midway, shipwreck ensues. And as a vessel of immense burden, if it reach not the harbor in time, but founder in the midst of the sea, gains nothing from the length of the voyage,

but even makes the calamity greater, in proportion as it has endured more toils; so are those souls which fall back when near the end of their labors, and faint in the midst of the struggle. Wherefore Paul said, that glory, and honor, and peace, should meet those who ran their course with patient continuance in well-doing. A thing which Christ now effecteth in the case of the

---

[1] al. "no time for."     [2] ἀλόγοις.

[3] Τοὺς ὀχετοὺς τῶν ἁμαρῶν ἕλκειν. An instance of employment requiring skill and practice. v. Iliad xxi. 257.
[4] Ἐπωλεῖτο. So Morel. Ben. and MSS. Sav. reads ἐπολεμεῖτο, "was warred against."

disciples. (Rom. ii. 7.) For since He had accepted them, and they rejoiced in Him, and then the sudden coming of the Passion and His sad words were likely to cut short their pleasure; after having conversed with them sufficiently to soothe them, He addeth, "These things have I spoken unto you, that My joy might remain in you, and that your joy might be fulfilled"; that is, "that ye might not be separated from Me, that ye might not cut short your course. Ye were rejoicing in Me, and ye were rejoicing exceedingly, but despondency hath fallen upon you. This then I remove, that joy may come at the last, showing that your present circumstances are fit cause, not for pain, but for pleasure. I saw you offended; I despised you not; I said not, 'Why do ye not continue noble?' But I spake to you words which brought comfort with them. And so I wish ever to keep you in the same love. Ye have heard concerning a kingdom, ye rejoiced. In order therefore that your joy might be fulfilled, I have spoken these things unto you." But "this is the commandment, that ye love one another as I have loved you." Seest thou that the love of God is intertwined with our own, and connected like a sort of chain? Wherefore it sometimes saith that there are two commandments, sometimes only one. For it is not possible that the man who hath taken hold on the first should not possess the second also. For at one time He said, "On this the Law and the Prophets hang"[1] (Matt. xxii. 40); and at another, "Whatsoever ye would that men should do to you, do ye even so to them, for this is the Law and the Prophets." (Matt. vii. 12.) And, "Love is the fulfilling of the Law." (Rom. xiii. 10.) Which He saith also here; for if to abide proceeds from love, and love from the keeping of the commandments, and the commandment is that we love one another, then the abiding in God proceeds from love towards each other. And He doth not simply speak of love, but declareth also the manner, "As I have loved you." Again He showeth, that His very departure was not of hatred but of love. "So that I ought rather to be admired on this account, for I lay down My life for you."[2] Yet nowhere doth He say this in these words, but in a former place, by sketching the best shepherd, and here by exhorting them, and by showing the greatness of His love, and Himself, who He is. But wherefore doth He everywhere exalt love? Because this is the mark of the disciples, this the bond of virtue.[3] On this account Paul saith such great things of it, as being a genuine disciple of Christ, and having had experience of it.

Ver. 14, 15. "Ye are My friends[4] — henceforth I call you not servants, for the servant knoweth not what his lord doeth. Ye are My friends, for[5] all things which I have heard of My Father I have made known unto you."

How then saith He, "I have many things to tell you, but ye cannot bear them now"? (c. xvi. 12.) By the "all" and the "hearing" He showeth nothing else, but that He uttered nothing alien, but only what was of the Father. And since to speak of secrets appears to be the strongest proof of friendship, "ye have," He saith, "been deemed worthy even of this communion." When however He saith "all," He meaneth, "whatever things it was fit that they should hear." Then He putteth also another sure proof of friendship, no common one. Of what sort was that?

Ver. 16. "Ye have not chosen Me, but I have chosen you."

That is, I ran upon your friendship. And He stayed not here, but,

"I set you,"[6] He saith, (that is, "I planted you,") "that ye should go," (He still useth the metaphor of the vine,) that is, "that ye should extend yourselves"; "and bring forth fruit, and that your fruit should remain."

"Now if your fruit remain, much more shall ye. For I have not only loved you," He saith, "but have done you the greatest benefits, by extending your branches through all the world." Seest thou in how many ways He showeth His love? By telling them things secret, by having in the first instance run to meet their friendship, by granting them the greatest blessings, by suffering for them what then He suffered. After this, He showeth that He also remaineth continually with those who shall bring forth fruit; for it is needful to enjoy His aid, and so to bear fruit.

"That whatsoever ye shall ask of the Father in My Name, He may give it you."

Yet it is the part of the person asked to do the thing asked; but if the Father is asked, how is it that the Son doeth it? It is that thou mayest learn that the Son is not inferior to the Father.

Ver. 17. "These things I command you, that ye love one another."

That is, "It is not to upbraid, that I tell you that I lay down My life for you, or that I ran to meet you, but in order to lead you into friendship." Then, since the being persecuted and insulted by the many was a grievous and intolerable thing, and enough to humble even a lofty soul, therefore, after having said ten thousand things first, Christ entered upon this matter.[7]

---

[1] "On these two commandments," &c.
[2] Ver. 13. "Greater love hath no man than this, that a man lay down his life for his friends." N. T.
[3] τὸ συγκροτοῦν τὴν ἀρ.
[4] "if ye do whatsoever I command you," N. T.
[5] "But I have called you friends, for," &c. N. T.
[6] "ordained," E. V.
[7] What follows seems to be a commentary on ver. 18, omitted. "If the world hate you, ye know that it hated Me before it hated you."

Having first smoothed their minds, He thus proceedeth to these points, showing that these things too were for their exceeding advantage, as He had also shown that the others were. For as He had told them that they ought not to grieve, but rather to rejoice, "because I go to the Father," (since He did this not as deserting but as greatly loving them,) so here also He showeth that they ought to rejoice, not grieve. And observe how He effecteth this. He said not, "I know that the action is grievous, but bear for My sake, since for My sake also ye suffer," for this reason was not yet sufficient to console them ; wherefore letting this pass, He putteth forward another. And what is that? It is that this thing[1] would be a sure proof of their former virtue. "And, on the contrary, ye ought to grieve, not because ye are hated now, but if ye were likely to be loved " ; for this He implieth by saying,

Ver. 19. "If ye were of the world, the world would love its own."[2]

So that had ye been loved it would be very clear that ye had shown forth signs of wickedness. Then, when by saying this first, He did not effect his purpose, He goeth on again with the discourse.

Ver. 20. "The servant is not greater than his lord. If they have persecuted Me, they will also persecute you."[3]

He showed that in this point they would be most His imitators. For while Christ was in the flesh, men had war with Him, but when He was translated, the battle came in the next place upon them. Then because owing to their fewness they were terrified at being about to encounter the attack of so great a multitude, He raiseth their souls by telling them that it was an especial subject of joy that they were hated by them ; "For so ye shall share My sufferings. Ye should not therefore be troubled, for ye are not better than I," as I before told you, "The servant is not greater than his lord." Then there is also a third source of consolation, that the Father also is insulted together with them.

Ver. 21. "But all these things will they do unto you for My Name's sake, because they know not Him that sent Me."

That is, "they insult Him also." Besides this, depriving those others of excuse, and putting also another source of comfort, He saith,

Ver. 22. "If I had not come and spoken unto them, they had not had sin."[4]

Showing that they shall do unjustly both what they do against Him and against them. "Why

then didst Thou[5] bring us into such calamities? Didst Thou not foreknow the wars, the hatred?" Therefore again He saith,

Ver. 23. "He that hateth Me, hateth My Father also."

From this also proclaiming beforehand no small punishment against them. For, since they continually pretended that they persecuted Him on account of the Father, to deprive them of this excuse He spake these words. "They have no excuse. I gave them the teaching which is by words, that by works I added, according to the Law of Moses, who bade all men obey one speaking and doing such things, when he should both lead to piety, and exhibit the greatest miracles."[6] And He spake not simply of " signs," but,

Ver. 24. "Which none other man did."[7]

And of this they themselves are witnesses, speaking in this way ; "It was never so seen in Israel " (Matt. ix. 33) ; and, "Since the world began was it not heard that any man opened the eyes of one that was born blind " (c. ix. 32) ; and the matter of Lazarus was of the same kind, and all the other acts the same, and the mode of wonder-working new, and all beyond[8] thought. "Why then," saith one, "do they persecute both Thee and us?" "Because ye are not of the world. If ye were of the world, the world would love its own." (Ver. 19.) He first remindeth them of the words which He spake also to His own brethren (c. vii. 7) ; but there he spake more by way of a reflection,[9] lest He should offend them, while here, on the contrary, He revealed all. "And how is it clear that it is on this account that we are hated?" "From what was done to Me. For, tell Me, which of My words or deeds could they lay hold on, that they would not receive Me?" Then since the thing would be astounding to us, He telleth the cause ; that is, their wickedness. And He stayeth not here either, but introduceth the Prophet (Ps. xxxv. 19 ; lxix. 4), showing him proclaiming before of old time, and saying, that,

Ver. 25. "They hated Me without a cause."[10]

[3.] Which Paul doth also. For when many wondered how that the Jews believed not, he brings in Prophets foretelling it of old, and declaring the cause ; that their wickedness and pride were the cause of their unbelief. "Well then ; if they kept not Thy saying, neither will they keep ours ; if they persecuted Thee, therefore they will persecute us also ; if they saw signs, such as none other man wrought ; if they

---

[1] i.e. persecution.
[2] "But because ye are not of the world, but I have chosen you out of the world, therefore the world hateth you." N. T.
[3] Ver. 20. "Remember the word that I said unto you, The servant," &c., adding, "If they have kept My saying, they will keep yours also." N. T.
[4] " but now they have no cloke for their sin," N. T.

[5] al. " did He."
[6] Implied in Deut. xiii. where it is written, that the prophet or dreamer who teaches idolatry is not to be followed.
[7] Ver. 24. "If I had not done among them the works that none other man did, they had not had sin; but now have they both seen and hated both Me and My Father." N. T.
[8] Ben. " new and beyond." [9] ἠθικώτερον.
[10] Ver. 25. "But that the word might be fulfilled that is written in their law, They," &c, N. T.

heard words such as none other spake, and profited nothing; if they hate Thy Father and Thee with Him, wherefore," saith one, "hast Thou sent us in among them? How after this shall we be worthy of belief? which of our kindred will give-heed to us?" That they may not therefore be troubled by such thoughts, see what sort of comfort he addeth.

Ver. 26, 27. "When the Comforter is come, whom I will send unto you from the Father, even the Spirit of Truth, which proceedeth from the Father, He shall testify of Me. And ye also shall bear witness, because ye have been with Me from the beginning."

"He shall be worthy of belief, for He is the Spirit of Truth." On this account He called It not "Holy Spirit," but "Spirit of Truth." But the, "proceedeth from the Father," showeth that He[1] knoweth all things exactly, as Christ also saith of Himself, that "I know whence I come and whither I go" (c. viii. 14), speaking in that place also concerning truth. "Whom I will send." Behold, it is no longer the Father alone, but the Son also who sendeth. "And ye too," He saith, "have a right to be believed, who have been with Me, who have not heard from others." Indeed, the Apostles confidently rely on this circumstance, saying, "We who did eat and drink with Him." (Acts x. 41.) And to show that this was not merely said to please, the Spirit beareth witness to the words spoken. (Acts x. 44.)

Ch. xvi. ver. 1. "These things have I spoken unto you, that ye should not be offended."

That is, "when ye see many disbelieve, and yourselves ill-treated."

Ver. 2. "They shall put you out of the synagogues."

(For "the Jews had already agreed, that if any one should confess Christ, he should be put out of the synagogues" — c. ix. 22.)

"Yea, the time cometh, that whosoever killeth you will think that he doeth God service."

"They shall so seek after[2] your murder, as of an action pious and pleasing to God." Then again He addeth the consolation,

Ver. 3. "And these things will they do,[3] because they have not known the Father, nor Me."

"It is sufficient for your comfort that ye endure these things for My sake, and the Father's." Here He remindeth them of the blessedness of which He spake at the beginning, "Blessed are ye, when men shall revile you, and persecute you, and shall say all manner of evil against you falsely, for My sake. Rejoice, and be exceeding glad; for great is your reward in heaven." (Matt. v. 11, 12.)

Ver. 4. "These things have I told you, that

when the time shall come, ye may remember them."[4]

"So, judging from these words, deem the rest also trustworthy. For ye will not be able to say, that I flatteringly told you only those things which would please you, nor that the words were words of deceit; for one who intended to deceive, would not have told you beforehand of matters likely to turn you away. I have therefore told you before, that these things might not fall upon you unexpectedly, and trouble you; and for another reason besides, that ye might not say, that I did not foreknow that these things would be. Remember then that I have told you." And indeed the heathen always covered their persecutions of them by a pretense of their wickedness, driving them out as corrupters; but this did not trouble the disciples who had heard beforehand, and knew for what they suffered. The cause of what took place was sufficient to rouse their courage. Therefore He everywhere handleth this, saying, "they have not known Me"; and, "for My sake they shall do it"; and, "for My Name's sake, and for the Father's sake"; and, "I suffered first"; and, "from no just cause they dare these things."

[4.] Let us too consider these things in our temptations, when we suffer anything from wicked men, "looking to the Beginner[5] and Finisher of our faith" (Heb. xii. 2), and considering that it is by wicked men, and that it is for virtue's sake, and for His sake. For if we reflect on these things, all will be most easy and tolerable. Since if one suffering for those he loves is even proud of it, what feeling of things dreadful will he have who suffers for the sake of God? For if He, for our sake, calleth that shameful thing, the Cross, "glory" (c. xiii. 31), much more ought we to be thus disposed. And if we can so despise sufferings, much more shall we be able to despise riches, and covetousness. We ought then, when about to endure anything unpleasant, to think not of the toils but of the crowns; for as merchants take into account not the seas only, but also the profits, so ought we to reckon on heaven and confidence towards God. And if the getting more seem a pleasant thing, think that Christ willeth it not, and straightway it will appear displeasing. And if it be grievous to you to give to the poor, stay not your reckoning at the expense, but straightway transport your thoughts to the harvest which results from the sowing; and when it is hard to despise the love of a strange woman, think of the crown which comes after the struggle, and thou shalt easily bear the struggle. For if fear diverts a man from unseemly things, much more should the

---

[1] i.e. the Holy Ghost.
[2] al. "think of."
[3] "do unto you," N. T.
[4] "may remember that I told you of them," N. T.
[5] ἀρχηγὸν, so rendered in margin of E. V.

love of Christ. Difficult is virtue; but let us cast around her form the greatness of the promise of things to come. Indeed those who are virtuous, even apart from these promises, see her beautiful in herself, and on this account go after her, and work because it seems good to God, not for hire; and they think it a great thing to be sober-minded, not in order that they may not be punished, but because God hath commanded it. But if any one is too weak for this, let him think of the prizes. So let us do in respect of alms-doing, let us pity our fellow-men, let us not, I entreat,[1] neglect them when perishing with hunger. How can it be otherwise than an unseemly thing, that we should sit at the table laughing and enjoying ourselves, and when we hear others wailing as they pass through the street, should not even turn at their cries, but be wroth with them, and call them "cheat"? "What meanest thou, man? Doth any one plan a cheat for a single loaf of bread?" "Yes," saith some one. Then in this case above all let him be pitied; in this case above all let him be delivered from his need. Or if thou art not minded to give, do not insult either; if thou wilt not save the wreck, do not thrust it into the gulf. For consider, when thou thrustest away the poor man who comes to thee, who thou wilt be when thou callest upon God. "With what measure ye mete, it shall be measured to you again." (Matt. vii. 2.) Consider how he departs, crushed, bowed down, lamenting; besides his poverty having received also the blow from your insolence. For if ye count the begging a curse, think what a tempest it makes, begging to get nothing, but to go away insulted. How long shall we be like wild beasts, and know not nature itself through greediness? Many groan at these words; but I desire them not now, but always, to have this feeling of compassion. Think, I pray you, of that day when we shall stand before the judgment-seat of Christ, when we shall beg for mercy, and Christ, bringing them forward, shall say, "For the sake of a single loaf, of a single obol, so great a surge did ye raise in these souls!" What shall we reply? What defense shall we make? To show that He will bring them forward, hear what He saith; "Inasmuch as ye did it not to one of these, ye did it not to Me." (Matt. xxv. 45.) They will no more say anything to us, but God on their behalf will upbraid us. Since the rich man saw Lazarus too,[2] and Lazarus said nothing to him, but Abraham spake for him; and thus it will be in the case of the poor who are now despised by us. We shall not see them stretching out their hands in pitiful state, but being in rest; and we shall take the state which

was theirs (and would that it were that state only, and not one much more grievous) as a punishment. For neither did the rich man desire to be filled with crumbs "there," but was scorched and tormented sharply, and was told, "Thou in thy lifetime receivedst thy good things, and likewise Lazarus evil things." (Luke xvi. 25.) Let us not then deem wealth any great thing; it will help us on our way to punishment, if we take not heed, just as, if we take heed, poverty also becomes to us an addition of enjoyment and rest. For we both put off our sins if we bear it with thankfulness, and gain great boldness before God.

[5.] Let us then not be ever seeking security here, in order that we may enjoy security there; but let us accept the labors which are in behalf of virtue, and cut off superfluities, and seek nothing more than we need, and spend all our substance on those who want. Since what excuse can we have, when God promiseth heaven to us, and we will not even give Him bread? when He indeed for thee maketh the sun to rise, and supplieth all the ministry of the Creation, but thou dost not even give Him a garment, nor allow Him to share thy roof? But why speak I of sun and moon? He hath set His Body before thee, He hath given thee His Precious Blood; and dost thou not even impart to Him of thy cup? But hast thou done so for once? This is not mercy; as long as, having the means, thou helpest not, thou hast not yet fulfilled the whole duty. Thus the virgins who had the lamps, had oil, but not in abundance. Why, thou oughtest, even didst thou give from thine own, not to be so miserly, but now when thou givest what is thy Lord's, why countest thou every little? Will ye that I tell you the cause of this inhumanity? When men get together their wealth through greediness, these same are slow to give alms; for one who has learnt so to gain, knows not how to spend. For how can a man prepared for rapine adapt himself to its contrary? He who takes from others, how shall he be able to give up his own to another? A dog accustomed to feed on flesh cannot guard the flock; therefore the shepherds kill such. That this be not our fate, let us refrain from such feasting. For these men too feed on flesh, when they bring on death by hunger. Seest thou not how God hath allowed to us all things in common? If amid riches He hath suffered men to be poor, it is for the consolation of the rich, that they may be able by showing mercy towards them to put off their sins. But thou even in this hast been cruel and inhuman; whence it is evident, that if thou hadst received this same power in greater things, thou wouldest have committed ten thousand murders, and wouldest have debarred men from light,

---

and from life altogether.[1] That this might not take place, necessity hath cut short insatiableness in such matters.

If ye are pained when ye hear these things, much more I when I see them taking place. How long shalt thou be rich, and that man poor? Till evening, but no farther; for so short is life, and all things so near their end,[2] and all things henceforth so stand at the door, that the whole must be deemed but a little hour. What need hast thou of bursting[3] storehouses, of a multitude of domestics and house-keepers? Why hast thou not ten thousand proclaimers of thy almsdoing? The storehouse utters no voice, yet will it bring upon thee many robbers; but the storehouses of the poor will go up to God Himself, and will make thy present life sweet, and put away all thy sins, and thou shalt gain glory from God, and honor from men. Why then grudgest thou thyself such good things? For thou wilt not do so much good to the poor, as to thyself, when thou benefitest them. Thou wilt right their present state; but for thyself thou wilt lay up beforehand the glory and confidence which shall be hereafter. And this may we all obtain, by the grace and lovingkindness of our Lord Jesus Christ, to whom with the Father and the Holy Ghost be the glory and the might for ever. Amen.

# HOMILY LXXVIII.

## John xvi. 4–6.

"These things I said not unto you at the beginning, because I was with you. But now I go My way to Him that sent Me; and none of you asketh Me, Whither goest Thou? But because I have said these things unto you, sorrow hath filled your heart."

[1.] GREAT is the tyranny of despondency, and much courage do we need so as to stand manfully against the feeling, and after gathering from it what is useful, to let the superfluous go. It hath somewhat useful; for when we ourselves or others sin, then only is it good to grieve; but when we fall into human vicissitudes, then despondency is useless. And now when it has overthrown the disciples who were not yet perfect, see how Christ raiseth them again by His rebuke. They who before this had asked Him ten thousand questions, (for Peter said, "Whither goest Thou?" [c. xiii. 36]; and Thomas, "We know not whither Thou goest, and how can we know the way?" [c. xiv. 5 and 8]; and Philip, "Show us Thy Father";) these men, I say, now hearing, "they will put you out of the synagogues," and "will hate you," and "whosoever killeth you will think that he doeth God service," were so cast down as to be struck dumb, so that they spake nothing to Him. This then He maketh a reproach to them, and saith, "These things I said not unto you at the beginning, because I was with you; but now I go unto Him that sent Me, and none of you asketh Me, Whither goest Thou? but because I have said these things unto you, sorrow hath filled your heart." For a dreadful thing is immoderate sorrow, dreadful and effective of death. Wherefore Paul said, "Lest perhaps such a one should be swallowed up by overmuch sorrow." (2 Cor. ii. 7.)

"And these things," saith He, "I told you not at the beginning." Why did He not tell them at the beginning? That none might say that He spake guessing from the ordinary course of events. And why did He enter on a matter of such unpleasantness? "I knew these things," He saith, "from the beginning, and spake not of them; not because I did not know them, but 'because I was with you.'" And this again was spoken after a human manner, as though He had said, "Because ye were in safety, and it was in your power to question Me when ye would, and all the storm blew upon Me, and it was superfluous to tell you these things at the beginning." "But did He not tell them this? Did He not call the twelve, and say unto them, 'Ye shall be brought before governors and kings for My sake,' and, 'they shall scourge you in the synagogues'? (Matt. x. 18, 17). How then saith He, 'I told you not at the beginning'?" Because He had proclaimed before the scourgings and bringing before princes, still not that their death should appear so desirable that the action should even be deemed a service to God. For this more than anything was suited to terrify them, that they were to be judged as impious and corrupters. This too may be said, that in that place He spake of what they should suffer from the Gentiles, but here He hath added in a stronger way the acts of the Jews also, and told them that it was at their doors.

---

[1] lit. "all life."  [2] Ben. omits "all things so near their end."
[3] ἐρευγομένων.

" But now I go to Him that sent Me, and no man of you saith, Whither goest Thou? But because I have said these things unto you, sorrow hath filled your heart." It was no slight comfort to them to learn that He knew the excess of their despondency. For they were beside themselves from the anguish caused by their being left by Him, and from their awaiting the terrible things which were to come, since they knew not whether they should be able to bear them manfully. " Why then after this did He not tell them that they had been vouchsafed the Spirit?" That thou mightest learn that they were exceedingly virtuous. For if, when they had not yet been vouchsafed the Spirit, they started not back, though overwhelmed with sorrow, consider what sort of men they were likely to be after having enjoyed the grace.[1] If they had heard this at that time, and so had endured, we should have attributed the whole to the Spirit, but now it is entirely the fruit of their own state of mind, it is a clear manifestation of their love for Christ, who applieth a touchstone to their mind as yet defenseless.

Ver. 7. " But I tell you the truth."[2]

Observe how He consoleth them again. " I speak not," He saith, " to please you, and although you be grieved ten thousand fold, yet must ye hear what is for your good; it is indeed to your liking that I should be with you, but what is expedient for you is different. And it is the part of one caring for others, not to be over gentle with his friends in matters which concern their interests, or to lead them away from what is good for them."

" For if I go not away, the Comforter will not come."[3]

What here say those who hold not the fitting opinion concerning the Spirit? Is it " expedient " that the master depart, and the servant come? Seest thou how great is the honor of the Spirit?

" But if I depart, I will send Him unto you." And what the gain?

Ver. 8. " He, when He is come, will reprove[4] the world."[5]

That is, " they shall not do these things unpunished if He come. For indeed, the things that have been already done, are sufficient to stop their mouths; but when these things are also done by Him, when doctrines are more perfect and miracles greater, much more shall they be condemned when they see such things done in My Name, which make the proof of the Resurrection more certain. For now they are able to say, ' this is the carpenter's son, whose father and mother we know '; but when they see the bands of death loosed, wickedness cast out, natural lameness straightened, devils expelled, abundant supply of the Spirit, and all this effected by My being called on, what will they say? The Father hath borne witness of Me, and the Spirit will bear witness also." Yet He bare witness at the beginning. Yea, and shall also do it now. But the, " will convince,"

Ver. 9. " Of sin."[6]

This meaneth, " will cut off all their excuses, and show that they have transgressed unpardonably."

Ver. 10. " Of righteousness, because I go to the[7] Father, and ye see Me no more."

That is, " I have exhibited a blameless[8] life, and this is the proof, that, ' I go to the Father.' " For since they continually urged this against Him, that He was not from God, and therefore called Him a sinner and transgressor, He saith, that the Spirit shall take from them this excuse also. " For if My being deemed not to be from God, showeth Me to be a transgressor, when the Spirit shall have shown that I am gone thither, not merely for a season, but to abide there, (for the, ' Ye see Me no more,' is the expression of one declaring this,) what will they say then?" Observe how by these two things, their evil suspicion is removed; since neither doth working miracles belong to a sinner, (for a sinner cannot work them,) nor doth the being with God continually belong to a sinner. " So that ye can[9] no longer say, that ' this man is a sinner,' that ' this man is not from God.' "

Ver. 11. " Of judgment, because the prince of this world is judged."

Here again He mooteth the argument concerning righteousness, that He had overthrown His opponent. Now had He been a sinner, He could not have overthrown him; a thing which not even any just man had been strong enough to do. " But that he hath been condemned through Me, they shall know who trample on him hereafter, and who clearly know My Resurrection, which is the mark of Him who condemneth him. For he was not able to hold Me. And whereas they said that I had a devil, and that I was a deceiver, these things also shall hereafter appear to be false;[10] for I could not have prevailed against him, had I been subject to sin; but now he is condemned and cast out."

[2.] Ver. 12. " I have yet many things to say unto you, but ye cannot bear them now."

" Therefore it is expedient for you that I depart, if ye then will bear them when I am departed." " And what hath come to pass? Is the Spirit greater than Thou, that now indeed

---

[1] or, " gift."
[2] " The truth; it is expedient for you that I go away." N. T.
[3] " come unto you," N. T.　　　[4] or, " convince."
[5] " Will reprove the world of sin, and of righteousness, and of judgment." N. T.

[6] " Of sin, because they believe not in Me." N. T.
[7] " My," N. T.
[8] ἄληπτον.　　　[9] al. " he can."　　　[10] ἕωλα, lit. " stale."

we bear not, but It will fit us to bear? Is It working more powerful and more perfect?" " Not so; for He too shall speak My words." Wherefore He saith,

Ver. 13–15. [1] " He shall not speak of Himself; but whatsoever He shall hear, that shall He speak; and He will show you things to come. He shall glorify Me; for He shall receive of Mine, and shall show it unto you. All things that the Father hath are Mine." [2]

For since He had told them, that " ' He shall teach you, and bring to your remembrance ' (c. xiv. 26), and shall comfort you in your afflictions," (which He Himself did not,) and that " it is expedient for you that I should depart " (ver. 7), and that He should come, and, " ' now ye are not able to bear' (ver. 12), but then ye shall be able," and, that " He shall lead you into all truth " (ver. 13); lest hearing these things they should suppose the Spirit to be the greater, and so fall into an extreme opinion of impiety, therefore He saith, " He shall receive of Mine," that is, " whatsoever things I have told you, He shall also tell you." When He saith, " He shall speak nothing of Himself," He meaneth, " nothing contrary, nothing of His own opposed to My words." As then in saying respecting Himself, " I speak not of Myself " (c. xiv. 10), He meaneth that He speaketh nothing beside what the Father saith, nothing of His own against Him, or differing from Him, so also with respect to the Spirit. But the, " of Mine," meaneth, " of what I know," " of My own knowledge "; " for the knowledge of Me and of the Spirit is one."

" And He will tell you things to come." He excited their minds, for the race of man is for nothing so greedy,[3] as for learning the future. This, for instance, they continually asked Him, " Whither goest Thou?" " Which is the way?" To free them therefore from this anxiety, He saith, " He shall foretell you all things, so that ye shall not meet with them without warning."

" He shall glorify Me." How? " In My name He shall grant His inward workings." For since at the coming of the Spirit they were about to do greater miracles, therefore, again introducing the Equality of Honor, He saith, " He shall glorify Me."

What meaneth He by, " all truth "? for this also He testifieth of Him, that " He shall guide us into all truth." (Ver. 13.) Because He was clothed with the flesh, and because He would not seem to speak concerning Himself, and because they did not yet know clearly concerning the Resurrection, and were too imperfect, and also because of the Jews, that they might

not think they were punishing Him as a transgressor; therefore He spake no great thing continually, nor plainly drew them away from the Law. But when the disciples were cut off from them,[4] and were for the future without; and when many were about to believe, and to be released from their sins; and when there were others who spake of Him, He with good reason spake not great things concerning Himself. " So that it proceeded not from ignorance of Mine," He saith, " that I told you not what I should have told you, but from the infirmity of the hearers." On this account having said, " He shall lead you into all truth," He added, " He shall not speak of Himself." For to show that the Spirit needeth not teaching, hear Paul saying, " So also the things of God knoweth no man, but the Spirit of God." (1 Cor. ii. 11.) " As then the spirit of man, not learning from another, knoweth; so also the Holy Spirit ' shall receive of Mine,' " that is, " shall speak in unison with what is Mine."

" All things that the Father hath are Mine." " Since then those things are Mine, and He shall speak from the things of the Father, He shall speak from Mine."

[3.] " But why did not the Spirit come before He departed?" Because the curse not having yet been taken away, sin not yet loosed, but all being yet subject to vengeance, He could not come. " It is necessary then," saith He, " that the enmity be put away, that we be reconciled to God, and then receive that Gift." But why saith He, " I will send Him "? (Ver. 7.) It meaneth, " I will prepare you beforehand to receive Him." For, how can that which Is everywhere, be " sent"? Besides, He also showeth the distinction of the Persons. On these two accounts He thus speaketh; and also, since they were hardly to be drawn away from Himself, exhorting them to hold fast to the Spirit, and in order that they might cherish It. For He Himself was able to have wrought these things, but He concedeth to the Spirit[5] the working of miracles,[6] on this account, that they might understand His[7] dignity. For as the Father could have brought into being things which are, yet the Son did so, that we might understand His power, so also is it in this case. On this account He Himself was made Flesh, reserving the inward working[8] for the Spirit, shutting up the mouths of those who take the argument of His ineffable love for an occasion of impiety. For when they say that the Son was made flesh because He was inferior to the Father, we will reply to them, " what then will ye say of the Spirit?" He took not the flesh, and yet certainly on this account

<hr>

[1] Ver. 13. " Howbeit when He, the Spirit of Truth, is come, He will guide you into all truth; for He shall not speak," &c. N. T.
[2] " are Mine, therefore said I, that He shall take of Mine, and shall show it unto you." N. T.
[3] λίχνον.

[4] i.e. the Jews.          [5] ἐκείνῳ.
[6] al. " concedeth that It should work," &c.
[7] i.e. the Spirit's.          [8] al. " nobleness."

ye will not call Him greater than the Son, nor the Son inferior to Him  Therefore, in the case of baptism also the Trinity is included. The Father is able to effect the whole, as is the Son, and the Holy Ghost; yet, since concerning the Father no man doubts, but the doubt was concerning the Son, and the Holy Ghost, They are included in the rite, that by Their community in supplying those unspeakable blessings, we may also fully learn Their community in dignity. For that both the Son is able by Himself to do that which in the case of baptism[1] He is able to do with the Father, and the Holy Ghost the same, hear these things said plainly. For to the Jews He said, "That ye may know that the Son of Man hath power on earth to forgive sins" (Mark ii. 10); and again, "That ye may become children of light" (c. xii. 36): and, "I give to them eternal life." (c. x. 28.) Then after this, "That they might have life, and might have it more abundantly." (c. x. 10.) Now let us see the Spirit also performing the same thing. Where can we see it? "But the manifestation of the Spirit," it saith, "is given to every man to profit withal" (1 Cor. xii. 7; c. vi. 63); He then that giveth these things, much more remitteth sins. And again, "It is the Spirit that quickeneth"; and, "Shall quicken you[2] by His Spirit which dwelleth in you" (Rom. viii. 11); and, "The Spirit is Life because of righteousness" (Rom. viii. 10); and, "If ye are led by the Spirit, ye are not under the Law." (Gal. v. 18.) "For ye have not received the Spirit of bondage again to fear, but ye have received the Spirit of adoption." (Rom. viii. 15.) All the wonders too which they then wrought, they wrought at the coming of the Spirit. And Paul writing to the Corinthians, said, "But ye have been washed, but ye have been sanctified in the name of our Lord Jesus Christ,[3] and by the Spirit of our God." (1 Cor. vi. 11.) Since then they had heard many things of the Father, and had seen the Son work many things, but as yet knew nothing clearly of the Spirit, that Spirit doeth miracles, and bringeth in the perfect knowledge. But (as I said before) that He may not thence be supposed to be greater, on this account Christ saith, "Whatsoever He shall hear, that shall He speak; and He will show you things to come." Since, if this be not so, how could it be otherwise than absurd, if He was about to hear then, and on account of those who were being made disciples? For according to you,[4] He would not even then know, except on account of those who were about to hear. What could be more unlawful than this saying? Besides, what would He have to hear? Did He not speak[5] all these

things by the Prophets? For if He was about to teach concerning the dissolution of the Law, it had been spoken of: if concerning Christ, His Divinity and the Dispensation, these had been spoken of also. What could He say more clearly after this?

"And shall show you things to come." Here most of all Christ showeth His[6] Dignity, for to foretell things to come is especially the property of God. Now if He[7] also learn this from others, He will have nothing more than the Prophets, but here Christ declareth a knowledge brought into exact accordance with God, that it is impossible that He should speak anything else. But the, "shall receive of Mine," meaneth, "shall receive, either of the grace[8] which came into My Flesh, or of the knowledge which I also have, not as needing it, nor as learning it from another, but because it is One and the same." "And wherefore spake He thus, and not otherwise?" Because they understand not yet the word concerning the Spirit, wherefore He provideth for one thing only, that the Spirit should be believed and received by them, and that they should not be offended. For since He had said, "One is your Teacher, even Christ" (Matt. xxiii. 10), that they might not deem that they should disobey Him in obeying the Spirit, He saith, "His teaching and Mine are One; of what I should have taught, of those things shall He also speak. Do not suppose His words are other than Mine, for those words are Mine, and confirm My opinion.[9] For One is the will of the Father, and of the Son, and of the Holy Ghost." Thus also He willeth us to be, when He saith, "That they may be one, as Thou and I are One."[10] (c. xvii. 11.)

[4.] There is nothing equal to unanimity and concord; for so one is manifold. If two or ten are of one mind, the one is one no longer, but each one is multiplied tenfold, and thou wilt find the one in the ten, and the ten in the one; and if they have an enemy, he who attacks the one, as having attacked the ten, is vanquished; for he is the mark not for one, but for ten opponents.[11] Is one in want? No, he is not in want, for he is wealthy in his greater part, that is, in the nine; and the needy part, the lesser, is concealed by the wealthy part, the greater. Each of these hath twenty hands, twenty eyes, and as many feet. For he sees not with his own eyes alone, but with those of others; he walks[12] not with his own feet alone, but with those of others; he works not with his own hands alone, but with theirs. He hath ten souls, for not only doth he take thought for himself, but those souls also for

---

1 al. "upon the Throne" (βήματος).    4 i.e. heretical objectors.
2 "your mortal bodies," N. T.    5 al. "foretell."
3 "Lord Jesus," N. T.

6 i.e. the Spirit's.    10 "as We," N. T.
7 Gr. "It."    11 or, "edges," στομάτων.
8 χαρίσματος.    12 al. "bears."
9 or, "maintain my glory."

him. And if they be made a hundred, it will still be the same, and their power will be extended. Seest thou the excess of love, how it makes the one both irresistible and manifold, how one can even be in many places, the same both in Persia and in Rome, and that what nature cannot do, love can? for one part of him will be here, and one there, or rather he will be wholly here and wholly there. If then he have a thousand or two thousand friends, consider again whither his power will extend. Seest thou what an increase-giving thing is love? for the wonderful thing is this, its making one a thousand. Why then do we not acquire this power and place ourselves in safety? This is better than all power or riches,[1] this is more than health, than light itself, it is the groundwork of good courage. How long do we set our love on one or two? Consider also the action in the contrary way. Suppose a man without a friend, a mark of the utmost folly, (for a fool will say, "I have no friend,") what sort of life will such a one lead? For though he be infinitely rich, in plenty and luxury, possessed of ten thousand good things, yet is he desolate and bare of all. But in the case of friends not so; though they be poor men, yet are they better provided than the wealthy; and the things which a man undertakes not to say for himself, a friend will say for him, and whatever gratifications he is not able to procure for himself, he will be enabled to obtain by means of another, and much more; and it will be to us the groundwork of all enjoyment and safety, since one who is guarded by so many spearmen cannot suffer harm. For the king's body guards are not equal in their strictness to these. The one perform their watch through compulsion and fear, the others through kindness and love; and love is far mightier than fear. The king fears his own guards; the friend is more confident in them than in himself, and by reason of them fears none of those that plot against him. Let us then engage in this traffic; the poor man, that he may have consolation in his poverty; the rich, that he may possess his wealth in safety; the ruler, that he may rule with safety;[2] the

ruled, that he may have benevolent rulers. This is the source of kindness, this the groundwork of gentleness; since even among beasts, those are the most fierce and untamable which are not gregarious. For this cause we dwell in cities, and have public places, that we may converse with one another. This also Paul commanded, saying, "Not forsaking the assembling of ourselves together" (Heb. x. 25); for no evil is so great as solitariness, and the state which is without compact and intercourse. "What then," saith some one, "of the solitaries, and of those who have occupied the summits of the mountains?" That neither are they without friends; they have indeed fled from the turmoil of common life, but they have many of one soul with them, and closely bound together one to another; and they have retired that they might rightly accomplish this thing.[3] For since the rivalry of business causes many disputes, therefore, removing from among men, they cultivate[4] love with much exactness. "But how," saith some one, "if a man be alone can he have ten thousand friends?" I, for my part, desire, if it be possible, that men should know how to dwell one with another; but for the present let the properties of friendship remain unshaken.[5] For it is not place which makes friends. They, for instance, have many who admire them; now these would not have admired had they not loved them. Again, they pray for all the world, which is the greatest proof of friendship. For this cause we salute one another at the Mysteries, that being many we may become one; and in the case of the uninitiated,[6] we make our prayers common, supplicating for the sick, and for the produce of the world, for land and sea. Seest thou all the power of love? in the prayers, in the Mysteries, in the exhortations? This is that which causeth all good things. If we hold carefully to this, we shall both rightly dispense things present, and also obtain the Kingdom; which may we all obtain through the grace and lovingkindness of our Lord Jesus Christ, by whom and with whom, to the Father and the Holy Ghost, be glory, for ever and ever. Amen.

---

[1] al. "than all riches."

[2] Sav. edition has, ἵνα μετὰ ἀσφαλείας ἀσφαλείᾳ ἀρχῇ, which seems to be an error of the press.

[3] i.e. might perfect love.    [4] γεωργοῦσι, lit. "till."

[5] i.e. the objection does not shake my argument.

[6] i.e. non-communicants.

# HOMILY LXXIX.

JOHN xvi. 16, 17.

"A little while, and ye shall not see[1] Me: and again, a little while, and ye shall see Me, because I go to the Father. Then said some of His disciples among themselves, What is this that He saith?" [And what follows.[2]]

[1.] NOTHING is wont so to cast down the soul that is anguished and possessed by deep despondency, as when words which cause pain are continually dwelt upon. Why then did Christ, after saying, "I go," and, "Hereafter I will not speak with you," continually dwell on the same subject, saying, "A little while, and ye shall not see Me, because I go to Him that sent Me"?[3] When He had recovered them by His words concerning the Spirit, He again casteth down their courage. Wherefore doth He this? He testeth their feelings, and rendereth them more proved, and well accustometh them by hearing sad things, manfully to bear separation from Him; for they who had practiced this when spoken of in words, were likely in actions also easily to bear it afterwards. And if one enquire closely, this very thing is a consolation,[4] the saying that, "I go to the Father." For it is the expression of One, who declares that He shall not perish, but that His end is a kind of translation. He addeth too another consolation; for He saith not merely, "A little while, and ye shall not see Me," but also, "A little while, and ye shall see Me"; showing that He will both come to them again, and that their separation would be but for a little while, and His presence with them continual. This, however, they did not understand. Whence one may with reason wonder how, after having often heard these things, they doubt, as though they had heard nothing. How then is it that they did not understand? It was either through grief, as I suppose, for that drove what was said from their understanding; or through the obscurity of the words. Because He seemed to them to set forth two contraries, which were not contrary. "If," saith one of them, "we shall see Thee, whither goest Thou? And if Thou goest, how shall we see Thee?" Therefore they say, "We cannot tell what He saith." That He was about to depart, they knew; but they knew not that He would shortly come to them. On which

account He rebuketh them, because they did not understand His saying. For, desiring to infix in[5] them the doctrine concerning His death, what saith He?

Ver. 20.[6] "Verily, verily, I say unto you, That ye shall weep and lament"—which belonged to the Death and the Cross—"but the world shall rejoice."

Because by reason of their not desiring His death, they quickly ran into the belief that He would not die, and then when they heard that He would die, cast about, not knowing what that "little" meant, He saith, "Ye shall mourn and lament."

"But your sorrow shall be turned into joy."[7]

Then having shown that after grief comes joy, and that grief gendereth joy, and that grief is short, but the pleasure endless, He passeth to a common[8] example; and what saith He?

Ver. 21. "A woman when she is in travail hath sorrow."[9]

And He hath used a comparison which the Prophets also use continually, likening despondencies to the exceeding pains of childbirth. But what He saith is of this kind: "Travail pains shall lay hold on you, but the pang of childbirth is the cause of joy"; both confirming His words relative to the Resurrection, and showing that the departing hence is like passing from the womb into the light of day. As though He had said, "Marvel not that I bring you to your advantage through such sorrow, since even a mother to become a mother, passeth in like manner through pain." Here also He implieth something mystical, that He hath loosened the travail pangs of death, and caused a new man to be born of them.[10] And He said not, that the pain shall pass away only, but, "she doth not even remember it," so great is the joy which succeedeth; so also shall it be with the Saints. And yet the woman doth not rejoice because "a man hath come into the world," but because a son hath been born to her; since, had this been the case, nothing would have hindered the barren from rejoicing over another who beareth.

---

[1] al. "ye no longer see."
[2] Part of ver. 17 and ver. 18. "A little while, and ye shall not see Me: and again, a little while, and ye shall see Me: and, Because I go to the Father. They said therefore, What is this that He saith, A little while? we cannot tell what He saith."
[3] "to the Father," N. T.     [4] al. "is of consolation."
[5] al. "to strike into."
[6] Ver. 19, omitted. "Now Jesus knew that they were desirous to ask Him, and said unto them, Do ye enquire among yourselves of that I said, A little while, and ye shall not see Me: and again, a little while, and ye shall see Me? N. T.
[7] "And ye shall be sorrowful, but," &c., N. T.
[8] lit. "worldly."
[9] "hath sorrow, because her hour is come; but as soon as she is delivered of the child, she remembereth no more the anguish, for joy that a man is born into the world." N. T.
[10] ἀπογεννηθῆναι.

Why then spake He thus? Because He introduced this example for this purpose only, to show that sorrow is for a season, but joy lasting : and to show that (death) is a translation unto life ; and to show the great profit of their pangs. He said not, " a child hath been born," but, " A man." For to my mind He here alludeth to His own Resurrection, and that He should be born not unto that death which bare the birth-pang, but unto the Kingdom. Therefore He said not, " a child hath been born unto her," but, " A man hath been born into the world."

Ver. 22, 23.[1] " And ye now therefore have sorrow — [but I will see you again, and your sorrow shall be turned into joy]."[2] Then, to show that He shall die no more, He saith, " And no man taketh it from you. And in that day ye shall ask Me nothing."

Again He proveth nothing else by these words, but that He is from God. " For then ye shall for the time to come know all things." But what is, " Ye shall not ask Me " ? " Ye shall need no intercessor, but it is sufficient that ye call on My Name, and so gain all things."

" Verily, verily, I say unto you, Whatsoever ye shall ask My Father in My Name."[3]

He showeth the power of His Name, if at least being neither seen nor called upon, but only named, He even maketh us approved[4] by the Father. But where hath this taken place? Where they say, " Lord, behold their threatenings, and grant unto Thy servants that with boldness they may speak Thy word " (Acts iv. 29, 31), " and work miracles in Thy Name." " And the place was shaken where they were."

Ver. 24. " Hitherto ye have asked nothing."[5]

[2.] Hence He showeth it to be good that He should depart, if hitherto they had asked nothing, and if then they should receive all things whatsoever they should ask. " For do not suppose, because I shall no longer be with you, that ye are deserted ; My Name shall give you greater boldness." Since then the words which He had used had been veiled, He saith,

Ver. 25. " These things have I spoken unto you in proverbs, but the time cometh when I shall no more speak unto you in proverbs."

" There shall be a time when ye shall know all things clearly." He speaketh of the time of the Resurrection. " Then,"

" I shall tell you plainly of the Father."

(For He was with them, and talked with them forty days, being assembled with them, and speaking of the things concerning the kingdom of God — Acts i. 3, 4,) — " because now being in fear, ye give no heed to My words ; but then when ye see Me risen again, and converse with Me, ye will be able to learn all things plainly, for the Father Himself will love you, when your faith in Me hath been made firm."

Ver. 26. " And I will not ask the Father."[6]

" Your love for Me sufficeth to be your advocate."

Ver. 27, 28. " Because[7] ye have loved Me, and have believed that I came out from God. I came forth from the Father, and am come into the world ; again I leave the world, and go to the Father."

For since His discourse concerning the Resurrection, and together with this, the hearing that " I came out from God, and thither I go," gave them no common comfort, He continually handleth these things. He gave a pledge, in the first place, that they were right in believing on Him ; in the second, that they should be in safety. When therefore He said, " A little while, and ye shall not see Me ; and again a little while, and ye shall see Me " (ver. 17), they with reason did not understand Him. But now it is no longer so. What then is, " Ye shall not ask Me " ? " Ye shall not say, ' Show us the Father,' and, ' Whither goest Thou ? ' for ye shall know all knowledge, and the Father shall be disposed towards you even as I am." It was this especially which made them breathe again, the learning that they should be the Father's friends ; wherefore they say,

Ver. 30.[8] " Now we know that Thou knowest all things."

Seest thou that He made answer to what was secretly harboring[9] in their minds?

" And needest not that any man should ask Thee."[10]

That is, " Before hearing, Thou knowest the things which made us stumble, and Thou hast given us rest, since Thou hast said, ' The Father loveth you, because ye have loved Me.' " After so many and so great matters, they say, " Now we know." Seest thou in what an imperfect state they were? Then, when, as though conferring a favor upon Him, they say, " Now we know," He replieth, " Ye still require many other things to come to perfection ; nothing is as yet achieved by you. Ye shall presently betray Me to My enemies, and such fear shall seize you, that ye shall not even be able to retire one with another, yet from this I shall suffer nothing dreadful." Seest thou again how con-

---

[1] Ver. 22. " And ye now therefore have sorrow, but I will see you again, and your heart shall rejoice, and your joy no man," &c. N. T.
[2] from ver. 10.    [3] " In My Name, He will give it you." N. T.
[4] lit. " admired."
[5] " nothing in My Name; ask, and ye shall receive, that your joy may be full," N. T. The words, " Hitherto," &c., are inserted by Savile.

[6] Ver. 26. " At that day ye shall ask in My Name; and I say not unto you, that I will pray the Father for you." N. T.
[7] " For the Father Himself loveth you, because," &c. N. T.
[8] Ver. 29. " His disciples said unto Him, Lo, now speakest Thou plainly, and speakest no parable." N. T.
[9] ὑφορμοῦν.
[10] " ask Thee ; by this we believe that Thou camest forth from God." N. T.

descending His speech is? And indeed He makes this a charge against them, that they continually needed condescension. For when they say, "Lo, now Thou speakest plainly, and speakest no parable" (ver. 29), "and therefore we believe Thee," He showeth them that now, when they believe, they do not yet believe, neither doth He accept their words. This He saith, referring them to another season. But the,

Ver. 32.[1] "The Father is with Me,"

He hath again put on their account; for this they[2] everywhere wished to learn. Then, to show that He did not give them perfect knowledge by saying this, but in order that their reason might not rebel, (for it was probable that they might form some human ideas, and think that they should not enjoy any assistance from Him,) He saith,

Ver. 33. "These things I have spoken unto you, that in Me ye might have peace."[3]

That is, "that ye should not cast Me from your thoughts, but receive Me." Let no one, then, drag these words into a doctrine; they are spoken for our comfort and love. "For not even when we suffer such things as I have mentioned shall your troubles stop there,[4] but as long as ye are in the world ye shall have sorrow, not only now when I am betrayed, but also afterwards. But rouse your minds, for ye shall suffer nothing terrible. When the master hath gotten the better of his enemies, the disciples must not despond." "And how," tell me, "hast Thou 'conquered the world'?" I have told you already, that I have cast down its ruler, but ye shall know hereafter, when all things yield and give place to you.

[3.] But it is permitted to us also to conquer, looking to the Author of our faith, and walking on that road which He cut for us. So neither shall death get the mastery of us. "What then, shall we not die?" saith some one. Why, from this very thing[5] it is clear that he shall not gain the mastery over us. The champion truly will then be glorious, not when he hath not closed with his opponent, but when having closed he is not holden by him. We therefore are not mortal, because of our struggle with death, but immortal, because of our victory; then should we have been mortal, had we remained with him always. As then I should not call the longest-lived animals immortal, although they long remain free from death, so neither him who shall rise after death mortal, because he is dissolved by death. For, tell me, if a man blush a little, should we say that he was continu-

ally ruddy? Not so, for the action is not a habit. If one become pale, should we call him jaundiced? No, for the affection is but temporary. And so you would not call him mortal, who hath been for but a short time in the hands of death. Since in this way we may speak of those who sleep, for they are dead, so to say, and without action. But doth death corrupt our bodies? What of that? It is not that they may remain in corruption, but that they be made better. Let us then conquer the world, let us run to immortality, let us follow our King, let us too set up a trophy,[6] let us despise the world's pleasures. We need no toil to do so; let us transfer our souls to[7] heaven, and all the world is conquered. If thou desirest it not, it is conquered; if thou deride it, it is worsted. Strangers are we and sojourners, let us then not grieve at any of its painful things. For if, being sprung from a renowned country, and from illustrious ancestors, thou hadst gone into some distant land, being known to no one, having with thee neither servants nor wealth, and then some one had insulted thee, thou wouldest not grieve as though thou hadst suffered these things at home. For the knowing clearly that thou wast in a strange and foreign land, would persuade thee to bear all easily, and to despise hunger, and thirst, and any suffering whatever. Consider this also now, that thou art a stranger and a sojourner, and let nothing disturb thee in this foreign land; for thou hast a City whose Artificer and Creator is God, and the[8] sojourning itself is but for a short and little time. Let whoever will strike, insult, revile; we are in a strange land, and live but meanly; the dreadful thing would be, to suffer so in our own country, before our fellow-citizens, then is the greatest unseemliness and loss. For if a man be where he had none that knows him, he endures all easily, because insult becomes more grievous from the intention of those who offer it. For instance, if a man insult the governor, knowing that he is governor, then the insult is bitter; but if he insult, supposing him to be a private man, he cannot even touch him who undergoeth the insult. So let us reason also. For neither do our revilers know what we are, as, that we are citizens of heaven, registered for the country which is above, fellow-choristers of the Cherubim. Let us not then grieve nor deem their insult to be insult; had they known, they would not have insulted us. Do they deem us poor and mean? Neither let us count this an insult. For tell me, if a traveler having got before his servants, were sitting a little space in the inn waiting for them, and then the innkeeper, or some travelers, should behave rudely to him, and revile him, would he not laugh at the other's

---

[1] Ver. 31, 32. "Jesus answered them, Do ye now believe? Behold, the hour cometh, yea, is now come, that ye shall be scattered every man to his own, and shall leave Me alone; but I am not alone, because," &c. N. T.    [2] al. "he," or, "one."

[3] "have peace. In the world ye shall have tribulation; but be of good cheer, I have overcome the world." N. T.

[4] "shall I stay your dangers."    [5] i.e. our death.

[6] al. "a trophy for Him."    [8] al. "and if the."
[7] al. "into."

ignorance? would not their mistake rather give him pleasure? would he not feel a satisfaction as though not he but some one else were insulted? Let us too behave thus. We too sit in an inn, waiting for our friends who travel the same road; when we are all collected, then they shall know whom they insult. These men then shall hang[1] their heads; then they shall say, "This is he whom we" fools "had in derision." (Wisd. v. 3.)

[4.] With these two things then let us comfort ourselves, that we are not insulted, for they know not who we are, and that, if we wish to obtain satisfaction, they shall hereafter give us a most bitter one. But God forbid that any should have a soul so cruel and inhuman. "What then, if we be insulted by our kinsmen? For this is the burdensome thing." Nay, this is the light thing. "Why, pray?" Because we do not bear those whom we love when they insult us, in the same way as we bear those whom we do not know. For instance, in consoling those who have been injured, we often say, "It is a brother who hath injured you, bear it nobly; it is a father; it is an uncle." But if the name of "father" and "brother" puts you to shame, much more if I name to you a relationship more intimate than these; for we are not only brethren one to another, but also members, and one body. Now if the name of brother shame you, much more that of member. Hast thou not heard that Gentile proverb, which saith, that "it behooveth to keep friends with their defects"? Hast thou not heard Paul say, "Bear ye one another's burdens"? Seest thou not lovers? For I am compelled, since I cannot draw an instance from you, to bring my discourse to that ground of argument. This also Paul doth, thus saying, "Furthermore we have had fathers in our flesh, which corrected us, and we gave them reverence." (Heb. xii. 9.) Or rather, that is more apt which he saith to the Romans, "As ye have yielded your members servants to uncleanness and to iniquity unto iniquity, even so now yield your members servants to righteousness." For this reason let us confidently keep hold of[2] the illustration. Now dost thou not observe lovers, what miseries these suffer when inflamed with desire for harlots, cuffed, beaten, and laughed at, enduring a harlot, who turns away from and insults them in ten thousand ways; yet if they see but once anything sweet or gentle, all is well to do with them, all former things are gone, all goes on with a fair wind, be it poverty, be it sickness, be it anything else besides these. For they count their own life as miserable or blessed, according as they may have her whom they love disposed towards them. They know nothing of mortal honor or disgrace, but

even if one insult, they bear all easily through the great pleasure and delight which they receive from her; and though she revile, though she spit in their face, they think, when they are enduring this, that they are being pelted with roses. And what wonder, if such are their feelings as to her person? for her very house they think to be more splendid than any, though it be but of mud, though it be falling down. But why speak I of walls? when they even see the places which they frequent in the evening, they are excited. Allow me now for what follows to speak the word of the Apostle. As he saith, "As ye have yielded your members servants to uncleanness, so yield your members servants unto righteousness"; so in like manner now I say, "as we have loved these women, let us love one another, and we shall not think that we suffer anything terrible."[3] And why say I, "one another"? Let us so love God. Do ye shudder, when ye hear that I require as much love in the case of God, as we have shown towards a harlot? But I shudder that we do not show even thus much. And, if you will, let us go on with the argument, though what is said be very painful. The woman beloved promises her lovers nothing good, but dishonor, shame, and insolence. For this is what the waiting upon a harlot makes a man, ridiculous, shameful, dishonored. But God promiseth us heaven, and the good things which are in heaven; He hath made us sons, and brethren of the Only-begotten, and hath given thee ten thousand things while living, and when thou diest, resurrection, and promiseth that He will give us such good things as it is not possible even to imagine, and maketh us honored and revered. Again, that woman compels her lovers to spend all their substance for the pit and for destruction; but God biddeth us sow the heaven, and giveth us an hundred-fold, and eternal life. Again, she uses her lover like a slave, giving commands more hardly than any tyrant; but God saith, "I no longer call you servants, but friends." (c. xv. 15.)

[5.] Have ye seen the excess both of the evils here and the blessings there[4]? What then comes next? For this woman's sake, many lie awake, and whatever she commands, readily obey; give up house, and father, and mother, and friends, and money, and patronage, and leave all that belongs to them in want and desolation; but for the sake of God, or rather for the sake of ourselves, we often do not choose to expend even the third portion of our substance, but we look on the hungry, we overlook him, and run past the naked, and do not even bestow a word upon him. But the lovers, if they see but a little servant girl of their mistress, and her

---

[1] al. "then hang."        [2] al. "we touch."        [3] i.e. in being insulted.        [4] al. "thence."

a barbarian, they stand in the middle of the market-place, and talk with her, as if they were proud and glad to do so, unrolling an interminable round of words;[1] and for her sake they count all their living as nothing, deem rulers and rule nothing, (they know it, all who have had experience of the malady,) and thank her more when she commands, than others when they serve. Is there not with good reason a hell? Are there not with good reason ten thousand punishments? Let us then become sober, let us apply to the service of God as much, or half, or even the third part of what others supply to the harlot. Perhaps again ye shudder; for so do I myself. But I would not that ye should shudder at words only, but at the actions; as it is, here indeed our[2] hearts are made orderly, but we go forth and cast all away. What then is the gain? For there, if it be required to spend money, no one laments his poverty, but even borrows it to give, perchance, when smitten. But here, if we do but mention almsgiving, they pretend to us children, and wife, and house, and patronage, and ten thousand excuses. "But," saith some one, "the pleasure is great there." This it is that I lament and mourn. What if I show that the pleasure here is greater? For there shame, and insult, and expense, cut away no little of the pleasure, and after these the quarreling and enmity; but here there is nothing of the kind. What is there, tell me, equal to this pleasure, to sit expecting heaven and the kingdom there, and the glory of the saints, and the life that is endless? "But these things," saith some one, "are in expectation, the others in experience." What kind of experience? Wilt thou that I tell thee the pleasures which are here also by experience? Consider what freedom thou enjoyest, and how thou fearest and tremblest at no man when thou livest in company with virtue, neither en-

emy, nor plotter, nor informer, nor rival in credit or in love, nor envious person, nor poverty, nor sickness, nor any other human thing. But there, although ten thousand things be according to thy mind, though riches flow in as from a fountain, yet the war with rivals, and the plots, and ambuscades, will make more miserable than any the life of him who wallows with those women.[3] For when that abominable one is haughty, and insolent, you needs must kindle quarrel to flatter her. This therefore is, more grievous than ten thousand deaths, more intolerable than any punishment. But here there is nothing of the kind. For "the fruit," it saith, "of the Spirit is love, joy, peace." (Gal. v. 22.) Here is no quarreling, nor unseasonable pecuniary expense, nor disgrace and expense too; and if thou give but a farthing, or a loaf, or a cup of cold water, He will be much beholden to thee, and He doth nothing to pain or grieve thee, but all so as to make thee glorious, and free thee from all shame. What defense therefore shall we have, what pardon shall we gain, if, leaving these things, we give ourselves up to the contrary, and voluntarily cast ourselves into the furnace that burns with fire? Wherefore I exhort those who are sick of this malady, to recover themselves, and return to health, and not allow themselves to fall into despair. Since that son[4] also was in a far more grievous state than this, yet when he returned to his father's house, he came to his former honor, and appeared more glorious than him who had ever been well-pleasing. Let us also imitate him, and returning to our Father, even though it be late, let us depart from that captivity, and transfer ourselves to freedom, that we may enjoy the Kingdom of heaven, through the grace and lovingkindness of our Lord Jesus Christ, to whom with the Father and the Holy Ghost be glory, for ever and ever. Amen.

---

[1] μακρῶν λόγων ἀνελίττοντες διαύλους. The δίαυλος was the double course, which ended where it began.     [2] al. "your."

[3] This seems to be the meaning of τοῦ μετ' ἐκείνων πλυνομένου.
[4] the prodigal, Luke xv.

# HOMILY LXXX.

JOHN xvii. 1.

"These words spake Jesus, and lifted up His eyes to heaven, and saith, Father, the hour is come; glorify Thy Son, that Thy Son also may glorify Thee."

[1.] " HE that hath done and taught,"[1] it saith, "the same shall be called great in the Kingdom of heaven." And with much reason ; for to show true wisdom in words, is easy, but the proof which is by works is the part of some noble and great one. Wherefore also Christ, speaking of the endurance of evil, putteth Himself forth, bidding us take example from Him. On this account too, after this admonition, He betaketh Himself to prayer, teaching us in our temptations to leave all things, and flee to God. For because He had said, " In the world ye shall have tribulation," and had shaken their souls, by the prayer He raiseth them again. As yet they gave heed unto Him as to a man ; and for their sake He acteth thus, just as He did in the case of Lazarus, and there telleth the reason ; " Because of the people that stand by I said it, that they might believe that Thou hast sent Me." (c. xi. 42.) " Yea," saith some one, " this took place with good cause in the case of the Jews ; but wherefore in that of the disciples ? " With good cause in the case of the disciples also. For they who, after all that had been said and done, said, " Now we know that Thou knowest " (c. xvi. 30), most of all needed to be established. Besides, the Evangelist doth not even call the action prayer ; but what saith he ? " He lifted up His eyes to heaven," and saith rather that it was a discoursing with the Father. And if elsewhere he speaks of prayer, and at one time shows Him kneeling on His knees, at another lifting His eyes to heaven, be not thou troubled ; for by these means we are taught the earnestness which should be in our petitions, that standing we should look up, not with the eyes of the flesh only, but of the mind, and that we should bend our knees, bruising our own hearts. For Christ came not merely to manifest Himself, but also about to teach virtue ineffable. But it behooveth the teacher to teach, not by words only, but also by actions. Let us hear then what He saith in this place.

" Father, the hour is come ; glorify Thy Son, that Thy Son also may glorify Thee."

Again He showeth us, that not unwilling He cometh to the Cross. For how could He be unwilling, who prayed that this might come to pass, and called the action " glory," not only for Himself the Crucified, but also for the Father ? since this was the case, for not the Son only, but the Father also was glorified. For before the Crucifixion, not even the Jews knew Him ;[2] " Israel," it saith, " hath not known Me " (Isa. i. 3) ; but after the Crucifixion, all the world ran to Him. Then He speaketh also of the manner of the glory, and how He will glorify Him.

Ver. 2. " As Thou hast given Him power over all flesh," " that nothing which Thou hast given Him should perish." [3]

For to be always doing good, is glory to God. But what is, " As Thou hast given Him power over all flesh "? He now showeth, that what belongs to the preaching is not confined to the Jews alone, but is extended to all the world, and layeth down beforehand the first invitations to the Gentiles. And since He had said, " Go not into the way of the Gentiles " (Matt. x. 5), and after this time is about to say, " Go ye, and make disciples of all nations " (Matt. xxviii. 19), He showeth that the Father also willeth this. For this greatly offended the Jews, and the disciples too ; nor indeed after this did they easily endure to lay hold on the Gentiles, until they received the teaching of the Spirit ; because hence arose no small stumblingblock for the Jews. Therefore, when Peter after such a manifestation of the Spirit came to Jerusalem, he could scarcely, by relating the vision of the sheet, escape the charges brought against him. But what is, " Thou hast given Him power over all flesh "? I will ask the heretics, " When did He receive this power ? was it before He formed them, or after ? " He himself saith, that it was after that He had been crucified,[4] and had risen again ; at least then He said, " All power is given unto Me " (Matt. xxviii. 18), and, " Go ye and make disciples of all nations." What then, had He not authority over His own works ? Did He make them, and had He not authority over them after having made them ? Yet He is seen doing all in times of old, punishing some as sinners,[5] (for, " Surely I will not hide," it saith, " from My servant Abraham, that which I am about to do " —Gen. xviii. 17, LXX.,) and honoring others as righteous. Had He then the power at that time, and now had He lost it, and did He again receive

---

[1] " Whosoever shall do," &c., N. T.

[2] i.e. the Father.
[3] N. T. " That He should give eternal life to as many as Thou hast given Him." [4] Morel. " had been made flesh."
[5] Some MSS. add, " and setting right some who turn."

it? What devil could assert this? But if His power was the same both then and now, (for, saith He, "as the Father raiseth up the dead and quickeneth them, even so the Son quickeneth whom He will"—c. v. 21,) what is the meaning of the words? He was about to send them to the Gentiles; in order therefore that they might not think that this was an innovation, because He had said, "I am not sent, save unto the lost sheep of the house of Israel" (Matt. xv. 24), He showeth that this seemeth good to the Father also. And if He saith this with great meanness of circumstance, it is not wonderful. For so He edified both those at that time, and those who came afterwards; and as I have before said, He always by the excess of meanness firmly persuaded them that the words were those of condescension.

[2.] But what is, "Of all flesh"? For certainly not all believed. Yet, for His part, all believed; and if men gave no heed to His words, the fault was not in the teacher, but in those who received them not.

"That He should give eternal life to as many as Thou hast given Him."

If here also He speaketh in a more human manner, wonder not. For He doth so both on account of the reasons I have given, and to avoid the saying anything great concerning Himself; since this was a stumblingblock to the hearers, because as yet they imagined nothing great concerning Him. John, for example, when He speaks in his own person, doth not so, but leadeth up his language to greater sublimity, saying, "All things were made by Him, and without Him was not anything made" (c. i. 3, 4, 9, 11); and that He was "Life"; and that He was "Light"; and that "He came to His own": he saith not, that He would not have had power, had He not received it, but that He gave to others also "power to become sons of God." And Paul in like manner calleth Him equal with God. But He Himself asketh in a more human way, saying thus, "That He should give eternal life to as many as Thou hast given Him." (Phil. ii. 6.)

Ver. 3. "And this is life eternal, that they might know Thee the only true God, and Jesus Christ whom Thou hast sent."

"The only true God," He saith, by way of distinction from those which are not gods; for He was about to send them to the Gentiles. But if they[1] will not allow this, but on account of this word "only" reject the Son from being true God, in this way as they proceed they reject Him from being God at all.[2] For He also saith, "Ye seek not the glory which is from the only God." (c. v. 44.) Well then; shall not the Son be God? But if the Son be God, and the Son of the Father

who is called the Only God, it is clear that He also is true, and the Son of Him who is called the Only true God. Why, when Paul saith, "Or I only and Barnabas" (1 Cor. ix. 6), doth he exclude Barnabas? Not at all; for the "only" is put by way of distinction from others. And, if He be not true God, how is He "Truth"? for truth far surpasses what is true. What shall we call the not being a "true" man, tell me? shall we not call it the not being a man at all? so if the Son is not true God, how is He God? And how maketh He us gods and sons, if He is not true? But on these matters we have spoken more particularly in another place; wherefore let us apply ourselves to what follows.

Ver. 4. "I have glorified Thee on the earth."

Well said He, "on the earth"; for in heaven He had been already glorified, having His own natural glory, and being worshiped by the Angels. Christ then speaketh not of that glory which is bound up with His[3] Essence, (for that glory, though none glorify Him, He ever possesseth in its fullness,) but of that which cometh from the service of men. And so the, "Glorify Me," is of this kind; and that thou mayest understand that He speaketh of this manner of glory, hear what follows.

"I have finished the work which Thou gavest Me that I should do it."

And yet the action was still but beginning, or rather was not yet beginning. How then said He, "I have finished"? Either He meaneth, that "I have done all My part"; or He speaketh of the future, as having already come to pass; or, which one may say most of all, that all was already effected, because the root of blessings had been laid, which fruits would certainly and necessarily follow, and from His being[4] present at and assisting in those things which should take place after these. On this account He saith again in a condescending way, "Which Thou gavest Me." For had He indeed waited to hear and learn, this would have fallen far short of His glory. For that He came to this[5] of His own will, is clear from many passages. As when Paul saith, that "He so loved us, as to give Himself for us" (Eph. v. 2); and, "He emptied Himself, and took upon Him the form of a servant" (Phil. ii. 7); and, "As the Father hath loved Me, so have I loved you." (c. xv. 9.)

Ver. 5. "And now, O Father, glorify Thou Me with Thine Own Self,[6] with the glory which I had with Thee before the world was."

Where is that glory? For allowing that He was[7] with reason unhonored among men, because of the covering[8] which was put around

---

1 i.e. the heretics: some MSS. τὸ μόνον.
2 al. "even reject God."
3 i.e. the Father's.
4 Ben. "and His being."
5 i.e. to His death.
6 παρὰ σεαυτῷ.
7 al. "Thou wast."
8 i.e. the flesh.

Him ; how seeketh He[1] to be glorified with the Father? What then saith He here? The saying refers to the Dispensation ; since His fleshly nature had not yet been glorified, not having as yet enjoyed incorruption, nor shared the kingly throne. Therefore He said not " on earth," but " with Thee."

[3.] This glory we also shall enjoy according to our measure, if we be sober. Wherefore Paul saith, " If so be that we suffer with Him, that we may also be glorified together." (Rom. viii. 17.) Ten thousand tears then do they merit, who through sluggishness and sleep plot against themselves when such glory is set before them ; and, were there no hell, they would be more wretched than any, who, when it is in their power to reign and to be glorified with the Son of God, deprive themselves of so great blessings. Since if it were necessary to be cut in pieces, if to die ten thousand deaths, if to give up every day ten thousand lives and as many bodies, ought we not to submit to such things[2] for such glory? But now we do not even despise money, which hereafter, though unwilling, we shall leave : we do not despise money, which brings about us ten thousand mischiefs, which remains here, which is not our own. For we are but stewards of that which is not our own, although we receive it from our fathers. But when there is hell besides, and the worm that dieth not, and the fire that is not quenched, and the gnashing of teeth, how, tell me, shall we bear these things? How long will we refuse to see clearly, and spend our all on daily fightings, and contentions, and unprofitable talk, feeding, cultivating earth, fattening the body and neglecting the soul, making no account of necessary things, but much care about things superfluous and unprofitable? And we build splendid tombs, and buy costly houses, and draw about with us herds of all kinds of servants, and devise different stewards, appointing managers of lands, of houses, of money, and managers of those managers ; but as to our desolate soul, we care nothing for that. And what will be the limit to this? Is it not one belly that we fill, is it not one body that we clothe? What is this great bustle of business? Why and wherefore do we cut up and tear to pieces the one[3] soul, which we have had assigned to us,[4] in attending to the service of such things, contriving for ourselves a grievous slavery? For he who needs many things is the slave of many things, although he seem to be their master. Since the lord is the slave even of his domestics, and brings in another and a heavier mode of service ; and in another way also he is their slave, not daring without them to enter the agora, nor the bath, nor the field,

but they frequently go about in all directions without him. He who seems to be master, dares not, if his slaves be not present, to go forth from home, and if whilst unattended he do but put his head out of his house, he thinks that he is laughed at. Perhaps some laugh at us when we say this, yet on this very account they would be deserving of ten thousand tears. For to show that this is slavery, I would gladly ask you, wouldest thou wish to need some one to put the morsel to thy mouth, and to apply the cup to thy lips? Wouldest thou not deem such a service worthy of tears? What if thou didst require continually supporters to enable thee to walk, wouldest thou not think thyself pitiable, and in this respect more wretched than any? So then thou oughtest to be disposed now. For it matters nothing whether one is so treated by irrational things,[5] or by men.

Why, tell me, do not the Angels differ from us in this respect, that they do not want so many things as we do? Therefore the less we need, the more we are on our way to them ; the more we need, the more we sink down to this perishable life. And that thou mayest learn that these things are so, ask those who have grown old which life they deem happiest, that when they were helplessly[6] mastered, or now when they are masters of these things? We have mentioned these persons, because those who are intoxicated with youth, do not even know the excess of their slavery. For what of those in fever, do they call themselves happy when, thirsting much, they drink much and need more, or when, having recovered their health, they are free from the desire? Seest thou that in every instance the needing much is pitiable, and far apart from true wisdom, and an aggravation of slavery and desire? Why then do we voluntarily increase to ourselves wretchedness? For, tell me, if it were possible to live uninjured without roof or walls, wouldest thou not prefer this ; wherefore then dost thou increase the signs of thy weakness? Do we not for this call Adam happy, that he needed nothing, no house, no clothes? " Yes," saith some one, " but now we are in need of them." Why then do we make our need greater? If many persons curtail many of the things actually needed, (servants, I mean, and houses, and money,) what excuse can we have if we overstep the need? The more thou puttest about thee, the more slavish dost thou become ; for by whatever proportion thou requirest more, in that proportion thou hast trenched upon thy freedom. For absolute[7] freedom is, to want nothing at all ; the next is, to want little ; and this the Angels and their imitators especially

[5] i.e. receives so much help from them.
[6] τὸν ὅτε ἐκρατοῦντο μάτην, ἢ τὸν ὅτε αὐτῶν κρατοῦσι νῦν. There may be some words omitted.
[7] ἀκριβῆς.

possess. But for men to succeed in this while tarrying in a mortal body, think how great praise this hath. This also Paul said, when writing to the Corinthians, " But I spare you," and, " lest such should have trouble in the flesh." [1] (1 Cor. vii. 28.) Riches are called " usables," [2] that we may " use " them rightly, and not keep and bury them ; for this is not to possess them, but to be possessed by them. Since if we are going to make this our aim how to multiply them, not that we may employ them rightly, the order is reversed, and they possess us, not we them. Let us then free ourselves from this grievous bondage, and at last become free. Why do we devise ten thousand different chains for ourselves? Is not the bond of nature enough for thee, and the ne-

cessity of life, and the crowd of ten thousand affairs, but dost thou twine also other nets for thyself, and put them about thy feet? And when wilt thou lay hold on heaven, and be able to stand on [6] that height? For a great thing, a great thing is it, that even having cut asunder all these cords, thou shouldest be able to lay hold on the city which is above. So many other hindrances are there ; all which that we may conquer, let us keep to the mean estate [7] [and having put away superfluities, let us keep to what is necessary.] Thus shall we lay hold on eternal life, through the grace and lovingkindness of our Lord Jesus Christ, to whom be glory for ever and ever. Amen.

---

# HOMILY LXXXI.

## John xvii. 6.

" I have manifested Thy Name unto the men which Thou gavest Me out of the world; Thine they were, and Thou gavest them Me, and they have kept Thy word."

[1.] " MESSENGER of great counsel " (Isa. ix. 6, LXX.), the Son of God is called, because of the other things which He taught, and principally because He announced the Father to men, as also now He saith, " I have manifested Thy Name unto the men." For after having said, " I have finished Thy work," He next explaineth it in detail, telling what sort of work. Now the Name indeed was well known. For Esaias said, " Ye shall swear [3] by the true God." (Isa. lxv. 16.) But what I have often told you I tell you now, that though it was known, yet it was so only to Jews, and not to all of these : but now He speaketh concerning the Gentiles. Nor doth He declare this merely, but also that they knew Him as the Father. For it is not the same thing to learn that He is Creator, and that He hath a Son. But He " manifested His [4] Name " both by words and actions.

" Whom Thou gavest Me out of the world." As He saith above, " No man cometh unto Me except it be given him " (c. vi. 65) ; and, " Except My Father [5] draw him " (c. vi. 64) ; so here too, " Whom thou gavest Me." (c. xiv. 6.) Now He calleth Himself " the Way "; whence it is clear that He establisheth two things by what is said here, that He is not opposed to

the Father, and that it is the Father's will to entrust them to the Son.

" Thine they were, and Thou gavest them Me."
Here He desireth to teach [8] that He is greatly loved by the Father. For that He needed not to receive them, is clear from this, He made them, He careth for them continually. How then did He receive them? This, as I said before, showeth His unanimity with the Father. Now if a man choose to enquire into the matter in a human manner, and as the words are spoken, they [9] will no longer belong to the Father. For if when the Father had them, the Son had them not, it is evident that when He gave them to the Son, He withdrew from His dominion over them. And again, there is a yet more unseemly conclusion ; for they will be found to have been imperfect while they yet were with the Father, but to have become perfect when they came to the Son. But it is mockery even to speak thus. What then doth He declare by this? [10] " That it hath seemed good to the Father also that they should believe on the Son."

" And they have kept Thy word."
Ver. 7. " Now they have known that all things whatsoever Thou hast given Me are of Thee."

How did they " keep Thy word "? " By believing in Me, and giving no heed to the Jews. For he that believeth in Him, it saith, ' hath set

---

1 " such shall have," &c., N. T.　　3 [ὁμοῦνται] LXX.
2 χρήματα.　　4 i.e. the Father's.
5 " The Father which hath sent Me," &c., N. T.

6 al. " rise up to."　　7 εὐτελείας.
8 βούλεται διδάξαι, Ben. and MSS. Savile omits βούλεται.
9 i.e. those given.
10 al. " by these words then He declareth."

to his seal that God is true.'" (c. iii. 33.) Some read, "Now I know that all things whatsoever Thou hast given Me are of Thee." But this would have no reason; for how would the Son be ignorant of the things of the Father? No, the words are spoken of the disciples. "From the time," He saith, "that I told them these things, they have learnt that all that Thou hast given Me is from Thee; nothing is alien, nothing peculiar to Me, with Thee."[1] (For whatever is peculiar, puts most things in the condition of being alien.[2] "They therefore have known that all things, whatsoever I teach, are Thy doctrines and teachings." "And whence have they learnt it?" From My words;[3] for so have I taught them. And not only this have I taught them, but also that "I came out from Thee." For this He was anxious to prove through all the Gospel.

Ver. 9. "I pray for them."[4]

"What sayest Thou?" "Dost Thou teach the Father, as though He were ignorant? Dost Thou speak to Him as to a man who knoweth not?" "What then meaneth this distinction?" Seest thou that the prayer is for nothing else than that they may understand the love which He hath towards them? For He who not only giveth what He hath of His own, but also calleth on Another to do the same, showeth greater love. What then is, "I pray for them"? "Not for all the world," He saith, but "for them whom Thou hast given·Me." He continually putteth the "hast given," that they might learn that this seemeth good to the Father. Then, because He had said continually, "they are Thine," and, "Thou gavest them unto Me," to remove any evil suspicion, and lest any one should think that His authority was recent, and that He had but now received them, what saith He?

[2.] Ver. 10. "All Mine are Thine, and Thine are Mine; and I am glorified in them."

Seest thou the equality of honor? For lest on hearing, "Thou hast given them Me," thou shouldest deem that they were alienated from the authority of the Father, or before this from that of the Son, He removed both difficulties by speaking as He did. It was as though He said, "Do not when thou hearest that 'Thou hast given them to Me,' deem that they are alienated from the Father, for what is Mine is His; nor when thou hearest, 'Thine they were,' think that they were aliens from Me, for what is

His is Mine." So that the, "Thou hast given," is said only for condescension; for what the Father hath is the Son's, and what the Son hath is the Father's. But this cannot even be said of a son after the manner of man, but because They[5] are upon a greater Equality of honor.[6] For that what belongs to the less, belongs to the greater also, is clear to every one, but the reverse not so; but here He converteth[7] these terms, and the conversion declares[8] Equality. And in another place, declaring this, He said, "All things that the Father hath are Mine," speaking of knowledge. And the "hast given Me," and the like expressions, are to show that He did not come as an alien and draw them to Him, but received them as His own. Then He putteth the cause and the proof, saying, "And I am glorified in them," that is, either that "I have power over them," or, that "they shall glorify Me, believing in Thee and Me, and shall glorify Us alike." But if He is not glorified equally in them, what is the Father's is no longer His. For no one is glorified in those over whom he hath no authority. Yet how is He glorified equally? All die for Him equally as for the Father; they preach Him as they do the Father; and as they say that all things are done in His Name, so also in the Name of the Son.

Ver. 11. "And now I am no more in the world, but these are in the world."[9]

That is, "Although I appear no longer in the flesh, yet by these am I glorified." But why doth He say continuously, that, "I am not in the world"; and that, "because I leave them I commit them to Thee"; and that, "when I was in the world I kept them"? for if one should take these words in their simple sense, many absurdities will follow. For how could it be reasonable to say, that He is no longer in the world, and that when He departeth He committeth them to another? since these are the words of a mere man parting from them forever. Seest thou how He speaketh for the most part like a man, and in a way adapted to their state of mind, because they thought that they had a greater degree of safety from His presence? Wherefore He saith, "While I was with them, I kept them." (c. xiv. 28.) Yet He telleth them, "I come to you"; and, "I am with you till the end." (Matt. xxviii. 20.) How then[10] saith He these words, as if about to be parted from them? He addresseth Himself, as I said before, to their thoughts,[11] that they may take breath a little when

[1] παρὰ σοί, i.e. in the Godhead, or with God. However, one Vatican MS. and Catena favor Savile's conjecture, παρὰ σε, "beside Thee," since the Father is in a peculiar manner His own.

[2] τὸ γὰρ ἴδιον ὡς ἐπ' ἀλλοτρίῳ τὰ πολλὰ τίθησι, i.e. when one thing is specified as peculiar to a person, it is implied that other things not specified do not belong to him.

[3] Ver. 8. "For I have given unto them the words which Thou gavest Me; and they have received them, and have known surely that I came out from Thee, and they have believed that Thou didst send Me."

[4] Ver. 9. "I pray for them; I pray not for the world, but for them which Thou hast given Me; for they are Thine."

[5] i.e. the Father and the Son.

[6] μείζονός εἰσιν ἰσοτιμίας. If this be the right reading, the sense is, that the Father and the Son are more Equal in honor than human father and son. Sav. reads μεῖζον. Ben. μείζονός ἐστιν, omitting ισ.

[7] ἀντιστρέφει.      [8] al. "shows."

[9] "in the world, and I come to Thee. Holy Father, keep through Thine own Name those whom Thou hast given Me, that they may be one as we are." N. T.

[10] al. "how now."      [11] Ben. "suspicion."

they hear Him speaking thus, and delivering them over to the care of the Father. For since, after hearing many exhortations from Him, they were not persuaded, He then holdeth converse with the Father, manifesting His affection for them. As though He had said, "Since Thou callest Me to Thyself, place these in safety ; for I come to Thee." "What sayest Thou? Art Thou not able to keep them?" "Yea, I am able." "Wherefore then speakest Thou thus?" "That they may have My joy fulfilled"[1] (ver. 13) ; that is, "may not be confounded, as being imperfect." And by these words He showed that He had spoken all these things so, to give them rest and joy. For the saying appears to be contradictory. "Now I am no longer in the world, and these are in the world." This was what they were suspecting. For a while therefore He condescendeth to them, because had He said, "I keep them," they would not have so well believed ; wherefore He saith, "Holy Father, keep them through Thine own Name"; that is, "by thy help."

Ver. 12. "While I was with them in the world, I kept them in Thy Name."

Again He speaketh as a man and as a Prophet, since nowhere doth He appear to have done anything by the Name of God.

"Those that Thou gavest Me I have kept, and none of them is lost, but the son of perdition, that the Scripture might be fulfilled."

And in another place He saith, "Of all that Thou gavest Me, I will surely lose nothing."[2] (c. vi. 39.) Yet not only was he[3] lost, but also many afterwards ; how then saith He, "I will in nowise lose"?[4] "For My part, I will not lose." So in another place, declaring the matter more clearly, He said, "I will in nowise cast out." (c. vi. 37.) "Not through fault of Mine, not because I either instigate or abandon them; but if they start away of themselves, I draw them not by necessity."

Ver. 13. "But now I come to thee."

Seest thou that the discourse is composed rather in a human manner? So that should any wish from these words to lower the Son, he will lower the Father also. Observe, in proof of this, how from the beginning He speaketh[5] partly as though informing and explaining to Him, partly as enjoining. Informing, as when He saith, "I pray not for the world"; enjoining, as, "I have kept them until now," "and none of them is lost"; and, "do Thou therefore now keep them," He saith. And again, "Thine they were, and Thou hast given them unto Me," and, "While I was in the world I kept them." But

the solution of all is, that the words were addressed to their infirmity.

But after having said that "none of them was lost but the son of perdition," He added, "that the Scripture might be fulfilled." Of what Scripture doth He speak? That which foretelleth many things concerning Him. Not that He perished on that account, in order that the Scripture might be fulfilled. But we have before spoken at length on this point, that this is the peculiar manner of Scripture, which puts things which fall out in accordance with it, as though they were caused by it.[6] And it is needful to enquire exactly into all, both the manner of the speaker, his argument, and the laws of Scripture, if at least we are minded not to draw wrong conclusions. For, "Brethren, be not children in your minds." (1 Cor. xiv. 20.)

[3.] This it is necessary to consider well,[7] not only for the understanding the Scriptures, but also for earnestness in one's way of life. For so little children do not desire great things, but are wont to admire those which are worth nothing ; they are pleased at seeing chariots, and horses, and the muleteer, and wheels, all made out of earthenware ; but if they see a king sitting upon a chariot, and a pair of white mules, and great magnificence, they do not even[8] turn their heads. And they deck out as brides dolls made of the same material, but the actual brides, real and beautiful, they do not even notice ; and this is their case in many other matters. Now this many men also undergo at this time ; for when they hear of heavenly things, they do not even give heed to them, but toward all the things of clay they are as eager as children, and stupidly admire the wealth which is of earth, and honor the glory and luxury of the present life. Yet these are just as much toys as those ; but the other are the causes of life, and glory, and repose. But as children deprived of their playthings cry, and do not know how even to desire the realities, so also are many of those who seem to be men. Wherefore it saith, "Be not children in your minds." (1 Cor. xiv. 20.) Desirest thou riches, tell me, and desirest thou not the wealth that lasteth, but childish toys? If thou shouldest see a man admiring a leaden coin, and stooping to pick it up, thou wouldest pronounce his penury to be extreme ; and dost thou, who collectest more worthless things than this, number thyself among the rich? How can this consist with reason? We will call him rich who despises all present things. For no one, no one will choose to laugh at these little things, silver and gold, and other things of show, unless he have the desire of greater things ; just as the man would

---

[1] " to Thee, and these things I speak in the world, that they might have My joy fulfilled in themselves." N. T.
[2] " which He hath given," N. T.       [4] οὐ μὴ ἀπ.
[3] i.e. the traitor.       [5] Ben. "is."

[6] ὡς αἰτιολογίαν τιθεμένης τὰ ἐκ τῆς ἐκβάσεως συμβαίνοντα.
[7] or, "to read (and understand)," ἀναγινώσκειν.
[8] Ben. "not at all."

not despise the leaden coin,[1] unless he possessed coins of gold. Do thou, therefore, when thou seest a man running by all worldly things, deem that he doth so from no other motive than because he looks to a greater world. So the husbandman despises a few grains of wheat, when he expects a larger harvest. But if, when the hope is uncertain, we despise things which are, much more ought we to do so in a case where the expectation is sure. Wherefore I pray and beseech you not to bring loss on yourselves, nor, keeping hold of mire, rob yourselves of the treasures which are above, bringing your vessel to port laden with straw and chaff. Let each say what he will concerning us, let him be angry at our continual admonitions, let him call us silly, tedious, tiresome, still we will not desist from exhorting you on these matters continually, and from continually repeating to you that of the Prophet, "'Break off thy sins by almsgiving, and thine iniquities by showing mercy to the poor' (Dan. iv. 27), and bind them upon thy neck."[2] Do not act in this way to-day, and desist to-morrow. For even this body has need of daily food; and so too hath the soul, or rather that much more; and if it give not,[3] it becomes weaker and more vile. Let us then not neglect it when it is perishing, choking. Many wounds it receives each day, by being lustful, angry, slothful, reviling, revengeful, envious. It is therefore necessary to prepare also remedies for it, and no small remedy is that of almsgiving, which can be placed on every wound. For, "Give alms," it saith, "of such things as ye have, and behold all things are clean unto you." (Luke xi. 41.) "Alms," not covetousness, for that which proceeds from covetousness endures not, though thou give to those who need. For almsgiving is that which is free from all injustice, "this" makes all things clean. This is a thing better even than fasting, or lying on the ground; they may be more painful and laborious, but this more profitable. It enlightens the soul, makes it sleek,[4] beautiful, and vigorous. Not so doth the fruit of the olive hold up the athletes, as this oil recovers the combatants of piety. Let us then anoint our hands, that we may lift them up well against our adversary. He that practiceth showing mercy to him that needeth, will soon cease from covetousness, he who continues in giving to the poor, will soon cease from anger, and will never even be high-minded. For as the physician continually tending wounded persons is easily sobered, beholding human nature in the calamities of others; so we, if we enter upon the work of aiding the poor, shall easily become truly wise, and shall not admire riches, nor deem present things any great matter, but despise them all, and soaring aloft to heaven, shall easily obtain the eternal blessings, through the grace and lovingkindness of our Lord Jesus Christ; to whom, with the Father and the Holy Ghost, be glory for ever and ever. Amen.

# HOMILY LXXXII.

### JOHN xvii. 14.

"I have given them Thy word; and the world hath hated them, because they are not of the world, even as I am not of the world."

[1.] WHEN having become virtuous we are persecuted by the wicked, or when being desirous of virtue we are mocked at by them, let us not be distracted or angry. For this is the natural course of things, and everywhere virtue is wont to engender hatred from wicked men. For envying those who desire to live properly, and thinking to prepare an excuse for themselves if they can overthrow the credit of others, they hate them as having pursuits opposite to their own, and use every means to shame their way of life. But let not us grieve, for this is a mark of virtue. Wherefore Christ also saith, "If ye were of the world, the world would love its own." (c. xv. 19.) And in another place again, "Woe unto you when all men shall speak well of you." (Luke vi. 26.) Wherefore also He saith here, "I have given them Thy word, and the world hath hated them." Again He telleth the reason for which they were worthy to obtain much care from the Father; "For Thy sake," He saith, "they have been hated, and for Thy word's sake"; so that they would be entitled to all providential care.

Ver. 15. "I pray not that Thou shouldest take them out of the world, but that Thou shouldest keep them from the evil."

Again He simplifieth[5] His language; again He rendereth it more clear; which is the act of one

---

[1] al. "the lead.".     [2] not found in the Chald. or LXX.
[3] κἂν μὴ καταβάλῃ. One MS. καταλάβῃ, "if it get it not."     [4] λιπαίνει.     [5] σαφηνίζει.

showing, by making entreaty for them with exactness, nothing else but this, that He hath a very
tender care for them. Yet He Himself had told
them, that the Father would do all things whatsoever they should ask. How then doth He
here pray for them? As I said, for no other
purpose than to show His love.

Ver. 16. "They are not of the world, even as
I am not of the world."

How then saith He in another place, "Which
Thou gavest Me out of the world; Thine they
were"? (Ver. 6.) There He speaketh of their
nature; here of wicked actions. And He putteth together a long encomium of them; first,
that "they were not of the world"; then, that
"the Father Himself had given them"; and
that "they had kept His word;" and that on
this account "they were hated." And if He
saith, "As I am not of the world," be not troubled; for the "as" is not here expressive of unvarying exactness. For as, when in the case of
Him and the Father the "as" is used, a great
Equality is signified, because of the Relationship
in Nature; so when it is used of us and Him,
the interval is great, because of the great and
infinite interval between the respective natures.
For if He "did no sin, neither was guile found
in His mouth" (1 Pet. ii. 22), how could the
Apostles be reckoned equal to Him? What is
it then that He saith, "They are not of the
world"? "They look to another world, they
have nothing common with earth, but are become citizens of heaven." And by these words
He showeth His love, when He commendeth
them to the Father, and committeth them to
Him who begat Him. When He saith, "Keep
them," He doth not speak merely of delivering
them from dangers, but also with regard to their
continuance in the faith. Wherefore He addeth,

Ver. 17. "Sanctify them through Thy truth."
"Make them holy by the gift of the Spirit, and
of right doctrines." As when He saith, "Ye
are clean through the word which I spake unto
you" (c. xv. 3), so now He saith the same thing,
"Instruct them, teach them the truth." "And
yet He saith that the Spirit doth this. How
then doth He now ask it from the Father?"
That thou mayest again learn their equality of
Honor. For right doctrines asserted concerning
God sanctify the soul. And if He saith that
they are sanctified by the word, marvel not. And
to show that He speaketh of doctrines, He addeth,

"Thy word is truth."

That is, "there is no falsehood in it, and all
that is said in it must needs come to pass"; and
again, it signifieth nothing typical or bodily. As
also Paul saith concerning the Church, that He
hath sanctified it by the Word. For the Word
of God is wont also to cleanse. (Eph. v. 26.)

Moreover, the, "sanctify them," seems to me to
signify something else, such as this, "Set them
apart for the Word and for preaching." And
this is made plain from what follows. For, He
saith,

Ver. 17. "As Thou hast sent Me into the
world, even so have I also sent them into the
world."

As Paul also saith, "Having put in us the
word of reconciliation." (2 Cor. v. 19.) For
the same end for which Christ came, for the
same did these take possession of the world. In
this place again the "as" is not put to signify
resemblance in the case of Himself and the
Apostles; for how was it possible for men to be
sent otherwise? But it was His custom to speak
of the future as having come to pass.[1]

Ver. 19. "And for their sakes I sanctify Myself, that they also might be sanctified in the
truth."

What is, "I sanctify Myself"? "I offer to
Thee a sacrifice." Now all sacrifices are called
"holy," and those are specially called "holy
things," which are laid up for God. For whereas
of old in type the sanctification was by the sheep,
but now it is not[2] in type, but by the truth itself,
He therefore saith, "That they may be sanctified
in Thy truth." "For I both dedicate them to
Thee, and make them an offering"; this He
saith, either because their Head was being made
so,[3] or because they also were sacrificed; for,
"Present," it saith, "your bodies a living sacrifice, holy" (Rom. xii. 1); and, "We were
counted as sheep for the slaughter." (Ps. xliv.
22.) And He maketh them, without death, a
sacrifice and offering; for that He alluded to
His own sacrifice, when He said, "I sanctify,"
is clear from what follows.

Ver. 20. "Neither pray I for these alone, but
for them also who shall believe."[4]

[2.] For since He was dying for them, and
said, that "For their sakes I sanctify Myself,"
lest any one should think that He did this for
the Apostles only, He added, "Neither pray I
for these only, but for them also who believe on
Me through their word." By this again He
revived their souls, showing that the disciples
should be many. For because He made common what they possessed peculiarly, He comforteth them by showing that they were being made
the cause of the salvation of others.

After having thus spoken concerning their salvation, and their being sanctified by faith and
the Sacrifice, He afterwards speaketh of concord, and finally closeth his discourse with this,
having begun with it and ended[5] in it. For at

---

[1] i.e. the words refer to the mission of the Ap. on the day of
Pentecost.        [2] al. "is no longer."
[3] διὰ τὸ τὴν κεφαλὴν τοῦτο γίνεσθαι, al. γίνεται.
[4] "believe on Me through their word," N. T.
[5] καταλύσας, al. τελευτήσας.

the beginning He saith, "A new commandment
I give unto you" (c. xiii. 34) ; and here,

Ver. 21. "That they all may be one, as Thou,
Father, art in Me and I in Thee."

Here again the "as" doth not denote exact
similarity in their case, (for it was not possible
for them in so great a degree,) but only as far
as was possible for men. Just as when He saith,
"Be ye merciful, as your Father." (Luke vi. 36.)
But what is, "In Us"?[1] In the faith which is
on Us. Because nothing so offends all men as
divisions, He provideth that they should be
one. "What then," saith some one, "did He
effect this?" Certainly He effected it. For
all who believe through the Apostles are one,
though some from among them were torn away.
Nor did this escape His knowledge, He even
foretold it, and showed that it proceeded from
men's slack-mindedness.

"That the world may believe that Thou hast
sent Me."

As He said in the beginning, "By this shall
all men know that ye are My disciples, if ye
love one another." And how should they hence
believe? "Because," He saith, "Thou art a
God of peace." If therefore they observe the
same as those of whom they have learnt, their
hearers shall know the teacher by the disciples,
but if they quarrel, men shall deny that they are
the disciples of a God of peace, and will not
allow that I, not being peaceable, have been
sent from Thee. Seest thou how, unto the end,
He proveth His unanimity with the Father?

Ver. 22. "And the glory which Thou gavest
Me, I have given them."[2]

That by miracles, that by doctrines,[3] and, that
they should be of one soul; for this is glory,
that they should be one, and greater even than
miracles. As men[4] admire God because there
is no strife or discord in That Nature, and this
is His greatest glory, "so too let these," He
saith, "from this cause become glorious." "And
how," saith some one, "doth He ask the Father
to give this to them, when He saith that He
Himself giveth it?" Whether His discourse be
concerning miracles, or unanimity, or peace, He
is seen Himself to have given these things to
them; whence it is clear that the petition is
made for the sake of their comfort.

Ver. 23. "I in them, and Thou in Me."

"How gave He the glory?" By being in
them, and having the Father with Him, so as to
weld them[5] together. But in another place He
speaketh not so; He saith not that the Father
cometh by Him, but, "that He and the Father
come, and take up their abode with him,"[6]

"there" removing the suspicion of Sabellius,
"here" that of Arius.[7]

"That they may be made perfect in one, and
that the world may know that Thou hast sent
Me." (c. xiv. 23.)

He saith these latter words immediately after
the other, to show that peace hath more power
to attract men than a miracle; for as it is the
nature of strife[8] to separate, so it is that of
agreement to weld together.

"And I have[9] loved them as Thou hast loved
Me."

Here again the "as" means, as far as it is
possible for a man to be loved; and the sure
proof of His love is His giving Himself for
them. After having told them that they shall
be in safety, that they shall not be overturned,
that they shall be holy, that many shall believe
through them, that they shall enjoy great glory,
that not He alone loved them, but the Father
also; He next telleth them of what shall be after
their sojourning here,[10] concerning the prizes and
crowns laid up for them.

Ver. 24. "Father," He saith, "I will that they
also whom Thou hast given Me, be with Me
where I am."

"Then dost Thou gain by prayer, and dost
Thou not yet possess that concerning which they
enquired continually, saying, 'Whither goest
Thou?' What sayest Thou? How then didst
Thou say to them, 'Ye shall sit upon twelve
thrones'? (Matt. xix. 28.) How didst Thou
promise other things more and greater?" Seest
thou that He saith all[11] in the way of condescension? since how would He have said, "Thou
shalt follow afterwards"? (c. xiii. 36.) But
He speaketh thus with a view to a fuller conviction and demonstration of His love.

"That they may behold My glory which Thou
hast given Me."

This again is a sign of His being of one mind
with the Father, of a higher character than those
former, for He saith, "Before[12] the foundation
of the world," yet hath it also a certain condescension; for, "Thou hast given Me," He saith.
Now if this be not the case, I would gladly ask
the gainsayers a question. He that giveth, giveth
to one subsisting;[13] did the Father then, having
first begotten the Son, afterwards give Him
glory, having before allowed Him to be without
glory? And how could this be reasonable?
Seest that the "He gave," is, "He begat"?

[3.] But why said He not, "That they may
share My glory," instead of, "That they may be-

---

[1] "that they also may be one in Us," N. T.
[2] "given them, that they may be one, even as We are One,"
N. T.     [4] al. "we."
[3] al. "teaching."     [5] al. "hold them."
[6] i.e. with him who keeps the commandments.

[7] al. "there stopping the mouths of the Sabellians, here removing the folly of Arius." The earlier passage, c. xiv. 23, proves
the distinct Personality, the latter, c. xvii. 23, the Consubstantiality
of the Son.
[8] al. "division."     [9] "and hast loved," N. T.
[10] Sav. conject. "departure hence."
[11] al. "all is said."
[12] "For Thou lovedst Me before," &c., N. T.     [13] ὑφεστῶτι.

hold My glory"? Here He implieth, that all that rest is, the looking on the Son of God. This certainly it is which causes them to be glorified; as Paul saith, "With open face mirroring the glory of the Lord." (2 Cor. iii. 18.) For as they who look on the sunbeams, and enjoy a very clear atmosphere, draw their enjoyment from their sight, so then also, and in much greater degree, this will cause us pleasure.[1] At the same time also He showeth, that what they should behold was not the body then seen, but some awful Substance.

Ver. 25. "O righteous Father, the world hath not known Thee."[2]

What meaneth this? What connection hath it? He here showeth that no man knoweth God, save those only who have come to know the Son. And what He saith is of this kind: "I wished all to be so,[3] yet they have not known Thee, although they had no complaint against Thee." For this is the meaning of, "O righteous Father." And here He seemeth to me to speak these words, as vexed that they would not know One so just and good. For since the Jews had said that they knew God, but that He knew Him not, at this He aimeth, saying, "For Thou lovedst Me before the foundation of the world"; thus putting together a defense against the accusations of the Jews. For how could He who had received glory, who was loved before the foundation of the world, who desired to have them as witnesses of that glory, how could He be opposed to the Father? "This then is not true which the Jews say, that they know Thee, and that I know Thee not; on the contrary, I know Thee, and they have not known Thee."

"And these have known that Thou hast sent Me."

Seest thou that He alludeth to those, who said that He was not from God, and all is finally summed up to meet this argument?

Ver. 26. "And I have declared unto them Thy Name, and will declare it."

"Yet thou sayest that perfect knowledge is from the Spirit." "But the things of the Spirit are Mine."

"That the love wherewith Thou hast loved Me may remain[4] in them, and I in them."

"For if they learn who Thou art, then they shall know that I am not separated from Thee, but one of the greatly beloved, and a true Son, and closely knit to Thee. And those who are rightly persuaded of this, will keep both the faith which is on Me and perfect love; and while they love as they ought, I remain in them."

Seest thou how He hath arrived[5] at a good end, finishing off the discourse with love, the mother of all blessings?

[4.] Let us then believe and love God, that it may not be said of us, "They profess that they know God, but in their works they deny Him." (Tit. i. 16.) And again, "He hath denied the faith, and is worse than an infidel." (1 Tim. v. 8.) For when he[6] helps his domestics and kinsmen and strangers, while thou dost not even succor those who are related to thee by family, what will henceforth be thy excuse, when God is blasphemed and insulted by reason of thee? Consider what opportunities of doing good God hath given to us. "Have mercy on one," He saith, "as a kinsman, on another as a friend, on another as a neighbor, on another as a citizen, on another as a man." And if none of these things hold thee, but thou breakest through all bonds, hear from Paul, that thou art "worse than an infidel"; for he having heard nothing of almsgiving, or of heavenly things, hath overshot thee in love for man; but thou who art bidden to love thy very enemies, lookest upon thy friends as enemies, and art more careful of thy money than of their bodies. Yet the money by being spent will sustain no injury, but thy brother if neglected will perish. What madness then to be careful of money, and careless about one's kindred? Whence hath this craving for riches burst in upon us?[7] Whence this inhumanity and cruelty? For if any one could, as though seated on the highest bench of a theater, look down upon all the world, — or rather, if you will, let us for the present take in hand a single city, — if then a man seated on an elevated spot could take in at a glance all the doings of the men there, consider what folly he would condemn, what tears he would weep, what laughter he would laugh, with what hatred he would hate; for we commit such actions as deserve both laughter, and the charge of folly, and tears, and hatred. One man keeps dogs to catch[8] brute animals, himself sinking into brutality; another keeps oxen and asses to transport stones, but neglects men wasting with hunger; and spends gold without limit to make men of stone, but neglects real men, who are becoming like stones through their evil state. Another, collecting with great pains golden quarries,[9] puts them about his walls, but when he beholds the naked bellies of the poor, is not moved.[10] Some again contrive garments over their very garments, while their brother hath not even wherewithal to cover his naked body. Again, one hath swallowed up another in the

---

[1] al. "will cause us greater pleasure."
[2] "known Thee; but I know Thee," N. T.
[3] i.e. knowing the Father.
[4] "may be," N. T.

[5] ἀπήντησεν, according to Sav. conject. and some MSS. for ἀπήρτησεν.
[6] i.e. the infidel.        [7] εἰσεκώμασε.
[8] σαγηνεύῃ, "sweep as with a seine net."
[9] for mosaic work, ψηφῖδας.        [10] lit. "bent."

law-courts; another hath spent his money on women and parasites, another on stage-players and theatrical bands,[1] another on splendid edifices, on purchases of fields and houses. Again, one man is counting interest, another interest of interest; another is putting together[2] bands full of many deaths, and doth not enjoy rest even at night, lying awake for others' harm. Then, when it is day, they run, one to his unjust gain, another to his wanton expense, others to public robbery.[3] And great is the earnestness about things superfluous and forbidden, but of things necessary no account is taken; and they who decide questions of law have indeed the name of jurymen, but are really[4] thieves and murderers. And if one should enquire into law suits and wills, he would find there again ten thousand mischiefs, frauds, robberies, plots, and about these things is all time spent; but for spiritual things there is no care, and they all inconvenience the Church, for the sake of seeing only. But this is not what is required; we need works, and a pure mind.[5] But if thou spendest all the day in grasping after riches, and then coming in sayest a few words, thou hast not only not propitiated God, but hast even angered Him more. Wouldest thou conciliate thy Lord, exhibit works, make thyself acquainted with the mass of woes, look upon the naked, the hungry, the wronged; He hath cut out for thee ten thousand ways of showing love for men. Let us not then deceive ourselves by living aimlessly and to no purpose, nor presume, because we now are in health; but bearing in mind, that often when we have fallen into sickness, and have reached the extreme of debility, we have been dead with fear and the looking for things to come, let us expect to fall again into the same state, let us get again the same fear, and let us become better men; since what is done now deserves infinite condemnation. For those in the courts of justice are like lions and dogs; those in the public places like foxes; and those who lead a life of leisure, even they do not use their leisure as they ought, speeding all their time on theaters and the mischiefs arising from them. And there is no one to reprove what is being done; but there are many who envy, and are vexed that they are not in the like condition,[7] so that these in their turn are punished, though not actually doing wicked things. For they "not only do these things, but also have pleasure in them that do them." Because what belongs to their will is alike[8] corrupt; whence it is plain, that the intention also will be punished. These things I say each day, and I will not cease to say them. For if any listen, it is gain; but if none give heed, ye shall *then* hear these things, when it will avail you nothing, and ye shall blame yourselves, and we shall be free from fault. But may it never come to pass that we should only have this excuse, but that you may be our boast before the judgment-seat of Christ, that together we may enjoy the blessings, through the grace and lovingkindness of our Lord Jesus Christ, with whom to the Father and the Holy Ghost be glory, for ever and ever. Amen.

# HOMILY LXXXIII.

## John xviii. 1.

"When Jesus had spoken these words, He went forth with His disciples over the brook Cedron, where was a garden, into the which He entered, and His disciples."

[1.] An awful thing is death, and very full of terror, but not to those who have learnt the true wisdom which is above. For he that knows nothing certain concerning things to come, but deems it[6] to be a certain dissolution and end of life, with reason shudders and is afraid, as though he were passing into non-existence. But we who, by the grace of God, have learnt the hidden and secret things of His wisdom, and deem the action to be a departure to another place, should have no reason to tremble, but rather to rejoice and be glad, that leaving this perishable life we go to one far better and brighter, and which hath no end. Which Christ teaching by His actions, goeth to His Passion, not by constraint and necessity, but willingly. "These things," it saith, "Jesus spake, and departed 'beyond the brook Cedron, where was a garden, into the which He entered, and His disciples.'"

Ver. 2. "Judas also, which betrayed Him, knew the place; for Jesus ofttimes resorted thither with His disciples."

He journeyeth at midnight, and crosseth a

---

[1] ὀρχήστρας, al. ὀρχηστὰς, "dancers."   [2] al. "putting."
[3] or, "robbing the State," κλοπὴν δεδημοσιευμένην.
[4] lit. "have the reality of."   [5] or, "intention."
[6] i.e. death, lit. "the action."

[7] or, "do not things like them."
[8] i.e. "no less than the actions."

river, and hasteth to come to a place known to the traitor, lessening the labor to those who plotted against Him, and freeing them from all trouble ; and showeth to the disciples that He came willingly to the action, (a thing which was most of all sufficient to comfort them,) and placeth Himself in the garden as in a prison.

"These things spake Jesus unto them." "What sayest thou?[1] Surely He was speaking with the Father, surely He was praying. Why then dost thou not say that, 'having ceased from the prayer,' He came there?" Because it was not prayer, but a speech made on account of the disciples. "And the disciples entered into the garden." He had so freed them from fear, that they no longer resisted, but entered with Him into the garden. But how came Judas there, or whence had he gained his information when he came? It is evident from this circumstance, that Jesus generally[2] passed the night out of doors.[3] For had He been in the habit of spending it at home, Judas would not have come to the desert, but to the house, expecting there to find Him asleep. And lest, hearing of a "garden," thou shouldest think that Jesus hid Himself, it addeth, that "Judas knew the place"; and not simply so,[4] but that He "often resorted thither with His disciples." For ofttimes He was with them apart, conversing on necessary matters, and such as it was not permitted to others to hear. And He did this especially in mountains and gardens, seeking a place free from disturbance, that their attention might not be distracted from listening.

Ver. 3. "Judas then, having received a band of men and officers from the Chief Priests and Pharisees, cometh thither with lanterns, and torches, and weapons."

And these men had often at other times sent to seize Him, but had not been able ; whence it is plain, that at this time He voluntarily surrendered Himself. And how did they persuade the band? They were soldiers,[5] who had made it their practice to do anything for money.

Ver. 4. "Jesus therefore, knowing all things that should come upon Him, went forth, and said, Whom seek ye?"

That is, He did not wait to learn this from their coming, but spake and acted without confusion, as knowing all these things. "But why come they with weapons, when about to seize Him?" They feared His followers, and for this reason they came upon Him late at night. "And He went forth, and said unto them, Whom seek ye?"

Ver. 5. "They answered Him, Jesus of Nazareth."[6]

Seest thou His invincible power, how being in the midst of them He disabled their eyes? for that the darkness was not the cause of their not knowing Him, the Evangelist hath shown, by saying, that they had torches also. And even had there been no torches, they ought at least to have known Him by His voice; or if they did not know it, how could Judas be ignorant, who had been so continually with Him? for he too stood with them, and knew Him no more than they, but with them fell backward. And Jesus did this to show, that not only they could not seize Him, but could not even see Him when in the midst, unless He gave permission.

Ver. 7. "He saith again, Whom seek ye?"[7]

What madness ! His word threw them backward, yet not even so did they turn, when they had learnt that His power was so great, but again set themselves to the same attempt. When therefore He had fulfilled all that was His, then He gave Himself up.

Ver. 8. "He answered, I told you that I Am." (Ver. 5. "And Judas also which betrayed Him stood with them.")

See the forbearance[8] of the Evangelist, how he doth not insult over the traitor, but relates what took place, only desiring to prove one thing, that the whole took place with His own consent. Then, lest any one should say that He Himself brought them to this, by having placed Himself into their hands, and revealed Himself to them ; after having shown to them all things which should have been sufficient to repulse them, when they persevered in their wickedness, and had no excuse, He put Himself in their hands, saying,

"If therefore ye seek Me, let these go their way."

Manifesting until the last hour His lovingkindness towards them. "If," He saith, "ye want Me, have nothing to do with these, for, behold, I give Myself up."

Ver. 9. "That the saying might be fulfilled which He spake, Of those which Thou gavest Me have I lost none."

By "loss"[9] He doth not here mean that which is of death, but that which is eternal ; though the Evangelist in the present case includes the former also. And one might wonder why they did not seize them with Him, and cut them to pieces, especially when Peter had exasperated them by what he did to the servant. Who then restrained them? No other than that Power which cast them backward. And so the Evangelist, to show that it did not come to pass through their intention, but by the power and

---

[1] addressed to St. John.    [4] or, "not once, but often," &c.
[2] τὰ πολλά.    [5] στρατιῶται, mercenaries.
[3] ἔξω.
[6] Ver. 5, 6. "They answered Him, Jesus of Nazareth. Jesus

saith unto them, I Am. And Judas also which betrayed Him stood with them. As soon then as He had said unto them, I Am, they went backward, and fell to the ground." N. T.

[7] "Whom seek ye? And they said, Jesus of Nazareth." N. T.
[8] τὸ ἀνεπαχθὲς.    [9] more exactly, "perdition."

decree of Him whom they had seized, has added, "That the saying might be fulfilled which He spake," that "not one, &c." (c. xvii. 12.)

[2.] Peter, therefore, taking courage from His voice, and from what had already happened, arms himself against the assailants.[1] "And how," saith some one, "doth he who was bidden not to have a scrip, not to have two coats, possess a sword?" Methinks he had prepared it long before, as fearing this very thing which came to pass. But if thou sayest, "How doth he, who was forbidden even to strike a blow with the hand, become a man-slayer?" He certainly had been commanded not to defend himself, but here he did not defend himself, but his Master. And besides, they were not as yet perfect or complete. But if thou desirest to see Peter endued with heavenly wisdom, thou shalt after this behold him wounded, and bearing it meekly, suffering ten thousand dreadful things, and not moved to anger. But Jesus here also worketh a miracle, both showing that we ought to do good to those who do evil to us, and revealing His own power. He therefore restored the servant's ear, and said to Peter, that "All they that take the sword shall perish by the sword" (Matt. xxvi. 52); and as He did in the case of the basin, when He relaxed his vehemence[2] by a threat, so also here. The Evangelist adds the name of the servant, because the thing done was very great, not only because He healed him, but because He healed one who had come against Him, and who shortly after would buffet Him, and because He stayed the war which was like to have been kindled from this circumstance against the disciples. For this cause the Evangelist hath put the name, so that the men of that time might search and enquire diligently whether these things had really come to pass. And not without a cause doth he mention the "right ear," but as I think desiring to show the impetuosity of the Apostle, that he almost aimed at the head itself. Yet Jesus not only restraineth him by a threat, but also calmeth him by other words, saying,

Ver. 11. "The cup which My Father hath given Me, shall I not drink it?"[3]

Showing, that what was done proceeded not from their power, but from His consent, and declaring that He was not one opposed to God, but obedient to the Father even unto death.

Ver. 12, 13. "Then Jesus was taken; and they bound Him, and led Him away to Annas."[4]

Why to Annas? In their pleasure they made a show of[5] what had been done, as though forsooth they had set up a trophy.

"And he was father-in-law to Caiaphas."

Ver. 14. "Now Caiaphas was he which gave counsel to the Jews, that it was expedient that one man should die for the people."

Why doth the Evangelist again remind us of his prophecy? To show that these things were done for our salvation. And such is the exceeding force of truth, that even enemies proclaimed these things beforehand. For lest the listener, hearing of bonds, should be confounded, he reminds him of that prophecy, that the death of Jesus was the salvation of the world.

Ver. 15. "And Simon Peter followed Jesus, and so did another disciple."[6]

Who is that other disciple? It is the writer himself. "And wherefore doth he not name himself? When he lay on the bosom of Jesus, he with reason concealed his name; but now why doth he this?" For the same reason, for here too he mentions a great good deed, that when all had started away,[7] he followed. Therefore he conceals himself, and puts Peter before him. He was obliged to mention himself, that thou mightest understand that he narrates more exactly than the rest what took place in the hall, as having been himself within. But observe how he detracts from his own praise; for, lest any one should ask, "How, when all had retreated, did this man enter in farther than Simon?" he saith, that he "was known to the high priest." So that no one should wonder that he followed, or cry him up for his manliness. But the wonder was that matter of Peter, that being in such fear, he came even as far as the hall, when the others had retreated. His coming thither was caused by love, his not entering within by distress and fear. For the Evangelist hath recorded these things, to clear a way for excusing his denial; with regard to himself, he doth not set it down as any great matter that he was known to the high priest, but since he had said that he alone with Jesus went in, lest thou shouldest suppose that the action proceeded from any exalted feelings, he puts also the cause. And that Peter would have also entered had he been permitted, he shows by the sequel; for when he went out, and bade the damsel who kept the door bring in Peter, he straightway came in. But why did he not bring him in himself? He clung to Christ, and followed Him; on this

---

[1] Ver. 10. "Then Simon Peter, having a sword, drew it, and smote the high priest's servant, and cut off his right ear. The servant's name was Malchus."        [2] lit. "tension."
[3] Ver. 11. "Then said Jesus unto Peter, Put up thy sword into the sheath; the cup," &c. N. T.
[4] Ver. 12, 13. "Then the band and the captain and officers of the Jews took Jesus, and bound Him, and led Him away to Annas

first; for he was father-in-law to Caiaphas, which was the high priest that same year." N. T.
[5] or, "made a show of Him in."
[6] Ver. 15, 16. "And Simon Peter followed Jesus, and so did that other disciple: that disciple was known unto the high priest, and went in with Jesus into the palace of the high priest. But Peter stood at the door without. Then went out that other disciple, which was known unto the high priest, and spake unto her that kept the door, and brought in Peter." N. T.        [7] al. "retired."

account he bade[1] the woman bring him in. What then saith the woman?

Ver. 17. "Art not thou also one of this man's disciples? And he saith, I am not."[2]

What sayest thou, Peter? Didst thou not declare but now, "If need be that I lay down my life for Thee, I will lay it down"? What hath happened then, that thou canst not even endure the questioning of a door-keeper? Is it a soldier who questions thee? Is it one of those who seized Him? No, it is a mean and abject door-keeper, nor is the questioning of a rough kind.[3] She saith not, "Art thou a disciple of that cheat and corrupter," but, "of that man," which was the expression rather of one pitying and relenting.[4] But Peter could not bear any of these words. The, "Art not thou also," is said on this account, that John was within. So mildly did the woman speak. But he perceived none of this, nor took it into his mind, neither the first time, nor the second, nor the third, but when the cock crew; nor did this even bring him to his senses, till Jesus gave him the bitter look. And he stood warming himself[5] with the servants of the high priest, but Christ was kept bound within. This we say not as accusing Peter, but showing the truth of what had been said by Christ.

Ver. 19. "The high priest then asked Jesus of His disciples, and of His doctrine."

[3.] O the wickedness! Though he had continually heard Him speaking in the temple and teaching openly, he now desires to be informed. For since they had no charge to bring, they enquired concerning His disciples, perhaps where they were, and why He had collected them, and with what intention, and on what terms. And this he said, as desiring to prove Him to be a seditious person and an innovator, since no one gave heed to Him, except them alone, as though His were some factory of wickedness. What then saith Christ? To overthrow this, He saith,

Ver. 20. "I spake openly to the world, (not to the disciples privately,) I taught openly in the temple."[6]

"What then, said He nothing in secret?" He did, but not, as they thought, from fear, and to make conspiracies, but if at any time His sayings were too high for the hearing of the many.

Ver. 21. "Why askest thou Me? Ask them which heard Me."[7]

These are not the words of one speaking arrogantly, but of one confiding in the truth of what He had said. What therefore He said at the beginning, "If I bear witness of Myself, My witness is not true" (c. v. 31), this He now implieth, desiring to render His testimony abundantly credible. For when Annas mentioned the disciples,[8] what saith He? "Dost thou ask Me concerning Mine? Ask Mine enemies, ask those who have plotted against Me, who have bound Me; let them speak." This is an unquestionable proof of truth, when one calls his enemies to be witnesses to what he saith. What then doth the high priest? When it would have been right thus to have made the enquiry, that person did not so.

Ver. 22. "And when He had thus spoken, one of the officers which stood by smote Him with the palm of his hand."[9]

What could be more audacious than this? Shudder, O heaven, be astounded, O earth, at the long-suffering of the Lord, and the senselessness of the servants! Yet what was it that He said? He said not, "Why askest thou Me," as if refusing to speak, but wishing to remove every pretext for senseless behavior; and being upon this buffeted, though He was able to shake, to annihilate, or to remove all things, He doth not any one of these, but speaketh words able to relax any brutality.

Ver. 23. "And He saith, If I have spoken evil, bear witness of the evil."[10]

That is, "If thou canst lay hold on My words, declare it; but if thou canst not, why strikest thou Me?" Seest thou that the judgment-hall is full of tumult, and trouble, and passion, and confusion? The high priest asked deceitfully and treacherously, Christ answered in a straightforward manner, and as was meet. What then was next to be done? Either to refute, or to accept what He said. This however is not done, but a servant buffets Him. So far was this from being a court of justice, and the proceedings those of a conspiracy, and a deed of tyranny. Then not having even so made any farther discovery, they send Him bound to Caiaphas.[11]

Ver. 25. "And Simon Peter stood and warmed himself."

Wonderful, by what a lethargy[12] that hot and furious one was possessed, when Jesus was being led away! After such things as had taken place, he doth not move, but still warms himself, that thou mayest learn how great is the weakness of

---

[1] al. "gave in charge."
[2] Ver. 17. "Then saith the damsel that kept the door unto Peter, Art not," &c. N. T.
[3] θρασεία.    [4] lit. "bent," κατακαμπτομένης.
[5] Ver. 18. "And the servants and officers stood there, who had made a fire of coals; and they warmed themselves; and Peter stood with them, and warmed himself."
[6] "Jesus answered him, I spake openly to the world; I ever taught in the synagogue, and in the temple, whither the Jews always resort; and in secret have I said nothing." N. T.
[7] "which heard Me, what I have said unto them; behold, they know what I said." N. T.

[8] al. "the disciples as disciples."
[9] "of his hand, saying, Answerest thou the high priest so?" N. T.
[10] "of the evil; but if well, why smitest thou Me?" N. T.
[11] Ver. 24. "Annas sent (ἀπέστειλεν) Him bound to Caiaphas the high priest." St. C. makes this the order of the narrative, but most commentators refer the words to an earlier period.
[12] κάρῳ.

our nature if God abandoneth. And, being questioned, he denies again.[1]

Ver. 26. Then saith "the kinsman[2] of him whose ear Peter cut off, (grieving at what had taken place,) Did I not see thee in the garden?"[3]

But neither did the garden bring him to remember what had taken place,[4] nor the great affection which Jesus there had shown by those words, but all these from pressure of anxiety he banished from his mind. But why have the Evangelists with one accord written concerning him? Not as accusing the disciple, but as desiring to teach us, how great an evil it is not to commit all to God, but to trust to one's self. But do thou admire the tender care of his Master, who, though a prisoner and bound, took great forethought for His disciple, raising Peter up, when he was down, by His look, and launching him into a sea of tears.[5]

"They lead Him therefore from Caiaphas to Pilate."[6]

This was done, in order that the number of His judges might show, even against their will, how fully tested was His truth. "And it was early." Before cock crow He was brought to Caiaphas, early in the morning to Pilate; whence the Evangelist shows, that being questioned by Caiaphas during an entire half of the night, He was in nothing proved guilty; wherefore Caiaphas sent Him on to Pilate. But leaving these things for the others to relate, John speaks of what follows next. And observe the ridiculous conduct of the Jews. They who had seized the innocent, and taken up arms, do not enter into the hall of judgment, "lest they should be polluted." And tell me, what kind of pollution was it to set foot in a judgment-hall, where wrong-doers suffer justice? They who paid tithes of mint and anise, did not think they were polluted when bent on killing unjustly, but thought that they polluted themselves by even treading in a court of justice. "And why did they not kill Him, instead of bringing Him to Pilate?" In the first place, the greater part of their rule and authority had been cut away, when their affairs were placed under the power of the Romans; and besides, they feared lest they should afterwards be accused and punished by Him. "But what is, 'That they might eat the Passover?'" For He had done this on the first day of unleavened bread." Either he calls the whole feast "the Passover," or means, that they were then keeping the Passover, while He delivered it to His followers one day sooner, reserving His own Sacrifice for[7] the Preparation-day, when also of old the Passover was celebrated. But they, though they had taken up arms, which was unlawful, and were shedding blood, are scrupulous about the place, and bring forth Pilate to them.

Ver. 29. "And having gone out, he said, What accusation bring ye against this man?"

[4.] Seest thou that he was free from[8] fondness for rule and from malice? For seeing Jesus bound, and led by so many persons, he did not think that they had unquestionable proof of their accusation, but questions them, thinking it a strange thing that they should take for themselves the judgment, and then commit the punishment without any judgment to him. What then say they?

Ver. 30. "If he were not a malefactor, we would not have delivered him up unto thee."

O madness! for why do ye not mention His evil deeds, instead of concealing them? Why do ye not prove the evil? Seest thou that they everywhere avoid a direct accusation, and that they can say nothing? That Annas questioned Him about His doctrine, and having heard Him, sent Him to Caiaphas; and he having in his turn questioned Him, and discovered nothing, sent Him to Pilate. Pilate saith, "What accusation bring ye against this man?" Nor here have they anything to say, but again employ certain[9] conjectures. At which Pilate being perplexed saith,

Ver. 31, 32. "Take ye him and judge him according to your law. They therefore said, It is not lawful for us to put any man to death." But this they said, "that the saying of the Lord might be fulfilled, which He spake, signifying by what death He should die."

"And how did the expression, 'It is not lawful for us to put any man to death,' declare this?" Either the Evangelist means that He was about to be slain not by the Jews only, but by[10] the Gentiles also, or that it was not lawful for them to crucify. But if they say, "It is not lawful for us to put any man to death," they say it with reference to that season. For that they did slay men, and that they slew them in a different way, Stephen shows, being stoned. But they desired to crucify Him, that they might make a display of the manner of His death. Pilate, wishing to be freed from trouble, doth not dismiss Him for a long trial, but,

Ver. 33, 34. "Having entered in, he asked Jesus, and said,[11] Art thou the King of the Jews?

---

[1] Part of ver. 25. "They said therefore unto him, Art not thou also one of his disciples? He denied it, and said, I am not."
[2] Ver. 26. "one of the servants of the high priest, being his kinsman," &c., "saith." N. T.
[3] "in the garden with him?" ver. 27. "Peter then denied again; and immediately the cock crew." N. T.
[4] al. "had been said."    [5] εἰς δάκρυα καθέλκων.
[6] Ver. 28. "Then led they Jesus from Caiaphas unto the hall of judgment; and it was early; and they themselves went not into the judgment-hall, lest they should be defiled; but that they might eat the Passover." N. T.

[7] or, "waiting for His," &c., "on."   [8] al. "from their."
[9] al. "but in certain."   [10] Ben. "not for," &c., "but for."
[11] "Then Pilate entered into the judgment hall again, and called Jesus, and said unto Him." N. T.

Jesus answered him, Sayest thou this thing of thyself, or did others tell it thee of Me?"

Wherefore did Christ ask this? Because He desired to expose the evil intentions of the Jews. Pilate had heard this saying from many, and, since the accusers had nothing to say, in order that the enquiry might not be a long one, he desires to bring forward that which was continually reported. But when he said to them, "Judge him according to your law," wishing to show that His offense was not a Jewish one, they replied, "It is not lawful for us." "He hath not sinned against our law, but the indictment is general."[1] Pilate •then, having perceived this, saith, as being (himself) likely to be endangered, "Art thou the King of the Jews?" Then Jesus, not from ignorance, but from a desire that the Jews should be accused even by him, asked him, saying, "Did others tell it thee?"[2] On this point then declaring himself, Pilate replied,

Ver. 35. "Am I a Jew? Thine own nation and the chief priests have delivered thee unto me; what hast thou done?"

Here desiring to clear himself of the matter. Then because he had said, "Art thou the King?" Jesus reproving him answereth, "This thou hast heard from the Jews. Why dost thou not make accurate enquiry? They have said that I am a malefactor; ask them what evil I have done. But this thou doest not, but art simply framing charges against Me." "Jesus answered him, Sayest thou this thing of thyself," or from others? Pilate then cannot at once say that he had heard it, but simply goes along with[3] the people, saying, "They have delivered thee unto me." "I must needs therefore ask thee what thou hast done." What then saith Christ?

Ver. 36. "My Kingdom is not of this world."

He leadeth upwards Pilate who was not a very wicked man, nor after their fashion, and desireth to show that He is not a mere man, but God, and the Son of God And what saith He?

"If My Kingdom were of this world, then would My servants fight, that I should not be delivered to the Jews."[4]

He undoeth that which Pilate for a while had feared, namely, the suspicion of seizing kingly power, "Is then His kingdom not of this world also?"[5] Certainly it is. "How then saith He it 'is not'?" Not because He doth not rule here, but because He hath his empire from above, and because it is not human, but far greater than this and more splendid. "If then

it be greater, how was He made captive by the other?" By consenting, and giving Himself up. But He doth not at present reveal[6] this, but what saith He? "If I had been of this world, 'My servants would fight, that I should not be delivered.'" Here He showeth the weakness of kingship among us, that its strength lies in servants; but that which is above is sufficient for itself, needing nothing. From this the heretics taking occasion say, that He is different from the Creator. What then, when it saith, "He came to His own"? (c. i. 11.) What, when Himself saith, "They are not of this world, as I am not of this world"? (c. xvii. 14.) So also He saith that His kingdom is not from hence, not depriving the world of His providence and superintendence, but showing, as I said, that His power was not human or perishable. What then said Pilate?

Ver. 37. "Art thou a king then? Jesus answered, Thou sayest that I am a King. To this end was I born."

If then He was born a king, all His other attributes are by Generation, and He hath nothing which He received in addition. So that when thou hearest that, "As the Father hath life in Himself, so hath He given to the Son also to have life" (c. v. 26), deem of nothing else but His generation, and so of the rest.

"And for this cause came I,[7] that I should bear witness unto the truth."

That is, "that I should speak this very thing, and teach it, and persuade all men."

[5.] But do thou, O man, when thou hearest these things, and seest thy Lord bound and led about, deem present things to be nought. For how can it be otherwise than strange, if Christ bore such things for thy sake, and thou often canst not endure even words? He is spit upon, and dost thou deck thyself with garments and rings, and, if thou gain not good report from all, think life unbearable? He is insulted, beareth mockings, and scornful blows upon the cheek; and dost thou wish everywhere to be honored, and bearest thou not the reproaching of Christ? Hearest thou not Paul saying, "Be ye imitators[8] of me, even as I also am of Christ"? (1 Cor. xi. 1.) When therefore any one makes a jest of thee, remember thy Lord, that in mockery they bowed the knee before Him, and worried[9] Him both by words and deeds, and treated Him with much irony; but He not only did not defend Himself, but even repaid them with the contraries, with mildness and gentleness. Him now let us emulate; so shall we be enabled even to be delivered from all insult. For it is not the insulter that gives effect to acts of insult, and makes them biting, but he who is little of soul,

---

[1] i.e. against heathen law also.
[2] Ver. 30. "Jesus answered him, Sayest thou this thing of thyself, or did others tell it thee of Me?" N. T.
[3] ἕπεται.
[4] "to the Jews: but now in My kingdom not from hence," N. T.
[5] Ben. omits "also."
[6] al. "hide."
[7] "came I into the world," N. T.
[8] μιμηταί.
[9] διέσυρον.

and is pained by them. If thou art not pained, thou hast not been insulted; for the suffering from injuries depends not on those who inflict, but on those who undergo them. Why dost thou grieve at all? If a man hath insulted thee unjustly, in this case surely thou oughtest not to grieve at all, but to pity him; if justly, much more oughtest thou to keep quiet. For should any one address thee, a poor man, as though thou wert rich, the praise contained in his words is nothing to thee, but his encomium is rather mockery; and so if one insulting thee utter things that are untrue, the reproach is nothing to thee either. But if conscience takes hold of what hath been said, be not grieved at the words, but make correction in deeds. This I say with regard to what really are insults. For if one reproach thee with poverty or low birth, laugh at him.[1] These things are a reproach not to the hearer, but to the speaker, as not knowing true wisdom. "But," saith some one, "when these things are said in the presence of many who are ignorant of the truth, the wound becomes unbearable." Nay, it is most bearable, when you have an audience present of witnesses praising and applauding you, scoffing at and making a jest of him. For not he that defends himself, but he that saith nothing, is applauded by sensible persons. And if none of those present be a sensible person, then laugh at him most of all, and delight thyself in the audience of heaven. For there all will praise and applaud and welcome thee. For one Angel is as good as all the world. But why speak I of Angels, when the Lord Himself proclaimeth[2] thee? Let us exercise ourselves with these reasonings. For it is no loss to be silent when insulted, but it is, on the contrary, to defend one's self when insulted. Since were it a fault silently to bear what is said, Christ would never have told us, "If one smite thee on the right cheek, turn to him the other also."

(Matt. v. 39.)[3] If then our enemy say what is not true, let us on this account even pity him, because he draws down upon him the punishment and vengeance of the accusers,[4] being unworthy even to read the Scriptures. For to the sinner God saith, "Why declarest thou My statutes, and takest My covenant in thy mouth? Thou satest and spakest against thy brother." (Ps. l. 16 and 20, LXX.) And if he speak the truth, so also he is to be pitied; since even the Pharisee spake the truth; yet he did no harm to him who heard him, but rather good, while he deprived himself of ten thousand blessings, enduring shipwreck by this accusation. So that either way it is he that suffers injury, not thou; but thou, if thou art sober, wilt have double gain; both the propitiating God by thy silence, and the becoming yet more discreet, the gaining an opportunity from what hath been said to correct what has been done, and the despising mortal glory. For this is the source of our pain, that many gape upon the opinion of men. If we are minded to be thus truly wise, we shall know well that human things are nothing. Let us learn then, and having reckoned up our faults, let us accomplish their correction in time, and let us determine to correct one this month, another next month, and a third in that which follows. And so mounting as it were by steps, let us get to heaven by a Jacob's ladder. For the ladder seems to me to signify in a riddle by that vision the gradual ascent by means of virtue, by which it is possible for us to ascend from earth to heaven, not using material steps, but improvement and correction of manners. Let us then lay hold on this means of departure and ascent, that having obtained heaven, we may also enjoy all the blessings there, through the grace and lovingkindness of our Lord Jesus Christ; to whom be glory for ever and ever. Amen.

---

[1] al. "this is to be laughed at."
[2] Sav. conj. "shall proclaim."

[3] "whosoever shall," &c., N. T.
[4] Sav. conj. "evil speaking."

# HOMILY LXXXIV.

## John xviii. 37.

"To this end was I born, and for this cause came I into the world, that I should bear witness unto the truth. Every one that is of the truth heareth My Voice."

[1.] A MARVELOUS thing is longsuffering; it places the soul as in a quiet harbor, freeing it from tossings [1] and evil spirits. And this everywhere Christ hath taught us, but especially now, when He is judged, and dragged, and led about. For when He was brought to Annas, He answered with great gentleness, and, to the servant who smote Him, said what had power to bring down all his insolence; thence having gone to Caiaphas, then to Pilate, and having spent the whole night in these scenes, He all through exhibiteth His own mildness; and when they said that He was a malefactor, and were not able to prove it, He stood silent; but when He was questioned concerning the Kingdom, then He spake to Pilate, instructing him, and leading him in to [2] higher matters. But why was it that Pilate made the enquiry not in their presence, but apart, having gone into the judgment hall? He suspected something great respecting Him, and wished, without being troubled by the Jews, to learn all accurately. Then when he said, "What hast thou done?" on this point Jesus made no answer; but concerning that of which Pilate most desired to hear, namely, His Kingdom, He answered, saying, "My Kingdom is not of this world." That is, "I am indeed a King, yet not such an one as thou suspectest, but far more glorious," declaring [3] by these words and those which follow, that no evil had been done by Him. For one who saith, "To this end was I born, and for this cause came I into the world, that I should bear witness unto the truth," showeth, that no evil hath been done by Him. Then when He saith, "Every one that is of the truth heareth My voice," He draweth him on by these means, and persuadeth him to become a listener to the words. "For if," saith He, "any one is true, and desireth these things, [4] he will certainly hear Me." And, in fact, He so took him by these short words, that he said,

Ver. 38. "What is truth?"

But for the present he applieth himself to what was pressing, for he knew that this question needed time, and desired to rescue Him from the violence of the Jews. Wherefore he went out, and what said he?

"I find no fault in him." [5]

Consider how prudently he acted. He said not, "Since he hath sinned, and is deserving of death, forgive him on account of the Feast"; [6] but having first acquitted Him of all guilt, he asks them over and above, if they were not minded to dismiss Him as innocent, yet as guilty to forgive Him on account of the time. Wherefore he added,

Ver. 39, 40. "Ye have a custom that I should release unto you one at the Passover"; then in a persuasory way, "Will ye therefore that I release the king of the Jews? Then cried they all, Not this man, but Barabbas." [7]

O accursed decision! They demand those like mannered with themselves, and let the guilty go; but bid him punish the innocent. For this was their custom from old time. But do thou all through observe the lovingkindness of the Lord in these circumstances. Pilate scourged Him, [8] perhaps desiring to exhaust and to soothe the fury of the Jews. For when he had not been able to deliver Him by his former measures, being anxious to stay the evil at this point, he scourged Him, and permitted to be done what was done, the robe and crown to be put on Him, so as to relax their anger. Wherefore álso he led Him forth to them crowned (ver. 5), that, seeing the insult which had been done to Him, they might recover a little from their passion, and vomit their venom. "And how would the soldiers have done this, had it not been the command of their ruler?" To gratify the Jews. Since it was not by his command that they at first went in [9] by night, but to please the Jews; they dared anything for money. But He, when so many and such things were done, yet stood silent, as He had done during the enquiry, and answered nothing. And do thou not merely hear these things, but keep them continually in thy mind, and when thou beholdest the King of the world and of all Angels, mocked of the soldiers, by words and by actions, and bearing all silently, do thou imitate Him by deeds thyself. For when Pilate had called Him the King of the Jews, and they now put about Him the ap-

---

[1] or, "waves," or, "winds."
[2] Sav. conj. "up."
[3] al. "hinting."
[4] i.e. the things of truth.
[5] "And when he had said this, he went out again unto the Jews and saith unto them, I find in him no fault at all." N. T.
[6] lit. "grant him to the feast."
[7] "Barabbas. Now Barabbas was a robber." N. T.
[8] Chap. xix. 1-3. "Then Pilate therefore took Jesus, and scourged Him. And the soldiers plaited a crown of thorns, and put it on His head, and they put on Him a purple robe, and said, Hail, King of the Jews! and they smote Him with their hands."
[9] i.e. to the garden.

parel of mockery, then Pilate having led Him out, said,

Ver. 4, 5. " I find no fault against him. He therefore went forth, wearing the crown."[1]

But not even so was their rage quenched, but they cried out,

Ver. 6. " Crucify him, crucify him."[2]

Then Pilate, seeing that all was done in vain, said,

" Take ye him, and crucify him."

Whence it is clear that he had permitted what had been done before, because of their madness.

" For I," he saith, " find no fault in him."

[2.] See in how many ways the judge makes His defense, continually acquitting Him of the charges ; but none of these things shamed the dogs from their purpose. For the, " Take ye him and crucify him," is the expression of one clearing himself of the guilt, and thrusting them forward to an action not permitted to them. They therefore had brought Him, in order that the thing might be done by the decision of the governor ; but the contrary fell out, that He was rather acquitted than condemned by the governor's decision. Then, because they were ashamed,

Ver. 7. "We have," they said, " a law, and by our law he ought to die, because he made himself the Son of God."

" How then when the judge said, ' Take ye him, and judge him according to your law,' did ye reply, ' It is not lawful for us to put any man to death,' while here ye fly to the law? And consider the charge, 'He made himself the Son of God.' Tell me, is this a ground of accusation, that He who performed the deeds of the Son of God should call Himself the Son of God?" What then doth Christ? While they held this dialogue one with the other, He held His peace, fulfilling that saying of the Prophet, that " He openeth not his mouth : in His humiliation His judgment was taken away." (Isa. liii. 7, 8, LXX.)

Then Pilate is alarmed[3] when he hears from them, that He made Himself the Son of God, and dreads lest the assertion may possibly be true, and he should seem to transgress ; but these men who had learnt this, both by His deeds and words, did not shudder, but are putting Him to death for the very reasons for which they ought to have worshiped Him. On this account he no more asks Him, " What hast thou done?" but, shaken by fear, he begins the enquiry again, saying, "Art thou the Christ?" But He answered not. For he who had heard, " To this end was I born, and for this came I," and, " My Kingdom is not of this world," he, when he ought to have opposed His enemies and delivered Him, did not so, but seconded the fury of the Jews. Then they being in every way silenced, make their cry issue in a political charge, saying, " He that maketh himself a king, speaketh against Cæsar." (Ver. 12.) Pilate ought therefore to have accurately enquired, whether He had aimed at sovereignty, and set His hand to expel Cæsar from the kingdom. But he makes not an exact enquiry, and therefore Christ answered him nothing, because He knew that he asked all the questions idly.[4] Besides, since His works bare witness to Him, He would not prevail by word, nor compose any defense, showing that He came voluntarily to this condition. When He was silent, Pilate saith,

Ver. 10. " Knowest thou not that I have power to crucify thee?"[5]

Seest thou how he condemned himself beforehand ; for, " if the whole rests with thee, why dost not thou let Him go, when thou hast found no fault in Him?" When then Pilate had uttered the sentence against himself, then He saith,

Ver. 11. " He that delivered Me unto thee hath the greater sin."

Showing that he also was guilty of sin. Then, to pull down his pride and arrogance, He saith,

" Thou wouldst have no power except it were given thee."[6]

Showing that this did not come to pass merely in the common order of events,[7] but that it was accomplished mystically. Then lest, when thou hearest, " Except it were given thee," thou shouldest deem that Pilate was exempt from all blame, on this account therefore He said, "Therefore he that delivered Me unto thee hath the greater sin." " And yet if it was given, neither he nor they were liable to any charge." " Thou objectest idly; for the 'given' in this place means what is 'allowed'; as though He had said, 'He hath permitted these things to be, yet not for that are ye clear of the wickedness.' " He awed Pilate by the words, and proffered a clear defense. On which account that person sought to release Him; but they again cried out, saying,[8]

unto Jesus, Whence art thou? But Jesus gave him no answer." N. T.

[4] εἰκῇ πάντα ἐρωτῶντα. Savile reads ἐρωτῶν, with the conjecture ἐρῶν. The reading rendered above best suits the sense, and is supported by MSS.

[5] Ver. 10. "Then saith Pilate unto Him, Speakest thou not unto me? Knowest thou not that I have power to crucify thee, and have power to release thee?" N. T.

[6] " no power against Me, except it were given thee from above: therefore he that," &c. N. T.

[7] τὴν τῶν πολλῶν ἀκολουθίαν, al. τῶν ἄλλων.

[8] Ver. 12. "And from thenceforth Pilate sought to release Him; but the Jews cried out, saying." N. T.

[1] Ver. 4, 5. "Pilate therefore went forth again, and saith unto them, Behold, I bring him forth to you, that ye may know that I find no fault in him. Then came Jesus forth, wearing the crown of thorns and the purple robe, and Pilate saith unto them, Behold the man." N. T.

[2] Ver. 6. "When the chief priests therefore and officers saw Him, they cried out, saying, Crucify Him." N. T.

[3] Ver. 8, 9. "When Pilate therefore heard that saying, he was the more afraid; and went again into the judgment-hall, and saith

Ver. 12. "If thou let this man go, thou art not Cæsar's friend."

For when they profited nothing by bringing charges drawn from their own law, they wickedly betook themselves to external laws, saying,

"Every one that maketh himself a king speaketh against Cæsar."

And where hath this Man appeared as a tyrant? Whence can ye prove it? By the purple robe? By the diadem? By the dress?[1] By the soldiers? Did not He ever walk unattended, save by His twelve disciples, following in every point a humble mode of living, both as to food, and clothing, and habitation? But O what shamelessness and ill-time cowardice! For Pilate, deeming that he should now incur some danger were he to overlook these words, comes forth as though to enquire into the matter,[2] (for the "sitting down" showed this,) but without making[3] any enquiry, he gave Him up to them, thinking to shame them. For to prove that he did it for this purpose, hear what he saith.

Ver. 14, 15. "Behold your king!" But when they said, "Crucify him," he added again, "Shall I crucify your king?" But they cried out, "We have no king but Cæsar."[4]

Of their own will they subjected themselves to punishment; therefore also God gave them up, because they were the first to cast themselves out from His providence and superintendence; and since with one voice they rejected His sovereignty, He allowed them to fall by their own suffrages. Still what had been said should have been sufficient to calm their passion, but they feared, lest, being let go, He should again draw the multitudes, and they did all they could to prevent this. For a dreadful thing is love of rule, dreadful and able to destroy the soul; it was on account of this that they had never heard Him. And yet Pilate, in consequence of a few words, desired to let Him go, but they pressed on, saying, "Crucify him." And why did they strive to kill Him in this manner? It was a shameful death. Fearing therefore lest there should afterwards be any remembrance of Him, they desired to bring Him to the accursed punishment, not knowing that truth is exalted by hindrances. To prove that they had this suspicion, listen to what they say;[5] "We have heard that that deceiver said, After three days I will rise again" (Matt. xxvii. 63); on this account they made all this stir, turning things

upside down,[6] that they might ruin matters in after time.[7] And the ill-ordered people, corrupted by their rulers, cried out continually, "Crucify him!"

[3.] But let us not merely read of these things, but bear them in our mind; the crown of thorns, the robe, the reed, the blows, the smiting on the cheek, the spittings, the irony. These things, if continually meditated on, are sufficient to take down all anger; and if we be mocked at, if we suffer injustice, let us still say, "The servant is not greater than his Lord" (c. xiii. 16); and let us bring forward the words of the Jews, which they uttered in their madness, saying, "Thou art a Samaritan, and hast a devil" (c. viii. 48); and, "He casteth out devils by Beelzebub." (Luke xi. 15.) For on this account He bare all these things, in order that we might walk in His footsteps, and endure those mockings which disturb more than any other kind of reproach. Yet nevertheless He not only bare these things, but even used every means to save and deliver from the appointed punishment those who did them. For He sent the Apostles also for their salvation, at least thou hearest them saying, that, "We[8] know that through ignorance ye did it" (Acts iii. 17); and by these means drawing them to repentance. This let us also imitate; for nothing so much maketh God propitious as the loving enemies, and doing good to those who despitefully use us. When a man insults thee, look not to him, but to the devil who moves him, and against him empty all thy wrath, but pity the man who is moved by him. For if lying is from the devil, to be angry without a cause is much more so. When thou seest one turning another into ridicule, consider that it is the devil who moves him, for mockings belong not to Christians. For he who hath been bidden to mourn, and hath heard, "Woe, ye that laugh" (Luke vi. 25), and who after this insults, and jests, and is excited, demands not reproach from us, but sorrow, since Christ also was troubled when He thought on Judas. All these things therefore let us practice in our actions, for if we act not rightly in these, we have come to no purpose and in vain into the world. Or rather we have come to our harm, for faith is not sufficient to bring men to the Kingdom, nay, it even hath power[9] in this way most to condemn those who exhibit an ill life; for He "which knew his Lord's will, and did it not, shall be beaten with many stripes" (Luke xii. 47); and again, "If I had not come and spoken unto them, they had not had sin." (c. xv. 22.) What excuse then shall we have, who have been set within

---

[1] al. "the chariot."
[2] Ver. 13. "When Pilate therefore heard that saying, he brought Jesus forth, and sat down in the judgment seat in a place that is called the Pavement, but in the Hebrew, Gabbatha." N. T.
[3] al. "taking pains for."
[4] Ver. 14, 15. "And it was the preparation of the Passover, and about the sixth hour; and he saith unto the Jews, Behold your king! But they cried out, Away with him, away with him, crucify him! Pilate saith unto them, Shall I crucify your king? The chief priests answered, We have no king but Cæsar." N. T.
[5] al. "one saith."

[6] or, "using every means."
[7] ὥστε τὰ μετὰ ταῦτα λυμήνασθαι.
[8] "I," N. T.     [9] or, "the case admits," ἔχει.

the palace, and deemed worthy to stoop[1] down and enter into the sanctuary, and have been made partakers of the releasing Mysteries,[2] and who yet are worse than the Greeks, who have shared in none of these things? For if they for the sake of vainglory have shown so much true wisdom, much more ought we to go after all virtue, because it is pleasing to God. But at present we do not even despise wealth; while they have often been careless of their life, and in wars have given up their children to their madness about devils,[3] and have despised nature for the sake of their devils, but we do not even despise money for the sake of Christ, nor anger on account of God's will, but are inflamed, and in no better state than the fevered. And just as they, when possessed by their malady, are all burning, so we, suffocated as by some fire, can stop at no point of desire, increasing both anger and avarice. On this account I am ashamed and astonished, when I behold among the Greeks men despising riches, but all mad among ourselves. For even if we could find some despising riches, we should find that they have been made[4] captive by other vices, by passion or envy; and a hard thing it is to discover true wisdom without a blemish.[5] But the reason is, that we are not earnest to get our remedies from the Scriptures, nor do we apply ourselves to those Scriptures with compunction, and sorrow, and groaning, but carelessly, if at any time we chance to be at leisure. Therefore when a great rush of worldly matters comes, it overwhelms all; and if there hath been any profit, destroys it. For if a man have a wound, and after putting on a plaster, do not tie it tight,

but allow it to fall off, and expose his sore to wet, and dust, and heat, and ten thousand other things able to irritate it, he will get no good; yet not by reason of the inefficacy of the remedies, but by reason of his own carelessness. And this also is wont to happen to us, when we attend but little to the divine oracles, but give ourselves up wholly and incessantly to things of this life; for thus all the seed is choked, and all is made unfruitful. That this may not be the case, let us look carefully a little, let us look up to heaven, let us bend down to the tombs and coffins of the departed. For the same end awaiteth us, and the same necessity of departure will often come upon us before the evening. Prepare we then for this expedition;[9] there is need of many supplies for the journey,[10] for great is the heat there, and great the drought, and great the solitude. Henceforth there is no reposing at an inn, there is no buying anything, when one hath not taken all from hence. Hear at least what the virgins say, "Go ye to them that sell" (Matt. xxv. 9); but they who went found not. Hear what Abraham saith, "A gulf between us and you." (Luke xvi. 26.) Hear what Ezekiel saith concerning that day, that Noah, and Job, and Daniel shall in nowise deliver their sons. (Ezek. xiv. 14.) But may it never come to pass that we hear these words, but that having taken hence sufficient provision for our way to eternal life, we may behold with boldness our Lord Jesus Christ, with whom to the Father and the Holy Ghost be glory, dominion, honor, now and ever, and world without end. Amen.

# HOMILY LXXXV.

### John xix. 16–18.

"Then delivered he Him therefore unto them to be crucified. And they took Jesus, and led Him away. And He, bearing His Cross, went forth into a place called the place of a skull,[6] where they crucified Him."[7]

[1.] Successes have terrible power to cast down or draw aside those who take not heed. Thus the Jews, who at first enjoyed the influence[8]

of God, sought the law of royalty from the Gentiles, and in the wilderness after the manna remembered the onions. In the same way here, refusing the Kingdom of Christ, they invited to themselves that of Cæsar. Wherefore God set a king over them, according to their own decision. When then Pilate heard these things, he delivered Him to be crucified. Utterly without reason. For when he ought to have enquired whether Christ had aimed at sovereign power, he pronounced the sentence through fear alone. Yet that this might not befall him, Christ said beforehand, "My kingdom is not of this world";

---

¹ or, " to peep," διακύψαι.
² Ben. " mysteries releasing from sins."
³ i.e. their heathen worship.
⁴ al. " they are made."          ⁵ καθαράν.
⁶ " place of a skull, which is called in the Hebrew, Golgotha." N. T.
⁷ " Him, and two others with Him, on either side one, and Jesus in the midst." N. T.          ⁸ ῥοπῆς.

⁹ ἔξοδον.          ¹⁰ ἐφοδίων.

but he having given himself wholly up to present things, would practice no great amount of wisdom. And yet his wife's dream should have been sufficient to terrify him; but by none of these things was he made better, nor did he look to heaven, but delivered Him up. And now they laid the cross upon Him as a malefactor. For even the wood they abominated, and endured not even to touch it. This was also the case in the type; for Isaac bare the wood. But then the matter stopped at the will of his father,[1] for it was the type; while here it proceeded to action, for it was the reality.

"And He came to the place of a skull." Some say that Adam died there, and there lieth; and that Jesus in this place where death had reigned, there also set up the trophy. For He went forth bearing the Cross as a trophy over the tyranny of death: and as conquerors do, so He bare upon His shoulders the symbol of victory. What matter if the Jews did[2] these things with a different intent. They crucified Him too with thieves, in this also unintentionally fulfilling prophecy; for what they did for insult contributed to the truth, that thou mayest learn how great is its power, since the Prophet had foretold of old, that "He was numbered with the transgressors." (Isa. liii. 12.) The devil therefore wished to cast a veil over what was done, but was unable; for the three were crucified, but Jesus alone was glorious, that thou mayest learn, that His power effected all. Yet the miracles took place when the three had been nailed to the cross; but no one attributed anything of what was done to either of those others, but to Jesus only; so entirely was the plot of the devil rendered vain,[3] and all returned upon his own head. For even of these two, one was saved. He therefore did not insult the glory of the Cross,[4] but contributed to it not a little. For it was not a less matter than shaking the rocks, to change a thief upon the cross, and to bring him unto Paradise.

Ver. 19. "And Pilate wrote a title."[5]

At the same time requiting the Jews, and making a defense for Christ. For since they had given Him up as worthless, and attempted to confirm this sentence by making Him share the punishment of the robbers, in order that for the future it might be in no man's power to prefer evil charges against him, or to accuse him as a worthless and wicked person, to close moreover their mouths and the mouths of all who might desire to accuse Him, and to show that they had risen up against their own King, Pilate thus placed, as on a trophy, those letters, which utter a clear voice, and show forth His victory, and proclaim His Kingdom, though not in its completeness. And this he made manifest not in a single tongue, but in three languages; for since it was likely that there would be a mixed multitude among the Jews on account of the Feast, in order that none might be ignorant of the defense, he publicly recorded[6] the madness of the Jews, in all the languages. For they bore malice against Him even when crucified.[7] "Yet what did this harm you?[8] Nothing. For if He was a mortal and weak, and was about to become extinct, why did ye fear the letters asserting that He is the King of the Jews?" And what do they ask? "Say that 'he said.'" For now it is an assertion, and a general sentence, but if 'he said' be added, the charge is shown to be one arising from his own rashness and arrogance." Still Pilate was not turned aside, but stood to his first decision. And it is no little thing that is dispensed even from this circumstance, but the whole matter. For since the wood of the cross was buried, because no one was careful to take it up, inasmuch as fear was pressing, and the believers were hurrying to other urgent matters; and since it was in after times to be sought for, and it was likely that the three crosses would lie together, in order that the Lord's might not be unknown, it was made manifest to all, first by its lying in the middle, and then by the title. For those of the thieves had no titles.

[2.] The soldiers parted the garments, but not the coat.[9] See the prophecies in every instance fulfilled by their wickednesses; for this also had been predicted of old; yet there were three crucified, but the matters of the prophecies[10] were fulfilled in Him. For why did they not this in the case of the others, but in His case only? Consider too, I pray you, the exactness of the prophecy. For the Prophet saith not only, that they "parted," but that they "did not part." The rest therefore they divided, the coat they divided not, but committed the matter to a decision by lot. And the, "Woven from the top" (ver. 23) is not put without a purpose; but some say that a figurative assertion is declared by it, that the Crucified was not simply man, but had also the Divinity from above.[11] Others say that the Evangelist describes the very form

---

[1] i.e. only showed Abraham's willingness.
[2] al. "ordered."                    [3] ἕωλος, lit. "stale."
[4] al. "the Crucified."
[5] Ver. 19, 20. "And Pilate wrote a title, and put it on the Cross, and the writing was, Jesus of Nazareth the King of the Jews. This title then read many of the Jews, for the place where Jesus was crucified was nigh to the city, and it was written in Hebrew, and Greek, and Latin."

[6] lit. "inscribed on a pillar."
[7] Ver. 21, 22. "Then said the chief priests of the Jews to Pilate, Write not, The King of the Jews, but that he said, I am King of the Jews. Pilate answered, What I have written, I have written." N. T.        [8] to the Jews.
[9] Ver. 23, 24. "Then the soldiers, when they had crucified Jesus, took His garments, and made four parts, to every soldier a part; and also His coat; now the coat was without seam, woven from the top throughout. They said therefore among themselves, Let us not rend it, but cast lots for it, whose it shall be, that the Scripture might be fulfilled which saith, They parted My raiment among them, and for My vesture they did cast lots." N. T.
[10] al. "of the prophetical."        [11] or, "from the first," ἄνωθεν.

of the coat.[1] For since in Palestine they put together two strips of cloth and so weave their garments, John, to show that the coat was of this kind, saith, "Woven from the top"; and to me he seems to say this, alluding to the poorness of the garments, and that as in all other things, so in dress also, He followed a simple[2] fashion.

Ver. 24. "These things the soldiers did."

But He on the Cross, committeth His mother to the disciple,[3] teaching us even to our last breath to show every care for our parents. When indeed she unseasonably troubled Him, He said, "Woman, what have I to do with thee?" (c. ii. 4.) And, "Who is My mother?" (Matt. xii. 48.) But here He showeth much loving affection, and committeth her to the disciple whom He loved. Again John conceals himself, in modesty; for had he desired to boast, he would have also put in the cause for which he was loved, since probably it was some great and wonderful one. But wherefore doth He converse on nothing else with John, nor comfort him when desponding? Because it was no time for comforting by words; besides, it was no little thing for him to be honored with such honor, and to receive the reward of steadfastness. But do thou consider, I pray, how even on the cross He did everything without being troubled, speaking with the disciple concerning His mother, fulfilling prophecies, holding forth good hopes to the thief. Yet before He was crucified He appeareth sweating, agonized, fearing. What then can this mean? Nothing difficult, nothing doubtful. There indeed the weakness of nature had been shown, here was being shown the excess of Power. Besides, by these two things He teacheth us, even if before things terrible we be troubled, not on that account to shrink from things terrible, but when we have embarked in the contest to deem all things[4] possible and easy. Let us then not tremble at death. Our soul hath by nature the love of life, but it lies with us either to loose the bands of nature, and make this desire weak; or else to tighten them, and make the desire more tyrannous. For as we have the desire of sexual intercourse, but when we practice true wisdom we render the desire weak, so also it falls out in the case of life; and as God hath annexed carnal desire to the generation of children, to maintain a succession among us, without however forbidding us from traveling the higher road of continence; so also He hath implanted in us the love of life, forbidding us

from destroying ourselves, but not hindering our despising the present life. And it behooves us, knowing this, to observe due measure, and neither to go at any time to death of our own accord, even though ten thousand terrible things possess us; nor yet when dragged to it, for the sake of what is pleasing to God, to shrink back from and fear it, but boldly to strip for it, preferring the future to the present life.

But the women stood by the Cross, and the weaker sex then appeared the manlier (ver. 25); so entirely henceforth were all things transformed.

[3.] And He, having committed His mother to John, said, "Behold thy Son." (Ver. 26.) O the honor! with what honor did He honor the disciple! when He Himself was now departing, He committed her to the disciple to take care of. For since it was likely that, being His mother, she would grieve, and require protection, He with reason entrusted her to the beloved. To him He saith, "Behold thy mother." (Ver. 27.) This He said, knitting them together in charity; which the disciple understanding, took her to his own home. "But why made He no mention of any other woman, although another stood there?" To teach us to pay more than ordinary respect to our mothers. For as when parents oppose us on spiritual matters, we must not even own them, so when they do not hinder us, we ought to pay them all becoming respect, and to prefer them before others, because they begat us, because they bred us up, because they bare for us ten thousand terrible things. And by these words He silenceth the shamelessness of Marcion; for if He were not born according to the flesh, nor had a mother, wherefore taketh He such forethought for her alone?

Ver. 28. "After this, Jesus knowing that all things were now accomplished."

That is, "that nothing was wanting to the Dispensation." For He was everywhere desirous to show, that this Death was of a new kind, if indeed the whole lay in the power of the Person dying, and death came not on the Body before He willed it; and He willed it after He had fulfilled all things. Therefore also He said, "I have power to lay down My life; and I have power to take it again." (c. x. 18.) Knowing therefore that all things were fulfilled, He saith, "I thirst."[5]

Here again fulfilling a prophecy. But consider, I pray, the accursed nature of the bystanders. Though we have ten thousand enemies, and have suffered intolerable things at their hands, yet when we see them perishing, we relent; but they did not even so make peace with

---

[1] lit. "little coat."          [2] λιτόν.
[3] Ver. 25–27. "Now there stood by the Cross of Jesus His mother, and His mother's sister, Mary the wife of Cleophas, and Mary Magdalene. When Jesus therefore saw His mother, and the disciple standing by whom He loved, He saith unto His mother, Woman, behold thy son. Then saith He to the disciple, Behold thy mother. And from that hour that disciple took her to his own home."          [4] al. "all things are."

[5] "that the Scripture might be fulfilled, saith, I thirst," N. T.

Him, nor were tamed by what they saw, but rather became more savage, and increased their irony ; and having brought to Him vinegar on a sponge,[1] as men bring it to the condemned, thus they gave Him to drink ; since it is on this account that the hyssop is added.

Ver. 30. "Having therefore received it, He saith, It is finished."

Seest thou how He doth all things calmly, and with power? And what follows shows this. For when all had been completed,

"He bowed His head, (this had not been nailed,) and gave up[2] the ghost."

That is, "died." Yet to expire does not come[3] after the bowing the head ; but here, on the contrary, it doth. For He did not, when He had expired, bow His head, as happens with us, but when He had bent His head, then He expired. By all which things the Evangelist hath shown, that He was Lord of all.

But the Jews, on the other hand, who swallowed the camel and strained at the gnat, having wrought so atrocious a deed, are very precise concerning the day.

Ver. 31. "Because it was the Preparation, that the bodies should not remain upon the cross[4]—they besought Pilate that their legs might be broken."[5]

Seest thou how strong a thing is truth? By means of the very things which are the objects of their zeal, prophecy is fulfilled, for by occasion of those things, this plain prediction, unconnected with them,[6] receives its accomplishment. For the soldiers[7] when they came, brake the legs of the others, but not those of Christ. Yet these to gratify the Jews pierced His side with a spear, and now insulted the dead body. O abominable and accursed purpose ! Yet, beloved, be not thou confounded, be not thou desponding ; for the things which these men did from a wicked will, fought on the side of the truth. Since there was a prophecy, saying, (from this circumstance,[8]) "They shall look on Him whom they pierced." (Ver. 37 ; Zech. xii. 10.) And not this only, but the deed then dared was a demonstration of the faith, to those who should afterwards disbelieve ; as to Thomas, and those like him. With this too an ineffable mystery was accomplished. For "there came forth water and blood." Not without a purpose, or by

chance, did those founts come forth, but because by means of these two together the Church consisteth.[9] And the initiated know it, being by water indeed regenerate, and nourished by the Blood and the Flesh. Hence the Mysteries take their beginning ; that[10] when thou approachest to that awful cup, thou mayest so approach, as drinking from the very side.

Ver. 35. "And he that saw it bare record, and his record is true."[11]

That is, "I heard it not from others, but was myself present and saw it, and the testimony is true." As may be supposed. For he relates an insult done ; he relates not anything great and admirable, that thou shouldest suspect his narrative ; but securing the mouths of heretics, and loudly proclaiming beforehand the Mysteries that should be, and beholding the treasure laid up in them, he is very exact concerning what took place. And that prophecy also is fulfilled,

Ver. 36. "A bone of Him shall not be broken."[12]　(Ex. xii. 46 ; Num. ix. 12.)

For even if this was said with reference to the lamb of the Jews, still it was for the sake of the reality that the type preceded, and in Him the prophecy was more fully accomplished. On this account the Evangelist brought forward the Prophet. For since by continually producing himself as witness he would have seemed unworthy of credit, he brings Moses to help him, and saith, that neither did this come to pass without a purpose, but was written before of old. And this is the meaning of the words, " A bone of Him shall not be broken." Again he confirms the Prophet's words by his own witness. "These things," saith he, "I have told you, that ye might learn that great is the connection of the type with the reality." Seest thou what pains he takes to make that believed which seemed to be matter of reproach, and bringing shame? For that the soldier should insult even the dead body, was far worse than being crucified. "But still, even these things," he saith, "I have told, and told with much earnestness, ' that ye might believe.' (Ver. 35.) Let none then be unbelieving, nor through shame injure our cause. For the things which appear to be most shameful, are the very venerable records[13] of our good things."

Ver. 38. "After this came Joseph of Arimathæa, being a disciple."[14]

---

[1] Ver. 29. "Now there was set a vessel full of vinegar: and they filled a sponge with vinegar, and put it upon hyssop, and put it to His mouth."

[2] ἀφῆκε, [παρέδωκε,] G. T.　　　[3] i.e. naturally.

[4] "Upon the cross on the Sabbath day, (for that day was a high day.)" N. T.

[5] "Be broken, and that they might be taken away." N. T.

[6] ἑτέρα αὐτοῖς αὕτη προαναφώνησις.

[7] Ver. 32–34. "Then came the soldiers and brake the legs of the first, and of the other which was crucified with him. But when they came to Jesus, and saw that He was dead already, they brake not His legs, but one of the soldiers with a spear pierced His side, and forthwith came thereout blood and water." N. T.

[8] ἐντεῦθεν.

[9] ἐξ ἀμφοτέρων τούτων ἡ Ἐκκλησία συνέστηκε.

[10] i.e. to teach thee that.

[11] "is true: and he knoweth that he saith true, that ye might believe," N. T.

[12] Ver. 36, 37. "For these things were done, that the Scripture should be fulfilled, A bone," &c. "And again another Scripture saith, They shall look on Him whom they pierced." N. T.

[13] σεμνολογήματα.

[14] Ver. 38–40. "And after this Joseph of Arimathæa, being a disciple of Jesus, but secretly for fear of the Jews, besought Pilate that he might take away the body of Jesus; and Pilate gave him leave. He came therefore, and took the body of Jesus. And there came also Nicodemus, which at the first came to Jesus by night, and

Not one of the twelve, but perhaps one of the seventy. For now deeming that the anger of the Jews was quenched by the Cross, they approached without fear, and took charge of His funeral. Joseph therefore came and asked the favor from Pilate, which he granted; why should he not? Nicodemus also assists him, and furnishes a costly burial. For they were still disposed to think of Him as a mere man. And they brought those [1] spices whose especial nature is to preserve the body for a long time, and not to allow it quickly to yield to corruption, which was an act of men imagining nothing great respecting Him; but anyhow, they exhibited very loving affection. But how did no one of the twelve come, neither John, nor Peter, nor any other of the more distinguished disciples? Nor doth the writer conceal this point. If any one say that it was from fear of the Jews, these men also [2] were occupied by the same fear; for Joseph too was, it saith, "A secret (disciple) for fear of the Jews." And not one can say that Joseph acted thus because he greatly despised them,[3] but though himself afraid, still he came. But John who was present, and had seen Him expire, did nothing of the kind. It seems to me that Joseph was a man of high rank, (as is clear from the funeral,) and known [4] to Pilate, on which account also he obtained the favor; and then he buried Him, not as a criminal, but magnificently, after the Jewish fashion, as some great and admirable one.

[4.] And because they were straitened by the time, (since the Death took place at the ninth hour, and it is probable, that what with going to Pilate and what with taking down the body, evening would come upon them when it was not lawful to work,) they laid Him in the tomb that was near.[5] And it is providentially ordered,[6] that He should be placed in a new tomb, wherein no one had been placed before, that His Resurrection might not be deemed to be that of some other who lay there with Him; and that the disciples might be able easily to come and be spectators of what came to pass, because the place was near; and that not they alone should be witnesses of His burial, but His enemies also, for the placing seals on the tomb, and the sitting by of the soldiers to watch it, were the actions of men testifying to the burial. For Christ earnestly desired that this should be confessed, no less than the Resurrection. Where-

fore also the disciples are very earnest about this, the showing that He died. For the Resurrection all succeeding time would confirm, but the Death, if at that time it had been partially concealed, or not made very manifest, was likely to harm the account of the Resurrection. Nor was it for these reasons only that He was laid near, but also that the story about the stealing might be proved false.

"The first day of the week" (that is, the Lord's day) "cometh Mary Magdalene, very early in the morning,[7] and seeth the stone taken away from the sepulcher." (Ch. xx. ver. 1.)

For He arose while both stone and seals lay over Him; but because it was necessary that others should be fully satisfied, the tomb was opened after the Resurrection, and thus what had come to pass was confirmed. This then was what moved Mary. For being entirely full of loving affection towards her Master, when the Sabbath was past, she could not bear to rest, but came very early in the morning, desiring to find some consolation from the place. But when she saw the place, and the stone [8] taken away, she neither entered in nor stooped down, but ran to the disciples,[9] in the greatness of her longing; for this was what she earnestly desired, she wished very speedily to learn what had become of the body. This was the meaning of her running, and her words declare it.

Ver. 2. "They have taken away," she saith, "my Lord,[10] and I know not where they have laid Him."

Seest thou how she knew not as yet anything clearly concerning the Resurrection, but thought there had been a removal of the body, and tells all simply to the disciples? And the Evangelist hath not deprived the woman of such a praise, nor thought it shame that they should have learnt these things first from her who had passed the night in watching. Thus everywhere doth the truth-loving nature of his disposition shine forth. When then she came and said these things, they hearing them, draw near with great eagerness to the sepulcher,[11] and see the linen clothes lying, which was a sign of the Resurrection. For neither, if any persons had removed the body, would they before doing so have stripped it; nor if any had stolen it, would they have taken the trouble to remove the napkin,

---

brought a mixture of myrrh and aloes, about an hundred pound weight. Then took they the body of Jesus, and wound it in the linen clothes with the spices, as the manner of the Jews is to bury."
　　[1] al. "such."　　　　　　[2] i.e. Joseph and Nicodemus.
　　[3] al. "that the greatly despising them effected this."
　　[4] al. "known in some way."
　　[5] Ver. 41, 42. "Now in the place where He was crucified there was a garden, and in the garden a new sepulcher, wherein was never man yet laid. There laid they Jesus therefore because of the Jews' preparation; for the sepulcher was nigh at hand."
　　[6] lit. "dispensed."

　　[7] ὄρθρου βαθέος om. in Ben. N. T. "early, when it was yet dark, unto the sepulcher, and seeth," &c.
　　[8] al. "saw the stone."
　　[9] Ver. 2. "Then she runneth, and cometh to Simon Peter, and to the other disciple whom Jesus loved."
　　[10] "the Lord out of the sepulcher," N. T.
　　[11] Ver. 3–7. "Peter therefore went forth, and that other disciple, and came to the sepulcher. So they ran both together: and the other disciple did outrun Peter, and came first to the sepulcher. And he stooping down, saw the linen clothes lying; yet went he not in. Then cometh Simon Peter following him, and went into the sepulcher, and seeth the linen clothes lie; and the napkin that was about His head, not lying with the linen clothes, but wrapped together in a place by itself." N. T.

and roll it up, and lay it in a place by itself; but how? they would have taken the body as it was. On this account John tells us by anticipation that it was buried with much myrrh, which glues linen to the body not less firmly than lead; in order that when thou hearest that the napkins lay apart, thou mayest not endure those who say that He was stolen. For a thief would not have been so foolish as to spend so much trouble on a superfluous matter. For why should he undo the clothes? and how could he have escaped detection if he had done so? since he would probably have spent much time in so doing, and be found out by delaying and loitering. But why do the clothes lie apart, while the napkin was wrapped together by itself? That thou mayest learn that it was not the action of men in confusion or haste, the placing some in one place, some in another, and the wrapping them together. From this they believed in the Resurrection. On this account Christ afterwards appeared to them, when they were convinced by what they had seen. Observe too here again the absence of boastfulness in the Evangelist, how he witnesses to the exactness of Peter's search. For he himself having gotten before Peter, and having seen the linen clothes, enquired not farther, but withdrew; but that fervent one passing farther in, looked at everything carefully, and saw somewhat more, and then the other too was summoned to the sight.[1] For he entering after Peter, saw the grave-clothes lying, and separate. Now to separate, and to place one thing by itself, and another, after rolling it up, by itself, was the act of some one doing things carefully, and not in a chance way, as if disturbed.

[5.] But do thou, when thou hearest that thy Lord arose naked, cease from thy madness about funerals; for what is the meaning of that superfluous and unprofitable[2] expense, which brings much loss to the mourners, and no gain to the departed, or (if we must say that it brings anything) rather harm? For the costliness of burial hath often caused the breaking open of tombs, and hath caused him to be cast out naked and unburied, who had been buried with much care. But alas for vainglory! How great the tyranny which it exhibits even in sorrow! how great the folly! Many, that this may not happen, having cut in pieces those fine clothes, and filled them with many spices, so that they may be doubly useless to those who would insult the dead, then commit them to the earth. Are not these the acts of madmen? of men beside themselves? to make a show of their ambition, and then to destroy it? "Yea," saith some one, "it is in order that they may lie safely with the dead

that we use all these contrivances." Well then, if the robbers do not get them, will not the moths get them, and the worms? Or if the moths and worms get them not, will not time and the moisture of putrefaction[3] destroy them? But let us suppose that neither tomb-breakers, nor moths, nor worms, nor time, nor anything else, destroy what lies in the tomb, but that the body itself remains untouched until the Resurrection, and these things are preserved new and fresh and fine; what advantage is there from this to the departed, when the body is raised naked, while these remain here, and profit us nothing for those accounts which must be given? "Wherefore then," saith some one, "was it done in the case of Christ?" First of all, do not compare these with human matters, since the harlot poured even ointment upon His holy feet. But if we must speak on these things, we say, that they were done when the doers knew not the word of the Resurrection; therefore it saith, "As was the manner of the Jews." For they who honored Christ[4] were not of the twelve, but were those who did not honor Him greatly. The twelve honored Him not in this way, but by death and massacre and dangers for His sake. That other indeed was honor, but far inferior to this of which I have spoken. Besides, as I began by saying, we are now speaking of men, but at that time these things were done with relation to the Lord. And that thou mayest learn that Christ made no account of these things, He said, "Ye saw Me an hungered, and ye fed Me; thirsty, and ye gave Me drink; naked, and ye clothed Me" (Matt. xxv. 35); but nowhere did He say, "dead, and ye buried Me." And this I say not as taking away the custom of burial, (that be far from me,) but as cutting short its extravagance and unseasonable vanity. "But," saith some one, "feeling and grief and sympathy for the departed persuade to this practice." The practice doth not proceed from sympathy for the departed, but from vainglory. Since if thou desirest to sympathize with the dead, I will show thee another way of mourning, and will teach thee to put on him garments which shall rise again with him, and make him glorious. For these garments are not consumed by worms, nor wasted by time, nor stolen by tomb-breakers. Of what sort then are these? The clothing of almsdoing; for this is a robe that shall rise again with him, because the seal of almsdoing is with him. With these garments shine they who then hear, "Hungering ye fed Me." These make men distinguished, these make them glorious, these place them in safety; but those used now are only something for moths to consume, and a table for worms. And this I say, not forbid-

---

[1] Ver. 8, 9. "Then went in also that other disciple which came first to the sepulcher, and he saw, and believed. For as yet they knew not the Scripture, that He must rise again from the dead." N. T.          [2] al. "senseless."

[3] ἰχώρ.          [4] i.e. in His burial.

ding to use funeral observance, but bidding you to do it with moderation, so as to cover the body, and not commit it naked to the earth. For if living He biddeth us have no more than enough to cover us, much more when dead; since the dead body[1] hath not so much need of garments as when it is living and breathing. For when alive, on account of the cold, and for decency's sake, we need the covering of garments, but when dead we require grave-clothes for none of these reasons, but that the body may not lie naked; and better than grave-clothes we have the earth, fairest of coverings, and more suited for the nature of such bodies as ours. If then where there are so many needs we must not search for anything superfluous, much more, where there is no such necessity, is the ostentation unseasonable.

[6.] "But the lookers-on will laugh," saith some one. Most certainly if there be any laughter, we need not care much for one so exceedingly foolish; but at present there are many who rather admire and accept our true wisdom. For these are not the things which deserve laughter, but those which we do at present, weeping, and wailing, and burying ourselves with the departed; these things deserve ridicule and punishment. But to show true wisdom, both in these respects and in the modesty of the attire used, prepares crowns and praises for us, and all will applaud us, and will admire the power of Christ, and will say, "Amazing! How great is the power of the Crucified One! He hath persuaded those who are perishing and wasting, that death is not death; they therefore do not act as perishing men, but as men who send the dead before them to a distant and better dwelling-place. He hath persuaded them that this corruptible and earthy body shall put on a garment more glorious than silk or cloth of gold, the garment of immortality; therefore they are not very anxious about their burial, but deem a virtuous life to be an admirable winding-sheet." These things they will say, if they see us showing true wisdom; but if they behold us bent down with grief, playing the woman, placing around troops of female mourners, they will laugh, and mock, and find fault in ten thousand ways, pulling to pieces our foolish expense, our vain labor. With these things we hear all finding fault; and very reasonably. For what excuse can we have, when we adorn a body, which is consumed by[2] cor-

ruption and worms, and neglect Christ when thirsting, going about naked, and a stranger? Cease we then from this vain trouble. Let us perform the obsequies of the departed, as is good both for us and them, to the glory of God: let us do much alms for their sake, let us send with them the best provision for the way. For if the memory of admirable men, though dead, hath protected the living, (for, "I will defend," it saith, "this city for Mine Own sake, and for My servant David's sake"— 2 Kings xix. 34,) much more will alms-doing effect this; for this hath raised even the dead, as when the widows stood round[3] showing what things Dorcas had made while she was with them. (Acts ix. 39.) When therefore one is about to die, let the friend of that dying person prepare the obsequies,[4] and persuade[5] the departing one to leave somewhat to the needy. With these garments let him send him to the grave, leaving[6] Christ his heir. For if they who write kings among their heirs, leave a safe portion to their relations,[7] when one leaves Christ heir with his children, consider how great good he will draw down upon himself and all his. These are the right[8] sort of funerals, these profit both those who remain and those who depart. If we be so buried, we shall be glorious at the Resurrection-time. But if caring for the body we neglect the soul, we then shall suffer many terrible things, and incur much ridicule. For neither is it a common unseemliness to depart without being clothed with virtue, nor is the body, though cast out without a tomb, so disgraced, as a soul appearing bare of virtue in that day. This let us put on, this let us wrap around us; it is best to do so during all our lifetime; but if we have in this life been negligent, let us at least in our end be sober, and charge our relations to help us when we depart by alms-doing; that being thus assisted by each other, we may attain[9] to much confidence, through the grace and lovingkindness of our Lord Jesus Christ, with whom to the Father and the Holy Ghost be glory, dominion, and honor, now and ever and world without end. Amen.

---

[1] al. "body of the dead."
[2] or, "given over to," lit. "spent upon."

[3] al. "stood by."
[4] or, "burial dress," τὰ ἐντάφια.
[5] i.e. by persuading.
[6] Sav. reads, κληρονόμον ἀφιέναι τὸν X. ἀφίεντα may be conjectured. The Ben. ed. reads, πειθέτω καὶ κλ. κ.τ.λ.
[7] Ben. "leave very great safety." One MS. has a slight variety of sense: "If they who write kings their heirs among their relations, leave that portion for the safety of the children."
[8] καλὰ.
[9] ἐπιτύχωμεν, without any conjunction preceding. Sav. conject. ἐπιτευξόμεθα.

# HOMILY LXXXVI.

JOHN xx. 10, 11.

"Then the disciples went away again unto their own home. But Mary stood without at the sepulcher, weeping."

[1.] FULL of feeling somehow is the female sex, and more [1] inclined to pity. I say this, lest thou shouldest wonder how it could be that Mary wept bitterly at the tomb, while Peter was in no way so affected. For, "The disciples," it saith, "went away unto their own home"; but she stood shedding tears. Because hers was a feeble nature, and she as yet knew not accurately the account of the Resurrection; whereas they having seen the linen clothes and believed, departed to their own homes in astonishment. And wherefore went they not straightway to Galilee, as had been commanded them before the Passion? They waited for the others, perhaps, and besides they were yet at the height of their amazement. These then went their way: but she stood at the place, for, as I have said, even the sight of the tomb tended greatly to comfort her. At any rate, thou seest her, the more to ease her grief, stooping down,[2] and desiring to behold the place where the body lay. And therefore she received no small reward for this her great zeal. For what the disciples saw not, this saw the woman first, Angels[3] sitting, the one at the feet, the other at the head, in white; even the dress[4] was full of much radiance[5] and joy. Since the mind of the woman was not sufficiently elevated to accept the Resurrection from the proof of the napkins, something more takes place, she beholdeth something more; Angels sitting in shining garments, so as to raise her thus awhile from her passionate sorrow, and to comfort her. But they said nothing to her concerning the Resurrection, yet is she gently led forward in this doctrine. She saw countenances bright and unusual; she saw shining garments, she heard a sympathizing voice. For what saith (the Angel)?

Ver. 13. "Woman, why weepest thou?"

By all these circumstances, as though a door was being opened for her, she was led by little and little to the knowledge of the Resurrection. And the manner of their sitting invited her to question them, for they showed that they knew what had taken place; on which account they did not sit together either, but apart from one another. For because it was not likely that she would dare at once to question them, both by questioning her, and by the manner of their sitting, they bring her to converse. What then saith she? She speaks very warmly and affectionately;

"They[6] have taken away my Lord, and I know not where they have laid Him."

"What sayest thou? Knowest thou not yet anything concerning the Resurrection, but dost thou still form fancies about His being laid[7]?" Seest thou how she had not yet received the sublime doctrine?

Ver. 14. "And when she had thus said, she turned herself back."[8]

And by what kind of consequence is it, that she having spoken to them, and not having yet heard anything from them, turned back? Methinks that while she was speaking, Christ suddenly appearing behind her, struck the Angels with awe; and that they having beheld their Ruler,[9] showed immediately by their bearing, their look, their movements, that they saw the Lord;[10] and this drew the woman's attention, and caused her to turn herself backwards. To them then He appeared on this wise, but not so to the woman, in order not at the first sight to terrify her, but in a meaner and ordinary form, as is clear from her supposing that He was the gardener. It was meet to lead one of so lowly a mind to high matters, not all at once, but gently. He therefore in turn asketh her,

Ver. 15. "Woman, why weepest thou? whom seekest thou?"

This showed that He knew what she wished to ask, and led her to make answer. And the woman, understanding this, doth not again mention the name of Jesus, but as though her questioner knew the subject of her enquiry, replies,

"Sir,[11] if thou have borne him hence, tell me where thou hast laid him, and I will take him away."

Again she speaks of laying down, and taking away, and carrying, as though speaking of a corpse. But her meaning is this; "If ye have borne him hence for fear of the Jews, tell me,

---

[1] i.e. more than men.
[2] Ver. 11, latter part. "And as she wept, she stooped down, and looked into the sepulcher." N. T.
[3] Ver. 12. "And seeth two Angels in white sitting, the one at the head, and the other at the feet, where the body of Jesus had lain." N. T.
[4] or, and the appearance, τὸ σχῆμα.　　[5] φαιδρότητος.

[6] "because they," N. T.　　[7] θέσιν.
[8] "Turned herself back, and saw Jesus standing, and knew not that it was Jesus." N. T.
[9] Δεσπότην.　　[10] Κύριον.
[11] "She, supposing Him to be the gardener, saith unto Him, Sir," &c. N. T.

and I will take him." Great is the kindness and loving affection of the woman, but as yet there is nothing lofty with her.[1] Wherefore He now setteth the matter before her, not by appearance, but by Voice. For as He was at one time known to the Jews, and at another time unperceived[2] though present; so too in speaking, He, when He chose, then made Himself known; as also when He said to the Jews, "Whom seek ye?" they knew neither the Countenance nor the Voice until He chose. And this was the case here. And He named her name only,[3] reproaching and blaming her that she entertained such fancies concerning One who lived. But how was it that,

Ver. 16. "She turned herself, and saith,"[4] if so be that He was speaking to her? It seems to me, that after having said, "Where have ye laid him?" she turned to the Angels to ask why they were astonished, and that then Christ, by calling her by name, turned her to Himself from them, and revealed Himself by His Voice; for when He called her "Mary," then she knew Him; so that the recognition was not by His appearance, but by His Voice. And if any say, "Whence is it clear that the Angels were awestruck, and that on this account the woman turned herself," they will in this place say, "whence is it clear that she would have touched Him, and fallen at His feet?" Now as this is clear from His saying, "Touch Me not," so is the other clear from its saying, that she turned herself. But wherefore, said He,

Ver. 17. "Touch Me not"?

[2.] Some assert, that she asked for spiritual grace, because she had heard Him when with the disciples say, "If I go to the Father, 'I will ask Him, and He shall give you another Comforter.'" (c. xiv. 3, 16.) But how could she who was not present with the disciples have heard this? Besides, such an imagination is far from the meaning here. And how should she ask, when He had not yet gone to the Father? What then is the sense? Methinks that she wished still to converse with Him as before, and that in her joy she perceived nothing great in Him, although He had become far more excellent in the Flesh. To lead her therefore from this idea, and that she might speak to Him with much awe, (for neither with the disciples doth He henceforth appear so familiar as before,) He raiseth her thoughts, that she should give more reverent heed to Him. To have said, "Approach Me not as ye did before, for matters are not in the same state, nor shall I henceforth be with you in the same way," would have been harsh and high-sounding; but the saying,

"I am not yet ascended to the[5] Father," though not painful to hear, was the saying of One declaring the same thing. For by saying, "I am not yet ascended," He showeth that He hasteth and presseth thither; and that it was not meet that One about to depart thither, and no longer to converse with men, should be looked on with the same feelings as before. And the sequel shows that this is the case.

"Go and say unto the brethren, that I go[6] unto My Father, and your Father, unto My God and your God."

Yet He was not about to do so immediately, but after forty days. How then saith He this? With a desire to raise their minds, and to persuade them that He departeth into the heavens. But the, "To My Father and your Father, to My God, and your God," belongs to the Dispensation,[7] since the "ascending" also belongs to His Flesh. For He speaketh these words to one who had no high thoughts. "Is then the Father His in one way, and ours in another?" Assuredly then He is. For if He is God of the righteous in a manner different from that in which He is God of other men, much more in the case of the Son and us. For because He had said, "Say to the brethren," in order that they might not imagine any equality from this, He showed the difference. He was about to sit on His Father's throne, but they to stand by.[8] So that albeit in His Subsistence according to the Flesh He became our Brother, yet in Honor He greatly differed from[9] us, it cannot even be told how much.

Ver. 18. "She therefore departeth, bearing these tidings to the disciples."[10]

So great a good is perseverance and endurance. But how was it that they did not any more grieve when He was about to depart, nor speak as they had done before? At that time they were affected in such a way, as supposing that He was about to die; but now that He was risen again, what reason had they to grieve? Moreover, Mary reported His appearance and His words, which were enough to comfort them. Since then it was likely that the disciples on hearing these things would either not believe the woman, or, believing, would grieve that He had not deemed them worthy of the vision, though He promised to meet them in Galilee; in order that they might not by dwelling on this be unsettled,[11] He let not a single day pass, but having brought them to a state of longing, by their knowledge that He was risen, and by what

---

[1] al. "but nothing lofty from her."          [2] ἄδηλος.
[3] Ver. 16. "Jesus saith unto her, Mary."
[4] "and saith unto Him, Rabboni, which is to say, Master," N. T.

[5] "to My," N. T.
[6] "Go to My brethren, and say unto them, I ascend," &c. N. T.
[7] i.e. the Incarnation.
[8] παρέσταναι. So Ben. and MSS. and it seems the best reading. Savile reads περιστῆναι.          [9] or, "surpassed."
[10] Ver. 18. "Mary Magdalene came and told the disciples that she had seen the Lord, and that He had spoken these things unto her." N. T.          [11] or, "distracted."

they heard from the woman, when they were thirsting to see Him, and were greatly afraid, (which thing itself especially made their yearning greater,) He then, when it was evening, presented[1] Himself before them, and that very marvelously.[2] And why did He appear in the "evening"? Because it was probable that they would then especially be very fearful. But the marvel was, why they did not suppose Him to be an apparition; for He entered, "when the doors were shut," and suddenly. The chief cause was, that the woman beforehand had wrought great faith in them; besides, He showed His countenance to them clear and mild. He came not by day, in order that all might be collected together. For great was the amazement; for neither did He knock at the door, but all at once stood in the midst, and showed His side and His hands.[3] At the same time also by His Voice He smoothed their tossing thought, by saying,

Ver. 19. "Peace be unto you."

That is, "Be not troubled"; at the same time reminding them of the word which He spake to them before the Crucifixion, "My peace I leave[4] unto you" (c. xiv. 27); and again, "In me ye have[5] peace, but" "in the world ye shall have tribulation." (c. xvi. 33.)

Ver. 20. "Then were the disciples glad when they saw the Lord."

Seest thou the words issuing in deeds? For what He said before the Crucifixion, that "I will see you again, and your heart shall rejoice, and your joy no man taketh from you" (c. xvi. 22), this He now[6] accomplished in deed; but all these things led them to a most exact faith. For since they had a truceless war with the Jews, He continually repeated the, "Peace be unto you,"[7] giving them, to counterbalance the war, the consolation. And so this was the first word that He spake to them after the Resurrection, (wherefore also Paul continually saith, "Grace be unto you and peace,") and to women He giveth good tidings of joy,[8] because that sex was in sorrow, and had received this as the first curse. Therefore He giveth good tidings suitable respectively, to men, peace, because of their war; joy to women, because of their sorrow. Then having put away all painful things, He telleth of the successes[9] of the Cross, and these were the "peace." "Since then all hin-

drances have been removed," He saith, "and I have made My[10] victory glorious, and all hath been achieved," (then He saith afterwards,)

Ver. 21. "As My Father hath sent Me, so send I you."

"Ye have no difficulty, owing to what hath already come to pass, and to the dignity of Me who send you." Here He lifteth up their souls, and showeth them their great cause of confidence, if so be that they were about to undertake His work. And no longer is an appeal made to the Father, but with authority He giveth to them the power. For,

Ver. 22, 23. "He breathed on them, and said,[11] Receive ye the Holy Ghost. Whosoever sins ye remit, they are remitted unto them, and whosoever sins ye retain, they are retained."

As a king sending forth governors, gives power to cast[12] into prison and to deliver from it, so in sending these forth, Christ investeth them with the same power. But how saith He, "If I go not away, He[13] will not come" (c. xvi. 7), and yet giveth them the Spirit? Some say that He gave not the Spirit, but rendered them fit to receive It, by breathing on them. For if Daniel when he saw an Angel was afraid, what would not they have suffered when they received that unspeakable Gift, unless He had first made them learners? Wherefore He said not, "Ye have received the Holy Ghost," but, "Receive ye the Holy Ghost." Yet one will not be wrong in asserting that they then also received some spiritual power and grace; not so as to raise the dead, or to work miracles, but so as to remit sins. For the gifts of the Spirit are of different kinds; wherefore He added, "Whosoever sins ye remit, they are remitted unto them," showing what kind of power He was giving. But in the other case,[14] after forty[15] days, they received the power of working miracles. Wherefore He saith, "Ye shall receive power, after that the Holy Ghost is come[16] upon you, and ye shall be My witnesses both in Jerusalem, and in all Judæa." (Acts i. 8.) And witnesses they became by means of miracles, for unspeakable is the grace of the Spirit and multiform the gift. But this comes to pass, that thou mayest learn that the gift and the power of the Father, the Son, and the Holy Ghost, is One. For things which appear to be peculiar to the Father, these are seen also to belong to the Son, and to the Holy Ghost. "How then," saith some one, "doth none come to the Son, 'except the Father draw him'?" (c. vi. 44.) Why, this very

---

[1] al. "presents."
[2] Ver. 19. "Then the same day at evening, being the first day of the week, when the doors were shut where the disciples were assembled for fear of the Jews, came Jesus and stood in the midst." N. T.
[3] Ver. 20. "And when He had so said, He showed unto them His hands and His side." 　[4] "give."
[5] "that in Me ye might have," N. T.
[6] al. "this therefore He."
[7] Ver. 21. "Then said Jesus to them again, Peace," &c.
[8] Matt. xxviii. 9. "Jesus met them (the women) saying, Rejoice." G. T. Χαίρετε. E. V. "All hail."
[9] or, "perfect actions," κατορθώματα.

[10] al. "all hindrances had been removed, and He had made His."
[11] Ver. 22. "And when He had said this, He breathed on them, and saith unto them," &c. N. T.
[12] al. "having the power of casting," &c., "gives it."
[13] "The Comforter," N. T. 　[14] ἐκεῖ.
[15] The sense seems to require "fifty," but there is no other reading than the above.
[16] or, "of the Holy Ghost coming."

thing is shown to belong to the Son also. "I," He saith, "am the Way: no man cometh unto the Father but by Me." (c. xiv. 6.) And observe that it belongeth to the Spirit also; for "No man can call Jesus Christ Lord,[1] but by the Holy Ghost." (1 Cor. xii. 3.) Again, we see that the Apostles were given to the Church at one time by the Father, at another by the Son, at another by the Holy Ghost, and that the "diversities of gifts" (1 Cor. xii. 4) belong to the Father, the Son, and the Holy Ghost.

[4.] Let us then do all we can to have the Holy Spirit with ourselves, and let us treat with much honor those into whose hands its operation hath been committed. For great is the dignity of the priests. "Whosesoever sins," it saith, "ye remit, they are remitted unto them"; wherefore also Paul saith, "Obey them that have the rule over you, and submit yourselves." (Heb. xiii. 17.) And hold them very exceedingly in honor; for thou indeed carest about thine own affairs, and if thou orderest them well, thou givest[2] no account for others, but the priest even if he rightly order his own life, if he have not an anxious care for thine, yea and that of all those around him, will depart with the wicked into hell; and often when not betrayed by his own conduct, he perishes by yours, if he have not rightly performed all his part. Knowing therefore the greatness of the danger, give them a large share of your goodwill; which Paul also implied when he said, "For they watch for your souls," and not simply so, but, "as they that shall give account." (Heb. xiii. 17.) They ought therefore to receive great attention from you; but if you join with the rest in trampling upon them, then neither shall your affairs be in a good condition. For while the steersman continues in good courage, the crew also will be in safety; but if he be tired out by their reviling him and showing ill-will against him, he cannot watch equally well, or retain his skill, and without intending it, throws them into ten thousand mischiefs. And so too the priest, if he enjoy honor[3] from you, will be able well to order your affairs; but if ye throw them into despondency, ye weaken their hands, and render them, as well as yourselves, an easy prey to the waves, although they be very courageous. Consider what Christ saith concerning the Jews. "The Scribes and the Pharisees sit on Moses' seat; all therefore whatsoever they bid[4] you to do, do ye." (Matt. xxiii. 2, 3.) Now we have not to say, "the priests sit on Moses' seat," but "on that of Christ"; for they have successively received His doctrine. Wherefore also Paul saith, "We are ambassadors for Christ, as though God did be-

seech you by us." (2 Cor. v. 20.) See ye not that in the case of Gentile rulers, all bow to them, and oftentimes even persons superior in family, in life, in intelligence, to those who judge them? yet still because of him who hath given them, they consider none of these things, but respect the decision of their governor, whosoever he be that receives the rule over them. Is there then such fear when man appoints, but when God appointeth do we despise him who is appointed, and abuse him, and besmirch him with ten thousand reproaches, and though forbidden to judge our brethren, do we sharpen our tongue against our priests? And how can this deserve excuse, when we see not the beam in our own eye, but are bitterly over-curious about the mote in another's? Knowest thou not that by so judging thou makest thine own judgment the harder? And this I say not as approving of those who exercise their priesthood unworthily, but as greatly pitying and weeping for them; yet do I not on this account allow that it is right that they should be judged by those over whom they are set.[5] And although their life be very much spoken against, thou, if thou take heed to thyself, wilt not be harmed at all[6] in respect of the things committed to them[7] by God. For if He caused a voice to be uttered by an ass, and bestowed spiritual blessings by a diviner, working by the foolish mouth and impure tongue of Balaam, in behalf of the offending Jews, much more for the sake of you the right-minded[8] will He, though the priests be exceedingly vile, work all the things that are His, and will send the Holy Ghost. For neither doth the pure draw down that Spirit by his own purity, but it is grace that worketh all. "For all," it saith, "is for your sake,[9] whether it be Paul, or Apollos, or Cephas." (1 Cor. iii. 22, 23.) For the things which are placed in the hands of the priest it is with God alone to give; and however far human wisdom may reach, it will appear inferior to that grace. And this I say, not in order that we may order our own life carelessly, but that when some of those set over you are careless livers, you the ruled may not often heap up evil for yourselves. But why speak I of priests? Neither Angel nor Archangel can do anything with regard to what is given from God; but the Father, the Son, and the Holy Ghost, dispenseth all, while the priest lends his tongue and affords his hand. For neither would it be just that through the wickedness of another, those who come in faith to the symbols of their salvation should be harmed. Knowing all these things, let us fear God, and hold His priests in honor, paying them all reverence; that both for our own good deeds, and

---

1 " call Jesus Lord," N. T.     2 al. " wilt give."
3 al. " attention."
4 " bid you observe, that observe and do," N. T.

5 Sav. adds in brackets, " and especially by those altogether the simplest." The words found in some MSS.
6 al. " not even be harmed a little."     7 Sav. " to him."
8 al. " ill-minded," or, " ungrateful."     9 " is yours," N. T.

the attention shown to them, we may receive a great return from God, through the grace and lovingkindness of our Lord Jesus Christ, with whom to the Father and the Holy Ghost be glory, dominion, and honor, now and ever, and world without end. Amen.

---

# HOMILY LXXXVII.

### John xx. 24, 25.

"But Thomas, one of the twelve, called Didymus, was not with them when Jesus came. The other disciples therefore said unto him, We have seen the Lord. But he said, Except I shall see in His hands[1] — I will not believe."

[1.] As to believe carelessly and in a random way, comes of an over-easy temper; so to be beyond measure curious and meddlesome, marks a most gross understanding. On this account Thomas is held to blame. For he believed not the Apostles when they said, "We have seen the Lord"; not so much mistrusting them, as deeming the thing to be impossible, that is to say, the resurrection from the dead. Since he saith not, "I do not believe you," but, "Except I put my hand — I do not[2] believe." But how was it, that when all were collected together, he alone was absent? Probably after the dispersion which had lately taken place, he had not returned even then. But do thou, when thou seest the unbelief of the disciple, consider the lovingkindness of the Lord, how for the sake of a single soul He showed Himself with His wounds, and cometh in order to save even the one, though he was grosser than the rest; on which account indeed he sought proof from the grossest of the senses, and would not even trust his eyes. For he said not, "Except I see," but, "Except I handle," he saith, lest what he saw might somehow be an apparition. Yet the disciples who told him these things, were at the time worthy of credit, and so was He that promised; yet, since he desired more, Christ did not deprive him even of this.

And why doth He not appear to him straightway, instead of "after eight days"?[3] (Ver. 26.) In order that being in the mean time continually instructed by the disciples, and hearing the same thing, he might be inflamed to more eager desire, and be more ready to believe for the future. But whence knew he that His side had been opened? From having heard it from the disciples. How then did he believe partly, and partly not believe? Because this thing was very strange and wonderful. But observe, I pray you, the truthfulness of the disciples, how they hide no faults, either their own or others', but record them with great veracity.

Jesus again presenteth himself to them, and waiteth not to be requested by Thomas, nor to hear any such thing, but before he had spoken, Himself prevented him, and fulfilled his desire; showing that even when he spake those words to the disciples, He was present. For He used the same words, and in a manner conveying a sharp rebuke, and instruction for the future. For having said,

Ver. 26. "Reach hither thy finger, and behold My hands; and reach hither thy hand, and thrust it into My side"; He added,

"And be not faithless, but believing."

Seest thou that his doubt proceeded from unbelief? But it was before he had received the Spirit; after that, it was no longer so, but, for the future, they were perfected.

And not in this way only did Jesus rebuke him, but also by what follows; for when he, being fully satisfied, breathed again, and cried aloud,

Ver. 28. "My Lord, and my God," He saith,

Ver. 29. "Because thou hast seen Me, thou hast believed; blessed are they who have not seen, and yet have believed."

For this is of faith, to receive things not seen; since, "Faith is the substance of things hoped for, the evidence of things not seen." (Heb. xi. 1.) And here He pronounceth blessed not the disciples only, but those also who after them should believe. "Yet," saith some one, "the disciples saw and believed." Yes, but they sought nothing of the kind, but from the proof of the napkins, they straightway received the word concerning the Resurrection, and before they saw the body, exhibited all faith. When therefore any one in the present day say, "I would that I had lived in those times, and had seen Christ working miracles," let them reflect, that, "Blessed are they who have not seen, and yet have believed."

---

[1] "But he said unto them, Except I shall see in His hands the print of the nails, and put my finger into the print of the nails, and thrust my hand into His side." N. T.

[2] "will not," N. T.

[3] Ver. 26. "And after eight days again His disciples were within, and Thomas with them; then came Jesus, the door being shut, and stood in the midst, and said, Peace be unto you." N. T.

It is worth enquiring, how an incorruptible body showed the prints of the nails, and was tangible by a mortal hand. But be not thou disturbed ; what took place was a matter of condescension. For that which was so subtle and light as to enter in when the doors were shut, was free from all density[1] ; but this marvel was shown, that the Resurrection might be believed, and that men might know that it was the Crucified One Himself, and that another rose not in His stead. On this account He arose[2] bearing the signs of the Cross, and on this account He eateth. At least the Apostles everywhere made this a sign of the Resurrection, saying, "We, who did eat and drink with Him." (Acts x. 41.) As therefore when we see Him walking on the waves before the Crucifixion, we do not say, that that body is of a different nature, but of our own ; so after the Resurrection, when we see Him with the prints of the nails, we will no more say, that he is therefore[3] corruptible. For He exhibited these appearances on account of the disciple.

Ver. 30. "And many other signs truly did Jesus."

[2.] Since this Evangelist hath mentioned fewer than the others, he tells us that neither have all the others mentioned them all, but as many as were sufficient to draw the hearers to belief. For, "If," it saith, "they should be written every one, I suppose that even the world itself could not contain the books." (c. xxi. 25.) Whence it is clear, that what they have mentioned they wrote not for display, but only for the sake of what was useful. For how could they who omitted the greater part, write these others[4] for display? But why went they not through them all? Chiefly on account of their number ; besides, they also considered, that he who believed not those they had mentioned, would not give heed to a greater number ; while he who received these, would have no need of another in order to believe. And here too he seems to me to be for the time speaking of the miracles after the Resurrection. Wherefore He saith,

"In the presence of His disciples."[5]

For as before the Resurrection it was necessary that many should be done, in order that they might believe that He was the Son of God, so was it also after the Resurrection, in order that they might admit that He had arisen. For another reason also he has added, "In the presence of His disciples," because He conversed with them alone after the Resurrection ; wherefore also He said, "The world seeth Me no

more." (c. xiv. 19.) Then, in order that thou mayest understand that what was done was done only for the sake of the disciples, he added,

Ver. 31. "That believing ye might have life in His Name."[6]

Speaking generally to mankind, and showing that not on Him who is believed on, but on ourselves, he bestows a very great favor. "In His Name," that is, "through Him" ; for He is the Life.

Chap. xxi. ver. 1. "After these things, Jesus showed Himself again to the disciples at the sea of Tiberias."[7]

Seest thou that He remaineth not with them continually, nor as before? He appeared, for instance, in the evening, and flew away ; then after eight days again once, and again flew away ; then after these things by the sea, and again with great terror. But what is the, "showed"? From this it is clear that He was not seen unless He condescended, because His body was henceforth incorruptible, and of unmixed purity.[8] But wherefore hath the writer mentioned the place? To show that he had now taken away the greater part of their fear, so that they now ventured forth from their dwelling, and went about everywhere. For they were no longer shut up at home, but had gone into Galilee, avoiding the danger from the Jews. Simon, therefore, comes to fish. For since neither was He with them continually, nor was the Spirit yet given, nor they at that time yet entrusted with anything, having nothing to do, they went after their trade.

Ver. 2. "There were together Simon Peter, and Thomas,[9] and Nathanael,"[10] (he that was called by Philip,) "and the sons of Zebedee, and two others."[11]

Having then nothing to do, they went to their fishing,[12] and this same they did by night, because they were greatly afraid. This Luke also mentions ;[13] but this is not the same occasion, but a different one. And the other disciples followed, because they were henceforth bound to one another, and at the same time desired to see the fishing, and to bestow[14] their leisure well. As they then were laboring and wearied, Jesus presenteth Himself before them, and doth not at once reveal Himself, so that they enter into converse with Him. He therefore saith to them,

Ver. 5. "Have ye[15] any meat[16]?"

For a time He speaketh rather after a human

---

[1] παχύτητος.  [2] al. "raiseth Himself," or, "is raised."
[3] οτ, "henceforth," λοιπὸν.
[4] According to Savile's conject. and two MSS. πῶς ἂν ταῦτα for πῶς ἐνταῦθα.
[5] "of His disciples, which are not written in this book," N. T.

[6] Ver. 31. "But these are written, that ye might believe that Jesus is the Christ, the Son of God, and that," &c. N. T.
[7] "of Tiberias; and on this wise showed He Himself," N. T.
[8] ἀκήρατον.  [9] "Thomas, called Didymus."
[10] "Nathanael of Cana in Galilee."
[11] "two other of His disciples," N. T.
[12] Ver. 3, 4. "Simon Peter saith unto them, I go a fishing. They say unto him, We also go with thee. They went forth, and entered into a ship immediately; and that night they caught nothing. But when the morning was now come, Jesus stood on the shore, but the disciples knew not that it was Jesus." N. T.
[13] Luke xxiv. 37. "But they were terrified and affrighted."
[14] al. "dispose."  [15] "Children, have ye," N. T.
[16] or, "fish," προσφάγιον, that which is eaten with the bread.

manner, as if about to buy somewhat of them. But when they made signs that they had none, He bade them cast their nets to the right; and on casting they obtained a haul.[1] But when they recognized Him, the disciples Peter and John again exhibited the peculiarities of their several tempers. The one was more fervent, the other more lofty; the one more keen, the other more clear-sighted. On this account John first recognized Jesus, Peter first came to Him.[2] For no ordinary signs were they which had taken place. What were they? First, that so many fish were caught; then, that the net did not break;[3] then, that before they landed, the coals had been found, and fish laid thereon, and bread.[4] For He no longer made things out of matter already subsisting, as, through a certain dispensation, He did before the Crucifixion. When therefore Peter knew Him, he threw down all, both fish and nets, and girded himself. . Seest thou his respect and love? Yet they were only two hundred cubits off; but not even so could Peter wait to go to Him in the boat, but reached the shore by swimming. What then doth Jesus?

Ver. 12. "Come," He saith, "dine." "And none of them durst ask Him."[5]

For they no longer had the same boldness, nor were they so confident, nor did they now approach Him with speech, but with silence and great fear and reverence, sat down giving heed to Him.

"For they knew that[6] it was the Lord."

And therefore they did not ask Him, "Who art Thou?" But seeing that His form was altered, and full of much awfulness, they were greatly amazed, and desired to ask somewhat concerning it; but fear, and their knowledge that He was not some other, but the Same, checked the enquiry, and they only ate what He created for them[7] with a greater exertion of power than before. For here He no more looketh to heaven, nor performeth those human acts, showing that those also which He did were done by way of condescension. And to show that He remained not with them continually, nor in like manner as before, It saith that,

Ver. 14. "This was the third time that Jesus appeared to them,[8] after that He arose from the dead."

And He biddeth them "to bring of the fish," to show that what they saw was no appearance. But here indeed it saith not that He ate with them, but Luke, in another place, saith that He did; for "He was eating together with them."[9] (Acts i. 4.) But the, "how," it is not ours to say; for these things came to pass in too strange a manner, not as though His nature now needed food, but from an act of condescension, in proof of the Resurrection.

[3.] Perhaps when ye heard these things, ye glowed, and called those happy who were then with Him, and those who shall be with Him at the day of the general Resurrection. Let us then use every exertion that we may see that admirable Face. For if when now we hear we so burn, and desire to have been in those days which He spent upon earth, and to have heard His Voice, and seen His face, and to have approached, and touched, and ministered unto Him; consider how great a thing it is to see Him no longer in a mortal body, nor doing human actions, but with a body guard of Angels, being ourselves also in a form of unmixed purity, and beholding Him, and enjoying the rest of that bliss which passes all language. Wherefore, I entreat, let us use every means, so as not to miss such glory. For nothing is difficult if we be willing, nothing burdensome if we give heed. "If we endure, we shall also reign with Him." (2 Tim. ii. 12.) What then is, "If we endure"? If we bear tribulations, if persecutions, if we walk in the strait way. For the strait way is by its nature laborious, but by our will it is rendered light, from the hope of things to come. "For our present light affliction worketh for us a far more exceeding and eternal weight of glory; while we look not at the things which are seen, but at those which are not seen." (2 Cor. iv. 17, 18.) Let us then transfer our eyes to heaven, and continually imagine "those" things, and behold them. For if we always spend our time with them, we shall not be moved to desire the pleasures of this world, nor find it hard to bear its sorrows; but we shall laugh at these and the like, and nothing will be able to enslave or lift us up, if only we direct our longing thither,[10] and look to that love.[11] And why say I that we shall not grieve at present troubles? We shall henceforth not even appear to see them. Such a thing is strong desire.[12] Those, for instance, who

---

[1] Ver. 5, 6, and 8. "They answered Him, No. And He said unto them, Cast the net on the right side of the ship, and ye shall find. They cast therefore, and now they were not able to draw it for the multitude of fishes. And the other disciples came in a little ship, for they were not far from land, but as it were two hundred cubits, dragging the net with fishes." N. T.

[2] Ver. 7. "Therefore that disciple whom Jesus loved saith unto Peter, It is the Lord. Now when Simon Peter heard that it was the Lord, he girt his fisher's coat unto him, (for he was naked,) and did cast himself into the sea." N. T.

[3] Ver. 11. "Simon Peter went up, and drew the net to land full of great fishes, an hundred and fifty and three: and for all there were so many, yet was not the net broken." N. T.

[4] Ver. 9, 10. "As soon then as they were come to land, they saw a fire of coals there, and fish laid thereon, and bread. Jesus saith unto them, Bring of the fish which ye have now caught." N. T.

[5] "ask him, Who art Thou?" N. T.

[6] "knowing that," N. T.

[7] Ver. 13. "Jesus then cometh, and taketh bread, and giveth them, and fish likewise." N. T.

[8] "was manifested to His disciples." N. T.

[9] συναλιζόμενος αὐτοῖς ἦν. The words are rendered as above in the margin of the Auth. Version, and St. Chrys. seems to have so understood them. The Vulgate has, "convescens." The literal sense is either "eating salt with them," or, as in the text of Auth. Version, "being assembled with."

[10] al. "increase that longing."

[11] ἀγάπην.

[12] ὁ ἔρως.

are not at present with us, but being absent are loved, we image every day. For mighty is the sovereignty of love,[1] it alienates the soul from all things else, and chains to the desired object. If thus we love Christ, all things here will seem to be a shadow, an image, a dream. We too shall say, "Who shall separate us from the love of Christ? Shall tribulation, or distress?" (Rom. viii. 35.) He said not, "money, or wealth, or beauty," (these are very mean and contemptible,) but he hath put the things which seem to be grievous, famines, persecutions, deaths. He then spat on these even, as being nought; but we for the sake of money separate ourselves from our life, and cut ourselves off from the light. And Paul indeed prefers "neither death, nor life, nor things present, nor things to come, nor any other creature," to the love which is towards Him; but we, if we see a little portion of gold, are fired, and trample on His laws. And if these things are intolerable when spoken of, much more are they so when done.[2] For the terrible thing is this, that we shudder to hear, but do not shudder to do: we swear readily, and perjure ourselves, and plunder, and exact usury, care nothing for sobriety, desist from exactness in prayer, transgress most of the commandments, and for the sake of money make no account of our own members.[3] For he that loves wealth will work ten thousand mischiefs to his neighbor, and to himself as well. He will easily be angry with him, and revile him, and call him fool, and swear and perjure himself, and does not[4] even preserve the measures of the old law. For he that loves gold will not love his neighbor; yet we, for the Kingdom's sake, are bidden to love even our enemies. Now if by fulfilling the old commandments, we shall not be able to enter the Kingdom of heaven, unless our righteousness exceed and go beyond them, when we transgress even these, what excuse shall we obtain? He that loves money, not only will not love his enemies, but will even treat his friends as enemies.

[4.] But why speak I of friends? the lovers of money have often ignored nature itself. Such a one knows not kindred, remembers not companionship, reverences not age, has no friend, but will be ill-disposed towards all, and above all others to himself, not only by destroying his soul, but by racking himself with ten thousand cares, and toils, and sorrows. For he will endure foreign travels, hatreds, dangers, plots, anything whatever, only that he may have in his house the root of all evil, and may count much gold. What then can be more grievous than this disease? It is void of any luxury or pleasure, for the sake of which men often sin, it is void of honor or glory. For the lover of money suspects that he has tens of thousands, and really has many, who accuse, and envy, and slander, and plot against him. Those whom he has wronged hate him as having been ill-used; those who have not yet suffered, fearing least they may suffer, and sympathizing with those who have, manifest the same hostility; while the greater and more powerful, being stung and indignant on account of the humbler sort, and at the same time also envying him, are his enemies and haters. And why speak I of men? For when one hath God also made his enemy, what hope shall there then be for him? what consolation? what comfort? He that loves riches will[5] never be able to use them; he will be their slave and keeper, not their master. For, being ever anxious to make them more, he will never be willing to spend them; but he will cut short himself, and be in poorer state than any poor man, as nowhere stopping in his desire. Yet riches are made not that we should keep, but that we should use them; but if we are going to bury them for others, what can be more miserable than we, who run about desiring to get together the possessions of all men,[6] that we may shut them up within, and cut them off from common use? But there is another malady not less than this. Some men bury their money in the earth, others in their bellies, and in pleasure and drunkenness; together with injustice adding to themselves the punishment of wantonness. Some minister with their substance to parasites and flatterers, others to dice and harlots, others to different expenses of the same kind, cutting out for themselves ten thousand roads that lead to hell, but leaving the right and sanctioned road which leads to heaven. And yet it hath not greater gain only, but greater pleasure than the things we have mentioned. For he who gives to harlots is ridiculous and shameful, and will have many quarrels, and brief pleasure; or rather, not even brief, because, give what he will to the women his mistresses, they will not thank him for it; for, "The house of a stranger is a cask with holes." (Prov. xxiii. 27, LXX.) Besides, that sort of persons is impudent,[7] and Solomon hath compared their love to the grave; and then only do they stop, when they see their lover stripped of all. Or rather, such a woman doth not stop even then, but tricks herself out the more, and tramples on him when he is down, and excites much laughter against him, and works him so much mischief, as it is not possible even to describe by words. Not such is the pleasure of the saved; for neither hath any one there a rival, but all rejoice and are glad, both they that receive blessings, and they that look

---

[1] ἀγάπης.

[2] al. "much more those (i.e. the opposite) when not done."

[3] i.e. our members in Christ.        [4] al. "will not."

[5] al. "From his riches? he will."        [7] lit. "forward."

[6] al. "get together all."

on. No anger, no despondency, no shame, no disgrace, besiege the soul of such a one, but great is the gladness of his conscience, and great his hope of things to come; bright his glory, and great his distinction; and more than all is the favor and safety which is from God, and not one precipice, nor suspicion, but a waveless harbor, and calm. Considering therefore all these things, and comparing pleasure with pleasure, let us choose the better,[6] that we may obtain the good things to come, through the grace and lovingkindness of our Lord Jesus Christ, to whom be glory and dominion for ever and ever. Amen.

# HOMILY LXXXVIII.

## John xxi. 15.

"So when they had dined, Jesus saith to Simon Peter, Simon, son of Jonas, lovest thou Me more than these? He saith unto Him, Yea, Lord, Thou knowest that I love Thee."

[1.] THERE are indeed many other things which are able to give us boldness towards God, and to show us bright and approved, but that which most of all brings good will from on high, is tender care for our neighbor. Which therefore Christ requireth of Peter. For when their eating was ended, Jesus saith to Simon Peter, "Simon, son of Jonas, lovest thou Me more than these? He saith unto Him, Yea, Lord, Thou knowest that I love Thee."

"He saith unto him, Feed My sheep."[1]

And why, having passed by the others, doth He speak with Peter on these matters? He was the chosen one of the Apostles, the mouth of the disciples, the leader of the band; on this account also Paul went up upon a time to enquire of him rather than the others. And at the same time to show him that he must now be of good cheer, since the denial was done away,[2] Jesus putteth into his hands the chief authority[3] among the brethren; and He bringeth not forward the denial, nor reproacheth him with what had taken place, but saith, "If thou lovest Me, preside over thy brethren, and the warm love which thou didst ever manifest, and in which thou didst rejoice, show thou now; and the life which thou saidst thou wouldest lay down for Me, now give for My sheep."

When then having been asked once and again, he called Him to witness who knoweth the secrets of the heart,[4] and then was asked even a third time,[5] he was troubled, fearing a repetition of what had happened before, (for then, having been strong in assertion, he was afterwards convicted,) and therefore he again betaketh himself to Him. For the saying,

Ver. 17. "Thou knowest all things,"

meaneth, "things present, and things to come." Seest thou how he had become better and more sober, being no more self-willed, or contradicting? For on this account he was troubled, "lest perchance I think that I love, and love not, as before when I thought and affirmed much, yet I was convicted at last." But Jesus asketh him the third time, and the third time giveth him the same injunction, to show at what a price He setteth the care[7] of His own sheep, and that this especially is a sign of love towards Him. And having spoken to him concerning the love towards Himself, He foretelleth to him the martyrdom which he should undergo, showing that He said not to Him what he said as distrusting, but as greatly trusting him; wishing besides to point out a proof of love towards Him, and to instruct us in what manner especially we ought to love Him. Wherefore He saith,

Ver. 18. "When thou wast young, thou girdedst thyself, and walkedst whither thou wouldest; but when thou art old, others shall gird thee,[8] and carry thee whither thou willest not."

And yet this he did will, and desired; on which account also He hath revealed it to him. For since Peter had continually said, "I will lay down my life for Thee" (c. xiii. 37), and, "Though I should die with Thee, yet will I not deny Thee" (Matt. xxvi. 35): He hath given him back[9] his desire. What then is the, "Whither thou willest not"? He speaketh of natural feeling, and the necessity of[10] the flesh, and that the soul is unwillingly torn away from the body. So that even though the will were firm, yet still even then nature would be found

---

[1] "My lambs," N. T.	[2] lit. "driven away."
[3] προστασίαν.
[4] Ver. 16. "He saith to him again the second time, Simon, son of Jonas, lovest thou Me? He saith unto Him, Yea, Lord, Thou knowest that I love Thee. He saith unto him, Feed my sheep." N. T.
[5] Ver. 17. "He saith unto him the third time, Simon, son of Jonas, lovest thou Me? Peter was grieved because He said unto him the third time, Lovest thou Me; and he said unto Him, Lord, Thou knowest all things; Thou knowest that I love Thee. Jesus saith unto him, Feed my sheep." N. T.

[6] al. "the better things."	[7] προστασίαν.
[8] "when thou art old thou shalt stretch forth thy hands, and another shall gird thee," &c. N. T. and some MSS.
[9] al. "given him."	[10] i.e. weakness inseparable from.

in fault. For no one lays aside the body without feeling, God, as I said before, having suitably ordained this, that violent deaths might not be many. For if, as things are, the devil has been able to effect this, and has led ten thousand to precipices and pits; had not the soul felt such a desire for the body, the many would have rushed to this under any common discouragement. The, "whither thou willest not," is then the expression of one signifying natural feeling.

But how after having said, "When thou wast young," doth He again say, "When thou art old"? For this is the expression of one declaring that he was not then young; (nor was he; nor yet old, but a man of middle age.[1]) Wherefore then did He recall to his memory his former life? Signifying, that this is the nature of what belongeth to Him. In things of this life the young man is useful, the old useless; "but in Mine," He saith, "not so; but when old age hath come on, then is excellence brighter, then is manliness more illustrious, being nothing hindered by the time of life." This He said not to terrify, but to rouse Him; for He knew his love, and that he long had yearned for this blessing. At the same time He declareth the kind of death. For since Peter ever desired to be in the dangers which were for His sake, "Be of good cheer," He saith, "I will so satisfy thy desire, that, what thou sufferedst not when young, thou must suffer when thou art old." Then the Evangelist, to rouse the hearer, has added,

Ver. 19. "This spake He, signifying by what death he should glorify God."

He said not, "Should die," but, "Should glorify God," that thou mayest learn, that to suffer for Christ, is glory and honor to the sufferer.

"And when He had spoken this, He saith,[2] Follow Me."

Here again He alludeth to his tender carefulness, and to his being very closely attached to Himself. And if any should say, "How then did James receive the chair at Jerusalem?" I would make this reply, that He appointed Peter[3] teacher, not of the chair, but of the world.

Ver. 20, 21. "Then Peter turning about, seeth the disciple whom Jesus loved following; who also leaned on His breast at supper; and saith,[4] Lord, and what shall this man do?"

[2.] Wherefore hath he reminded us of that reclining? Not without cause or in a chance way, but to show us what boldness Peter had after the denial. For he who then did not dare to question Jesus, but committed the office to another, was even entrusted with the chief authority over the brethren, and not only doth not commit to another what relates to himself, but himself now puts a question to his Master concerning another. John is silent, but Peter speaks. He showeth also here the love which he bare towards him; for Peter greatly loved John, as is clear from what followed, and their close union is shown through the whole Gospel, and in the Acts. When therefore Christ had foretold great things to him, and committed the world to him, and spake beforehand of his martyrdom, and testified that his love was greater than that of the others, desiring to have John also to share with him, he said, "And what shall this man do?" "Shall he not come the same way with us?" And as at that other time not being able himself to ask, he puts John forward, so now desiring to make him a return, and supposing that he would desire to ask about the matters pertaining to himself, but had not courage, he himself undertook the questioning. What then saith Christ?

Ver. 22. "If I will that he tarry till I come, what is that to thee?"[5]

Since he spake from strong affection, and wishing not to be torn away from him,[6] Christ, to show that however much he might love, he could not go beyond His love, saith, "If I will that he tarry — what is that to thee?" By these words teaching us not to be impatient, nor curious beyond what seemeth good to Him. For because Peter was ever hot, and springing forward to enquiries such as this, to cut short his warmth, and to teach him not to enquire farther, He saith this.

Ver. 23. "Then went this saying abroad among the brethren, that that disciple should not die; yet Jesus said not[7] that he shall not die; but, If I will that he tarry till I come, what is that to thee?"

"Do not thou on any account suppose," He saith, "that I order your matters after a single rule." And this He did to withdraw them from[8] their unseasonable sympathy for each other; for since they were about to receive the charge of the world, it was necessary that they should no longer be closely associated together; for assuredly this would have been a great loss to the world. Wherefore He saith unto him, "Thou hast had a work entrusted to thee, look to it, accomplish it, labor and struggle. What if I will that he tarry here? Look thou to and care for thine own matters." And observe, I pray thee, here also the absence of pride in the Evangelist; for having mentioned the opinion of the disciples, he corrects it, as though they had not comprehended what Jesus meant. "Jesus

---

[1] lit. "a perfect man."   [2] "saith unto him," N. T.
[3] lit. "this man."
[4] "at supper, and said, Lord, which is he that betrayeth Thee? Peter seeing him saith." N. T.

[5] "to thee? Follow thou Me." N. T.
[6] i.e. St. John.
[7] "said not unto him," N. T.   [8] al. "on account of."

said not," he tells us, "that ' he shall not die, but, If I will that he tarry.' "

Ver. 24. "This is the disciple which testifieth of these things, and wrote these things, and we know that his testimony is true."

Why is it, that then, when none of the others do so, he alone uses these words, and that for the second time, witnessing to himself? for it seems to be offensive to the hearers. What then is the cause? He is said to have been the last who came to writing, Christ[1] having moved and roused him to the work; and on this account he continually sets forth his love, alluding to the cause by which he was impelled to write. Therefore also he continually makes mention of it, to make his record trustworthy, and to show, that, moved from thence,[2] he came to this work. "And I know," he saith, "that the things are true which he saith. And if the many believe not, it is permitted them to believe from this." " From what?" From that which is said next.

Ver. 25. "There are also many other things which Jesus did, the' which, if they should be written every one, I suppose that even the world itself could not contain the books that should be written."

" Whence it is clear that I could not have written to court favor; for I who, when the miracles were so many, have not even related so many as the others have, but omitting most of them, have brought forward the plots of the Jews, the stonings, the hatred, the insults, the revilings, and have shown how they called Him a demoniac and a deceiver, certainly could not have acted to gain favor. For it behooved one who courted favor to do the contrary, to reject[3] the reproachful, to set forth the glorious." Since then he wrote what he did from full assurance, he does not decline to produce his own testimony, challenging men separately to enquire into and scrutinize the circumstances. For it is a custom with us, when we think that we are speaking exactly true, never to refuse our testimony; and if we do this, much more would he who wrote by the Spirit. What then the other Apostles when they preached declared, he also saith; "We are witnesses of the things spoken,[4] and the Spirit which He hath given[5] to them that obey Him." (Acts v. 32.) And besides, he was present at all, and did not desert Him even when being crucified, and had His mother entrusted to him; all which things are signs of his love for Him, and of his knowing all things exactly. And if he has said that so many miracles had taken place, marvel thou not, but, considering the ineffable power of the Doer, receive with

faith what is spoken. For it was as easy for Him to do whatever He would, as it is for us to speak, or rather much easier; for it sufficed that He should will only, and all followed.

[3.] Let us then give exact heed to the words, and let us not cease to unfold and search them through, for it is from continual application that we get some advantage. So shall we be able to cleanse our life, so to cut up the thorns; for such a thing is sin and worldly care, fruitless and painful. And as the thorn whatever way it is held pricks the holder, so the things of this life, on whatever side they be laid hold of, give pain to him who hugs and cherishes them. Not such are spiritual things; they resemble a pearl, whichever way thou turn it, it delights the eyes. As thus. A man hath done a deed of mercy; he not only is fed with hopes of the future, but also is cheered by the good things here, being everywhere full of confidence, and doing all with much boldness. He hath got the better of an evil desire; even before obtaining the Kingdom, he hath already received the fruit here, being praised and approved,[6] before all others,[7] by his own conscience. And every good work is of this nature; just as conscience also punishes wicked deeds here, even before the pit. For if, after sinning, thou considerest the future, thou becomest afraid and tremblest, though no man punish thee; if the present, thou hast many enemies, and livest in suspicion, and canst not henceforth even look in the face those who have wronged thee, or rather, those who have not wronged thee.[8] For we do not in the case of those evil deeds reap so much pleasure, as we do despondency, when conscience cries out against us, men, without, condemn us, God is angered, the pit travailing to receive us, our thoughts not at rest. A heavy, a heavy and a burdensome thing is sin, harder to bear than any lead. He at least who hath any sense of it will not be able to look up ever so little, though he be very dull. Thus, for instance, Ahab, though very impious, when he felt this, walked bending downwards, crushed and afflicted. On this account he clothed himself in sackcloth, and shed fountains of tears. (1 Kings xxi. 27.) If we do this, and grieve as he did, we shall put off our faults as did Zacchæus, and we too shall obtain some pardon. (Luke xix. 9.) For as in the case of tumors,[9] and fistulous ulcers,[10] if one stay not first the discharge which runs over and inflames the wound, how many soever remedies he applies, while the source of the evil is not stopped, he doth all in vain; so too if we stay not our hand from covetousness, and check not that evil afflux of wealth, although we give alms, we do all to no

---

[1] al. "God."
[2] i.e. by his love.
[3] al. "conceal."
[4] "His witnesses of these words."
[5] "Holy Spirit which God hath given." N. T.
[6] lit. "admired."
[7] or, "all other things."
[8] i.e. in wronging thee, have not wronged thee, because thou deservest punishment.
[9] al. "diseases."
[10] συρίγγων.

purpose. For that which was healed by it,[1] covetousness coming after is wont to overwhelm[2] and spoil, and to make harder to heal than before. Let us then cease from rapine, and so do alms. But if we betake ourselves to precipices, how shall we be able to recover ourselves?[3] for if one party (that is, alms-doing) were to pull at a falling man from above, while another was forcibly dragging him from below, the only result of such a struggle would be, that the man would be torn asunder. That we may not suffer this, nor, while covetousness weighs us down from below, alms-doing depart and leave us, let us lighten ourselves, and spread our wings,[4] that having been perfected by the riddance of evil things, and the practice of good,[5] we may obtain the goods everlasting, through the grace and lovingkindness of our Lord Jesus Christ, with whom to the Father and the Holy Ghost be glory, dominion, and honor, now and ever and world without end. Amen.

---

[1] i.e. by the alms. [2] al. "undo."
[3] lit. "recover breath."

[4] lit. "expand ourselves."
[5] Sav. and Ben. "everlasting goods." But MSS. omit αἰωνίων.

# THE HOMILIES OF ST. JOHN CHRYSOSTOM,

ARCHBISHOP OF CONSTANTINOPLE,

ON THE

## EPISTLE TO THE HEBREWS

*The Oxford Translation Revised, with Introduction and Notes, by*

## REV. FREDERIC GARDINER, D.D.,

LATE PROFESSOR IN THE BERKELEY DIVINITY SCHOOL, MIDDLETOWN, CONN.

# PREFACE.

THIS volume completes the series of St. Chrysostom's Homilies on the New Testament. Translated a quarter of a century ago by the Rev. T. Keble, Vicar of Bisley, and revised with great labor in the use of the then existing editions by his brother, the Vicar of Hursley, it was thought best to delay the publication until Dr. Field had completed the long-delayed publication of the Greek Text. This appeared in 1862.

The editing of the text of St. Chrysostom's Homilies is attended with peculiar difficulties. Written sermons,[1] if ever preached in those days, were the exception. Those which have been preserved to us have been generally taken down by some hearer. St. Augustine afterwards revised his, when brought to him for the purpose. In the case of St. Chrysostom's Homilies on the Acts of the Apostles, as well as of the present volume, there are two distinct texts still extant: that originally taken down by the short-hand writer, and another, when this had been polished and made neat at a subsequent time. Dr. Field's great labor then in the Greek Text of the present volume had been to restore the older form of these Homilies. He had ample material, both in Greek MSS., in a Catena published not many years ago by our Dr. CRAMER, Principal of New Inn Hall, which exhibit the older text (the former half of a second Catena, compiled by Niketas,[2] Archbishop of Heraclea in Thrace in the eleventh century, and published by the same Dr. Cramer, appears to use both) ; and, of yet more importance, in Latin versions.

Cassiodorus, an Italian, who lived about 150 years after St. Chrysostom, in the earlier part of his treatise, *de Institutione Divinarum Litterarum*, cap. 8. (opp. t. ii. p. 543, ed. Rotom. 1679) in describing a volume of St. Paul's Epistles, in which 13 of the Epistles had a good commentary, goes on, " But in regard to the Epistle to the Hebrews which St. John Bishop of Constantinople treated of in Greek in 34 homilies, we have caused Mutianus, a most eloquent man, to translate them into Latin, that the order of the Epistles might not be unduly broken off."

To Cassiodorus then we owe the Latin version of Mutianus which has come down to us, and which, translated from the older form of text, has been a great assistance in the editing. It is often quoted in the foot-notes. In p. 167 there is also given an extract from the 13th Homily by Facundus, an African Bishop, who lived about the same time with Mutianus, but who apparently translated the passage into Latin for himself.

The short-hand writer, who took down these Homilies and thus preserved them to us, is not unknown to us. It is St. Chrysostom's dearly-loved friend the Priest Constantine or Constantius.[3] For the title is, " Homilies of St. John Chrysostom Archbishop of Constantinople on the Epistle to the Hebrews, published after his decease, from notes by Constantine, Presbyter of Antioch."

---

[1] See an animadversion of St. Cyril Alex. on those who committed to writing other people's sermons and thus preserved what might have been less deliberately uttered as though it had been thoroughly well weighed. *De Ador*. viii. t. i. 267. See also the constantly occurring expressions in St. Augustine, which belong to the natural extemporaneous delivery, but which would be untrue in the delivery of written sermons. The Preface to the first volume of St. Augustine on St. John, in this Library, written by the Rev. H. Browne, contains interesting details of St. Augustine's preaching. Fleury remarks of Atticus, Archbishop of Constantinople, in the beginning of the fifth century, just after St. Chrysostom's decease, " His sermons were indifferent, so that no one took the trouble to take them down in writing." Fleury, *Eccles. Hist.* xxii. 9, p. 133, Oxford translation. The extract, however, which St. Cyril has preserved of Atticus (*de recta fide ad Arcadiam Marinamque*, repeated in his *Apol. adv. Episcopos Orientales*, cap. 4) is eloquent and pious.

[2] Dr. Cramer had published this from the Paris MS. Cod. Reg. 238, which contains the first half only: but the whole catena is extant in the Library of St. Ambrose at Milan (E. 63 part inf.).

[3] Montfaucon observes that the Manuscripts frequently interchange the name.

At the beginning of St. Chrysostom's exile in 404, when he was in Nicæa, in a Letter which he wrote to Constantius about a mission which he had set on foot at Phœnicia (Ep. 121 t. iii. pp. 721, 722, ed. Montf.), he begs him "not to cease having a care for the Churches of Phœnicia and Arabia and the east, and to write to" St. Chrysostom "quite often, and tell him how many Churches had been built in a year and what holy men had gone into Phœnicia." Soon after, Constantius seems to have asked leave of St. Chrysostom to join him; for in his 13th letter to Olympias on arriving at Cocussus or Cucusus in Cappadocia, now Goksyn, his bitter place of exile, St. Chrysostom says (ib. p. 594), "My Lord, the most pious priest Constantius, would fain have been here long ago, for he wrote to me begging that I would let him come." About this time, perhaps while Constantius was on his actual journey to Cucusus, St. Chrysostom writes to him (Ep. 225, p. 724), grieved at not having heard from him, and speaks of their great love for each other and of Constantius' goodness to the poor, the fatherless and widows: soon after he writes from Cucusus to Elpidius bishop of Laodicea (Ep. 114, p. 656), "the most reverend priests Constantius and Euethius are here with us." There are extant two Letters of Constantius, one of them to his mother, written while he was companion of St. Chrysostom there (pp. 731 and 734). In the course of this banishment St. Chrysostom writes (Ep. 123, pp. 663, 664) about this Phœnician mission to "the priests and monks in Phœnicia, who were instructing the Gentiles there," encouraging them in their work, and saying that he had given orders that all their expenses " in clothing, shoes, and support of the brethren should be bountifully supplied," and adds that they will know about his affairs from Constantius' letter. In a letter to Gerontius (Ep. 54, p. 623) written during this exile about the mission in Phœnicia, St. Chrysostom says that he had intrusted Constantius to give Gerontius all he needed whether " for building or for the needs of the brethren."

To Constantius' piety we owe the preservation of these Homilies. One very special value of them lies in the pious fervent exhortation at the end of each, on Penitence, Almsgiving, or whatever St. Chrysostom had at the time chiefly in mind, breathing forth words from a heart, filled with the love of GOD and that longed for his flock to partake it.

HOM. 1 on sin and Almsgiving
2 on high thoughts and on poverty and wealth
3 on God's gifts to each
4 on heathen practices at funerals
5 on temptation
6 on Heaven
7 on old age
8 on study of Scriptures
9 on Penitence and confession of our sins
10 on relieving distress
11 on Almsgiving and giving to beggars
12 on free-will and Penitence
13 on not postponing Baptism and on a right life
14 on Thought of GOD and earnest prayer
15 on sin-enslavement and on untimely laughter
16 on dwelling in Heaven
17 on worthily receiving Holy Communion
18 on the Might of Poverty
19 on the great Gain of loving one's neighbor
20 on slavery to possessions and on Thankfulness
21 on gossip
22 on seeking GOD, on His protection and enduring Temptation
23 on the loss of GOD
24 on the acquirement of Virtue

25 on not caring for things of the world nor partaking with the covetous
26 on loyalty to GOD
27 on the might of Prayer and on minding us that we are sinners
28 value of Affliction and on simplicity of life and adornment of the soul
29 on the Peril of Luxury
30 on helping each other in way of salvation
31 on Penitence and keeping in mind our sins
32 on the Might of mercifulness to others
33 on the value of affliction, trial, poverty, and on Thankfulness
34 on using with intensity of mind and purpose, the Grace of the SPIRIT.

After the publication of Dr. Field's text (*Bibliotheca Patrum Ecclesiae Catholicae Qui ante Orientis et Occidentis schisma floruerunt,* tom vii. Oxonii 1862) the translation was again very carefully revised by that text by the Rev. Dr. BARROW, Principal of St. Edmund Hall : he also wrote heads for the present Preface. The headings were given (as far as could be done) in the MS. and many of them have been retained ; others, fitting in less well with the printed page, seemed to need a little modification. For an occasional note enclosed in brackets, the son of the one remaining Editor of the Library is responsible.

P. E. PUSEY.

OXFORD, May, 1877.

[It has seemed better in this edition to conform the translation of the Scripture texts to some one standard. St. Chrysostom used the current text of his day, which, on the whole, was more like the *Textus Receptus,* the basis of the A. V., than the more critical text followed by the R. V. It has therefore seemed best to take the A. V. as the standard (except where St. Chrysostom has followed a different text), but note has been made of any variations of the R. V. materially affecting the sense. There remain a number of loose quotations and combinations of different texts, and in these the English translation is retained.

Effort has been made to simplify the language and remove involved constructions in the translation of the Homilies. The English translation was originally made from the Benedictine, and afterwards revised from Field's more accurate text, and the differences between these have sometimes been overlooked. Besides this, it has often been possible to give St. Chrysostom's meaning more accurately, — sometimes even reversing the sense. There are, however, many very felicitous translations in the English edition which have been retained. It is a revision, and not a new translation.

All the notes in the English edition have been scrupulously retained, additions being enclosed in square brackets, with the initials of the reviser. An introduction on the authorship of this Epistle has been inserted. — F. G.]

[Published after his decease. — F. G., jr.]

# INTRODUCTION.

## BY THE AMERICAN REVISER.

In the following Homilies St. Chrysostom assumes throughout St. Paul's authorship of the Epistle, and in his opening Homily deals with considerable ingenuity with several of the most obvious objections to the Pauline authorship.

The Epistle, however, is anonymous, and is not attributed to St. Paul by the most ancient historical testimony which has come down to us, nor is his authorship generally recognized by modern criticism. It is interesting, therefore, to enquire whether St. Chrysostom, in adopting the prevailing view of his time, did so on sufficient grounds.

The history of the matter is very curious. At the close of the second century Tertullian speaks positively and unhesitatingly of the Epistle to the Hebrews as written by Barnabas, the early and long-continued companion of St. Paul.[1] But there happened to be current in the ancient Church another epistle ascribed to Barnabas, and then commonly received as his, though generally considered spurious. The two epistles were so entirely unlike that no one could well receive them both as from the same author. The result was different in different parts of the Church. In the West, although the Epistle to the Hebrews had been used very largely by Clement of Rome, it came to be discredited altogether, and did not secure general recognition until the fourth century; it was then gradually acknowledged and attributed, at first doubtfully, but afterwards by common consent, to St. Paul. In the East, on the other hand, the Epistle itself was firmly accepted from the first, but with no certain tradition and much questioning in regard to its author. The suggestion of its Pauline authorship seems to have been made by Pantænus, the teacher of Clement of Alexandria, and a contemporary of Tertullian. We have his opinion, however, only at third hand, in a quotation preserved by Eusebius[2] from a lost work of Clement, and it is impossible to tell on what grounds he rested his opinion, or whether it was a mere personal speculation, like the reason he gives for the omission of the name of St. Paul in connection with the Epistle.

His disciple Clement adopted the suggestion not without hesitation. No one familiar with Greek, which was still the current language of the East, and especially of Alexandria, could fail to be struck by the extreme difference of style between this Epistle and those of St. Paul. Clement, therefore, conjectured that it might have been originally written by St. Paul in Hebrew and translated into Greek by St. Luke. This again is second-hand opinion preserved to us by Eusebius.[3] Nevertheless, in other works, which are still extant, he frequently cites the Epistle as St. Paul's.

---

[1] Tertull. *De Pud.* c. 20, Ed. Migne, 1021. *Exstat enim et Barnabae titulus ad Hebraeos, adeo satis auctoritatis viro [viri], ut quem Paulus juxta se constituerit in abstinentiae tenore: . . . [1 Cor. ix. 6]. . . . Et utique receptior apud Ecclesias Epistola Barnabae illo apocrypho Pastore moechorum. Monens itaque discipulos, omissis omnibus initiis, ad perfectionem magis tendere,* . . . [After quoting Heb. vi. 4-8, he goes on] *Hoc qui ab Apostolis didicit et cum Apostolis docuit,* etc.

[2] Eusebius' *Eccl. Hist.* vi. 14 (Crusé's translation, p. 213). "But now, as the blessed presbyter used to say, 'since the Lord who was the Apostle of the Almighty, was sent to the Hebrews, Paul by reason of his inferiority, as if sent to the Gentiles, did not subscribe himself an apostle of the Hebrews; both out of reverence for the Lord, and because he wrote of his abundance to the Hebrews, as a herald and apostle of the Gentiles.'"

[3] *Ibid.* The Epistle to the Hebrews he asserts was written by Paul to the Hebrews in the Hebrew tongue, but that it was carefully translated by Luke and published among the Greeks. Therefore one finds the same character of style and of phraseology in the Epistle as in the Acts. "But it is probable that the title, Paul the Apostle, was not prefixed to it. For as he wrote to the Hebrews, who had imbibed prejudices against him and suspected him, he wisely guards against diverting them from the perusal by giving his name."

Clement was succeeded in his catechetical office at Alexandria by Origen, a profound thinker and scholar. He was strongly impressed with the difference between the Greek of this and of the Pauline Epistles, and speaks of the matter in different parts of his voluminous works, sometimes suggesting the Clementine hypothesis, sometimes speaking of the variety of opinions and traditions on the subject, sometimes speaking of St. Luke or of Clement of Rome as the probable author, but summing up his perplexity (in language, quoted fully by Eusebius), by saying that who really was the author, God only knows.[1]

Thus far the question of authorship was evidently an open one on which every one was free to hold his own opinion, or uncertainty of opinion. Tertullian speaks of the authorship of Barnabas simply as a fact, without an allusion to any doubt on the matter. But as the time went on, the attention of the masters of thought in the Church became more and more engrossed with doctrinal questions, while those of exegesis and criticism more and more lost their interest, especially in the East. In the West there is no trace of any reference of the authorship of the Epistle to St. Paul until the middle of the fourth century; but after this the opinion spread rapidly, and under the influence of Augustine, in the year 393 somewhat hesitatingly, but in 419 positively, the provincial council of Carthage reckoned it among the Pauline Epistles. Augustine himself, however, sometimes expressed himself doubtfully, and although it had now become customary to quote the Epistle as St. Paul's, yet scholars like Jerome, when distinctly treating of the question, express the old doubts and uncertainties of Origen. The assumption of the Pauline authorship was a convenience in maintaining the authority of the Epistle, and there being almost no one to call it in question, had come to be generally adopted in St. Chrysostom's time, and remained almost unquestioned until the revival of learning at the period of the Reformation. Since then, while still remaining a popular impression, it has come to be rejected by the great majority of careful students.

In this variety of opinion from the earliest times, and in the absence of any consistent external evidence, we are plainly left free to form our own conclusions from internal evidence. Among the great number of authors suggested by different writers, the only names entitled to especial consideration are those of St. Paul (Chrysostom, Augustine, and later writers generally until modern times, but at present the only scholar of weight is Hofmann), St. Luke (besides the views of ancients given above, Calvin, Ebrard, Döllinger, and to a certain extent Delitzsch), Clement of Rome (Erasmus, Reithmaier, Bisping), Silas (Mynster, Böhme, Godet), Apollos (Luther, Semler, De Wette, Tholuck, Bunsen, Kurtz, Farrar, De Pressensé, Bleek, Hilgenfeld, Lünemann, Alford), and Barnabas (Ullmann, Wieseler, Ritschl, Grau, Thiersch, Weiss, Renan, Keil). Of the three first we have genuine writings with which to make a comparison; of the three last—assuming the spuriousness of the so-called Epistles of Barnabas—nothing remains.

The supposition of the authorship of St. Paul, although so long carelessly held, seems almost forbidden by an expression in the Epistle itself. St. Paul was always most strenuous in asserting that he had received his apostleship and his knowledge of the truth "not of man, neither by man, but by Jesus Christ, and God the Father" (Gal. i. 1), while the author of this Epistle ranks himself among those who had received through the medium of others that Gospel "which at the first began to be spoken by the Lord, and was confirmed unto us by them that heard Him" (ii. 3). All attempts to weaken the force of this evidence by considering the passage as merely an instance of the rhetorical figure *koinosis*, in which the writer identifies himself with his readers, and thus attributes to himself what properly belongs only to them, have been unsuccessful. Delitzsch considers that if the Epistle were the joint work of St. Paul and St. Luke, in which the former only supplied the general course of thought, leaving its expression entirely to

---

[1] Eusebius' *Eccl. Hist.* vi. 25. Extended quotations from the various writers above referred to, and from many others, may be found in almost any of the innumerable treatises on the subject, and are given with especial fullness and clearness in Alford's *Prolegomena*.

the latter, even this expression, so singularly like Luke i. 1, 2, might have been used; but this can only be by a practical surrender of the Pauline authorship. St. Paul everywhere lays such emphasis on the fact that his presentation of Christian truth was in no way whatever derived from man, but was from express divine instruction given to himself personally, that this passage must form a presumption against the Pauline authorship so strong as to be set aside only by clear and positive evidence. It has already appeared that there is no such external evidence; the internal will be examined below.

The authorship of Clement of Rome may also be set aside on two grounds: (1) That he quotes largely from this Epistle with the whole air of one citing from a higher authority to confirm his own teachings; and (2) that his own manner and style, as well as intellectual power, is so unlike as to make the supposition of a common authorship scarcely conceivable.

The early suggestion that the Epistle may have been written in Hebrew by St. Paul, more or less fully, and translated by St. Luke or St. Clement, or some other of his companions more or less paraphrastically, can find no favor with the modern scholar. If such a supposition is meant to leave the work essentially a translation, it encounters all the difficulties already mentioned against the Pauline authorship, and besides is opposed to abundant evidence that the work was originally written in Greek. "It abounds in compound words which are essentially Greek, which have no analogues in Aramaic or in Hebrew,"[1] and it contains *paronomasia*, entering into the thought, which could only be possible in Greek. If, on the other hand, it is meant to express merely some connection of St. Paul with the thought and line of argument of the Epistle, it really gives up the Pauline authorship, and even this thread of connection may be found in the sequel difficult to retain.

In favor of the authorship of St. Paul so far as the ideas and essential argument of the Epistle are concerned, Origen urges the beauty of the thoughts, and there must be some force in this argument, or the Epistle could hardly have been so long and so widely attributed to him. Perhaps it may be summed up in the words of an eminent and now departed divine,[2] "If the Epistle were not written by St. Paul, then we have the remarkable phenomenon that there were two men among the Christians of that age who were capable of writing it." The theory has also a certain *primâ facie* probability, and offers a convenient way of reconciling the conflict of the external evidence. But of course it cannot be accepted merely on these grounds.

At the outset, on a general view of the Epistle, every one must be struck with the marked difference in its construction from any of St. Paul's Epistles. The omission of his name at the beginning has been more or less satisfactorily accounted for from ancient times, but the reasons for this do not apply to the absence of any sort of salutation, "any heading or introductory thanksgiving," by which St. Paul always takes pains to conciliate his readers, and of which there was especial need if he were writing to Hebrews disposed to prejudice against him. On the contrary, after the manner of St. Mark in his Gospel, the writer strikes directly into his subject, without any sort of preface. Another striking feature of difference is, that St. Paul always keeps close to his argument until it is completed, and then adds practical exhortations founded upon it, while in our Epistle each short division of the argument is separated from that which follows by its appropriate practical application. This indicates quite a different habit of mind, and it is difficult to fancy such a severely logical reasoner as St. Paul thus pausing in the flow of his argument. The style of the Epistle is so markedly different from that of St. Paul that attention has been drawn to this point from the time of Origen down. The "rounded oratorical periods" of the Hebrews are very unlike the "unstudied, broken, abrupt phraseology" of St. Paul. This difference might, in part at least, be accounted for as the work of the translator; only in that case, the translator could have been neither St. Luke, whose style is clear and smooth enough, but not at all oratorical, nor Clement, whose style is very unlike.

---

[1] Godet in *The Expositor*, April, 1888, p. 262.  [2] Bp. George Burgess.

When we come to details, there are two passages which have been thought to favor a Pauline authorship. There is a quotation in Heb. x. 30, which, it is alleged, agrees precisely with the same quotation in Rom. xii. 19, but differs from either the Hebrew or the Greek of Deut. xxxii. 35. The A. V. makes a slight variation in language between Romans and Hebrews, but the *Textus Receptus* of the original is the same : "Vengeance is mine ; I will recompense, saith the Lord." Now the LXX reads, "In the day of vengeance I will recompense"; the Hebrew, "mine [are] vengeance and recompense." If, however, we examine any critical text, we shall find that the clause "saith the Lord," is rejected as a gloss in this Epistle, while undisputed in Romans, thus constituting a difference between them. It is still true, however, that they both differ in the same way from the Hebrew and the LXX. This might be a difficulty were it not that the quotation as it is in this Epistle is found exactly in the Targum, and from that had probably passed into familiar use. Everywhere else the author of Hebrews quotes very closely from the LXX, and from that in what is known as its Alexandrine form, while St. Paul uses the Vatican text, quotes far more loosely, and often follows the Hebrew rather than the Greek.

The other passage really gives no clear indication at all, and as far as it goes, is rather at variance with Pauline authorship. In xii. 23 the writer says, "Know ye that our brother Timothy is set at liberty ; with whom, (if he come shortly,) I will see you." It is of course possible that Timothy may have been imprisoned, at Rome or elsewhere, when St. Paul was with him ; but as far as we know the history of the two, it seems unlikely. The passage might quite as well have been written by almost any of the companions of St. Paul who were also associated with Timothy.

When now, enquiry is made as to the indications to be found in the choice of words and construction of sentences, there is certainly room for some difference of opinion. Delitzsch has endeavored throughout his commentary on this Epistle to show that there is such a striking similarity between it and the writings of St. Luke as to favor decidedly the view that it was written by him ; Lünemann, on the other hand, in the introduction to his commentary, has collected the instances of Delitzsch and remarks upon them, "So soon as we separate therefrom that which is not exclusively peculiar to Luke and the Epistle to the Hebrews ; so soon as we also put out of the account that which Luke has only taken up out of the sources employed by him, and cease to lay any weight upon isolated expressions and turns of discourse which were the common property either of the Greek language in general, or of the later Greek in particular, and are only accidentally present in Luke and the Epistle to the Hebrews, — there is nothing whatever left of an actual affinity, such as must of necessity admit of being traced out between the works of the same author." The fact seems to be that there is between these two writers as compared with the other New Testament writers a certain similarity, not so much of particular words and constructions, as of the general cast, both of the phraseology and the structure of the sentences ; but that this similarity arises, not from the identity of the writers, but from the fact that both wrote in somewhat better Greek than is found in the rest of the New Testament. The grammars of the New Testament Greek continually refer to the fact, that certain classical constructions are found only, or at least more frequently, in these writers than elsewhere. But this does not prove more than that the author of this Epistle, as might easily have been the case with several of the companions of St. Paul, like St. Luke, was more accustomed to classical Greek usage than most of the earliest Christian writers.

An examination of the vocabulary of this Epistle in comparison with that of St. Paul, St. Luke, and the other New Testament writers will throw some light upon the question. In another place [1] I have made such an examination with some care, and will here give a summary of its results. It is to be borne in mind that this Epistle is much shorter than the collective writings of St. Paul, or St. Luke, or of the other New Testament writers taken together. By a careful

---

[1] *Journal of the Soc. of Bibl. Literature and Exegesis* for June, 1887, pp. 1-27.

estimate of the actual length of these four groups it is found that, taking the longest as the standard, in order to determine the relative use of any word in them, it is necessary to multiply the number of its occurrences in St. Luke by 1.57, in St. Paul by 1.86, in Hebrews by 11.56. The results may in many instances prove fallacious. Any writer may use a word several times, even in a short passage, which he would not have used again had his writing been greatly extended; or he may not use a particular word once in twenty pages, when he will employ it several times in the twenty-first. Such facts must be borne in mind, but the above process seems to be the only means of making a comparative statement in figures; and when it is applied to a large number of words, and especially to whole groups of words which correspond to certain classes of ideas, the general result must have a decided bearing upon the question of authorship.

It has often been noticed that the number of words peculiar to any New Testament writer is an index of the number freely at his command. Peculiar words, it is true, are often required by peculiarity of subject, and may sometimes be what is called accidental. Still, when the number of them in any writer is unusually large, the fact has its value, and such words do abound in the writings of St. Luke and in the Epistle to the Hebrews above all others.[1] No great importance perhaps should be attached to this point; yet as it is often brought forward, the exact facts should be ascertained. Excluding words occurring only in quotations from the LXX (which can have no bearing upon the characteristics of the writer), and also excluding words which depend on doubtful readings, the number of words found in the New Testament only in the Gospel of St. Luke is 249, in the Acts 414, in both taken together 724; the similar number in the much shorter Epistle to the Hebrews is 147, while even the Apocalypse, with all its peculiar subjects and imagery, has but 116, and none of the other books (except Matthew 114) reach as high as 100. This suggests that the writer of this Epistle was like St. Luke in having at his command a peculiarly rich vocabulary. But if the facts be looked at in another way, and the comparative length of the various books taken into consideration, a different result is reached. St. Luke's Gospel has one peculiar word to every 9.76 lines; Acts, one to every 5.77; Hebrews, one to 4.45; but 1 Timothy has one to every three lines; 2 Timothy, one to 3.22; Titus, one to 2.97; James, one to 3.5; and so on with several of the shorter epistles. The result of such statistics appears to depend much upon how they are manipulated. Nevertheless, in no book of nearly equal, or of greater length, is the proportion so large as in this Epistle, except in the Acts. If the writings of various authors be taken collectively, —

> St. Luke has 724 peculiar words = 1 to every  6.66 lines.
> St. Paul has 777 peculiar words = 1 to every  5.25 lines.
> Hebrews has 147 peculiar words = 1 to every  4.45 lines.
> St. John has 244 peculiar words = 1 to every 13.46 lines.
> All others taken together have 378 peculiar words = 1 to every 11.38 lines.

On the whole, then, the first impression of every reader is confirmed: St. Paul, St. Luke, and the author of Hebrews are alike distinguished from the other New Testament writers by the comparative richness of their vocabulary; yet, in view of the peculiar subjects treated in this Epistle, this fact has less significance than it might be entitled to under other circumstances.

Another question may be asked of the same kind. May not some indication of authorship be found in the number and character of the words common only to the Hebrews with St. Paul, with St. Luke, and with the other writers respectively? There are 34 words common to St. Luke and Hebrews, and found nowhere else; to St. Paul and Hebrews, 46; to all others and Hebrews, 28. Or, proportioning these numbers to the length of the several books, common to Luke and Hebrews, 53.5; to St. Paul and Hebrews, 85.56; to other writers and Hebrews, 28; or nearly twice as many common to Hebrews with St. Luke, and more than three times as many

---

[1] See Thayer's *Grimm's N. T. Lexicon*, Appendix iv. pp. 698–710, for lists of words peculiar to each New Testament writer.

common to Hebrews with St. Paul, as there are common to Hebrews with other writers. This examination tends like the other, but much more strongly, to connect this Epistle both with St. Luke and St. Paul, but especially with the latter. It falls in with the vacillating opinion of Origen, already given, and with his report of the current traditions of his time.

But much more important than the mere numerical statement, is the character of some of these words, used in common by these writers and by no others. Most of them, indeed, have nothing characteristic, and many are used but once by each of the writers, and that apparently without any special design. There are several, however, worthy of more consideration. The noun καταπαύσις and the verb καταπαύω, which might be expected to be common enough, are used only in Luke and Hebrews, the noun once in Luke, eight times in Hebrews; the verb 11 times in Luke, three times in Hebrews; or together, 12 times and 11 times. The noun μέτοχος is used once in Luke, five times in Hebrews, and nowhere else, while the verb μετέχω is used five times by St. Paul, three times in Hebrews, and by no other writer. Διατίθεμαι occurs three times in Luke, twice in Hebrews, and nowhere else. Συναντάω is used four times in Luke, twice in Hebrews, and not elsewhere. The word for *star* in Greek has either form, ἄστρον or ἀστήρ, and both are common in the LXX; but the former is used exclusively by St. Luke (three times) and also in Hebrews, where, however, it occurs but once; but ἀστήρ is used exclusively by all the other New Testament writers, by St. Paul three times, by others 21 times. On the other hand, ἐνδείκνυμι occurs twice in Hebrews, nine times in St. Paul, and in no other writer. The verb εὐαρεστέω (occurring three times) is peculiar to Hebrews, as is also the adverb εὐαρέστως, while the adjective εὐάρεστος occurs once in Hebrews, and seven times in St. Paul, being found nowhere else in the New Testament. The striking adverb ἐφάπαξ, not found in any other New Testament writer, occurs three times in Hebrews and twice in St. Paul. The verb λειτουγέω with the nouns λειτουγία and λειτουργός and the adjective λειτουργικός, though common enough in the LXX, and apparently sufficiently often called for, are used in the New Testament only by St. Luke, St. Paul, and in Hebrews. The verb occurs once in each of them; λειτουργία is used once by St. Luke, three times by St. Paul, twice in Hebrews; λειτουργός three times by St. Paul, twice in Hebrews; while the adjective occurs only once in the last; *i.e.* taking the whole group together, it is employed twice by St. Luke, seven times by St. Paul, and six times in Hebrews, and never elsewhere. The much more important word μεσίτης is used only in St. Paul and Hebrews, three times in each. The same is true of ὁμολογία, a word which might have been expected more frequently. There seems to be nothing peculiar about ὀνειδισμός which yet happens to be found only in St. Paul (three times) and in Hebrews (twice). The words παιδεία and παιδευτής also occur only in these writers, the former four times, the latter once in St. Paul; the former twice, the latter once in Hebrews; or together, five times and three times. We are surprised to find such a word as πληροφορία only in these writers, in each of them twice. The remarkable word ὑπόστασις, afterwards in another sense of so much importance theologically, is found only in these writers, in St. Paul three times, in Hebrews twice.

The results of this comparison have a positive value, unless they can be, at least in some good degree, paralleled by words common to Hebrews and the other New Testament writers. I do not find this to be the case. There seem to be but two words common only to Hebrews and to any of them occurring more than once in each. One of these is the purely accidental word ἕβδομος, used twice in Hebrews, and seven times elsewhere (five times in Revelation); and the other is the more important word βαπτισμός (always in the plural = purifying ablutions) used twice each in Mark and Hebrews. Whatever value, therefore, there may be in this examination of common words, it is much increased by the almost entire absence of any such relation between this Epistle and the other writings of the New Testament. It certainly points, as far as it goes, to some sort of relation between the three writers, St. Luke, St. Paul, and the author of Hebrews, and especially between the two last.

We now turn to common words of wider range which yet have something in their usage tending to show the style of the writer. The verb ἔρχομαι with its compounds ἀπ'-, ἐπ'-, ἐξ-, εἰσ-, κατ-, παρ-, and προσ-, is naturally more common in narrative. Making allowance for this, we are surprised at its relative frequency in Hebrews and infrequency in the Pauline Epistles, while the word is in such common use as to make this difference significant. The proportionate numbers are : Hebrews, 519 ; St Luke, 656 ; St. Paul, 169 ; all others, 708. For the particular compound εἰσέρχομαι, the same numbers are : Hebrews, 196 ; St. Luke, 133 ; St. Paul, 7 ; all others, 91. While it is relatively much the most frequent in Hebrews, it is yet common in St. Luke, but almost entirely avoided by St. Paul.

Λαμβάνω with its compounds ἐπι-, παρα-, and ὑπο-, have a similar variable usage. They are all relatively much more frequent in Hebrews than elsewhere, less common in St. Luke, and still less so in St. Paul ; taking the simple verb and its compounds separately, St. Luke alone uses that with ὑπό (four times actually, or relatively, six times), and almost entirely avoids that with παρά, and St. Paul, like the other writers, that with ἐπί ; while Hebrews uses them all (except ὑπό) with peculiar frequency. The proportionate numbers are : —

|  | HEBREWS. | ST. LUKE. | ST. PAUL. | ALL OTHERS. |
|---|---|---|---|---|
| λαμβάνω . . . . | 196 | 80 | 61 | 157 |
| ἐπι- . . . . . | 34 | 19 | 4 | 4 |
| παρα- . . . . | 139 | 1 | 20 | 25 |
| ὑπο- . . . . . | — | 6 | — | — |
| Total . . . | 369 | 106 | 85 | 186 |

The verbs employed for *request* or *prayer* are numerous, and their employment by the different writers varies much. The following list of their relative frequency shows the principal facts : —

|  | HEBREWS. | ST. LUKE. | ST. PAUL. | ALL OTHERS. |
|---|---|---|---|---|
| αἰτέω . . . . . | 11 | 330 | 7 | 46 |
| ἀπ- . . . . . | — | 3 | — | — |
| ἐξ- . . . . . | — | 2 | — | — |
| ἐπ- . . . . . | — | 3 | — | — |
| παρ- . . . . . | 35 | 6 | 7 | — |
| προσ- . . . . | — | 1 | — | 2 |
| δεόμαι . . . . | — | 8 | 9 | 1 |
| ἐπιθυμέω . . . . | 11 | 23 | 11 | 5 |
| ἐρωτάω . . . . | — | 31 | 7 | 37 |
| εὐχόμαι . . . . | — | 3 | 6 | 2 |
| Total . . . | 57 | 410 | 47 | 93 |

While St. Matthew habitually designates heavenly things by the *plural* (gen. or dat.) of οὐρανός, and is somewhat followed by the other writers, the author of Hebrews and St. Paul employ these forms very little, and are almost alone in availing themselves of the compound adjective ἐπουράνιος for the same purpose. St. Luke uses this word only once ; Hebrews, six times ; St. Paul, twelve times ; all others, twice. On the other hand, the simple οὐράνιος is not used at all in Hebrews and St. Paul, but occurs twice in St. Luke, and four times elsewhere.

The words λαλεῖν and λέγειν are both common enough, and the distinction between them is well recognized. The point to be noticed is the frequency of their use relatively to each other. Hebrews uses them in the proportion of 1 : 2 ; St. Paul the same ; St. Luke, 1 : 3½ ; all others, 1 : 7 nearly. St. Luke here varies considerably from Hebrews and St. Paul, but far less than the others.

The Hebraistic πρόσωπον, so frequent in the LXX, is found but once in Hebrews, and then in an allusion to the LXX; but curiously occurs 27 times in St. Luke, as many in St. Paul, and in all others 22. So also ῥῆμα is a common enough word; but in its Hebraistic sense, corresponding to *dabar, a thing*, the subject-matter of speech or command, its use is confined to St. Luke, and it does not occur either in Hebrews or elsewhere. Both ὑπάρχω and ὑποστρέφω are favorite words with St. Luke. The former occurs in his writings 34 times, is not found at all in Hebrews; is used by St. Paul 11 times, and only four times elsewhere; the latter is used by St. Luke 31 times, and elsewhere only once each in Hebrews, St. Paul, and St. Mark. Κατεργάζομαι is a Pauline word (21 times), never used in Hebrews, and but three times elsewhere (Jas. 2, Pet. 1). On the other hand, the use of the comparatives κρείσσων and πλείων, with the superlative πλεῖστος, is far more common in Hebrews. The comparative numbers are: for κρείσσων, Hebrews, 150; St. Luke, 0; St. Paul, 7 (he also used the adverb κρεῖσσον once); all others, 2. For πλείων πλεῖστος, Heb. 46; St. Luke, 42; St. Paul, 19; all others, 17.

I do not recall any other words of this kind, the usage of which affects our enquiry. Such inferences as may be drawn from this examination are somewhat contradictory. They certainly do not point to the author of this Epistle as either St. Paul or St. Luke, as they might be expected to do if such were the fact. There are some striking similarities of diction; but the differences are, at least, quite as important.

It is time now to turn to those adverbs, particles and prepositions, which bring out the grammatical form in which a writer is accustomed to clothe his ideas. But before speaking of these, mention must be made of one grammatical form peculiarly characteristic of the nicety and subtlety of thought of the classic Greek writers — the optative mood. This subject has been investigated by Dr. Harman with great care. He finds that this mode is used in the whole New Testament 66 times, 32 of them in the Pauline Epistles, 28 in the writings of St. Luke, once in Hebrews, and five times in all other writers. "In nearly all the cases in which the optative occurs in the New Testament it is used to express a *wish* or *prayer*, except in the writings of Luke." "In the *Epistle to the Hebrews* we find one instance of the optative, καταρτίσαι, '*May* God *make* you perfect' (xiii. 21). This is presumptive proof that an Alexandrian did not write this Epistle, as it is not likely that the use of this mode in but one instance would have satisfied his fine Greek taste." [1]

The usage of the particles, adverbs and prepositions, require so much detail that only a summary can here be given with a reference to the paper on the "Language of the Epistles to the Hebrews," already mentioned.

The particles μέν and δέ would naturally be more common in narrative; but as between Hebrews, St. Paul, and the other Epistles, they are relatively most frequent in Hebrews. The same is true of the conjunction τε, which is more common in St. Luke and St. Paul than in other New Testament writers. The adversative ἀλλά is common enough everywhere, not even the shortest epistle being without more than one instance of its use. St. Luke and Hebrews employ it very much more seldom; but again, St. Luke uses it far less than Hebrews. The three writers, St. Luke, St. Paul, and the author of Hebrews, are distinguished from the other writers by the (comparatively) sparing use of ἄν and ἐάν, but of the three, St. Luke employs it most, and St. Paul least. Hebrews alone uses ἐάνπερ, but never ἐάν μή, which is employed in St. Luke with moderate freedom, by St. Paul twice as often, and still more frequently by the other writers. In the case of διό, St. Paul uses it relatively only half as often as Hebrews, but three times as often as St. Luke, and the last more than twice as often as the other writers. In the use of διότι, a much less common word, there is a less difference, but still a marked one and in the same order.

---

[1] "The Optative Mode in Hellenistic Greek," by Prof. H. M. Harman, D.D., LL.D. *Journal of Soc. of Bibl. Lit. and Exegesis,* Dec. 1886, p. 10.

The pronouns of the first and second person are used, as might be expected, most abundantly by St. Paul; but Hebrews is singularly shy of them. This fact has been noticed and an explanation offered on the ground that the work has more the character of a treatise than of a personal epistle; but this explains too much, since these personal pronouns, though relatively infrequent, are still very common in our epistle. The author was not disposed to bring forward the personality of either himself or his hearers. St. Paul, on the contrary, used these pronouns more than twice as often as our author, and indeed far more frequently than any other New Testament writer.

The case of the third person of the pronoun is peculiar, since its frequent redundant use is one of the marked characteristics of the New Testament diction; yet St. Paul uses it less than half as often as Hebrews. The same is true of the demonstrative ἐκεῖνος; but in the use of the reflective ἑαυτός, St. Paul is largely in excess. The difference in the use of these pronouns between Hebrews and St. Luke is not very great; but, in regard to the two first particularly, the difference from the other writers is marked, and St. Paul's usage of all of them is very different. On the other hand, in the use of οὗτος, Hebrews is strongly separated from St. Luke and less so from St. Paul.

The words ἀλλήλων, ἄλλος, ἕτερος, τίς (interrog.), and τις (indef.) have marked peculiarities in their frequency of employment by the different writers, but it is enough to instance here ἄλλος, employed oftener by St. Paul than by St. Luke and Hebrews put together, and yet by the other writers collectively twice as often as by him; and ἕτερος used with exactly the same frequency by St. Luke and St. Paul, less than one quarter as often by other writers, but far oftener in Hebrews than in any of them. So also with ἕκαστος, τοιοῦτος, and τοσοῦτος: they are all used with exactly the same frequency in Hebrews; but while the first is used by St. Paul much oftener, the last is used only one-fourteenth as often. The usage of St. Luke is markedly different from that of either.

Further and more detailed examination of words of this class would be out of place here. Suffice it to say that such an examination shows a marked individuality in the usage of the several writers; and it is to be remembered that Hebrews, Acts, and the latter Epistles of St. Paul must have been written with no great interval of time between them.

The same things are true in whatever way we test the forms of expression of these writers. If we take the particle εἰ with its various combinations εἰ καί, εἰ μή, εἴγε, εἰ δὲ μή, εἰ μή τε, εἴ περ, εἴ πως, εἴ τε, εἴ τις, we shall find that only the first two of these combinations occur in Hebrews at all, and those only once each, while all of them are found in the Pauline Epistles, and all but three of them in the writings of St. Luke. The whole group together is used more than twice as often by St. Paul as by any other writer.

Adverbs of space are very sparingly used by St. Paul, with an approach to equality between Hebrews and St. Luke, but twice as often by other writers. In the various particles and adverbs of negation, there do not seem to be, on the whole, very noticeable peculiarities, although μηδείς and μηδέ occur but once each in Hebrews, while the former is everywhere else common, and the latter also in St. Paul and other writers, though less frequent in St. Luke. But the word χωρίς is frequent enough in Hebrews to be considered characteristic, is used far less by St. Paul, only once by St. Luke, and comparatively seldom by other writers. Πάλιν is quite rare in St. Luke, equally common in Hebrews and St. Paul, and a little less so in the other writers. The use of ἤ is very rare in Hebrews whether as a disjunctive conjunction, or as a term of comparison. In the latter sense it occurs but once, and in the former only four times, two of which are in quotations from the LXX, and a third in a more than doubtful reading. In all the other New Testament writers it is very common, but most of all in St. Paul. In the use of μᾶλλον, however, though St. Paul still exceeds, Hebrews most nearly approaches his usage. The causal ἐπεί is five times as frequent in Hebrews as in St. Paul, and yet four times more frequent in his writings than in the others, and is still less common in St. Luke than in them. The word πῶς is used but once in Hebrews (interrogatively), while it is common enough everywhere else. Both ἵνα and ὅτι are used very often by St. Paul and the other writers, and much more sparingly in Hebrews; but St. Luke uses ἵνα much less than half as often as Hebrews, while he employs ὅτι much more than half as often again. The un-Attic particle καθώς, the adverbs οὕτως, ὡσεί, ὥσπερ, and the conjunction ὥστε, are all appropriate to trains of reasoning, but their usage in the different writers, particularly in the three we are especially considering, is very various. The same may be said of the prepositions, among which σύν is never used in Hebrews (except in composition), while it is employed much oftener by St. Luke than by St. Paul or any other writer.

It may be thought that all this examination — still tedious, though much condensed — is not worth the trouble. It goes to show, what has always been noticed by every reader, that the style of this Epistle is unlike that of St. Paul; but if it show, as it seems to do quite as clearly, that it is unlike that of St. Luke as well, something has been gained. It makes it at least improbable that St. Luke wrote the Epistle to give expression to the ideas of St. Paul.

It remains to examine some words of another class. There are many words and groups of words so peculiarly appropriated to certain ideas or shades of thought, that the use or non-use of them becomes a fair index of the habitual tone of thought of the writer. If he use them frequently, the phase of truth which they represent must have been prominent in his mind; or if he seldom employ them, then that aspect of truth was not the predominant one from his point of view. Such words or groups of words may be of different degrees of importance; but even those of inferior significance help to complete the picture of the writer's mental habits, and it is therefore well to examine all that are at all characteristic. As the force of the evidence from these words can only be brought out by a more careful examination of them, I venture to copy some pages of the paper referred to above.

The group ἀγαπάω, ἀγάπη, and ἀγαπητός is noteworthy. They are very common in the Pauline writings, but are rare both in St. Luke and in Hebrews. In fact only one of them, ἀγαπητός, occurs at all in the Acts, and none of them are ever used by St. Luke except in recording the words of others. So also of the Hebrews. Of the five instances of their use, two are in quotations from the LXX. They are common enough in other writers, but are especial favorites of St. John. Of the 154 instances in "other writers," 109 are in St. John, so that the words may be called Pauline and Johannean. Their rarity in St. Luke and Hebrews may be partly explained by the fact that ἀγάπη is an exclusively biblical word, and that ἀγαπάω also is used in a higher sense in the sacred than in profane writings. Still they were common words in the Christian community, and they mark a distinction in thought between St. Luke and Hebrews on the one side, and St. Paul and the rest of the New Testament on the other. The actual number of instances of their use is: Hebrews, 5 times; St. Luke, 15; St. Paul, 135; all others (John, 109), 154; but if we exclude from the enumeration all quotations from the LXX, and all record of the words of others, the numbers become: Hebrews, 3; St. Luke, 0; St. Paul, 132; all others (John, 43), 87. The comparison is too obvious to call for proportionate numbers. As an appendix to this group it may be mentioned that φιλέω never occurs in Hebrews, is used only twice by St. Luke, twice by St. Paul, and 21 times elsewhere, 15 of which are in St. John.

A word especially appropriate to Hebrews, and one which might have been expected there very often, ἁγιασμός, occurs but once, while it is used eight times by St. Paul, and is not found in the rest of the New Testament. On the other hand, αἷμα, which we might have expected frequently in St. Paul as well as in Hebrews, is very common in the latter and not at all so in the former. Proportionate numbers are: Hebrews, 231 times; St. Luke, 31; St. Paul, 24; all others, 44. Here, from the nature of the writings, we may not be surprised at the commonness of the word in Hebrews; but its comparative rarity in St. Paul is remarkable. His subjects led to it, and had it come to his mind as readily as it did to that of the author of Hebrews, it must have occurred in his writings much oftener.

The group of words, ἀλήθεια, ἀληθής, ἀληθινός, ἀληθῶς, and ἀληθεύω, which we are accustomed to consider peculiarly Johannean, is also very frequent in St. Paul, but comparatively rare in St. Luke and Hebrews. The actual numbers are : Hebrews, 4 (ἀληθινός three times, ἀλήθεια once) ; St. Luke, 12 ; St. Paul, 55 ; all others, 114 (of which St. John, 95).

Of the group ἀσθενεία, ἀσθενέω, ἀσθένημα, and ἀσθενής, only two occur in Hebrews — ἀσθενεία (four times) and ἀσθενής (once). The actual occurrences of the whole together are : Hebrews, 5 times ; St. Luke, 15 ; St. Paul, 43; all others, 21 ; or proportionately, Hebrews, 58 ; St. Luke, 23 ; St. Paul, 90 ; all others, 21. This is evidently an especially Pauline class of words.

The words of opposite signification, βέβαιος, βεβαιόω, βεβαίωσις, — very infrequent in the LXX, — do not occur at all in St. Luke, and are relatively far more frequent in Hebrews than anywhere else. The proportionate numbers are : Hebrews, 92 times ; St. Luke, 0 ; St. Paul, 15 ; elsewhere, 3. Evidently St. Paul preferred to dwell upon weakness, the author of Hebrews upon strength.

There is a similar contrast between the verb ἐλπίζω and the noun ἐλπίς on the one hand, and the verb ἐπαγγέλλομαι and the noun ἐπαγγελία on the other. Κληρονομέω, κληρονομία, and κληρονόμος are most common in Hebrews. The proportionate numbers are : —

|  | HEBREWS. | ST. LUKE. | ST. PAUL. | ALL OTHERS. |
|---|---|---|---|---|
| ἐλπίζω and ἐλπίς . . . . . . . | 69 | 20 | 100 | 10 |
| ἐπαγγέλλομαι and ἐπαγγελία . . . | 208 | 16 | 57 | 9 |
| κληρονομέω, κληρονομία, κληρονόμος . | 104 | 11 | 33 | 8 |
| Together . . . . | 381 | 47 | 190 | 27 |

It is plain that while the author of Hebrews dwelt much more upon the brightness of the future than any other writer, he preferred to speak of it in the light of *promise* and of *inheritance*, while it rested in St. Paul's mind more as a *hope*. This is the more noteworthy because the ideas of sonship and of adoption are very common in St. Paul. He alone uses the word υἱοθεσία five times.

The words ἡμέρα and σήμερον are curiously infrequent in a writer of the present urgency of St. Paul, and are relatively most common in St. Luke and Hebrews, but most so in the last. In proportion the numbers are : Hebrews, 278 ; St. Luke, 207 ; St. Paul, 100 ; all others, 153. That is, Hebrews uses them nearly three times as often as St. Paul.

The names for God and for our Lord are used by the various writers with much difference, and with an evident preference in each of them for his own accustomed word. The proportionate numbers (which can take no note of periphrases) are as follows : —

|  | HEBREWS. | ST. LUKE. | ST. PAUL. | ALL OTHERS. |
|---|---|---|---|---|
| θεός . . . . . . . . . . . . | 774 | 463 | 1016 | 419 |
| Κύριος . . . . . . . . . . . | 185 | 335 | 524 | 213 |
| Ἰησοῦς . . . . . . . . . . . | 150 | 255 | 405 | 519 |
| Χριστός . . . . . . . . . . | 150 | 69 | 562 | 102 |

In all cases St. Paul uses these words most freely (about twice as often as anybody else), except that in the case of Ἰησοῦς he is exceeded by "other writers" as a result of the large amount of narrative contained in them. Θεός is used in Hebrews next in frequency to St. Paul, but with a long interval between them, and very much more often than elsewhere. Κύριος is used least frequently in Hebrews, while Ἰησοῦς and Χριστός are employed there, one with exactly the same frequency as the other, though St. Luke, St. Paul, and the other writers employ them very unequally, one preferring one and another the other. The use of these words is so much a matter of habit, habit alike of writing and of mode of thinking, that these go far to differentiate the writers.

Κήρυγμα, κῆρυξ, and κηρύσσω are none of them ever used in Hebrews. For the others proportionate numbers are : St. Luke, 27 times ; St. Paul, 35 ; all others, 20.

The group καυχάομαι, καύχημα, and καύχησις is almost exclusively Pauline, occurring in his writings 58 times, while it is nearly absent from Hebrews, only καύχημα being used, and that but once. These words do not occur in the other New Testament writers except three times in James. So also λογίζομαι and μακροθυμία are especially Pauline. They each occur only once in Hebrews. The first is found twice, the second not at all in St. Luke ; but λογίζομαι occurs 34 times in St. Paul, four times in other writers, while μακροθυμία is used by St. Paul ten times, and only three times elsewhere.

Μανθάνω is used 16 times by St. Paul, only once each by Hebrews and St. Luke, and seven times elsewhere. Παρακαλέω and παράκλησις are much more frequent in St. Paul's writings than elsewhere, but in this case he is more nearly approached by Hebrews than by others — yet with a great difference. Proportionate numbers are : Hebrews, 81 ; St. Luke, 54 ; St. Paul, 137 ; all others, 22. The word προσευχή occurs in Hebrews but once, and προσεύχομαι not at all. This is a noteworthy omission in our epistle, although it is also true that they are not used by St. John, except προσευχή three times in Revelation. The two words are found in St. Luke and St. Paul each 33 times, and in the other writers 43 times. The words σάρξ and σαρκικός are favorites of St. Paul. They occur seven times in Hebrews, six times in St. Luke, 102 times in St. Paul, and 46 times (of which one-half are in St. John) elsewhere. Proportionately Hebrews uses them about two-thirds as often as St. Paul, and nearly twice as often as all other writers together. The group φρονέω, φρόνημα, and φρόνησις is characteristic. None of them are found at all in Hebrews, and they occur but twice in St. Luke, and twice in the other writers (Matthew, 1, Mark, 1, in parallel passages), both in the record of the words of others ; but St. Paul uses them 31 times. (He uses φρόνημα, however, only in Romans — four times.) A word used in a figurative sense especially characteristic of St. John (31 times), φῶς, never occurs in Hebrews. It is used 16 times by St. Luke, 12 times by St. Paul, and ten times by other writers. It is more or less used by every New Testament writer except the author of Hebrews, and St. Jude in his very short epistle. Χαίρω is also used by every other writer (St. Luke, 19 times ; St. Paul, 27 times), except Hebrews and St. Jude. St. Paul greatly delights in the word χάρις, and in the idea conveyed by it ; he never wrote an epistle without it, and uses it 101 times. In Hebrews it is found eight times, in St. Luke 24, and in all others 22, not occurring in the first two Gospels.

The foregoing list is somewhat long of words characteristic of phases of thought which are especially favorite with St. Paul, and either wholly unused or much less frequently employed in Hebrews. A corresponding list may be made of other words especially common in Hebrews, but less used by St. Luke and St. Paul. Before going to this, however, a few words are to be considered which in their frequency of usage are characteristic of all three, or of two of these writers as distinguished from others, although with some differences between them.

Most prominent in this latter class is νόμος, which we are accustomed to think especially Pauline. It is indeed used much oftener by St. Paul than by any other writer, yet it also occurs in Hebrews with a frequency distinguishing that Epistle from any other writing. The proportionate numbers are : Hebrews, 162 ; St. Luke, 44 ; St. Paul, 227 ; all others, 33. Nevertheless, the assimilation here is more apparent than real ; for St. Paul employs it chiefly of a method of salvation, while it refers in Hebrews mostly to a definite collection of statutes. In the same way πίστις is usually regarded as a characteristically Pauline word. It is relatively much more common in Hebrews ; for the proportionate numbers are : Hebrews, 369 ; St. Luke, 42 ; St. Paul, 262 ; all others, 43. But here also there is a shade of distinction in the force of the word as used by the two writers ; St. Paul's πίστις is reliance upon Christ as the means of salvation in opposition to the law and the works of the law, while in the Hebrews it is only a general reliance on God's grace and promises. Of course, it is not denied that St. Paul sometimes uses a word, so common, in such varied shades of meaning, in a more general way as in 1 Cor. xiii. 2, 13 ; xvi. 13 ; 2 Cor. v.

7, etc.; but the distinction in the shade of meaning between his habitual employment of the word, and that common in the Epistle to the Hebrews is easily recognized. In this connection πιστεύω must be mentioned, though belonging in the former category. The proportionate instances of its use are: Hebrews, 23; St. Luke, 76; St. Paul, 100; all others (of which St. John, 99), 143. It is therefore a comparatively rare word in Hebrews. The adjective πιστός, which ought perhaps hardly to be considered in this connection, is used proportionately, in Hebrews, 58 times; St. Luke, 6; St. Paul, 61; all others, 23. Πείθω somewhat associates the three writers together, although most frequent in Hebrews, occurring proportionately, in Hebrews, 58 times; St. Luke, 33; St. Paul, 43; all others, 6. Συνειδέω and συνείδησις are used proportionately: Hebrews, 58; St. Luke, 8 (all in Acts); St. Paul, 37 (but συνειδέω only once); all others, 4. The word σωτήρ, though used by St. Luke four times, St. Paul 12, and by others eight times, never occurs in Hebrews; but this is not remarkable, as it is not found in the much larger books of Matthew, Mark, and Revelation; moreover, it should be taken in connection with σωτηρία and σωτήριον, which also do not occur in the first two Gospels, but are found in Hebrews 7 times, St. Luke 13, St. Paul 19, and all others 9 times. This would give them a relatively greater frequency in Hebrews; but they are also common words in St. Luke and St. Paul. The word ψυχή, while a little more common relatively in Hebrews, is yet frequent enough in St. Luke and other writers, though not a favorite with St. Paul. Proportionate numbers are: Hebrews, 69; St. Luke, 57; St. Paul, 29; all others, 54.

This leads to the third class of words — those which, embodying certain sets of ideas, are characteristic of Hebrews in distinction from other writers, especially St. Luke and St. Paul. One of these is the idea of *witness*, expressed by μάρτυρ, μάρτυς, μαρτυρία, μαρτύριον, μαρτυρέω, and μαρτύρομαι. This group of words is especially common in Hebrews, and much less frequent in St. Luke and St. Paul. It is also very common in St. John. The proportionate numbers are: Hebrews, 127; St. Luke, 45; St. Paul, 50; all others (of which St. John, 80), 96. The word τάξις is so naturally called for in the argument of Hebrews that there is nothing remarkable in its occurring there seven times, while in all the rest of the New Testament it is found but three times (St. Paul twice, St. Luke once). The group τέλειος, τελειότης, τελειόω, τελείως, τελείωσις, and τελειωτής, is more significant. The words do not occur with great frequency, but they mark a distinct Christian thought, and are relatively far more common in Hebrews than anywhere else. The proportionate numbers are: Hebrews, 162; St. Luke, 8; St. Paul, 19; all others, 20 (one-half of which are in St. John). The perfection and finality of Christian truth as set forth in this epistle comes out in the frequency of the use of these words as clearly as in its general scope; it is difficult to suppose that the Epistle to the Galatians, e.g., which does not contain any of these words, could have been written by the same author.

But by far the most important word in this connection is ἱερεύς, with its various derivatives, ἀρχιερεύς, ἱερατεία, ἱεράτευμα, and ἀρχιερατικός. The last two of these are of little importance, as ἱεράτευμα occurs only twice, in St. Peter, and ἀρχιερατικός only once, in Acts; also ἱερατεία occurs only once each in St. Luke and Hebrews, and nowhere else. Altogether, ἱερεύς and its compounds and derivatives occur 159 times, but are never once used by St. Paul.[1] The actual numbers are, for ἱερεύς: Hebrews, 14 times; St. Luke, 9; St. Paul, 0; all others, 9; for ἀρχιερεύς, Hebrews, 17; St. Luke, 37; St. Paul, 0; the other Gospels, 68, but never elsewhere. This is a remarkable fact. In view of St. Paul's arguments in the epistles to the Romans and to the Galatians, and in view of the frequency and emphasis with which he insists in all his Epistles, upon the sacrificial character of Christ's death, it seems to show that his mind was so absorbed in dwelling upon the value and power of the sacrifice that he was not in the habit of thinking or speaking of Christ as also Himself the Sacrificer. Redemption came to his thought through the medium of the Victim by whom it was obtained, but not through that of the Priest who offered the Victim. This is the more

---

[1] The word ἱερουργοῦντα (ἀπ. λεγ.) in the highly figurative passage, Rom. xv. 16, is no exception, being derived not from ἱερεύς, but from ἱερός.

striking from the fact that he often speaks of Christ as giving Himself, offering Himself, and the like; but always for the purpose of bringing out the voluntariness and the love of the act, and never with any allusion to its priestly character. The line of reasoning in the Epistle to the Hebrews was thus quite foreign to the habitual thought of St. Paul. Such similarity of language to his acknowledged writings as exists must be accounted for in some other way.

On looking back over these various words, with their difference of usage, it is plain that they are not perfectly of accord in their indications. This was to be expected. I have endeavored, in this part of the examination, to select only words characteristic of thought, and to note every word of this kind in regard to which there is any considerable difference of usage; yet so many words are used by every writer accidentally, as it were, and not because they are characteristic, that much allowance is to be made. Still, the investigation seems to me to afford a sufficient basis for some probable conclusions. The Epistle contains both style-words and thought-words, characteristic alike of St. Luke and St. Paul, sometimes of one, sometimes of the other, sometimes of both; and these must be taken into account in any theory of the authorship. But they are not more than might be expected in any writer belonging among the companions of a leader of such magnetism and power as St. Paul. I see nothing in them to prove, hardly even to suggest, actual authorship. On the other hand, there are many words and groups of words expressing ideas very prominently in the mind of the author of this Epistle, which must have appeared also in the writings of St. Paul had the thoughts of this Epistle been derived from him, but which are not found there. Of course, no man expresses all his ideas in any one epistle, nor the same ideas in every one he writes; but the difference here is more radical. As one mind now is affected by one, and another by another of the various aspects of Christian truth, so the differences here go to show that the mind of the author of Epistle to the Hebrews was not affected in the same way as St. Paul; for Hebrews is scarcely more unlike the Epistles in which St. Paul addressed believing Jews than the speeches recorded in Acts xiii., xxii., and xxviii., in which he spoke to his still unbelieving countrymen. This leaves us free to accept the author's own statement, that instead of being, like St. Paul, one who had received his apostleship "not of man, neither by man, but by Jesus Christ, and God the Father" (Gal. i. 1), he was of that number who had received through the medium of others that Gospel "which at the first began to be spoken by the Lord, and was confirmed unto us by them that heard Him" (Heb. ii. 3).

It thus appears that neither are the thoughts of this Epistle Pauline, nor is its language that of St. Luke. It may be well to say a few words in conclusion as to the person to whom such facts as we have point as the probable author.

It is plain from what has been said, as well as from the common consent of students, that the author must be looked for among those companions of St. Paul who, through prolonged intercourse, were likely to have their modes of expression somewhat affected by his language. The number of these is considerable, and after so many ages of uncertainty, beginning with the earliest discussion of the subject, it is not likely that the right one can ever be pointed out with certainty. Many modern critics have selected Apollos as the most probable author, chiefly because of the facts recorded of him in Acts xviii. 24–28, that he "was born at Alexandria, an eloquent man and mighty in the Scriptures," and that after receiving further instruction from Aquila and Priscilla, "he mightily convinced the Jews, and that publicly, showing by the Scriptures that Jesus was Christ." He was certainly personally known to St. Paul (1 Cor. xvi. 12), although of the length of time they may have been together we have no information. His being an Alexandrian is thought to explain what some are pleased to consider an Alexandrian tone of thought in the Epistle, and also the fact that its quotations are from the LXX, and accord rather with its Alexandrian than its Vatican recension. The force of the last point is not obvious. In the meagreness of our knowledge of the original LXX, it appears probable that the so-called Alexandrian recension was the one generally current in the Levant, and therefore that this indication, whatever it may be worth, simply points to an Oriental author. And so also whatever there may be of an Alexandrian caste of thought in the Epistle only indicates some one familiar with Jewish-Alexandrian literature, and this would include almost every educated Jew living in the Levant.[1] At all events, neither of these considerations seemed to have occurred to any of those early Alexandrian scholars, Pantænus, Clement, or Origen, who all speak of the authorship, the last at some length and with discrimination. The theory of Apollos' authorship has, however, this great advantage : that no line of his remains to compare with our Epistle. It has also these disadvantages : that it never occurred to any ancient author, but was first suggested by Luther ; that there is no evidence of any prolonged personal intercourse between him and St. Paul ; and that there is nothing to connect him with any especial interest in, or familiarity with, the Jewish ritual and temple beyond the simple fact that he was a Jew, as was also almost every other writer who has ever been suggested. The non-use of the optative is also strongly against the authorship of the Alexandrian Apollos. Moreover, it is clear from such passages as vii. 12 ; x. 32–36 ; xiii. 7, 17–19, 23–25, that this Epistle was addressed to some particular community, a fact now generally recognized, and that the author was personally and favorably known to his readers. There is a difference of opinion in regard to the locality of that community ; but if, as seems altogether probable, it was Palestinian, we have no reason to suppose that Apollos was ever known to them ; and although this evidence is only negative, it suggests looking for some other names positively in accord with it.

Of the other names suggested in ancient and modern times St. Luke and St. Clement of Rome seem to be sufficiently excluded by a comparison of the Epistle with their acknowledged writings ; the former also by the probability that he was a Gentile, the latter by the very use he makes of the Epistle, apparently as quoting words of another.[2]

Silas has also been suggested as a possible author. Of him we know even less than of Apollos. He was a prophet in the early Church at Jerusalem (Acts xv. 32), and was the companion of St. Paul on his second missionary journey and subsequently in his labors at Corinth, and was also associated with the work of St. Peter (1 Pet. v. 12). In all this there is nothing to mark him out as the one likely to have written this Epistle beyond several others of the companions of St. Paul. The only point which really gives plausibility to the suggestion of his authorship is the fact that he was much associated with Timothy (1 Thess. i. 1 ; 2 Thess. i. 1 ; 2 Cor. i. 19), and this may explain the reference to Timothy in Hebrews xiii. 23. On that ground the suggestion of his name might be adopted if there were not much more to be said in favor of another, and also if there were not the same very serious objection as in the case of Apollos — that he was never so much as named in all antiquity.

There is a person, however, to whose authorship one of the very earliest witnesses, Tertullian, as already noted, positively and unhesitatingly testifies, — Barnabas.[3] He has the same advantage with Apollos in having transmitted to us no writing with which to institute a comparison

---

[1] But that the *style* indicates that the Epistle was not actually written by an Alexandrian may be gathered from the non-use of the optative mood. See the reference to Dr. Harman on p. 348.

[2] If the question be asked how Clement of Rome should have been so familiar with this Epistle, the sufficient answer is, that if this Clement be the same with the Clement mentioned in Phil. iv. 3, as is altogether probable and as is generally asserted in the fathers, they were both companions of St. Paul, though whether they were with him at the same time is not known, and so one of them was likely to know and value the work of the other. Moreover, nearly all the varying traditions about Barnabas concur in speaking of his preaching at Rome, where he would have become personally known to Clement, and whence he may have written this Epistle. If he planted the Church at Milan, as is asserted in the title and proper preface for St. Barnabas Day, in the Ambrosian liturgy, he must have passed through Rome on his way.

[3] Tertullian *De Pudicitia*, c. 20, Tom. II., fol. 1021, ed. Migne. It is well known that the Pauline authorship of the Epistle was rejected by many of the ancients. Eusebius (*Eccl. Hist.* vi. 20) mentions that in the list of Caius, Presbyter at Rome (cir. 200), only thirteen epistles of Paul are enumerated, and this is omitted. It is also omitted in the Muratonian fragment, if that be not the same. The *Codex Claromontanus* (6th cent.) was copied from a MS. not containing Hebrews, but gives at the end of Philemon a stichometrical catalogue of all the books of the Old and New Testaments, and then gives our Epistle. In the catalogue, however, before Revelations and Acts, and immediately after Jude, is mentioned the " Epistle of Barnabas," having 850 lines. It has been conjectured that by this may be meant the Epistle to the Hebrews; for 1 Corinthians is put down at 1060 lines, and this would give, in proportion, very nearly the right length for our Epistle, making Hebrews 826 instead of 850 lines, whereas the spurious " Epistle of Barnabas " is nearly one-half longer. (See Salmon, *Introd. to the N. T.*, note at end of xxi., 2d ed., pp. 453, 454.) This conclusion is controverted by Lünemann, *Introd. to Heb.*, sect. i., p. 23, ed. T. & T. Clark.

(the spuriousness of the epistle attributed to him being admitted,)[1] and in having been a Hellenistic Jew, likely to have written somewhat better Greek than St. Paul. His birthplace also was in the Levant, in Cyprus, where he could have had the full benefit of Alexandrian literature. Being at Jerusalem he became one of the very early converts to Christianity, long before St. Paul, and he was a man of property and benevolence; for although a Cypriote, he had land in Jerusalem and sold it to relieve the necessities of the early Christian community (Acts iv. 36, 37). He must have been known from the first very generally in the Hebrew-Christian community, and he must have been endeared to them, not merely by this act of benevolence, but by that kindly sympathy which led to his surname, "Son of consolation." A very few writers, indeed, have identified him with "Joseph called Barsabas, who was surnamed Justus," of Acts i. 23, and this is countenanced by the Codex Bezæ and the Æthiopic reading βαρνάβαν; and in this case he must have been an original disciple, and would be excluded by the language of Heb. ii. 3. But there seems to be no ground for the identification. In Acts iv. 36 the language implies that Barnabas is there spoken of for the first time, the names themselves are different, and Barsabas was known by the surname of Justus, which does not appear to have been ever given to Barnabas. He is next heard of as bringing Saul, of whom all were afraid, to the apostles, and telling the story of his conversion (Acts ix. 26, 27), showing at once the position he occupied and his own moral courage. When tidings of the conversion of many Gentiles at Antioch came to the Church at Jerusalem, they sent forth Barnabas to take charge of the matter, and by his labors "much people was added to the Lord." The work growing too great for him, he sought out Saul at Tarsus and brought him to his assistance (Acts xi. 25, 26). Then after a year, the Church at Antioch sent Barnabas and Saul to carry their alms to the Church at Jerusalem. Having returned to Antioch, they were divinely selected to go forth upon a wider missionary work, in the course of which they visited "Lystra and Derbe," when probably the young Timothy received his first knowledge of Christianity. On St. Paul's second visit to these cities he is spoken of as already "a disciple." Barnabas must, therefore, have known him from the very beginning of his Christian life, and it is, therefore, entirely natural that he should speak of him in the way recorded in Heb. xiii. 23. After Barnabas and Paul returned from this, when disputes arose between the Jews and Gentiles, they were sent to Jerusalem together, and having obtained a favorable hearing before the Council again returned to Antioch. Here are years of closest companionship between Barnabas and St. Paul, during all the earlier part of which Barnabas appears as the leader, Paul as the assistant. They had often stood together in the synagogue to tell to their fellow-countrymen the story of the cross, and probably had often discussed with one another the best way of presenting truth to the Jewish mind, and they had shared together the charge of the numerous Jewish converts. Barnabas must have been a man of dignity, for when the people of Lystra took them for gods, they selected Barnabas as Jupiter (Acts xiv. 11, 12). The companionship was broken up at the entrance upon another missionary journey, by a difference of opinion about taking Mark with them. In this case Barnabas, although doubtless influenced by his kinship, appears to have been the better judge of character, since at a later date St. Paul writes from Rome to Timothy, " Take Mark and bring him with thee; for he is profitable to me in the minis-

---

[1] The following memorandum of the authorities for and against the genuineness of the Epistle of Barnabas, and for its date, has been kindly furnished by the Rev. E. C. Richardson, Librarian of the Hartford Theological Seminary: —

*Genuineness, etc. For:* Origen, Clement of A., Eusebius, Hieron., Apost. const., Voss, Hammond, Pearson, Bull, Cave, Du Pin, Grynaeus, Wake, Lardner, Fleury, Le Nourry, Russel, Galland, Less, Rosenmüller, Muenscher, Stäudlin, Danz, Bertholdt, Hemsen, Schmidt, Henke, Bleek, Rördam, Gieseler, Näbe, Credner, Bretschneider, Guericke, Francke, Gfrörer, Möhler, Baumgarten-Crusius, De Wette (?), Rysewyk, Schneckenburger, Sprinzl, Alzog, Nirschl, Sharpe. *Against:* Rivet, Usher, Menard, Daillé, Papebroch, Calmet, Cotelerius, Le Moyne, Tenzel, Natalis Alex., Ittig, Spanheim, Tillemont, Basnage, Oudin, Ceillier, Stolle, Pertsch, Baumgarten, Walch, Mosheim, Semler, Schroekh, Rössler, Starke, Lumper, Michaelis, Gaab, Lange, Hänlein, Winter, Neander, Ullmann, Mynster, Hug, Baur, Winer, Hase, Ebrard, Semisch, Kayser, Reithmayr, Hefele, MacKenzie, Lipsius, Weizäcker, Donaldson, Roberts and D., Riggenbach, Westcott, Braunsberger, Cunningham, Funk, Alford. *Interpolated:* Schenkel, Heydecke.

*Date:* Reign of Vespasian, Menardus, Ewald, Weizäcker, Milligan; 71-73, Galland; 70-100, Tischendorf (at first); reign of Domitian, Wieseler, Hilgenfeld, Riggenbach. Donaldson, Reuss, Ewald, Dressel, and Ritschl also put it in the first century. Papebroch pronounces for some time later than 97, Hefele for 107-120. Volkmar, Tischendorf (later), Baur, and others, for 119; Tentzel for the reign of Trajan; and Hug, Ullmann, Lücke, Neander, Winer, Zeller, and Köstlin for some time early in the 2d century, while Heydecke distinguishes into a genuine B., 70-71, and an interpolator, 119-121.

try " (2 Tim. iv. 11) ; but however this may be, Barnabas showed in the matter independence and determination. He is called by the name of " Apostle " (Acts xiv. 14), and altogether held such a position in the Christian community as would make his writing such an Epistle a proper act. In all that is related of him there is but one faulty act, and even this points him out as especially interested in the Hebrews. When St. Peter behaved so ill at Antioch and received the sharp reproof of St. Paul, in his account of the matter St. Paul says, " the other Jews dissembled likewise with him " ; and adds as evidence of the strength and danger of the defection, " insomuch that Barnabas also was carried away with their dissimulation" (Gal. ii. 13, 14). Barnabas then was not only a Jew by birth, but had strong sympathies with his race.

More than this : he was a Levite. The particular line of argument adopted in the main part of the Epistle to the Hebrews is one which would have occurred to few, and scarcely to any who was not familiar with the temple ritual. There is no evidence that this was the case with Apollos ; but with Barnabas the temple service was a matter of professional duty, as well as the prompting of his devout heart. Indeed, an objection to the authorship of Barnabas has been based on this very point ; — it is said that the author does not show that nicely accurate precision in his statements which might be expected from one personally familiar with the temple. The points referred to admit of easy explanation on other grounds ; but were they better taken, considering that the service of the Levites was altogether subordinate to that of the priests, and did not lead them into the ναός itself, the objection seems hypercritical. But one of the actual duties of the Levites, and a very prominent one, was that of chanting in the Levitical choirs in the courts of the temple. This would have led to a special familiarity with the Psalms. Now it is a curious fact that about one-half of all the quotations from the Old Testament in the Epistle to the Hebrews are taken from the Psalms, and that the author cites that book, relatively, nearly four times as often as St. Paul, and eight times as often as St. Luke or the other writers. This fact is at once explained by the supposition that the author of the Epistle was a Levite.[1] It is not unlikely that when that " great company of the priests were obedient to the faith " (Acts vi. 7), Barnabas, as one of their attending Levites, was influenced by their example and with them accepted the faith of Christ.

The only important objection urged against the authorship of Barnabas is, that since the time of Tertullian until recently, there has never been any considerable weight of opinion in its favor. But this is accounted for by the almost universal acceptance in the meantime of the spurious Epistle of Barnabas as his genuine work. The two certainly could not have been written by the same person. The fact, however, that the spurious Epistle was attributed to him may be an indication of a belief that he had left to the Church some legacy of written teaching. Since that Epistle has been found not to be his, and is probably of a somewhat later date, there remains nothing to hinder the belief that the devout Levite of Cyprus, the early convert to Christianity while still in strong sympathy with the Christian Jews, the man of benevolence and wealth, and therefore probably of education, by birth the appointed servant of the temple, the man of independence and dignity, and yet of such tender sympathy as to be surnamed " Son of consolation," the long and intimate companion of St. Paul, and for years in the position of his superior, —there is nothing to hinder the acceptance of the early ecclesiastical statement that he was also the author of the Epistle to the Hebrews.

FREDERIC GARDINER.

---

[1] The large proportion of quotations from the Psalms in this Epistle is noticed in the article upon it in Smith's Bible Dictionary (where the proportion is stated as 16 out of 32) ; but my attention was first called to the bearing of this upon the question of authorsnip by the quick observation of Rev. Hermann Lilienthal. It is not easy to give a precise numerical statement of the proportion because of the large number of historical allusions which can hardly be reckoned as quotations, and also because the New Testament writers often clothe their thoughts in the familiar words of the Old Testament, apparently without any conscious quotation. This matter, however, which cannot be tabulated, is quite in accord with the rest, and the whole Epistle is saturated with the language and the historical allusions of the Psalms. Taking only what may fairly be considered as designed quotations, the relative numbers taken from the Psalms are: Hebrews, 200; St. Luke, 25; St. Paul, 39; all others, 25. The Apocalypse is omitted from the calculation. In the comparatively few quotations in St. Luke less than one-third (17 out of 55) are from the Psalms, and every one of these in recording the words of others; less than one-fifth in St. Paul (16 out of 89) ; and in the others 22 out of 116. In Hebrews almost exactly one-half.

# CONTENTS.

## HOMILIES ON EPISTLE TO HEBREWS.

# HOMILIES OF ST. JOHN CHRYSOSTOM,

## ARCHBISHOP OF CONSTANTINOPLE,

### ON THE

## EPISTLE TO THE HEBREWS,

PUBLISHED AFTER HIS FALLING ASLEEP, FROM NOTES BY CONSTANTINE, PRESBYTER OF ANTIOCH.

---

## ARGUMENT,

### AND SUMMARY OF THE EPISTLE.

[1.] THE blessed Paul, writing to the Romans, says, " Inasmuch then as I am the Apostle of the Gentiles, I magnify mine office : if by any means I may provoke to emulation them that are my flesh " :[1] and again, in another place, " For He that wrought effectually in Peter to the apostleship of the circumcision, the same was mighty in me toward the Gentiles."[2] If therefore he were the Apostle of the Gentiles, (for also in the Acts, God said to him, " Depart ; for I will send thee far hence unto the Gentiles,"[3]) what had he to do with the Hebrews? and why did he also write an Epistle to them?

And especially as besides, they were ill-disposed towards him, and this is to be seen from many places. For hear what James says to him, " Thou seest, brother, how many thousands of Jews there are which believe . . . and these all have been informed of thee that thou teachest men to forsake the law."[4] And oftentimes he had many disputings concerning this.

Why therefore, one might ask, as he was so learned in the law (for he was instructed in the law at the feet of Gamaliel,[5] and had great zeal in the matter, and was especially able to con-

found them in this respect) — why did not God send him to the Jews? Because on this very account they were more vehement in their enmity against him. " For they will not endure thee,"[6] God says unto him ; " But depart far hence to the Gentiles, for they will not receive thy testimony concerning me."[7] Whereupon he says, " Yea, Lord, they know that I imprisoned and beat in every synagogue them that believed on thee ; and when the blood of thy martyr Stephen was shed, I also was standing by and consenting unto his death, and kept the raiment of them that slew him."[8]

And this he says[9] is a sign and proof of their not believing him. For thus it is : when a man goes away from any people,[10] if he be one of the least of those who are nothing worth, he does not much vex those from whom he went ; but if he be among the distinguished and earnest partisans and those who care for these things, he exceedingly grieves and vexes them beyond measure, in that[11] he especially overthrows their system with the multitude.

And besides this, there was something else.[12] What now might this be? That they who were about Peter were also with Christ, and saw signs

---

[1] Rom. xi. 13, 14.
[2] Gal. ii. 8.
[3] Acts xxii. 21.

[4] Acts xxi. 20, 21.
[5] Acts xxii. 3.

[6] " Wherefore God foreseeing this, that they would not receive Him," Ben. K. Sav.
[7] Acts xxii. 21, 18.
[8] Acts xxii. 19, 20.
[9] " they show," K. Ben.
[10] ἔθνους.
[11] " Departing from them, going to others," K. Ben. Sav.
[12] Add : " Which should make them incredulous," Bened. K. Sav.

and wonders; but he [Paul] having had the benefit of none of these, but being with Jews, suddenly deserted and became one of them. This especially promoted our cause. For while they indeed, seemed to testify even from gratitude, and one might have said that they bore witness to those things in love for their Master; he, on the other hand, who testifies to the resurrection, this man was rather one who heard a voice only. For this cause thou seest them waging war passionately with him, and doing all things for this purpose, that they might slay him, and raising seditions.[1]

The unbelievers, then, were hostile to him for this reason; but why were the believers? Because in preaching to the Gentiles he was constrained to preach Christianity purely; and if haply even in Judæa he were found [doing so], he cared not. For Peter and they that were with him, because they preached in Jerusalem, when there was great fierceness, of necessity enjoined the observance of the law; but this man was quite at liberty. The [converts] too from the Gentiles were more than the Jews because they were without.[2] And this[3] enfeebled the law, and they had no such great reverence for it, although[4] he preached all things purely. Doubtless in this matter they think to shame him by numbers, saying, "Thou seest, brother, how many ten thousands of Jews there are which[5] are come together."[6] On this account they hated him and turned away from him, because "They are informed of thee, he says, that thou teachest men to forsake the law."[7]

[2.] Why, then, not being a teacher of the Jews, does he send an Epistle to them? And where were those to whom he sent it? It seems to me in Jerusalem and Palestine. How then does he send them an Epistle? Just as he baptized, though he was not commanded to baptize. For, he says, "I was not sent to baptize":[8] not, however, that he was forbidden, but he does it as a subordinate matter. And how could he fail to write to those, for whom he was willing even to become accursed?[9] Accordingly he said,[10] "Know ye that our brother Timothy is set at liberty; with whom, if he come shortly, I will see you."[11]

For as yet he was not arrested. Two years then he passed bound, in Rome; then he was set free; then, having gone into Spain, he saw Jews[12] also in like manner; and then he returned to Rome, where also he was slain by Nero. The Epistle to Timothy then was later[13] than this Epistle. For there he says, "For I am now ready to be offered"[14]; there also he says, "In my first answer no man stood with me."[15] In many places they [the Hebrew Christians] had to contend[16] with persecution, as also he says, writing to the Thessalonians, "Ye became followers of the churches of Judæa":[17] and writing to these very persons he says, "Ye took joyfully the spoiling of your goods."[18] Dost thou see them contending? And if men had thus treated the Apostles, not only in Judæa, but also wherever they were among the Gentiles, what would they not have done to the believers? On this account, thou seest, he was very careful for them. For when he says, "I go unto Jerusalem to minister unto the saints";[19] and again, when he exhorts the Corinthians to beneficence, and says that the Macedonians had already made their contribution,[20] and says, "If it be meet that I go also,"[21] —he means this. And when he says, "Only that we should remember the poor; the same which I also was forward to do,"[22] —he declares this. And when he says, "They gave to me and Barnabas the right hands of fellowship; that we should go unto the heathen, and they unto the circumcision,"[23] —he declares this.

But this was[24] not for the sake of the poor who were there, but that by this we might be partakers in the beneficence. For not as the preaching did we apportion the care for the poor to each other (we indeed to the Gentiles, but they to the circumcision). And everywhere thou seest him using great care for them: as was reasonable.

Among the other nations indeed, when there were both Jews and Greeks, such was not the case; but then, while they still seemed to have authority and independence and to order many things by their own laws, the government not being yet established nor brought perfectly under the Romans, they naturally exercised great tyranny. For if in other cities, as in Corinth, they beat the Ruler of the synagogue before the Deputy's judgment seat, and Gallio "cared for none of these things,"[25] but it was not so in

---

[1] "For this purpose, and raising seditions that they might slay him," Bened. A. K.

[2] "The chosen people being *fewer than all people*, encircled on all sides by the heathen"; see Mic. v. 7, 8.

[3] "By this he enfeebled," Ben.

[4] "Because," Ben. Sav. K. Q. R.

[5] Acts xxi. 20.

[6] "which believe," Ben. Sav. K. Q.

[7] Acts xxi. 21.

[8] 1 Cor. i. 17.

[9] Rom. ix. 3.

[10] St. Chrys. introduces this as an instance of St. Paul's interest in the Hebrews: that he not only wrote to them, but also intended to visit them; and on that digresses to the events of his history and the relative date of his Epistles.    [11] Heb. xiii. 23.

[12] [The text might perhaps leave it uncertain whether St. Chrys. meant to state that St. Paul saw Jews in Spain, or that, after visiting Spain, he went into Judæa. Ben. Sav. K. Q. are express, "Spain; then he went into Judæa, where also he saw the Jews." εἰς τὰς Σπανίας ἦλθεν· εἶτα εἰς Ἰουδαίαν ἔβη ὅτε καὶ Ἰουδαίους εἶδε.—F. G.]

[13] πρεσβυτέρα. The word is elsewhere used in this sense by St. Chrys. See Mr. Field's notes. St. Chrys. often points out that the Ep. ii. to Timothy is the last of all St. Paul's Epistles.

[14] 2 Tim. iv. 6.

[15] 2 Tim. iv. 16.

[16] ἤθλησαν, see ἠθέλησιν, Heb. x. 32.

[17] 1 Thess. ii. 14.

[18] Heb. x. 34.

[19] Rom. xv. 25.

[20] 2 Cor. viii. 1–3.

[21] 1 Cor. xvi. 4.

[22] Gal. ii. 10.

[23] Gal. ii. 9.

[24] "But these things he does not say merely for," &c., Ben. Sav. K. Q.

[25] Acts xviii. 17.

Judæa.[1] Thou seest indeed, that while in other cities they bring them to the magistrates, and need help from them. and from the Gentiles, here they took no thought of this, but assemble a Sanhedrim themselves and slay whom they please. Thus in fact they put Stephen to death, thus they beat the Apostles, not taking them before rulers. Thus also they were about to put Paul to death, had not the chief captain thrown himself[2] [upon them]. For this took place while the priests, while the temple, while the ritual, the sacrifices were yet standing. Look indeed at Paul himself being tried before the High Priest, and saying, " I wist not that he was the High Priest,"[3] and this in the presence of the Ruler.[4] For they had then great power. Consider then what things they were likely to suffer who dwelt in Jerusalem and Judæa.

[3.] He then who prays to become accursed for those who were not yet believers, and who so ministers to the faithful, as to journey himself, if need be, and who everywhere took great care of them ; — let us not wonder if he encourage and comfort them by letters also, and if he set them upright when tottering and fallen. For in a word, they were worn down[5] and despairing on account of their manifold afflictions. And this he shows near the end, saying, " Wherefore lift up the hands that hang down, and the feeble knees " ;[6] and again, " Yet a little while, he that shall come will come, and will not tarry " ;[7] and again, " If ye be without chastisement, . . . then are ye bastards and not sons."[8]

For since they were Jews and learned from the fathers that they must expect both their good and their evil immediately and must live accordingly, but then [when the Gospel came] the opposite was [taught] — their good things being in hope and after death, their evils in hand, though they had patiently endured much, it was likely that many would be fainthearted ; — hereon he discourses.

But we will unfold these things at a fit opportunity. At present : he of necessity wrote to those for whom he cared so greatly. For while the reason why he was not sent to them is plain, yet he was not forbidden to write. And that they were becoming fainthearted he shows when he says, " Lift up the hands which hang down, and the feeble knees, and make straight paths " ;[9] and again, " God is not unrighteous to forget your work and love."[10] For the soul overtaken

by many trials, was turned aside even from the faith.[11] Therefore he exhorts them to " Give heed to the things which they have heard, and that there should not be an evil heart of unbelief."[12] On this account also, in this Epistle, especially, he argues at length concerning faith, and after much [reasoning] shows at the end that to them [of old] also He promised good things in hand, and yet gave nothing.

And besides these things, he establishes two points that they might not think themselves forsaken : the one, that they should bear nobly whatever befalls them ; the other, that they should look assuredly for their recompense. For truly He will not overlook those with Abel and the line of unrewarded righteous following him.

And he draws comfort in three ways : first, from the things which Christ suffered : as He Himself says, " The servant is not greater than his Lord."[13] Next, from the good things laid up for the believers. Thirdly, from the evils ; and this point he enforces not only from the things to come (which would be less persuasive), but also from the past and from what had befallen their fathers. Christ also does the same, at one time saying, " The servant is not greater than his Lord " ;[14] and again, " There are many mansions with the Father " ;[15] and He denounces innumerable woes on the unbelievers.

But he speaks much of both the New and the Old Covenant ; for this was useful to him for the proof of the Resurrection. Lest they should disbelieve that [Christ] rose on account of the things which He suffered, he confirms it from the Prophets, and shows that not the Jewish, but ours are the sacred [institutions]. For the temple yet stood and the sacrificial rites ; therefore he says, " Let us go forth therefore without, bearing His reproach."[16] But this also was made an argument against him : " If these things are a shadow, if these things are an image, how is it that they have not passed away or given place when the truth was manifested, but these things still flourish ? " This also he quietly intimates shall happen, and that at a time close at hand.

Moreover, he makes it plain that they had been a long time in the faith and in afflictions, saying, " When for the time ye ought to be teachers,"[17] and, " Lest there be in any of you an evil heart of unbelief,"[18] and ye became " Followers of them who through patience inherit the promises."[19]

---

[1] i.e. in Judæa, they beat and scourged, not through the indifference of the judge, but by their own authority.
[2] Acts xxi. 31–33.      [3] Acts xxiii. 5.
[4] i.e. before Lysias.
[5] " having lost their freshness and vigor like salted fish." See many instances of its use in this sense in Mr. Field's note on St. Chrys. on 1 Cor. Hom. xxviii. (p. 255, A). [See p. 390, O. T.]
[6] Heb. xii. 12.      [8] Heb. xii. 8.
[7] Heb. x. 37.      [9] Heb. xii. 12, 13.
[10] Heb. vi. 10 [St. Chrys. here follows the better reading, omitting τοῦ κόπου. — F. G.].

[11] Heb. ii. 1.      [16] Heb. xiii. 13.
[12] Heb. iii. 12.      [17] Heb. v. 12.
[13] John xiii. 16.      [18] Heb. iii. 12.
[14] John xiii. 16.      [19] Heb. vi. 12.
[15] John xiv. 2.

# HOMILY I.

Hebrews i. 1, 2.

"God who at sundry times and in divers manners spake in time past unto the fathers by the Prophets, hath at the end of the days[1] spoken unto us by His Son: whom He hath appointed heir of all things, by whom also He made the worlds."

[1.] TRULY, "where sin abounded, grace did much more abound." (Rom. v. 20.) This at least the blessed Paul intimates here also, in the very beginning of his Epistle to the Hebrews. For since as it was likely that afflicted, worn out by evils, and judging of things thereby, they would think themselves worse off than all other men, — he shows that herein they had rather been made partakers of greater, even very exceeding, grace ; arousing the hearer at the very opening of his discourse. Wherefore he says, " God who at sundry times and in divers manners spake in times past unto the fathers by the Prophets, hath at the end of the days spoken unto us by His Son."

Why did he [Paul] not oppose " himself " to " the prophets " ? Certainly, he was much greater than they, inasmuch as a greater trust was committed to him. Yet he doth not so. Why? First, to avoid speaking great things concerning himself. Secondly, because his hearers were not yet perfect. And thirdly, because he rather wished to exalt them, and to show that their superiority was great. As if he had said, What so great matter is it that He sent prophets to our fathers? For to us [He has sent] His own only-begotten Son Himself.

And well did he begin thus, " At sundry times and in divers manners," for he points out that not even the prophets themselves saw God ; nevertheless, the Son saw Him. For the expressions, " at sundry times and in divers manners " are the same as " in different ways." " For I "(saith He) " have multiplied visions, and used similitudes by the ministry of the Prophets." (Hos. xii. 10.) Wherefore the excellency consists not in this alone, that to them indeed prophets were sent, but to us the Son ; but that none of them saw God, but the Only-begotten Son saw Him. He doth not indeed at once assert this, but by what he says afterwards he establishes it, when he speaks concerning His human nature ; " For to which of the

Angels said He, Thou art My Son," (ver. 5), and, " Sit thou on My right hand " ? (Ver. 13.)

And look on his great wisdom. First he shows the superiority from the prophets. Then having established this as acknowledged, he declares that to them indeed He spake by the prophets, but to us by the Only-begotten. Then [He spake] to them by Angels, and this again he establishes, with good reason (for angels also held converse with the Jews) : yet even herein we have the superiority, inasmuch as the Master [spake] to us, but to them servants, and prophets, fellow-servants.

[2.] Well also said he, " at the end of the days," for by this he both stirs them up and encourages them desponding of the future. For as he says also in another place, " The Lord is at hand, be careful for nothing " (Phil. iv. 5, 6), and again, " For now is our salvation nearer than when we believed " (Rom. xiii. 11) : so also here. What then is it which he says? That whoever is spent in the conflict, when he hears of the end thereof, recovers his breath a little, knowing that it is the end indeed of his labors, but the beginning of his rest.

" Hath in the end of the days spoken unto us in [His] Son." Behold again he uses the saying, " in [His] Son,"[2] for " through the Son,"[3] against those who assert that this phrase is proper to the Spirit.[4] Dost thou see that the [word] " in " is " through " ?[5]

And the expression, " In times past," and this, " In the end of the days," shadows forth some other meaning : — that when a long time had intervened, when we were on the edge of punishment, when the Gifts had failed, when there was no expectation of deliverance, when we were expecting to have less than all — then we have had more.

And see how considerately he hath spoken it. For he said not, " Christ spake " (albeit it was He who did speak), but inasmuch as their souls were weak, and they were not yet able to hear the things concerning Christ, he says, " God hath spoken by Him." What meanest thou?

---

[1] ἐσχάτου τῶν ἡμερῶν. ἐσχάτων τ. ἡ. (in these last days) Sav. Ben. here and throughout the Homily. The former is considered to be the true reading of the Sacred Text. It is throughout the reading of St. Chrys. as is clear from his argument. [It is the reading of all the uncials ; the cursives and the versions are divided. The R. V. follows the correct text. — F. G.]

[2] ἐν υἱῷ.　　　[3] διὰ τοῦ υἱοῦ.
[4] That is, the Macedonians or Pneumatomachi, who about the year 373 found great fault with St. Basil for using indifferently the two forms of doxology, sometimes μετὰ τοῦ Υἱοῦ σὺν τῷ Πνεύματι τῷ Ἁγίῳ, sometimes διὰ τοῦ Υἱοῦ ἐν τῷ Πνεύματι τῷ Ἁγίῳ. They said that the latter, by which they meant to imply inferiority in the Third Person especially, was the only proper form. This gave occasion to St. Basil's writing his Tract De Spiritu Sancto, in which he refutes them at large, proving among other things that ἐν is in Scripture often equivalent to σύν. c. 25. t. iii. 49. That ἐν is put for διὰ is also said by St. Chrys. Hom. on 1 Cor. i. 4 (p. 13, O T.) and elsewhere.　　　[5] [τὸ, ἐν, διά ἐστι. — F. G.]

did God speak through the Son? Yes. What then? Is it thus thou showest the superiority? for here thou hast but pointed out that both the New and the Old [Covenants] are of One and the same : and that this superiority is not great. Wherefore he henceforth follows on upon this argument, saying, "He spake unto us by [His] Son."

(Note, how Paul makes common cause, and puts himself on a level with the disciples, saying, He spake "to us": and yet He did not speak to him, but to the Apostles, and through them to the many. But he lifts them [the Hebrews] up, and declares that He spake also to them. And as yet he doth not at all reflect on the Jews. For almost all to whom the prophets spake, were a kind of evil and polluted persons. But as yet the discourse is not of these : but hitherto of the gifts derived from God.)

"Whom He appointed," saith he, "heir of all." What is "whom He appointed heir of all"? He speaks here of the flesh [the human nature]. As He also says in the second Psalm, "Ask of Me, and I will give Thee the heathen for Thine inheritance." (Ps. ii. 8.) For no longer is "Jacob the portion of the Lord" nor "Israel His inheritance" (Deut. xxxii. 9), but all men : that is to say, He hath made Him Lord of all : which Peter also said in the Acts, "God hath made Him both Lord and Christ." (Acts ii. 36.) But he has used the name "Heir," declaring two things : His proper sonship[1] and His indefeasible sovereignty. "Heir of all," that is, of all the world.

[3.] Then again he brings back his discourse to its former point. "By whom also He made the worlds [the ages]."[2] Where are those who say, There was [a time] when He was not?

Then, using degrees of ascent, he uttered that which is far greater than all this, saying,

Ver. 3, 4. "Who, (being the brightness of His glory, and the express image of His person, and upholding all things by the word of His power,) when He had by Himself purged our sins, sat down on the right hand of the Majesty on high ; being made[3] so much better than the Angels as He hath by inheritance obtained a more excellent name than they."

O! the wisdom of the Apostle! or rather, not the wisdom of Paul, but the grace of the Spirit is the thing to wonder at. For surely he uttered not these things of his own mind, nor in that way did he find his wisdom. (For whence could it be? From the knife, and the skins, or the workshop?) But it was from the working of God. For his own understanding did not give birth to these thoughts, which was

then so mean and slender as in nowise to surpass the baser sort ; (for how could it, seeing it spent itself wholly on bargains and skins?) but the grace of the Spirit shows forth its strength by whomsoever it will.

For just as one, wishing to lead up a little child to some lofty place, reaching up even to the top of Heaven, does this gently and by degrees, leading him upwards by the steps from below, — then when he has set him on high, and bidden him to gaze downwards, and sees him turning giddy and confused, and dizzy, taking hold of him, he leads him down to the lower stand, allowing him to take breath ; then when he hath recovered it, leads him up again, and again brings him down ; — just so did the blessed Paul likewise, both with the Hebrews and everywhere, having learnt it from his Master. For even He also did so ; sometimes He led His hearers up on high, and sometimes He brought them down, not allowing them to remain very long.

See him, then, even here — by how many steps he led them up, and placed them near the very summit of religion, and then or ever they grow giddy, and are seized with dizziness, how he leads them again lower down, and allowing them to take breath, says, "He spake unto us by [His] Son," "whom He appointed Heir of all things."[4] For the name of Son is so far common. For where a true[5] [Son] it is understood of, He is above all : but however that may be, for the present he proves that He is from above.

And see how he says it: "Whom He appointed," saith he, "heir of all things." The phrase, "He appointed Heir," is humble. Then he placed them on the higher step, adding, "by whom also He made the worlds." Then on a higher still, and after which there is no other, "who being the brightness of His glory, and the express image of His person." Truly he has led them to unapproachable light, to the very brightness itself. And before they are blinded see how he gently leads them down again, saying, "and upholding all things by the word of His power, when He had by Himself purged our sins, sat down on the right hand of the Majesty." He does not simply say, "He sat down," but "after the purifying, He sat down," for he hath touched on the Incarnation, and his utterance is again lowly.

Then again having said a little by the way (for he says, "on the right hand of the Majesty on high"), [he turns] again to what is lowly ; "being made so much better than the angels,

---

[1] τὸ γνήσιον τῆς υἱότητος.
[2] τοὺς αἰῶνας, "the ages," "duration beyond time."
[3] [R. V. "having become." — F. G.]

[4] That is for the moment St. Paul does not argue the dignity of Christ from the title " Son " — from His being the *true* Son of God, and therefore God, but condescending to the weakness of his hearers, at first uses the word in a general sense, and establishes His Divinity by other considerations.
[5] γνήσιος.

as He hath by inheritance obtained a more excellent name than they." Henceforward then he treats here of that which is according to the flesh, since the phrase "being made better" doth not express His essence according to the Spirit,[1] (for that was not "made" but "begotten,") but according to the flesh: for this was "made." Nevertheless the discourse here is not about being called into[2] existence. But just as John says, "He that cometh after me, is preferred before me" (John i. 15, 30), that is, higher in honor and esteem; so also here, "being made so much better than the angels"—that is, higher in esteem and better and more glorious, "by how much He hath obtained by inheritance a more excellent name than they." Seest thou that he is speaking of that which is according to the flesh? For this Name,[3] God the Word ever had; He did not afterwards "obtain it by inheritance"; nor did He afterwards become "better than the Angels, when He had purged our sins"; but He was always "better," and better without all comparison.[4] For this is spoken of Him according to the flesh.

So truly it is our way also, when we talk of man, to speak things both high and low. Thus, when we say, "Man is nothing," "Man is earth," "Man is ashes," we call the whole by the worse part. But when we say, "Man is an immortal animal," and "Man is rational, and of kin to those on high," we call again the whole by the better part. So also, in the case of Christ, sometimes Paul discourseth from the less and sometimes from the better; wishing both to establish the economy, and also to teach about the incorruptible nature.

[4.] Since then "He hath purged our sins," let us continue pure; and let us receive no stain, but preserve the beauty which He hath implanted in us, and His comeliness undefiled and pure, "not having spot or wrinkle or any such thing." (Eph. v. 27.) Even little sins are "a spot and a wrinkle," such a thing, I mean, as Reproach, Insult, Falsehood.

Nay, rather not even are these small, but on the contrary very great: yea so great as to deprive a man even of the kingdom of Heaven. How, and in what manner? "He that calleth his brother fool, is in danger" (He saith) "of hell-fire." (Matt. v. 22.) But if it be so with him who calls a man "fool," which seems to be the slightest of all things, and rather mere children's talk; what sentence of punishment will not he incur, who calleth him malignant and crafty and envious, and casteth at him ten thousand other reproaches? What more fearful than this?

Now suffer, I beseech you, the word [of exhortation].[5] For if he that "doeth" [aught] to "one of the least, doeth it to Him" (Matt. xxv. 40), and he that "doeth it not to one of the least doeth it not to Him" (Matt. xxv. 45), how is it not the same also in the matter of good or evil speaking? He that reviles his brother, reviles God: and he that honors his brother, honors God. Let us train therefore our tongue to speak good words. For "refrain," it is said, "thy tongue from evil." (Ps. xxxiv. 13.) For God gave it not that we should speak evil, that we should revile, that we should calumniate one another; but to sing hymns to God withal, to speak those things which "give grace to the hearers" (Eph. iv. 29), things for edification, things for profit.

Hast thou spoken evil of a man? What is thy gain, entangling thyself in mischief together with him? For thou hast obtained the reputation of a slanderer. For there is not any, no not any evil, which stops at him that suffers it, but it includes the doer also. As for instance, the envious person seems indeed to plot against another, but himself first reaps the fruit of his sin, wasting and wearing himself away, and being hated of all men. The cheat deprives another of his money; yea and himself too of men's good will: and causes himself to be evil spoken of by all men. Now reputation is much better than money, for the one it is not easy to wash out, whereas it is easy to gain possession of the other. Or rather, the absence of the one doth no hurt to him that wanteth it; but the absence of the other makes you reproached and ridiculed, and an object of enmity and warfare to all.

The passionate man again first punishes and tears himself in pieces, and then him with whom he is angry.

Just so the evil speaker disgraces first himself and then him who is evil-spoken of: or, it may be, even this hath proved beyond his power, and while he departs with the credit of a foul and detestable kind of person, he causes the other to be loved the more. For when a man hearing a bad name given him, doth not requite the giver in the same kind, but praises and admires, he doth not praise the other, but himself. For I before observed that, as calumnies against our neighbors first touch those who de-

---

[1] κατὰ πνεῦμα is the reading adopted by Mr. Field, following herein an ancient Catena [compiled by Niketas Archbishop of Heraclea in Thrace who flourished in the 11th century] which has preserved it: κατὰ τὸν πατέρα is found in all other MSS. and Editions, and was probably the reading in Mutianus' text, who translates "essentiæ paternæ." Of the use of πνεῦμα for the Divine Nature of the Son, see many instances brought together in the note to the Oxford Translation of St. Athanasius against the Arians, p. 196 d. [See also in Tertullian, O. T. note H, pp. 322 sqq.]

[2] οὐσιώσεως, "communication of Being." Cf. in 1 Cor. Hom. v. § 4, p. 56, Oxf. Tr.

[3] That is the Name Son. The passage is thus rightly pointed by Mr. Field in accordance with the addition of the explanatory word "Son" in [Niketas'] Catena (Supp.). According to the pointing of the other editions, the translation would be, "For this Name, God the Word, He ever had."   [4] ἀσυγκρίτως.

[5] Comp. Heb. xiii. 22. It seems as if the hearers were showing themselves surprised at the severity of what he was saying.

vise the mischief, so also good works done towards our neighbors, gladden first those who do them. The parent either of good, or evil, justly reaps the fruit of it first himself. And just as water, whether it be brackish or sweet, fills the vessels of those who resort to it, but lessens not the fountain which sends it forth ; so surely also, both wickedness and virtue, from whatever person they proceed, prove either his joy or his ruin.

So far as to the things of this world ; but what speech may recount the things of that world, either the goods or the evils? There is none. For as to the blessings, they surpass all thought, not speech only ; for their opposites are expressed indeed in terms familiar to us. For fire, it is said, is there, and darkness, and bonds, and a worm that never dieth. But this represents not only the things which are spoken of, but others more intolerable. And to convince thee, consider at once this first : if it be fire, how is it also darkness? Seest thou how that fire is more intolerable than this? For it hath no light. If it be fire, how is it forever burning? Seest thou how something more intolerable than this happens? For it is not quenched. Yea, therefore it is called unquenchable. Let us then consider how great a misery it must be, to be forever burning, and to be in darkness, and to utter unnumbered groanings, and to gnash the teeth, and not even to be heard. For if here any one of those ingeniously brought up, should he be cast into prison, speaks of the mere ill savor, and the being laid in darkness, and the being bound with murderers, as more intolerable than any death : think what it is when we are burning with the murderers of the whole world, neither seeing nor being seen, but in so vast a multitude thinking that we are alone. For the darkness and gloom doth not allow our distinguishing those who are near to us, but each will burn as if he were thus suffering alone. Moreover, if darkness of itself afflicteth and terrifieth our souls, how then will it be when together with the darkness there are likewise so great pains and burnings?

Wherefore I entreat you to be ever revolving these things with yourselves, and to submit to the pain of the words, that we may not undergo the punishment of the things. For assuredly, all these things shall be, and those whose doings have deserved those chambers of torture no man shall rescue, not father, nor mother, nor brother.

" For a brother redeemeth not," He saith ; " shall a man redeem ? " (Ps. xlix. 7, LXX.), though he have much confidence, though he have great power with God. For it is He Himself who rewards every one according to his works, and upon these depends our salvation or punishment.

Let us make then to ourselves " friends of the mammon of unrighteousness " (Luke xvi. 9), that is : Let us give alms ; let us exhaust our possessions upon them, that so we may exhaust that fire : that we may quench it, that we may have boldness there. For there also it is not they who receive us, but our own work : for that it is not simply their being our friends which can save us, learn from what is added. For why did He not say, " Make to yourselves friends, that they may receive you into their everlasting habitations," but added also the manner ? For saying, " of the mammon of unrighteousness," He points out that we must make friends of them by means of our possessions, showing that mere friendship will not protect us, unless we have good works, unless we spend righteously the wealth unrighteously gathered.

Moreover, this our discourse, of Almsgiving I mean, fits not only the rich, but also the needy. Yea even if there be any person who supporteth himself by begging, even for him is this word. For there is no one, so poverty-stricken, however exceeding poor he may be, as not to be able to provide " two mites." (Luke xxi. 2.) It is therefore possible that a person giving a small sum from small means, should surpass those who have large possessions and give more ; as that widow did. For not by the measure of what is given, but by the means and willingness of the givers is the extent of the alms-deed estimated. In all cases the will is needed, in all, a right disposition ; in all, love towards God. If with this we do all things, though having little we give little, God will not turn away His face, but will receive it as great and admirable : for He regards the will, not the gifts : and if He see that to be great, He assigneth His decrees and judges accordingly, and maketh them partakers of His everlasting benefits.

Which may God grant us all to obtain, by the grace and love of our Lord Jesus Christ, with whom to the Father together with the Holy Ghost, be glory, power, honor, now and for ever, and world without end. Amen.

# HOMILY II.

Hebrews i. 3.

"Who being the brightness of His Glory and the express Image of His person, and upholding all things by the word of His power, when He had by Himself purged our sins."

[1.] Everywhere indeed a reverential mind is requisite, but especially when we say or hear anything of God: Since neither can tongue speak nor thought[1] hear anything suitable to our God. And why speak I of tongue or thought?[1] For not even the understanding[2] which far excels these, will be able to comprehend anything accurately, when we desire to utter aught concerning God. For if "the peace of God surpasseth all understanding" (Phil. iv. 7), and "the things which are prepared for them that love Him have not entered into the heart of man" (1 Cor. ii. 9); much more He Himself, the God of peace, the Creator of all things, doth by a wide measure exceed our reasoning. We ought therefore to receive all things with faith and reverence, and when our discourse[3] fails through weakness, and is not able to set ·forth accurately the things which are spoken, then especially to glorify God, for that we have such a God, surpassing both our thought and our conception.[4] For many of our conceptions[5] about God, we are unable to express, as also many things we express, but have not strength to conceive of them. As for instance: —That God is everywhere, we know; but how, we no longer understand.[6] That there is a certain incorporeal power the cause of all our good things, we know: but how it is, or what it is, we know not. Lo! we speak, and do not understand. I said, That He is everywhere, but I do not understand it. I said, That He is without beginning, but I do not understand it. I said, That He begat from Himself, and again I know not how I shall understand it. And some things there are which we may not even speak — as for instance, thought conceives[7] but cannot utter.

And to show thee that even Paul is weak and doth not put out his illustrations with exactness; and to make thee tremble and refrain from searching too far, hear what he says, having called Him Son and named Him Creator, "Who being the brightness of His Glory, and the express image of His person."

This we must receive with reverence and clear of all incongruities. "The brightness of His glory," saith he. But observe in what reference he understands this, and so do thou receive it: — that He is of Him:[8] without passion: that He is neither greater, nor less; since there are some, who derive certain strange things from the illustration. For, say they, "the brightness" is not substantial,[9] but hath its being in another. Now do not thou, O man, so receive it, neither be thou sick of the disease of Marcellus[10] and Photinus.[11] For he hath a remedy for thee close at hand, that thou fall not into that imagination, nor doth he leave thee to be hurried down into that fatal malady. And what saith he? "And the express image of His person" [or "subsistence"[12]]: that is, just as He [the Father] is personally subsisting, being in need of nothing,[13] so also the Son. For he saith this here, showing the undeviating similitude[14] and the peculiar image of the Prototype, that He [the Son] is in subsistence by Himself.

For he who said above, that "by Him He made all things" here assigns to Him absolute authority. For what doth he add? "And upholding all things by the word of His power".; that we might hence infer not merely His being the express image of His Person, but also His governing all things with absolute authority.

See then, how he applies to the Son that which is proper to the Father. For on this account he did not say simply, "and upholding all things," nor did he say, "by His power," but, "by the word of His power." For much as just now we saw him gradually ascend and descend; so also now, as by steps, he goes up on high, then again descends, and saith, "by whom also He made the worlds."

Behold how here also he goes on two paths, by the one leading us away from Sabellius, by the other from Arius, yea and on another, that He [Christ] should not be accounted un-

---

[1] διάνοια οὖς, Sav. Ben. in both places.
[2] ὁ νοῦς.
[3] λόγος.
[4] τὴν ἔννοιαν, τὸν λόγον, Sav. Ben.
[5] ὧν νοοῦμεν.
[6] νοοῦμεν.
[7] νοεῖ ἡ διάνοια.

[8] ὅτι ἐξ αὐτοῦ, "that He [Christ] is of Him [the Father]."
[9] ἐνυπόστατον.
[10] Marcellus Bishop of Ancyra lapsed towards Sabellianism, holding, as it seems, virtually at least, that our Lord is not a Person eternally distinct from the Father, but, a Manifestation of the Father, lasting from the Incarnation to the Judgment. His views are anathematized in 1 Conc. Constantinop. Canon 1.
[11] Photinus Bishop of Sirmium, who had been Deacon under Marcellus, and carried his theory out, maintaining our Lord to have had no distinct existence before His Birth of Mary. Socr. E. H. 2. 29. His doctrine too was condemned at Constantinople, ubi sup.
[12] ὑποστάσεως. St. Chrys. understands the word to mean here neither "substance" nor "Person," but, if we may use such a word, "substantiality," or "substantive existence," which in speaking de Divinis we call "Personality." See below, page 371, note 5.
[13] Sav. Ben. add πρὸς ὑπόστασιν.　　[14] ἀπαράλλακτον

originated,[1] which he does also throughout, nor yet alien from God. For if, even after so much, there are some who assert that He is alien, and assign to Him another father, and say that He is at variance with Him ; — had [Paul] not declared these things, what would they not have uttered ?

How then does he this? When he is compelled to heal, then is he compelled also to utter lowly things : as for instance, " He appointed Him " (saith he) " heir of all things," and " by Him He made the worlds." (*Supra*, ver. 2.) But that He might not be in another way dishonored, he brings Him up again to absolute authority and declares Him to be of equal honor with the Father, yea, so equal, that many thought Him to be the Father.

And observe thou his great wisdom. First he lays down the former point and makes it sure accurately. And when this is shown, that He is the Son of God, and not alien from Him, he thereafter speaks out safely all the high sayings, as many as he will. Since any high speech concerning Him, led many into the notion just mentioned, he first sets down what is humiliating and then safely mounts up as high as he pleases. And having said, " whom He appointed heir of all things," and that " by Him He made the worlds," he then adds, " and upholding all things by the word of His power." For He that by a word only governs all things, could not be in need of any one, for the producing all things.

[2.] And to prove this, mark how again going forward, and laying aside the " by whom," he assigns to Him absolute power. For after he had effected what he wished by the use of it, thenceforward leaving it, what saith he ? " Thou Lord in the beginning hast laid the foundation of the earth, and the heavens are the works of Thine hands." (*Infra*, ver. 10.) Nowhere is there the saying " by whom," or that " by Him He made the worlds." What then? Were they not made by Him? Yes, but not, as thou sayest or imaginest, " as by an instrument " : nor as though He would not have made them unless the Father had reached out a hand to Him. For as He " judgeth no man " (John v. 22), and is said to judge by the Son, in that He begat Him a judge ; so also, to create by Him, in that He begat Him a Creator. And if the Father be the original cause of Him, in that He is Father, much more of the things which have been made by Him. When therefore he would show that He is of Him, he speaks of necessity lowly things. But when he would utter high

things, Marcellus takes a handle, and Sabellius ; avoiding however the excess of both, he holds a middle [way]. For neither does he dwell on the humiliation, lest Paul of Samosata should obtain a standing place, nor yet does he for ever abide in the high sayings ; but shows on the contrary His abundant nearness, lest Sabellius rush in upon him. He names Him " Son," and immediately Paul of Samosata comes on him, saying that He is a son, as the many are. But he gives him a fatal wound, calling Him " Heir." But yet, with Arius, he is shameless. For the saying, " He appointed Him heir," they both hold : the former one saying, it comes of weakness ; the other still presses objections, endeavoring to support himself by the clause which follows. For by saying, " by whom also He made the worlds," he strikes backwards the impudent Samosatene : while Arius still seems to be strong. Nevertheless see how he smites him likewise, saying again, " who being the brightness of His glory." But behold ! Sabellius again springs on us, with Marcellus, and Photinus : but on all these also he inflicts one blow, saying, " and the express image of His person and upholding all things by the word of His power." Here again he wounds Marcion too ;[2] not very severely, but however he doth wound him. For through the whole of this Epistle he is fighting against them.

But the very thing which he said, " the brightness of the glory," hear also Christ Himself saying, " I am the Light of the world." (John viii. 12.) Therefore he [the Apostle] uses the word " brightness," showing that this was said in the sense of " Light of Light." Nor is it this alone which he shows, but also that He hath enlightened our souls ; and He hath Himself manifested the Father, and by " the brightness " he has indicated the nearness of the Being [of the Father and the Son[3]]. Observe the subtlety of his expressions. He hath taken one essence and subsistence to indicate two subsistences. Which he also doth in regard to the knowledge of the Spirit[4] ; for as he saith that the knowledge of the Father is one with that of the Spirit, as being indeed one, and in nought varying from itself (1 Cor. ii. 10-12) : so also here he hath taken hold of one certain [thing] whereby to express the subsistence of the Two.[5]

And he adds that He is " the express Image."

---

2 Because Marcion, holding the Creation to be evil, denied the Son's preserving Power.

3 καὶ διὰ τοῦ ἀπαυγάσματος τῆς οὐσίας τὴν ἐγγύτητα ἔδειξεν. Sav. and Ben. read διὰ δὲ τοῦ ἀ. τὸ ἴσον ἐσήμανε τῆς οὐσίας, καὶ τὴν πρὸς τὸν πατέρα ἐγγύτητα. " By &c. he indicated the equality of His Substance and His nearness to the Father."

4 Cf. *forsitan.*

5 εἰς τὴν τῶν δυὸ ὑπόστασιν. Sav. and Ben. read ἐ. τ. τ. δ. ὑποστάσεων δήλωσιν, " whereby to show the two Subsistencies." Mr. Field says that the old translation of Mutianus in some degree confirms this latter reading, which is easier. The word ὑπόστασιν in the singular is used in the sense of " Personality," as above, p. 370, note 12.

---

1 ἄναρχον. On this third heresy respecting the Holy Trinity, see St. Greg. Naz. *Orat.* ii. 37 ; xx. 6 ; in both which places it is, as here, mentioned as the third form of error with Sabellianism and Arianism. See also Bp. Bull, *Def. Fid. N.* iv. 1. 8. The mention of this is not found in the Common text, in which the whole passage is recast.

For the "express Image" is something other[1] than its Prototype: yet not Another in all respects, but as to having real subsistence. Since here also the term, "express image," indicates there is no variation from that whereof it is the "express image": its similarity in all respects. When therefore he calls Him both Form,[2] and express Image, what can they say? "Yea," saith he, "man is also called an Image of God."[3] What then! is he so [an image of Him] as the Son is? No (saith he) but because the term, image, doth not show resemblance. And yet, in that man is called an Image, it showeth resemblance, as in man. For what God is in Heaven, that man is on earth, I mean as to dominion. And as he hath power over all things on earth, so also hath God power over all things which are in heaven and which are on earth. But otherwise, man is not called "Express image," he is not called Form: which phrase declares the substance, or rather both substance and similarity in substance. Therefore just as "the form of a slave" (Phil. ii. 6, 7) expresses no other thing than a man without variation[4] [from human nature], so also "the form of God" expresses no other thing than God.

"Who being" (saith he) "the brightness of His glory." See what Paul is doing. Having said, "Who being the brightness of His glory," he added again, "He sat down on the right hand of the Majesty": what names he hath used, nowhere finding a name for the Substance. For neither "the Majesty," nor "the Glory" setteth forth the Name, which he wishes to say, but is not able to find a name. For this is what I said at the beginning, that oftentimes we think something, and are not able to express [it]: since not even the word GOD is a name of substance, nor is it at all possible to find a name of that Substance.

And what marvel, if it be so in respect of God, since not even in respect of an Angel, could one find a name expressive of his substance? Perhaps too, neither in respect of the soul. For this name [soul] doth not seem to me to be significative of the substance thereof, but of breathing. For one may see that the same [thing] is called both Soul and Heart and Mind: for, saith he, "Create in me a clean heart, O God" (Ps. li. 10), and one may often see that it [the soul] is called spirit.

"And upholding all things by the word of His power." Tell me, "God said" (it is written), "Let there be light" (Gen. i. 3): "the Father, saith one,[5] commanded, and the Son obeyed"? But behold here He also [the Son] acts by word.

For (saith he), "And upholding all things"—that is, governing; He holds together what would fall to pieces; For, to hold the world together, is no less than to make it, but even greater (if one must say a strange thing). For the one is to bring forward something out of things which are not: but the other, when things which have been made are about to fall back into non-existence, to hold and fasten them together, utterly at variance as they are with each other: this is indeed great and wonderful, and a certain proof of exceeding power.

Then showing the easiness, he said, "upholding": (he did not say, governing,[6] from the figure of those who simply with their finger move anything, and cause it to go round.) Here he shows both the mass of the creation to be great, and that this greatness is nothing to Him. Then again he shows the freedom from the labor, saying, "By the word of His power." Well said he, "By the word." For since, with us, a word is accounted to be a bare thing, he shows that it is not bare with God. But, how "He upholdeth by the word," he hath not further added: for neither is it possible to know. Then he added concerning His majesty: for thus John also did: having said that "He is God" (John i. 1), he brought in the handiwork of the Creation. For the same thing which the one indirectly expressed, saying, "In the beginning was the Word," and "All things were made by Him" (John i. 3), this did the other also openly declare by "the Word," and by saying "by whom also He made the worlds." For thus he shows Him to be both a Creator, and before all ages. What then? when the prophet saith, concerning the Father, "Thou art from everlasting and to everlasting" (Ps. xc. 2), and concerning the Son, that He is before all ages, and the maker of all things—what can they say? Nay rather, when the very thing which was spoken of the Father,—"He which was before the worlds,"—this one may see spoken of the Son also? And that which one saith, "He was life" (John i. 4), pointing out the preservation of the creation, that Himself is the Life of all things,—so also saith this other, "and upholding all things by the word of His power": not as the Greeks who defraud Him, as much as in them lies, both of Creation itself, and of Providence, shutting up His power, to reach only as far as to the Moon.

"By Himself" (saith he) "having purged our sins." Having spoken concerning those marvelous and great matters, which are most above us, he proceeds to speak also afterwards concerning His care for men. For indeed the former expression, "and upholding all things," also was universal: nevertheless this is far greater, for it

---

[1] ἄλλος τις.  
[2] Phil. ii. 6, see below.  
[3] εἰκόνος εἰκών, Ben.: εἰκών (only), Sav.  
[4] ἀπαράλλακτον.  
[5] This is an heretical objection, as is expressed by the reading in the editions of Sav. and Ben.  

[6] κυβερνῶν.

also is universal: for, for His part, "all" men believed.[1]. As John also, having said, "He was life," and so pointed out His providence, saith again, and "He was light."

"By Himself," saith he, "having purged our sins, He sat down on the right hand of the Majesty on high." He here setteth down two very great proofs of His care: first the "purifying us from our sins," then the doing it "by Himself." And in many places, thou seest him making very much of this,—not only of our reconciliation with God, but also of this being accomplished through the Son. For the gift being truly great, was made even greater by the fact that it was through the Son.

For[2] in saying, "He sat on the right hand," and, "having by Himself purged our sins,"—though he had put us in mind of the Cross, he quickly added the mention of the resurrection and ascension. And see his unspeakable wisdom: he said not, "He was commanded to sit down," but "He sat down." Then again, lest thou shouldest think that He standeth, he subjoins, "For to which of the angels said He at any time, Sit thou on My right hand."

"He sat" (saith he) "on the right hand of the Majesty on high." What is this "on high"? Doth he enclose God in place? Away with such a thought! but just as, when he saith, "on the right hand," he did not describe Him as having figure, but showed His equal dignity with the Father; so, in saying "on high," he did not enclose Him there, but expressed the being higher than all things, and having ascended up above all things. That is, He attained even unto the very throne of the Father: as therefore the Father is on high, so also is He. For the "sitting together" implies nothing else than equal dignity. But if they say, that He said, "Sit Thou," we may ask them, What then? did He speak to Him standing? Moreover, he said not that He commanded, nor that He enjoined, but that "He said": for no other reason, than that thou mightest not think Him without origin and without cause. For that this is why he said it, is evident from the place of His sitting. For had he intended to signify inferiority, he would not have said, "on the right hand," but on the left hand.

Ver. 4. "Being made," saith he, "so much better than the angels, as He hath by inheritance obtained a more excellent name than they." The "being made," here, is instead of "being shown forth," as one may say. Then also from what does he reason confidently? From the Name. Seest thou that the name Son is wont to declare true relationship? And indeed if He

were not a true Son (and "true" is nothing else than "of Him"), how does he reason confidently from this? For if He be Son only by grace, He not only is not "more excellent than the angels," but is even less than they. How? Because righteous men too were called sons; and the name son, if it be not a genuine son, doth not avail to show the "excellency." When too he would point out that there is a certain difference between creatures and their maker, hear what he saith:

Ver. 5. "For to which of the Angels said He at any time, Thou art My Son, this day have I begotten Thee. And again, I will be to Him a Father, and He shall be to Me a Son"? For these things indeed are spoken with reference also to the flesh: "I will be to Him a Father, and He shall be to Me a Son"—while this,[3] "Thou art My Son, this day have I begotten Thee," expresses nothing else than "from [the time] that God is." For as He is said to be,[4] from the time present (for this befits Him more than any other), so also the [word] "To-day" seems to me to be spoken here with reference to the flesh. For when He hath taken hold of it, thenceforth he speaks out all boldly. For indeed the flesh partakes of the high things, just as the Godhead of the lowly. For He who disdained not to become man, and did not decline the reality, how should He have declined the expressions?

Seeing then that we know these things, let us be ashamed of nothing, nor have any high thoughts. For if He Himself being God and Lord and Son of God, did not decline to take the form of a slave, much more ought we to do all things, though they be lowly. For tell me, O man, whence hast thou high thoughts? from things of this life? but these or ever they appear, run by. Or, from things spiritual? nay, this is itself one spiritual excellency,—to have no high thoughts.

Wherefore then dost thou cherish high thoughts? because thou goest on aright? hear Christ saying, "When ye have done all things, say, we are unprofitable servants, for we have done that which was our duty to do." (Luke xvii. 10.)

Or because of thy wealth hast thou high thoughts? Dost thou not see those before thee, how they departed naked and desolate? did we not come naked into life, and naked also shall depart? who hath high thoughts on having what is another's? for they who will use it to their own enjoyment alone, are deprived of it how-

---

[1] [i.e. so far as Christ's work for men was concerned, it was universal. He put it in the power of all to believe. — F. G.]
[2] γὰρ, om. S.
[3] Sav. and Ben. omit the words σήμερον . . . σε, and for ἐξ οὗ ἐστιν ὁ θεός. ὥσπερ γὰρ have ἐξ αὐτοῦ ἐστιν· ὥσπερ δὲ, so that the passage runs; "but this, 'Thou art My Son,' expresses nothing else than that He is of Him. And just as," &c. . . The corrector seems to have misapprehended the meaning of ἐξ οὗ in this place.
[4] ὤν.

ever unwillingly, often before death, and at death certainly. But (saith one) while we live we use them as we will. First of all, one doth not lightly see any man using what he hath as he will. Next, if a man do even use things as he will, neither is this a great matter: for the present time is short compared with the ages without end. Art thou high-minded, O man, because thou art rich? on what account? for what cause? for this befalleth also robbers, and thieves, and man-slayers, and effeminate, and whoremongers, and all sorts of wicked men. Wherefore then art thou high-minded? Since if thou hast made meet use of it, thou must not be high-minded, lest thou profane the commandment: but if unmeet, by this indeed [it has come to pass that] thou art become a slave of money, and goods, and art overcome by them. For tell me, if any man sick of a fever should drink much water, which for a short space indeed quencheth his thirst, but afterwards kindleth the flame, ought he to be high-minded? And what, if any man have many cares without cause, ought he therefore to be high-minded? tell me, wherefore? because thou hast many masters? because thou hast ten thousand cares? because many will flatter thee? [Surely not.] For thou art even their slave. And to prove that to thee, hear plainly. The other affections which are within us, are in some cases useful. For instance, Anger is often useful. For (saith he) "unjust wrath shall not be innocent" (Ecclus. i. 22): wherefore it is possible for one to be justly in wrath. And again, "He that is angry with his brother without cause,[1] shall be in danger of hell." (Matt. v. 22.) Again for instance, emulation, desire, [are useful]: the one when it hath reference to the procreation of children, the other when he directs his emulation to excellent things. As Paul also saith, "It is good to be zealously affected always in a good thing" (Gal. iv. 18) and, "Covet earnestly the best gifts." (1 Cor. xii. 31.) Both therefore are useful: but an insolent spirit is in no case good, but is always unprofitable and hurtful.

However, if a man must be proud, [let it be] for poverty, not for wealth. Wherefore? Because he who can live upon a little, is far greater and better than he who cannot. For tell me, supposing certain persons called to the Imperial City, if some of them should need neither beasts, nor slaves, nor umbrellas, nor lodging-places, nor sandals, nor vessels, but it should suffice them to have bread, and to take water from the wells, — while others of them should say, "unless ye give us conveyances, and a soft bed, we cannot come; unless also we have many followers, unless we may be allowed con-

tinually to rest ourselves, we cannot come, nor unless we have the use of beasts, unless too we may travel but a small portion of the day — and we have need of many other things also": whom should we admire? those or these? plainly, these who require nothing. So also here: some need many things for the journey through this life; others, nothing. So that it would be more fitting to be proud, for poverty if it were fitting at all.

"But the poor man," they say, "is contemptible." Not he, but those who despise him. For why do not I despise those who know not how to admire what they ought? Why, if a person be a painter, he will laugh to scorn all who jeer at him, so long as they are uninstructed; nor doth he regard the things which they say, but is content with his own testimony. And shall we depend on the opinion of the many? Therefore, we are worthy of contempt when men despise us for our poverty, and we do not despise them nor call them miserable.

And I say not how many sins are produced by wealth, and how many good things by poverty. But rather, neither wealth nor poverty is excellent in itself, but through those who use it. The Christian shines out in poverty rather than in riches. How? He will be less arrogant, more sober-minded, graver, more equitable, more considerate: but he that is in wealth, hath many impediments to these things. Let us see then what the rich man does, or rather, he who useth his wealth amiss. Such an one practiceth rapine, fraud, violence. Men's unseemly loves, unholy unions, witchcrafts, poisonings, all their other horrors, — wilt thou not find them produced by wealth? Seest thou, that in poverty rather than in wealth the pursuit of virtue is less laborious? For do not, I beseech thee, think that because rich men do not suffer punishment here, neither do they sin. Since if it were easy for a rich man to suffer punishment, thou wouldest surely have found the prisons filled with them. But among its other evils, wealth hath this also, that he who possesseth it, transgressing in evil with impunity, will never be stayed from doing so, but will receive wounds without remedies, and no man will put a bridle on him.

And if a man choose, he will find that poverty affords us more resources even for pleasure. How? Because it is freed from cares, hatred, fighting, contention, strife, from evils out of number.

Therefore let us not follow after wealth, nor be forever envying those who possess much. But let those of us who have wealth, use it aright; and those who have not, let us not grieve for this, but give thanks for all things unto God, because He enableth us to receive with little labor the same reward with the rich, or even (if we will) a greater: and from small means we shall

---

[1] [St. Chrys. here follows a text having the gloss εἰκῆ now rejected by nearly all critical editors. — F. G.]

have great gains. For so he that brought the two talents, was admired and honored equally with him who brought the five. Now why? Because he was entrusted with [but] two talents, yet he accomplished all that in him lay, and brought in what was entrusted to him, doubled. Why then are we eager to have much entrusted to us, when we may by a little reap the same fruits, or even greater? when the labor indeed is less, but the reward much more? For more easily will a poor man part with his own, than a rich man who hath many and great possessions. What, know ye not, that the more things a man hath, the more he setteth his love upon? There-fore, lest this befall us, let us not seek after wealth, nor let us be impatient of poverty, nor make haste to be rich : and let those of us who have [riches] so use them as Paul commanded. ("They that have," saith he, "as though they had not, and they that use this world as not abusing it "— 1 Cor. vii. 29, 31) : that we may obtain the good things promised. And may it be granted to us all to obtain them, by the grace and love of our Lord Jesus Christ, with whom to the Father together with the Holy Ghost, be glory, power, honor, now, and for ever, and world without end. Amen.

# HOMILY III.

## HEBREWS i. 6–8.

"And again when He bringeth in the First-Begotten into the world, He saith, And let all the angels of God worship Him. And of the Angels He saith, Who maketh His angels spirits, and His ministers a flame of fire. But unto the Son He saith, Thy throne, O God, is for ever and ever."

[1.] OUR Lord Jesus Christ calls His coming in the flesh an exodus [or going out] : as when He saith, "The sower went out to sow." (Matt. xiii. 3.) And again, "I went out from the Father, and am come." (John xvi. 28.) And in many places one may see this. But Paul calls it an [eisodus or] coming in, saying, "And when again He bringeth in the First-Begotten into the world," meaning by this Bringing in, His taking on Him flesh.

Now why has he so used the expression? The things signified [thereby] are manifest, and in what respect it is [thus] said. For Christ indeed calls it a Going out, justly; for we were out from God. For as in royal palaces, prison-ers and those who have offended the king, stand without, and he who desires to reconcile them, does not bring them in, but himself going out discourses with them, until having made them meet for the king's presence, he may bring them in, so also Christ hath done. Having gone out to us, that is, having taken flesh, and having dis-coursed to us of the King's matters, so He brought us in, having purged the sins, and made reconciliation. Therefore he calls it a Going out.

But Paul names it a Coming in, from the metaphor of those who come to an inheritance and receive any portion or possession. For the saying, "and when again He bringeth in the First-Begotten into the world," means this, "when he putteth the world into His hand." For when He was made known, then also He obtained possession of the whole thereof, He saith not these things concerning God The Word, but concerning that which is according to the flesh. For if according to John, "He was in the world, and the world was made by Him" (John i. 10) : how is He "brought in," otherwise than in the flesh?

"And," saith he, "Let all the angels of God worship Him." Whereas he is about to say something great and lofty, he prepares it before-hand, and makes it acceptable, in that he rep-resents the Father as "bringing in" the Son. He had said above, that "He spake to us not by prophets but by His Son"; that the Son is superior to angels ; yea and he establishes this from the name [SON]. And here, in what fol-lows, from another fact also. What then may this be? From worship. And he shows how much greater He is, as much as a Master is than a slave ; just as any one introducing another into a house straightway commands those having the care thereof to do him reverence ; [so] say-ing in regard to the Flesh, "And let all the Angels of God worship Him."

Is it then Angels only? No ; for hear what follows : "And of His Angels He saith, Which maketh His Angels spirits, and His ministers a flame of fire : but unto the Son, Thy Throne, O God, is for ever and ever." Behold, the greatest difference ! that they are created, but He un-created. While of His angels He saith, who "maketh" ; wherefore of the Son did He not say "Who maketh"? Although he might have expressed the difference as follows : "Of His Angels He saith, Who maketh His Angels spirits, but of the Son, 'The Lord created Me': 'God hath made Him Lord and Christ.'" (Prov. viii. 22; Acts ii. 36.) But neither was the one spoken concerning the Son, nor the other concerning God The Word, but concerning the flesh. For when he desired to express the true difference, he no longer included angels only, but the whole ministering power above. Seest thou how he distinguishes, and with how great clearness, between creatures and Creator, ministers and Lord, the Heir and true Son, and slaves?

[2.] "But unto the Son he saith, Thy throne, O God, is for ever and ever." Behold a symbol of Kingly Office. ·"A scepter of righteousness is the scepter of Thy kingdom." Behold again another symbol of Royalty.

Then again with respect to the flesh (ver. 9) "Thou hast loved righteousness and hated iniquity, therefore God, even Thy God, hath anointed Thee."

What is, "Thy God"? Why, after that he hath uttered a great word, he again qualifieth it. Here he hits both Jews, and the followers of Paul of Samosata, and the Arians, and Marcellus, and Sabellius, and Marcion. How? The Jews, by his indicating two Persons, both God and Man;[1] the other Jews,[2] I mean the followers of Paul of Samosata, by thus discoursing concerning His eternal existence, and uncreated essence: for by way of distinction, against the word, "He made," he put, "Thy throne, O God, is for ever and ever." Against the Arians there is both this same again, and also that He is not a slave; but if a creature, He is a slave. And against Marcellus and the others, that these are two Persons, distinguished in reference to their subsistence.[3] And against the Marcionites, that the Godhead is not anointed, but the Manhood.

Next he saith, "Above Thy fellows." But who are these His "fellows" other than men? that is Christ received "not the Spirit by measure." (John iii. 34.) Seest thou how with the doctrine concerning His uncreated nature he always joins also that of the "Economy"? what can be clearer than this? Didst thou see how what is created and what is begotten are not the same? For otherwise he would not have made the distinction, nor in contrast to the word, "He made" [&c.], have added, "But unto the Son He said, Thy throne, O God, is for ever and ever." Nor would he have called the name, "Son, a more

excellent Name," if it is a sign of the same thing. For what is the excellence? For if that which is created, and that which is begotten be the same, and they [the Angels] were made,·what is there [in Him] "more excellent"? Lo! again ὁ Θεὸς, "God," with the Article.[4]

[3.] And again he saith (ver. 10–12): "Thou Lord in the beginning hast laid the foundation of the earth, and the heavens are the works of Thine hands. They shall perish, but Thou remainest, and they shall all wax old as a garment, and as a vesture shalt Thou fold them up, and they shall be changed: but Thou art the same and Thy years shall not fail."

Lest hearing the words, "and when He bringeth in the First-Begotten into the world"; thou shouldest think it as it were a Gift afterwards super-added to Him; above, he both corrected this beforehand, and again further corrects, saying, "in the beginning": not now, but from the first. See again he strikes both Paul of Samosata and also Arius a mortal blow, applying to the Son the things which relate to the Father. And withal he has also intimated another thing by the way, greater even than this. For surely he hath incidentally pointed out also the transfiguration of the world, saying, "they shall wax old as a garment, and as a vesture Thou shalt fold them up, and they shall be changed." Which also he saith in the Epistle to the Romans, that he shall transfigure the world. (See Rom. viii. 21.) And showing the facility thereof, he adds, as if a man should fold up a garment so shall He both fold up and change it. But if He with so much ease works the transfiguration and the creation to what is better and more perfect, needed He another for the inferior creation? How far doth your shamelessness go? At the same time too this is a very great consolation, to know that things will not be as they are, but they all shall receive change, and all shall be altered, but He Himself remaineth ever existing, and living without end: "and Thy years," he saith, "shall not fail."

[4.] Ver. 13. "But to which of the Angels said He at any time, Sit thou on My right hand until I make thine enemies thy footstool?" Behold, again he encourages them, inasmuch as their enemies were to be worsted, and their enemies are the same also with Christ's.

This again belongs to Sovereignty, to Equal Dignity, to Honor and not weakness, that the Father should be angry for the things done to the Son. This belongs to His great Love and honor towards the Son, as of a father towards a son. For He that is angry in His behalf how is He a stranger to Him? Which also he saith in

---

[1] δυὸ πρόσωπα δεικνὺς, καὶ Θεὸν καὶ ἄνθρωπον. That is *both* two distinct Persons in the Godhead, and also the Divine and human natures of the Christ. The corrector would seem to have understood it "two Persons, both God and man"; the common texts read δυὸ τὸν αὐτὸν δεικνὺς, κ. θ. κ. ἁ. "showing the same [Person] to be two, both God and man." [The first καὶ may well be translated *both*. It seems to have been omitted by the corrector simply as superfluous, not as altering the sense. — F. G.]

[2] Sav. and Ben. omit Ἰουδαίους. The teaching of Paul of Samosata was regarded as closely connected with Judaism, and he and his followers were called Jews.

[3] κατὰ τὴν ὑπόστασιν, see above, pp. 370, 371, notes.

[4] The Ben. editor observes that it had been said that ὁ θεός with the article is used in Scripture only of the Father, and that St. Chrys. here as in other places argues that it is used of the Son.

the second Psalm, " He that dwelleth in heaven shall laugh them to scorn, and the Lord shall have them in derision. Then shall He speak unto them in His wrath, and vex them in His sore displeasure." (Ps. ii. 4, 5.) And again He Himself saith, "Those that would not that I should reign over them, bring hither before Me, and slay them." (Luke xix. 27.) For that they are His own words, hear also what He saith in another place, "How often would I have gathered thy children together, and ye would not ! Behold, your house is left desolate." (Luke xiii. 34, 35.) And again, " The kingdom shall be taken from you, and shall be given to a nation bringing forth the fruits thereof." (Matt. xxi. 43.) And again, " He that falleth upon that stone shall be broken, but on whomsoever It shall fall, It will grind him to powder." (Matt. xxi. 44.) And besides, He who is to be their Judge in that world, much more did He Himself repay them in this. So that the words " Till I make thine enemies thy footstool " are expressive of honor only towards the Son.

Ver. 14. " Are they not all ministering spirits, sent forth to minister for them who shall be heirs of salvation?" What marvel (saith he) if they minister to the Son, when they minister even to our salvation? See how he lifts up their minds, and shows the great honor which God has for us, since He has assigned to Angels who are above us this ministration on our behalf. As if one should say, for this purpose (saith he) He employs them ; this is the office of Angels, to minister to God for our salvation. So that it is an angelical work, to do all for the salvation of the brethren : or rather it is the work of Christ Himself, for He indeed saves as Lord, but they as servants. And we, though servants, are yet Angels' fellow-servants. Why gaze ye so earnestly on the Angels (saith he) ? They are servants of the Son of God, and are sent many ways for our sakes, and minister to our salvation. And so they are partners in service with us.

Consider ye how he ascribes no great difference to the kinds of creatures. And yet the space between angels and men is great ; nevertheless he brings them down near to us, all but saying, For us they labor, for our sake they run to and fro : on us, as one might say, they wait. This is their ministry, for our sake to be sent every way.

And of these examples both the Old [Testament] is full, and the New. For when Angels bring glad tidings to the shepherds, or to Mary, or to Joseph ; when they sit at the sepulcher, when they are sent to say to the disciples, "Ye men of Galilee, why stand ye gazing up into heaven?" (Acts i. 11), when they release

Peter out of the prison, when they discourse with Philip, consider how great the honor is ; when God sends His Angels for ministers as to friends, when to Cornelius [an Angel] appears, when [an Angel] brings forth all the apostles from the prison, and says, " Go, stand and speak in the temple to the people the words of this life " (Acts v. 20) ; and to Paul himself also an Angel appears. Dost thou see that they minister to us on God's behalf, and that they minister to us in the greatest matters? wherefore Paul saith, " All things are yours, whether life or death, or the world, or things present, or things to come." (1 Cor. iii. 22.)

Well then the Son also was sent, but not as a servant, nor as a minister, but as a Son, and Only-Begotten, and desiring the same things with the Father. Rather indeed, He was not " sent " : for He did not pass from place to place, but took on Him flesh : whereas these change their places, and leaving those in which they were before, so come to others in which they were not.

And by this again he incidentally encourages them, saying, What fear ye? Angels are ministering to us.

[5.] And having spoken concerning the Son, both what related to the Economy, and what related to the Creation, and to His sovereignty, and having shown His co-equal dignity, and that as absolute Master He ruleth not men only but also the powers above, he next exhorts them, having made out his argument, that we ought to give heed to the things which have been heard. (c. ii. 1.) " Wherefore we ought to give more earnest heed " (saith he) " to the things which we have heard." Why " more earnest "? Here he meant " more earnest " than to the Law : but he suppressed the actual expression of it, and yet makes it plain in the course of reasoning, not in the way of counsel, nor of exhortation. For so it was better.

Ver. 2, 3. " For if the word spoken by Angels " (saith he) " was steadfast, and every transgression and disobedience received a just recompense of reward ; how shall we escape if we neglect so great salvation, which at the first began to be spoken to us by the Lord, and was confirmed unto us by them that heard Him?"

Why ought we to " give more earnest heed to the things which we have heard "? were not those former things of God, as well as these? Either then he meaneth " more earnest " than [to] the Law, or " very earnest " ; not making comparison, God forbid. For since, on account of the long space of time, they had a great opinion of the Old Covenant, but these things had been despised as yet new, he proves (more than his argument required) that we ought rather to give heed to these. How? By saying in effect, Both these and those are of God, but not in a like manner. And this he shows us afterwards : but for the present he treats it somewhat superficially, but afterwards more clearly, saying ; "For if that first covenant had been faultless" (c. viii. 7), and many other such things : "for that which decayeth and waxeth old is ready to vanish away." (c. viii. 13.) But as yet he ventures not to say any such thing in the beginning of his discourse, nor until he shall have first occupied and possessed his hearer by his fuller [arguments].

Why then ought we "to give more earnest heed"? "Lest at any time," saith he, "we should let them slip"— that is, lest at any time we should perish, lest we should fall away. And here he shows the grievousness of this falling away, in that it is a difficult thing for that which hath fallen away to return again, inasmuch as it hath happened through wilful negligence. And he took this form of speech from the Proverbs. For, saith he, "my son [take heed] lest thou fall away" (Prov. iii. 21, LXX.), showing both the easiness of the fall, and the grievousness of the ruin. That is, our disobedience is not without danger. And while by his mode of reasoning he shows that the chastisement is greater, yet again he leaves it in the form of a question, and not in the conclusion. For indeed this is to make one's discourse inoffensive, when one does not in every case of one's self infer the judgment, but leaves it in the power of the hearer himself to give sentence : and this would render them more open to conviction. And both the prophet Nathan doth the same in the Old [Testament], and in Matthew Christ, saying, "What will He do to the husbandmen" (Matt. xxi. 40) of that vineyard? so compelling them to give sentence themselves : for this is the greatest victory.

Next, when he had said, "For if the word which was spoken by Angels was steadfast"— he did not add, much more that by Christ : but letting this pass, he said what is less, "How shall we escape, if we neglect so great salvation?" And see how he makes the comparison. "For if the word which was spoken by Angels," saith he. There, "by Angels," here, "by the Lord"— and there "a word," but here, "salvation."

Then lest any man should say, Thy sayings, O Paul, are they Christ's? he proves their trustworthiness both from his having heard these things of Him, and from their being now spoken by God ; since not merely a voice is wafted, as in the case of Moses, but signs are done, and facts bear witness.

[6.] But what is this, "For if the word spoken by Angels was steadfast"? For in the Epistle to the Galatians also he saith to this effect, "Being ordained by angels in the hand of a Mediator." (Gal. iii. 19.) And again, "Ye received a law by the disposition of Angels, and have not kept it." (Acts vii. 53.) And everywhere he saith it was given by angels. Some indeed say that Moses is signified ; but without reason. For here he says Angels in the plural : and the Angels too which he here speaks of, are those in Heaven. What then is it? Either he means the Decalogue only (for there Moses spake, and God answered him — Ex. xix. 19), — or that angels were present, God disposing them in order, — or that he speaks thus in regard of all things said and done in the old Covenant, as if Angels had part in them. But how is it said in another place, "The Law was given by Moses" (John i. 17), and here "by Angels"? For it is said, "And God came down in thick darkness."[1] (Ex. xix. 16, 20.)

"For if the word spoken by angels was steadfast." What is "was steadfast"? True, as one may say ; and faithful in its proper season ; and all the things which had been spoken came to pass. Either this is his meaning, or that they prevailed, and the threatenings were coming to be accomplished. Or by "the word" he means injunctions. For apart from the Law, Angels sent from God enjoined many things : for instance at Bochim, in the Judges, in [the history of] Samson. (Judg. ii. 1 ; xiii. 3.) For this is the cause why he said not "the Law" but "the word." And he seems to me haply rather to mean this, viz., those things which are committed to the management of angels. What shall we say then? The angels who were entrusted with the charge of the nation were then present, and they themselves made the trumpets, and the other things, the fire, the thick darkness. (Ex. xix. 16.)

"And every transgression and disobedience," saith he. Not this one and that one, but "every" one. Nothing, he saith, remained unavenged, but "received a just recompense of reward," instead of [saying] punishment. Why now spake he thus? Such is the manner of Paul, not to make much account of his phrases, but indifferently to put down words of evil sound, even in matters of good meaning. As also in another place he saith, "Bringing into captivity every thought to the obedience of Christ."[2] (2 Cor. x. 5.) And again he hath put "the recompense" for punishment,[3] as here he calleth punishment "reward." "If it be a righteous thing," he saith, "with God to recompense tribulation to them that trouble you, and to you

---

[1] This last clause seems unconnected as it stands here. If there were MS. authority one should be glad to transfer it a few lines lower, after the management of Angels: τὰ διὰ τῶν ἀγγέλων οἰκονομηθέντα, or to place here the words "What shall we say," down to "thick darkness."
[2] See St. Chrys. on the passage, 2 Cor. x. 5 [p. 242, O. T.]. The expression "captivity" was the "word of evil sound."
[3] Rom. i. 27.

who are troubled rest." (2 Thess. i. 6, 7.) That is, justice was not violated, but God went forth against them, and caused the penalty to come round on the sinners, though not all their sins are made manifest, but only where the express ordinances were transgressed.

"How then shall we," he saith, "escape if we neglect so great salvation?" Hereby he signified, that that other salvation was no great thing. Well too did he add the "So great." For not from wars (he saith) will He now rescue us, nor bestow on us the earth and the good things that are in the earth, but it will be the dissolution of death, the destruction of the devil, the kingdom of Heaven, everlasting life. For all these things he hath briefly expressed, by saying, "if we neglect so great salvation."

[7.] Then he subjoins what makes this worthy of belief. "Which at the first began to be spoken by the Lord": that is, had its beginning from the fountain itself. It was not a man who brought it over [1] into the earth, nor any created power, but the Only-Begotten Himself.

"And was confirmed unto us by them that heard [Him]." What is "confirmed"? It was believed,[2] or, it came to pass. For (he saith) we have the earnest;[3] that is, it hath not been extinguished, it hath not ceased, but it is strong and prevaileth. And the cause is, the Divine power works therein. It means they who heard from the Lord, themselves confirmed us. This is a great thing and trustworthy: which also Luke saith in the beginning of his Gospel, "As they delivered unto us, which from the beginning were eyewitnesses and ministers of the Word." (Luke i. 2.)

How then was it confirmed? What if those that heard were forgers? saith some one. This objection then he overthrows, and shows that the grace was not human. If they had gone astray, God would not have borne witness to them; for he subjoined (ver. 4), "God also bearing witness with them." Both they indeed bear witness, and God beareth witness too. How doth He bear witness? not by word or by voice, (though this also would have been worthy of belief): but how? "By signs, and wonders, and divers miracles." (Well said he, "divers

miracles," declaring the abundance of the gifts: which was not so in the former dispensation, neither so great signs and so various.) That is, we did not believe them simply, but through signs and wonders: wherefore we believe not them, but God Himself.

"And by gifts of the Holy Ghost, according to His own will."

What then, if wizards also do signs, and the Jews said that He "cast out devils through Beelzebub"? (Luke xi. 15.) But they do not such kind of signs: therefore said he "divers miracles": for those others were not miracles, [or powers,[4]] but weakness and fancy, and things altogether vain. Wherefore he said, "by gifts of the Holy Ghost according to His own will."

[8.] Here he seems to me to intimate something further. For it is not likely there were many there who had gifts, but that these had failed, upon their becoming more slothful. In order then that even in this he might comfort them, and not leave them to fall away, he referred all to the will of God. He knows (he says) what is expedient, and for whom, and apportions His grace accordingly. Which also he [Paul] does in the Epistle to the Corinthians, saying, "God hath set every one of us, as it pleased Him." (1 Cor. xii. 18.) And again, "The manifestation of the Spirit is given to every man to profit withal." (1 Cor. xii. 7.)

"According to His will." He shows that the gift is according to the will of the Father. But oftentimes on account of their unclean and slothful life many have not received a gift, and sometimes also those whose life is good and pure have not received one. Why, I pray you? Lest they might be made haughty, that they might not be puffed up, that they might not grow more negligent, that they might not be more excited. For if even without a gift, the mere consciousness of a pure life be sufficient to lift a man up, much more when the grace is added also. Wherefore to the humble, to the simple, it was rather given, and especially to the simple: for it is said, "in singleness and gladness of heart." (Acts ii. 46.) Yea, and hereby also he rather urged them on, and if they were growing negligent gave them a spur. For the humble, and he who imagines no great things concerning himself, becomes more earnest when he has received a gift, in that he has obtained what is beyond his deserts, and thinks that he is not worthy thereof. But he who thinks he hath done well, reckoning it to be his due, is puffed up. Wherefore God dispenseth this profitably: which one may see taking place also in the Church: for one hath the word of teaching, another hath not power to open his

---

[1] lit. *ferried* it over: διεπόρθμευσεν, the word is specially applied to messages between earth and heaven, by Pseudo-Dionys. *Areop. de Celesti Hierarchia*, c. xv. 6. "The Angels are called Winds, to express their rapid power of making things, how it reaches almost to all things without time; and their motion in the manner of those who ferry over, from above downwards, and again from the lower parts up the steep, both drawing out the things of secondary order towards that loftier height, and moving those of the first order to come forth in the way of sympathy and care for their inferiors."

[2] ἐπιστεύθη. Dunæus suggested ἐπιστώθη, "it was accredited," but there is no MS. authority for the change.

[3] St. Chrys. seems to have had in view 2 Cor. i. 21, 22, where "confirming" is connected with the earnest of "the Spirit." [The passage is, "how he which stablishes us with you in Christ, and hath anointed us, is God; who hath also sealed us, and given the earnest of the Spirit in our hearts."—F. G.]

[4] δυνάμεις.

mouth. Let not this man (he says) be grieved because of this. For " the manifestation of the Spirit is given to every man to profit withal." (1 Cor. xii. 7.) For if a man that is an householder knoweth to whom he should entrust anything, much more God, who understands the mind of men, " who knoweth all things or ever they come into being."[1] One thing only is worthy of grief, Sin : there is nothing else.

Say not, Wherefore have I not riches? or, If I had, I would give to the poor. Thou knowest not, if thou hadst them, whether thou wouldest not the rather be covetous. For now indeed thou sayest these things, but being put to the trial thou wouldest be different. Since also when we are satisfied, we think that we are able to fast ; but when we have gone without a little space, other thoughts come into us. Again, when we are out of the way of strong drink, we think ourselves able to master our appetite, but no longer so, when we are caught by it.

Say not, Wherefore had I not the gift of teaching? or, If I had had it, I should have edified innumerable souls. Thou knowest not, if thou hadst it, whether it would not be to thy condemnation, — whether envy, whether sloth, would not have disposed thee to hide thy talent. Now, indeed, thou art now free from all these, and though thou give not "the portion of meat" (Luke xii. 42), thou art not called to account : but then, thou wouldest have been responsible for many.

[9.] And besides, neither now art thou without the gift. Show in the little, what thou wouldst have been, if thou hadst had the other. " For if " (he says) " ye are not faithful in that which is little, how shalt any one give you that which is great? " (Luke xvi. 11.) Give such proof as did the widow ; she had two farthings,[2] and she cast in all, whatsoever she possessed.

Dost thou seek riches? Prove that thou thinkest lightly of the few things, that I may trust thee also concerning the many things. But if thou dost not think lightly even of these, much less wilt thou do so of the other.

Again, in speech, prove that thou canst use fitly exhortation and counsel. Hast thou not external eloquence? hast thou not store of thoughts? But nevertheless thou knowest these common things. Thou hast a child, thou hast a neighbor, thou hast a friend, thou hast a brother, thou hast kinsmen. And though publicly before the Church, thou art not able to draw out a long discourse, these thou canst exhort in private. Here, there is no need of rhetoric, nor of elaborate discourse : prove in these, that if thou hadst skill of speech, thou wouldest not have neglected it. But if in the small matter thou art not in earnest, how shall I trust thee concerning the great?

For, that every man can do this, hear what Paul saith, how he charged even lay people ; " Edify," he says, " one another, as also ye do." (1 Thess. v. 11.) And, " Comfort one another with these words." (1 Thess. iv. 18.) God knoweth how He should distribute to every man. Art thou better than Moses? hear how he shrinks from the hardship. " Am I," saith he, " able to bear them? for Thou saidst to me, Bear them up, as a nursing-father would bear up the sucking-child." (Num. xi. 12.) What then did God? He took of his spirit and gave unto the others, showing that neither when he bare them was the gift his own, but of the Spirit. If thou hadst had the gift, thou wouldst perchance[3] have been lifted up, perchance wouldst thou have been turned out of the way. Thou knowest not thyself as God knoweth thee. Let us not say, To what end is that? on what account is this? When God dispenseth, let us not demand an account of Him : for this [is] of the uttermost impiety and folly. We are slaves, and slaves far apart from our Master, knowing not even the things which are before us.

[10.] Let us not then busy ourselves about the counsel of God, but whatsoever He hath given, this let us guard, though it be small, though it be the lowest, and we shall be altogether approved. Or rather, none of the gifts of God is small : art thou grieved because thou hast not the gift of teaching? Then tell me, which seems to you the greater, to have the gift of teaching, or the gift of driving away diseases? Doubtless the latter. But what? Tell me ; doth it not seem to thee greater to give eyes to the blind than even to drive away diseases? But what? Tell me ; doth it not seem to thee greater to raise the dead than to give eyes to the blind? What again, tell me ; doth it not seem to thee greater to do this by shadows and napkins, than by a word? Tell me then, which wouldst thou? Raise the dead with shadows and napkins, or have the gift of teaching? Doubtless thou wilt say the former, to raise the dead with shadows and napkins. If then I should show to thee, that there is another gift far greater than this, and that thou dost not receive it when it is in thy power to receive it, art not thou justly deprived of those others? And this gift not one or two, but all may have. I know that ye open wide your mouths and are amazed, at being to hear that it is in your power to have a greater gift than raising the dead, and giving eyes to the blind, doing the same things which were done in the time of the Apostles. And it seems to you past belief.

---

[1] *Hist. Sus.* 42.    [2] ὀβολούς.    [3] πολλάκις, see Mr. Field's note.

What then is this gift? charity. Nay, believe me; for the word is not mine, but Christ's, speaking by Paul. For what saith he? "Covet earnestly the best gifts: and yet show I unto you a more excellent way." (1 Cor. xii. 31.) What is this, "yet more excellent"? What he means is this. The Corinthians were proud over their gifts, and those having tongues, the least gift, were puffed up against the rest. He saith therefore, Do ye by all means desire gifts? I show unto you a way of gifts not merely excelling but far more excellent. Then he saith, "Though I speak with the tongues of Angels, and have not charity, I am nothing. And though I have faith so as to remove mountains, and have not charity, I am nothing." (1 Cor. xiii. 1, 2.)

Hast thou seen the gift? Covet earnestly this gift. This is greater than raising the dead. This is far better than all the rest. And that it is so, hear what Christ Himself saith, discoursing with His disciples, "By this shall all men know that ye are My disciples." (John xiii. 35.) And showing how, He mentioned not the miracles, but what? "If ye have love one with another." And again He saith to the Father, "Hereby shall they know that Thou hast sent Me, if they be one." (John xvii. 21.) And He said to His disciples, "A new commandment I give to you, that ye love one another." (John xiii. 34.) Such an one therefore is more venerable and glorious than those who raise the dead; with reason. For that indeed is wholly of God's grace, but this, of thine own earnestness also. This is of one who is a Christian indeed: this shows the disciple of Christ, the crucified, the man that hath nothing common with earth. Without this, not even martyrdom can profit.

And as a proof, see this plainly. The blessed Paul took two of the highest virtues, or rather three; namely, those which consist in miracles, in knowledge, in life. And without this the others, he said, are nothing. And I will say how these are nothing. "Though I give my goods to feed the poor," he says, "and have not charity, I am nothing." (1 Cor. xiii. 3.) For it is possible not to be charitable even when one feeds the poor and exhausts one's means.

[11.] And indeed these things have been sufficiently declared by us, in the place concerning Charity:[1] and thither we refer the readers. Meanwhile, as I was saying, let us covet earnestly the Gift, let us love one another; and we shall need nothing else for the perfect acquisition of virtue, but all will be easy to us without toils and we shall do all perfectly with much diligence.

But see, even now, it is said, we love one another. For one man hath two friends, and another three. But this is not to love for God's sake, but for the sake of being beloved. But to love for God's sake hath not this as its principle of Love; but such an one will be disposed towards all men as towards brethren; loving those that are of the same faith as being true brothers; heretics and Heathen and Jews, brothers indeed by nature, but vile and unprofitable, — pitying and wearing himself out and weeping for them. Herein we shall be like God if we love all men, even our enemies; not, if we work miracles. For we regard even God with admiration when He worketh wonders, yet much more, when He showeth love towards man, when He is long-suffering. If then even in God this is worthy of much admiration, much more in men is it evident that this rendereth us admirable.

This then let us zealously seek after: and we shall be no way inferior to Paul and Peter and those who have raised innumerable dead, though we may not be able to drive away a fever. But without this [Love]; though we should work greater miracles even than the Apostles themselves, though we should expose ourselves to innumerable dangers for the faith: there will be to us no profit from any. And these things it is not I that say, but he, the very nourisher of Charity, knoweth these things. To him then let us be obedient; for thus we shall be able to attain to the good things promised, of which may we all be made partakers, by the grace of our Lord Jesus Christ, with whom to the Father with the Holy Ghost, be the glory, now and for ever and world without end. Amen.

---

[1] His Homily on 1 Cor. xiii. 3 [pp. 444 sqq. O. T.] is referred to.

# HOMILY IV.

HEBREWS ii. 5–7.

" For unto Angels He hath not put in subjection the world to come, whereof we speak. But one in a certain place testified, saying, What is man that Thou art mindful of him, or the son of man that Thou visitest him? Thou madest him a little lower than the Angels."

[1.] I COULD have wished to know for certain whether any hear with fitting earnestness the things that are said, whether we are not casting the seeds by the wayside : for in that case I should have made my instructions with more cheerfulness. For we shall speak, though no one hear, for the fear which is laid on us by our Saviour. For, saith He, testify to this people ; even if they hear not, thou shalt thyself be guiltless. (See Ezek. iii. 19.) If however I had been persuaded of your earnestness, I should have spoken not for fear only, but should have done it with pleasure also. For now indeed, even if no man hear, even if my work, so long as I fulfill my own part, brings no danger, still the labor is not altogether pleasant. For what profit is it, when though I be not blamed, yet no one is benefited? But if any would give heed we shall receive advantage not so much from avoiding punishment ourselves as from your progress.

How then shall I know this? Having taken notice of some of you, who are not very attentive, I shall question them privately, when I meet them. And if I find that they retain any of the things that have been spoken (I say not all, for this would not be very easy for you), but even if [they retain] a few things out of many, it is plain I should have no further doubts about the rest. And indeed we ought, without giving notice beforehand, to have attacked you when off your guard. However it will suffice, if even in this way I should be able to attain my purpose. Nay rather, even as it is, I can attack you when you are off your guard. For that I *shall* question you, I have forewarned you ; but *when I* shall question you I do not as yet make evident. For perhaps it may be to-day ; perhaps to-morrow, perhaps after twenty or thirty days, perhaps after fewer, perhaps after more. Thus has God also made uncertain the day of our death. Nor hath He allowed it be clear to us, whether it shall befall us to-day, or to-morrow, or after a whole year, or after many years ; that through the uncertainty of the expectation we may through all time keep ourselves firm in virtue. And that we shall indeed depart, He hath said,

— but when, He hath not yet said. Thus too I have said that I shall question you, but I have not added when, wishing you always to be thoughtful.

And let no man say, I heard these things four or five weeks ago, or more, and I cannot retain them. For I wish the hearer so to retain them as to have his recollection perpetual and not apt to fade, nor yet that he should disown what is spoken. For I wish you to retain them, not, in order to tell them to me, but that ye may have profit ; and this is of most serious interest to me. Let no one then say this.

[2.] However, I must now begin with what follows in the epistle. What then is set before us to speak on to-day?

" For not to angels," he says, " did He put in subjection the world to come,[1] whereof we speak." Is he then discoursing concerning some other world? No, but concerning this. Therefore he added " whereof we speak," that he might not allow the mind to wander away in search of some other. How then does he call it " the world to come "? Exactly as he also says in another place, " Who is the figure of him that was to come,"[2] (Rom. v. 14,) when he is speaking about Adam and Christ in the Epistle to the Romans ; calling Christ according to the flesh " Him that was to come " in respect of the times of Adam, (for [then] He was to come). So now also, since he had said, " but when he bringeth in the First-Begotten into the world " : that thou mightest not suppose that he is speaking of another world, it is made certain from many considerations and from his saying " to come." For the world was to come, but the Son of God always was. This world then which was about to come, He put in subjection not to Angels but to Christ. For that this is spoken with reference to the Son (he says) is evident : for surely no one would assert the other alternative, that it had reference to Angels.

Then he brings forward another testimony also and says, " but one in a certain place testified, saying." Wherefore did he not mention the name of the prophet, but hid it? Yea, and in other testimonies also he doth this : as when he saith, " but when He bringeth in again the First-Begotten into the world, He saith, And let all the Angels of God worship Him. And again, I will be to Him a Father. And of the Angels

---

[1] τὴν μέλλουσαν.    [2] τοῦ μέλλοντος.

He saith, Who maketh His angels spirits. And, Thou, Lord, in the beginning hast laid the foundations of the earth " (c. i. 6, 5, 7, 10) : — so also here he saith, " but one in a certain place testified, saying." And this very thing (I conceive) is the act of one that conceals himself, and shows that they were well skilled in the Scriptures ; his not setting down him who uttered the testimony, but introducing it as familiar and obvious.

"What is man that Thou art mindful of him, or the son of man that Thou visitest him? Thou madest him a little lower than the angels : Thou crownedst him with glory and honor." [1] (Ver. 8.) " Thou hast put all things in subjection under his feet."

Now although these things were spoken of human nature generally, they would nevertheless apply more properly to Christ according to the flesh. For this, "Thou hast put all things in subjection under his feet," belongs to Him rather than to us. For the Son of God visited us when we were nothing : and after having assumed our [nature],[2] and united it 'to Himself, He became higher than all.

"For," he says, "in that He hath put all things in subjection under Him, He left nothing not put under Him : but now we see not yet all things put under Him." What he means is this : — since he had said, " Until I make Thine enemies Thy footstool" (c. i. 13), — and it was likely that they would still be grieved, — then having inserted a few things after this parenthetically, he added this testimony in confirmation of the former. For that they might not say, How is it that He hath put His enemies under His feet, when we have suffered so much? he sufficiently hinted at it in the former place indeed (for the word " until " showed, not what should take place immediately, but in course of time) but here he followeth it up. For do not suppose (he says) that because they have not yet been made subject, they are not to be made subject : for that they must be made subject, is evident ; for, on this account was the prophecy spoken. " For," he says, " in that He hath put all things under Him, He left nothing not put under Him." How then is it that all things have not been put under Him? Because they are hereafter to be put under Him.

If then all things must be made subject to Him, but have not yet been made subject, do not grieve, nor trouble thyself. If indeed when the end were come, and all things were made subject, thou wert still suffering these things, with reason wouldst thou repine : " But now we

see not yet all things put under Him." The King has not yet clearly conquered. Why then art thou troubled when suffering affliction? the preaching [of the Gospel] hath not yet prevailed over all ; it is not yet time that they should be altogether made subject.

[3.] Then again there is another consolation ; if indeed He who is hereafter to have all put in subjection under Him, hath Himself also died and submitted to sufferings innumerable. (Ver. 9.) " But," he says, " we see Him who was made a little [3] lower than the angels, even Jesus, for the suffering of death " — then the good things again, — " crowned with glory and honor." Seest thou, how all things apply to Him? For the [expression], " a little," would rather suit Him, who was only three days in Hades, but not ourselves who are for a long time in corruption. Likewise also the [expression] " with glory and honor " will suit Him much more than us.

Again, he reminds them of the Cross, thereby effecting two things ; both showing His care [for them] and persuading them to bear all things nobly, looking to the Master. For (he would say) if He who is worshiped of Angels, for thy sake endured to have a little less than the Angels, much more oughtest thou who art inferior to the Angels, to bear all things for His sake. Then he shows that the Cross is " glory and honor," as He Himself also always calls it, saying, " That the Son of Man might be glorified " (John xi. 5) ; and, " the Son of Man is glorified." (John xii. 23.) If then He calls the [sufferings] for His servants' sake " glory," much more shouldest thou the [sufferings] for the Lord.

Seest thou the fruit of the Cross, how great it is? fear not the matter : for it seemeth to thee indeed to be dismal, but it brings forth good things innumerable. From these considerations he shows the benefit of trial. Then he says, " That He by the grace of God should taste death for every man."

" That by the grace of God," he says. And He indeed because of the grace of God towards us suffered these things. " He who spared not His Own Son," he says, " but delivered Him up for us all." (Rom. viii. 32.) Why? He did not owe us this, but has done it of grace. And again in the Epistle to the Romans he says, " Much more the grace of God, and the gift by grace which is by one man Jesus Christ, hath abounded unto many." (Rom. v. 15.)

" That by the grace of God He should taste death for every man," not for the faithful only, but even for the whole world : for He indeed died for all ; But what if all have not believed? He hath fulfilled His own [part].

Moreover he said rightly " taste death for

---

[1] S. B. add καὶ κατέστησας αὐτὸν ἐπὶ τὰ ἔργα τῶν χειρῶν σου. This clause is omitted from the text of the Epistle by critical editors of the New Testament, and is not commented on by St. Chrysostom. [It is bracketed by Lu., Tr., W. H., and the Basle ed., but retained in the Revision. — F. G.]     [2] τὸ ἐξ ἡμῶν.

[3] or, " for a short time."

every man," he did not say "die." For as if He really was tasting it, when He had spent a little time therein, He immediately arose.

By saying then "for the suffering of death," he signified real death, and by saying "superior to angels," he declared the resurrection. For as a physician though not needing to taste the food prepared for the sick man, yet in his care for him tastes first himself, that he may persuade the sick man with confidence to venture on the food, so since all men were afraid of death, in persuading them to take courage against death, He tasted it also Himself though He needed not. "For," He says, "the prince of this world cometh and findeth nothing in Me." (John xiv. 30.) So both the words "by grace" and "should taste death for every man," establish this.

[4.] Ver. 10. "For it became Him, for whom are all things, and by whom are all things, in bringing many sons unto glory, to make the Captain of their salvation perfect through sufferings." He speaks here of the Father. Seest thou how again he applies the [expression] "by whom"[1] to Him? Which he would not have done, had it been [an expression] of inferiority, and only applicable to the Son. And what he says is this : — He has done what is worthy of His love towards mankind, in showing His First-born to be more glorious than all, and in setting Him forth as an example to the others, like some noble wrestler that surpasses the rest.

"The Captain of their salvation," that is, the Cause of their salvation. Seest thou how great is the space between? Both He is a Son, and we are sons; but He saves, we are saved. Seest thou how He both brings us together and then separates us; "bringing," he says, "many sons unto glory": here he brings us together, — "the Captain of their salvation," again he separates.

"To make perfect through sufferings."[2] Then sufferings are a perfecting, and a cause of salvation. Seest thou that to suffer affliction is not the portion of those who are utterly forsaken; if indeed it was by this that God first honored His Son, by leading Him through sufferings? And truly His taking flesh to suffer what He did suffer, is a far greater thing than making the world, and bringing it out of things that are not. This indeed also is [a token] of His loving-kindness, but the other far more. And [the Apostle] himself also pointing out this very thing, says, "That in the ages to come He might show forth the exceeding riches of His goodness, He both raised us up together, and made us sit together in the heavenly places in Christ Jesus." (Eph. ii. 7, 6.)

" "For it became Him for whom are all things and by whom are all things in bringing many sons to glory, to make the Captain of their salvation perfect through sufferings." For (he means) it became Him who taketh tender care, and brought all things into being, to give up the Son for the salvation of the rest, the One for the many. However he did not express himself thus, but, "to make perfect through sufferings," showing the suffering for any one, not merely profits "him," but he himself also becomes more glorious and more perfect. And this too he says in reference to the faithful, comforting then by the way : for Christ was glorified then when He suffered. But when I say, He was glorified, do not suppose that there was an accession of glory to Him : for that which is of nature He always had, and received nothing in addition.

[5.] "For," he says, "both He that sanctifieth, and they who are sanctified, are all of one, for which cause He is not ashamed to call them brethren." Behold again how he brings [them] together, honoring and comforting them, and making them brethren of Christ, in this respect that they are "of one."[3] Then again guarding himself and showing that he is speaking of that which is according to the flesh, he introduces, "For He who sanctifieth," [i.e.] Christ, "and they who are sanctified," ourselves. Dost thou see how great is the difference?[4] He sanctifies, we are sanctified. And above he said, "the Captain of their salvation. For there is one God, of whom are all things."[5] (1 Cor. viii. 6.)

"For which cause He is not ashamed to call them brethren." Seest thou how again he shows the superiority? For by saying, "He is not ashamed," he shows that the whole comes not of the nature of the thing, but of the loving affection of Him who was "not ashamed" of anything, [yea] of His great humility. For though we be "of one," yet He sanctifieth and we are sanctified : and great is the difference.[6] Moreover "He" is of the Father, as a true Son, that is, of His substance; "we," as created, that is, brought out of things that are not, so that the difference is great. Wherefore he says, "He is not ashamed to call them brethren" (ver. 12), "saying, I will declare Thy name unto My brethren." (Ps. xxii. 22.) For when He clothed Himself with flesh, He clothed Himself also with the brotherhood, and at the same time came in the brotherhood.

This indeed he brings forward naturally. But this (ver. 13) "I will put my trust in Him" (2 Sam. xxii. 3), what does it mean? For what follows this is also [introduced] naturally. "Behold, I and the children which God hath given Me." (Isa.

---

[1] δι' οὗ, see above, note 4, p. 366.
[2] suffering perfects and works salvation.

[3] ἐξ ἑνός.　　　　[4] τὸ μέσον.
[5] This citation is connected with "they are of one," the intervening words, "Then again ... salvation," being introduced parenthetically.　　　　[6] τὸ μέσον.

viii. 18.) For as here He shows Himself a Father, so before, a Brother. "I will declare Thy name unto My brethren," He saith.

And again he indicates the superiority and the great interval [between us], by what follows (ver. 14): "Since then the children," he saith, "are partakers of flesh and blood" (thou seest where he saith the likeness is? in reference to the flesh), "in like manner He also Himself took part of the same." Let all the Heretics be ashamed, let those hide their faces who say that He came in appearance and not in reality.[1] For he did not say, "He took part of these" only, and then say no more; although had he said thus, it would have been sufficient, but he asserted something more, adding "in like manner," not in appearance, he means, or by an image (since in that case "in like manner" is not preserved) but in reality; showing the brotherhood.

[6.] Next he sets down also the cause of the economy.[2] "That through death," he says, "He might destroy him that had the power of death, that is, the devil."

Here he points out the wonder, that by what the devil prevailed, by that was he overcome, and the very thing which was his strong weapon against the world, [namely], Death, by this Christ smote him. In this he exhibits the greatness of the conqueror's power. Dost thou see how great good death hath wrought?

Ver. 15. "And should deliver them," he says, "who through fear of death were all their life-time subject to bondage." Why (he means) do ye shudder? Why do you fear him that hath been brought to nought? He is no longer terrible, but has been trodden under foot, hath been utterly despised; he is vile and of no account. (2 Tim. i. 10.)

But what is "through fear of death were all their life-time subject to bondage"? He either means this, that he who fears death is a slave, and submits to all things rather than die; or this, that all men were slaves of death and were held under his power, because he had not yet been done away; or that men lived in continual fear, ever expecting that they should die, and being afraid of death, could have no sense of pleasure, while this fear was present with them. For this he hinted at in saying, "All their life-time." He here shows that the afflicted, the harassed, the persecuted, those that are deprived of country and of substance and of all other things, spend their lives more sweetly and more freely than they of old time who were in luxury, who suffered no such afflictions, who were in continual prosperity, if indeed these "all their life-time"

were under this fear and were slaves; while the others have been made free and laugh at that which they shudder at. For this is now as if, when one was being led away to a captivity leading to death, and in continual expectation of it, one should feed him up with abundant dainties (something such as this was Death of old); but now, as if some one taking away that fear together with the dainties, were to promise a contest, and propose a combat that should lead no longer to death, but to a kingdom. Of which number wouldst thou have wished to be — those who are fed up in the prison-house, while every day looking for their sentence, or those who contend much and labor willingly, that they may crown themselves with the diadem of the kingdom? Seest thou how he has raised up their soul, and made them elated? He shows too, that not death alone has been put an end to, but that thereby he also who is ever showing that war without truce against us, I mean the devil, hath been brought to nought; since he that fears not death is out of reach of the devil's tyranny. For if "skin for skin, yea all things a man would give for his life" (Job ii. 4) — when any one has determined to disregard even this, of what henceforward will he be the slave? He fears no one, he is in terror of no one, he is higher than all, and more free than all. For he that disregards his own life, much more [doth he disregard] all other things. And when the devil finds a soul such as this, he can accomplish in it none of his works. For what? tell me, shall he threaten the loss of property, and degradation, and banishment from one's country? But these are small matters to him who "counteth not even his life dear" (Acts xx. 24) unto him, according to the blessed Paul. Thou seest that in casting out the tyranny of death, he also overthrew the strength of the devil. For he who has learnt to study innumerable [truths] concerning the resurrection,[3] how should he fear death? How should he shudder any more?

[7.] Therefore be ye not grieved, saying, why do we suffer such and such things? For so the victory becomes more glorious. And it would not have been glorious, unless by death He had destroyed death; but the most wonderful thing is that He conquered him by the very means by which he was strong, showing in every point the abundance of His means, and the excellence of His contrivances. Let us not then prove false to the gift bestowed on us. "For we," he says, "have received not a spirit of fear, but a spirit of power, and of love, and of a sound mind." (Rom. viii. 15; 2 Tim. i. 7.) Let us stand then nobly, laughing death to scorn.

But [I pause] for it comes over me to groan

---

[1] Cf. St. Iren. pp. 450, 482, 497, O. T.
[2] i.e. the Incarnation. [οἰκονομία is not so much the Incarnation as the whole arrangement of the Christian dispensation — here with especial reference to Christ's death. — F. G.]

[3] μυρία φιλοσοφεῖν.

bitterly [at the thought of] whither Christ hath raised us up, and whither we have brought ourselves down. For when I see the wailings in the public places, the groanings over those departing life, the howlings, the other unseemly behavior, believe me, I am ashamed before those heathen, and Jews, and heretics who see it, and before all who for this cause openly laugh us to scorn. For whatever I may afterwards say, I shall talk to no purpose, when philosophizing concerning the resurrection. Why? Because the heathen do not attend to what is said by me, but to what is done by you. For they will say at once, 'when will any of these [fellows] be able to despise death, when he is not able to see another dead?'

Beautiful things were spoken by Paul, beautiful and worthy of Heaven, and of the love of God to man. For what does he say? "And He shall deliver them who through fear of death, were all their life-time subject to bondage." But ye do not allow these things to be believed, fighting against them by your deeds. And yet many things exist for this very end, God building a stronghold against it, that He might destroy this same evil custom. For tell me, what mean the bright torches? Do we not send them before as athletes? And what [mean] the hymns? Do we not glorify God, and give thanks that at last He has crowned the departed one, that He has freed him from his labors, that taking away uncertainty, He has him with Himself? Are not the Hymns for this? Is not Psalmody for this? All these are the acts of those rejoicing. "For," it is said, "is any merry? let him sing psalms." (Jas. v. 13.) But to these things the heathen give no heed. For (one will say) do not tell me of him who is philosophical[1] when out of the affliction, for this is nothing great or surprising;— show me a man who in the very affliction itself is philosophical, and then I will believe the resurrection,

And indeed, that women engaged in the affairs of this life[2] should act thus is no way surprising. And yet indeed this even is dreadful; for from them also is the same philosophy required. Wherefore also Paul says, "But concerning them which are asleep, I would not have you ignorant, that ye sorrow not even as the rest who have no hope." (1 Thess. iv. 13.) He wrote not this to solitaries, nor to perpetual virgins, but to women and men in the world.[3] But however this is not so dreadful. But when any man or woman, professing to be crucified to the world, he tears his hair, and she shrieks violently — what can be more unseemly than this?

Believe me when I say if things were done as

they ought, such persons should be excluded for a long time from the thresholds of the Church. For those who are indeed worthy of being grieved for, are these who still fear and shudder at death, who have no faith in the resurrection.

'But I do not disbelieve the resurrection' (one says) 'but I long after his society.' Why then, tell me, when he goes from home, and that for a long absence, dost not thou do the same? 'Yea, but I do weep then also' (she says) 'and mourn as I long after him.' But that is the conduct of those that really long after their associates, this that of her who despairs of his return.

Think, what thou singest on that occasion, "Return unto thy rest, O my soul, for the Lord hath dealt bountifully with thee." (Ps. cxvi. 7.) And again, "I will fear no evil, for Thou art with me." (Ps. xxiii. 4.) And again, "Thou art my refuge from the affliction which encompasseth me." (Ps. xxxii. 7.) Think what these Psalms mean. But thou dost not give heed, but art drunk from grief.

Consider carefully the funeral lamentations of others that thou mayest have a remedy in thine own case. "Return, O my soul, to thy rest, for the Lord hath dealt bountifully with thee." Tell me, sayest thou that the Lord hath dealt bountifully with thee, and weepest? Is not this mere acting, is it not hypocrisy? For if indeed thou really believest the things thou sayest, thy sorrow is superfluous: but if thou art in sport and acting a part, and thinkest these things fables, why dost thou sing psalms? Why dost thou even endure the attendants? Why dost thou not drive away the singers? But this would be the act of madmen. And yet far more the other.

For the present, then, I advise you: but as time goes on, I shall treat the matter more seriously: for indeed I am greatly afraid that by this practice some grievous disease may make its way into the Church. The case of the wailings then we will hereafter correct. And meanwhile I charge and testify, both to rich and poor, both to women and men.

May God indeed grant that you all depart out of life unwailed, and according to the fitting rule fathers now grown old may be attended to their graves by sons, and mothers by daughters, and grand-children, and great grand-children, in a green old age, and that untimely death may in no case occur. May this then be, and this I pray, and I exhort the prelates and all of you to beseech God for each other, and to make this prayer in common. But if (which God forbid, and may it never happen) any bitter death should occur, bitter, I mean, not in its nature (for henceforth there is no bitter death, for it differs not at all from sleep), but bitter in regard of your disposition, if it should happen, and any

---

[1] The word includes the ideas of being patient, as well as of thinking and speaking deep things.
[2] βιωτικὰς.
[3] κοσμικαῖς καὶ κοσμικοῖς.

should hire these mourning women, believe me when I say (I speak not without meaning [1] but as I have resolved, let him who will, be angry), that person we will exclude from the Church for a long time, as we do the idolater. For if Paul calls "the covetous man an idolater" (Eph. v. 5), much more him who brings in the practices of the idolaters over a believer.

For, tell me, for what cause dost thou invite presbyters, and the singers? Is it not to afford consolation? Is it not to honor the departed? Why then dost thou insult him? And why dost thou make him a public show? And why dost thou make game as on a stage? We come, discoursing of the things concerning the resurrection, instructing all, even those who have not yet been smitten, by the honor shown to him, to bear it nobly if any such thing should happen: and dost thou bring those who overthrow our [teachings] as much as in them lieth? What can be worse than this ridicule and mockery? What more grievous than this inconsistency?

[8.] Be ashamed and show reverence: but if ye will not, we cannot endure the bringing in upon the Church of practices so destructive. For, it is said, "them that sin rebuke before all." (1 Tim. v. 20.) And as to those miserable and wretched women, we through you forbid them [2] ever to introduce themselves into the funerals of the faithful, lest we should oblige them in good earnest to wail over their own evils, and teach them not to do these things in the ills of others, but rather to weep for their own misfortunes. For an affectionate father too, when he has a disorderly son, not only advises him not to draw near to the wicked, but puts them in fear also. Behold then, I advise you, and those women through you, that you do not invite such persons, and that they do not attend. And may God grant that my words may produce some effect, and that my threat may avail. But if (which God forbid) we should be disregarded, we have no choice henceforward but to put our threat into execution, chastising you by the laws of the Church, and those women as befits them.

Now if any man is obstinate and contemptuous, let him hear Christ saying even now, "If any one trespass against thee, go, tell him his fault between thee and him alone"; but if he will not be persuaded, "take with thee one or two." But if even so he contradict, "tell it to the Church, but if he shall also refuse to hear the Church, let him be unto thee as a heathen man and a publican." (Matt. xviii. 15, 16, 17.) Now if when a man trespasses against me, and will not be persuaded, [the Lord] commands me thus to turn away from him, judge

ye in what light I ought to hold him who trespasses against himself, and against God. For do not you yourselves condemn us when we come down so gently upon you?

If however any man disregard the bonds which we inflict, again let Christ instruct him, saying, "Whatsoever ye shall bind on earth shall be bound in heaven; and whatsoever ye shall loose on earth shall be loosed in heaven." (Matt. xviii. 18.) For though we ourselves be miserable and good for nothing and worthy to be despised, as indeed we are; yet are we not avenging ourselves nor warding off anger, but are caring for your salvation.

Be influenced by reverence, I beseech you, and respect. For if a man bear with a friend when he attacks him more vehemently than he ought, ascertaining his object, and that he does it with kind intention, and not out of insolence; much more [should he bear with] a teacher when rebuking him, and a teacher who does not himself say these things as of authority, nor as one in the position of a ruler, but in that of a kindly guardian. For we do not say these things as wishing to exhibit our authority, (for how could we, praying that we may never come to the trial of them?) but grieving and lamenting for you.

Forgive me then, and let no man disregard the bonds of the Church. For it is not man who binds, but Christ who has given unto us this authority, and makes men lords of this so great dignity. For we indeed wish to use this power for loosing; or rather, we wish to have no need even of that, for we wish that there should not be any bound among us — we are not so miserable and wretched [as that] even though some of us are extreme good-for-nothings. If however we be compelled [so to act], forgive us. For it is not of our own accord, nor wishing it, but rather out of sorrow for you that are bound that we put the chains around you. But if any man despise these chains, the time of judgment will come, which shall teach him. And what comes after I do not wish to speak of, lest I should wound your minds. For in the first place indeed we do not wish to be brought into this necessity; but if we are so brought, we fulfill our own part, we cast around the chains. And if any man burst through them, I have done my part, and am henceforth free from blame, and thou wilt have to give account to Him who commanded me to bind.

For neither, when a king is sitting in public, if any of the guard who stand beside him be commanded to bind one of the attendants, and to put the chains around [him], and he should not only thrust this man away, but also break the bonds in pieces, is it the guard who suffers the insult, and not much more the King who gave the order. For if He claim as His own, the things which are done to the faithful, much more will He feel as if Himself insulted when he is insulted who has been appointed to teach.

But God grant that none of those who are over this Church should be driven to the necessity of [inflicting] these bonds. For as it is a good thing not to sin, so is it profitable to endure reproof. Let us then endure the rebuke, and earnestly endeavor not to sin; and if we should sin let us bear the rebuke. For as it is an excellent thing not to be wounded, but, if this should happen, to apply the remedy to the wound, so also in this case.

But God forbid that any man should need such remedies as these. "But we are persuaded better things of you, and things that accompany salvation, though we thus speak." (c. vi. 9.) But we have discoursed more vehemently for the sake of greater security. For it is better that I should be suspected by you of being a harsh, and severe, and self-willed person, than that you should do things not approved of God. But we trust in God, that this reproof will not be unserviceable to you, but that ye will be so changed, that these discourses may be devoted to encomiums on you and to praises: that we may all be counted worthy to attain to those good things, which God hath promised to them that love Him in Christ Jesus our Lord, with whom to the Father together with the Holy Ghost be glory, might, honor, now and for ever and world without end. Amen.

# HOMILY V.

### Hebrews ii. 16, 17.

" For verily He taketh not hold of Angels, but of the seed of Abraham He taketh hold.[1] Wherefore in all things it behooved Him to be made like unto His brethren."

[1.] Paul wishing to show the great kindness of God towards man, and the Love which He had for the human race, after saying: "Forasmuch then as the children were partakers of blood and flesh, He also Himself likewise took part of the same" (c. v. 14) — follows up the subject in this passage. For do not regard lightly what is spoken, nor think this merely a slight [matter], His taking on Him our flesh. He granted not this to Angels; "For verily He taketh not hold of Angels, but of the seed of Abraham." What is it that he saith? He took not on Him an Angel's nature, but man's. But what is "He taketh hold of"? He did not (he means) grasp that nature, which belongs to Angels, but ours. But why did he not say, "He took on Him," but used this expression, "He taketh hold of"? It is derived from the figure of persons pursuing those who turn away from them, and doing everything to overtake them as they flee, and to take hold of them as they are bounding away. For when human nature was fleeing from Him, and fleeing far away (for we "were far off" — Eph. ii. 13), He pursued after and overtook us. He showed that He has done this only out of kindness, and love, and tender care. As then when he saith, "Are they not all ministering spirits, sent forth to minister for them who shall be heirs of salvation" (c. i.

14) — he shows His extreme interest in behalf of human nature, and that God makes great account of it, so also in this place he sets it forth much more by a comparison, for he says, "He taketh not hold of angels." For in very deed it is a great and a wonderful thing, and full of amazement that our flesh should sit on high, and be adored by Angels and Archangels, by the Cherubim and the Seraphim. For myself having oftentimes thought upon this, I am amazed at it, and imagine to myself great things concerning the human race. For I see that the introductions are great and splendid, and that God has great zeal on behalf of our nature.

Moreover he said not "of men (simply) He taketh hold," but wishing to exalt them [the Hebrews] and to show that their race is great and honorable, he says, "but of the seed of Abraham He taketh hold."

"Wherefore it behooved [Him] in all things to be made like unto His brethren." What is this, "in all things"? He was born (he means), was brought up, grew, suffered all things necessary, at last He died. This is, "in all things to be made like unto His brethren." For after he had discoursed much concerning His majesty and the glory on high, he then begins concerning the dispensation. And consider with how great power [he doth this]. How he represents Him as having great zeal "to be made like unto us": which was a sign of much care. For having said above, "Inasmuch then as the children were partakers of flesh and blood, He also Himself in like manner took part of the same";

---

[1] marg. of E. V.

in this place also he says, "in all things to be made like unto His brethren." Which is all but saying, He that is so great, He that is "the brightness of His glory," He that is "the express image of His person," He that "made the worlds," He that "sitteth on the right hand of the Father," He was willing and earnest to become our brother in all things, and for this cause did He leave the angels and the other powers, and come down to us, and took hold of us, ·and wrought innumerable good things. He destroyed Death, He cast out the devil from his tyranny, He freed us from bondage : not by brotherhood alone did He honor us, but also in other ways beyond number. For He was willing also to become our High Priest with the Father : for he adds,

[2.] "That He might become a merciful and faithful High Priest in things pertaining to God." For this cause (he means) He took on Him our flesh, only for Love to man, that He might have mercy upon us. For neither is there· any other cause of the economy, but this alone. For He saw us, cast on the ground, perishing, tyrannized over by Death, and He had compassion on us. "To make reconciliation," he says, "for the sins of the people. That He might be a merciful and faithful High Priest."

What is "faithful"? True, able. For the Son is a faithful High Priest, able to deliver from their sins those whose High Priest He is. In order then that He might offer a sacrifice able to purify us, for this cause He has become man.

Accordingly he added, "in things pertaining to God," — that is, for the sake of things in relation to God. We were become altogether enemies to God, (he would say)· condemned, degraded, there was none who should offer sacrifice for us. He saw us in this condition, and had compassion on us, not appointing a High Priest for us, but Himself becoming a High Priest. In what sense He was "faithful," he added [viz.], "to make reconciliation for the sins of the people."

Ver. 18. "For," he says, "in that He hath suffered Himself being tempted, He is able to succor them that are tempted." This is altogether low and mean, and unworthy of God. "For in that He hath suffered Himself," he says. It is of Him who was made flesh that he here speaks, and it was said for the full assurance of the hearers, and on account of their weakness. That is (he would say) He went through the very experience of the things which we have suffered ; "now" He is not ignorant of our sufferings ; not only does He know them as God, but as man also He has known them, by the trial wherewith He was tried ; He suffered much, He knows how to sympathize. And yet God is incapable of suffering : but he describes here what belongs to the Incarnation, as if he had said, Even the very flesh of Christ suffered many terrible things. He knows what tribulation is ; He knows what temptation is, not less than we who have suffered, for He Himself also has suffered.

(What then is this, "He is able to succor them that are tempted"? It is as if one should say, He will stretch forth His hand with great eagerness, He will be sympathizing.)

[3.] Since they wished for something great, and to have an advantage over the [converts] from the Gentiles, he shows that they have an advantage in this while he did not hurt those from the Gentiles at all. In what respect now is this? Because of them is the salvation, because He took hold of them first, because from that race He assumed flesh. "For," he says, "He taketh not hold of angels, but of the seed of Abraham He taketh hold." Hereby he both gives honor to the Patriarch, and shows also what "the seed of Abraham" is. He reminds them of the promise made to him, saying, "To thee and to thy seed will I give this land" (Gen. xiii. 15) ; showing by the very least thing, the nearness [of the relationship] in that they were "all of one." But that nearness was not great : [so] he comes back to this, and thenceforward dwells upon the dispensation which was after the flesh, and says, Even the mere willing to become man was a proof of great care and love ; but now it is not this alone, but there are also the undying benefits which are bestowed on us through Him, for, he says, "to make reconciliation for the sins of the people."

Why said he not, of the world, instead of " the people"? for He bare away the sins of all. Because thus far his discourse was concerning them [the Hebrews]. Since the Angel also said to Joseph, "Thou shalt call His name JESUS, for He shall save His people." (Matt. i. 21.) For this too ought to have taken place first, and for this purpose He came, to save them and then through them the rest, although the contrary came to pass. This also the Apostles said at the first, "To you [God] having raised up His Son, sent [Him] to bless you" (Acts iii. 26) : and again, "To you was the word of this Salvation sent." (Acts xiii. 26.) Here he shows the noble birth of the Jews, in saying, "to make reconciliation for the sins of the people." For a while he speaks in this way. For that it is He who forgives the sins of all men, He declared both in the case of the paralytic, saying, "Thy sins are forgiven" (Mark ii. 5) ; and also in that of Baptism : for He says to the disciples, "Go ye and teach all nations, baptizing them in the Name of the Father, and of the Son, and of the Holy Ghost." (Matt. xxviii. 19.)

[4.] But when Paul has once taken in hand the flesh, he proceeds to utter all the lowly things, without any fear : for see what he says next :

C. iii. 1, 2. "Wherefore, holy brethren, partakers of the heavenly calling, consider the Apostle and High Priest of our profession, Christ Jesus, who was faithful to Him that appointed [*or* made] Him, as also Moses [was faithful] in all His house."

Being about to place Him before Moses in comparison, he led his discourse to the law of the high-priesthood ; for they all had a high esteem for Moses : moreover, he is already beforehand casting down the seeds of the superiority. Therefore he begins from the flesh, and goes up to the Godhead, where there was no longer any comparison. He began from the flesh [from His Human nature], by assuming for a time the equality, and says, "as also Moses in all His house" : nor does he at first show His superiority lest the hearer should start away, and straightway stop his ears. For although they were believers, yet nevertheless they still had strong feeling of conscience as to Moses. "Who was faithful," he says, "to Him that made Him"—made [Him] what? "Apostle and High Priest." He is not speaking at all in this place of His Essence, nor of His Godhead ; but so far concerning human dignities.

"As also Moses in all His house," that is, either among the people, or in the temple. But here he uses the expression "in His house," just as one might say, concerning those in the household ; even as some guardian and steward of a household, so was Moses to the people. For that by "house" he means the people, he added, "whose house we are" (c. iii. 6) ; that is, we are in His creation. Then [comes] the superiority.

Ver. 3. "For this man was counted worthy of more glory than Moses," (Again [he is speaking] of the Flesh), "inasmuch as he who hath builded[1] [the house] hath more honor than the house" ; [Moses] himself also (he means) was of the house. (Moreover he did not say, For this one was a servant, but the Other a master, but he covertly intimated it.) If the people were the house and he was of the people, then he certainly was of the household. For so also we are accustomed to say, such an one is of such an one's house. For here he is speaking of a house, not of the temple, for the temple was not constructed by God, but by men. But He that made[2] him [is] God. Moses he means. And see how he covertly shows the superiority. "Faithful," he says, "in all His house," being himself also of

the house, that is, of the people. The builder has more honor than the house, yet he did not say "the artificer hath more honor than his works," but "he that hath builded the house, than the house." (Ver. 4.) "But He that built all things is God." Thou seest that he is speaking not about the temple but about the whole people.

Ver. 5. "And Moses verily [was] faithful in all His house, as a servant, for a testimony of those things which were to be spoken." See also another point of superiority, that [which is derived] from the Son and the servants. You see again that by the appellation of The Son, he intimates true relationship. (Ver. 6.) "But Christ as a Son over His own house." Perceivest thou how he separates the thing made and the maker, the servant and the son ? Moreover He indeed enters into His Father's property as a master, but the other as a servant.

"Whose" [i.e.] God's "house are we, if we hold fast the confidence and the rejoicing of the hope firm unto the end." Here again he encourages them to press forward nobly, and not to fall : for we shall be the "house" of God (he says), as Moses was, "if we hold fast our confidence and our rejoicing firm unto the end." He however (he would say) that is distressed in his trials, and who falls, doth not glory : he that is ashamed, he that hideth himself, has no confidence, he that is perplexed doth not glory.

And then he also commends them, saying, "if we hold fast the confidence and the rejoicing of the hope firm unto the end," implying that they had even made a beginning ; but that there is need of the end, and not simply to stand, but to have their hope firm "in full assurance of faith," without being shaken by their trials.

[5.] And be not astonished, that the [words] "Himself being tempted" (c. ii. 18) are spoken more after the manner of men. For if the Scripture says of the Father, who was not made flesh, "The Lord looked down from heaven, and beheld all the sons of men" (Ps. xiv. 2), that is, accurately acquainted Himself with all things ; and again, "I will go down, and see whether they do altogether according to the cry of them" (Gen. xviii. 21) ; and again, "God cannot endure the evil ways of men" (Gen. vi. 5 ?), the divine Scripture shows forth the greatness of His wrath : much more, who even suffered in the flesh, these things are said of Christ. For since many men consider experience the most reliable means of knowledge, he wishes to show that He that has suffered knows what human nature suffers.

"Whence[3] holy brethren" (he says "whence" instead of "for this cause"), "partakers of an

---

[1] κατασκευάσας.
[2] ποιήσας. Referring to what is implied in ver. 2, that Moses was faithful to Him that made him.

[3] ὅθεν.

heavenly calling" — (seek nothing here, if ye have been called yonder — yonder is the reward, yonder the recompense. What then?) "Consider the Apostle and High Priest of our profession, Christ JESUS, who was faithful to Him that appointed Him, as also Moses [was faithful] in all His house." (What is "who was faithful to Him that appointed Him?" it is, well disposed, protecting what belongs to Him, not allowing them to be lightly carried away, "as also Moses in all His house") that is, know who your High Priest is, and what He is, and ye will need no other consolation nor encouragement. Now he calls Him "Apostle," on account of His having been "sent," and "high priest of our profession," that is of the Faith. This One also was entrusted with a people, as the other with the leadership of a people, but a greater one, and upon higher grounds.

"For a testimony of those things which shall be spoken." What meanest thou? Doth God receive the witness of man? Yes, certainly. For if He call to witness heaven and earth and hills (saying by the prophet, "Hear, O heaven, and give ear, O earth, for the Lord hath spoken" — Isa. i. 2 — and "Hear ye ravines,[1] foundations of the earth, for the Lord hath a controversy with His people" — Mic. vi. 2·), much more men; that is, that they may be witnesses, when themselves [the Jews] shameless.

Ver. 6. "But Christ as a Son." The one takes care of the property of others, but this One of His own. "And the rejoicing of the hope." Well said he "of the hope." For since the good things were all in hope, and yet we ought so "to hold it fast," as even now to glory as for things which had already come to pass: for this cause he says, "the rejoicing of the hope."

And adds, "let us hold it firm unto the end." (Rom. viii. 24.) For "by hope we are saved"; if therefore "we are saved by hope," and "are waiting with patience" (Rom. viii. 25), let us not be grieved at present things, nor seek now those that have been promised afterwards; "For" (he says) "hope which is seen is not hope." For since the good things are great, we cannot receive them here in this transitory life. With what object then did He even tell us of them beforehand, when He was not about to give them here? In order that by the promise He might refresh our souls, that by the engagement He might strengthen our zeal, that He might anoint [preparing us for our contests] and stir up our mind. For this cause then all these things were done.

[6.] Let us not then be troubled, let no man be troubled, when he seeth the wicked prospering. The recompense is not here, either of wickedness or of virtue; and if in any instance there be either of wickedness or of virtue, yet is it not according to desert, but merely as it were a taste of the judgment, that they who believe not the resurrection may yet even by things that happen here be brought to their senses. When then we see a wicked man rich, let us not be cast down; when we see a good man suffering, let us not be troubled. For yonder are the crowns, yonder the punishments.

Yea and in another point of view, it is not possible either that a bad man should be altogether bad, but he may have some good things also: nor again that a good man should be altogether good, but he may also have some sins. When therefore the wicked man prospers, it is for evil on his own head, that having here received the reward of those few good things, he may hereafter be utterly punished yonder; for this cause does he receive his recompense in this life. And happy is he most of all who is punished here, that having put away all his sins, he may depart approved, and pure, and without having to be called to account. And this Paul teacheth us when he says, "For this cause many [are] weak and sickly among you, and many sleep." (1 Cor. xi. 30.) And again, "I have delivered such an one to Satan." (1 Cor. v. 5.) And the prophet says, "for she hath received of the Lord's hand her sins double " (Isa. xl. 2); and again David, "Behold mine enemies that they are multiplied above the hairs of my head,[2] and [with] an unjust hatred have they hated me": "and forgive Thou all my sins." (Ps. xxv. 19, 18.) And again another: "O Lord, our God, give peace unto us; for Thou hast rendered all things to us again." (Isa. xxvi. 12.)

These however are [the words] of one showing that good men receive here the punishments of their sins. But where are the wicked [mentioned] who receive their good things here, and there are utterly punished? Hear Abraham saying to the rich man, "Thou didst receive good things," and "Lazarus evil things." (Luke xvi. 25.) What good things? For in this place by saying "thou receivest,[3]" and not thou "hadst taken,[4]" he shows that it was according to what was due to him that each was treated, and that the one was in prosperity, and the other in adversity. And he says, "Therefore he is comforted" here (for thou seest him pure from sins) "and thou art tormented." Let us not then be perplexed when we see sinners well off here; but when we ourselves are afflicted, let us rejoice.

---

[1] St. Chrys. had mentioned hills (βουνοὶ) as called to witness by God: in the verse preceding this (Mic. vi. 1) occur the words, "let *the hills* hear Thy voice"; and this verse itself runs, "Hear ye hills" (βουνοὶ) according to the Alexandrine MSS. of the LXX. or "ye mountains" (ὄρη according to the Vatican), "the judgment of the Lord, and ye ravines," &c.

[2] The words "above the hairs of my head" are part of another Psalm, xl. 12, or lxix. 4.
[3] ἀπέλαβες.　　　　[4] ἔλαβες.

For this very thing is paying off the penalty[1] of sins.

[7.] Let us not then seek relaxation: for Christ promised tribulation to His disciples: and Paul says, "All who will live godly in Christ Jesus, shall suffer persecution." (2 Tim. iii. 12.) No noble-spirited wrestler, when in the lists,[2] seeks for baths, and a table full of food and wine. This is not for a wrestler, but for a sluggard. For the wrestler contendeth with dust, with oil, with the heat of the sun's ray, with much sweat, with pressure and constraint. This is the time for contest and for fighting, therefore also for being wounded, and for being bloody and in pain. Hear what the blessed Paul says, "So fight I, not as one that beateth the air." (1 Cor. ix. 26.) Let us consider that our whole life is in combats, and then we shall never seek rest, we shall never feel it strange when we are afflicted: no more than a boxer feels it strange, when he combats. There is another season for repose. By tribulation we must be made perfect.

And even if there be no persecution, nor tribulation, yet there are other afflictions which befall us every day. And if we do not bear these, we should scarcely endure those. "There hath no temptation taken you," it is said, "but such as is common to man." (1 Cor. x. 13.) Let us then pray indeed to God that we may not come into temptation; but if we come into it, let us bear it nobly. For that indeed is the part of prudent men, not to throw themselves upon dangers; but this of noble men and true philosophers. Let us not then lightly cast ourselves upon [dangers], for that is rashness; nor yet, if led into them, and called by circumstances, let us give in, for that is cowardice. But if indeed the Gospel[3] call us, let us not refuse; but in a simple case, when there is no reason, nor need, nor necessity which calls us in the fear of God, let us not rush in. For this is mere display, and useless ambition. But should any of those things which are injurious to religion occur, then though it be necessary to endure ten thousand deaths, let us refuse nothing. Challenge not trials, when thou findest the things that concern godliness prosper as thou desirest. Why draw down needless dangers which bring no gain?

These things I say, because I wish you to observe the laws of Christ who commands us to "pray that we enter not into temptation" (Matt. xxvi. 41), and commands us to "take up the cross and follow" Him. (Matt. xvi. 24.) For these things are not contradictory, nay they are rather exceedingly in harmony. Do thou be so prepared as is a valiant soldier, be continually in thine armor, sober, watchful, ever looking for the enemy: do not however breed wars, for this is not [the act] of a soldier but of a mover of sedition. But if on the other hand the trumpet of godliness call thee, go forth immediately, and make no account of thy life, and enter with great eagerness into the contests, break the phalanx of the adversaries, bruise the face of the devil, set up thy trophy. If however godliness be in nowise harmed, and no one lay waste our doctrines (those I mean which relate to the soul), nor compel us to do anything displeasing to God, do not be officious.

The life of the Christian must be full of bloodsheddings; I say not in shedding that of others, but in readiness to shed one's own. Let us then pour out our own blood, when it is for Christ's sake, with as great readiness as one would pour out water (for the blood which flows about the body is water), and let us put off our flesh with as much good temper, as one even would a garment. And this shall we do, if we be not bound to riches, if not to houses, if not to affections, if we be detached from all things. For if they who live this life of [earthly] soldiers bid farewell to all things, and whithersoever war calls them there present themselves, and make journeys, and endure all things with ready mind; much more ought we, the soldiers of Christ, so to have prepared ourselves, and to set ourselves firm against the war of the passions.

[8.] There is no persecution now, and God grant there may never be: but there is another war, that of the desire of money, of envy, of the passions. Paul, describing this war, says, "We wrestle not against flesh and blood." (Eph. vi. 12.) This war is ever at hand. Therefore he wishes us to stand ever armed. Because he wishes us to stand ever armed, he says, "Stand, having girded yourselves about." (Eph. vi. 14.) Which itself also belongs to the time present, and expresses that we ought ever to be armed. For great is the war through the tongue, great that through the eyes; this then we must keep down — great [too] is that of the lusts.

Therefore he begins at that point to arm the soldier of Christ: for "stand," saith he, "having your loins girt about," and he added "with truth." (Eph. vi. 14.) Why "with truth"? Because lust is a mockery and a lie: wherefore the prophet says, "My loins are filled with mockings." (Ps. xxxviii. 7.) The thing is not pleasure, but a shadow of pleasure. "Having your loins," he says, "girt about with truth"; that is, with true pleasure, with temperance, with orderly behavior. For this cause he gives this advice, knowing the unreasonableness of sin, and wishing that all our members should be hedged round; for "unjust anger," it is said, "shall not be guiltless." (Ecclus. i. 22.)

<hr>

[1] ἔκτισις.    [2] σκάμματι.    [3] κήρυγμα.

Moreover he wishes us to have around us a breastplate and a buckler. For desire is a wild beast which easily springs forth, and we shall have need of walls and fences innumerable, to overcome, and to restrain it. And for this cause God has built this part [of our body] especially with bones, as with a kind of stones, placing around it a support, so that [desire] might not at any time, having broken or cut through, easily injure the whole man. For it is a fire (it is said) and a great tempest, and no other part of the body could endure this violence. And the sons of the physicians too say that for this cause the lungs have been spread under the heart, so that the heart being itself [put] into something soft and tender, by beating as it were into a sort of sponge, may continually be rested, and not [by striking] against the resisting and hard sternum, receive hurt through the violence of its beatings. We have need therefore of a strong breastplate, so as to keep this wild beast alway quiet.

We have need also of an helmet; for since the reasoning faculty is there, and from this it is possible for us either to be saved, when what is right is done, or it is possible for us to be ruined — therefore he says, "the helmet of salvation." (Eph. vi. 17.) For the brain is indeed by nature tender, and therefore is covered above with the skull, as with a kind of shell. And it is to us the cause of all things both good and evil, knowing what is fitting, or what is not so. Yea and our feet too and our hands need armor, not these hands, nor these feet, but as before those of the soul — the former by being employed about what is right, the latter, that they may walk where they ought. Thus then let us thoroughly arm ourselves, and we shall be able to overcome our enemies, and to wreathe ourselves with the crown in Christ Jesus our Lord, with whom to the Father together with the Holy Ghost be glory, might, honor, now and for ever and world without end. Amen.

---

# HOMILY VI.

### HEBREWS iii. 7–11.

" Wherefore, as the Holy Ghost saith, To-day if ye will hear His voice, harden not your hearts, as in the provocation in the day of temptation in the wilderness, when your fathers tempted Me, proved Me, and saw My works forty years. Wherefore I was grieved with that generation, and said, They do alway err in their heart, and they have not known My ways. So[1] I sware in My wrath they shall not enter into My rest."

[1.] PAUL, having treated of hope, and having said that "We are His house, if we hold fast the confidence and the rejoicing of the hope firm unto the end " (c. iii. ver. 6) ; next shows that we ought to look forward with firmness, and he proves this from the Scriptures. But be attentive, because he has expressed this in a manner somewhat difficult and not readily to be comprehended. And therefore we must first make our own statements, and after we have briefly explained the whole argument, then make clear the words of the Epistle. For you will no longer need us, if you have understood the scope of the Apostle.

His discourse was concerning Hope, and that it behooves us to hope for the things to come, and that for those who have toiled here there will assuredly be some reward and fruit and refreshment. This then he shows from the prophet ; and what says he? " Wherefore as

the Holy Ghost saith, To-day if ye will hear His voice, harden not your hearts, as in the provocation, in the day of temptation in the wilderness : when your fathers tempted Me, proved Me, and saw My works forty years. Wherefore I was grieved with that generation, and said, they do alway err in their heart, and they have not known My ways. So[2] I sware in My wrath, they shall not enter into My rest."

He says that there are " three " rests : one, that of the Sabbath, in which God rested from His works ; the second, that of Palestine, into which when the Jews had entered they would be at rest from their hardships and labors ; the third, that which is Rest indeed, the kingdom of Heaven ; which those who obtain, do indeed rest from their labors and troubles. Of these three then he makes mention here.

And why did he mention the three, when he is treating of the one only? That he might show that the prophet is speaking concerning this one. For he did not speak (he says) concerning the first. For how could he, when that had taken place long before? Nor yet again concerning the second, that in Palestine. For how could he? For he says, " They shall not enter into My rest." It remains therefore that it is this third.

[2.] But it is necessary also to unfold the

---

[1] as.

[2] as.

history, to make the argument more clear. For when they had come forth out of Egypt, and had accomplished a long journey, and had received innumerable proofs of the power of God, both in Egypt, and in the Red Sea (cf. Acts vii. 36), and in the wilderness, they determined to send spies to search out the nature of the land; and these went and returned, admiring indeed the country, and saying that it abounded in noble fruits, nevertheless it was a country of strong and invincible men: and the ungrateful and senseless Jews, when they ought to have called to mind the former blessings of God, and how when they were hemmed in in the midst of the armies of so many Egyptians, He rescued them from their perils, and made them masters of their enemies' spoils; and again, in the wilderness He clave the rock, and bestowed on them abundance of waters, and gave them the manna, and the other wonderful things which He wrought; [when they ought, I say, to have remembered this,] and to have trusted in God, they considered none of these things, but being struck with terror, just as if nothing had been done, they said, we wish to go back again into Egypt, "for God hath brought us out thither" (it is said) "to slay us, with our children and wives." (Cf. Num. xiv. 3.) God therefore being angry that they had so quickly cast off the memory of what had been done, sware that that generation, which had said these things, should not enter into the Rest; and they all perished in the wilderness. When David then, he says, speaking at a later period, and after these events, after that generation of men, said, "To-day, if ye will hear His voice, harden not your hearts," that ye may not suffer the same things which your forefathers did, and be deprived of the Rest; he evidently [said this] as of some [future] rest. For if they had received their Rest (he says) why does He again say to them, "To-day if ye will hear His voice harden not your hearts," as your fathers did? What other rest then is there, except the kingdom of Heaven, of which the Sabbath was an image and type?

[3.] Next having set down the whole testimony (and this is, "To-day if ye will hear His voice, harden not your hearts, as in the provocation in the day of temptation in the wilderness, when your fathers tempted Me, proved Me, and saw My works forty years. Wherefore I was grieved with that generation, and said, They do alway err in their heart, and they have not known My ways. So I sware in My wrath, they shall not enter into My rest"), he then adds:

Ver. 12. "Take heed, brethren, lest there be in any of you an evil heart of unbelief in departing from the living God." For from hardness unbelief ariseth: and as in bodies, the parts that have become callous and hard do not yield

to the hands of the physicians, so also souls that are hardened yield not to the word of God. For it is probable besides that some even disbelieved as though the things which had been done were not true.

Therefore he says, "Take heed lest there be in any of you an evil heart of unbelief in departing from the living God." For since the argument from the future is not so persuasive as from the past, he reminds them of the history, in which they had wanted faith. For if your fathers (he says) because they did not hope as they ought to have hoped, suffered these things, much more will you. Since to them also is this word addressed: for, "To-day" (he says) is "ever," so long as the world lasts.

[4.] Ver. 13. Wherefore "exhort ye one another daily, while it is called to-day." That is, edify one another, raise yourselves up: lest the same things should befall you. "Lest any one of you be hardened by the deceitfulness of sin." Seest thou that sin produces unbelief? For as unbelief brings forth an evil life, so also a soul, "when it is come into a depth of evils, becometh contemptuous"[1] (Prov. xviii. 3), and having become contemptuous it endures not even to believe, in order thereby to free itself from fear. For "they said" (one says), "The Lord shall not see, neither shall the God of Jacob regard." (Ps. xciv. 7.) And again, "Our lips are our own: who is Lord over us?" (Ps. xii. 4); and again, "Wherefore hath the wicked man provoked God to wrath?" (Ps. x. 13); and again, "The fool hath said in his heart, there is no God; they are corrupt and become abominable in their doings." (Ps. xiv. 1.) "There is no fear of God before his eyes, for he was deceitful before Him, to find out[2] his iniquity and to hate." (Ps. xxxvi. 1, 2.) Yea and Christ also says this same thing, "Every one that doeth evil, hateth the light and cometh not to the light." (John iii. 20.)

Then he adds (ver. 14), "For we have been made partakers of Christ." What is this, "We have been made partakers of Christ"? We partake of Him (he means); we were made One, we and He — since He is the Head and we the body, "fellow-heirs and of the same body; we are one body, of His flesh and of His bones." (Eph. iii. 6; Rom. xii. 5; Eph. v. 30.)

"If we hold fast the beginning of our confidence [or, the principle of our subsistence[3]] steadfast unto the end." What is "the principle of our subsistence"? The faith by which we stand, and have been brought into being and were made to exist, as one may say.

[5.] Then he adds (ver. 15), "When it is

---

[1] καταφρονεῖ.　　　[2] τοῦ εὑρεῖν.
[3] ἀρχὴν τῆς ὑποστάσεως. St. Chrys. understands ὑπόστασις in its prior sense, as "subsistence," "subsisting," "being brought into real existence."

said,[1] To-day if ye hear His voice, harden not your hearts, as in the provocation." This is a transposition,[2] "when it is said, To-day if ye hear His voice, harden not your hearts." [It must be read thus :]

(Ch. iv. 1, 2.) "Let us fear lest a promise being left us of entering into His rest, any of you should seem to come short of it ; for to us was the Gospel preached[3] as well as unto them, when it is said, To-day if ye hear His voice" (for "To-day" is "at every time "[4]).

Then [he adds] "but the word of hearing did not profit them, as they were not mixed[5] by faith with them that heard." How did it not profit? Then wishing to alarm them, he shows the same thing by what he says :

(Ch. iii. 16–19.) "For some when they had heard did provoke, howbeit not all that came out of Egypt by Moses : And with whom was He grieved forty years? Was it not with them that had sinned, whose carcasses fell in the wilderness? And to whom swear He that they should not enter into His rest, but to them that believed not? So[6] we see, that they could not enter in because of unbelief." After again repeating the testimony, he adds also the question, which makes the argument clear. For he said (he repeats), "To-day if ye hear His voice, harden not your hearts, as. in the provocation." Of whom does he speak (he says) [as] having been hardened? Of whom [as] not believing? Is it not of the Jews?

Now what he says is to this effect. They also heard, as we hear : but no profit came to them. Do not suppose then that by " hearing " what is proclaimed ye will be profited ; seeing that they also heard, but derived no benefit because they did not believe.

Caleb then and Joshua, because they agreed not with those who did not believe, escaped the vengeance that was sent forth against them. And see how admirably he said, not, They did not agree, but, "they were not mixed " — that is, they stood apart, but not factiously when all the others had one and the same mind. Here it seems to me that a faction too is hinted at.[7]

[6.] (Ch. iv. 3.) For " we who have believed," he says, " do enter into rest." From what this is evident, he adds : " as He said, as I have sworn in My wrath, if they shall enter into My rest : although the works were finished from the foundation of the world." This indeed, is not evidence that we shall enter in, but that they did not enter in. What then? Thus far he aims to show that as that rest does not hinder the speaking of another rest, so neither does this [exclude] that of Heaven. Up to this point then, he wishes to show that they [the Israelites] did not attain to the rest. For because he means this, he says (ver. 4, 5), " For he spake in a certain place of the seventh day on this wise, And God did rest the seventh day from all His works. And in this place again, If they shall enter into My rest." Thou seest how that doth not hinder this from being a rest?

Ver. 6, 7. "Seeing therefore it remaineth " (he says) " that some must enter therein, and they to whom it was first preached entered not in because of unbelief : again he limiteth a certain day, saying in David, To-day, after so long a time ; as it has been said before."[8] But what is it that he means? " Seeing then " (he means) that " some must " certainly " enter in," and " they did not enter in." And that an entrance is proclaimed, and that " some must enter in," let us hear from what this is clear. Because after so many years (he says) David again says : " To-day if ye will hear His voice, harden not your hearts " (ver. 8), " For if Joshua had given them rest he would not afterward have spoken of another day." It is evident, that he says these things, as of persons who are to attain some recompense.

[7.] Ver. 9. " There remaineth therefore a rest[9] for the people of God." Whence [does this appear]? From the exhortation, " Harden not your hearts ": for if there were no rest, these exhortations would not have been given. Neither would they have been exhorted not to do the same things [with the Jews] lest they should suffer the same things, unless they were about to suffer the same. But how were they who were in possession of Palestine about to suffer the same things [i.e. exclusion from the rest] unless there were some other rest?

And well did he conclude the argument. For he said not rest but " Sabbath-keeping " ; calling the kingdom " Sabbath-keeping," by the appropriate name, and that which they rejoiced in and were attracted by. For as, on the Sabbath He commands to abstain from all evil things ; and that those things only which relate to the Service of God should be done, which things the Priests were wont to accomplish, and whatsoever profits the soul, and nothing else ; so also [will it be] then. However it is not he

---

[1] ἐν τῷ λέγεσθαι, " in its being said."　　[2] καθ' ὑπέρβατον.
[3] That is, these words are addressed to us as well as to them.
[4] ἀεί.
[5] συγκεκραμένους. Sav. and Ben. have συγκεκραμένης (i.e. ἀκοῆς). The received text of the New Testament has συγκεκραμένος, " the word not being mixed." [This is also given in the margin of W. H. and of the Revisers.] Lachmann [and Tisch., W. H., and the Revisers] read συγκεκερασμένους, which is the reading of some MSS. of St. Chrys.　　[6] And.
[7] αἰνίττεσθαι. That is, is indirectly condemned, by the contrast of the conduct of Caleb and Joshua. St. Chrys. reverses the expression of the Epistle, and says, " Caleb and Joshua were not mixed with the unbelievers," when the Apostle had said, " the unbelievers were not mixed with them."

[8] προείρηται. This is the correct reading of the sacred text Heb. iv. 7: for which the common editions [i.e. the Textus Receptus. All critical editors have προείρ. — F. G.] have εἴρηται, " it is said."
[9] σαββατισμός.

who spoke thus, but what? (Ver. 10), " For he that is entered into his rest, he also hath ceased from his own works, as God [did] from His." As God ceased from His works, he says, so he that hath entered into His rest [hath ceased]. For since his discourse to them was concerning rest, and they were desirous to hear when this would be, he concluded the argument with this.

[8.] And [he said] "To-day,"[1] that they might never be without hope. " Exhort one another daily," he says, [" while it is called to-day,"] that is, even if a man have sinned, as long as it is " To-day," he has hope : let no man then despair so long as he lives. Above all things indeed, he says, " let there not be an evil heart of unbelief." (c. iii. 12.) But even suppose there should be, let no man despair, but let him recover himself ; for as long as we are in this world, the " To-day " is in season. But here he means not unbelief only, but also murmurings : " whose carcasses," he says, " fell in the wilderness."[2]

Then, lest any think that they will simply be deprived of rest only, he adds also the punishment, saying (c. iv. 12), " For the Word of God is quick, and powerful ; and sharper than any two-edged sword, and pierceth even to the dividing asunder of soul and spirit, and of the joints and marrow : and is a discerner of the thoughts and intents of the heart." Here he is speaking of Hell and of punishment. " It pierceth " (he says) into the secrets of our heart, and cutteth asunder the soul. Here it is not the falling of carcasses nor, as there, the being deprived of a country, but of a heavenly kingdom ; and being delivered to an everlasting hell, and to undying punishment and vengeance.

(Ch. iii. 13.) " But exhort[3] one another." Observe the gentleness and mildness [of the expression] : he said not " Rebuke," but " Exhort." Thus we are required to bear ourselves towards those who are straightened by affliction. This he says also in writing to the Thessalonians, " Warn them that are unruly " (1 Thess. v. 14), but in speaking of the feeble-minded, not so, but what? " Comfort the feeble-minded, support the weak, be patient toward all men " ; that is, do not cease to hope ; do not despair. For he that does not encourage one who is straightened by affliction, makes him more hardened.

[9.] " Lest any of you," he says, " be hardened by the deceitfulness of sin." He means either the deceit of the devil (for it is indeed a deceit, not to look for the things to come, to

think that we are without responsibility, and that we shall not pay the penalty for our deeds here, neither will there be a resurrection) ; or in another sense insensibility [or] despairing is deceit. For to say, ' What is there left? I have sinned once for all, I have no hope of recovering myself,' is deceit.

Then he suggests hopes to them, saying (ver. 14), " We are made partakers of Christ " ; All but saying, He that so loved us, He that counted us worthy of so great things, as to make us His Body, will not suffer us to perish. Let us consider (he says) of what we have been thought worthy : we and Christ are One : let us not then distrust Him. And again, he hints at that which had been said in another place, that " If we suffer, we shall also reign with Him." (2 Tim. ii. 12.) For this is [implied in] " We are made partakers," we partake of the same things whereof Christ also partakes.

He urges them on from the good things ; " for we are," he says, " partakers of Christ." Then, again, from gloomy ones (c. iv. 1), " Let us fear, lest at any time a promise being left us of entering into His rest, any of you should seem to come short of it." For that is manifest and confessed.

(Ch. iii. 9.) " They proved Me," He says, " and saw My works forty years." Seest thou that it is not right to call God to account, but whether He defend [our cause] or not, to trust Him? For against those [of old] he now brings this charge, that " they tempted God." For he that will have proof either of His power, or of His providence, or of His tender care, does not yet believe, either that He is powerful or kind to man. This he hints also in writing to these [Hebrews] who probably already wished, in their trials, to obtain experience and positive evidence of His power and His providential care for them. Thou seest that in all cases the provocation and the angering arises from unbelief.

What then does he say? (c. iv. 9.) " There remaineth therefore a rest for the people of God." And see how he has summed up the whole argument. " He sware," saith he, to those former ones, " that they should not enter into " the " rest," and they did not enter in. Then long after their time discoursing to the Jews, he says, " Harden not your hearts," as your fathers, showing that there is another rest. For of Palestine we have not to speak : for they were already in possession of it. Nor can he be speaking of the seventh [day] ; for surely he was not discoursing about that which had taken place long before. It follows therefore that he hints at some other, that which is rest indeed.

[10.] For that is indeed rest, where " pain, sorrow and sighing are fled away " (Isa. xxxv. 10) : where there are neither cares, nor labors,

---

[1] St. Chrys. returns here to c. iii. 13, connecting the " To-day if ye hear His voice, harden not your heart," with " Exhort one another daily while it is called To-day": as he had said, " to-day is at every time."

[2] The words of the Apostle, c. iii. 17, are those of Num. xiv. 29, &c., where murmuring is the sin specified.

[3] παρακαλεῖτε. The word includes the idea of comforting and encouraging as well as of exhorting.

nor struggle, nor fear stunning and shaking the soul; but only that fear of God which is full of delight. There there is not, "In the sweat of thy face thou shalt eat thy bread," nor "thorns and thistles" (Gen. iii. 19, 18); no longer, "In sorrow thou shalt bring forth children, and to thy husband shall be thy desire and he shall rule over thee." (Gen. iii. 16.) All is peace, joy, gladness, pleasure, goodness, gentleness. There is no jealousy, nor envy, no sickness, no death whether of the body, or that of the soul. There is no darkness nor night; all [is] day, all light, all things are bright. It is not possible to be weary, it is not possible to be satiated: we shall always persevere in the desire of good things.[1]

Would you that I should also give you some image of the condition there? It is impossible. But yet, so far as it is possible, I will try to give you some image. Let us look up into the heaven, when without any intervening cloud it shows forth its crown [of stars]. Then when we have dwelt long on the beauty of its appearance, let us think that we too shall have a pavement, not indeed such [as this], but as much more beautiful as the gold is than the clay, and [let us think] on the higher roof which is again beyond; then on the Angels, the Archangels, the infinite multitude of unbodied powers, the very palace of God itself, the Throne of the Father.

But language is too weak (as I said) to set forth the whole. Experience is necessary, and the knowledge which [cometh] by experience. Tell me, how was it (think you) with Adam in Paradise? This course of life is far better than that, as much as heaven [is better] than earth. [11.] But however let us search after another image still. If it happened that he who now reigns was master of the whole world, and then was troubled neither by wars nor by cares, but was honored only and lived delicately; and had large tributes, and on every side gold flowed in to him, and he was looked up to, what feelings do you think he would have, if he saw that all the wars in all parts of the world had ceased? Something such as this will it be. But rather I have not even yet arrived at that image [which I seek]; therefore I must search after another too.

Consider then, I pray you: for as some royal child, so long as he is in the womb, has no sense of anything, but should it happen that he suddenly came forth from thence, and ascended the royal throne, not gradually, but all at once received possession of all things; so is it as regards this [present] and that [future] state. Or, if some captive, having suffered innumerable evils, should be caught up at once to the royal throne.

But not even thus have I attained to the image exactly. For here indeed whatever good things a person may obtain, even shouldst thou say the kingdom itself, during the first day indeed his desires are in full vigor, and for the second too, and the third, but as time goes on, he continues indeed to have pleasure, but not so great. For whatever it be, it always ceases from familiarity with it. But yonder it not only does not diminish, but even increases. For consider how great a thing it is, that a soul after departing thither, should no longer look for an end of those good things, nor yet change, but increase, and life that has no end, and life set free from all danger, and from all despondency and care, full of cheerfulness and blessings innumerable.

For if when we go out into a plain, and there see the soldiers' tents fixed with curtains, and the spears, and helmets, and bosses of the bucklers glittering, we are lifted up with wonder; but if we also chance to see the king himself running in the midst or even riding with golden armor, we think we have everything; what thinkest thou [it will be] when thou seest the everlasting tabernacles of the saints pitched in heaven? (For it is said, "They shall receive you into their everlasting tabernacles"—Luke xvi. 9) when thou seest each one of them beaming with light above the rays of the sun, not from brass and steel, but from that glory whose gleamings the eye of man cannot look upon? And this indeed with respect to the men. But what, if one were to speak of the thousands of Angels, of Archangels, of Cherubim, of Seraphim, of thrones, of dominions, of principalities, of powers, whose beauty is inimitable, passing all understanding?

But how far shall I go in pursuing what cannot be overtaken? "For eye hath not seen," it is said, "nor ear heard, neither have entered into the heart of man, the things which God hath prepared for them that love Him." (1 Cor. ii. 9.) Therefore nothing is more pitiable than those who miss, nor anything more blessed than those who attain. Let us then be of the blessed, that we may attain to the everlasting good things that are in Christ Jesus our Lord, with whom to the Father together with the Holy Ghost be glory, might, honor, now and for ever and world without end. Amen.

---

[1] [The insatiate yet satisfied; The full yet craving still.
*Rhythm of Bernard de Morlaix*, translated by Dr. Neale, p. 15.]

# HOMILY VII.

Hebrews iv. 11–13.

" Let us labor therefore to enter into that rest, lest any man fall after the same example of unbelief. For the word of God is quick [i.e. living] and powerful, and sharper than any two-edged sword, piercing even to the dividing asunder of soul and spirit, and of the joints and marrow, and is a discerner of the thoughts and intents of the heart, neither is there any creature that is not manifest in His sight, but all things are naked and opened unto the eyes of Him with whom we have to do."

[1.] Faith is indeed great and bringeth salvation, and without it, it is not possible ever to be saved. It suffices not however of itself to accomplish this, but there is need of a right conversation also. So that on this account Paul also exhorts those who had already been counted worthy of the mysteries ; saying, " Let us labor to enter into that rest." " Let us labor " (he says), Faith not sufficing, the life also ought to be added thereto, and our earnestness to be great ; for truly there is need of much earnestness too, in order to go up into Heaven. For if they who suffered so great distress in the Wilderness, were not counted worthy of [the promised] land, and were not able to attain [that] land, because they murmured and because they committed fornication : how shall we be counted worthy of Heaven, if we live carelessly and indolently? We then have need of much earnestness.

And observe, the punishment does not extend to this only, the not entering in (for he said not, " Let us labor to enter into the rest," lest we fail of so great blessings), but he added what most of all arouses men. What then is this? " Lest any man fall, after the same example of unbelief." What means this? It means that we should have our mind, our hope, our expectation, yonder, lest we should fail. For that [otherwise] we shall fail, the example shows, " lest [&c.] after the same," he says.

[2.] In the next place, lest hearing [the words] " after the same [example]," thou shouldest think that the punishment is the same, hear what he adds ; " For the Word of God is quick and powerful, and sharper than any two-edged sword, and pierceth even to the dividing asunder of soul and spirit, and of the joints and marrow, and is a discerner of the thoughts and intents of the heart." In these words he shows that He, the Word of God, wrought the former things also, and lives, and has not been quenched.[1]

Do not then when hearing the Word, think of it lightly. For " He is sharper," he says, " than a sword." Observe His condescension ; and hence consider why the prophets also needed to speak of saber [2] and bow and sword.[3] " If ye turn not," it is said, " He will whet His sword, He hath bent His bow and made it ready." (Ps. vii. 12.) For if now, after so long a time, and after their being perfected,[4] He cannot smite down by the name of the Word alone, but needs these expressions in order to show the superiority [arising] from the comparison [of the Gospel with the law] : much more then [of old].

" Piercing," he says, " even to the dividing asunder of soul and spirit." What is this? He hinted at something more fearful. Either that He divides the spirit from the soul, or that He pierces even through them disembodied, not as a sword through bodies only. Here he shows, that the soul also is punished, and that it thoroughly searches out the most inward things, piercing wholly through the whole man.

" And is a discerner of the thoughts and intents of the heart, neither is there any creature that is not manifest in His sight." In these words most of all he terrified them. For do not (he says) be confident if ye still stand fast in the Faith, but without full assurance. He judges the inner heart, for there He passes through, both punishing and searching out.

And why speak I of men? he says. For even if thou speak of Angels, of Archangels, of the Cherubim, of the Seraphim, even of any " creature " whatsoever : all things are laid open to that Eye, all things are clear and manifest ; there is nothing able to escape it ; " All things are naked and opened unto the eyes of Him, with whom we have to do."

But what is " opened "[5]? [It is] a metaphor from the skins which are drawn off from the victims. For as in that case, when a man has killed them, and has drawn aside the skin from the flesh, he lays open all the inward parts, and makes them manifest to our eyes ; so also do all things lie open before God. And observe, I pray thee, how he constantly needs bodily im-

---

[1] [St. Chrys. here understands the λόγος of the Second Person of the Trinity. It is now generally interpreted as a personification of the spoken or written word sent forth by Him. — F. G.]
[2] μάχαιραν.
[3] ῥομφαίαν.
[4] μετὰ τελείωσιν, i.e. by Baptism. [The meaning of τελείωσις can hardly here be restricted to the baptism of the individual, but rather refers to the perfection of the means of salvation under the Gospel, which the Apostle so often expresses in this Epistle by τελείωσις. — F. G.]
[5] τετραχηλισμένα.

ages; which arose from the weakness of the hearers. For that they were weak, he made plain, when he said that they were " dull," and " had need of milk, not of strong meat." " All things are naked," he says, " and opened unto the eyes of Him, with whom we have to do." (c. v. 11, 12.)

[3.] But what is, " after the same example of unbelief " ? As if one should say, why did they of old not see the land? They had received an earnest of the power of God; they ought to have believed, but yielding too much to fear, and imagining nothing great concerning God, and being faint-hearted, — so they perished. And there is also something more to be said, as, that after they had accomplished the most part of the journey, when they were at the very doors, at the haven itself, they were sunk into the sea. This I fear (he says) for you also. This is [the meaning of] " after the same example of unbelief."

For that these also [to whom he is writing] had suffered much, he afterwards testifies, saying, " Call to mind the former days, in which after that ye had been enlightened, ye endured a great fight of afflictions." (c. x. 32.) Let no man then be faint-hearted, nor fall down near the end through weariness. For there are, there are those who at the beginning engage in the fight with the full vigor of zeal; but a little after, not being willing to add to all, they lose all. Your forefathers (he says) are sufficient to instruct you not to fall into the same [sins], not to suffer the same things which they suffered. This is, " After the same example of unbelief." Let us not faint, he means (which he says also near the end [of the Epistle]. " Lift up the hands which hang down, and the feeble knees ") : " lest any man," he says, " fall after the same example." (c. xii. 12.) For this is to fall indeed.

Then, lest when thou hearest, " any man fall after the same example," thou shouldest conceive of the same death which they also underwent, see what he says : " For the Word of God is quick and powerful and sharper than any two-edged sword." For the Word falls upon the souls of these [men] more severely than any sword, causing grievous wounds; and inflicts fatal blows. And of these things he need not give the proof, nor establish them by argument, having a history so fearful. For (he would say) what kind of war destroyed them? What sort of sword? Did they not fall simply of themselves? For let us not be careless because we have not suffered the same things. While " it is called. To-day," it is in our power to recover ourselves.

For lest on hearing the things that belong to the soul we should grow negligent, he adds .also

what concerns the body. For then it is as a king, when his officers are guilty of some great fault, first strips them (say) of their command, and after depriving them of their belt, and their rank, and their herald,[1] then punishes them : so also in this case the sword of the Spirit works.

[4.] Next he discourses of the Son, " with whom we have to do," he says. What is " with whom we have to do "? To Him (he would say) we have to render account for the things we have done? Even so. How then [must we act] that we fall not, nor be faint-hearted?

These things indeed (he would say) are sufficient to instruct us. But we have also " a great High Priest, that is passed into the heavens, Jesus the Son of God." Because he added [it], for this reason he went on, " For we have not an High Priest who cannot be touched with the feeling of our infirmities." Therefore he said above, " In that He hath suffered Himself being tempted, He is able to succor them which are tempted." See then how here also he does the same. And what he says is to this effect : He went (he says) the road which we also [are going] now, or rather even a more rugged one. For He had experience of all human [sufferings].

He had said above " There is no creature that is not manifest in His sight," intimating His Godhead ; then, since he had touched on the flesh, he again discourses more condescendingly, saying (ver. 14), " Having then a great High Priest, that is passed into the heavens ": and shows that His care is greater and that He protects them as His own, and would not have them fall away. For Moses indeed (he says) did not enter into the rest, while He [Christ] did enter in. And it is wonderful how he has nowhere stated the same, lest they might seem to find an excuse ; he however implied it, but that he might not appear to bring an accusation against the man,[2] he did not say it openly. For if, when none of these things had been said, they yet brought forward these [charges], saying, This man hath spoken against Moses and against the law (see Acts xxi. 21, 28) ; much more, if he had said, It is not Palestine but Heaven,[3] would they have said stronger things than these.

[5.] But he attributes not all to the Priest, but requires also what is [to come] from us, I mean our profession. For " having," he says, " a great High Priest, who is passed into the heavens, Jesus the Son of God, let us hold fast our profession " [or " confession "[4]]. What sort

---

[1] Having a κῆρυξ was a special mark of dignity, belonging to certain offices. See Mr. Field's notes.     [2] i.e. Moses.
[3] There are two points of superiority over Moses implied in the words " that is passed into the Heavens." 1. That Christ entered into the rest which He promised His people, while Moses did not. 2. That that rest is Heaven, not the earthly Canaan.
[4] ὁμολογία used of the Creed [and more generally of the profession of a Christian. — F. G.].

of profession does he mean? That there is a Resurrection, that there is a retribution : that there are good things innumerable ; that Christ is GOD, that the Faith is right. These things let us profess, these things let us hold fast. For that they are true, is manifest from the fact, that the High Priest is within. We have not failed of [our hopes], let us confess ; although the realities are not present, yet let us confess : if already they were present they were but a lie. So that this also is true, that [our good things] are deferred. For our High Priest also is Great.

Ver. 15. "For we have not an High Priest, who cannot be touched with the feeling of our infirmities." He is not (he means) ignorant of what concerns us, as many of the High Priests, who know not those in tribulations, nor that there is tribulation at any time. For in the case of men it is impossible that one should know the affliction of the afflicted who has not had experience, and gone through the actual sensations. Our High Priest endured all things. Therefore He endured first and then ascended, that He might be able to sympathize with us.

But was "in all points tempted like as we are, yet without sin." Observe how both above he has used the word "in like manner,"[1] and here "after the likeness." (c. ii. 14.) That is, He was persecuted, was spit upon, was accused, was mocked at, was falsely informed against, was driven out, at last was crucified.

"After our likeness, without sin." In these words another thing also is suggested, that it is possible even for one in afflictions to go through them without sin. So that when he says also "in the likeness of flesh" (Rom. viii. 3), he means not that He took on Him [merely] "the likeness of flesh," but "flesh." Why then did he say "in the likeness"? Because he was speaking about "sinful flesh" :[2] for it was "like" our flesh, since in nature it was the same with us, but in sin no longer the same.

[6.] Ver. 16. "Let us come then boldly [with confidence] unto the throne of His grace, that we may obtain mercy, and find grace to help in time of need."

What "throne of grace" is he speaking of? that royal throne concerning which it is said, "The LORD said unto my Lord, Sit Thou on My right hand." (Ps. cx. 1.)

What is "let us come boldly"? Because "we have a sinless High Priest" contending with the world. For, saith He, "Be of good cheer, I have overcome the world" (John xvi. 33) ; for, this is to suffer all things, and yet to be pure from sins. Although we (he means) are under sin, yet He is sinless.

How is it that we should "approach boldly"? Because *now* it is a throne of Grace, not a throne of Judgment. Therefore boldly, "that we may obtain mercy," even such as we are seeking. For the affair is [one of] munificence, a royal largess.

"And may find grace to help in time of need [for help in due season]." He well said, "for help in time of need." If thou approach now (he means) thou wilt receive both grace and mercy, for thou approachest "in due season" ; but if thou approach *then*,[3] no longer [wilt thou receive it]. For *then* the approach is unseasonable, for it is not "then a throne of Grace." Till that time He sitteth granting pardon, but when the end [is come], then He riseth up to judgment. For it is said, "Arise, O God, judge the earth." (Ps. lxxxii. 8.) ("Let us come boldly," or he says again having no "evil conscience," that is, not being in doubt, for such an one cannot "come with boldness.") On this account it is said, "I have heard thee in an accepted time and in a day of salvation have I succored thee." (2 Cor. vi. 2.) Since even *now* for those to find repentance who sin after baptism is of grace.

But lest when thou hearest of an High Priest, thou shouldst think that He standeth, he forthwith leads to the throne.[4] But a Priest doth not sit, but stands. Seest thou that [for Him] to be made High Priest, is not of nature,[5] but of grace and condescension, and humiliation?

This is it seasonable for us also now to say, "Let us draw near" asking "boldly" : let us only bring Faith and He gives all things. Now is the time of the gift ; let no man despair of himself. Then [will be] the time of despairing, when the bride-chamber is shut, when the King is come in to see the guests, when they who shall be accounted worthy thereof, shall have received as their portion the Patriarch's bosom : but now it is not as yet so. For still are the spectators assembled, still is the contest, still is the prize in suspense.

[7.] Let us then be earnest. For even Paul saith, "I so run not as uncertainly." (1 Cor. ix. 26.) There is need of running, and of running vehemently. He that runneth [a race] seeth none of those that meet him ; whether he be passing through meadows, or through dry places : he that runneth looketh not at the specta-

---

[1] παραπλησίως.
[2] The words of Rom. viii. 3, to which St. Chrys. alludes, are "God sending His own Son in the likeness of sinful flesh," &c.

[3] τότε, "at the Day of Judgment," opposed to "now." "in this life"; as ἐκεῖ, "there," "yonder," is the usual expression for the future state, opposed to ἐνταῦθα, "here," "in this world."
[4] "The throne of grace," as he has said, is that of Christ, on which He sits at the right hand of the Father.
[5] The Arians maintained that our Lord was Priest in His Divine Nature antecedent to the Incarnation. See the Oxford translation of St. Athanasius against Arianism, p. 292, note m. [add p. 267, note l.; cf. also S. Cyril, Book 3 against Nestorius].

tors, but at the prize. Whether they be rich or whether they be poor, whether one mock at him, or praise him, whether one insult, or cast stones at him, or plunder his house, whether he see children, or wife, or anything whatever. He is occupied in one thing alone, in running, in gaining the prize. He that runneth, never standeth still, since even if he slacken a little, he has lost the whole. He that runneth, not only slackens nothing before the end, but then even especially straineth his speed.

This have I spoken for those who say; In our younger days we used discipline,[1] in our younger days we fasted, *now* we are grown old. *Now* most of all it behooves you to make your carefulness more intense. Do not count up to me the old things especially done well: be now youthful and vigorous. For he that runneth this bodily race, when gray hairs have overtaken him, probably is not able to run as he did before: for the whole contest depends on the body; but thou — wherefore dost thou lessen thy speed? For in this race there is need of a soul, a soul thoroughly awakened: and the soul is rather strengthened in old age; then it is in its full vigor, then is it in its pride.

For as the body, so long as it is oppressed by fevers and by one sickness after another, even if it be strong, is exhausted, but when it is freed from this attack, it recovers its proper force, so also the soul in youth is feverish, and is chiefly possessed by the love of glory, and luxurious living, and sensual lusts, and many other imaginations; but old age, when it comes on, drives away all these passions, some through satiety, some through philosophy. For old age relaxes the powers of the body, and does not permit the soul to make use of them even if it wish, but repressing them as enemies of various kinds, it sets her in a place free from troubles and produces a great calm, and brings in a greater fear.

For if none else does, it is said, yet they who are grown old know, that they are drawing to their end, and that they certainly stand near to death. When therefore the desires of this life are withdrawing, and the expectation of the judgment-seat is coming on, softening the stubbornness of the soul, does it not become more attentive, if one be willing?

[8.] What then (you allege) when we see old men more intractable than young ones? Thou tellest me of an excess of wickedness. For in the case of madmen too, we see them going over precipices, when no man pushes them. When therefore, an old man has the diseases of the young, this is an excess of wickedness; besides not even in youth would such an one have an excuse: since he is not able to say, "Remem-

ber not the sins of my youth, and my ignorances." (Ps. xxv. 7.) For he who in old age remains the same, shows that even in youth, he was what he was not from ignorance, nor from inexperience, nor from the time of life, but from slothfulness. For that man may say, "Remember not the sins of my youth, and mine ignorances," who does such things as become an old man, who changes in old age. But if even in age he continue the same unseemly courses, how can such an one be worthy of the name of an old man, who has no reverence even for the time of life? For he who says, "Remember not the sins of my youth, nor my ignorances," utters this, as one doing right in his old age. Do not then, by the deeds of age, deprive thyself also of pardon for the sins of youth.

For how can what is done be otherwise than unreasonable, and beyond pardon? An old man sits in taverns. An old man hurries to horse-races — an old man goes up into theaters, running with the crowd like children. Truly it is a shame and a mockery, to be adorned outside with gray hairs, but within to have the mind of a child.

And indeed if a young man insult [him], he immediately puts forward his gray hairs. Reverence them first thyself; if however thou dost not reverence thy own even when old, how canst thou demand of the young to reverence them? Thou dost not reverence the gray hairs, but puttest them to shame. God hath honored thee with whiteness of hairs: He hath given thee high dignity. Why dost thou betray the honor? How shall the young man reverence thee, when thou art more wanton than he? For the hoary head is then venerable, when it acts worthily of the gray head; but when it plays youth, it will be more ridiculous than the young. How then will you old men be able to give these exhortations to the young man when you are intoxicated by your disorderliness?

[9.] I say not these things as accusing the old, but the young. For in my judgment they who act thus even if they have come to their hundredth year, are young; just as the young if they be but little children, yet if they are soberminded, are better than the old. And this doctrine is not my own, but Scripture [2] also recognizes the same distinction. "For," it says, "honorable age is not that which standeth in length of time, and an unspotted life is old age." (Wisd. iv. 8, 9.)

For we honor the gray hair, not because we esteem the white color above the black, but because it is a proof of a virtuous life; and when we see them we conjecture therefrom the inward hoariness. But if men continue to do

---

[1] ἠσκήσαμεν.

[2] [ἡ γραφή, the same form of quotation as in the case of the canonical Scriptures. — F. G.]

what is inconsistent with the hoary head, they will on that account become the more ridiculous. Since we also honor the Emperor, and the purple and the diadem, because they are symbols of his office. But if we should see him, with the purple, spitted on, trodden under foot by the guards, seized by the throat, cast into prison, torn to pieces, shall we then reverence the purple or the diadem, and not rather weep over the pomp itself? Claim not then to be honored for thy hoary head, when thou thyself wrongest it. For it ought indeed itself to receive satisfaction from thee, because thou bringest disgrace on a form so noble and so honorable.

We say not these things against all [old persons], nor is our discourse against old age simply (I am not so mad as that), but against a youthful spirit bringing dishonor on old age. Nor is it concerning those who are grown old that we sorrowfully say these things, but concerning those who disgrace the hoary head.

For the old man is a king, if you will, and more royal than he who wears the purple, if he master his passions, and keep them under subjection, in the rank of guards. But if he be dragged about and thrust down from his throne, and become a slave of the love of money, and vainglory, and personal adornment, and luxuriousness, and drunkenness, anger, and sensual pleasures, and has his hair dressed out with oil, and shows an age insulted by his way of life, of what punishment would not such an one be worthy?

[10.] But may ye not be such, O young men! for not even for you is there the excuse for sinning. Why so? Because it is possible to be old in youth: just as there are youths in old age, so also the reverse. For as in the one case the white hair saves no one, so in the other the black is no impediment. For if it is disgraceful for the old man to do these things of which I have spoken, much more than for the young man, yet still the young man is not freed from accusation. For a young man can have an excuse only, in case he is called to the management of affairs, when he is still inexperienced, when he needs time and practice; but no longer when it is necessary to display temperance and courage, nor yet when it is needful to keep his property.

For it sometimes happens that the young man is blamed more than the old. For the one needs much service, old age making him feeble: but the other being able, if he will, to provide for himself, what sort of excuse should he meet with, when he plunders more than the old, when he remembers injuries, when he is contemptuous, when he does not stand forward to protect others more than the old man, when he utters many things unseasonably, when he is insolent, when he reviles, when he is drunken?

And if in the [matter of] chastity he think that he cannot be impleaded,[1] consider that here also he has many helps, if he will. For although desire trouble him more violently than it doth the old, yet nevertheless there are many things which he can do more than an old man, and so charm that wild beast. What are these things? Labors, readings, watchings through the night, fastings.

[11.] What then are these things to us (one says) who are not monastics? Sayest thou this to me? Say it to Paul, when he says, "Watching with all perseverance and supplication" (Eph. vi. 18), when he says, "Make not provision for the flesh, to fulfill the lusts thereof." (Rom. xiii. 14.) For surely he wrote not these things to solitaries only, but to all that are in cities. For ought the man who lives in the world to have any advantage over the solitary, save only the living with a wife? In this point he has allowance, but in others none, but it is his duty to do all things equally with the solitary.

Moreover the Beatitudes [pronounced] by Christ, were not addressed to solitaries only: since in that case the whole world would have perished, and we should be accusing God of cruelty. And if these beatitudes were spoken to solitaries only, and the secular person cannot fulfill them, yet He permitted marriage, then He has destroyed all men. For if it be not possible, with marriage, to perform the duties of solitaries, all things have perished and are destroyed, and the [functions] of virtue are shut up in a strait.

And, how can marriage be honorable, which so hinders us? What then? It is possible, yea very possible, even if we have wives, to pursue after virtue, if we will. How? If having "wives," we "be as though we had none," if we rejoice not over our "possessions," if we "use the world as not abusing it." (1 Cor. vii. 29, 31.)

And if any persons have been hindered by marriage state, let them know that marriage is not the hindrance, but their purpose which made an ill use of marriage. Since it is not wine which makes drunkenness, but the evil purpose, and the using it beyond due measure. Use marriage with moderation, and thou shalt be first in the kingdom, and shalt enjoy all good things, which may we all attain by the grace and love of our Lord Jesus Christ with whom to the Father together with the Holy Ghost be glory, might, honor, now and for ever and world without end. Amen.

---

1 that is, if he have fallen into sin in this respect.

# HOMILY VIII.

Hebrews v. 1–3.

"For every high priest taken from among men, is ordained for men in things pertaining to God, that he may offer both gifts and sacrifices for sins: who can have compassion on[1] the ignorant and on them that are out of the way, for that he himself also is compassed with infirmity; and by reason hereof he ought, as for the people so also for himself to offer for sins."

[1.] THE blessed Paul wishes to show in the next place that this covenant is far better than the old. This then he does by first laying down remote considerations. For inasmuch as there was nothing bodily or that made a show,[2] no temple for instance, nor Holy of Holies, nor Priest with so great apparel, no legal observances, but all things higher and more perfect, and there was nothing of bodily things, but all was in things spiritual, and things spiritual did not attract the weak, as things bodily; he thoroughly sifts this whole matter.

And observe his wisdom: he makes his beginning from the priest first, and continually calls Him an High Priest, and from this first [point] shows the difference [of the two Dispensations]. On this account he first of all defines what a Priest is, and shows whether He has any things proper to a Priest, and whether there are any signs of priesthood. It was however an objection in his way that He [Christ] was not even well-born, nor was He of the sacerdotal tribe, nor a priest on earth. How then was He a Priest? some one may say.

And just as in the Epistle to the Romans, having taken up an argument of which they were not easily persuaded, that Faith effects that which the labor of the Law could not, nor the sweat of the daily life, he betook himself to the Patriarch and referred the whole [question] to that time: so now here also he opens out the other path of the Priesthood, showing its superiority from the things which happened before. And as, in [the matter of] punishment, he brings before them not Hell alone, but also what happened to their fathers,[3] so now here also, he first establishes this position from things present. For it were right indeed that earthly things should be proved from heavenly, but when the hearers are weak, the opposite course is taken.

[2.] Up to a certain point he lays down first the things which are common [to Christ and their High Priests], and then shows that He is superior. For comparative[4] excellence arises thus, when in some respects there is community, in others superiority; otherwise it is no longer comparative.

"For every High Priest taken from among men," this is common to Christ; "is ordained for men in things pertaining to God," and this also; "that he may offer both gifts and sacrifices for the people," and this too, [yet] not entirely: what follows however is no longer so: "who can have compassion[5] on the ignorant, and on them that are out of the way," from this point forward is the superiority, "inasmuch as himself also is encompassed with infirmity; and by reason hereof he ought as for the people, so also for himself, to offer for sins."

Then also [there are] other [points]: He is made [Priest] (he says) by Another and does not of Himself intrude into [the office]. This too is common (ver. 4), "And no man taketh this honor to himself, but he that is called of God as was Aaron."

Here again he conciliates[6] them in another point, because He was sent from God: which Christ was wont to say throughout to the Jews. "He that sent Me is greater than I," and, "I came not of Myself." (John xii. 49; xiv. 28; viii. 42.)

He appears to me in these words also to hint at the priests of the Jews, as being no longer priests, [but] intruders and corrupters of the law of the priesthood; (ver. 5) "So Christ also glorified not Himself to be made an High Priest."

How then was He appointed (one says)? For Aaron was many times appointed as by the Rod, and when the fire came down and destroyed those who wished to intrude into the priesthood. But in this instance, on the contrary, they [the Jewish Priests] not only suffered nothing, but even are in high esteem. Whence then [His appointment]? He shows it from the prophecy. He has nothing [to allege] perceptible by sense, nothing visible. For this cause he affirms it from prophecy, from things future; "But He that said unto Him Thou art My Son, to-day have I begotten Thee." What has this to do with the Son? Yea (he says) it is a preparation for His being appointed by God.

---

[1] μετριοπαθεῖν.
[2] φανταστικὸν.
[3] c. iii. 7, &c.
[4] ἡ κατὰ σύγκρισιν.
[5] [St. Chrys. has not drawn attention to the nice distinction between μετριοπαθεῖν equal "to bear reasonably with," applied to the earthly High Priest, and συμπαθεῖν equal "to sympathize with," applied to Christ.—F. G.]
[6] θεραπεύει.

Ver. 6. "As He saith also in another place, Thou art a Priest forever after the order of Melchisedech." Unto whom now was this spoken? Who is "after the order of Melchisedech"? No other [than He]. For they all were under the Law, they all kept sabbaths, they all were circumcised; one could not point out any other [than Him].

[3.] Ver. 7, 8. "Who in the days of His flesh, when He had offered up prayers and supplications with strong crying and tears, to Him that was able to save Him from death, and was heard in that He feared; though He were a Son, yet learned He obedience by the things which He suffered." Seest thou that he sets forth nothing else than His care and the exceeding greatness of His love? For what means the [expression] "with strong crying"? The Gospel nowhere says this, nor that He wept when He prayed, nor yet that He uttered a cry. Seest thou that it was a condescension? For he could not [merely] say that He prayed, but also "with strong crying."

"And was heard," (he says), "in that He feared; though He were a Son, yet learned He obedience by the things which He suffered." (Ver. 9, 10), "And being made perfect He became the Author of eternal salvation unto all them that obey Him: called of God an High Priest after the order of Melchisedech."

Be it with "crying," why also "strong [crying] and tears"?

"Having offered," (he says), "and having been heard in that He feared." What sayest thou? Let the Heretics[1] be ashamed. The Son of God "was heard in that He feared." And what more could any man say concerning the prophets? And what sort of connection is there, in saying, "He was heard in that He feared, though He were Son, yet learned He obedience by the things which He suffered"? Would any man say these things concerning God? Why, who was ever so mad? And who, even if he were beside himself, would have uttered these things? "Having been heard," (he says), "in that He feared, He learned obedience by the things which He suffered." What obedience? He that before this had been obedient even unto death, as a Son to His Father, how did He afterwards learn? Seest thou that this is spoken concerning the Incarnation?

Tell me now, did He pray the Father that He might be saved from death? And was it for this cause that He was "exceeding sorrowful, and said, If it be possible, let this cup pass from Me"? (Matt. xxvi. 38, 39.) Yet He nowhere prayed the Father concerning His resurrection, but on the contrary He openly declares, "Destroy this temple and within three days I will raise it up." (John. ii. 19.) And, "I have power to lay down My life, and I have power to take it again. No man taketh it from Me, I lay it down of Myself." (John x. 18.) What then is it; why did He pray? (And again He said, "Behold we go up to Jerusalem, and the Son of Man shall be betrayed unto the chief priests and scribes, and they shall condemn Him to death. And they shall deliver Him to the Gentiles, to mock, and to scourge, and to crucify Him; and the third day He shall rise again" (Matt. xx. 18, 19), and said not, "My Father shall raise Me up again.") How then did He pray concerning this? But for whom did He pray? For those who believed on Him.

And what he means is this, 'He is readily listened to.' For since they had not yet the right opinion concerning Him, he said that He was heard. Just as He Himself also when consoling His disciples said, "If ye loved Me, ye would rejoice, because I go to My Father" (John xiv. 28), and "My Father is greater than I." But how did He not glorify Himself, He who "made Himself of no reputation" (Phil. ii. 7), He who gave Himself up? For, it is said, "He gave Himself" up "for our sins." (See Gal. i. 4.) And again, "Who gave Himself a ransom for us all." (1 Tim. ii. 6.) What is it then? Thou seest that it is in reference to the flesh that lowly things are spoken concerning Himself: So also here, "Although He were Son, He was heard in that He feared," it is said. He wishes to show, that the success was of Himself, rather than of God's favor. So great (he says) was His reverence, that even on account thereof God had respect unto Him.

"He learned," he saith, to obey God. Here again he shows how great is the gain of sufferings. "And having been made perfect," he says, "He became the Author of salvation to them that obey Him." (Cf. supra, pp. 384, 391.) But if He, being the Son, gained obedience from His sufferings, much more shall we. Dost thou see how many things he discourses about obedience, that they might be persuaded to it? For it seems to me that they would not be restrained. "From the things," he says, "which He suffered He" continually "learned" to obey God. And being "made perfect" through sufferings. This then is perfection, and by this means must we arrive at perfection. For not only was He Himself saved, but became to others also an abundant supply of salvation. For "being made perfect He became the Author of salvation to them that obey Him."

[4.] "Being called," he says, "of God an High Priest after the order of Melchisedech": (ver. 11) "Of whom we have many things to say and hard to be uttered [or explained]."

---

[1] Heretics who denied the reality of our Lord's human nature.

When he was about to proceed to the difference of the Priesthood, he first reproves them, pointing out both that such great condescension was " milk," and that it was because they were children that he dwelt longer on the lowly subject, relating to the flesh, and speaks [about Him] as about any righteous man.  And see, he neither kept silence as to the doctrine altogether, nor did he utter it ; that on the one hand, he might raise their thoughts, and persuade them to be perfect, and that they might not be deprived of the great doctrines ; and on the other, that he might not overwhelm their minds.

" Of whom," he says, " we have many things to say and hard to be explained, seeing ye are dull of hearing." Because they do not hear, the doctrine is " hard to be explained." For when one has to do with men who do not go along with him nor mind the things that are spoken, he cannot well explain the subject to them.

But perhaps some one of you that stand here, is puzzled, and thinks it a hard case, that owing to the Hebrews, he himself is hindered from hearing the more perfect doctrines. Nay rather, I think that perhaps here also except a few, there are many such [as they], so that this may be said concerning yourselves also : but for the sake of those few I will speak.

Did he then keep entire silence, or did he resume the subject again in what follows ; and do the same as in the Epistle to the Romans ? For there too, when he had first stopped the mouths of the gainsayers, and said, " Nay but, O man, who art thou that repliest against God ? " (Rom. ix. 20), he then subjoined the solution. And for my own part I think that he was not even altogether silent, and yet did not speak it out, in order to lead the hearers to a longing [for the knowledge]. For having mentioned [the subject], and said that certain great things were stored up in the doctrine, see how he frames his reproof in combination with panegyric.

For this is ever a part of Paul's wisdom, to mix painful things with kind ones. Which he also does in the Epistle to the Galatians, saying, " Ye did run well ; who did hinder you ? " (Gal. v. 7.) And, " Have ye suffered so many things in vain ? if it be yet in vain " (Gal. iii. 4), and, " I have confidence in you in the Lord." (Gal. v. 10.) Which he says also to these [Hebrews], " But we are persuaded better things of you, and things that accompany salvation." (c. vi. 9.) For these two things he effects, he does not overstrain them, nor suffer them to fall back ; for if the examples of others are sufficient to arouse the hearer, and to lead him to emulation ; when a man has himself for an example and is bidden to emulate himself, the possibility follows at the same time. He therefore shows this also, and does

not suffer them to fall back as men utterly condemned, nor as being alway evil, but [says] that they were once even good ; (ver. 12) for " when for the time ye ought to be teachers," he says. Here he shows that they had been believers a long while, and he shows also that they ought to instruct others.

[5.] At all events observe him continually travailing to introduce the discourse concerning the High Priest, and still putting it off. For hear how he began : " Having a great High Priest that is passed into the heavens " (c. iv. 14) ; and omitting to say how He was great, he says again, " For every High Priest taken from among men, is appointed for men in things pertaining to God." (c. v. 1.) And again, " So Christ also glorified not Himself to be made an High Priest." (c. v. 5.) And again after saying, " Thou art a Priest for ever after the order of Melchisedech " (c. v. 6), he again puts off [the subject], saying, " Who in the days of His Flesh offered prayers and supplications." (c. v. 7.) When therefore he had been so many times repulsed, he says, as if excusing himself, The blame is with you. Alas ! how great a difference ! When they ought to be teaching others, they are not even simply learners, but the last of learners. (Ver. 12), " For when for the time ye ought to be teachers, ye have need again that some one [1] teach you again which be the first principles [2] of the oracles of God." Here he means the Human Nature [of Christ]. For as in external literature it is necessary to learn the elements first, so also here they were first taught concerning the human nature.

Thou seest what is the cause of his uttering lowly things. So Paul did to the Athenians also, discoursing and saying, " The times of this ignorance God winked at : but now commandeth all men everywhere to repent, because He hath appointed a day in the which He will judge the world in righteousness by that Man whom He hath ordained, whereof He hath given assurance unto all men, in that He hath raised Him from the dead." (Acts xvii. 30, 31.) Therefore, if he says anything lofty, he expresses it briefly, while the lowly statements are scattered about in many parts of the Epistle. And thus too he shows the lofty ; since the very lowliness [of what is said] forbids the suspicion that these things relate to the Divine Nature. So here also the safe ground was kept.[3]

But what produces this dullness ? This he pointed out especially in the Epistle to the Corinthians, saying, " For whereas there is

---

[1] τινα. The common editions have τίνα, " that one teach you which be," &c., as is read in the received version of the Epistle, where Lachman adopts the reading τινα.
[2] " the elements of the beginning."
[3] That is, he took care to provide against being understood to refer to His Divine Nature, when he said lowly things concerning Christ.

among you envy and strife and divisions, are ye not carnal?" (1 Cor. iii. 3.) But observe, I beseech you, his great wisdom, how he always deals according to the distempers before him. For there the weakness arose more from ignorance, or rather from sin; but here not from sins only, but also from continual afflictions. Wherefore he also uses expressions calculated to show the difference, not saying, "ye are become carnal," but "dull" : in that case "carnal," but in this the pain is greater. For they [the Corinthians] indeed were not able to endure [his reproof], because they were carnal: but these were able. For in saying, "Seeing ye are become dull of hearing" (c. v. 11), he shows that formerly they were sound in health, and were strong, fervent in zeal, which he also afterwards testifies respecting them.

[6.] "And are become such as have need of milk, not of strong meat." He always calls the lowly doctrine "milk," both in this place and in the other. "When," he says, "for [i.e. "because of"] the time ye ought to be teachers": because of that very thing, namely the time, for which ye ought especially to be strong, for this especially ye are become backsliding. Now he calls it "milk," on account of its being suited to the more simple. But to the more perfect it is injurious, and the dwelling on these things is hurtful. So that it is not fitting that matters of the Law should be introduced[1] now or the comparison made from them, [such as] that He was an High Priest, and offered sacrifice, and needed crying and supplication. Wherefore see how these things are unhealthful[2] to "us"; but at that time they nourished them being by no means unhealthful to them.

So then the oracles of God are true nourishment. "For I will give unto them," he saith, "not a famine of bread, nor a thirst of water, but a famine of hearing the word of the Lord." (Amos viii. 11.)

"I gave you milk to drink, and not meat" (1 Cor. iii. 2); He did not say, I fed you, showing that such [nourishment] as this is not food, but that [the case is] like that of little children who cannot be fed with bread. For such have not drink given them, but their food is to them instead of drink.

Moreover he did not say, "ye have need," but "ye are become such as have need of milk and not of strong meat." That is, ye willed [it]; ye have reduced yourselves to this, to this need.

Ver. 13. "For every one that partaketh of milk is unskilled in the word of righteousness: for he is a babe." What is "the Word [doctrine] of righteousness"? He seems to me here to hint at conduct also. That which Christ also said, "Except your righteousness shall exceed the righteousness of the Scribes and Pharisees" (Matt. v. 20), this he says likewise, "unskilled in the word of righteousness," that is, he that is unskilled in the philosophy that is above, is unable to embrace a perfect and exact life.[3] Or else by "righteousness" he here means Christ, and the high doctrine concerning Him.

That they then were "become dull," he said; but from what cause, he did not add, leaving it to themselves to know it, and not wishing to make his discourse hard to bear. But in the case of the Galatians he both "marveled" (Gal. i. 6) and "stood in doubt" (Gal. iv. 20), which tends much more to encourage, as [it is the language] of one who would never have expected that this should happen. For this is [what] the doubting [implies].

Thou seest that there is another infancy. Thou seest that there is another full age.[4] Let us become of "full age" in this sense: It is in the power even of those who are children, and the young to come to that "full age": for it is not of nature, but of virtue.

[7.] Ver. 14. "But strong meat belongeth to them that are of full age [perfect], even them who by reason of use have their senses exercised to discern both good and evil." Those had not "their senses exercised," nor did they "know good and evil." He is not speaking now concerning life [conduct], when he says "to discern good and evil," for this is possible and easy for every man to know, but concerning doctrines that are wholesome and sublime, and those that are corrupted and low. The babe knows not how to distinguish bad and good food. Oftentimes at least it even puts dirt into its mouth, and takes what is hurtful; and it does all things without judgment; but not [so] the full grown man. Such [babes] are they who lightly listen to everything, and give up their ears indiscriminately: which seems to me to blame these [Hebrews] also, as being lightly "carried about," and now giving themselves to these, now to those. Which he also hinted near the end [of the Epistle], saying, "Be not carried aside by divers and strange doctrines." (c. xiii. 9.) This is the meaning of "to discern good and evil." "For the mouth tasteth meat, but the soul trieth words." (Job xxxiv. 3.)

[8.] Let us then learn this lesson. Do not, when thou hearest that a man is not a Heathen nor a Jew, straightway believe him to be a Christian; but examine also into all the other points; for even Manichæans, and all the heresies, have

---

[1] The allowing the observances of the law, as well as the dwelling thus on the human characteristics of our Lord, were suited for the beginners, but would be injurious to us.
[2] προσίσταται. Said of that which cannot be digested or causes nausea.
[3] ἄκρον καὶ ἠκριβωμένον.
[4] τελειότης.

put on this mask, in order thus to deceive the more simple. But if we "have the senses" of the soul "exercised to discern both good and evil," we are able to discern such [teachers].

But how do our "senses" become "exercised"? By continual hearing; by experience of the Scriptures. For when we set forth the error of those [Heretics], and thou hearest to-day and to-morrow; and provest that it is not right, thou hast learnt the whole, thou hast known the whole: and even if thou shouldest not comprehend to-day, thou wilt comprehend to-morrow.

"That have," he says, their "senses exercised." Thou seest that it is needful to exercise our hearing by divine studies, so that they may not sound strangely. "Exercised," saith he, "for discerning," that is, to be skilled.

One man says, that there is no Resurrection; and another looks for none of the things to come; another says there is a different God; another that He has His beginning from Mary. And see at once how they have all fallen away from want of moderation,[1] some by excess, others by defect. As for instance, the first Heresy of all was that of Marcion; this introduced another different God, who has no existence.[2] See the excess. After this that of Sabellius, saying that the Son and the Spirit and the Father are One.[3] Next that of Marcellus and Photinus, setting forth the same things. Moreover that of Paul of Samosata, saying that He had His beginning from Mary. Afterwards that of the Manichæans; for this is the most modern of all. After these the heresy of Arius. And there are others too.

And on this account have we received the Faith, that we might not be compelled to attack innumerable heresies, and to deal with them, but whatever any man might have endeavored either to add or take away, that we might consider spurious. For as those who give the standards do not oblige [people] to busy themselves about measures innumerable, but bid them keep to what is given them; so also in the case of doctrines.

[9.] But no man is willing to give heed to the Scriptures. For if we did give heed, not only should we not be ourselves entangled by deceit, but we should also set others free who are deceived, and should draw them out of dangers. For the strong soldier is not only able to help himself, but also to protect his comrade, and to free him from the malice of the enemy. But as it is, some do not even know that there are any Scriptures. Yet the Holy Spirit indeed made so many wise provisions in order that they might be safely kept.

And look at it from the first, that ye may learn the unspeakable love of God. He inspired the blessed Moses; He engraved the tables, He detained him on the mount forty days; and again as many [more] to give the Law. And after this He sent prophets who suffered woes innumerable. War came on; they slew them all, they cut them to pieces, the books were burned. Again, He inspired another admirable man to publish them, Ezra I mean, and caused them to be put together from the remains. And after this He arranged that they should be translated by the seventy. They did translate them. Christ came, He receives them; the Apostles disperse them among men. Christ wrought signs and wonders.

What then after so great painstaking? The Apostles also wrote, even as Paul likewise said, "they were written for our admonition, upon whom the ends of the world are come." (1 Cor. x. 11.) And again Christ said, "Ye do err not knowing the Scriptures" (Matt. xxii. 29): and again Paul said, "That through patience and comfort of the Scriptures we may have hope." (Rom. xv. 4.) And again, "All Scripture is given by inspiration of God, and is profitable." (2 Tim. iii. 16.) And "let the word of Christ dwell in you richly." (Col. iii. 16.) And the prophet, "he shall meditate in His Law day and night" (Ps. i. 2), and again in another place, "Let all thy communication be in the law of the Most High." (Ecclus. ix. 15.) And again, "How sweet are Thy words unto my throat." (He said not to my hearing, but to my "throat"); "more than honey and the honeycomb to my mouth." (Ps. cxix. 103.) And Moses says, "Thou shalt meditate in them continually, when thou risest up, when thou sittest, when thou liest down." (Deut. vi. 7.) "Be in them" (1 Tim. iv. 15), saith he. And innumerable things one might say concerning them. But notwithstanding, after so many things there are some who do not even know that there are Scriptures at all. For this cause, believe me, nothing sound, nothing profitable comes from us.

[10.] Yet, if any one wished to learn military affairs, of necessity he must learn the military laws. And if any one sought to learn navigation or carpentry or anything else, of necessity he must learn the [principles] of the art. But in this case they will not do anything of the kind, although this is a science which needs much wakeful attention. For that it too is an art which needs teaching, hear the prophet saying, "Come, ye children, hearken unto me, I will teach you the fear of the Lord." (Ps. xxxiv. 11.) It follows therefore certainly that the fear of God needs teaching. Then he says, "What man is he that desireth life?" (Ps. xxxiv. 12.) He means the life yonder; and again, "Keep thy tongue from evil and thy lips from speaking guile; de-

---

[1] ἐξ ἀμετρίας.　　　[2] Cf. St. Irenæus, iv. 33. 2, p, 405, O. T.
[3] ἕν. The common texts add πρόσωπον, "one person."

part from evil and do good, seek peace and pursue it." (Ps. xxxiv. 13, 14.)

Do you know indeed who said these things, a prophet or a historian, or an apostle, or an evangelist? For my own part I do not think you do, except a few. Yea and these themselves again, if we bring forward a testimony from some other place, will be in the same case as the rest of you. For see, I repeat the same statement expressed in other words. "Wash ye, make you clean, put away your wickedness from your souls before Mine eyes, learn to do well, seek out judgment. Keep thy tongue from evil, and do good : learn to do well." (Isa. i. 16, 17.) Thou seest that virtue needs to be taught? For this one says, "I will teach you the fear of the Lord," and the other, "Learn to do well."

Now then do you know where these words are? For myself I do not think you do, except a few. And yet every week these things are read to you twice or even three times : and the reader when he goes up [to the desk] first says whose the book is, [the book] of such a prophet, and then says what he says, so that it shall be more intelligible to you and you may not only know the contents of the Book, but also the reason of the writings, and who spake these things. But all in vain ; all to no purpose. For your zeal is spent on things of this life, and of things spiritual no account is made. Therefore not even those matters turn out according to your wishes, but there also are many difficulties. For Christ says, "Seek ye the Kingdom of God, and all these things shall be added unto you." (Matt. vi. 33.) These things He said, shall also be given in the way of addition : but we have inverted the order and seek the earth and the good things which are in the earth, as if those other [heavenly] things were to be given us in addition. Therefore we have neither the one nor the other. Let us then at last wake up and become coveters of the things which shall be hereafter ; for so these also will follow. For it is not possible that he who seeks the things that relate to God, should not also attain human [blessings]. It is the declaration of the Truth itself which says this. Let us not then act otherwise, but let us hold fast to the counsel of Christ, lest we fail of all. But God is able to give you compunction and to make you better, in Christ Jesus our Lord, with whom to the Father together with the Holy Ghost be glory, power, honor, now and for ever and world without end. Amen.

# HOMILY IX.

## HEBREWS vi. 1–3.

"Therefore leaving the principles of the Doctrine of Christ,[1] let us go on unto perfection, not laying again the foundation of repentance from dead works, and of faith toward God; of the doctrine of baptisms, and of laying on of hands; and of resurrection of the dead, and of eternal judgment. And this we will do, if God permit."

[1.] You have heard how much Paul found fault with the Hebrews for wishing to be always learning about the same things. And with good reason : "For when for the time ye ought to be teachers, ye have need again that some one teach you the elements of the first principles[2] of the oracles of God." (c. v. 12.)

I am afraid that this might fitly be said to you also, that "when for the time ye ought to be teachers," ye do not maintain the rank of learners, but ever hearing the same things, and on the same subjects, you are in the same condition as if you heard no one. And if any man should question you, no one will be able to answer, except a very few who may soon be counted.

But this is no trifling loss. For oftentimes when the teacher wishes to go on further, and to touch on higher and more mysterious themes, the want of attention in those who are to be taught prevents.

For just as in the case of a grammar-master, if a boy though hearing continually the first elements does not master them, it will be necessary for him to be continually dinning the same things into the boy, and he will not leave off teaching, until the boy has been able to learn them accurately ; for it is great folly to lead him on to other things, without having put the first well into him ; so too in the Church, if while we constantly say the same things you learn nothing more, we shall never cease saying the same things.

For if our preaching were a matter of display and ambition, it would have been right to jump from one subject to another and change about continually, taking no thought for you, but only

---

[1] τὸν λόγον τῆς ἀρχῆς τοῦ Χριστοῦ. Literally, "the discourse of the beginning of Christ"; but presently St. Chrys. substitutes for this, ἡ ἀρχὴ τοῦ λόγου, "the beginning of the doctrine," as the words are translated in our version.
[2] τὰ στοιχεῖα τῆς ἀρχῆς.

for your applauses. But since we have not devoted our zeal to this, but our labors are all for your profit, we shall not cease discoursing to you on the same subjects, till you succeed in learning them. For I might have said much about Gentile superstition, and about the Manichæans, and about the Marcionists, and by the grace of God have given them heavy blows, but this sort of discourse is out of season. For to those who do not yet know accurately their own affairs, to those who have not yet learned that to be covetous is evil, who would utter such discourses as those, and lead them on to other subjects before the time?

We then shall not cease to say the same things, whether ye be persuaded or not. We fear however, that by continually saying the same things, if ye hearken not, we may make the condemnation heavier for the disobedient.

I must not however say this in regard to you all; for I know many who are benefited by their coming here, who might with justice cry out against those others, as insidiously injuring them[1] by their ignorance and inattention. But not even so will they be injured. For hearing the same things continually is useful even to those who know them, since by often hearing what we know, we are more deeply affected. We know, for instance, that Humility is an excellent thing, and that Christ often discoursed about it; but when we listen to the words themselves and the reflections made upon them, we are yet more affected, even if we hear them ten thousand times.

[2.] It is then a fitting time for us also to say now to you, "Wherefore leaving the beginning of the doctrine of Christ, let us go unto perfection." What is "the beginning of the doctrine"?[2] He goes on to state it himself, saying, "not laying again" (these are his words) "the foundation of repentance from dead works, and faith toward God, of the doctrine of baptisms and of laying on of hands, of the resurrection of the dead, and of eternal judgment."

But if this be "the Beginning," what else is our doctrine save to repent "from dead works," and through the Spirit to receive "the faith,"[3] in "the resurrection of the dead, and eternal judgment"? But what is "the Beginning"? "The Beginning," he says, is nothing else than this, when there is not a strict life. For as it is necessary to instruct one who is entering on the study of grammar, in the Elements[4] first, so also must the Christian know these things accurately, and have no doubt concerning them. And should he again have need of teaching, he has

not yet the foundation. For one who is firmly grounded ought to be fixed and to stand steady, and not be moved about. But if one who has been catechised and baptized is going ten years afterwards to hear again about the Faith, and that we ought to "believe" in "the resurrection of the dead," he does not yet have the foundation, he is again seeking after the beginning of the Christian religion. For that the Faith is the foundation, and the rest the building, hear him [the Apostle] saying; "I have laid the foundation and another buildeth thereupon." (1 Cor. iii. 10.) "If any man build upon this foundation, gold, silver, precious stones, wood, hay, stubble." (1 Cor. iii. 12.)

"Not laying again" (he says) "the foundation of repentance from dead works."

[3.] But what is, "let us go on unto perfection"? Let us henceforth proceed (he means) even to the very roof, that is, let us have the best life. For as in the case of the letters the Alpha[5] involves the whole, and as the foundation, the whole building, so also does full assurance concerning the Faith involve purity of life. And without this it is not possible to be a Christian, as without foundations there can be no building; nor skill in literature without the letters. Still if one should be always going round about the letters, or if about the foundation, not about the building, he will never gain anything.

Do not however think that the Faith is depreciated by being called elementary: for it is indeed the whole power: for when he says, "For every one that useth milk is unskilled in the word of righteousness, for he is a babe" (c. v. 13), it is not this which he calls "milk." But to be still doubting about these things is [a sign] of a mind feeble, and needing many discourses. For these are the wholesome doctrines. For we call him "a perfect man" [i.e. "of full age"] who with the faith has a right life; but if any one have faith, yet does evil, and is in doubt concerning [the faith] itself, and brings disgrace on the doctrine, him we shall with reason call "a babe," in that he has gone back again to the beginning. So that even if we have been ten thousand years in the faith, yet are not firm in it, we are babes; when we show a life not in conformity with it; when we are still laying a foundation.

[4.] But besides [their way of] life he brings another charge also against these [Hebrews], as being shaken to and fro, and needing "to lay a foundation of repentance from dead works." For he who changes from one to another, giving up this, and choosing that, ought first to condemn this, and to be separated from the system, and then to pass to the other. But if he intends

---

[1] ἐνεδρευόντων αὐτούς.　　[2] ἡ ἀρχὴ τοῦ λόγου.
[3] The Faith; πίστις with the article in this place and a little below means the Creed; as we say "the Belief." [Yet it would be impossible to substitute the word "Creed"—"Creed in the resurrection." &c. What is meant is that Christian belief which finds expression in the Creed, as well as elsewhere.—F. G.]
[4] or "the letters."

[5] τὸ ἄλφα.

again to lay hold on the first, how shall he touch the second?

What then of the Law (he says)? We have condemned it, and again we run back to it. This is not a shifting about, for here also [under the Gospel] we have a law. "Do we then" (he says) "make void the law through faith? God forbid, yea we establish the Law." (Rom. iii. 31.) I was speaking concerning evil deeds. For he that intends to pursue virtue ought to condemn wickedness first, and then go in pursuit of it. For repentance cannot prove[1] them clean. For this cause they were straightway baptized, that what they were unable to accomplish by themselves, this might be effected by the grace of Christ. Neither then does repentance suffice for purification, but men must first receive baptism. At all events, it was necessary to come to baptism, having condemned the sins thereby and given sentence against them.

But what is "the doctrine of baptisms"? Not as if there were many baptisms, but one only.[2] Why then did he express it in the plural? Because he had said, "not laying again a foundation of repentance." For if he again baptized them and catechised them afresh, and having been baptized at the beginning[3] they were again taught what things ought to be done and what ought not, they would remain perpetually incorrigible.

"And of laying on of hands." For thus did they receive the Spirit, "when Paul had laid his hands on them" (Acts xix. 6), it is said.

"And of the resurrection of the dead." For this is both effected in baptism, and is affirmed in the confession.

"And of eternal judgment." But why does he say this? Because it was likely that, having already believed, they would either be shaken [from their faith], or would lead evil and slothful lives, he says, "be wakeful."[4]

It is not open to them to say, If we live slothfully we will be baptized again, we will be catechised again, we will again receive the Spirit; even if now we fall from the faith, we shall be able again by being baptized, to wash away our sins, and to attain to the same state as before. Ye are deceived (he says) in supposing these things.

[5.] Ver. 4, 5. "For it is impossible for those who were once enlightened and have tasted of the heavenly gift, and were made partakers of the Holy Ghost, and have tasted the good word of God, and the powers of the world to come, if they shall fall away, to renew them again unto repentance, crucifying[5] to themselves the Son

of God afresh, and putting Him to an open shame."

And see how putting them to shame,[6] and forbiddingly he begins. "Impossible." No longer (he says) expect that which is not possible; (For he said not, It is not seemly, or, It is not expedient, or, It is not lawful, but "impossible," so as to cast [them] into despair), if ye have once been altogether enlightened.

Then he adds, "and have tasted of the heavenly gift. If ye have tasted" (he says) "of the heavenly gift," that is, of forgiveness. "And been made partakers of the Holy Ghost, and tasted the good word of God" (he is speaking here of the doctrine) "and the powers of the world to come" (what powers is he speaking of? either the working of miracles, or "the earnest of the Spirit" — 2 Cor. i. 22) "and have fallen away, to renew them again unto repentance, seeing they crucify to themselves the Son of God afresh and put Him to an open shame." "Renew them," he says, "unto repentance," that is, by repentance, for unto repentance is by repentance. What then, is repentance excluded? Not repentance, far from it! But the renewing again by the laver.[7] For he did not say, "impossible" to be renewed "unto repentance," and stop, but added how "impossible, [by] crucifying afresh."

To "be renewed," that is, to be made new, for to make men new is [the work] of the laver only: for (it is said) "thy youth shall be renewed as the eagle's." (Ps. ciii. 5.) But it is [the work of] repentance, when those who have been made new, have afterwards become old through sins, to set them free from this old age, and to make them strong.[8] To bring them to that former brightness however, is not possible; for there the whole was Grace.

[6.] "Crucifying to themselves," he says, "the Son of God afresh, and putting Him to an open shame." What he means is this. Baptism is a Cross, and "our old man was crucified with [Him]" (Rom. vi. 6), for we were "made conformable to the likeness of His death" (Rom. vi. 5; Phil. iii. 10), and again, "we were buried therefore with Him by baptism into death." (Rom. vi. 4.) Wherefore, as it is not possible that Christ should be crucified a second time, for that is to "put Him to an open shame."[9] For "if death shall no more have dominion over Him" (Rom. vi. 9), if He rose again, by His resurrection becoming superior to death; if by death He wrestled with and overcame death, and then is crucified again, all those things become a fable and a mockery.[10] He

---

[1] δεῖξαι.
[2] That is, the Apostle repudiates the teaching of more than one baptism.
[3] ἐξ ἀρχῆς.   [4] νήψατε.
[5] St. Chrys.'s exposition requires this literal translation of the participle. He gives two explanations of it, " to renew them by crucifying afresh," and " seeing they crucify afresh."

[6] ἐντρεπτικῶς.   [7] διὰ λουτροῦ.
[8] στερροὺς καινοὺς, Sav. Ben.
[9] The common editions add οὕτως οὐδὲ βαπτισθῆναι, " so neither [is it possible] to be baptized [a second time]." The apodosis is wanting in the older text, as it is in several other places.
[10] [The original has a *paronomasia* hardly to be reproduced in

then that baptizeth[1] a second time, crucifies Him again.

But what is "crucifying afresh"? [It is] crucifying over again. For as Christ died on the cross, so do we in baptism, not as to the flesh, but as to sin. Behold two deaths. He died as to the flesh; in our case the old man was buried, and the new man arose, made conformable to the likeness of His death. If therefore it is necessary to be baptized [again[2]], it is necessary that this same [Christ] should die again. For baptism is nothing else than the putting to death of the baptized, and his rising again.

And he well said, "crucifying afresh unto themselves." For he that does this, as having forgotten the former grace,[3] and ordering his own life carelessly, acts in all respects as if there were another baptism. It behooves us therefore to take heed and to make ourselves safe.

[7.] What is, "having tasted of the heavenly gift"? it is, "of the remission of sins": for this is of God alone to bestow, and the grace is a grace once for all. "What then? shall we continue in sin that grace may abound? Far from it!" (Rom. vi. 1, 2.) But if we should be always going to be saved by grace we shall never be good. For where there is but one grace, and we are yet so indolent, should we then cease sinning if we knew that it is possible again to have our sins washed away? For my part I think not.

He here shows that the gifts are many: and to explain it, Ye were counted worthy (he says) of so great forgiveness; for he that was sitting in darkness, he that was at enmity, he that was at open war, that was alienated, that was hated of God, that was lost, he having been suddenly enlightened, counted worthy of the Spirit, of the heavenly gift, of adoption as a son, of the kingdom of heaven, of those other good things, the unspeakable mysteries; and who does not even thus become better, but while indeed worthy of perdition, obtained salvation and honor, as if he had successfully accomplished great things; how could he be again baptized?

On two grounds then he said that the thing was impossible, and he put the stronger last: first, because he who has been deemed worthy of such [blessings], and who has betrayed all that was granted to him, is not worthy to be again renewed; neither[4] is it possible that

[Christ] should again be crucified afresh: for this is to "put Him to an open shame."

There is not then any second laver: there is not [indeed]. And if there is, there is also a third, and a fourth; for the former one is continually disannulled by the later, and this continually by another, and so on without end.

"And tasted," he says, "the good word of God"; and he does not unfold it; "and the powers of the world to come," for to live as Angels and to have no need of earthly things, to know that this is the means of our introduction to the enjoyment of the worlds to come; this may we learn through the Spirit, and enter into those sacred recesses.

What are "the powers of the world to come"? Life eternal, angelic conversation. Of these we have already received the earnest through our Faith from the Spirit. Tell me then, if after having been introduced into a palace, and entrusted with all things therein, thou hadst then betrayed all, wouldest thou have been entrusted with them again?[5]

[8.] What then (you say)? Is there no repentance? There is repentance, but there is no second baptism: but repentance there is, and it has great force, and is able to set free from the burden of his sins, if he will, even him that hath been baptized much in sins, and to establish in safety him who is in danger, even though he should have come unto the very depth of wickedness. And this is evident from many places. "For," says one, "doth not he that falleth rise again? or he that turneth away, doth not he turn back to [God]?" (Jer. viii. 4.) It is possible, if we will, that Christ should be formed in us again: for hear Paul saying, "My little children of whom I travail in birth again, until Christ be formed in you." (Gal. iv. 19.) Only let us lay hold on repentance.

For behold the love of God to man! We ought on every ground to have been punished at the first; in that having received the natural law, and enjoyed innumerable blessings, we have not acknowledged our Master, and have lived an unclean life. Yet He not only has not punished us, but has even made us partakers of countless blessings, just as if we had accomplished great things. Again we fell away, and not even so does He punish us, but has given medicine of repentance, which is sufficient to put away and blot out all our sins; only if we knew the nature of the medicine, and how we ought to apply it.

What then is the medicine of Repentance? and how is it made up? First, of the condemnation of our own sins;[6] "For" (it is said) "mine iniquity have I not hid" (Ps. xxxii. 5); and

---

English. The word is παραδειγματισμός, of which the παραδειγματίσαι = "put to an open shame," above is the verb.—F. G.

[1] The later texts add ἑαυτὸν, "that baptizeth himself." St. Chrys. however is speaking of a bishop who repeats baptism.

[2] S. B. add πάλιν.

[3] χάρις. The word is used throughout this passage in the sense of remission, as explained in the next clause.

[4] The longer text in Sav. and Ben. adds, δευτέρῳ δὲ ὅτι οὐ, "and secondly because it is not," &c.: the shorter text has only οὐδὲ, omitting "secondly." There are many other instances of a similar negligence of style in the genuine text, as also in other works of St. Chrys.

[5] The common texts add τὰ ἐκεῖ, "the things in heaven." But St. Chrys. is speaking of present privileges here on earth.

[6] The common texts add καὶ ἀπὸ ἐξαγορεύσεως, "and [of] from confession."

again, " I will confess against myself my lawlessness unto the Lord, and Thou forgavest the iniquity of my heart." And " Declare thou at the first thy sins, that thou mayest be justified." (Isa. xliii. 26.) And, " The righteous man is an accuser of himself at the first speaking." (Prov. xviii. 17.)

Secondly, of great humbleness of mind : For it is like a golden chain ; if one have hold of the beginning, all will follow. Because if thou confess thy sin as one ought to confess, the soul is humbled. For conscience turning it on itself[1] causeth it to be subdued.

Other things too must be added to humbleness of mind if it be such as the blessed David knew, when he said, " A broken and a contrite heart God will not despise." (Ps. li. 17.) For that which is broken does not rise up, does not strike, but is ready to be ill-treated and itself riseth not up. Such is contrition of heart : though it be insulted, though it be evil entreated, it is quiet, and is not eager for vengeance.

And after humbleness of mind, there is need of intense prayers, of many tears, tears by day, and tears by night : for, he says, " every night will I wash my bed, I will water my couch with my tears. I am weary with my groaning." (Ps. vi. 6.) And again, " For I have eaten ashes as it were bread, and mingled my drink with weeping." (Ps. cii. 9.)

And after prayer thus intense, there is need of much almsgiving : for this it is which especially gives strength to the medicine of repentance. And as there is a medicine among the physicians' helps which receives many herbs, but one is the essential, so also in case of repentance this is the essential herb, yea, it may be everything. For hear what the Divine Scripture says, " Give alms, and all things shall be clean." (Luke xi. 41.) And again, " By almsgiving and acts of faithfulness[2] sins are purged away." (Prov. xvi. 6.) And, " Water will quench a flaming fire, and alms will do away with great sins." (Ecclus. iii. 30.)

Next not being angry with any one, not bearing malice ; the forgiving all their trespasses. For, it is said, " Man retaineth wrath against man, and yet seeketh healing from the Lord." (Ecclus. xxviii. 3.) " Forgive that ye may be forgiven." (Mark xi. 25.)

Also, the converting our brethren from their wandering. For, it is said,[3] " Go thou, and convert thy brethren, that thy sins may be forgiven thee." And from one's being in close relations with[4] the priests, " and if," it is said, " a man hath committed sins it shall be forgiven him." (Jas. v. 15.) To stand forward in defense of those who are wronged. Not to retain anger : to bear all things meekly.

[9.] Now then, before you learned that it is possible to have our sins washed away by means of repentance, were ye not in an agony, because there is no second laver, and were ye not in despair of yourselves? But now that we have learned by what means repentance and remission is brought to a successful issue, and that we shall be able entirely to escape, if we be willing to use it aright, what forgiveness can we possibly obtain, if we do not even enter on the thought of our sins? since if this were done, all would be accomplished.

For as he who enters the door, is within ; so he who reckons up his own evils will also certainly come to get them cured. But should he say, I am a sinner, without reckoning them up specifically,[5] and saying, This and this sin have I committed, he will never leave off, confessing indeed continually, but never caring in earnest for amendment. For should he have laid down a beginning, all the rest will unquestionably follow too, if only in one point[6] he have shown a beginning : for in every case the beginning and the preliminaries are difficult. This then let us lay as a foundation, and all will be smooth and easy.

Let us begin therefore, I entreat you, one with making his prayers intense : another with continual weeping : another with downcast[7] countenance. For not even is this, which is so small, unprofitable : for " I saw " (it is said) " that he was grieved and went downcast, and I healed his ways." (Isa. lvii. 17, 18.)

But let us all humble our own souls by almsgiving and forgiving our neighbors their trespasses, by not remembering injuries, nor avenging ourselves. If we continually reflect on our sins, no external circumstances can make us elated : neither riches, nor power, nor authority, nor honor ; nay, even should we sit in the imperial chariot itself, we shall sigh bitterly : Since even the blessed David was a King, and yet he said, " Every night I will wash my bed," [&c.] (Ps. vi. 6) : and he was not at all hurt by the purple robe and the diadem : he was not puffed up ; for he knew himself to be a man, and inasmuch as his heart had been made contrite, he went mourning.

[10.] For what are all things human? Ashes and dust, and as it were spray before the wind ; a smoke and a shadow, and a leaf driven here and there ; and a flower ; a dream, and a tale, and a fable, wind and air vainly puffed out and

---

[1] συστρέφον.

[2] καὶ πίστεσιν. [These same two words, ἐλεημοσύναι καὶ πίστεις, "almsgiving and acts of faithfulness," are used by the Septuagint to translate " mercy and truth " in Prov. iii. 3 also, as if πίστεις were the distinct acts of faithfulness which go to make up truth, comp. true of heart throughout the Psalms.]

[3] This seems to be an expression of the doctrine of James v. 19, 20, partially in the language of our Lord, Luke xxii. 33. [Cf. Acts iii. 19.]

[4] ἔχειν οἰκείως.

[5] κατ' εἶδος.

[6] εἰς ἕν, or, " once for all."

[7] κατηφεῖν, " seriousness."

wasting away; a feather that hath no stay, a stream flowing by, or if there be aught of more nothingness than these.

For, tell me, what dost thou esteem great? What dignity thinkest thou to be great? is it that of the Consul? For the many think no greater dignity than that. He who is not Consul is not a whit inferior to him who is in so great splendor, who is so greatly admired. Both one and the other are of the same dignity; both of them alike, after a little while, are no more.

When was he made [Consul]? For how long a time? tell me: for two days? Nay, this takes place even in dreams. But that is [only] a dream, you say. And what is this? For (tell me) what is by day, is it [therefore] not a dream? Why do we not rather call these things a dream? For as dreams when the day comes on are proved to be nothing: so these things also, when the night comes on, are proved to be nothing. For night and day have received each an equal portion of time, and have equally divided all duration. Therefore as in the day a person rejoices not in what happened at night, so neither in the night is it possible for him to reap the fruit of what is done in the day. Thou hast been made Consul? So was I in the night; only I in the night, thou in the day. And what of this? Not even so hast thou any advantage over me, except

haply its being said, Such an one is Consul, and the pleasure that springs from the words, gives him the advantage.

I mean something of this kind, for I will express it more plainly: if I say "Such an one is Consul," and bestow on him the name, is it not gone as soon as it is spoken? So also are the things themselves; no sooner doth the Consul appear, than he is no more. But let us suppose [that he is Consul] for a year, or two years, or three or four years. Where are they who were ten times Consul? Nowhere.

But Paul is not so. For he was, and also is living continually: he did not live one day, nor two, nor ten, and twenty, nor thirty; nor ten and twenty, nor yet thirty years — and die. Even the four hundredth year is now past, and still even yet is he illustrious, yea much more illustrious than when he was alive. And these things indeed [are] on earth; but the glory of the saints in heaven what word could set forth?

Wherefore I entreat you, let us seek this glory; let us pursue after it, that we may attain it. For this is the true glory. Let us henceforth stand aloof from the things of this life, that we may find grace and mercy in Christ Jesus our Lord: with whom to the Father, together with the Holy Ghost, be glory, power, honor and worship, now and for ever, and world without end. Amen.

# HOMILY X.

## Hebrews vi. 7, 8.

"For the Earth which drinketh in the rain that cometh oft upon it, and bringeth forth herbs meet for them by whom it is dressed, receiveth blessing from God. But if it bear[1] thorns and briars it is rejected, and nigh unto cursing, whose end is to be burned."

[I.] Let us hear the oracles of God with fear, with fear and much trembling. For (it is said) "Serve the Lord with fear, and rejoice unto Him with trembling." (Ps. ii. 11.) But if even our joy and our exultation ought to be "with trembling," of what punishment are we not worthy, if we listen not with terror to what is said, when the things spoken, as now, are themselves fearful?

For having said that "it is impossible for those who have fallen away" to be baptized a

second time, and to receive remission through the laver, and having pointed out the awfulness of the case, he goes on: "for the earth which drinketh in the rain that cometh oft upon it, and bringeth forth herbs meet for them by whom it is dressed, receiveth blessing from God. But if it bear thorns and thistles, it is rejected,[2] and nigh unto cursing; whose end is to be burned."

Let us then fear, beloved! This threat is not Paul's, these words are not of man: they are of the Holy Ghost, of Christ that speaketh in him. Is there then any one that is clear from these thorns? And even if we were clear, not even so ought we to be confident, but to fear and tremble lest at any time thorns should spring up in us. But when we are "thorns and thistles" through and through, whence (tell me) are we confident? And are becoming supine? What is it which makes us inert? If "he that thinketh he standeth" ought to fear "lest he fall"; for

---

[1] The received version is necessarily altered here: St. Chrysostom's commentary will be more readily understood if it is kept in mind that the exact translation would be as below: "the land which hath drunk in," &c., "partaketh of blessing," &c. "But if it bear thorns and thistles, it is reprobate, and nigh unto a curse, whose end is for burning." [There seems to be no need of this slight correction: the present participle of the Greek is even more closely represented by the A. V. than by the above translation. But in view of this note, it must be allowed to stand. — F. G.]

[2] ἀδόκιμος, "reprobate."

(he says) " Let him that thinketh he standeth, take heed lest he fall " (1 Cor. x. 12) ; he that falleth, how anxious ought he to be that he may rise up again ! If Paul fears, " lest that by any means, when he had preached to others, he himself should be a castaway " (1 Cor. ix. 27) ; and he who had been so approved is afraid lest he should become disapproved :[1] what pardon shall we have who are already disapproved, if we have no fear, but fulfill our Christianity as a custom, and for form's sake. Let us then fear, beloved : " For the wrath of God is revealed from heaven." (Rom. i. 18.) Let us fear, for it " is revealed " not " against impiety " only, but " against all unrighteousness." What is " against all unrighteousness "? [Against all] both small and great.

[2.] In this passage he intimates the loving-kindness of God towards man : and the teaching [of the Gospel] he calls " rain " : and what he said above, " when for the time ye ought to be teachers " (c. v. 12), this he says here also. Indeed in many places the Scripture calls the teaching " rain." For (it says) " I will command the clouds that they rain no rain upon it " (Isa. v. 6), speaking of " the vineyard." The same which in another place it calls " a famine of bread, and a thirst of water." (Amos viii. 11.) And again, " The river of God is full of waters." (Ps. lxv. 9.)

" For land," he says, " which drinketh in the rain that cometh oft upon it." Here he shows that they received and drank in the word, yea and often enjoyed this, and yet even so they were not profited. For if (he means) thou hadst not been tilled, if thou hadst enjoyed no rains, the evil would not have been so great. For (it is said) " If I had not come and spoken unto them they had not had sin." (John xv. 22.) But if thou hast often drunk and received [nourishment], wherefore hast thou brought forth other things instead of fruits? For (it is said) " I waited that it should bring forth grapes, and it brought forth thorns." (Isa. v. 2.)

Thou seest that everywhere the Scripture calleth sins " thorns." For David also saith, " I was turned into mourning when a thorn was fixed in me." (Ps. xxxii. 4, so LXX.) For it does not simply come on us, but is fixed in ; and even if but a little of it remain in, even if we take it not out entirely, that little of itself in like manner causes pain, as in the case of a thorn. And why do I say, ' that little of itself '? Even after it has been taken out, it leaves therein for a long time the pain of the wound. And much care and treatment is necessary, that we may be per-

fectly freed from it. For it is not enough merely to take away the sin, it is necessary also to heal the wounded place.

But I fear however lest the things said apply to us more than to others. " For," he says, " the earth which drinketh in the rain that cometh oft upon it." We are ever drinking, ever hearing, but " when the sun is risen " (Matt. xiii. 6) we straightway lose our moisture, and therefore bring forth thorns. What then are the thorns? Let us hear Christ saying, that " the care of this world, and the deceitfulness of riches, choke the word, and it becometh unfruitful." (Matt. xiii. 22.)

[3.] " For the earth which drinketh in the rain that cometh oft upon it," he says, " and bringeth forth meet herbs." Because nothing is so meet as purity of life, nothing so suitable as the best life, nothing so meet as virtue.

" And bringeth forth " (saith he) " herbs meet for them by whom it is dressed, receiveth blessing from God." Here he says that God is the cause of all things, giving the heathen a blow, who ascribed the production of fruits to the power of the earth. For (he says) it is not the hands of the husbandman which stir up the earth to bear fruits, but the command from God. Therefore he says, " receives blessing from God."

And see how in speaking of the thorns, he said not, " bringing forth[2] thorns," nor did he use this word expressive of what is useful; but what? " Bearing "[3] [literally " putting out "] " thorns," as if one should say, " forcing out," " throwing out."

" Rejected " (he says) " and nigh unto cursing." Oh ! how great consolation in this word ! For he said " nigh unto cursing," not " a curse." Now he that hath not yet fallen into a curse, but is come to be near [thereto], may also come to be far off [therefrom].

And not by this only did he encourage them, but also by what follows. For he did not say " rejected and nigh unto cursing," " which shall be burned," but what? " Whose end is to be burned," if he continue [such] (he means) unto the end. So that, if we cut out and burn the thorns, we shall be able to enjoy those good things innumerable and to become approved, and to partake of blessing.

And with good reason did he call sin " a thistle,"[4] saying " that which beareth thorns and thistles " ; for on whatever side you lay hold on it, it wounds and stings, and it is unpleasant even to look at.

[4.] Having therefore sufficiently rebuked them, and alarmed and wounded them, he in turn heals them, so as not to cast them down too much, and make them supine. For he that

---

[1] ἀδόκιμος. In the original it is one and the same word which in the text, Heb. vi. 8, is translated " rejected," in 1 Cor. ix. 27; " a castaway "; it is in this clause opposed to δόκιμος, " approved," " accepted." It means rejected after testing, as in case of metals: which may take place, as St. Chrys. implies in this passage, either here or hereafter; either for a time or for eternity.

[2] τίκτουσα.   [3] ἐκφέρουσα.
[4] [τρίβολον, " a burr."]

strikes one that is "dull," makes him more dull. So then he neither flatters them throughout, lest he should make them supine, nor does he wound them throughout, but having inserted a little to wound them, he applies much to heal in what follows.

For what does he say? We speak not these things, as having condemned you, nor as thinking you to be full of thorns, but fearing lest this should come to pass. For it is better to terrify you by words, that ye may not suffer by the realities. And this is specially of Paul's wisdom.

Moreover he did not say, We think, or, we conjecture, or, we expect, or, we hope, but what? (Ver. 9) "But beloved, we are persuaded better things of you, and things that accompany salvation, though we thus speak." Which word he also used in writing to the Galatians: "But I am persuaded of you in the Lord, that ye will be none otherwise minded." (Gal. v. 10.) For in that instance, inasmuch as they were greatly to be condemned, and he could not praise them from things present, he does it from things future ("that ye will be none otherwise minded," he says): he said not, ye are, but "ye will be none otherwise minded." But here he encourages them from things present. "We are persuaded better things of you, beloved, and things that accompany to salvation, though we thus speak." And since he was not able to say so much from things present, he confirms his consolation from things past; and says,

Ver. 10. "For God is not unrighteous to forget your work, and[1] the love, which ye have showed toward His name, in that ye have ministered unto the saints and do minister." O how did he here restore their spirit, and give them fresh strength, by reminding them of former things, and bringing them to the necessity of not supposing that God had forgotten. (For he cannot but sin who is not fully assured concerning his hope, and says that God is unrighteous. Accordingly he obliged them by all means to look forward to those future things. For one who despairs of present things, and has given up exerting himself, may be restored by [the prospect of] things future.) As he himself also said in writing to the Galatians, "Ye did run well" (Gal. v. 7): and again, "Have ye suffered so many things in vain? if it be yet in vain." (Gal. iii. 4.)

And as in this place he puts the praise with the reproof, saying, "When for the time ye ought to be teachers" (c. v. 12), so also there, "I marvel that ye are so soon removed." (Gal. i. 6.) With the reproof is the praise. For respecting great things we marvel, when they

fail. Thou seest that praise is concealed under the accusation and the blame. Nor does he say this concerning himself only, but also concerning all. For he said not, I am persuaded, but "we are persuaded better things of you," even good things (he means). He says this either in regard to matters of conduct, or to the recompense.

In the next place, having said above, that it is "rejected and nigh unto a curse," and that it "shall be for burning," he says, we do not by any means speak this of you. "For God is not unrighteous to forget your work, and love." (Ver. 10.)

[5.] Why then did we say these things? (Ver. 11, 12) "But we desire that every one of you do show the same diligence to the full assurance of hope unto the end; that ye be not slothful, but followers of them who through faith and patience inherit the promises."

"We desire," he says, and we do not therefore merely labor for, or even so far as words go, wish this. But what? "We desire" that ye should hold fast to virtue, not as condemning your former conduct (he means), but fearing for the future. And he did not say, 'not as condemning your former conduct, but your present; for ye have fainted, ye are become too indolent'; but see how gently he indicated it, and did not wound them.

For what does he say? "But we desire that every one of you do show the same diligence unto the end." For this is the admirable part of Paul's wisdom, that he does not expressly show that they "had" given in, that they "had" become negligent. For when he says, "We desire that every one of you" — it is as if one should say, I wish thee to be always in earnest; and such as thou wert before, such to be now also, and for the time to come. For this made his reproof more gentle and easy to be received.

And he did not say, "I will," which would have been expressive of the authority of a teacher, but what is expressive of the affection of a father, and what is more than "willing," "we desire." All but saying, Pardon us, even if we say what is distasteful.

"We desire that every one of you do show the same diligence to the full assurance of your hope unto the end." Hope (he means) carries us through: it recovers us again. Be not wearied out, do not despair, lest your hope be in vain. For he that worketh good hopeth also good, and never despairs of himself.

"That ye may not become dull."[2] Still[3] "become"; and yet he said above, "seeing ye are become dull[2] of hearing." (c. v. 11.) Ob-

---

[1] Sav. and Ben. here, and in other places where the text is cited, insert τοῦ κόπου, "the labor of love," &c. These words are probably not part of the sacred text. They are not referred to by St. Chrysostom.

[2] νωθροὶ. The same word is translated "slothful" and "dull" in these two passages. It means "sluggish," "stupid," "without quickness in perception or energy in action." [3] ἀκμὴν.

serve however how he limited the dullness to the hearing. And here he hints the very same thing ; instead of 'that ye may not continue in it,' he says [this]. But again he leads on to that future time for which they were not yet responsible ; saying in effect "that ye may not become too slothful" : since for that which is not yet come we could not be responsible. For he who in regard to the present time is exhorted to be in earnest, as being remiss, will perhaps become even more slothful, but he who is exhorted with reference to the future, not so.

"We desire" (he says) "that every one of you." Great is his affection for them : he cares equally for great and small ; moreover he knows all, and overlooks no one, but shows the same tender care for each, and equal value for all : from which cause also he the rather persuaded them to receive what was distasteful in his words.

"That ye be not slothful," he says. For as inactivity hurts the body, so also inactivity as to what is good renders the soul more supine and feeble.

[6.] "But followers" (he says) " of them, who through faith and patience inherit the promises." And who they are, he tells afterwards. He said before, "Imitate your own former well-doings." Then, lest they should say, What? He leads them back to the Patriarch : bringing before them examples of well-doing indeed from their own history,[1] but of the thought of being forsaken, from the Patriarch ; that they might not suppose that they were disregarded and forsaken as worthy of no account, but might know that it is [the portion] of the very noblest men to make the journey of life through trials ; and that God has thus dealt with great and admirable men.

Now we ought (he says) to bear all things with patience : for this also is believing : whereas if He say that He gives and thou immediately receivest, how hast thou also believed? Since in that case this is no longer of thy faith, but of Me, the Giver. But if I say that I give, and give after an hundred years, and thou hast not despaired ; then hast thou accounted Me worthy to be believed, then thou hast the right opinion concerning Me. Thou seest that oftentimes unbelief arises not from want of hope only, but also from faintheartedness, and want of patience, not from condemning him who made the promise.

"For God" (he says) "is not unrighteous to forget your love" and the zeal "which ye have showed toward His Name, in that ye have ministered unto the saints, and do minister." He testifies great things of them, not deeds only, but deeds done with alacrity, which he says also in another place, " and not only so, but they gave themselves also to the Lord and to us." (2 Cor. viii. 5.)

"Which " (he says) "ye have showed toward His Name, in that ye have ministered to the saints, and do minister." See how again he soothes them, by adding "and do minister." Still even at this time (he says) ye are ministering, and he raises them up by showing that they had done [what they did] not to them [the saints], but to God. "Which ye have showed" (he says) ; and he said not "unto the saints," but "towards God," for this is "toward His Name." It is for His Name's sake (he means) that ye have done all. He therefore who has the enjoyment from you of[2] so great zeal and love, will never despise you nor forget you.

[7.] Hearing these things, let us, I beseech you, "minister to the saints." For every believer is a saint in that he is a believer. Though he be a person living in the world, he is a saint. "For" (he says) "the unbelieving husband is sanctified by the wife, and the unbelieving wife by the husband." (1 Cor. vii. 14.) See how the faith makes the saintship. If then we see even a secular person in misfortune, let us stretch out a hand [to him]. Let us not be zealous for those only who dwell in the mountains ; they are indeed saints both in manner of life and in faith ; these others however are saints by their faith, and many of them also in manner of life. Let us not, if we see a monk [cast] into prison, in that case go in ; but if it be a secular person, refuse to go in. He also is a saint and a brother.

What then (you say) if he be unclean and polluted? Listen to Christ saying, "Judge not that ye be not judged." (Matt. vii. 1.) Do thou act for God's sake. Nay, what am I saying? Even if we see a heathen in misfortune, we ought to show kindness to him, and to every man without exception who is in misfortunes, and much more to a believer who is in the world. Listen to Paul, saying, "Do good unto all men, but especially to those who are of the household of faith." (Gal. vi. 10.)

But I know not whence this [notion] has been introduced, or whence this custom hath prevailed. For he that only seeks after the solitaries, and is willing to do good to them alone, and with regard to others on the contrary is over-curious in his enquiries, and says, 'unless he be worthy,[3] unless he be righteous, unless he work miracles, I stretch out no hand' ; [such an one] has taken away the greater part of charity,[4] yea and in time he will in turn destroy the very thing itself. And yet that is charity,[4] [which is shown]

---

[1] οἴκοθεν.

[2] ἀπολαύων.

[3] ἐὰν μὴ ᾖ ἄξιος, ἐὰν μὴ ᾖ δίκαιος. Mr. Field retains μὴ in these clauses, in accordance with the common editions, though all the MSS. omit the negative in the first clause, and the best MSS. in the second also, and it was not read by Mutianus. If it be omitted, the passage would run thus, "and says, If he be worthy, if he be righteous [I will help him]. Unless he work miracles I stretch out no hand," &c.; which seems to give a good sense.

[4] ἐλεημοσύνη, "mercifulness," or "almsgiving."

towards sinners, towards the guilty. For this is charity,[1] not the pitying those who have done well, but those who have done wrong.

[8.] And that thou mayest understand this, listen to the Parable : "A certain man" (it is said) "went down from Jerusalem to Jericho, and fell among thieves" (Luke x. 30, &c.) ; and when they had beaten him, they left him by the way-side, having badly bruised him. A certain Levite came, and when he saw him, he passed by ; A priest came, and when he saw him, he hastened past ; a certain Samaritan came, and bestowed great care upon him. For he "bound up his wounds" (Luke x. 34), dropped oil on them, set him upon his ass, "brought him to the inn, said to the host, Take care of him" (Luke x. 35) ; and (observe his great liberality), "and I," he says, "will give thee whatsoever thou shalt expend." Who then is his neighbor? "He," it is said, "that showed mercy on him. Go thou then also," He says, "and do likewise." (Luke x. 37.) And see what a parable He spake. He said not that a Jew did [so and so] to a Samaritan, but that a Samaritan showed all that liberality. Having then heard these things, let us not care only for "those that are of the household of faith" (Gal. vi. 10), and neglect others. So then also thou, if thou see any one in affliction, be not curious to enquire further. His being in affliction involves a just claim on thy aid.[2] For if when thou seest an ass choking thou raisest him up, and dost not curiously enquire whose he is, much more about a man one ought not to be over-curious in enquiring whose he is. He is God's, be he heathen or be he Jew ; since even if he is an unbeliever, still he needs help. For if indeed it had been committed to thee to enquire and to judge, thou wouldst have well said thus, but, as it is, his misfortune does not suffer thee to search out these things. For if even about men in good health it is not right to be over-curious, nor to be a busybody in other men's matters, much less about those that are in affliction.

[9.] But on another view what [shall we say]? Didst thou see him in prosperity, in high esteem, that thou shouldst say that he is wicked and worthless? But if thou seest him in affliction, do not say that he is wicked. For when a man is in high credit, we fairly say these things ; but when he is in calamity, and needs help, it is not right to say that he is wicked. For this is cruelty, inhumanity, and arrogance. Tell me what was ever more iniquitous than the Jews. But nevertheless while God punished them, and that justly, yea, very justly, yet He approved of those who had compassion on them, and those who rejoiced over them He punished. (Amos vi. 6.) For "they were not grieved," it is said, "at the affliction of Joseph."

And again it is said "Redeem [Ransom] those who are ready to be slain : spare not." (Prov. xxiv. 11.) (He said not, enquire curiously, and learn who he is ; and yet, for the most part, they who are led away to execution are wicked,) for this especially is charity. For he that doeth good to a friend, doeth it not altogether for God's sake : but he that [doeth good] to one unknown, this man acts purely for God's sake. "Do not spare" thy money, even if it be necessary to spend all, yet give.

But we, when we see persons in extreme distress,[3] bewailing themselves, suffering things more grievous than ten thousand deaths, and oftentimes unjustly, we [I say] are sparing of our money, and unsparing of our brethren ; we are careful of lifeless things, but neglect the living soul. And yet Paul says, "in meekness instruct those that oppose themselves, if peradventure God should give them repentance to the acknowledging of the truth, and they may recover themselves out of the snare of the devil who are taken captive by him, at His will." (2 Tim. ii. 25, 26.) "If peradventure," he says ; thou seest of how great long-suffering the word is full.

Let us also imitate Him, and despair of no one. For the fishermen too, when they have cast many times [suppose it], have not succeeded ; but afterwards having cast again, have gained all. So we also expect that ye will all at once show to us ripe fruit. For the husbandman too, after he has sown, waits one day or two days, and is a long while in expectation : and all at once he sees the fruits springing up on every side. This we expect will take place in your case also by the grace and lovingkindness of our Lord Jesus Christ, with whom to the Father and also to the Holy Ghost be glory, might, honor, now and for ever and·world without end. Amen.

---

[1] ἐλεημοσύνη, "mercifulness," or "almsgiving."
[2] τὸ δικαίωμα τῆς βοηθείας.

[3] ἀγχομένους.

# HOMILY XI.

HEBREWS vi. 13–16.

" For when God made promise to Abraham, because He could swear by no greater, He sware by Himself, saying, Surely blessing I will bless thee, and multiplying I will multiply thee. And so after he had patiently endured, he obtained the promise. For men verily swear by the greater, and an oath for confirmation is to them an end of all strife."

[1.] HAVING boldly reflected on the faults of the Hebrews, and sufficiently alarmed them, he consoles them, first, by praises, and secondly (which also is the stronger ground), by the [thought] that they would certainly attain the object of their hope. Moreover he draws his consolation, not from things future, but again from the past, which indeed would the rather persuade them. For as in the case of punishment, he alarms them rather by those [viz. things future], so also in the case of the prizes [set before them], he encourages them by these [viz. by things past], showing [herein] God's way of dealing. And that is, not to bring in what has been promised immediately, but after a long time. And this He does, both to present the greatest proof of His power, and also to lead us to Faith, that they who are living in tribulation without having received the promises, or the rewards, may not faint under their troubles.

And omitting all [the rest], though he had many whom he might have mentioned, he brought forward Abraham both on account of the dignity of his person, and because this had occurred in a special way in his case.

And yet at the end of the Epistle he says, that " all these, having seen the promises afar off, and having embraced them, received them not, that they without us should not be made perfect." (c. xi. 13.) " For when God made promise to Abraham " (he says) " because He could swear by no greater, He sware by Himself, saying, Surely blessing I will bless thee, and multiplying I will multiply thee. And so after he had patiently endured, he obtained the promise." (c. xi. 39, 40.) How then does he say at the end [of the Epistle] that " he received not the promises," and here, that " after he had patiently endured he obtained the promise " ? How did he not receive ? How did he obtain ? He is not speaking of the same things in this place and in the other, but makes the consolation twofold. God made promises to Abraham, and after a long space of time He gave the things [spoken of] in this place, but those others not yet.

"And so after he had patiently endured, he obtained the promise." Seest thou that the promise alone did not effect the whole, but the patient waiting as well? Here he alarms them, showing that oftentimes a promise is thwarted through faintheartedness.[1] And this he had indeed shown through [the instance of] the [Jewish] people : for since they were fainthearted, therefore they obtained not the promise. But now he shows the contrary by means of Abraham. Afterwards near the end [of the Epistle] he proves something more also : [viz.] that even though they had patiently endured, they did not obtain ; and yet not even so are they grieved.

[2.] " For men verily swear by the greater, and an Oath for confirmation is to them an end of all strife. But God because He could swear by no greater, sware by Himself." Well, who then is He that sware unto Abraham ? Is it not the SON? No, one says. Certainly indeed it was He : however, I shall not dispute [thereon]. So when He [the Son] sweareth the same oath, " Verily, verily, I say unto you," is it not plain that it was because He could not swear by any greater ? For as the Father sware, so also the Son sweareth by Himself, saying, " Verily, verily, I say unto you." He here reminds them also of the oaths of Christ, which He was constantly uttering. " Verily, verily, I say unto thee, he that believeth on Me shall never die." (John xi. 26.)

What is, " And an oath for confirmation is to them an end of all strife " ? it is instead of, " by this every doubtful question is solved " : not this, or this, but every one.

God, however, ought to have been believed even without an oath : (ver. 17) " wherein " (he says) " God willing more abundantly to show unto the heirs of promise the immutability of His counsel, confirmed it [lit. " mediated "[2]] by an oath." In these words he comprehends also the believers, and therefore mentions this " promise " which was made to us in common [with them]. " He mediated " (he says) " by an oath." Here again he says that the Son was mediator between men and God.

Ver. 18. " That by two immutable things, in which it was impossible that God should lie." What are these two ? The speaking and promising ; and the adding an oath to the promise.

---

¹ ὀλιγοψυχίαν.　　　　　² ἐμεσίτευσεν.

For since among men that which is [confirmed] by an oath is thought more worthy of credit, on this account He added that also.

Seest thou that He regardeth not His own dignity, but how He may persuade men, and endures to have unworthy things said concerning Himself. That is He wishes to impart full assurance. And in the case of Abraham indeed [the Apostle] shows that the whole was of God, not of his patient endurance, since He was even willing to add an oath, for He by whom men swear, by Him also God "sware," that is "by Himself." They indeed as by one greater, but He not as by one greater. And yet He did it. For it is not the same thing for man to swear by himself, as for God. For man has no power over himself. Thou seest then that this is said not more for Abraham than for ourselves : "that we " (he says) "might have strong consolation, who have fled for refuge to lay hold on the hope set before us." Here too again,[1] "after he had patiently endured he obtained the promise."

"Now" he means, and he did not say "when[2] He swore." But what the oath is, he showed, by speaking of swearing by a greater. But since the race of men is hard of belief, He condescends to the same [things] with ourselves. As then for our sake He swears, although it be unworthy of Him that He should not be believed, so also did [the Apostle] make that other statement : "He learned from the things which He suffered" (c. v. 8), because men think the going through experience more worthy of reliance.

What is "the hope set before us"? From these [past events] (he says) we conjecture the future. For if these came to pass after so long a time, so certainly the others will. So that the things which happened in regard to Abraham give us confidence also concerning the things to come.

[3.] (Ver. 19, 20) "Which [hope] we have as an anchor of the soul both sure and steadfast, and which entereth into that within the veil : whither the forerunner is for us entered, even JESUS, made High Priest forever after the order of Melchisedec." He shows, that while we are still in the world, and not yet departed from [this] life, we are already among the promises. For through hope we are already in heaven. He said, "Wait ; for it shall surely be." Afterwards giving them full assurance, he says, "nay rather by hope."[3] And he said not, "We are within," but 'It hath entered within,' which was more true and more persuasive. For as the anchor, dropped from the vessel, does not

allow it to be carried about, even if ten thousand winds agitate it, but being depended upon makes it steady, so also does hope.

And see how very suitable an image he has discovered : For he said not, Foundation ; which was not suitable ; but, "Anchor." For that which is on the tossing sea, and seems not to be very firmly fixed, stands on the water as upon land, and is shaken and yet is not shaken. For in regard to those who are very firm, and philosophic, Christ with good reason made that statement, saying, "Whosoever hath built his house on a rock." (Matt. vii. 24.) But in respect of those who are giving way, and who ought to be carried through by hope, Paul hath suitably set down this. For the surge and the great storm toss the boat ; but hope suffers it not to be carried hither and thither, although winds innumerable agitate it : so that, unless we had this [hope] we should long ago have been sunk. Nor is it only in things spiritual, but also in the affairs of this life, that one may find the power of hope great. Whatever it may be, in merchandise, in husbandry, in a military expedition, unless one sets this before him, he would not even touch the work. But he said not simply "Anchor," but "sure and steadfast" [i.e.] not shaken. "Which entereth into that within the veil" ; instead of 'which reacheth through even to heaven.'

[4.] Then after this he led on to Faith also, that there might not only be hope, but a very true [hope]. For after the oath he lays down another thing too, even proof by facts, because "the forerunner is for us entered in, even JESUS." But a forerunner is a forerunner of some one, as John was of Christ.

Now he did not simply say, "He is entered in," but "where He is entered in a forerunner for us," as though we also ought to attain. For there is no great interval between the forerunner and those who follow : otherwise he would not be a forerunner ; for the forerunner and those who follow ought to be in the same road, and to arrive after [each other].

"Being made an High Priest forever after the order," he says, "of Melchisedec." Here is also another consolation, if our High Priest is on high, and far better than those among the Jews, not in the kind [of Priesthood] only, but also in the place, and the tabernacle, and the covenant, and the person. And this also is spoken according to the flesh.

[5.] Those then, whose High Priest He is, ought to be greatly superior. And as great as the difference is between Aaron and Christ, so great should it be between us and the Jews. For see, we have our victim[4] on high, our priest on

---

[1] This observation seems to be suggested by the words "the hope set before us" : i.e. this is another instance of obtaining a future blessing by patient waiting. The next clause bears on the Apostle's statement that this oath was made "that we might have consolation," we, "now," at this time ; not Abraham, to whom the oath was originally made.

[2] ἐπειδή, "at the very time that."

[3] Sav. and Ben. add ἤδη ἐτύχετε, "ye have already attained it."

[4] ἱερεῖον.

high, our sacrifice[1] on high: let us bring such sacrifices as can be offered on that altar, no longer sheep and oxen, no longer blood and fat. All these things have been done away; and there has been brought in in their stead "the reasonable service." (Rom. xii. 1.) But what is "the reasonable service"? The [offerings made] through the soul; those made through the spirit. ("God," it is said, "is a Spirit, and they that worship Him must worship Him in spirit and in truth" — John iv. 24); things which have no need of a body, no need of instruments, nor of special places, whereof each one is himself the Priest, such as, moderation, temperance, mercifulness, enduring ill-treatment, long-suffering, humbleness of mind.

These sacrifices one may see in the Old [Testament] also, shadowed out beforehand. "Offer to God," it is said, "a sacrifice of righteousness" (Ps. iv. 5); "Offer a sacrifice of praise" (Ps. l. 14); and, "a sacrifice of praise shall glorify Me" (Ps. l. 23), and, "the sacrifice of God is a broken spirit" (Ps. li. 17); and "what doth the Lord require of thee but" to hearken to Him? (Mic. vi. 8.) "Burnt-offerings and sacrifices for sin Thou hast had no pleasure in: then I said, Lo I come to do Thy will, O God!" (Ps. xl. 6, 7), and again, "To what purpose do ye bring the incense from Sheba?" (Jer. vi. 20.) "Take thou away from Me the noise of thy songs, for I will not hear the melody of thy viols." (Amos v. 23.) But instead of these "I will have mercy and not sacrifice." (Hosea vi. 6.) Thou seest with what kind of "sacrifices God is well pleased." (c. xiii. 16.) Thou seest also that already from the first the one class have given place, and these have come in their stead.

These therefore let us bring, for the other indeed are [the offerings] of wealth and of persons who have [possessions], but these of virtue: those from without, these from within: those any chance person even might perform; these only a few. And as much as a man is superior to a sheep, so much is this sacrifice superior to that; for here thou offerest thy soul as a victim.

[6.] And other sacrifices also there are, which are indeed whole burnt-offerings, the bodies of the martyrs: there both soul and body [are offered]. These have a great savor of a sweet smell. Thou also art able, if thou wilt, to bring such a sacrifice.

For what, if thou dost not burn thy body in the fire? Yet in a different fire thou canst; for instance, in that of voluntary poverty, in that of affliction. For to have it in one's power to spend one's days in luxury and expense, and yet to take up a life of toil and bitterness, and to mortify the body, is not this a whole burnt-offer-

ing? Mortify thy body, and crucify it, and thou shalt thyself also receive the crown of this martyrdom. For what in the other case the sword accomplishes, that in this case let a willing mind effect. Let not the love of wealth burn, or possess you, but let this unreasonable appetite itself be consumed and quenched by the fire of the Spirit; let it be cut in pieces by the sword of the Spirit.

This is an excellent sacrifice, needing no priest but him who brings it. This is an excellent sacrifice, performed indeed below, but forthwith taken up on high. Do we not wonder that of old time fire came down and consumed all? It is possible now also that fire may come down far more wonderful than that, and consume all the presented offerings:[2] nay rather, not consume, but bear them up to heaven. For it does not reduce them to ashes, but offers them as gifts to God.

[7.] Such were the offerings of Cornelius. For (it is said) "thy prayers and thine alms are come up for a memorial before God." (Acts x. 4.) Thou seest a most excellent union. Then are we heard, when we ourselves also hear the poor who come to us. "He" (it is said) "that stoppeth his ears that he may not hear the poor" (Prov. xxi. 13), his prayer God will not hearken to. "Blessed is he that considereth the poor and needy: the Lord will deliver him in the evil day." (Ps. xl. 1.) But what day is evil except that one which is evil to sinners?

What is meant by "he that considereth"? He that understandeth what it is to be a poor man, that has thoroughly learned his affliction. For he that has learned his affliction, will certainly and immediately have compassion on him. When thou seest a poor man, do not hurry by, but immediately reflect what thou wouldest have been, hadst thou been he. What wouldest thou not have wished that all should do for thee? "He that considereth" (he says). Reflect that he is a free-man like thyself, and shares the same noble birth with thee, and possesses all things in common with thee; and yet oftentimes he is not on a level even with thy dogs. On the contrary, while they are satiated, he oftentimes lies, sleeps, hungry, and the free-man is become less honorable than thy slaves.

But they perform needful services for thee. What are these? Do they serve thee well? Suppose then I show that this [poor man] too performs needful services for thee far greater than they do. For he will stand by thee in the Day of judgment, and will deliver thee from the fire. What do all thy slaves do like this? When Tabitha died, who raised her up? The slaves who stood around or the poor? But thou art not

---

[1] θυσία, "the act of sacrificing." [θυσία commonly has the meaning given in the text, not that in the note. — F. G.]

[2] τὰ προκείμενα.

even willing to put the free-man on an equality with thy slaves. The frost is hard, and the poor man is cast out in rags, well-nigh dead, with his teeth chattering, both by his looks and his air fitted to move thee : and thou passeth by, warm and full of drink ; and how dost thou expect that God should deliver thee when in misfortune?

And oftentimes thou sayest this too : ' If it had been myself, and I had found one that had done many wrong things, I would have forgiven him ; and does not God forgive?' Say not this. Him that has done thee no wrong, whom thou art able to deliver, him thou neglectest. How shall He forgive thee, who art sinning against Him? Is not this deserving of hell?

And how amazing ! Oftentimes thou adornest with vestments innumerable, of varied colors and wrought with gold, a dead body, insensible, no longer perceiving the honor ; whilst that which is in pain, and lamenting, and tormented, and racked by hunger and frost, thou neglectest ; and givest more to vainglory, than to the fear of God.

[8.] And would that it stopped here ; but immediately accusations are brought against the applicant. For why does he not work (you say) ? And why is he to be maintained in idleness? But (tell me) is it by working that thou hast what thou hast, didst thou not receive it as an inheritance from thy fathers? And even if thou dost work, is this a reason why thou shouldest reproach another? Hearest thou not what Paul saith? For after saying, " He that worketh not, neither let him eat " (2 Thess. iii. 10), he says, " But ye be not weary in well doing." (2 Thess. iii. 13.)

But what say they? He is an impostor.[1] What sayest thou, O man? Callest thou him an impostor, for the sake of a single loaf or of a garment? But (you say) he will sell it immediately. And dost thou manage all thy affairs well? But what? Are all poor through idleness? Is no one so from shipwreck? None from lawsuits? None from being robbed? None from dangers? None from illness? None from any other difficulties? If however we hear any one bewailing such evils, and crying out aloud, and looking up naked toward heaven, and with long hair, and clad in rags, at once we call him, The impostor ! The deceiver ! The swindler ! Art thou not ashamed? Whom dost thou call impostor? Give nothing, and do not accuse the man.

But (you say) he has means, and pretends. This is a charge against thyself, not against him. He knows that he has to deal with the cruel, with wild beasts rather than with men, and that, even if he utter a pitiable story, he attracts no one's attention : and on this account he is forced to assume also a more miserable guise,

that he may melt thy soul. If we see a person coming to beg in a respectable dress, This is an impostor (you say), and he comes in this way that he may be supposed to be of good birth. If we see one in the contrary guise, him too we reproach. What then are they to do? O the cruelty, O the inhumanity !

And why (you say) do they expose their maimed limbs? Because of thee. If we were compassionate, they would have no need of these artifices : if they persuaded us at the first application, they would not have contrived these devices. Who is there so wretched, as to be willing to cry out so much, as to be willing to behave in an unseemly way, as to be willing to make public lamentations, with his wife destitute of clothing, with his children, to sprinkle ashes on [himself]. How much worse than poverty are these things? Yet on account of them not only are they not pitied, but are even accused by us.

[9.] Shall we then still be indignant, because when we pray to God, we are not heard? Shall we then still be vexed, because when we entreat we do not persuade? Do we not tremble for fear, my beloved?

But (you say) I have often given. But dost thou not always eat? And dost thou drive away thy children often begging of thee? O the shamelessness ! Dost thou call a poor man shameless? And thou indeed art not shameless when plundering, but he is shameless when begging for bread ! Considerest thou not how great are the necessities of the belly? Dost not thou do all things for this? Dost thou not for this neglect things spiritual? Is not heaven set before thee and the kingdom of heaven? And thou fearing the tyranny of that [appetite] endurest all things, and thinkest lightly of that [kingdom]. This is shamelessness.

Seest thou not old men maimed? But O what trifling ! ' Such an one' (you say) ' lends out so many pieces of gold, and such an one so many, and yet begs.' You repeat the stories and trifles of children ; for they too are always hearing such stories from their nurses. I am not persuaded of it. I do not believe this. Far from it. Does a man lend money, and beg when he has abundance? For what purpose, tell me? And what is more disgraceful than begging? It were better to die than to beg. Where does our inhumanity stop? What then? Do all lend money? Are all impostors? Is there no one really poor? " Yea " (you say) " and many." Why then dost thou not assist those persons, seeing thou art a strict enquirer into their lives? This is an excuse and a pretense.

" Give to every one[2] that asketh of thee, and

---

[1] ἐπιθέτης.

[2] [St. Chrys. here supplies πάντι, equals " every one," from the

from him that would borrow of thee turn not thou away." (Matt. v. 42.) Stretch out thy hand, let it not be closed up. We have not been constituted examiners into men's lives, since so we should have compassion on no one. When thou callest upon God why dost thou say, Remember not my sins? So then, if that person even be a great sinner, make this allowance in his case also, and do not remember his sins. It is the season of kindness, not of strict enquiry; of mercy, not of account. He wishes to be maintained: if thou art willing, give; but if not willing, send him away without raising doubts.[1] Why art thou wretched and miserable? Why dost thou not even thyself pity him, and also turnest away those who would? For when such an one hears from thee, This [fellow] is a cheat; that a hypocrite; and the other lends out money; he neither gives to the one nor to the other; for he suspects all to be such. For you know that we easily suspect evil, but good, not [so easily].

[10.] Let us "be merciful," not simply so, but "as our heavenly Father is." (Luke vi. 36.) He feeds even adulterers, and fornicators, and sorcerers, and what shall I say? Those having every kind of wickedness. For in so large a world there must needs be many such. But nevertheless He feeds all; He clothes all. No one ever perished of hunger, unless one did so of his own choice. So let us be merciful. If one be in want and in necessity, help him.

But now we are come to such a degree of unreasonableness, as to act thus not only in regard to the poor who walk up and down the alleys, but even in the case of men that live in [religious] solitude.[2] Such an one is an impostor, you say. Did I not say this at first, that if we give to all indiscriminately, we shall always be compassionate; but if we begin to make over-curious enquiries, we shall never be compassionate? What dost thou mean? Is a man an impostor in order to get a loaf? If indeed he asks for talents of gold and silver, or costly clothes, or slaves, or anything else of this sort, one might with good reason call him a swindler. But if he ask none of these things, but only food and shelter, things which are suited to a philosophic life,[3] tell me, is this the part of a swindler? Cease we from this unseasonable fondness for meddling, which is Satanic, which is destructive.

For indeed, if a man say that he is on the list of the Clergy, or calls himself a priest, then busy thyself [to enquire], make much ado: since in that case the communicating[4] without enquiry is not without danger. For the danger is about matters of importance, for thou dost not give but receivest. But if he want food, make no enquiry.

Enquire, if thou wilt, how Abraham showed hospitality towards all who came to him. If he had been over-curious about those who fled to him for refuge, he would not have "entertained angels." (c. xiii. 2.) For perhaps not thinking them to be angels, he would have thrust them too away with the rest. But since he used to receive all, he received even angels.

What? Is it from the life of those that receive [thy bounty] that God grants thee thy reward? Nay [it is] from thine own purpose, from thy abundant liberality; from thy lovingkindness; from thy goodness. Let this be [found], and thou shalt attain all good things, which may we all attain, through the grace and lovingkindness of our Lord Jesus Christ, with whom to the Father and together with the Holy Ghost, be glory, power, honor, now and for ever and world without end. Amen.

---

parallel place in Luke vi. 30, though the form of quotation is from Matt. v. 42. — F. G.]

[1] ἐπαπορήσας.  [2] μοναζόντων ἀνδρῶν.

[3] ἃ φιλοσοφίας ἐστί, i.e. of the ascetics or solitary life.
[4] κοινωνία.

# HOMILY XII.

HEBREWS vii. 1–3.

"For this Melchisedec, King of Salem, Priest of the most High God, who met Abraham returning from the slaughter of the Kings, and blessed him: to whom also Abraham gave a tenth part of all; first being by interpretation King of Righteousness, and after that also King of Salem, which is, King of Peace, without father, without mother, without genealogy, having neither beginning of days, nor end of life, but made like unto the Son of God, abideth a Priest continually."

[1.] PAUL wishing to show the difference between the New and Old [Covenant], scatters it everywhere; and shoots from afar, and noises it abroad,[1] and prepares beforehand. For at once, even from the introduction, he laid down this, saying, that "to them indeed He spake by prophets, but to us by the Son" (c. i. 1, 2), and to them "at sundry times and in divers manners," but to us through the Son. Afterwards, having discoursed concerning the Son, who He was and what He had wrought, and given an exhortation to obey Him, lest we should suffer the same things as the Jews; and having said that He is "High Priest after the order of Melchisedec" (c. vi. 20), and having oftentimes wished to enter into [the subject of] this difference, and having used much preparatory management; and having rebuked them as weak, and again soothed and restored them to confidence; then at last he introduces the discussion on the difference [of the two dispensations] to ears in their full vigor. For he who is depressed in spirits would not be a ready hearer. And that you may understand this, hear the Scripture saying, "They hearkened not to Moses for anguish of spirit."[2] (Ex. vi. 9.) Therefore having first cleared away their despondency by many considerations, some fearful, some more gentle, he then from this point enters upon the discussion of the difference [of the dispensations].

[2.] And what does he say? "For this Melchisedec, King of Salem, Priest of the Most High God." And, what is especially noteworthy, he shows the difference to be great by the Type itself. For as I said, he continually confirms the truth from the Type, from things past, on account of the weakness of the hearers. "For" (he says) "this Melchisedec, King of Salem, Priest of the Most High God, who met Abraham returning from the slaughter of the Kings, and blessed him, to whom also Abraham

gave a tenth part of all." Having concisely set down the whole narrative, he looked at[3] it mystically.

And first from the name. "First" (he says) "being by interpretation King of righteousness": for Sedec means "righteousness"; and Melchi, "King": Melchisedec, "King of righteousness." Seest thou his exactness even in the names? But who is "King of righteousness," save our Lord Jesus Christ? "King of righteousness. And after that also King of Salem," from his city, "that is, King of Peace," which again is [characteristic] of Christ. For He has made us righteous, and has "made peace" for "things in Heaven and things on earth." (Col. i. 20.) What man is "King of Righteousness and of Peace"? None, save only our Lord JESUS Christ.

[3.] He then adds another distinction, "Without father, without mother, without genealogy, having neither beginning of days nor end of life, but made like unto the Son of God, abideth a Priest continually." Since then there lay in his way [as an objection] the [words] "Thou art a Priest for ever, after the order of Melchisedec," whereas he [Melchisedec] was dead, and was not "Priest for ever," see how he explained it mystically.

'And who can say this concerning a man?' I do not assert this in fact (he says); the meaning is, we do not know when[4] [or] what father he had, nor what mother, nor when he received his beginning, nor when he died. And what of this (one says)? For does it follow, because we do not know it, that he did not die, [or] had no parents? Thou sayest well: he both died and had parents. How then [was he] "without father, without mother"? How "having neither beginning of days nor end of life"? How? [Why] from its not being expressed.[5] And what of this? That as this man is so, from his genealogy not being given, so is Christ from the very nature of the reality.

See the "without beginning"; see the "without end." As in case of this man, we know not either "beginning of days," or "end of life," because they have not been written; so we know [them] not in the case of JESUS, not because they have not been written, but because

---

[1] διακωδωνίζει.   [2] ὀλιγοψυχίαν, "faint-heartedness."

[3] ἐθεώρησε, "drew out the mystical senses."
[4] Mr. Field reads πότε, making a double question. The other editions have ποτε, "at all."
[5] ἐμφέρεσθαι.

they do not exist. For that indeed is a type,[1] and therefore [we say] ' because it is not written,' but this is the reality,[2] and therefore [we say] ' because it does not exist.' For as in regard to the names also (for there " King of Righteousness" and " of Peace " are appellations, but here the reality) so these too are appellations in that case, in this the reality. How then hath He a beginning? Thou seest that the Son is " without beginning," [3] not in respect of His not having a cause ;[4] (for this is impossible : for He has a Father, otherwise how is He Son?) but in respect of His " not having beginning or end of life."

" But made like unto the Son of God." Where is the likeness? That we know not of the one or of the other either the end or the beginning. Of the one because they are not written ; of the other, because they do not exist. Here is the likeness. But if the likeness were to exist in all respects, there would no longer be type and reality ; but both would be type. [Here] then just as in representations[5] [by painting or drawing], there is somewhat that is like and somewhat that is unlike. By means of the lines indeed there is a likeness of features,[6] but when the colors are put on, then the difference is plainly shown, both the likeness and the unlikeness.

[4.] Ver. 4. " Now consider" (saith he) " how great this man is to whom even the Patriarch Abraham gave the tenth of the spoils."[7] Up to this point he has been applying the type : henceforward he boldly shows him [Melchisedec] to be more glorious than the Jewish realities. But if he who bears a type of Christ is so much better not merely than the priests, but even than the forefather himself of the priests, what should one say of the reality? Thou seest how superabundantly he shows the superiority.

" Now consider" (he says) " how great this man is to whom even the Patriarch Abraham gave a tenth out of the choice portions." Spoils taken in battle are called " choice portions."[8] And it cannot be said that he gave them to him as having a part in the war, because (he said) he met him " returning from the slaughter of the kings," for he had staid at home (he means), yet [Abraham] gave him the first-fruits of his labors.

Ver. 5. " And verily they that are of the sons of Levi who receive the office of Priesthood, have a commandment to take tithes of the people according to the law, that is, of their

brethren, though they come out of the loins of Abraham." So great (he would say) is the superiority of the priesthood, that they who from their ancestors are of the same dignity, and have the same forefather, are yet far better than the rest. At all events they " receive tithes " from them. When then one is found, who receives tithes from these very persons, are not they indeed in the rank of laymen, and he among the Priests?

And not only this ; but neither was he of the same dignity with them, but of another race : so that he would not have given tithes to a stranger unless his dignity had been great. Astonishing ! What has he accomplished? He has made quite clear a greater point than those relating to faith which he treated in the Epistle to the Romans. For there indeed he declares Abraham to be the forefather both of our polity and also of the Jewish. But here he is exceeding bold against him, and shows that the uncircumcised person is far superior. How then did he show that Levi paid tithes? Abraham (he says) paid them. ' And how does this concern us?' It especially concerns you : for you will not contend that the Levites are superior to Abraham. (Ver. 6) " But he whose descent is not counted from them, received tithes of Abraham."

And after that he did not simply pass on, but added, " and blessed him that had the promises." Inasmuch as throughout, this was regarded with reverence, he shows that [Melchisedec] was to be reverenced more than Abraham, from the common judgment of all men. (Ver. 7) " And without all contradiction," he says, " the less is blessed of the better," i.e. in the opinion of all men it is the inferior that is blessed by the superior. So then the type of Christ is superior even to " him that had the promises."

(Ver. 8) " And here men that die receive tithes : but there he of whom it is testified that he liveth." But lest we should say, Tell us, why goest thou so far back? He says, (ver. 9) " And as I may so say " (and he did well in softening it) " Levi also who receiveth tithes payed tithes in Abraham." How? (Ver. 10) " For he was yet in his loins when Melchisedec met him," i.e. Levi was in him, although he was not yet born. And he said not the Levites but Levi.

Hast thou seen the superiority? Hast thou seen how great is the interval between Abraham and Melchisedec, who bears the type of our High Priest? And he shows that the superiority had been caused by authority, not necessity. For the one paid the tithe, which indicates the priest : the other gave the blessing, which indicates the superior. This superiority passes on also to the descendants.

In a marvelous and triumphant way he cast out the Jewish [system]. On this account he

---

[1] τύπος.
[2] ἀλήθεια.
[3] ἄναρχον.
[4] αἴτιον.
[5] εἰκόσιν. The comparison is not between the living object and the picture, but between representations in drawing and in painting: the word εἰκων, as our " likeness," being applicable to both. The passage is considerably altered in the common editions so as to avoid an apparent difficulty.
[6] χαρακτήρων.
[7] " choice portions."
[8] ἀκροθίνια.

said, "Ye are become dull," (c. v. 12), because he wished to lay these foundations, that they might not start away. Such is the wisdom of Paul, first preparing them well, he so leads[1] them into what he wishes. For the human race is hard to persuade, and needs much attention, even more than plants. Since in that case there is [only] the nature of material bodies, and earth, which yields to the hands of the husbandmen: but in this there is will, which is liable to many alterations, and now prefers this, now that. For it quickly turns to evil.

[5.] Wherefore we ought always to "guard" ourselves, lest at any time we should fall asleep. For "Lo" (it is said) "he that keepeth Israel shall neither slumber nor sleep" (Ps. cxxi. 4), and "Do not suffer[2] thy foot to be moved." (Ps. cxxi. 3.) He did not say, 'be not moved' but "do not thou suffer," &c. The suffering depends then on ourselves, and not on any other. For if we will stand "steadfast and unmoveable" (1 Cor. xv. 58), we shall not be shaken.

What then? Does nothing depend on God? All indeed depends on God, but not so that our free-will is hindered. 'If then it depend on God,' (one says), 'why does He blame us?' On this account I said, 'so that our free-will is not hindered.' It depends then on us, and on Him. For we must first choose the good; and then He leads us to His own.[3] He does not anticipate our choice,[4] lest our free-will should be outraged. But when we have chosen, then great is the assistance he brings to us.

How is it then that Paul says, "not of him that willeth," if it depend on ourselves also "nor of him that runneth, but of God that showeth mercy." (Rom. ix. 16.)

In the first place, he did not introduce it as his own opinion, but inferred it from what was before him and from what had been put forward[5] [in the discussion]. For after saying, "It is written, I will have mercy on whom I will have mercy, and I will have compassion on whom I will have compassion" (Rom. ix. 15), he says, "It follows then[6] that it is not of him that willeth, nor of him that runneth, but of God that show-

eth mercy." "Thou wilt say then unto me, why doth He yet find fault?" (Rom. ix. 16, 19.)

And secondly the other explanation may be given, that he speaks of all as His, whose the greater part is. For it is ours to choose[7] and to wish; but God's to complete and to bring to an end. Since therefore the greater part is of Him, he says all is of Him, speaking according to the custom of men. For so we ourselves also do. I mean for instance: we see a house well built, and we say the whole is the Architect's [doing], and yet certainly it is not all his, but the workmen's also, and the owner's, who supplies the materials, and many others', but nevertheless since he contributed the greatest share, we call the whole his. So then [it is] in this case also. Again, with respect to a number of people, where the many are, we say All are: where few, nobody. So also Paul says, "not of him that willeth, nor of him that runneth, but of God that showeth mercy."

And herein he establishes two great truths: one, that we should not be lifted up:[8] even shouldst thou run (he would say), even shouldst thou be very earnest, do not consider that the well doing[9] is thine own. For if thou obtain not the impulse[10] that is from above, all is to no purpose. Nevertheless that thou wilt attain that which thou earnestly strivest after is very evident; so long as thou runnest, so long as thou willest.

He did not then assert this, that we run in vain, but that, if we think the whole to be our own, if we do not assign the greater part to God, we run in vain. For neither hath God willed that the whole should be His, lest He should appear to be crowning us without cause: nor again our's, lest we should fall away to pride. For if when we have the smaller [share], we think much of ourselves, what should we do if the whole depended on us?

[6.] Indeed God hath done away many things for the purpose of cutting away our boastfulness, and still there is the[11] high hand. With how many afflictions hath He encompassed us, so as to cut away our proud spirit! With how many wild beasts hath He encircled us! For indeed when some say, 'why is this?' 'Of what use is this?' They utter these things against the will of God. He hath placed thee in the midst of so

---

[1] ἐμβάλλει.

[2] In Psalm cxxi. 3 (cxx. 3, LXX.) where we have "He shall not suffer," &c., the LXX. have, μὴ δῷης εἰς σάλον τὸν πόδα σου, μηδὲ νυστάξῃ (Vat.) ὁ φυλάσσων σε, "Lest thou suffer," &c., and "lest he that keepeth thee slumber." St. Chrys. substitutes δῷς for δῷης, making the sense, "Do not suffer," &c., "and let not him that keepeth thee slumber." This he applies to the Christian keeping guard over himself (his words are χρὴ πάντοτε φυλάττειν ἑαυτούς, μήποτε ἀπονυστάξωμεν): and so he seems to have understood ver. 4, of the Christian: that a watchman of Israel ought not to slumber or sleep. The Alex. MS. has νυστάξει in the third verse.

[3] εἰσάγει τὰ παρ' ἑαυτοῦ, Hi· part.

[4] βουλήσεις. Those acts of the soul whereby we desire and aim at what is good.

[5] προκειμένου . . . προβληθέντος. The former word is used by St. Chrys. to express the portion of Scripture on which he is treating: the latter is a received term in the dialectical method of the Greeks to express a proposition put forward to be argued from, to see what consequences follow from it, with a view of showing it to be untrue, or determining the sense in which it is true. St. Chrys. means to say that this proposition was only thus argumentatively inferred by St. Paul.

[6] Ἄρα οὖν.

[7] or, "purpose and will," προελέσθαι καὶ βουληθῆναι.

[8] In the genuine text here as in some other places, there is no mention of the second point. The longer text has "one that we should not be lifted up by what we do well: the other that when we do well, we should attribute to God the cause of our well-doing. Therefore," &c. Mr. Field thinks that either the thread of the discourse is broken, and the second point not mentioned, or (which seems more probable) that it is contained in the words "Nevertheless," &c.

[9] κατόρθωμα.

[10] ῥοπή: "The inclining of the balance"; or, "the weight which makes it turn."

[11] Sav. and Ben. add αὐτοῦ, "His hand is high"; but the reference is to our sinning "with a high hand," as appears from what follows in the next paragraph.

great fear, and yet not even so art thou lowly-minded; but if thou ever attain a little success, thou reachest to Heaven itself in pride.

For this cause [come] rapid changes and reverses; and yet not even so are we instructed. For this cause are there continual and untimely deaths, but are minded as if we were immortal, as if we should never die. We plunder, we over-reach, as though we were never to give account. We build as if we were to abide here always. And not even the word of God daily sounded into our ears, nor the events themselves instruct us. Not a day, not an hour can be mentioned, in which we may not see continual funerals. But all in vain: and nothing reaches our hardness [of heart]: nor are we even able to become better by the calamities of others; or rather, we are not willing. When we ourselves only are afflicted, then we are subdued, and yet if God take off His hand, we again lift up our hand: no one considers what is proper for man,[1] no one despises the things on earth; no one looks to Heaven. But as swine turn their heads downwards, stooping towards their belly, wallowing in the mire; so too the great body of mankind defile themselves with the most intolerable filth, without being conscious of it.

[7.] For better were it to be defiled with unclean mud than with sins; for he who is defiled with the one, washes it off in a little time, and becomes like one who had never from the first fallen into that slough; but he who has fallen into the deep pit of sin has contracted a defilement that is not cleansed by water, but needs long time, and strict repentance, and tears and lamentations, and more wailing, and that more fervent, than we show over the dearest friends. For this defilement attaches to us from without, wherefore we also speedily put it away; but the other is generated from within, wherefore also we wash it off with difficulty, and cleanse ourselves from it. "For from the heart" (it is said) "proceed evil thoughts, fornications, adulteries, thefts, false witnesses." (Matt. xv. 19.) Wherefore also the Prophet said, "Create in me a clean heart, O God." (Ps. li. 10.) And another, "Wash thine heart from wickedness,

O Jerusalem." (Jer. iv. 14.) (Thou seest that it is both our [work] and God's.) And again, "Blessed are the pure in heart, for they shall see God." (Matt. v. 8.)

Let us become clean to the utmost of our power. Let us wipe away our sins. And how to wipe them away, the prophet teaches, saying, "Wash you, make you clean, put away your wickedness from your souls, before Mine eyes." (Isa. i. 16.) What is "before Mine eyes"? Because some seem to be free from wickedness, but only to men, while to God they are manifest as being "whited sepulchers." Therefore He says, so put them away as I see. "Learn to do well, seek judgment, do justice for the poor and lowly." "Come now, and let us reason together, saith the Lord: and though your sins be as scarlet, I will make you white as snow, and if they be as crimson, I will make you white as wool." (Isa. i. 17, 18.) Thou seest that we must first cleanse ourselves, and then God cleanses us. For having said first, "Wash you, make you clean," He then added "I will make you white."

Let no one then, [even] of those who are come to the extremest wickedness, despair of himself. For (He says) even if thou hast passed into the habit, yea and almost into the nature of wickedness itself, be not afraid. Therefore taking [the instance of] colors that are not superficial but almost of the substance of the materials, He said that He would bring them into the opposite state. For He did not simply say that He would "wash" us, but that He would "make" us "white, as snow and as wool," in order to hold out good hopes before us. Great then is the power of repentance, at least if it makes us as snow, and whitens us as wool, even if sin have first got possession and dyed our souls.

Let us labor earnestly then to become clean; He has enjoined nothing burdensome. "Judge the fatherless, and do justice for the widow." (Isa. i. 17.) Thou seest everywhere how great account God makes of mercy, and of standing forward in behalf of those that are wronged. These good deeds let us pursue after, and we shall be able also, by the grace of God, to attain to the blessings to come: which may we all be counted worthy of, in Christ Jesus our Lord, with whom to the Father together with the Holy Ghost, be glory, power, honor, now and for ever and world without end. Amen.

---

[1] οὐδεὶς ἀνθρώπινα φρονεῖ. This is the reading also of Savile and Morell. It is supported by one MS. and the pr. m. of another: which had been corrected to οὐδ. οὐράνια φ., the reading of the Verona edition. Mutianus has *nemo divina sapit;* and the later translator *cælestia.* The other MSS. have ἀνθρώπινα περιφρονεῖ. ταπεινὰ φρονεῖ, ταπεινοφρονεῖ. Montfaucon conjectured τὰ ἄνω φρονεῖ.

# HOMILY XIII.

### Hebrews vii. 11–14.

"If therefore perfection were by[1] the Levitical priest-hood; (for under it the people have received the law[2]) what further need was there that another priest should arise after the order of Melchisedec, and not be called after the order of Aaron? For the priesthood being changed, there is[3] made of necessity a change also of the law. For He of whom these things are spoken, pertained to another. tribe, of[4] which no man gave attendance at the altar. For it is evident that our Lord sprang out of Judah, of which tribe Moses spake nothing concern-ing priests."[5]

[1.] "If therefore" (he says) "perfection were by the Levitical priesthood." Having spoken concerning Melchisedec, and shown how much superior he was to Abraham, and having set forth the great difference between them, he begins from this point forward to prove the wide difference as to the covenant itself, and how the one is imperfect and the other perfect. How-ever he does not even yet enter on the matters themselves, but first contends on the ground of the priesthood, and the tabernacle. For these things would be more easily received by the unbelieving, when the proof was derived from things already allowed, and believed.

He had shown that Melchisedec was greatly superior both to Levi and to Abraham, being to them in the rank of the priests. Again he argues from a different point. What then is this? Why (he says) did he not say, "after the order of Aaron"? And observe, I pray you, the great superiority [of his argument]. For from the very circumstance which naturally excluded His priesthood, viz. that He was not "after the order of Aaron," from that he establishes Him, and excludes the others. For this is the very thing that I say (he declares); why has He "not been made after the order of Aaron"?

And the [saying] "what further need" has much emphasis. For if Christ had been "after the order of Melchisedec" according to the flesh, and then afterwards the law had been in-troduced, and all that pertained to Aaron, one might reasonably say that the latter as being more perfect, annulled the former, seeing that it had come in after it. But if Christ comes later, and takes a different type, as that of His

priesthood, it is evident that it is because those were imperfect. For (he would say) let us sup-pose for argument's sake, that all has been ful-filled, and that there is nothing imperfect in the priesthood. "What need" was there in that case that He should be called "after the order of Melchisedec and not after the order of Aaron"? Why did He set aside Aaron, and introduce a different priesthood, that of Melchisedec? "If then perfection," that is the perfection of the things themselves, of the doctrines, of life,[6] "had been by the Levitical priesthood."

And observe how he goes forward on his path. He had said that [He was] "after the order of Melchisedec," implying that the [priesthood] "after the order of Melchisedec" is superior : for [he was][7] far superior. Afterwards he shows this from the time also, in that He was after Aaron ; evidently as being better.

[2.] And what is the meaning of what follows? "For" (he says) "under [or "upon"] it the people have received the Law [or "have been legislated for"]."[8] What is "under it" [&c.]? Ordereth itself[9] by it ; through it does all things. You cannot say that it was given to others, "the people under it have received the law," that is, have used it, and did use it. You cannot say indeed that it was perfect, it did not govern the people ; "they have been legislated for upon it," that is, they used it.

What need was there then of another priest-hood? "For the priesthood being changed, there is of necessity a change of the law also." But if there must be another priest, or rather another priesthood, there must needs be also another law. This is for those who say, What need was there of a new Covenant? For he could indeed have alleged a testimony from prophecy also. "This is the covenant which I made with your fathers" [&c.]. (c. viii. 10.) But for the present he contends on the ground of the priesthood. And observe, how he says this from the first. He said, "According to the order of Melchisedec." By this he excluded the order of Aaron. For he would not have said "After the order of Melchisedec," if the other had been better. If therefore another priesthood has been brought in, there must be

---

[1] "by means of."
[2] νενομοθέτηται is the reading of the best MSS. of St. Chrys. here and throughout the Homily. The common editions had νενομοθέ-τητο. So while the common editions [Textus Rec.] of the N. T. read νενομοθέτητο, the critical editors have νενομοθέτηται.
[3] "takes place."　　　[4] "from."
[5] ἱερέων. The editions had ἱερωσύνης; so the common text of the New Test. read ἱερωσύνης, the critical editions have ἱερέων.

[6] εἰ μὲν οὖν τελείωσις, τουτέστι τῆς τῶν πραγμάτων, τῆς τῶν δογμάτων, τοῦ βίου ἡ τελείωσις. It is not clear, as Mr. Field re-marks, to what the articles τῆς, τῆς are to be referred.
[7] or ["it is"]. S. B. have ἐκεῖνος in the text.
[8] [have been subjected to the law. — F. G.]
[9] στοιχεῖ.

also [another] Covenant; for neither is it possible that there should be a priest, without a covenant and laws and ordinances, nor that having received a different priesthood He should use the former [covenant].

In the next place, as to the ground of objection: "How could He be a priest if He were not a Levite?" Having overthrown this by what had been said above, he does not even think it worth answering, but introduces it in passing. I said (he means) that the priesthood was changed, therefore also the Covenant is. And it was changed not only in its character,[1] or in its ordinances, but also in its tribe. For of necessity [it must be changed] in its tribe also. How? "For the priesthood being changed [or "transferred"]," from tribe to tribe, from the sacerdotal to the regal [tribe], that the same might be both regal and sacerdotal.

And observe the mystery. First it was royal, and then it is become sacerdotal: so therefore also in regard to Christ: for King indeed He always was, but has become Priest from the time that He assumed the Flesh, that He offered the sacrifice. Thou seest the change, and the very things which were ground of objection these he introduces, as though the natural order of things required them. "For" (he says) "He of whom these things are spoken pertained to another tribe." I myself also say it, I know that this tribe [of Judah] had nothing of priesthood. For there is a transferring.

[3.] Yea and I am showing another difference also (he would say): not only from the tribe, nor yet only from the Person, nor from the character [of the Priesthood], nor from the covenant, but also from the type itself. (Ver. 16) "Who was made ["became" so], not according to the law of a carnal commandment, but according to the power of an endless life. He became" (he says) "a priest not according to the law of a carnal commandment": for that law was in many respects unlawful.[2]

What is, "of a carnal commandment"? Circumcise the flesh, it says; anoint the flesh; wash the flesh; purify the flesh; shave the flesh; bind upon the flesh;[3] cherish the flesh; rest as to the flesh. And again its blessings, what are they? Long life for the flesh; milk and honey for the flesh; peace for the flesh; luxury for the flesh. From this law Aaron received the priesthood; Melchisedec however not so.

Ver. 15. "And it is yet far more evident, if after the similitude of Melchisedec there ariseth another priest." What is evident? The interval between the two priesthoods, the difference; how much superior He is "who was made not

according to the law of a carnal commandment." (Who? Melchisedec? Nay; but Christ.) "But according to the power of an endless[4] life. For He testifieth, Thou art a Priest for ever after the order of Melchisedec"; that is, not for a time, nor having any limit, "but according to the power of an endless life," that is, by means of power, by means of "endless life."

And yet this does not follow after, "who was made not according to the law of a carnal commandment": for what would follow would be to say, "but according to that of a spiritual one." However by "carnal," he implied temporary. As he says also in another place, carnal ordinances imposed until the time of reformation." (c. ix. 10.)

"According to the power of life," that is, because He lives by His own power.

[4.] He had said, that there is also a change of law, and up to this point he has shown it; henceforward he enquires into the cause, that which above all gives full assurance to men's minds, [I mean] the knowing the cause thoroughly; and it leads us more to faith[5] when we have learned also the cause, and the principle according to which [the thing] comes to pass.

Ver. 18. "For there is verily" (he says) "a disannulling of the commandment going before, for the weakness and unprofitableness thereof." Here the Heretics[6] press on. But listen attentively. He did not say "for the evil," nor, "for the viciousness," but "for the weakness and unprofitableness [thereof]," yea and in other places also he shows the weakness; as when he says "In that it was weak through the flesh." (Rom. viii. 3.) [The law] itself then is not weak, but we.

Ver. 19. "For the Law made nothing perfect." What is, "make nothing perfect"? Made no man perfect, being disobeyed. And besides, even if it had been listened to, it would not have made one perfect and virtuous. But as yet he does not say this here, but that it had no strength: and with good reason. For written precepts were there set down, Do this and Do not that, being enjoined only, and not giving power within.[7] But "the Hope" is not such.

What is "a disannulling"? A casting out. A "disannulling" is a disannulling of things which are of force. So that he implied, that it [once] was of force, but henceforward was of no account, since it accomplished nothing. Was the Law then of no use? It was indeed of use; and of great use: but to make men perfect it was of no use. For in this respect he says, "The Law made nothing perfect." All were figures, all shadows; circumcision, sacrifice, sabbath. There-

---

[1] τρόπῳ.      [2] ἄνομος.
[3] See Deut. vi. 8.

[4] ἀκαταλύτου, "indestructible."     [5] or, "conviction."
[6] The early Heretics denied the divine character of the Mosaic dispensation.     [7] ἐντιθέντα.

fore they could not reach through the soul, wherefore they pass away and gradually withdraw. "But the bringing in of a better hope did, by which we draw nigh unto God."

[5.] (Ver. 20) "And forasmuch as not without the taking of an oath."[1] Thou seest that the matter of the oath becomes necessary for him here. Accordingly for this reason he previously treated much [hereon], how that God sware; and sware for the sake of [our] fuller assurance.

"But the bringing in of a better hope." For that system also had a hope, but not such as this. For they hoped that, if they were well pleasing [to God], they should possess the land, that they should suffer nothing fearful. But in this [dispensation] we hope that, if we are well pleasing [to God], we shall possess not earth, but heaven; or rather (which is far better than this) we hope to stand near to God, to come unto the very throne of the Father, to minister unto Him with the Angels. And see how he introduces these things by little and little. For above he says "which entereth into that within the veil" (c. vi. 19), but here, " by which we draw nigh unto God."

"And inasmuch as not without an oath." What is "And inasmuch as not without an oath"? That is, Behold another difference also. And these things were not merely promised (he says). " For those priests were made without an oath," (ver. 21, 22) " but This with an oath, by Him that said unto Him, The Lord sware and will not repent, Thou art Priest for ever after the order of Melchisedec.[2] By so much was Jesus made a surety of a better covenant."[3] He lays down two points of difference, that it hath no end as the [covenant] of the Law had;[4] and this he proves from [its being] Christ who exercises [the priesthood]; for he says " according to the power of an endless life." And he proves it also from the oath, because "He sware," &c., and from the fact; for if the other was cast out, because it was weak, this stands firm, because it is powerful. He proves it also from the priest. How? Because He is One [only]; and there would not have been One [only], unless He had been immortal. For as there were many priests, because they were mortal, so [here is] The One, because He is immortal. "By so much was Jesus made a surety of a better covenant," inasmuch as He sware to Him that He should

always be [Priest]; which He would not have done, if He were not living.

[6.] (Ver. 25) "Wherefore He is able also to save them to the uttermost, that come unto God by Him, seeing He ever liveth to make intercession for them." Thou seest that he says this in respect of that which is according to the flesh. For when He [appears] as Priest, then He also intercedes. Wherefore also when Paul says, " who also maketh intercession for us " (Rom. viii. 34), he hints the same thing; the High Priest maketh intercession. For He " that raiseth the dead as He will, and quickeneth them," (John v. 21), and that " even as the Father " [doth], how [is it that] when there is need to save, He " maketh intercession '? (John v. 22.) He that hath " all judgment," how [is it that] He " maketh intercession "? He that " sendeth His angels " (Matt. xiii. 41, 42), that they may " cast " some into " the furnace," and save others, how [is it that] He " maketh intercession "? Wherefore (he says) " He is able also to save." For this cause then He saves, because He dies not. Inasmuch as " He ever liveth," He hath (he means) no successor : And if He have no successor, He is able to aid all men. For there [under the Law] indeed, the High Priest although he were worthy of admiration during the time in which he was [High Priest] (as Samuel for instance, and any other such), but, after this, no longer ; for they were dead. But here it is not so, but "He " saves " to the uttermost."[5]

What is " to the uttermost "? He hints at some mystery. Not here[6] only (he says) but there[7] also He saves them that " come unto God by Him." How does He save? " In that He ever liveth " (he says) " to make intercession for them." Thou seest the humiliation? Thou seest the manhood? For he says not, that He obtained this, by making intercession once for all, but continually, and whensoever it may be needful to intercede for them.

"To the uttermost." What is it? Not for a time only, but there also in the future life. ' Does He then always need to pray? Yet how can [this] be reasonable? Even righteous men have oftentimes accomplished all by one entreaty, and is He always praying? Why then is He throned with [the Father]?' Thou seest that it is a condescension. The meaning is : Be not afraid, nor say, Yea, He loves us indeed, and He has confidence towards the Father, but He cannot live always. For He doth live alway.

[7.] (Ver. 26) "For such an High Priest also[8] became us, who is holy, harmless, unde-

---

[1] ὀρκωμοσίας.

[2] [The words " after the order of Melchisedec " are in the text of St. Chrys. and in the *Textus Rec.* They are omitted in recent critical editions, but are implied in the context. — F. G.]

[3] The common editions add here ver. 23, 24, " and they truly were many priests, because they were not suffered to continue by reason of death; but this [man] because he continueth ever, hath an unchangeable priesthood." St. Chrys. alludes to these words in what follows: but without citing them.

[4] The common texts add here " and that it is with oath-taking ": this is probably to be understood: as if he had said, He lays down a second point of difference that, &c.

[5] εἰς τὸ παντελές.　　　　　[6] in this world.

[7] in the other world.

[8] In Mr. Field's ed. καὶ is read here, and where the words are cited afterwards, in the common texts it is omitted. So critical editors consider that the sacred text is τοιοῦτος γὰρ ἡμῖν καὶ ἔπρεπεν κ. λ. [The critical editors are not agreed; some insert the καὶ, others place it in brackets. — F. G.]

filed, separate from the sinners." Thou seest that the whole is said with reference to the manhood. (But when I say 'the manhood,' I mean [the manhood] having Godhead; not dividing [one from the other], but leaving [you] to suppose¹ what is suitable.) Didst thou mark the difference of the High Priest? He has summed up what was said before, "in all points tempted like as we are yet without sin." (c. iv. 15.) "For" (he says) "such an High Priest also became us, who is holy, harmless." "Harmless": what is it? Without wickedness: that which another² Prophet says: "guile was not found in His mouth" (Isa. liii. 9), that is, [He is] not crafty. Could any one say this concerning God? And is one not ashamed to say that God is not crafty, nor deceitful? Concerning Him, however, in respect of the Flesh, it might be reasonable [to say it]. "Holy, undefiled." This too would any one say concerning God? For has He a nature capable of defilement? "Separate from sinners."

[8.] Does then this alone show the difference, or does the sacrifice itself also? How? (Ver. 27) "He needeth not" (he says) "daily, as the High Priest,³ to offer up sacrifices for his sins, for this He did once for all, when He offered up Himself." "This," what? Here what follows sounds a prelude concerning the exceeding greatness of the spiritual sacrifice and the interval [between them]. He has mentioned the point of the priest; he has mentioned that of the faith; he has mentioned that of the Covenant; not entirely indeed, still he has mentioned it. In this place what follows is a prelude concerning the sacrifice itself. Do not then, having heard that He is a priest, suppose that He is always executing the priest's office. For He executed it once, and thenceforward "sat down." (c. x. 12.) Lest thou suppose that He is standing on high, and is a minister, he shows that the

matter is [part] of a dispensation [or economy]. For as He became a servant, so also [He became] a Priest and a Minister. But as after becoming a servant, He did not continue a servant, so also, having become a Minister, He did not continue a Minister. For it belongs not to a minister to sit, but to stand.

This then he hints at here, and also the greatness of the sacrifice, if being [but] one, and having been offered up once only, it affected that which all [the rest] were unable to do. But he does not yet [treat] of these points.

"For this He did," he says. "This"; what? "For" (he says) "it is of necessity that this [Man] have somewhat also to offer" (c. viii. 3); not for Himself; for how did He offer Himself? But for the people. What sayest thou? And is He able to do this? Yea (he says). "For the Law maketh men high priests, which have infirmity." (c. vii. 28.) And doth He not need to offer for Himself? No, he says. For, that you may not suppose that the [words, "this"] "He did once for all," are said respecting Himself also, hear what he says: "For the law maketh men high priests, which have infirmity." On this account they both offer continually, and for themselves. He however who is mighty, He that hath no sin, why should He offer for Himself, or oftentimes for others?

"But the word of the oath which was since the Law [maketh] the Son who has been consecrated for evermore." "Consecrated":⁴ what is that? Paul does not set down the common terms of contradistinction;⁵ for after saying "having Infirmity," he did not say "the Son" who is mighty, but "consecrated":⁴ i.e. mighty, as one might say. Thou seest that the name Son is used in contradistinction to that of servant. And by "infirmity" he means either sin or death.

What is, "for evermore"? Not now only without sin but always. If then He is perfect, if He never sins, if He lives always, why shall He offer many sacrifices for us? But for the present he does not insist strongly on this point: but what he does strongly insist upon is, His not offering on His own behalf.

[9.] Since then we have such an High Priest, let us imitate Him; let us walk in His footsteps. There is no other sacrifice: one alone has cleansed us, and after this, fire and hell. For indeed on this account he repeats it over and over, saying, "one Priest," "one Sacrifice," lest any one supposing that there are many [sacrifices] should sin without fear. Let us then, as many as have been counted worthy of The Seal,⁶

---

¹ ὑποπτεύειν.

² As this passage is cited by Facundus Hermianensis, an African Bishop, writing about the year 547, it may be well to give his words and also the two Greek texts corresponding to them, as an evidence that the text which he had was of the short and simple form now restored in Mr. Field's edition.

"In interpretatione quoque Epistolæ ad Hebræos, Sermone xiv, de eo quod scriptum est, *Sicut consummatio per Leviticum sacerdotium erat,* ita locutus est: Dicit alter propheta, Dolus non est inventus in ore ejus, hoc est nulla calliditas. Hoc forsitan quisquam de Deo dicat, et non erubescit dicens, quia Deus non est callidus, neque dolosus. De eo vero qui secundum carnem est, habebit forsitan rationem." (pro def. trium capp. lib. xi. c. 5, p. 488, ed. Sirm.) [*Gall. Bibl. Patr.* xi. 789.]

Mr. Field's text is, ὁ (ὁ om. MS. R.) λέγει ἕτερος προφήτης· δόλος οὐχ εὑρέθη ἐν τῷ στόματι αὐτοῦ (τουτέστιν, οὐχ ὕπουλος· τοῦτο ἄν τις περὶ Θεοῦ εἴποι; καὶ οὐκ αἰσχύνεται λέγων, ὅτι ὁ θεὸς οὐκ ἔστιν ὕπουλος, οὐδὲ δολερός; περὶ μέντοι τοῦ κατὰ σάρκα ἔχοι ἂν λόγον.

The text of Savile and the Benedictines οὐχ ὕπουλος· καὶ ὅτι τοιοῦτος, ἄκουε τοῦ προφήτου λεγοντος· οὐδὲ εὑρέθη δόλος ἐν τῷ στόματι αὐτοῦ, τοῦτο οὖν ἄν τις περὶ Θεοῦ εἴποι; ὁ δὲ οὐκ αἰσχύνεται λέγων, ὅτι ὁ θεὸς οὐκ ἔστιν ὕπουλος, οὐδὲ δολερός; περὶ μὲν οὖν τοῦ κατὰ σάρκα ἔχοι ἂν λόγον.

³ This is the reading adopted by Mr. Field. The common texts give the passage as it stands in the text of the Epistle [where there is no *var. lect.* of importance.— F. G.] Indeed what is omitted must plainly be intended to be supplied.

⁴ [τετελειωμένον. This is the common Levitical term for priestly *consecration.* It is also used in the Classics in a corresponding sense of *initiation* into the mysteries. The English edition takes it in the common sense of *perfected.*— F. G.]

⁵ τὰς ἀντιδιαστολὰς κυρίας.        ⁶ i.e. Baptism.

as many as have enjoyed The Sacrifice, as many as have partaken of the immortal Table, continue to guard our noble birth and our dignity: for falling away is not without danger.

And as many as have not yet been counted worthy these [privileges], let not these either be confident on that account. For when a person goes on in sin, with the view of receiving holy baptism at the last gasp, oftentimes he will not obtain it. And, believe me, it is not to terrify you that I say what I am going to say. I have myself known many persons, to whom this has happened, who in expectation indeed of the enlightening[1] sinned much, and on the day of their death went away empty. For God gave us baptism for this cause, that He might do away our sins, not that He might increase our sins. Whereas if any man have employed it as a security for sinning more, it becomes a cause of negligence. For if there had been no Washing, they would have lived more warily, as not having [the means of] forgiveness. Thou seest that we are the ones who cause it to be said "Let us do evil, that good may come." (Rom. iii. 8.)

Wherefore, I exhort you also who are uninitiated, be sober. Let no man follow after virtue as an hireling, no man as a senseless[2] person, no man as after a heavy and burdensome thing. Let us pursue it then with a ready mind, and with joy. For if there were no reward laid up, ought we not to be good? But however, at least with a reward, let us become good. And how is this anything else than a disgrace and a very great condemnation? Unless thou give me a reward (says one), I do not become self-controlled. Then am I bold to say something: thou wilt never be self-controlled, no not even when thou livest with self-control, if thou dost it for a reward. Thou esteemest not virtue at all, if thou dost not love it. But on account of our great weakness, God was willing that for a time it should be practiced even for reward, yet not even so do we pursue it.

But let us suppose, if you will, that a man dies, after having done innumerable evil things, having also been counted worthy of baptism (which however I think does not readily happen), tell me, how will he depart thither? Not indeed called to account for the deeds he had done, but yet without confidence;[3] as is reasonable. For when after living a hundred years, he has no good work to show,[4] but only that he has not sinned, or rather not even this, but that he was saved by grace[5] only, and when he sees others crowned, in splendor, and highly approved: even

if he fall not into hell, tell me, will he endure his despondency?

[10.] But to make the matter clear by an example, Suppose there are two soldiers, and that one of them steals, injures, overreaches, and that the other does none of these things, but acts the part of a brave man, does important things well, sets up trophies in war, stains his right hand with blood; then when the time arrives, suppose that (from the same rank in which the thief also was) he is at once conducted to the imperial throne and the purple; but suppose that the other remains there where he was, and merely of the royal kindness does not pay the penalty of his deeds, let him however be in the last place, and let him be stationed under the King. Tell me, will he be able to endure his despair when he sees him who was [ranked] with himself ascended even to the very highest dignities, and made thus glorious, and master of the world, while he himself still remains below, and has not even been freed from punishment with honor, but through the grace and kindness of the King? For even should the King forgive him, and release him from the charges against him, still he will live in shame; for surely not even will others admire him: since in such forgiveness, we admire not those who receive the gifts, but those who bestow them. And as much as the gifts are greater, so much the more are they ashamed who receive them, when their transgressions are great.

With what eyes then will such an one be able to look on those who are in the King's courts, when they exhibit their sweatings out of number and their wounds, whilst he has nothing to show, but has his salvation itself of the mere lovingkindness of God? For as if one were to beg off a murderer, a thief, an adulterer, when he was going to be arrested, and were to command him to stay at the porch of the King's palace, he will not afterwards be able to look any man in the face, although he has been set free from punishment: so too surely is this man's case.

For do not, I beseech you, suppose that because it is called a palace,[6] therefore all attain the same things. For if here in Kings' courts there is the Prefect, and all who are about the King, and also those who are in very inferior stations, and occupy the place of what are called Decani[7] (though the interval be so great between the Prefect and the Decanus) much more shall this be so in the royal court above.

---

[1] Baptism.　　[2] ἀγνώμων.　　[3] ἀπαρρησίαστος.
[4] [St. Cyril Alex. speaks too of those who put off baptism till they are old and receive forgiveness through it, but have nought to bring to their Master. Glaph. 273.]
[5] i.e mercy [χάριτι, the common word for "grace."—F. G.]

[6] βασίλεια, but Sav. βασιλεία, a kingdom.
[7] "The Δεκανοὶ at Constantinople were lictors, and had the charge of burying the dead: they are otherwise called *funerum elatores, lecticarii, vespillones, libitinarii,* κοπιᾶται. Corippus, lib. iii., says

　　　　　　Jamque ordine certo
　　Turba *decanorum*, cursorum, in rebus agentum,
　　Cumque palatinis stans candida turba tribunis."
Suicer, *Thes. Eccles.* p. 835, cited by Mr. Field.

And this I say not of myself. For Paul layeth down another difference greater even than these. For (he says) as many differences as there are between the sun and the moon and the stars, and the very smallest star, so many also between those in the kingdom [of Heaven]. And that the difference between the sun and the smallest star is far greater than that between the Decanus (as he is called) and the Prefect, is evident to all. For while the sun shines upon all the world at once, and makes it bright, and hides the moon and the stars, the other often does not appear, not even in the dark. For there are many of the stars which we do not see. When then we see others become suns, and we have the rank of the very smallest stars, which are not even visible, what comfort shall we have?

Let us not, I beseech you, let us not be so slothful, not so inert, let us not barter away the salvation of God for an easy life, but let us make merchandise of it, and increase it. For even if one be a Catechumen, still he knows Christ, still he understands the Faith, still he is a hearer of the divine oracles, still he is not far from the knowledge; he knows the will of his Lord. Wherefore does he procrastinate? wherefore does he delay and postpone? Nothing is better than a good life whether here or there, whether in case of the Enlightened or of the Catechumens.

[11.] For tell me what burdensome command have we enjoined? Have a wife (it is said) and be chaste. Is this difficult? How? when many, not Christians only but heathens also, live chastely without a wife. That which the heathen surpasses [1] for vainglory, thou dost not even keep for the fear of God.

Give (He says) to the poor out of what thou hast. Is this burdensome? But in this case also heathen condemn us who for vainglory only have emptied out their whole possessions.

Use not filthy communication. Is this difficult? For if it had not been enjoined, ought we not to have done right in this, to avoid appearing degraded? For that the contrary conduct is troublesome, I mean the using filthy communication, is manifest from the fact that the soul is ashamed and blushes if it have been led to say any such thing and would not unless perhaps it were drunk. For when sitting in a public place, even if thou doest it at home, why dost thou not do it there? Because of those that are present. Why dost thou not readily do the same thing before thy wife? That thou mayest not insult her. So then thou dost it not, lest thou shouldest insult thy wife; and dost thou not blush at insulting God? For He is everywhere present, and heareth all things.

Be not drunken, He says. For this very thing of itself, is it not a chastisement? He did not say, Put thy body on the rack, but what? Do not give it free rein [2] so as to take away the authority of the mind: on the contrary "make not provision for the lusts thereof." (Rom. xiii. 14.)

Do not (He says) seize by violence what is not thine own; do not overreach; do not forswear thyself. What labors do these things require! what sweatings!

Speak evil of no man (He says) nor accuse falsely. The contrary indeed is a labor. For when thou hast spoken ill of another, immediately thou art in danger, in suspicion, [saying] Did he of whom I spake, hear? whether he be great or small. For should he be a great man, immediately thou wilt be indeed in danger; but if small, he will requite thee with as much, or rather with what is far more grievous; for he will say evil of thee in a greater degree. We are enjoined nothing difficult, nothing burdensome, if we have the will. And if we have not the will, even the easiest things will appear burdensome to us. What is easier than eating? but from great effeminacy many feel disgust even at this, and I hear many say, that it is weariness even to eat. None of these things is wearisome if thou hast but the will. For everything depends on the will after the grace from above. Let us will good things that we may attain also to the good things eternal, in Christ Jesus our Lord, whom to the Father together with the Holy Ghost be glory, might, honor, now and for ever, and world without end. Amen.

---

[1] ὑπερβαίνει.

[2] ἐκτραχηλίσῃς.

# HOMILY XIV.

## Hebrews viii. 1, 2.

"Now of the things which we have spoken this is the sum: We have such an High Priest; who is set down on the right hand of the throne of the majesty in the heavens: a minister of the sanctuary and of the true tabernacle which the Lord pitched, and not man."

[1.] Paul mixes the lowly things with the lofty, ever imitating his Master, so that the lowly become the path to the lofty, and through the former we are led to the latter, and when we are amid the great things we learn that these [lowly ones] were a condescension. This accordingly he does here also. After declaring that "He offered up Himself," and showing Him to be a "High Priest," what does he say? "Now of the things which we have spoken this is the sum: we have such an High Priest who is set down on the right hand of the throne of the majesty." And yet this is not [the office] of a Priest, but of Him whom the Priest should serve.

"A minister of the sanctuary," not simply a minister, but "a minister of the sanctuary. And of the true Tabernacle, which the Lord pitched and not man." Thou seest the condescension. Did he not a little before make a separation,[1] saying: "Are they not all ministering spirits?" (supra, i. 14) and therefore (he says) it is not said to them, "Sit thou on my right hand," (supra, i. 13) for He that sitteth is not a minister. How is it then that it is here said, "a minister," and "a minister of the Sanctuary"? for he means here the Tabernacle.

See how he raised up the minds of the believing Jews. For as they would be apt to imagine that we have no such tabernacle [as they had], see here (he says) is the Priest, Great, yea, much greater than the other, and who has offered a more wonderful sacrifice. But is not all this mere talk? is it not a boast, and merely said to win over our minds? on this account he established it first from the oath, and afterwards also from "the tabernacle." For this difference too was manifest: but the Apostle thinks of another also, "which" (he says) "the Lord pitched [or "made firm"] and not man." Where are they who say that the heaven whirls around?[2] where are they who declare that it is spherical? for both of these notions are overthrown here.

"Now" (he says) "of the things which we have spoken this is the sum." By "the sum" is always meant what is most important. Again he brings down his discourse; having said what is lofty, henceforward he speaks fearlessly.

[2.] In the next place that thou mayest understand that he used the word "minister" of the manhood, observe how he again indicates it: "For" (ver. 3) (he says) "every high priest is ordained to offer both gifts and sacrifices, wherefore it is of necessity that this man have somewhat also to offer."

Do not now, because thou hearest that He sitteth, suppose that His being called High Priest is mere idle talk.[3] For the former, viz. His sitting, belongs to the dignity of the Godhead,[4] but this to His great lovingkindness, and His tender care for us. On this account he repeatedly urges[5] this very thing, and dwells more upon it: for he feared lest the other [truth] should overthrow it.[6] Therefore he again brings down his discourse to this: since some were enquiring why He died. He was a Priest. But there is no Priest without a sacrifice. It is necessary then that He also should have a sacrifice.

And in another way; Having said that He is on high, he affirms and proves that He is a Priest from every consideration, from Melchisedec, from the oath, from offering sacrifice. From this he also frames another and necessary syllogism. "For if" (he says) "He had been on earth, He would not be a Priest, seeing that there are priests who offer the gifts according to the Law." If then He is a Priest (as He really is), we must seek some other place for Him. "For if He were" indeed "on earth, He should not be a priest." For how [could He be]? He offered no sacrifice, He ministered not in the Priest's office. And with good reason, for there were the priests. Moreover he shows, that it was impossible that [He] should be a priest upon earth. For how [could He be]? There was no rising up against [the appointed Priests], he means.

[3.] Here we must apply our minds attentively, and consider the Apostolic wisdom; for again he shows the difference of the Priesthood.

---

1 See Hom. iii.
2 δινεῖσθαι. The common editions read κινεῖσθαι. Savile observes that it was the opinion of St. Chrys. that the heaven was stationary, and that the sun, moon and stars moved through it. [Such may have been St. Chrysostom's opinion, but it does not appear in this passage. — F. G.]

3 ὕθλον.
4 τῆς ἀξίας τοῦ Θεοῦ.
5 λιπαίνει.
6 That is, lest the belief of His Godhead should undermine our belief in His true manhood.

"Who" (he says) "serve unto the example[1] and shadow of heavenly things."

What are the heavenly things he speaks of here? The spiritual things. For although they are done on earth, yet nevertheless they are worthy of the Heavens. For when our Lord Jesus Christ lies slain[2] [as a sacrifice], when the Spirit is with us,[3] when He who sitteth on the right hand of the Father is here,[4] when sons are made by the Washing, when they are fellow-citizens of those in Heaven, when we have a country, and a city, and citizenship there, when we are strangers to things here, how can all these be other than "heavenly" things"? But what! Are not our Hymns heavenly? Do not we also who are below utter in concert with them the same things which the divine choirs of bodiless powers sing above? Is not the altar also heavenly? How? It hath nothing carnal, all spiritual things become the offerings.[5] The sacrifice does not disperse into ashes, or into smoke, or into steamy savor, it makes the things placed there bright and splendid. How again can the rites which we celebrate be other than heavenly? For when He says, "Whose soever sins ye retain they are retained, whose soever sins ye remit, they are remitted" (John xx. 23): when they have the keys of heaven, how can all be other than heavenly?

"Who" (he says) "serve unto the example and shadow of heavenly things, as Moses was admonished of God,[6] when he was about to make the tabernacle, for see, saith He, that thou make all things according to the pattern showed to thee in the mount." Inasmuch as our hearing is less ready of apprehension than our sight (for the things which we hear we do not in such wise lay up in our soul, as those which we see with our very eyes), He showed him all. Either then he means this by "the example and shadow," or else he [speaks] of the Temple. For, he went on to say, "See" (His words are), that "thou make all things according to the pattern[7] showed to thee in the mount." Was it then only what concerned the furniture of the temple that he saw, or was it also what related to the sacrifices, and all the rest? Nay, one would not be wrong in saying even this; for The Church is heavenly, and is nothing else than Heaven.

[4.] (Ver. 6) "But now hath He obtained a more excellent ministry,[8] by how much also He is the Mediator of a better covenant." Thou seest (he means) how much better is the one ministration than the other, if one be an example and type, and the other truth [reality]. But this did not profit the hearers, nor cheer them. Therefore he says what especially cheered them: "Which was established upon better promises." Having raised them up by speaking of the place, and the priest, and the sacrifice, he then sets forth also the wide difference of the covenant, having also said before that it was "weak and unprofitable." (See Heb. vii. 18.)

And observe what safeguards he lays down, when intending to find fault with it. For in the former place after saying, "according to the power of an endless life" (Heb. vii. 16), he then said that "there is a disannulling of the commandment going before" (Heb. vii. 18); and then after that, he set forth something great, saying, "by which we draw nigh unto God." (Heb. vii. 19.) And in this place, after leading us up into Heaven, and showing that instead of the temple, we have Heaven, and that those things were types of ours, and having by these means exalted the Ministration [of the New Covenant], he then proceeds suitably to exalt the priesthood.

But (as I said) he sets down that which especially cheers them, in the words, "Which was established upon better promises." Whence does appear? In that this the one was cast out, and the other introduced in its place: for it is therefore of force because it is better. For as he says, "If perfection were by" it, "what further need was there, that another priest should rise, after the order of Melchisedec?" (Heb. vii. 11); so also here he used the same syllogism, saying (ver. 7) "For if that first covenant had been faultless, then should no place have been sought for the second"; that is, if it made men "faultless." For it is because he is speaking of this that he did not say, "But finding fault with" it, but (ver. 8, 9) "But finding fault with them, He saith, Behold, the days come, saith the Lord, when I will make a new covenant with the house of Israel and with the house of Judah: not according to the covenant that I made with their fathers in the day when I took them by the hand to lead them out of the land of Egypt: because they continued not in My covenant, and I regarded them not, saith the Lord."

Yea, verily. And whence does it appear that [the first Covenant] came to an end? He showed it indeed also from the Priest, but now he shows more clearly by express words that it has been cast out.

But how is it "upon better promises"? For

---

[1] ὑποδείγματι ... λατρεύουσι. i.e. "do service to and minister in that system which is a sample and shadow."
[2] ἐσφαγμένος, see Rev. v. 6, 9, 12; xiii. 8.
[3] παραγίνηται.　　　[4] ἐνταῦθα ᾖ.
[5] τὰ προκείμενα. The Sacred Elements there set before God. [The English edition has here missed the sense of πάντα πνευματικὰ γίνεται τὰ προκείμενα. προκείμενα is predicate rather than subject, and πάντα is to be taken with πνευματικά, not with προκείμενα. The idea is (as shown by the context) that our spiritual things (hymns, praises, &c.) answer to the parts of the victim laid upon the carnal altar of old.— F. G.]
[6] [κεχρημάτισται—a word always used of Divine communications.— F. G.]　　　[7] τύπον.
[8] λειτουργίας, "service as priest."

how, tell me, can earth and heaven be equal? But do thou consider,[1] how he speaks of promises there [in that other covenant] also, that thou mayest not bring this charge against it. For there also, he says "a better hope, by which we draw nigh unto God" (Heb. vii. 19), showing that a Hope was *there* also; and in this place "better promises," hinting that *there* also He had made promises.

But inasmuch as they were forever making objections, he says, "Behold! the days come, saith the Lord, when I will make a new covenant with the house of Israel and with the house of Judah." He is not speaking of any old Covenant: for, that they might not assert this, he determined the time also. Thus he did not say simply, "according to the covenant which I made with their fathers," lest thou shouldest say [it was] the one made with Abraham, or that with Noah: but he declares what [covenant it was], "not according to the covenant which I made with their fathers" in the Exodus. Wherefore he added also, "in the day that I took them by the hand, to lead them out of the land of Egypt; because they continued not in My covenant, and I regarded them not, saith the Lord." Thou seest that the evils begin first from ourselves ("they" themselves first, saith he, "continued not in [the "covenant"]") and the negligence is from ourselves, but the good things from Him; I mean the [acts] of bounty. He here introduces, as it were, an apology showing the cause why He forsakes them.

[5.] (Ver. 10) "For this," he says, "is the covenant that I will make with the house of Israel after those days, saith the Lord; I will put[2] My laws into their mind, and write them in their hearts, and I will be to them a God, and they shall be to Me a people." Thus He says this concerning the New [covenant] because His words are "not according to the covenant which I covenanted."

But what other difference is there beside this?[3] Now if any person should say that "the difference is not in this respect, but in respect to its being put into their hearts; He makes no mention of any difference of ordinances, but points out the mode of its being given: for no longer" (he says) "shall the covenant be in writings, but in hearts;" let the Jew in that case show that this was ever carried into effect; but he could not, for it was made a second time in writings after the return from Babylon. But I show that

the Apostles received nothing in writing, but received [it] in their hearts through the Holy Ghost. Wherefore also Christ said, "When He cometh, He will bring all things to your remembrance, and He shall teach you." (John xiv. 26.)

[6.] (Ver. 11, 12) "And they shall not teach" (he says) "every man his neighbor,[4] and every man his brother, saying, Know the Lord: for all shall know Me from the least to the greatest. For I will be merciful to their unrighteousness, and their sins and their iniquities will I remember no more." Behold also another sign. "From the least even to the greatest of them" (he says) "they shall know Me, and they shall not say, Know the Lord." When hath this been fulfilled save now? For our [religion][5] is manifest: but theirs [i.e. the Jews'] was not manifest, but had been shut up in a corner.

[A covenant] is then said to be "new," when it is different and shows some advantage over the old. "Nay surely," says one,[6] "it is new also when part of it has been taken away, and part not. For instance, when an old house is ready to fall down, if a person leaving the whole, has patched up the foundation, straightway we say, he has made it new, when he has taken some parts away, and brought others into their place. For even the heaven also is thus called 'new,'[7] when it is no longer 'of brass,' but gives rain;[8] and the earth likewise is new when it is not un-

---

[1] θεωρεῖ used of contemplating and discerning the mystical sense of the Old Testament.

[2] "give."

[3] That is, besides the covenant being in itself a new one, different from the Mosaic, there is also, he says, the difference in the mode of giving it, the one being written, the other put into the heart. The Jew is supposed to allege that this second is the only difference, and that the promise in the Prophecy is that the Mosaic law shall be given into the heart, and that this was fulfilled by the reformation of the people: as for instance after the Captivity.

[4] πολίτην. The common editions have πλησίον, as has the common text of the New Testament, but there also Scholz, Lachmann, Tischendorf [Tregelles, W. and H.] read πολίτην, which is the word used in Jeremiah, according to the Vatican MS. It is used by the LXX. to translate the Hebrew for "neighbor."

[5] τὸ ἡμέτερον.

[6] Ἰδού, φησί, καὶ αὕτη καινὴ τυγχάνει. This is the argument of an objector, who alleges that the promise of a New Covenant was fulfilled by the modification and renewed efficacy of the Mosaic system, such as occurred after the Captivity. He alleges two senses in which the word "New" might be applied without implying the substitution of another system in place of the old, (i) as a repaired house is said to be new, and (ii) according to his interpretation, as the Heavens are new, when after long drought they again give rain. St. Chrys. replies. i. That after the Captivity the Covenant was still, as of old, unfruitful. ii. That this interpretation of the "new heaven" is incorrect. iii. That the Prophecy distinctly foretells a substitution. The common editions have changed the character of the passage by substituting ἄλλως δὲ καινὴ for καινὴ two lines above, and καινὴ δὲ καὶ αὕτη τ. for Ἰδού . . . καινὴ τ. in this place; by omitting φησὶ at the end of the objection; and substituting ἵνα δείξῃ for ἐὰν οὖν δείξω.

[7] See Isa. lxv. 17; Deut. xxviii. 23.

[8] The Verona edition, one Catena, the MSS. which Mr. Field usually follows, and the Latin versions of Mutianus and the later translator, all give the text which is here translated: ὅταν μηκέτι χαλκοῦς ᾖ, ἀλλ᾽ ὑετὸν διδῷ · ὅταν μὴ ἄκαρπος, οὐχ ὅταν μεταβληθῇ, οὐχ ὅταν τὰ μὲν αὐτοῦ ἐξαιρεθῇ, τὰ δὲ μένῃ. Mr. Field says that he has *nolens volens* admitted into the text the "amended" readings of the common editions, ὅταν μηκέτι χ. ᾖ. ἀ. ὑ. διδῷ, καὶ ἡ γῆ ὁμοίως καινή, ὅταν μὴ ἀ. ᾖ, οὐχ ὅταν μεταβληθῇ, καὶ οἶκος οὕτω καινὸς ὅταν τὰ μὲν κ. λ. "when it is no longer of brass, but gives rain: [and the earth in like manner is new,] when it is not unfruitful, not when it has been changed: [and in this sense the house is new], when portions of it have been," &c. There does not however appear to be any need for this: on the contrary, while the old text is simple and intelligible, the additions bring in matters which are out of place. [The other Catena, however, that of Niketas, Archbishop of Heraklea, one of Mr. Field's valuable authorities, has the bracketed bits.]

The words ὅταν μὴ ἄκαρπος apply naturally to the heaven, when it does not supply the moisture necessary for producing fruit. This argument from the "new heaven" is alleged by the objector as distinct from that of the "new house": it is an instance, he would say, of the word "new" being applied, when there was neither change nor substitution, as St. Chrys. interprets the prophecy; nor even partial alteration as in the analogy of the "new house"; but

fruitful, not when it has been changed ; and the house is likewise new, when portions of it have been taken away, and portions remain. And thus, he says,[1] he hath well termed it ' a New Covenant.' "

If then I show that that covenant had become "Old" in this respect, that it yielded no fruit? And that thou mayest know this exactly, read what Haggai says, what Zechariah, what the Messenger,[2] when the return from the Captivity had not yet fully taken place ; and what Esdras charges. How then did [the people] receive him?[3] And how no man enquired of the Lord, inasmuch as they [the priests] themselves also transgressed, and knew it not even themselves?[4] Dost thou see how thy [interpretation] is broken down,[5] whilst I maintain my own : that this [covenant] must be called " New " in the proper sense of the word?

And besides, I do not concede that the words " the heaven shall be new " (Isa. lxv. 17), were spoken concerning this. For why, when saying in Deuteronomy " the heaven shall be of brass," did he not set down this in the contrasted passage,[6] " but if ye. hearken, it shall be new."

And further on this account He says that He will give "another Covenant, because they did not continue in the first." This I show by what he says (" For what the law could not do in that it was weak through the flesh," Rom. viii. 3; and again, " Why tempt ye God, to put a yoke upon the neck of the disciples, which neither our fathers nor we were able to bear?" Acts xv. 10.) But " they did not continue therein," he says.

Here he shows that [God] counts us worthy of greater and of spiritual [privileges] : for it is said " their sound went out into all the earth, and their words unto the ends of the world." (Ps. xix. 5 ; Rom. x. 18.) That is [the meaning of] " they shall not say each man to his neighbor, Know the Lord." And again, " the earth

shall be filled with the knowledge of the Lord as much water to cover the seas." (Isa. xi. 9.)

[7.] " In calling it new " (he says), " He hath made the first old : but that which decayeth and waxeth old is ready to vanish away." See what was hidden, how he hath laid open the very mind of the prophet ! He honored the law, and was not willing to call it " old " in express terms : but nevertheless, this he did call it. For if the former had been new, he would not have called this which came afterwards " new " also. So that by granting something more and different, he declares that " it was waxen old." Therefore it is done away and is perishing, and no longer exists.

Having taken boldness from the prophet, he attacks it more suitably,[7] showing that our [dispensation] is now flourishing. That is, he showed that [the other] was old : then taking up the word " old," and adding of himself another [circumstance], the [characteristic] of old age, he took up what was omitted by the others, and says " ready to vanish away."

The New then has not simply caused the old to cease, but because it had become aged, as it was not [any longer] useful. On this account he said, " for the weakness and unprofitableness thereof " (Heb. vii. 18), and, " the law made nothing perfect " (Heb. vii. 19) ; and that " if the first had been faultless, then should no place have been sought for the second." (Heb. viii. 7.) And " faultless " ; that is, useful ; not as though it [the old Covenant] was obnoxious to any charges, but as not being sufficient. He used a familiar form of speech. As if one should say, the house is not faultless, that is, it has some defect, it is decayed : the garment is not faultless, that is, it is coming to pieces. He does not therefore here speak of it as evil, but only as having some fault and deficiency.

[8.] So then we also are new, or rather we were made new, but now are become old ; therefore we are " near to vanishing away," and to destruction. Let us scrape off[8] this old age. It is indeed no longer possible to do it by Washing, but by repentance it is possible here [in this life].[9] If there be in us anything old, let us cast it off ; if any " wrinkle," if any stain, if any " spot," let us wash it away and become fair (Eph. v. 27) : that " the King may desire our beauty." (Ps. xlv. 11.)

It is possible even for him who has fallen into the extremest deformity[10] to recover that beauty of which David says that the King shall desire

---

only a renewal of fertilizing action which had been previously suspended.

On the other hand the introduction of " the new earth " by the interpolator is out of place: inasmuch as unfruitful ground would represent the people not the Law: neither does St. Chrys. in the refutation which follows refer at all to this point of " new earth." The introduction of the " house " is simply needless repetition. [It has seemed better to follow in the translation Field's text than to follow the alterations of the English edition — both because the passage is thus much clearer, and because this is professedly a translation of Field's text, and his critical sagacity must be considered on such a point of higher value. — F. C.]

[1] ὥστε, φησί. Sav. &c. om. φησί.
[2] ὁ 'Αγγελος Malachi.
[3] πῶς οὖν ἔλαβεν αὐτόν ; The Catena has πῶς συνέλαβον αὐτόν ; which Mutianus read, translating it, " Quomodo corripuerunt eum?" Mr. Field thinks that neither reading gives a suitable meaning. If the reading adopted by Mr. F. and followed in the translation be the true one, it must be supposed that St. Chrys. had in mind the condition in which Ezra, or perhaps Nehemiah, found the Jews. The words τί δὲ 'Εσδρας ἐγκαλεῖ ; seem more appropriate to Nehemiah than to Ezra: and the reception of Nehemiah on his second visit to Jerusalem may have been the circumstance of which the orator was thinking.
[4] See Mal. i. 6, and c. ii., iii.
[5] βεβίασται τὸ σόν ; or, " how forced it is."
[6] ἐν τῇ διαστολῇ. See Deut. xxviii. 12.

[7] μᾶλλον αὐτοῦ καθάπτεται συμφερόντως.
[8] ἀποξύσωμεν: alluding to the poetic phrase ξῦσαι ἀπὸ γήρας ὀλοιόν.     [9] ἐνταῦθα.
[10] [There was one who sold his patrimony,
A dear-bought dower
That had come down from high
In a golden shower,

thy beauty. "Hearken, O daughter, and consider; forget also thine own people and thy father's house: so shall the King greatly desire thy beauty." (Ps. xlv. 10, 11.) And yet forgetting doth not produce beauty. Yea, beauty is of the soul. What sort of forgetting? That of sins. For he is speaking about the Church from among the Gentiles, exhorting her not to remember the things of her fathers, that is [of] those that sacrificed to idols; for from such was it gathered.

And he said not, "Go not after them," but what is more, Do not admit them into thy mind; which he says also in another place, "I will not mention their names through my lips." (Ps. xvi. 4.) And again, "That my mouth may not talk of the deeds of men." (Ps. xvii. 3, 4.) As yet is this no great virtue; nay, rather, it is indeed great, but not such as this [which is here spoken of]. For what does he say there? He says not; "Talk not of the things of men, neither speak of the things of thy fathers"; but, neither remember them, nor admit them into thy mind. Thou seest to how great a distance he would have us keep away from wickedness. For he that remembers not [a matter] will not think of it, and he that does not think, will not speak of it: and he that does not speak of it, will not do it. Seest thou from how many paths he hath walled us off? by what great intervals he hath removed us, even to a very great [distance]?

[9.] Let us then also "hearken and forget" our own evils. I do not say our sins, for (He says) "Remember thou first, and I will not remember." (Isa. xliii. 26, 25, LXX.) I mean for instance, Let us no longer remember rapacity, but even restore the former [plunder]. This is to forget wickedness, and to cast out the thought of rapacity, and never at any time to admit it, but to wipe away also the things already done amiss.

Whence may the forgetfulness of wickedness come to us? From the remembrance of good things, from the remembrance of God. If we continually remember God, we cannot remember those things also. For (he says) "When I remembered Thee upon my bed, I thought upon Thee in the morning dawn." (Ps. lxiii. 6.) We ought then to have GOD always in remembrance, but then especially, when thought is undisturbed, when by means of that remembrance [a man] is able to condemn himself, when he can retain [things] in memory. For in the daytime indeed, if we do remember, other cares and troubles entering in, drive the thought out again: but in the night it is possible to remember continually, when the soul is calm and at rest; when it is in the haven, and under a serene sky. "The things which you say in your hearts be ye grieved for on your beds," he says. (Ps. iv. 4, LXX.) For it were indeed right to retain this remembrance through the day also. But inasmuch as you are always full of cares, and distracted amidst the things of this life, at least then remember God on your bed; at the morning dawn meditate upon Him.

If at the morning dawn we meditate on these things, we shall go forth to our business with much security. If we have first made God propitious by prayer[1] and supplication, going forth thus we shall have no enemy. Or if thou shouldest, thou wilt laugh him to scorn, having God propitious. There is war in the market place; the affairs of every day are a fight, they are a tempest and a storm. We therefore need arms: and prayer is a great weapon. We need favorable winds; we need to learn everything, so as to go through the length of the day without shipwrecks and without wounds. For every single day the rocks are many, and oftentimes the boat strikes and is sunk. Therefore have we especially need of prayer early and by night.

[10.] Many of you have often beheld the Olympic games: and not only have beheld but have been zealous partisans and admirers of the combatants, one of this [combatant], one of that. You know then that both during the days of the contests, and during those nights, all night long the herald[2] thinks of nothing else, has no other anxiety, than that the combatant should not disgrace himself when he goes forth. For those who sit by the trumpeter admonish him not to speak to any one, that he may not spend his breath and get laughed at. If therefore he who is about to strive before men, uses such forethought, much more will it befit us to be continually thoughtful, and careful, since our whole life is a contest. Let every night then be a vigil,[3] and let us be careful that when we go out in the day we do not make ourselves ridiculous. And would it were only making ourselves ridiculous. But now the Judge of the contest is

It was a loss that gold could never mend,
　　The heart-blood of a Friend,
From out the world's dark den he came aside,
　　A monster for the sun to see,
All hideous soiled with foulest leprosy,
And he sat down upon the grass and cried,

Is there no fountain that can wash again?
·　·　·　·　·　·　·　·　·

There is a fount where holy men do say
　　He that doth look for aye
He shall become like that he doth behold,
Borrowing a light more pure than gold.
There is a glass whereon he that doth bend
　　Shall see portrayed the Heaven,
Till he forget what earth hath best to lend
In the sweet hope that he may be forgiven.

The Rev. Isaac Williams, *Thoughts in Past Years*, "The Penitent," p. 151, ed. 2, 1842.]

---

[1] ἐντεύξει.　　　[2] κῆρυξ.
[3] παννυχίς. The term applied by Christians to whole nights spent in Psalmody and Prayer; "vigils."

seated on the right hand of the Father, hearkening diligently that we utter not any false note, anything out of tune. For He is not the Judge of actions only, but of words also. Let us keep our vigil,[1] beloved ; we also have those that are eager for our success, if we will. Near each one of us Angels are sitting ; and yet we snore through the whole night. And would it were only this. But many do even many licentious things, some indeed going to the very brothels,[2] and others making their own houses places of whoredom by taking courtesans thither. Yes most certainly. For is it not so? They care well for their contest. Others are drunken and speak amiss ;[3] others make an uproar. Others keep

evil vigil through the night weaving, and worse than those who sleep, schemes of deceit ; others by calculating usury ; others by bruising themselves with cares, and doing anything rather than what is suited to the contest. Wherefore, I exhort you, let us lay aside all [other] things, and look to one only, how we may obtain the prize, [how we may] be crowned with the Chaplet ; let us do all by which we shall be able to attain to the promised blessings. Which may we all attain in Christ Jesus our Lord, with whom to the Father and also to the Holy Ghost be glory, might, honor, now and for ever and world without end. Amen.

---

# HOMILY XV.

### HEBREWS ix. 1–5.

" Then verily the first [covenant] had also ordinances of divine service, and a[4] worldly Sanctuary. For there was a tabernacle made; the first, wherein was the Candlestick, and the Table, and the Shew-bread, which is called the Sanctuary. And after the second veil, the tabernacle which is called the Holiest of all; which had the golden censer and the Ark of the Covenant overlaid round about with gold: wherein was the golden pot that had[5] manna, and Aaron's rod that budded, and the tables of the covenant: and over it the Cherubim of glory, shadowing the Mercy-seat: of which we cannot now speak particularly."

[1.] HE has shown from the Priest, from the Priesthood, from the Covenant, that that [dispensation] was to have an end. From this point he shows it from the fashion of the tabernacle itself. How? This, he says, [was] the " Holy "[6] and the " Holy of Holies."[7] The holy place then is a symbol of the former period (for there all things are done by means of sacrifices) ; but the Holy of Holies of this that is now present.

And by the Holy of Holies he means Heaven; and by the veil, Heaven, and the Flesh[8] " entereth[9] into that within the veil " : that is to say, " through the veil of His flesh." (*Supra*, vi. 19 ; Heb. x, 20.)

And it were well to speak of this passage, taking it up from the beginning. What then does he say? " Then verily the first had also " (the first what? " The Covenant "). " Ordinances of Divine service." What are " ordinances "? symbols or rights. Then ;[10] as (he means) it has not now. He shows that it had already given place, for (he says) it *had* at that time ; so that now, although it stood, it is not.

" And the worldly Sanctuary." He calls it " worldly," inasmuch as it was permitted to all to tread it, and in the same house the place was manifest where the priests stood, where the Jews, the Proselytes, the Grecians, the Nazarites. Since therefore even Gentiles were permitted to tread it, he calls it " worldly." For surely the Jews were not " the world."

" For " (he says) " there was a tabernacle made ; the first, which is called holy, wherein was the Candlestick, and the Table, and the Shew-bread." These things are symbols of the world.

" And after the second veil " (There was then not one veil [only], but there was a veil without also) " the tabernacle, which is called holy of holies." Observe how everywhere he calls it a tabernacle in regard of [God's] encamping there.[11]

" Which had " (he says) " a golden Censer, and the ark of the Covenant overlaid round about with gold : wherein was the golden pot that held the manna, and Aaron's rod that budded, and

---

[1] πανννχίσωμεν.
[2] χαμαιτυπεία.
[3] παραφθέγγονται.
[4] the.
[5] held the.
[6] [ἄγια, " the sanctuary."]
[7] [ἄγια τῶν ἁγίων, " the holiest of all."]
[8] [Cf. St. Cyr. *Quod Unus Christus* t. v. i. 761 c d.]
[9] This passage is translated [in the English edition] as if there was a point between τὴν σάρκα and εἰσερχομένην: and as if in the next clause τουτέστι was a part of the citation, being put by St. Chrys. before the words διὰ τοῦ καταπετάσματος, instead of after them, as in Heb. x. 20. St. Chrys. says that " the veil " represents both Heaven and " the Flesh " of our Lord; and cites the two places where it is so interpreted by the Apostle, vi. 19, x. 20. See below [4], p. 440. [The simple translation of the Greek (as given in the text) seems far better than this curious modification. The clause τὴν σάρκα εἰσερχομένην εἰς τὸ ἐσώτ. τ. καταπετ. is closely connected together, and it is hardly tolerable to separate σάρκα from the participle agreeing with it. There is no " which " in the Greek. — F. G.]

[10] τότε. Mr. Field seems to think that the Expositor read τότε in the sacred text: though, as he observes, he presently has τό τε. Perhaps the difficulty is avoided by supposing that the word εἶχε, " had," with which the clause begins, was emphasized in delivery, the explanation of the word " ordinances " being parenthetical, and the τότε being implied in the past tense εἶχε.
[11] παρὰ τὸ σκηνοῦν ἐκεῖ.

the tables of the covenant." All these things were venerable and conspicuous memorials of the Jewish obstinacy; "and the tables of the covenant" (for they brake them) "And the manna" (for they murmured; and therefore handing on the memory thereof to posterity, He commanded it to be laid up in a golden pot). "And Aaron's rod that budded. And over it, the Cherubim of glory." What is, "the Cherubim of glory"? He either means "the glorious," or those which are under God.[1] "Shadowing the mercy-seat."

But in another point of view also he extols these things in his discourse, in order to show that those which come after them are greater. "Of which" (he says) "we cannot now speak particularly." In these words he hints that these were not merely what was seen, but were a sort of enigmas.[2] "Of which" (he says) "we cannot now speak particularly," perhaps because they needed a long discourse.

[2.] Ver. 6. "Now when these things were thus ordained, the priests went always into the first tabernacle accomplishing the service [of God]." That is, these things indeed were [there], but the Jews did not enjoy them: they saw them not. So that they were no more theirs than [ours] for whom they prophesied.[3]

(Ver. 7) "But into the second the High Priest went alone once[4] every year, not without blood, which he offered for himself, and for the errors of the people."[5] Thou seest that the types were already laid down beforehand? for, lest they should say, "how is there [but] one sacrifice?" he shows that this was so from the beginning, since at least the more holy and the awful [sacrifice] was [but] one. And how did the High Priest offer once for all? Thus were they wont [to do] from the beginning, for then also (he says) "the High Priest" offered "once for all."

And well said he, "not without blood." (Not indeed without blood, yet not this blood, for the business was not so great.) He signifies that there shall be a sacrifice, not consumed by fire, but rather distinguished by blood. For inasmuch as he called the Cross a sacrifice, though it had neither fire, nor logs, nor was offered many times, but had been offered in blood once for all; he shows that the ancient sacrifice also was of this kind, was offered "once for all" in blood.

"Which he offers for himself;" again, "for

himself; and for the errors of the people." He said not "sins"; but "errors," that they might not be high-minded. For even if thou hast not sinned intentionally, yet unintentionally thou hast erred,[6] and from this no man is pure.

And everywhere [he adds] the "for himself," showing that Christ is much greater. For if He be separated from our sins, how did He "offer for Himself"? Why then saidst thou these things (one says)? Because this is [a mark] of One that is superior.

[3.] Thus far there is no speculation.[7] But from this point he philosophizes[8] and says, (ver. 8) "The Holy Ghost this signifying, that the way into the Holiest of all was not yet made manifest, while as the first tabernacle was yet standing." For this cause (he says) have these things been thus "ordained," that we might learn that "the Holy of Holies," that is, Heaven, is as yet inaccessible. Let us not then think (he says) that because we do not enter them, they have no existence: inasmuch as neither did we enter the Most Holy [place].

Ver. 9. "Which" (he says) "was established[9] as a figure for the time then present."[10] What does he mean by "the time present"? That before the coming of Christ: For after the coming of Christ, it is no longer a time present: For how [could it be], having arrived, and being ended?

There is too something else which he indicates, when he says this, "which [was] a figure for the time then present," that is, became the Type. "In which[11] were offered both gifts and sacrifices, that could not make him that did the service perfect, as pertaining to the conscience." Thou seest now what is [the meaning of] "The Law made nothing perfect," (Heb. vii. 19,) and "If that first [covenant] had been faultless." (Heb. viii. 7.) How? "As pertaining to the conscience." For the sacrifices did not put away[12] the defilement from the soul, but still were concerned with the body: "after the law of a carnal commandment." (Heb. vii. 16.) For certainly they could not put away[13] adultery, nor murder, nor sacrilege. Seest thou? Thou hast eaten this, Thou hast not eaten that, which are matters of indifference. ["Which stood] only in meats and drinks, and divers washings." "Thou hast drunk this," he says: and yet nothing has been ordained concerning drink, but he said this, treating them as trifles.[14]

Ver. 10. "And [in] divers washings, and carnal ordinances imposed on them until the

---

[1] τὰ ὑποκάτω τοῦ Θεοῦ.　　[2] αἰνίγματα.
[3] ἢ οἷς προεφητεύετο, or, "for whom they were foreshown," &c.: for this the common editions have προετυποῦτο, "the foreshadowing as in a type."　　[4] ἅπαξ, "once for all."
[5] [One is disposed to think that in this and the following paragraphs there must be some serious corruption of the text. As it stands there is a confusion between the words of the Epistle relating to the Jewish High Priest and those that refer to Christ. It is only possible, however, to translate the text as it has come down to us. — F. G.]

[6] ἠγνόησας.
[7] θεωρία.
[8] θεωρεῖ.
[9] καθέστηκε.
[10] ἐνεστηκότα, or "close at hand."
[11] καθ᾽ ὃν [καιρὸν].
[12] ἠφίεσαν, or "forgive."
[13] ἀφιέναι.
[14] ἐξευτελίζων. As if they were so immaterial that he did not think it worth while to be accurate, and mentioned "drinks," about which there were no precepts. St. Chrys. had perhaps overlooked the law of the Nazarites, Numb. vi. 3.

time of reformation."[1] For this is the righteousness of the flesh. Here he depreciates
the sacrifices, showing that they had no efficacy,
and that they existed "till the time of reformation," that is, they waited for the time that
reformeth all things.

[4.] Ver. 11. "But Christ being come an
High Priest of good things that are come[2] by a
greater and more perfect tabernacle not made
with hands." Here he means the flesh. And
well did he say, "greater and more perfect,"
since God The Word and all the power of The
Spirit dwells therein ; "For God giveth not the
Spirit by measure [unto Him]." (John iii. 34.)
And "more perfect," as being both unblamable,
and setting right greater things.

"That is, not of this creation." See how [it
was] "greater." For it would not have been
"of the Spirit" (Matt. i. 20), if man had constructed it. Nor yet is it "of this creation";
that is, not of these created things, but spiritual,
of[3] the Holy Ghost.

Seest thou how he calls the body tabernacle
and veil and heaven.[4] "By a greater and more
perfect tabernacle. Through the veil, that is,
His flesh." (Heb. x. 20.) And again, "into
that within the veil." (Heb. vi. 19.) And
again, "entering into[5] the Holy of Holies, to
appear before the face of God." (Heb. ix.
24.) Why then doth he this? According as
one thing or a different one is signified. I mean
for instance, the Heaven is a veil, for as a veil
it walls off the Holy of Holies ; the flesh [is a
veil] hiding the Godhead ;[6] and the tabernacle
likewise holding the Godhead. Again, Heaven
[is] a tabernacle : for the Priest is there within.

"But Christ" (he says) "being come an
High Priest": he did not say, "become," but
"being come," that is, having come for this very
purpose, not having been successor to another.
He did not come first and then become [High

Priest], but came and became at the same time.[7]
And he did not say "being come an High Priest"
of things which are sacrificed, but "of good things
that are come," as if his discourse had not power
to put the whole before us.

Ver. 12. "Neither by the blood," he says, "of
goats and calves" (All things are changed) "but by
His own Blood " (he says) "He entered in once
for all[8] into the Holy Place." See thus he called
Heaven. "Once for all " (he says) "He entered
into the Holy Place, having obtained eternal
redemption." And this [expression] "having
obtained," was [expressive] of things very difficult, and that are beyond expectation, how by
one entering in, He "obtained everlasting redemption."

[5.] Next [comes] that which is calculated
to persuade.

Ver. 13, 14. "For if the blood of bulls and of
goats, and the ashes of an heifer sprinkling the
unclean, sanctifieth to the purifying of the flesh ;
how much more shall the Blood of Christ, who
through the Holy[9] Spirit offered Himself without spot to God, purge your conscience from
dead works, to serve the living God."

For (he says) if "the blood of bulls " is able
to purify the flesh, much rather shall the Blood
of Christ wipe away the defilement of the soul.
For that thou mayest not suppose when thou
hearest [the word] "sanctifieth," that it is some
great thing, he marks out[10] and shows the difference between each of these purifyings, and how the
one of them is high and the other low. And says
it is [so] with good reason, since that is "the
blood of bulls," and this "the Blood of Christ."

Nor was he content with the name, but he sets
forth also the manner of the offering. "Who "
(he says) "through the Holy[11] Spirit offered Himself without spot to God," that is, the victim was
without blemish, pure from sins. For this is
[the meaning of] "through the Holy Spirit,"
not through fire, nor through any other things.

"Shall purge your conscience " (he says)
"from dead works." And well said he "from
dead works " ; if any man touched a dead body,
he was polluted ; and here, if any man touch a
"dead work," he is defiled through his conscience. "To serve" (he says) "the Living
and true God." Here he declares that it is not
[possible] while one has "dead works to serve the
Living and true God," for they are both dead
and false ; and with good reason [he says this].

[6.] Let no man then enter in here with "dead
works." For if it was not fit that one should
enter in who had touched a dead body, much

---

1 διορθώσεως, "setting right."
2 γενομένων: Here and afterwards μελλόντων has been substituted in the modern editions of St. Chrys. γενομένων is considered
by Lachmann to be the true reading in the Epistle.
3 ἐκ.
4 A slight alteration of Mr. Field's text seems needed here. The
text of the Homily which he gives in accordance with all the authorities is: ὁρᾶς πῶς καὶ σκηνὴν καὶ καταπέτασμα καὶ οὐρανὸν τὸ
σῶμα καλεῖ. But there is no appearance that the Apostle called
Christ's body heaven, nor do any of the texts cited show it. If, however, we introduce καὶ before τὸ σῶμα, or substitute it for τὸ, we
have a good sense, in accordance with the four texts cited by St.
Chrys. and the explanations which he afterwards gives. [The criticism of the English editor is not without some force; yet it seems
best to adhere to the text of St. Chrys., as is here done. The proposed alteration does not remove the difficulty, which is merely negative. The rendering in the English edition is "he calls heaven
and the body both tabernacle and veil." But τὸ σῶμα should be the
subject and σκηνὴν καὶ καταπέτασμα καὶ οὐρανόν predicates.—F. G.]
5 εἰσερχομένην; probably used by St. Chrys. as if τὴν σάρκα had
preceded.
6 The pointing has been changed in this place. In Mr. Field's
edition the passage stands thus: καταπέτασμα ὁ οὐρανός · ὥσπερ
γὰρ ἀποτειχίζει τὰ ἅγια καταπέτασμα, ἡ σὰρξ κρύπτουσα τὴν θεό-
τητα. The translation is made as if the pointing was τὰ ἅγια ·
καταπέτασμα ἡ σὰρξ, κρύπτουσα τὴν θ. Otherwise we must supply
ἡ σὰρξ before ὥσπερ. [The pointing is better as it stands; at most,
it is only necessary to understand καταπέτασμα after σὰρξ, which
the contrast plainly suggests.—F. G.]

7 ἀλλ' ἅμα ἦλθε, or, "but [became so] as soon as He came."
8 ἐφάπαξ. 9 ἁγίου; so also Sav. and Ben. 10 ἐπισημαίνεται.
11 Here and again below the Catena and Mutianus read " eternal," and so one MS. a priori manu. [The reading αἰωνίου of the
Textus Receptus is far better supported, and is retained by all
critical editors. It is also the reading of one of Field's MSS., although with ἁγίου written above it.—F. G.]

more one that hath "dead works": for this is the most grievous pollution. And "dead works" are, all which have not life, which breathe forth an ill odor. For as a dead body is useful to none of the senses, but is even annoying to those who come near it, so sin also at once strikes the reasoning faculty,[1] and does not allow the understanding itself to be calm, but disturbs and troubles it.

And it is said too that a plague at its very commencement corrupts[2] the living bodies; such also is sin. It differs in nothing from a plague, not [indeed] corrupting the air first, and then the bodies, but darting at once into the soul. Seest thou not how persons affected with the plague, are inflamed: how they writhe about, how they are full of an ill scent, how disfigured are their countenances: how wholly unclean they are? Such are they also that sin, though they see it not. For, tell me, is not he who is possessed by the desire of riches or carnal lust, worse than any one that is in a fever? Is he not more unclean than all these, when he does and submits to all shameless things?

[7.] For what is baser than a man who is in love with money? Whatever things women that are harlots or on the stage refuse not to do, neither does he [refuse]. Rather it is likely that they would refuse [to do] a thing, rather than he. He even submits to do things fit for slaves, flattering those whom he ought not; again he is overbearing where he ought not to be, being inconsistent in every respect. He will sit by flattering wicked people, and oftentimes depraved old men, that are of much poorer and meaner condition than himself; and will be insolent and overbearing to others that are good and in all respects virtuous. Thou seest in both respects the baseness, the shamelessness: he is both humble beyond measure, and boastful.

Harlots however stand in front of their house, and the charge against them is that they sell their body for money: yet, one may say, poverty and hunger compel them (although at the most this is no sufficient excuse: for they might gain a livelihood by work). But the covetous man stands, not before his house, but before the midst of the city, making over to the devil not his body but his soul; so that he [the devil] is in his company, and goes in unto him, as verily to a harlot: and having satisfied all his lusts, departs; and all the city sees it, not two or three persons only.

And this again is the peculiarity of harlots, that they are his who gives the gold. Even if he be a slave or a gladiator,[3] or any person what-

ever, yet if he offers their hire, they receive him. But the free, even should they be more noble than all, they do not accept without the money. These men also do the same. They turn away right thoughts when they bring no money; but they associate with the abominable, and actually with those that fight with wild beasts,[4] for the sake of the gold, and associate with them shamelessly and destroy the beauty of the soul. For as those women are naturally of odious appearance[5] and black, and awkward and gross, and formless and ill-shaped, and in all respects disgusting, such do the souls of these men become, not able to conceal their deformity by their outward paintings.[6] For when the ill look[7] is extreme, whatever they may devise, they cannot succeed in their feigning.

For that shamelessness makes harlots, hear the prophet saying, "Thou wert shameless towards all; thou hadst a harlot's countenance." (Jer. iii. 3.) This may be said to the covetous also: "Thou wert shameless towards all," not towards these or those, but "towards all." How? Such an one respects neither father, nor son, nor wife, nor friend, nor brother, nor benefactor, nor absolutely any one. And why do I say friend, and brother, and father? He respects not God Himself, but all [we believe] seems to him a fable; and he laughs, intoxicated by his great lust, and not even admitting into his ears any of the things which might profit him.

But O! their absurdity! and then what things they say! "Woe to thee, O Mammon, and to him that has thee not." At this I am torn to pieces with indignation: for woe to those who say these things, though they say them in jest. For tell me, has not God uttered such a threat as this, saying, "Ye cannot serve two masters"? (Matt. vi. 24.) And dost thou set at nought[8] the threat? Does not Paul say that it is Idolatry, and does he not call "the covetous man an Idolater"? (Eph. v. 5.)

[8.] And thou standest laughing, raising a laugh after the manner of women of the world who are on the stage. This has overthrown, this has cast down everything. Our affairs,[9] both our business[10] and our politeness, are turned into laughing; there is nothing steady, nothing grave. I say not these things to men of the world only; but I know those whom I am hinting at. For the Church has been filled with laughter. Whatever clever thing one may say, immediately there

---

of the passage had inserted καὶ ἐλεύθερος. Mr. Field many years ago in earlier volumes of his edition, suggested the true reading here, as also the word θηριομάχοις (bestialibus Mut.) just below, for which θεομάχοις had been substituted in the common texts. Both conjectures are now confirmed by MS. authority. The gladiators, especially the bestiarii, who fought with wild beasts, were regarded as a most degraded class.

[4] θηριομάχοις.     [5] φύσει εἰδεχθεῖς.
[6] ἐπιτρίμμασι, what they rub on.
[7] δυσειδία. Mut. and one MS. have δυσωδία, "ill savor."
[8] ἐκλύεις.   [9] τὰ ἡμέτερα.   [10] πολιτισμός.

---

[1] τὸ λογιστικόν.     [2] τικτόμενος διαφθείρει.
[3] μονομάχος. The reading of the common editions is [κἂν δοῦλος ᾖ] κἂν ἐλεύθερος, κἂν μόναχος. The word μόναχος had been at a very early period written by some copyists for μονομάχος (Mutianus has monachus), and the interpolator misapprehending the drift

is laughter among those present: and the marvelous thing is that many do not leave off laughing even during the very time of the prayer.

Everywhere the devil leads the dance,[1] he has entered into all, is master of all. Christ is dishonored, is thrust aside; the Church is made no account of. Do ye not hear Paul saying, Let "filthiness and foolish talking and jesting" (Eph. v. 4) be put away from you? He places "jesting" along with "filthiness," and dost thou laugh? What is "foolish talking"? that which has nothing profitable. And dost thou, a solitary, laugh at all and relax thy countenance? thou that art crucified? thou that art a mourner? tell me, dost thou laugh? Where dost thou hear of Christ doing this? Nowhere: but that He was sad indeed oftentimes. For even when He looked on Jerusalem, He wept; and when He thought on the Traitor He was troubled; and when He was about to raise Lazarus, He wept; and dost thou laugh? If he who grieves not over the sins of others deserves to be accused, of what consideration will he be worthy, who is without sorrow for his own sins, yea laughs at them? This is the season of grief and tribulation, of bruising and bringing under [the body], of conflicts and sweatings, and dost thou laugh? Dost not thou see how Sarah was rebuked? dost thou not hear Christ saying, "Woe to them that laugh, for they shall weep"? (Luke vi. 25.) Thou chantest these things every day, for, tell me, what dost thou say? "I have laughed?" By no means; but what? "I labored in my groaning." (Ps. vi. 6.)

But perchance there are some persons so dissolute and silly as even during this very rebuke to laugh, because forsooth we thus discourse about laughter. For indeed such is their derangement, such their madness, that it does not feel the rebuke.

The Priest of God is standing, offering up the prayer of all: and art thou laughing, having no fears? And while he is offering up the prayers in trembling for thee, dost thou despise all? Hearest thou not the Scripture saying, "Woe, ye despisers!" (cf. Acts xiii. 41 from Hab. i. 5); dost thou not shudder? dost thou not humble thyself? Even when thou enterest a royal palace, thou orderest thyself in dress, and look, and gait, and all other respects: and here where there is the true Palace, and things like those of heaven, dost thou laugh? Thou indeed, I know, seest [them] not, but hear thou that there are angels present everywhere, and in the house of God especially they stand by the King, and all is filled by those incorporeal Powers.

This my discourse is addressed to women also, who in the presence of their husbands indeed do not dare readily to do this, and even if they do it, it is not at all times, but during a season of relaxation, but here they do it always. Tell me, O woman, dost thou cover thine head and laugh, sitting in the Church? Didst thou come in here to make confession of sins, to fall down before God, to entreat and to supplicate for the transgressions thou hast wretchedly committed, and dost thou do this with laughter? How then wilt thou be able to propitiate Him?

[9.] But (one says) what harm is there in laughter? There is no harm in laughter; the harm is when it is beyond measure, and out of season. Laughter has been implanted in us, that when we see our friends after a long time, we may laugh; that when we see any persons downcast and fearful, we may relieve them by our smile; not that we should burst out violently[2] and be always laughing. Laughter has been implanted in our soul, that the soul may sometimes be refreshed, not that it may be quite relaxed. For carnal desire also is implanted in us, and yet it is not by any means necessary that because it is implanted in us, therefore we should use it, or use it immoderately: but we should hold it in subjection, and not say, Because it is implanted in us, let us use it.

Serve God with tears, that thou mayest be able to wash away your sins. I know that many mock us,[3] saying, "Tears directly." Therefore it is a time for tears. I know also that they are disgusted, who say, "Let us eat and drink, for to-morrow we die." (1 Cor. xv. 32.) "Vanity of vanities, all is vanity." (Eccles. i. 2.) It is not I that say it, but he who had had the experience of all things saith thus: "I builded for me houses, I planted vineyards, I made me pools of water, [I had] men servants and women servants." (Eccles. ii. 4, 6, 7.) And what then after all these things? "Vanity of vanities, all is vanity." (Eccles. xii. 8.)

Let us mourn therefore, beloved, let us mourn in order that we may laugh indeed, that we may rejoice indeed in the time of unmixed joy. For with this joy [here] grief is altogether mingled: and never is it possible to find it pure. But that is simple and undeceiving joy: it has nothing treacherous, nor any admixture. In that joy let us delight ourselves; that let us pursue after. And it is not possible to obtain this in any other way, than by choosing here not what is pleasant, but what is profitable, and being willing to be afflicted a little, and bearing all things with thanksgiving. For thus we shall be able to attain even to the Kingdom of Heaven, of which may we all be counted worthy, in Christ Jesus our Lord, with whom to the Father be glory, together with the Holy Ghost, now and for ever and world without end. Amen.

---

[1] χορεύει.          [2] ἀνακαγχάζωμεν.          [3] διαμωκῶνται.

# HOMILY XVI.

HEBREWS ix. 15–18.

"And for this cause He is the Mediator of the New Testament, that by means of death for the redemption of the transgressions that were under the first Testament, they which are called might receive the promise of an eternal inheritance. For where a testament is, there must also of necessity be the death of the testator.[1] For a testament is of force after men are dead,[2] otherwise it is of no strength at all while the testator liveth. Whereupon [3] neither the first [testament] was dedicated [4] without blood."

[1.] IT was probable that many of those who were more weakly would especially distrust the promises of Christ because He had died. Paul accordingly out of a superabundance introduced this illustration,[5] deriving it from common custom. Of what kind is it? He says, "indeed, on this very account we ought to be of good courage." On what account? Because testaments are established and obtain their force when those who have made them are not living, but dead. "And for this cause," he says, "He is the Mediator of the New Testament." A Testament is made towards the last day, [the day] of death.

And a testament is of this character: It makes some heirs, and some disinherited. So in this case also: "I will that where I am," Christ says, "they also may be." (John xvii. 24.) And again of the disinherited, hear Him saying, "I pray not for" all, "but for them that believe on Me through their word." (John xvii. 20.) Again, a testament has relation both to the testator, and to the legatees; so that they have some things to receive, and some to do. So also in this case. For after having made promises innumerable, He demands also something from them, saying, "a new commandment I give unto you." (John xiii. 34.) Again, a testament ought to have witnesses. Hear Him again saying, "I am one that bear witness of Myself, and He that sent Me beareth witness of Me." (John viii. 18.) And again, "He shall testify of Me" (John xv. 26), speaking of the Comforter. The twelve Apostles too He sent, saying, "Bear ye witness before God."[6]

[2.] "And for this cause" (he says) "He is the Mediator of the New Testament." What is a "Mediator"? A mediator is not lord of the thing of which he is mediator, but the thing belongs to one person, and the mediator is another: as for instance, the mediator of a marriage is not the bridegroom, but one who aids him who is about to be married. So then also here: The Son became Mediator between the Father and us. The Father willed not to leave us this inheritance, but was wroth against us, and was displeased [with us] as being estranged [from Him]; He accordingly became Mediator between us and Him, and prevailed with Him.

And what then? How did He become Mediator? He brought words from [Him] and brought [them to us], conveying over[7] what came from the Father to us, and adding His own death thereto. We had offended: we ought to have died: He died for us and made us worthy of the Testament. By this is the Testament secure, in that henceforward it is not made for the unworthy. At the beginning indeed, He made His dispositions as a father for sons; but after we had become unworthy, there was no longer need of a testament, but of punishment.

Why then (he would say) dost thou think upon the law? For it placed us in a condition of so great sin, that we could never have been saved, if our Lord had not died for us;[8] the law would not have had power, for it is weak.

[3.] And he established this no longer from common custom only, but also from what happened under the old [Testament]: which especially influenced them. There was no one who died there: how then could that [Testament] be firm? In the same way (he says). How? For blood was there also, as there is blood here. And if it was not the blood of the Christ, do not be surprised; for it was a type. "Whereupon," he says, "neither was the first [Testament] dedicated without blood." What is "was dedicated"? was confirmed,

---

[1] "of him that made it."
[2] "in the case of the dead."　　　[3] "whence."
[4] "inaugurate." [ἐγκεκαίνισται. It cannot be denied that the word in the classics bears both the closely related meanings of *inaugurate* and *consecrate*. The English editor has adopted the former throughout this homily; but as the common meaning in the LXX. is *consecrate*, and as the common name of the festival of the dedication of the restored temple was ἐγκαίνια, it seems better to keep to the word adopted both by the A. V. and the Revision. — F. G.]　　　[5] ὑπόδειγμα.
[6] This is not a citation of any words of our Lord: but probably John xv. 27, which is substantially equivalent, was the passage in-

tended; the words are those of 1 Tim. v. 21 [I charge thee before God, Διαμαρτύρομαι ἐνώπιον τοῦ Θεοῦ] thrown into the imperative form.
[7] [διαπορθμεύων, see above, p. 379, note 1.]
[8] Mr. Field points the passage thus: "we could never have been saved: if our Lord had not died for us, the Law would not have had power," &c. The translation follows the Bened. pointing, as giving the meaning most in accordance with St. Chrys.'s teaching. [This pointing of the English edition is allowed to stand as making the sense more obvious to the English reader; but Mr. Field's pointing gives essentially the same sense and is more in St. Chrysostom's style. — F. G.]

was ratified. The word "whereupon"[1] means "for this cause." It was needful that the symbol of the Testament should be also that of death.

For why (tell me) is the book of the testament sprinkled? (Ver. 19, 20) "For" (he says) "when Moses had spoken every precept to all the people according to the law, he took the blood of calves, with water, and scarlet wool, and hyssop, and sprinkled both the book itself and all the people, saying, This is the blood of the testament, which God hath enjoined unto you." Tell me then why is the book of the testament sprinkled, and also the people, except on account of the precious blood, figured from the first? Why "with hyssop"? It is close and retentive.[2] And why the "water"? It shows forth also the cleansing by water. And why the "wool"? this also [was used], that the blood might be retained. In this place blood and water show forth the same thing,[3] for baptism is His passion.[4]

[4.] Ver. 21, 22. "Moreover he sprinkled with blood both the tabernacle and all the vessels of the ministry. And almost[5] all things are by the law purged with blood, and without shedding of blood is no remission." Why the "almost"? why did he qualify it? Because those [ordinances] were not a perfect purification, nor a perfect remission, but half-complete and in a very small degree. But in this case He says, "This is the blood[6] of the New Testament, which is shed for you, for the remission of sins." (Matt. xxvi. 28.)

Where then is "the book"? He purified their minds. They themselves then were the books of the New Testament. But where are "the vessels of the ministry"? They are themselves. And where is "the tabernacle"? Again, they are; for "I will dwell in them," He says, "and walk in them." (2 Cor. vi. 16.)

[5.] But they were not sprinkled with "scarlet wool," nor yet "with hyssop." Why was this? Because the cleansing was not bodily but spiritual, and the blood was spiritual. How? It flowed not from the body of irrational animals, but from the Body prepared by the Spirit. With this blood not Moses but Christ sprinkled us, through the word which was spoken; "This is the blood of the New Testament, for the remission of sins." This word, instead of hyssop, having been dipped in the blood, sprinkles

all. And there indeed the body was cleansed outwardly, for the purifying was bodily; but here, since the purifying is spiritual, it entereth into the soul,·and cleanseth it, not being simply sprinkled over, but gushing forth in our souls. The initiated understand what is said. And in their case indeed one sprinkled just the surface; but he who was sprinkled washed it off again; for surely he did not go about continually stained with blood. But in the case of the soul it is not so, but the blood is mixed with its very substance, making it vigorous and pure, and leading it to the very unapproachable beauty.

[6.] Henceforward then he shows that His death is the cause not only of confirmation, but also of purification. For inasmuch as death was thought to be an odious thing, and especially that of the cross, he says that it purified, even a precious purification, and in regard to greater things. Therefore the sacrifices preceded, because of this blood. Therefore the lambs; everything was for this cause.

Ver. 23. "It was therefore necessary that the Patterns"[7] (he says) "of the things in the heavens should be purified with these, but the heavenly things themselves with better sacrifices than these."

And how are they "patterns[8] of things in the heavens"? And what does he mean now by "the things in the heavens"? Is it Heaven? Or is it the Angels? None of these, but what is ours.[9] It follows then that our things are in Heaven, and heavenly things are ours, even though they be accomplished on earth; since although angels are on earth, yet they are called Heavenly. And the Cherubim appeared on earth, but yet are heavenly. And why do I say "appeared"? nay rather they dwell on earth, as indeed in Paradise: but this is nothing; for they are heavenly.[10] And, "Our conversation is in Heaven" (Phil. iii. 20), and yet we live here.

"But these are the heavenly things," that is, the philosophy which exists amongst us; those who have been called thereto.[11]

"With better sacrifices than these." What is "better" is better than something [else] that is good. Therefore "the patterns also of things in the heavens" have become good; for not even the patterns were evil: else the things whereof they are patterns would also have been evil.

---

[1] ὅθεν. so Hom. v. 5, p. 69 on c. iii. 1.

[2] κρατητικόν. The common text, besides other additions, adds the explanatory words τοῦ αἵματος, "of the blood."

[3] The common editions add ὄν, determining the meaning to be "he [or it] shows that blood and water are the same thing."

[4] See above on ch. vi. 6.

[5] or, "and we may almost say that according," &c.

[6] Or as the position of φησὶ after αἵμα would seem to imply was the interpretation of St. Chrys.: "This blood is that of the New Testament," &c.

[7] ὑποδείγματα.

[8] or, "samples," "means of showing."

[9] The Greek is τὰ ἡμέτερα, including all our sacraments, services, relations, life and conversation. See Hom. xiv. [3]. [S. Chrys. there describes the heavenly things as "spiritual," and here, in accordance with the whole context, he must refer more to the spiritual than to the outward and ceremonial side of our religion. — F. G.]

[10] [There is a paronomasia here which is difficult of expression in English; lit. "our citizenship is in heaven, yet we live as citizens here."— F. G.]

[11] [This passage is obscure; but the meaning seems to be, "This teaching, given above, is the philosophy of those Christians who are called to such studies." — F. G.]

[7.] If then we are heavenly, and have obtained such a sacrifice,[1] let us fear. Let us no longer continue on the earth; for even now it is possible for him that wishes it, not to be on the earth. For to be and not to be on the earth is the effect of moral disposition and choice. For instance; God is said to be in Heaven. Wherefore? not because He is confined by space,[2] far from it, nor as having left the earth destitute of His presence, but by His relation to and intimacy with[3] the Angels. If then we also are near to God, we are in Heaven. For what care I about Heaven when I see the Lord of Heaven, when I myself am become a Heaven? "For," He says, "We will come," I and the Father, "and will make our abode with him." (John xiv. 23.)

Let us then make our soul a Heaven. The heaven is naturally bright; for not even in a storm does it become black, for it does not itself change its appearance, but the clouds run together and cover it. Heaven has the Sun; we also have the Sun of Righteousness. I said it is possible to become a Heaven; and I see that it is possible to become even better than Heaven. How? when we have the Lord of the Sun. Heaven is throughout pure and without spot; it changes not either in a storm or in the night. Neither let us then be so influenced, either by tribulations or by "the wiles of the devil" (Eph. vi. 11), but let us continue spotless and pure. Heaven is high and far from the earth. Let us also effect this [as regards ourselves]; let us withdraw ourselves from the earth, and exalt ourselves to that height, and remove ourselves far from the earth. Heaven is higher than the rains and the storms, and is reached by none of them. This we also can do, if we will.

It does appear to be, but is not really so affected. Neither then let us be affected, even if we appear to be so. For as in a storm, most men know not the beauty of [heaven,] but think that it is changed, while philosophers know that it is not affected at all, so with regard to ourselves also in afflictions; most men think that we are changed with them, and that affliction has touched our very heart, but philosophers know that it has not touched us.

[8.] Let us then become heaven, let us mount up to that height, and so we shall see men differing nothing from ants. I do not speak of the poor only, nor the many, but even if there be a general there, even if the emperor be there,

we shall not distinguish the emperor, nor the private person. We shall not know what is gold, or what is silver, or what is silken or purple raiment: we shall see all things as if they were flies, if we be seated in that height. There is no tumult there, no disturbance, nor clamor.

And how is it possible (one says) for him who walks on the earth, to be raised up to that height? I do not tell it thee in words, but I show thee in fact those who have attained to that height. Who then are they?

I mean such as Paul, who being on earth, spent their lives in heaven. But why do I say "in heaven"? They were higher than the Heaven, yea than the other heaven, and mounted up to God Himself. For, "who" (he says) "shall separate us from the love of Christ? shall tribulation, or distress, or persecution, or famine, or nakedness, or peril, or sword?" (Rom. viii. 35.) And again, "while we look not at the things which are seen, but at the things which are not seen." (2 Cor. iv. 18.) Seest thou that he did not even see the things here? But to show thee that he was higher than the heavens, hear him saying himself, "For I am persuaded that neither death, or life, nor things present, nor things to come, nor height, nor depth, nor any other creature, shall be able to separate us from the love of Christ." (Rom. viii. 38, 39.)

Seest thou how thought, hurrying past all things, made him higher not than this creation only, not than these heavens, but even [than any other also] if any other there were? Hast thou seen the elevation of his mind? Hast thou seen what the tent-maker became, because he had the will, he who had spent his whole life in the market-place?

[9.] For there is no hindrance, no not any, but that we may rise above all men, if we have the will. For if we are so successful in arts that are beyond the reach of the generality, much more in that which does not require so great labor.

For, tell me, what is more difficult than to walk along a tight rope, as if on level ground, and when walking on high to dress and undress, as if sitting on a couch? Does not the performance seem to us to be so frightful, that we are not even willing to look at it, but are terrified and tremble at the very sight? And tell me, what is more difficult than to hold a pole upon your face, and when you have put up a child upon it, to perform innumerable feats and delight the spectators? And what is more difficult than to play at ball[4] with swords? And tell me what is harder than thoroughly to search out the bottom of the sea? And one might mention innumerable other arts.

---

[1] θυσίας. Mr. Field adopts the reading of the later MSS. (and common editions) οὐσίας, "substance," or "possession." But the three MSS. which he usually follows and the old translation read θυσίας, which has been followed in the translation. [There are, however, as many MSS. on the other side, and whether οὐσίας be translated "possession" or "reality," it would give an excellent sense and one well in accordance with the context. — F. G.]

[2] τόπῳ ἀποκλειόμενος.          [3] σχέσει καὶ οἰκειώσει.          [4] σφαιρίζειν.

But easier than all these, if we have the will, is virtue, and the going up into Heaven. For here it is only necessary to have the will, and all [the rest] follows. For we may not say, I am unable, neither accuse the Creator. For if He made us unable, and then commands, it is an accusation against Himself.

[10.] How is it then (some one says) that many are not able? How is it then that many are not willing? For, if they be willing, all will be able. Therefore also Paul says, " I would that all men were even as I myself " (1 Cor. vii. 7), since he knew that all were able to be as himself. For he would not have said this, if it had been impossible. Dost thou wish to become [such]? only lay hold on the beginning.

Tell me now, in the case of any arts, when we wish to attain them, are we content with wishing, or do we also engage with the things themselves?[1] As for instance, one wishes to become a pilot; he does not say, I wish, and content himself with that, but he also puts his hand to the work. He wishes to become a merchant; he does not merely say, I wish, but he also puts his hand to the work. Again he wishes to travel abroad, and he does not say, I wish, but he puts his hand to the work. In everything then, wishing alone is not sufficient, but work must also be added; and when thou wishest to mount up to heaven, dost thou merely say, " I wish "?

How then (he says) saidst thou that willing is sufficient? [I meant] willing joined with deeds, the laying hold on the thing itself, the laboring. For we have God working with us, and acting with us. Only let us make our choice, only let us apply ourselves to the matter as to work, only let us think earnestly about it, only let us lay it to heart, and all follows. But if we sleep on, and as we snore expect to enter into heaven, how shall we be able to obtain the heavenly inheritance?

Let us therefore be willing, I exhort you, let us be willing. Why do we carry on all our traffic with reference to the present life, which to-morrow we shall leave? Let us choose then that Virtue which will suffice us through all eternity: wherein we shall be continually, and shall enjoy the everlasting good things; which may we all attain, in Christ Jesus our Lord, with whom to the Father together with the Holy Ghost be glory, power, honor, now and for ever and world without end. Amen.

# HOMILY XVII.

## HEBREWS ix. 24–26.

" For Christ is not entered into the holy places made with hands, which are the figures[2] of the true, but into Heaven itself, now to appear in the presence of God for us. Nor yet that He should offer Himself often, as the High Priest entereth into the Holy Place every year with blood of others, for then must He often have suffered since the foundation of the world. But now, once,[3] in the end of the world, hath He appeared to put away[4] sin by the sacrifice of Himself."

[1.] THE Jews greatly prided themselves on the temple and the tabernacle. Wherefore they said, " The temple of the Lord, The temple of the Lord, The temple of the Lord." (Jer. vii. 4.) For nowhere else in the earth was such a temple constructed as this, either for costliness, or beauty, or anything else. For God who ordained it, commanded that it should be made with great magnificence, because they also were more attracted and urged on by material things. For it had bricks of gold in the walls; and any one who wishes may learn this in the second [book] of Kings, and in Ezekiel, and how many talents of gold were then expended.

But the second [temple] was a more glorious building, both on account of its beauty, and in all other respects. Nor was it reverenced for this reason only, but also from its being One. For they were wont to resort thither from the uttermost parts of the earth, whether from Babylon or from Ethiopia. And Luke shows this when he says in the Acts: " There were dwelling " there " Parthians, and Medes, and Elamites, and the dwellers in Mesopotamia, in Judea and Cappadocia, in Pontus and Asia, Phrygia and Pamphylia, in Egypt and in the parts of Libya about Cyrene." (Acts ii. 5, 9, 10.) They then who lived in all parts of the world assembled there, and the fame of the temple was great.

What then does Paul do? What [he did] in regard to the sacrifices, that also he does here. For as there he set against [them] the death of Christ, so here also he sets the whole heaven against the temple.

---

[1] ἁπτόμεθα τῶν πραγμάτων. The expression (τοῦ πράγματος ἅπτεται) is repeated in each of the three instances that follow: in the translation it is varied.

[2] ἀντίτυπα.

[3] ἅπαξ, " once for all." [The English editor seems to have regarded ἅπαξ as the equivalent for the more emphatic ἐφάπαξ of vii. 27, ix. 12, x. 10, both here and throughout this Homily. It seems better to retain the distinction of the Greek words. — F. G.]

[4] or, " annul."

[2.] And not by this alone did he point out the difference, but also by adding that The Priest is nearer to God : for he says, " to appear in the presence[1] of God." So that he made the matter august, not only by the [consideration of] heaven, but also by [that of Christ's] entering in [there]. For not merely through symbols as here, but He sees God Himself there.

Seest thou that condescension through the lowly things have been said throughout? Why dost thou then any longer wonder that He intercedes there, where He places Himself as a High Priest? " Nor yet, that He should offer Himself often, as the High Priest."

" For Christ is not entered into the Holy Places made with hands " (he says) " which are the figures[2] of the True." (These then are true ; and those are figures,[3] for the temple too has been so arranged,[4] as the Heaven of Heavens.)

What sayest thou? He who is everywhere present, and who filleth all things, doth not He " appear "[5] unless He enter into Heaven? Thou seest that all these things pertain to the flesh.

" To appear," he says, " in the presence of God for us." What is " for us " ? He went up (he means) with a sacrifice which had power to propitiate the Father. Wherefore (tell me) ? Was He an enemy? The angels were enemies, He was not an enemy. For that the Angels were enemies, hear what he says, " He made peace as to things on earth and things in Heaven."[6] (Col. i. 20.) So that He also " entered into Heaven, now to appear in the presence of God for us." He " now appeareth," but " for us."

[3.] " Nor yet that He should offer Himself often, as the High Priest entereth into the Holy place every year with blood of others." Seest Thou how many are the differences? The " often " for the " once " ; " the blood of others," for " His own."[7] Great is the distance. He is Himself then both victim and Priest and sacrifice. For if it had not been so, and it had been necessary to offer many sacrifices, He must have been many times crucified. " For then," he says, " He must often have suffered since the foundation of the world."

In this place he has also veiled over[8] something. " But now once more in the end of the world." Why " at the end of the world " ? After the many sins. If therefore, it had taken place at the beginning, then no one would have believed ; and He must not die a second time, all would have been useless. But since later, there were many transgressions, with reason He then appeared : which he expresses in another place also, " Where sin abounded, grace did much more abound. But now once in the end of the world, hath He appeared to put away sin by the sacrifice of Himself." (Rom. v. 20.)

[4.] (Ver. 27) " And as it is appointed[9] unto men once to die, but after this, the Judgment." He next says also why He died once [only] : because He became a ransom by one death. " It had been appointed " (he says) " unto men once to die." This then is [the meaning of] " He died once,"[10] for all.[11] (What then? Do we no longer die that death? We do indeed die, but we do not continue in it : which is not to die at all. For the tyranny of death, and death indeed, is when he who dies is never more allowed to return to life. But when after dying is living, and that a better life, this is not death, but sleep.) Since then death was to have possession of all, therefore He died that He might deliver us.

Ver. 28. " So Christ was once[12] offered." By whom offered? evidently by Himself. Here he says that He is not Priest only, but Victim also, and what is sacrificed.[13] On this account are [the words] " was offered." " Was once offered " (he says) " to bear[14] the sins of many." Why " of many," and not " of all " ? Because not all believed. For He died indeed for all, that is His part : for that death was a counterbalance[15] against the destruction of all men. But He did not bear the sins of all men, because they were not willing.

And what is [the meaning of] " He bare the sins " ? Just as in the Oblation we bear up our sins and say, " Whether we have sinned voluntarily or involuntarily, do Thou forgive,"[16] that is, we make mention of them first, and then ask for their forgiveness. So also was it done here. Where has Christ done this? Hear Himself saying, " And for their sakes I sanctify[17] Myself." (John xvii. 19.) Lo! He bore the sins. He took them from men, and bore them to the Father ; not that He might determine anything

---

[1] τῷ προσώπῳ, " before the Face."    [3] τύποι.
[2] ἀντίτυπα.                          [4] κατεσκεύασται.
[5] ἐμφανίζεται. " He makes Himself visible," " apparent"; so " presents Himself," or " appears in presence": in His Human Nature.
[6] St. Chrys. understands this passage as meaning that peace was made between things on earth and those in Heaven, between us and the Angels. See his Homily on Col. i. 20 [pp. 212 sqq. O. T.]. By introducing this subject of the Father not being inimical to us, he seems to guard against any misinterpretation of what he had said, Hom. xvi. [2].
[7] See ver. 12.
[8] The Apostle has here stated something covertly. What this is St. Chrys. proceeds to explain.

[9] ἀπόκειται, " laid up."
[10] ἅπαξ.
[11] ὑπὲρ ἁπάντων.
[12] ἅπαξ.
[13] θῦμα καὶ ἱερεῖον.
[14] ἀνενεγκεῖν. Lit. to bring or bear up: hence to refer to or bring before a person, to present. The word is used in the Epistle to the Hebrews for " offer " as a sacrifice; vii. 27; xiii. 15. [This secondary meaning is brought out in 1 Pet. ii. 24, ὃς ἁμαρτίας ἡμῶν αὐτὸς ἀνήνεγκεν ἐν τῷ σώματι αὐτοῦ ἐπὶ τὸ ξύλον, " Who bore up our sins in His body upon the cross," viz. to expiate them. It is a common word in the LXX. for offering sacrifice. both its primary and secondary meanings corresponding to those of the Hebrew word which it translates.— F. G.]    [15] ἀντίρροπος.
[16] [This occurs, not absolutely verbally in the " prayer of Trisagion," in St. Chrys.'s liturgy. See Dr. Neale's Liturgies of Mark, &c., p. 121, Hayes, 1859.]
[17] ἁγιάζω, " devote as a Sacrifice." See St. Chrys. Homily on the words, John xvii. 19.

against them [mankind], but that He might forgive them.

"Unto them that look for Him shall He appear" (he says) "the second time without sin unto salvation." What is "without sin"? it is as much as to say, He sinneth not. For neither did He die as owing the debt of death, nor yet because of sin. But how "shall He appear"? To punish, you say. He did not however say this, but what was cheering; "shall He appear unto them that look for Him, without sin unto salvation." So that for the time to come they no longer need sacrifices to save themselves, but to do this by deeds.

[5.] (Chap. x. 1.) "For" (he says) "the Law having a shadow of the good things to come, not the very image of the things"; i.e. not the very reality. For as in painting, so long as one [only] draws the outlines, it is a sort of "shadow": but when one has added the bright paints and laid in the colors, then it becomes "an image." Something of this kind also was the Law.

"For" (he says) "the Law having a shadow of the good things to come, not the very image of the things," i.e. of the sacrifice, of the remission: "can never by those sacrifices[1] with[2] which they offered continually make the comers thereunto perfect." (Ver. 2-9) "For then would they not have ceased to be offered? because that the worshipers once purged, should have had no more conscience of sins? But in those sacrifices there is a remembrance again made of sins every year. For it is not possible that the blood of bulls and of goats should take away sins. Wherefore when He cometh into the world, He saith, Sacrifice and offering Thou wouldest not, but a body hast Thou prepared Me. In burnt-offerings and sacrifices for sin Thou hast had no pleasure. Then said I, Lo! I come, in the volume of the book it is written of Me, to do Thy will, O God. Above when He said, Sacrifice, and offering, and burnt-offerings, and [offering] for sin Thou wouldest not, neither hadst pleasure therein, which are offered by the Law, then He said, Lo! I come to do Thy will, O God! He taketh away the first that He may establish the second."

Thou seest again the superabundance [of his proofs]? This sacrifice (he says) is one; whereas the others were many: therefore they had no strength, because they were many. For, tell me, what need of many, if one had been sufficient? so that their being many, and offered "continually," proves that they [the worshipers] were never made clean. For as a medicine, when it is poweful and productive of health,

and able to remove the disease entirely, effects all after one application; as, therefore, if being once applied it accomplishes the whole, it proves its own strength in being no more applied, and this is its business, to be no more applied; whereas if it is applied continually, this is a plain proof of its not having strength. For it is the excellence of a medicine to be applied once, and not often. So is it in this case also. Why forsooth are they continually cured with the "same sacrifices"? For if they were set free from all their sins, the sacrifices would not have gone on being offered every day. For they had been appointed to be continually offered in behalf of the whole people, both in the evening and in the day. So that there was an arraignment of sins, and not a release from sins; an arraignment of weakness, not an exhibition of strength. For because the first had no strength, another also was offered: and since this effected nothing, again another; so that it was an evidence of sins. The "offering" indeed then, was an evidence of sins, the "continually," an evidence of weakness. But with regard to Christ, it was the contrary: He was "once offered." The types[3] therefore contain the figure only, not the power; just as in images, the image has the figure of the man, not the power. So that the reality and the type have [somewhat] in common with one another. For the figure exists equally in both, but not the power. So too also is it in respect of Heaven and of the tabernacle, for the figure was equal: for there was the Holy of Holies, but the power and the other things were not the same.

What is, "He hath appeared to put away sin by the sacrifice of Himself"?[4] What is this "putting away"? it is making contemptible. For sin has no longer any boldness; for it is made of no effect in that when it ought to have demanded[5] punishment, it did not demand it: that is, it suffered violence: when it expected to destroy all men, then it was itself destroyed.

"He hath appeared by the sacrifice of Himself" (he says), that is, "He hath appeared," unto God, and drawn near [unto Him]. For do not [think] because the High Priest was wont to do this oftentimes in the year . . . .[6] So that henceforward this is done in vain, although

---

[1] The common editions have κατ᾽ ἐνιαυτὸν, "year by year," before ταῖς αὐταῖς θυσίαις, as has the old translation of Mutian.; but it is omitted in the best MSS.

[2] αἷς: ἃς, "which," Ben. Sav.

[3] ἀντίτυπα.

[4] St. Chrys. here reverts to ch. ix. 26, to supply an explanation of the words εἰς ἀθέτησιν τῆς ἁμαρτίας διὰ τῆς θυσίας αὐτοῦ πεφανέρωται, which he had omitted before: ἀθέτησις is properly ["setting aside." — F. G.] "annulling," "rendering invalid and of no effect," thence it is used for "despising," "treating as nothing worth."

[5] ὀφείλουσα ἀπολαβεῖν.

[6] This is an imperfect sentence: the interpolator substitutes for the lacuna and the next sentence the following: "that it was done simply and not because of weakness. For if it were not done because of weakness, why was it done at all? For if there are no wounds, neither is there afterwards need of medicines for the patient." Mr. Field prefers leaving it as it stands without conjecturing what is omitted: only observing that the words "this is done" refer to the Levitical sacrifices continued after the completion of that on the Cross.

it is done; for what need is there of medicines where there are no wounds? On this account He ordained offerings "continually," because of their want of power, and that a remembrance of sins might be made.

[6.] What then? do not we offer every day? We offer indeed, but making a remembrance of His death, and this [1] [remembrance] is one and not many. How is it one, and not many? Inasmuch as that [2] [Sacrifice] was once for all offered, [and] carried into the Holy of Holies. This is a figure of that [sacrifice] and this remembrance of that. [3] For we always offer the same, [4] not one sheep now and to-morrow another, but always the same thing: [5] so that the sacrifice is one. And yet by this reasoning, since the offering is made in many places, are there many Christs? but Christ is one everywhere, being complete here and complete there also, one Body. As then while offered in many places, He is one body and not many bodies; so also [He is] one sacrifice. He is our High Priest, who offered the sacrifice that cleanses us. That we offer now also, which was then offered, which cannot be exhausted. This is done in remembrance of what was then done. For (saith He) "do this in remembrance of Me." (Luke xxii. 19.) It is not another sacrifice, as the High Priest, but we offer [6] always the same, or rather we perform a remembrance of a Sacrifice.

[7.] But since I have mentioned this sacrifice, I wish to say a little in reference to you who have been initiated; little in quantity, but possessing great force and profit, for it is not our own, but the words of Divine SPIRIT. What then is it? Many partake of this sacrifice once in the whole year, others twice; others many times. Our word then is to all; not to those only who are here, but to those also who are settled in the desert. [7] For they partake once in the year, and often indeed at intervals of two years.

What then? which shall we approve? those [who receive] once [in the year]? those who [receive] many times? those who [receive] few times? Neither those [who receive] once, nor those [who receive] often, nor those [who receive] seldom, but those [who come] with a pure conscience, from a pure heart, with an irreproachable life. Let such draw near continually; but those who are not such, not even once. Why, you will ask? Because they receive to themselves judgment, yea and condemnation, and punishment, and vengeance. And do not wonder. For as food, nourishing by nature, if received by a person without appetite, ruins and

corrupts all [the system], and becomes an occasion of disease, so surely is it also with respect to the awful mysteries. Dost thou feast at a spiritual table, a royal table, and again pollute thy mouth with mire? Dost thou anoint thyself with sweet ointment, and again fill thyself with ill savors?

Tell me, I beseech thee, when after a year thou partakest of the Communion, dost thou think that the Forty Days [8] are sufficient for thee for the purifying of the sins of all that time? And again, when a week has passed, dost thou give thyself up to the former things? Tell me now, if when thou hast been well for forty days after a long illness, thou shouldest again give thyself up to the food which caused the sickness, hast thou not lost thy former labor too? For if natural things are changed, much more those which depend on choice. As for instance, by nature we see, and naturally we have healthy eyes; but oftentimes from a bad habit [of body] our power of vision is injured. If then natural things are changed, much more those of choice. Thou assignest forty days for the health of the soul, or perhaps not even forty, and dost thou expect to propitiate God? Tell me, art thou in sport?

These things I say, not as forbidding you the one and annual coming, but as wishing you to draw near continually.

[8.] These things have been given to the holy. This the Deacon also proclaims when he calls on the holy; [9] even by this call searching the faults of all. For as in a flock, where many sheep indeed are in good health, but many are full of the scab, it is needful that these should be separated from the healthy; so also in the Church: since some sheep are healthy, and some diseased, by this voice he separates the one from the other, the priest [I mean] going round on all sides by this most awful cry, and calling and drawing on [10] the holy. For it is not possible that a man should know the things of his neighbor, (for "what man," he says, "knoweth the things of a man, save the spirit of man which is in him?"—1 Cor. ii. 11): he utters this voice after the whole sacrifice has been completed, that no person should come to the spiritual fountain carelessly and in a chance way. For in the case of the flock also (for nothing prevents us from again using the same example), the sickly ones we shut up within, and keep them in the dark, and give them different food, not permitting them to partake either of pure air, or of simple grass, or of the fountain without [the fold]. In this case then also this voice is instead of fetters.

---

1 αὕτη.
2 ἐκείνη.
3 τοῦτο ἐκείνης τύπος ἐστὶ, καὶ αὕτη ἐκείνης.
4 τὸν αὐτὸν.
5 τὸ αὐτὸ.
6 ποιοῦμεν, or "make."
7 The Eremites.

8 Lent; devoted to preparation for the Easter Communion.
9 After the Oblation was made and before the Communion the deacon proclaimed τὰ ἅγια τοῖς ἁγίοις, "The Holy things for the holy."
10 ἕλκων.

Thou canst not say, 'I did not know, I was not aware that danger attends the matter.' Nay surely Paul too especially testified this. But wilt thou say, 'I never read it'? This is not an apology, but even an accusation. Dost thou come into the Church every day and yet art ignorant of this?

However, that thou mayest not have even this excuse to offer, for this cause, with a loud voice, with an awful cry, like some herald lifting up his hand on high, standing aloft, conspicuous to all, and after that awful silence crying out aloud, he invites some, and some he forbids, not doing this with his hand, but with his tongue more distinctly than with his hand. For that voice, falling on our ears, just like a hand, thrusts away and casts out some, and introduces and presents others.

Tell me then, I beseech [you], in the Olympic games does not the herald stand, calling out with loud and uplifted voice, saying, " Does any one accuse this man? Is he a slave? Is he a thief? Is he one of wicked manners?" And yet, those contests for prizes are not of the soul, nor yet of good morals, but of strength and the body. If then where there is exercise of bodies, much examination is made about character, how much rather here, where the soul is alone the combatant. Our herald then even now stands, not holding each person by the head, and drawing him forward, but holding all together by the head within; he does not set against them other accusers, but themselves against themselves. For he says not, " Does any one accuse this man?" but what? " If any man accuse himself." For when he says, The Holy things for the holy, he means this: " If any is not holy, let him not draw near."

He does not simply say, " free from sins," but, " holy." For it is not merely freedom from sins which makes a man holy, but also the presence of the Spirit, and the wealth of good works. I do not merely wish (he says) that you should be delivered from the mire, but also that you should be bright and beautiful. For if the Babylonian King, when he made choice of the youths from the captives, chose out those who were beautiful in form, and of fair countenance: much more is it needful that we, when we stand by the royal table, should be beautiful in form, [I mean] that of the soul, having adornment of gold, our robe pure, our shoes royal, the face of our soul well-formed, the golden ornament put around it, even the girdle of truth. Let such an one as this draw near, and touch the royal cups. But if any man clothed in rags, filthy, squalid,

wish to enter in to the royal table, consider how much he will suffer, the forty days not being sufficient to wash away the offenses which have been committed in all the time. For if hell is not sufficient, although it be eternal (for therefore also it *is* eternal), much more this short time. For we have not shown a strong repentance, but a weak.

[9.] Eunuchs especially ought to stand by the King: by eunuchs, I mean those who are clear in their mind, having no wrinkle nor spot, lofty in mind, having the eye of the soul gentle and quick-sighted, active and sharp, not sleepy nor supine; full of much freedom, and yet far from impudence and overboldness, wakeful, healthful, neither very gloomy and downcast, nor yet dissolute and soft.

This eye we have it in our own power to create, and to make it quicksighted and beautiful. For when we direct it, not to the smoke nor to the dust (for such are all human things), but to the delicate breeze, to the light air, to things heavenly and high, and full of much calmness and purity, and of much delight, we shall speedily restore it, and shall invigorate it, as it luxuriates in such contemplation. Hast thou seen covetousness and great wealth? do not thou lift up thine eye thereto. The thing is mire, it is smoke, an evil vapor, darkness, and great distress and suffocating cares. Hast thou seen a man cultivating righteousness, content with his own, and having abundant space for recreation, having anxieties, not fixing his thoughts on things here? Set [thine eye] there, and lift [it] up on high; and thou wilt make it far the most beautiful, and more splendid, feasting it not with the flowers of the earth, but with those of virtue, with temperance, moderation, and all the rest. For nothing so troubles the eye as an evil conscience (" Mine eye," it is said, " was troubled by reason of anger " — Ps. vi. 7) ; nothing so darkens it. Set it free from this injury, and thou wilt make it vigorous and strong, ever nourished with good hopes.

And may we all make both it and also the other energies of the soul, such as Christ desires, that being made worthy of the Head who is set over us, we may depart thither where He wishes. For He saith, " I will that where I am, they also may be with Me, that they may behold My glory." (John xvii. 24.) Which may we all enjoy in Christ Jesus our Lord, with whom to the Father together with the Holy Ghost be glory, might, honor, now and for ever and world without end. Amen.

# HOMILY XVIII.

## Hebrews x. 8–13.

"Above when He said, Sacrifice and offering, and burnt-offerings, and [offering] for sin, Thou wouldest not, neither hadst pleasure [therein], which are offered by[1] the Law, then said He, Lo! I come to do Thy will, O God. He taketh away the first, that He may establish the second. By the which will we are[2] sanctified, by the offering of the body of Jesus Christ, once for all.[3] And every Priest standeth daily ministering, and offering oftentimes the same sacrifices, which can never take away sins. But this [man] after He had offered one sacrifice for sins for ever, sat down on the right hand of God, from henceforth expecting till His enemies be made His footstool."[4]

[1.] In what has gone before he had shown that the sacrifices were unavailing for perfect purification, and were a type, and greatly defective. Since then there was this objection to his argument, If they are types, how is it that, after the truth is come, they have not ceased, nor given place, but are still performed? he here accordingly labors at this very point, showing that they are no longer performed, even as a figure, for God does not accept them. And this again he shows not from the New [Testament], but from the prophets, bringing forward from times of old the strongest testimony, that it [the old system] comes to an end, and ceases, and that they do all in vain, "alway resisting the Holy Ghost." (Acts vii. 51.)

And he shows over and above that they cease not now [only], but at the very coming of the Messiah, nay rather, even before His coming: and how it was that Christ did not abolish them at the last, but they were abolished first, and then He came; first they were made to cease, and then He appeared. That they might not say, Even without this sacrifice, and by means of those, we could have been well pleasing unto God, He waited for these sacrifices to be convicted [of weakness], and then He appeared; for (He says) "sacrifice and offering Thou wouldest not." Hereby He took all away; and having spoken generally, He says also particularly, "In burnt-offerings and [sacrifice] for sin Thou hadst no pleasure." But "the offering" was everything except the sacrifice. "Then said I, Lo! I come." Of whom was this spoken? of none other than the Christ.

Here he does not blame those who offer, showing that it is not because of their wickednesses that He does not accept them, as He says else-where, but because the thing itself has been convicted for the future and shown to have no strength, nor any suitableness to the times.[5] What then has this to do with the "sacrifices" being offered "oftentimes"? Not only from their being "oftentimes" [offered] (he means) is it manifest that they are weak, and that they effected nothing; but also from God's not accepting them, as being unprofitable and useless. And in another place it is said, "If Thou hadst desired sacrifice I would have given it." (Ps. li. 16.) Therefore by this also he makes it plain that He does not desire it. Therefore sacrifices are not God's will, but the abolition of sacrifices. Wherefore they sacrifice contrary to His will.

What is "To do Thy will"? To give up Myself, He means: This is the will of God. "By which Will we are sanctified." Or he even means something still further, that the sacrifices do not make men clean, but the Will of God. Therefore to offer sacrifice is not the will of God.

[2.] And why dost thou wonder that it is not the will of God now, when it was not His will even from the beginning? For "who," saith He, "hath required this at your hands?" (Isa. i. 12.)

How then did He Himself enjoin it? In condescension. For as Paul says, "I would[6] that all men were even as I myself" (1 Cor. vii. 7), in respect of continence, and again says, "I will[7] that the younger women marry, bear children" (1 Tim. v. 14); and lays down two wills, yet the two are not his own, although he commands; but the one indeed is his own, and therefore he lays it down without reasons; while the other is not his own, though he wishes it, and therefore it is added with a reason. For having previously accused them, because "they had waxed wanton against Christ" (1 Tim. v. 11), he then says, "I will that the younger women marry, bear children." (1 Tim. v. 14.) So in this place also it was not His leading will that the sacrifices should be offered. For, as He says, "I wish not the death of the sinner, as that he should turn unto [Me] and live" (Ezek. xxxiii. 11): and in another place He says that He not only wished, but even desired[8] this: and yet these are contrary to each other: for intense

---

1 "according to."            3 ἐφάπαξ.
2 "have been."               4 "a footstool for His feet."

5 προσήκοντα καιρὸν.    6 θέλω.    7 βούλομαι.
8 St. Chrys. seems to refer to some place where it is said that God desired (ἐπεθύμησε) the death of the wicked. It does not appear what passage he had in view.

wishing is desire. How then dost Thou "not wish"? how dost Thou in another place "desire," which is a sign of vehement wishing? So is it in this case also.

"By the which will we are sanctified," he says. How sanctified? "by the offering of the Body of JESUS Christ once for all."

[3.] "And every priest standeth daily ministering and offering oftentimes the same sacrifice." (To stand therefore is a sign of ministering; accordingly to sit, is a sign of being ministered unto.) "But this [man] after He had offered one sacrifice for sins for ever, sat down on the right hand of God, from henceforth expecting till His enemies be made His footstool." (Ver. 14, 15) "For by one offering He hath perfected forever them that are sanctified. Whereof the Holy Ghost also is a witness to us." He had said that those [sacrifices] are not offered; he reasoned from what is written, [and] from what is not written;[1] moreover also he put forward the prophetic word which says, "sacrifice and offering Thou wouldest not." He had said that He had forgiven their sins. Again this also He proves from the testimony of what is written, for "the Holy Ghost" (he says) "is a witness to us: for after that He had said," (ver. 16–18) "This is the covenant, that I will make with them, after those days, saith the Lord: I will put My laws into their hearts, and in their minds will I write them, and their sins and iniquities will I remember no more. Now where remission of these is there is no more offering for sin." So then He forgave their sins, when He gave the Covenant, and He gave the Covenant by sacrifice. If therefore He forgave the sins through the one sacrifice, there is no longer need of a second.

"He sat down on the right hand of God, from henceforth expecting." Why the delay? "that His enemies be put under His feet. For by one offering He hath perfected for ever them that are sanctified." But perhaps some one might say; Wherefore did He not put them under at once? For the sake of the faithful who should afterwards be brought forth and born. Whence then [does it appear] that they shall be put under? By the saying "He sat down." He called to mind again that testimony which saith, "until I put the enemies under His feet." (See above, i. 13.) But His enemies are the Jews. Then since he had said, "Till His enemies be put under His feet," and they [these enemies[2]] were vehemently urgent, therefore he introduces all his discourse concerning faith after this. But who are the enemies? All unbelievers: the dæmons. And intimating the greatness of their subjection, he said not "are subjected," but "are put under His feet."

[4.] Let us not therefore be of [the number of] His enemies. For not they alone are enemies, the unbelievers and Jews, but those also who are full of unclean living. "For the carnal mind is enmity against God: for it is not subject to the law of God, for neither can it be." (Rom. viii. 7.) What then (you say)? this is not a ground of blame. Nay rather, it is very much a ground of blame. For the wicked man as long as he is wicked, cannot be subject [to God's law]; he can however change and become good.

Let us then cast out carnal minds. But what are carnal? Whatever makes the body flourish and do well, but injures the soul: as for instance, wealth, luxury, glory (all these things are of the flesh), carnal love. Let us not then love gain, but ever follow after poverty: for this is a great good.

But (you say) it makes one humble and of little account. [True:] for we have need of this, for it benefits us much. "Poverty" (it is said) "humbles a man." (Prov. x. 4, LXX.) And again Christ [says], "Blessed are the poor in spirit." (Matt. v. 3.) Dost thou then grieve because thou art upon a path leading to virtue? Dost thou not know that this gives us great confidence?

But, one says, "the wisdom of the poor man is despised." (Eccles. ix. 16.) And again another says, "Give me neither riches nor poverty" (Prov. xxx. 8), and, "Deliver me from the furnace of poverty."[3] (See Isa. xlviii. 10.) And again, if riches and poverty are from the Lord, how can either poverty or riches be an evil? Why then were these things said? They were said under[4] the Old [Covenant], where there was much account made of wealth, where there was great contempt of poverty, where the one was a curse and the other a blessing. But now it is no longer so.

But wilt thou hear the praises of poverty? Christ sought after it, and saith, "But the Son of Man hath not where to lay His head." (Matt. viii. 20.) And again He said to His disciples, "Provide[5] neither gold, nor silver, nor two coats." (Matt. x. 9, 10.) And Paul in writing said, "As having nothing and yet possessing all things." (2 Cor. vi. 10.) And Peter said to him who was lame from his birth, "Silver and gold have I none." (Acts iii. 6.) Yea and under the Old [Covenant] itself, where wealth was held in admiration, who were the admired?

---

[1] That is from other arguments than the words of the Old Testament.

[2] [The English editor supplies this ellipsis with the words "to whom he wrote." The reference seems rather to be to "the enemies," and such was apparently the understanding of Mutianus and of the Benedictine editor. — F. G.]

[3] The words of the LXX. are "He took me out of the furnace of poverty."

[4] or "in," ἐν.

[5] or "get."

Was not Elijah, who had nothing save the sheep-skin? Was not Elisha? Was not John?

Let no man then be humiliated on account of his poverty: It is not poverty which humiliates, but wealth, which compels us to have need of many, and forces us to be under obligations to many?

And what could be poorer than Jacob (tell me), who said, "If the Lord give me bread to eat, and raiment to put on"? (Gen. xxviii. 20.) Were Elijah and John then wanting in boldness?[1] Did not the one reprove Ahab, and the other Herod? The latter said, "It is not lawful for thee to have thy brother Philip's wife." (Mark vi. 18.) And Elias said to Ahab with boldness, "It is not I that trouble Israel, but thou and thy father's house." (1 Kings xviii. 18.) Thou seest that this especially produces boldness, poverty [I mean]? For while the rich man is a slave, being subject to loss, and in the power of every one wishing to do him hurt, he who has nothing, fears not confiscation, nor fine. So, if poverty had made men wanting in boldness Christ would not have sent His disciples with poverty to a work requiring great boldness. For the poor man is very strong, and has nothing wherefrom he may be wronged or evil entreated. But the rich man is assailable on every side: just in the same way as one would easily catch a man who was dragging many long ropes after him, whereas one could not readily lay hold on a naked man. So here also it falls out in the case of the rich man: slaves, gold, lands, affairs innumerable, innumerable cares, difficult circumstances, necessities, make him an easy prey to all.

[5.] Let no man then henceforth esteem poverty a cause of disgrace. For if virtue be there, all the wealth of the world is neither clay, nor even a mote in comparison of it. This then let us follow after, if we would enter into the kingdom of heaven. For, He saith, "Sell that thou hast, and give to the poor, and thou shalt have treasure in Heaven." (Matt. xix. 21.) And again, "It is hard for a rich man to enter into the Kingdom of Heaven." (Matt. xix. 23.) Dost thou see that even if we have it not, we ought to draw it to us? So great a good is Poverty. For it guides us by the hand, as it were, on the path which leads to Heaven, it is an anointing for the combat, an exercise great and admirable, a tranquil haven.

But (you say) I have need of many [things], and am unwilling to receive a favor from any. Nevertheless, even in this respect the rich man is inferior to thee; for thou perhaps askest the favor for thy support, but he shamelessly [asks] for ten thousand things for covetousness' sake.

So that it is the rich that are in need of many [persons], yea oftentimes those who are unworthy of them. For instance, they often stand in need of those who are in the rank of soldiers, or of slaves: but the poor man has no need even of the Emperor himself, and if he should need him, he is admired because he has brought himself down to this, when he might have been rich.

Let no man then accuse poverty as being the cause of innumerable evils, nor let him contradict Christ, who declared it to be the perfection of virtue, saying, "If thou wilt be perfect." (Matt. xix. 21.) For this He both uttered in His words, and showed by His acts, and taught by His disciples. Let us therefore follow after poverty, it is the greatest good to the sober-minded.

Perhaps some of those who hear me, avoid it as a thing of ill omen. I do not doubt it.[2] For this disease is great among most men, and such is the tyranny of wealth, that they cannot even as far as words endure the renunciation of it, but avoid it as of ill omen. Far be this from the Christian's soul: for nothing is richer than he who chooses poverty of his own accord, and with a ready mind.

[6.] How? I will tell you, and if you please, I will prove that he who chooses poverty of his own accord is richer even than the king himself. For he indeed needs many [things], and is in anxiety, and fears lest the supplies for the army should fail him; but the other has enough of everything, and fears about nothing, and if he fears, it is not about so great matters. Who then, tell me, is the rich man? he who is daily asking, and earnestly laboring to gather much together, and fears lest at any time he should fall short, or he who gathers nothing together, and is in great abundance and hath need of no one? For it is virtue and the fear of God, and not possessions which give confidence. For these even enslave. For it is said, "Gifts and presents blind the eyes of the wise, and like a muzzle on the mouth turn away reproofs." (Ecclus. xx. 29.)

Consider how the poor man Peter chastised the rich Ananias. Was not the one rich and the other poor? But behold the one speaking with authority and saying, "Tell me whether ye sold the land for so much" (Acts v. 8), and the other saying with submission, "Yea, for so much." And who (you say) will grant to me to be as Peter? It is open to thee to be as Peter if thou wilt; cast away what thou hast. "Disperse, give to the poor" (Ps. cxii. 9), follow Christ, and thou shalt be such as he. How? he (you say) wrought miracles. Is it this then, tell me,

---

[1] ἀπαρρησίαστοι.

[2] οὐκ ἀπιστῶ.

which made Peter an object of admiration, or the boldness which arose from his manner of life? Dost thou not hear Christ saying, "Rejoice not because the devils are subject unto you; If thou wilt be perfect [&c]." (Luke x. 20.) Hear what Peter says: "Silver and gold have I none, but what I have I give thee." (Acts iii. 6.) If any man have silver and gold, he hath not those other gifts.

Why is it then, you say, that many have neither the one nor the other? Because they are not voluntarily poor: since they who are voluntarily poor have all good things. For although they do not raise up the dead nor the lame, yet, what is greater than all; they have confidence towards God. They will hear in that day that blessed voice, "Come, ye blessed of My Father," (what can be better than this?) "inherit the kingdom prepared for you from the foundation of the world: for I was an hungered and ye gave Me meat: I was thirsty and ye gave Me drink: I was a stranger and ye took Me in: I was naked and ye clothed Me: I was sick and in prison and ye visited Me. Inherit the kingdom prepared for you from the foundation of the world." (Matt. xxv. 34–36.) Let us then flee from covetousness, that we may attain to the kingdom [of Heaven]. Let us feed the poor, that we may feed Christ: that we may become fellow-heirs with Him in Christ Jesus our Lord, with whom to the Father together with the Holy Ghost, be glory, power, honor, now and for ever and world without end. Amen.

# HOMILY XIX.

## Hebrews x. 19–23.

" Having therefore, brethren, boldness to enter into the holiest by the blood of Jesus, by a new and living way which He hath consecrated [1] for us, through the Veil, that is to say, His flesh, and having an High Priest [2] over the house of God, let us draw near with a true heart, in full assurance of faith, having our hearts sprinkled from an evil conscience, and our bodies washed with pure water. Let us hold fast the profession [3] of our hope without wavering."

[1.] " Having therefore, brethren, boldness to enter into the holiest by the blood of Jesus, by a new and living way which He hath consecrated for us." Having shown the difference of the High Priest, and of the sacrifices, and of the tabernacle, and of the Covenant, and of the promise, and that the difference is great, since those are temporal, but these eternal, those "near to vanishing away," these permanent, those powerless, these perfect, those figures, these reality, for (he says) "not according to the law of a carnal commandment, but according to the power of an endless life." (c. vii. 16.) And "Thou art a Priest for ever." (c. v. 6.) Behold the continuance of the Priest. And concerning the Covenant, That (he says) is old (for "that which decayeth and waxeth old is ready to vanish away"—c. viii. 13), but this is new; and has remission of sins, while that [has] nothing of the kind: for (he says) "the Law made nothing perfect." (c. vii. 19.) And again, "sacrifice and offering Thou wouldest not." (c. x. 5.) That is made with hands, while this is "not made with hands" (c. ix. 11): that "has the blood of goats" (c. ix. 12), this of the Lord; that has the Priest "standing," this "sitting." Since therefore all those are inferior and these greater, therefore he says, "Having therefore, brethren, boldness."

[2.] "Boldness": from whence? As sins (he means) produce shame, so the having all things forgiven us, and being made fellow-heirs, and enjoying so great Love, [produces] boldness.

"For the entrance into the holiest." What does he mean here by "entrance"? Heaven, and the access to spiritual things.

"Which he hath inaugurated," [4] that is, which He prepared, and which He began; for the beginning of using is thenceforth called the inaugurating; which He prepared (he means) and by which He Himself passed.

" A new and living way." Here He expresses " the full assurance of hope." "New," he says. He is anxious to show that we have all things greater; since now the gates of Heaven have been opened, which was not done even for Abraham. "A new and living way," he says, for the first was a way of death, leading to Hades, but this of life. And yet he did not say, " of life," but called it " living," (the ordinances, that is,) that which abideth. [5]

---

[1] " new made" or " inaugurated."
[2] " a great Priest."
[3] " confession."

[4] ἐνεκαίνισε, " consecrated."
[5] ἀλλὰ ζῶσαν αὐτὴν ἐκάλεσε· τουτέστι, τὰ προστάγματα, τὴν μένουσαν. This is the reading of all the best MSS., the Catena and ancient Translation. The later editions omit τουτέστι, τὰ προστάγ-

"Through the veil" (he says) "of His flesh." For this flesh first cut that way, by this He inaugurated it [the way] by which He walked. And with good reason did he call [the flesh] "a veil."[1] For when it was lifted up on high, then the things in heaven appeared.

"Let us draw near" (he says) "with a true heart." To what should we "draw near"? To the holy things, the faith, the spiritual service. "With a true heart, in full assurance of faith," since nothing is seen; neither the priest henceforward, nor the sacrifice, nor the altar. And yet neither was that priest visible, but stood within, and they all without, the whole people. But here not only has this taken place, that the priest has entered into the holy of holies, but that we also enter in. Therefore he says, "in full assurance of faith." For it is possible for the doubter to believe in one way, as there are even now many who say, that of some there is a resurrection and of others not. But this is not faith. "In full assurance of faith" (he says); for we ought to believe as concerning things that we see, nay, even much more; for "here" it is possible to be deceived in the things that are seen, but there not: "here" we trust to the senses, but there to the Spirit.

"Having our hearts sprinkled from an evil conscience." He shows that not faith only, but a virtuous life also is required, and the consciousness to ourselves of nothing evil. Since the holy of holies does not receive "with full assurance" those who are not thus disposed. For they are holy, and the holy of holies; but here no profane person enters. They were sprinkled as to the body, we as to the conscience, so that we may even now be sprinkled over with virtue itself. "And having our body washed with pure water." Here he speaks of the Washing, which no longer cleanses the bodies, but the soul.

"For He is faithful that promised." "That promised" what? That we are to depart thither and enter into the kingdom. Be then in nothing over-curious, nor demand reasonings. Our [religion][2] needs faith.

[3.] (Ver. 24, 25) "And" (he says) "let us consider one another to provoke unto love and to good works. Not forsaking the assembling of ourselves together, as the manner of some is, but exhorting[3] one another and so much the more as ye see the day approaching." And again in other places, "The Lord is at hand; be careful for nothing." (Phil. iv. 5, 6.) "For now is our salvation nearer: Henceforth the time is short." (Rom. xiii. 11.)

What is, "not forsaking the assembling of ourselves together"? (1 Cor. vii. 29.) He knew that much strength arises from being together and assembling together. "For where two or three" (it is said) "are gathered together in My name, there am I in the midst of them" (Matt. xviii. 20); and again, "That they may be One, as we" also are (John xvii. 11); and, "They had all one heart and [one] soul." (Acts iv. 32.) And not this only, but also because love is increased by the gathering [of ourselves] together; and love being increased, of necessity the things of God must follow also. "And earnest prayer" (it is said) was "made by" the people. (Acts xii. 5.) "As the manner of some is." Here he not only exhorted, but also blamed [them].

"And let us consider one another," he says, "to provoke unto[4] love and to good works." He knew that this also arises from "gathering together." For as "iron sharpeneth iron" (Prov. xvii. 17), so also association increases love. For if a stone rubbed against a stone sends forth fire, how much more soul mingled with soul! But not unto emulation (he says) but "unto the sharpening of love." What is "unto the sharpening of love"? Unto the loving and being loved more. "And of good works"; that so they might acquire zeal. For if doing has greater force for instruction than speaking, ye also have in your number many teachers, who effect this by their deeds.

What is "let us draw near with a true heart"? That is, without hypocrisy; for "woe be to a fearful heart, and faint hands" (Ecclus. ii. 12): let there be (he means) no falsehood among us; let us not say one thing and think another; for this is falsehood; neither let us be fainthearted, for this is not [a mark] of a "true heart." Faintheartedness comes from not believing. But how shall this be? If we fully assure ourselves through faith.

"Having our hearts sprinkled": why did he not say "having been purified"? [Because] he wished to point out the difference of the sprinklings: the one he says is of God, the other our own. For the washing and sprinkling the conscience is of God; but "the drawing near with" truth and "in full assurance of faith" is our own. Then he also gives strength to their faith from the truth of Him that promised.

What is "and having our bodies washed with pure water"? With water which makes pure; or which has no blood.

Then he adds the perfect thing, love. "Not forsaking the assembling of ourselves together," which some (he says) do, and divide the assemblies.[5]

---

ματα and add οὕτω δηλῶν. Mr. Field thinks the passage may be corrupt; the parenthetic words seem added to explain that it is the Christian *ordinances*, which he understands by the "way that abideth."

[1] [See above, p. 438 and St. Cyril Alex. *Quod Unus Christus*, 761.]

[2] τὰ ἡμέτερα.        [3] or, "encouraging."

[4] εἰς παροξυσμὸν, "to the sharpening" or "exciting of."

[5] [The English edition here inserts, "This he forbids them [to do]," from τοῦτο αὐτοῖς ἀπαγορεύει of the Benedictine text, supported by some MSS., but omitted by Mr. Field.—F. G.]

For " a brother helped by a brother is as a strong city." (Prov. xviii. 19, LXX.)

" But let us consider one another to provoke unto love." What is, " let us consider one another"? For instance if any be virtuous, let us imitate him, let us look on him so as to love and to be loved. For from Love good works proceed. For the assembling is a great good : since it makes love more warm ; and out of love all good things arise. For nothing is good which is not done through love.

[4.] This then let us " confirm "[1] towards each other. "For love is the fulfilling of the law." (Rom. xiii. 10.) We have no need of labors or of sweatings if we love one another. It is a pathway leading of itself towards virtue. For as on the highway, if any man find the beginning, he is guided by it, and has no need of one to take him by the hand ; so is it also in regard to Love : only lay hold on the beginning, and at once thou art guided and directed by it. " Love worketh no ill to his neighbor " (Rom. xiii. 10) ; "thinketh no evil." (1 Cor. xiii. 5.) Let each man consider with himself, how he is disposed toward himself. He does not envy himself ; he wishes all good things for himself ; he prefers himself before all ; he is willing to do all things for himself. If then we were so disposed towards others also, all grievous things are brought to an end ; there is no enmity ; there is no covetousness : for who would choose to overreach himself? No man ; but on the contrary we shall possess all things in common, and shall not cease assembling ourselves together. And if we do this, the remembrance of injuries would have no place : for who would choose to remember injuries against himself? Who would choose to be angry with himself? Do we not make allowances for ourselves most of all? If we were thus disposed towards our neighbors also, there will never be any remembrance of injuries.

And how is it possible (you say) that one should so love his neighbor as himself? If others had not done this, you might well think it impossible : but if they have done it, it is plain that from indolence it is not done by ourselves.

And besides, Christ enjoins nothing impossible, seeing that many have even gone beyond His commands. Who has done this? Paul, Peter, all the company of the Saints. Nay, indeed if I say that they loved their neighbors, I say no great matter : they so loved their enemies as no man would love those who were likeminded with himself. For who would choose for the sake of those likeminded, to go away into Hell, when he was about to depart unto a

kingdom? No man. But Paul chose this for the sake of his enemies, for those who stoned him, those who scourged him. What pardon then will there be for us, what excuse, if we shall not show towards our friends even the very smallest portion of that love which Paul showed towards his enemies?

And before him too, the blessed Moses was willing to be blotted out of God's book for the sake of his enemies who had stoned him. David also when he saw those who had stood up against him slain, saith, " I, the shepherd, have sinned, but these, what have they done ? " (See 2 Sam. xxiv. 17.) And when he had Saul in his hands, he would not slay him, but saved him ; and this when he himself would be in danger. But if these things were done under the Old [Covenant] what excuse shall we have who live under the New, and do not attain even to the same measure with them? For if, " unless our righteousness exceed that of the Scribes and Pharisees, we shall not enter into the kingdom of Heaven " (Matt. v. 20), how shall we enter in when we have even less than they?

[5.] " Love your enemies," He says. (Matt. v. 44.) Love thou therefore thy enemy : for thou art doing good not to him, but to thyself. How? Thou art becoming like God. He, if he be beloved of thee, hath no great gain, for he is beloved by a fellow-slave ; but thou, if thou love thy fellow-slave, hast gained much, for thou art becoming like God. Seest thou that thou art doing a kindness not to him but to thyself? For He appoints the prize not for him, but for thee.

What then if he be evil (you say) ? So much the greater is the reward. Even for his wickedness thou oughtest to feel grateful to him : even should he be evil after receiving ten thousand kindnesses. For if he were not exceedingly evil, thy reward would not have been exceedingly increased ; so that the reason [thou assignest] for not loving him, the saying that he is evil, is the very reason for loving him. Take away the contestant and thou takest away the opportunity for the crowns. Seest thou not the athletes, how they exercise when they have filled the bags with sand? But there is no need for thee to practice this. Life is full of things that exercise thee, and make thee strong. Seest thou not the trees too, the more they are shaken by the winds, so much the more do they become stronger and firmer? We then, if we be long-suffering, shall also become strong. For it is said, " a man who is long-suffering abounds in wisdom, but he that is of a little soul is strongly foolish." (Prov. xiv. 29.) Seest thou how great is his commendation of the one, seest thou how great his censure of the other ? " Strongly foolish," i.e. very [foolish].

---

[1] See 2 Cor. ii. 8.

Let us not then be faint-hearted[1] one towards another : for this does not rise from enmity, but from having a small soul. As if the soul be strong, it will endure all things easily, and nothing will be able to sink it, but will lead it into tranquil havens. To which may we all attain, by the grace and lovingkindness of our Lord Jesus Christ, with whom to the Father together with the Holy Ghost, be glory, power, honor, now and for ever and world without end. Amen.

# HOMILY XX.

## Hebrews x. 26, 27.

" For if we sin willfully, after we have received the knowledge of the truth, there remaineth no more[2] sacrifice for sins, but a certain fearful looking for of judgment, and fiery indignation[3] which shall devour the adversaries."

[1.] TREES which have been planted, and have had the advantage of all other care, and the hands and the labors of the cultivator, and yet yield no return for the labors, are pulled up by the roots, and handed over to the fire. So somewhat of this kind takes place also in the case of our Illumination.[4] For when Christ has planted us, and we have enjoyed the watering of the Spirit, and then show no fruit ; fire, even that of Hell, awaits us, and flame unquenchable.

Paul therefore having exhorted them to love, and to bringing forth the fruit of good works, and having urged them from the kindlier [considerations] (What are these? That we have an entrance into the holy of holies, " the new way which He hath inaugurated for us." — c. x. 20), does the same again from the more gloomy ones, speaking thus. For having said, " not forsaking the assembling of ourselves together, as the manner of some is, but exhorting[5] one another, and so much the more, as ye see the day approaching" (c. x. 25), this being sufficient for consolation, he added, " For if we sin willfully after we have received the knowledge of the truth." There is need, he means, of good works, yea, very great need, " For if we sin willfully after we have received the knowledge of the truth, there remaineth no more sacrifice for sins." Thou wast cleansed ; thou wast set free from the charges against thee, thou hast become a son. If then thou return to thy former vomit, there awaits thee on the other hand excommunication and fire and whatever such things there are. For there is no second sacrifice.

[2.] At this place we are again assailed by those who take away repentance,[6] and by those who delay to come to baptism. The one saying, that it is not safe for them to come to baptism, since there is no second remission : And the other asserting that it is not safe to impart the mysteries[7] to those who have sinned, if there is no second remission.

What shall we say then to them both? That he does not take away repentance, nor the propitiation through repentance, nor does he thrust away and cast down with despair the fallen. He is not thus an enemy of our salvation ; but what? He takes away the second Washing. For he did not say, no more[8] is there repentance, or no more is there remission, but " no more " is there a " sacrifice," that is, there is no more a second Cross.[9] For this is what he means by sacrifice. " For by one sacrifice," he says, " He hath perfected forever them that are sanctified " (c. x. 14) ; not like the Jewish [rites]. For this reason he has treated· so much throughout concerning the Sacrifice, that it is one, even one ; not wishing to show this only, that herein it differed from the Jewish [rites], but also to make [men] more steadfast, so that they might no longer expect another sacrifice according to the Jewish law.

" For," saith he, " if we sin willfully." See how he is disposed to pardon. He says, " if we sin willfully," so that there is pardon for those [who sin] not willfully. " After the knowledge of the truth " : He either means, of Christ, or of all doctrines. " There remaineth no more sacrifice for sins," but what? " A certain fearful looking for of judgment and fiery indignation which shall devour the adversaries." By " Adversaries " he means not the unbelievers, but those also who do what is against virtue ; or [else he means] that the same fire shall receive them of the household also, which [receives] " the adversaries." Then expressing its devouring nature, he says, as if giving it life, " fiery indignation which shall devour the adversaries." For as a wild beast when irritated and very fierce and savage, would

---

[1] μικροψυχῶμεν.
[2] οὐκέτι.
[3] lit. " indignation of fire."
[4] i.e. Baptism.
[5] " encouraging."
[6] The Novatians, who refused to admit to Penitence and the Sacraments those who had fallen into deadly sin after Baptism.
[7] The Holy Eucharist.
[8] οὐκέτι.
[9] Compare Hom. ix. [5], p. 410.

not rest till it could lay hold on some one and eat him up ; so also that fire, like one goaded by indignation, whatever it can lay hold of does not let go, but devours and tears it to pieces.

[3.] Next he adds also the reason of the threat, that it is on good grounds, that it is just ; for this contributes to confidence, when we show that it is just.

For, he says, (ver. 28) "He that hath despised Moses' law dies without mercy, under two or three witnesses." "Without mercy," he says ; so that there is no pardon, no pity there ; although the law is of Moses ; for he ordained the most of it.

What is "under two or three"? If two or three bore witness, he means, they immediately suffered punishment.

If then under the Old [Covenant], when the law of Moses is set at nought, there is so great punishment, (ver. 29) "Of how much sorer punishment, suppose ye, shall he be thought worthy, who hath trodden under foot the Son of God, and hath counted the blood of the covenant an unholy [a common] thing, and hath done despite unto the Spirit of grace?"

And how does a man "tread under foot the Son of God"? When partaking of Him in the mysteries (he would say) he has wrought sin, has he not trodden Him under foot? Has he not despised Him? For just as we make no account of those who are trodden under foot, so also, they who sin have made no account of Christ ; and so they have sinned. Thou art[1] become the Body of Christ, and givest thou thyself to the devil, so that he treads thee under foot.

"And accounted the blood a common thing," he says. What is "common"? It is "unclean," or the having nothing beyond other things.

"And done despite unto the Spirit of grace." For he that accepts not a benefit, does despite to the benefactor. He made thee a son : and thou wishest to become a slave. He came to dwell with thee, and thou bringest in wicked imaginations to Him. Christ wished to stay with thee : and thou treadest Him down by surfeiting, by drunkenness.

Let us listen, whoever partake of the mysteries unworthily : let us listen, whoever approach that Table unworthily. "Give not" (He says) "that which is holy unto the dogs, lest in time they trample them under their feet" (Matt. vii. 6), that is, lest they despise, lest they repudiate [them]. Yet he did not say this, but what was more fearful than this. For he constrains their souls by what is fearful. For this also is adapted to convert, no less than consolation. And at the same time he shows both the difference, and the chastisement, and sets forth the judgment upon them, as though it were an evident matter. "Of how much sorer punishment, suppose ye, shall he be thought worthy?" Here also he appears to me to hint at the mysteries.

[4.] Next he adds testimony, saying, (ver. 31, 30) "It is a fearful thing to fall into the hands of the Living God." "For." it is written : "Vengeance [belongeth] unto Me, I will recompense, saith the Lord. And again, The Lord shall judge His people." "Let us fall," it is said, "into the hands of the Lord, and not into the hands of men." (Ecclus. ii. 18.[2]) But if ye repent not, ye shall "fall into the hands of" God : that is fearful : it is nothing, to "fall into the hands of men." When, he means, we see any man punished here, let us not be terrified at the things present, but shudder at the things to come. "For according to His mercy, so is His wrath."[3] And, "His indignation will rest upon sinners." (Ecclus. v. 6.)

At the same time too he hints at something else. For "Vengeance [belongeth] unto Me," he says, "I will recompense." This is said in regard to their enemies, who are doing evil, not to those who are suffering evil. Here he is consoling them too, all but saying, God abideth for ever and liveth, so that even if they receive not [their reward] now, they will receive it hereafter. They ought to groan, not we : for we indeed shall fall into their hands, but they into the hands of God. For neither is it the sufferer who suffers the ill, but he that does it ; nor is it he who receives a benefit that is benefited, but the benefactor.

[5.] Knowing then these things, let us be patient as to suffering evil, forward as to kindnesses. And this will be, if we think lightly of wealth and honor. He that hath stripped himself of those affections, is of all men most generous, and more wealthy even than he who wears the purple. Seest thou not how many evils come through money? I do not say how many through covetousness, but merely by our attachment to these things. For instance, if a man has lost his money, he leads a life more wretched than any death. Why grievest thou, O man? why weepest thou? Because God has delivered Thee from excessive watching? Because thou dost not sit trembling and fearful? Again, if any one chain thee to a treasure, commanding thee to sit there perpetually, and to keep watch for other people's goods, thou art grieved, thou art disgusted ; and dost thou, after thou hast bound thyself with most grievous chains, grieve when thou art delivered from the slavery?

---

[1] or, "Art thou . . . dost thou give?"

[2] [Or better, 2 Sam. xxiv. 14. — F. G.]

[3] St. Chrys. may have had in mind the latter part of the verse just cited, Ecclus. ii. 18, "for as His majesty is, so is His mercy," and combined it with the first part of the verse he next cites, Ecclus. v. 6, "For mercy and wrath come from Him," &c.

Truly sorrows and joys are [matters] of fancy.[1] For we guard them as if we had another's.

Now my discourse is for the women. A woman often has a garment woven with gold, and this she shakes, wraps up in linen, keeps with care, trembles for it, and has no enjoyment of it. For either she dies, or she becomes a widow. Or, even if none of these things happen, yet from fear lest wearing it out by continual use, she should deprive herself of it, she deprives herself of it in another way, by sparing it. But she passes it on [you say] to another. But neither is this clear: and even if she should pass it on, the other again will also use it in the same way. And if any one will search their houses, he will find that the most costly garments and other choice things, are tended with special honor, as if they were living masters. For she does not use them habitually, but fears and trembles, driving away moths and the other things that are wont to eat them, and laying most of them in perfumes and spices, nor permitting all persons to be counted worthy of the sight of them, but oftentimes carefully putting them in order herself with her husband.

Tell me: did not Paul with reason call covetousness "idolatry"? (Col. iii. 5.) For these show as great honor to their garments, their gold, as they to their idols.

[6.] How long shall we stir up the mire? How long shall we be fixed to the clay and the brickmaking? For as they toiled for the King of the Egyptians, so do we also toil for the devil, and are scourged with far more grievous stripes. For by how much the soul surpasses the body, by so much does anxiety the weals of scourging. We are scourged every day, we are full of fear, in anxiety, in trembling. But if we will groan, if we will look up to God, He sendeth to us, not Moses, nor Aaron, but His own Word, and compunction. When this [word] has come, and taken hold of our souls, He will free from the bitter slavery, He will bring us forth out of Egypt, from unprofitable and vain zeal, from slavery which brings no gain. For they indeed went forth after having at least received golden [ornaments], the wages for building, but we [receive] nothing: and would it were nothing. For indeed we also receive, not golden ornaments, but the evils of Egypt, sins and chastisements and punishments.

Let us then learn to be made use of, let us learn to be spitefully treated; this is the part of a Christian. Let us think lightly of golden raiment, let us think lightly of money, that we may not think lightly of our salvation. Let us think lightly of money and not think lightly of

the soul. For this is chastised, this is punished: those things remain here, but the soul departeth yonder. Why, tell me, dost thou cut thyself to pieces, without perceiving it?

[7.] These things I say to the overreaching. And it is well to say also to those who are overreached. Bear their overreachings generously; they are ruining themselves, not you. You indeed they defraud of your money, but they strip themselves of the good will and help of God. And he that is stripped of that, though he clothe himself with the whole wealth of the world, is of all men most poor: and so he who is the poorest of all, if he have this, is the wealthiest of all. For "the Lord" (it is said) "is my shepherd, and I shall lack nothing." (Ps. xxiii. 1.)

Tell me now, if thou hadst had a husband, a great and admirable man, who thoroughly loved thee and cared for thee, and then knewest that he would live always, and not die before thee, and would give thee all things to enjoy in security, as thine own: wouldst thou then have wished to possess anything? Even if thou hadst been stripped of all, wouldst thou not have thought thyself the richer for this?

Why then dost thou grieve? Because thou hast no property? But consider that thou hast had the occasion of sin taken away. But is it because thou hadst [property] and hast been deprived of it? But thou hast acquired the good will of God. And how have I acquired it (you say)? He has said, "Wherefore do ye not rather suffer wrong?" (1 Cor. vi. 7.) He hath said, "Blessed are they who bear all things with thankfulness."[2] Consider therefore how great good will thou wilt enjoy, if thou showest forth those things by [thy] works. For one thing only is required from us, "in all things to give thanks" to God, and [then] we have all things in abundance. I mean, for instance: hast thou lost ten thousand pounds of gold? Forthwith give thanks unto God, and thou hast acquired ten times ten thousand, by that word and thanksgiving.

[8.] For tell me when dost thou account Job blessed? When he had so many camels, and flocks, and herds, or when he uttered that saying: "The Lord gave, the Lord hath taken away"? (Job i. 21.) Therefore also the devil causes us losses, not that he may take away our goods only, for he knows that is nothing, but that through them he may compel us to utter some blasphemy. So in the case of the blessed Job too, he did not strive after this only, to make him poor, but also to make him a blasphemer. At any rate, when he had stripped him of every-

---

[2] It does not appear what passage of Scripture St. Chrys. referred to: the altered text has, "He hath said: 'In everything give thanks.' He hath said, 'Blessed are the poor in spirit.'"

thing, observe what he says to him through his wife, "Say some word against the Lord, and die." (Job ii. 9.) And yet, O accursed one, thou hadst stripped him of everything. ' But ' (he says) ' this is not what I was striving for; for I have not yet accomplished that for which I did all. I was striving to deprive him of God's help : for this cause I deprived him of his goods too. This is what I wish, that other is nothing. If this be not gained, he not only has not been injured at all, but has even been benefited.' Thou seest that even that wicked demon knows how great is the loss in this matter?

And see him plotting the treachery through the wife. Hear this, ye husbands, as many as have wives that are fond of money, and compel you to blaspheme God. Call Job to mind. But let us see, if it please you, his great moderation, how he silenced her. "Wherefore" (he says) "hast thou spoken as one of the foolish women [speaketh]?" (Job ii. 10.) Of a truth "evil communications corrupt good manners" (1 Cor. xv. 33), at all times indeed, but particularly in calamities : then they who give evil advice have strength. For if the soul is even of itself prone to impatience, how much more, when there is also an adviser. Is it not thrust into a pit? A wife is a great good, as also a great evil. For because a wife is a great [good], observe from what point he [Satan] wishes to break through the strong wall. ' The depriving him of his property' (he says) ' did not take him ; the loss has produced no great effect.' Therefore he says, ' If indeed he will curse thee to thy face.' (Job ii. 5.) You see whither he was aspiring.[1]

If then we bear [losses] thankfully, we shall recover even these things ; and if we should not recover them, our reward will be greater. For when he had wrestled nobly, then God restored to him these things also. When He had shown the devil, that it is not for these things that he serves Him, then He restored them also to him.

[9.] For such is He. When God sees that we are not riveted to things of this life, then He gives them to us. When He sees that we set a higher value on things spiritual, then He also bestows on us things carnal. But not first,

lest we should break away from things spiritual : and to spare us He does not give carnal things, to keep us away from them, even against our will.

Not so (you say) but if I receive [them], I am satisfied, and am the more thankful. It is false, O man, for then especially wilt thou be thoughtless.

Why then (you say) does He give [them] to many? Whence is it clear, that He gives [them]? But who else, you say, gives? Their overreaching, their plundering. How then does He allow these things? As He also [allows] murders, thefts, and violence.

What then (you will say) as to those who receive by succession an inheritance from their fathers, being themselves full of evils innumerable? And what of this? How does God suffer them (you say) to enjoy these things? Surely just as He allows thieves, and murderers, and other evil doers. For it is not now the time of judgment, but of the best course of life.

And what I just now said, that I repeat, that they shall suffer greater punishment, who, when they have enjoyed all good things, do not even so become better. For all shall not be punished alike ; but they who, even after His benefits, have continued evil, shall suffer a greater punishment, while they who after poverty [have done this] not so. And that this is true, hear what He says to David, "Did I not give thee all thy master's goods?" (2 Sam. xii. 8.) Whenever then thou seest a young man that has received a paternal inheritance without labor and continues wicked, be assured that his punishment is increased and the vengeance is made more intense. Let us not then emulate these ; but if any man has succeeded to virtue, if any man has obtained spiritual wealth, [him let us emulate]. For (it is said) "Woe to them that trust in their riches" (cf. Ps. xlix. 6) : "Blessed are they that fear the Lord." (Ps. cxxviii. 1.) To which of these, tell me, wouldst thou belong? Doubtless to those who are pronounced blessed. Therefore emulate these, not the other, that thou also mayest obtain the good things which are laid up for them. Which may we all obtain, in Christ Jesus our Lord, with whom to the Father be glory together with the Holy Ghost, now and for ever, and world without end. Amen.

---

[1] που ἔπνει.

# HOMILY XXI.

### HEBREWS x. 32-34.

" But call to remembrance the former days, in which after
ye were illuminated, ye endured a great fight of
afflictions;[1] partly, whilst ye were made a gazing
stock both by reproaches and afflictions,[2] and partly
whilst ye became companions of them that were so
used.　For ye had compassion on those who were
in bonds,[3] and took joyfully the spoiling of your
goods, knowing that ye have for yourselves[4] in heaven
a better and an enduring substance."

[1.] THE best Physicians after they have
made a deep incision, and have increased the
pains by the wound, soothing the afflicted part,
and giving rest and refreshment to the disturbed
soul, proceed not to make a second incision, but
rather soothe that which has been made with
gentle remedies, and such as are suited to remove
the violence of the pain.　This Paul also did,
after he had shaken their souls, and pierced
them with the recollection of Hell, and convinced then, that he must certainly perish, who
does despite to the grace of God, and after he
had shown from the laws of Moses, that they
also shall perish, and the more [fearfully], and
confirm it by other testimonies, and had said,
" It is a fearful thing to fall into the hands of
the Living God" (c. x. 31) : then, lest the
soul desponding through excessive fear, should
be swallowed up with grief, he soothes them
by commendations and exhortation, and gives
them zeal derived from their own conduct.　For,
he says, " call to remembrance the former days,
in which after ye had been enlightened, ye endured a great fight of afflictions."　Powerful is
the exhortation from deeds [already done] :
for he who begins a work ought to go forward
and add to it.　As if he had said, when ye were
brought in[5] [to the Church], when ye were in
the rank of learners, ye displayed so great readiness, so great nobleness ; but now it is no longer
so.　And he who encourages, does thus especially encourage them from their own example.

And he did not simply say, " ye endured a
fight "[6] but a " great " [fight].　Moreover he did
not say " temptations " but " fight," which is an
expression of commendation and of very great
praise.

Then he also enumerates them particularly,
amplifying his discourse, and multiplying his
praise.　How?　" Partly " (he says) " whilst ye
were made a gazing-stock by reproaches and
afflictions " ; for reproach is a great thing, and
calculated to pervert the soul, and to darken the
judgment.　For hear what the prophet says :[7]
" While they daily say unto me, Where is thy
God?" (Ps. xlii. 10.)　And again, " If the enemy
had reproached me, I would have borne it."
(Ps. lv. 12.)　For since the human race is exceedingly vainglorious, therefore it is easily
overcome by this.

And he did not simply say " by reproaches,"
but that even with great intensity, being " made
a gazing-stock."[8]　For when a person is reproached alone, it is indeed painful, but far more
so when in presence of all.　For tell me how great
the evil was when men who had left the meanness of Judaism, and gone over, as it were, to
the best course of life, and despised the customs
of their fathers, were ill treated by their own
people, and had no help.

[2.] I cannot say (he says) that ye suffered
these things indeed and were grieved, but ye
even rejoiced exceedingly.　And this he expressed by saying, " Whilst ye became companions of them that were so used," and he brings
forward the Apostles themselves.　Not only (he
means) were ye not ashamed of your own sufferings, but ye even shared with others who were
suffering the same things.　This too is the language of one who is encouraging them.　He said
not, ' Bear my afflictions, share with me,' but
respect your own.

" Ye had compassion on them that were in
bonds."[9]　Thou seest that he is speaking concerning himself and the rest who were in prison.
Thus ye did not account " bonds " to be bonds :
but as noble wrestlers so stood ye : for not
only ye needed no consolation in your own
[distresses], but even became a consolation to
others.

And " ye took joyfully the spoiling of your
goods."　O ! what " full assurance of faith " !
(c. x. 22.)　Then he also sets forth the motive, not only consoling them for their strug-
gles, but also that they might not be shaken
from the Faith.　When ye saw your property

---

[1] παθημάτων.　　　　　[2] θλίψεσι.
[3] τοῖς δεσμίοις.　This is held to be the true reading of the sacred
text: τοῖς δεσμοῖς μου was substituted here, but not in the body of
the Homily, in some MSS. and in the editions of St. Chrys. before
the Benedictine.
[4] ἑαυτοῖς without ἐν is the approved reading of the sacred text,
and is found in all the MSS. and Edd. of St. Chrys.　[It is the reading in the margin of the A. V. and of the R. V.　There is but slight
authority for the ἐν.　" In heaven " is also omitted by the more important authorities, the critical editors, and by the R. V. — F. G.]
[5] ἐνήγεσθε.　　　[6] ἄθλησιν,'a contest, as that of wrestlers.

[7] The common editions have the entire text, " My tears have
been my meat day and night, while," &c.
[8] θεατριζόμενοι.
[9] A catena, the Verona editions, and perhaps one MS. have " with
my bonds."

plundered (he means) ye endured ; for already ye saw Him who is invisible, as visible : which was the effect of genuine faith, and ye showed it forth by your deeds themselves.

Well then, the plundering was perhaps from the force of the plunderers, and no man could prevent it ; so that as yet it is not clear, that ye endured the plundering for the faith's sake. (Although this too is clear. For it was in your power if you chose, not to be plundered, by not believing.) But ye did what is far greater than this ; the enduring such things even " with joy " ; which was altogether apostolical, and worthy of those noble souls, who rejoiced when scourged. For, it says, " they departed from the presence of the council, rejoicing that they were counted worthy to suffer shame for the Name." [1] (Acts v. 41.) But he that endures " with joy," shows that he has some reward, and that the affair is no loss but a gain.

Moreover the expression " ye took " [2] shows their willing endurance, because, he means, ye chose and accepted.

" Knowing " (he says) " that ye have for yourselves in heaven a better and an enduring substance " ; instead of saying, firm, not perishing like this.

[3.] In the next place, having praised them, he says, (ver. 35) " Cast not away therefore your confidence, which hath great recompense of reward." What meanest thou ? He did not say, ' ye have cast it away, and recover it ' : but, which tended more to strengthen them, " ye have it," he says. For to recover again that which has been cast away, requires more labor : but not to lose that which is held fast does not. But to the Galatians he says the very opposite : " My children of whom I travail in birth again, till Christ be formed in you " (Gal. iv. 19) ; and with reason ; for they were more supine, whence they needed a sharper word ; but these were more faint-hearted, so that they rather needed what was more soothing.

" Cast not away therefore " (he says) " your confidence," so that they were in great confidence towards God. " Which hath " (he says) " great recompense of reward." " And when shall we receive them (some one might say) ? Behold ! All things on our part have been done." Therefore he anticipated them on their own supposition, saying in effect, If ye know that ye have in heaven a better substance, seek nothing here.

" For ye have need of patience," not of any addition [to your labors], that ye may continue in the same state, that ye may not cast away what has been put into your hands. Ye need nothing else, but so to stand as ye have stood, that when ye come to the end, ye may receive the promise.

(Ver. 36) " For " (he says) " ye have need of patience, that after ye have done the will of God, ye might receive the promise." Ye have need of one thing only, to bear with the delay ; not that ye should fight again. Ye are at the very crown (he means) ; ye have borne all the combats of bonds, of afflictions ; your goods have been spoiled. What then ? Henceforward ye are standing to be crowned : endure this only, the delay of the crown. O the greatness of the consolation ! It is as if one should speak to an athlete who had overthrown all, and had no antagonist, and then was to be crowned, and yet endured not that time, during which the president of the games comes, and places the crown [upon him] ; and he impatient, should wish to go out, and escape as though he could not bear the thirst and the heat.

He then also hinting this, what does he say ? (Ver. 37) " Yet a little while and He that shall come will come, and will not tarry." For lest they should say, And when will He come ? He comforts them from the Scriptures. For thus also when he says in another place, " Now is our salvation nearer " (Rom. xiii. 11), he comforts them because the remaining time is short. And this he says not of himself but from the Scriptures. [3] But if from that time it was said, " Yet a little while, and He that shall come will come, and will not tarry," it is plain that now He is nearer. Wherefore also waiting is no small reward.

(Ver. 38) " Now the just " (he says) " shall live by faith, but if any man draw back, My soul shall have no pleasure in him." This is a great encouragement when one shows that they have succeeded in the whole matter and are losing it through a little indolence. (Ver. 39) " But we are not of them that draw back unto perdition, but of them that believe to the saving of the soul."

[4.] (c. xi. 1, 2) " Now faith is the substance [4] of things hoped for, the evidence of things not seen. For by it the elders obtained a good report." O what an expression has he used, in saying, " an evidence of things not seen." For [we say] there is " evidence," in the case of things that are very plain. [5] Faith then is the seeing things not plain (he means), and brings what are not seen to the same full

[1] κατηξιώθησαν ὑπὲρ τοῦ ὀνόματος ἀτιμασθῆναι. The common editions of St. Chrys. as the common text of the New Testament, add αὐτοῦ, " His Name," in this and in other places.

[2] προσεδέξασθε.

[3] It is to be observed that the words " He that cometh will come and will not tarry," are from the prophet Habakkuk ii. 3: where the LXX. has, ἐὰν ὑστερήσῃ ὑπόμεινον αὐτὸν (" Him " not " it.") ὅτι ἐρχόμενος ἥξει, καὶ οὐ μὴ χρονίσῃ, &c. The Apostle interprets this by adding the article: ὁ ἐρχόμενος, the well-known designation of the Messiah. [4] " substantiality."

[5] δῆλων. Savile and Morell following some MSS. read ἀδήλων, " obscure " : but St. Chrys. means that we use the word ἔλεγχος of a proof which makes things most certain and evident [and so Mutianus read. — F. G.].

assurance with what are seen. So then neither is it possible to disbelieve in things which are seen, nor, on the other hand can there be faith, unless a man be more fully assured with respect to things invisible, than he is with respect to things that are most clearly seen. For since the objects of hope seem to be unsubstantial, Faith gives them substantiality,[1] or rather, does not give it, but is itself their substance.[2] For instance, the Resurrection has not come, nor does it exist substantially, but hope makes it substantial in our soul. This is [the meaning of] "the substance of things."

If therefore it is an "evidence of things not seen," why forsooth do you wish to see them, so as to fall away from faith, and from being just?[3] Since "the just shall live by faith," whereas ye, if ye wish to see these things, are no longer faithful. Ye have labored (he says), ye have struggled: I too allow this, nevertheless, wait; for this is Faith: do not seek the whole "here."

[5.] These things were indeed said to the Hebrews, but they are a general exhortation also to many of those who are here assembled. How, and in what way? To the faint-hearted; to the mean-spirited. For when they see the wicked prospering, and themselves faring ill, they are troubled, they bear it impatiently: while they long for the chastisement, and the inflicting vengeance on others; while they wait for the rewards of their own sufferings. "For yet a little time, and He that shall come will come."

Let us then say this to the slothful: Doubtless there will be punishment; doubtless He will come, henceforth the events of the[4] Resurrection are even at the doors.

Whence [does] that [appear] (you say)? I do not say, from the prophets; for neither do I now speak to Christians only; but even if a heathen be here, I am perfectly confident, and bring forward my proofs, and will instruct him. How (you say)?

Christ foretold many things. If those former things did not come to pass, then do not believe them; but if they all came to pass, why doubt concerning those that remain? And indeed, it were very unreasonable,[5] nothing having come to pass, to believe the one, or when all has come to pass, to disbelieve the others.

But I will make the matter more plain by an example. Christ said, that Jerusalem should be taken, and should be so taken as no city ever was before, and that it should never be raised up: and in fact this prediction came to pass. He said, that there should be "great tribulation" (Matt. xxiv. 21), and it came to pass. He said that a grain of mustard seed is sown, so should

the preaching [of the Gospel] be extended: and every day we see this running over the world. He said, that they who left father or mother, or brethren, or sisters, should have both fathers and mothers; And this we see fulfilled by facts. He said, "in the world ye shall have tribulation, but be of good cheer, I have overcome the world" (John xvi. 33), that is, no man shall get the better of you. And this we see by the events has come to pass. He said that "the gates of hell shall not prevail against the Church" (Matt. xvi. 18), even though persecuted, and that no one shall quench the preaching [of the Gospel]: and the experience of events bears witness to this prediction also: and yet when He said these things, it was very hard to believe Him. Why? Because all these were words, and He had not as yet given proof of the things spoken. So that they have now become far more credible. He said that "when the Gospel should have been preached among all the nations, then the end shall come" (Matt. xxiv. 14); lo! now ye have arrived at the end: for the greater part of the world hath been preached to, therefore the end is now at hand. Let us tremble, beloved.

[6.] But what, tell me? Art thou anxious about the end? It indeed is itself near, but each man's life and death is nearer.[6] For it is said, "the days of our years are seventy years; but if [one be] in strength, fourscore years." (Ps. xc. 10; [LXX. lxxxix. 10].) The day of judgment is near. Let us fear. "A brother doth not redeem; shall man redeem?" (Ps. xlix. 7; [LXX. xlviii. 8].) There we shall repent much, "but in death no man shall praise Him." (Ps. vi. 5; [LXX. 6].) Wherefore he saith, "Let us come before His presence with thanksgiving" (Ps. xcv. 2; [LXX. xciv.]), that is, his coming. For here [in this life] indeed, whatever we do has efficacy; but there, no longer. Tell me, if a man placed us for a little while in a flaming furnace, should we not submit to anything in order to escape, even were it necessary to part with our money, nay to undergo slavery? How many have fallen into grievous diseases, and would gladly give up all, to be delivered from them, if the choice were offered them? If in this world then, a disease of short duration so afflicts us, what shall we do yonder, when repentance will be of no avail?

[7.] Of how many evils are we now full, without being conscious of them? We bite one another, we devour one another, in wronging, accusing, calumniating, being vexed by the credit of our neighbors. (Cf. Gal. v. 15.)

And see the difficulty.[7] When a man wishes

---

[1] ὑπόστασιν.
[2] οὐσία.
[3] or, "righteous."

[4] τὰ τῆς ἀ.
[5] ἀπίθανον.

[6] ἡ δὲ ἑκάστου ζωὴ ἐγγυτέρα πολλῷ καὶ ἡ τελευτή. But Mut. "sed et vitæ finis uniuscujuscunque prope est."
[7] τὸ χαλεπόν.

to undermine the reputation of a neighbor, he says, 'Such an one said this of him ; O God, forgive me, do not examine me strictly, I must give account of what I have heard.'[1] Why then dost thou speak of it at all, if thou dost not believe it? Why dost thou speak of it? Why dost thou make it credible by much reporting? Why dost thou pass on the story which is not true? Thou dost not believe it, and thou entreatest God not to call thee to strict account? Do not say it then, but keep silence, and free thyself from all fear.

But I know not from whence this disease has fallen upon men. We have become tattlers, nothing remains[2] in our mind. Hear the exhortation of a wise man who says, " Hast thou heard a word? Let it die in[3] thee, be bold ; it will not burst thee." (Ecclus. xix. 10.) And again, " A fool heareth a word, and travaileth, as a women in labor of a child." (Ecclus. xix. 11.) We are ready to make accusations, prepared for condemning. Even if no other evil thing had been done by us, this were sufficient to ruin us, and to carry us away to Hell, this involves us in ten thousand evils. And that thou mayest know this certainly, hear what the prophet says, " Thou satest and spakest against thy brother." (Ps. l. 20.)

But it is not I, you say, but the other [who told me]. Nay rather, it is thyself; for if *thou* hadst not spoken, another would not have heard : or even if he should hear it, yet *thou* wouldest not have been to blame for the sin. We ought to shade over and conceal the failings of neighbors, but thou paradest them under a cloak of zeal for goodness. Thou becomest, not an accuser, but a gossip, a trifler, a fool. O what cleverness ! Without being aware of it, thou bringest disgrace upon thyself as well as on him.

And see what great evils which arise from this. Thou provokest the wrath of God. Dost thou not hear Paul saying about widows, " they not only " (these are his words) " learn to be idle, but tattlers also and busybodies, wandering about from house to house, and speaking things which they ought not." (1 Tim. v. 13.) So that even when thou believest the things which are said against thy brother, thou oughtest not even in that case to speak of them ; much less, when thou dost not believe them.

But thou [forsooth] lookest to thine own interest? Thou fearest to be called to account by God? Fear then, lest even for thy tattling thou be called to account. For here, thou canst not say, ' O God, call me not to account for light

talking ' : for the whole matter is light talking. Why didst thou publish it? Why didst thou increase the evil? This is sufficient to destroy us. On this account Christ said, " Judge not, that ye be not judged." (Matt. vii. 1.)

But we pay no regard to this, neither are we brought to our senses by what happened to the Pharisee. He said what was true, " I am not as this Publican " (Luke xviii. 11), he said it too in no man's hearing ; yet was he condemned. If he were condemned when he said what was true, and uttered it in no man's hearing, what fearful [punishment] shall not they suffer, who like gossiping women, carry about everywhere lies which they do not even themselves believe? What shall they not endure?

[8.] Henceforward let us set "a door and a bolt before the mouth." (Ecclus. xxviii. 25.) For innumerable evils have arisen from tattling ; families have been ruined, friendships torn asunder, innumerable other miseries have happened. Busy not thyself, O man, about the affairs of thy neighbor.

But thou art talkative and hast a weakness. Talk of thine own [faults] to God : thus the weakness will be no longer a weakness, but an advantage. Talk of thy own [faults] to thy friends, those who are thorough friends and righteous men, and in whom thou hast confidence, that so they may pray for thy sins. If thou speak of the [sins] of others, thou art nowise profited, neither hast thou gained anything, but hast ruined thyself. If thou confessest thy own [sins] to the Lord, thou hast great reward : for one says, " I said, I will confess against myself mine iniquity to the Lord, and Thou forgavest the impiety of my heart." (Ps. xxxii. 5.)

Dost thou wish to judge? Judge thine own [sins]. No one will accuse[4] thee, if thou condemn thyself : but he will accuse if thou do not condemn ; he will accuse thee, unless thou convict thyself ; will accuse thee of insensibility. Thou hast seen such an one angry, irritated, doing something else out of place? Think at once, even thou on thy own [faults] : and thus thou wilt not greatly condemn him, and wilt free thyself from the load of thy past transgressions. If we thus regulate our own conduct, if we thus manage our own life, if we condemn ourselves, we shall probably not commit many sins, and we shall do many good things, being fair and moderate ; and shall enjoy all the promises to them that love God : to which may all attain, by the grace and lovingkindness of our Lord Jesus Christ, with whom to the Father together with the Holy Ghost, be glory, power, honor, now and for ever and world with end. Amen.

---

[1] Or might it be read, ἀκοῆς λόγον ὀφείλω ; " am I responsible for what I hear, for common reports? "
[2] ἐναπομένει.
[3] ἐναποθανέτω.
[4] ἐγκαλεῖ.

# HOMILY XXII.

## Hebrews xi. 3, 4.

"Through faith we understand that the worlds were framed by the word of God; so that things which are seen were not made of things which do appear. By faith Abel offered unto God a more excellent sacrifice than Cain, by which he obtained witness[1] that he was righteous, God testifying of his gifts: and by it he being dead yet speaketh."[2]

[1.] FAITH[3] needs a generous and vigorous soul, and one rising above all things of sense, and passing beyond the weakness of human reasonings. For it is not possible to become a believer, otherwise than by raising one's self above the common customs [of the world].

Inasmuch then as the souls of the Hebrews were thoroughly weakened, and though they had begun from faith, yet from circumstances, I mean sufferings, afflictions, they had afterwards become faint-hearted, and of little spirit, and were shaken from [their position], he encouraged them first indeed from these very things, saying, "Call to remembrance the former days" (c. x. 32); next from the Scripture saying, "But the just shall live by faith" (c. x. 38); afterwards from arguments, saying, "But Faith is the substance of things hoped for, the evidence of things not seen." (c. xi. 1.) And now again from their forefathers, those great and admirable men, as much as saying; If where the good things were close at hand, all were saved by faith, much more are we.

For when a soul finds one that shares the same sufferings with itself, it is refreshed and recovers breath. This we may see both in the case of Faith, and in the case of affliction: "that there may be comfort for you[4] it is said through our mutual faith." (Rom. i. 12.) For mankind are very distrustful, and cannot place confidence in themselves, are fearful about whatever things they think they possess, and have great regard for the opinion of the many.

[2.] What then does Paul do? He encourages them by the fathers; and before that by the common notions [of mankind].[5] For tell me, he says, since Faith is calumniated[6] as being a thing without demonstration[7] and rather a matter of deceit, therefore he shows that the greatest things are attained through faith and not through reasonings. And how does he show this, tell me?[8] It is manifest, he saith, that God made the things which are, out of things which are not,[9] things which appear, out of things which appear not, things which subsist, out of things which subsist not. But whence [is it shown] that He did this even "by a Word"? For reason suggests nothing of this kind; but on the contrary, that the things which appear are [formed] out of things which appear.

Therefore the philosophers expressly say that 'nothing comes out of things that are not'[10] being "sensual" (Jude 19), and trusting nothing to Faith. And yet these same men, when they happen to say anything great and noble, are caught entrusting it to Faith. For instance, that "God is without beginning,[11] and unborn"[12]: for reason does not suggest this, but the contrary. And consider, I beseech you, their great folly. They say[13] that God is without beginning; and yet this is far more wonderful than the [creation] out of things that are not. For to say, that He is without beginning, that He is unborn, neither begotten by Himself nor by another is more full of difficulties,[14] than to say that God made the things which are, out of things which are not. For here there are many things uncertain: as, that some one made it, that what was made had a beginning, that, in a word, it was made. But in the other case, what? He is self-existing,[15] unborn, He neither had beginning nor time; tell me, do not these things require faith? But he did not assert this, which was far greater, but the lesser.

Whence [does it appear], he would say, that God made these things? Reason does not suggest it; no one was present when it was done. Whence is it shown? It is plainly the result of faith. "Through faith we understand that the worlds were made." Why "through faith"? Because "the things that are seen were not made of things which do appear." For this is Faith.

[3.] Having thus stated the general [princi-

---

[1] "was testified of."

[2] λαλεῖ, with the most approved MSS. of the Epistle; the editions have λαλεῖται; which is the reading of the common texts of the N. T.

[3] τὸ τῆς πίστεως.

[4] ὥστε εἶναι παράκλησιν ὑμῖν: the common editions follow MSS. in which the very words of Rom. i. 12 have been substituted.

[5] κοινῆς ἐννοίας.

[6] Thus the sentence is inconsequent, as it stands in the best texts: in the common editions it is altered to, "For inasmuch as the Faith was at that time calumniated," &c.　　[7] ἀναπόδεικτον.

[8] At this place and generally throughout the Homily: the later texts and the common editions insert the words of the Epistle, but not so the best MSS. or the old translation.

[9] ἐξ οὐκ ὄντων, i.e. "out of nothing."

[10] "De nihilo nihil" is probably referred to.

[11] ἄναρχος.　　　　　　　　　[12] ἀγέννητος.

[13] λέγοντες, an irregular construction: the common texts substitute λέγουσιν.

[14] ἀπορώτερον.　　　　　　　　[15] αὐτόματος.

ple],[1] he afterwards tests[2] it by individuals. For a man of note is equivalent to the world. This at all events he afterwards hinted. For when he had matched it against one or two hundred persons, and then saw the smallness of the number, he afterwards says, "by whom the world was outweighed in worth."[3] (c. xi. 38.)

And observe whom he puts first, him who was ill-treated, and that by a brother. It was their own affliction,[4] "For you also" (he says) "have suffered like things of your own countrymen." (1 Thess. ii. 14.) And by a brother who had been nothing wronged, but who envied him on God's account; showing that they also are looked on with an evil eye and envied. He honored God, and died because he honored Him: and has not yet attained to a resurrection. But his readiness is manifest, and his part[5] has been done, but God's part has not yet been carried out towards him.

And by a "more excellent sacrifice" in this place, he means that which is more honorable, more splendid, more necessary.

And we cannot say (he says) that it was not accepted. He did accept it, and said unto Cain, ["Hast thou] not [sinned], if thou rightly offer, but dost not rightly divide?" (Gen. iv. 7, LXX.) So then Abel both rightly offered, and rightly divided. Nevertheless for this, what recompense did he receive? He was slain by his brother's hand: and that sentence which his father endured on account of sin, this he first received who was upright. And he suffered so much the more grievously because it was from a brother, and he was the first [to suffer].

And he did these things rightly looking to no man. For to whom could he look, when he so honored God? To his father and his mother? But they had outraged Him in return for His benefits. To his brother then? But he also had dishonored [God]. So that by himself he sought out what was good.

And he that is worthy of so great honor, what does he suffer? He is put to death. And how too was he otherwise "testified of that he was righteous"? It is said, that fire came down and consumed the sacrifices. For instead of ["And the Lord] had respect to Abel and to his sacrifices" (Gen. iv. 4), the Syriac[6] said, "And He set them on fire." He therefore who both by word and deed bare witness to the righteous

man and sees him slain for His sake, did not avenge him, but left him to suffer.

But your case is not such: for how could it be? You who have both prophets and examples, and encouragements innumerable, and signs and miracles accomplished? Hence that was faith indeed. For what miracles did he see, that he might believe he should have any recompense of good things? Did he not choose virtue from Faith alone?

What is, "and by it he being dead yet speaketh"? That he might not cast them into great despondency, he shows that he has in part obtained a recompense. How? 'The influence coming from him[7] is great, he means, "and he yet speaketh"; that is, [Cain] slew him, but he did not with him slay his glory and memory. He is not dead; therefore neither shall ye die. For by how much the more grievous a man's sufferings are, so much the greater is his glory.'

How does he "yet speak"? This is a sign both of his being alive, and of his being by all celebrated, admired, counted blessed. For he who encourages others to be righteous, speaks. For no speech avails so much, as that man's suffering. As then heaven by its mere appearance speaks, so also does he by being had in remembrance. Not if he had made proclamation of himself, not if he had ten thousand tongues, and were alive, would he have been so admired as now. That is, these things do not take place with impunity, nor lightly, neither do they pass away.

[4.] (Ver. 5) "By faith Enoch was translated, that he should not see death, and was not found, because God had translated him." This man displayed greater faith than Abel. How (you ask)? Because, although he came after him, yet what befell [Abel] was sufficient to guide him back.[8] How? God foreknew that [Abel] would be killed. For He said to Cain: "Thou hast sinned: do not add thereto."[9] Honored by him, He did not protect him. And yet neither did this throw him [Enoch] into indifference. He said not to himself, 'What need of toils and dangers? Abel honored God, yet He did not protect him. For what advantage had he that was departed, from the punishment

---

[1] τὸ κοίνον.　　　[2] γυμνάζει.
[3] ἄξιος. St. Chrys. takes the word in its primary sense, " of like value," " worth as much as." See Hom. xxvii. [6], pp. 489 sqq.
[4] οἰκεῖον τὸ πάθος.　　　[5] τὰ παρ' αὐτοῦ.
[6] The reading of some MSS. and of the editions except Savile's was ὁ κύριος instead of ὁ Σύρος. On this Montfaucon has the note: "This sentence is imperfect. Mutianus's rendering is, 'On Abel (saith he) He looked, and on his sacrifices.' But in the Syrian language it has, 'And set [them] on fire.' It would seem, therefore, that we should read, ὁ Σύρος, καὶ ἐνεπύρισεν, εἶπεν. The Hebrew words are וישע יהוה, which (not the Syriac translator, but) Theodotion renders καὶ ἐνεπύρισεν ὁ Θεός, 'And God set [them] on fire,'

as may be seen in our edition of the Hexapla, and is proved by Jerome's testimony on the passage. For the Syriac translation is, 'and God was well pleased.' So perhaps it might be an error of Chrysostom." Four of the six MSS. mentioned by Mr. Field [but not the Catena] have Σύρος. [Field's MSS. A and O have κύριος. — F. G.]　　　[7] ἡ ἐπισκοπὴ ἡ παρ' αὐτοῦ.
[8] [ἀποστρέψαι. Some of Field's MSS. read ἐπιστρέψαι. The sentence is not clear, but the meaning seems to be, "to guide him back from the evil ways of the world around." The Bened. translator has ad eum avertendum; Mutianus, ad revocandum eum et dehortandum. The English edition, "to turn him away from [serving God]," is certainly wrong. — F. G.]
[9] The words of the Septuagint, Gen. iv. 7, are ἥμαρτες; ἡσύχασον: for which St. Chrys. substitutes the words of Ecclus. xxi. 1, ἥμαρτες; μὴ προσθῇς ἔτι. He combines these two texts (either from confusing them or by way of explanation) in three other places. See Mr. Fields' note. The words were addressed to Cain before he killed his brother.

of his brother? And what benefit could he reap therefrom? Let us allow that he suffers severe punishment: what is that to him who has been slain?' He neither said nor thought anything of this kind, but passing beyond all these things, he knew that if there is a God, certainly there is a Rewarder also: although as yet they knew nothing of a resurrection. But if they who as yet know nothing of a resurrection, and see contradictory things here, thus pleased [God], how much more should we? For they neither knew of a resurrection, nor had they any examples to look to. This same thing then made [Enoch] well-pleasing [to God], namely, that he received nothing. For he knew that [God] "is a rewarder." Whence [knew he this]? "For He recompensed Abel," do you say? So that reason suggested other things, but faith the opposite of what was seen. Even then (he would say) if you see that you receive nothing here, be not troubled.

How was it "by faith" that "Enoch was translated"? Because his pleasing [God] was the cause of his translation, and faith [the cause] of his pleasing [Him]. For if he had not known that he should receive a reward, how could he have pleased [Him]? "But without faith it is impossible to please" Him. How? If a man believe that there is a God and a retribution, he will have the reward. Whence then is the well-pleasing?

[5.] It is necessary to "believe that He is," not 'what He is.'[1] If "that He .is" needs Faith, and not reasonings; it is impossible to comprehend by reasoning 'what He is.' If that "He is a rewarder" needs Faith and not reasonings, how is it possible by Reasoning to compass His essence?[2] For what Reasoning can reach this? For some persons say that the things that exist are self-caused.[3] Seest thou that unless we have Faith in regard to all things, not only in regard to retribution, but also in regard to the very being of God, all is lost to us?

But many ask whither Enoch was translated, and why he was translated, and why he did not die, neither he nor Elijah, and, if they are still alive, how they live, and in what form. But to ask these things is superfluous. For that the one was translated, and that the other was taken up, the Scriptures have said; but where they are, and how they are, they have not added: For they say nothing more than is necessary. For this indeed took place, I mean his translation, immediately at the beginning, the human soul [thereby] receiving a hope of the destruction of death, and of the overthrow of the devil's

tyranny, and that death will be done away; for he was translated, not dead, but "that he should not see death."

Therefore he added, he was translated alive, because he was well-pleasing [unto God]. For just as a Father when he has threatened his son, wishes indeed immediately after he has threatened, to relax his threat, but endures and continues resolute, that for a time he may chasten and correct him, allowing the threat to remain firm; so also God, to speak as it were after the manner of men, did not continue resolute, but immediately showed that death is done away. And first He allows death to happen, wishing to terrify the father through the son: For wishing to show that the sentence is verily fixed, He subjected to this punishment not wicked men at once, but him even who was well-pleasing, I mean, the blessed Abel; and almost immediately after him, He translated Enoch. Moreover, He did not raise the former, lest they should immediately grow bold; but He translated the other being yet alive: having excited fear by Abel, but by this latter giving zeal to be well-pleasing unto Him. Wherefore they who say that all things are ruled and governed of themselves,[4] and do not expect a reward, are not well-pleasing; as neither are the heathen. For "He becomes a rewarder of them that diligently seek Him" by works and by knowledge.

[6.] Since then we have "a rewarder," let us do all things that we may not be deprived of the rewards of virtue. For indeed the neglecting such a recompense, the scorning such a reward, is worthy of many tears. For as to "those who diligently seek Him," He is a rewarder, so to those who seek Him not, the contrary.

"Seek" (He says) "and ye shall find" (Matt. vii. 7): but how can we find the Lord? Consider how gold is found; with much labor. ["I sought the Lord] with my hands" (it is said) "by night before Him, and I was not deceived" (Ps. lxxvii. 2. See LXX [Ps. lxxvi. 3]), that is, just as we seek what is lost, so let us seek God. Do we not concentrate our mind thereon? Do we not enquire of every one? Do we not travel from home? Do we not promise money?

For instance, suppose that any among us has lost his son, what do we not do? What land, what sea do we not make the circuit of? Do we not reckon money, and houses, and everything else as secondary to the finding him? And should we find him, we cling to him, we hold him fast, we do not let him go. And when we are going to seek anything whatever, we busy ourselves in all ways to find what is sought. How

---

[1] That is, what the substance of God is, is not a part of what we muſt believe in order to please Him: nor can it be ascertained by reasonings.
[2] τὰ τῆς οὐσίας.　　　[3] αὐτόματα.　　　[4] αὐτόματα.

much more ought we to do this in regard to God, as seeking what is indispensable ; nay rather, not in the same way, but much more ! But since we are weak, at least seek God as thou seekest thy money or thy son. Wilt thou not leave thy home for Him ? Hast thou never left thy home for money ? Dost thou not busy thyself in all ways ? When thou hast found [it], art thou not full of confidence ?

[7.] "Seek" (He says) "and ye shall find." For things sought after need much care, especially in regard of God. For many are the hindrances, many the things that darken, many that impede our perception. For as the sun is manifest, and set forth publicly before all, and we have no need to seek it ; but if on the other hand we bury ourselves and turn everything upside down, we need much labor to look at the sun ; so truly here also, if we bury ourselves in the depth of evil desires, in the darkness of passions and of the affairs of this life, with difficulty do we look up, with difficulty do we raise our heads, with difficulty do we see clearly. He that is buried underground, in whatever degree he sees upwards, in that degree does he come towards the sun. Let us therefore shake off the earth, let us break through the mist which lies upon us. It is thick, and close, and does not allow us to see clearly.

And how, you say, is this cloud broken through ? If we draw to ourselves the beams of "the sun of righteousness." "The lifting up of my hands" (it is said) "is an evening sacrifice." (Ps. cxli. 2.) With our hands let us also lift up our mind : ye who have been initiated know what I mean,[1] perhaps too ye recognize the expression, and see at a glance what I have hinted at. Let us raise up our thoughts on high.

I myself know many men almost suspended apart from the earth, and beyond measure stretching up their hands, and out of heart because it is not possible to be lifted into the air, and thus praying with earnestness. Thus I would have you always, and if not always, at least very often ; and if not very often, at least now and then, at least in the morning, at least in the evening prayers.[2] For, tell me, canst thou not stretch forth the hands ? Stretch forth the will, stretch forth as far as thou wilt, yea even to heaven itself. Even shouldst thou wish to touch the very summit, even if thou wouldst ascend higher and walk thereon, it is open to thee. For our mind is lighter, and higher than any winged creature. And when it receives grace from the Spirit, O ! how swift is it ! How quick is it ! How does it compass all things ! How does it never sink down or fall to the ground ! These wings

let us provide for ourselves : by means of them shall we be able to fly even across the tempestuous sea of this present life. The swiftest birds fly unhurt over mountains, and woods, and seas, and rocks, in a brief moment of time. Such also is the mind ; when it is winged, when it is separated from the things of this life, nothing can lay hold of it, it is higher than all things, even than the fiery darts of the devil.

The devil is not so good a marksman, as to be able to reach this height ; he sends forth his darts indeed, for he is void of all shame, yet he does not hit the mark ; the dart returns to him without effect, and not without effect only, but it [falls] upon his own head. For what is sent forth by him must of necessity strike [something]. As then, that which has been shot out by men, either strikes the person against whom it is directed, or pierces bird, or fence, or garment, or wood, or the mere air, so does the dart of the devil also. It must of necessity strike ; and if it strike not him that is shot at, it necessarily strikes him that shoots it. And we may learn from many instances, that when we are not hit, without doubt he is hit himself. For instance, he plotted against Job : he did not hit him, but was struck himself. He plotted against Paul, he did not hit him, but was struck himself. If we watch, we may see this happening everywhere. For even when he strikes, he is hit ; much more then [when he does not hit].

[8.] Let us turn his weapons then against himself, and having armed and fortified ourselves with the shield of faith, let us keep guard with steadfastness, so as to be impregnable. Now the dart of the devil is evil concupiscence. Anger especially is a fire, a flame ; it catches, destroys, consumes ; let us quench it, by longsuffering, by forbearance. For as red-hot iron dipped into water, loses its fire, so an angry man falling in with a patient one does no harm to the patient man, but rather benefits him, and is himself more thoroughly subdued.

For nothing is equal to longsuffering. Such a man is never insulted ; but as bodies of adamant are not wounded, so neither are such souls. For they are above the reach of the darts. The longsuffering man is high, and so high as not to receive a wound from the shot. When one is furious, laugh ; but do not laugh openly, lest thou irritate him : but laugh mentally on his account. For in the case of children, when they strike us passionately, as though forsooth they were avenging themselves, we laugh. If then thou laugh, there will be as great difference between thee and him, as between a child and a man : but if thou art furious thou hast made thyself a child. For the angry are more senseless than children. If one look at a furious child, does he not laugh at him ? "The poor-spirited"

<sup></sup>

---

[1] The words of the Liturgy which were said throughout the Church Catholic, "Lift up your hearts," &c.

[2] ἐν ταῖς ἑωθιναῖς, ἐν ταῖς ἑσπεριναῖς.

(it is said) "is mightily simple." (Prov. xiv. 29.) The simple then is a child : and "he who is longsuffering" (it is said) "is abundant in wisdom." This "abundant wisdom" then let us follow after, that we may attain to the good things promised us in Christ Jesus our Lord, with whom to the Father together with the Holy Ghost, be glory, power, honor, now and for ever and world without end. Amen.

# HOMILY XXIII.

## HEBREWS xi. 7.

"By faith Noah, being warned of God[1] of things not seen as yet, moved with fear, prepared an ark to the saving of his house; by the which he condemned the world, and became heir of the righteousness which is by Faith."

[1.] "By faith" (he says) "Noah being warned of God." As the Son of God, speaking of His own coming, said, "In the days of Noah they married and were given in marriage" (Luke xvii. 26, 27), therefore the Apostle also recalled to their mind an appropriate image. For the example of Enoch, was an example only of Faith; that of Noah, on the other hand, of unbelief also. And this is a complete consolation and exhortation, when not only believers are found approved, but also unbelievers suffer the opposite.

For what does he say? "By faith being warned of God."[2] What is "being warned of God"? It is, "It having been foretold to him." But why is the expression "divine communication"[3] (Luke ii. 26) used? for in another place also it is said, "and it was communicated[4] to him by the Spirit," and again, "and what saith the divine communication?"[3] (Rom. xi. 4.) Seest thou the equal dignity of the Spirit? For as God reveals,[5] so also does the Holy Spirit. But why did he speak thus? The prophecy is called "a divine communication."

"Of things not seen as yet," he says, that is of the rain.

"Moved with fear, prepared an ark." Reason indeed suggested nothing of this sort; For "they were marrying and being given in marriage"; the air was clear, there were no signs [of change] : but nevertheless he feared: "By faith" (he says) "Noah being warned of God of things not seen as yet, moved with fear, prepared an ark to the saving of his house."

How is it, "By the which he condemned the world"? He showed them to be worthy of punishment, since they were not brought to their senses even by the preparation.

"And he became" (he says) "heir of the righteousness which is by Faith" : that is, by his believing God he was shown to be righteous. For this is the [part] of a soul sincerely disposed towards Him and judging nothing more reliable than His words, just as Unbelief is the very contrary. Faith, it is manifest, works righteousness. For as we have been warned of God respecting Hell, so was he also : and yet at that time he was laughed at; he was reviled and ridiculed; but he regarded none of these things.

[2.] (Ver. 8, 9) "By faith Abraham when he was called to go out into a place which he should after receive for an inheritance, obeyed; and he went out not knowing whither he went. By faith he sojourned in the land of promise, as in a strange country, dwelling in tabernacles, with Isaac and Jacob, the heirs with him of the same promise." ["By faith"] : for (tell me) whom did he see to emulate?[6] He had for father a Gentile, and an idolater; he had heard no prophets; he knew not whither he was going. For as they of the Hebrews who believed, looked to these [patriarchs] as having enjoyed blessings innumerable, he shows that none of them obtained anything as yet; all are unrewarded; no one as yet received his reward. "He" escaped from his country and his home, and "went out not knowing whither he went."

And what marvel, if he himself [were so], when his seed also dwelt in this same way? For seeing the promise disproved[7] (since He had said, "To thee will I give this land, and to thy seed" — Gen. xii. 7; xiii. 15), he saw his son dwelling there; and again his grandson saw himself dwelling in a land not his own; yet was he nowise troubled. For the affairs of Abraham happened as we might have expected, since the promise was to be accomplished afterwards in his family (although it is said even to himself,

---

[1] χρηματισθείς.
[2] χρηματισθείς.
[3] χρηματισμός.
[4] ἦν κεχρηματισμένον.
[5] χρᾷ. This word is properly used of quasi-Divine communications made through oracles: the words χρηματίζω and χρηματισμός have the same meaning. Hence the emphatic character of the words "of God" in our version of the text, Rom. xi. 4; and so in the other passage which St. Chrys. cites (Luke ii. 26), the Divinity of the Holy Spirit (he says) is implied in the use of the word ἦν κεχρηματισμένον ὑπὸ (not διὰ) τοῦ Πνεύματος, "a divine communication was made by the Spirit."

[6] "To endeavor to imitate, or even surpass."
[7] ἐλεγχομένην.

"To thee, and to thy seed," not, "to thee through thy seed," but "to thee and to thy seed") : still neither he, nor Isaac, nor Jacob, enjoyed the promise. For one of them served for hire, and the other was driven out: and he himself even was failing[1] through fear: and while he took some things indeed in war, others, unless he had had the aid of God, would have been destroyed. On this account [the Apostle] says, "with the heirs of the same promise "; not himself alone, he means ; but the heirs also.

[3.] (Ver. 13) "These all died in faith," he says, "not having obtained[2] the promises." At this place it is worth while to make two enquiries ; how, after saying that [God] "translated Enoch, and he was not found, so that he did not see death," does he say, "These all *died* in Faith." And again, after saying, "they not having obtained the promises," he declares that Noah had received a reward, "to the saving of his house," and that Enoch had been "translated," and that Abel "yet speaks," and that Abraham had gained a hold on the land, and yet he says, "These all died in Faith, not having obtained the promises." What then is [meant]?

It is necessary to solve the first [difficulty], and then the second. "These all" (he says) "*died* in faith." The word "all" is used here not because all had died, but because with that one exception "all these had died," whom we know to be dead.

And the [statement] "not having obtained the promises," is true : for surely the promise to Noah was not to be this [which is here spoken of]. But further, of what kind of "promises" is he speaking? For Isaac and Jacob received the promises of the land ; but as to Noah and Abel and Enoch, what kind of promises did they receive? Either then he is speaking concerning these three ; or if concerning those others also, the promise was not this, that Abel should be admired, nor that Enoch should be translated, nor that Noah should be preserved ;[3] but these things came to them for their virtue's sake, and were a sort of foretaste of things to come. For God from the beginning, knowing that the human race needs much condescension, bestows on us not only the things in the world to come, but also those here ; as for instance, Christ said even to the disciples, "Whosoever hath left houses, or brethren, or sisters, or father, or mother, shall receive an hundredfold and

shall inherit everlasting life." (Matt. xix. 29.) And again, "Seek ye the kingdom of God, and all these things shall be added unto you." (Matt. vi. 33.) Seest thou that these things are given by Him in the way of addition, that we might not faint?[4] For as the athletes have the benefit of careful attention, even when engaged in the combat, but do not then enjoy entire ease, living under rules, yet afterwards they enjoy it entire : so God also does not grant us here to partake of "entire" ease. For even here He does give [some].

[4.] "But having seen them afar off," he says,[5] "and embraced them." Here he hints at something mystical : that they received beforehand all the things which have been spoken concerning things to come ; concerning the resurrection, concerning the Kingdom of Heaven, concerning the other things, which Christ proclaimed when He came, for these are "the promises" of which he speaks. Either then he means this, or, that they did not indeed receive them, but died in confidence respecting them, and they were [thus] confident through Faith only.

"Having seen them afar off" : four generations before ; for after so many [generations], they went up out of Egypt.

"And embraced them," saith he, and were glad. They were so persuaded of them as even to "embrace [or "salute"] them," from the metaphor of persons on ship-board seeing from afar the longed-for cities : which, before they enter them, they take and occupy by words of greeting.

(Ver. 10) "For they looked" (he says) "for the[6] city which hath foundations, whose builder and maker is God." Seest thou that they received them in this sense, in their already accepting them and being confident respecting them. If then to be confident is to receive, it is in your power also to receive. For these, although they enjoyed not those [blessings], yet still saw them by their longing desire. Why now do these things happen? That we might be put to shame, in that they indeed, when things on earth were promised them, regarded them not, but sought the future "city" : whereas God again and again speaks to us of the city[7] which is above, and yet we seek that which is here. He said to them, I will give you the things of the present [world]. But when He saw, or rather, when they showed themselves worthy of greater things, then He no longer suffers them to receive these, but those greater ones ; wishing to show us that they are worthy

---

[1] ἐξέπιπτε: i.e. τῆς ὑποσχέσεως, "of the promise," is Mr. Field's interpretation; Mutianus has *pæne exciderat*.
[2] κομισάμενοι. This word is used by St. Chrys. throughout this passage without any variation of reading. The text of the Epistle here has λαβόντες, but in ver. 39, οὐκ ἐκομίσαντο. [St. Chrys. in another work has the reading λαβόντες, but κομισάμενοι is generally adopted by the critical editors as the true text in the Epistle.—F. G.]
[3] We must probably understand also, "nor that the Patriarchs should live in Canaan": the argument seems to require this; besides, in the statement of the difficulty, Abraham's having "got a hold on the land" is mentioned together with the blessings bestowed on Abel, Enoch, and Noah, as something already given them.

[4] See above, p. 408.
[5] St. Chrys. does not cite nor yet refer to the words καὶ πεισθέντες, "and were persuaded of them." They are found in the common editions of the Epistle, but are not supposed to be a genuine part of the Sacred Text. [They are rejected by all critical editors. and have very little support from the authorities for this text.—F. G.]
[6] τὴν πόλιν.
[7] πόλιν.

of greater things, being unwilling to be bound to these. As if one should promise playthings to an intelligent child, not that he might receive them, but by way of exhibiting his philosophy, when he asks for things more important. For this is to show, that they held off from the land with so great earnestness, that they did not even accept what was given. Wherefore their posterity receive it on this account, for themselves were worthy of the land.

What is, "the city which hath foundations"? For are not these [which are visible] "foundations"? In comparison of the other, they are not. "Whose Builder and Maker is God." O! What an encomium on that city!

[5.] (Ver. 11) "By faith also Sarah herself," he says. Here he began [speaking] in a way to put them to shame, in case, that is, they should show themselves more faint-hearted than a woman. But possibly some one might say, How "by faith," when she laughed? Nay, while her laughter indeed was from unbelief, her fear [was] from Faith, for to say, "I laughed not" (Gen. xviii. 15), arose from Faith. From this then it appears that when unbelief had been cleared out, Faith came in its place.

" By faith also Sarah received strength to conceive seed even when she was past age."[1] What is, "to conceive seed"?[2] She who was become dead, who was barren, received power for the retaining of seed, for conception. For her imperfection was two-fold ; first from her time of life, for she was really old ; secondly from nature, for she was barren.

(Ver. 12) "Wherefore even from one they" all " sprang, as the stars of the sky, and as the sand which is by the sea-shore." " Wherefore " (he says) "even from one they" all "sprang." Here he not only says that she bare [a child], but that she also became mother of so many as not even fruitful wombs [are mothers of]. "As the stars," He says. How then is it that He often numbers them, although He said, "As the stars of the heaven shall not be numbered, so neither shall your seed"? (Gen. xv. 5.) He either means the excess, or else [speaks of] those who are continually being born. For is it possible, tell me, to number their forefathers of one family as, such an one son of such an one, and such an one son of such an one? But here such are the promises of God, so skillfully arranged are His undertakings.

[6.] But if the things which He promised as additional, are so admirable, so beyond expectation, so magnificent, what will those be, to which these are an addition, to which these are some-

what over and above? What then can be more blessed than they who attain them? What more wretched than those who miss them? For if a man when driven out from his native country, is pitied by all ; and when he has lost an inheritance is considered by all as an object of compassion, with what tears ought he to be bewailed, who fails of Heaven, and of the good things there stored up? Or rather, he is not even to be wept for : for one is wept for, when he suffers something of which he is not himself the cause ; but when of his own choice he has entangled himself in evil, he is not worthy[3] of tears, but of wailings ;[4] or rather then of mourning ;[5] since even our Lord JESUS Christ mourned and wept for Jerusalem, impious as it was. Truly we are worthy of weepings innumerable, of wailings innumerable. If the whole world should receive a voice, both stones, and wood, and trees, and wild beasts, and birds, and fishes, and in a word, the whole world, if receiving a voice it should bewail us who have failed of those good things, it would not bewail and lament enough. For what language, what intellect, can represent that blessedness and virtue, that pleasure, that glory, that happiness, that splendor? "What eye hath not seen, and ear hath not heard, and what hath not entered into the heart of man" (1 Cor. ii. 9), (he did not say, that they simply surpass [what we imagine] ; but none hath ever conceived) " the things which God hath prepared for them that love Him." For of what kind are those good things likely to be, of which God is the Preparer and Establisher? For if immediately after He had made us, when we had not yet done anything, He freely bestowed so great [favors], Paradise, familiar intercourse with Himself, promised us immortality, a life happy and freed from cares ; what will He not bestow on those who have labored and struggled so greatly, and endured on His behalf? For us He spared not His Only Begotten, for us when we were enemies He gave up His own SON to death ; of what will He not count us worthy, having become His friends? what will He not impart to us, having reconciled us to Himself?

[7.] He both is abundantly and infinitely rich ; and He desires and earnestly endeavors to obtain our friendship ; we do not thus earnestly endeavor. What am I saying, 'do not earnestly endeavor'? We do not wish to obtain the good things as He wishes it. And what He has done shows that He wishes it more [than we]. For while, for our own sake, we with difficulty think lightly of a little gold : He, for our sake, gave even the Son who was His own. Let us make use of the love of God as we ought ; let us reap the fruits of His friendship. For "ye are

---

[1] καὶ παρὰ καιρὸν ἡλικίας. The common texts of St. Chrys. add here ἔτεκεν, in accordance with the common editions of the New Testament; but in neither case is it supposed to be genuine. [Field's text omits it, and it is not in critical editions of the text of Heb. — F. G.] [2] εἰς καταβολὴν σπέρματος.

[3] ἄξιος. [4] θρήνων. [5] πένθους.

My friends" (he says) "if ye do what I say to you." (John xv. 14.) How wonderful! His enemies, who were at an infinite distance from Him, whom in all respects He excels by an incomparable superiority, these He has made His friends and calls them friends. What then should not one choose to suffer for the sake of this friendship? For the friendship of men we often incur danger, but for that of God, we do not even give up money. Our [condition] does indeed call for mourning, for mourning and tears and wailings, and loud lamentation and beating of the breast. We have fallen from our hope, we are humbled from our high estate, we have shown ourselves unworthy of the honor of God; even after His benefits we are become unfeeling, and ungrateful. The devil has stripped us of all our good things. We who were counted worthy to be sons; we His brethren and fellow-heirs, are come to differ nothing from His enemies that insult Him.

Henceforward, what consolation shall there be for us? He called us to Heaven, and we have thrust ourselves down to hell. "Swearing and lying and stealing and adultery, are poured out upon the earth." (Hos. iv. 2.) Some "mingle blood upon blood"; and others do deeds worse than blood-shedding. Many of those that are wronged, many of those that are defrauded prefer ten thousand deaths to the suffering such things: and except they had feared God, would even have killed themselves, being so murderously disposed against themselves. Are not these things then worse than blood-shedding?

[8.] "Woe is me, my soul! For the godly man is perished from the earth, and there is none upright among men" (Mic. vii. 1, 2, LXX.); let us also now cry out, first about our own selves: but aid me in my lamentation.

Perhaps some are even disgusted and laugh. For this very cause ought we to make our lamentations the more intense, because we are so mad and beside ourselves, that we do not know that we are mad, but laugh at things for which we ought to groan. O man! "There is wrath revealed from heaven against all ungodliness and unrighteousness of men" (Rom. i. 18); "God will come manifestly: a fire will burn before Him, and round about Him will be a mighty tempest." (Ps. l. 3.) "A fire will burn before Him, and consume His enemies on every side." (Ps. xcvii. 3.) "The day of the Lord is as a burning oven." (Mal. iv. 1.) And no man lays up these things in his mind, but these tremendous and fearful doctrines are more despised than fables, and are trodden under foot. He that heareth, — there is no one: while they who laugh and make sport are — all. What resource will there be for us? Whence shall we find safety? "We are undone, we are utterly consumed"

(Num. xvii. 12), we are become the laughing-stock of our enemies, and a mockery for the heathen and the Demons. Now is the devil greatly elated; he glories and is glad. The angels to whom we had been entrusted are all ashamed and in sadness: there is no man to convert [you]: all means have been used by us in vain, and we seem to you as idle talkers. It is seasonable even now to call on the heaven, because there is no man that heareth; to take to witness the elements: "Hear, O heaven! and give ear, O earth! for the Lord hath spoken." (Isa. i. 2.)

Give a hand, stretch it forth, O ye who have not yet been overwhelmed, to them who are undone through their drunkenness: ye that are whole to them that are sick, ye that are sober-minded to them that are mad, that are giddily whirling round.

Let no man, I beseech you, prefer the favor of his friend to his salvation; and let violence and rebuke look to one thing only, — his benefit. When one has been seized by a fever, even slaves lay hold of their Masters. For when that is pressing on him, throwing his mind into confusion, and a swarm of slaves are standing by, they recognize not the law of Master and Servant, in the calamity of the Master.

Let us collect ourselves, I exhort you: there are daily wars, submersions [of towns], destructions innumerable all around us, and on every side the wrath of God is enclosing us as in a net. And we, as though we were well-pleasing to Him, are in security. We all make our hands ready for unjust gains, none for helping others: all for plundering, none for protecting: each one is in earnest as to how he shall increase his possessions; no one as to how he shall aid the needy: each one has much anxiety how he may add to his wealth; no one how he may save his own soul. One fear possesses all, lest (you say) we should become poor; no man is in anguish and trembling lest we should fall into hell. These things call for lamentations, these call for accusation, these call for reprobation.

[9.] But I do not wish to speak of these things, but I am constrained by my grief. Forgive me: I am forced by sorrow to utter many things, even those which I do not wish. I see that our wound is grievous, that our calamity is beyond comfort, that woes have overtaken us greater than the consolation. We are undone. "O that my head were waters and mine eyes a fountain of tears" (Jer. ix. 1), that I might lament. Let us weep, beloved, let us weep, let us groan.

Possibly there may be some here who say, He talks to us of nothing but lamentation, nothing but tears. It was not my wish, believe me, it was not my wish, but rather to go through a course of commendations and praises : but now it is not the season for these. Beloved, it is not lamenting which is grievous, but the doing things which call for lamentations. Sorrow is not the thing to shrink from, but the committing things that call for sorrow. Do not thou be punished, and I will not mourn. Do not die, and I will not weep. If the body indeed lies dead, thou callest on all to grieve with thee, and thinkest those without sympathy who do not mourn : And when the soul is perishing, dost thou tell us *not* to mourn?

But I cannot be a father, if I do not weep. I am a father full of affection. Hear how Paul exclaims, " My little children, of whom I travail in birth again " (Gal. iv. 19) : what mother in child-birth utters cries so bitter as he ! Would that it were possible for thee to see the very fire that is in my heart, and thou wouldest know, that I burn [with grief] more intense than any woman, or girl that suffers untimely widowhood. She does not so mourn over her husband, nor any father over his son, as I do over this multitude that is here with us.

I see no progress. Everything turns to calumnies and accusations. No man makes it his business to please God ; but (he says) ' let us speak evil of such an one or such an one.' ' Such an one is unfit to be among the Clergy.' ' Such an one does not lead a respectable life.'

When we ought to be grieving for our own evils, we judge others, whereas we ought not to do this, even when we are pure from sins. " For who maketh thee to differ " (he says) " and what hast thou which thou didst not receive? But if thou hast received it, why dost thou glory, as though thou hadst not received it?" (1 Cor. iv. 7.) " And thou, why dost thou judge thy brother " (Rom. xiv. 10), being thyself full of innumerable evils? When thou sayest, Such an one is a bad man, and a spendthrift, and vicious, think of thyself, and examine strictly thy own [condition], and thou wilt repent of what thou hast said. For there is no, no not any, such powerful stimulus to virtue, as the recollecting of our sins.

If we turn over these two things in our minds, we shall be enabled to attain the promised blessings, we shall be enabled to cleanse ourselves and wipe away [what is amiss]. Only let us take serious thought sometime ; let us be anxious about the matter, beloved. Let us grieve here in reflection, that we may not grieve yonder in punishment, but may enjoy the everlasting blessings, where " pain and sorrow and sighing are fled away " (Isa. xxxv. 10), that we may attain to the good things which surpass man's understanding, in Christ Jesus our Lord, for to Him is glory and power for ever and ever. Amen.

# HOMILY XXIV.

### Hebrews xi. 13–16.

" These all died in faith,[1] not having received the promises, but having seen them afar off,[2] and embraced them, and confessed that they were strangers and pilgrims on the earth. For they that say such things, declare plainly that they seek a country. And truly if they had been mindful of that country from whence they came out, they might have had opportunity to have returned. But now they desire a better country, that is, an heavenly; wherefore God is not ashamed [3] to be called their God, for He hath prepared for them a city."

[1.] THE first virtue, yea the whole of virtue, is to be a stranger to this world, and a sojourner, and to have nothing in common with things here, but to hang loose from them, as from things strange to us ; As those blessed disciples did, of whom he says, " They wandered about in sheep-skins, and in goat-skins, being destitute, afflicted,

tormented : [4] of whom the world was not worthy." (c. xi. 37, 38.)

They called themselves therefore " strangers " ; but Paul said somewhat much beyond this : for not merely did he call himself a stranger, but said that he was dead to the world, and that the world was dead to him. " For the world " (he says) " has been crucified to me and I to the world." (Gal. vi. 14.) But we, both citizens [5] and quite alive, busy ourselves about everything here as citizens. And what righteous men were to the world, " strangers " and " dead," that we are to Heaven. And what they were to Heaven, alive and acting as citizens, that we are to the world. Wherefore we are dead, because we have refused that which is truly life, and have chosen this which is but for a time. Wherefore we have provoked God to wrath, because when the enjoyments of Heaven have been set before

---

[1] κατὰ πίστιν.

[2] [The words of the A. V. " and were persuaded of them," καὶ πεισθέντες, are not in St. Chrysostom's text or in that of any critical edition. In the R. V. they are omitted. — F. G.]

[3] lit. " ashamed of them, to be," &c.

[4] " ill-treated."

[5] πολίτας.

us, we are not willing to be separated from things on earth, but, like worms, we turn about from the earth to the earth, and again from this to that ; [1] and in short are not willing to look up even for a little while, nor to withdraw ourselves from human affairs, but as if drowned in torpor and sleep and drunkenness, we are stupefied with imaginations.

[2.] And as those who are under the power of sweet sleep lie on their bed not only during the night, but even when the morning has overtaken them, and bright day has come, and are not ashamed to indulge in pleasure, and to make the season of business and activity a time of slumber and indolence, so truly we also, when the day is drawing near, when the night is far spent, or rather the day ; for " work " (it is said) " while it is day " (John ix. 4) ; when it is day we practice all that belongs to the night, sleeping, dreaming, indulging in luxurious fancies ; and the eyes of our understanding are closed as well as those of our body ; we speak amiss, we talk absurdly ; even if a person inflict a deep wound upon us, if he carry off all our substance, if he set the very house on fire, we are not so much as conscious of it.

Or rather, we do not even wait for others to do this, but we do it ourselves, piercing and wounding ourselves every day, lying in unseemly fashion, and stripped bare of all credit, all honor, neither ourselves concealing our shameful deeds, nor permitting others to do so, but lying exposed to public shame, to the ridicule, the numberless jests of spectators and passers-by.

[3.] Do ye not suppose that the wicked themselves laugh at those who are of like characters to themselves, and condemn them? For since God has placed within us a tribunal which cannot be bribed nor ever utterly destroyed, even though we come to the very lowest depth of vice ; therefore even the wicked themselves give sentence against themselves, and if one call them that which they are, they are ashamed, they are angry, they say that it is an insult. Thus they condemn what they do, even if not by their deeds, yet by their words, by their conscience, nay rather even by their deeds. For when they carry on their practices out of sight and secretly, they give the strongest proof of the opinion they hold concerning the thing itself. For wickedness is so manifest, that all men are its accusers, even those who follow after it, while such is the quality of virtue, that it is admired even by those who do not emulate it. For even the fornicator will praise chastity, and the covetous will condemn injustice, and the passionate will admire patience, and blame quarrelsomeness, and the wanton [will blame] wantonness.

How then (you say) does he pursue these things? From excessive indolence, not because he judges it good ; otherwise he would not have been ashamed of the thing itself, nor would he have denied it when another accused him. Nay many when caught, not enduring the shame, have even hanged themselves. So strong is the witness within us in behalf of what is good and becoming. Thus what is good is brighter than the sun, and the contrary more unsightly than anything.

[4.] The saints were " strangers and sojourners." How and in what way? And where does Abraham confess himself " a stranger and a sojourner "? Probably indeed he even himself confessed it : [2] but David both confessed " I am a stranger " and what ? " As all my fathers were." (Ps. xxxix. 12.) For they who dwell in tents, they who purchase even burial places for money, evidently were in some sense strangers, as they had not even where to bury their dead.

What then? Did they mean that they were " strangers " from the land that is in Palestine? By no means : but in respect of the whole world : and with reason ; for they saw therein none of the things which they wished for, but everything foreign and strange. They indeed wished to practice virtue : but here there was much wickedness, and things were quite foreign to them. They had no friend, no familiar acquaintance, save only some few.

But how were they " strangers "? They had no care for things here. And this they showed not by words, but by their deeds. In what way?

He said to Abraham, " Leave that which seems thy country and come to one that is foreign " : And he did not cleave to his kindred, but gave it up as unconcernedly as if he were about to leave a foreign land. He said to him, " Offer up thy son," and he offered him up as if he had no son ; as if he had divested himself of his nature, so he offered him up. The wealth which he had acquired was common to all passers-by, and this he accounted as nothing. He yielded the first places to others : he threw himself into dangers ; he suffered troubles innumerable. He built no splendid houses, he enjoyed no luxuries, he had no care about dress, which all are things of this world ; but lived in all respects as belonging to the City yonder ; he showed hospitality, brotherly love, mercifulness, forbearance, contempt for wealth and for present glory, and for all else.

And his son too was such as himself : when he was driven away, when war was made on him, he yielded and gave way, as being in a foreign land. For foreigners, whatever they suffer, endure it, as not being in their own country. Even when his wife was taken from him, he endured this also as being in a strange land: and lived in all respects as one whose home was above, showing sobermindedness and a well-ordered life.[1] For after he had begotten a son, he had no more commerce with his wife, and it was when the flower of his youth had passed that he married her, showing that he did it not from passion, but in subservience to the promise of God.

And what did Jacob? Did he not seek bread only and raiment, which are asked for by those who are truly strangers, by those that have come to great poverty? When he was driven out, did he not as a stranger give place? Did he not serve for hire? Did he not suffer afflictions innumerable, everywhere, as a stranger?

[5.] And these things (he says) they said, "seeking" their "own country." Ah! how great is the difference! They indeed were in travail-pains each day, wishing to be released from this world, and to return to their country. But we, on the contrary, if a fever attack us, neglecting everything, weeping like little children, are frightened at death.

Not without reason are we thus affected. For since we do not live here like strangers, nor as if hastening to our country, but are like persons that are going away to punishment, therefore we grieve, because we have not used circumstances as we ought, but have turned order upside down. Hence we grieve when we ought to rejoice: hence we shudder, like murderers or robber chiefs, when they are going to be brought before the judgment-seat, and are thinking over all the things they have done, and therefore are fearful and trembling.

They, however, were not such, but pressed on. And Paul even groaned; "And we" (he says) "that are in this tabernacle do groan, being burdened." (2 Cor. v. 4.) Such were they who were with Abraham; "strangers," he says, they were in respect of the whole world, and "they sought a country."

What sort of "country" was this? Was it that which they had left? By no means. For what hindered them if they wished, from returning again, and becoming citizens? but they sought that which is in Heaven? Thus they desired their departure hence, and so they pleased God; for "God was not ashamed to be called their God."

[6.] Ah! how great a dignity! He vouchsafed "to be called their God." What dost thou say? He is called the God of the earth, and the God of Heaven, and hast thou set it down as a great thing that "He is not ashamed to be

called their God"? Great and truly great this is, and a proof of exceeding blessedness. How? Because He is called God of earth and of heaven as also of the Gentiles: in that He created and formed them: but [God] of those holy men, not in this sense, but as some true friend.

And I will make it plain to you by an example; as in the case of [slaves] in large households, when any of those placed over the household are very highly esteemed, and manage everything themselves, and can use great freedom towards their masters, the Master is called after them, and one may find many so called. But what do I say? As we might say the God, not of the Gentiles but of the world, so we might say "the God of Abraham." But you do not know how great a dignity this is, because we do not attain to it. For as now He is called the Lord of all Christians, and yet the name goes beyond our deserts: consider the greatness if He were called the God of one [person]! He who is called the God of the whole world is "not ashamed to be called" the God of three men: and with good reason: for the saints would turn the scale, I do not say against the world[2] but against ten thousand such. "For one man who doeth the will of the Lord,[3] is better than ten thousand transgressors." (Ecclus. xvi. 3.)

Now that they called themselves "strangers" in this sense is manifest. But supposing that they said they were "strangers" on account of the strange land, why did David also [call himself a stranger]? Was not he a king? Was not he a prophet? Did he not spend his life in his own country? Why then does he say, "I am a stranger and a sojourner"? (Ps. xxxix. 12.) How art thou a stranger? "As" (he says) "all my fathers were." Seest thou that they too were strangers? We have a country, he means, but not really our country. But how art thou thyself a stranger? As to the earth. Therefore they also [were strangers] in respect of the earth: For "as they were," he says, so also am I; and as he, so they too.

[7.] Let us even now become strangers; that God may "not be ashamed of us to be called our God." For it is a shame to Him, when He is called the God of the wicked, and He also is ashamed of them; as He is glorified when He is [called the God] of the good and the kind, and of them that cultivate virtue. For if "we" decline to be called the masters of our wicked slaves, and give them up; and should any one

---

[1] σωφροσύνην κοσμιότητα.

[2] See on ver. 36, pp. 488 sqq.

[3] Mr. Field observes that St. Chrys. repeatedly cites Ecclus. xvi. 3, thus; and that while the Greek is simply, "for one is better than a thousand," the Syriac seems to have read ὅτι κρείσσων εἷς ποιῶν θέλημα, &c. So the English version has "for one *that is just*."

come to us and say, 'such a one does innumerable bad things, he is your slave, is he not?' We immediately say, "by no means," to get rid of the disgrace: for a slave has a close relation to his master, and the discredit passes from the one to the other.[1] — But they were so illustrious, so full of confidence, that not only was He "not ashamed to be called" from them, but He even Himself says, "I am the God of Abraham, and the God of Isaac, and the God of Jacob." (Ex. iii. 6.)

Let us also, my beloved, become "strangers"; that God may "not be ashamed of us"; that He may not be ashamed, and deliver us up to Hell. Such were they who said, "Lord, have we not prophesied in Thy Name, and in Thy Name have done many wonderful works!" (Matt. vii. 22.) But see what Christ says to them: "I know you not:" the very thing which masters would do, when wicked slaves run to them, wishing to be rid of the disgrace. "I know you not," He says. How then dost Thou punish those whom Thou knowest not? I said, "I know not," in a different sense: that is, "I deny you, and renounce you." But God forbid that we should hear this fatal and terrible utterance. For if they who cast out demons and prophesied, were denied, because their life was not suitable thereto; how much more we!

[8.] And how (you ask) is it possible that they should be denied, who have shown prophetic powers, and wrought miracles, and cast out demons? Is it probable they were afterwards changed, and became wicked; and therefore were nothing benefited, even by their former virtue. For not only ought we to have our beginnings splendid, but the end also more splendid still.

For tell me, does not the Orator take pains to make the end of his speech splendid, that he may retire with applause? Does not the public officer make the most splendid display at the close of his administration? The wrestler, if he do not make a more splendid display and conquer unto the end, and if after vanquishing all he be vanquished by the last, is not all unprofitable to him? Should the pilot have crossed the whole ocean, yet if he wreck his vessel at the port, has he not lost all his former labor? And what [of] the Physician? If, after he has freed the sick man from his disease, when he is on the point of discharging him cured, he should then destroy him, has he not destroyed everything? So too in respect of Virtue, as many as have not added an end suitable to the beginning, and in unison and harmony with it, are ruined, and undone. Such are they who have sprung forth from the starting place bright and

exulting, and afterwards have become faint and feeble. Therefore they are both deprived of the prize, and are not acknowledged by their master.

Let us listen to these things, those of us who are in love of wealth: for this is the greatest iniquity. "For the love of money is the root of all evil." (1 Tim. vi. 10.) Let us listen, those of us who wish to make our present possessions greater, let us listen, and sometime cease from our covetousness, that we may not hear the same things as they [will hear]. Let us listen to them now, and be on our guard, that we may not hear them then. Let us listen now with fear, that we may not then listen with vengeance: "Depart from Me" (He says); "I never knew you" (Matt. vii. 23), no not even then (He means) when ye made a display of prophesyings, and were casting out demons.

It is probable that He also here hints at something else, that even then they were wicked; and from the beginning, grace wrought even by the unworthy. For if it wrought through Balaam, much more through the unworthy, for the sake of those who shall profit [by it].

But if even signs and wonders did not avail to deliver from punishment; much more, if a man happen to be in the priestly dignity:[2] even if he reach the highest honor, even if grace work in him to ordination, even if unto all the other things, for the sake of those who need his leadership,[3] he also shall hear, "I never knew thee," no, not even then when grace wrought in thee.

[9.] O! how strict shall the search be there as to purity of life! How does that, of itself, suffice to introduce us into the kingdom? While the absence of it gives up the man [to destruction], though he have ten thousand miracles and signs to show. For nothing is so pleasing to God as an excellent course of life. "If ye love Me" (John xiv. 15), He declares; He did not say, "work miracles," but what? "Keep My commandments." And again, "I call you friends" (John xv. 14), not when ye cast out demons, but "if ye keep My words." For those things come of the gift of God: but these after the gift of God, of our own diligence also. Let us strive to become friends of God, and not remain enemies to Him.

These things we are ever saying, these exhortations we are ever giving, both to ourselves and to you: but nothing more is gained. Wherefore also I am afraid. And I would have wished indeed to be silent, so as not to increase your danger. For when a person often hears, and even so does not act, this is to provoke the Lord to anger. But I fear also myself that other danger, that of silence, if when I am ap-

---

[1] The sentence is left incomplete: The common editions add, "much more does God."

[2] ἀξιώματι ἱερατικῷ.　　　[3] τῆς προστασίας.

pointed to the ministering of the word, I should hold my peace.

What shall we then do that we may be saved? Let us begin [the practice of] virtue, as we have opportunity: let us portion out the virtues to ourselves, as laborers do their husbandry; in this month let us master evil-speaking, injuriousness, unjust anger; and let us lay down a law for ourselves, and say, To-day let us set this right. Again, in this month let us school ourselves in forbearance, and in another, in some other virtue: And when we have got into the habit of this virtue let us go to another, just as in the things we learn at school, guarding what is already gained, and acquiring others.

After this let us proceed to contempt for riches. First let us restrain our hands from grasping, and then let us give alms. Let us not simply confound everything, with the same hands both slaying and showing mercy forsooth. After this, let us go to some other virtue, and from that, to another. " Filthiness and foolish talking and jesting, let it not be even named among you." (Eph. v. 4, 3.) Let us be thus far in the right way.

There is no need of spending money, there is no need of labor, none of sweat, it is enough to have only the will, and all is done. There is no need to travel a long way, nor to cross a boundless ocean, but to be in earnest and of ready mind, and to put a bridle on the tongue. Unseasonable reproaches, anger, disorderly lusts, luxuriousness, expensiveness, let us cast off; and the desire of wealth also from our soul, perjury and habitual oaths.

If we thus cultivate ourselves, plucking out the former thorns, and casting in the heavenly seed, we shall be able to attain the good things promised. For the Husbandman will come and will lay us up in His Garner, and we shall attain to all good things, which may we all attain, by the grace and lovingkindness of our Lord Jesus Christ, with whom to the Father together with the Holy Ghost, be glory, power, honor, now and for ever, and world without end. Amen.

# HOMILY XXV.

### Hebrews xi. 17–19.

" By faith [Abraham],[1] when he was tried, offered up Isaac; and he that had received the promises offered up his only-begotten son, of whom it was said, That in Isaac shall thy seed be called: accounting that God was able to raise him up even from the dead; from whence also he received him in a figure."

[1.] Great indeed was the faith of Abraham. For while in the case of Abel, and of Noah, and of Enoch, there was an opposition of reasonings only, and it was necessary to go beyond human reasonings; in this case it was necessary not only to go beyond human reasonings, but to manifest also something more. For what was of God[2] seemed to be opposed to what was of God; and faith opposed faith, and command promise.

I mean this: He had said, " Get thee out of thy country, and from thy kindred, and I will give thee this land." (Gen. xii. 1, 7.) " He gave him none inheritance in it, no not so much as to set his foot on." (Acts vii. 5.) Seest thou how what was done was opposed to the promise? Again He said, " In Isaac shall thy seed be called" (Gen. xxi. 12), and he believed: and again He says, Sacrifice to Me this one, who was to fill all the world from his seed. Thou seest the opposition between the commands and the promise? He enjoined things that were in contradiction to the promises, and yet not even so did the righteous man stagger, nor say he had been deceived.

For you indeed, he means, could not say this, that He promised ease and gave tribulation. For in our case, the things which He promised, these also He performs. How so? " In the world " (He says), " ye shall have tribulation." (John xvi. 33.) " He that taketh not his cross and followeth Me, is not worthy of Me." (Matt. x. 38.) " He that hateth not his life shall not find it." (John xii. 25.) And, " He that forsaketh not all that he hath, and followeth after Me, is not worthy of Me." (Luke xiv. 27, 33.) And again, " Ye shall be brought before rulers and kings for My sake." (Matt. x. 18.) And again, " A man's foes shall be they of his own household." (Matt. x. 36.) But the things which pertain to rest are yonder.

But with regard to Abraham, it was different. He was enjoined to do what was opposed to the promises; and yet not even so was he troubled, nor did he stagger, nor think he had been deceived. But you endure nothing except what was promised, yet you are troubled.

---

[1] Mr. Field's text omits Ἀβραάμ, and has δεξάμενος for ἀναδεξάμενος.
[2] τὰ τοῦ Θεοῦ, the acts and words of God.

[2.] He heard the opposite of the promises from Him who had made them ; and yet he was not disturbed, but did them as if they had been in harmony [therewith]. For they were in harmony ; being opposed indeed according to human calculations, but in harmony [when viewed] by Faith. And how this was, the Apostle himself has taught us, by saying, " accounting[1] that God was able to raise Him up, even from the dead." By the same faith (he means) by which he believed that God gave what was not,[2] and raised up the dead, by the same was he persuaded that He would also raise him up after he had been slain in sacrifice. For it was alike impossible (to human calculation, I mean) from a womb which was dead and grown old and already become useless for child-bearing to give a child, and to raise again one who had been slain. But his previous faith prepared the way for things to come.

And see ; the good things came first, and the hard things afterwards, in his old age. But for you, on the contrary, (he says) the sad things are first, and the good things last. This for those who dare to say, ' He has promised us the good things after death ; perhaps He has deceived us.' He shows that " God is able to raise up even from the dead," and if God be able to raise from the dead, without all doubt He will pay all [that He has promised].

But if Abraham so many years before, believed " that God is able to raise from the dead," much more ought we to believe it. Thou seest (what I at first said) that death had not yet entered in, ₄nd yet He drew them at once to the hope of the resurrection, and led them to such full assurance, that when bidden, they even slay their own sons, and readily offer up those from whom they expected to people the world.

And he shows another thing too, by saying, that " God tempted Abraham." (Gen. xxii. 1.) What then ? Did not God know that the man was noble and approved ? Why then did He tempt him ? Not that He might Himself learn, but that He might show to others, and make his fortitude manifest to all.[3] And here also he shows the cause of trials, that they may not suppose they suffer these things as being forsaken [of God]. For in their case indeed, it was necessary that they should be tried, because there were many who persecuted or plotted against them : but in Abraham's case, what need was there to devise trials for him which did not

exist ? Now this trial, it is evident, was by His command. The others indeed happened by His allowance, but this even by His command. If then temptations make men approved in such wise that, even where there is no occasion, God exercises His own athletes ; much more ought we to bear all things nobly.

And here he said emphatically, " By faith, when he was tried, he offered up Isaac," for there was no other cause for his bringing the offering but that.

[3.] After this he pursues the same thought. No one (he says) could allege, that he had another son, and expected the promise to be fulfilled from him, and therefore confidently offered up this one. " And " (his words are) " he offered up his only-begotten, who had received the promises." Why sayest thou " only-begotten "? What then ? Of whom was Ishmael sprung ? I mean " only-begotten " (he would say) so far as relates to the word of the promise. Therefore after saying, " Only-begotten," showing that he says it for this reason, he added, " of whom it was said, In Isaac shall thy seed be called," that is, " from " him. Seest thou how he admires what was done by the Patriarch ? " In Isaac shall thy seed be called," and that son he brought to be sacrificed.

Afterwards, that no one may suppose he does this in despair, and in consequence of this command had cast away that Faith,[4] but may understand that this also was truly of faith, he says that he retained that faith also, although it seem to be at variance with this. But it was not at variance. For he did not measure the power of God by human reasonings, but committed all to faith. And hence he was not afraid to say, that God was " able to raise him up, even from the dead."

" From whence also he received him in a figure,"[5] that is in idea,[6] by the ram, he means. How ? The ram having been slain, he was saved : so that by means of the ram he received him again, having slain it in his stead. But these things were types : for here it is the Son of God who is slain.

And observe, I beseech you, how great is His lovingkindness. For inasmuch as a great favor was to be given to men, He, wishing to do this, not by favor, but as a debtor, arranges that a man should first give up his own son on account of God's command, in order that He Himself might seem to be doing nothing great in giving up His own Son, since a man had done this before Him ; that He might be supposed to do it not of grace, but of debt. For we wish to do this kindness also to those whom we love, others, to appear first to have received some little thing

---

[1] λογισάμενος. The cognate word λογισμὸς is used throughout for our " reasoning," " calculation."
[2] οὐκ ὄντα ἐχαρίσατο, i.e. Isaac. See Rom. iv. 17, " Before God, in whom he believed, who quickeneth the dead, and calleth those things which he not as though they were (τὰ μὴ ὄντα ὡς ὄντα) ; and for the next clause, see ib. ver. 19, " He considered not his own body, now dead, nor yet the deadness of Sarah's womb ": to which, so to say, life was restored.
[3] [See St. Cyr. Alex. Glaph. 87.]
[4] conviction [?].      [5] ἐν παραβολῇ.
[6] ἐν ὑποδείγματι, see c. ix. 9, 23.

from them, and so give them all : and we boast more of the receiving than of the giving ; and we do not say, We gave him this, but, We received this from him.

"From whence also" (are his words) "he received him in a figure," i.e. as in a riddle[1] (for the ram was as it were a figure of Isaac) or, as in a type. For since the sacrifice had been completed, and Isaac slain in purpose,[2] therefore He gave him to the Patriarch.

[4.] Thou seest, that what I am constantly saying, is shown in this case also? When we have proved that our mind is made perfect, and have shown that we disregard earthly things, then earthly things also are given to us ; but not before ; lest being bound to them already, receiving them we should be bound still. Loose thyself from thy slavery first (He says), and then receive, that thou mayest receive no longer as a slave, but as a master. Despise riches, and thou shalt be rich. Despise glory, and thou shalt be glorious. Despise the avenging thyself on thine enemies, and then shalt thou attain it. Despise repose, and then thou shalt receive it : that in receiving thou mayest receive not as a prisoner, nor as a slave, but as a freeman.

For as in the case of little children, when the child eagerly desires childish playthings, we hide them from him with much care, as a ball, for instance, and such like things, that he may not be hindered from necessary things ; but when he thinks little of them, and no longer longs for them, we give them fearlessly, knowing that henceforth no harm can come to him from them, the desire no longer having strength enough to draw him away from things necessary ; so God also, when He sees that we no longer eagerly desire the things of this world, thenceforward permits us to use them. For we possess them as freemen and men, not as children.

For [in proof] that if thou despise the avenging thyself on thine enemies, thou wilt then attain it, hear what he says, "If thine enemy hunger, feed him ; if he thirst, give him drink," and he added, "for in so doing, thou shalt heap coals of fire on his head." (Rom. xii. 20.) And again, that if thou despise riches, thou shalt then obtain them, hear Christ saying, "There is no man which hath left father, or mother, or house, or brethren, who shall not receive an hundredfold, and shall inherit everlasting life." (Matt. xix. 29.) And that if thou despise glory, thou shalt then attain it, again hear Christ Himself saying, "He that will be first among you, let him be your minister." (Matt. xx. 26.) And

again, "For whosoever shall humble himself, he shall be exalted." (Matt. xxiii. 12.)

What sayest thou? If I give drink to mine enemy, do I then punish him? If I give up my goods, do I then possess them? If I humble myself, shall I then be exalted? Yea, He says, for such is My power, to give contraries by means of contraries. I abound in resources and in contrivances : be not afraid. The 'Nature of things' follows My will : not I attend upon Nature. I do all things : I am not controlled by them : wherefore also I am able to change their form and order.

[5.] And why dost thou wonder if [it is so] in these instances? For thou wilt find the same also in all others. If thou injure, thou art injured ;[3] if thou art injured, then thou art uninjured ; if thou punish, then thou hast not punished another, but hast punished thyself. For "he that loveth iniquity," it is said, "hateth his own soul." (Ps. xi. 5, LXX.) Seest thou that thou dost not injure, but art injured?[4] Therefore also Paul says, "Why do ye not rather take wrong?" (1 Cor. vi. 7.) Dost thou see that this is not to be wronged?

When thou insultest, then art thou insulted. And most persons partly know this : as when they say one to another, "Let us go away, do not disgrace yourself." Why? Because the difference is great between thee and him : for however much thou insultest him, he accounts it a credit. Let us consider this in all cases, and be above insults. I will tell you how.

Should we have a contest with him who wears the purple, let us consider that in insulting him, we insult ourselves, for we become worthy to be disgraced. Tell me, what dost thou mean? When thou art a citizen of Heaven, and hast the Philosophy that is above, dost thou disgrace thyself with him "that mindeth earthly things"? (Phil. iii. 19.) For though he be in possession of countless riches, though he be in power, he does not as yet know the good that is therein. Do not in insulting him, insult thyself. Spare thyself, not him. Honor thyself, not him. Is there not some Proverb such as this, He that honoreth,[5] honoreth himself? With good reason : for he honors not the other, but himself. Hear what a certain wise man says, "Do honor to thy soul according to the dignity thereof." (Ecclus. x. 28.) "According to the dignity thereof," what is this? If he have defrauded

---

[1] ἐν αἰνίγματι, where one thing is said, and another covertly meant: as the expression is used 1 Cor. xiii. 12, of our present knowledge of the Blessedness of Heaven.    [2] τῇ προαιρέσει.

[3] ἠδικήθης.
[4] This reading, adopted by Mr. Field, is found only in one MS. followed by Savile and the later editions: the other authorities, including Mutianus' version, have, "Seest thou that thou hast not been injured, but injurest?" Perhaps this may be the true reading, St. Chrys. in these words turning his address to those who are suffering worldly wrong: and saying that if they patiently endure, they are not the sufferers, but inflict suffering on their oppressors, though the expression ἀδικεῖς is very strong.
[5] or, "respects [another], respects," &c.

(it means), do not thou defraud; if he has insulted, do not thou insult.

[6.] Tell me, I pray thee, if some poor man has taken away clay thrown out of thy yard, wouldst thou for this have summoned a court of justice? Surely not. Why? Lest thou shouldst disgrace thyself; lest all men should condemn thee. The same also happens in this case. For the rich man is poor, and the more rich he is, the poorer is he in that which is indeed poverty. Gold is clay, cast out in the yard, not lying in thy house, for thy house is Heaven. For this, then, wilt thou summon a Court of Justice, and will not the citizens on high condemn thee? Will they not cast thee out from their country, who art so mean, who art so shabby, as to choose to fight for a little clay? For if the world were thine, and then some one had taken it, oughtest thou to pay any attention to it?

Knowest thou not, that if thou wert to take the world ten times or an hundred times, or ten thousand times, and twice that, it is not to be compared with the least of the good things in Heaven? He then who admires the things here slights those yonder, since he judges these worthy of exertion, though so far inferior to the other. Nay, rather indeed he will not be able to admire those other. For how [can he], whilst he is passionately excited towards these earthly things? Let us cut through the cords and entanglements: for this is what earthly things are.

How long shall we be stooping down? How long shall we plot one against another, like wild beasts; like fishes? Nay rather, the wild beasts do not plot against each other, but [against] animals of a different tribe. A bear for instance does not readily kill a bear, nor a serpent kill a serpent, having respect for the sameness of race. But thou, with one of the same race, and having innumerable claims,[1] as common origin, rational faculties, the knowledge of God, ten thousand other things, the force of nature, him who is thy kinsman, and partaker of the same nature — him thou killest, and involvest in evils innumerable. For what, if thou dost not thrust thy sword, nor plunge thy right hand into his neck, other things more grievous than this thou doest, when thou involvest him in innumerable evils. For if thou hadst done the other, thou wouldst have freed him from anxiety, but now thou encompassest him with hunger, with slavery, with feelings of discouragement, with many sins. These things I say, and shall not cease to say, not [as] preparing you to commit murder: nor as urging you to some crime short of that; but that you may not be confident, as if you were not to give account. "For" (it says) "he that

taketh away a livelihood" (Ecclus. xxxiv. 22) and asketh bread, it says.[2]

[7.] Let us at length keep our hands to ourselves, or rather, let us not keep them, but stretch them out honorably, not for grasping, but for alms-giving. Let us not have our hand unfruitful nor withered; for the hand which doeth not alms is withered; and that which is also grasping, is polluted and unclean.

Let no one eat with such hands; for this is an insult to those invited. For, tell me, if a man when he had made us lie down on tapestry[3] and a soft couch and linen interwoven with gold, in a great and splendid house, and had set by us a great multitude of attendants, and had prepared a tray[4] of silver and gold, and filled it with many dainties of great cost and of all sorts, then urged us to eat, provided we would only endure his besmearing his hands with mire or with human ordure, and so sitting down to meat with us — would any man endure this infliction? Would he not rather have considered it an insult? Indeed I think he would, and would have gone straightway off. But now in fact, thou seest not hands filled with what is indeed filth, but even the very food, and yet thou dost not go off, nor flee, nor find fault. Nay, if he be a person in authority, thou even accountest it a grand affair, and destroyest thine own soul, in eating such things. For covetousness is worse than any mire; for it pollutes, not the body but the soul, and makes it hard to be washed. Thou therefore, though thou seest him that sitteth at meat defiled with this filth both on his hands and his face, and his house filled with it, nay and his table also full of it (for dung, or if there be anything more unclean than that, it is not so unclean and polluted as those viands), dost thou feel as if forsooth thou wert highly honored, and as if thou wert going to enjoy thyself?

And dost thou not fear Paul who allows us to go without restraint to the Tables of the heathen if we wish, but not even if we wish to those of the covetous? For, "if any man who is called a Brother" (1 Cor. v. 11), he says, meaning here by Brother every one who is a believer simply, not him who leads a solitary life. For what is it which makes brotherhood? The Washing of regeneration; the being enabled to call God our Father. So that he that is a Monk, if he be a Catechumen, is not a Brother,[5] but

---

[1] δικαιώματα.

[2] καὶ ἄρτον αἰτῶν, φησί. There is great variation in the MSS. of this passage: and possibly the true reading is lost. St. Chrys. partly quotes Ecclus. xxxi. 22 of the Septuagint (xxxiv. 22 of our Version), "He that taketh away his living slayeth his neighbor, and he that defraudeth the hireling of his hire is a blood-shedder." As the text stands we must suppose that he is alluding to sayings which had become proverbial, and that his hearers would supply the words, "is a murderer"; or "is the same."

[3] ταπήτων.          [4] πίνακα.

[5] It will be observed that the word πιστὸς, "believer," means "one who believes and is baptized": as opposed to the unbaptized,

the believer though he be in the world, is a Brother. "If any man," saith he, "that is called a Brother." (1 Cor. v. 11.) For at that time there was not even a trace of any one leading a Monastic life, but this blessed [Apostle] addressed all his discourse to persons in the world. "If any man," he says, "that is called a Brother, be a fornicator, or covetous, or a drunkard, with such an one, no not to eat." But not so with respect to the heathen: but "If any of them that believe not," meaning the heathen, "bid you and ye be disposed to go, whatsoever is set before you eat." (1 Cor. x. 27.)

[8.] "If any man that is called Brother be" (he says) "a drunkard." Oh! what strictness! Yet we not only do not avoid drunkards, but even go to their houses, partaking of what they set before us.

Therefore all things are upside down, all things are in confusion, and overthrown, and ruined. For tell me, if any such person should invite thee to a banquet, thee who art accounted poor and mean, and then should hear thee say, "Inasmuch as the things set before me are [the fruit] of overreaching, I will not endure to defile my own soul," would he not be mortified? Would he not be confounded? Would he not be ashamed? This alone were sufficient to correct him, and to make him call himself wretched for his wealth, and admire thee for thy poverty, if he saw himself with so great earnestness despised by thee.

But we "are become" (I know not why) "servants of men" (1 Cor. vii. 23), though Paul cries aloud throughout, "Be not ye the servants of men." Whence then have we become "servants of men"? Because we first became servants of the belly, and of money, and of glory, and of all the rest; we gave up the liberty which Christ bestowed on us.

What then awaiteth him who is become a servant (tell me)? Hear Christ saying, "The servant abideth not in the house for ever." (John viii. 35.) Thou hast a declaration complete in itself, that he never entereth into the Kingdom; for this is what "the House" means. For, He says, "in My Father's House are many mansions." (John xiv. 2.) "The servant" then "abideth not in the House for ever." By a servant He means him who is "the servant of sin." But he that "abideth not in the House for ever," abideth in Hell for ever, having no consolation from any quarter.

Nay, to this point of wickedness are matters come, that they even give alms out of these [ill-gotten gains], and many receive [them]. Therefore our boldness has broken down, and we are not able to rebuke any one. But however, henceforward at least, let us flee the mischief arising from this; and ye who have rolled yourselves in this mire, cease from such defilement, and restrain your rage for such banquets, if even now we may by any means be able to have God propitious to us, and to attain to the good things which have been promised: which may we all obtain in Christ Jesus our Lord, with whom to the Father together with the Holy Ghost, be glory, power, honor, now and for ever, and world without end. Amen.

---

# HOMILY XXVI.

## Hebrews xi. 20—22.

"By faith, Isaac blessed Jacob and Esau concerning things to come. By faith, Jacob when he was a dying blessed both the sons of Joseph, and worshiped[1] leaning on the top of his staff. By faith, Joseph when he died made mention of the departing of the children of Israel; and gave commandment concerning his bones."

[1.] "Many prophets and righteous men" (it is said) "have desired to see those things which ye see, and have not seen them; and to hear those things which ye hear and have not heard them." (Matt. xiii. 17.) Did then those righteous men know all the things to come? Yea, most certainly. For if because of the weakness of those who were not able to receive Him, the Son was not revealed, — He was with good reason revealed to those conspicuous in virtue. This Paul also says, that they knew "the things to come," that is the resurrection of Christ.

Or he does not mean this: but that "By faith, concerning things to come" [means] not [concerning] the world to come, but "concerning things to come" in this world. For how [except by faith] could a man sojourning in a strange land, give such blessings?

---

even though they believed and were so religious as to devote themselves to an ascetic life. Also, that at this time there were those who had given themselves up to an ascetic life and still deferred their Baptism, see St. Greg. Naz. Hom. xl. 18. In the later form of the text, this clause has been altered to "So that a Catechumen, even though he be a Monk, is not a brother."

[1] or, "bowed himself, made obeisance."

But on the other hand he obtained the blessing, and yet did not receive it.[1] Thou seest that what I said with regard to Abraham, may be said also of Jacob, that they did not enjoy[2] the blessing, but the blessings went to his posterity, while he himself obtained the "things to come." For we find that his brother rather enjoyed the blessing. For [Jacob] spent all his time in servitude and working as a hireling, and [amid] dangers, and plots, and deceits, and fears; and when he was asked by Pharaoh, he says, "Few and evil have my days been" (Gen. xlvii. 9); while the other lived in independence and great security, and afterwards was an object of terror to [Jacob]. Where then did the blessings come to their accomplishment, save in the [world] to come?

Seest thou that from the beginning the wicked have enjoyed things here, but the righteous the contrary? Not however all. For behold, Abraham was a righteous man, and he enjoyed things here as well, though with affliction and trials. For indeed wealth was all he had, seeing all else relating to him was full of affliction. For it is impossible that the righteous man should not be afflicted, though he be rich: for when he is willing to be overreached, to be wronged, to suffer all other things, he must be afflicted. So that although he enjoy wealth, [yet is it] not without grief. Why? you ask. Because he is in affliction and distress. But if at that time the righteous were in affliction, much more now.

"By Faith," he says, "Isaac blessed Jacob and Esau concerning things to come" (and yet Esau was the elder; but he puts Jacob first for his excellence). Seest thou how great was his Faith? Whence did he promise to his sons so great blessings? Entirely from his having faith in God.

[2.] "By Faith, Jacob when he was a dying, blessed both the sons of Joseph." Here we ought to set down the blessings entire, in order that both his faith and his prophesying may be made manifest. "And worshiped leaning,"[3] he says, "upon the top of his staff." Here, he means, he not only spoke, but was even so confident about the future things, as to show it also by his act. For inasmuch as another King was about to arise from Ephraim, therefore it is said, "And he bowed himself upon the top of his staff." That is, even though he was now an old man, "he bowed himself" to Joseph, showing the obeisance of the whole people which was to be [directed] to him. And this indeed had al-

ready taken place, when his brethren "bowed down" to him: but it was afterwards to come to pass through the ten tribes. Seest thou how he foretold the things which were to be afterwards? Seest thou how great faith they had? How they believed "concerning the things to come"?

For some of the things here, the things present, are examples of patience only, and of enduring ill-treatment, and of receiving nothing good; for instance, what is mentioned in the case of Abraham, in the case of Abel. But others are [examples] of Faith, as in the case of Noah, that there is a God, that there is a recompense. (For Faith in this place is manifold,[4] both of there being a recompense, and of awaiting it, not under the same conditions,[5] and of wrestling before the prizes.) And the things also which concern[6] Joseph are of Faith only. Joseph heard that [God] had made a promise to Abraham, that He had engaged His word "to thee and to thy seed will I give this land;" and though in a strange land, and not yet seeing the engagement fulfilled, but never faltered even so, but so believed as even to "speak of the Exodus, and to give commandment concerning his bones." He then not only believed himself, but led on the rest also to Faith: that having the Exodus always in mind (for he would not have "given commandment concerning his bones," unless he had been fully assured [of this]), they might look for their return [to Canaan].

Wherefore, when some men say, 'See! Even righteous men had care about their sepulchers,' let us reply to them, that it was for this reason: for he knew that "the earth is the Lord's and all that therein is."[7] (Ps. xxiv. 1.) He could not indeed have been ignorant of this, who lived in so great philosophy, who spent his whole life in Egypt. And yet if he had wished, it was possible for him to return, and not to mourn or vex himself. But when he had taken up his father thither, why did he enjoin them to carry up thence his own bones also? Evidently for this reason.

But what? Tell me, are not the bones of Moses himself laid in a strange land? And those of Aaron, of Daniel, of Jeremiah? And as to those of the Apostles we do not know where those of most of them are laid. For of Peter indeed, and Paul, and John, and Thomas, the sepulchers are well known; but those of the rest, being so many, have nowhere become known.[8] Let us not therefore lament at all about this, nor be so little-minded. For wherever we may be buried, "the earth is the Lord's

---

[1] That is, Jacob obtained the blessing from Isaac, but did not himself receive the good things bestowed by the blessing. Therefore the good things to come were not those of this world. This is a reply to the second, the alternative, interpretation suggested.

[2] ἀπώναντο. This is the reading of the best MSS. and the oldest translation. There seems no reason to adopt the later reading ἀπώναντο, "he did not enjoy."

[3] προσεκύνησεν, as Gen. xlvii. 31. The same word also is used in the LXX. in Gen. xxxvii. 7, 9, 10, of Joseph's dreams, where our version has "made obeisance" and "bow down ourselves."

[4] πολύτροπος.

[5] καὶ τοῦ μὴ ἐπὶ τοῖς αὐτοῖς αὐτὴν ἀναμένειν.

[6] τὰ κατά.    [7] τὸ πλήρωμα αὐτοῦ.

[8] οὐδαμοῦ γνώριμοι γεγόνασι.

and all that therein is." (Ps. xxiv. 1.) Certainly what must take place, does take place: to mourn however, and lament, and bewail the departed, arises from littleness of mind.

[3.] (Ver. 23) "By faith, Moses when he was born, was hid three months of his parents." Dost thou see that in this case they hoped for things on the earth after their death?[1] And many things were fulfilled after their death. This is for some who say, 'After death those things were done for them, which they did not obtain while alive; nor did they believe [would be] after their death.'

Moreover Joseph did not say, He gave not the land to me in my life-time, nor to my father, nor to my grandfather, whose excellence too ought to have been reverenced; and will He vouchsafe to these wretched people what He did not vouchsafe to them? He said nothing of all this, but by Faith he both conquered and went beyond all these things.

He has named Abel, Noah, Abraham, Isaac, Jacob, Joseph, all illustrious and admirable men. Again he makes the encouragement greater, by bringing down the matter to ordinary persons. For that the admirable should feel thus, is nothing wonderful, and to appear inferior to them, is not so dreadful: but to show oneself inferior even to people without names, this is the dreadful thing. And he begins with the parents of Moses, obscure persons, who had nothing so great as their son [had]. Therefore also he goes on to increase the strangeness of what he says by enumerating even women that were harlots, and widows. For "by Faith" (he says) "the harlot Rahab perished not with them that believed not, when she had received the spies with peace." And he mentions the rewards not only of belief but also of unbelief; as in [the case of] Noah.

But at present we must speak of the parents of Moses. Pharaoh gave orders that all the male children should be destroyed, and none had escaped the danger. Whence did these expect to save their child? From faith. What sort of Faith? "They saw" (he says) "that he was a proper child." The very sight drew them on to Faith: thus from the beginning, yea from the very swaddling-clothes, great was the Grace that was poured out on that righteous man, this being not the work of nature. For observe, the child immediately on its birth appears fair and not disagreeable to the sight. Whose [work] was this? Not that of nature, but of the Grace of God, which also stirred up and strengthened that

barbarian woman, the Egyptian, and took and drew her on.

And yet in truth Faith had not a sufficient foundation in their case. For what was it to believe from sight? But you (he would say) believe from facts and have many pledges of Faith. For "the receiving with joyfulness the spoiling of their goods" (c. x. 34), and other such [things], were [evidences] of Faith and of Patience. But inasmuch as these [Hebrews] also had believed, and yet afterwards had become faint-hearted, he shows that the Faith of those [saints of old] also was long continued,[2] as, for instance, that of Abraham, although the circumstances seemed to contend against it.

"And" (he says) "they were not afraid of the king's commandment," although that was in operation,[3] but this [their hope respecting their child] was simply a kind of bare expectation. And this indeed was [the act] of his parents; but Moses himself what did he contribute?

[4.] Next again an example appropriate to them, or rather greater than that. For, saith he, (ver. 24–26) "by faith Moses when he was come to years, refused to be called the son of Pharaoh's daughter, choosing rather to suffer affliction with the people of God than to enjoy the pleasures of sin for a season; esteeming the reproach of Christ greater riches than the treasures of Egypt;[4] for he had respect unto the recompense of the reward." As though he had said to them, 'No one of you has left a palace, yea a splendid palace, nor such treasures; nor, when he might have been a king's son, has he despised this, as Moses did.' And that he did not simply leave [these things], he expressed by saying, "he refused," that is, he hated, he turned away. For when Heaven was set before him, it was superfluous to admire an Egyptian Palace.

And see how admirably Paul has put it. He did not say, 'Esteeming heaven, and the things in heaven,' 'greater riches than the treasures of Egypt,' but what? "The reproach of Christ." For the being reproached for the sake of Christ he accounted better than being thus at ease; and this itself by itself was reward.

"Choosing rather" (he says) "to suffer affliction with the people of God." For ye indeed suffer on your own account, but he "chose" [to suffer] for others; and voluntarily threw himself into so many dangers, when it was in his power both to live religiously, and to enjoy good things.

"Than" (he says) "to enjoy the pleasures of sin for a season." He called unwillingness "to

---

[1] i.e. they hoped that through their child, when they were dead, the promised blessings upon earth (or in the land of Canaan) would be given. In the next sentence St. Chrys. seems to return to the conduct of Joseph, in order to add an observation, which he had omitted before.

[2] εἰς πολὺ παρετείνετο.　　　[3] ἐκεῖνο ἐνηργεῖτο.
[4] Αἰγύπτου. This is the approved reading of the sacred text and of St. Chrys. The common editions have ἐν Αἰγύπτῳ, "in Egypt," in each of the three places where the words recur.

suffer affliction with the" rest "sin": this, he says, [Moses] accounted to be "sin." If then he accounted it "sin" not to be ready to "suffer affliction with" the rest, it follows that the suffering affliction must be a great good; since he threw himself into it from the royal palace.

But this he did, seeing some great things before him. "Esteeming the reproach of Christ greater riches than the treasures of Egypt." What is, "the reproach of Christ"? It is, being reproached in such ways as ye are, the reproach which Christ endured; Or that he endured for Christ's sake: for "that rock was Christ"[1] (1 Cor. x. 4); the being reproached as you are.

But what is "the reproach of Christ"? That [because] we repudiate the [ways] of our fathers we are reproached; that we are evil-entreated when we have run to God. It was likely that he also was reproached, when it was said to him, "Wilt thou kill me as thou killedst the Egyptian yesterday?" (Ex. ii. 14.) This is "the reproach of Christ," to be ill-treated to the end, and to the last breath: as He Himself was reproached and heard, "If Thou be the Son of God" (Matt. xxvii. 40), from those who were of the same race. This is "the reproach of Christ" when a man is reproached by those of his own family, or by those whom he is benefiting. For [Moses] also suffered these things from the man who had been benefited [by him].

In these words he encouraged them, by showing that even Christ suffered these things, and Moses also, two illustrious persons. So that this is rather "the reproach of Christ" than of Moses, inasmuch as He suffered these things from "His own." (John i. 11.) But neither did the one send forth lightnings, nor the Other feel any [anger],[2] but He was reviled and endured all things, whilst they "wagged their heads." (Matt. xxvii. 39.) Since therefore it was probable that they [the readers] also would hear such things, and would long for the Recompense, he says that even Christ and Moses had suffered the like. So then ease[3] is [the portion] of sin; but to be reproached, of Christ. For what then dost thou wish? "The reproach of Christ," or ease?

[5.] (Ver. 27) "By faith he forsook Egypt not fearing the wrath of the king; for he endured as seeing Him who is Invisible." What dost thou say? That he did not fear? And yet the Scripture says, that when he heard, he "was afraid"[4] (Ex. ii. 14), and for this cause provided for safety by flight, and stole away, and secretly withdrew himself; and afterwards he was exceedingly afraid. Observe the expressions with care: he said, "not fearing the wrath of the king," with reference to his even presenting himself again. For it would have been [the part] of one who was afraid, not to undertake again his championship, nor to have any hand in the matter. That he did however again undertake it, was [the part] of one who committed all to God: for he did not say, 'He is seeking me, and is busy [in the search], and I cannot bear again to engage in this matter.'

So that even flight was [an act of] faith. Why then did he not remain (you say)? That he might not cast himself into a foreseen danger. For this finally would have been tempting [God]: to leap into the midst of dangers, and say, 'Let us see whether God will save me.' And this the devil said to Christ, "Cast Thyself down." (Matt. iv. 6.) Seest thou that it is a diabolical thing, to throw ourselves into danger without cause and for no purpose, and to try whether God will save us? For he [Moses] could no longer be their champion when they who were receiving benefits were so ungrateful. It would therefore have been a foolish and senseless thing to remain there. But all these things were done, because, "he endured as seeing Him who is Invisible."

[6.] If then we too always see God with our mind, if we always think in remembrance of Him, all things will appear endurable to us, all things tolerable; we shall bear them all easily, we shall be above them all. For if a person seeing one whom he loves, or rather, remembering him is roused in spirit, and elevated in thought, and bears all things easily, while he delights in the remembrance; one who has in mind Him who has vouchsafed to love us in deed, and remembers Him, when will he either feel anything painful, or dread anything fearful or dangerous? When will he be of cowardly spirit? Never.

For all things appear to us difficult, because we do not have the remembrance of God as we ought; because we do not carry Him about alway in our thoughts. For surely He might justly say to us, "Thou hast forgotten Me, I also will forget thee." And so the evil becomes twofold, both that we forget Him and He us. For these two things are involved in each other, yet are two. For great is the effect of God's remembrance, and great also of His being remembered by us. The result of the one is that we choose good things; of the other that we

---

[1] The later MSS. and common editions add some explanatory words, thus: "he suffered for Christ's sake when he was reviled in the matter of the rock, from which he brought out water: and 'that rock' (he says) 'was Christ'"; they omit the clause next following.
[2] ἔπαθέ τι.   [3] ἄνεσις.

[4] See Ex. ii. 14, 15. St. Chrys. is speaking of Moses' flight after killing the Egyptian.

accomplish them, and bring them to their end.[1] Therefore the prophet says, " I will remember Thee from the land of Jordan, and from the little hill of Hermon." (Ps. xlii. 6.) The people which were in Babylon say this : being there, I will remember Thee.

[7.] Therefore let us also, as being in Babylon, [do the same]. For although we are not sitting among warlike foes, yet we are among enemies. For some [of them] indeed were sitting as captives, but others did not even feel their captivity, as Daniel, as the three children (cf. Ps. cxxxvii. 1) ; who even while they were in captivity became in that very country more glorious even than the king who had carried them captive. And he who had taken them captive does obeisance to[2] the captives.

Dost thou see how great virtue is? When they were in actual captivity he waited on them as masters. He therefore was the captive, rather than they. It would not have been so marvelous if when they were in their native country, he had come and done them reverence in their own land, or if they had been rulers there. But the marvelous thing is, that after he had bound them, and taken them captive, and had them in his own country, he was not ashamed to do them reverence in the sight of all, and to " offer an oblation."[3] (Dan. ii. 46.)

Do you see that the really splendid things are those which relate to God, whereas human things are a shadow? He knew not, it seems, that he was leading away masters for himself, and that he cast into the furnace those whom he was about to worship. But to them, these things were as a dream.

Let us fear God, beloved, let us fear [Him] : even should we be in captivity, we are more glorious than all men. Let the fear of God be present with us, and nothing will be grievous, even though thou speak of poverty, or of disease, or of captivity, or of slavery, or of any other grievous thing : Nay even these very things will themselves work together for us the other way. These men were captives, and the king worshiped them : Paul was a tent-maker, and they sacrificed to him as a God.

[8.] Here a question arises : Why, you ask, did the Apostles prevent the sacrifices, and rend their clothes, and divert them from their attempt, and say with earnest lamentation, " What are ye doing? we also are men of like passions with you " (Acts xiv. 15) ; whereas Daniel did nothing of this kind.

For that he also was humble, and referred [the] glory to God no less than they, is evident from many places. Especially indeed is it evident, from the very fact of his being beloved by God. For if he had appropriated to himself the honor belonging to God, He would not have suffered him to live, much less to be in honor. Secondly, because even with great openness he said, " And as to me, O King, this secret hath not been revealed to me through any wisdom that is in me." (Dan. ii. 30.) And again ; he was in the den for God's sake, and when the prophet brought him food, he saith, " For God hath remembered me." (Bel and the Dragon, ver. 38.) Thus humble and contrite was he.

He was in the den for God's sake, and yet he counted himself unworthy of His remembrance, and of being heard. Yet we though daring [to commit] innumerable pollutions, and being of all men most polluted, if we be not heard at our first prayer, draw back. Truly, great is the distance between them and us, as great as between heaven and earth, or if there be any greater.

What sayest thou? After so many achievements, after the miracle which had been wrought in the den, dost thou account thyself so humble? Yea, he says ; for what things soever we have done, " we are unprofitable servants." (Luke xvii. 10.) Thus by anticipation did he fulfill the evangelical precept, and accounted himself nothing. For " God hath remembered me," he said. His prayer again, of how great lowliness of mind it is full. And again the three children said thus, " We have sinned, we have committed iniquity." (Song of the Three Children, ver. 6.) And everywhere they show their humility.

And yet Daniel had occasions innumerable for being puffed up ; but he knew that these also came to him on account of his *not* being puffed up, and he did not destroy his treasure. For among all men, and in the whole world he was celebrated, not only[4] because the king cast himself on his face and offered sacrifice to him, and accounted him to be a God, who was himself honored as God in all parts of the world : for he ruled over the whole [earth] ; (and this is evident from Jeremiah. " Who putteth on the earth," saith he, " as a garment." (See Jer. xliii. 12 and Ps. civ. 2.) And again, " I have given it to Nebuchadnezzar My servant " (Jer. xxvii. 6), and again from what he [the King] says in his letter).[5] And because he was held in admiration not only in the place where he was, but everywhere, and was greater than if the rest of the nations had been present and seen him ; when even by letters [the King] confessed his submission[6] and the miracle. But yet again for his wisdom he was also held in admiration,

---

[1] Probably this is to be understood according to that said Hom. xii. 5 [*supra*, pp. 425, 426] of the co-operation of Grace and the human will.

[2] προσκυνεῖ, Dan. ii. 46.

[3] μαναὰ, Dan. ii. 46, according to the translation of Theodotion, and the Vatican MS. The Alex. has μαννὰ, as has one MS. of St. Chrys.

[4] The apodosis seems to be, " But yet again for his wisdom," &c., which comes after some parentheses.

[5] See Dan. iv. 1, &c.　　　[6] τὴν δουλείαν.

for it is said, "Art thou wiser than Daniel?" (Ezek. xxviii. 3.) And after all these things he was thus humble, dying ten thousand times for the Lord's sake.

Why then, you ask, being so humble did he not repel either the adoration which•was paid him by the king, or the offerings?

[9.] This I will not say, for it is sufficient for me simply to mention the question, and the rest I leave to you, that at least in this way I may stir up your thoughts. (This however I conjure you, to choose all things for the fear of God, having such examples; and because in truth we shall obtain the things here also, if we sincerely lay hold on the things which are to come.) For that he did not do this out of arrogance, is evident from his saying, "Thy gifts be to thyself." (Dan. v. 17.)

For besides this also again is another question, how while in words he rejected it, in deed he received the honor, and wore the chain[1] [of gold]. (Dan. v. 29.)

Moreover while Herod on hearing the cry "It is the voice of a god and not of a man," inasmuch as "he gave not God the glory, burst in sunder, and all his bowels gushed out" (Acts xii. 22, 23 ; see i. 18), this man received to himself even the honor belonging to God, not words only.

However it is necessary to say what this is. In that case [at Lystra] the men were falling into greater idolatry, but in this [of Daniel] not so. How? For his being thus accounted of, was an honor to God. Therefore he said in anticipation, "And as to me, not through any wisdom that is in me." (Dan. ii. 30.) And besides he does not even appear to have accepted the offerings. For he [the king] said (as it is written) that they should offer sacrifice, but it did not appear that the act followed. But there [at Lystra] they carried it even to sacrificing the bulls, and "they called" the one "Jupiter and" the other "Mercurius." (Acts xiv. 12.)

The chain [of gold] then he accepted, that he might make himself known; the offering however why does it not appear that he rejected it? For in the other case too they did not do it, but they attempted it, and the Apostles hindered them; wherefore here also he ought at once to have rejected [the adoration]. And there it was the entire people : here the King. Why he did not divert him [Daniel] expressed by anticipation, [viz.] that [the king] was not making an offering [to him] as to a God, to the overthrow of religious worship, but for the greater wonder. How so? It was on God's account that [Nebuchadnezzar] made the decree; wherefore [Daniel] did not mutilate[2] the honor [offered]. But those others [at Lystra] did not act thus, but supposed them to be indeed gods. On this account they were repelled.

And •here, after having done him reverence, he does these things : for he did not reverence him as a God, but as a wise man.

But it is not clear that he made the offering : and even if he did make it, yet not that it was with Daniel's acceptance.

And what [of this], that he called him "Belteshazzar, the name of" his own "god"?[3] Thus [it seems] they accounted their gods to be nothing wonderful, when he called even the captive thus ; he who commands all men to worship the image,[4] manifold and of various colors, and who adores the dragon.[5]

Moreover the Babylonians were much more foolish than those at Lystra. Wherefore it was not possible at once to lead them on to this. And many [more] things one might say : but thus far these suffice.

If therefore we wish to obtain all good things, let us seek the things of God. For as they who seek the things of this world fail both of them and of the others, so they who prefer the things of God, obtain both. Let us then not seek these but those, that we may attain also to the good things promised in Christ Jesus our Lord, with whom to the Father together with the Holy Ghost, be glory, power, honor, now and for ever and world without end. Amen.

---

[1] μανιάκην.

[2] ἠκρωτηρίαζε.
[3] See Dan. iv. 8.

[4] Dan. iii. 1, &c.
[5] Bel and the Dragon 24.

# HOMILY XXVII.

## HEBREWS xi. 28–31.

"Through faith, he kept the Passover and the sprinkling of blood, lest he that destroyed the first-born should touch them. By faith they passed through the Red Sea, as by dry land; which the Egyptians assaying to do, were drowned.[1] By faith, the walls of Jericho fell down, after they had been compassed about seven days. By faith, the harlot Rahab perished not with them that believed not, when she had received the spies with peace."

[1.] PAUL is wont to establish many things incidentally, and is very full[2] of thoughts. For such is the grace of The Spirit. He does not comprehend a few ideas in a multitude of words, but includes great and manifold thought in brevity of expressions. Observe at least how, in the midst[3] of exhortation, and when discoursing about faith, of what a type and mystery he reminds us, whereof we have the reality. "Through faith" (he says) "he kept the Passover and the sprinkling of blood, lest he that destroyed the first-born should touch them."

But what is "the sprinkling of blood"?[4] A lamb was slain in every household, and the blood was smeared on the door-posts, and this was a means of warding off the Egyptian destruction. If then the blood of a lamb preserved the Jews unhurt in the midst of the Egyptians, and under so great a destruction, much more will the blood of Christ save us, who have had it sprinkled[5] not on the door-posts, but in our souls. For even now also the Destroyer is going about in this depth of night: but let us be armed with that Sacrifice. (He calls the "sprinkling"[6] anointing.) For God has brought us out from Egypt, from darkness, from idolatry.

Although what was done, was nothing, what was achieved was great. For what was done was blood; but was achieved, was salvation, and the stopping, and preventing of destruction. The angel feared the blood; for he knew of what it was a Type; he shuddered, thinking on the Lord's death; therefore he did not touch the door-posts.

Moses said, Smear, and they smeared, and were confident. And you, having the Blood of the Lamb Himself, are ye not confident?

[2.] "By faith, they passed through the Red Sea as by dry land." Again he compares one whole people with another, lest they should say, we cannot be as the saints.

"By faith" (he says) "they passed through the Red Sea, as by dry land, which the Egyptians assaying to do, were drowned." Here he leads them also to a recollection of the sufferings in Egypt.

How, "by faith"? Because they had hoped to pass through the sea, and therefore they prayed: or rather it was Moses who prayed. Seest thou that everywhere Faith goes beyond human reasonings, and weakness and lowliness? Seest thou that at the same time they both believed, and feared punishment, both in the blood on the doors, and in the Red Sea?

And he made it clear that it was [really] water, through those that fell into it, and were choked; that it was not a mere appearance: but as in the case of the lions those who were devoured proved the reality of the facts, and in the case of the fiery furnace, those who were burnt; so here also thou seest that the same things become to the one a cause of salvation[7] and glory, and to the other of destruction.

So great a good is Faith. And when we fall into perplexity, then are we delivered, even though we come to death itself, even though our condition be desperate. For what else was left [for them]? They were unarmed, compassed about by the Egyptians and the sea; and they must either be drowned if they fled, or fall into the hands of the Egyptians. But nevertheless [He] saved them from impossibilities. That which was spread under the one as land, overwhelmed the others as sea. In the former case it forgot its nature: in the latter it even armed itself against them. (Cf. Wisd. xix. 20.)

[3.] "By faith, the walls of Jericho fell down, after they had been compassed about for seven days." For assuredly the sound of trumpets is not able to throw down stones, though one blow for ten thousand years; but Faith can do all things.

Seest thou that in all cases it is not by natural sequence, nor yet by any law of nature that it was changed, but all is done contrary to expectation? Accordingly in this case also all is done contrary to expectation. For inasmuch as he had said again and again, that we ought to trust to the future hopes, he introduced all this argument with reason, showing that not now [only], but even from the beginning all the miracles have been accomplished and achieved by means of it.

"By faith, the harlot Rahab perished not with

---

[1] κατεποντίσθησαν is the reading adopted by Mr. Field, but κατεπόθησαν, "swallowed up," seems to be the reading of his MSS. See his annotation.     [2] πυκνός.
[3] ἐν τάξει.     [4] πρόσχυσις.
[5] ἐπιχριομένους, "been anointed with it."
[6] πρόσχυσιν, the word used by St. Paul, which we translate "sprinkling."

[7] πρὸς σωτηρίας.

them that believed not, having received the spies with peace." It would then be disgraceful, if you should appear more faithless even than a harlot. Yet she [merely] heard what the men related, and forthwith believed. Whereupon the end also followed; for when all perished, she alone was preserved. She did not say to herself, I shall be with my many friends.[1] She did not say, Can I possibly be wiser than these judicious men who do not believe, — and shall I believe? She said no such thing, but believed what had taken place,[2] which it was likely that they would suffer.

[4.] (Ver. 32) "And what shall I more say? For the time would fail me to tell." After this he no longer puts down the names: but having ended with an harlot, and put them to shame by the quality of the person, he no longer enlarges on the histories, lest he should be thought tedious. However he does not set them aside, but runs over them, [doing] both very judiciously, avoiding satiety, and not spoiling the closeness of arrangement; he was neither altogether silent, nor did he speak so as to annoy; for he effects both points. For when a man is contending vehemently [in argument], if he persist in contending, he wearies out the hearer, annoying him when he is already persuaded, and gaining the reputation of vain ambitiousness. For he ought to accommodate himself to what is expedient.

"And what do I more say" (he says)? "For the time would fail me to tell of Gideon, and of Barak, and of Samson, and of Jephthah, of David also and Samuel, and of the prophets."

Some find fault with Paul, because he puts Barak, and Samson, and Jephthah in these places. What sayest thou? After having introduced the harlot, shall he not introduce these? For do not tell me of the rest of their life, but only whether they did not believe and shine in Faith.

"And the prophets," he says, (ver. 33) "who through faith subdued kingdoms." Thou seest that he does not here testify to their life as being illustrious; for this was not the point in question: but the enquiry thus far was about their faith. For tell me whether they did not accomplish all by faith?

"By faith," he says, "they subdued kingdoms;" those with Gideon. "Wrought righteousness;" who? The same. Plainly he means here, kindness.[3]

I think it is of David that he says "they obtained promises." But of what sort were these? Those in which He said that his "seed should sit upon" his "throne." (Ps. cxxxii. 12.)

"Stopped the mouths of lions," (ver. 34) "quenched the violence of fire, escaped the edge of the sword." See how they were in death itself, Daniel encompassed by the lions, the three children abiding in the furnace, the Israelites,[4] Abraham, Isaac, Jacob, in divers temptations; and yet not even so did they despair. For this is Faith; when things are turning out adversely, then we ought to believe that nothing adverse is done, but all things in due order.

"Escaped the edge of the sword." I think that he is again speaking of the three children.

"Out of[5] weakness were made strong." Here he alludes to what took place at their return from Babylon. For "out of weakness," is out of captivity. When the condition of the Jews had now become desperate, when they were no better than dead bones, who could have expected that they would return from Babylon, and not return only, but also "wax valiant" and "turn to flight armies of aliens"? 'But to us,' some one says,[6] 'no such thing has happened.' But these are figures of "the things to come."

(Ver. 35) "Women received their dead raised to life again." He here speaks of what occurred in regard to the prophets, Elisha, [and] Elijah; for they raised the dead.

[5.] (Ver. 35) "And others were tortured,[7] not accepting deliverance, that they might obtain a better resurrection." But we have not obtained a Resurrection. I am able however, he means, to show that they also were cut off, and did "not accept [deliverance], that they might obtain a better resurrection." For why, tell me, when it was open to them to live, did they not choose it? Were they not evidently looking for a better life? And they who had raised up others, themselves chose to die; in order "to obtain a better resurrection," not such as the children of those women.[8]

Here I think he alludes both to John and to James. For beheading is called "torturing."[9] It was in their power still to behold the sun. It was in their power to abstain from reproving[10] [sinners], and yet they chose to die; even they who had raised others chose to die themselves, "that they might obtain a better resurrection."

(Ver. 36) "And others had trial of cruel mockings and scourgings, yea moreover of bonds and imprisonment." He ends with these; with things that come nearer home. For these [ex-

[1] μετ' ἐμῶν.
[2] τοῖς γενομένοις; probably the destruction of the Egyptians and the Amorites, &c., Josh. ii. 10. The common texts have τοῖς λεγομένοις.     [3] φιλανθρωπίαν.
[4] i.e. "when crossing the Red Sea." Field.
[5] ἀπὸ, "from" or "after."
[6] i.e. some Hebrew Christian.
[7] ἀποτυμπανίσθησαν.
[8] The children of the widow of Sarepta, and the Shunamite, had been brought back to continue this life of temptation and sorrow; it was a "better" kind of "Resurrection" which the prophets sought to obtain themselves.
[9] ἀποτυμπανισμός. For instances of this meaning of the word, see Mr. Field's annot.
[10] ἐλέγξαι, the word used by St. John Baptist reproving Herod, Luke iii. 19.

amples] especially bring consolation, when the distress is from the same cause, since even if you mention something more extreme, yet unless it arise from the same cause, you have effected nothing.   Therefore he concluded his discourse with this, mentioning "bonds, imprisonments, scourges, stonings," alluding to the case of Stephen, also to that of Zacharias.

Wherefore he added, "They were slain with the sword." What sayest thou? Some "escaped the edge of the sword," and some "were slain by the sword." (Ver. 34.) What is this? Which dost thou praise? Which dost thou admire? The latter or the former? Nay, he says: the former indeed, is appropriate to you, and the latter, because Faith was strong even unto death itself, and it is a type of things to come. For the wonderful qualities of Faith are two, that it both accomplishes great things, and suffers great things, and counts itself to suffer nothing.

And thou canst not say (he says) that these were sinners and worthless. For even if you put the whole world against them, I find that they weigh down the beam and are of greater value.[1] What then were they to receive in this life? Here he raises up their thoughts, teaching them not to be riveted to things present, but to mind[2] things greater than all that are in this present life, since the "world is not worthy" of them. What then dost thou wish to receive here? For it were an insult to thee, shouldst thou receive thy reward here.

[6.] Let us not then mind[3] worldly things, nor seek our recompense here, nor be so beggarly. For if "the" whole "world is not worthy of" them, why dost thou seek after a part of it? And with good reason; for they are friends of God.

Now by "the world" does he mean here the people, or the creation itself? Both: for the Scripture is wont to use the word of both. If the whole creation, he would say, with the human beings that belong to it, were put in the balance, they yet would not be of equal value with these; and with reason. For as ten thousand measures of chaff and hay would not be of equal value to ten pearls, so neither they; for "better is one that doeth the will of the Lord, than ten thousand transgressors" (Ecclus. xvi. 3);[4] meaning by "ten thousand" not [merely] many, but an infinite multitude.

Consider of how great value is the righteous man. Joshua the son of Nun said, "Let the sun stand still at Gibeon, the moon at the valley of Elom" (Josh. x. 12), and it was so. Let then the whole world come, or rather two or three, or four, or ten, or twenty worlds, and let them say

and do this; yet shall they not be able. But the friend of God commanded the creatures of his Friend, or rather he besought his Friend, and the servants yielded, and he below gave command to those above. Seest thou that these things are for service fulfilling their appointed course?

This was greater than the [miracles] of Moses. Why (I ask)? Because it is not a like thing to command the sea and the heavenly [bodies]. For that indeed was also a great thing, yea very great, nevertheless it was not at all equal [to the other].

Why was this? The name of Joshua [JESUS],[5] was a type. For this reason then, and because of the very name, the creation reverenced him. What then! Was no other person called Jesus? [Yes]; but this man was on this account so called in type; for he used to be called Hoshea. Therefore the name was changed: for it was a prediction and a prophecy. He brought in the people into the promised land, as JESUS [does] into heaven; not the Law; since neither did Moses [bring them in], but remained without. The Law has not power to bring in, but grace. Seest thou the types which have been before sketched out from the beginning? He laid his commands on the creation, or rather, on the chief[6] part of the creation, on the very head itself as he stood below; that so when thou seest JESUS in the form of Man saying the same, thou mayest not be disturbed, nor think it strange. He, even while Moses was living, turned back wars. Thus, even while the Law is living, He directs[7] all things; but not openly.

[7.] But let us consider how great is the virtue of the saints. If here they work such things, if here they do such things, as the angels do, what then above? How great is the splendor they have?

Perhaps each of you might wish to be such as to be able to command the sun and moon. (At this point what would they say who assert that the heaven is a sphere?[8] For why did he not [merely] say, "Let the sun stand still," but added "Let the sun stand still at the valley of Elom," that is, he will make the day longer? This was done also in the time of Hezekiah. The sun went back. This again is more wonderful than the other, to go the contrary way, not having yet gone round his course.)

We shall attain to greater things than these if we will. For what has Christ promised us? Not that we shall make the sun stand still, or the moon, nor that the sun shall retrace his steps, but what? "I and the Father will come unto him," He says, "and We will make our abode with him." (John xiv. 23.) What need have I

---

[1] The common texts add the explanatory words, "For this cause also he said, ' Of whom the world was not worthy.'"
[2] φρονεῖν μείζω.
[3] φρονῶμεν.
[4] See above, p. 475, note 3.

[5] [The two names being the same in Greek. Cf. Heb. iv. 8, Ἰησοῦς. — F. G.]        [6] καιρίῳ.
[7] διοικεῖ: so Tertullian in the well-known words: Adv. Prax. 16.
[8] See above, p. 314.

of the sun and the moon, and of these wonders, when the Lord of all Himself comes down and abides with me? I need these not. For what need I any of these things? He Himself shall be to me for Sun and for Light. For, tell me, if thou hadst entered into a palace, which wouldst thou choose, to be able to re-arrange some of the things which have been fixed there, or so to make the king a familiar friend, as to persuade him to take up his abode with thee? Much rather the latter than the former.

[8.] But what wonder is it, says some one, that what a man commands, Christ should also? But Christ (you say) needs not the Father, but acts of His own authority, you say. Well. Therefore first confess and say, that he needs not the Father, and acts of His own authority: and then I will ask thee, whether His prayer is not in the way of condescension and arrangement (for surely Christ was not inferior to Joshua the son of Nun), and that He might teach us? For as, when thou hearest a teacher lisping,[1] and saying over the alphabet, thou dost not say that he is ignorant; and when he asks, Where is such a letter? thou knowest that he does not ask in ignorance, but because he wishes to lead on the scholar; in like manner Christ also did not make His prayer as needing prayer, but desiring to lead thee on, that thou mayest continually apply thyself to prayer, that thou mayest do it without ceasing, soberly, and with great watchfulness.

And by watching, I do not mean, merely the rising at night, but also the being sober[2] in our prayers during the day. For such an one is called watchful.[3] Since it is possible both in praying by night to be asleep, and in praying by day to be awake, when the soul is stretched out towards God, when it considers with whom it holds converse, to whom its words are addressed, when it has in mind that angels stand by with fear and trembling, while he approaches gaping and scratching himself.

[9.] Prayer is a mighty weapon if it be made with suitable mind. And that thou mayest learn its strength, continued entreaty has overcome shamelessness, and injustice, and savage cruelty, and overbearing rashness. For He says, "Hear what the unjust judge saith." (Luke xviii. 6.) Again it has overcome sloth also, and what friendship did not effect, this continued entreaty did: and "although he will not give him because he is his friend" (He says), "yet because of his importunity he will rise and give to him." (Luke xi. 8.) And continued assiduity made her worthy who was unworthy. "It is not meet" (He says) "to take the children's bread and to cast it to the dogs. Yea! Lord!" she says, "for even the dogs eat [the crumbs] from their master's table." (Matt. xv. 26, 27.) Let us apply ourselves to Prayer. It is a mighty weapon if it be offered with earnestness, if without vainglory, if with a sincere mind. It has turned back wars, it has benefited an entire nation though undeserving. "I have heard their groaning" (He says) "and am come down to deliver them." (Acts vii. 34.) It is itself a saving medicine, and has power to prevent sins, and to heal misdeeds. In this the desolate widow was assiduous. (1 Tim. v. 5.)

If then we pray with humility, smiting our breast as the publican, if we utter what he did, if we say, "Be merciful to me a sinner" (Luke xviii. 13), we shall obtain all. For though we be not publicans, yet have we other sins not less than his.

For do not tell me, that thou hast gone wrong in some small matter [only], since the thing has the same nature. For as a man is equally called a homicide whether he has killed a child or a man, so also is he called overreaching whether he be overreaching in much or in little. Yea and to remember injuries too, is no small matter, but even a great sin. For it is said, "the ways of those who remember injuries [tend] to death." (Prov. xii. 28, LXX.) And "He that is angry with his brother without a cause, shall be in danger of hell," and he that "calleth his brother a fool" (Matt. v. 22), and senseless, and numberless such things.

But we partake even of the tremendous mysteries unworthily, and we envy, and we revile. And some of us have even oftentimes been drunk. But each one of these things, even itself by itself, is enough to cast us out of the kingdom, and when they even come all together, what comfort shall we have? We need much penitence, beloved, much prayer, much endurance, much perseverance, that we may be enabled to attain the good things which have been promised to us.

[10.] Let us then say, even we, "Be merciful to me a sinner," nay rather, let us not say it only, but let us also be thus minded; and should another call us so, let us not be angry. He heard the words, "I am not as this Publican" (Luke xviii. 11), and was not provoked thereby, but filled with compunction. He accepted the reproach, and he put away the reproach. The other spoke of the wound, and he sought the medicine. Let us say then, "Be merciful to me a sinner" (Luke xviii. 13); but even if another should so call us, let us not be indignant.

But if we say ten thousand evil things of ourselves, and are vexed when we hear them from others, then there is no longer humility, nor confession, but ostentation and vainglory. Is it ostentation (you say) to call one's self a sinner? Yes; for we obtain the credit of humility,

---

[1] ψελλίζοντος.  [2] νήφειν.
[3] ἄγρυπνος.

we are admired, we are commended; whereas if we say the contrary of ourselves, we are despised. So that we do this too for the sake of credit. But what is humility? It is when another reviles us, to bear it, to acknowledge our fault, to endure evil speakings. And yet even this would not be [a mark] of humility but of candor. But now we call ourselves sinners, unworthy, and ten thousand other such names, but if another apply one of them to us, we are vexed, we become savage. Seest thou that this is not confession, nor even candor? Thou saidst of thyself that thou art such an one: be not indignant if thou hearest it also said by others, and art reproved.

In this way thy sins are made lighter for thee, when others reproach thee: for they lay a burden on themselves indeed, but thee they lead onwards into philosophy. Hear what the blessed David says, when Shimei cursed him, "Let him alone" (he says) "the Lord hath bidden him, that He might look on my humiliation" (he says): "And the Lord will requite me good for his cursing on this day." (2 Sam. xvi. 11, 12.)

But thou while saying evil things of thyself, even in excess, if thou hearest not from others the commendations that are due to the most righteous, art enraged. Seest thou that thou art trifling with things that are no subjects for trifling? For we even repudiate praises in our desire for other praises, that we may obtain yet higher panegyrics, that we may be more admired. So that when we decline to accept commendations, we do it that we may augment them. And all things are done by us for credit, not for truth. Therefore all things are hollow, all impracticable. Wherefore I beseech you now at any rate to withdraw from this mother of evils, vainglory, and to live according to what is approved by God, that so you may attain to the good things to come, in Christ Jesus our Lord, with whom to the Father be glory, together with His Holy and good Spirit, now and ever and world without end. Amen.

---

# HOMILY XXVIII.

## Hebrews xi. 37, 38.

"They wandered about in sheep-skins, and goat-skins, being destitute, afflicted, tormented (of whom this[1] world was not worthy); wandering in deserts, and in mountains, and in dens, and caves of the earth."

[1.] At all times indeed, but especially then when I reflect upon the achievements of the saints, it comes over me to feel despondency concerning my own condition,[2] because we have not even in dreams experienced the things among which those men spent their whole lives, not paying the penalty of sins, but always doing rightly and yet always afflicted.

For consider, I beseech you, Elijah, to whom our discourse has come round to-day, for he speaks of him in this passage, and in him his examples end: which [example] was appropriate to their case. And having spoken of what befell the Apostles, that "they were slain with the sword, were stoned," he goes back again to Elijah, who suffered the same things with them. (See 2 Kings i. 8.) For since it was probable that they would not as yet hold the Apostles in so great estimation, he brings his exhortation and consolation from him who had been taken up [into Heaven] and who was held in special admiration.

For "they wandered about" (he says) "in sheep-skins, and goat-skins, being destitute, afflicted, tormented,[3] of whom this world was not worthy."

They had not even raiment, he says, through the excess of affliction, no city, no house, no lodging-place; the same which Christ said, "but the Son of Man hath not where to lay His head." (Matt. viii. 20.) Why do I say "no lodging-place"? No standing-place: for not even when they had gained the wilderness, were they at rest. For he said not, They sat down in the wilderness, but even when they were there, they fled, and were driven thence, not out of the inhabited world only, but even out of that which was uninhabitable. And he reminds them of the places where they were set, and of things which there befell [them].

Then next, he says, they bring accusations against you for Christ's sake. What accusation had they against Elijah, when they drove him out, and persecuted him, and compelled him to struggle with famine? Which these [Hebrews] were then suffering. At least, the brethren, it is said, decided to send [relief] to those of the disciples who were afflicted. "Every man according to his ability, determined to send relief unto

---

[1] οὗτος. Mr. F. observes that St. Chrys. more usually cites the text without οὗτος.
[2] ἀπαγορεύειν τὰ καθ' ἑ.

[3] "ill-treated," κακουχούμενοι.

the brethren that dwelt in Judea" (Acts xi. 29), which was [the case] of these also.

"Tormented" [or "ill-treated"], he says; that is, suffering distress, in journeyings, in dangers.

But "They wandered about," what is this? "Wandering," he says, "in deserts and in mountains and in dens and caves of the earth," like exiles and outcasts, as persons taken in the basest [of crimes], as those not worthy to see the sun, they found no refuge from the wilderness, but must always be flying, must be seeking hiding-places, must bury themselves alive in the earth, always be in terror.

[2.] What then is the reward of so great a change?[1]  What is the recompense?

They have not yet received it, but are still waiting; and after thus dying in so great tribulation, they have not yet received it.  They gained their victory so many ages ago, and have not yet received [their reward].  And you who are yet in the conflict, are you vexed?

Do you also consider what a thing it is, and how great, that Abraham should be sitting, and the Apostle Paul, waiting till thou hast been perfected, that then they may be able to receive their reward.  For the Saviour has told them before that unless we also are present, He will not give it them.  As an affectionate father might say to sons who were well approved, and had accomplished their work, that he would not give them to eat, unless their brethren came.  And art thou vexed, that thou hast not yet received the reward?  What then shall Abel do, who was victor before all, and is sitting uncrowned?  And what Noah?  And what, they who lived in those [early] times: seeing that they wait for thee and those after thee?

Dost thou see that we have the advantage of them?  For "God" (he says) "has provided some better thing for us."  In order that they might not seem to have the advantage of us from being crowned before us, He appointed one time of crowning for all; and he that gained the victory so many years before, receives his crown with thee.  Seest thou His tender carefulness?

And he did not say, "that they without us might not be crowned," but "that they without us might not be made perfect"; so that at that time they appear perfect also.  They were before us as regards the conflicts, but are not before us as regards the crowns.  He wronged not them, but He honored us.  For they also wait for the brethren.  For if we are "all one body," the pleasure becomes greater to this body, when it is crowned altogether, and not part by part.  For the righteous are also worthy

of admiration in this, that they rejoice in the welfare of their brethren, as in their own.  So that for themselves also, this is according to their wish, to be crowned along with their own members.  To be glorified all together, is a great delight.

[3.] (C. xii. 1)  "Wherefore" (he says) "we also being compassed about with so great a cloud of witnesses."  In many places the Scripture derives its consolation in evils from corresponding things.  As when the prophet says, "From burning heat, and from storm, and rain."  (Isa. iv. 6.)  This at least he says here also, that the memory of those holy men, reestablishes and recovers the soul which had been weighed down by woes, as a cloud does him who is burnt by the too hot rays [of the sun].

And he did not say, "lifted on high above us," but, "compassing us about," which was more than the other; so that we are in greater security.

What sort of "cloud"?  "A load of witnesses."[2]  With good reason he calls not those in the New [Testament] only, but those in the Old also, "witnesses" [or "martyrs"].  For they also were witnesses to the greatness of God, as for instance, the Three Children, those with Elijah, all the prophets.

"Laying aside all things."  "All": what? That is, slumber, indifference, mean reasonings, all human things.

"And the sin which doth [so] easily beset us"; εὐπερίστατον, that is either, "which easily circumvents us," or "what can easily be circumvented,"[3] but rather this latter.  For it is easy, if we will, to overcome sin.

"Let us run with patience" (he says) "the race that is set before us."  He did not say, Let us contend as boxers, nor, Let us wrestle, nor, Let us do battle: but, what was lightest of all, the [contest] of the foot-race, this has he brought forward.  Nor yet did he say, Let us add to the length of the course; but, Let us continue patiently in this, let us not faint.  "Let us run" (he says) "the race that is set before us."

[4.] In the next place as the sum and substance of his exhortation, which he puts both first and last, even Christ.  (Ver. 2)  "Looking" (he says) "unto JESUS the Author and Finisher of our Faith";  The very thing which Christ Himself also continually said to His disciples, "If they have called the Master of the house

---

[1] ἀμοιβῆς, i.e. the accepting sufferings instead of an easy life.

[2] μαρτύρων ὄγκον.  St. Chrys. connects ὄγκον with μαρτύρων and takes πάντα as a neuter plural; the words of the Apostle, τοσοῦτον ἔχοντες περικείμενον ἡμῖν νέφος, μαρτύρων ὄγκον, ἀποθέμενοι πάντα, he would understand thus, " Seeing we are compassed about with so great a cloud, a load of witnesses, let us lay aside all things," &c. [But previously he has connected with γέφος, so that the present connection with ὄγκον was probably an afterthought on the spur of the moment. — F. G.]

[3] περίστασιν παθεῖν.

Beelzebub, how much more them of His house-hold?" (Matt. x. 25.) And again, "The disciple is not above his Master, nor the servant above his Lord." (Matt. x. 24.)

"Looking" (he says), that is, that we may learn to run. For as in all arts and games, we impress the art upon our mind by looking to our masters, receiving certain rules through our sight, so here also, if we wish to run, and to learn to run well, let us look to Christ, even to JESUS "the author and finisher of our faith." What is this? He has put the Faith within us. For He said to His disciples, "Ye have not chosen Me, but I have chosen you" (John xv. 16); and Paul too says, "But then shall I know, even as also I have been known."[1] (1 Cor. xiii. 12.) He put the Beginning into us, He will also put on the End.

"Who," he says, "for the joy that was set before Him, endured the Cross, despising the shame." That is, it was in His power not to suffer at all, if He so willed. For "He did no sin, neither was guile found in His mouth" (1 Pet. ii. 22); as He also says in the Gospels, "The Prince of the world cometh and hath nothing in Me." (John xiv. 30.) It lay then in His power, if so He willed, not to come to the Cross. For, "I have power," He says, "to lay down My life; and I have power to take it again." (John x. 18.) If then He who was under no necessity of being crucified, was cruci-fied for our sake, how much more is it right that we should endure all things nobly!

"Who for the joy that was set before Him" (he says) "endured the cross, despising the shame." But what is, "Despising the shame"? He chose, he means, that ignominious death. For suppose that He died. Why [should He] also [die] ignominiously? For no other reason, but to teach us to make no account of glory from men. Therefore though under no obliga-tion He chose it, teaching us to be bold against it, and to set it at nought. Why did he say not "pain," but "shame"? Because it was not with pain[2] that He bore these things.

What then is the end? "He is set down at the right hand of the throne of God." Seest thou the prize which Paul also says in an epistle, "Wherefore God also hath highly exalted Him, and given Him a Name which is above every name, that at the Name of JESUS Christ every knee should bow." (Phil. ii. 9, 10.) He speaks in respect to the flesh.[3] Well then, even if there were no prize, the example would suffice to per-suade us to accept all [such] things. But now prizes also are set before us, and these no com-mon ones, but great and unspeakable.

[5.] Wherefore let us also, whenever we suf-

fer anything of this kind, before the Apostles con-sider Christ. Why? His whole life was full of insults. For He continually heard Himself called mad, and a deceiver, and a sorcerer; and at one time the Jews said, "Nay," (it says) "but He deceiveth the people." (John vii. 12.) And again, "That deceiver said while He was yet alive, after three days I will rise again." (Matt. xxvii. 63.) As to sorcery too they calumniated Him, saying, "He casteth out the devils by Beelzebub." (Matt. xii. 24.) And that "He is mad and hath a devil." (John x. 20.) "Said we not well" (it says) "that He hath a devil and is mad?" (John viii. 48.)

And these things He heard from them, when doing them good, performing miracles, showing forth the works of God. For indeed, if He had been so spoken of, when He did nothing, it would not have been so wonderful: But [it is wonderful] that when He was teaching what pertained to Truth He was called "a deceiver," and when He cast out devils, was said to "have a devil," and when He was overthrowing all that was opposed [to God], was called a sorcerer. For these things they were continually alleging against Him.

And if thou wouldst know both the scoffs[4] and the ironical jeerings,[5] which they made against Him (what particularly wounds our souls), hear first those from His kindred. "Is not this" (it says) "the carpenter's son, whose father and mother we know? Are not his brethren all with us?" (Matt. xiii. 55; Mark vi. 3; John vi. 42.) Also scoffing at Him from His country, they said He was "of Nazareth." And again, "search," it says, "and see, for out of Galilee hath no prophet arisen." (John vii. 52.) And He en-dured being so greatly calumniated. And again they said, "Doth not the Scripture say, that Christ cometh from the town of Bethlehem?" (John vii. 42.)

Wouldst thou see also the ironical jeerings they made? Coming, it says, to the very cross they worshiped Him; and they struck Him and buffeted Him, and said, "Tell us who it is that smote Thee" (Matt. xxvi. 68); and they brought vinegar to Him, and said, "If Thou be the Son of God, come down from the Cross." (Matt. xxvii. 40.) And again, the servant of the High Priest struck Him with the palm of his hand; and He says, "If I have spoken evil, bear witness of the evil; but if well, why smit-eth thou Me?" (John xviii. 23.) And in derision they put a robe about Him; and they spat in His face; and they were continually applying their tests, tempting Him.

Wouldest thou see also the accusations, some secret, some open, some from disciples? "Will ye

---

[1] ἐπεγνώσθην.
[2] λύπης.
[3] the human nature.
[4] σκώμματα.
[5] εἰρωνείας.

also go away?" (John vi. 67) He says. And that saying, "Thou hast a devil" (John viii. 48, vii. 20), was uttered by those who already believed.

Was He not continually a fugitive, sometimes in Galilee, and sometimes in Judea? Was not His trial great, even from the swaddling clothes? When He was yet a young child, did not His mother take Him and go down into Egypt? For all these reasons he says, "Looking unto JESUS the Author and Finisher of our Faith, who for the joy that was set before Him endured the cross, despising the shame, and is set down at the right hand of the throne of God."

To Him then let us look, also to the [sufferings [1]] of His disciples, reading the [writings [2]] of Paul, and hearing him say, "In much patience, in afflictions, in necessities, in persecutions,[3] in distresses, in stripes, in imprisonments." (2 Cor. vi. 4, 5.) And again, "Even to this present hour, we both hunger, and thirst, and are naked, and are buffeted, and have no certain dwelling-place, and labor, working with our own hands. Being reviled, we bless; being persecuted, we suffer it; being defamed, we entreat." (1 Cor. iv. 11–13.) Has any one [of us] suffered the smallest part of these things? For, he says, [we are] "As deceivers, as dishonored, as having nothing." (2 Cor. vi. 8, 10.) And again, "Of the Jews five times received I forty stripes save one; thrice was I beaten with rods, once was I stoned, a night and a day have I been in the deep; in journeyings often, in tribulations, in distress, in hunger." (2 Cor. xi. 24–26.) And that these things seem good to God, hear him saying, "For this I besought the Lord thrice, and He said to me, My Grace is sufficient for thee; for My strength is made perfect in weakness." (2 Cor. xii. 8–10.) "Wherefore," he says, "I take pleasure in infirmities, in afflictions, in necessities, in distresses, in stripes, in imprisonments, that the power of Christ may rest upon me." Moreover, hear Christ Himself saying, "In the world ye shall have tribulation." (John xvi. 33.)

[6.] Ver. 3. "For consider," saith he, "Him that endured such contradiction of sinners against Himself, lest ye be wearied and faint in your minds." For if the sufferings of those near us arouse us, what earnestness will not those of our Master give us! What will they not work in us!

And passing by all [else], he expressed the whole by the [word] "Contradiction"; and by adding "such." For the blows upon the cheek, the laughter, the insults, the reproaches, the mockeries, all these he indicated by "contradiction." And not these only, but also the things which befell Him during His whole life, of teaching.

For a great, a truly great consolation are both the sufferings of Christ, and those of the Apostles. For He so well knew that this is the better way of virtue, as even to go that way Himself, not having need thereof: He knew so well that tribulation is expedient for us, and that it becomes rather a foundation for repose. For hear Him saying, "If a man take not his cross, and follow after Me, he is not worthy of Me." (Matt. x. 38.) If thou art a disciple, He means, imitate the Master; for this is [to be] a disciple. But if while He went by [the path of] affliction, thou [goest] by that of ease, thou no longer treadest the same path, which He trod, but another. How then dost thou follow, when thou followest not? How shalt thou be a disciple, not going after the Master? This Paul also says, "We are weak, but ye are strong; we are despised, but ye are honored." (1 Cor. iv. 10.) How is it reasonable, he means, that we should be striving after opposite things, and yet that you should be disciples and we teachers?

[7.] Affliction then is a great thing, beloved, for it accomplishes two great things; It wipes out sins, and it makes men strong.

What then, you say, if it overthrow and destroy? Affliction does not do this, but our own slothfulness. How (you say)? If we are sober and watchful, if we beseech God that He would not "suffer us to be tempted above that we are able" (1 Cor. x. 13), if we always hold fast to Him, we shall stand nobly, and set ourselves against our enemy. So long as we have Him for our helper, though temptations blow more violently than all the winds, they will be to us as chaff and a leaf borne lightly along. Hear Paul saying, "In all these things" (are his words) "we are more than conquerors." (Rom. viii. 37.) And again, "For I reckon that the sufferings of this present time are not worthy to be compared with the glory which shall be revealed in us." (Rom. viii. 18.) And again, "For the light affliction which is but for a moment, worketh for us a far more exceeding and eternal weight of glory." (2 Cor. iv. 17.)

Consider what great dangers, shipwrecks, afflictions one upon another, and other such things, he calls "light"; and emulate this inflexible one, who wore this body simply and heedlessly.[4] Thou art in poverty? But not in such as Paul, who was tried by hunger, and thirst, and nakedness. For he suffered this not for one day, but endured it continually. Whence does this appear? Hear himself saying, "Even unto this present hour we both hunger and thirst and are naked." (1 Cor. iv. 11.) Oh!

---

[1] τὰ.			[2] τὰ.
[3] [The insertion of ἐνδιωγμοῖς here appears to be entirely without authority, and was probably a slip of memory. — F. G.]

[4] ἁπλῶς καὶ εἰκῆ.

How great glory did he already have in preaching, when he was undergoing so great [afflictions]! Having now [reached] the twentieth year [thereof], at the time when he wrote this. For he says, "I knew a man fourteen years ago, whether in the body, or out of the body, I know not." (2 Cor. xii. 2.) And again, "After three years" (he says) "I went up to Jerusalem." (Gal. i. 18.) And again hear him saying, "It were better for me·to die, than that any man should make my glorying void." (1 Cor. ix. 15.) And not only this, but again also in writing he said, "We are become as the filth of the world." (1 Cor. iv. 13.) What is more difficult to endure than hunger? What than freezing cold? What than plottings made by brethren: whom he afterwards calls "false brethren"? (2 Cor. xi. 26.) Was he not called the pest of the world? An Impostor? A subverter? Was he not cut with scourging?

[8.] These things let us take into our mind, beloved, let us consider them, let us hold them in remembrance, and then we shall never faint, though we be wronged, though we be plundered, though we suffer innumerable evils. Let it be granted us to be approved in Heaven, and all things [are] endurable. Let it be granted us to fare well there, and things here are of no account. These things are a shadow, and a dream; whatever they may be, they are nothing either in nature or in duration, while those are hoped for and expected.

For what wouldst thou that we should compare with those fearful things? What with the unquenchable fire? With the never-dying worm? Which of the things here canst thou name in comparison with the "gnashing of teeth," with the "chains," and the "outer darkness," with the "wrath," the "tribulation," the "anguish"? But as to duration? Why, what are ten thousand years· to ages boundless and without end? Not so much as a little drop to the boundless ocean.

But what about the good things? There, the superiority is still greater. "Eye hath not seen," (it is said,) "ear hath not heard, neither have entered into the heart of man" (1 Cor. ii. 9), and these things again shall be during boundless ages. For the sake of these then were it not well to be cut [by scourging] times out of number, to be slain, to be burned, to undergo ten thousand deaths, to endure everything whatsoever that is dreadful both in word and deed? For even if it were possible for one to live when burning in the fire, ought one not to endure all for the sake of attaining to those good things promised?

[9.] But why do I trifle in saying these things to men who do not even choose to disregard riches, but hold fast to them as though they were immortal? And if they give a little out of much,

think they have done all? This is not Almsgiving. For Almsgiving is that of the Widow who emptied out "all her living." (Mark xii. 44.) But if thou dost not go on to contribute so much as the widow, yet at least contribute the whole of thy superfluity: keep what is sufficient, not what is superfluous.

But there is no one who contributes even his superabundance. For so long as thou hast many servants,[1] and garments of silk, these things are all superfluities. Nothing is indispensable or necessary, without which we are able to live; these things are superfluous, and are simply superadded.[2] Let us then see, if you please, what we cannot live without. If we have only two servants, we can live. For whereas some live without servants, what excuse have we, if we are not content with two? We can also have a house built of brick of three rooms,[3] and this were sufficient for us. For are there not some with children and wife who have but one room?[4] Let there be also, if you will, two serving boys.

[10.] And how is it not a shame (you say) that a gentlewoman[5] should walk out with [only] two servants? It is no shame, that a gentlewoman should walk abroad with two servants, but it is a shame that she should go forth with many. Perhaps you laugh when you hear this. Believe me it *is* a shame. Do you think it a great matter to go out with many servants, like dealers in sheep, or dealers in slaves? This is pride and vainglory, the other is philosophy and respectability. For a gentlewoman ought not to be known from the multitude of her attendants. For what virtue is it to have many slaves? This belongs not to the soul, and whatever is not of the soul does not show gentility. When she is content with a few things, then is she a gentlewoman indeed; but when she needs many, she is a servant and inferior to slaves.

Tell me, do not the angels go to and fro about the world alone, and need not any one to follow them? Are they then on this account inferior to us? They who need no [attendants] to us who need them? If then not needing an attendant at all, is angelic, who comes nearer to the angelic life, she who needs many [attendants], or she who [needs] few? Is not this a shame? For a shame it is to do anything out of place.

Tell me who attracts the attention of those who are in the public places,[6] she who brings many in her train, or she who [brings but] few? And is not she who is alone, less conspicuous even than she who is attended by few? Seest thou that this [first-named conduct] is a shame? Who attracts the attention of those in the public

---

1 i.e. slaves.
2 ἁπλῶς ἔξω πρόσκειται.
3 οἰκημάτων.
4 οἶκον.
5 τὴν ἐλευθέραν.
6 the open spaces of the streets where idlers gathered.

places, she who wears beautiful garments, or she who is dressed simply and artlessly? Again who attracts those in the public places, she who is borne on mules, and with trappings ornamented with gold, or she who walks out simply, and as it may be, with propriety? Or we do not even look at this latter, if we even see her; but the multitudes not only force their way to see the other, but also ask, Who is she, and Where from? And I do not say how great envy is hereby produced. What then (tell me), is it disgraceful to be looked at or not to be looked at? When is the shame greater, when all stare at her, or when no one [does]? When they inform themselves about her, or when they do not even care? Seest thou that we do everything, not for modesty's sake but for vainglory?

However, since it is impossible to draw you away from that, I am content for the present that you should learn that this [conduct] is no disgrace. Sin alone is a disgrace, which no one thinks to be a disgrace, but everything rather than this.

[11.] Let your dress be such as is needful, not superfluous. However, that we may not shut you up too narrowly, this I assure you, that we have no need of ornaments of gold, or of lace.[1] And it is not I who say this. For that the words are not mine, hear the blessed Paul saying, and solemnly charging women "to adorn themselves, not with plaitings [of the hair], or gold, or pearls, or costly apparel." (1 Tim. ii. 9.) But with what kind, O Paul, wouldest thou tell us? For perhaps they will say, that only golden things are costly; and that silks are not costly. Tell us with what kind thou wouldest? "But having food and raiment,[2] let us therewith" (he says) "be content."[3] (1 Tim. vi. 8.) Let our garment be such as merely to cover us. For God hath given them to us for this reason, that we may cover our nakedness; and this any sort of garment can do, though but of trifling cost. Perhaps ye laugh, who wear dresses of silk; for in truth one may well laugh, considering what Paul enjoined and what we practice!

But my discourse is not addressed to women only, but also to men. For the rest of the things, which we have are all superfluous; only the poor possess no superfluities; and perhaps they too from necessity: since, if it had been in their power, even they would not have abstained [from them]. Nevertheless, "whether in pretense or in truth" (Phil. i. 18), so far they have no superfluities.

[12.] Let us then wear such clothes as are sufficient for our need. For what does much gold mean? To those on the stage these things are fitting, this apparel belongs to them, to har-

lots, to those who do everything to be looked at. Let her beautify herself, who is on the stage or the dancing platform. For she wishes to attract all to her. But a woman who professes godliness, let her not beautify herself thus, but in a different way. Thou hast a means of beautifying thyself far better than that. Thou also hast a theater:[4] for that theater make thyself beautiful: clothe thyself with those ornaments. What is thy theater? Heaven, the company of Angels. I speak not of Virgins only, but also of those in the world. All as many as believe in Christ have that theater. Let us speak such things that we may please those spectators. Put on such garments that thou mayest gratify them.

For tell me, if a harlot putting aside her golden ornaments, and her robes, and her laughter, and her witty and unchaste talk, clothe herself with a cheap garment, and having dressed herself simply come [on the stage], and utter religious words, and discourse of chastity, and say nothing indelicate, will not all rise up? Will not this theater be dispersed? Will they not cast her out, as one who does not know how to suit herself to the crowd, and speaks things foreign to that Satanic theater? So thou also, if thou enter into the Theater of Heaven clad with her garments, the spectators will cast thee out. For there, there is no need of these garments of gold, but of different ones. Of what kind? Of such as the prophet names, "clothed in fringed work of gold, and in varied colors" (Ps. xlv. 13), not so as to make the body white and glistering, but so as to beautify the soul. For the soul it is, which is contending and wrestling in that Theater. "All the glory of the King's daughter is from within" (Ps. xlv. 13), it says. With these do thou clothe thyself; for [so] thou both deliverest thyself from other evils innumerable, and thy husband from anxiety and thyself from care.

For so thou wilt be respected by thy husband, when thou needest not many things. For every man is wont to be shy towards those who make requests of him; but when he sees that they have no need of him, then he lets down his pride, and converses with them as equals. When thy husband sees that thou hast no need of him in anything, that thou thinkest lightly of the presents which come from him, then, even though he be very arrogant,[5] he will respect thee more, than if thou wert clad in golden ornaments; and thou wilt no longer be his slave. For those of whom we stand in need, we are compelled to stoop to. But if we restrain ourselves we shall no longer be regarded as criminals,[6] but he knows that we pay him obedience from the fear of God, not for what is given by him. For now, when that he confers great favors on us, whatever

---

[1] λεπτῶν ὀθονίων.
[2] σκεπάσματα.
[3] ἀρκεσθησόμεθα.
[4] "body of spectators."
[5] φρονημάτων.
[6] ὑπόδικοι.

honor he receives, he thinks he has not received all [that is due to him] : but then, though he obtain but a little, he will account it a favor; he does not reproach, nor will he be himself compelled to overreach on thy account.

[13.] For what is more unreasonable, than to provide golden ornaments, to be worn in baths, and in market places? However, in baths and in market places it is perhaps no wonder, but that a woman should come into Church so decked out is very ridiculous. For, for what possible reason does she come in here wearing golden ornaments, she who ought to come in that she may hear [the precept] "that they adorn not themselves with gold, nor pearls, nor costly array"? (1 Tim. ii. 9.) With what object then, O woman, dost thou come? Is it indeed to fight with Paul, and show that even if he repeat these things ten thousand times thou regardest them not? Or is it as wishing to put us your teachers to shame as discoursing on these subjects in vain? For tell me; if any heathen and unbeliever, after he has heard the passage read where the blessed Paul says these things, having a believing wife, sees that she makes much account of beautifying herself, and puts on ornaments of gold, that she may come into Church and hear Paul charging [the women] that they adorn themselves, neither with "gold" (1 Tim. ii. 9), nor with "pearls," nor with "costly array," will he not indeed say to himself, when he sees her in her little room,[1] putting on these things, and arranging them beautifully, "Why is my wife staying within in her little room? Why is she so slow? Why is she putting on her golden ornaments? Where has she to go to? Into the Church? For what purpose? To hear? 'not with costly array';" will he not smile, will he not burst out into laughter? will he not think our religion[2] a mockery and a deceit? Wherefore, I beseech [you], let us leave golden ornaments to processions, to theaters, to signs on the shops.[3] But let not the image of God be decked out with these things: let the gentlewoman be adorned with gentility, and gentility is the absence of pride, and of boastful display.

Nay even if thou wish to obtain glory from men, thou wilt obtain it thus. For we shall not wonder so much that the wife of a rich man wears gold and silk (for this is the common practice of them all), as when she is dressed in a plain and simple garment made merely of wool. This all will admire, this they will applaud. For in that adorning indeed of ornaments of gold and of costly apparel, she has many to share with her. And if she surpass one, she is surpassed by another. Yea, even if she surpass all, she must yield the palm to the Empress her-

self. But in the other case, she outdoes all, even the Emperor's wife herself. For she alone in wealth, has chosen the [dress] of the poor. So that even if we desire glory, here too the glory is greater.

[14.] I say this not only to widows, and to the rich; for here the necessity of widowhood seems to cause this : but to those also who have a husband.

But, you say, I do not please my husband [if I dress plainly]. It is not thy husband thou wishest to please, but the multitude of poor women; or rather not to please them, but to make them pine [with envy], and to give them pain, and make their poverty greater. How many blasphemies are uttered because of thee ! 'Let there be no poverty' (say they). 'God hates the poor.' 'God loves not those in poverty.' For that it is not thy husband whom thou wishest to please, and for this reason thou deckest thyself out, thou makest plain to all by what thou thyself doest. For as soon as thou hast passed over the threshold of thy chamber,[4] thou immediately puttest off all, both the robes, and the golden ornaments, and the pearls; and at home of all places thou dost not wear them.

But if thou really wishest to please thy husband, there are ways of pleasing him, by gentleness, by meekness, by propriety. For believe me, O woman, even if thy husband be infinitely debased,[5] these are the things which will more effectually win him, gentleness, propriety, freedom from pride and expensiveness and extravagance. For even if thou devise ten thousand such things, thou wilt not restrain the profligate. And this they know who have had such husbands. For however thou mayest beautify thyself, he being a profligate will go off to a courtesan; while [the husband] that is chaste and regular thou wilt gain not by these means, but by the opposite : yea by these thou even causest him pain, clothing thyself with the reputation of a lover of the world. For what if thy husband out of respect, and that as a sober-minded man, does not speak, yet inwardly he will condemn thee, and will not conceal[6] ill-will[7] and jealousy. Wilt thou not drive away all pleasure for the future, by exciting ill-will against thyself?

[15.] Possibly you are annoyed at hearing what is said, and are indignant, saying, 'He irritates husbands still more against their wives.' I say this, not to irritate your husbands, but I wish that these things should be done by you willingly, for your own sakes, not for theirs; not to free them from envy but to free you from the parade of this life.

Dost thou wish to appear beautiful? I also wish it, but with beauty which God seeks, which

---

[1] κοιτωνίσκῳ.    [2] τὰ ἡμέτερο.
[3] ταῖς προθήκαις ταῖς ἐπὶ τῶν ἐργαστηρίων.

[4] θαλάμου.
[5] κατωφερὴς.
[6] or, "conceal," περιστελεῖται.
[7] φθόνους.

"the King desires."[1] (Ps. xlv. 11.) Whom wouldst thou have as a Lover? God or men? Shouldest thou be beautiful with that beauty, God will "desire thy beauty"; but if with the other apart from this, He will abominate thee, and thy lovers will be profligates. For no man who loves a married woman is good. Consider this even in regard to the adorning that is external. For the other adorning, I mean that of the soul, attracts God; but this again, profligates. Seest thou that I care for you, that I am anxious for you, that ye may be beautiful, really beautiful, splendid, really splendid, that instead of profligate men, ye may have for your Lover God the Lord of all? And she who has Him for her Lover, to whom will she be like? She has her place among the choirs of Angels. For if one who is beloved of a king is accounted happy above all, what will her dignity be who is beloved of God with much love? Though thou put the whole world [in the balance against it], there is nothing equivalent to that beauty.

This beauty then let us cultivate; with these embellishments let us adorn ourselves, that we may pass into the Heavens, into the spiritual chambers, into the nuptial chamber that is undefiled. For this beauty is liable to be destroyed by anything; and when it lasts well, and neither disease nor anxiety impair it (which is impossible), it does not last twenty years. But the other is ever blooming, ever in its prime. *There*, there is no change to fear; no old age coming brings a wrinkle, no undermining disease withers it; no desponding anxiety disfigures it; but it is far above all these things. But this [earthly beauty] takes flight before it appears, and if it appears it has not many admirers. For those of well-ordered minds do not admire it; and those who do admire it, admire with wantonness.

[16.] Let us not therefore cultivate this [beauty], but the other: let us have that, so that with bright torches we may pass into the bridal chamber. For not to virgins only has this been promised, but to virgin souls. For had it belonged merely to virgins, those five would not have been shut out. This then belongs to all who are virgins in soul, who are freed from worldly imaginations: for these imaginations corrupt our souls. If therefore we remain unpolluted, we shall depart thither, and shall be accepted. "For I have espoused you," he says, "to one husband, to present you a chaste virgin unto Christ." (2 Cor. xi. 2.) These things he said, not with reference to Virgins, but to the whole body of the entire Church. For the uncorrupt soul is a virgin, though she have a husband: she is a virgin as to that which is Virginity indeed, that which is worthy of admiration. For this of the body is but the accompaniment and shadow of the other: while that is the True Virginity. This let us cultivate, and so shall we be able with cheerful countenance to behold the Bridegroom, to enter in with bright torches, if the oil do not fail us, if by melting down our golden ornaments we procure such oil as makes our lamps bright. And this oil is lovingkindness.

If we impart what we have to others, if we make oil therefrom, then it will protect us, and we shall not say at that time, "Give us oil, for our lamps are going out" (Matt. xxv. 8), nor shall we beg of others, nor shall we be shut out when we are gone to them that sell, nor shall we hear that fearful and terrible voice, while we are knocking at the doors, "I know you not." (Matt. xxv. 12.) But He will acknowledge us, and we shall go in with the Bridegroom, and having entered into the spiritual Bride-chamber we shall enjoy good things innumerable.

For if here the bride-chamber is so bright, the rooms so splendid, that none is weary of observing them, much more there. Heaven is the chamber,[2] and the bride-chamber[3] better than Heaven; then we shall enter. But if the Bride-chamber is so beautiful, what will the Bridegroom be?

And why do I say, 'Let us put away our golden ornaments, and give to the needy'? For if ye ought even to sell yourselves, if ye ought to become slaves instead of free women, that so ye might be able to be with that Bridegroom, to enjoy that Beauty, [nay] merely to look on that Countenance, ought you not with ready mind to welcome all things? We look at and admire a king upon the earth, but when [we see] a king and a bridegroom both, much more ought we to welcome him with readiness. Truly these things are a shadow, while those are a reality. And a King and a Bridegroom in Heaven! To be counted worthy also to go before Him with torches, and to be near Him, and to be ever with Him, what ought we not to do? What should we not perform? What should we not endure? I entreat you, let us conceive some desire for those blessings, let us long for that Bridegroom, let us be virgins as to the true Virginity. For the Lord seeks after the virginity of the soul. With this let us enter into Heaven, "not having spot, or wrinkle, or any such thing" (Eph. v. 27); that we may attain also to the good things promised, of which may we all be partakers through the grace and mercy of Jesus Christ our Lord, with whom to the Father together with the Holy Ghost, be glory, power, honor, now and ever, and world without end. Amen.

---

# HOMILY XXIX.

HEBREWS xii. 4–6.

"Ye have not yet resisted unto blood, striving against sin. And ye have forgotten the exhortation which speaketh unto you as unto children, My son, despise not thou the chastening of the Lord, nor faint when thou art rebuked of Him. For whom the Lord loveth, He chasteneth: and scourgeth every son whom He receiveth." [1]

[1.] THERE are two kinds of consolation, apparently opposed to one another, but yet contributing great strength each to the other; both of which he has here put forward. The one is when we say that persons have suffered much: for the soul is refreshed, when it has many witnesses of its own sufferings, and this he introduced above, saying, "Call to mind the former days, in which after ye had been illuminated, ye endured a great fight of afflictions." (c. x. 32.) The other is when we say, "Thou hast suffered no great thing." The former, when [the soul] has been exhausted refreshes it, and makes it recover breath: the latter, when it has become indolent and supine, turns it again [2] and pulls down pride. Thus that no pride may spring up in them from that testimony [to their sufferings], see what he does. "Ye have not yet" (he says) "resisted unto blood, [striving] against sin." And he did not at once go on with what follows, but after having shown them all those who had stood "unto blood," and then brought in the glory of Christ, His sufferings, [3] he afterwards easily pursued his discourse. This he says also in writing to the Corinthians, "There hath no temptation taken you, but such as is common to man" (1 Cor. x. 13), that is, small. For this is enough to arouse and set right the soul, when it considers that it has not risen to the whole [trial], and encourages itself from what has already befallen it.

What he means is this: Ye have not yet submitted to death; your loss has extended to money, to reputation, to being driven from place to place. Christ however shed His blood for you, while you have not [done it] for yourselves. He contended for the Truth even unto death, fighting for you; while ye have not yet entered upon dangers that threaten death.

"And ye have forgotten the exhortation." That is, And ye have slackened your hands, ye have become faint. "Ye have not yet," he said, "resisted unto blood, striving against sin."

Here he indicates that sin is both very vigorous, [4] and is itself armed. For the [expression] "Ye have resisted [stood firm against]," is used with reference to those who stand firm. [5]

[2.] "Which" (he says) "speaketh unto you as unto sons, My son, despise not thou the chastening of the Lord, nor faint when thou art rebuked of Him." He has drawn his encouragement from the facts themselves; over and above he adds also that which is drawn from arguments, from this testimony.

"Faint not" (he says) "when thou art rebuked of Him." It follows that these things are of God. For this too is no small matter of consolation, when we learn that it is God's work that such things have power, [6] He allowing [them]; even as also Paul says; "He said unto me, My grace is sufficient for thee: for My strength is made perfect in weakness." (2 Cor. xii. 9.) He it is who allows [them].

"For whom the Lord loveth He chasteneth, and scourgeth every son whom He receiveth." Thou canst not say that any righteous man is without affliction: even if he appear to be so, yet *we* know not his other afflictions. So that of necessity every righteous man. must pass through affliction. For it is a declaration of Christ, that the wide and broad way leads to destruction, but the strait and narrow one to life. (Matt. vii. 13, 14.) If then it is possible to enter into life by that means, and is not by any other, then all have entered in by the narrow [way], as many as have departed unto life.

Ver. 7. "Ye endure chastisement" [7] (he says); not for punishment, nor for vengeance, nor for suffering. See, from that from which they supposed they had been deserted [of God], from these he says they may be confident, that they have not been deserted. It is as if he had said, Because ye have suffered so many evils, do you suppose that God has left you and hates you? If ye did not suffer, then it were right to suppose this. For if "He scourgeth every son whom He receiveth," he who is not scourged, perhaps is not a son. What then, you say, do not bad men suffer distress? They suffer indeed; how then? He did not say, Every one

---

[1] or, "accepteth."

[2] ἐπιστρέφει, or, "turns, converts to God."

[3] τὸ καύχημα τοῦ Χριστοῦ τὰ παθήματα, or, "our glory — our boast — the sufferings of Christ."

[4] σφόδρα πνέουσαν.

[5] [There is a paronomasia here, Τὸ ἀντικατέστητε, πρὸς τοὺς ἑστῶτας εἴρηται, which cannot easily be reproduced in English. — F. G.]

[6] τὸ τοιαῦτα δυνηθῆναι.

[7] εἰς παιδείαν. εἰς παιδείαν ὑπομένετε is the reading of the best MSS. &c. of St. Chrys. as it is the approved reading of the Epistle. The later [printed] texts have the later reading εἰ π. ὑπ.

who is scourged is a son, but every son is scourged. For in all cases He scourges His son: what is wanted then is to show, whether any son is not scourged. But thou wouldest not be able to say : there are many wicked men also who are scourged, such as murderers, robbers, sorcerers, plunderers of tombs. These however are paying the penalty of their own wickedness, and are not scourged as sons, but punished as wicked : but ye as sons.

[3.] Then again [he argues] from the general custom. Seest thou how he brings up arguments from all quarters, from facts in the Scripture, from its words, from our own notions, from examples in ordinary life? (Ver. 8.) " But if ye be without chastisement " [&c.]. Seest thou that he said what I just mentioned, that it is not possible to be a son without being chastened? For as in families, fathers care not for bastards, though they learn nothing, though they be not distinguished, but fear for their legitimate sons, lest they should be indolent, [so here]. If then not to be chastised is [a mark] of bastards, we ought to rejoice at chastisement, if this be [a sign] of legitimacy. " God dealeth with you as with sons " ; for this very cause.

Ver. 9. " Furthermore, we have had fathers of our flesh which corrected us, and we gave them reverence." Again, [he reasons] from their own experiences, from what they themselves suffered. For as he says above, " Call to mind the former days " (c. x. 32), so here also, " God " (he saith) " dealeth with you as with sons," and ye could not say, We cannot bear it : yea, " as with sons " tenderly beloved. For if they reverence their " fathers of the flesh," how shall not you reverence your heavenly Father?

However the difference arises not from this alone, nor from the persons, but also from the cause itself, and from the fact. For it is not on the same grounds that He and they inflict chastisement : but they [did it] with a view to " what seemed good to them," that is, fulfilling [their own] pleasure oftentimes, and not always looking to what was expedient. But here, that cannot be said. For He does this not for any interest of His own but for you, and for your benefit alone. They [did it] that ye might be useful to themselves also, oftentimes without reason ; but here there is nothing of this kind. Seest thou that this also brings consolation? For we are most closely attached to those [earthly parents], when we see that not for any interests of their own they either command or advise us : but their earnestness is, wholly and solely, on our account. For this is genuine love, and love in reality, when we are beloved though we be of no use to him who loves us,— not that he may receive, but that he may impart. He

chastens, He does everything, He uses all diligence, that we may become capable of receiving His benefits. (Ver. 10.) " For they verily " (he says) " for a few days chastened us after their own pleasure, but He for our profit, that we might be partakers of His holiness."

What is " of his holiness " ? It is, of His purity, so as to become worthy of Him, according to our power. He earnestly desires that ye may receive, and He does all that He may give you : do ye not earnestly endeavor that ye may receive? " I said unto the Lord " (one says) " Thou art my Lord, for of my good things Thou hast no need." (Ps. xvi. 2.)

" Furthermore," he saith, " we have had fathers of our flesh which corrected us and we gave them reverence : shall we not much rather be in subjection to the Father of spirits, and live?" (" To the Father of spirits," whether of spiritual gifts, or of prayers, or of the incorporeal powers.) If we die thus, then " we shall live. For they indeed for a few days chastened us after their own pleasure," for what seems [so] is not always profitable, but " He for our profit."

[4.] Therefore chastisement is " profitable " ; therefore chastisement is a " participation of holiness." Yea and this greatly : for when it casts out sloth, and evil desire, and love of the things of this life, when it helps the soul, when it causes a light esteem of all things here (for affliction [does] this), is it not holy? Does it not draw down the grace of the Spirit?

Let us consider the righteous, from what cause they all shone brightly forth. Was it not from affliction? And, if you will, let us enumerate them from the first and from the very beginning : Abel, Noah himself ; for it is not possible that he, being the only one in that so great multitude of the wicked, should not have been afflicted ; for it is said, " Noah being " alone " perfect in his generation, pleased God." (Gen. vi. 9.) For consider, I beseech you, if now, when we have innumerable persons whose virtue we may emulate, fathers, and children, and teachers, we are thus distressed, what must we suppose he suffered, alone among so many? But should I speak of the circumstances of that strange and wonderful rain? Or should I speak of Abraham, his wanderings one upon another, the carrying away of his wife, the dangers, the wars, the famines? Should I speak of Isaac,[1] what fearful things he underwent, driven from every place, and laboring in vain, and toiling for others? Or of Jacob? for indeed to enumerate all his [afflictions] is not necessary, but it is reasonable to

---

[1] The common texts substitute Jacob for Isaac here, omitting the following clause where Jacob is mentioned (as they also in the preceding sentence have " temptations " instead of " families ") ; to correct the apparent inaccuracies of the text. But Mr. Field shows from other passages of St. Chrys. that he really means Isaac, having in view Gen. xxvi. 18–22, 27.

bring forward the testimony, which he himself [gave] when speaking with Pharaoh ; " Few and evil are my days, and they have not attained to the days of my fathers." (Gen. xlvii. 9.) Or should I speak of Joseph himself? Or of Moses? Or of Joshua? Or of David? Or of Elijah? Or of Samuel? Or wouldest thou [that I speak] of all the prophets? Wilt thou not find that all these were made illustrious from their afflictions? Tell me then, dost *thou* desire to become illustrious from ease and luxury? But thou canst not.

Or should I speak of the Apostles? Nay but they went beyond all. And Christ said this, " In the world ye shall have tribulation." (John xvi. 33.) And again, "Ye shall weep and lament, but the world shall rejoice." (John xvi. 20.) And, that " Strait and narrow is the way¹ that leadeth unto life." (Matt. vii. 14.) The Lord of the way said, that it is " narrow and strait " ; and dost thou seek the " broad " [way]? How is this not unreasonable? In consequence thou wilt not arrive at life, going another [way], but at destruction, for thou hast chosen the [path] which leads thither.

Wouldst thou that I bring before you those [that live] in luxury? Let us ascend from the last to the first. The rich man who is burning in the furnace ; the Jews who live for the belly, " whose god is their belly " (Phil. iii. 19), who were ever seeking ease in the wilderness, were destroyed ; as also those in Sodom, on account of their gluttony ; and those in the time of Noah, was it not because they chose this soft and dissolute life? For " they luxuriated," it says, " in fullness of bread." (Ezek. xvi. 49.) It speaks of those in Sodom. But if " fullness of bread " wrought so great evil, what should we say of other delicacies? Esau, was not he in ease? And what of those who being of " the sons of God " (Gen. vi. 2), looked on women, and were borne down the precipice? And what of those who were maddened by inordinate lust? and all the kings of the nations, of the Babylonians, of the Egyptians, did they not perish miserably? Are they not in torment?

[5.] And as to things now, tell me, are they not the same? Hear Christ saying, " They that wear soft clothing are in kings' houses " (Matt. xi. 8), but they who do not [wear] such things, are in Heaven. For the soft garment relaxes even the austere soul, breaks it and enervates it : yea, even if it meet with a body rough and hard, it speedily by such delicate treatment makes it soft and weak.

For, tell me, for what other reason do you suppose women are so weak? Is it from their sex only? By no means : but from their way of living, and their bringing up. For their avoiding exposure,² their inactivity, their baths, their unguents, their multitude of perfumes, the delicate softness of their couches, makes them in the end such as they are.

And that thou mayest understand, attend to what I say. Tell me ; take from a garden a tree from those standing in the uncultivated³ part and beaten by the winds, and plant it in a moist and shady place, and thou wilt find it very unworthy of that from which thou didst originally take it. And that this is true, [appears from the fact that] women brought up in the country are stronger than citizens of towns : and they would overcome many such in wrestling. For when the body becomes more effeminate, of necessity the soul also shares the mischief, since, for the most part, its energies are affected in accordance with the [body]. For in illness we are different persons owing to weakness, and when we become well, we are different again. For as in the case of a string when the tones⁴ are weak and relaxed, and not well arranged, the excellence of the art is also destroyed, being obliged to serve the ill condition of the strings : so in the case of the body also, the soul receives from it many hurts, many necessities.⁵ For when it needs much nursing, the other endures a bitter servitude.

[6.] Wherefore, I beseech you, let us make it strong by work, and not nurse it as an invalid.⁶ My discourse is not to men only but to women also. For why dost thou, O woman, continually enfeeble⁷ [thy body] with luxury and exhaust it?⁷ Why dost thou ruin thy strength with fat? This fat is flabbiness, not strength. Whereas, if thou break off from these things, and manage thyself differently, then will thy personal beauty also improve according to thy wish, when strength and a good habit of body are there. If however thou beset it with ten thousand diseases, there will neither be bloom of complexion, nor good health ; for thou wilt always be in low spirits. And you know that as when the air is smiling it makes a beautiful house look splendid, so also cheerfulness of mind when added to a fair countenance, makes it better : but if [a woman] is in low spirits and in pain she becomes more illlooking. But diseases and pains produce low spirits ; and diseases are produced from the body too delicate through great luxury. So that even for this you will flee luxury, if you take my advice.

' But, you will say, luxury gives pleasure.' Yes, but not so great as the annoyances. And besides, the pleasure goes no further than the

---

¹ St. Chrys. seems to have read this text without the words ἡ πύλη.

² " to the heat," σκιατροφία.
³ ἐν τῇ ἐρήμῳ, " dry and open part? "
⁴ φθόγγοι.
⁵ ἀνάγκας.
⁶ νοσηλεύωμεν.
⁷ ἐκπλύνεις . . . ἐξίτηλον, lit. " washed out," and " faded," as when colors are washed out of dresses.

palate and the tongue. For when the table has been removed, and the food swallowed, thou wilt be like one that has not partaken, or rather much worse, in that thou bearest thence oppression, and distension, and headache, and a sleep like death, and often too, sleeplessness from repletion, and obstruction of the breathing, and eructation. And thou wouldest curse bitterly thy belly, when thou oughtest to curse thy immoderate eating.

[7.] Let us not then fatten the body, but listen to Paul saying, "Make not provision for the flesh, to fulfill the lusts thereof." (Rom. xiii. 14.) As if one should take food and throw it into a drain, so is he who throws it into the belly: or rather it is not so, but much worse. For in the one case he uses[1] the drain without harm to himself: but in the other he generates innumerable diseases. For what nourishes is a sufficiency which also can be digested: but what is over and above our need, not only does not nourish, but even spoils the other. But no man sees these things, owing to some prejudice and unseasonable pleasure.

Dost thou wish to nourish the body? Take away what is superfluous; give what is sufficient, and as much as can be digested. Do not load it, lest thou overwhelm it. A sufficiency is both nourishment and pleasure. For nothing is so productive of pleasure, as food well digested: nothing so [productive of] health: nothing [so productive of] acuteness of the faculties, nothing tends so much to keep away disease. For a sufficiency is both nourishment, and pleasure, and health; but excess is injury, and unpleasantness and disease. For what famine does, that also satiety does; or rather more grievous evils. For the former indeed within a few days carries a man off and sets him free; but the other eating into and putrefying the body, gives it over to long disease, and then to a most painful death. But *we*, while we account famine a thing greatly to be dreaded, yet run after satiety, which is more distressing than that.

Whence is this disease? Whence this madness? I do not say that we should waste ourselves away, but that we should eat as much food as also gives us pleasure, that is really pleasure, and can nourish the body, and furnish it to us well ordered and adapted for the energies of the soul, well joined and fitted together. But when it comes to be water-logged[2] by luxury, it cannot in the flood-wave, keep fast the bolts[3] themselves, as one may say, and joints which hold the frame together. For the flood-wave coming in, the whole breaks up and scatters.

"Make not provision for the flesh" (he says) "to fulfill the lusts thereof." (Rom. xiii. 14.) He said well. For luxury is fuel for unreasonable lusts; though the luxurious should be the most philosophical of all men, of necessity he must be somewhat affected by wine, by eating, he must needs be relaxed, he must needs endure the greater flame. Hence [come] fornications, hence adulteries. For a hungry belly cannot generate lust, or rather not one which has used just enough. But that which generates unseemly lusts, is that which is relaxed[4] by luxury. And as land which is very moist and a dung-hill which is wet through and retains much dampness, generates worms, while that which has been freed from such moistness bears abundant fruits, when it has nothing immoderate: even if it be not cultivated, it yields grass, and if it be cultivated, fruits: [so also do we].

Let us not then make our flesh useless, or unprofitable, or hurtful, but let us plant in it useful fruits, and fruit-bearing trees; let us not enfeeble them by luxury, for they too put forth worms instead of fruit when they are become rotten. So also implanted desire, if thou moisten it above measure, generates unreasonable pleasures, yea the most exceedingly unreasonable. Let us then remove this pernicious evil, that we may be able to attain the good things promised us, in Christ Jesus our Lord, with whom to the Father, together with the Holy Spirit, be glory now and ever and world without end. Amen.

---

[1] ἐργάζεται.

[2] ὑπέραντλον.
[3] γόμφους.
[4] πλαδῶσα, "wet and soft."

# HOMILY XXX.

## HEBREWS xii. 11–13.

"No chastening for the present seemeth to be joyous,[1] but grievous,[2] nevertheless, afterward it yieldeth the peaceable fruit of righteousness unto them which are [3] exercised thereby. Wherefore lift up the hands which hang down, and the feeble knees: and make straight paths for your feet, lest that which is lame be turned out of the way, but let it rather be healed."

[1.] THEY who drink bitter medicines, first submit to some unpleasantness, and afterwards feel the benefit. For such is virtue, such is vice. In the latter there is first the pleasure, then the despondency: in the former first the despondency, and then the pleasure. But there is no equality; for it is not the same, to be first grieved and afterwards pleased, and to be first pleased and afterwards grieved. How so? because in the latter case the expectation of coming despondency makes the present pleasure less: but in the former the expectation of coming pleasure cuts away the violence of present despondency; so that the result is that in the one instance we never have pleasure, in the latter we never have grief. And the difference does not lie in this only, but also in other ways. As how? That the duration is not equal, but far greater and more ample. And here too, it is still more so in things spiritual.

From this [consideration] then Paul undertakes to console them; and again takes up the common judgment of men, which no one is able to stand against, nor to contend with the common decision, when one says what is acknowledged by all.

Ye are suffering, he says. For such is chastisement; such is its beginning. For "no chastening for the present seemeth to be joyous but grievous." Well said he, "seemeth not." Chastisement he means is not grievous but "seemeth" so. "All chastisement": not this and that, but "all," both human and spiritual. Seest thou that he argues from our common notions? "Seemeth" (he says) "to be grievous," so that it is not [really so]. For what sort of grief brings forth joy? So neither does pleasure bring forth despondency.

"Nevertheless, afterward it yieldeth the peaceable fruits of righteousness to them which have been exercised thereby." Not "fruit" but "fruits," [4] a great abundance.

"To them" (he says) "which have been exercised thereby." What is "to them which have been exercised thereby"? To them that have endured for a long while, and been patient. And he uses an auspicious [5] expression. So then, chastisement is exercise, making the athlete strong, and invincible in combats, irresistible in wars.

If then "all chastisement" be such, this also will be such: so that we ought to look for good things, and for a sweet and peaceful end. And do not wonder if, being itself hard, it has sweet fruits; since in trees also the bark is almost destitute of all quality,[6] and rough; but the fruits are sweet. But he took it from the common notion. If therefore we ought to look for such things, why do ye vex yourselves? Why, after ye have endured the painful, do ye despond as to the good? The distasteful things which ye had to endure, ye endured: do not then despond as to the recompense.

He speaks as to runners, and boxers, and warriors.[7] Seest thou how he arms them, how he encourages them? "Walk straight," he says. Here he speaks with reference to their thoughts; that is to say, not doubting. For if the chastisement be of love, if it begin from loving care, if it end with a good result (and this he proves both by facts and by words, and by all considerations), why are ye dispirited? For such are they who despair, who are not strengthened by the hope of the future. "Walk straight," he says, that your lameness may not be increased, but brought back to its former condition. For he that runs when he is lame, galls the sore place. Seest thou that it is in our power to be thoroughly healed?

[2.] Ver. 14. "Follow peace with all men, and holiness, without which no man shall see the LORD." What he also said above, "Not forsaking the assembling of yourselves together" (c. x. 25), he hints at in this place also. For nothing so especially makes persons easily vanquished and subdued in temptations, as isolation. For, tell me, scatter a phalanx in war, and the enemy will need no trouble, but will take them prisoners, coming on them separately, and thereby the more helpless.

"Follow peace with all men, and holiness" [8]

---

[1] "of joy."  [2] "of grief."
[3] [The Revision has here correctly "have been exercised," and it is so commented upon by St. Chrys. below. — F. G.]
[4] καρπούς. [At the head of the homily the word is in the singular, as in the text of Hebrews; it is here commented upon as if in the plural. — F. G.]

[5] εὐφήμῳ.   [6] ἄποιος.
[7] These words refer to ver. 13, "Wherefore lift up the hands which hang down, and the feeble knees, and make straight paths for your feet, lest that which is lame be turned out of the way, but let it rather be healed," which is inserted in the text of the common editions.
[8] "the sanctification." [It is the same word as above and is rendered in the R. V. "the sanctification." — F. G.]

(he says). Therefore with the evil-doers as well? "If it be possible," he says, "as much as lieth in you, live peaceably with all men." (Rom. xii. 18.) For thy part (he means) "live peaceably," doing no harm to religion: but in whatever thou art ill-treated, bear it nobly. For the bearing with evil is a great weapon in trials. Thus Christ also made His disciples strong by saying, "Behold I send you forth as sheep in the midst of wolves: be ye therefore wise as serpents, and harmless as doves." (Matt. x. 16.) What dost Thou say? Are we "among wolves," and dost Thou bid us to be "as sheep," and "as doves"? Yea, He says. For nothing so shames him that is doing us evil, as bearing nobly the things which are brought upon us: and not avenging ourselves either by word or by deed. This both makes us more philosophical ourselves and procures a greater reward, and also benefits them. But has such an one been insolent? Do thou bless [him]. See how much thou wilt gain from this: thou hast quenched the evil, thou hast procured to thyself a reward, thou hast made him ashamed, and thou hast suffered nothing serious.

[3.] "Follow peace with all men, and holiness." What does he mean by "holiness"[1]? Chaste, and orderly living in marriage. If any person is unmarried (he says) let him remain pure, let him marry: or if he be married, let him not commit fornication, but let him live with his own wife: for this also is "holiness." How? Marriage is not "holiness," but marriage preserves the holiness which [proceeds] from Faith, not permitting union with a harlot. For "marriage is honorable" (c. xiii. 4), not holy. Marriage is pure: it does not however also give holiness, except by forbidding the defilement of that [holiness] which has been given by our Faith.

"Without which" (he says) "no man shall see the Lord." Which he also says in the [Epistle] to the Corinthians. "Be not deceived: neither fornicators, nor adulterers, nor idolaters, nor effeminate, nor abusers of themselves with mankind, nor covetous persons, nor thieves, nor drunkards, nor revilers, nor extortioners, shall inherit the kingdom of God." (1 Cor. vi. 9, 10.) For how shall he who has become the body of a harlot, how shall he be able to be the body of Christ?

[4.] Ver. 15. "Looking diligently[2] lest any man come short of the grace of God; lest any root of bitterness springing up trouble you, and thereby many be defiled: lest there be any fornicator or profane person." Dost thou see how everywhere he puts the common salvation into the hands of each individual? "Exhorting one

another daily" (he says) "while it is called To-day." (c. iii. 13.) Do not then cast all [the burden] on your teachers; do not [cast] all upon them who have the rule over you: ye also (he means) are able to edify one another. Which also he said in writing to the Thessalonians, "Edify one another, even as also ye do." (1 Thess. v. 11.) And again, "Comfort one another with these words." (1 Thess. iv. 18.) This we also now exhort you.

[5.] If ye be willing, ye will have more success with each other than we can have. For ye both are with one another for a longer time, and ye know more than we of each other's affairs, and ye are not ignorant of each other's failings, and ye have more freedom of speech, and love, and intimacy; and these are no small [advantages] for teaching, but great and opportune introductions for it: ye will be more able than we both to reprove and to exhort. And not this only, but because I am but one, whereas ye are many; and ye will be able, however many, to be teachers. Wherefore I entreat you, do not "neglect this gift." (1 Tim. iv. 14.) Each one of you has a wife, has a friend, has a servant, has a neighbor; let him reprove him, let him exhort him.

For how is it not absurd, with regard to [bodily] nourishment, to make associations for messing together, and for drinking together, and to have a set day whereon to club with one another, as they say, and to make up by the association what each person being alone by himself falls short of — as for instance, if it be necessary to go to a funeral, or to a dinner, or to assist a neighbor in any matter — and not to do this for the purpose of instruction in virtue? Yea, I entreat you, let no man neglect it. For great is the reward he receives from God. And that thou mayest understand, he who was entrusted with the five talents is the teacher: and he with the one is the learner. If the learner should say, I am a learner, I run no risk, and should hide the reason,[3] which he received of God, that common and simple [reason], and give no advice, should not speak plainly, should not rebuke, should not admonish, if he is able, but should bury [his talents] in the earth (for truly that heart is earth and ashes, which hides the gift of God): if then he hides it either from indolence, or from wickedness, it will be no defense to him to say, 'I had but one talent.' Thou hadst one talent. Thou oughtest then to have brought one besides, and to have doubled the talent. If thou hadst brought one in addition, thou wouldst not have been blamed. For neither did He say to him who brought the two, Wherefore hast thou not brought five? But He

---

[1] "sanctification," as 1 Thess. iv. 3, &c.
[2] ἐπισκοποῦντες.

[3] τὸν λόγον, includes "word," and "doctrine."

accounted him of the same worth with him who brought the five. Why? Because he gained as much as he had. And, because he had received fewer than the one entrusted with the five, he was not on this account negligent, nor did he use the smallness [of his trust, as an excuse] for idleness. And thou oughtest not to have looked to. him who had the two ; or rather, thou oughtest to have looked to him, and as he having two imitated him who had five, so oughtest thou to have emulated him who had two. For if for him who has means and does not give, there is punishment, how shall there not be the greatest punishment for him who is able to exhort in any way, and does it not? In the former case the body is nourished, in the latter the soul ; there thou preventest temporal death, here eternal.

[6.] But I have no [skill of] speech,[1] you say. But there is no need of [skill of] speech nor of eloquence. If thou see a friend going into fornication, say to him, Thou art going after an evil thing ; art thou not ashamed? Dost thou not blush? This is wrong. 'Why, does he not know' (you say) 'that it is wrong?' Yes, but he is dragged on by lust. They that are sick also know that it is bad to drink cold water, nevertheless they need persons who shall hinder [them from it]. For he who is suffering, will not easily be able to help himself in his sickness. There is need therefore of thee who art in health, for his cure. And if he be not persuaded by thy words, watch for him as he goes away and hold him fast ; peradventure he will be ashamed.

'And what advantage is it' (you say), 'when he does this for my sake, and because he has been held back by me?' Do not be too minute in thy calculations. For a while, by whatever means, withdraw him from his evil practice ; let him be accustomed not to go off to that pit, whether through thee, or through any means whatever. When thou hast accustomed him not to go, then by taking him after he has gained breath a little thou wilt be able to teach him that he ought to do this for God's sake, and not for man's. Do not wish to make all right at once, since you cannot : but do it gently and by degrees.

If thou see him going off to drinking, or to parties where there is nothing but drunkenness, then also do the same ; and again on the other hand intreat him, if he observe that thou hast any failing, to help thee and set thee right. For in this way, he will even of himself, bear reproof, when he sees both that thou needest reproofs as well, and that thou helpest him, not as one that had done everything right, nor as a teacher, but

as a friend and a brother. Say to him, I have done thee a service, in reminding thee of things expedient : do thou also, whatever failing thou seest me have, hold me back,[2] set me right. If thou see me irritable, if avaricious, restrain me, bind me by exhortation.

This is friendship ; thus "brother aided by brother becomes a fortified city." (Prov. xviii. 19.) For not eating and drinking makes friendship : such friendship even robbers have and murderers. But if we are friends, if we truly care for one another, let us in these respects help one another. This leads us to a profitable friendship : let us hinder those things which lead away to hell.

[7.] Therefore let not him that is reproved be indignant : for we are men and we have failings ; neither let him who reproves do it as exulting over him and making a display, but privately, with gentleness. He that reproves has need of greater gentleness, that thus he may persuade [them] to bear the cutting. Do you not see surgeons, when they burn, when they cut, with how great gentleness they apply their treatment? Much more ought those who reprove others to act thus. For reproof is sharper even than fire and knife, and makes [men] start. On this account surgeons take great pains to make them bear the cutting quietly, and apply it as tenderly as possible, even giving in[3] a little, then giving time to take breath.

So ought we also to offer reproofs, that the reproved may not start away. Even if therefore, it be necessary to be insulted, yea even to be struck, let us not decline it. For those also who are cut [by the surgeons] utter numberless cries against those who are cutting them ; they however heed none of these things, but only the health of the patients. So indeed in this case also we ought to do all things that our reproof may be effectual, to bear all things, looking to the reward which is in store.

"Bear ye one another's burdens," saith he, "and so fulfill the law of Christ." (Gal. vi. 2.) So then, both reproving and bearing with one another, shall we be able to fulfill edification. And thus will ye make the labor light for us, in all things taking a part with us, and stretching out a hand, and becoming sharers and partakers, both in one another's salvation, and each one in his own. Let us then endure patiently, both bearing "one another's burdens," and reproving : that we may attain to the good things promised in Christ Jesus our Lord, with whom to the Father together with the Holy Ghost, be glory, might, honor, now and for ever and world without end. Amen.

---

[1] λόγου.

[2] ἀναχαίτισον.                    [3] ἐνδιδόντες.

# HOMILY XXXI.

Hebrews xii. 14.

" Follow peace with all men, and holiness,[1] without which no one shall see the LORD."

[1.] THERE are many things characteristic of Christianity : but more than all, and better than all, Love towards one another, and Peace. Therefore Christ also saith, " My peace I give unto you." (John xiv. 27.) And again, " By this shall all men know that ye are My disciples, if ye love one another." (John xiii. 35.) Therefore Paul too says, " Follow peace with all men, and holiness," that is, purity,[2] " without which no man shall see the LORD."

" Looking diligently lest any man fail of the grace of God." As if they were traveling together on some long journey, in a large company, he says, Take heed that no man be left behind : I do not seek this only, that ye should arrive yourselves, but also that ye should look diligently after the others.

" Lest any man " (he says) " fail of the grace of God." (He means the good things to come, the faith of the gospel, the best course of life : for they all are of " the Grace of God.") Do not tell me, It is [but] one that perisheth. Even for one Christ died. Hast thou no care for him " for whom Christ died "? (1 Cor. viii. 11.)

" Looking diligently," he saith, that is, searching carefully, considering, thoroughly ascertaining, as is done in the case of sick persons, and in all ways examining, thoroughly ascertaining. " Lest any root of bitterness springing up trouble you." (Deut. xxix. 18.) This is found in Deuteronomy ; and he derived it from the metaphor of plants. " Lest any root of bitterness," he says ; which he said also in another place when he writes, " A little leaven leaveneth the whole lump." (1 Cor. v. 6.) Not for his sake alone do I wish this, he means, but also on account of the harm arising therefrom. That is to say, even if there be a root of this kind, do not suffer any shoot to come up, but let it be cut off, that it may not bear its proper fruits, that so it may not defile and pollute the others also. For he saith, " Lest any root of bitterness springing up trouble you ; and by it many be defiled."

And with good reason did he call sin " bitter " : for truly nothing is more bitter than sin, and they know it, who after they have committed it pine away under their conscience, who endure much bitterness. For being exceedingly bitter, it perverts the reasoning faculty itself. Such is the nature of what is bitter : it is unprofitable.

And well said he, " root of bitterness." He said not, " bitter," but " of bitterness." For it is possible that a bitter root might bear sweet fruits ; but it is not possible that a root and fountain and foundation of bitterness, should ever bear sweet fruit ; for all is bitter, it has nothing sweet, all are bitter, all unpleasant, all full of hatred and abomination.

" And by this " (he says) " many be defiled." That is, Cut off the lascivious persons.

[2.] Ver. 16. " Lest there be any fornicator : or profane person, as Esau, who for one morsel of meat sold his birthright." [3]

And wherein was Esau a " fornicator "? He does not say that Esau was a fornicator. " Lest there be any fornicator," he says, then, " follow after holiness : lest there be any, as Esau, profane " ; that is, gluttonous, without self-control, worldly, selling away things spiritual.

" Who for one morsel of meat sold his birthright," who through his own slothfulness sold this honor which he had from God, and for a little pleasure, lost the greatest honor and glory. This was suitable to them. This [was the conduct] of an abominable, of an unclean person. So that not only is the fornicator unclean, but also the glutton, the slave of his belly. For he also is a slave of a different pleasure. He is forced to be overreaching, he is forced to be rapacious, to behave himself unseemly in ten thousand ways, being the slave of that passion, and oftentimes he blasphemes. So he accounted " his birthright " to be nothing worth. That is, providing for temporary refreshment, he went even to the [sacrifice of his] " birthright." So henceforth " the birthright " belongs to us, not to the Jews. And at the same time also this is added to their calamity, that the first is become last, and the second, first : the one, for courageous endurance ; the other last for indolence.

[3.] Ver. 17. " For ye know " (he says) " how that afterward, when he would have inherited the blessing, he was rejected. For he found no place of repentance, though he sought it carefully with tears." What now is this? Doth he indeed exclude repentance? By no means. ' But how, you say, was it that " he found no

---

[1] or, " the sanctification."
[2] σεμνότητα, properly a disposition and conduct which creates respect or reverence: so specially (here as in other places) chastity. See Hom. xxx. [3], above, p. 504.

[3] πρωτοτόκια, " birthright privileges."

place of repentance"?' For if he condemned himself, if he made a great wailing, why did he "find no place of repentance"? Because it was not really a case of repentance. For as the grief of Cain was not of repentance, and the murder proved it; so also in this case, his words were not those of repentance, and the murder afterwards proved it. For even he also in intention slew Jacob. For "The days of mourning for my father," he said, "are at hand; then will I slay my brother Jacob." (Gen. xxvii. 41.) "Tears" had not power to give him "repentance." And [the Apostle] did not say "by repentance" simply, but even "with tears, he found no place of repentance." Why now? Because he did not repent as he ought, for this is repentance; he repented not as it behoved him.

For how is it that he [the Apostle] said this? How did he exhort them again after they had become "sluggish" (c. vi. 12)? How, when they were become "lame"? How, when they were "paralyzed"[1] (ver. 13)? How, when they were "relaxed"[1] (ver. 12)? For this is the beginning of a fall. He seems to me to hint at some fornicators amongst them, but not to wish at that time to correct them: but feigns ignorance that they might correct themselves. For it is right at first indeed to pretend ignorance: but afterwards, when they continue [in sin], then to add reproof also, that so they may not become shameless. Which Moses also did in the case of Zimri and the daughter of Cosbi.

"For he found" (he says) "no place of repentance," he found not repentance; or that he sinned beyond[2] repentance. There are then sins beyond repentance. His meaning is, Let us not fall by an incurable fall. So long as it is a matter of lameness, it is easy to become upright: but if we turn out of the way, what will be left? For it is to those who have not yet fallen that he thus discourses, striking them with terror, and says that it is not possible for him who is fallen, to obtain consolation; but to those who have fallen, that they may not fall into despair, he says the contrary, speaking thus, "My little children, of whom I travail in birth again, until Christ be formed in you." (Gal. iv. 19.) And again, "Whosoever of you are justified by the Law, are fallen from Grace." (Gal. v. 4.) Lo! he testifies that they had fallen away. For he that standeth, hearing that it is not possible to obtain pardon after having fallen, will be more zealous, and more cautious about his standing: if however thou use the same violence towards one also who is fallen, he will never rise again. For by what hope will he show forth the change?

But he not only wept (you say), but also

"sought earnestly." He does not then exclude repentance; but makes them careful not to fall.

[4.] As many then as do not believe in Hell, let them call these things to mind: as many as think to sin without being punished, let them take account of these things. Why did Esau not obtain pardon? Because he repented not as he ought. Wouldest thou see perfect repentance? Hear of the repentance of Peter after his denial. For the Evangelist in relating to us the things concerning him, says, "And he went out and wept bitterly." (Matt. xxvi. 75.) Therefore even such a sin was forgiven him, because he repented as he ought. Although the Victim had not yet been offered, nor had The Sacrifice as yet been made, nor was sin as yet taken away, it still had the rule and sovereignty.

And that thou mayest learn, that this denial [arose] not so much from sloth, as from His being forsaken of God, who was teaching him to know the measures of man and not to contradict the sayings of the Master, nor to be more high-minded than the rest, but to know that nothing can be done without God, and that "Except the Lord build the house, they labor in vain who build it" (Ps. cxxvii. 1): therefore also Christ said to him alone, "Satan desired to sift thee as wheat," and I allowed it not, "that thy faith may not fail." (Luke xxii. 31, 32.) For since it was likely that he would be high-minded, being conscious to himself that he loved Christ more than they all, therefore "he wept bitterly"; and he did other things after his weeping, of the same character. For what did he do? After this he exposed himself to dangers innumerable, and by many means showed his manliness and courage.

Judas also repented, but in an evil way: for he hanged himself. Esau too repented, as I said; or rather, he did not even repent; for his tears were not [tears] of repentance, but rather of pride and wrath. And what followed proved this. The blessed David repented, thus saying, "Every night will I wash my bed: I will water my couch with my tears." (Ps. vi. 6.) And the sin which had been committed long ago, after so many years, after so many generations he bewailed, as if it had recently occurred.

[5.] For he who repents ought not to be angry, nor to be fierce, but to be contrite, as one condemned, as not having boldness, as one on whom sentence has been passed, as one who ought to be saved by mercy alone, as one who has shown himself ungrateful toward his Benefactor, as unthankful, as reprobate, as worthy of punishments innumerable. If he considers these things, he will not be angry, he will not be indignant, but will mourn, will weep, will groan, and lament night and day.

He that is penitent ought never to forget his

---

[1] [παραλυθέντας . . . παρειμένους, as in ver. 12.]
[2] μείζονα, "committed sins too great for repentance."

sin, but on the one hand, to beseech God not to remember it; while on the other, he himself never forgets it. If we remember it, God will forget it. Let us exact punishment from ourselves; let us accuse ourselves; thus shall we propitiate the Judge. For sin confessed becomes less, but not confessed worse. For if sin add to itself shamelessness and ingratitude, how will he who does not know that he sinned before be at all able to guard himself from falling again into the same [evils]?

Let us then not deny [our sins], I beseech you, nor be shameless, that we may not unwillingly pay the penalty. Cain heard God say, "Where is Abel thy brother? And he said, I know not; am I my brother's keeper?" (Gen. iv. 9.) Seest thou how this made his sin more grievous? But his father did not act thus. What then? When he heard, "Adam, where art thou?" (Gen. iii. 9), he said, "I heard Thy voice, and I was afraid, because I am naked, and I hid myself." (Gen. iii. 10.) It is a great good to acknowledge our sins, and to bear them in mind continually. Nothing so effectually cures a fault, as a continual remembrance of it. Nothing makes a man so slow to wickedness.

[6.] I know that conscience starts back, and endures not to be scourged by the remembrance of evil deeds; but hold tight thy soul and place a muzzle on it. For like an ill-broken[1] horse, so it bears impatiently [what is put upon it], and is unwilling to persuade itself that it has sinned: but all this is the work of Satan.[2] But let us persuade it that it has sinned; let us persuade it that it has sinned, that it may also repent, in order that having repented it may escape torment. How dost thou think to obtain pardon for thy sins, tell me, when thou hast not yet confessed them? Assuredly he is worthy of compassion and kindness who has sinned. But thou who hast not yet persuaded thyself [that thou hast sinned], how dost thou think to be pitied, when thou art thus without shame for some things?[3]

Let us persuade ourselves that we have sinned. Let us say it not with the tongue only, but also with the mind. Let us not call ourselves sinners, but also count over our sins, going over them each specifically.[4] I do not say to thee, Make a parade of thyself, nor accuse thyself before others: but be persuaded by the prophet when he saith, "Reveal thy way unto the Lord." (Ps. xxxvii. 5.) Confess these things before God. Confess before the Judge thy sins with prayer; if not with tongue, yet in memory, and be worthy of mercy.

If thou keep thy sins continually in remembrance, thou wilt never bear in mind the wrongs of thy neighbor. I do not say, if thou art persuaded that thou art thyself a sinner; this does not avail so to humble the soul, as sins themselves [taken] by themselves, and examined specifically.[5] Thou wilt have no remembrance of wrongs [done thee], if thou hast these things continually in remembrance; thou wilt feel no anger, thou wilt not revile, thou wilt have no high thoughts, thou wilt not fall again into the same [sins], thou wilt be more earnest towards good things.

[7.] Seest thou how many excellent [effects] are produced from the remembrance of our sins? Let us then write them in our minds. I know that the soul does not endure a recollection which is so bitter: but let us constrain and force it. It is better that it should be gnawed with the remembrance now, than at that time with vengeance.

Now, if thou remember them, and continually present them before God (see p. 448), and pray for them, thou wilt speedily blot them out; but if thou forget them now, thou wilt then be reminded of them even against thy will, when they are brought out publicly before the whole world, displayed before all, both friends and enemies, and Angels. For surely He did not say to David only, "What thou didst secretly, I will make manifest to" (2 Sam. xii. 12) all, but even to us all. Thou wert afraid of men (he said) and respected them more than God; and God seeing thee, thou caredst not, but wert ashamed before men. For it says,[6] "the eyes of men, this is their fear." Therefore thou shalt suffer punishment in that very point; for I will reprove thee, setting thy sins before the eyes of all. For that this is true, and that in that day the sins of us all are [to be] publicly displayed, unless we now do them away by continual remembrance, hear how cruelty and inhumanity are publicly exposed, "I was an hungered" (He says) "and ye gave Me no meat." (Matt. xxv. 42.) When are these things said? Is it in a corner? Is it in a secret place?[7] By no means. When then? "When the Son of Man shall come in His glory" (Matt. xxv. 31, 32), and "all the nations" are gathered together, when He has separated the one from the other, then will He speak in the audience of all, and will "set" them "on His right hand" and "on" His "left" (Matt. xxv. 33): "I was an hungered and ye gave Me no meat."

See again the five virgins also, hearing before all, "I know you not." (Matt. xxv. 12.) For the five and five do not set forth the number of five only, but those virgins who are wicked and cruel and inhuman, and those who are not such.

---

1 δυσήνιος.
2 σατανικόν.
3 ἐπὶ τίσιν.
4 κατ' εἶδος, see above. p. 412.
5 κατ' εἶδος.
6 This seems to be alleged as a citation from Holy Scripture, but it does not appear what passage St. Chrysostom had in view.
7 ἐν παραβύστῳ.

So also he that buried his one talent, heard before all, even of those who had brought the five and the two, "Thou wicked and slothful servant." (Matt. xxv. 26.) But not by words alone, but by deeds also does He then convict them: even as the Evangelist also says, "They shall look on Him whom they pierced." (John xix. 37.) For the resurrection shall be of all at the same time, of sinners and of the righteous. At the same time shall He be present to all in the judgment.

[8.] Consider therefore who they are who shall then be in dismay, who in grief, who dragged away to the fire, while the others are crowned. "Come" (He says), "ye blessed of My Father, inherit the kingdom which hath been prepared for you from the foundation of the world." (Matt. xxv. 34.) And again, "Depart from Me into the fire which hath been prepared for the devil and his angels." (Matt. xxv. 41.)

Let us not merely hear the words but write them also before our sight, and let us imagine Him to be now present and saying these things, and that we are led away to that fire. What heart shall we have? What consolation? And what, when we are cut asunder? And what when we are accused of rapacity? What excuse shall we have to utter? What specious argument? None: but of necessity bound, bending down, we must be dragged to the mouths of the furnace, to the river of fire, to the darkness, to the never-dying punishments, and entreat no one. For it is not, it is not possible, He says, to pass across from this side to that: for "there is a great gulf betwixt us and you" (Luke xvi. 26), and it is not possible even for those who wish it to go across, and stretch out a helping hand: but we must needs burn continually, no one aiding us, even should it be father or mother, or any whosoever, yea though he have much boldness toward God. For, it says, "A brother doth not redeem; shall man redeem?" (Ps. xlix. 8.)

Since then it is not possible to have one's hopes of salvation in another, but [it must be] in one's self after the lovingkindness of God, let us do all things, I entreat you, so that our conduct may be pure, and our course of life the best, and that it may not receive any stain even from the beginning. But if not, at all events, let us not sleep after the stain, but continue always washing away the pollution by repentance, by tears, by prayers, by works of mercy.

What then, you say, if I cannot do works of mercy?[1] But thou hast "a cup of cold water" (Matt. x. 42), however poor thou art. But thou hast "two mites" (Mark xii. 42), in whatever poverty thou art; but thou hast feet, so as to visit the sick, so as to enter into a prison; but thou hast a roof, so as to receive strangers. For there is no pardon, no, none for him who does not do works of mercy.

These things we say to you continually, that we may effect if it be but a little by the continued repetition: these things we say, not caring so much for those who receive the benefits, as for yourselves. For ye give to them indeed things here, but in return you receive heavenly things: which may we all obtain, in Christ Jesus our Lord, with whom to the Father be glory, together with the Holy Ghost, now and ever, and world without end. Amen.

---

[1] ἐλετημοσύνην ἐργάζεσθαι.

# HOMILY XXXII.

" For ye are not come unto a fire[1] that might be touched and that burned, and unto blackness, and darkness, and tempest, and the sound of a trumpet, and the voice of words, which voice they that heard entreated that the word should not be spoken to them any more.[2] (For they could not endure that which was commanded, And if so much as a beast touch the mountain, it shall be stoned.[3] And so terrible was the sight, that Moses said, I exceedingly fear and quake.) . But ye are come unto Mount Sion, and unto the city of the living God, the Heavenly Jerusalem; and to an innumerable company of Angels, to the general assembly,[4] and Church of the first-born which are written in Heaven; and to God the Judge of all; and to the spirits of just men made perfect: and to JESUS the Mediator of the New Covenant: and to the blood of sprinkling that speaketh better things than[5] that of Abel."

[1.] WONDERFUL indeed were the things in the Temple, the Holy of Holies; and again awful were those things also that were done at Mount Sina, "the fire, the darkness, the blackness, the tempest." (Cf. Deut. xxxiii. 2.) For, it says, "God appeared in Sina," and long ago were these things celebrated.[6] The New Covenant, however, was not given with any of these things, but has been given in simple discourse by God.[7]

See then how he makes the comparison in these points also. And with good reason has he put them afterwards. For when he had persuaded them by innumerable [arguments], when he had also shown the difference between each covenant, then afterwards, the one having been already condemned, he easily enters on these points also.

And what says he? " For ye are not come unto a fire that might be touched, and that burned, and unto blackness, and darkness, and tempest, and the sound of a trumpet, and the voice of words; which they that heard entreated that the word should not be spoken to them any more."

These things, he means, are terrible; and so terrible that they could not even bear to hear them, that not even "a beast" dared to go up. (But things that come hereafter[8] are not such. For what is Sina to Heaven? And what the "fire which might be touched" to God who cannot be touched? For "God is a consuming fire." — c. v. 29.) For it is said, "Let not God speak, but let Moses speak unto us. And so fearful was that which was commanded, Though even a beast touch the mountain, it shall be stoned; Moses said, I exceedingly fear and quake." (Ex. xx. 19.) What wonder as respects the people? He himself who entered into "the darkness where God was," saith, " I exceedingly fear and quake." (Ex. xx. 21.)

[2.] "But ye are come unto Mount Sion and unto the city of the living God, the heavenly Jerusalem : and to an innumerable company of angels and to the general assembly and Church of the first-born which are written in Heaven, and to God the Judge of all, and to the spirits of just men made perfect, and to JESUS the Mediator of the New Covenant, and to the blood of sprinkling, that speaketh better [things] than that of Abel."

Instead of "Moses," JESUS. Instead of the people, "myriads of angels."

Of what "first-born" does he speak? Of the faithful.

"And to the spirits of just men made perfect." With these shall ye be, he says.

"And to Jesus the mediator of the New Covenant, and to the blood of sprinkling that speaketh better [things] than that of Abel." Did then the [blood] "of Abel" speak? "Yea," he saith, "and by it he being dead yet speaketh." (c. xi. 4.) And again God says, "The voice of thy brother's blood crieth unto Me." (Gen. iv. 10.) Either this [meaning] or that; because it is still even now celebrated: but not in such way as that of Christ. For this has cleansed all men, and sends forth a voice more clear and more distinct, in proportion as it has greater testimony, namely that by facts.

Ver. 25–29. "See that ye refuse not Him that speaketh. For if they escaped not, who refused him that spake[9] on earth, much more shall not we escape, if we turn away from Him that speaketh from heaven. Whose voice then shook the earth : but now hath He promised,

---

[1] ὅρει is omitted in Mr. Field's text, as by some [all — F. G.] critical editors of the New Test. It is not referred to by St. Chrys.

[2] " that not a word more should be spoken to them."

[3] [The words ἢ βολίδι κατατοξευθήσεται are omitted by St. Chrys., as by all critical editors of the N. T., and are not given in the R. V. — F. G.]

[4] πανηγύρει. See next column. This word is connected with the preceding μυρίασιν ἀγγέλων by St. Chrys. as appears from his interpretation. So the Latin Vulgate has *et multorum millium angelorum frequentiam, et ecclesiam primitivorum*, &c. [The English edition translates " to myriads of angels in festive gathering." Whether πανηγύρει should be connected with the preceding or following clause is merely a question of punctuation. It is joined to the latter both in the A. V. and the R. V. — F. G.]

[5] " in comparison of."

[6] ᾔδετο, e.g. Ps. xviii., lxviii., Habak. iii. as well as Ex. xix.

[7] παρὰ Θεοῦ. The reading of the common edition is Χριστοῦ: which was that of Mutianus.

[8] τὰ μετὰ ταῦτα.

[9] χρηματίζοντα, " that made a revelation ": see above, p. 469.

saying, Yet once more I shake not the earth only, but also heaven. And this word, Yet once more, signifieth the removing of those things that are shaken, as of things that are made, that those which cannot be shaken may remain. Wherefore we receiving a kingdom which cannot be moved, let us have grace whereby we[1] serve God acceptably with reverence and godly fear. For our God is a consuming fire."

[3.] Fearful were those things, but these are far more admirable and glorious. For here there is not " darkness," nor " blackness," nor "tempest." It seems to me that by these words he hints at the obscurity of the Old [Testament], and the overshadowed and veiled[2] character of the Law. And besides the Giver of the Law appears in fire terrible, and apt to punish those who transgress.

But what are " the sounds of the trumpet"? Probably it is as though some King were coming. This at all events will also be at the second coming. " At the last trump " (1 Cor. xv. 52) all must be raised. But it is the trumpet of His voice which effects this. At that time then all things were objects of sense, and sights, and sounds ; now all are objects of understanding, and invisible.

And, it says, "there was much smoke." (See Ex. xix. 18.) For since God is said to be fire, and appeared thus in the bush, He indicates the fire even by the smoke. And what is " the blackness and the darkness"? He again expresses its fearfulness. Thus Isaiah also says ; "And the house was filled with smoke." (Isa. vi. 4.) And what is the object of " the tempest "? The human race was careless. It was therefore needful that they should be aroused by these things. For no one was so dull as not to have had his thoughts raised up, when these things were done, and the Law ordained.[3]

" Moses spake, and God answered him by a voice " (Ex. xix. 19) :[4] for it was necessary that the voice of God should be uttered. Inasmuch as He was about to promulgate His Law through Moses, therefore He makes him worthy of confidence. They saw him not, because of the thick darkness : they heard him not, because of the weakness of his voice. What then? " God answered by a voice," addressing the multitude :[5] yea and his name shall be called.[6]

" They entreated " (he says) " that the word should not be spoken to them any more."[7]

From the first therefore they were themselves the cause of God's being manifested through the Flesh.[8] Let Moses speak with us, and " Let not God speak with us." (Ex. xx. 9.) They who make comparisons elevate the one side the more, that they may show the other to be far greater. In this respect also our [privileges][9] are more gentle and more admirable. For they are great in a twofold respect : because while they are glorious and greater, they are more accessible. This he says also in the Epistle to the Corinthians : " with unveiled countenance " (2 Cor. iii. 18), and, " not as Moses put a veil over his face." (2 Cor. iii. 13.) They, he means, were not counted worthy of what we [are]. For of what were they thought worthy? They saw " darkness, blackness "; they heard " a voice." But thou also hast heard a voice, not through darkness, but through flesh. Thou hast not been disturbed, neither troubled, but thou hast stood and held discourse with the Mediator.

And in another way, by the " darkness " he shows the invisibleness.[10] " And darkness " (it says) " was under His feet." (Ps. xviii. 9.)

*Then* even Moses feared, but now no one.

As the people then stood below, so also do we. They were not below, but below Heaven. The Son is near to God, but not as Moses.[11]

*There* was a wilderness, here a city.

[4.] " And to an innumerable company of angels." Here he shows the joy, the delight, in place of the " blackness " and " darkness " and " tempest."

" And to the general assembly and church of the first-born which are written in Heaven, and to GOD the Judge of all." They did not draw near, but stood afar off, even Moses : but " ye are come near."

Here he makes them fear, by saying, " And to God the Judge of all " ; not of the Jews alone, and the faithful, but even of the whole world.

" And to the spirits of just men made perfect." He means the souls of those who are approved.

" And to JESUS the Mediator of the New Covenant : and to the blood of sprinkling," that is, of purification, " which speaketh better things

---

[1] [The reading of St. Chrys. here and below (Hom. xxxiii.) is λατρεύομεν, but elsewhere he concurs with nearly all the critical editors, the A. V. and the R. V. in reading λατρεύωμεν. — F. G.]

[2] τὸ συνεσκιασμένον καὶ συγκεκαλυμμένον.

[3] νομοθετουμένων.

[4] St. Chrys. says this referring to, without expressly citing, the φωνῇ ῥημάτων of the text.

[5] δημηγορῶν.

[6] ἀλλ' ὄνομα αὐτοῦ καλέσεται. Mr. Field with hesitation adopts here the reading of the Catena καλέσεται, in the sense here given. The MSS. have καλέσαι and (excepting one) not any stop after it. St. Chrys. probably has in view the fact of Moses being called up to the top of the Mount, Ex. xix. 20.

[7] " that not a word more should be spoken to them."

[8] φανῆναι διὰ τῆς σ.

[9] τὰ ἡμέτερα.     [10] τὸ ἀόρατον.

[11] This passage, Mr. Field observes, is difficult and probably corrupt. St. Chrysostom seems to mean, that we are like the people in that we are still here below, not in heaven: for they were " below " only in the sense of being below in reference to the mountain and heaven to which Moses had been called up. At the same time as being sons of God we are near to Him with a special nearness — a spiritual and so most intimate nearness — of the soul, not like that bodily nearness with which Moses was called to draw near.

If, however, " the Son " be understood of the Only-Begotten, it may be supposed that there is some latent connection of thought, as, that in His nearness His people also are brought near to the Father in a manner far more intimate than was granted to Moses.

than that of Abel." And if the blood speaks, much more does He who, having been slain, lives. But what does it speak? "The Spirit also" (he says) "speaketh with groanings which cannot be uttered." (Rom. viii. 26.) How does He speak? Whenever He falls into a sincere mind, He raises it up and makes it speak.

[5.] "See that ye refuse not Him that speaketh"; that is, that ye reject[1] [Him] not. "For if they escaped not who refused Him that spake[2] on earth." Whom does he mean? Moses, I suppose. But what he says is this: if they, having "refused Him" when He gave laws "on earth, did not escape," how shall we refuse Him, when He gives laws from Heaven? He declares here not that He is another; far from it. He does not set forth One and Another, but He appears terrible, when uttering His Voice "from Heaven."[3] It is He Himself then, both the one and the other: but the One is terrible. For he expresses not a difference of Persons but of the gift. Whence does this appear? "For if they escaped not," he says, "who refused Him that spake on earth, much more shall not we escape, if we turn away from Him that speaketh from heaven." What then? Is this one different from the other? How then does he say, "whose voice then shook the earth"? For it was the "voice" of Him who "then" gave the Law, which "shook the earth. But now hath He promised, saying, Yet once more I shake not the earth only, but also heaven. And this word Yet once more, signifieth the removing of those things which are shaken, as of things that are made." All things therefore will be taken away, and will be compacted anew for the better. For this is what he suggests here. Why then dost thou grieve when thou sufferest in a world that abideth not; when thou art afflicted in a world which will very shortly have passed away? If our rest were [to be] in the latter period of the world, then one ought to be afflicted in looking to the end.

"That" (he says) "those which cannot be shaken may remain." But of what sort are "those things which cannot be shaken"? The things to come.

[6.] Let us then do all for this, that we may attain that [rest], that we may enjoy those good things. Yea, I pray and beseech you, let us be earnest for this. No one builds in a city which is going to fall down. Tell me, I pray you, if

any one said that after a year, this city would fall, but such a city not at all, wouldest thou have built in that which was about to fall? So I also now say this, Let us not build in this world; it will fall after a little, and all will be destroyed. But why do I say, It will fall? Before its fall we shall be destroyed, and suffer what is fearful; we shall be removed from them.

Why build we upon the sand? Let us build upon the rock: for whatsoever may happen, that building remains impregnable, nothing will be able to destroy it. With good reason. For to all such attacks that region is inaccessible, just as this is accessible. For earthquakes, and fires, and inroad of enemies, take it away from us even while we are alive: and oftentimes destroy us with it.

And even in case it remains, disease speedily removes us, or if we stay, suffers us not to enjoy it fairly. For what pleasure [is there], where there are sicknesses, and false accusations, and envy, and intrigues? Or should there be none of these things, yet oftentimes if we have no children, we are disquieted, we are impatient, not having any to whom we may leave houses and all other things; and thenceforward we pine away as laboring for others. Yea oftentimes too the inheritance passes away to our enemies, not only after we are gone, but even while we live. What is more miserable then than to toil for enemies, and ourselves to be gathering sins together in order that they may have rest? And many are the instances of this that are seen in our cities. And yet [I say no more] lest I should grieve those who have been despoiled. For I could have mentioned some of them even by name, and have had many histories to tell, and many houses to show you, which have received for masters the enemies of those who labored for them: nay not houses only, but slaves also and the whole inheritance have oftentimes come round to enemies. For such are things human.

But in Heaven there is nothing of this to fear, —lest after a man is dead, his enemy should come, and succeed to his inheritance. For there there is neither death nor enmity; the tabernacles of the saints are permanent abodes; and among those saints is exultation, joy, gladness. For "the voice of rejoicing" (it is said) is "in the tabernacles of the righteous." (Ps. cxviii. 15.) They are eternal, having no end. They do not fall down through age, they do not change their owners, but stand continually in their best estate. With good reason. For there is nothing corruptible, nor perishable there, but all is immortal, and undefiled. On this building let us exhaust all our wealth. We have no need of carpenters nor of laborers. The hands of the poor build such houses; the lame, the blind, the

---

[1] ἀπογνῶτε.
[2] χρηματίζοντα. The word is used of God's speaking. See above, Hom. xxiii. [1], p. 469. St. Chrysostom's argument seems to oblige us to understand in the next clause something equivalent to "you say," which words have been inserted for clearness' sake. The supposition that Moses was meant by τὸν χρηματίζοντα is mentioned only to be rejected. [The words "you say" are omitted in this edition as unnecessary. χρηματίζοντα does not refer so much to God's speaking as to Moses' speaking by God's direction. — F. G.]
[3] Comp. St. Iren. pp. 330, 338, 403, O. T.

maimed, they build those houses. And wonder not, since they procure even a kingdom for us, and give us confidence towards God.

[7.] For mercifulness[1] is as it were a most excellent art, and a protector of those who labor at it. For it is dear to God, and ever stands near Him readily asking favor for whomsoever it will, if only it be not wronged by us; And it is wronged, when we do it by extortion. (See p. 481.) So, if it be pure, it gives great confidence to those who offer it up. It intercedes even for those who have offended, so great is its power, even for those who have sinned. It breaks the chains, disperses the darkness, quenches the fire, kills the worm, drives away the gnashing of teeth. The gates of heaven open to it with great security: And as when a Queen is entering, no one of the guards stationed at the doors dares to inquire who she is, and whence, but all straightway receive her; so also indeed with mercifulness. For she is truly a queen indeed, making men like God. For, he says, "ye shall be merciful, as your Heavenly Father is merciful." (Luke vi. 36.)

She is winged and buoyant, having golden pinions, with a flight which greatly delights the angels. There, it is said, are "the wings of a dove covered with silver, and her back with the yellowness of gold." (Ps. lxviii. 13.) As some dove golden and living, she flies, with gentle look, and mild eye. Nothing is better than that eye. The peacock is beautiful, but in comparison of her, is a jackdaw. So beautiful and worthy of admiration is this bird. She continually looks upwards; she is surrounded abundantly with God's glory: she is a virgin with golden wings, decked out, with a fair and mild countenance. She is winged, and buoyant, standing by the royal throne. When we are judged, she suddenly flies in, and shows herself, and rescues us from punishment, sheltering us with her own wings.

God would have her rather than sacrifices. Much does He discourse concerning her: so He loves her. "He will relieve" (it is said) "the widow" and "the fatherless" (Ps. cxlvi. 9) and the poor. God wishes to be called from her. "The Lord is pitiful and merciful,[2] long-suffering, and of great mercy" (Ps. cxlv. 8), and true. The mercy of God is over all the earth. She hath saved the race of mankind (see Ps. cxlv. 9): For unless she had pitied us, all things would have perished. "When we were enemies" (see Rom. v. 10), she "reconciled" us, she wrought innumerable blessings; she persuaded the Son of God to become a slave, and to empty Himself [of His glory].[3] (Phil. ii. 7.)

Let us earnestly emulate her by whom we have been saved; let us love her, let us prize her before wealth, and apart from wealth, let us have a merciful soul. Nothing is so characteristic of a Christian, as mercy. There is nothing which both unbelievers and all men so admire, as when we are merciful. For oftentimes we are ourselves also in need of this mercy, and say to God "Have mercy upon us, after Thy great goodness." (Ps. li. 1.) Let us begin first ourselves: or rather it is not we that begin first. For He has Himself already shown His mercy towards us: yet at least let us follow second. For if men have mercy on a merciful man, even if he has done innumerable wrongs, much more does God.

[8.] Hear the prophet saying, "But I" (his words are) "am like a fruitful olive tree in the house of God." (Ps. lii. 8.) Let us become such: let us become "as an olive tree": let us be laden on every side with the commandments. For it is not enough to be as an olive tree, but also to be fruitful. For there are persons who in doing alms give little, [only once] in the course of the whole year, or in each week, or who give away a mere chance matter. These are indeed olive trees, but not fruitful ones, but even withered. For because they show compassion they are olive trees, but because they do it not liberally, they are not fruitful olive trees. But let us be fruitful.

I have often said and I say now also: the greatness of the charity[4] is not shown by the measure of what is given, but by the disposition of the giver. You know the case of the widow. It is well continually to bring this example [forward], that not even the poor man may despair of himself, when he looks on her who threw in the two mites. Some contributed even hair in the fitting up of the temple, and not even these were rejected. (Ex. xxxv. 23.) But if when they had gold, they had brought hair, they [would have been] accursed: but if, having this only, they brought it, they were accepted. For this cause Cain also was blamed, not because he offered worthless things, but because they were the most worthless he had. "Accursed" (it is said) "is he which hath a male, and sacrificeth unto God a corrupt thing." (Mal. i. 14.) He did not speak absolutely, but, "he that hath" (he says) and spareth [it]. If then a man have nothing, he is freed from blame, or rather he has a reward. For what is of less value than two farthings, or more worthless than hair? What than a pint of meal? But nevertheless these were approved equally with the calves and the gold. For "a man is accepted according to that he hath, not according to that he hath not."

---

[1] or, "charity," ἐλεημοσύνη.　　See above, p. 509.
[2] [ἐλεήμων, akin to ἐλεημοσύνη, which St. Chrysostom is here describing.]　　　[3] κενῶσαι ἑαυτὸν.
[4] ἐλεημοσύνης.

(2 Cor. viii. 12.) And, it says, "according as thy hand hath, do good." (Prov. iii. 27.)

Wherefore, I entreat you, let us readily empty out what we have for the poor. Even if it be little we shall receive the same reward with them who have cast the most; or rather, more than those who cast in ten thousand talents. If we do these things we shall obtain the unspeakable treasures of God; if we not only hear, but practice also, if we do not praise [charity], but also show [it] by our deeds. Which may we all attain, in Christ Jesus our Lord, with whom to the Father together with the Holy Ghost, be glory, might, honor, now and for ever and world without end. Amen.

---

# HOMILY XXXIII.

## HEBREWS xii. 28, 29.

"Wherefore we receiving a kingdom which cannot be moved, let us have grace [or gratitude,][1] whereby we serve[2] God acceptably with reverence and godly fear. For our God is a consuming fire."

[1.] IN another place he says the same, "for the things which are seen are temporal, but the things which are not seen are eternal" (2 Cor. iv. 18); and from this makes an exhortation with regard to the evils which we endure in this present life; and here he does this, and says, let us continue steadfast; "let us have thankfulness," i.e., let us give thanks unto God. For not only we ought not to be discouraged at present things, but even to show the greatest gratitude to Him, for those to come.

"Whereby we serve God acceptably," that is to say, 'for thus is it possible to serve God acceptably,' by giving him thanks in all things. "Do all things" (he says) "without murmurings and disputings." (Phil. ii. 14.) For whatever work a man does with murmuring, he cuts away and loses his reward; as the Israelites — how great a penalty they paid for their murmurings. Wherefore he says, "Neither murmur ye." (1 Cor. x. 10.) It is not therefore possible to "serve" Him "acceptably" without a sense of gratitude to Him for all things, both for our trials, and the alleviations of them. That is, let us utter nothing hasty, nothing disrespectful, but let us humble ourselves that we may be reverential. For this is "with reverence and godly fear."

C. xiii. 1, 2. "Let brotherly love continue. Be not forgetful of hospitality,[3] for hereby some have entertained angels unawares." See how he enjoins them to preserve what they had: he does not add other things. He did not say, "Be loving as brethren," but, "Let brotherly love continue." And again, he did not say, "Be hospitable," as if they were not, but, "Be not forgetful of hospitality," for this was likely to happen owing to their afflictions.

Therefore[4] (he says) "some have entertained angels unawares." Seest thou how great was the honor, how great the gain! What is "unawares"?[5] They entertained them without knowing it. Therefore the reward also was great, because he entertained them, not knowing that they were Angels. For if he had known it, it would have been nothing wonderful. Some say that he here alludes to Lot also.

[2.] Ver. 3-5. "Remember them that are in bonds, as bound with them, them which suffer adversity as being yourselves also in the body. Marriage is honorable in all,[6] and the bed undefiled; but whoremongers and adulterers God will judge. Let your conversation be without covetousness: being content with such things as ye have."

See how large is his discourse concerning chastity. "Follow peace," he said, "and holiness; Lest there be any fornicator or profane person" (c. xii. 14); and again, "Fornicators and adulterers God will judge." (c. xii. 16.) In every case, the prohibition is with a penalty. "Follow peace with all men," he says, "and holiness, without which no man shall see the Lord: But fornicators and adulterers God will judge."

And having first set down "Marriage is honorable in all men, and the bed undefiled," he shows that he rightly added what follows. For if marriage has been conceded, justly is the fornicator punished, justly does the adulterer suffer vengeance.

Here he strips for[7] the heretics. He did not say again, Let no one be a fornicator; but having said it once for all, he then went on as

---

[1] χάριν ἔχωμεν. St. Chrys. understands the expression in this sense; which it has elsewhere: as in Luke xvii. 9; 2 Tim. i. 3.

[2] λατρεύομεν is the reading of all the MSS., the common texts have λατρεύωμεν.

[3] φιλοξενίας, see below, [5]. [Neither the A. V. "to entertain strangers," nor the R. V. "to show love to strangers," have hit upon the natural meaning of φιλοξενία, adopted throughout by St. Chrys. — F. G.]

[4] διὰ τοῦτο, or διὰ ταύτης, "thereby." [5] ἔλαθον.

[6] [The R. V. puts this and the following clause in the imperative, "Let marriage be had in honor among all." The Greek has simply the adjective and noun which would naturally be connected by the simple copula. — F. G.]

[7] ἀποδύεται πρὸς.

with a general exhortation, and not as directing himself against them.

"Let your conversation be without covetousness," he says. He did not say, Possess nothing, but, "Let your conversation be without covetousness": that is, let it show forth the philosophical character of your mind.[1] [And it will show it, if we do not seek superfluities, if we keep only to what is necessary.][2] For he says above also, "And ye took joyfully the spoiling of your goods." (c. x. 34.) He gives these exhortations, that they might not be covetous.

"Being content" (he says) "with such things as ye have." Then here also the consolation; (ver. 5) "For He" (he says) "hath said, I will never leave thee nor forsake thee"; (ver. 6) "so that we may boldly say, the Lord is my helper, and I will not fear what man shall do unto me." Again consolation in their trials.

[3.] Ver. 7. "Remember them which have the rule over you." This he was laboring to say above: therefore "Follow peace with all men." (c. xii. 14.) He gave this exhortation also to the Thessalonians, to "hold them in honor exceedingly." (1 Thess. v. 13.)

"Remember" (he says) "them which have the rule over you,[3] who have spoken unto you the word of God, whose faith follow, considering the end of their conversation." What kind of following is this? Truly the best: for he says, beholding their life, "follow their faith." For from a pure life [cometh] faith.

Or else by "faith," he means steadfastness. How so? Because they believe in the things to come. For they would not have shown forth a pure life, if they had questioned about the things to come, if they had doubted. So that here also he is applying a remedy to the same [evil].[4]

Ver. 8, 9. "JESUS CHRIST the same yesterday and to-day and for ever. Be not carried about with divers and strange doctrines. For it is good that the heart be established with grace, not with meats, which have not profited them that have been occupied therein."

In these words, "Jesus Christ the same yesterday and to-day and for ever," "yesterday" means all the time that is past: "to-day," the present: "for ever," the endless which is to come. That is to say: Ye have heard of an High Priest, but not an High Priest who fails. He is always the same. As though there were some who said, 'He is not, another will come,' he says this, that He who was "yesterday and to-day," is "the same also for ever." For even now the Jews say, that

another will come; and having deprived themselves of Him that is will fall into the hands of Antichrist.

"Be not carried about with divers and strange doctrines." Not "with strange doctrines" only, but neither with "divers ones."

"For it is a good thing that the heart be established with grace, not with meats which have not profited them that have been occupied[5] therein." Here he gently hints at those who introduce the observance of "meats." For by Faith all things are pure. There is need then of Faith, not of "meats."

For (ver. 10) "we have an altar whereof they have no right to eat which serve[6] the Tabernacle." Not as the Jewish [ordinances], are those among us, as it is not lawful even for the High Priest to partake of them. So that since he had said, "Do not observe,"[7] and this seemed to be [the language] of one who is throwing down his own building, he again turns it round. What, have not we then observances as well (he says)? [Yea we have], and we observe them very earnestly too, not sharing them even with the priests themselves.

[4.] Ver. 11, 12. "For the bodies of those beasts whose blood is brought into the sanctuary by the High Priest for sin, are burned without the camp. Wherefore JESUS also, that He might sanctify the people with His own blood, suffered" (he says) "without the gate." Seest thou the type shining forth? "For sin," he says, and "suffered without the gate." (Ver. 13) "Let us go forth therefore to Him without the camp, bearing His reproach," that is, suffering the same things; having communion with Him in His sufferings. He was crucified without as a condemned person: neither let us then be ashamed to "go forth out" [of the world].

Ver. 14, 15. "For we have here no continuing city" (he says) "but we seek one to come. By Him therefore let us offer the sacrifice of praise to God continually, that is, the fruit of our lips giving thanks to His Name."

"By Him," as by an High Priest, according to the flesh.[8] "Giving thanks"[9] (he says) "to His Name." (See p. 514.) Let us utter nothing blasphemous, nothing hasty, nothing bold, nothing presumptuous, nothing desperate. This is "with reverence and godly fear." (c. xii. 28.) For a soul in tribulations becomes desponding, and reckless.[10] But let not us [be so]. See here he again says the same thing which he said before, "not forsaking the assembling of ourselves together," for so shall we be able to do all things

---

[1] [The R. V. translates, "Be ye free from the love of money," with the margin, "Let your turn of mind be free."—F. G.]

[2] [This passage is omitted in Field's text, though contained in the Benedictine, and should of course be omitted here.—F. G.]

[3] ἡγουμένων, "spiritual leaders and guides."

[4] τὸ αὐτὸ θεραπεύει, "unchastity."

[5] οἱ περιπατήσαντες, i.e. "that have walked in them": "lived in the observance of rules respecting them."

[6] "perform the service of."

[7] παρατηρεῖτε, see Gal. iv. 10.

[8] His human nature.

[9] [R. V. "which make confession."—F. G.]

[10] ἀπαναισχυντεῖ, "loses respect."

with reverence. For oftentimes even out of respect for men, we refrain from doing many evil things.

Ver. 16. "But to do good and to communicate forget not." I speak not [merely] with reference to the brethren present, but to those absent also. But if others have plundered your property, display your hospitality out of such things as ye have. What excuse then shall we have henceforward, when they, even after the spoiling of their goods, were thus admonished?

[5.] And he did not say, "Be not forgetful" of the entertaining of strangers,[1] but "of hospitality":[2] that is, do not merely entertain strangers, but [do it] with love for the strangers. Moreover he did not speak of the recompense that is future, and in store for us, lest he should make them more supine, but of that already given. For "thereby some" (he says) "have entertained angels unawares."

But let us see in what sense "Marriage is honorable in all and the bed undefiled." Because (he means) it preserves the believer in chastity. Here he also alludes to the Jews, because they accounted the woman after childbirth[3] polluted: and "whosoever comes from the bed," it is said, "is not clean."[4] Those things are not polluted[5] which arise from nature, O ungrateful and senseless Jew,[6] but those which arise from choice.[7] For if "marriage is honorable" and pure, why forsooth dost thou think that one is even polluted by it?

"Let your conversation" (he says) "be without covetousness": since many after having exhausted[8] their property, afterwards wish to recover it again under the guise of alms, therefore he says, "Let your conversation be without covetousness"; that is, that we should be [desirous only] of what is necessary[9] and indispensable. What then (you say) if we should not have a supply even of these? This is not possible; indeed it is not. "For He hath said," and He doth not lie, "I will never leave thee, nor forsake thee. So that we boldly say, The Lord is my Helper, and I will not fear what man shall do unto me." Thou hast the promise from Himself: do not doubt henceforward. He has promised; make no question. But this, "I will never leave thee," he says not concerning money only, but concerning all other things

also. "The Lord is my Helper, and I will not fear what man shall do unto me"; with good reason.

This then also let us say in all temptations; let us laugh at human things, so long as we have God favorable to us. For as, when He is our enemy, it is no gain, though all men should be our friends, so when He is our friend, though all men together war against us, there is no harm. "I will not fear what man shall do unto me."

[6.] "Remember them which have the rule over you, who have spoken unto you the word of God." In this place I think that he is speaking about assistance also.[10] For this is [implied in the words] "who have spoken unto you the word of God."

"Whose faith follow considering the end of their conversation." What is, "considering"?[11] Continually revolving, examining it by yourselves, reasoning, investigating accurately, testing it as you choose. "The end of their conversation," that is, their conversation to the end: for "their conversation" had a good end.

"JESUS Christ the same yesterday and to-day and for ever." Do not think that then indeed He wrought wonders, but now works no wonders. He is the same. This is, "remember them that have the rule over you."[12]

"Be not carried about with divers and strange doctrines." "Strange," that is, different from those ye heard from us; ["Divers"] that is, of all sorts: for they have no stability, but are different [one from another]. For especially manifold[13] is the doctrine of meats.

"For it is a good thing that the heart be established with grace; not with meats." These are the "divers," these the "strange"[14] [doctrines]: especially as Christ has said, "not that which entereth into the mouth defileth the man, but that which cometh out." (Matt. xv. 11.) And observe that he does not make bold to say this openly, but as it were by a hint.[15] "For it is a good thing that the heart be established with grace, not with meats."

Faith is all. If that establishes [it], the heart stands in security. It follows that Faith establishes: consequently reasonings shake. For Faith is contrary to reasoning.

"Which." (he says) "have not profited them that have been occupied therein." For what is the gain from the observance[16] [of them], tell me. Does it not rather destroy? Does it not make such an one to be under sin? If it be

---

[1] St. Chrys. here reverts to ver. 2, and goes over again the portion on which he has already commented.
[2] "Love of the stranger," φιλοξενία.
[3] τὴν λεχώ: Edd. τὴν κοίτην.
[4] See Lev. xv. 18.　　　[5] βδελυρά.
[6] [St. Chrys. might seem here to be casting contempt upon the laws of the Old Dispensation; but he probably means that while they were fitting enough as parts of the temporary ceremonial law, they have no such foundation in nature as to remain of any force under the Christian Dispensation. — F. G.]
[7] τῆς προαιρέσεως.
[8] κενῶσαι. This word is used commonly by St. Chrys. for giving away one's whole property in charity, and probably that is its meaning here.　　　[9] τῆς χρείας ὦμεν.

[10] ἐπικουρία: see 1 Tim. v. 17, &c.　　[11] ἀναθεωροῦντες.
[12] That is, Remember them, because of the continual presence and working of Christ in His Church.
[13] or, "intricate and complicated," πολύπλοκον.
[14] "foreign to us."　　　[15] ἐν αἰνίγματι.
[16] παρατήρησις; see Gal. iv. 10, "Ye observe (παρατηρεῖσθε) days," &c.

necessary to observe [them], we must guard ourselves.[1]

"Which" (he says) "have not profited them that have been occupied therein." That is, who have always diligently kept them.

There is one observance, abstaining from sin. For what profit is it, when some are so polluted, as not to be able to partake of the sacrifices? So that it did not save them at all; although they were zealous about the observances. But because they had not faith, even thus they profited nothing.

[7.] In the next place he takes away[2] the sacrifice from the type, and directs his discourse to the prototype, saying, "The bodies of those beasts whose blood is brought into the sanctuary by the High Priest, are burned without the camp." Then those things were a type of these, and thus Christ, suffering "without," fulfilled all.

Here he makes it plain too that He suffered voluntarily, showing[3] that those things were not accidental, but even the [Divine] arrangement itself was of a suffering "without." [He suffered] without, but His Blood was borne up into Heaven. Thou seest then that we partake of Blood which has been carried into the Holy Place, the True Holy Place; of the Sacrifice of which the Priest alone had the privilege. We therefore partake of the Truth [the Reality]. If then we partake not of "reproach" [only] but of sanctification,[4] the "reproach" is the cause of the sanctification. For as He was reproached, so also are we. If we go forth "without" therefore, we have fellowship with Him.

But what is, "Let us go forth to Him"? Let us have fellowship with Him in His sufferings; let us bear His reproach. For He did not simply bid us dwell "outside the gate," but as He was reproached as a condemned person, so also we.

And "by Him let us offer a sacrifice to God." Of what kind of sacrifice does he speak? "The fruit of lips giving thanks to His Name." They [the Jews] brought sheep, and calves, and gave them to the Priest: let "us" bring none of these things, but thanksgiving. This "fruit" let "our lips" put forth.

"For with such sacrifices God is well pleased." Let us give such a sacrifice to Him, that He may offer [it] to The Father. For in no other way it is offered except through the Son, or rather also through a contrite mind. All these things [are said] for the weak. For that the thanks belong to the Son is evident: since otherwise, how is the honor equal? "That all men" (He says) "should honor the Son even as they honor

the Father." (John v. 23.) Wherein is the honor equal? "The fruit of our lips giving thanks to His Name."[5]

[8.] Let us bear all things thankfully, be it poverty, be it disease, be it anything else whatever: for He alone knows the things expedient for us. "For we know not what we should pray for as we ought." (Rom. viii. 26.) We then who do not know even how to ask for what is fitting, unless we have received of[6] the Spirit, let us take care to offer up thanksgiving for all things, and let us bear all things nobly. Are we in poverty? Let us give thanks. Are we in sickness? Let us give thanks. Are we falsely accused? Let us give thanks: when we suffer affliction, let us give thanks.

This brings us near to God: then we even have God for our debtor. But when we are in prosperity, it is we who are debtors and liable to be called to account. For when we are in prosperity, we are debtors to God: and oftentimes these things bring a judgment upon us, while those are for a payment of sins.[7] Those [afflictions] draw down mercy, they draw down kindness: while these on the other hand lift up even to an insane pride, and lead also to slothfulness, and dispose a man to fancy great things concerning himself; they puff up. Therefore the prophet also said, "It is good for me, Lord, that Thou hast afflicted[8] me; that I may learn Thy statutes." (Ps. cxix. 71.) When Hezekiah had received blessings and been freed from calamities, his heart was lifted up on high; when he fell sick, then was he humbled, then he became near to God. "When He slew them," it says, "then they sought Him diligently, and turned, and were early in coming to[9] God." (Ps. lxxviii. 34.) And again, "When the beloved waxed gross and fat, then he kicked." (Deut. xxxii. 15.) For "the Lord is known when He executeth judgments." (Ps. ix. 16.)

[9.] Affliction is a great good. "Narrow is the way" (Matt. vii. 14), so that affliction[10] thrusts us into the narrow [way]. He who is not pressed by affliction cannot enter. For he who afflicts himself in the narrow [way], is he who also enjoys ease; but he that spreads himself out,[11] does not enter in, and suffers from being so to say wedged in.[12] See how Paul enters into this narrow way. He "keeps under" his "body" (1 Cor. ix. 27), so as to be able to enter. Therefore, in all his afflictions, he continued giving thanks unto God. Hast thou lost thy property? This hath lightened thee of the most of thy wideness. Hast thou fallen from glory? This is

---

[1] ἐστι παρατηρεῖσθαι: *potius sibi cavendum est*, is Mr. Field's translation; "to be guarded," as we say.
[2] ἀναιρεῖ.
[3] δεικνὺς ὅτι οὐκ ἐκεῖνα ἁπλῶς ἦν, ἀλλὰ καὶ αὐτὴ ἡ οἰκονομία ἔξω πάθους ἦν.
[4] ἁγιασμοῦ. The effect of the sprinkling with blood. See c. ix. 12, 13, &c.; x. 10, 14.

[5] That is, "to the Name of the Son."
[6] ἐπιλαβώμεθα, "taken hold of."
[7] ἔκτισις, see above, Hom. v. [6.] p. 391.
[8] or, "humbled."    [9] ὤρθριζον πρὸς.
[10] θλίψις, literally "pressing": probably St. Chrys. had in mind a word of the text which he does not cite, τεθλιμμένη ἡ ὁδός.
[11] ἐμπλατύνων ἑαυτόν.    [12] θλίβεται σφηνούμενος.

another sort of wideness. Hast thou been falsely accused? Have the things said against thee, of which thou art nowise conscious to thyself been believed? "Rejoice and leap for joy." For "blessed are ye" (He says) "when men reproach you, and say all manner of evil against you, falsely, for My sake. Rejoice and be exceeding glad, for great is your reward in Heaven." (Matt. v. 11, 12.)

Why dost thou marvel, if thou art grieved, and wish to be set free from temptations? Paul wished to be set free, and oftentimes entreated God, and did not obtain. For the "thrice for this I besought the Lord," is oftentimes; "and He said unto me, My grace is sufficient for thee, for My strength is made perfect in weakness." (2 Cor. xii. 8, 9.) By "weakness," he here means "afflictions." What then? When he heard this he received it thankfully, and says, "Wherefore I take pleasure in infirmities" (2 Cor. xii. 10); that is, I am pleased, I rest in my afflictions. For all things then let us give thanks, both for comfort, and for affliction.[1] Let us not murmur: let us not be unthankful. "Naked came I out of my mother's womb, naked also shall I depart." (Job i. 21.) Thou didst not come forth glorious, do not seek glory. Thou wast brought into life naked, not of money alone, but also of glory, and of honorable name.

Consider how great evils have oftentimes arisen from wealth. For "It is easier" (it is said) "for a camel to go through the eye of a needle, than for a rich man to enter into the kingdom of Heaven." (Matt. xix. 24.) Seest thou to how many good things wealth is a hindrance, and dost thou seek to be rich? Dost thou not rejoice that the hindrance has been overthrown? So narrow is the way which leadeth into the Kingdom. So broad is wealth, and full of bulk and swelling out. Therefore He says, "Sell that thou hast" (Matt. xix. 21), that that way may receive thee. Why dost thou yearn after wealth? For this cause He took it away from thee, that He might free thee from slavery. For true fathers also, when a son is corrupted by some mistress, and having given him much exhortation they do not persuade him to part from her, send the mistress into banishment. Such also is abundance of wealth. Because the Lord cares for us, and delivers us from the harm [which arises] therefrom, He takes away wealth from us.

Let us not then think poverty an evil: sin is the only evil. For neither is wealth a good thing by itself: to be well-pleasing to God is the only good. Poverty then let us seek, this let us pursue: so shall we lay hold on heaven, so shall we attain to the other good things. Which may we all attain by the grace and lovingkindness of our Lord Jesus Christ, with whom to the Father together with the Holy Ghost be glory, power, honor, now and ever and world without end. Amen.

---

# HOMILY XXXIV.

## Hebrews xiii. 17.

"Obey them that have the rule over you, and submit yourselves. For they watch for your souls, as they that must give account, that they may do it with joy, and not with grief,[2] for this is unprofitable for you."

[1.] ANARCHY[3] is an evil, and the occasion of many calamities, and the source of disorder and confusion. For as, if thou take away the leader from a chorus, the chorus will not be in tune and in order; and if from a phalanx of an army thou remove the commander, the evolutions will no longer be made in time and order, and if from a ship thou take away the helmsman, thou wilt sink the vessel; so too if from a flock thou remove the shepherd, thou hast overthrown and destroyed all.

Anarchy then is an evil, and a cause of ruin. But no less an evil also is the disobedience to rulers. For it comes again to the same. For a people not obeying a ruler, is like one which has none; and perhaps even worse. For in the former case they have at least an excuse for disorder, but no longer in the latter, but are punished.

But perhaps some one will say, there is also a third evil, when the ruler is bad. I myself too know it, and no small evil it is, but even a far worse evil than anarchy. For it is better to be led by no one, than to be led by one who is evil. For the former indeed are oftentimes saved, and oftentimes are in peril,[4] but the latter

---

[1] [See above, pp. 442, 459, 460, 517. St. Chrysostom in his bitter banishment finished his last prayer "with his usual thanksgiving, 'Glory to God for all things,' and sealed it with a final Amen." *Dr. Bright, Hist. of Church, between A.D. 313 and 451,* chapter ix. end, p. 255 and Dr. Bright's note b. on the same page.]

[2] "lamenting," στενάζοντες.

[3] It will be observed that St. Chrysostom uses "rulers" (ἄρχοντες) and the cognate words, of spiritual rulers.

[4] "suffer," ἐκινδύνευσεν.

will be altogether in peril, being led into the pit [of destruction].

How then does Paul say, "Obey them that have the rule over you, and submit yourselves"? Having said above, "whose faith follow, considering the end of their conversation" (c. ver. 7), he then said, "Obey them that have the rule over you, and submit yourselves."

What then (you say), when he is wicked should we obey?

Wicked? In what sense? If indeed in regard to Faith, flee and avoid him; not only if he be a man, but even if he be an angel come down from Heaven; but if in regard to life, be not over-curious. And this instance I do not allege from my own mind, but from the Divine Scripture. For hear Christ saying, "The Scribes and the Pharisees sit on Moses' seat." (Matt. xxiii. 2.) Having previously spoken many fearful things concerning them, He then says, "They sit on Moses' seat: all therefore whatsoever they tell you observe, do; but do not ye after their works." (Matt. xxiii. 2, 3.) They have (He means) the dignity of office, but are of unclean life. Do thou however attend, not to their life, but to their words. For as regards their characters, no one would be harmed [thereby]. How is this? Both because their characters are manifest to all, and also because though he were ten thousand times as wicked, he will never teach what is wicked. But as respects Faith, [the evil] is not manifest to all, and the wicked [ruler] will not shrink from teaching it.

Moreover, "Judge not that ye be not judged" (Matt. vii. 1) concerns life, not faith : surely what follows makes this plain. For "why" (He says) "beholdest thou the mote that is in thy brother's eye, but considerest not the beam that is in thine own eye?" (Matt. vii. 3.)

"All things therefore" (He says) "which they bid you observe, do ye" (now to "do" belongs to works not to Faith) "but do not ye after their works." Seest thou that [the discourse] is not concerning doctrines, but concerning life and works?

[2.] Paul however previously commended them,[1] and then says, "Obey them that have the rule over you, and submit yourselves, for they watch for your souls, as they that shall give account."

Let those who rule also hear, and not only those who are under their rule; that as the subjects ought to be obedient, so also the rulers ought to be watchful and sober. What sayest thou? He watches; he imperils his own head; he is subject to the punishments of thy sins, and for thy sake is amenable to what is so fear-

ful, and art thou slothful, and affectedly indifferent, and at ease? Therefore he says, "That they may do this with joy, and not with grief :[2] for this is unprofitable for you."

Seest thou that the despised ruler ought not to avenge himself, but his great revenge is to weep and lament? For neither is it possible for the physician, despised by his patient, to avenge himself, but to weep and lament. But if [the ruler] lament (he means), God inflicts vengeance on thee. For if when we lament for our own sins we draw God to us, shall we not much rather [do this], when we lament for the arrogance and scornfulness of others? Seest thou that he does not suffer him to be led on to reproaches? Seest thou how great is his philosophy? He ought to lament who is despised, is trodden under foot, is spit upon.

Be not confident because he does not avenge himself on thee, for lamenting is worse than any revenge. For when of himself he profits nothing by lamenting, he calls on the Lord: and as in the case of a teacher and nurse, when the child does not listen to him, one is called in who will treat him more severely, so also in this case.

[3.] Oh! how great the danger! What should one say to those wretched men, who throw themselves upon so great an abyss of punishments? Thou hast to give account of all over whom thou rulest, women and children and men; into so great a fire dost thou put thy head. I marvel if any of the rulers can be saved, when in the face of[3] such a threat, and of the present indifference, I see some still even running on, and casting themselves upon so great a burden of authority.

For if they who are dragged by force[4] have no refuge or defense, if they discharge duty ill and are negligent; since even Aaron was dragged by force, and yet was imperiled;[5] and Moses again was imperiled, although he had oftentimes declined; and Saul having been entrusted with another kind of rule, after he had declined it, was in peril, because he managed it amiss; how much more they who take so great pains to obtain it, and cast themselves upon it? Such an one much more deprives himself of all excuse. For men ought to fear and to tremble, both because of conscience, and because of the burden of the office; and neither when dragged to it should they once for all decline, nor, when not dragged cast themselves upon it, but should even flee, foreseeing the greatness of the dignity; and

---

[2] στενάζοντες. It will be observed that St. Chrys. dwells much on this word: and also that he understands the "do this" of "watching for souls"; not as the English version might lead us to understand it, of the "giving account."
[3] πρὸς.
[4] Those who are ordained against their will by actual force; as frequently occurred in the age of St. Chrysostom.
[5] κινδυνεύω seems here as elsewhere in writers of this age to imply actual suffering as well as danger; so in this discourse. [1.]

when they have been seized, they ought again to show their godly fear.[1] Let there be nothing out of measure. If thou hast perceived it beforehand, retire ; convince thyself that thou art unworthy of the office. Again, if thou hast been seized, in like manner be thou reverential,[2] always showing rightmindedness.[3]

[4.] Ver. 18. "Pray for us" (he says) ; "for we trust we have a good conscience among all,[4] willing to live honestly."

Thou seest that he used these apologies, as writing to persons grieved with him, as to those who turned away, who were disposed as towards a transgressor, not enduring even to hear his name? Inasmuch then as he asked from those who hated him what all others ask from those who love them [their prayers for him], therefore he here introduces this ; saying, "We trust that we have a good conscience." For do not tell me of accusations ; our conscience, he says, in nothing hurts[5] us ; nor are we conscious to ourselves that we have plotted against you. "For we trust," he says, "that we have a good conscience among all," not among the Gentiles only, but also among you. We have done nothing with deceitfulness,[6] nothing with hypocrisy : for it was probable that these [calumnies] were reported respecting him. "For they have been informed concerning thee" (it is said) "that thou teachest apostasy." (Acts xxi. 21.) Not as an enemy, he means, nor as an adversary I write these things, but as a friend. And this he shows also by what follows.

Ver. 19. "But I beseech you the rather to do this, that I may be restored to you the sooner." His thus praying was [the act] of one who loved them greatly, and that not simply, but with all earnestness, that so, he says, I may come to you speedily. The earnest desire to come to them is [the mark] of one conscious to himself of nothing [wrong], also the entreating them to pray for him.

Therefore having first asked their prayers, he then himself also prays for all good things on them. (Ver. 20) "Now the God of peace," he says (be ye not therefore at variance one with another), "that brought again from the earth the Shepherd of the sheep" (this is said concerning the resurrection) "the Great [Shepherd]" (another addition : here again he confirms to them even to the end, his discourse concerning the Resurrection) "through the blood of the everlasting covenant, our Lord

Jesus Christ," (ver. 21) "make you perfect in every good work, to do His will, working in you[7] that which is well-pleasing in His sight."

Again he bears high testimony to them. For that is made "perfect" which having a beginning is afterwards completed. And he prays for them which is the act of one who yearns for them. And while in the other Epistles, he prays in the prefaces, here he does it at the end. "Working in you," he says, "that which is well-pleasing in His sight through Jesus Christ, to whom be glory for ever and ever. Amen."

[5.] Ver. 22. "And I beseech you, brethren, suffer the word of exhortation, for indeed I have written a letter unto you in few words." Seest thou that what he wrote to no one [else], he writes to them? For (he means) I do not even trouble you with long discourse.

I suppose that they were not at all unfavorably disposed towards Timothy : wherefore he also put him forward.[8] For (ver. 23) "know ye," he says, "that our brother Timothy is set at liberty,[9] with whom, if he come shortly, I will see you." "Set at liberty," he says ; from whence? I suppose he had been cast into prison : or if not this, that he was sent away from Athens. For this also is mentioned in the Acts.[10]

Ver. 24, 25. "Salute all them that have the rule over you, and all the saints. They of Italy salute you. Grace be with you all. Amen."

[6.] Seest[11] thou how he shows that virtue is born[12] neither wholly from God, nor yet from ourselves alone? First[13] by saying, "make you perfect in every good work" ; Ye have virtue indeed, he means, but need to be made complete. What is "good work and word"?[14] So as to have both life and doctrines right. "According to His will, working in you that which is well-pleasing in His sight."

"In His sight," he says. For this is the highest virtue, to do that which is well-pleasing in the sight of God, as the Prophet also says, "And according to the cleanness of my hands in His eye-sight." (Ps. xviii. 24.)

And having written thus much, he said this was little, in comparison with what he was going to say. As he says also in another place, "As I wrote to you in few words : whereby when ye read, ye may understand my knowledge in the mystery of Christ." (Eph. iii. 3, 4.)

---

[1] εὐλάβειαν. That is, by submitting to the will of God thus manifested, and receiving ordination.
[2] have a godly fear.　　　　[3] εὐγνωμοσύνην.
[4] ἐν πᾶσιν, see below. [The construction of ἐν πᾶσι with what follows, "in all things willing (wishing) to live honestly," both in the A. V. and the R. V. is undoubtedly correct; but St. Chrysostom has taken it as connected with the preceding clause. — F. G.]
[5] καταβλάπτει.
[6] καπηλείας, see St. Chrys. on 2 Cor. ii. 17.

[7] [The R. V. here follows the reading ἐν ἡμῖν adopted by many critical authorities. — F. G.]
[8] By saying that he would come with Timothy, as if Timothy were his superior; see the further comment, in the next section.
[9] or, "released," "gone," or, "come away," ἀπολελυμένον.
[10] See Acts xvii. 16; xviii. 5.　　[12] γεγενημένην . . . ἐκ.
[11] St. Chrys. here recurs to ver. 21.
[13] Here as elsewhere St. Chrys. does not expressly mention any "secondly," but after treating the remaining verses recurs to the subject in speaking on the words "Grace be with you": and there indicates a second evidence.
[14] See 2 Thess. ii. 17. "Stablish you in every good word and work." Probably St. Chrys. had this in his mind.

And observe his wisdom. He says not, "I beseech you, suffer the word of" admonition, but "the word of exhortation,"[1] that is, of consolation, of encouragement. No one, he means, can be wearied at the length of what has been said (Did this then make them turn away from him? By no means: he does not indeed wish to express this) : that is, even if ye be of little spirit, for it is the peculiarity of such persons not to endure a long discourse.

"Know ye that our brother Timothy is set at liberty, with whom if he come shortly I will see you." This is enough to persuade them to submit themselves, if he is ready to come with his disciple.

"Salute them that have the rule over you, and all the saints." See how he honored them, since he wrote to them instead of to those [their rulers].

"They of Italy salute you. Grace be with you all. Amen." Which was for them all in common.

But how does "Grace" come to be "with" us? If we do not do despite to the benefit, if we do not become indolent in regard to the Gift. And what is "the grace"? Remission of sins, Cleansing : this is "with" us. For who (he means) can keep the Grace despitefully, and not destroy it? For instance ; He freely forgave thee thy sins. How then shall the "Grace be with" thee, whether it be the good favor, or the effectual working of the SPIRIT? If thou draw it to thee by good deeds. For the cause of all good things is this, the continual abiding with us of the "grace" of the Spirit. For this guides us to all [good things], just as when it flies away from us, it ruins us, and leaves us desolate.

[7.] Let us not then drive it from us. For on ourselves depends, both its remaining, and its departing. For the one results, when we mind heavenly things ; the other, when [we mind] the things of this life. "Which the world" (He says) "cannot receive because it seeth Him not, neither knoweth Him." (John xiv. 17.) Seest thou that a worldly soul cannot have Him? We need great earnestness that so there He may be held fast by us, so as to direct all our affairs, and do them in security, and in much peace.

For as a ship sailing with favorable winds is neither to be hindered nor sunk, so long as it enjoys a prosperous and steady breeze, but also causes great admiration according to the march of its progress, both to the mariners, and to the passengers, giving rest to the one, and not forcing them to toil on at their oars, and setting the others free from all fear, and giving them the most delightful view of her course ; so too a soul strengthened by the Divine Spirit, is far above

all the billows of this life, and more strongly than the ship, cuts the way bearing on to Heaven, since it is not sent along by wind, but has all the pure sails filled by the Paraclete Himself : and He casts out of our minds all that is slackened and relaxed.

For as the wind if it fall upon a slackened sail, would have no effect ; so neither does the SPIRIT endure to continue in a slack soul ; but there is need of much tension, of much vehemence, so that our mind may be on fire, and our conduct under all circumstances on the stretch, and braced up. For instance when we pray, we ought to do it with much intentness,[2] stretching forth the soul toward Heaven, not with cords, but with great earnestness. Again when we do works of mercy, we have need of intentness, lest by any means, thought for our household, and care for children, and anxiety about wife, and fear of poverty entering in, should slacken our sail. For if we put it on the stretch on all sides by the hope of the things to come, it receives well the energy[3] of the SPIRIT ; and none of those perishable and wretched things will fall upon it, yea, and if any of them should fall, it does it no harm, but is quickly thrown back by the tightness, and is shaken off and falls down.

Therefore we have need of much intentness. For we too are sailing over a great and wide sea, full of many monsters, and of many rocks, and bringing forth for us many storms, and from the midst of serene weather raising up a most violent tempest. It is necessary then if we would sail with ease, and without danger, to stretch the sails, that is, our determination : for this is sufficient for us. For Abraham also, when he had stretched forth his affections towards God and set before Him his fixed resolution,[4] what else had he need of? Nothing : but "he believed God, and it was counted unto him for righteousness." (Gen. xv. 6.) But Faith [comes] of a sincere will.[5] He offered up his son, and though he did not slay him, he received a recompense as if he had slain him, and though the work was not done the reward was given.

Let our sails then be in good order,[6] not grown old (for everything "that is decayed and waxen old is nigh to vanishing away"[7]) (c. viii. 13), not worn into holes, that so they may bear the energy of the SPIRIT. "For the natural man,"[8] it is said, "receiveth not the things of the Spirit." (1 Cor. ii. 14.) For as the webs of spiders could not receive a blast of wind, so neither will the soul devoted to this life, nor the natural man ever be able to receive the grace of the SPIRIT : for our reasonings differ nothing

---

[1] [παρακλήσεως.]

[2] tension.
[3] ἐνέργειαν.
[4] [προαίρεσιν.]
[5] [προαιρέσεως.]

[6] καθαρά.
[7] ἐγγὺς ἀφανισμοῦ.
[8] ψυχικὸς.

from them,[1] preserving a connection in appearance only but destitute of all power.

[8.] Our condition, however, is not such, if we are watchful: but whatever may fall upon [the Christian], he bears all, and is above all, stronger than any whirlpool.[2] For suppose there be a spiritual man, and that innumerable calamities befall him, yet is he overcome by none of them. And what do I say? Let poverty come upon him, disease, insults, revilings, mockings, stripes, every sort of infliction, every sort of mocking, and slanders, and insults: yet, as though he were outside the world, and set free from the feelings of the body, so will he laugh all to scorn.

And that my words are not mere boasting, I think many [such] exist even now; for instance, of those who have embraced the life of the desert. This however, you say, is nothing wonderful. But I say that of those also who live in cities,

there are such men unsuspected. If thou wish however, I shall be able to exhibit some among those of old. And that thou mayest learn, consider Paul, I pray thee. What is there fearful that he did not suffer, and that he did not submit to? But he bore all nobly. Let us imitate him, for so shall we be able to land in the tranquil havens with much merchandise.

Let us then stretch our mind towards Heaven, let us be held fast by that desire, let us clothe ourselves with spiritual fire, let us gird ourselves with its flame. No man who bears flame fears those who meet him; be it wild beast, be it man, be it snares innumerable, so long as he is armed with fire, all things stand out of his way, all things retire. The flame is intolerable, the fire cannot be endured, it consumes all.

With this fire let us clothe ourselves, offering up glory to our Lord JESUS Christ, with whom to the Father, together with the Holy Ghost, be glory, might, honor, now and ever and world without end. Amen.

---

[1] the cobwebs.          [2] ἴλιγγος.

**Thanks be to God.**

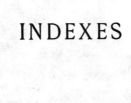

INDEXES

# HOMILIES ON THE GOSPEL OF JOHN

## INDEX OF SUBJECTS

# HOMILIES ON THE GOSPEL OF JOHN.

## INDEX OF TEXTS.

# HOMILIES ON THE EPISTLE TO THE HEBREWS.

## INDEX OF SUBJECTS.

Sepulchres, see *Tombs.*

Sermons, applause at, 409.

Servants, two are enough, 495; lady walking out should not be attended by many, *ib.;* angels do not have, *ib.*

Service in church, every day, 450; increases love, 455, 456; benefit of being together in, 504, 516.

Seventy, the, translated (ordered of the Holy Ghost) Scriptures into Greek, 407.

Shame, in the wicked their own witness against themselves, 474; before men, not before God, 508.

Sheep, treatment of the sickly, 450.

Silence, peril of, to ministers of the Word, 476.

Silk, a superfluity, 496.

Sin, a very plague, 441; in Heb. xi. 25, holding back from affliction, 483; to, belongs ease, 484; its bitterness causes some to pine away, 506; easily overcome if we will, 493; the sole disgrace, though none think so, 496; the sole evil, 518; it is a duty to keep others from sin even if by force, after in other ways and by begging his help for one's self, 505; King David long bewailed his, 507; may be hindered even from a lower motive, by degrees leading to a higher, 505; abstaining from, a due observance, 516.

Sins, the lesser not a spot or wrinkle, but far worse, 368; not small, 490; recoil on the doer, 368; parent of unbelief, 394; notwithstanding, hope remains, while to-day lasts, 396; we may not despair after, 396, 426; he who seeks pardon for sins of youth must not sin when old, 401; they who are old in, repentance frees, 410; all can be blotted out by right repentance, 412; must be

confessed one by one, 412, 508; affliction wipes out, 494; confession lessens, 508; we must remember our, 412, 437, 507 *sqq.;* if we remember, God forgets, 508; remembering, helps cure, *ib.;* great help of remembering, 473, 508, 509; punishment if we deny, 508; pity if we confess, *ib.;* called *thorns,* 414, 415; not enough to remove, treatment also needed, 414; if we cut out, may enjoy the good things innumerable, 415; difficulty of cleansing away, 426; almsgiving and defending the wronged do it, *ib.; cf.* 412; if we begin, God cleanses, 426; of ignorance none is free from, 439; we should mourn over others', 442; and keep silence as to them, 464; to tell our own to God and our friends, *ib.;* prevented or healed by prayer, 490; one enough to cast us out of the kingdom, and they are many, *ib.;* to confess, not humility but candor, *ib.;* some too great for repentance, 507; remembering always our own, we forget wrongs from others, 508; we must offer to God, 447, 508; penitence, prayer, deeds of mercy, wash away, 509; by mourning our, we draw God to us, 519; putting away, what, 448.

Sinners, if others call us, we must not be angry, 491; *cf.* 507.

Slave-dealers, 495.

Slaves, esteemed, the Master sometimes called after, 475, 476; two suffice for a family willing to part with superfluities, 495.

Sleep, some indulge in by day, we spiritually, 474.

Son, force of the word, 367, 368, 373, 375, 385, 390, 430; the Son and sons contrasted, 384, 385.

Soul, punished, 398, 459; suffers, 396; in its vigor when a person is aged, 401; when one is young it is subject to fevers, *ib.;* purified by Blood of Christ, 440; its eye, how to make quick and beautiful, 450; mingled with soul increases love, 455; might of a great, 456; in calamity apt to be impatient, 459; reproach a sore trial of the, 461; and scorning and jests, 493; covetousness degrades, 480; eating at banquets of the overreaching destroys, *ib.;* and defiles, 481; striving in prayer to God, 490; wrestles in theater of Heaven, 496; the well-adorned, has God for its Lover, and place with the choirs of angels, 498; virgin if pure, even though married, 496, 498; it the Lord seeks after, 498; exhausted, how refreshed, 499; made collected through affliction, 500; enervated through luxury, 501; shares it if body be effeminate,

*ib.;* must be forced to remember its sins, 508; in tribulation liable to despond, 516; must be braced to receive the impulses of the Spirit, 521, 522.

Spirit, Holy, see *God the Holy Ghost.*

Starvation, no one dies of, except by his own will, 422.

Strangers, Patriarchs, to this world, 471, 473 *sqq.;* King David 475; we to our own country, 473, 475; to the world if we, God to be called our God, 475, 476.

Substance, no word will express, even of angel, far less of God, 372.

Suffering, perfects, 384, 392, 404; is a cause of salvation, 384; *cf.* 404; we are to rejoice in our own, as paying the penalty of sins, 391; helps to wipe them out, 494; use of, 426, 494; it is only our own which moves us, 426; amid, we may be calm within, as the sky when overclouded, 445; of Abel preaches beyond all speech, 466; of them of old during their whole lives we have no idea of, 491, 494; all can be borne if we be approved of Heaven, 494, 495.

Suicide, some long for death, and only the fear of God withholds them, 512.

Surgeons, their mingled gentleness and firmness, 505.

Suspect, we are apt to, 422.

Swearing, 477.

Talents, teacher has five, learner one, 504; earth wherein single talent is buried, the bad heart, *ib.*

Teacher, of grammar, must make boy master the things to be learnt, 409; if he repeat the alphabet, it is not to teach himself, 490; has five talents, learner one, 504; if he teach a child heedless, one is called who punishes the child, 519.

Tears, help wash away sins, 442, 509; one ingredient in medicine of repentance, 412, 426; of wailing and mourning, they worthy who choose to fail of the things to come, 471; St. Chrysostom calls for, 472; of Christ, 442.

Temple, its magnificence, 446; its wonders, 510; its being One, 446; as the Jewish was for whole world, so is Christ our Priest in the temple of Heaven, 447; offering even of hair accepted for, 514.

Temporal things, we seek first, and lose both them and Heaven, 408; God gives, when He sees us prefer spiritual things, 460, 479; given as a refreshment, 470; often possessed, not as His gift, but by fraud, 460; Patriarchs of old loved their Home, cared not for these, 471; so magnificent, *ib.;* who seek, lose them and Divine things; who prefer Divine obtain both, 486; soon go, 512; when

# HOMILIES ON THE EPISTLE TO THE HEBREWS.

## INDEX OF TEXTS.

* See same form of citation in St. Chrysostom on Romans, p. 459.